Oxfo
South African
School
Dictionary

3rd Edition

Oxford University Press is a department of the University of Oxford.
It furthers the University's objective of excellence in research, scholarship,
and education by publishing worldwide. Oxford is a registered trade mark of
Oxford University Press in the UK and in certain other countries

Published in South Africa by
Oxford University Press Southern Africa (Pty) Limited

Vasco Boulevard, Goodwood, N1 City, Cape Town, South Africa, 7460
P O Box 12119, N1 City, Cape Town, South Africa, 7463

First published in 1996
Second edition published in 2004
Third edition (completely revised) published in 2010

Oxford South African School Dictionary 3rd edition

ISBN 978 0 19 598396 8 Paperback edition
ISBN 978 0 19 904064 3 Paperback edition with CD-ROM
ISBN 978 0 19 599133 8 Hardback edition

Ninth impression 2014

Printed on 60 gsm woodfree paper

Acknowledgements
See Acknowledgements: South African edition on page v
Typesetters: CBT Typesetting & Design CC (A–Z) and
Baseline Publishing Services and Peter Burgess (extra matter)
Printed and bound by: ABC Press, Cape Town

121558

Contents

Introduction

Based on unique research by Oxford University Press into the words South African learners need to understand their textbooks in all subjects, this edition of the best-selling *South African School Dictionary* is now even more helpful and easier to use.

Completely revised, it was developed with three main aims:

- to support Intermediate and Senior Phase learners across the curriculum, by including the vocabulary they need to understand their textbooks better
- to be even easier and quicker to use than previous editions
- to cover every dictionary-related requirement of the curriculum.

Curriculum support

For most users, the main reason for using a dictionary is to look up the meanings of words. To ensure that we included the words learners need to study and communicate effectively, we used a **corpus** (or database) made up of a range of approved textbooks for all subjects from Grades 4 to 9.

Using special software, we analysed the database and identified important words to include, from words that are the foundations of much other learning (e.g. *angle, cross section, mammal*), to more advanced curriculum terms (e.g. *algorithm, coulomb, GPS, ordinate, tectonic*).

We developed clear definitions for all of these words, and commissioned illustrations for many of them, because we know that illustrations boost learners' understanding quickly.

We also used the database to identify South African words that are useful for school, or are a normal part of South African English vocabulary (e.g. *Khoisan, spaza, Strandloper, tik*).

We paid special attention to almost 100 exam and test instruction words (e.g. *classify*, *compare* and *define*), because we know that if learners don't understand these terms, they will struggle to succeed at school.

Throughout the dictionary, there are thousands of example sentences to show learners how to use these words in real sentences. We know from research that example sentences are the support that teachers and learners want.

Easy and quick to use

Oxford's research in schools shows that:

- learners want to find words quickly ➜ This dictionary's clear design will help users find the words they want, faster than ever.
- learners want straightforward definitions that they understand first time ➜ Every definition in this dictionary uses only familiar words, drawn from a list of 3 000 basic words that are widely understood.

The language curriculum

This dictionary covers features of the language curriculum in far more ways than we can list here. These are some of the most important:

Learners should use dictionaries to develop vocabulary:
HL Gr 4–5 LO3 & LO4, Gr 4–9 LO6; FAL Gr 4–9 LO3 & LO6
The dictionary includes synonyms, opposites and word building notes, plus

a detailed section on using prefixes and suffixes to build words in the Study pages (in the middle of the dictionary).

Learners should use dictionaries to check meanings and spellings of words, and grammar, and to proofread and revise drafts of their work:
HL & FAL Gr 4–9 LO4; HL Gr 6–9 LO6
Learners will find the plurals of all nouns and the tenses of all verbs at each relevant entry – great support for spelling. The dictionary also guides learners on good usage (e.g. at *borrow* and *lend*), while clear summaries of grammar in the Study pages are ideal for quick reference.

Learners should know how to pronounce words accurately:
HL & FAL Gr 4–9 LO2; FAL Gr 4–9 LO6
Throughout, there are easy guides to the standard way of saying words in English. These include familiar words that are often mispronounced, such as *mischievous* (say **miss**-chiv-uhss), and more difficult words like *pneumatic* (say nyoo-**mat**-ik).

Learners should use appropriate words for different purposes and audiences:
HL Gr 4–6 LO 2; Gr 4–9 LO6; FAL Gr 4–6 LO2, Gr 7–9 LO3 & LO4
The 'formal' and 'informal' labels as well as notes in many entries guide learners to choose the right word for their purpose.

Learners should explore the origins of words:
HL Gr 4–9 LO6
Hundreds of entries include the origins of words that came into English from Latin, Greek, French and many other languages, for example, at *algorithm* and *assassin*. The Study pages include a history of English.

We want learners to get the most they can out of this dictionary, so we have included ready-to-use photocopiable lessons (with answers) in the Study pages, to build dictionary skills (SP22–32).

The separate Workbook with its activities, games, and links to curriculum outcomes helps build a wider and deeper range of dictionary skills.

We hope learners using this dictionary will become confident and effective users of English, who fulfil their potential to succeed.

Acknowledgements: South African edition

Publishing manager: Megan Hall
Chief editor and publisher: Mary Reynolds
Final editors: Phillip Louw, Dorothy Mantzel and Fred Pheiffer, with Lorna Hiles
Development editors: Lorna Hiles, Dorothy Mantzel, Daphne Paizee, Fred Pheiffer, Pippa Tsilik
Science and Maths development editor: Julie van der Vlugt
South African pronunciation development editor: David Merrington
South African inflections development editor: Jessica Kew
Etymology development editor: Pippa Tsilik
Editorial development assistant: Susan Dorrington
Corpus developers: Phillip Louw, Mary Reynolds
Study pages writer: Daphne Paizee
Study pages editor: Jacqueline de Vos
Proofreaders: John Linnegar, Judy Norton, Elbert Visser
Researchers: Rodney Nesbitt, Mary Reynolds
Computational lexicographic consultants: David Joffe, Malcolm Macleod (TshwaneDJe)
Dictionary development software: TshwaneLex
Designer (A–Z, extra matter): Peter Burgess
Cover designer: Sharna Sammy
Illustrators: John Dickin, Wayne Jones, Val Myburgh, Walter Pichler
Typesetter (A–Z): CBT Typesetting & Design CC
Typesetter (extra matter): Baseline Publishing Services

How to use this dictionary

Find words quickly

Guide words show which entries are covered on each page, helping you find the right page quickly.

An **alphabet guide** on each page shows which letter you are on.

Words that can be more than one part of speech are usually in **different entries**, helping you find the right meaning quickly.

When a separate entry isn't needed, words are given as **derivatives** of the main headword.

Short entries tell you where to find the main entries for words.

Say words correctly

Easy guides show you how to **pronounce** words in the standard way. Stress the part that is printed bold.

See the key to the pronunciation guide on page viii.

Check your grammar

The **plural** is given for every noun that has a plural form.

Nouns that **do not have plurals** have a label to show this.

For every verb, the **past tense** and the **present participle** (-ing form) is given.

If the verb has an irregular **past participle**, this is also shown.

A **part of speech** (or word class) is given for each headword.

---

ally → tik

A B C D E F G H I J K L M N O P Q R S T U V W X Y Z

ally[1] (say **al**-y) *noun* (*plural* **allies**)
a person or country that agrees to help another person or country, for example in a war

ally[2] (say uh-**ly**) *verb* (**allying, allied**)
to make an agreement with another country or organization to work together and support each other: *Britain **allied** itself to France.*
▸ **allied** (*adjective*): ***allied** nations*

almost (say **awl**-mohst) *adverb*
nearly but not quite: *It's **almost** three o'clock.* ◇ *I **almost** fell into the river!*

alphabetical (say al-fuh-**bet**-i-kuhl) *adjective*
in the order of the alphabet: *Put these words in **alphabetical** order* (= with words beginning with A first, then B, then C, etc.).
▸ **alphabetically** (*adverb*): *The books are listed **alphabetically**.*

am form of **be**

a.m. (say ay-**em**) *abbreviation*
You add this abbreviation to a time to show that it is between midnight and midday: *I start work at 9 **a.m.*** ❶ **a.m.** is short for 'ante meridiem' which means 'before midday' in Latin. ➲ See **p.m.**

caught (say **kawt**) form of **catch**

colonel (say **kur**-nuhl) *noun* (*plural* **colonels**)
an officer of a high level in the army

PRONUNCIATION Notice that the sound of this word is very different from the spelling.

fungus (say **fung**-guhss) *noun* (*plural* **fungi** or **funguses**) (*biology*)
a type of organism that is neither a plant nor an animal, and that lives on **organic** matter. **Mushrooms** and **moulds** are fungi.

furniture (say **furn**-i-tshuh) *noun* (*no plural*)
tables, chairs, beds, etc.: *They've bought some **furniture** for their new house.* ◇ *I'm cleaning all the **furniture** in our flat.*

USAGE **Furniture** does not have a plural. If you are talking about one item, you say **a piece of furniture**.

lend *verb* (**lending, lent**)
to give something to somebody for a short time: *I **lent** the book to Jo.* ◇ *Rick **lent** me his car for an hour.* ➲ See note at **borrow** ➲ SYNONYM **loan**[2]

mow (*rhymes with* **go**) *verb* (**mowing, mowed, has mown**)
to cut grass with a machine: *She is **mowing** the grass.*

2

muzzle (say **muz**-l) *noun* (*plural* **muzzles**)
1 the nose and mouth of some animals such as dogs
2 a leather or wire cover for an animal's mouth to stop it biting
3 the open end of a gun where the bullets come out

myth (say **mith**) *noun* (*plural* **myths**)
1 a very old story: *Greek myths*
2 a story or belief that is not true: *It's a* ***myth*** *that money makes you happy.*

octopus (say **ok**-tuh-puhss) *noun* (*plural* **octopuses**)
a sea animal with eight long parts (called **tentacles**).

octopus

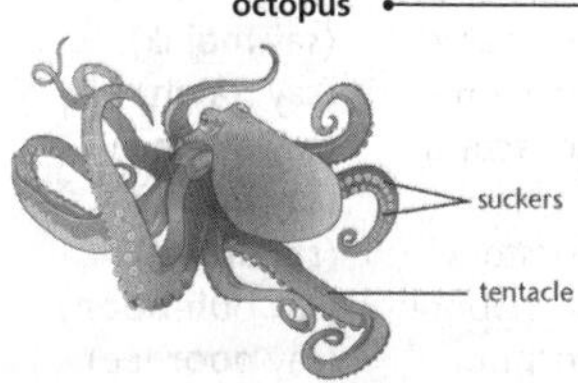

scissors (say **siz**-uhz) *plural noun*
a tool for cutting that has two flat sharp parts that are joined together: *These* ***scissors*** *aren't sharp enough to cut the paper.* ◇ *I need two pairs of* ***scissors****.*

USAGE Be careful! You cannot say 'a scissor' nor 'a scissors'. You say a **pair of scissors**: *I need a* ***pair of scissors*** (or: *I need some scissors*).

sufficient (say suh-**fish**-uhnt) *adjective*
as much or as many as you need or want: *We had* ***sufficient*** *food to last two weeks.*
➲ SYNONYM **enough** ➲ OPPOSITE **insufficient**

sulphur (say **sul**-fuh) *noun* (also **sulfur**) (symbol S) (*no plural*)
a natural yellow substance that smells like bad eggs

SPELLING For many years this word was spelt in two ways: **sulphur** and **sulfur**. Scientists have agreed that in scientific writing the word must be spelt **sulfur**, not **sulphur**.

tik (say **tik**) *noun* (*no plural*) (*S. African, informal*)
a dangerous illegal drug that increases your energy, prevents sleep, and causes violent behaviour ➲ SYNONYM **methamphetamine**
ℹ ORIGIN: 20th century, from the crackling sound that tik makes when it is heated, usually in a thin glass container or a light bulb

Understand what words mean

When a word has more than one meaning, **each meaning** (or sense) is **numbered** to help you find the right one quickly.

Illustrations with labels and captions help to make the meanings of words clear.

Use words correctly

Example sentences and phrases show you how to use words correctly in sentences.

Notes help you to avoid hundreds of common mistakes in **pronunciation, spelling, grammar** and **usage.**

Build your vocabulary

Synonyms and **opposites** help you to write more effectively.

Find out more

Labels tell you if a word is **informal** or **formal,** showing you when it is appropriate to use it.

Notes on **word origins** tell you where words come from (a requirement in the language curriculum) and when they came into English.

The entries on these pages have been drawn together from different pages of the dictionary, to show its features.

Pronunciation

The headwords in the dictionary have guides to the standard way of saying them. Most of these use an easy respelling system. The part of the word that is printed bold should be said with extra stress. Examples are:

- at **chemist** (say **kem**-ist)
- at **psalm** (say **saam**)
- at **pneumatic** (say nyoo-**mat**-ik)
- at **weigh** (say **way**)

In a few cases, it is more helpful to say what the word rhymes with, for example:

- at **barrow** (rhymes with **narrow**)
- at **prow** (rhymes with **cow**)

Where the pronunciation of a short word follows its spelling exactly (as it does with **bag** and **mud**) a guide is unnecessary, and has therefore been left out.

Key to pronunciation guides

a	as in 'camp'	(say **kamp**)
aa	as in 'farm'	(say **faam**)
air	as in 'care'	(say **kair**)
aw	as in 'ball'	(say **bawl**)
ay	as in 'daylight'	(say **day**-lite)
b	as in 'back'	(say **bak**)
ch	as in 'chart'	(say **chaat**)
d	as in 'dark'	(say **daak**)
e	as in 'egg'	(say **eg**)
ee	as in 'feeling'	(say **feel**-ing)
eer	as in 'here'	(say **heer**)
f	as in 'fact'	(say **fakt**)
g	as in 'game'	(say **gaym**)
h	as in 'help'	(say **help**)
i	as in 'dinner'	(say **din**-uh)
ibe	as in 'tribe'	(say **tribe**)
ide	as in 'sideways'	(say **side**-wayz)
ife	as in 'lifebelt'	(say **life**-belt)
ike	as in 'likely'	(say **like**-lee)
ile	as in 'smile'	(say **smile**)
ime	as in 'time'	(say **time**)
ine	as in 'line'	(say **line**)
ise	as in 'nice'	(say **nise**)
ite	as in 'write'	(say **rite**)
ive	as in 'five'	(say **five**)
ize	as in 'baptize'	(say **bap**-tize)
j	as in 'jeans'	(say **jeenz**)
k	as in 'key'	(say **kee**)
kh	as in 'gogga'	(say ***khaw***-*kh*uh)
l	as in 'ladder'	(say **lad**-uh)
m	as in 'magic'	(say **maj**-ik)
n	as in 'name'	(say **naym**)
ng	as in 'acting'	(say **ak**-ting)
o	as in 'box'	(say **bokss**)
oh	as in 'stone'	(say **stohn**)
oo	as in 'baboon'	(say buh-**boon**)
oor	as in 'poorly'	(say **poor**-lee)
ow	as in 'how'	(say **how**)
oy	as in 'boyfriend'	(say **boy**-frend)
p	as in 'pack'	(say **pak**)
r	as in 'rain'	(say **rayn**)
s	as in 'sak'	(say **sak**)
sh	as in 'shade'	(say **shayd**)
ss	as in 'mass'	(say **mass**)
t	as in 'take'	(say **tayk**)
th	as in 'thing'	(say **thing**)
th	as in 'that'	(say ***th*at**)
tsh	as in 'capture'	(say **kap**-tshuh)
u	as in 'buck'	(say **buk**)
uh	as in 'farmer'	(say **faam**-uh)
	and 'abandon'	(say uh-**ban**-duhn)
ur	as in 'furnish'	(say **furn**-ish)
uu	as in 'bush'	(say **b*uu*sh**)
v	as in 'visit'	(say **viz**-it)
w	as in 'wake'	(say **wayk**)
y	as in 'yard'	(say **yaad**)
y	as in 'cry'	(say **kr*y***)
z	as in 'zigzag'	(say **zig**-zag)
zh	as in 'Asian'	(say **ay**-*zh*uhn)

Help! I can't find the word I want

Sometimes it is difficult to know where to look for a word in the dictionary, if it is pronounced differently from the way it is spelt. These are useful tips to remember if you cannot find a word:

if it starts with a **f-** sound	try **ph-**	*pharmacy, phone*
if it starts with a **ge-** sound	try **gue-**	*guess, guest*
if it starts with a **h-** sound	try **wh-**	*who, whole*
if it starts with a **j-** sound	try **g-**	*germ, gym*
if it starts with a **k-** sound	try **c-**	*cart, cat*
if it starts with a **k-** sound	try **ch-**	*chemist, Christmas*
if it starts with a **kw-** sound	try **qu-**	*queen, queer*
if it starts with a **kyoo-** sound	try **cu-**	*cube, curious*
if it starts with a **mi-** sound	try **my-**	*mystery, myth*
if it starts with a **myoo-** sound	try **mu-**	*music, mutate*
if it starts with a **n-** sound	try **gn-**	*gnaw, gnome*
if it starts with a **n-** sound	try **kn-**	*knee, knife*
if it starts with a **nyoo-** sound	try **pn-**	*pneumatic, pneumonia*
if it starts with an **o-** or **ow-** sound	try **h-**	*honest, hour*
if it starts with a **r-** sound	try **wr-**	*wrap, wrong*
if it starts with a **s-** sound	try **c-**	*cell, cent*
if it starts with a **s-** sound	try **ps-**	*psalm, psychology*
if it starts with a **s-** sound	try **sc-**	*scent, science*
if it starts with a **sh-** sound	try **ch-**	*champagne, chandelier*
if it starts with a **shoo-** sound	try **su-**	*sure*
if it starts with a **si-** sound	try **sy-**	*symbol, syrup*
if it starts with a **sk-** sound	try **sch-**	*scheme, school*
if it starts with a **skw-** sound	try **squ-**	*square, squint*
if it starts with a **w-** sound	try **o-**	*one, once*
if it starts with a **wo-** sound	try **wa-**	*wallet, watch*
if it starts with a **yoo-** sound	try **u-**	*unit, utensil*
if it starts with a **z-** sound	try **x-**	*xylophone*

Aa

a (say **uh**) *article* (also **an**)
1 one or any: *Would you like **a** drink?* ◇ ***A** dog has four legs.* ◇ *He's **a** teacher.*
2 each, or for each: *She phones her mother three times **a** week.* ◇ *Calls cost 70c **a** minute.*

WHICH WORD? A or an?
- You use **an** before words that start with a vowel sound. Be careful! It is the sound that is important, not the spelling.
- For example, words like *uniform* and *eucalyptus* take **a** instead of **an**.
- Words that begin with a silent 'h', like *hour*, take **an** instead of **a**.
- Look at these examples: ***a** box, **an** apple, **a** singer, **an** hour, **a** university, **an** NGO, **a** eucalyptus, **an** uncle.*

WHICH WORD? A or the?
- If you say '*I saw **the** dog*' you mean one particular dog – not just any dog.
- If you say '*I saw **a** dog*', you mean any dog.

@ *symbol* (say **at**)
1 (used in email addresses) at: *My email address is susan@hotmail.com.*
2 (used to show the cost of each thing) at: *3 apples @ R2 = R6* ◇ *ten mugs @ R3,50 each*

aardvark (say **aad**-faak) *noun* (*plural* **aardvarks**)
a wild African mammal with a long nose and a long tongue that it uses to catch ants and other small insects that it eats
ℹ **ORIGIN**: 18th century, from South African Dutch *aarde* meaning 'earth' + *vark* meaning 'pig'

abacus (say **ab**-uh-kuhss) *noun* (*plural* **abacuses**)
a frame holding wires with beads that move along them, used for counting

abakhwetha (say ub-uh-**kwair**-tuh) plural of **umkhwetha**

abalone (say **ab**-uh-lohn-ee or **ab**-uh-lohn) *noun* (*plural* **abalones** or **abalone**)
a large shellfish that you can eat
➲ **SYNONYM perlemoen**

abandon[1] (say uh-**ban**-duhn) *verb* (**abandoning, abandoned**)
1 to leave a person or thing completely: *He **abandoned** his broken bike by the road.*
2 to stop doing something before it is finished: *When the rain started, we **abandoned** our game.*

abandon[2] (say uh-**ban**-duhn) *noun* (*no plural*)
a casual and careless manner: *He danced with **abandon**.*

abattoir (say **ab**-uh-twaa) *noun* (*plural* **abattoirs**)
a building where people kill animals and cut up their meat for food

abbey (say **ab**-ee) *noun* (*plural* **abbeys**)
a church and buildings where religious men or women (called **monks** and **nuns**) live or lived

abbr. *abbreviation* **abbreviation**

abbreviate (say uh-**breev**-i-ayt) *verb* (**abbreviating, abbreviated**)
to make a word shorter by not saying or writing some of the letters: *The word 'telephone' is often **abbreviated** to 'phone'.*

abbreviation (say uh-breev-i-**ay**-shuhn) *noun* (*plural* **abbreviations**)
a short form of a word: *TV is an **abbreviation** for 'television'.*

abdicate (say **ab**-di-kayt) *verb* (**abdicating, abdicated**)
1 to choose to stop being a king, queen or chief
2 to stop being responsible for something: *The government **abdicated** its responsibility to the flood victims.*

abdomen (say **ab**-duh-muhn) *noun* (*plural* **abdomens**)
1 the front middle part of your body, which contains your stomach ➲ See illustration at **body**
2 the end part of an insect's body ➲ See illustration at **insect**
► **abdominal** (*adjective*): *an **abdominal** pain*

abduct (say ab-**dukt**) *verb* (**abducting, abducted**)
to take someone away illegally ➲ **SYNONYM kidnap**
► **abduction** (*noun*)

abhor (say uhb-**haw**) *verb* (**abhorring, abhorred**)
to hate: *I **abhor** cruelty to animals.*

ability (say uh-**bil**-uh-tee) *noun* (*plural* **abilities**)
the power and knowledge to do something: *She has the **ability** to pass the exam, but she must work harder.*

abject (say **ab**-jekt) *adjective*
1 very bad and without hope: *The family lived in **abject** poverty.*
2 without any pride or respect for yourself: *He gave an **abject** apology.*

ablaze (say uh-**blayz**) *adjective*
burning strongly, and completely on fire: *The building was **ablaze** when the fire engine got there.*

able (say **ayb**-l) *adjective*
be able to do something to have the power and knowledge to do something: *Will you be **able** to come to the party?* ◇ *Is Thato **able** to swim?* ➲ OPPOSITE **unable** ➲ See **can**[1]

abnormal (say ab-**nawm**-l) *adjective*
different from what is normal or usual, in a way that worries you or that is unpleasant: *They thought the boy's behaviour was **abnormal**.*
▸ **abnormally** (*adverb*): *an **abnormally** heavy rainfall*

aboard (say uh-**bawd**) *adverb, preposition*
on or onto a ship, train, bus or plane: *Welcome **aboard**!* ◇ *Are all the passengers **aboard** the ship?*

abode (say uh-**bohd**) *noun* (*plural* **abodes**) (*formal*)
the place where you live: *This is my humble **abode**.*

abolish (say uh-**bol**-ish) *verb* (**abolishing, abolished**)
to stop or end something by law: *The Americans **abolished** slavery in 1865.*

abolition (say ab-uh-**lish**-uhn) *noun* (*no plural*)
the act of ending a law or system officially: *the **abolition** of smoking in public places*

abominable (say uh-**bom**-in-uhb-l) *adjective*
so bad that it shocks you: *Your behaviour was **abominable**.*

aborigine (say ab-uh-**rij**-uh-nee) *noun* (*plural* **aborigines**)
1 a member of a people that has lived in a place from the earliest times
2 Aborigine (also **Aboriginal**) a member of the people who were the original inhabitants of Australia
▸ **aboriginal** (*adjective*): ***aboriginal** beliefs*

abort (say uh-**bawt**) *verb* (**aborting, aborted**)
1 to end something before it is complete: *He **aborted** the project.*
2 to cause a baby to die before it is born

abortion (say uh-**baw**-shuhn) *noun* (*plural* **abortions**)
1 a medical operation that causes a baby to die inside its mother before it is fully developed: *She had an **abortion**.*
2 a **miscarriage**

abound (say uh-**bownd**) *verb* (**abounding, abounded**)
1 to exist in large numbers: *Flowers **abound** on the mountain.*
2 to contain large numbers of something: *The sea **abounds** with fish.*

about (say uh-**bowt**) *preposition, adverb*
1 a little more or less than or a little before or after: *She's **about** 30 years old.* ◇ *There were **about** 2 000 people at the concert.* ◇ *Go at **about** four o'clock.* ➲ SYNONYM **approximately**
2 of, or on the subject of: *a book **about** cats* ◇ *We talked **about** the problem.*
3 (also **around**) in a lot of different directions or places: *The children were running **about** in the garden.*
4 almost or nearly: *Dinner is just **about** ready.*
be about to do something to be going to do something very soon: *The film is **about** to start.*

above (say uh-**buv**) *preposition, adverb*
1 in or to a higher place, or higher than a person or thing: *We flew **above** the clouds.* ◇ *There is a picture on the wall **above** the fireplace.* ➲ OPPOSITE **below** 1
2 more than a number or price: *children aged ten and **above*** ➲ OPPOSITES **below** 1, **under** 2
above all what is most important, more than any other thing: *He's handsome and intelligent and, **above** all, he's kind!*

abrasive (say uh-**bray**-siv) *adjective*
1 rough and likely to scratch: *Don't use an **abrasive** cleaner on the pot.*
2 (about a person) rude and quite aggressive: *She has an **abrasive** personality.*
▸ **abrasive** (*noun*): *Don't use that cleaner on the pot; it's an **abrasive**.*

abreast (say uh-**brest**) *adverb*
next to or level with somebody and going in the same direction: *The soldiers marched two **abreast**.*

abridge (say uh-**brij**) *verb* (**abridging, abridged**)
to make a book shorter by removing parts of it: *We will **abridge** the book.*
▸ **abridged** (*adjective*) *an **abridged** edition of Macbeth*

abroad (say uh-**brawd**) *adverb*
in or to another country, or overseas: *She lives **abroad**.*

abrupt (say uh-**brupt**) *adjective*
1 sudden and unexpected: *an **abrupt** change of plan*

2 seeming rude and unfriendly: *I'm sorry for being so **abrupt** with you.*
▶ **abruptly** (*adverb*): *The conversation ended **abruptly**.*

abscess (say **ab**-sess) *noun* (*plural* **abscesses**)
a swelling on or in the body, containing a yellow liquid (called **pus**)

abscond (say uhb-**skond**) *verb* (**absconding, absconded**)
to run away from somewhere, sometimes with something you should not take: *They **absconded** with the money.*

absence (say **ab**-suhnss) *noun* (*plural* **absences**)
a time when a person or thing is not there: *I am doing Julie's job in her **absence**.*

absent (say **ab**-suhnt) *adjective*
not there: *He was **absent** from work yesterday because he was ill.* ➲ OPPOSITE **present**[1] 1
➲ SYNONYM **away** 3

absentee (say ab-suhn-**tee**) *noun* (*plural* **absentees**)
a person who is not in the place where they should be: *There were three **absentees** from school today.*

absent-minded (say ab-suhnt-**mine**-did) *adjective*
often forgetting or not noticing things, perhaps because you are thinking about something else: *Grandma is getting more **absent-minded** as she gets older.* ➲ SYNONYM **forgetful**

absolute (say **ab**-suh-loot) *adjective*
complete: *I've never played chess before. I'm an **absolute** beginner.* ◇ *The whole trip was an **absolute** disaster.*

absolutely (say **ab**-suh-loot-lee) *adverb*
completely: *The bottle is **absolutely** empty.*

absorb (say uhb-**zawb**) *verb* (**absorbing, absorbed**)
to take in something such as liquid or heat, and hold it: *The dry ground **absorbed** all the rain.*
ℹ ORIGIN: 15th century, from Latin *absorbere*, from *ab-* meaning 'from' + *sorbere* meaning 'suck in'

absorbent (say uhb-**zaw**-buhnt) *adjective*
able to take in and hold something, especially liquid: *An **absorbent** cloth soaks up water.*

absorbing (say uhb-**zawb**-ing) *adjective*
very interesting: *an **absorbing** book*

abstain (say uhb-**stayn**) *verb* (**abstaining, abstained**)
1 to stop yourself from doing something that you enjoy: *I'll **abstain** from watching TV.*
2 not to vote for something: *In the class vote, 21 people said 'yes', 22 said 'no', and three **abstained**.*

abstinence (say **ab**-stin-uhnss) *noun* (*no plural*)
not doing or having something that you enjoy: *The doctor advised total **abstinence** from alcohol.*

abstract[1] (say **ab**-strakt) *adjective*
1 about an idea, not a real thing: ***abstract** thought*
2 not like a real thing: *an **abstract** painting*

abstract[2] (say **ab**-strakt) *noun* (*plural* **abstracts**)
a summary: *Write an **abstract** of your essay.*

absurd (say uhb-**surd**) *adjective*
so silly that it makes you laugh: *The guards look **absurd** in that new uniform.* ◇ *Don't be **absurd**! I can't possibly do all this work in one day.*
➲ SYNONYM **ridiculous**

abundant (say uh-**bun**-duhnt) *adjective*
existing in such quantities that there is more than enough: *an **abundant** supply of water.*
▶ **abundance** (*noun*): *an **abundance** of food*

abuse[1] (say uh-**byooz**) *verb* (**abusing, abused**)
1 to use something in a wrong or bad way: *The manager often **abuses** her power.*
2 to say rude things to somebody: *The player got a red card for **abusing** the referee.*
3 to be cruel or unkind to somebody: *The children were **abused** by their father.*

abuse[2] (say uh-**byooss**) *noun* (*no plural*)
1 using something in a wrong or bad way: *the dangers of drug **abuse***
2 rude words: *The truck driver shouted **abuse** at the cyclist.* ◇ *racial **abuse***
3 being cruel or unkind to somebody: *The child had suffered verbal and physical **abuse**.*

abysmal (say uh-**biz**-muhl) *adjective*
very bad: *Your homework is **abysmal**!*

abyss (say uh-**biss**) *noun* (*plural* **abysses**)
a very deep hole that seems to have no bottom

AC (say ay-**see**) *noun*
a flow of electricity that changes direction regularly many times a second ℹ **AC** is short for 'alternating current'. ➲ See **DC**

acacia (say uh-**kay**-shuh) *noun* (*plural* **acacias**)
a tree or shrub of warm climates with yellow or white flowers. It typically has thorns.

academic (say ak-uh-**dem**-ik) *adjective*
connected with education, especially in schools and universities: *Our **academic** year begins in January.*

academy (say uh-**kad**-uh-mee) *noun* (*plural* **academies**)
1 a school or college for special training: *a language **academy***

2 (also **Academy**) an official group of people who are important in art, science or literature: *South African **Academy** of Engineering*

a cappella (say aah ka-**pel**-uh) *adjective, adverb* (*music*)
making music with singing, without musical instruments: *an **a cappella** concert*

accelerate (say uhk-**sel**-uh-rayt) *verb* (**accelerating, accelerated**)
to go faster or to make something go faster: ***Accelerate** and pass that car.*
▸ **acceleration** (*noun*)

accelerator (say uhk-**sel**-uh-ray-tuh) *noun* (*plural* **accelerators**)
(in a vehicle) the **pedal**[1] that you press when you want the vehicle to go faster: *She put her foot down on the **accelerator** and overtook the bus.*

accent (say **ak**-sent) *noun* (*plural* **accents**)
1 the way a person from a certain place or country speaks a language: *She speaks English with an Afrikaans **accent**.*
2 saying one word or part of a word more strongly than another: *In the word 'because', the **accent** is on the second part of the word.*
3 (in writing) a mark, usually above a letter, that changes the sound of the letter: *Café has an **accent** on the 'e'.*

accept (say uhk-**sept**) *verb* (**accepting, accepted**)
1 to say 'yes' when somebody asks you to have or do something: *I **accepted** the invitation to his party.* ➲ OPPOSITE **refuse**[1]
2 to believe that something is true: *She can't **accept** that her son is dead.*

SPELLING Be careful! Don't confuse **accept** and **except**, which sound similar but have different spellings and different meanings.

acceptable (say uhk-**sep**-tuhb-l) *adjective*
allowed by most people as being good enough: *It's not **acceptable** to make so many mistakes.*

acceptance (say uhk-**sep**-tuhnss) *noun* (*no plural*)
taking something that somebody offers you or asks you to have: *Her quick **acceptance** of the job offer surprised me.* ➲ OPPOSITE **refusal**

access[1] (say **ak**-sess) *noun* (*no plural*)
a way to go into a place or to use something: *We don't have **access** to the river from our garden.* ◇ *Do you have **access** to a computer?*

access[2] (say **ak**-sess) *verb* (**accessing, accessed**) (*computing*)
to find information on a computer: *Click on the icon to **access** a file.*

accessible (say uhk-**sess**-uhb-l) *adjective*
1 possible to be reached: *The park is **accessible** by dirt road.*
2 easy to understand, get or use: *This book makes maths **accessible** to learners.*
▸ **accessibility** (*noun*): *the **accessibility** of a good textbook*

accessory (say uhk-**sess**-suh-ree) *noun* (*plural* **accessories**)
1 an extra item that is added to something and is useful or attractive but not essential: *bicycle **accessories***
2 a thing that you can wear or carry that matches your clothes, for example a belt or a bag
3 (in law) a person who helps somebody to commit a crime: *He was charged with being an **accessory** to murder.*

accident (say **ak**-si-duhnt) *noun* (*plural* **accidents**)
something bad that happens unexpectedly or by chance: *I had a car **accident** and two people were hurt.* ◇ *I'm sorry I broke your watch – it was an **accident**.*
by accident by chance, not because you planned it: *I took Jane's book by **accident**. I thought it was mine.*

accidental (say ak-si-**den**-tuhl) *adjective*
that happens by chance and is not planned: *Police do not know whether the plane crash was **accidental** or caused by a bomb.*
▸ **accidentally** (*adverb*): *He **accidentally** broke the window.*

acclaim (say uh-**klaym**) *verb* (**acclaiming, acclaimed**)
to say that something or someone is excellent: *This novel has been **acclaimed** as the best book of the year.*
▸ **acclaim** (*noun*): *He's received **acclaim** for his work.*

acclimatize (say uh-**klime**-uh-tize) *verb* (**acclimatizing, acclimatized**) (also **acclimatise**)
to get used to a new climate or situation so that it is not a problem: *We **acclimatized** to the new school quickly.*

accommodate (say uh-**kom**-uh-dayt) *verb* (**accommodating, accommodated**)
1 to have enough space for a certain number of people: *This room can **accommodate** three people.*
2 to give a person a place to stay: *You will be **accommodated** in tents.*
3 to do or give a person what they want or need: *We will try to **accommodate** your requests.*
▸ **accommodating** (*adjective*): *She is such an **accommodating** person.*

accommodation (say uh-kom-uh-**day**-shuhn) *noun* (*no plural*)
a place to stay or live: *It's difficult to find cheap **accommodation** in Johannesburg.*

USAGE **Accommodation** has no plural. We cannot say 'cheap accommodations' or 'I'll help you find an accommodation'. We can say *'I'll help you to find **accommodation**'*.

SPELLING Remember! You spell **accommodation** with **cc** and **mm**.

accompany (say uh-**kum**-puh-nee) *verb* (**accompanying, accompanied**)
1 (*formal*) to go with somebody to a place: *Four teachers **accompanied** the class on their trip.*
2 to happen at the same time as something else: *Lightning is **accompanied** by thunder.*
3 to play music while somebody sings or plays another instrument: *You sing and I'll **accompany** you on the piano.*

accomplice (say uh-**kum**-pliss) *noun* (*plural* **accomplices**)
a person who helps another person commit a crime or do something bad: *Matt and two **accomplices** stole the car.*

accomplish (say uh-**kum**-plish) *verb* (**accomplishing, accomplished**)
to succeed in doing something difficult that you planned to do: *The first part of the plan has been safely **accomplished**.* ➲ SYNONYM **achieve**

accord (say uh-**kawd**) *noun* (*plural* **accords**)
an agreement, especially between two countries: *The two sides signed a peace **accord** last July.*
of your own accord because you want to, not because somebody has asked you: *She left the job of her own **accord**.*

according to (say uh-**kaw**-ding tuh) *preposition*
as somebody or something says: ***According to** Lunga, this film is really good.* ◇ *The church was built in 1895, **according to** this book.*

accordion (say uh-**kaw**-di-uhn) *noun* (*plural* **accordions**)
a musical instrument that you hold with both hands and pull and squeeze while pressing buttons

accost (say uh-**kost**) *verb* (**accosting, accosted**)
to walk up to and speak to someone in a way that is rude or aggressive: *The man **accosted** me in the street.*

account¹ (say uh-**kownt**) *noun* (*plural* **accounts**)
1 words that somebody says or writes about something that happened: *She gave the police a full **account** of the robbery.*
2 an arrangement with a bank which lets you keep your money there: *I paid the money into my **account**.*
3 (usually **accounts**) lists of all the money that a person or business receives and pays: *Who keeps the **accounts** for your business?*
on account of something because of something: *Our school was closed on **account** of bad weather.*
on no account not for any reason: *On no **account** should you walk home on your own.*
take account of something, take something into account to remember one or many things when you are deciding something: *Judges must take all the facts into **account**.*

account² (say uh-**kownt**) *verb* (**accounting, accounted**)
account for something
1 to explain or give a reason for something: *How can you **account** for the missing pieces?*
2 to be a particular amount or part of something: *Sales to African countries **accounted** for 60% of our total sales last year.*

accountable (say uh-**kownt**-uhb-l) *adjective*
responsible or expected to explain or give a reason for something: *Who is **accountable** for the mess in the classroom?*
▸ **accountability** (*noun*)

accountant (say uh-**kownt**-uhnt) *noun* (*plural* **accountants**)
a person whose job is to calculate and keep records of the money that people or businesses receive and pay: *Zanele is an **accountant**.*

accounting (say uh-**kownt**-ing) *noun* (*no plural*)
1 the work of an **accountant**: *A system of **accounting** or bookkeeping helps a business to organize its financial data properly.*
2 a subject that students study to learn about managing financial accounts

accumulate (say uh-**kyoom**-yuh-layt) *verb* (**accumulating, accumulated**)
1 to collect: *We **accumulated** a lot of books.*
2 to increase over time: *The interest in my savings account **accumulated** during the year.*
▸ **accumulation** (*noun*): *There was an **accumulation** of post on the table.*

accuracy (say **ak**-yuh-ruh-see) *noun* (*no plural*)
the quality of being exactly right, with no mistakes: *drawn with great **accuracy***

accurate (say **ak**-yuh-ruht) *adjective*
exactly right, with no mistakes: *He gave an **accurate** description of the thief.*
➲ OPPOSITE **inaccurate**
▸ **accurately** (*adverb*): *The map was **accurately** drawn.*

A B C D E F G H I J K L M N O P Q R S T U V W X Y Z

A B C D E F G H I J K L M N O P Q R S T U V W X Y Z

accusation (say **ak**-kyoo-zay-shuhn) *noun* (*plural* **accusations**)
a statement saying that somebody has done something wrong: *The **accusations** were not true.*

accuse (say uh-**kyooz**) *verb* (**accusing, accused**)
to say that somebody has done something wrong or broken the law: *His classmates **accused** him of cheating in the exam.* ◇ *She was **accused** of murder.* ◇ *Don't **accuse** me!*
▸ **accusing** (*adjective*): *She gave him an **accusing** look.*

accustomed (say uh-**kuss**-tuhm-d) *adjective*
familiar with something and accepting it as normal or usual: *My eyes slowly grew **accustomed** to the dark.*

ace (say **ayss**) *noun* (*plural* **aces**)
1 a **playing card** that has only one picture on it. It has either the lowest or the highest value in a game of cards: *the **ace** of hearts*
2 (*informal*) a person who is very good at something: *a soccer **ace***
3 in tennis, a first hit that is so good that your opponent cannot reach the ball: *She served an **ace**.*

acetylene (say uh-**set**-uh-leen) *noun* (*no plural*)
a gas that burns with a very hot bright flame, often used for cutting or joining metal: *an **acetylene** torch*

ache[1] (say **ayk**) *verb* (**aching, ached**)
to hurt or to give you pain: *She was **aching** all over.* ◇ *My legs **ached** after the long walk.*

ache[2] (say **ayk**) *noun* (*plural* **aches**)
a pain that lasts for a long time: *If you eat all those sweets, you'll get a stomach **ache**.*

WORD BUILDING We can combine **ache** with some parts of the body, for example **earache**, **headache**, **stomach ache** and **toothache**.

achieve (say uh-**cheev**) *verb* (**achieving, achieved**)
to do or finish something well after trying hard: *He worked hard and **achieved** his aim of becoming a doctor.*
▸ **achiever** (*noun*): *She's a top **achiever** in her class.*

achievement (say uh-**cheev**-muhnt) *noun* (*plural* **achievements**)
something that somebody has done after trying hard: *Winning the marathon was her greatest **achievement**.*

acid (say **ass**-id) *noun* (*plural* **acids**) (*science*)
a substance with a **pH** less than seven. Strong acids can burn things and make holes in metal: *hydrochloric **acid*** ➲ See **alkali**, **base**[1] 5
▸ **acid** (*adjective*): ***acid** soil*

acid rain *noun* (*no plural*)
rain that has chemicals in it from factories, for example. It causes damage to trees, rivers and buildings.

acknowledge (say uhk-**nol**-ij) *verb* (**acknowledging, acknowledged**)
1 to agree or accept that something is true: *He **acknowledged** that he had made a mistake.*
2 to write to somebody who has sent you a present or a letter, to say that you have received it: *She never **acknowledged** my letter.*
▸ **acknowledgement** (*noun*): *I received **acknowledgement** of my letter.*

acne (say **ak**-nee) *noun* (*no plural*)
a skin problem, common among young people, that causes red spots, especially on the face

acorn (say **ay**-kawn) *noun* (*plural* **acorns**)
a small nut with a base like a cup. **Acorns** grow on **oak** trees.

acoustic (say uh-**kooss**-tik) *adjective*
1 relating to sound or hearing
2 a musical instrument that is not electric: *an **acoustic** guitar*

acquaint (say uh-**kwaynt**) *verb* (**acquainting, acquainted**)
to make someone familiar with something: *I **acquainted** myself with my new computer.*
▸ **acquainted** (*adjective*): *I'm not **acquainted** with my new neighbours yet.*

acquaintance (say uh-**kwayn**-tuhnss) *noun* (*plural* **acquaintances**)
a person who you know a little but who is not a close friend: *He's an **acquaintance** of mine.*

acquire (say uh-**kwy**-uh) *verb* (**acquiring, acquired**) (*formal*)
to get or buy something: *I **acquired** an old coat from my uncle.*

acquit (say uh-**kwit**) *verb* (**acquitting, acquitted**)
to say formally in a court that someone is not guilty of a crime: *The court **acquitted** her of the murder.*
▸ **acquittal** (*noun*): *The lawyer was very pleased with the **acquittal**.*

acrid (say **ak**-rid) *adjective*
having a strong and bitter unpleasant smell or taste

acrimonious (say ak-ri-**moh**-ni-uhss) *adjective*
with angry and bitter feelings or words: *Arnold had an **acrimonious** relationship with his cousin.*
▸ **acrimoniously** (*adverb*)

acrobat (say **ak**-ruh-bat) *noun* (*plural* **acrobats**)
a person who performs difficult acts such as walking on high ropes, especially in a **circus**

acronym (say **ak**-ruh-nim) *noun* (*plural* **acronyms**)
a short word that is made up from the first letters of a group of words: *AIDS is an* ***acronym*** *for Acquired Immune Deficiency Syndrome.*

across (say uh-**kross**) *adverb, preposition*
1 from one side to the other side of something: *We walked* ***across*** *the playground.* ◇ *A smile spread* ***across*** *her face.* ◇ *The river was about twenty metres* ***across****.*
2 on the other side of something: *There is a bank just* ***across*** *the road.*

acrostic (say uh-**kross**-tik) *noun* (*plural* **acrostics**)
a word game or poem where the first or last letters of each line make a word or words

acrylic (say a-**kril**-ik) *noun* (*plural* **acrylics**)
an artificial material that is used in making clothes and paint

act[1] (say **akt**) *verb* (**acting, acted**)
1 to do something, or to behave in a certain way: *Stop* ***acting*** *like a child!* ◇ *Doctors* ***acted*** *quickly to save the boy's life after the accident.*
2 to play the role of somebody else in a play, film or television programme ➲ SYNONYM **perform** 2
act as something to do the job of another person, usually for a short time: *He* ***acted*** *as manager while his boss was ill.*

act[2] (say **akt**) *noun*
1 (*plural* **acts**) a thing that you do: *an* ***act*** *of kindness*
2 (*plural* **acts**) one of the main parts of a play or an **opera**: *This play has five* ***acts****.*
3 (*plural* **acts**) a law that a government makes: *an* ***act*** *of Parliament*
4 (*no plural*) behaviour that hides your true feelings: *She seems very happy, but she's just putting on an* ***act****.*
in the act (of doing something) while doing something wrong: *I caught him in the* ***act*** *of stealing the money.*

acting (say **ak**-ting) *noun* (*no plural*)
being in plays or films: *Have you ever done any* ***acting****?*

action (say **ak**-shuhn) *noun*
1 (*no plural*) doing things, especially for a particular purpose: *Now is the time for* ***action****!* ◇ *If we don't take* ***action*** *quickly, it'll be too late!*
2 (*plural* **actions**) something that you do: *The little girl copied her mother's* ***actions****.*
3 (*no plural*) exciting things that happen: *I like films with a lot of* ***action*** *in them.* ◇ *an* ***action****-packed film*
in action doing something, or working: *We watched the machine in* ***action****.*

activate (say **ak**-ti-vayt) *verb* (**activating, activated**)
to make something start working: *Don't forget to* ***activate*** *the alarm before you go out.*

active (say **ak**-tiv) *adjective*
1 describing a person who is always busy and able to do a lot of things: *My grandmother is 75 but she's still very* ***active****.* ➲ OPPOSITE **inactive**
2 (*grammar*) when the person or thing doing the action is the subject of a sentence or verb: *In the sentence 'The dog bit him', the verb is an* ***active*** *verb.* ➲ OPPOSITE **passive[1]**

activist (say **ak**-ti-vist) *noun* (*plural* **activists**)
a person who takes action to encourage political or social change: *Environmental* ***activists*** *protested against mining.*

activity (say ak-**tiv**-uh-tee) *noun*
1 (*no plural*) a lot of things happening and people doing things: *On the day of the festival there was a lot of* ***activity*** *in the streets.*
2 (*plural* **activities**) something that you do, usually regularly and because you enjoy it: *At school we do a range of sporting* ***activities****.*

actor (say **ak**-tuh) *noun* (*plural* **actors**)
a man, woman or child who acts in plays, films or television programmes

actress (say **ak**-truhss) *noun* (*plural* **actresses**)
a woman or girl who acts in plays, films or television programmes

actual (say **ak**-tshuu-uhl) *adjective*
that really happened or is real: *The* ***actual*** *damage to the car was not as bad as we'd feared.* ◇ *They seemed to be good friends but in* ***actual*** *fact they hated each other.*

actually (say **ak**-tshuu-uh-lee) *adverb*
1 really, in fact: *You don't* ***actually*** *believe her, do you?* ◇ *I can't believe I'm* ***actually*** *going to Australia!*
2 a word that you use to disagree politely or when you say something new: *I don't agree. I thought the film was very good,* ***actually****.*

acupuncture (say **ak**-yuu-punk-tshuh) *noun* (*no plural*)
a way of healing a person by putting thin needles into certain parts of their body
► **acupuncturist** (*noun*): *The* ***acupuncturist*** *used needles to treat my neck pain.*

A B C D E F G H I J K L M N O P Q R S T U V W X Y Z

acute (say uh-**kyoot**) *adjective*
very serious or very great: *an **acute** shortage of food*
▸ **acutely** (*adverb*): *I felt the pain **acutely**.*

acute angle *noun* (*plural* **acute angles**) (*maths*)
an angle of less than 90 degrees. ➲ See illustration at **angle** ➲ See **obtuse angle**

AD (say ay-**dee**) *abbreviation*
used in dates for showing the number of years after the time when Jesus Christ was born: *They invaded in* AD *150.* ❶ AD is short for the Latin words 'anno domini' meaning 'in the year of the Lord'. ➲ See **BC**, **CE**

USAGE Note that AD comes before the date: *The bridge was built in* AD *390*. Compare this with BC, which you write after the date: *She was born in 540* BC.

ad (say **ad**) *noun* (*plural* **ads**) (*informal*) short for **advertisement**

adamant (say **ad**-uh-muhnt) *adjective*
very sure or certain: *She was **adamant** that the holiday was on a Thursday.*

adapt (say uh-**dapt**) *verb* (**adapting**, **adapted**)
1 to change the way that you do things because you are in a new situation: *He has **adapted** very well to being at a new school.*
2 to change something so that you can use it in a different way: *The car was **adapted** for use as a taxi.*
▸ **adaptation** (*noun*): *This film is an **adaptation** of a book.*

adaptable (say uh-**dap**-tuhb-l) *adjective*
able to change in a new situation: *He's **adaptable** and will soon get used to his new school.*

adaptor (say uh-**dap**-tuh) *noun* (*plural* **adaptors**)
a device that allows you to connect more than one piece of electrical equipment to an electricity supply point

add (say **ad**) *verb* (**adding**, **added**)
1 to put something with something else: *Mix the flour with the milk and then **add** the eggs.* ◇ *Add your name to the list.*
2 to put numbers together so that you get a total: *If you **add** 2 and 5 together, you get 7.* ◇ *Add R10 to the total.* ➲ OPPOSITE **subtract**
3 to say something more: *'Go away – and don't come back again,' she **added**.*
add up to find the total of several numbers: *The waiter hadn't **added** up the bill correctly.*

addendum (say uh-**den**-duhm) *noun* (*plural* **addenda**)
extra information that is added, especially to a book

adder (say **ad**-uh) *noun* (*plural* **adders**)
a type of poisonous snake: *We get puff **adders** and night **adders** in South Africa.*

addict (say **ad**-ikt) *noun* (*plural* **addicts**)
a person who cannot stop wanting something that is bad for them: *a drug **addict***

addicted (say uh-**dik**-tuhd) *adjective*
not able to stop wanting something that is bad for you: *He is **addicted** to heroin.*

addictive (say uh-**dik**-tiv) *adjective*
difficult to stop taking or doing: *Many drugs are **addictive**, which makes them so dangerous.*

addition (say uh-**di**-shuhn) *noun*
1 (*no plural*) putting numbers together: *We learnt **addition** and subtraction at primary school.*
2 (*plural* **additions**) a thing or person that is added to something: *They have a new **addition** to their family* (= a new baby).
in addition, in addition to something as well as: *He speaks five languages in **addition** to English.*
▸ **additional** (*adjective*): *A new baby means **additional** expenses.*

additive (say **ad**-uh-tiv) *noun* (*plural* **additives**)
something that is added to something else in small amounts: *Some foods contain **additives** like flavouring or colouring.*

address[1] (say uh-**dress**) *noun* (*plural* **addresses**)
1 the number of the building and the name of the street and town where somebody lives or works: *Her **address** is 18 Hill Street, Nelspruit 1201.* ◇ *Are you still living at that **address**?*
2 (*computing*) a group of words and symbols that tells you where you can find somebody or something using a computer: *What's your email **address**?* ◇ *a website **address***

SPELLING Remember! You spell **address** with **dd** and **ss**.

PRONUNCIATION When you say **address**, the stress is on the second syllable in standard English.

address[2] (say uh-**dress**) *verb* (**addressing**, **addressed**)
1 to write on a letter or package the name and address of the person you are sending it to: *The letter was **addressed** to Alison Waters.*
2 to make a formal speech to a group of people: *The President will **address** the assembly.*

adequate (say **ad**-i-kwuht) *adjective*
enough for what you need: *They are very poor and do not have* ***adequate*** *food or clothing.*
➲ OPPOSITE **inadequate**
▸ **adequately** (*adverb*): *They were* ***adequately*** *paid.*

adhere (say ad-**heer**) *verb* (**adhering, adhered**)
1 to stick to something: *Make sure your pictures* ***adhere*** *to the poster.*
2 to follow a rule: ***Adhere*** *to the rules.*

adhesion (say ad-**hee**-zhuhn) *noun* (*no plural*)
the process of sticking or the ability to stick to something

adhesive (say ad-**hee**-siv) *noun* (*plural* **adhesives**)
a substance that makes things stick together: *Use* ***adhesive*** *to stick the photos to your poster.*
▸ **adhesive** (*adjective*): *I need* ***adhesive*** *tape to wrap the presents.*

adjacent (say uh-**jay**-suhnt) *adjective*
next to or near something: *The police station is* ***adjacent*** *to the bus station.*

adjective (say **aj**-ek-tiv) *noun* (*plural* **adjectives**) (*grammar*)
a word that you use with a noun or pronoun, that tells you more about it: *In the sentence 'This soup is hot', 'hot' is an* ***adjective***. ➲ See Study pages 4 and 10

adjourn (say uh-**jurn**) *verb* (**adjourning, adjourned**)
to stop something, especially a meeting or a trial, for a short time and start it again later: *The meeting was* ***adjourned*** *until the following week.*

adjudicate (say uh-**joo**-di-kayt) *verb* (**adjudicating, adjudicated**)
1 to judge a competition
2 to decide who is right in an argument
▸ **adjudication** (*noun*): *the* ***adjudication*** *of a contest* ▸ **adjudicator** (*noun*): *an independent* ***adjudicator***

adjust (say uh-**just**) *verb* (**adjusting, adjusted**)
to make a small change to something, to make it better: *You can* ***adjust*** *the height of this chair.*
▸ **adjustment** (*noun*): *a price* ***adjustment***

ad lib (say ad **lib**) *verb* (**ad libbing, ad libbed**)
to do or say something without preparing first: *Celia left the notes for her speech at home, so she had to* ***ad lib***. ➲ SYNONYM **improvise** 2
▸ **ad lib** (*adjective*): *It was an* ***ad lib*** *performance.*

administer (say ad-**min**-i-strayt) *verb* (**administering, administered**)
1 to control or manage something: *The secretary* ***administers*** *the sports teams.*
2 to give someone something, especially medicine: *The nurse* ***administered*** *medicine to the patient.*

administration (say ad-min-i-**stray**-shuhn) *noun* (*no plural*)
controlling or managing something, for example a business, an office or a school

administrator (say ad-**min**-i-stray-tuh) *noun* (*plural* **administrators**)
a person whose job is to organize or manage a system or business: *a sports* ***administrator***

admiral (say **ad**-muh-ruhl) *noun* (*plural* **admirals**)
the most important officer in the navy

admire (say ad-**my**-uh) *verb* (**admiring, admired**)
to think or say that somebody or something is very good: *I* ***admire*** *you for doing such a difficult job.* ◇ *He was* ***admiring*** *the view from the window.*
▸ **admiration** (*noun*): *I have great* ***admiration*** *for her work.*

admission (say uhd-**mish**-uhn) *noun*
1 (*no plural*) (also **admittance**) allowing somebody to go into a school, club or public place: *There is no* ***admission*** *to the park after 8 p.m.* ◇ *All those who were not wearing a tie were refused* ***admission*** *to the club.*
2 (*no plural*) the amount of money that you have to pay to go into a place: ***Admission*** *to the zoo is R45.*
3 (*plural* **admissions**) when you agree that you did something wrong or bad: *an* ***admission*** *of guilt*

admit (say uhd-**mit**) *verb* (**admitting, admitted**)
1 to say that you have done something wrong or that something bad is true: *He* ***admitted*** *stealing the money.* ◇ *I* ***admit*** *that I made a mistake.* ➲ OPPOSITE **deny**
2 to allow somebody or something to go into a place: *This ticket* ***admits*** *one person to the museum.*

ado (say uh-**doo**) *noun* (*no plural*)
without further ado without delaying: *We left without further* ***ado***.

adolescence (say ad-uh-**less**-uhnss) *noun* (*no plural*)
the period of a person's life between being a child and becoming an adult

adolescent (say ad-uh-**less**-uhnt) *noun* (*plural* **adolescents**)
a young person who is developing from a child into an adult ➲ SYNONYM **teenager**

adopt (say uh-**dopt**) *verb* (**adopting, adopted**)
to take the child of another person into your

family and treat them as your own child by law: *They **adopted** him after his parents died.*

adore (say uh-**daw**) *verb* (**adoring, adored**)
to love somebody or something very much: *She **adores** her grandchildren.*

adrenalin (say uh-**dren**-uh-lin) *noun* (*no plural*)
a substance that your body produces that makes your heart go faster when you are very frightened, excited or angry: *I felt an **adrenalin** rush when the elephant charged our car.*

adrift (say uh-**drift**) *adjective*
floating on water and not tied to anything or controlled by anything: *We saw a boat **adrift** at sea.*

adult (say **ad**-ult) *noun* (*plural* **adults**)
a person or an animal that has grown to the full size: ***Adults** as well as children will enjoy this film.*
▸ **adult** (*adjective*): *an **adult** elephant* ◇ ***adult** education*

adultery (say uh-**dul**-tuh-ree) *noun* (*no plural*)
sex between a person who is married and another person who they are not married to: *They committed **adultery**.*

advance[1] (say uhd-**vaanss**) *noun* (*plural* **advances**)
progress or a new development in something: *major **advances** in computer technology*
in advance before something happens: *You should book tickets for the concert well in **advance**.*

advance[2] (say uhd-**vaanss**) *verb* (**advancing, advanced**)
1 to move forward: *The army **advanced** overnight.*
2 to make progress: *Discover how technology **advanced** farming methods.*

advanced (say uhd-**vaanst**) *adjective*
1 of or for somebody who is already good at something: *an **advanced** learner* ◇ *This Maths book is very **advanced**.*
2 highly developed: ***advanced** technology*

advantage (say uhd-**vaan**-tij) *noun* (*plural* **advantages**)
something that helps you or that is useful: *There are many **advantages** to living close to school.* ➲ OPPOSITE **disadvantage**
take advantage of something to make good use of something to help yourself: *Buy now and take **advantage** of our prices!*

adventure (say uhd-**ven**-tshuh) *noun* (*plural* **adventures**)
something exciting that you do or that happens to you: *She wrote a book about her **adventures** in Africa.*

adventurous (say uhd-**ven**-tshuh-ruhss) *adjective*
describing a person who likes to do exciting, dangerous things

adverb (say **ad**-vurb) *noun* (*plural* **adverbs**)
(*grammar*)
a word that tells you how, when or where something happens: *In the sentence 'Please speak slowly', 'slowly' is an **adverb**.* ➲ See Study pages 4 and 11

adverse (say **ad**-vurss) *adjective*
making something difficult: *Your fighting has an **adverse** effect on our teamwork.*

advert (say **ad**-vurt) *noun* (*plural* **adverts**)
(*informal*) short for **advertisement**

advertise (say **ad**-vuh-tize) *verb* (**advertising, advertised**)
to put information in a newspaper, on television or on a wall to make people want to buy something or do something: *I saw those trainers **advertised** in a magazine.* ◇ *It's very expensive to **advertise** on television.*

advertisement (say ad-**vur**-tiss-muhnt) *noun* (*plural* **advertisements**)
information in a newspaper, on television, on the Internet or on a wall that makes people want to buy something or do something: *an **advertisement** for a new kind of chocolate bar*

> PRONUNCIATION Notice how to say **advertisement**. There is no **-ize** sound here, though you do use **-ize** when saying **advertise**.

advertising (say **ad**-vuh-tize-ing) *noun* (*no plural*)
telling people about things to buy: *He works in **advertising**.* ◇ *The magazine gets a lot of money from **advertising**.*

advice (say uhd-**vise**) *noun* (*no plural*)
words that you say to help somebody decide what to do: *The book gives some good **advice** on travelling abroad.* ◇ *I took the doctor's **advice*** (= I did what the doctor told me to do) *and stayed in bed.*

> SPELLING Be careful! Don't confuse **advice**, which is a noun, with **advise**, which is a verb: *She gave me some useful **advice**.* ◇ *He **advised** me to tell the police.*

advise (say uhd-**vize**) *verb* (**advising, advised**)
to tell somebody what you think they should do: *The doctor **advised** him to lose weight.*
▸ **adviser** (*noun*): *an **adviser** to the President*

advocate[1] (say **ad**-vuh-kayt) *verb* (**advocating, advocated**)
to recommend something: *He **advocates** sport at schools.*

advocate[2] (say **ad**-vuh-kuht) *noun* (*plural* **advocates**)
1 a person who supports something: *He is an **advocate** of children's rights.*
2 a lawyer who defends somebody in the higher courts: *My grandfather's **advocate** told him to tell the truth in court.* ➲ See **attorney**

aerate (say **air**-rayt) *verb* (**aerating, aerated**)
to get air into something: *Earthworms help to **aerate** the soil.*

aerial[1] (say **air**-ri-uhl) *noun* (*plural* **aerials**)
a long metal **rod**, usually on a building or car, that receives radio or television signals

aerial[2] (say **air**-ri-uhl) *adjective*
in or from the air: *We took **aerial** photographs from the helicopter.*

aerobics (say air-**roh**-bikss) (*no plural*)
physical exercises that make the heart and lungs stronger, and that people often do in classes, with music: ***Aerobics** is fun!*

aerodynamic (say air-roh-dy-**nam**-ik) *adjective*
shaped in a way that makes something travel faster through air: *Racing cars are more **aerodynamic** than they used to be.*
▸ **aerodynamics** (*noun*): *This bike's shape is better for **aerodynamics**.*

aeronautics (say air-ruh-**naw**-tikss) (*no plural*)
the science and practice of building or flying aircraft. ***Aeronautics** is a practical science.*
▸ **aeronautical** (*adjective*): *Martin wants to be an **aeronautical** engineer.*

aerophone (say **air**-ruh-fohn) *noun* (*plural* **aerophones**) (*music*)
a wind instrument

aeroplane (say **air**-ruh-playn) *noun* (*plural* **aeroplanes**)
a vehicle with wings and one or more engines that can fly through the air ➲ See **plane**[1]

aerosol (say **air**-ruh-sol) *noun* (*plural* **aerosols**)
a container in which liquid is kept under pressure. When you press a button the liquid comes out in a fine spray.

aesthetic (say ess-**thet**-ik) *adjective*
about beauty or art: *She has good **aesthetic** sense.*
▸ **aesthetics** (*plural noun*): *The **aesthetics** in this room are modern.*

affair (say uh-**fair**) *noun*
1 (*plural* **affairs**) something that happens, or an event: *The wedding was a very quiet **affair**.*
2 affairs (*plural noun*) important events and situations: *the Minister of Foreign **Affairs*** ◇ *We talked about current **affairs*** (= the political and social events that are happening at the present time).
3 (*no plural*) something private that you do not want other people to know about: *What happened between us is my **affair**. I don't want to talk about it.*
4 (*plural* **affairs**) a sexual relationship between two people, usually one that is secret: *Her husband was having an **affair**.*

affect (say uh-**fekt**) *verb* (**affecting, affected**)
to make something or somebody change in a particular way, especially a bad way: *Smoking can **affect** your health.* ◇ *His parents' divorce **affected** the child deeply.*

> SPELLING Be careful! Don't confuse **affect**, which is a verb, with **effect**, which is a noun: *The weather **affects** our crops.* ◇ *The weather has an **effect** on farmers' crops.*

affection (say uh-**fek**-shuhn) *noun* (*no plural*)
the feeling of loving or liking somebody: *She has great **affection** for her aunt.*

affectionate (say uh-**fek**-shuh-nuht) *adjective*
showing that you love or like somebody very much: *a very **affectionate** child*
▸ **affectionately** (*adverb*): *He smiled at his son **affectionately**.*

affidavit (say af-uh-**day**-vit) *noun* (*plural* **affidavits**)
a written statement that you say officially is true, and that can be used in a court of law: *She signed an **affidavit** to say where she was last night.*

affiliated (say uh-**fil**-i-ayt-uhd) *adjective*
connected to an organization: *This programme is **affiliated** to Wits University.*

affinity (say uh-**fin**-uh-tee) *noun* (*plural* **affinities**)
a strong feeling that you like and understand something or somebody, because you feel similar to them in some way: *He has an **affinity** for children.*

affirm (say uh-**furm**) *verb* (**affirming, affirmed**)
to say clearly that something is true, or that you support something strongly: *I can **affirm** our commitment to peace.*
▸ **affirmation** (*noun*): ***affirmation** of hope*

affirmative (say uh-**furm**-uh-tiv) *adjective*
meaning 'yes': *an **affirmative** answer*
affirmative action a practice or policy that supports people who have been unfairly treated

A B C D E F G H I J K L M N O P Q R S T U V W X Y Z

in the past: *When we employ people, our company practises **affirmative** action.*

affluent (say **af**-luu-uhnt) *adjective*
having a lot of money: *Only **affluent** people live here.* ➲ SYNONYM **rich** 1
▸ **affluence** (*noun*)

afford (say uh-**fawd**) *verb* (**affording, afforded**)
can afford something to have enough money or time to be able to do something: *I can't **afford** a holiday this year.*

afloat (say uh-**floht**) *adjective, adverb*
floating on water: *Keep yourself **afloat**.*

afraid (say uh-**frayd**) *adjective*
having or showing fear: *Some people are **afraid** of snakes.* ◇ *I was **afraid** to open the door.*
➲ SYNONYMS **frightened, scared**
I'm afraid ... a polite way of saying that you are sorry: *I'm **afraid** that I can't come to your party.*

Africana (say uf-ri-**kaa**-nuh) *plural noun*
valuable art, furniture and books from southern Africa

African Union *noun*
an organization of African countries that encourages its members to work together

Afrikaans (say uf-ri-**kaanss**) *noun* (*no plural*)
a southern African language. It grew from seventeenth-century Dutch (= the language of the Netherlands) through influence from **aboriginal** languages and the languages of **slaves**.

Afro- (say **af**-roh) *prefix*
African

after[1] (say **aaf**-tuh) *preposition*
1 later than a person or thing: *They arrived **after** dinner.* ◇ ***After** doing my homework, I went out.*
2 behind or following a person or thing: *Ten comes **after** nine.* ◇ *Close the door **after** you.*
3 trying to get or catch a person or thing: *The police officer ran **after** her.*
after all
1 used when you thought something different would happen: *I was worried about the exam, but it wasn't difficult **after** all.*
2 used to mean 'do not forget': *She doesn't understand. **After** all, she's only two.*

after[2] (say **aaf**-tuh) *conjunction, adverb*
at a time later than a person or thing: *We arrived **after** the film had started.* ◇ *Lumka left at ten o'clock and I left soon **after**.*

afternoon (say **aaf**-tuh-noon) *noun* (*plural* **afternoons**)
the part of a day between midday and the evening: *We had lunch and went for a walk in the **afternoon**.* ◇ *I saw him this **afternoon**.* ◇ *Yesterday **afternoon** I went shopping.* ◇ *He left on Friday **afternoon**.*

> USAGE We usually say **in the afternoon**: *We went to town **in the afternoon**.* If we include a day or date then we use **on**: *We went shopping **on Monday afternoon**.*

afterwards (say **aaf**-tuh-wuhdz) *adverb*
later or after another thing has happened: *We had supper and went to see a film **afterwards**.*

again (say uh-**gayn**) *adverb*
1 one more time or once more: *Could you say that **again**, please?* ◇ *I will never see him **again**.*
2 in the way that a person or thing was before: *You'll soon feel well **again**.*
again and again many times: *I've told you **again** and **again** not to do that!*

against (say uh-**gaynst**) *preposition*
1 on the other side in a game or fight: *They played **against** a tennis team from another town.*
2 not in agreement with something: *Many people are **against** the plan.* ➲ OPPOSITE **for[1]** 8
3 touching a person or thing for support: *I put the ladder **against** the wall.*
4 to stop something: *Have you had an injection **against** the disease?*

age (say **ayj**) *noun*
1 (*plural* **ages**) the amount of time that a person or thing has been in the world: *She is seven years of **age**.* ◇ *I started work at the **age** of sixteen.*
2 (*no plural*) being old: *Her hair was grey with **age**.*
3 (*plural* **ages**) a certain time in history: *the computer **age*** ◇ *the Stone **Age*** (= when people used stone tools)
4 ages (*plural noun*) (*informal*) a very long time: *She's lived here for **ages**.*

aged (say **ayj**-d) *adjective*
of the age mentioned: *They have two children, **aged** three and five.*

agency (say **ay**-juhn-see) *noun* (*plural* **agencies**)
the work or office of a person who does business for others: *A travel **agency** plans holidays for people.*

agenda (say uh-**jen**-duh) *noun* (*plural* **agendas**)
a list of all the things to be talked about in a meeting: *The next item on the **agenda** is the school sports day.*

agent (say **ay**-juhnt) *noun* (*plural* **agents**)
a person who does business for another person or for a company: *An actor's **agent** tries to find work for actors and actresses.* ◇ *a travel **agent***

aggravate (say **ag**-ruh-vayt) *verb* (**aggravating, aggravated**)
1 to make something worse: *This weather will* ***aggravate*** *my cold.*
2 to make a person or animal angry: *Don't* ***aggravate*** *the bull.*
▶ **aggravation** (*noun*)

aggregate (say **ag**-ri-guht) *noun* (*plural* **aggregates**)
a total number or amount made up of smaller amounts that are put together

aggressive (say uh-**gress**-iv) *adjective*
ready to argue or fight: *He often gets* ***aggressive*** *after drinking alcohol.*
▶ **aggression** (*noun*): *You shouldn't use* ***aggression*** *to solve your problems.*

aghast (say uh-**gaast**) *adjective*
filled with horror and surprise: *We were* ***aghast*** *when we saw what he'd done.*

agile (say **aj**-ile) *adjective*
able to move quickly and easily: *an* ***agile*** *cat*
➲ SYNONYM **nimble**
▶ **agility:** *You can improve your* ***agility****.*

agitate (say **aj**-i-tayt) *verb* (**agitating, agitated**)
1 to make someone worried or nervous: *Stop* ***agitating*** *me!*
2 to make people feel strongly about something: *We need to* ***agitate*** *for better housing.*
▶ **agitation** (*noun*)

agitated (say **aj**-i-tay-tid) *adjective*
worried or excited: *My aunt gets* ***agitated*** *at the airport.*

AGM (say ay-jee-**em**) *abbreviation* (*plural* **AGMs**)
Annual General Meeting

agnostic (say ag-**noss**-tik) *noun* (*plural* **agnostics**)
a person who is not sure whether God exists or not

ago (say uh-**goh**) *adverb*
in the past, before now: *I learned to ride a bike a long time* ***ago****.* ◇ *five years* ***ago***
long ago a very long time in the past: *Long ago there were no cars or aeroplanes.*

agony (say **ag**-uh-nee) *noun* (*plural* **agonies**)
very great pain: *He screamed in* ***agony****.*

agree (say uh-**gree**) *verb* (**agreeing, agreed**)
1 to have the same opinion as another person about something: *Dad thinks we should go by train but I don't* ***agree****.* ◇ *I* ***agree*** *with you.*
➲ OPPOSITE **disagree**
2 to say 'yes' when somebody asks you to do something: *She* ***agreed*** *to give me the money.*
➲ OPPOSITE **refuse**[1]
3 to decide something with another person: *We* ***agreed*** *to meet on Monday.* ◇ *Neo and I* ***agreed*** *on a meeting place.*

agreement (say uh-**gree**-muhnt) *noun*
1 (*no plural*) the state of sharing an opinion or feeling with someone: *She nodded her head in* ***agreement****.* ➲ OPPOSITE **disagreement**
2 (*plural* **agreements**) a plan or decision that two or more people have made together: *The leaders reached an* ***agreement*** *after five days of talks.*

agriculture (say **ag**-ri-kul-tshuh) *noun* (*no plural*)
keeping animals and growing plants for food
➲ SYNONYM **farming**
▶ **agricultural** (*adjective*): ***agricultural*** *workers*
ℹ ORIGIN: 15th century, from Latin *agricultura*, from *ager* meaning 'field' + *cultura* meaning 'growing'

ahead (say uh-**hed**) *adverb*
1 in front of a person or thing: *We could see a light* ***ahead*** *of us.*
2 before or more advanced than another person or thing: *Our friends arrived a few minutes* ***ahead*** *of us.* ◇ *The other class is further* ***ahead*** *than we are.*
3 into the future: *He's got a difficult time* ***ahead*** *of him.* ◇ *We must think* ***ahead****.*
4 winning in a game or competition: *Ghana was one goal* ***ahead*** *at half-time.*
go ahead used to give somebody permission to do something: *'Can I borrow your bike?' 'Sure, go* ***ahead****.'*

aid (say **ayd**) *noun*
1 (*plural* **aids**) help, or something that gives help: *He walks with the* ***aid*** *of a stick.* ◇ *She wears a hearing* ***aid*** (= a small thing that you put in your ear so you can hear better).
2 (*no plural*) money, food or clothes sent to a country or to people in order to help them: *We sent* ***aid*** *to the flood victims.*
in aid of a person or **thing** for a person or thing, especially for a charity: *a concert in* ***aid*** *of children in need*

AIDS (say **aydz**) *noun* (*no plural*) (also **Aids**)
a very serious illness which destroys the body's ability to fight other illnesses: *the* ***AIDS*** *virus*
ℹ **AIDS** is short for 'Acquired Immune Deficiency Syndrome'. ➲ See **HIV**

ailment (say **ayl**-muhnt) *noun* (*plural* **ailments**)
an illness that is not very serious

aim[1] (say **aym**) *noun* (*plural* **aims**)
a purpose or something that you want and plan to do: *Her* ***aim*** *is to find a good job.* ➲ SYNONYM **object**[1] 2

aim[2] (say **aym**) *verb* (**aiming, aimed**)
1 to try or plan to do something: *He's **aiming** to leave at nine o'clock.*
2 to plan something for a certain person or group: *This book is **aimed** at teenagers.*
3 to point something, for example a gun, at a person or thing that you want to hit: *He **aimed** the gun and fired.*

aimless (say **aym**-luhss) *adjective*
having no plan or purpose
▸ **aimlessly:** *They wandered around **aimlessly** until the show started.*

air (*rhymes with* **share**) *noun* (*no plural*)
1 the mixture of gases that surrounds the Earth and that you take in through your nose and mouth when you breathe: *Please open a window — I need some fresh **air**.*
2 the space around and above things: *He threw the ball up into the **air**.*
3 travel or transport in an aircraft: *It's more expensive to travel by **air** than by train.* ◇ *an **air** ticket*
on air, on the air on the radio or on television: *This radio station is on the **air** 24 hours a day.*

air conditioning *noun* (*no plural*)
a system that keeps the air cool and dry in a room, building or car
▸ **air-conditioned** (*adjective*): ***air-conditioned** offices*

aircraft (say **air**-kraft) *noun* (*plural* **aircraft**)
any vehicle that can fly in the air, for example a plane

air force *noun* (*plural* **air forces**)
the aircraft that a country uses for military purposes such as defence and **patrol**, and the people who fly them

airline (say **air**-line) *noun* (*plural* **airlines**)
a company that takes people or things to different places by plane: *Which **airline** are you flying with?*

airliner (say **air**-line-uh) *noun* (*plural* **airliners**)
a large plane that carries passengers

airlock (say **air**-lok) *noun* (*plural* **airlocks**)
1 a bubble of air that blocks the flow of liquid in a pipe
2 a small room with a tightly closed door at each end, which you go through to reach another area at a different air pressure, for example on a spacecraft or **submarine**

airmail (say **air**-mayl) *noun* (*no plural*)
the system of sending letters and packages by plane: *I sent the parcel by **airmail**.*

airport (say **air**-pawt) *noun* (*plural* **airports**)
a place where people get on and off planes, with buildings where passengers can wait: *I'll meet you at the **airport**.*

airtight (say **air**-tite) *adjective*
closed so tightly that air cannot get in or out: *Store it in an **airtight** container.*

aisle (*rhymes with* **pile**) *noun* (*plural* **aisles**)
a way between lines of seats in a place such as a hall, church or plane

> **PRONUNCIATION** Don't pronounce the **s** in **aisle**.

ajar (say uh-**jaa**) *adjective*
(used about a door) slightly open: *Leave the door **ajar** so the cat can come in.*

AK-47 (say ay-kay-faw-tee-**sev**-uhn) *noun* (*plural* **AK-47s**)
a military **rifle** made in Russia that fires bullets automatically and is used for attack

aka (say ay-kay-**ay**) *abbreviation*
also known as: *Rapper Shawn Carter, **aka** Jay-Z.*

alarm[1] (say uh-**laam**) *noun*
1 (*no plural*) a sudden feeling of fear: *He heard a noise, and jumped out of bed in **alarm**.*
2 (*plural* **alarms**) something that tells you about danger, for example by making a loud noise: *a burglar **alarm*** ◇ *a fire **alarm***
3 (*plural* **alarms**) an **alarm clock**

alarm[2] (say uh-**laam**) *verb* (**alarming, alarmed**)
to make a person or thing feel suddenly frightened or worried: *The noise **alarmed** the bird and it flew away.*

alarm clock *noun* (*plural* **alarm clocks**) (also **alarm**)
a clock that makes a noise to wake you up: *She set the **alarm clock** for half past six.*

alas (say uh-**lass**) *exclamation* (*old-fashioned*) used for showing sadness: ***Alas**, we were too late.*

albino (say ul-**bee**-noh) *noun* (*plural* **albinos**)
a person or animal with very pale skin and hair or fur and pink eyes

album (say **ul**-buhm) *noun* (*plural* **albums**)
1 a collection of songs on one CD, tape or record: *The band is about to release its third **album**.* ➲ See **single**[2] 1
2 a book in which you can keep things that you have collected, such as stamps or photographs: *a photograph **album***

albumen (say **al**-byoo-muhn) *noun* (*no plural*) (*biology*)
the clear inside part of an egg that turns white when you cook it

alchemy (say **al**-kuh-mee) *noun* (*no plural*)
a type of chemistry in the Middle Ages which involved trying to discover how to change ordinary metals into gold
▸ **alchemist** (*noun*)

alcohol (say **al**-kuh-hol) *noun* (*no plural*)
1 the clear liquid in drinks such as beer and wine that can make people drunk
2 drinks that contain alcohol, for example wine and beer

alcoholic[1] (say al-kuh-**hol**-ik) *adjective*
containing alcohol: *an **alcoholic** drink*

WORD BUILDING Drinks without alcohol are called **soft drinks** or **cooldrinks**.

alcoholic[2] (say al-kuh-**hol**-ik) *noun* (*plural* **alcoholics**)
a person with a very strong desire to drink too much alcohol: *This clinic helps **alcoholics** to overcome their addiction to alcohol.*

alcove (say **al**-kohv) *noun* (*plural* **alcoves**)
an area on a wall which is further back than the rest of the wall

ale (*rhymes with* **sale**) *noun* (*plural* **ales**)
a type of beer

alert[1] (say uh-**lurt**) *adjective*
watching and listening for something with all your attention: *A good driver is always **alert**.*

alert[2] (say uh-**lurt**) *verb* (**alerting, alerted**)
to warn someone of danger or a problem: *They **alerted** the fire brigade.*
▸ **alert** (*noun*): *a bomb **alert***

alfalfa (say al-**fal**-fuh) *noun* (*no plural*) = **lucerne**

alga (say **al**-guh) (*plural* **algae**)
a simple type of plant that grows in water, with no true stems, leaves or roots

algebra (say **al**-ji-bruh) *noun* (*no plural*)
a type of mathematics in which letters and symbols are used to represent numbers

algorithm (say **al**-guh-ri*th*-uhm) *noun* (*plural* **algorithms**)
a process or set of rules that must be followed when solving certain problems or doing certain calculations, especially by a computer: *a basic **algorithm** for division*

ORIGIN: 17th century, via French and Latin, from Arabic *al-Kwarizmi* meaning 'the man of Kwarizm', a name given to the mathematician Abu Ja'far Muhammad ibn Musa, who lived in the ninth century and who was the author of widely translated works on algebra and arithmetic.

alias (say **ay**-li-uhss) *noun* (*plural* **aliases**)
a false or different name: *He used an **alias** to get a library card.*
▸ **alias** (*adverb*): *The bank robber was Mike Jones, **alias** Andrew Maxwell.*

alibi (say **al**-uh-by) *noun* (*plural* **alibis**)
a statement by a person that says they were in a different place at the time of a crime and so cannot be guilty of the crime: *He said he had an **alibi**.*

alien[1] (say **ay**-li-uhn) *noun* (*plural* **aliens**)
1 a plant or an animal that comes from another area or another country: *Eucalyptus trees are **aliens** in South Africa.* ➲ See **indigenous**
2 (in science fiction) a person or an animal that comes from another planet: ***aliens** from outer space*
3 a person who comes from another country: *an illegal **alien***

alien[2] (say **ay**-li-uhn) *adjective*
strange and different to your normal experience: *Writing letters instead of emails is **alien** to me.*

alienate (say **ay**-li-uhn-ayt) *verb* (**alienating, alienated**)
to make somebody feel that they do not belong somewhere, or are not part of something: *He was **alienated** from his family.*
➲ SYNONYM **ostracize**
▸ **alienation** (*noun*): ***alienation** from her parents*

alight (say uh-**lite**) *adjective*
on fire or burning: *A cigarette set the petrol **alight**.*

align (say uh-**line**) *verb* (**aligning, aligned**)
to arrange things in a straight line or so that they are parallel to something else: ***Align** the numbers under each other.*
▸ **alignment** (*noun*)

alike (say uh-**like**) *adjective, adverb*
1 very similar: *The two sisters are very **alike**.*
2 in the same way: *The book is popular with adults and children **alike**.*

A B C D E F G H I J K L M N O P Q R S T U V W X Y Z

alimentary canal (say ali-men-tuh-ree kuh-**nal**) *noun* (*plural* **alimentary canals**)
the passage in your body that food moves along, from your mouth to where it leaves your body

alimentary canal

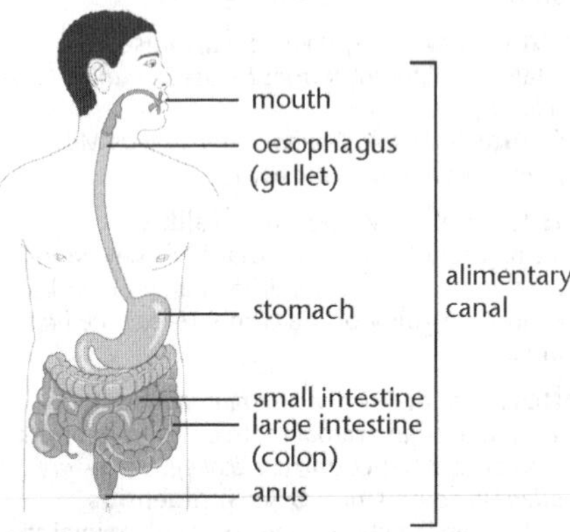

alive (say uh-**live**) *adjective*
not dead but living: *Are your grandparents* ***alive****?*

alkali (say **al**-kuh-ly) *noun* (*plural* **alkalis**) (*science*)
a substance that be dissolved in water and has a **pH** greater than seven: *Baking soda is an alkali.* ➲ See **acid**, **base**[1] 5
▸ **alkaline** (*adjective*): *an* ***alkaline*** *battery*

all[1] (say **awl**) *adjective, pronoun*
1 every part or the whole of something: *She's eaten* ***all*** *the bread.*
2 every one of a group: ***All*** *cats are animals but not* ***all*** *animals are cats.* ◇ *I invited ten people, but not* ***all*** *of them came.*
3 the only thing that, or everything that: ***All*** *I've eaten today is one banana.*
(not) at all in any way: *I didn't enjoy it at* ***all****.*

all[2] (say **awl**) *adverb*
completely: *She lives* ***all*** *alone.* ◇ *He was dressed* ***all*** *in black.*
all along from the beginning: *I knew* ***all*** *along that she was lying.*

Allah (say **ul**-uh) *noun*
the Muslim name for God

allay (say uh-**lay**) *verb* (**allaying, allayed**)
to make something less strong: *Her fears were* ***allayed*** *when she turned on the light.*

allegation (say al-uh-**gay**-shuhn) *noun* (*plural* **allegations**)
a statement that you make without proof: *There were* ***allegations*** *that she had lied.* ◇ *several* ***allegations*** *of theft*

allege (say uh-**lej**) *verb* (**alleging, alleged**)
to make a statement without proof: *He* ***alleges*** *that she took the book.*

allegiance (say uh-**lee**-juhnss) *noun* (*plural* **allegiances**)
support for a leader, government or belief: *She showed* ***allegiance*** *to the ruling party.*

allegory (say **al**-uh-guh-ree) *noun* (*plural* **allegories**)
a story that is a symbol for an idea
▸ **allegorical** (*adjective*): *an* ***allegorical*** *story*

allergic (say uh-**lur**-jik) *adjective*
1 having an **allergy**: *He's* ***allergic*** *to cow's milk.*
2 caused by an **allergy**: *an* ***allergic*** *reaction*

allergy (say **al**-uh-jee) *noun* (*plural* **allergies**)
a medical condition that makes you ill when you eat, touch or breathe something that does not normally make other people ill: *She has an* ***allergy*** *to cats.*

alleviate (say uh-**leev**-i-ayt) *verb* (**alleviating, alleviated**)
to make something less strong or bad: *You can* ***alleviate*** *the pain by lying down.*

alley (say **al**-ee) *noun* (*plural* **alleys**)
a narrow path between buildings

alliance (say uh-**ly**-uhnss) *noun* (*plural* **alliances**)
an agreement between countries or groups of people to work together and help each other

allied (say **al**-ide) *adjective* ➲ See **ally**[2]

alligator (say **al**-i-gay-tuh) *noun* (*plural* **alligators**)
a large reptile with a long tail and a big mouth with sharp teeth. They live in the lakes and rivers of America and China.
🛈 **ORIGIN:** 16th century, from Spanish *el lagarto* meaning 'the lizard'

alliteration (say uh-lit-uh-**ray**-shuhn) *noun* (*no plural*)
using the same letter or sound at the beginning of words that are close together: *'An ant ate an apple' is an example of* ***alliteration****.* ➲ See Study page 17 ➲ See **assonance**

allocate (say **al**-uh-kayt) *verb* (**allocating, allocated**)
to give something to a person or organization as their share: *Our government* ***allocates*** *a large sum of money to education each year.*

allot (say uh-**lot**) *verb* (**allotting, allotted**)
to give a share of work, space or time to somebody or something: *I've* ***allotted*** *this job to you.*

► **allotment** (*noun*): *an* ***allotment*** *of land*

SPELLING Be careful! Don't confuse **allot** with **a lot. A lot** is always two words: *I need* ***a lot*** *of paper.*

allow (say uh-**low**) *verb* (**allowing, allowed**)
to say that somebody can have or do something: *My parents* ***allow*** *me to stay out late at weekends.* ◇ *Smoking is not* ***allowed*** *in most cinemas.* ➲ OPPOSITE **forbid** ➲ See **let** 1, **permit**[1]

PRONUNCIATION The second part of **allow** rhymes with **cow**, not with **no**.

allowance (say uh-**low**-uhnss) *noun* (*plural* **allowances**)
1 an amount of something that you are allowed: *a baggage* ***allowance*** *of 20 kg*
2 an amount of money you get every month: *I usually spend my* ***allowance*** *by the middle of the month.*

alloy (say **al**-oy) *noun* (*plural* **alloys**)
a metal made by mixing two or more types of metal together: *Bronze is an* ***alloy*** *of copper and tin.*

all right (say awl **rite**) *adjective, adverb, exclamation*
1 good, or good enough: *Is everything* ***all right?***
2 not hurt, but well: *I was ill, but I'm* ***all right*** *now.*
3 used to say 'yes, I agree' when somebody asks you to do something: *'Can you get me some stamps?'* ***'All right.'*** ➲ SYNONYMS **OK**[1], **OK**[2]

alluvium (say uh-**loo**-vi-uhm) *noun* (*no plural*) (*geography*)
sand and earth that is left by rivers or floods

ally[1] (say **al**-y) *noun* (*plural* **allies**)
a person or country that agrees to help another person or country, for example in a war

ally[2] (say uh-**ly**) *verb* (**allying, allied**)
to make an agreement with another country or organization to work together and support each other: *Britain* ***allied*** *itself to France.*
► **allied** (*adjective*): ***allied*** *nations*

almighty (say awl-**my**-tee) *adjective*
1 having the power to do anything
2 (*informal*) very great: *We heard an* ***almighty*** *crash.*

almond (say **aa**-muhnd) *noun* (*plural* **almonds**)
a flat brown nut that you can eat and use in cooking

PRONUNCIATION Don't pronounce the **l** in **almond**.

almost (say **awl**-mohst) *adverb*
nearly but not quite: *It's* ***almost*** *three o'clock.* ◇ *I* ***almost*** *fell into the river!*

aloe (say **al**-oh) *noun* (*plural* **aloes**)
a plant that grows in hot regions and has thick juicy leaves with sharp points

alone (say uh-**lohn**) *adjective, adverb*
1 without any other person: *I don't like being* ***alone*** *in the house.* ◇ *I want to be* ***alone*** *for a while.* ◇ *My grandmother lives* ***alone.***
2 only: *You* ***alone*** *can help me.*

WHICH WORD? **Alone** or **lonely**?
- With sense 1 above, **alone** means that you are not with other people: *She lived* ***alone*** *in a flat.* ◇ *She enjoys being* ***alone.***
- **Lonely** means that you are unhappy because you are not with other people: *He felt* ***lonely*** *without his old friends.*

along[1] (say uh-**long**) *preposition*
1 from one end of something towards the other end: *We walked* ***along*** *the road.*
2 in a line next to something long: *There are trees* ***along*** *the river bank.*

along[2] (say uh-**long**) *adverb*
1 forward: *He drove* ***along*** *very slowly.*
2 (*informal*) with somebody: *We're going for a walk. Why don't you come* ***along*** *too?*

alongside (say uh-long-**side**) *preposition, adverb*
next to something: *Put your bike* ***alongside*** *mine.*

aloof (say uh-**loof**) *adjective*
not friendly to other people: *The new learner seemed* ***aloof*** *and unfriendly.*

aloud (say uh-**lowd**) *adverb*
in a normal speaking voice that other people can hear: *I read the story* ***aloud*** *to my sister.*

alphabet (say **al**-fuh-buht) *noun* (*plural* **alphabets**)
all the letters of a language: *The English* ***alphabet*** *starts with A and ends with Z.*

alphabetical (say al-fuh-**bet**-i-kuhl) *adjective*
in the order of the alphabet: *Put these words in* ***alphabetical*** *order* (= with words beginning with A first, then B, then C, etc.).
► **alphabetically** (*adverb*): *The books are listed* ***alphabetically.***

already (say awl-**red**-ee) *adverb*
before now or before then: *'Would you like some lunch?' 'No, thank you – I've* ***already*** *eaten.'*

WHICH WORD? **Already** or **all ready**?
Be careful not to confuse these.
- **All ready** means that everyone is ready: *The boys are* ***all ready*** *to go.*
- **Already** has a different meaning: *The boys have* ***already*** *gone.*

WHICH WORD? **Already** or **yet**?
- **Yet** means the same as **already**, but you use **yet** only in questions and in negative sentences: *'I've finished that book* ***already****.'* ◇ *'Have you finished the book* ***yet****?' 'No, not yet.'*

alright (say awl-**rite**) (*informal*) another word for **all right**

WHICH WORD? **All right** or **alright**?
Alright is informal. Use **all right** in schoolwork and formal writing.

Alsatian (say al-**say**-shuhn) *noun* (*plural* **Alsatians**)
a large dog that is often trained for police work ➲ SYNONYM **German shepherd**

also (say **awl**-soh) *adverb*
as well, too: *He plays several instruments and* ***also*** *writes music.*

altar (say **awl**-tuh) *noun* (*plural* **altars**)
a high table that is the centre of a religious ceremony

alter (say **awl**-tuh) *verb* (**altering, altered**)
to make something different in some way or to change: *The dress was too big so my mother* ***altered*** *it.*

alteration (say awl-tuh-**ray**-shuhn) *noun* (*plural* **alterations**)
a small change: *We want to make a few* ***alterations*** *to the house.*

altercation (say awl-tuh-**kay**-shun) *noun* (*plural* **altercations**)
a noisy argument or disagreement

alternate[1] (say awl-**turn**-uht) *adjective*
1 with first one thing, then the other, then the first thing again, and so on: *The cake had* ***alternate*** *layers of fruit and cream.*
2 one out of every two: *He works* ***alternate*** *weeks* (= he works the first week, he doesn't work the second week, he works again the third week, etc.).

alternate[2] (say **awl**-tuh-nayt) *verb* (**alternating, alternated**)
(two types of events or things) to happen or follow regularly one after the other: *She* ***alternated*** *between loving him and hating him.*

alternative[1] (say awl-**turn**-uh-tiv) *adjective*
that you can use or do instead of something else: *The road was closed so we had to find an* ***alternative*** *route.*

WHICH WORD? **Alternate** or **alternative?**
Be careful! These words mean different things.
- *Let's visit my gran on* ***alternate*** *days. I'll go on Monday, you go on Tuesday, I'll go on Wednesday, etc.*
- I can't visit her at midday, so I'll have to find an ***alternative*** *time.*

alternative[2] (say awl-**turn**-uh-tiv) *noun* (*plural* **alternatives**)
a thing that you can choose instead of another thing: *We could go by train – the* ***alternative*** *is to take the car.*

alternatively (say awl-**turn**-uh-tiv-lee) *adverb*
used to talk about a second possible thing you can do: *We can go by bus.* ***Alternatively****, I could take the car.*

although (say awl-***thoh***) *conjunction*
1 in spite of something: ***Although*** *she was ill, she went to work.*
2 but: *I love dogs,* ***although*** *I wouldn't have one as a pet.* ➲ SYNONYM **though**[1]

PRONUNCIATION The second sound in this word rhymes with **go**.

altimeter (say **al**-ti-mee-tuh) *noun* (*plural* **altimeters**)
an instrument that shows **altitude** 1

altitude (say **al**-ti-tyood) *noun* (*plural* **altitudes**)
1 height above sea level: *The plane flew at an* ***altitude*** *of 4 000 metres.*
2 a place that is high above sea level: *Snow leopards live at high* ***altitudes****.*

alto (say **al**-toh) *noun*
1 (*no plural*) the lowest singing voice for a woman and the highest for a man
2 (*plural* **altos**) a man or woman with this voice ➲ See **baritone, soprano, tenor**

altogether (say awl-tuu-**ge*th***-uh) *adverb*
1 completely: *I don't* ***altogether*** *agree.*
2 counting everything or everybody: *There were ten of us* ***altogether****.*

WHICH WORD? **Altogether** or **all together**?
Be careful not to confuse these.
- **All together** is used to talk about people or things that are all in the same place: *Her four children are **all together** on the beach.*
- Compare this sentence: *She has four children **altogether*** (i.e. in total), *but they live in different towns.*

altruistic (say al-troo-**iss**-tik) *adjective*
caring about the needs of other people more than your own
▸ **altruism** (*noun*)

aluminium (say al-*uu*-**min**-i-uhm or al-uh-**min**-i-uhm) *noun* (*no plural*) (symbol Al)
a light, silver-coloured metal

always (say **awl**-wayz) *adverb*
1 at all times or every time: *I have **always** lived in East London.* ◇ *The train is **always** late.*
2 for ever: *I will **always** remember that day.*
3 again and again: *My sister is **always** borrowing my clothes!*

am form of **be**

a.m. (say ay-**em**) *abbreviation*
You add this abbreviation to a time to show that it is between midnight and midday: *I start work at 9 a.m.* ❶ **a.m.** is short for 'ante meridiem' which means 'before midday' in Latin. ➲ See **p.m.**

WORD BUILDING You use **p.m.** for times between midday and midnight.

amakhosi (also **amakosi**) plural of **inkosi**

amakhosikazi (also **amakosikazi**) plural of **inkosikazi**

amalgamate (say uh-**mal**-guh-mayt) *verb* (**amalgamating, amalgamated**)
to join together to form one organization, group or substance
▸ **amalgamation** (*noun*)

amandla (say uh-**mun**-dluh) *exclamation*
power or strength
❶ ORIGIN: from isiXhosa and isiZulu *amandla* meaning 'power, strength'

amasi (say u-**maa**-si) *noun* (*no plural*)
thickened sour milk
❶ ORIGIN: from isiXhosa and isiZulu *amasi* meaning 'sour milk that has become thick'

amateur (say **am**-uh-tuh) *noun* (*plural* **amateurs**)
a person who does a sport or an activity because they enjoy it, but not for money or as a job: *Only **amateurs** can take part in the tournament.* ➲ OPPOSITE **professional**[2] 1
▸ **amateur** (*adjective*): *an **amateur** photographer*

amaze (say uh-**mayz**) *verb* (**amazing, amazed**)
to surprise somebody very much or to be difficult for somebody to believe: *It **amazes** me that anyone could be so stupid!*

amazed (say uh-**mayz**-d) *adjective*
very surprised: *She was **amazed** to discover the truth about her father.*

amazement (say uh-**mayz**-muhnt) *noun* (*no plural*)
great surprise: *She looked at me in **amazement**.*

amazing (say uh-**mayz**-ing) *adjective*
very surprising and difficult to believe: *He has shown **amazing** courage.* ◇ *an **amazing** story*
➲ SYNONYM **incredible** 1
▸ **amazingly** (*adverb*): *She plays the violin **amazingly** well.*

ambassador (say am-**bass**-uh-duh) *noun* (*plural* **ambassadors**)
an important official who represents his or her country in a foreign country: *the South African **ambassador** to Italy*

WORD BUILDING An **ambassador** works in an **embassy**.

amber (say **am**-buh) *noun* (*no plural*)
1 a hard, clear, yellow-brown substance used for making jewellery and other objects
2 the colour of this substance

ambidextrous (say am-bi-**dekss**-truhss) *adjective*
being able to use your left hand and right hand equally well

ambience (say **am**-bi-uhnss) *noun* (*no plural*)
the character of a place or the feeling that it gives you: *This restaurant has a wonderful **ambience**.*

ambiguous (say am-**big**-yoo-uhss) *adjective*
having more than one meaning: *The message was **ambiguous** so we didn't know what to do.*
▸ **ambiguity** (*noun*) ▸ **ambiguously** (*adverb*)
❶ ORIGIN: 16th century, from Latin *ambiguus* meaning 'doubtful', from *ambi-* meaning 'both ways' + *agere* meaning 'to drive'

ambition (say am-**bi**-shuhn) *noun*
1 (*plural* **ambitions**) something that you really want to do: *My **ambition** is to become a doctor.*
2 (*no plural*) a very strong wish to be successful or to have power: *Dimako is intelligent, but she has no **ambition**.*

A B C D E F G H I J K L M N O P Q R S T U V W X Y Z

ambitious (say am-**bi**-shuhss) *adjective*
1 having a strong desire to be successful or to have power: *an **ambitious** young manager*
2 needing a lot of effort, money or time to succeed: *The company has announced **ambitious** plans for expansion.*

ambivalent (say am-**biv**-uh-luhnt) *adjective*
not being sure about something or having a mixture of feelings: *I am **ambivalent** about the play we saw.*
▸ **ambivalence** (*noun*)

amble (say **am**-buhl) *verb* (**ambling, ambled**)
to walk at a relaxed speed: *We **ambled** along the beach.*

ambulance (say **am**-byoo-luhnss) *noun* (*plural* **ambulances**)
a vehicle that takes people who are ill or hurt to hospital

ambush (say **am**-buush) *noun* (*plural* **ambushes**)
a surprise attack by someone that is hiding: *They were caught in an **ambush** along the road.*
▸ **ambush** (*verb*): *We **ambushed** my brother as he walked past.*

amen (say aa-**men** or ay-**men**) *exclamation*
a word that Christians and Jews say at the end of a prayer

amenable (say uh-**meen**-uhb-l) *adjective*
happy to accept something: *I am **amenable** to the idea.*

amend (say uh-**mend**) *verb* (**amending, amended**)
to change something to make it better: *We **amended** the class rules.*
▸ **amendment** (*noun*)

amenity (say uh-**meen**-i-tee) *noun* (*plural* **amenities**)
something that makes a place easy and pleasant to live in: *The **amenities** in this campsite include a pool and a braai area.*

amiable (say **ay**-mi-uhb-l) *adjective*
friendly and pleasant: *Graham is an **amiable** captain.*

amicable (say **am**-ik-uhb-l) *adjective*
made or done in a friendly way, without argument: *It was an **amicable** debate.*
▸ **amicably** (*adverb*): *The argument was settled **amicably**.*

amid (say uh-**mid**) *adjective* (also **amidst**)
in the middle of: *We cut down electricity use **amid** fears of another crisis.*

amiss (say uh-**miss**) *adjective, adverb*
wrong or faulty: *Is anything **amiss**?*

ammeter (say **am**-ee-tuh) *noun* (*plural* **ammeters**) (*science*)
an instrument used for measuring the strength of an electric current

ammonia (say uh-**moh**-ni-uh) *noun* (*no plural*)
a colourless gas with a strong smell. Dissolved in water, it is used for cleaning.

ammunition (say am-yoo-**ni**-shuhn) *noun* (*no plural*)
a supply of rounds such as bullets to be fired from guns: *They had no more **ammunition**.*

amnesia (say am-**neez**-i-uh) *noun* (*no plural*)
loss of memory: *She suffered from **amnesia** after the brain injury.*

amnesty (say **am**-nuhss-tee) *noun* (*no plural*)
1 a time when a government forgives prisoners for political crimes and allows them to go free
2 a time when people can admit to a crime or give up weapons without being punished

amoeba (say uh-**mee**-buh) *noun* (*plural* **amoebas** or **amoebae**)
a very small organism consisting of one cell

among (say uh-**mung**) *preposition* (also **amongst**)
1 in the middle of a group of people or things: *I often feel nervous when I'm **among** strangers.*
2 in a particular group of people or things: *There is a lot of anger **among** teachers about the new law.*
3 for or by three or more things or people: *He divided the money **among** his six children.*

WHICH WORD? **Among** or **between**?
- We use **among** when we are talking about three or more people or things: *You're **among** friends here.*
- If there are only two people or things, we use **between**: *Lerato and I divided the cake **between** us.* ◇ *I was standing **between** Bongi and Tiyani.*

among and between

a house among trees | **a small house between two big houses**

amoral (say ay-**mo**-ruhl) *adjective*
(used about people or their behaviour) not following any moral rules or not caring about

right or wrong: *The film is about an **amoral** killer.*

amorous (say **am**-uh-ruhss) *adjective*
showing strong loving feelings or sexual desire for someone

amorphous (say uh-**maw**-fuhss) *adjective*
having no definite shape, form or structure

amount[1] (say uh-**mownt**) *noun* (*plural* **amounts**)
1 a quantity, or how much of something there is: *the **amount** of meat that people eat*
2 a total or sum of money: *I calculated the **amount** of the bill.*

WHICH WORD? **Amount** or **number**?
- Only use **amount** with things that you cannot count, for example: *a large **amount** of sand* ◇ *a small **amount** of money*
- Don't use **amount** with things that you can count. Instead, say, for example: *a large **number** of people* ◇ *a small **number** of coins*

amount[2] (say uh-**mownt**) *verb* (**amounting, amounted**)
amount to something to add up to something or to make a certain total: *The cost of the repairs **amounted** to R500.*

amp *abbreviation* (*plural* **amps**)
1 ampere
2 amplifier

ampere (say **am**-pair) *noun* (*plural* **amperes**)
(abbr. A or amp)
a unit for measuring the strength of an electric current: *a 15-**ampere** battery charger*
ORIGIN: 19th century, named after André-Marie Ampère (1775–1836), a French physicist and mathematician

ampersand (say **am**-puh-sand) *noun* (*plural* **ampersands**)
the symbol & (meaning 'and')

amphibian (say am-**fib**-i-uhn) *noun* (*plural* **amphibians**)
any of a class of animals that live both on land and in water: *Frogs and toads are **amphibians**.*

amphibious (say am-**fib**-i-uhss) *adjective*
able to live or be used on both land and in water: *Frogs are **amphibious**.* ◇ *an **amphibious** vehicle*

amphitheatre (say **am**-fi-theer-tuh) *noun* (*plural* **amphitheatres**)
a theatre without a roof, and with rows of seats that rise in steps away from the central open space

ample (say **amp**-l) *adjective*
enough or more than enough: *Our car has **ample** space for all our luggage.*

amplifier (say **amp**-li-fy-uh) *noun* (*plural* **amplifiers**)
an electrical machine that makes sounds louder

amplify (say **amp**-li-fy) *verb* (**amplifying, amplified**)
1 to increase the volume of a sound
2 to make larger, stronger or more important: *Her fear was **amplified** by the sudden noise.*
3 to add details to something in order to explain it more fully: *He **amplified** his argument with the examples he gave.*

amplitude (say **amp**-li-tyood) *noun* (*plural* **amplitudes**)
the greatest height that a wave, especially a sound wave or a radio wave, **vibrates** (= moves up and down) ➲ See illustration at **wavelength**

amputate (say **am**-pyoo-tayt) *verb* (**amputating, amputated**)
to cut off a person's arm or leg, especially for medical reasons: *His leg was **amputated** below the knee.*
▸ **amputation** (*noun*) ▸ **amputee** (*noun*): *There are many **amputees** as a result of landmines.*

amuse (say uh-**myooz**) *verb* (**amusing, amused**)
1 to make somebody smile or laugh: *Msizi's joke did not **amuse** his mother.*
2 to keep somebody happy and busy: *We sang songs to **amuse** ourselves on the trip.*
▸ **amused** (*adjective*): *He was **amused** by the jokes in the newspaper.*

amusement (say uh-**myooz**-muhnt) *noun* (*no plural*)
the feeling that you have when something makes you laugh or smile: *We watched in **amusement** as the dog chased its tail.*

amusing (say uh-**myooz**-ing) *adjective*
(of a person or thing) that makes you smile or laugh: *an **amusing** story* ➲ SYNONYM **funny** 1

an (say **an** or **uhn**) *article*
1 one or any: *I ate **an** apple.*
2 each, or for each: *It costs R5 **an** hour to park your car here.*

anachronism (say uh-**nak**-ruh-niz-uhm) *noun* (*plural* **anachronisms**)
1 a person or custom that seems old-fashioned and in the wrong time
2 something that does not belong in the period of time of a particular book or film: *The Roman*

*soldier's digital watch was an **anachronism** in the film.*
▸ **anachronistic** (*adjective*)

anaemia (say uh-**neem**-i-uh) *noun* (*no plural*)
a medical condition in which there are not enough red blood cells in the blood
▸ **anaemic** (*adjective*): ***Anaemic** people are often pale and lack energy.*

anaesthetic (say an-uhss-**thet**-ik) *noun* (*plural* **anaesthetics**)
a drug that a doctor gives you so that you will not feel any pain during an operation: *The patient is under **anaesthetic** now.*

anaesthetist (say uh-**neess**-thuh-tist) *noun* (*plural* **anaesthetists**)
a medical doctor who is trained to give patients an **anaesthetic**

anagram (say **an**-uh-gram) *noun* (*plural* **anagrams**)
a word or phrase that is made of letters from another word or phrase that have been arranged differently: *'Evil' is an **anagram** of 'live' and 'garden' is an **anagram** of 'danger'.*

anal (say **ay**-nuhl) *adjective*
1 relating to the **anus**: *an **anal** examination*
2 (also **anal-retentive**) (*informal*) extremely orderly and **fussy**

analgesic (say an-uhl-**jee**-zik) *noun* (*plural* **analgesics**)
a medicine that reduces pain
➲ SYNONYM **painkiller**

analogue (say **an**-uh-log) *adjective*
1 using an electronic system that uses changing physical quantities to measure or store information
2 (used about a clock or watch) showing the time using hands that move around a **dial**[2]
➲ See **digital**

analogy (say uh-**nal**-uh-jee) *noun* (*plural* **analogies**)
a comparison between two things that shows how they are similar: *The minister used an **analogy** of a tree to explain marriage.*
▸ **analogous** (*adjective*)

analyse (say **an**-uh-lize) *verb* (**analysing, analysed**)
to look at or think about the different parts of something carefully so that you can understand it: *They will **analyse** the statistics.*
🛈 ORIGIN: 16th century, through Latin from Greek *analuein* meaning 'to loosen'

analysis (say uh-**nal**-uh-suhss) *noun* (*plural* **analyses**)
the process of carefully examining the different parts of something: *Samples of the water were sent away for **analysis**.* ➲ See Study page 19

anarchy (say **an**-aa-kee) *noun* (*no plural*)
a situation in which people do not obey rules and laws: *They suffered years of civil war and **anarchy**.*
▸ **anarchist** (*noun*): ***Anarchists** attacked the police station.*

anatomy (say uh-**nat**-uh-mee) *noun*
1 (*no plural*) the scientific study of the structure of human or animal bodies
2 (*plural* **anatomies**) the structure of an animal or a plant: *human **anatomy** ◇ the **anatomy** of the knee*
▸ **anatomical** (*adjective*): ***anatomical** research*

ancestor (say **an**-sess-tuh) *noun* (*plural* **ancestors**)
a person from whom you are **descended**, typically one from the **generations** before your **grandparents**: *My **ancestors** came from the Karoo.*

anchor[1] (say **ang**-kuh) *noun* (*plural* **anchors**)
a heavy metal thing that you drop into the water from a boat to stop the boat moving away

anchor[2] (say **ang**-kuh) *verb* (**anchoring, anchored**)
1 to keep a boat in place in the water by using the anchor
2 to fix firmly in place: *You can **anchor** the mat in place with nails.*

anchovy (say **an**-chuh-vee) *noun* (*plural* **anchovies**)
a very small fish with a strong flavour

ancient (say **ayn**-shuhnt) *adjective*
very old, from a long time ago: ***ancient** buildings*

and (say **and** or **uhnd**) *conjunction*
a word that joins words or parts of sentences together: *fish **and** chips ◇ The cat was black **and** white. ◇ They sang **and** danced all night.*

anecdote (say **an**-ik-doht) *noun* (*plural* **anecdotes**)
a short, interesting, true story: *She tells very funny **anecdotes** about her travels.*

anemometer (say an-i-**mom**-uh-tuh) *noun* (*plural* **anemometers**) (*technology*)
an instrument that measures wind speed

angel (say **ayn**-juhl) *noun* (*plural* **angels**)
a spirit who is believed to carry messages from God. In pictures, they are usually dressed in white and have wings.
🛈 ORIGIN: from Old English *engel*, through Latin from Greek *angelos* meaning 'messenger'.

anger (say **ang**-guh) *noun* (*no plural*)
the strong feeling that you have when something has happened or somebody has done something that you do not like: *She was shaking with* ***anger***.

angiosperm (say **an**-ji-oh-spurm) *noun* (*plural* **angiosperms**) (*biology*)
a plant that has flowers and produces seeds that are contained in a fruit or a **pod**: *Many plants that live on land are* ***angiosperms***. ➲ See **gymnosperm**

angle (say **ang**-guhl) *noun* (*plural* **angles**)
the space between two lines that meet. It is measured in degrees: *an* ***angle*** *of 30 degrees* ◇ *an* ***angle*** *of 40°*

WORD BUILDING A **right angle** measures exactly 90°. An **acute angle** measures less than 90° and an **obtuse angle** measures more than 90°.

SPELLING Be careful! Don't confuse **angle** and **angel**. Look closely at the difference in spelling.

angles

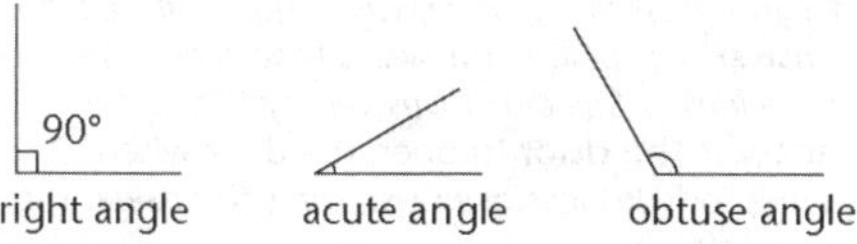

angler (say **ang**-gluh) *noun* (*plural* **anglers**)
a person who catches fish as a hobby

Anglo- (say **ang**-gloh) *prefix*
relating to England or Britain

Anglo-Boer War (say **ang**-gloh-buur **waw**) *noun* = **South African War**

angry (say **ang**-gree) *adjective* (**angrier**, **angriest**)
feeling or showing anger: *My father was* ***angry*** *with me when I got home late.*
▸ **angrily** (*adverb*): *'Somebody has taken my book!' she shouted* ***angrily***.

anguish (say **ang**-gwish) *noun* (*no plural*)
great sorrow or mental pain

angular (say **ang**-gyuh-luh) *adjective*
with sharp points or corners: *The car has an* ***angular*** *shape.*

animal (say **an**-i-muhl) *noun* (*plural* **animals**)
1 (*biology*) any living thing that can move and feel, including mammals, birds, reptiles, fish and **invertebrates**: *Humans are social* ***animals***.
2 (*informal*) any mammal, but not a human being: *Cats, horses and rats are* ***animals***.

animate (say **an**-i-muht) *adjective*
having life: *an* ***animate*** *object*
➲ OPPOSITE **inanimate**

animated (say **an**-i-mayt-uhd) *adjective*
1 full of interest and energy: *an* ***animated*** *discussion* ➲ SYNONYM **lively**
2 (used about films) using a process or method which makes pictures or models appear to move: ***animated*** *cartoons*

animation (say an-i-**may**-shuhn) *noun* (*no plural*)
the process of making films, videos and computer games in which drawings or models of people and animals seem to move: *computer* ***animation***

ankle (say **ang**-kuhl) *noun* (*plural* **ankles**)
the part of your leg where it joins your foot
➲ See illustration at **foot**

annex (say uh-**nekss**) *verb* (**annexing**, **annexed**)
to take control of something, such as a country: *Germany* ***annexed*** *Austria in 1938.*

annexe (say **an**-ekss) *noun* (*plural* **annexes**)
a building that is attached to a larger one: *I live in an* ***annexe*** *next to the house.*

annihilate (say uh-**ny**-uh-layt) *verb* (**annihilating**, **annihilated**)
to destroy or defeat something completely: *The soldiers were ordered to* ***annihilate*** *the city.* ◇ *The Springboks* ***annihilated*** *England in the rugby match.*
▸ **annihilation** (*noun*)

anniversary (say an-i-**vur**-suh-ree) *noun* (*plural* **anniversaries**)
a day that is exactly a year or a number of years after a special or important event: *Today is their 25th wedding* ***anniversary***.

annotate (say **an**-uh-tayt) *verb* (**annotating**, **annotated**)
to add notes to a book or text, giving explanations or comments: ***Annotate*** *your map to show where you have been.*
▸ **annotated** (*adjective*): *an* ***annotated*** *drawing*

announce (say uh-**nownss**) *verb* (**announcing**, **announced**)
to tell a lot of people something important: *She* ***announced*** *the winner of the race.* ◇ *She* ***announced*** *that she was leaving.*
▸ **announcement** (*noun*): *Ladies and gentlemen, I'd like to make an* ***announcement***.

announcer (say uh-**nown**-suh) *noun* (*plural* **announcers**)
a person whose job is to tell us about programmes on radio or television

annoy (say uh-**noy**) *verb* (**annoying, annoyed**)
to make somebody a little angry: *It **annoys** me when he leaves his clothes on the floor.* ◇ *Close the door if the noise is **annoying** you.*

annoyance (say uh-**noy**-uhnss) *noun* (*no plural*)
the feeling of being a little angry: *She could not hide her **annoyance** when I arrived late.*

annoyed (say uh-**noyd**) *adjective*
a little angry: *I was **annoyed** when he forgot to phone me.* ◇ *My dad is **annoyed** with me.*

annoying (say uh-**noy**-ing) *adjective*
making you feel a little angry: *It's **annoying** when people don't listen to you.*

annual (say **an**-yuu-uhl) *adjective*
1 that happens or comes once every year: *There is an **annual** meeting in June.*
2 for a period of one year: *Their **annual** income* (= the money they earn in a year) *is less than R20 000.*
▸ **annually** (*adverb*): *Payment will be made **annually**.*

annul (say uh-**nul**) *verb* (**annulling, annulled**)
to say officially that something is no longer legally valid: *They **annulled** their marriage after a week.*

anode (say **an**-ohd) *noun* (*plural* **anodes**) (*science*)
the positive pole in an electric current system: *An **anode** is a positively charged electrode.*
➲ See **cathode**, **electrode**

anon. (say uh-**non**) *abbreviation* **anonymous**

anonymous (say uh-**non**-i-muhss) *adjective*
1 (used about a person) whose name is not known or made public: *An **anonymous** caller told the police about the bomb.*
2 done or written by a person whose name is not known or made public: *She received an **anonymous** letter.*
▸ **anonymously** (*adverb*): *The letter was sent **anonymously**.*

anorak (say **an**-uh-rak) *noun* (*plural* **anoraks**)
a short coat with a covering for your head (called a **hood**) that protects you from rain, wind and cold

anorexia (say an-uh-**rek**-si-uh) *noun* (*no plural*) (also **anorexia nervosa**)
a mental illness in which someone is afraid of being fat and so they do not eat. It especially affects young women.
▸ **anorexic** (*adjective*): *She was **anorexic** for a few years.*

another (say uh-**nu*th***-uh) *adjective, pronoun*
1 one more thing or person of the same kind: *Would you like **another** drink?* ◇ *I like these cakes – can I have **another** one?*
2 a different thing or person: *I can't see you tomorrow – can we meet **another** day?*

answer[1] (say **aan**-suh) *noun* (*plural* **answers**)
1 something that you say or write when you **respond** to somebody or something: *Thanks for the offer but the **answer** is still no.* ◇ *Have you had an **answer** to your letter?*
2 when somebody opens the door or picks up the telephone because somebody has knocked or rung: *I knocked on the door and waited but there was no **answer**.*
3 a way of stopping a problem: *I didn't have any money so the only **answer** was to borrow some.*
4 the correct reply to a question in a test or an exam: *What was the **answer** to question 4?* ◇ *All the **answers** are at the back of the book.*

PRONUNCIATION Don't pronounce the **w** in **answer**.

answer[2] (say **aan**-suh) *verb* (**answering, answered**)
to say or write something back when somebody has asked you something or written to you: *I asked him if he was hungry but he didn't **answer**.* ◇ *I couldn't **answer** all the exam questions.* ◇ *She didn't **answer** my letter.*
answer the door to open the door when somebody knocks or rings: *Can you **answer** the door, please?*
answer the telephone to pick up the telephone when it rings, and speak

ant *noun* (*plural* **ants**)
a very small insect that lives in big groups in the ground and is known for being **industrious**

antagonism (say an-**tag**-uhn-i-zuhm) *noun* (*no plural*)
a feeling of hate and of being against someone or something
▸ **antagonistic** (*adjective*)

antagonize (say an-**tag**-uhn-ize) *verb* (**antagonizing, antagonized**) (also **antagonise**)
to annoy or make somebody angry

Antarctic (say ant-**aak**-tik) *noun* (*no plural*)
the very cold regions in the most southern part of the world ➲ See **Arctic**

anteater (say **ant**-eet-uh) *noun* (*plural* **anteaters**)
a wild mammal with a long nose and long sticky tongue that it uses to catch ants

antelope (say **ant**-i-lohp) *noun* (*plural* **antelope** or **antelopes**)
a wild mammal from Africa and Asia that has long thin legs and can run fast. All male **antelope** and many female **antelope** have horns: *Springbok and gemsbok are two types of antelope.* ➲ SYNONYM **buck**[1] 1

examples of antelope

springbok gemsbok

antenatal (say an-tee-**nay**-tuhl) *adjective*
relating to the care of pregnant women: *an **antenatal** clinic* ➲ See **post-natal**

antenna (say an-**ten**-uh) *noun*
1 (*biology*) (*plural* **antennae**) one of the two long thin parts on the head of some **arthropods**, especially on that of an insect and a **crustacean**, which they use to touch, smell and taste things ➲ SYNONYM **feeler** ➲ See illustrations at **crayfish**, **insect**
2 (*plural* **antennas** or **antennae**) an **aerial**

anterior (say an-**teer**-ri-uh) *adjective*
at or near the front of the body: *The fish has **anterior** gills.* ➲ OPPOSITE **posterior**

anthem (say **an**-thuhm) *noun* (*plural* **anthems**)
a song that is usually sung on special occasions: *We sing our school **anthem** on important days.* ◇ *Our national **anthem** is made up of two songs.*

anther (say **an**-thuh) *noun* (*plural* **anthers**) (*biology*)
the male part of a flower that produces **pollen** ➲ See illustration at **flower**

anthology (say an-**thol**-uh-jee) *noun* (*plural* **anthologies**)
a book that has a collection of poems or other writing by different authors

anthracite (say **an**-thruh-site) *noun* (*no plural*)
a very hard type of coal that burns slowly without much smoke

anthrax (say **an**-thrakss) *noun* (*no plural*)
a serious disease that affects animals, especially sheep and cows and sometimes people, and can cause death

anthropology (say an-thruh-**pol**-uh-jee) *noun* (*no plural*)
the study of people and their customs and beliefs

anti- (say **an**-ti) *prefix*
against, or not: *an **anti-smoking** campaign*
ℹ ORIGIN: from Greek *anti* meaning 'against'

antibiotic (say an-ti-by-**ot**-ik) *noun* (*plural* **antibiotics**)
a medicine that can destroy bacteria and cure infections: *The doctor gave me some **antibiotics**.*
ℹ ORIGIN: 19th century, from Greek *anti-* meaning 'against' + *biotikos* meaning 'fit for life' (from *bios* meaning 'life')

antibody (say **an**-ti-bod-ee) *noun* (*plural* **antibodies**)
a substance that the body produces to fight infections: ***Antibodies** are a type of protein.*

anticipate (say an-**tiss**-i-payt) *verb* (**anticipating**, **anticipated**)
to think that something will happen and be ready for it: *We **anticipated** this problem.*

anticipation (say an-tiss-i-**pay**-shuhn) *noun* (*no plural*)
excited feelings about something that is going to happen: *They queued outside the stadium in excited **anticipation**.*

anticlimax (say an-ti-**kly**-makss) *noun* (*plural* **anticlimaxes**)
an event that is not as exciting as you expected, that becomes a disappointment ➲ See Study page 17

anticline (say **an**-ti-kline) *noun* (*plural* **anticlines**) (*geography*)
folded layers of rock shaped like a hill ➲ See **syncline**

anticline

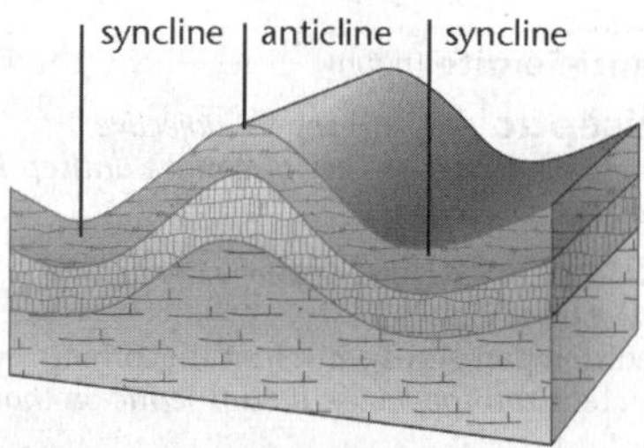

anticlockwise (say an-ti-**klok**-wize) *adjective, adverb*
in the opposite direction to the hands of a clock: *Turn the handle **anticlockwise**.*
➲ OPPOSITE **clockwise**

A B C D E F G H I J K L M N O P Q R S T U V W X Y Z

A B C D E F G H I J K L M N O P Q R S T U V W X Y Z

antics (say **an**-tikss) *plural noun*
funny, strange or silly ways of behaving: *Despite their clownish* ***antics****, the bears are extremely dangerous.*

anticyclone (say an-ti-**sike**-lohn) *noun* (*plural* **anticyclones**)
an area of high air pressure that often produces calm weather conditions with clear skies: *Rotating winds move outwards from the centre of an* ***anticyclone****.*

antidote (say **an**-ti-doht) *noun* (*plural* **antidotes**)
1 a substance that is used to prevent a poison from having an effect
2 anything that helps you deal with something unpleasant: *A letter from my friend gave me the* ***antidote*** *I needed.*

antihistamine (say an-ti-**hiss**-tuh-meen) *noun* (*plural* **antihistamines**)
a medicine used to treat an **allergy**

antipathy (say an-**ti**-puh-thee) *noun* (*no plural*)
a strong feeling of not liking a person or thing

antique (say an-**teek**) *noun* (*plural* **antiques**)
an old thing that is worth a lot of money: *These chairs are* ***antiques****.*
► **antique** (*adjective*): *an* ***antique*** *vase*

antiquity (say an-**tik**-wuh-tee) *noun*
1 (*no plural*) the ancient past, especially the times of the Ancient Greeks and Romans
2 (*plural* **antiquities**) objects from ancient times

antiretroviral (say an-ti-ret-roh-**vy**-ruhl) *adjective* (abbr. ARV)
referring to a class of medicines that slow the activity of a **retrovirus** such as HIV
► **antiretroviral** (*noun*)

anti-Semitic (say an-ti-suh-**mit**-ik) *adjective*
against Jewish people: *Your* ***anti-Semitic*** *views are unfair.*
► **anti-Semite** (*noun*)

antiseptic[1] (say an-ti-**sep**-tik) *adjective*
able to kill bacteria: *They also make* ***antiseptic*** *pads to heal wounds.*

antiseptic[2] (say an-ti-**sep**-tik) *noun* (*plural* **antiseptics**)
medicine that stops a cut from becoming infected: *You should use an* ***antiseptic*** *on that cut.*

antisocial (say an-ti-**soh**-shuhl) *adjective*
unfriendly and not liking to be with other people

antithesis (say an-**ti**-thuh-siss) *noun* (*plural* **antitheses**)
the opposite of something: *They are the* ***antithesis*** *of the democratic government we voted for.*

antler (say **ant**-luh) *noun* (*plural* **antlers**)
a bone shaped like a branch that grows on the head of a **deer**

antonym (say **an**-tuh-nim) *noun* (*plural* **antonyms**)
a word or phrase that means the opposite of another word or phrase in the same language: *'Tall' and 'short' are* ***antonyms****.*
➲ OPPOSITE **synonym**

anus (say **ay**-nuhss) *noun* (*plural* **anuses**)
the opening through which solid waste substances leave the body ➲ See illustration at **alimentary canal**
► **anal** (*adjective*): ***anal*** *cancer*

anvil (say **an**-vil) *noun* (*plural* **anvils**)
1 a flat iron block on which a **blacksmith** beats heated metal into a required shape with a hammer
2 a very small bone inside the ear

anxiety (say ang-**zy**-uh-tee) *noun* (*plural* **anxieties**)
a feeling of worry and fear

anxious (say **ank**-shuhss) *adjective*
1 worried and afraid: *She's* ***anxious*** *because her daughter hasn't arrived yet.*
2 wanting something very much: *My family are* ***anxious*** *to meet you.* ◇ *The teacher is* ***anxious*** *for her class to do well.*
► **anxiously** (*adverb*): *We waited* ***anxiously****.*

any[1] (say **en**-ee) *pronoun, adjective*
1 a word that you use instead of 'some' in questions and after 'not' and 'if': *'No, I don't want* ***any****.'* ◇ *I want some chocolate but there isn't* ***any****.* ➲ See note at **some**
2 used for saying that it does not matter which thing or person you choose: *Come* ***any*** *day next week.* ◇ *Take* ***any*** *book you want.*

any[2] (say **en**-ee) *adverb*
used in negative sentences or questions to make an adjective or an adverb stronger: *I can't walk* ***any*** *faster.* ◇ *Is your dad feeling* ***any*** *better?* ◇ *I don't want* ***any*** *more.*

anybody (say **en**-ee-bod-ee) another word for **anyone**

anyhow (say **en**-ee-how) another word for **anyway**

any more (say en-ee **maw**) *adverb* (also **anymore**)
used at the end of negative sentences and questions to mean 'now': *She doesn't live here **any more**.* ◇ *Why doesn't he speak to me **any more**?*

anyone (say **en**-ee-wun) *pronoun* (also **anybody**)
1 used in questions and negative sentences to mean 'any person': *There wasn't **anyone** there.* ◇ *Did you see **anyone** you know?*
2 any person, it does not matter who: ***Anyone** can learn to swim.*

anything (say **en**-ee-thing) *pronoun*
1 used in questions and negative sentences to mean 'a thing of any kind': *Is there **anything** in that box?* ◇ *I can't see **anything**.* ◇ *'Would you like **anything** else?' 'No, thanks.'*
2 any thing or things, it does not matter what: *I'm so hungry, I could eat **anything**!* ◇ *I'll do **anything** you say.*
not anything like somebody or **something** not the same as any person or thing in any way: *She isn't **anything** like her sister.*

anyway (say **en**-ee-way) *adverb* (also **anyhow**)
1 a word that you use when you give a second, more important reason for something: *I don't want to go out tonight and **anyway** I haven't got any money.*
2 in spite of something else: *It was very expensive but she bought it **anyway**.*
3 a word that you use when you start to talk about something different or when you go back to something you talked about earlier: ***Anyway**, how are you?*

anywhere (say **en**-ee-wair) *adverb*
1 used in negative sentences and in questions instead of 'somewhere': *I can't find a pen **anywhere**.* ◇ *Are you going **anywhere**?*
2 in, at or to any place, when it does not matter where: *Put the box down **anywhere**.*

aorta (say ay-**aw**-tuh) *noun* (*plural* **aortas**)
the main **artery** that carries blood from the heart to the rest of the body ➲ See illustration at **heart**

apart (say uh-**paat**) *adverb*
1 away from the others or each other: *The two houses are 500 metres **apart**.* ◇ *My mother and father live **apart** now.*
2 into parts: *He took my radio **apart** to repair it.*
apart from a person or **thing** except for: *There's nobody here, **apart** from me.* ◇ *I like all vegetables **apart** from carrots.*

apartheid (say uh-**paat**-hayt) *noun* (*no plural*)
the former government policy in South Africa which kept people of different races separate, and allowed only white people to have full political and economic rights
🛈 **ORIGIN**: 20th century, from Afrikaans *apartheid* meaning 'separateness'

apartment (say uh-**paat**-muhnt) *noun* (*plural* **apartments**)
a group of rooms for living in, usually in a big building: *We live in a two-bedroomed **apartment**.* ➲ **SYNONYM flat**[3]

apathy (say **ap**-uh-thee) *noun* (*no plural*)
a feeling of not caring about something or not being enthusiastic about something: *There was **apathy** about the elections at school.*
▸ **apathetic** (*adjective*): *Why are you so **apathetic** about school this year?*

ape (say **ayp**) *noun* (*plural* **apes**)
an animal like a big monkey, with long arms and no tail: *Gorillas and chimpanzees are **apes**.*

aperture (say **ap**-uh-tshuh) *noun* (*plural* **apertures**)
1 (*formal*) a small opening in something
2 (*technology*) the small opening that allows light onto the **lens** of a camera to take a photo

apex (say **ay**-pekss) *noun* (*plural* **apexes**)
the top or highest part of something: *A tile has come off the **apex** of our roof.*

aphid (say **ay**-fid) *noun* (*plural* **aphids**)
a very small insect that sucks the juice from plants

aphorism (say **ay**-fuh-riz-uhm) *noun* (*plural* **aphorisms**)
a short phrase that says something true in a clever way

apiary (say **ay**-pi-uh-ree) *noun* (*plural* **apiaries**)
a place where bees are kept in **hives**

apocalypse (say uh-**pok**-uh-lipss) *noun* (*no plural*)
1 the complete destruction of the world
2 a situation causing very serious damage
▸ **apocalyptic** (*adjective*)

apocryphal (say uh-**pok**-ri-fuhl) *adjective*
(used about a story) well known but probably not true

apologize (say uh-**pol**-uh-jize) *verb* (**apologizing, apologized**) (also **apologise**)
to say that you are sorry about something that you have done: *I **apologized** to Themba for losing his book.*

apology (say uh-**pol**-uh-jee) *noun* (*plural* **apologies**)
words that you say or write to show that you are sorry about something you have done: *Please accept my **apologies**.*

A B C D E F G H I J K L M N O P Q R S T U V W X Y Z

apostle (say uh-**poss**-uhl) *noun* (*plural* **apostles**)
1 Apostle one of the twelve men that Jesus Christ chose to tell people about him and what he taught
2 someone who strongly believes in something and tries to make other people believe in it too
🛈 ORIGIN: from Old English *apostol*, through Latin from Greek *apostolos* meaning 'messenger'

apostrophe (say uh-**poss**-truh-fee) *noun* (*plural* **apostrophes**)
the sign ' that you use in writing ➲ See Study page 16

USAGE You use an **apostrophe** to show that you have left a letter out of a word, for example in **I'm** (= I am) and **we're** (= we are).

USAGE You also use an **apostrophe** to show that something belongs to somebody or something.
- If the noun is singular, write the apostrophe before the s: *one boy's homework*
- If the noun is plural and ends in -s, write the apostrophe after the s: *three boys' homework*
- If the noun is plural and doesn't end in -s, use the apostrophe like this: *ten men's hats* ◇ *three women's bikes* ◇ *people's history*
- Note that **its, hers** and **theirs** have no apostrophe in these situations, e.g. *The dog hurt its foot.* ◇ *The book is hers.*

apothem (say **ap**-oh-them) *noun* (*plural* **apothems**) (*maths*)
a line from the centre of a regular **polygon** that forms a 90-degree angle with any one of its sides

appalling (say uh-**pawl**-ing) *adjective*
very bad, terrible: ***appalling** cruelty*

apparatus (say ap-uh-**ray**-tuhss) *noun* (*plural* **apparatuses**)
the set of tools, instruments or equipment used for doing an experiment or an activity: *the **apparatus** in our laboratory* ◇ *breathing **apparatus***

apparent (say uh-**pa**-ruhnt) *adjective*
clear, or easy to see or understand: *It was **apparent** that she didn't like him.*
➲ SYNONYM **obvious**

apparently (say uh-**pa**-ruhnt-lee) *adverb*
according to what you have heard or read or according to the way something appears, but perhaps not true: ***Apparently**, he's already been married twice.* ◇ *She was **apparently** undisturbed by the news.*

apparition (say ap-uh-**rish**-uhn) *noun* (*plural* **apparitions**)
a ghost

appeal[1] (say uh-**peel**) *noun*
1 (*no plural*) a quality that makes a person or thing attractive or interesting: *I can't understand the **appeal** of stamp collecting.*
2 (*plural* **appeals**) asking a lot of people for money, help or information: *The police made an **appeal** for witnesses to come forward.*

appeal[2] (say uh-**peel**) *verb* (**appealing, appealed**)
1 to ask in a serious way for something that you want very much: *Aid workers in the disaster area **appealed** for food and clothing.*
2 to be attractive or interesting to somebody: *Pop music doesn't **appeal** to me.*

appear (say uh-**peer**) *verb* (**appearing, appeared**)
1 to seem: *She **appears** to be very happy at her new school.* ◇ *It **appears** that I was wrong.*
2 to suddenly be seen or to come into sight: *The sun **appeared** from behind a cloud.* ◇ *We waited for an hour but he didn't **appear**.*
➲ OPPOSITE **disappear**

appearance (say uh-**peer**-ruhnss) *noun* (*plural* **appearances**)
1 the way that a person or thing looks or seems: *A new hairstyle can completely change your **appearance**.*
2 the coming of a person or thing or when a person or thing is seen: *Her **appearance** at the party surprised us.* ◇ *Is this your first **appearance** on television?*

appease (say uh-**peez**) *verb* (**appeasing, appeased**)
1 to make somebody calmer or less angry by agreeing to do what they want: *I gave my little brother a biscuit to **appease** him.*
2 to give a country what it wants to stop a war from happening

append (say uh-**pend**) *verb* (**appending, appended**)
to add something at the end: *We **appended** a poem to our project.*

appendage (say uh-**pend**-ij) *noun* (*plural* **appendages**)
a smaller or less important part of something bigger: *Your appendix is a useless **appendage** of your intestine.*

appendicitis (say uh-pen-duh-**sy**-tiss) *noun* (*no plural*)
a swelling of the **appendix**, often causing pain and sometimes needing to be removed

appendix (say uh-**pen**-dikss) *noun*
1 (*plural* **appendixes**) a small organ, with no known function, joined to your **intestine**
2 (*plural* **appendices**) a section at the end of a book or other writing that gives extra information

appetite (say **ap**-uh-tite) *noun* (*plural* **appetites**) the feeling that you want to eat: *Swimming always gives me an **appetite*** (= makes me hungry).

applaud (say uh-**plawd**) *verb* (**applauding, applauded**) to make a noise by hitting your hands together (called **clapping**) to show that you like something: *We all **applauded** loudly at the end of the song.*
▸ **applause** (*noun*): *There was loud **applause** from the audience.*

apple (say **ap**-l) *noun* (*plural* **apples**) a hard round fruit with green or red skin
🛈 **ORIGIN**: from Old English *æppel*, related to Dutch *appel*

appliance (say uh-**ply**-uhnss) *noun* (*plural* **appliances**) a useful machine for doing something in the house: *Washing machines and irons are electrical **appliances**.*

applicable (say **ap**-lik-uhb-l) *adjective* concerning someone or something: *The rules are **applicable** to everybody taking part in the competition.*

applicant (say **ap**-li-kuhnt) *noun* (*plural* **applicants**) a person who makes a formal request for a job, or a place at university, for example: *There were six **applicants** for the job.*

application (say ap-li-**kay**-shuhn) *noun* (*plural* **applications**)
1 writing to ask for something, for example a job: ***Applications** for the job should be made to the Personnel Manager.*
2 (*computing*) a computer program that is designed to do a particular job
3 the practical use of something, especially of knowledge or something you have discovered: *The **application** of science is important in modern farming.* ◇ *the **application** of new technologies to teaching* ➲ See Study page 19
application form a special piece of paper that you write on when you are trying to get something, for example a job

apply (say uh-**ply**) *verb* (**applying, applied**)
1 to write to ask for something: *Sizwe has **applied** for a place at university.*
2 to be about a person or thing or to be important to a person or thing: *This law **applies** to children under sixteen.*
3 to use something or make something work in a particular situation: ***Apply** what you learnt in maths to your woodwork project.*

appoint (say uh-**poynt**) *verb* (**appointing, appointed**) to choose somebody for a job or position: *The bank has **appointed** a new manager.*

appointment (say uh-**poynt**-muhnt) *noun* (*plural* **appointments**)
1 an arrangement to see somebody at a particular time: *I've got an **appointment** with the doctor at ten o'clock.* ◇ *You can telephone to make an **appointment**.*
2 (*formal*) a job

appreciate (say uh-**pree**-shi-ayt) *verb* (**appreciating, appreciated**)
1 to enjoy something or understand how good somebody or something is: *My boss doesn't **appreciate** me.*
2 to understand that a situation is difficult: *I **appreciate** your problem, but I can't help you.*
3 to be grateful for something that somebody has done for you: *Thank you for your help. I **appreciate** it.*
4 to become more valuable over a period of time ➲ **OPPOSITE depreciate**

appreciation (say uh-pree-shi-**ay**-shuhn) *noun* (*no plural*)
1 understanding and enjoyment of how good somebody or something is: *She shows little **appreciation** of good music.*
2 the feeling of being grateful for something that somebody has done for you: *We gave her some flowers to show our **appreciation** for her hard work.*
3 an increase in value

apprehend (say ap-ri-**hend**) *verb* (**apprehending, apprehended**) to stop and catch a criminal: *The thief was **apprehended** before he could leave the property.*

apprehension (say ap-ri-**hen**-shuhn) *noun* (*no plural*) a feeling of worry about something: *You could hear the **apprehension** in her voice before she wrote the exam.*

apprentice (say uh-**pren**-tiss) *noun* (*plural* **apprentices**) a young person who is learning to do a job: *an **apprentice** electrician*

approach[1] (say uh-**prohch**) *verb* (**approaching, approached**) to come near to a person or thing in distance or time: *As you **approach** the village, you'll see a*

A B C D E F G H I J K L M N O P Q R S T U V W X Y Z

A B C D E F G H I J K L M N O P Q R S T U V W X Y Z

church on your right. ◇ *The exams were **approaching**.*

approach² (say uh-**prohch**) *noun*
1 (*plural* **approaches**) a way of doing something: *This is a new **approach** to learning languages.*
2 (*no plural*) coming near or nearer to a person or thing: *the **approach** of winter*

appropriate (say uh-**proh**-pri-uht) *adjective*
suitable or right for a particular situation or person: *Jeans and T-shirts are not **appropriate** for a job interview.* ➲ OPPOSITE **inappropriate**
▸ **appropriately** (*adverb*): *Please come **appropriately** dressed.*

approval (say uh-**proov**-l) *noun* (*no plural*)
feeling, showing or saying that something or somebody is good or right: *Palisa's parents gave the marriage their **approval**.* ➲ OPPOSITE **disapproval**

approve (say uh-**proov**) *verb* (**approving, approved**)
to think or say that something or somebody is good or right: *My parents don't **approve** of my friends.* ◇ *She doesn't **approve** of smoking.*
➲ OPPOSITE **disapprove**

approximate (say uh-**prokss**-i-muht) *adjective*
almost correct but not exact: *The **approximate** time of arrival is three o'clock.*

approximately (say uh-**prokss**-i-muht-lee) *adverb*
about or more or less: *I live **approximately** two kilometres from the station.*
➲ SYNONYMS **about** 1, **roughly** 1

apricot (say **ay**-pri-kot) *noun* (*plural* **apricots**)
a small, soft, yellow or orange fruit with a large stone inside

April (say **ay**-pruhl) *noun*
the fourth month of the year
ℹ ORIGIN: through Old English, from Latin *Aprilis*

apron (say **ay**-pruhn) *noun* (*plural* **aprons**)
a piece of clothing that you wear over the front of your clothes to keep them clean, especially when you are cooking

apt *adjective*
suitable and right for a certain situation: *That comment was very **apt**.*

aptitude (say **ap**-ti-tyood) *noun* (*plural* **aptitudes**)
a natural ability or skill: *My sister has an **aptitude** for maths and I have an **aptitude** for English.*

aquarium (say uh-**kwair**-ri-uhm) *noun* (*plural* **aquariums**)
1 a large glass container filled with water in which fish are kept
2 a building where people can go to see fish and other water animals

aquatic (say uh-**kwat**-ik) *adjective*
being in or near the water: *Dolphins and whales are **aquatic** mammals.*

aqueduct (say **ak**-wi-dukt) *noun* (*plural* **aqueducts**)
a structure like a bridge used for carrying water across a valley

Arabic (say **a**-ruh-bik) *noun* (*no plural*)
the language of the Arab people

Arabic number *noun* (*plural* **Arabic numbers**)
any of the numbers 1, 2, 3, 4, 5, 6, 7, 8, 9 and 0 that we use for counting and maths
➲ See Study page 20 ➲ See **Roman number**

arable (say **a**-ruhb-l) *adjective*
relating to land that is suitable for growing crops: ***arable** soil*

arachnid (say a-**rak**-nid) *noun* (*plural* **arachnids**)
any of the class of small creatures with eight legs, including spiders: *Scorpions, spiders and ticks belong to the **arachnid** class.*

arbitrary (say **aa**-bit-ruh-ree) *adjective*
not seeming to have a reason or plan: *It was an **arbitrary** decision, made without discussion.*

arbitrate (say **aa**-bi-trayt) *verb* (**arbitrating, arbitrated**)
(an outside person) to settle an argument between two people or groups by finding a solution that both can accept: *Our teacher had to **arbitrate** our disagreement.*
▸ **arbitration** (*noun*): *They called for **arbitration** to help settle the argument.*
▸ **arbitrator** (*noun*): *The **arbitrator** settled the dispute between the manager and his workers.*

Arbor Day (say **aa**-buh day) *noun*
a day in the year set aside to plant and **appreciate** trees

arc (say **aak**) *noun* (*plural* **arcs**) (*maths*)
any part of a curved line, especially of a circle

arcs

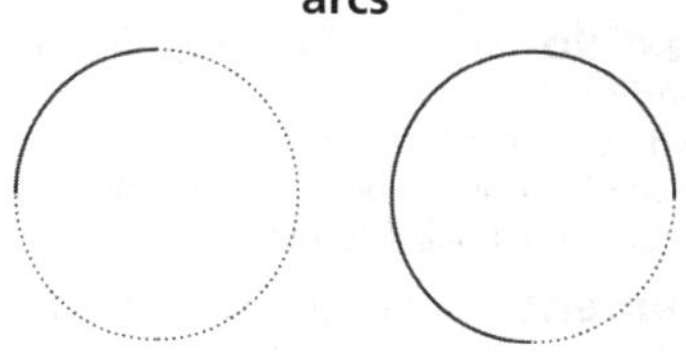

the solid lines show two different arcs of a circle

arcade (say aa-**kayd**) *noun* (*plural* **arcades**)
a covered passage with shops

arch[1] (say **aach**) *noun* (*plural* **arches**)
a part of a bridge, building or wall that is in the shape of a half-circle

arch

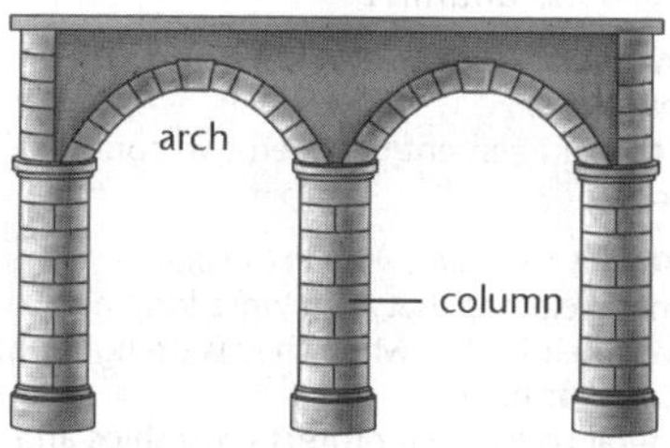

arch[2] (say **aach**) *verb* (**arching, arched**)
to make into an arch: *The cat* ***arched*** *his back when he stretched.*

arch- (say **aach**) *prefix*
most important, or most extreme: ***archbishop*** ◇ ***arch-enemy***

archaeologist (say aa-kee-**ol**-uh-jist) *noun* (*plural* **archaeologists**)
a person who studies or knows a lot about **archaeology**

archaeology (say aa-kee-**ol**-uh-jee) *noun* (*no plural*)
the study of the past by looking at objects or parts of old buildings that are found in the ground

archaic (say aa-**kay**-ik) *adjective*
very old-fashioned and not used any more

archbishop (say aach-**bish**-uhp) *noun* (*plural* **archbishops**)
a priest with a very high position, who is responsible for all the churches in an area

arch-enemy (say aach-**en**-uh-mee) *noun* (*plural* **arch-enemies**)
your main enemy

archer (say **aach**-uh) *noun* (*plural* **archers**)
a person who shoots arrows with a **bow[3]** 1

archetype (say **aa**-ki-tipe) *noun* (*plural* **archetypes**)
a typical example of something: *He is the* ***archetype*** *of a movie star, with a great body and good looks.*
▸ **archetypal** (*adjective*)

archipelago (say aa-ki-**pel**-uh-goh) *noun* (*plural* **archipelagos** or **archipelagoes**)
a group of islands or a sea with many islands

architect (say **aa**-ki-tekt) *noun* (*plural* **architects**)
a person whose job is to design and plan buildings

architecture (say **aa**-ki-tek-tshuh) *noun* (*no plural*)
1 the study of designing and making buildings: *He has a degree in* ***architecture****.*
2 the design or style of a building or buildings: *Do you like modern* ***architecture****?*

archive (say **aa**-kive) *noun* (*plural* **archives**)
1 a collection of documents which shows the history of a place, organization or period: *The library has an* ***archive*** *of World War I records.*
2 (usually **archives**) the place where they are kept: *Our class went to the* ***archives*** *to do research.*

Arctic (say **aak**-tik) *noun* (*no plural*)
the very cold regions in the most northern part of the world ➲ See **Antarctic**

ardent (say **aa**-duhnt) *adjective*
showing strong feelings: *He was an* ***ardent*** *supporter of the Proteas.*

arduous (say **aad**-yoo-uhss) *adjective*
full of difficulties: *Their journey was* ***arduous*** *and dangerous.*

are (say **aa**) form of **be**

area (say **air**-ri-uh) *noun* (*plural* **areas**)
1 a part of a town, country or the world: *Do you live in this* ***area****?* ◇ *the desert* ***areas*** *of North Africa*
2 the size of a flat place: *If a room is three metres wide and four metres long, it has an* ***area*** *of twelve square metres.*
3 a space that you use for a particular activity: *Learners are not allowed into this* ***area*** *of the school.*

arena (say uh-**ree**-nuh) *noun* (*plural* **arenas**)
a place with seats around it where you can watch sports or concerts

A B C D E F G H I J K L M N O P Q R S T U V W X Y Z

A B C D E F G H I J K L M N O P Q R S T U V W X Y Z

aren't (say **aant**) short for **are not**

argon (say **aa**-gon) *noun (no plural) (science)* (symbol Ar)
a colourless gas that does not react with other elements and is used in electric lights

argue (say **aa**-gyoo) *verb* (**arguing, argued**)
1 to talk angrily to somebody because you do not agree: *My parents **argue** about money.* ◇ *I often **argue** with my brother.*
2 to say why you think something is right or wrong: *He **argued** that war is not the answer.*

argument (say **aa**-gyoo-muhnt) *noun (plural* **arguments**)
1 an angry discussion between people who do not agree with each other: *They had an **argument** about where to go on holiday.*
2 the reason(s) that you give to support your opinion about something: *the **argument** for and against the death penalty*

argumentative (say aa-gyoo-**ment**-uh-tiv) *adjective*
often involved in arguments or enjoying arguments: *My brother is so **argumentative**.*

aria (say **aa**-ri-uh) *noun (plural* **arias**)
a song in an opera for one voice

arid (say **a**-rid) *adjective*
(describing a land or climate) very dry: *We live in the **arid** part of the Northern Cape.*

arise (say uh-**rize**) *verb* (**arising, arose, has arisen**) *(formal)*
(a problem or difficult situation) to happen or start to exist

aristocrat (say **a**-riss-tuh-krat) *noun (plural* **aristocrats**)
a person born in the highest social class, who often has a special title
▸ **aristocracy** *(noun)*
▸ **aristocratic** *(adjective)*

arithmetic (say uh-**rith**-muh-tik) *noun (no plural) (maths)*
the area of mathematics that deals with adding, subtracting, multiplying or dividing numbers: *I'm not very good at mental **arithmetic**.*

ark (say **aak**) *noun (plural* **arks**)
(in the Bible) a large boat that Noah built to save his family and two of every type of animal from the flood

arm¹ (say **aam**) *noun (plural* **arms**)
the part of your body from your shoulder to your hand: *Put your **arms** in the air.* ◇ *He was carrying a book under his **arm**.*
arm in arm with your arm holding another person's arm: *The two friends walked **arm** in **arm**.*

arm² (say **aam**) *verb* (**arming, armed**)
to give someone weapons: *The government **armed** the troops.*

armadillo (say aam-uh-**dil**-oh) *noun (plural* **armadillos**)
a wild South American mammal with a hard shell made of pieces of bone, that eats insects and rolls into a ball if something attacks it

armaments (say **aam**-uh-muhntss) *plural noun*
weapons and military equipment

armchair (say **aam**-chair) *noun (plural* **armchairs**)
a soft comfortable chair with side parts where you can put your arms: *She was asleep in an **armchair**.*

armed (say **aamd**) *adjective*
carrying a gun or other weapon: *an **armed** robber* ◇ *Are the police **armed** in your country?*
➲ OPPOSITE **unarmed**

armistice (say **aam**-uhss-tiss) *noun (plural* **armistices**)
a peace agreement between two countries at war

armour (say **aam**-uh) *noun (no plural)*
1 metal clothes that men wore long ago to cover their bodies when they were fighting: *a suit of **armour***
2 metal covers that protect navy ships and army vehicles such as tanks

armoury (say **aam**-uh-ree) *noun (plural* **armouries**)
a place where people store weapons

armpit (say **aam**-pit) *noun (plural* **armpits**)
the part of your body under your arm, where your arm joins your body

arms (say **aamz**) *plural noun*
guns, bombs and other weapons for fighting

army (say **aa**-mee) *noun (plural* **armies**)
a large organized group of soldiers who are trained to fight on land: *He joined the **army** when he was nineteen.* ◇ *the South African **Army***

WORD BUILDING A soldier who fights on land is in the **army**, one who fights at sea is in the **navy** and a soldier who fights in the air is in the **air force**. The **army**, the **navy** and the **air force** together are called **the armed forces**.

aroma (say uh-**roh**-muh) *noun (plural* **aromas**)
a smell, usually pleasant: *the **aroma** of baking bread*
▸ **aromatic** *(adjective)*

arose (say uh-**rohz**) form of **arise**

around (say uh-**rownd**) *preposition, adverb*
1 (also **round**) in or to different places or in different directions: *Her clothes were lying **around** the room.* ◇ *The children were running **around** the house.*
2 (also **round**) in the opposite direction or in another direction: *Turn **around** and go home.*
3 (also **round**) on or to all sides of something, often in a circle: *We sat **around** the table.* ◇ *He ran **around** the track.*
4 in a place, or near here: *Is there a bank **around** here?* ◇ *Is Tshedi **around**? I need her.*
5 (also **about**) a little more or less, or a little before or after than: *I'll see you **around** seven* (= at about 7 o'clock).

arouse (say uh-**rowz**) *verb* (**arousing, aroused**)
to make someone react in a certain way: *This will **arouse** her interest.* ◇ *His suspicion was **aroused**.*

arrange (say uh-**raynj**) *verb* (**arranging, arranged**)
1 to make a plan for the future: *I have **arranged** to meet him at six o'clock.* ◇ *We **arranged** a big party for her birthday.*
2 to put things in a certain order or place: ***Arrange** the chairs in a circle.*

arrangement (say uh-**raynj**-muhnt) *noun* (*plural* **arrangements**)
1 a plan or preparation that you make so that something can happen in the future: *They are making **arrangements** for a party.*
2 a group of things put together so that they look nice: *a flower **arrangement***

array (say uh-**ray**) *noun* (*plural* **arrays**)
an arrangement of things: *I had an **array** of bursaries to choose from.*

arrears (say uh-**reerz**) *plural noun*
money that you owe somebody and should have paid earlier: *rent **arrears** of R2 000.*
to be in arrears to be late in paying money that you owe

arrest[1] (say uh-**rest**) *verb* (**arresting, arrested**)
(used about the police) to take a person away and not allow them to leave, because they broke the law or because the police think they may have committed a crime: *The man was **arrested** for carrying a weapon.*

arrest[2] (say uh-**rest**) *noun* (*plural* **arrests**)
the act of arresting somebody: *The police made five **arrests**.* ◇ *The wanted man is now under **arrest*** (= has been arrested).

arrival (say uh-**rive**-uhl) *noun* (*plural* **arrivals**)
the action or process of arriving: *My brother met me at the airport on my **arrival**.*
➲ OPPOSITE **departure**

arrive (say uh-**rive**) *verb* (**arriving, arrived**)
1 to come to a place: *What time did you **arrive** home?* ◇ *They've **arrived** in Botswana.* ◇ *We **arrived** at the station ten minutes late.*
➲ OPPOSITES **leave[1] 1, depart**
2 to come or happen: *Summer has **arrived**!*

> USAGE Be careful! In sense 1 above, we use **arrive in** with the name of a town or country and **arrive at** with a building such as a station, an airport or a school.

arrogant (say **a**-ruh-guhnt) *adjective*
thinking that you are better and more important than other people: *leaders who are **arrogant** and do whatever they want*

arrow (say **a**-roh) *noun* (*plural* **arrows**)
1 a long thin piece of wood or metal with a point at one end: *She released the **arrow** from the bow and it flew straight to the target.*
2 the sign (←) that shows where something is or where you should go: *The **arrow** is pointing left.*

arsenal (say **aa**-suh-nuhl) *noun* (*plural* **arsenals**)
1 a collection of weapons
2 a building where weapons are stored

arsenic (say **aa**-suh-nik) *noun* (*no plural*) (*science*) (symbol As)
a very poisonous chemical element

arson (say **aa**-suhn) *noun* (*no plural*)
the crime of setting fire to a building
▸ **arsonist** (*noun*): *The **arsonist** was arrested.*

art (say **aat**) *noun*
1 (*no plural*) making beautiful things, such as paintings and drawings: *He's studying **art** at college.*
2 (*no plural*) beautiful things such as paintings and drawings that somebody has made: *modern **art*** ◇ *an **art** gallery*
3 the arts (*plural noun*) things such as films, plays and literature: *How much money does the government spend on the **arts**?*
4 (*no plural*) a skill, or something that needs skill: *the **art** of letter writing*
5 arts (*plural noun*) the subjects you can study at school or university which are not science subjects, for example history or languages: *She has an **arts** degree.*

artefact (say **aa**-ti-fakt) *noun* (*plural* **artefacts**)
an object that a person has made, especially one of historical or cultural interest: ***Artefacts** such as jewellery and pottery were found in an ancient burial site.*

artery (say **aa**-tuh-ree) *noun* (*plural* **arteries**)
one of the tubes in your body that carry blood

A B C D E F G H I J K L M N O P Q R S T U V W X Y Z

away from your heart to other parts of your body ➲ See **vein**

arthritis (say aa-**thry**-tiss) *noun* (*no plural*)
a disease that causes pain and swelling in the joints of your body, for example your wrists and elbows

arthropod (say **aa**-thruh-pod) *noun* (*plural* **arthropods**)
any of a large group of animals with a hard body, no **backbone**, and legs that are divided into sections: *Arachnids, insects and crustaceans are **arthropods**.*

artichoke (say **aa**-ti-chohk) *noun* (*plural* **artichokes**)
a green vegetable with a lot of thick pointed leaves that looks like a flower. You eat the bottom part of the leaves and its centre when it is cooked.

article (say **aa**-tik-l) *noun* (*plural* **articles**)
1 a piece of writing in a newspaper or magazine: *Did you read the **article** about young fashion designers?*
2 a thing: *Many of the **articles** in the shop are half-price.* ◇ ***articles** of clothing* (= things such as skirts, coats and trousers)
3 (*grammar*) the words *a* and *an* (called the **indefinite articles**), or *the* (called the **definite article**) ➲ See Study page 4

articulate¹ (say aa-**tik**-yuh-luht) *adjective*
good at saying what you mean clearly: *She was polite and **articulate** when explaining what she wanted.* ➲ OPPOSITE **inarticulate** 1

articulate² (say aa-**tik**-yuu-layt) *verb* (**articulating**, **articulated**)
1 to say what you mean clearly: *When you read aloud, you should **articulate** clearly.*
2 to connect with a joint: *bones that **articulate** with others*
▸ **articulated** (*adjective*): *an **articulated** truck*

artificial (say aa-ti-**fish**-uhl) *adjective*
not natural or real, but made by people: ***artificial** flowers* ➲ SYNONYMS **man-made**, **synthetic**

artillery (say aa-**til**-uh-ree) *noun* (*no plural*)
the part of the army that uses large heavy guns

artisan (say aa-ti-**zan**) *noun* (*plural* **artisans**)
a person who makes things skilfully, usually with their hands

artist (say **aa**-tist) *noun* (*plural* **artists**)
a person who paints or draws pictures: *Monet was a famous **artist**.*

artistic (say aa-**tiss**-tik) *adjective*
good at painting, drawing or making beautiful things: *He's very **artistic** – his drawings are excellent.*

artwork (say **aat**-wurk) *noun*
1 (*plural* **artworks**) drawings, photographs and other pieces of art: *Who created this **artwork**?*
2 (*no plural*) photographs and pictures prepared for books and magazines

ARV (say ay-aar-**vee**) *noun* (*plural* **ARVs**)
a medicine that is used to fight **HIV**, the virus that causes AIDS in a person ❶ **ARV** is short for 'antiretroviral'.

Aryan (say **air**-ri-uhn) *noun* (*plural* **Aryans**)
1 a member of the group of people who settled in South Asia around 1500 BC
2 a person with fair hair and blue eyes, who the German Nazi party believed was better than other people

as (say **az**) *conjunction, preposition*
1 while something else is happening: *Just **as** I was leaving the house, the phone rang.*
2 as ... as words that you use to compare people or things: *Musa is **as** tall **as** his father.* ◇ *I haven't got **as** many clothes **as** you have.*
3 used to say that a person or thing has a particular job or purpose: *She works **as** a secretary for a big company.*
4 in the same way: *Please do **as** I tell you!*
5 because: ***As** she was ill, she stayed in bed.*

asap (say ay-ess-ay-**pee**) *abbreviation* (*informal*)
as soon as possible: *I'd like the report on my desk **asap**.*

asbestos (say ass-**bess**-tuhss) *noun* (*no plural*)
a soft mineral that does not burn. **Asbestos** was used a lot in the past to protect against heat, but it was found to be very dangerous to people's health: *We no longer use **asbestos** to make roofs.*

asbestosis (say ass-bess-**toh**-siss) *noun* (*no plural*)
a serious lung disease caused by breathing in small pieces of **asbestos**

ascend (say uh-**send**) *verb* (**ascending**, **ascended**)
to go up ➲ OPPOSITE **descend**
▸ **ascending** (*adjective*)
▸ **ascension** (*noun*)

ascent (say uh-**sent**) *noun* (*plural* **ascents**)
1 the act of moving up: ***ascent** to fame* ◇ ***ascent** to power*
2 a path that goes up: *The **ascent** was difficult but we rested at the top.*

ascertain (say ass-uh-**tayn**) *verb* (**ascertaining**, **ascertained**) (*formal*)
to find something out or to make sure of

something: *Try to **ascertain** which group this insect belongs to.*

ascetic (say uh-**set**-ik) *adjective*
not allowing yourself any pleasure

ascribe (say uh-**skribe**) *verb* (**ascribing, ascribed**)
to say that something was written by someone, or belongs to someone, or was caused by something: *Some people **ascribe** their tiredness to the hot weather.*

asexual (say ay-**sek**-shuu-uhl) *adjective*
1 (*biology*) not having or not using sexual organs: ***asexual** parasites*
2 (*biology*) producing new plants without using seeds: *An example of **asexual** reproduction is when you plant a potato and it develops into a new plant.*
3 without sexual feelings or qualities: *He was always presented as an **asexual** figure.*
▸ **asexually** (*adverb*)

ash *noun* (also **ashes**)
the grey powder that is left after something has burned: *the **ashes** of the fire*

ashamed (say uh-**shaym**-d) *adjective*
feeling sorry and unhappy because you have done something wrong, or because you are not as good as other people: *I was **ashamed** about lying to my parents.* ◇ *She was **ashamed** of her old clothes.*

ashore (say uh-**shaw**) *adverb*
onto the land from the sea or a river: *We left the boat and went **ashore**.*

ashtray (say **ash**-tray) *noun* (*plural* **ashtrays**)
a small dish for cigarette **ash** and the ends of cigarettes

Asian (say **ay**-zhuhn) *adjective*
from or connected with Asia: ***Asian** food*
▸ **Asian** (*noun*): *There are some **Asians** and Australians at our school.*

aside (say uh-**side**) *adverb*
on or to one side or away: *He put the letter **aside** while he did his homework.*

ask (say **aask**) *verb* (**asking, asked**)
1 to try to get an answer by using a question: *I **asked** him what the time was.* ◇ *'What's your name?' she **asked**.* ◇ *She **asked** the teacher a question.*
2 to request somebody to do something for you: *I **asked** her to drive me to the station.*
3 to try to get permission to do something: *I **asked** my teacher if I could go home.*
4 to invite somebody to go somewhere with you: *Vuyani has **asked** me to his party.*
ask for something to request somebody to give you something: *He **asked** for a new bike for his birthday.*

asleep (say uh-**sleep**) *adjective*
sleeping: *The baby is **asleep** in the bedroom.* ◇ *He fell **asleep*** (= started sleeping) *in front of the fire.* ➲ OPPOSITE **awake**

asparagus (say uh-**spa**-ruh-guhss) *noun* (*no plural*)
thin green plants with pointed ends that are eaten as a vegetable

aspect (say **ass**-pekt) *noun* (*plural* **aspects**)
one of the qualities or parts of a situation, idea or problem: *Spelling is one of the most difficult **aspects** of learning English.*

asphalt (say **ass**-falt) *noun* (*no plural*)
a thick black substance that is used for making the surface of roads

asphyxiate (say uhs-**fikss**-i-ayt) *verb* (**asphyxiating, asphyxiated**) (*formal*)
to make someone unable to breathe or to be unable to breathe: *He was **asphyxiated** by the smoke.*

aspire (say uh-**spy**-uh) *verb* (**aspiring, aspired**)
to have the strong desire to do or have something: *I **aspire** to be an architect when I leave school.*
▸ **aspiration** (*noun*): *He supported our **aspirations** to be great athletes.*

aspirin (say **ass**-prin or **ass**-puh-rin) *noun*
1 (*no plural*) a medicine that stops pain
2 (*plural* **aspirins**) (*informal*) a tablet of this medicine: *I took an **aspirin** for my headache.*

ass (*rhymes with* **mass**) *noun* (*plural* **asses**)
a donkey

assassin (say uh-**sass**-in) *noun* (*plural* **assassins**)
a person who kills an important person for money or political reasons
🛈 ORIGIN: 16th century, through French, from Arabic *ḥašīšī* meaning 'someone who takes hashish (dagga)'. *Ḥašīšī* were members of a religious group in the 11th–13th centuries. People believed that they took hashish before they went to kill their enemies.

assassinate (say uh-**sass**-i-nayt) *verb* (**assassinating, assassinated**)
to kill an important or famous person: *John F. Kennedy was **assassinated** in 1963.*
▸ **assassination** (*noun*): *an **assassination** attempt*

assault (say uh-**sawlt**) *verb* (**assaulting, assaulted**)
to attack or hurt somebody: *He **assaulted** a policeman.*
▸ **assault** (*noun*): *an **assault** on an old lady*

assegai (say **ass**-uh-gy) *noun* (*plural* **assegais**)
a long stick with a metal point that is used as a weapon, mainly by southern African people
ℹ ORIGIN: 17th century, through French, originally from Arabic *al-zagaya* meaning 'the spear'

assemble (say uh-**semb**-l) *verb* (**assembling, assembled**)
1 to put parts of something together: *In this term you will* ***assemble*** *a portfolio.*
2 to come together: *We will* ***assemble*** *in the school hall after break.* ➲ SYNONYM **congregate**

assembly (say uh-**sem**-blee) *noun* (*plural* **assemblies**)
a meeting of a big group of people for a special reason: *Our school* ***assembly*** *is at 9.30.*

assent (say uh-**sent**) *noun* (*no plural*) (*formal*)
official agreement to or approval of something: *The director has given her* ***assent*** *to the proposals.*
▸ **assent** (*verb*): *I* ***assented*** *to being in the school play.*

assert (say uh-**surt**) *verb* (**asserting, asserted**)
1 to say something clearly and firmly: *He* ***asserted*** *that he was old enough to go.*
2 to behave in a way that shows you are confident: ***assert*** *yourself*

assertive (say uh-**sur**-tiv) *adjective*
when you behave in a way that shows that you are confident: *Be* ***assertive*** *in a job interview.*

assess (say uh-**sess**) *verb* (**assessing, assessed**)
to judge and measure how good, bad or important something is: *It's difficult to* ***assess*** *the effects of the price rises.* ◇ *Our teacher* ***assessed*** *each learner's work.* ➲ SYNONYM **rate**[2] 1
▸ **assessment** (*noun*): *I made a careful* ***assessment*** *of the risks involved.*

asset (say **ass**-et) *noun* (*plural* **assets**)
1 something that you own, that has value: *My* ***assets*** *include a house and a car.*
2 a thing or person that is useful: *Healthy citizens are the greatest* ***asset*** *to a country.* ◇ *His intelligence is a great* ***asset****.*

assign (say uh-**sine**) *verb* (**assigning, assigned**)
to give someone their share of something: *Each group was* ***assigned*** *a different topic.*

assignment (say uh-**sine**-muhnt) *noun* (*plural* **assignments**)
a job or piece of work that somebody is given to do: *You have to complete three written* ***assignments*** *each term.*

assimilate (say uh-**sim**-uh-layt) *verb* (**assimilating, assimilated**)
1 to become part of a group
2 to learn and understand something: *The test will show if you have* ***assimilated*** *the knowledge.*

assist (say uh-**sist**) *verb* (**assisting, assisted**) (*formal*)
to help somebody: *The driver* ***assisted*** *her with her suitcases.*

USAGE **Help** is the word that we usually use. **Assist** is quite formal.

assistance (say uh-**siss**-tuhnss) *noun* (*no plural*) (*formal*)
help: *I can't move this table without your* ***assistance****.*

assistant (say uh-**siss**-tuhnt) *noun* (*plural* **assistants**)
a person who helps somebody in a more important position: *The principal has an* ***assistant*** *who answers the phone for her.*
➲ See **shop assistant**

associate (say uh-**soh**-shi-ayt) *verb* (**associating, associated**)
to make a connection between things or people in your mind: *Many people* ***associate*** *Africa with heat and dust.*
▸ **associated** (*adjective*): *These illnesses are* ***associated*** *with smoking.*

association (say uh-soh-shi-**ay**-shuhn) *noun* (*plural* **associations**)
a group of people who join or work together for a special reason: *the Football* ***Association***

associative (say uh-**soh**-shi-uh-tiv) *adjective*
1 relating to the connection between ideas or things
2 (*maths*) giving the same result, no matter what order the parts of a calculation are done in: $(a \times b) \times c = a \times (b \times c)$ *is an* ***associative*** *operation.*

assonance (say **ass**-uh-nuhnss) *noun* (*no plural*)
the effect that is created when two words that are close to each other have the same vowel sounds but different consonants, for example 'seen' and 'beat': *'The round cloud' has* ***assonance*** *because the 'ou' sound is repeated.*
➲ See Study page 17 ➲ See **alliteration**

assorted (say uh-**saw**-tid) *adjective*
mixed or of different types: *There will be* ***assorted*** *prizes for the winners.* ➲ SYNONYMS **miscellaneous, various**

assume (say uh-**syoom**) *verb* (**assuming, assumed**)
to think that something is true although you are not really sure: *Hanli is not here today, so I* ***assume*** *that she is ill.*

▸ **assumption** (*noun*): *Our* ***assumption*** *is that she's ill.*

assurance (say uh-**shoor**-ruhnss) *noun*
1 (*plural* **assurances**) a promise that something will certainly happen or be true: *They gave me an* ***assurance*** *that the work would be done by Friday.*
2 (*no plural*) (also **self-assurance**) the confidence in what you can do or that you will succeed: *She drove with* ***assurance.***
3 (*no plural*) (also **life assurance**) a type of insurance in which money is paid out when a person dies or after an agreed period of time

assure (say uh-**shoor**) *verb* (**assuring, assured**)
to tell somebody what is true or certain so that they feel less worried: *I* ***assure*** *you that the dog isn't dangerous.*

asterisk (say **ass**-tuh-risk) *noun* (*plural* **asterisks**)
the symbol (*) that you use to make people notice something in a piece of writing

asteroid (say **ass**-tuh-royd) *noun* (*plural* **asteroids**)
a solid **rocky** object, smaller than a planet, that goes around the sun

asthma (say **ass**-muh) *noun* (*no plural*)
an illness which makes breathing difficult: *He had an* ***asthma*** *attack.*
▸ **asthmatic** (*noun*): *She's an* ***asthmatic.***
▸ **asthmatic** (*adjective*): ***asthmatic*** *patients*

astonish (say uh-**ston**-ish) *verb* (**astonishing, astonished**)
to surprise somebody very much: *The news* ***astonished*** *everyone.* ➲ SYNONYM **astound**

astonished (say uh-**ston**-isht) *adjective*
very surprised: *I was* ***astonished*** *to hear that she was getting married.*

astonishing (say uh-**ston**-ish-ing) *adjective*
very surprising: *an* ***astonishing*** *story*

astonishment (say uh-**ston**-ish-muhnt) *noun* (*no plural*)
a feeling of great surprise: *He looked at me in* ***astonishment*** *when I told him the news.*

astound (say uh-**stownd**) *verb* (**astounding, astounded**)
to surprise someone very much: *I was* ***astounded*** *by the surprise party my friends gave me.* ➲ SYNONYMS **astonish, surprise**[2]

astral (say **ass**-truhl) *adjective*
of the stars

astray (say uh-**stray**) *adverb*
go astray to become lost or be stolen: *Our luggage has gone* ***astray*** *at the airport.*

astride (say uh-**stride**) *adverb, preposition*
to sit or stand with one leg on either side of something: *The riders were sitting* ***astride*** *their horses.*

astrology (say uhss-**trol**-uh-jee) *noun* (*no plural*)
the study of stars and planets in the belief that they affect a person's personality according to when they were born: *According to* ***astrology,*** *my star sign is Sagittarius.*
▸ **astrologist** (*noun*): *The* ***astrologist*** *said I will meet a tall stranger this week.*
ⓘ ORIGIN: 15th century, through Old French and Latin, from Greek *astron* meaning 'star' + *-logia* meaning 'study'

astronaut (say **ass**-truh-nawt) *noun* (*plural* **astronauts**)
a person who works and travels in space
ⓘ ORIGIN: 20th century, from Greek *astron* meaning 'star' + *nautēs* meaning 'sailor'

astronomer (say uh-**stron**-uh-muh) *noun* (*plural* **astronomers**)
a person who studies or knows a lot about **astronomy**

astronomy (say uh-**stron**-uh-mee) *noun* (*no plural*)
the scientific study of the sun, moon, planets and stars
ⓘ ORIGIN: 13th–15th century, from Old French *astronomie*, through Latin from Greek *astronomos* meaning 'star-arranging'

astute (say uhss-**tyoot**) *adjective*
clever at judging people or a situation: *He's an* ***astute*** *businessman.* ➲ SYNONYM **shrewd**

asylum (say uh-**sile**-uhm) *noun*
1 (*no plural*) the protection that another country gives you when you have left your own country: *Some foreigners applied for* ***asylum*** *in South Africa.*
2 (*plural* **asylums**) (*old-fashioned*) a hospital where mentally ill people can stay

asymmetrical (say ay-si-**met**-rik-l) *adjective*
having two parts or sides that are not the same in size and shape: *an* ***asymmetrical*** *hairstyle*
➲ OPPOSITE **symmetrical** ➲ See illustration at **symmetrical**
▸ **asymmetric** (*adjective*)
▸ **asymmetry** (*noun*)

at *preposition*
1 a word that shows where: *They are* ***at*** *school.* ◇ ***at*** *the back of the book*
2 a word that shows when: *I go to bed* ***at*** *eleven o'clock.* ◇ ***At*** *night you can see the stars.*
3 towards a person or thing: *Look* ***at*** *the picture.* ◇ *I smiled* ***at*** *her.*

A B C D E F G H I J K L M N O P Q R S T U V W X Y Z

A B C D E F G H I J K L M N O P Q R S T U V W X Y Z

4 (*computing*) the symbol @ which is used in email addresses after a person's name

ate (say **ayt** or **et**) form of **eat**

atheist (say **ay**-thee-ist) *noun* (*plural* **atheists**)
a person who does not believe in a god
► **atheism** (*noun*)

athlete (say **ath**-leet) *noun* (*plural* **athletes**)
a person who is good at sports such as running or jumping, especially one who takes part in sports competitions: ***Athletes** from all over the world go to the Olympic Games.*

athletic (say ath-**let**-ik) *adjective*
having a fit, strong and healthy body

athletics (say ath-**let**-ikss) *plural noun*
sports such as running, jumping and throwing

atlas (say **at**-luhss) *noun* (*plural* **atlases**)
a book of maps: *an **atlas** of the world*
ORIGIN: 16th century, named after a Greek god, Atlas, who fought against the ruler of the gods. Many people believed that Atlas's punishment was to hold the weight of the world on his shoulders forever.

atmosphere (say **at**-muhss-feer) *noun* (*no plural*)
1 the atmosphere the layers of gas surrounding the Earth or another object in space: *pollution of the **atmosphere***
2 the air in a place: *a smoky **atmosphere***
3 the feeling that places or people give you: *The **atmosphere** in the school was very friendly.*
► **atmospheric** (*adjective*): ***atmospheric** conditions* ◇ ***atmospheric** lighting*

the Earth's atmosphere

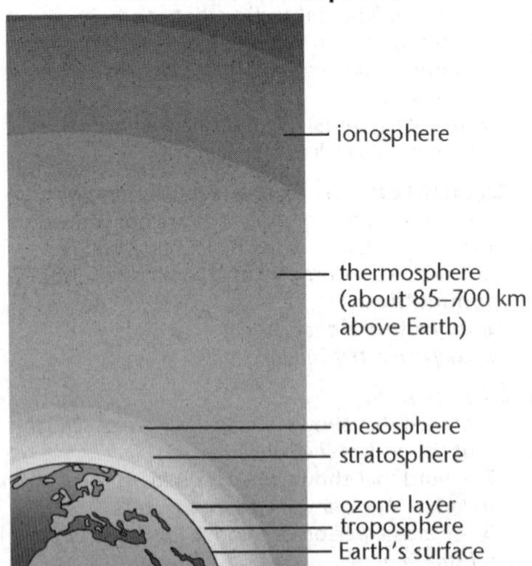

the layers of the Earth's atmosphere

atoll (say **at**-ol) *noun* (*plural* **atolls**)
an island shaped like a ring and nearly or completely surrounding a **lagoon** (=a lake of salt water): *Did you know that **atolls** are formed from coral?*

atom (say **at**-uhm) *noun* (*plural* **atoms**)
one of the very small things that everything is made of: *Water is made of **atoms** of hydrogen and oxygen.* ➲ See **molecule**

atomic (say uh-**tom**-ik) *adjective*
1 of or about atoms: ***atomic** physics*
2 using the energy that is produced by splitting atoms: *an **atomic** bomb* ◇ ***atomic** energy*

atrium (say **ay**-tri-uhm) *noun* (*plural* **atria** or **atriums**)
1 an open space with a high ceiling in the centre of a building
2 (*biology*) either of the two upper spaces in the heart ➲ See illustration at **heart**

atrocious (say uh-**troh**-shuss) *adjective*
extremely bad: *The weather was **atrocious** this weekend.* ➲ SYNONYMS **monstrous** 2, **terrible**
► **atrociously** (*adverb*)

atrocity (say uh-**tross**-i-tee) *noun* (*plural* **atrocities**)
a cruel thing done to somebody: ***Atrocities** were committed during the war.*

attach (say uh-**tach**) *verb* (**attaching, attached**)
to join or fix one thing to another thing: *I **attached** the photo to the letter.* ➲ OPPOSITE **detach**

attached (say uh-**tacht**) *adjective*
liking somebody or something very much: *We've grown very **attached** to this house.*

attachment (say uh-**tach**-muhnt) *noun* (*plural* **attachments**)
1 a strong feeling of love or liking for a person or thing: *the child's strong **attachment** to her parents*
2 (*computing*) a document that you send to somebody using email

attack[1] (say uh-**tak**) *noun* (*plural* **attacks**)
1 a violent act which is done in order to hurt somebody or damage something: *There was a terrorist **attack** on the city.*
2 a time when you are ill: *an **attack** of flu*

attack[2] (say uh-**tak**) *verb* (**attacking, attacked**)
to start fighting or hurting somebody or damaging something: *The army **attacked** the town.* ◇ *The old man was **attacked** and robbed.*

attain (say uh-**tayn**) *verb* (**attaining, attained**)
to get or achieve something: *I want to **attain** a good mark in this exam.*

attempt (say uh-**tempt**) *verb* (**attempting, attempted**)
to try to do something that is difficult: *He **attempted** to sail round the world.*
➲ SYNONYM **try**[1] 1
▸ **attempt** (*noun*): *She made no **attempt** to help.*

attend (say uh-**tend**) *verb* (**attending, attended**)
to go to or be present at a place where something is happening: *Did you **attend** the meeting?*

attendance (say uh-**tend**-uhnss) *noun*
1 (*no plural*) being present at a place, for example at school: *His **attendance** at school has been poor* (= he hasn't been coming to school regularly).
2 (*plural* **attendances**) the number of people who go to an organized event: *Cinema **attendances** have risen recently.*

attendant (say uh-**tend**-uhnt) *noun* (*plural* **attendants**)
a person whose job is to serve or help people in a public place: *a car park **attendant***

attention (say uh-**ten**-shuhn) *noun* (*no plural*)
looking or listening carefully and with interest: *I shouted in order to attract her **attention*** (= make her notice me). ◇ *Can I have your **attention**, please?* (= please listen to me)
pay attention to look or listen carefully: *Please pay **attention** to what I'm saying.*

attentive (say uh-**ten**-tiv) *adjective*
watching, listening to or thinking about something carefully: *The learner was **attentive** during the demonstration.*
▸ **attentively** (*adverb*): *The class listened **attentively** to the story.*

attic (say **at**-ik) *noun* (*plural* **attics**)
the room or space under the roof of a house: *My old clothes are in a box in the **attic**.*
➲ SYNONYM **loft**

attitude (say **at**-i-tyood) *noun* (*plural* **attitudes**)
the way you think or feel about something: *What's your **attitude** to marriage?*

attorney (say uh-**tur**-nee) *noun* (*plural* **attorneys**)
a lawyer who may advise somebody on legal matters, act on their behalf and defend them in the lower courts ➲ See **advocate**[2] 2

attract (say uh-**trakt**) *verb* (**attracting, attracted**)
1 to make somebody like a person or thing: *He was **attracted** to her.* ◇ *The idea of playing in a band **attracted** me.*
2 to make somebody or something come somewhere: *Moths are **attracted** to light.* ◇ *The new film has **attracted** a lot of publicity.*

attraction (say uh-**trak**-shuhn) *noun*
1 (*no plural*) a feeling of liking a person or thing very much: *I can't understand her **attraction** to snakes.*
2 (*plural* **attractions**) something that makes people come to a place: *Robben Island is a major tourist **attraction**.*

attractive (say uh-**trak**-tiv) *adjective*
1 describing a person who is nice to look at: *He's a very **attractive** boy.* ➲ See note at **beautiful**
2 describing something that pleases or interests you: *Her dress is very **attractive**.* ➲ OPPOSITE **unattractive**

attribute[1] (say **at**-ri-byoot) *noun* (*plural* **attributes**)
a feature or quality of a person or thing: *Kindness is one of her **attributes**.* ◇ *One of the **attributes** of this car is air conditioning.*

attribute[2] (say uh-**trib**-yoot) *verb* (**attributing, attributed**)
to believe that something was caused by a person or thing: *The painting of the new classroom is **attributed** to the Grade 7s.* ◇ *The cool, clear weather is **attributed** to a high pressure system.*

attributive (say uh-**trib**-yuh-tiv) *adjective* (*grammar*)
(used about adjectives or nouns) used before a noun to describe it: *In 'the blue sky' and 'a family business', 'blue' and 'family' are **attributive**.*
▸ **attributively** (*adverb*)

AU (say ay-**yoo**) *abbreviation* **African Union**

aubergine (say **oh**-buh-zheen) *noun* (*plural* **aubergines**) = **brinjal**

auburn (say **aw**-buhn) *adjective*
(used about hair) with a colour between red and brown: *She has pretty **auburn** hair.*

auction (say **awk**-shuhn) *noun* (*plural* **auctions**)
a sale where each thing is sold to the person who will give the most money for it
▸ **auction** (*verb*): *They **auctioned** all their furniture before they went overseas.*

audacious (say aw-**day**-shuss) *adjective*
not afraid to take risks or do something shocking
▸ **audaciously** (*adverb*): *He walked **audaciously** amongst the diners.*

audible (say **aw**-dib-l) *adjective*
that you can hear: *The music was barely **audible** above the wind.* ➲ OPPOSITE **inaudible**

audience (say **aw**-di-uhnss) *noun* (*plural* **audiences**)
the people who are watching or listening to a film, play, concert or programme

audio (say **aw**-di-oh) *adjective*
related to the recording of sound: ***audio** tapes*

audio-visual (say aw-di-oh-**vizh**-yuu-uhl) *adjective*
using both sound and pictures: ***audio-visual** aids for the classroom*

audit (say **aw**-dit) *noun* (*plural* **audits**)
an official examination of a company's financial statements
▶ **audit** (*verb*): *Will they **audit** our company?*
▶ **auditor** (*noun*): *My dad is an **auditor**.*

audition (say aw-**dish**-uhn) *noun* (*plural* **auditions**)
a short performance by an actor, singer or musician to see if they are good enough to be in a show: *There will be **auditions** for the school play this week.*
▶ **audition** (*verb*): *Which part will you **audition** for?*

auditorium (say aw-di-**taw**-ri-uhm) *noun* (*plural* **auditoriums** or **auditoria**)
the part of a theatre where the audience sits

August (say **aw**-guhst) *noun*
the eighth month of the year
🛈 ORIGIN: named after Augustus Caesar (63 BC–AD 14), the first Roman emperor. *Augustus* meant 'honoured, respected' in Latin.

aunt (say **aant**) *noun* (*plural* **aunts**) (also *informal* **auntie**, **aunty**)
the sister of your mother or father, or the wife of your uncle: ***Aunt** Marie*

au pair (say oh **pair**) *noun* (*plural* **au pairs**)
a young person who looks after the children and helps in the house of a family, sometimes in a foreign country

aura (say **aw**-ruh) *noun* (*plural* **auras**)
a particular quality that a person or thing has: *He has an **aura** of wisdom about him.*

aural (say **aw**-ruhl) *adjective*
relating to hearing

aurora (say aw-**raw**-ruh) *noun* (*plural* **auroras** or **aurorae**)
a natural show of light in the atmosphere, occurring near the North and South Poles

austere (say oss-**teer**) *adjective*
simple and plain: *She had an **austere** sense of fashion.* ◇ *We grew up in **austere** surroundings.*
▶ **austerely** (*adverb*)

Australasian (say oss-truh-**lay**-zhuhn) *adjective*
from or relating to Australia and the islands near Australia, including New Zealand

Australopithecus (say oss-truh-loh-**pith**-i-kuhss) *noun* (*no plural*)
a creature with both human and ape-like characteristics that lived in Africa between four and one million years ago
🛈 ORIGIN: 20th century, from Latin *australis* meaning 'southern' + Greek *pithekos* meaning 'ape'. Raymond Dart (1893–1988), a scientist, created this name for the type of early human whose fossilized bones were found at Taung in South Africa in 1924.

authentic (say aw-**then**-tik) *adjective*
real and true: *That's not an **authentic** Van Gogh painting – it's just a copy.*

author (say **aw**-thuh) *noun* (*plural* **authors**)
a person who writes books or stories: *Who is your favourite **author**?*

authoritarian (say aw-tho-ri-**tair**-ri-uhn) *adjective*
not giving people the freedom to decide things for themselves: *Our teacher has an **authoritarian** style of teaching.*

authoritative (say aw-**tho**-ruh-tu-tiv) *adjective*
1 demanding or expecting that people respect your authority: *an **authoritative** tone of voice*
2 that you can trust and respect as true and correct: *the most **authoritative** book on the subject*

authority (say aw-**tho**-ruh-tee) *noun*
1 (*no plural*) the power to tell people what they must do: *The police have the **authority** to stop cars.*
2 (*plural* **authorities**) a group of people who tell other people what they must do: *the city **authorities***

authorize (say **aw**-thuh-rize) *verb* (**authorizing**, **authorized**) (also **authorise**)
to give permission to someone to do something: *My parents **authorized** my trip to the zoo.*
▶ **authorization** (*noun*) (also **authorisation**)

autistic (say aw-**tiss**-tik) *adjective*
relating to a mental condition in which a person finds it difficult to communicate or form relationships with other people: *an **autistic** child*
▶ **autism** (*noun*)

autobiography (say awt-oh-by-**og**-ruh-fee) *noun* (*plural* **autobiographies**)
a book that a person has written about their life
➲ SYNONYM **memoir**

autocrat (say **aw**-toh-krat) *noun* (*plural* **autocrats**)
a ruler who has complete power
▸ **autocratic** (*adjective*)

autograph (say **aw**-toh-graaf) *noun* (*plural* **autographs**)
the signature of a famous person, which they themselves have written: *He asked Madonna for her **autograph**.*
▸ **autograph** (*verb*): *She **autographed** my poster.*

automatic (say aw-toh-**mat**-ik) *adjective*
1 (referring to a machine) that can work by itself, without people controlling it: ***automatic** doors*
2 that you do without thinking: *Breathing is **automatic**.*
▸ **automatically** (*adverb*): *This light comes on **automatically** at five o'clock.*

autonomy (say aw-**ton**-uh-mee) *noun* (*no plural*)
when a person or a country has the right to govern itself

autopsy (say **aw**-top-see) *noun* (*plural* **autopsies**)
an examination of a dead person to find out the cause of death

autotrophic (say aw-toh-**trof**-ik) *adjective*
relating to an organism that is able to feed itself using simple chemical substances such as **carbon dioxide**: ***autotrophic** nutrition*

autumn (say **aw**-tuhm) *noun* (*no plural*)
the part of the year (called a **season**) that comes between summer and winter: *In **autumn** the leaves begin to fall from the trees.*

auxiliary (say awg-**zil**-yuh-ree) *adjective*
giving extra help: *This hospital has staff nurses and **auxiliary** nurses.*

auxiliary verb *noun* (*plural* **auxiliary verbs**) (*grammar*)
a verb that you use with a main verb to show the tense or to form questions. Examples are 'be' and 'have' in these sentences: *I'll be leaving soon. I have finished the job. Have you finished?*
➲ See Study page 4

available (say uh-**vayl**-uhb-l) *adjective*
ready for you to use, have or see: *Are there any rooms **available**? ◇ The manager is not **available** right now.*
▸ **availability** (*noun*): *She will check the **availability** of rooms for next week.*

avalanche (say **av**-uh-laansh) *noun* (*plural* **avalanches**)
a very large amount of snow that falls quickly down the side of a mountain

avarice (say **av**-uh-riss) *noun* (*no plural*)
a strong desire for more money ➲ SYNONYM **greed**
▸ **avaricious** (*adjective*)

Ave. *abbreviation* **avenue**

avenge (say uh-**venj**) *verb* (**avenging, avenged**)
to punish someone for hurting you or someone you care about: *In this story, Alf wanted to **avenge** his mother's death.*

avenue (say **av**-uh-nyoo) *noun* (*plural* **avenues**) (abbr. Ave.)
a wide road or street, usually with trees along its sides: *I live in Fifth **Avenue**.*

average¹ (say **av**-uh-rij) *noun*
1 (*plural* **averages**) the result you get when you add two or more amounts together and then divide the total by the number of amounts you added: *The **average** of 2, 3 and 7 is 4 (2 + 3 + 7 = 12, and 12 ÷ 3 = 4).*
2 (*no plural*) the normal amount, quality or number, for example: *On **average**, I play sport about twice a week.*
🛈 **ORIGIN:** 15th century, through French, originally from Arabic *awār* meaning 'damage to goods'. When goods carried in a ship were damaged or lost at sea, the owner of the goods and the owner of the ship had to share the costs. The word came to mean 'calculating the average'.

average² (say **av**-uh-rij) *adjective*
1 (used about a number) found by calculating the average: *The **average** age of the learners is thirteen.*
2 normal or usual: *The **average** learner gets about five hours of homework a week.*

aversion (say uh-**vur**-zhuhn) *noun* (*plural* **aversions**)
a strong feeling of not liking a person or thing: *Ian has an **aversion** to seafood.*

avert (say uh-**vurt**) *verb* (**averting, averted**)
1 to prevent something unpleasant from happening: *An accident was **averted** when the driver swerved.*
2 turn away: *I **averted** my eyes.*

aviary (say **ay**-vi-uh-ree) *noun* (*plural* **aviaries**)
a large bird cage

aviation (say ay-vi-**ay**-shuhn) *noun* (*no plural*)
the designing, building and flying of aircraft

avid (say **av**-id) *adjective*
very interested and enthusiastic about something: *I am an **avid** reader.*
▸ **avidly** (*adverb*): *Sara follows the news **avidly**.*

A B C D E F G H I J K L M N O P Q R S T U V W X Y Z

A B C D E F G H I J K L M N O P Q R S T U V W X Y Z

avocado (say av-uh-**kaa**-doh) *noun* (*plural* **avocados**)
a dark green fruit that has an **oval** shape, soft, light-green flesh and a large seed inside
🛈 ORIGIN: 17th century, through Spanish *aguacate*, from Nahuatl *ahuacatl*. Nahuatl is a language spoken in southern Mexico and Central America. Spanish colonists and traders brought the word to Europe.

avoid (say uh-**voyd**) *verb* (**avoiding, avoided**)
1 to stop something happening or to try not to do something: *He always tried to* ***avoid*** *arguments.* ◇ *She has to* ***avoid*** *eating sweets.*
2 to stay away from a person or thing: *We crossed the road to* ***avoid*** *him.*

awake (say uh-**wayk**) *adjective*
not sleeping: *The children are still* ***awake***.
➲ OPPOSITE **asleep**

award[1] (say uh-**wawd**) *verb* (**awarding, awarded**)
to officially give a prize to somebody: *He was* ***awarded*** *first prize in the writing competition.*

award[2] (say uh-**wawd**) *noun* (*plural* **awards**)
a prize or money that you give to somebody who has done something very well: *She won the* ***award*** *for best actress.*

aware (say uh-**wair**) *adjective*
knowing of something: *He's not* ***aware*** *of the problem.* ◇ *I was* ***aware*** *that somebody was watching me.* ➲ OPPOSITE **unaware**
▸ **awareness** (*noun*): *She raised my* ***awareness*** *of the importance of exercise.*

away (say uh-**way**) *adverb*
1 to or in another place: *She ran* ***away*** *from him.* ◇ *He put his books* ***away***.
2 from a place: *The sea is two kilometres* ***away***.
3 not here: *She is* ***away*** *from school today because she is ill.* ➲ SYNONYM **absent**
4 in the future: *Our holiday is three weeks* ***away***.

awe (say aw) *noun* (*no plural*)
a feeling of respect and wonder: *Fagan was in* ***awe*** *of his older brother.* ◇ *The acrobat's performance filled us with* ***awe***.
awe-inspiring causing a feeling of respect and wonder: *Paula gave an* ***awe-inspiring*** *performance in the race.*

awesome (say **aw**-suhm) *adjective*
1 very impressive and perhaps rather frightening: *an* ***awesome*** *sight*
2 (*informal*) very good or enjoyable: *I've just bought this* ***awesome*** *new CD!* ➲ SYNONYMS **great** 5, **wonderful**

awful (say **aw**-fuhl) *adjective*
very bad: *The pain was* ***awful***. ◇ *What* ***awful*** *weather!* ➲ See note at **bad**

awfully (say **aw**-fuh-lee) *adverb* (*informal*)
very: *It was* ***awfully*** *hot.* ◇ *I'm* ***awfully*** *sorry!*
➲ SYNONYM **terribly** 1

awkward (say **awk**-wuhd) *adjective*
1 difficult or causing problems: *This box is* ***awkward*** *to carry.* ◇ *an* ***awkward*** *question*
2 uncomfortable and embarrassing: *I felt* ***awkward*** *at the party.*
3 not able to move your body in an easy way: *He's very* ***awkward*** *when he dances.*

awl (*rhymes with* **fall**) *noun* (*plural* **awls**)
a small pointed tool used to make holes in materials such as leather

awning (say **aw**-ning) *noun* (*plural* **awnings**)
a sheet of cloth or other material that stretches from a door or window over an outside area

AWOL (say **ay**-wol) *abbreviation*
used especially in the military when a member has left their group without permission: *He's gone* ***AWOL*** *from his base.* 🛈 **AWOL** is short for 'absent without (official) leave'.

axe (say **akss**) *noun* (*plural* **axes**)
a tool for cutting wood: *He chopped down the tree with an* ***axe***.

axis (say **ak**-siss) *noun* (*plural* **axes**)
1 an imaginary line through the middle of an object: *The Earth rotates on its* ***axis***. ◇ *the* ***axis*** *of symmetry*
2 a fixed line used for marking measurements on a graph. Most graphs have a **horizontal** axis (also called the ***x*-axis**) and a **vertical** axis (also called the ***y*-axis**).

axes

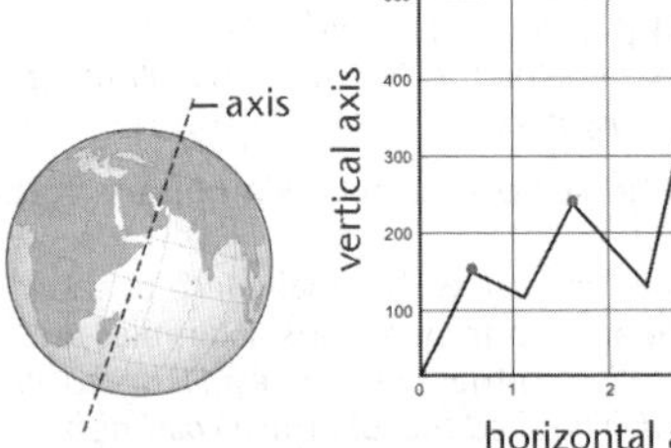

the Earth's axis **the axes on a graph**

axle (say **akss**-l) *noun* (*plural* **axles**)
a bar that connects a pair of wheels on a vehicle ➲ See illustration at **wheel**[1]

AZT (say ay-zed-**tee**) *noun* (*no plural*)
a medicine used for treating **AIDS** 🛈 **AZT** is short for 'Azidothymidine'.

Aztec (say **az**-tek) *noun* (*no plural*)
the language of the Aztec people of Mexico. This language is now **extinct**.

Bb

baboon (say buh-**boon**) *noun* (*plural* **baboons**)
a large monkey with a face like a dog's
ORIGIN: 13th–15th century, from Old French *babuin*, possibly from *baboue* meaning 'muzzle, grimace'

baby (say **bay**-bee) *noun* (*plural* **babies**)
a very young child: *She's going to have a **baby**.* ◇ *a **baby** boy* ◇ *a **baby** girl*

babysitter (say **bay**-bee-sit-uh) *noun* (*plural* **babysitters**)
a person who looks after a child while the parents are not at home

bachelor (say **ba**-chuh-luh) *noun* (*plural* **bachelors**)
1 a man who has never married
2 Bachelor a person who has completed a university degree: *a **Bachelor** of Science*

back[1] (say **bak**) *noun*
1 (*plural* **backs**) the part of a person or an animal that is between the neck and the bottom: *He lay on his **back** looking up at the sky.* ◇ *Don't talk about Sisanda behind her **back*** (= when she is not there and doesn't know about it).
2 the back (*no plural*) the part of something that is behind or furthest from the front: *The answers are at the **back** of the book.* ◇ *We sat in the **back** of the car.* ➲ OPPOSITE **front**
back to front with the **back**[2] part where the front should be: *You've got your sweater on **back** to front.*

back[2] (say **bak**) *adjective*
furthest from the front: *the **back** door*

back[3] (say **bak**) *adverb*
1 in or to the place where somebody or something was before: *Go **back** to sleep.* ◇ *We walked to the shops and **back**.*
2 away from the front: *I looked **back** to see if she was coming.* ◇ *Could everyone move **back** a bit, please?* ➲ OPPOSITE **forward**[1]
3 as a way of returning or answering something: *He paid me the money **back**.* ◇ *I can't talk now – can I phone you **back**?*
back and forth from one place to another and back again, many times: *She travels **back** and forth between Bhisho and Tshwane.*

back[4] (say **bak**) *verb* (**backing**, **backed**)
1 to move backwards or to make something move backwards: *She **backed** the car out of the garage.* ◇ *He **backed** away from the dog.*
2 to give help or support to somebody or something: *They're **backing** the school team.*
back out to not do something that you promised or agreed to do: *You said you would come. You can't **back** out now!*
back something up
1 to say or show that something is true: *All the evidence **backed** up what the woman had said.*
2 (*computing*) to make a copy of information in your computer that you do not want to lose

backbone (say **bak**-bohn) *noun* (*plural* **backbones**)
the line of bones down the back of your body ➲ SYNONYM **spine** 1

backdrop (say **bak**-drop) *noun* (*plural* **backdrops**)
1 a painted piece of cloth that hangs at the back of the stage in a theatre as part of the scenery
2 the background for a story or event: *Against a **backdrop** of racial tension, the war began.*

backfire (say **bak**-fy-uh) *verb* (**backfiring**, **backfired**)
to have an unexpected and unpleasant result, often the opposite of what was expected: *Our plan **backfired** and we didn't get the day off school.*

background (say **bak**-grownd) *noun* (*plural* **backgrounds**)
1 the things at the back in a picture: *This is a photo of my house with the mountains in the **background**.* ➲ OPPOSITE **foreground**
2 the type of family that a person comes from and the education and experience that they have: *I come from a poor **background**.*

backhand (say **bak**-hand) *noun* (*plural* **backhands**)
a way of hitting the ball in a game such as tennis, in which the back of your hand faces forward ➲ See **forehand**

backing (say **bak**-ing) *noun* (*no plural*)
help or support to do something: *Our captain has the **backing** of the whole team.*

backlog (say **bak**-log) *noun* (*plural* **backlogs**)
an amount of work that should have been done but has not been done yet

backpack[1] (say **bak**-pak) *noun* (*plural* **backpacks**)
a large bag that you carry on your back when you are travelling ➲ SYNONYM **rucksack**

A B C D E F G H I J K L M N O P Q R S T U V W X Y Z

backpack[2] (say **bak**-pak) *verb* (**backpacking**, **backpacked**)
to go walking or travelling with your clothes and things you need in a **backpack**[1]: *We went* ***backpacking*** *in India last summer.*

backside (say **bak**-side) *noun* (*plural* **backsides**) (*informal*)
the part of your body that you sit on
➲ SYNONYM **bottom** 4

backstroke (say **bak**-strohk) *noun* (*no plural*)
a way of swimming on your back

backup (say **bak**-up) *noun*
1 (*no plural*) extra help or support that you can get if necessary: *The police had* ***backup*** *from the army.*
2 (*plural* **backups**) (*computing*) a copy of information that you have put in your computer and which you do not want to lose

backward (say **bak**-wuhd) *adjective*
1 in the direction behind you: *a* ***backward*** *step*
2 slow to learn or change: *The transport system is* ***backward*** *compared to some countries.*

backwards (say **bak**-wuhdz) *adverb* (also **backward**)
1 towards a place or a position that is behind: *Could everybody take a step* ***backwards****?*
➲ OPPOSITE **forward**[1]
2 with the back or the end first: *If you say the alphabet* ***backwards****, you start with 'Z'.*
backwards and forwards first in one direction and then in the other, many times: *The dog ran* ***backwards*** *and forwards.*

backyard (say **bak**-yaad) *noun* (*plural* **backyards**)
1 an area at the back of a house
2 (*informal*) your neighbourhood: *Do you know what's going on in your own* ***backyard****?*

bacon (say **bay**-kuhn) *noun* (*no plural*)
long thin pieces of meat from a pig: *We had* ***bacon*** *and eggs for breakfast.*

bacteria (say bak-**teer**-ri-uh) plural of **bacterium**

bacterium (say bak-**teer**-ri-um) *noun* (*plural* **bacteria**)
a very small and simple organism that lives in large numbers in air, water, earth, plants and animals. Some **bacteria** can make us ill.

> USAGE Be careful! We usually use this word in the plural form, **bacteria**. Remember to treat **bacteria** as a plural, for example: *These* ***bacteria*** *are dangerous.*

bad *adjective* (**worse**, **worst**)
1 not good or nice: *The weather was very* ***bad****.* ◇ *a* ***bad*** *smell* ◇ *some* ***bad*** *news* ◇ *'What was the film like?' 'Not* ***bad****.'* ➲ SYNONYM **unpleasant**
2 serious: *She had a* ***bad*** *accident.*
3 not done or made well: ***bad*** *driving*
4 not able to work or do something well: *My eyesight is* ***bad****.* ◇ *He's a* ***bad*** *teacher.* ◇ *I'm very* ***bad*** *at sports.* ➲ SYNONYM **poor** 3
5 not fresh and too old to eat: ***bad*** *eggs*
➲ SYNONYM **rotten**
6 not behaving well: *That* ***bad*** *dog chewed my shoes!*
bad for you able to make you ill: *Smoking is* ***bad*** *for you.*

> WORD BUILDING There are many words that you can use instead of **bad**, but check their exact meanings first. Examples are: **atrocious**, **awful**, **dreadful**, **evil**, **horrible**, **immoral**, **lousy** (informal), **naughty**, **poor**, **rotten**, **sinful**, **terrible**, **unpleasant**, **wicked** and **vile**. See the Word Building note at **horrible** also.

badge (say **baj**) *noun* (*plural* **badges**)
a small piece of metal, cloth or plastic with a design or words on it that you wear on your clothes to show, for example, that you belong to an organization, have achieved something or have a particular rank: *We wear our school* ***badge*** *on our blazers.*

badger (say **baj**-uh) *noun* (*plural* **badgers**)
a wild mammal with black and white fur that lives in Europe

badly (say **bad**-lee) *adverb* (**worse**, **worst**)
1 in a way that is not good enough or not done well: *She played* ***badly****.* ◇ *These clothes are* ***badly*** *made.*
2 very much: *I* ***badly*** *need a holiday.* ◇ *He was* ***badly*** *hurt in the accident.*

bad-tempered (say **bad**-temp-uhd) *adjective*
often angry or impatient: *The* ***bad-tempered*** *old man often shouted at the children.*

Bafana Bafana (say buh-**faa**-nuh buh-**faa**-nuh) *plural noun*
the South African national soccer team
ⓘ ORIGIN: from isiXhosa *abafana* meaning 'young men'

baffle (say **baf**-l) *verb* (**baffling**, **baffled**)
to confuse somebody very much: *The puzzle* ***baffled*** *Mike.*

bag *noun* (*plural* **bags**)
a thing made of cloth, paper, leather or plastic for holding and carrying things: *He put the apples in a paper* ***bag****.* ◇ *a plastic* ***bag***
➲ See **carrier bag**, **handbag**

bagel (say **bay**-guhl) *noun* (*plural* **bagels**)
a type of bread roll in the shape of a ring

baggage (say **bag**-ij) *noun* (*no plural*)
bags and suitcases that you take with you when you travel: *We put all our **baggage** in the car.*
➲ SYNONYM **luggage**

baggy (say **bag**-ee) *adjective* (**baggier**, **baggiest**)
describing clothes that are big and loose: *He was wearing **baggy** trousers.*

bagpipes (say **bag**-pipe-ss) *plural noun*
a musical instrument that is often played in Scotland

bail[1] (say **bayl**) *noun*
1 (*no plural*) money that you pay to a court to get somebody out of jail: *He paid **bail** for his grandmother.*
2 (*plural* **bails**) (in cricket) one of two pieces of wood on top of the set of three wooden sticks (called **stumps**)

bail[2] (say **bayl**) *verb* (**bailing**, **bailed**)
bail out to get out of a difficult situation: *The pilot **bailed** out of the burning plane.*

bait (say **bayt**) *noun* (*no plural*)
food that is used to catch animals or fish with: *We used sardines for **bait**.*

bake (say **bayk**) *verb* (**baking**, **baked**)
to cook food, for example bread or cakes, in an oven: *My brother **baked** a cake.*

baker (say **bayk**-uh) *noun* (*plural* **bakers**)
a person who makes and sells bread and cakes

bakery (say **bayk**-uh-ree) *noun* (*plural* **bakeries**)
a place where bread and cakes are baked and sometimes sold

bakkie (say **buk**-ee) *noun* (*plural* **bakkies**)
(*S. African*)
1 a vehicle with an open back part, used for carrying loads
2 a dish or a small container with a lid
❶ ORIGIN: 20th century, from Afrikaans *bakkie* meaning 'small container'

balance[1] (say **bal**-uhnss) *noun*
1 (*no plural*) a situation in which different or opposite things are of equal importance or size: *You need a **balance** between work and play.*
2 (*no plural*) the ability to keep steady with an equal amount of weight on each side of the body: *I struggled to keep my **balance** on my new skates.*
3 (*plural* **balances**) the amount of money that is left after you have used some money: *I must check my bank **balance*** (= find out how much I have in my account).

balance[2] (say **bal**-uhnss) *verb* (**balancing**, **balanced**)
to put your body or something else into a position where it is steady and does not fall: *He **balanced** the bag on his head.* ◊ *She **balanced** on one leg.*

balcony (say **bal**-kuh-nee) *noun* (*plural* **balconies**)
a small platform on the outside wall of a building, above the ground, where you can stand or sit

bald (say **bawld**) *adjective* (**balder**, **baldest**)
with no hair or not much hair: *My dad is going **bald*** (= losing his hair).

bale (say **bayl**) *noun* (*plural* **bales**)
a quantity of something that is pressed together and tied up: *a **bale** of hay*
▸ **bale** (*verb*): *The farmer **baled** the straw.*

ball (say **bawl**) *noun* (*plural* **balls**)
1 a round thing that you use in games and sports: *Throw the **ball** to me.* ◊ *a **football***
2 any round thing: *a **ball** of string*
3 a big formal party where people dance

ballad (say **ba**-luhd) *noun* (*plural* **ballads**)
a poem or song that tells a story, often about love

ballast (say **ba**-luhst) *noun* (*no plural*)
heavy material kept in a ship to make it heavier and keep it steady

ball bearing (say **bawl** bair-ring) *noun* (*plural* **ball bearings**)
one of a number of small metal balls put between parts of a machine to make the parts move smoothly

ballerina (say **bal**-uh-ree-nuh) *noun* (*plural* **ballerinas**)
a woman who dances in a **ballet**

ballet (say **bal**-ay) *noun*
1 (*no plural*) a kind of dancing that tells a story with music but no words: *He wants to be a **ballet** dancer.*
2 (*plural* **ballets**) a performance or work that consists of this type of dancing: *I went to see a **ballet**.*

balloon (say buh-**loon**) *noun* (*plural* **balloons**)
1 a small coloured rubber bag that you blow air into and use as a toy or for decoration: *We are going to hang **balloons** around the room for the party.*
2 (also **hot-air balloon**) a large bag made of strong material that is filled with hot air or gas to make it rise in the air, usually carrying a basket for passengers underneath: *I would like to go up in a **balloon**.*

A B C D E F G H I J K L M N O P Q R S T U V W X Y Z

ballot (say **bal**-uht) *noun* (*plural* **ballots**)
1 a system that allows people to choose somebody or something by writing secretly on a piece of paper: *We held a* ***ballot*** *to choose new prefects.*
2 (also **ballot paper**) the piece of paper on which a person marks who they are voting for

ballpoint (say **bawl**-poynt) *noun* (*plural* **ballpoints**) (also **ballpoint pen**)
a pen that has a very small ball at the end that rolls the ink onto the paper

ballroom (say **bawl**-room) *noun* (*plural* **ballrooms**)
a large room where people have formal dances

balsa (say **bohl**-suh) *noun* (*no plural*)
a type of wood that weighs very little

balustrade (say **bal**-uh-strayd) *noun* (*plural* **balustrades**)
a row of short poles joined together at the top, built along the edge of a staircase or a **balcony**

bamboo (say bam-**boo**) *noun* (*plural* **bamboos**)
a tall plant that grows in hot countries and is often used for making furniture: *a* ***bamboo*** *chair* ◇ ***bamboo*** *shoots* (= young ***bamboo*** *plants that can be eaten)*
🛈 **ORIGIN:** 16th century, through Dutch *bamboes* from Malay *mambu*. Dutch colonists and traders brought the word to Europe.

bamboozle (say bam-**booz**-l) *verb* (**bamboozling**, **bamboozled**)
to cheat or trick someone

ban *verb* (**banning**, **banned**)
to say officially that something must not happen or is not allowed: *The film was* ***banned****.*
▸ **ban** (*noun*): *There is a* ***ban*** *on smoking in restaurants.*

banal (say buh-**naal**) *adjective*
not original or interesting: *I didn't want to finish this book; I found it* ***banal****.* ➲ **SYNONYMS** **boring**, **mundane**, **trite**

banana (say buh-**naa**-nuh) *noun* (*plural* **bananas**)
a long curved yellow fruit
🛈 **ORIGIN:** 16th century, through Portuguese and Spanish from Mande, a group of West African languages. Colonists and traders brought the word to Europe.

band *noun* (*plural* **bands**)
1 a group of people who play music together: *a rock* ***band*** ◇ *a jazz* ***band***
2 a thin flat piece of material that you put around something: *an elastic* ***band*** ◇ *The hat had a red* ***band*** *round it.*
3 a line of colour or material on something that is different from the rest of it: *Her T-shirt has a* ***band*** *of red across the middle.*

bandage[1] (say **ban**-dij) *noun* (*plural* **bandages**)
a long piece of white cloth that you tie around a part of your body that is hurt

bandage[2] (say **ban**-dij) *verb* (**bandaging**, **bandaged**)
to put a **bandage**[1] around a part of the body: *The nurse* ***bandaged*** *my foot.*

bandit (say **ban**-dit) *noun* (*plural* **bandits**)
a person who attacks and robs travellers in **isolated lawless** areas: *They were killed by* ***bandits*** *in the mountains.*

bandwagon (say **band**-wag-uhn) *noun* (*plural* **bandwagons**)
get on the bandwagon to copy what other people are doing because it is fashionable or successful: *Many politicians jumped on the environmental* ***bandwagon****.*

bandy (say **ban**-dee) *adjective*
(used about legs) bent, with the knees wide apart: *He's got* ***bandy*** *legs.*

bane (say **bayn**) *noun* (*no plural*)
a cause of trouble: *These cockroaches are the* ***bane*** *of my life.*

bang[1] *verb* (**banging**, **banged**)
to make a loud noise by hitting something hard or by closing something: *He* ***banged*** *his head on the ceiling.* ◇ *Don't* ***bang*** *the door!*

bang[2] *noun* (*plural* **bangs**)
1 a sudden very loud noise: *She shut the door with a* ***bang****.*
2 a short strong knock or hit, especially one that causes pain and injury: *He fell and got a* ***bang*** *on the head.*

bangle (say **bang**-guhl) *noun* (*plural* **bangles**)
a circular band that you wear around your wrist for decoration

banish (say **ban**-ish) *verb* (**banishing**, **banished**)
to send somebody away from a place, especially a country, as an official punishment: *The government* ***banished*** *the rebels from the city.*

banister (say **ban**-iss-tuh) *noun* (*plural* **banisters**)
a long piece of wood or metal that you hold on to when you go up or down stairs

banjo (say **ban**-joh) *noun* (*plural* **banjos**)
a musical instrument with a long neck, a round body and strings, that looks like a guitar

bank[1] (say **bangk**) *noun* (*plural* **banks**)
1 a place that keeps money safe for people: *I've got R500 in the* ***bank****.*
2 the land along the side of a river: *People were fishing along the* ***banks*** *of the river.*

bank[2] (say **bangk**) *verb* (**banking**, **banked**)
to keep your money in a particular bank: *Who do you* ***bank*** *with?*
bank on a person or thing to expect and trust someone to do something, or something to happen: *The boss might give you the day off but I wouldn't* ***bank*** *on it.*

bank account *noun* (*plural* **bank accounts**)
an arrangement that you have with a bank that lets you keep your money there: *I'd like to open a* ***bank account****.*

banker (say **bang**-kuh) *noun* (*plural* **bankers**)
a person who owns a bank or who has an important job in a bank

banknote (say **bangk**-noht) *noun* (*plural* **banknotes**)
a piece of paper money: *These are South African* ***banknotes****.*

bankrupt (say **bang**-krupt) *adjective*
not able to continue in business because you cannot pay the money that you owe:
His business went ***bankrupt*** *after a year.*
➲ SYNONYM **insolvent**
▸ **bankruptcy** (*noun*)

banner (say **ban**-uh) *noun* (*plural* **banners**)
a long piece of cloth with a message on it that people carry in a **demonstration** 1 or hang up in a public place to show support for something: *The* ***banner*** *said 'Stop the war'.*

banquet (say **bang**-kwuht) *noun* (*plural* **banquets**)
a formal dinner for a large number of people

banter (say **ban**-tuh) *noun* (*no plural*)
friendly comments and jokes: *There was* ***banter*** *between the competitors.*

Bantu (say **bun**-too) *adjective*
relating to a very large group of African languages that includes isiXhosa, isiZulu, Sesotho, Sesotho sa Leboa, Shona, Swahili, Tshivenda, Xitsonga, and many others
ⓘ ORIGIN: from the plural form of *-ntu* meaning 'person' in certain Bantu languages

> USAGE Some people find this word offensive, but it is used internationally by language experts as an official term for this group of languages.

baobab (say **bay**-uh-bab) *noun* (*plural* **baobabs**)
an African tree with a very large **trunk**
ⓘ ORIGIN: 17th century, probably from an African language

baptism (say **bap**-tiz-uhm) *noun* (*plural* **baptisms**)
a religious ceremony to **baptize** a person

baptize (say bap-**tize**) *verb* (**baptizing**, **baptized**) (also **baptise**)
to put water on somebody and give them a name, to show that they belong to the Christian Church

bar[1] (say **baa**) *noun* (*plural* **bars**)
1 a place where people can go and buy drinks, especially alcoholic drinks: *There's a* ***bar*** *in the hotel.*
2 a place where you can get a particular kind of food or drink: *a coffee* ***bar***
3 a small block of something hard: *a* ***bar*** *of soap* ◇ *a* ***bar*** *of chocolate*
4 a long thin piece of metal: *There were iron* ***bars*** *on the windows.*

bar[2] (say **baa**) *verb* (**barring**, **barred**)
1 to put something across a place so that people cannot pass: *Police* ***barred*** *the road.*
2 to say officially that somebody must not do something or go somewhere: *He was* ***barred*** *from the team for fighting.*

barb (say **baab**) *noun* (*plural* **barbs**)
the point of an arrow or a hook that is curved backwards to make it difficult to pull out: *a* ***barb*** *on a fish hook*

barbarian (say baa-**bair**-ri-uhn) *noun* (*plural* **barbarians**)
a wild person with no culture, who behaves very badly
ⓘ ORIGIN: 13th–15th century, through Old French or Latin from Greek *barbaros* meaning 'foreign'. When the word came into English, it was used in a negative way to describe a person with different customs and speech.

barbecue (say **baa**-buh-kyoo) *noun* (*plural* **barbecues**) another word for **braai**
ⓘ ORIGIN: 17th century, through Spanish *barbacoa*, possibly from Arawak *barbacoa* meaning 'wooden frame on posts'. Arawak is a group of South American languages. Spanish colonists and traders brought the word to Europe.

barbed wire (say baabd **wy**-uh) *noun* (*no plural*)
wire with a lot of sharp points on it

barber (say **baa**-buh) *noun* (*plural* **barbers**)
a person who works in a shop where men go to get their hair cut

bar code *noun* (*plural* **bar codes**)
a pattern of black lines that is printed on things that you buy. It contains information about the product and its price that a computer can read: *There is a **bar code** on the back cover of this dictionary.*

bare (say **bair**) *adjective* (**barer, barest**)
1 (used about a part of the body) with no clothes covering it: *He had **bare** feet* (= he wasn't wearing shoes or socks).
2 without anything covering it or in it: *The empty house had **bare** walls.*

barefoot (say **bair**-fuut) *adjective, adverb*
with no shoes or socks on your feet: *a **barefoot** athlete ◇ The children ran **barefoot** along the beach.*

barely (say **bair**-lee) *adverb*
only just or almost not: *She **barely** ate anything.*
➲ SYNONYM **hardly, scarcely**

bargain¹ (say **baa**-guhn) *noun* (*plural* **bargains**)
something that is cheaper than usual: *At just R40, the dress was a real **bargain**!*

bargain² (say **baa**-guhn) *verb* (**bargaining, bargained**)
to try to agree on the right price for something: *I think she'll sell the car for less if you **bargain** with her.*

barge¹ (say **baaj**) *noun* (*plural* **barges**)
a long boat with a flat bottom for carrying things or people on a river or canal

barge² (say **baaj**) *verb* (**barging, barged**)
to push people out of the way to move past them: *He just **barged** to the front of the queue.*

baritone (say **ba**-ri-tohn) *noun*
1 (*no plural*) a fairly low male singing voice
2 (*plural* **baritones**) a man with such a voice

bark¹ (say **baak**) *noun*
1 (*no plural*) the hard surface of a tree
2 (*plural* **barks**) the short loud sound that a dog makes

bark² (say **baak**) *verb* (**barking, barked**)
(used about a dog) to make a short loud sound: *The dog **barks** at people it doesn't know.*

barley (say **baa**-lee) *noun* (*no plural*)
a plant that produces grain that we use for making food, beer and some other drinks

bar mitzvah (say baa **mitss**-vuh) *noun* (*plural* **bar mitzvahs**)
a ceremony for a Jewish boy who has turned thirteen and is old enough to be called an adult
➲ See **bat mitzvah**
🛈 ORIGIN: from Hebrew *bar miṣwāh* meaning 'son of the commandment'

barn (say **baan**) *noun* (*plural* **barns**)
a large building on a farm for keeping crops or animals in

barnacle (say **baan**-ik-l) *noun* (*plural* **barnacles**)
a small sea creature with a hard shell that attaches itself to rocks

barometer (say buh-**rom**-i-tuh) *noun* (*plural* **barometers**)
an instrument that measures air pressure and indicates changes in weather

barometer

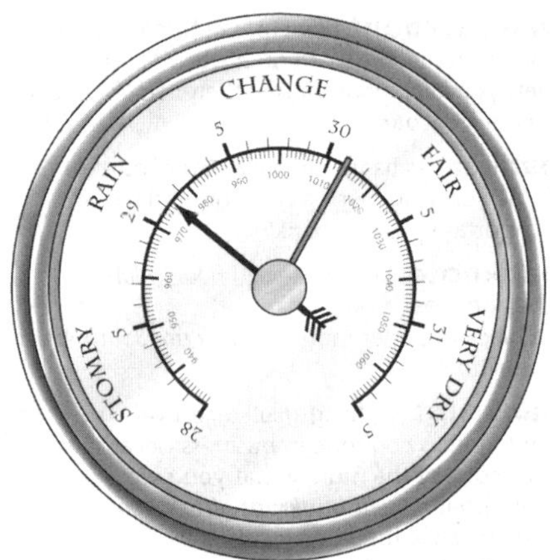

baron (say **ba**-ruhn) *noun* (*plural* **barons**)
1 a man who has a high social position, especially in Britain
2 a person who controls a large part of an industry: *a newspaper **baron***

baroque (say buh-**rok**) *adjective*
relating to a very decorative style of European architecture and music of the 17th and 18th centuries

barracks (say **ba**-ruhkss) *plural noun*
a building or group of buildings where soldiers live: *an army **barracks***

barrage (say **ba**-raazh) *noun* (*plural* **barrages**)
1 a continuous attack by many guns
2 many questions or comments directed at a person very quickly: *a **barrage** of criticism*

barrel (say **ba**-ruhl) *noun* (*plural* **barrels**)
1 a large container for liquids, with round sides and flat ends: *a **barrel** of oil*
2 the part of a gun that is like a tube, through which the bullets are fired

barren (say **ba**-ruhn) *adjective*
1 (used about land or soil) with no plants growing on it: *a **barren** desert ◇ a **barren** playground*

2 (used about plants) not producing fruit
3 (used about animals) not able to produce young animals

barricade (say ba-ri-**kayd**) *noun* (*plural* **barricades**)
a line of things arranged across a road to stop people from getting past
▸ **barricade** (*verb*): *He **barricaded** the door to keep the police out.*

barrier (say **ba**-ri-uh) *noun* (*plural* **barriers**)
a wall or fence that stops you going somewhere: *You must show your ticket at the **barrier** before you get on the train.*

barrow (*rhymes with* **narrow**) *noun* (*plural* **barrows**) short for **wheelbarrow**

barter (say **baa**-tuh) *verb* (**bartering, bartered**)
to exchange goods or services for something without using money: *They **bartered** cattle for tools.*
▸ **barter** (*noun*): ***Barter** is common here.*

base[1] (say **bayss**) *noun* (*plural* **bases**)
1 the bottom part of something, the part that something stands on: *The lamp has a heavy **base**.* ◇ *the **base** of a column*
2 an idea or a fact from which something develops or is made: *She used her family's history as a **base** for her novel.*
3 a person's or a company's main home or office: *She travels all over the world but Johannesburg is her **base**.*
4 a place where soldiers in the army live and work: *an army **base***
5 (*science*) a chemical substance with a pH value of more than seven that can combine with an acid to form a salt ➲ See **acid**, **alkali**
6 (*maths*) a number on which a system of counting and expressing numbers is built up, for example two in the **binary** 1 system

base[2] (say **bayss**) *verb* (**basing, based**)
be based somewhere (used about a person or a company) to have their main home or office in a particular place
base something on something to make or develop something, using another thing as a starting point: *The film is **based** on a true story.*

baseball (say **bayss**-bawl) *noun*
1 (*no plural*) a game in which two teams hit a ball with a wooden stick (called a **bat**) and then score points by running round four fixed points (called **bases**) on a large field: *We played **baseball** in the park.*
2 (*plural* **baseballs**) a ball for playing this game

basement (say **bayss**-muhnt) *noun* (*plural* **basements**)
part of a building that is under the level of the ground: *a **basement** flat*

bases[1] (say **bay**-suhz) plural of **base[1]**

bases[2] (say **bay**-seez) plural of **basis[1]**

bash *verb* (**bashing, bashed**) (*informal*)
to hit a person or thing very hard: *I fell and **bashed** my knee.*

bashful (say **bash**-fuul) *adjective*
shy and embarrassed

basic (say **bay**-sik) *adjective*
1 most important and necessary: *Our **basic** needs are food, clothes and a place to live.*
2 simple, and including only what is necessary: *We learnt some **basic** computer skills.*

basically (say **bay**-sik-lee) *adverb*
in the most important ways: *She's a little strange but **basically** a very nice person.*

basil (say **baz**-il) *noun* (*no plural*)
a plant with shiny green leaves that smell sweet and are used as a **herb** in cooking

basin (say **bay**-sin) *noun* (*plural* **basins**)
1 a **washbasin**
2 a round bowl for cooking or mixing food

basis (say **bay**-siss) *noun*
1 (*plural* **bases**) the most important part or idea, from which something grows: *Her notes formed the **basis** of a book.*
2 (*no plural*) the way something is done or organized: *We meet on a regular **basis*** (= often).

basket (say **baa**-skit) *noun* (*plural* **baskets**)
a container made of thin sticks or thin pieces of plastic or metal, that you use for holding or carrying things: *a shopping **basket***

basketball (say **baa**-skit-bawl) *noun*
1 (*no plural*) a game for two teams of five players who try to throw a ball into a high net
2 (*plural* **basketballs**) a ball for playing this game

bass[1] (say **bayss**) *adjective*
with a deep sound: *She plays the **bass** guitar.*

bass[2] (say **bayss**) *noun*
1 (*no plural*) the lowest tone or part in music, for instruments or voices
2 (*no plural*) a man's singing voice with a low range
3 (*plural* **basses**) a singer with such a voice
4 (*no plural*) (also **bass guitar**) an electric guitar that plays very low notes

A B C D E F G H I J K L M N O P Q R S T U V W X Y Z

bass³ (*rhymes with* **mass**) *noun* (*plural* **bass** or **basses**)
a sea or freshwater fish that is used for food

bassoon (say buh-**soon**) *noun* (*plural* **bassoons**)
a musical instrument of the **woodwind** group. It is shaped like a large wooden tube with a double reed that you blow into, and produces notes with a low sound.

bastard (say **baa**-stuhd) *noun* (*plural* **bastards**)
1 (*old-fashioned*) a person who was born when their parents were not married to each other
2 (*informal*) a rude word for a very unpleasant person

Baster (say **buss**-tuh) *noun* (*plural* **Basters**)
a member of a group of Afrikaans-speaking people, most of whom live in Namibia

bastion (say **bass**-ti-uhn) *noun* (*plural* **bastions**)
part of a **fort** from which soldiers can defend themselves from attack

bat¹ *noun* (*plural* **bats**)
1 a piece of wood for hitting the ball in a game such as cricket or **table tennis**
2 a small mammal with wings that comes out and flies at night

bats

cricket bat

fruit bat

> **WORD BUILDING** The thing that you use to hit the ball has different names in different sports. You use a **bat** in baseball, cricket and table tennis. You use a **racket** to play squash and tennis. To play golf, you use a **club** and to play hockey, you use a **stick**.

bat² *verb* (**batting**, **batted**)
to try to hit a ball in games such as cricket or **baseball**: *He **bats** very well.*

batch (say **bach**) *noun* (*plural* **batches**)
a group of things: *She made a **batch** of cakes.*

bath (say **baath**) *noun* (*plural* **baths**)
1 a large container that you fill with water and sit in to wash your body
2 the act of washing your body in a bath: *I had a **bath** this morning.*

bathe (say **bay*th***) *verb* (**bathing**, **bathed**)
1 to wash a part of your body carefully: *He **bathed** the cut on his finger.*
2 (*old-fashioned*) to swim in the sea or in a lake or river: *On hot days we often **bathe** in the lake.*

bathroom (say **baath**-ruum) *noun* (*plural* **bathrooms**)
1 a room where you can wash and have a bath or shower
2 a room with a toilet in it: *Can I go to the **bathroom** (= use the toilet)?* ➲ See note at **toilet**

batik (say ba-**teek**) *noun*
1 (*no plural*) a method of printing patterns on cloth
2 (*plural* **batiks**) a cloth made in this way

bat mitzvah (say but **mitss**-vuh) *noun* (*plural* **bat mitzvahs**)
a ceremony for a Jewish girl who has turned twelve and is old enough to be called an adult ➲ See **bar mitzvah**

baton (say **bat**-on) *noun* (*plural* **batons**)
1 a short thick stick that a police officer carries as a weapon ➲ SYNONYM **truncheon**
2 a short thin stick used by the leader of an orchestra
3 a stick which a runner in a **relay** race passes to the next runner

batsman (say **batss**-muhn) *noun* (*plural* **batsmen**)
(in cricket) a player who hits the ball with a bat

battalion (say buh-**tal**-i-uhn) *noun* (*plural* **battalions**)
a small unit of soldiers that is part of a larger unit in an army

batten (say **bat**-uhn) *noun* (*plural* **battens**)
a piece of thin wood or metal that you use to hold something in place

batter¹ (say **bat**-uh) *verb* (**battering**, **battered**)
to hit someone or something hard and quickly: *He **battered** the door until it broke* ◇ *Rain **battered** the town.*

batter² (say **bat**-uh) *noun* (*no plural*)
a mixture of flour, milk and egg used to cover

food such as fish and vegetables, before you fry them: *I love eating fried fish in **batter**.*
➲ See **fritter**[1]

battery (say **bat**-ree) *noun* (*plural* **batteries**)
a device that gives electricity, for example for a toy, radio or car: *a 1,5 volt **battery***

battle[1] (say **bat**-l) *noun* (*plural* **battles**)
1 a fight between armies in a war: *the **battle** of El Alamein*
2 a determined effort to solve a difficult problem or to succeed in a difficult situation: *In the end, she lost her **battle** against cancer.*

battle[2] (say **bat**-l) *verb* (**battling, battled**)
to try very hard to do something difficult: *The doctors **battled** to save her life.*

bauble (say **bawb**-l) *noun* (*plural* **baubles**)
1 a pretty ball that you hang on a Christmas tree as decoration
2 something that is pretty but has no value

bawl (*rhymes with* **tall**) *verb* (**bawling, bawled**) (*informal*)
to cry loudly: *The little boy is sitting outside and **bawling**.*

bay *noun* (*plural* **bays**)
a part of the coast where the land goes in to form a curve: *There was a ship in the **bay**.*

bayonet (say **bay**-oh-net) *noun* (*plural* **bayonets**)
a knife that can be fixed to the end of a gun

bazaar (say buh-**zaa**) *noun* (*plural* **bazaars**)
1 a market
2 a sale to make money for something: *a church **bazaar***
🛈 ORIGIN: 16th century, through Italian *bazarro*, through Turkish from Persian *bāzār* meaning 'market'

BC (say bee-**see**) *abbreviation*
used in dates for showing the number of years before the time when Jesus Christ was born: *Julius Caesar died in 44 BC.* 🛈 BC is short for 'before Christ'. ➲ See **AD, BCE, CE**

USAGE Note that BC comes after the date: *It was built in 250 BC.* Compare this with AD, which you write before the date: *She was born in about AD 350.*

BCE (say bee-see-**ee**) *abbreviation*
used in dates for showing the number of years before the time when Jesus Christ was born. It is another word for BC: *The Roman building was built in around 1450 BCE.* 🛈 BCE is short for 'before the Common Era'.

be (say **bee**) *verb* (**being, was** or **were, has been**)
1 to exist or be present in a place: *There **are** a lot of trees in our garden.* ◇ ***Is** there a post office near here?*
2 a word that you use to give the position of a person or thing or the place where they are: ***Jen's*** (= Jen is) *in her room.* ◇ *Where **are** the scissors?*
3 a word that you use when you are giving the name of people or things, describing them or giving more information about them: ***I'm*** (= I am) *Ben.* ◇ *The film **was** excellent.* ◇ *Danie **is** a doctor.* ◇ *Today **is** Friday.*
4 a word that you use to talk about the age of a person or thing or to talk about time: *'How old **is** she?' '**She's** twelve.'* ◇ *Her birthday **was** in May.* ◇ ***It's** six o'clock.*
5 a word that you use with another verb: *'What **are** you doing?' '**I'm*** (= I am) *reading.'*
6 a word that you use with part of another verb to show that something happens to somebody or something: *The house **was** built in 1910.*

USAGE A table on Study page 8 shows you how to use this verb.

beach (say **beech**) *noun* (*plural* **beaches**)
a piece of land next to the sea that is covered with sand or stones: *a sandy **beach***

beacon (say **bee**-kuhn) *noun* (*plural* **beacons**)
1 a fire or a light on a hill that people can see from far away
2 (*also* **trig beacon, trigonometrical beacon**) (*geography*) a structure on a hill or mountain or along the coast, used in the past by makers of maps to calculate distances and the height above the sea

bead (say **beed**) *noun* (*plural* **beads**)
a small ball of wood, glass or plastic with a hole in the middle. They are put on a string to make jewellery.
🛈 ORIGIN: from Old English *gebed* meaning 'prayer'. People used a string of beads to count the prayers they said; eventually the word came to mean the bead itself.

beading (say **beed**-ing) *noun* (*no plural*)
a decoration made of beads

beadwork (say **beed**-wurk) *noun* (*no plural*)
things such as jewellery and decorations made with beads: *Designers use **beadwork** to decorate clothing.*

beak (say **beek**) *noun* (*plural* **beaks**)
the hard pointed part of a bird's mouth

beaker (say **bee**-kuh) *noun* (*plural* **beakers**)
1 a cup without a handle

A B C D E F G H I J K L M N O P Q R S T U V W X Y Z

2 a glass container that you use in science experiments

beam[1] (say **beem**) *noun* (*plural* **beams**)
1 a line of light: *a laser* ***beam***
2 a long heavy piece of wood that holds up a roof or ceiling

beam[2] (say **beem**) *verb* (**beaming, beamed**) (*informal*)
to have a big happy smile on your face

bean (say **been**) *noun* (*plural* **beans**)
a seed, or a seed container, that we use as food: *green* ***beans*** ◇ *coffee* ***beans***

beanbag (say **been**-bag) *noun* (*plural* **beanbags**)
1 a large bag filled with light material that you sit on
2 a small bag filled with beans that you can throw and catch

bear[1] (say **bair**) *verb* (**bearing, bore, has borne**)
1 to be able to accept something unpleasant without complaining: *The pain was difficult to* ***bear***.
2 to hold a person or thing up so that they do not fall: *This ladder isn't strong enough to* ***bear*** *your weight.*
can't bear a person or **thing** to hate a person or thing: *I can't* ***bear*** *this music.* ◇ *He can't* ***bear*** *feeling bored.*

bear[2] (say **bair**) *noun* (*plural* **bears**)
a large wild mammal with thick brown fur, claws and sharp teeth: *a brown* ***bear*** ◇ *a polar* ***bear***

beard (say **beerd**) *noun* (*plural* **beards**)
the hair on a man's chin and cheeks: *He has got a* ***beard***.

bearing (say **bair**-ring) *noun*
1 (*no plural*) a connection to the thing being discussed: *This has no* ***bearing*** *on the matter we're discussing.*
2 (*no plural*) the way somebody stands or moves: *Dikeledi has a confident* ***bearing***.
3 (*plural* **bearings**) the direction measured from a fixed point, using a special instrument (called a **compass**)

beast (say **beest**) *noun* (*plural* **beasts**)
1 (*formal*) a wild animal
2 an unkind or cruel person

beat[1] (say **beet**) *verb* (**beating, beat, has beaten**)
1 to win a fight or game against a person or group of people: *Ebrahim always* ***beats*** *me at tennis.* ◇ *Our team was* ***beaten*** *2 – 1.*
2 to hit a person or thing very hard many times: *She* ***beats*** *her dog with a stick.* ◇ *The rain was* ***beating*** *on the roof.*
3 to make the same sound or movement many times: *His heart was* ***beating*** *fast.*
4 to mix food quickly with a fork, for example: ***Beat*** *the eggs and sugar together.*
beat somebody up to hit or kick somebody hard, many times: *He was badly* ***beaten*** *up by a gang of youths.*

beat[2] (say **beet**) *noun* (*plural* **beats**)
a sound that comes again and again: *We heard the* ***beat*** *of the drums.* ➲ See **heartbeat**

beautiful (say **byoo**-ti-fuul) *adjective*
1 very pretty or attractive: *a* ***beautiful*** *woman*
➲ OPPOSITE **ugly**
2 very nice to see, hear or smell: *Those flowers are* ***beautiful***. ◇ *What a* ***beautiful*** *song!*
➲ SYNONYM **lovely**
▶ **beautifully** (*adverb*): *He sang* ***beautifully***.

WORD BUILDING There are many words that you can use instead of **beautiful**, but check their exact meanings first. Examples are: **attractive**, **captivating**, **charming**, **delightful**, **elegant**, **exquisite**, **fine**1, **good-looking**, **glamorous**, **glorious** 2, **gorgeous**, **graceful**, **handsome**, **lovely**, **magnificient**, **pretty** 2, **ravishing**, **scenic**, **spectacular**, **splendid**, **stunning** and **superb**.

WORD BUILDING When we use sense 1 above to talk about people, we usually (but not always) say **beautiful** and **pretty** for women and girls, and **handsome** and **good-looking** for men and boys. **Attractive** is used for everyone.

beauty (say **byoo**-tee) *noun* (*no plural*)
the quality of being beautiful: *a woman of great* ***beauty*** ◇ *the* ***beauty*** *of nature*
🛈 ORIGIN: 13th–15th century, from Old French *beaute*, based on Latin *bellus*

beaver (say **beev**-uh) *noun* (*plural* **beavers**)
a wild mammal with brown fur that lives in and near rivers in North America and Europe

because (say bi-**kawz**) *conjunction*
for the reason that: *He was angry* ***because*** *I was late.*
because of something as a result of something or someone: *We stayed at home* ***because*** *of the rain.*

beckon (say **bek**-uhn) *verb* (**beckoning, beckoned**)
to move your finger to show that you want somebody to come nearer

become (say bi-**kum**) *verb* (**becoming, became, has become**)
to begin to be something: *She **became** a doctor in 1982.* ◇ *The weather is **becoming** colder.*
what became of ...? used to ask what has happened to a person or thing: *What **became** of your friend, Ashley?*

> USAGE In sentences with adjectives, we usually say **get** instead of **become**, because **get** is less formal: *The weather is **getting** colder.*

bed *noun* (*plural* **beds**)
1 a thing that you sleep on: *It was time to go to **bed**.* ◇ *The children are in **bed**.* ◇ *to make the **bed*** (= to make it ready for somebody to sleep in) ◇ *Would you prefer a single **bed** or a double **bed**?*
2 the bottom of a river or the sea

bedding (say **bed**-ing) *noun* (*no plural*)
everything that you put on a bed and need for sleeping: *I washed my **bedding** this morning.*

bedraggled (say bi-**drag**-uhld) *adjective*
very wet and untidy: *My poor **bedraggled** cat was lost in the rain.*

bedroom (say **bed**-ruum) *noun* (*plural* **bedrooms**)
a room where you sleep

bedtime (say **bed**-time) *noun* (*no plural*)
the time when somebody usually goes to bed

bee *noun* (*plural* **bees**)
a black and yellow flying insect that can sting. Bees live in large groups and make a sweet food that we eat (called **honey**).

beef *noun* (*no plural*)
meat from a cow: *roast **beef***
ℹ ORIGIN: 13th–15th century, through Old French *boef* meaning 'ox', from Latin *bos, bov*

beefburger (say **beef**-bur-guh) *noun* (*plural* **beefburgers**) another word for **hamburger**

beehive (say **bee**-hive) *noun* (*plural* **beehives**)
a type of box in which people keep **bees**

been
1 form of **be**: *I've **been** absent.*
2 form of **go**[1]: *I've **been** to your house.*
have been to to have gone to a place and come back again: *Have you ever **been** to Oudtshoorn?*

> WHICH WORD? **Been** or **gone**?
> ■ If you have **been** to a place, you have travelled there and returned: *'Hello! Where have you **been**?' 'I've **been** to Kimberley.'*
> ■ If you have **gone** to a place, you have travelled there and you are still there now: *'Mpho isn't here. He's **gone** to Polokwane.'*

> SPELLING Be careful! Don't confuse **been** and **being**.

beer (*rhymes with* **gear**) *noun*
1 (*no plural*) an alcoholic drink made from grain: *a pint of **beer***
2 (*plural* **beers**) a glass, bottle or can of beer: *Three **beers**, please.*

beet *noun* (*plural* **beets**)
a plant with a root that is used as a vegetable
➲ See **beetroot**

beetle (say **beet**-l) *noun* (*plural* **beetles**)
an insect with a shiny body and a hard case on its back, covering its wings

beetroot (say **beet**-root) *noun* (*plural* **beetroots**)
a round, dark red vegetable that you usually cook before eating it

befall (say bi-**fawl**) *verb* (**befalling, befell, has befallen**)
to happen to somebody: *This is the latest crisis to **befall** Max.*

before[1] (say bi-**faw**) *preposition, conjunction*
1 earlier than a person or thing, or earlier than the time that: *He arrived **before** me.* ◇ *I said goodbye **before** I left.* ◇ *She worked in a hospital **before** getting this job.* ➲ OPPOSITE **after**[1] 1
2 in front of a person or thing: *B comes **before** C in the alphabet.* ➲ OPPOSITE **after**[1] 2

before[2] (say bi-**faw**) *adverb*
at an earlier time or in the past: *I've never met them **before**.* ◇ *I've seen this film **before**.*

beforehand (say bi-**faw**-hand) *adverb*
at an earlier time than something: *Tell me **beforehand** if you are going to be late.*

befriend (say bi-**frend**) *verb* (**befriending, befriended**)
to become friends with someone: *I **befriended** my new neighbours.*

beg *verb* (**begging, begged**)
1 to ask somebody for something, especially in an anxious way, because you want or need it very much: *She **begged** me to stay with her.* ◇ *He **begged** for help.*
2 to ask for money or food because you are very poor: *He was **begging** in the street.*
I beg your pardon (*formal*)
1 I am sorry: *I **beg** your pardon, I didn't mean to bump you.*

A B C D E F G H I J K L M N O P Q R S T U V W X Y Z

A B C D E F G H I J K L M N O P Q R S T U V W X Y Z

2 (used when you have not heard what someone says) please repeat what you said

beggar (say **beg**-uh) *noun* (*plural* **beggars**)
a person who asks other people for money or food

begin (say bi-**gin**) *verb* (**beginning, began, has begun**)
1 to start to do something or to start to happen: *I'm **beginning** to feel cold.* ◇ *The film **begins** at 7.30.*
2 to start in a particular way: *The name John **begins** with a 'J'.* ➲ OPPOSITE **end²**
to begin with at first or at the beginning: *To **begin** with they were very happy.*

beginner (say bi-**gin**-uh) *noun* (*plural* **beginners**)
a person who is starting to do or learn something ➲ SYNONYM **novice**

beginning (say bi-**gin**-ing) *noun* (*plural* **beginnings**)
the time or place where something starts or the first part of something: *I didn't see the **beginning** of the film.* ➲ OPPOSITE **end¹**

begun (say bi-**gun**) form of **begin**

behalf (say bi-**haaf**) *noun*
on behalf of somebody, on somebody's behalf for somebody or in the place of somebody: *Mr Sigcawu is away, so I am writing to you on his **behalf**.*

behave (say bi-**hayv**) *verb* (**behaving, behaved**)
to do and say things in a certain way: *They **behaved** very kindly towards me.* ◇ *The children **behaved** badly all day.*
behave yourself to be good and to do and say the right things: *Did the children **behave** themselves?* ➲ OPPOSITE **misbehave**

behaviour (say bi-**hay**-vi-uh) *noun* (*no plural*)
the way you are or the way that you do and say things: *He was sent out of the class for bad **behaviour**.* ➲ SYNONYM **conduct²**

behead (say bi-**hed**) *verb* (**beheading, beheaded**)
to cut someone's head off

behind (say bi-**hynd**) *preposition, adverb*
1 at or to the back of a person or thing: *I hid **behind** the wall.*
2 slower or less good than a person or thing or than you should be: *She is **behind** with her work.*
3 in the place where a person or thing was before: *I got off the train and left my bag **behind*** (= on the train).

beige (say **bayzh**) *adjective*
with a light brown colour

being¹ (say **bee**-ing) form of **be**

being² (say **bee**-ing) *noun* (*plural* **beings**)
a person or living thing: *a **being** from another planet*

bel *noun* (*plural* **bels**)
a unit used in the measurement of sound

belch (say **belch**) *verb* (**belching, belched**)
1 to let out wind from your stomach through your mouth: *Dennis **belched** loudly after supper.* ➲ SYNONYM **burp**
2 to send out a lot of smoke: *The volcano **belched** smoke all night.*
▸ **belch** (*noun*): *a loud **belch***

belief (say bi-**leef**) *noun*
1 (*no plural*) a sure feeling that something is true or real, or morally good: *his **belief** in God*
2 (*no plural*) an opinion about something: *There is a general **belief** that things will soon get better.*
3 (*plural* **beliefs**) something that you believe, especially as part of your religion: *Divorce is against their religious **beliefs**.*

believable (say bi-**leev**-uhb-l) *adjective*
that you can believe ➲ OPPOSITE **unbelievable**

believe (say bi-**leev**) *verb* (**believing, believed**)
1 to feel sure that something is true, or that what somebody says is true: *Long ago, people **believed** that the Earth was flat.* ◇ *She says she didn't take the money. Do you **believe** her?*
2 to think that something is true or possible, although you are not certain: *'Does he still work here?' 'I **believe** so.'*
believe in a person or **thing** to feel sure that a person or thing exists: *Do you **believe** in ghosts?*

belittle (say bi-**lit**-l) *verb* (**belittling, belittled**)
to make someone feel unimportant: *Her comments **belittled** me.*

bell (say **bel**) *noun* (*plural* **bells**)
a metal object that makes a sound when something hits or touches it: *The church **bells** were ringing.* ➲ See **doorbell**

belligerent (say buh-**lij**-uh-ruhnt) *adjective*
unfriendly and aggressive: *We didn't like our **belligerent** old neighbour.*

bellow (say **bel**-oh) *verb* (**bellowing, bellowed**)
to shout loudly: *He **bellowed** angrily at us.*
▸ **bellow** (*noun*): *a loud **bellow***

> PRONUNCIATION Notice how **bellow** sounds different from **below**.

bellows (say **bel**-ohz) *plural noun*
an instrument that you use to blow air onto a fire

belly (say **bel**-ee) *noun* (*plural* **bellies**)
the part of your body between your chest and your legs ➲ SYNONYMS **stomach, tummy**

belong (say bi-**long**) *verb* (**belonging, belonged**)
1 to be somebody's: *'Who does this pen* ***belong*** *to?' 'It* ***belongs*** *to me.'*
2 to be a member of a group or an organization: *Do you* ***belong*** *to any clubs?*
3 to have its right or usual place: *That chair* ***belongs*** *in my room.*

belongings (say bi-**long**-ingz) *plural noun*
the things that you own: *They lost all their* ***belongings*** *in the fire.*

beloved (say bi-**luv**-id or bi-**luvd**) *adjective*
that is loved very much: *This is Sara's* ***beloved*** *horse.*
▸ **beloved** (*noun*): *My* ***beloved*** *phoned.*

PRONUNCIATION Use the first pronunciation when **beloved** comes before a noun.

below (say bi-**loh**) *preposition, adverb*
1 in or to a lower place than a person or thing: *From the plane we could see the mountains* ***below****. ◇ She dived* ***below*** *the surface of the water.* ➲ OPPOSITE **above** 1
2 less than a number or price: *The price was* ***below*** *R10.* ➲ SYNONYM **beneath**

belt[1] *noun* (*plural* **belts**)
a long narrow piece of cloth, plastic or leather that you wear around the middle of your body
➲ See **safety belt, seat belt**

belt[2] *verb* (**belting, belted**) (*informal*)
1 to hit someone very hard: *My son* ***belted*** *the class bully.*
2 to run or go somewhere very fast: *He* ***belted*** *round the corner before the gang could catch him.*

bench *noun* (*plural* **benches**)
a long seat for two or more people, usually made of wood: *They sat on a park* ***bench****.*

bend[1] *verb* (**bending, bent**)
1 to make something that was straight into a curved shape: ***Bend*** *your legs!*
2 to be or become curved: *The road* ***bends*** *to the left.*
bend down, bend over to move your body forward and down: *She* ***bent*** *down to put on her shoes.*

bend[2] *noun* (*plural* **bends**)
a part of a road or river that is not straight: *Drive slowly – there's a* ***bend*** *in the road.*

beneath (say bi-**neeth**) *preposition, adverb*
in or to a lower place than a person or thing: *From the tree, he looked at the ground* ***beneath*** *him. ◇* ***beneath*** *the sea* ➲ SYNONYMS **below** 1, **underneath** ➲ OPPOSITE **above** 1

benefactor (say **ben**-i-fak-tuh) *noun* (*plural* **benefactors**)
someone who helps or gives money to a person or organization: *A* ***benefactor*** *has donated money to the charity.*

beneficial (say ben-i-**fish**-uhl) *adjective*
good or useful: *Exercise is* ***beneficial*** *to your health.*

beneficiary (say ben-i-**fish**-uh-ree) *noun* (*plural* **beneficiaries**)
a person who receives something, such as money or property: *We are* ***beneficiaries*** *of her gifts.*

benefit[1] (say **ben**-i-fit) *noun* (*plural* **benefits**)
1 something that is good or helpful: *the* ***benefits*** *of having a computer ◇ I did it for your* ***benefit*** (= to help you).
2 money that the government gives to people who are ill or poor or who do not have a job: *unemployment* ***benefits***

benefit[2] (say **ben**-i-fit) *verb* (**benefiting** or **benefitting, benefited** or **benefitted**)
to be good or helpful for somebody: *The new law will* ***benefit*** *families with children.*
benefit from something to get something good or useful from something: *She will* ***benefit*** *from a holiday.*

benevolent (say buh-**nev**-uh-luhnt) *adjective*
kind and friendly: *a* ***benevolent*** *old man*
▸ **benevolence** (*noun*)

benign (say bi-**nine**) *adjective*
1 (used about a person) gentle and kind
2 (used about a disease) not dangerous
➲ OPPOSITE **malignant**

bent[1] form of **bend**[1]

bent[2] *adjective*
not straight but curved: *Do this exercise with your knees* ***bent****. ◇ This knife is* ***bent****.*
➲ OPPOSITE **straight**[2] 1

bereaved (say bi-**reevd**) *adjective*
having lost a relative or close friend who has recently died

bereft (say bi-**reft**) *adjective*
1 having lost something, not having something: *We were* ***bereft*** *of hope after the floods.*
2 sad and lonely because someone you loved died

beret (say **be**-ray) *noun* (*plural* **berets**)
a soft flat round hat

A **B** C D E F G H I J K L M N O P Q R S T U V W X Y Z

berg (say **burg**) *noun* (*plural* **bergs**) (*S. African*) a mountain
🛈 ORIGIN: 19th century, from Dutch *berg*

berry (*rhymes with* **very**) *noun* (*plural* **berries**) a small soft fruit with seeds in it: *Those **berries** are poisonous.* ◇ ***strawberries***

berserk (say buh-**zurk**) *adjective* very angry, often in a violent or uncontrolled way: *He went **berserk** when he saw his car after the crash.*
🛈 ORIGIN: 19th century, from *berserker*, meaning 'wild raging warrior' from Old Norse *berserkr*. The word originally meant a wild warrior from Norway or Scandinavia in ancient or medieval times.

berth (*rhymes with* **birth**) *noun* (*plural* **berths**)
1 a place to sleep on a ship or a train: *We slept in a **berth** on our train trip.*
2 a place where a ship can stop and stay
to give a person or thing a wide berth to stay well away from a person or thing: *I gave the snake a wide **berth**.*

beside (say bi-**side**) *preposition* at the side of a person or thing: *Come and sit **beside** me.*

besides[1] (say bi-**sy**dz) *adverb* also: *I don't really want to go. **Besides**, it's too late now.*

besides[2] (say bi-**sy**dz) *preposition* as well as a person or thing, or not counting a person or thing: *I have lots of things to do today **besides** homework.*

besiege (say bi-**seej**) *verb* (**besieging, besieged**)
1 to surround a place with an army
2 to surround a thing in large numbers

best[1] *adjective* (**good, better, best**) better than all others: *This is the **best** ice cream I have ever eaten!* ◇ *She is my **best** friend.* ◇ *Jo's the **best** player on the team.* ➲ OPPOSITE **worst**[1]

best[2] *noun* (*no plural*) the person or thing that is better than all others: *Sipho and Sello are good at tennis but Deneo is the **best**.*
all the best words that you use when you say goodbye to somebody, to wish them success
do your best to do all that you can: *I'll do my **best** to finish the work today.*

best[3] *adverb* (**well, better, best**)
1 most well: *I work **best** in the morning.*
2 more than all others: *Which picture do you like **best**?* ➲ SYNONYM **most**[2] ➲ OPPOSITE **least**

bet *verb* (**betting, betted**) to risk money on a race or a game by saying what the result will be. If you are right, you win money: *I **bet** you R5 that our team will win.*
I bet (*informal*) I am sure: *I **bet** it will rain tomorrow.* ◇ *I **bet** you can't climb that tree.*
▸ **bet** (*noun*): *I lost the **bet**.*

betray (say bi-**tray**) *verb* (**betraying, betrayed**) to harm your friends or your country by giving information to an enemy: *She **betrayed** the group to the secret police.*

betrothed (say bi-**troh*th*d**) *adjective* (*formal*), (*old-fashioned*) having promised to marry a person: *The couple are **betrothed** to each other.*
➲ SYNONYM **engaged** 1
▸ **betrothed** (*noun*): *How long have you known your **betrothed**?*

better[1] (say **bet**-uh) *adjective* (**good, better, best**)
1 of a higher standard or quality, or not as bad as something else: *This book is **better** than that one.*
2 less ill: *I was ill yesterday, but I feel **better** now.*
➲ OPPOSITE **worse**[1]

better[2] (say **bet**-uh) *adverb* (**good, better, best**) in a more excellent or pleasant way, or not as badly: *You speak English **better** than I do.*
be better off to be happier or richer: *I'm **better** off now that I've got a new job.*
you had better do something you should or ought to do something: *You'd **better** go now if you want to catch the train.*

better[3] (say **bet**-uh) *verb* (**bettering, bettered**) to improve something: *I **bettered** my position in the race.*

between (say bi-**tween**) *preposition, adverb*
1 in the space in the middle of two things or people: *The letter B comes **between** A and C.* ◇ *I sat **between** Jabu and Rendani.*
2 to and from two places: *The bus travels **between** the station and the airport.*
3 more than one thing but less than another thing: *It will cost **between** R25 and R40.*
4 after one time and before the next time: *I'll meet you **between** 4 and 4.30.*
5 for or by two or more people or things: *We divided the cake **between** us.*
➲ See note at **among**

beverage (say **bev**-uh-rij) *noun* (*plural* **beverages**) a drink: *Would you like a **beverage** with dinner?*

beware (say bi-**wair**) *verb*
beware of a person or thing to be careful because a person or thing is dangerous: ***Beware** of the dog!* (= words written on a sign)

bewilder (say bi-**wil**-duh) *verb* (**bewildering, bewildered**)
to confuse or surprise: *The new road names **bewilder** me.* ➲ SYNONYM **mystify**
▸ **bewildered** (*adjective*): *I was completely **bewildered** by his sudden change of mood.*

bewitch (say bi-**wich**) *verb* (**bewitching, bewitched**)
1 to use magic to make somebody behave differently: *He threatened to **bewitch** her husband.*
2 to attract and interest somebody very much: *He was **bewitched** by her beauty.*

beyond (say bi-**yond**) *preposition, adverb*
on the other side or further than something: *The road continues **beyond** the village into the hills.* ◇ *These birds migrate north to Canada and **beyond**.*

Bhagavad Gita (say **bug**-uh-vud **geet**-uh) *noun* (also **The Gita**)
an ancient poem about faith in God and about your duty, that is of great importance to **Hinduism**

bi- (say **by**) *prefix*
two or twice or double: *a **bicycle*** ◇ *A **bimonthly** newsletter comes twice a month.* ◇ *A **bilingual** person can speak two languages.*
ℹ ORIGIN: from Latin, meaning 'with two, having two'

biannual (say by-**an**-yuu-uhl) *adjective*
happening two times a year: *Our photography club has a **biannual** meeting.*

SPELLING Be careful! Don't confuse **biennial**, which means 'happening every two years' or 'lasting for two years', with **biannual**.

bias (say **by**-uhss) *noun* (*plural* **biases**)
1 a strong feeling of preferring a person or thing, not based on fair reasons: *The coach showed **bias** when she chose the team.*
2 (used about cloth) a direction that is diagonal to the weave of the cloth: *Cut this pattern on the **bias**.*
▸ **bias** (*verb*): *He **biased** the judges against the visiting team.*

bib *noun* (*plural* **bibs**)
a piece of cloth or plastic that a baby wears under its chin when it is eating

bible (say **by**-buhl) *noun*
1 the Bible (*no plural*) the most important book of the Christian religion, containing the Old and the New Testaments
2 the Bible (*no plural*) the most important book of the Jewish religion, containing the Torah
3 (*plural* **bibles**) (*informal*) a book with a lot of information on a subject: *an athlete's **bible***

biblical (say **bib**-lik-l) *adjective*
relating to the Bible

bibliography (say bib-li-**og**-ruh-fee) *noun* (*plural* **bibliographies**)
a list of books and articles that a writer used to write a particular book

biceps (say **by**-sepss) *noun* (*plural* **biceps**)
the large muscle at the front of your upper arm
➲ See **triceps**

bicker (say **bik**-uh) *verb* (**bickering, bickered**)
to argue about unimportant things: *Stop **bickering** or you can walk home!*

bicycle (say **by**-sik-l) *noun* (*plural* **bicycles**) (also *informal* **bike**)
a vehicle with two wheels that you ride by pushing the **pedals** with your feet: *Can you ride a **bicycle**?*

bid[1] *verb* (**bidding, bid**)
to offer some money because you want to buy something: *He **bid** R10 000 for the painting.*

bid[2] *noun* (*plural* **bids**)
an offer of money for something that you want to buy: *She made a **bid** of R50 for the vase.*

biennial (say by-**en**-i-uhl) *adjective*
1 lasting for two years
2 happening every two years: *The **biennial** event had taken over a year to plan.*

SPELLING Be careful! Don't confuse **biannual**, which means 'two times a year', with **biennial**.

big *adjective* (**bigger, biggest**)
1 not small, but large: *Durban is a **big** city.* ◇ *This shirt is too **big** for me.* ◇ *How **big** is your flat?* ➲ OPPOSITE **small**
2 great or important: *a **big** problem* ➲ OPPOSITE **small**
3 older: *She is my **big** sister.* ➲ OPPOSITE **little**[1] 1-2

WORD BUILDING There are many words that you can use instead of **big**, but check their exact meanings first. Examples are: **broad**, **bulky**, **colossal**, **enormous**, **extensive**, **giant**[2], **gigantic**, **great**1, **heavy**2, **huge**, **immense**, **jumbo** (informal), **large**, **massive**, **mighty**, **substantial**2, **tremendous**1 and **vast**.

bigamy (say **big**-uh-mee) *noun* (*no plural*)
the crime of being married to two people at the same time ➲ See **monogamy**, **polygamy**

A B C D E F G H I J K L M N O P Q R S T U V W X Y Z

bigot (say **big**-uht) *noun* (*plural* **bigots**)
a person who has unreasonable or unfair opinions and will not change them: *The **bigot** wouldn't let my family stay at the hotel.*

bike (*rhymes with* **like**) *noun* (*plural* **bikes**) (*informal*)
a bicycle or a motorbike: *I go to school by **bike**.*

bikini (say bi-**kee**-ni) *noun* (*plural* **bikinis**)
a piece of clothing in two pieces that women wear for swimming

bilateral (say by-**lat**-ruhl) *adjective*
1 involving two sides of the body or brain
2 involving two groups of people or countries: *They had a **bilateral** agreement.*

bile (*rhymes with* **tile**) *noun* (*no plural*)
a greenish-brown liquid that tastes bitter, that comes up from your stomach when you vomit

bilharzia (say bil-**haatss**-i-uh) *noun* (*no plural*)
a disease that makes people tired and weak, caused by a small worm in the blood
ORIGIN: 19th century, named after Theodor Bilharz (1825–1862), the German scientist who discovered the worm that causes bilharzia

bilingual (say by-**ling**-gwuhl) *adjective*
1 able to speak two languages equally well: *Many South Africans are **bilingual**.*
2 having or using two languages: *a **bilingual** dictionary*
ORIGIN: 19th century, from Latin *bilinguis*, from *bi-* meaning 'having two' + *lingua* meaning 'tongue'

bilious (say **bil**-i-uhss) *adjective*
feeling like you are going to vomit
➲ See **nausea**

bill (say **bil**) *noun* (*plural* **bills**)
a piece of paper that shows how much money you must pay for something: *Can I have the **bill**, please?*

billboard (say **bil**-bawd) *noun* (*plural* **billboards**)
a large board near a road which shows advertisements

billiards (say **bil**-i-uhdz) (*no plural*)
a game that you play by hitting three balls with a long stick (called a **cue**) on a table covered in cloth

billion (say **bil**-i-uhn) *number* (*plural* **billions**)
1 000 000 000 or one thousand million: *five **billion** rand* ◇ *The company is worth **billions** of rand.*
▸ **billionth** (*number*)

USAGE We say **five billion people** (without s), but **billions of people**.

billow (say **bil**-oh) *verb* (**billowing, billowed**)
to fill with air and move in the wind: *The sheets on the washing line were **billowing** in the wind.*

billy goat (say **bil**-ee-goht) *noun* (*plural* **billy goats**)
a male goat ➲ See **nanny goat**

biltong (say **bil**-tong) *noun* (*no plural*)
meat that has been dried and salted, that you eat as a snack

bin *noun* (*plural* **bins**)
a container that you put rubbish in: *Put your rubbish in the **bin**.* ➲ See **dustbin**

binary (say **by**-nuh-ree) *adjective*
1 (*maths*) relating to a number system that has two as its base, using only the symbols 0 and 1
2 consisting of two elements or parts: *a **binary** compound* ◇ *a **binary** star*

bind (*rhymes with* **find**) *verb* (**binding, bound**)
to tie string or rope round something to hold it firmly: *They **bound** the prisoner's arms and legs together.*

binge (say **binj**) *noun* (*plural* **binges**)
a short time of eating or drinking too much: *I had a chocolate **binge** before lunch.*
▸ **binge** (*verb*): *I **binged** on fruit in the holidays.*

binoculars (say bi-**nok**-yuh-luhz) *plural noun*
an instrument with a **lens** for each eye, that you use to see things that are far away
➲ See **telescope**

binomial (say by-**noh**-mi-uhl) *noun* (*plural* **binomials**) (*maths*)
an expression with two terms: *7xy + 2x is a **binomial**.*

bio- (say **by**-oh) *prefix*
relating to living things: ***biodegradable*** ◇ ***biology***
ORIGIN: Greek *bios* meaning 'human life'

biochemistry (say by-oh-**kem**-iss-tree) *noun* (*no plural*)
1 the study of the chemistry of living things
2 the chemical structure of a living thing: *the **biochemistry** of a cell*
▸ **biochemical** (*adjective*): ***biochemical** engineering* ▸ **biochemist** (*noun*)

biodegradable (say by-oh-di-**gray**-duhb-l) *adjective*
describing substances that can break down and go back into the earth and so do not damage the environment

biodiversity (say by-oh-di-**ver**-sit-ee) *noun* (*no plural*)
the number of different types of living organisms in an area: *It is important to conserve*

a high level of ***biodiversity*** *along our coastlines.*
🛈 ORIGIN: 20th century, from Greek *bios* meaning 'life' + *diversity* from Latin *divertere* meaning 'turn in separate ways'

biography (say by-**og**-ruh-fee) *noun* (*plural* **biographies**)
the story of a person's life, that another person writes: *a* ***biography*** *of Nelson Mandela*
➲ See **autobiography**

biology (say by-**ol**-uh-jee) *noun* (*no plural*)
the study of the life of animals and plants: *Biology is my favourite subject.*
▸ **biologist** (*noun*): *a marine* ***biologist*** (= someone who studies sea life)
🛈 ORIGIN: 19th century, through French from Greek *bios* meaning 'life' + *-logia* meaning 'study'

biomass (say **by**-oh-mass) *noun* (*no plural*)
the total mass of **organic** material, living or recently dead, in a particular area at a given time: *The* ***biomass*** *of tropical forests has decreased over the last ten years.*

biome (say **by**-ohm) *noun* (*plural* **biomes**)
a community of plants, animals and other organisms living in an area with a particular climate: *an aquatic* ***biome*** ◇ *a desert* ***biome***

biopsy (say **by**-op-see) *noun* (*plural* **biopsies**)
the removal and examination of some cells from a person's body in order to find out about an illness they might have: *The doctor performed a liver* ***biopsy*** *on her patient.*

biosphere (say **by**-ohss-feer) *noun* (*plural* **biospheres**)
the parts of the Earth's surface, water and atmosphere in which plants and animals live

biotic (say by-**ot**-ik) *adjective*
of or relating to living things: *a* ***biotic*** *community* ◇ ***biotic*** *resources*

biped (say **by**-ped) *noun* (*plural* **bipeds**)
any animal that walks on two feet
➲ See **quadruped**
▸ **bipedal** (*adjective*): *Humans and birds are* ***bipedal.***

birch (say **burch**) *noun*
1 (*plural* **birches**) a tree with smooth **bark**[1] 1 and thin branches
2 (*no plural*) the hard pale wood of this tree

bird (say **burd**) *noun* (*plural* **birds**)
an animal with feathers and wings: *Seagulls, pigeons and eagles are* ***birds.***

bird

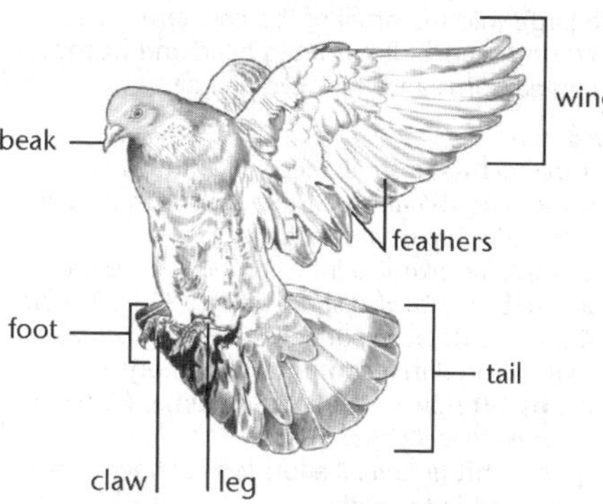

bird flu (say **burd** floo) *noun* (*no plural*)
a serious illness that birds, especially chickens, can catch and which can be spread from birds to humans, sometimes causing death

bird of prey *noun* (*plural* **birds of prey**)
a bird that catches and eats other birds and small animals: *Eagles are* ***birds of prey.***

biriani (say bi-ri-**aa**-nee) *noun* (*no plural*) (also **breyani**)
an Indian dish made with rice, spices, and meat, fish or vegetables

birth (say **burth**) *noun* (*plural* **births**)
the act of being born, when a baby comes out of its mother: *the* ***birth*** *of a baby* ◇ *What's your date of* ***birth*** (= the date when you were born)*?*
give birth to have a baby: *My sister gave* ***birth*** *to her second child last week.*

birthday (say **burth**-day) *noun* (*plural* **birthdays**)
the day each year that is the same as the date when you were born: *My* ***birthday*** *is on the 2nd of May.* ◇ *a* ***birthday*** *present* ◇ *Happy* ***birthday!***

biscuit (say **biss**-kuht) *noun* (*plural* **biscuits**)
a kind of small thin hard cake that is usually sweet: *a packet of* ***biscuits*** ◇ *a chocolate* ***biscuit***
➲ SYNONYM **cookie**
🛈 ORIGIN: 13th–15th century, from Old French *bescuit*, based on Latin *bis* meaning 'twice' + *coctus* meaning 'cooked'. Biscuits used to be baked twice.

bisect (say by-**sekt**) *verb* (**bisecting, bisected**)
1 to cut in two: *The path* ***bisects*** *the field.*
2 (*maths*) to divide into two equal parts: *to* ***bisect*** *an angle*
▸ **bisection** (*noun*)

bishop (say **bish**-uhp) *noun* (*plural* **bishops**)
an important priest in the Christian church, who looks after all the churches in a large area
🛈 ORIGIN: from Old English *biscop*, from Greek *episkopos* meaning 'looking from above'

A **B** C D E F G H I J K L M N O P Q R S T U V W X Y Z

bison (say **by**-suhn) *noun* (*plural* **bison**)
a large wild mammal of the cow family from North America. It has a big head and **hump**, curved horns and thick brown hair.

bit *noun*
1 (*plural* **bits**) a small piece or amount of something: *Would you like a **bit** of cake?* ◇ *Some **bits** of the film were very funny.*
2 a bit (*no plural*) a little: *You look a **bit** tired.*
3 a bit (*no plural*) a short time: *Let's wait a **bit**.*
4 (*plural* **bits**) (*computing*) a unit of information that is stored in a computer's memory
bit by bit slowly or a little at a time: ***Bit** by **bit**, I started to feel better.*
quite a bit (*informal*) a lot: *It must have rained quite a **bit** in the night.*

bitch (say **bich**) *noun* (*plural* **bitches**)
1 a female dog
2 (*informal*) a rude way to refer to a woman that has made you angry or whom you do not like

bite[1] *verb* (**biting**, **bit**, **has bitten**)
1 to cut something with your teeth: *That dog **bit** my leg!*
2 (used about an insect or other animal) to push a small sharp point into your skin and cause pain: *I've been **bitten** by mosquitoes.*

bite[2] *noun* (*plural* **bites**)
1 a piece of food that you can put in your mouth: *He took a **bite** of his sandwich.*
2 a painful place on your skin made by an insect or other animal: *a snake **bite***

bitter (say **bit**-uh) *adjective*
1 (used about food) with a sharp unpleasant taste: *The coffee was **bitter**.*
2 angry and sad about something that has happened: *He felt **bitter** about losing his job.*
3 very cold: *a **bitter** wind*
▸ **bitterness** (*noun*): *The new rule caused great **bitterness**.*

bitumen (say **bit**-shuh-muhn) *noun* (*no plural*)
a thick black substance, often made from petrol, used for covering roads or roofs

bizarre (say bi-**zaa**) *adjective*
very strange: *He has a **bizarre** sense of humour.*
➲ SYNONYM **weird**
▸ **bizarrely** (*adverb*): ***bizarrely** dressed teenagers*

black[1] (say **blak**) *adjective* (**blacker**, **blackest**)
1 with the colour of the sky at night: *a **black** dog*
2 belonging to a group of people with dark skins: *Martin Luther King was a famous **black** leader.*
3 without milk: ***black** coffee*

black[2] (say **blak**) *noun*
1 (*no plural*) the colour of the sky at night: *She was dressed in **black**.*
2 (*plural* **blacks**) a person who belongs to a group of people with dark skins
black and white with the colours black, white and grey only: *We watched a **black** and **white** film on TV.*

blackberry (say **blak**-buh-ree) *noun* (*plural* **blackberries**)
a small, soft, black fruit that grows on a bush

blackbird (say **blak**-burd) *noun* (*plural* **blackbirds**)
a bird with black feathers that lives in Europe

blackboard (say **blak**-bawd) *noun* (*plural* **blackboards**) (also **board**)
a black board that a teacher writes on with chalk: *Look at the **blackboard**.*
➲ See **chalkboard**

Black Consciousness *noun* (*no plural*)
a movement that made people aware of the rights of black people

blacklist (say **blak**-list) *verb* (**blacklisting**, **blacklisted**)
to put someone on a list of people who do not pay money that they owe to a company: *I didn't pay my account and was **blacklisted** by the telephone company.*
▸ **blacklist** (*noun*)

blackmail (say **blak**-mayl) *noun* (*no plural*)
1 the crime of threatening to tell a secret about a person if they do not give you money
2 the act of putting pressure on a person to do something they do not want to do, for example by making them feel guilty: *emotional **blackmail***
▸ **blackmail** (*verb*): *She **blackmailed** him into giving her thousands of rand.*

blacksmith (say **blak**-smith) *noun* (*plural* **blacksmiths**)
a person whose job is to make and repair things made of iron

bladder (say **blad**-uh) *noun* (*plural* **bladders**)
the organ in your body where liquid waste (**urine**) collects before leaving your body

blade (say **blayd**) *noun* (*plural* **blades**)
1 the flat sharp part of something such as a knife or a tool
2 a long thin leaf of a plant such as grass: *a **blade** of grass*

blame (say **blaym**) *verb* (**blaming**, **blamed**)
to say that a certain person or thing made something bad happen: *The other driver **blamed** me for the accident.*

▸ **blame** (*noun*): *She took the* ***blame*** *for the mistake.*

blameless (say **blaym**-luhss) *adjective*
not guilty: *Sonia was* ***blameless*** *in the incident.*

bland *adjective* (**blander**, **blandest**)
1 ordinary and not very interesting: *I find her songs rather* ***bland***. ➲ SYNONYM **insipid** 1
2 (used about food) without a strong taste: *a* ***bland*** *diet of rice and fish*
➲ SYNONYM **insipid** 2

blank *adjective*
1 with no writing, pictures or anything else on it: *a* ***blank*** *piece of paper*
2 describing a face that shows no feelings or understanding: *I asked her a question, but she just gave me a* ***blank*** *look.*

blanket (say **blang**-kuht) *noun* (*plural* **blankets**)
a thick cover that you put on a bed

blare (say **blair**) *verb* (**blaring**, **blared**)
to make a loud, unpleasant noise: *I cannot hear myself think with that music* ***blaring***!

blasé (say blaa-**zay**) *adjective*
not impressed by something because you are used to it: *They are rich and* ***blasé*** *about expensive restaurants.*

blaspheme (say blass-**feem**) *verb* (**blaspheming**, **blasphemed**)
to write or speak about God in a rude way

blast[1] (say **blaast**) *noun* (*plural* **blasts**)
1 an explosion, especially of a bomb: *Two people were killed in the* ***blast***.
2 a sudden movement of air: *a* ***blast*** *of cold air*
3 a sudden loud noise: *The driver gave a few* ***blasts*** *on his horn.*

blast[2] (say **blaast**) *verb* (**blasting**, **blasted**)
to make a hole in something with an explosion: *They* ***blasted*** *through the mountain to make a tunnel.*

blatant (say **blay**-tuhnt) *adjective*
very clear or obvious: *My brother told a* ***blatant*** *lie.*

blaze[1] (say **blayz**) *verb* (**blazing**, **blazed**)
to burn strongly and brightly: *The fire* ***blazed*** *all night.*

blaze[2] (say **blayz**) *noun* (*plural* **blazes**)
a large and often dangerous fire: *It took firefighters hours to put out the* ***blaze***.

blazer (say **blay**-zuh) *noun* (*plural* **blazers**)
a jacket, especially one that shows which school or club you belong to.

bleach[1] (say **bleech**) *verb* (**bleaching**, **bleached**)
to become white or to make something white by using a chemical or leaving it in the sun for a long time

bleach[2] (say **bleech**) *noun* (*plural* **bleaches**)
the chemical that you use to make something white

bleak (say **bleek**) *adjective* (**bleaker**, **bleakest**)
1 describing a situation that is not hopeful or encouraging: *The country's future looks* ***bleak***.
2 cold and grey: *It was a* ***bleak*** *winter's day.*

bleat (say **bleet**) *verb* (**bleating**, **bleated**)
to make the noise that a sheep or goat makes
▸ **bleat** (*noun*)

bleed *verb* (**bleeding**, **bled**)
to lose blood: *I cut my hand and it's* ***bleeding***.

bleep *noun* (*plural* **bleeps**)
a short high sound that is used as a signal
▸ **bleep** (*verb*)

blemish (say **blem**-ish) *noun* (*plural* **blemishes**)
a mark that spoils how something looks: *My new tablecloth has got a* ***blemish*** *on it.*

blend *verb* (**blending**, **blended**)
1 to mix: ***Blend*** *the sugar and the butter.*
2 to look or sound good together: *These colours* ***blend*** *very well.*
▸ **blend** (*noun*): *This is a* ***blend*** *of two different kinds of coffee.*

bless *verb* (**blessing**, **blessed**)
to ask for God's protection for a person or thing: *The priest* ***blessed*** *the couple.*
Bless you! words that you say to a person when they **sneeze**

blessing (say **bless**-ing) *noun* (*plural* **blessings**)
1 a prayer asking for God's help and protection: *A priest gave a* ***blessing*** *as the fishing boats set out.*
2 a thing that you are thankful for or that brings happiness: *It's a* ***blessing*** *that we finally got rain.*
3 support or approval: *My parents gave their* ***blessing***.

blew (say **bloo**) form of **blow**[1]

blight (say **blite**) *noun*
1 (*no plural*) a disease that kills plants
2 (*plural* **blights**) something that has a bad effect on something else: *This ugly building is a* ***blight*** *on the city's landscape.*

blind[1] (say **blynd**) *adjective*
not able to see: *My grandad is* ***blind***.
▸ **blindness** (*noun*): *The disease can cause* ***blindness***.

blind[2] (say **blynd**) *noun* (*plural* **blinds**)
a piece of cloth or other material that you pull down to cover a window

A B C D E F G H I J K L M N O P Q R S T U V W X Y Z

blindfold (say **blynd**-fohld) *noun* (*plural* **blindfolds**)
a piece of cloth that you put over a person's eyes so that they cannot see
▸ **blindfold** (*verb*): *The guards* ***blindfolded*** *the prisoners.*

blink (*rhymes with* **sink**) *verb* (**blinking, blinked**)
to shut and open your eyes very quickly
▸ **blink** (*noun*) ➲ See **wink**

bliss *noun* (*no plural*)
perfect happiness
▸ **blissful** (*adjective*) ▸ **blissfully** (*adverb*)

blister (say **bliss**-tuh) *noun* (*plural* **blisters**)
a small painful place on your skin caused by rubbing or burning. It looks like a bubble and is filled with liquid.: *My new shoes gave me* ***blisters.***

blitz (say **blitss**) *noun* (*plural* **blitzes**)
a sudden attack on something: *The crime* ***blitz*** *resulted in many arrests.*

blizzard (say **bliz**-uhd) *noun* (*plural* **blizzards**)
a very bad storm with snow and strong winds

bloated (say **bloht**-uhd) *adjective*
unusually large and uncomfortable because of food, liquid, or air inside: *I feel* ***bloated*** *after such a big lunch.*

blob *noun* (*plural* **blobs**)
a small amount of a thick liquid: *There are* ***blobs*** *of paint on the floor.*

block[1] (say **blok**) *noun* (*plural* **blocks**)
1 a big heavy piece of something, with flat sides: *a* ***block*** *of wood* ◇ *concrete* ***blocks***
2 a big building with a lot of rooms inside: *an office* ***block*** ◇ *a* ***block*** *of flats*
3 a group of buildings with streets all round it: *We drove round the* ***block.***
4 something that stops a person or thing from moving forward: *The police have put road* ***blocks*** *around the town.*

block[2] (say **blok**) *verb* (**blocking, blocked**)
to stop a person or thing from moving forward: *A fallen tree* ***blocked*** *the road.*

blockade (say blok-**ayd**) *noun* (*plural* **blockades**)
1 the action by military forces of surrounding a city or a port, to stop people or goods from coming in or out
2 a barrier that stops the movement of people or vehicles: *The police set up a* ***blockade*** *on the highway.*
▸ **blockade** (*verb*)

blog *noun* (*plural* **blogs**)
a personal record that somebody puts on their website saying what they do every day and what they think about things
▸ **blogger** (*noun*): ***Bloggers*** *use the Internet to explain their ideas.*

bloke (*rhymes with* **joke**) *noun* (*plural* **blokes**) (*informal*)
a man: *He's a really nice* ***bloke.***

blonde[1] (say **blond**) *adjective* (**blonder, blondest**) (also **blond**)
with light-coloured hair: *She is tall and* ***blonde.*** ◇ *He's got* ***blond*** *hair.*

WHICH WORD? **Blonde** or **blond**?
- In the past people used **blond** to describe men and **blonde** to describe women, but in modern English, you can use either spelling for men and women.
- The noun, **blonde**, should always be spelt with **e**.

blonde[2] (say **blond**) *noun* (*plural* **blondes**)
a woman with **blonde[1]** hair

blood (say **blud**) *noun* (*no plural*)
the red liquid inside your body
🛈 ORIGIN: from Old English *blod*, related to Dutch *bloed*

bloodbath (say **blud**-baath) *noun* (*plural* **bloodbaths**)
a violent act that kills many people

bloodshed (say **blud**-shed) *noun* (*no plural*)
the killing or harming of people: *The leaders must realize that* ***bloodshed*** *will not bring peace.*

bloodshot (say **blud**-shot) *adjective*
(used about eyes) red

bloodthirsty (say **blud**-thurss-tee) *adjective*
enjoying watching violence, or wanting to do something violent

blood vessel *noun* (*plural* **blood vessels**)
one of the tubes in your body that blood flows through

bloody (say **blud**-ee) *adjective* (**bloodier, bloodiest**)
1 covered with blood: *a* ***bloody*** *nose*
2 with a lot of killing: *It was a* ***bloody*** *war.*

bloom (*rhymes with* **doom**) *verb* (**blooming, bloomed**)
to produce flowers: *Roses* ***bloom*** *in the summer.*

blossom (say **bloss**-uhm) *noun* (*plural* **blossoms**)
the flowers on a tree, especially a fruit tree: *The apple tree is covered in* ***blossoms.***
▸ **blossom** (*verb*): *The cherry trees are* ***blossoming.***

blot[1] *noun* (*plural* **blots**)
1 a spot of something, especially one made by ink on paper, or a stain
2 a thing that spoils your happiness or other people's opinion of you: *His cheating in the exam has left a **blot** on his character.*

blot[2] *verb* (**blotting, blotted**)
1 to make a spot or mark on something, especially ink on paper
2 to wipe something off using short quick movements: *She sniffed and **blotted** her eyes with a tissue.*

blouse (say **blowz**) *noun* (*plural* **blouses**)
a piece of clothing like a shirt that a woman or girl wears

blow[1] (*rhymes with* **go**) *verb* (**blowing, blew, has blown**)
1 (used about air or wind) to move: *The wind was **blowing** from the sea.*
2 to move something through the air: *The wind **blew** my hat off.*
3 to send air out of your mouth: *Please **blow** into this tube.*
4 to send air out from your mouth into a musical instrument, for example, to make a noise: *The referee **blew** his whistle.*
blow your nose to clear your nose of **mucus** by forcing it out onto a piece of cloth or paper with air from your lungs
blow up, blow something up
1 to explode or make something explode, for example with a bomb: *The plane **blew** up.* ◇ *They **blew** up the station.*
2 to fill something with air: *We **blow** up some balloons for the party.*

blow[2] (*rhymes with* **go**) *noun* (*plural* **blows**)
1 a hard hit from somebody's hand or a weapon: *He felt a **blow** on his back.*
2 something that happens suddenly and that makes you very unhappy: *Her father's death was a terrible **blow**.*

blowlamp (say **bloh**-lamp) *noun* (*plural* **blowlamps**) (also **blowtorch**)
a tool with a very hot flame that you can point at a surface, for example to remove paint

blubber (say **blub**-uh) *noun* (*no plural*)
the fat from a **whale** and other large sea mammals

bludgeon (say **bluj**-uhn) *verb* (**bludgeoning, bludgeoned**)
to hit a person or thing very hard and often with a heavy object

blue (say **bloo**) *adjective* (**bluer, bluest**)
having the colour of a clear sky when the sun shines: *He wore a **blue** shirt.* ◇ *a dark **blue** cap*
▸ **blue** (*noun*): *She was dressed in **blue**.*

bluebottle (say **bloo**-bot-l) *noun* (*plural* **bluebottles**)
a sea creature that looks like a small blue balloon with a long tail that has a poisonous sting

blueprint (say **bloo**-print) *noun* (*plural* **blueprints**)
1 (*technology*) a photographic print of a plan for a building or a machine, with white lines on a blue background
2 a plan or map of how to make, build or achieve something

blues (say **blooz**) *plural noun*
1 a type of music that is slow and sad
2 a feeling of sadness: *I've got the **blues** today – I don't know why.*

bluff[1] (say **bluf**) *verb* (**bluffing, bluffed**)
to trick someone by saying something that is not true: *Don't worry, I was only **bluffing**.*

bluff[2] (say **bluf**) *noun* (*plural* **bluffs**) (*geography*)
a steep cliff that is next to the sea or a river

blunder (say **blun**-duh) *verb* (**blundering, blundered**)
1 to make a stupid mistake
2 to move in a careless way: *She **blundered** around in the dark, looking for the light switch.*
▸ **blunder** (*noun*): *Oh dear! That was a **blunder**.*

blunt *adjective* (**blunter, bluntest**)
1 with an edge or point that is not sharp: *This pencil is **blunt**.* ➲ OPPOSITE **sharp**[1] 1
2 saying what you think in a way that is not polite

blur (*rhymes with* **stir**) *verb* (**blurring, blurred**)
to make something less clear: *If you move while you are taking the photo, it will be **blurred**.*

blurt (*rhymes with* **flirt**) *verb* (**blurting, blurted**)
to say something without thinking: *Mpho **blurted** out the secret.*

blush (*rhymes with* **flush**) *verb* (**blushing, blushed**)
(used about your face) to suddenly become red, for example because you are shy: *She **blushed** when he looked at her.*

blustery (say **bluss**-tuh-ree) *adjective*
(used to describe the weather) with strong winds: *The day was cold and **blustery**.*

boar (say **baw**) *noun* (*plural* **boars**)
1 a male pig
2 (also **wild boar**) a wild pig

A
B
C
D
E
F
G
H
I
J
K
L
M
N
O
P
Q
R
S
T
U
V
W
X
Y
Z

board[1] (say **bawd**) *noun* (*plural* **boards**)
1 a long thin flat piece of wood: *I nailed a **board** across the broken window.* ◇ ***floorboards***
2 a flat piece of wood, for example, that you use for a special purpose: *There is a list of names on the **noticeboard**.* ◇ *a **chessboard*** ◇ *an ironing **board*** ➲ See **blackboard**
3 a group of people who have a special job, for example controlling a company: *the school **board***
on board on a ship or a plane: *How many passengers are on **board**?*

board[2] (say **bawd**) *verb* (**boarding, boarded**)
to get on a ship, bus, train or plane: *We **boarded** the plane at six o'clock.*

boarder (say **bawd**-uh) *noun* (*plural* **boarders**)
1 a child who lives at the school and goes home for weekends or holidays
2 a person who pays to live in a room in someone else's house

boarding school (say **bawd**-ing skool) *noun* (*plural* **boarding schools**)
a school where learners can live

boast (*rhymes with* **most**) *verb* (**boasting, boasted**)
to talk in a way that shows you are too proud of something that you have or something that you can do: *He's always **boasting** about what a good drummer he is.* ➲ SYNONYM **brag**

boat (*rhymes with* **goat**) *noun* (*plural* **boats**)
a small **vessel**: *a fishing **boat*** ◇ *a rowing **boat*** ◇ *We travelled by **boat**.* ➲ See **ship**

bob *verb* (**bobbing, bobbed**)
to move quickly up and down: *The boats **bobbed** up and down in the water.*

bobbin (say **bob**-in) *noun* (*plural* **bobbins**)
a small round thing that you put thread around, that you use in a machine such as a sewing machine

bobble (say **bob**-l) *noun* (*plural* **bobbles**)
a small round decoration

bobotie (say buh-**boor**-tee) *noun* (*no plural*) (*S. African*)
a dish made with very small bits of meat (called **mince**) with spices and a mixture of egg and milk on top
ⓘ ORIGIN: 19th century, through Afrikaans, probably from Malay

body (say **bod**-ee) *noun* (*plural* **bodies**)
1 the whole physical form of a person or an animal: *the human **body***
2 all of a person or animal except the legs, arms and head: *The baby mice have thin **bodies** and big heads.*
3 a dead person: *The police found a **body** in the river.*
4 the main part of something: *The **body** of your letter should be about two paragraphs long.*

human body

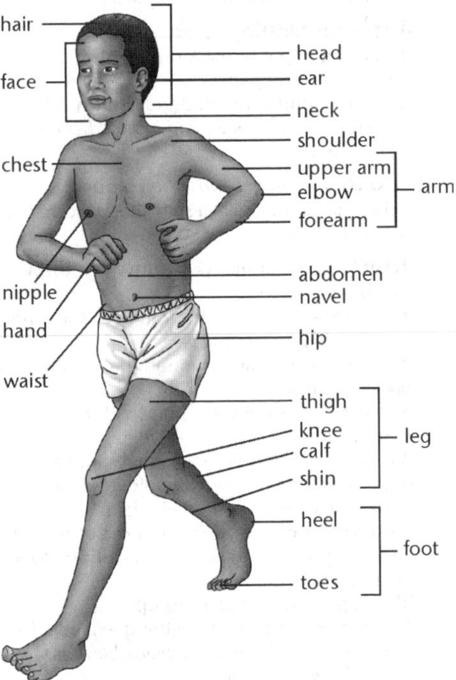

bodyguard (say **bod**-ee-gaad) *noun* (*plural* **bodyguards**)
a person or group of people whose job is to keep an important person safe: *The President's **bodyguards** all carry guns.*

boer (say **buu**-uh or **buur**) *noun* (*plural* **boere** or **boers**)
1 (also **Boer**) (*history*) one of the Dutch- or Afrikaans-speaking people who settled in southern Africa in the seventeenth century, or a descendant of these people
2 Boer a Dutch- or Afrikaans-speaking soldier who fought against the British in the **South African War**
3 (*informal, S. African*) a farmer, especially one who speaks Afrikaans: *My grandfather was a **boer** in the Free State.*
ⓘ ORIGIN: 18th century, from Dutch *boer* meaning 'farmer'

boere- (say **buu**-ruh) *prefix* (*S. African*)
associated with Afrikaner traditions: ***boeremusiek** and **boeresport***

boeremusiek (say **buu**-ruh-muu-sik) *noun* (*no plural*) (*S. African*)
traditional Afrikaans music

boeresport (say **buu**-ruh-spawt) *noun* (*no plural*) (*S. African*)
traditional Afrikaans games and sports

boerewors (say **buu**-ruh-vawss) *noun* (*no plural*) (*S. African*)
a sausage that is made with meat and spices
ORIGIN: 20th century, from Afrikaans *boerewors*, from *boere* meaning 'farmers' + *wors* meaning 'sausage'

bog *noun* (*plural* **bogs**)
an area of ground that is very soft and wet

bogus (say **boh**-guhss) *adjective*
pretending to be real: *The thief was a* ***bogus*** *salesman.* ➲ SYNONYM **fake**[1]

boil[1] (say **boyl**) *verb* (**boiling, boiled**)
1 (used about a liquid) to become very hot and make steam and bubbles: *Water* ***boils*** *at 100 °C.*
2 to heat a liquid until it makes bubbles and steams: *I* ***boiled*** *some water for the pasta.* ◇ *Don't let the milk* ***boil*** *over.*
3 to cook something in boiling water: ***Boil*** *the rice in a pan.* ◇ *a* ***boiled*** *egg*
▸ **boiling** (*adjective*): *It's* ***boiling*** (= very hot) *in here.*

boil[2] (say **boyl**) *noun*
1 (*no plural*) boiling point: *Bring the water to the* ***boil*** *then add the pasta.*
2 (*plural* **boils**) a sore red lump under your skin

boisterous (say **boyss**-tuh-ruhss) *adjective*
noisy and very active: *The* ***boisterous*** *children are playing outside.*
▸ **boisterously** (*adverb*)

bold (*rhymes with* **gold**) *adjective* (**bolder, boldest**)
brave and not afraid: *It was very* ***bold*** *of you to ask for more money.*
▸ **boldly** (*adverb*): *He* ***boldly*** *said that he disagreed.*

bollard (say **bol**-aad) *noun* (*plural* **bollards**)
a short thick post that is used to stop cars from going into a particular area

bolt[1] (say **bohlt**) *noun* (*plural* **bolts**)
1 a piece of metal that you move across a door to lock it
2 a thick metal pin that you screw into a metal **nut** 2 to fix things together

bolt[2] (say **bohlt**) *verb* (**bolting, bolted**)
1 to lock a door with a **bolt**[1] 1
2 to fasten something using a **bolt**[1] 2
3 to run away very fast: *He* ***bolted*** *round the corner.*

bomb[1] (say **bom**) *noun* (*plural* **bombs**)
a thing that explodes and hurts or damages people or things: *Aircraft* ***dropped*** *bombs on the city.* ◇ *A* ***bomb*** *went off* (= exploded) *at the station.*

PRONUNCIATION Don't pronounce the **b** at the end of **bomb**.

bomb[2] (say **bom**) *verb* (**bombing, bombed**)
to attack people or a place with **bombs**: *The city was* ***bombed*** *in the war.*

bombard (say bom-**baad**) *verb* (**bombarding, bombarded**)
1 to attack a place with bombs and guns
2 to give someone too much information or to ask too many questions: *He* ***bombarded*** *me with advice.*

bombshell (say **bom**-shel) *noun* (*plural* **bombshells**)
news that you were not expecting to get that is a big shock: *Naazneen dropped the* ***bombshell*** *that she's leaving for Paris.* ◇ *The newspaper dropped a* ***bombshell*** *with its report.*

bonanza (say buh-**nan**-zuh) *noun* (*plural* **bonanzas**)
sudden or unexpected luck

bond[1] *noun* (*plural* **bonds**)
1 something that joins people or groups together: *a* ***bond*** *of friendship* ◇ *The agreement strengthened the* ***bond*** *between the two countries.*
2 a legal agreement by which a bank lends you money to buy a house, which you pay back over many years ➲ SYNONYM **mortgage**
3 (*science*) the way in which atoms are held together in a chemical compound

bond[2] *verb* (**bonding, bonded**)
1 to join something together
2 to develop or create a relationship of trust with another person: *Parents need to* ***bond*** *with their children when they become teenagers.*

bondage (say **bon**-dij) *noun* (*no plural*) (*old-fashioned*), (*formal*)
the state of being a **slave**[1] or prisoner: *The Israelites were in* ***bondage*** *in Egypt.*

bone (*rhymes with* **stone**) *noun* (*plural* **bones**)
one of the hard white parts inside the body of a person or an animal: *She broke a* ***bone*** *in her foot.* ◇ *This fish has a lot of* ***bones*** *in it.*

bonfire (say **bon**-fy-uh) *noun* (*plural* **bonfires**)
a big fire that you make outside

bonnet (say **bon**-uht) *noun* (*plural* **bonnets**)
1 the front part of a car that covers the engine
➲ See illustration at **car**

A B C D E F G H I J K L M N O P Q R S T U V W X Y Z

A
B
C
D
E
F
G
H
I
J
K
L
M
N
O
P
Q
R
S
T
U
V
W
X
Y
Z

2 a soft hat tied with strings under the chin, worn by babies and, especially in the past, by women

bonny (say **bon**-ee) *adjective* (**bonnier, bonniest**) (*old-fashioned*)
looking healthy and attractive: *a* ***bonny*** *baby*

bontebok (say **bawn**-tuh-bawk) *noun* (*plural* **bontebok** or **bonteboks**)
a dark brown antelope with white marks that lives in southern Africa
🛈 **ORIGIN:** 18th century, from South African Dutch *bontebok* from *bont* meaning 'having two colours' + *bok* meaning 'antelope, buck'

bonus (say **boh**-nuhss) *noun* (*plural* **bonuses**)
1 payment that you get that is more than usual: *Everybody at work got a* ***bonus*** *this year.*
2 something good that is extra: *It was a* ***bonus*** *that the weather was good.*

book[1] (say **buuk**) *noun* (*plural* **books**)
a thing that you read or write in, that has many pages joined together inside a cover: *I'm reading a* ***book*** *by Alan Paton.* ◇ *an exercise* ***book*** (= a ***book*** *that you write in at school)*

book[2] (say **buuk**) *verb* (**booking, booked**)
to arrange to have or do something later: *We* ***booked*** *a table for six at the restaurant.* ◇ *The hotel is fully* ***booked*** (= all the rooms are full).
➲ **SYNONYM reserve**[1]

bookcase (say **buuk**-kayss) *noun* (*plural* **bookcases**)
a piece of furniture that you put books in

booking (say **buuk**-ing) *noun* (*plural* **bookings**)
an arrangement that you make for the future, for example to travel somewhere or go to a film: *When did you make your* ***booking****?*
➲ See **reservation**

bookkeeping (say **buuk**-keep-ing) *noun* (*no plural*)
the job of keeping records of the money in a business
▸ **bookkeeper** (*noun*)

booklet (say **buuk**-luht) *noun* (*plural* **booklets**)
a small thin book that gives information about something

Boolean (say **Boo**-li-uhn) *adjective* (*maths*), (*computing*)
connected with a system that uses only the numbers 1 (to show something is true) and 0 (to show something is false)
🛈 **ORIGIN:** 19th century, from the name of George Boole (1815–1864), an English mathematician

boom[1] (*rhymes with* **doom**) *noun* (*plural* **booms**) (*business*)
a period in which something increases or develops very quickly: *a* ***boom*** *in car sales*

boom[2] (*rhymes with* **doom**) *verb* (**booming, boomed**)
to make a loud deep sound: *We heard the guns* ***booming*** *in the distance.*

boomerang (say **boom**-uh-rang) *noun* (*plural* **boomerangs**)
a curved flat piece of wood that can be thrown so that it turns and comes back to you. Originally **boomerangs** were weapons used for hunting by **Aborigines**.
🛈 **ORIGIN:** 19th century, from Dharuk, an extinct Aboriginal language of Australia

boomslang (say **buu**-uhm-slung) *noun* (*plural* **boomslangs**)
a very poisonous tree snake found in southern Africa
🛈 **ORIGIN:** 18th century, from South African Dutch *boomslang*, from *boom* meaning 'tree' + *slang* meaning 'snake'

boost (*rhymes with* **roost**) *verb* (**boosting, boosted**)
to make something increase in number, value, or strength: *Lower prices have* ***boosted*** *sales.* ◇ *What can we do to* ***boost*** *her confidence* (= make her feel more confident)*?*

boot (*rhymes with* **shoot**) *noun* (*plural* **boots**)
1 a shoe that covers your foot and ankle and sometimes part of your leg
2 the part of a car in which you can put bags and boxes, usually at the back

booth (say **booth**) *noun* (*plural* **booths**)
a small room with thin walls: *a voting* ***booth*** ◇ *a phone* ***booth***

booty (say **boo**-tee) *noun* (*no plural*)
things that are taken by thieves: *They hid the* ***booty*** *in the bushes next to the river.*

booze (say **booz**) *noun* (*no plural*) (*informal*)
alcohol: *Bring your own* ***booze*** *to the party.*

border (say **baw**-duh) *noun* (*plural* **borders**)
1 a line between two countries: *You need a passport to cross the* ***border****.* ➲ See **boundary**
2 a line along the edge of something: *a white tablecloth with a blue* ***border***

borderline (say **baw**-duh-line) *noun* (*plural* **borderlines**)
1 the line that marks the border of two countries or areas
2 the line that is between two different conditions: *My mood is on the* ***borderline*** *between anger and disappointment.*

bore¹ (say **baw**) form of **bear¹**

bore² (say **baw**) *verb* (**boring, bored**)
1 to make somebody feel bored, especially by talking too much: *He **bores** everyone with his long stories.*
2 to make a thin round hole in something: *These insects **bore** holes in wood.*

bore³ (say **baw**) *noun* (*plural* **bores**)
a person who talks a lot in a way that is not interesting

bored (say **bawd**) *adjective*
not interested, or unhappy because you have nothing interesting to do: *I'm **bored** with this book.* ◇ *The children were **bored** stiff* (= extremely bored).
▸ **boredom** (*noun*): *I started to eat too much out of **boredom**.*

USAGE Note that we say **bored by** and **bored with**: *I'm **bored** by this film. I'm **bored** with this discussion.* It it not correct to say that you are 'bored of something'.

borehole (say **baw**-hohl) *noun* (*plural* **boreholes**)
a narrow and deep hole that you dig into the ground, usually for finding water, oil or gas: *I have a **borehole** in my garden which gives me plenty of water for my plants.*

boring (say **baw**-ring) *adjective*
not interesting: *That lesson was so **boring**!*

born (say **bawn**) *verb*
be born to start your life: *He was **born** in 1990.* ◇ *Where were you **born**?*

SPELLING Be careful! Don't confuse **born** and **borne**, which have different meanings: *I was **born** in Gauteng. He has **borne** a heavy load.*

borne (say **bawn**) form of **bear¹**

borrow (*rhymes with* **sorrow**) *verb* (**borrowing, borrowed**)
to take and use something that you will give back after a short time: *I **borrowed** some books from the library.*

WHICH WORD? **Borrow** or **lend**?
- If you **borrow** something, you have it for a short time and you must give it back: *I **borrowed** a CD from Zanele for the weekend.*
- If you **lend** something, you give it to someone for a short time: *Zanele* **lent** me a CD for the weekend.

bosom (say **buu**-zuhm) *noun* (*plural* **bosoms**)
(*formal*) a person's chest, especially a woman's breasts: *a woman with a large **bosom***

boss¹ *noun* (*plural* **bosses**) (*informal*)
a person who controls a place where people work and tells people what they must do: *I asked my **boss** for a holiday.*

boss² *verb* (**bossing, bossed**)
boss somebody about, **boss somebody around** to tell somebody what to do, in a way that annoys them: *I wish you'd stop **bossing** me about.*

bossy (say **boss**-ee) *adjective* (**bossier, bossiest**)
describing a person who likes to tell other people what to do: *My sister is very **bossy**.*

botany (say **bot**-uh-nee) *noun* (*no plural*)
the scientific study of plants ➲ See **biology**, **zoology**
▸ **botanical** (*adjective*): ***botanical** gardens*
▸ **botanist** (*noun*): *Linda wants to be a **botanist**, because she is interested in fynbos conservation.*

both (say **bohth**) *adjective, pronoun*
the two, not only one but also the other: *Hold it in **both** hands.* ◇ ***Both** her sisters are doctors.* ◇ ***Both** of us like dancing.* ◇ *We **both** like dancing.*
both … and … not only … but also …: *She is **both** rich and intelligent.*

bother¹ (say **bo*th***-uh) *verb* (**bothering, bothered**)
1 to spend extra time or energy doing something: *Don't **bother** about the washing-up.* ◇ *He didn't **bother** to say goodbye.*
2 to annoy or worry somebody, especially when they are doing something else: *Please don't **bother** me now.* ◇ *Is this music **bothering** you?* ◇ *Sorry to **bother** you.* ➲ SYNONYM **trouble²** 2

bother² (say **bo*th***-uh) *noun* (*no plural*)
something that causes you difficulty: *'Thanks for your help!' 'It was no **bother**.'* ➲ SYNONYM **trouble¹** 2

bottle (say **bot**-uhl) *noun* (*plural* **bottles**)
a glass or plastic container for liquids, with a narrow part at the top: *They drank two **bottles** of water.* ◇ *a **cooldrink** bottle*

bottleneck (say **bot**-uhl-nek) *noun* (*plural* **bottlenecks**)
1 a narrow piece of road that makes traffic slow down
2 anything in a process that makes things slow down behind it: *There was a **bottleneck** at the border because there was only one official on duty.*

bottom (say **bot**-uhm) *noun*
1 (*plural* **bottoms**) the lowest part of something: *They live at the **bottom** of the hill.* ◇ *Look at the picture at the **bottom** of the page.*

A B C D E F G H I J K L M N O P Q R S T U V W X Y Z

A B C D E F G H I J K L M N O P Q R S T U V W X Y Z

➲ OPPOSITE **top**[1] 1, ➲ SYNONYM **foot** 3
2 (*no plural*) the last part of something or the end: *The bank is at the **bottom** of the road.*
➲ OPPOSITE **top**[1] 1
3 (*no plural*) the lowest position compared to other people or groups: *They were at the **bottom** of the class in maths.* ➲ OPPOSITE **top**[1] 1
4 (*plural* **bottoms**) the part of your body that you sit on ➲ SYNONYM **backside**
▶ **bottom** (*adjective*): *Put the book on the **bottom*** (= the lowest) *shelf.*

bottomless (say **bot**-uhm-luhss) *adjective*
very deep and without limit: *a **bottomless** pit* ◇ *a **bottomless** cup of coffee* (= a cup that you can refill as often as you like, for the price of one cup)

bougainvillea (say boo-guhn-**vil**-i-uh) *noun* (*no plural*)
a climbing plant with many brightly coloured flower-like parts
🛈 **ORIGIN:** named after Louis Antoine de Bougainville (1729–1811), a French explorer

bough (*rhymes with* **cow**) *noun* (*plural* **boughs**)
a main branch of a tree

> PRONUNCIATION Don't pronounce the **gh** in **bough**.

bought (say **bawt**) form of **buy**

boulder (*rhymes with* **older**) *noun* (*plural* **boulders**)
a very big rock

boulevard (say **boo**-luh-vaad) *noun* (*plural* **boulevards**)
a wide street in a city that often has trees along the sides

bounce (say **bownss**) *verb* (**bouncing**, **bounced**)
1 (used about a ball) to move away quickly after hitting something hard, or to make a ball do this: *The ball **bounced** off the wall.* ◇ *The boy was **bouncing** a tennis ball.*
2 to jump up and down many times: *The children were **bouncing** on their beds.*

bound[1] (say **bownd**) form of **bind**

bound[2] (say **bownd**) *adjective*
bound to certain to do something: *She works very hard, so she is **bound** to pass the exam.*
bound for going to a place: *This ship is **bound** for Hong Kong.*

bound[3] (say **bownd**) *verb* (**bounding**, **bounded**)
to run with long steps: *The dog **bounded** up the steps.*

boundary (say **bown**-dree) *noun* (*plural* **boundaries**)
a line between two places: *This fence is the **boundary** between the two gardens.*
➲ See **border** 1

bounds (say **bowndz**) *plural noun*
limits that cannot or should not be passed: *Prices should stay within **bounds**.*
out of bounds not to be entered by somebody: *This area is out of **bounds** to learners.*

bounty (say **bown**-tee) *noun* (*plural* **bounties**)
1 something given or found in large amounts: *You can harvest the **bounty** of your own garden.*
2 money that someone gets for catching a criminal or killing somebody

bouquet (say buu-**kay**) *noun* (*plural* **bouquets**)
a group of flowers that is arranged in an attractive way: *He gave her a **bouquet** of roses.*

bout (say **bowt**) *noun* (*plural* **bouts**)
a short period of something, like illness or hard work: *a **bout** of flu*

boutique (say boo-**teek**) *noun* (*plural* **boutiques**)
a small shop that sells fashionable clothing or expensive gifts

bovine (say **boh**-vine) *adjective*
of or like **cattle**: ***bovine** tuberculosis*
▶ **bovine** (*noun*): *a young **bovine***

bow[1] (*rhymes with* **now**) *verb* (**bowing**, **bowed**)
to bend your head or body forward to show respect: *The actors **bowed** to the audience.*

> PRONUNCIATION Notice the difference in pronunciation between **bow**[1] (above) and **bow**[3] (below).

bow[2] (*rhymes with* **now**) *noun* (*plural* **bows**)
1 the act of bending your head or the upper part of your body forward to say hello or goodbye or to show respect: *He gave a **bow** and left the room.*
2 the front part of a boat or ship ➲ See illustration at **ship**

bow[3] (*rhymes with* **go**) *noun* (*plural* **bows**)
1 a curved piece of wood with a string between the two ends that you use to send arrows through the air.
2 a long thin piece of wood with string stretched across it that you use for playing some musical instruments: *a violin **bow***
➲ See illustration at **violin**
3 a knot with two loops (= round shapes made by something like string) and two loose ends that you use when you are tying your shoes or

wrapping a parcel: *She tied the ribbon with a bow.*

bowel (say **bow**-uhl) *noun* (*plural* **bowels**)
the tube in your body that carries food away from your stomach to the place where it leaves your body ➲ SYNONYM **intestine**

bowl[1] (*rhymes with* **hole**) *noun* (*plural* **bowls**)
a deep round dish that is used for holding food or liquids: *a sugar **bowl** ◇ a **bowl** of soup*

bowl[2] (*rhymes with* **hole**) *verb* (**bowling, bowled**)
(in games such as cricket) to throw a ball so that play can take place

bowler (say **boh**-luh) *noun* (*plural* **bowlers**)
1 (in cricket) the player who throws **(bowls)** the ball to the person with the bat
2 a round hard black hat

bow tie (say **boh**-ty) *noun* (*plural* **bow ties**)
a tie in the shape of a **bow[3]** 3 that men wear on formal occasions

box[1] (say **bokss**) *noun* (*plural* **boxes**)
a container that has straight sides and often a lid: *Put the books in a cardboard **box**. ◇ a **box** of chocolates ◇ a **box** of matches*

box[2] (say **bokss**) *verb* (**boxing, boxed**)
to fight with your hands, wearing thick gloves, as a sport

boxer (say **bokss**-uh) *noun*
1 (*plural* **boxers**) a person who does **boxing** as a sport: *Muhammad Ali was a famous **boxer**.*
2 boxers (also **boxer shorts**) men's underwear that looks like a pair of short trousers: *a pair of **boxers***

boxing (say **bokss**-ing) *noun* (*no plural*)
the sport of fighting with your hands, wearing thick gloves

box office *noun* (*plural* **box offices**)
a place where you buy tickets in a theatre or cinema

boy *noun* (*plural* **boys**)
a male child or a young male person: *They have three children, two **boys** and a girl.*

boycott (say **boy**-kot) *verb* (**boycotting, boycotted**)
to refuse to buy something from a certain shop or take part in an event because you disapprove of it: *Let's **boycott** the tuckshop.*
▸ **boycott** (*noun*): *The union organized **boycotts** and strikes.*
🛈 **ORIGIN:** from the name of Captain Charles *Boycott* (1832–1897), an Irish estate manager. The local community refused to deal with him when he would not reduce tenants' rents.

boyfriend (say **boy**-frend) *noun* (*plural* **boyfriends**)
a boy or man who somebody has a romantic relationship with: *Her **boyfriend** is in her class.*

bra (say **braa**) *noun* (*plural* **bras**)
a piece of clothing that a woman wears under her other clothes to cover and support her breasts

braai (say **bry**) *noun* (*plural* **braais**) (*S. African*)
1 a meal that is cooked on a fire outside: *We had a **braai** last night.*
2 the metal instrument that you use to cook on: *Please clean the **braai**.* ➲ SYNONYM **barbecue**
▸ **braai** (*verb*): *We **braaied** our meat.*
🛈 **ORIGIN:** 20th century, through Afrikaans *braai*, from Dutch *braden* meaning 'to roast, grill'

braaivleis (say **bry**-flayss) *noun* (*no plural*) (*S. African*)
a party where food is cooked outside on a fire
🛈 **ORIGIN:** 20th century, from Afrikaans *braaivleis* from *braai* meaning 'cook over an open fire, grill' + *vleis* meaning 'meat'

brace[1] (say **brayss**) *noun*
1 (*plural* **braces**) a device that holds things firmly together or supports them in position: *a neck **brace*** (= worn to support the neck after an injury)
2 braces (*plural noun*) a metal frame that is fixed to a child's teeth in order to make them straight
3 braces (*plural noun*) a pair of straps that go over your shoulders to hold your trousers up

brace[2] (say **brayss**) *verb* (**bracing, braced**)
to prepare for bad news: ***Brace** yourself for Marie's news.*

bracelet (say **brayss**-luht) *noun* (*plural* **bracelets**)
a pretty piece of metal, wood or plastic that you wear around your arm

bracket (say **brak**-it) *noun* (*plural* **brackets**)
one of two marks, ( ) or [ ], that you put round extra information in a piece of writing: *(This sentence is written in **brackets**.)* ➲ See Study page 16 ➲ SYNONYM **parenthesis**

brackish (say **brak**-ish) *adjective*
(used about water) containing some salt, but not as much as sea water: *The **brackish** water did not taste good.* ➲ SYNONYM **brak**

bract (say **brakt**) *noun* (*plural* **bracts**) (*biology*)
special leaves arranged around a small flower that are often larger and more colourful than the flower itself

A B C D E F G H I J K L M N O P Q R S T U V W X Y Z

brag (*rhymes with* **drag**) *verb* (**bragging, bragged**)
to talk in a way that shows you are too proud of something that you have or something that you can do: *She often **brags** about how clever she is.* ➲ SYNONYM **boast**

Brahman (say **braa**-muhn) *noun* (*plural* **Brahmans**) (also **Brahmin**)
1 a person at the highest level of Hindu people, that includes priests
2 one of a certain breed of cattle

braid (say **brayd**) *verb* (**braiding, braided**)
to cross three long pieces of hair over and under each other to make one thick piece: *Will you **braid** my hair?* ➲ SYNONYM **plait**
▸ **braid** (*noun*): *She has long **braids**.*

Braille (say **brayl**) *noun* (*no plural*) (also **braille**)
a system of printing using little round raised marks that blind people can read by touching the page
🛈 ORIGIN: from the name of Louis Braille (1809–1852), the Frenchman who invented the system

brain (say **brayn**) *noun* (*plural* **brains**)
the part inside the head of a person or an animal that thinks and feels: *The **brain** controls the rest of the body.* ➲ See illustration at **organ**

brainstorm (say **brayn**-stawm) *verb* (**brainstorming, brainstormed**)
to solve a problem or make a decision by thinking of many ideas in a short time: *Let's **brainstorm** a solution to the problem.*

brainwash (say **brayn**-wosh) *verb* (**brainwashing, brainwashed**)
to force somebody to believe something that they did not believe before: *The advertisers try to **brainwash** us into wanting their products.*
➲ SYNONYM **indoctrinate**

brainwave (say **brayn**-wayv) *noun* (*plural* **brainwaves**)
a sudden clever idea: *I've had a **brainwave**! Let's sell airtime.*

brainy (say **brayn**-ee) *adjective* (**brainier, brainiest**) (*informal*)
clever: *Palisa's even **brainier** than her sister.*

braise (say **brayz**) *verb* (**braising, braised**)
to cook meat or vegetables slowly in a little liquid in a covered dish

brak (say **bruk**) *adjective* (*S. African*)
(used about river water or soil) containing a lot of salt ➲ SYNONYM **brackish**

brake¹ (say **brayk**) *noun* (*plural* **brakes**)
the part of a vehicle that you use to make it go slower or stop: *I put my foot on the **brake**.*

brake² (say **brayk**) *verb* (**braking, braked**)
to make a vehicle go slower or stop by using a **brake¹**: *A child ran into the road and the driver **braked** suddenly.*

bramble (say **bramb**-l) *noun* (*plural* **brambles**)
a type of bush with thorns on it

bran *noun* (*no plural*)
the brown outer parts of wheat that people can eat

branch¹ (say **braanch**) *noun* (*plural* **branches**)
1 one of the parts of a tree that grow out from the thick main part (called the **trunk**)
2 an office or a shop that is part of a big company: *This bank has **branches** all over the country.*

branch² (say **braanch**) *verb* (**branching, branched**)
branch off (used about a road) to leave a larger road and go off in another direction: *The road **branches** off to the left.*
branch out to start something new: *It gave me the inspiration to **branch** out on my own.*

brand¹ *noun* (*plural* **brands**)
the name of a product that a certain company makes: *Which **brand** of coffee do you buy?*

brand² *verb* (**branding, branded**)
1 to mark an animal with a hot iron to show who owns it.
2 to say that someone has a bad character so that other people do not like them: *He was **branded** a lunatic.*

brandish (say **bran**-dish) *verb* (**brandishing, brandished**)
to wave something in the air in a fierce way: *The robbers **brandished** their weapons.*

brand new *adjective*
completely new: *a **brand new** car*

brandy (say **bran**-dee) *noun*
1 (*no plural*) a strong alcoholic drink made from wine
2 (*plural* **brandies**) a glass of this drink

brash *adjective* (**brasher, brashest**)
too confident and direct: *He was loud and **brash** at the party.*

brass (say **braass**) *noun* (*no plural*)
1 a yellow metal: ***brass** buttons*
2 the group of musical instruments that are made of brass, such as trumpets and horns

brat *noun* (*plural* **brats**)
a child who behaves badly

bravado (say bruh-**vaa**-doh) *noun* (*no plural*)
a confident way of behaving that is supposed

to impress people: *He was full of **bravado** when he was with his friends.*

brave (say **brayv**) *adjective* (**braver**, **bravest**)
ready to do dangerous or difficult things without fear: ***brave** soldiers* ◇ *Try to be **brave**.*
▶ **bravely** (*adverb*): *He fought **bravely** in the war.* ▶ **bravery** (*noun*): *He won a medal for **bravery**.*

brawl (*rhymes with* **call**) *noun* (*plural* **brawls**)
a noisy fight that is usually in a public place
▶ **brawl** (*verb*)

bray *verb* (**braying**, **brayed**)
to make the noise that a donkey makes
▶ **bray** (*noun*)

braze (say **brayz**) *verb* (**brazing**, **brazed**)
to join metal parts together using a type of metal (called **brass**)

brazen (say **bray**-zuhn) *adjective*
without embarrassment, especially in a way that shocks people: *The pirates have become more **brazen** in their attacks.*
▶ **brazenly** (*adverb*)

brazier (say **bray**-zi-uh) *noun* (*plural* **braziers**)
a large metal container that holds burning coals and is used to keep people warm

breach (say **breech**) *noun* (*plural* **breaches**)
1 something that breaks an agreement: *It was a **breach** of their contract.*
2 a hole broken in a wall that was built to protect or defend
▶ **breach** (*verb*): *She **breached** the terms of their agreement.* ◇ *The soldiers **breached** the wall.*

bread (say **bred**) *noun* (*no plural*)
food made from flour and baked in an oven: *I bought a loaf of **bread**.* ◇ *a slice of **bread*** ◇ *three loaves of **bread*** ◇ *She's baking **bread**.*
🛈 **ORIGIN**: from Old English *bread*, related to Dutch *brood*

> **USAGE** Notice how we use this word. It is correct to say: *I bought two **loaves of bread**.* But it is not correct English to say: 'I bought two breads'.

breadline (say **bred**-line) *noun* (*no plural*)
the smallest amount of money that people need to live
on the breadline having just enough money to support yourself
below the breadline not having enough money to support yourself

breadth (say **bredth**) *noun* (*plural* **breadths**)
how far it is from one side of something to the other ➲ **SYNONYM width**
➲ The adjective is **broad**

breadwinner (say **bred**-win-uh) *noun* (*plural* **breadwinners**)
the person in a family who earns most of the money that they need

break[1] (say **brayk**) *verb* (**breaking**, **broke**, **has broken**)
1 to go into smaller pieces or to make something go into smaller pieces: *The cup fell and **broke**.* ◇ *He **broke** the window.* ◇ *Food is **broken** down in the stomach and digestive system.*
2 to stop working or to damage a machine so that it stops working: *I **broke** my watch.*
3 to do something that is against the law or against what has been agreed or promised: *People who **break** the law must be punished.* ◇ *I never **break** my promises.*
break out
1 to start suddenly: *A fire **broke** out last night.*
2 to get free from a place such as a prison: *Four prisoners **broke** out of the jail last night.*
break up to start the school holidays: *We **break** up at the end of March.*

break[2] (say **brayk**) *noun* (*plural* **breaks**)
1 a short time when you stop doing something: *I worked without a **break**.*
2 a place where something opens or has broken: *The sun shone through a **break** in the clouds.* ◇ *a **break** in a pipe*
3 the time at school between lessons when you stop learning and go outside

breakdown (say **brayk**-down) *noun* (*plural* **breakdowns**)
1 a time when something such as a machine or a car stops working: *On the way we had a **breakdown**.*
2 a time when something stops because it did not succeed: *a **breakdown** in the peace talks*
3 a time when a person is so unhappy or worried that they cannot work normally

breaker (say **brayk**-uh) *noun* (*plural* **breakers**)
a large wave covered with white **foam** that is moving towards the beach

breakfast (say **brek**-fuhst) *noun* (*plural* **breakfasts**)
the first meal of the day: *I had **breakfast** at seven o'clock.*
🛈 **ORIGIN**: 14th–15th century, from Old English *brecan* meaning 'to break' + *faestan* meaning 'to fast, not eat', because breakfast is eaten after many hours without food

breakthrough (say **brayk**-throo) *noun* (*plural* **breakthroughs**)
an important discovery or development: *The police have made a **breakthrough** in the murder case.*

breast (say **brest**) *noun* (*plural* **breasts**)
1 one of the two soft round parts of a woman's body that can give milk
2 the front part of a bird's body

breastbone (say **brest**-bohn) *noun* (*plural* **breastbones**) (also **sternum**)
the long flat bone in the chest that the seven top pairs of ribs are connected to ➲ See illustration at **skeleton**

breastfeed (say **brest**-feed) *verb* (**breastfeeding**, **breastfed**)
to feed a baby with milk from the breast: *I **breastfed** my baby for two years.*

breaststroke (say **brest**-strohk) *noun* (*no plural*)
a way of swimming on your front, moving your arms and legs away from your body and then back towards it in a circle: *Can you do **breaststroke**?* ➲ See **backstroke**, **crawl**[2]

breath (say **breth**) *noun*
1 (*no plural*) the air that you take into and blow out of your lungs: *Climbing all those stairs made me gasp for **breath**.*
2 (*plural* **breaths**) an act of taking air into or blowing air out of your lungs: *Take a deep **breath**.*
hold your breath to stop breathing for a short time: *We all held our **breath** as the winner was announced.*
out of breath breathing very quickly: *She was out of **breath** after climbing the stairs.*

> SPELLING Be careful! Don't confuse **breath** which is a noun, with **breathe**, the verb. Note that they also sound different.

breathalyzer (say **breth**-uh-lize-uh) *noun* (*plural* **breathalyzers**) (also **breathalyser**)
a special machine that measures how much alcohol a person has drunk

breathe (say **bree*th***) *verb* (**breathing**, **breathed**)
to take air into your lungs and let it out again through your nose and mouth: *The doctor told me to **breathe** in and then **breathe** out again slowly.*

breathless (say **breth**-luhss) *adjective*
breathing quickly or with difficulty: *Running made them hot and **breathless**.*

breathtaking (say **breth**-tayk-ing) *adjective*
extremely beautiful: *The view from the mountain was **breathtaking**.* ➲ SYNONYM **spectacular**

breed[1] *verb* (**breeding**, **bred**)
1 (used about animals) to produce young animals: *Birds **breed** in the spring.*
2 to keep animals so that they will produce baby animals: *They **breed** sheep on their farm.*

breed[2] *noun* (*plural* **breeds**)
a kind of animal: *There are many different **breeds** of dog.*

breeze (say **breez**) *noun* (*plural* **breezes**)
a light wind

breve (say **breev**) *noun* (*plural* **breves**) (*music*)
a very long musical note

brevity (say **brev**-uh-tee) *noun* (*no plural*)
the state of being short or quick: *She was complimented on the **brevity** of her speech.*

brew[1] (say **broo**) *verb* (**brewing**, **brewed**)
1 to make beer or tea
2 to grow or develop: *Their anger was **brewing** all night.*

brew[2] (say **broo**) *noun* (*plural* **brews**)
a drink that has been standing or developing: *This is a strong **brew**.*

brewery (say **broo**-uh-ree) *noun* (*plural* **breweries**)
a place where beer is made

breyani (say bray-**aa**-nee) *noun* (*no plural*)
= **biriani**

bribe *noun* (*plural* **bribes**)
money or a present that you give to somebody to make them do something for you, especially something dishonest
▸ **bribe** (*verb*): *The prisoner **bribed** the guard to let him go free.*

brick (say **brik**) *noun* (*plural* **bricks**)
a small block of **clay** that has been baked until it is hard and that is used for building: *a **brick** wall*

bricklayer (say **brik**-lay-uh) *noun* (*plural* **bricklayers**)
a person whose job is to build things with bricks

bride (*rhymes with* **side**) *noun* (*plural* **brides**)
a woman on the day of her wedding

bridegroom (say **bride**-groom) *noun* (*plural* **bridegrooms**) (also **groom**)
a man on the day of his wedding

bridesmaid (say **brydz**-mayd) *noun* (*plural* **bridesmaids**)
a girl or woman who helps a **bride** at her wedding

bridge[1] (say **brij**) *noun* (*plural* **bridges**)
a structure that is built over a road, railway or river so that people, trains or cars can cross it: *We walked over the **bridge**.*

bridge[2] (say **brij**) *verb* (**bridging**, **bridged**)
to make a bridge over something: ***bridge** a gap*

bridle (say **bride**-l) *noun* (*plural* **bridles**)
the leather straps that you put over a horse's head so that you can control it when you ride it
➲ See illustration at **horse**

brief[1] (say **breef**) *adjective* (**briefer**, **briefest**)
short or quick: *a **brief** telephone call* ◇ *Please be **brief**.*
in brief in a few words: *This is the problem, in **brief**.*
▸ **briefly** (*adverb*): *He had spoken to her only **briefly**.*

brief[2] (say **breef**) *noun* (*plural* **briefs**)
instructions or information about a job or task: *My **brief** was to find out about ants.*

brief[3] (say **breef**) *verb* (**briefing**, **briefed**)
to give somebody instructions or information about a job or task: *I **briefed** the artist to draw a realistic picture.*

briefcase (say **breef**-kayss) *noun* (*plural* **briefcases**)
a flat case that you use for carrying papers, especially when you go to work

briefs (say **breefss**) *plural noun*
short pants that you wear under your clothes: *a pair of **briefs***

brigade (say bri-**gayd**) *noun* (*plural* **brigades**)
a group of people who work together for a certain job: *fire **brigade***

brigadier general (say **brig**-uh-deer **jen**-ruhl) *noun* (*plural* **brigadier generals**)
an important officer in the army or the **air force**

bright (say **brite**) *adjective* (**brighter**, **brightest**)
1 with a lot of light: *It was a **bright** sunny day.* ◇ *That lamp is very **bright**.*
2 with a strong colour: *a **bright** yellow shirt*
3 clever: *She is the **brightest** child in the class.*
▸ **brightly** (*adverb*): ***brightly** coloured clothes*
▸ **brightness** (*noun*): *the **brightness** of the sun*

brighten (say **brite**-uhn) *verb* (**brightening**, **brightened**) (also **brighten up**)
to become brighter or happier, or to make something brighter: *Her face **brightened** when she saw him.* ◇ *These flowers will **brighten** the room up.*

brilliant (say **bril**-i-uhnt) *adjective*
1 very bright, and with a lot of light: ***brilliant** sunshine*
2 very intelligent: *a **brilliant** student*
3 (*informal*) very good: *The film was **brilliant**!*
▸ **brilliance** (*noun*): *the **brilliance** of the light*
▸ **brilliantly** (*adverb*): *She played **brilliantly**.*

brim *noun* (*plural* **brims**)
1 the edge around the top of something such as a cup, bowl or glass: *The glass was full to the **brim**.*
2 the wide part around the bottom of a hat

brine (*rhymes with* **mine**) *noun* (*no plural*)
salt water that you store food in: *tuna in **brine***

bring *verb* (**bringing**, **brought**)
1 to take something or somebody with you to a place: *Could you **bring** me a glass of water?* ◇ *Can I **bring** a friend to the party?*
2 to make something happen: *Money doesn't always **bring** happiness.*
bring something back
1 to return something: *I've **brought** back the book you lent me.*
2 to make you remember something: *These photos **bring** back many memories.*
bring somebody up to look after a child until they are grown up: *He was **brought** up by his aunt after his parents died.*
bring something up
1 to be sick, so that food comes up from your stomach and out of your mouth
2 to start to talk about something: *She **brought** up the problem of litter.*

WHICH WORD? **Bring**, **take** or **fetch**?
- With sense 1 above, you **bring** something with you to the place where you are going: *He always **brings** me flowers.*
- You **take** something to a different place: ***Take** a jersey when you go out.*
- You go somewhere to **fetch** someone or something and **bring** them back: *I'm going to **fetch** Sisanda from the airport.*

brinjal (say **brin**-juhl) *noun* (*plural* **brinjals**)
a vegetable with a purple skin
🛈 ORIGIN: from Portuguese *berinjela*, from Arabic

brink *noun* (*plural* **brinks**)
the edge of something: *The company was on the **brink** of failure.*

brisk *adjective* (**brisker**, **briskest**)
quick and using a lot of energy: *We went for a **brisk** walk.*

bristle (say **briss**-l) *noun* (*plural* **bristles**)
a short thick hair like the hair on a brush

British (say **brit**-ish) *adjective*
relating to Britain: *I like **British** music.*
▸ **British** (*noun*): *What do the **British** think about this movie?*

A B C D E F G H I J K L M N O P Q R S T U V W X Y Z

brittle (say **brit**-l) *adjective*
hard but easily broken: *This glass is very* ***brittle.***

broach (*rhymes with* **coach**) *verb* (**broaching**, **broached**)
to start talking about a particular subject, especially when it is embarrassing or difficult: *I* ***broached*** *the subject of my birthday party with my parents.*

broad (say **brawd**) *adjective* (**broader**, **broadest**)
large from one side to the other: *a* ***broad*** *river* ➲ SYNONYM **wide**[1] 1 ➲ The noun is **breadth** ➲ OPPOSITE **narrow** 1

broadband (say **brawd**-band) *noun* (*no plural*) (*computing*)
(used about an Internet connection) a technology which allows you to send and receive a lot of information quickly: *Have you got* ***broadband?***

broadcast (say **brawd**-kaast) *verb* (**broadcasting**, **broadcast**)
to send out sound or pictures by radio or television: *The Olympics are* ***broadcast*** *live.*
▸ **broadcast** (*noun*): *a news* ***broadcast***
▸ **broadcaster** (*noun*): *The* ***broadcaster*** *said, 'Good morning. This is the news.'*

broad-minded (say brawd-**mine**-did) *adjective*
willing to accept ways of life and beliefs that are different from your own
➲ OPPOSITE **narrow-minded**

broccoli (say **brok**-uh-lee) *noun* (*no plural*)
a vegetable with very small green flowers that you eat

brochure (say **broh**-shuh) *noun* (*plural* **brochures**)
a thin book with pictures of things you can buy or places you can go to on holiday: *a travel* ***brochure***

broke (*rhymes with* **joke**) *adjective*
not having any money: *I'm always* ***broke*** *at the end of the month.*

broke, broken forms of **break**[1]

broken (say **broh**-kuhn) *adjective*
in pieces or not working: *a* ***broken*** *window* ◇ *'What's the time?' 'I don't know – my watch is* ***broken.'*** ◇ *The TV is* ***broken.*** ➲ The verb is **break**[1]

broker (say **broh**-kuh) *noun* (*plural* **brokers**)
a person who buys and sells things for another person: *insurance* ***broker***

bronchiole (say **brong**-ki-ohl) *noun* (*plural* **bronchioles**)
one of the very small branches into which a **bronchus** divides ➲ See illustration at **lung**

bronchitis (say brong-**ky**-tiss) *noun* (*no plural*)
a swelling of the tubes leading to the lungs, causing a very bad cough

bronchus (say **brong**-kuus) *noun* (*plural* **bronchi**)
one of the tubes that carry air to the **lungs**
▸ **bronchial** (*adjective*): *a* ***bronchial*** *infection*
➲ See illustration at **lung**

bronze (say **bronz**) *noun* (*no plural*)
a dark red-brown metal: *a* ***bronze*** *medal*

brooch (*rhymes with* **coach**) *noun* (*plural* **brooches**)
a piece of jewellery with a pin at the back that you wear on your clothes

brood[1] (say **brood**) *noun* (*plural* **broods**)
all the young birds that have the same mother and are the same age: *a* ***brood*** *of chicks*

brood[2] (say **brood**) *verb* (**brooding**, **brooded**)
1 to sit on eggs until the chicks are ready to come out
2 to think a lot about something that makes you sad or worried

broody (say **broo**-dee) *adjective* (**broodier**, **broodiest**)
1 (about a hen) ready to have eggs
2 (*informal*) (about a person) wanting to have a baby

brook (say **bruuk**) *noun* (*plural* **brooks**)
a small flow of water

broom (say **bruum** or **broom**) *noun* (*plural* **brooms**)
a brush on the end of a long handle that you use to **sweep** floors

broth (*rhymes with* **moth**) *noun* (*no plural*)
soup that is watery

brothel (say **broth**-l) *noun* (*plural* **brothels**)
a place where men pay to have sex with women

brother (say **bruth**-uh) *noun* (*plural* **brothers**)
a man or boy who has the same parents as you: *My younger* ***brother*** *is called Vuyo.* ◇ *Gavin and Nick are* ***brothers.*** ◇ *Have you got any* ***brothers*** *and sisters?*
ⓘ ORIGIN: from Old English *brothor*

brotherhood (say **bruth**-uh-huud) *noun* (*no plural*)
a feeling of friendship and understanding between people

brother-in-law (say **bru*th***-uh-in-law) *noun* (*plural* **brothers-in-law**)
1 the brother of your wife or husband
2 the husband of your sister
➲ See **sister-in-law**

brought (say **brawt**) form of **bring**

brow (*rhymes with* **cow**) *noun* (*plural* **brows**) (*formal*)
the part of your face above your eyes
➲ SYNONYM **forehead**

brown *adjective, noun* (**browner**, **brownest**)
having the colour of earth or wood: ***brown** eyes* ◇ *Toast the bread until it goes **brown**.*
▸ **brown** (*noun*): ***Brown** suits you* (= makes you look good).

Brownie (say **brown**-ee) *noun* (*plural* **Brownies**)
a young girl who is a member of the junior branch of the Guides Association. They wear brown uniforms. ➲ See **Guide**[1] 4

browse (say **browz**) *verb* (**browsing**, **browsed**)
1 to spend time in a shop looking at what they have for sale
2 to look through a book, magazine or the Internet without reading every part

browser (say **browz**-uh) *noun* (*plural* **browsers**) (*computing*)
a program that lets you look at pages on the Internet: *a Web **browser***

bruise (say **brooz**) *noun* (*plural* **bruises**)
a blue, brown or purple mark that appears on your skin after you have fallen or been hit: *He's covered in **bruises**.*
▸ **bruise** (*verb*): *She fell and **bruised** her leg.*

brunette (say broo-**net**) *noun* (*plural* **brunettes**)
a woman with brown hair: *There are three **brunettes** and two blondes in our team.*

brush[1] (*rhymes with* **crush**) *noun* (*plural* **brushes**)
a thing that you use for cleaning, painting or making your hair tidy: *a clothes **brush**.*

brush[2] (*rhymes with* **crush**) *verb* (**brushing**, **brushed**)
to clean or tidy something with a brush: *I **brush** my teeth twice a day.* ◇ ***Brush** your hair!*

Brussels sprout (say **bruss**-uhlz sprowt) *noun* (*plural* **Brussels sprouts**) (also **sprout**)
a very small, round green vegetable consisting of a tight ball of leaves

brutal (say **broot**-l) *adjective*
very cruel: *a **brutal** murder*
▸ **brutally** (*adverb*): *She was **brutally** attacked.*

brute[1] (say **broot**) *noun* (*plural* **brutes**)
a person who is very cruel and violent

brute[2] (say **broot**) *adjective*
(only before a noun) using strength to do something rather than thinking about it: *You're going to need **brute** force to get this window open.*

bubble[1] (say **bub**-l) *noun* (*plural* **bubbles**)
a small ball of air or gas inside a liquid: *The children blew **bubbles** under the water.*

bubble[2] (say **bub**-l) *verb* (**bubbling**, **bubbled**)
to make a lot of bubbles: *When water boils, it **bubbles**.*

bubonic plague (say byoo-bon-ik **playg**) *noun* (*no plural*)
a disease spread by rats that causes **fever**, swellings on the body and usually death

buchu (say **buu**-*khuu*) *noun* (*no plural*)
a type of bush with a strong pleasant smell
🛈 ORIGIN: 18th century, from Khoikhoi *buchu*

> PRONUNCIATION Pronounce the **ch** in this word like the **g** in the Afrikaans word **lag**.

buck[1] (say **buk**) *noun*
1 (*plural* **buck**) (*S. African*) a wild mammal with long thin legs that can run fast. Most **buck** have horns: *Springbok, impala and duiker are all types of **buck**.* ➲ SYNONYM **antelope**
2 (*plural* **bucks**) the male of some animals, for example rabbits and deer
3 (*plural* **bucks**) (*informal*) a dollar or a rand: *That will be four **bucks**.*
🛈 ORIGIN: 19th century, through Afrikaans and South African Dutch *bok* meaning 'antelope or goat', from Dutch *bok* meaning 'animal that has horns'

buck[2] (say **buk**) *verb* (**bucking**, **bucked**)
to jump with an arched back: *The horse **bucked** while Elize was riding it.*

bucket (say **buk**-uht) *noun* (*plural* **buckets**)
a round metal or plastic container with a handle that you use for carrying water, for example.

buckle (say **buk**-l) *noun* (*plural* **buckles**)
a piece of metal or plastic on the end of a belt or on a shoe that you use for fastening it
🛈 ORIGIN: 13th–15th century, through Old French from Latin *buccula* meaning 'cheek strap of a helmet'

bud *noun* (*plural* **buds**)
a leaf or flower before it opens: *The trees are covered with **buds**.* ➲ See illustration at **plant**[1]

Buddha (say **buud**-uh) *noun*
a title given to the founder of **Buddhism**, Siddartha Gautama

A B C D E F G H I J K L M N O P Q R S T U V W X Y Z

A B C D E F G H I J K L M N O P Q R S T U V W X Y Z

Buddhism (say **buud**-i-zuhm) *noun* (*no plural*)
a widespread Asian religion or philosophy, founded by Siddartha Gautama in India in the fifth century BC.
▸ **Buddhist** (*adjective*): *a **Buddhist** temple*
▸ **Buddhist** (*noun*): *She is a **Buddhist*** (= she follows the teachings of Buddha).

budding (say **bud**-ing) *adjective*
starting to develop and be successful: *Catherine is a **budding** artist.*

budge (say **buj**) *verb* (**budging, budged**)
to move a little or to make something move a little: *I pushed the rock but it didn't **budge**.*

budgerigar (say **bu**-juh-ri-gaa) *noun* (*plural* **budgerigars**) (also *informal* **budgie**)
a small brightly coloured bird that people often keep as a pet

budget (say **buj**-uht) *noun* (*plural* **budgets**)
a plan of how much money you will have and how you will spend it: *We have a weekly **budget** for food.*
▸ **budget** (*verb*): *If you **budget** carefully, you can save money.*
🛈 ORIGIN: 15th century, through Old French *bougette*, from Latin *bulga* meaning 'leather bag or wallet'. Later the word meant the money in a wallet and then a financial statement.

budgie (say **buj**-ee) *noun* (*plural* **budgies**) short for **budgerigar**

buff¹ (say **buf**) *adjective*
having an off-yellow colour

buff² (say **buf**) *verb* (**buffing, buffed**)
to polish

buffalo (say **buf**-uh-loh) *noun* (*plural* **buffalo** or **buffaloes**)
a large wild mammal of the cow family, with long curved horns

buffer (say **buf**-uh) *noun* (*plural* **buffers**)
a thing or person that reduces the unpleasant effects of something: *Save money so that you have a **buffer** for when you need extra money.*

buffet¹ (say **buu**-fay) *noun* (*plural* **buffets**)
a meal when all the food is on a big table and you take what you want: *a **buffet** lunch*

buffet² (say **buf**-uht) *verb* (**buffeting, buffeted**)
to hit or knock something: *The wind was **buffeting** the little boat in the waves.*

buffoon (say buf-**foon**) *noun* (*plural* **buffoons**)
a silly person

bug¹ *noun* (*plural* **bugs**)
1 a small insect
2 an illness that is not serious: *I've caught a **bug**.*
3 a fault in a machine, especially a computer system or program

bug² *verb* (**bugging, bugged**)
1 to hide a very small device somewhere so you can listen to someone's conversation without their knowing: *They **bugged** my phone.*
2 to annoy: *Stop **bugging** me!*

buggy (say **bug**-ee) *noun* (*plural* **buggies**)
1 a small car, often without a roof or doors: *a beach **buggy***
2 a **pushchair**

bugle (say **byoog**-l) *noun* (*plural* **bugles**)
a musical instrument like a small **trumpet**, used in the army for giving signals

bugle

build¹ (say **bild**) *verb* (**building, built**)
to make something by putting parts together: *He **built** a wall in front of the house.* ◇ *The bridge is **built** of stone.*

build² (say **bild**) *noun* (*plural* **builds**)
the shape and size of someone's body: *He exercises a lot and has a good **build**.*

builder (say **bild**-uh) *noun* (*plural* **builders**)
a person whose job is to make buildings

building (say **bild**-ing) *noun* (*plural* **buildings**)
a structure with a roof and walls, such as a house, school, church or shop

built (say **bilt**) form of **build¹**

bulb (say **bulb**) *noun* (*plural* **bulbs**)
1 (also **light bulb**) the glass part of an electric lamp that gives light
2 a round thing that some plants grow from: *a flower **bulb***

bulge (say **bulj**) *verb* (**bulging, bulged**)
to go out in a round shape from something that is usually flat: *My stomach is **bulging** – I have to get some exercise.*
▸ **bulge** (*noun*): *a **bulge** in the wall*

bulimia (say buu-**lim**-i-uh or buu-**leem**-i-uh) *noun* (*no plural*)
an illness in which a person keeps eating too much and then makes themselves vomit
➲ See **anorexia**
▸ **bulimic** (*adjective*)

bulk (*rhymes with* **sulk**) *noun* (*no plural*)
1 the main part of something: *I've done the **bulk** of my homework.*
2 the size of something: *Despite its **bulk**, this bike isn't heavy.*
in bulk in large quantities: *She buys most of her groceries in **bulk**.*

bulky (say **bul**-kee) *adjective* (**bulkier**, **bulkiest**)
big, heavy and difficult to carry: *a **bulky** parcel*

bull (say **buul**) *noun* (*plural* **bulls**)
the male of the cow and of some other animals
ⓘ ORIGIN: through Old English *bula* meaning 'bull', from Old Norse *boli*

bulldog (say **buul**-dog) *noun* (*plural* **bulldogs**)
a strong dog with short legs and a large head

bulldozer (say **buul**-doh-zuh) *noun* (*plural* **bulldozers**)
a big heavy machine that moves earth and makes land flat

bullet (say **buu**-luht) *noun* (*plural* **bullets**)
a small piece of metal that comes out of a gun: *The **bullet** hit him in the leg.*

bulletin (say **buu**-luh-tin) *noun* (*plural* **bulletins**)
a short news report on television or radio: *The news **bulletin** is at six tonight.*

bulletproof (say **buu**-luht-proof) *adjective*
made of a strong material that stops bullets from passing through it: *a **bulletproof** vest*

bullion (say **buu**-li-uhn) *noun* (*no plural*)
bars of gold or silver

bull's-eye (say **buul**-zy) *noun* (*plural* **bull's-eyes**)
the centre of a round object that you are aiming at (called a **target**)

bully (say **buu**-lee) *noun* (*plural* **bullies**)
a person who hurts or frightens a weaker person: *He's a terrible **bully**.*
▸ **bully** (*verb*): *She was **bullied** by the older girls.*

bum *noun* (*plural* **bums**) (*informal*)
1 the part of your body (your **bottom**) that you sit on
2 a lazy or useless person

bumble (say **bumb**-l) *verb* (**bumbling**, **bumbled**)
to move in an unsteady way: *He **bumbled** along the road.*

bump[1] *verb* (**bumping**, **bumped**)
1 to hit a person or thing when you are moving: *She **bumped** into a chair.*
2 to hit a part of your body against something hard: *I **bumped** my knee on the table.*
bump into somebody to meet somebody by chance: *I **bumped** into Mpho.*

bump[2] (say **bump**) *noun* (*plural* **bumps**)
1 the action or sound of something hitting a hard surface: *He fell and hit the ground with a **bump**.*
2 a round raised area on your body where you have hit it: *I've got a **bump** on my head.*
3 a small part on something flat that is higher than the rest: *The car hit a **bump** in the road.*

bumper[1] (say **bump**-uh) *adjective*
larger than usual: *We had a **bumper** crop of asparagus this year.*

bumper[2] (say **bump**-uh) *noun* (*plural* **bumpers**)
a bar on the front and back of a car which helps to protect the car if it hits something
➲ See illustration at **car**

bumpkin (say **bump**-kin) *noun* (*plural* **bumpkins**)
a person who is not comfortable in the city

bumpy (say **bump**-ee) *adjective* (**bumpier**, **bumpiest**)
not flat or smooth: *The road was **bumpy**.*
➲ OPPOSITE **smooth** 1

bun *noun* (*plural* **buns**)
a small round cake or piece of bread

bunch (*rhymes with* **lunch**) *noun* (*plural* **bunches**)
a group of things that grow together or that you tie or hold together: *a **bunch** of grapes* ◇ *two **bunches** of flowers*

bundle (say **bund**-l) *noun* (*plural* **bundles**)
a group of things that you tie or wrap together: *a **bundle** of old newspapers*

bundu (say **buun**-duu) *noun* (*no plural*)
the wild or the bush: *I spent my holiday in the **bundu**.*
ⓘ ORIGIN: 20th century, probably from Shona *bundo* meaning 'grasslands'. Shona is a language spoken in Zimbabwe.

bundu-bash *verb* (**bundu-bashing**, **bundu-bashed**)
to travel into the wild by forcing your way through rough **terrain**
▸ **bundu-basher** (*noun*)
▸ **bundu-bashing** (*noun*)

bungalow (say **bung**-guh-loh) *noun* (*plural* **bungalows**)
a low house that has only one floor, with no upstairs rooms

bungee jumping (say **bun**-jee jump-ing) *noun* (*no plural*)
a sport in which you jump from a high place, like a bridge, with a thick elastic rope around your feet

bungle (say **bung**-guhl) *verb* (**bungling, bungled**)
to do something badly: *The mechanic* ***bungled*** *the work on my car.*

bunk[1] (say **bungk**) *noun* (*plural* **bunks**)
1 a narrow bed that is fixed to a wall, for example on a ship or train
2 (also **bunk bed**) one of a pair of single beds built one on top of the other

bunk[2] (say **bungk**) *verb* (**bunking, bunked**) (*informal*)
to miss something important on purpose

bunker (say **bung**-kuh) *noun* (*plural* **bunkers**)
1 a strong underground shelter that people can stay in for protection during a war
2 a sandy area on a golf course

bunny (say **bun**-ee) *noun* (*plural* **bunnies**)
a child's word for rabbit

Bunsen burner (say **bun**-suhn burn-uh) *noun* (*plural* **Bunsen burners**)
an instrument used in scientific work that produces a hot gas flame
ⓘ **ORIGIN:** from the name of Robert Bunsen (1811–1899), the German chemist who designed the Bunsen burner

buoy (say **boy**) *noun* (*plural* **buoys**)
a thing that floats in the sea to show ships where there are dangerous places

buoyant (say **boy**-uhnt) *adjective*
1 (used about a material) floating or able to float: *It is important to make your boat out of* ***buoyant*** *material.*
2 happy and confident: *We were in a* ***buoyant*** *mood after we won the league.*

burden (say **bur**-duhn) *noun* (*plural* **burdens**)
something that you have to do that causes worry, difficulty or hard work: *I don't want to be a* ***burden*** *to my children when I'm old.*

bureau (say **byoo**-roh) *noun* (*plural* **bureaux** or **bureaus**)
1 an organization that gives information: *the weather* ***bureau*** ◇ *an information* ***bureau***
2 a writing desk with drawers and a lid

bureaucracy (say byoo-**rok**-ruh-see) *noun* (*plural* **bureaucracies**)
1 a system of government by a large number of officials
2 a system of official rules that make tasks complicated

bureaucrat (say **byoo**-ruh-krat) *noun* (*plural* **bureaucrats**)
an official in a government department
▶ **bureaucratic** (*adjective*)

burgeon (say **bur**-juhn) *verb* (**burgeoning, burgeoned**)
to grow quickly: *a* ***burgeoning*** *market*

burger (say **bur**-guh) *noun* (*plural* **burgers**)
meat cut into very small pieces and made into a flat round shape, that you eat between two pieces of bread: *a* ***burger*** *and chips*
➲ **SYNONYM hamburger**

burgher (say **bur**-guh) *noun* (*plural* **burghers**) (*history*) (*S. African*)
a citizen of a Boer Republic
ⓘ **ORIGIN:** 18th century, from Dutch *burgher* from *burg* meaning 'town'

burglar (say **burg**-luh) *noun* (*plural* **burglars**)
a person who goes into a building to steal things

burglary (say **burg**-luh-ree) *noun* (*plural* **burglaries**)
the crime of going into a building to steal things: *He was arrested for* ***burglary.***

burgle (say **burg**-l) *verb* (**burgling, burgled**)
to go into a building illegally, usually using force, and steal from it: *Our house was* ***burgled.***

burial (say **be**-ri-uhl) *noun* (*plural* **burials**)
the ceremony when a dead body is put in the ground ➲ **SYNONYM funeral**

buried, buries forms of **bury**

burly (say **bur**-lee) *adjective* (**burlier, burliest**)
(about a person's body) strong and heavy

burn[1] *verb* (**burning, burnt** or **burned, has burnt** or **has burned**)
1 to make flames and heat or to be on fire: *Paper* ***burns*** *easily.* ◇ *The building is* ***burning.***
2 to harm or destroy a person or thing with fire or heat: *I* ***burnt*** *my fingers on a match.* ◇ *We* ***burned*** *the wood on the fire.*
burn down, burn something down to burn, or to make a building burn, until there is nothing left: *Their house* ***burnt*** *down.*

burn[2] *noun* (*plural* **burns**)
a place on your body where fire or heat has hurt it: *I've got a* ***burn*** *on my arm.*

burnish (say **burn**-ish) *verb* (**burnishing, burnished**)
to polish something
▶ **burnished** (*adjective*): ***burnished*** *wood*

burnt *adjective*
damaged by burning: ***burnt*** *food* ◇ *Her hand was badly* ***burnt.***

burp *verb* (**burping**, **burped**)
to make a noise from your mouth when air suddenly comes up from your stomach: *He **burped** loudly.* ➲ SYNONYM **belch** 1
▶ **burp** (*noun*): *I heard a loud **burp**.*

burrow (say **bu**-roh) *noun* (*plural* **burrows**)
a hole in the ground where some animals, for example rabbits, live

bursar (say **bur**-suh) *noun* (*plural* **bursars**)
a person who manages the finances of a school or university

bursary (say **bur**-suh-ree) *noun* (*plural* **bursaries**)
money that a student receives to pay for their studies

burst[1] (say **burst**) *verb* (**bursting**, **burst**)
1 to break open suddenly or to make something do this: *The bag was so full that it **burst**.* ◇ *I **burst** the balloon.*
2 to go or come suddenly: *She **burst** into the room.*
burst into something to start doing something suddenly: *She read the letter and **burst** into tears* (= started to cry). ◇ *The car **burst** into flames* (= started to burn).
burst out laughing to suddenly start to laugh: *When she saw my hat, she **burst** out laughing.*

burst[2] (say **burst**) *noun* (*plural* **bursts**)
something that happens suddenly and quickly: *a **burst** of laughter*

bury (*rhymes with* **very**) *verb* (**burying**, **buried**)
1 to put a dead body in the ground ➲ The noun is **burial**
2 to put something in the ground or under something: *The dog **buried** the bone.*

bus (say **buss**) *noun* (*plural* **buses**)
a large vehicle that carries a lot of people along the road and stops often so they can get on and off: *We went to town by **bus**.* ◇ *Where do you get off the **bus**?* ◇ *'How do you get to school?' 'By **bus**.'*

bush (say **buush**) *noun*
1 (*plural* **bushes**) a plant like a small tree with many branches: *a rose **bush***
2 the bush (*no plural*) wild country with many small trees in Africa or Australia: *coastal **bush***
▶ **bushy** (*adjective*): *a **bushy** area* (= an area with many bushes) ◇ *a **bushy** tail* (= a tail that grows thickly like a bush)

Bushman (say **buush**-muhn) *noun* (*plural* **Bushmen**) (also **San**)
a member of the people who have lived in southern Africa since very early times ➲ See **San**
🛈 ORIGIN: 17th century, from Dutch *boschjesman*, from *bosch* meaning 'bush' + *man* meaning 'man'

> USAGE Some people think **Bushman** is offensive or old-fashioned and prefer to use the word **San** to refer to this group of people.

bushveld (say **buush**-felt) *noun* (*no plural*)
1 a large natural area with bushes
2 the Bushveld the hot dry areas of northern South Africa
🛈 ORIGIN: 19th century, through Afrikaans *bosveld* from *bos* meaning 'bush' + *veld* meaning 'open countryside'

business (say **biz**-nuhss) *noun*
1 (*no plural*) buying and selling things: *I want to go into **business** when I leave school.* ◇ ***Business** is not very good this year.*
2 (*plural* **businesses**) a place where people sell or make things, for example a shop or factory
3 (*no plural*) the work that you do as your job: *The manager will be away on **business** next week.* ◇ *a **business** trip*

businesslike (say **biz**-nuhss-like) *adjective*
being professional and practical, not friendly: *My aunt had a **businesslike** manner.*

businessperson (say **biz**-nuhss-pur-suhn) *noun* (*plural* **businesspeople**)
a person who works in business, especially at a senior level

busker (say **buss**-kuh) *noun* (*plural* **buskers**)
a person who plays music in the street for money

bust[1] *noun* (*plural* **busts**)
1 a model in stone, clay or wood of a person's head, shoulders and chest
2 a woman's chest

bust[2] *verb* (**busting**, **busted**) (*informal*)
to break: *You **bust** my cellphone!*
▶ **bust** (*adjective*): *My cellphone is **bust**.*

bustle (say **buss**-l) *verb* (**bustling**, **bustled**)
to move in a busy, noisy or excited way: *They **bustled** around the kitchen buttering scones.*
▶ **bustle** (*noun*): *I love the **bustle** of the market on a Saturday.*

busy (say **biz**-ee) *adjective* (**busier**, **busiest**)
1 working, not free and with a lot of things that you must do: *Dr Mahomed can't see you now – he's **busy**.*
2 with a lot of things happening: *I had a **busy** morning.* ◇ *The shops are always **busy**.*
3 (used about a telephone) being used: *The line is **busy** – I'll try again later.* ➲ SYNONYM **engaged** 2
▶ **busily** (*adverb*): *She was **busily** writing a letter.*

A B C D E F G H I J K L M N O P Q R S T U V W X Y Z

busybody (say **biz**-ee-bod-ee) *noun* (*plural* **busybodies**)
a person who is too interested in other people's private lives

but¹ *conjunction*
a word that you use to show something different: *I like sweets* ***but*** *I don't like chocolate.* ◇ *He worked hard* ***but*** *he didn't pass the exam.* ◇ *The weather was sunny* ***but*** *cold.*

but² *preposition*
except: *She eats nothing* ***but*** *chocolate.*

butcher (say **buu**-chuh) *noun* (*plural* **butchers**)
a person who works in a shop that sells meat: *Ask the* ***butcher*** *for some steak.*

butler (say **but**-luh) *noun* (*plural* **butlers**)
the main male servant in a large house, who organizes and serves food and wine

butt (say **but**) *noun* (*plural* **butts**)
1 the end of a cigarette that has been smoked
2 the thicker end of a tool or weapon

butter (say **but**-uh) *noun* (*no plural*)
a soft yellow food that is made from cream. You put it on bread or use it in cooking: *She spread* ***butter*** *on the bread.*
▸ **butter** (*verb*): *I* ***buttered*** *the toast.*
ORIGIN: from Old English *butere*, related to Dutch *boter*

butterfly (say **but**-uh-fly) *noun* (*plural* **butterflies**)
an insect with big coloured wings

butternut (say **but**-uh-nut) *noun* (*plural* **butternuts**)
a type of **pumpkin** with a round base and a narrower neck

buttock (say **but**-uhk) *noun* (*plural* **buttocks**)
one of the two parts of your body that you sit on

button (say **but**-uhn) *noun* (*plural* **buttons**)
1 a small round piece of plastic, wood or metal on clothes that holds them together: *There are five* ***buttons*** *on my shirt.*
2 a small thing on a machine, that you push: *Press this* ***button*** *to ring the bell.*

buttress (say **but**-ruhss) *noun* (*plural* **buttresses**)
a stone or brick structure that supports a wall or makes it stronger

buy (*rhymes with* **my**) *verb* (**buying, bought**)
to pay money to get something: *I* ***bought*** *a new watch.* ◇ *He* ***bought*** *the car from a friend.*
➲ See **sell**

buzz (say **buz**) *verb* (**buzzing, buzzed**)
to make the sound that a flying insect such as a bee makes: *A fly was* ***buzzing*** *against the window.*
▸ **buzz** (*noun*): *the* ***buzz*** *of insects*

by¹ (*rhymes with* **my**) *preposition*
1 very near: *The telephone is* ***by*** *the door.* ◇ *They live* ***by*** *the sea.* ➲ SYNONYM **beside**
2 a word that shows who or what did something: *a painting* ***by*** *Matisse* ◇ *She was caught* ***by*** *the police.*
3 using or doing something: *I go to work* ***by*** *train.* ◇ *You turn the TV on* ***by*** *pressing this button.*
4 as a result of something: *I got on the wrong bus* ***by*** *mistake.* ◇ *We met* ***by*** *chance.*
5 not later than: *I must finish this work* ***by*** *six o'clock.* ➲ SYNONYM **before¹** 1
6 from one side of a person or thing to the other: *He walked* ***by*** *me without speaking.* ➲ SYNONYM **past³** 2
7 used for showing the measurements of an area: *The table is two metres* ***by*** *one metre* (= two metres long and one metre wide).

> USAGE Be careful how you use **by** when you mean 'at or near a place'. It means 'right next to particular place': *I can see her standing* ***by*** *the gate.*
> - Don't say 'We live there, by Langa'. Instead, say: '*We live there,* ***in*** *Langa.*'
> - Don't say 'The meeting is by the school'. Instead, say: '*The meeting is* ***at*** *the school.*'
> - Don't say 'She's staying by her cousin.' Instead, say: '*She's staying* ***at*** *her cousin's home.*'

by² (*rhymes with* **my**) *adverb*
past: *She drove* ***by*** *without stopping.*

bye (*rhymes with* **my**) *exclamation* (also **bye-bye**) (*informal*)
goodbye: ***Bye!*** *See you tomorrow.*

bypass¹ (say **by**-paass) *noun* (*plural* **bypasses**)
a road that goes around a city or town instead of through it

bypass² (say **by**-paass) *verb* (**bypassing, bypassed**)
to go around something instead of through it: *We decided to* ***bypass*** *the beach on our way home.*

by-product (say **by**-prod-ukt) *noun* (*plural* **by-products**)
1 something that is formed during the making of something else
2 something that happens as a result of something else: *Poverty is a* ***by-product*** *of unemployment.*

byte (say **bite**) *noun* (*plural* **bytes**) (*computing*)
a unit of information in a computer

Cc

C *abbreviation*
1 Celsius, centigrade
2 century

c *abbreviation*
1 cent
2 circa

© *symbol* **copyright**

cab (say **kab**) *noun* (*plural* **cabs**)
1 a car that is used as a **taxi**
2 the part of a truck, train or bus where the driver sits

cabaret (say **kab**-uh-ray) *noun* (*plural* **cabarets**)
entertainment with singing, dancing and funny acts in a restaurant or club

cabbage (say **kab**-ij) *noun* (*plural* **cabbages**)
a large round vegetable with thick green, red or white leaves

cabin (say **kab**-in) *noun* (*plural* **cabins**)
1 a small bedroom on a ship
2 the part of a plane where people sit: *the passengers in the first-class* ***cabin***
3 a small simple house made of wood: *a log* ***cabin***

cabinet (say **kab**-i-nuht) *noun*
1 (*plural* **cabinets**) a piece of furniture that you can keep things in: *a bathroom* ***cabinet*** ◇ *a filing* ***cabinet*** (= one to keep documents in)
2 the Cabinet (*no plural*) a group of ministers working with the leader of a country, who are responsible for government policy

cable (say **kayb**-l) *noun* (*plural* **cables**)
1 a strong thick metal rope
2 a wire that carries electricity or messages

cache (say **kash**) *noun* (*plural* **caches**)
1 a collection of things such as drugs or weapons that have been hidden
2 (*computing*) the part of a computer's memory used for storing data that needs to be found quickly

cackle (say **kak**-l) *verb* (**cackling, cackled**)
1 to make a sound such as that of a chicken
2 to laugh in a high, loud and unpleasant way: *They all* ***cackled*** *with laughter.*
▸ **cackle** (*noun*): *the* ***cackle*** *of hens*

cacophony (say kuh-**kof**-uh-nee) *noun* (*plural* **cacophonies**)
a noisy mixture of sounds: *a* ***cacophony*** *of car alarms*

cactus (say **kak**-tuhss) *noun* (*plural* **cacti** or **cactuses**)
a plant with a thick stem and many small sharp points (called **prickles**) that grows in hot dry places

caddie (say **kad**-ee) *noun* (*plural* **caddies**)
a person who carries the bag with sticks (called **golf clubs**) during a game of golf

cadence (say **kay**-duhnss) *noun* (*plural* **cadences**) (*formal*)
1 the way in which your voice rises and falls when you speak
2 (*music*) the final notes in a musical passage

cadet (say kuh-**det**) *noun* (*plural* **cadets**)
a person who is training to be in the army, navy, air force or police

Caesarean (say suh-**zair**-ri-uhn) *noun* (*plural* **Caesareans**) (also **Caesarian**)
a medical operation in which an opening is cut in a mother's body in order to take out a baby: *an emergency* ***Caesarean***
🛈 **ORIGIN:** 17th century, from *Caesarian*, based on the story that Julius Caesar (100–44 BC), a Roman general and political leader, was born in this way

WORD BUILDING This operation is also called a **Caesarean section** or **Caesar**.

cafe (say **kaf**-ay or **kaf**-ee) *noun* (*plural* **cafes**) (also **café**)
1 a small restaurant
2 (*S. African*) a small shop that sells sweets, cigarettes, newspapers and some **groceries**

cafeteria (say kaf-uh-**teer**-ri-uh) *noun* (*plural* **cafeterias**)
a restaurant where you choose and pay for your meal and then carry it to a table. Places such as factories and hospitals often have **cafeterias**.

caffeine (say **kaf**-een) *noun* (*no plural*)
the substance in coffee and tea that makes you feel more active and awake ➲ See **decaffeinated**

cage (say **kayj**) *noun* (*plural* **cages**)
a place with bars round it where animals or birds are kept so that they cannot escape

cake¹ (say **kayk**) *noun* (*plural* **cakes**)
a sweet food that you make from flour, eggs, sugar and butter and bake in the oven: *a chocolate* ***cake*** ◇ *Would you like a piece of* ***cake****?*

A B C D E F G H I J K L M N O P Q R S T U V W X Y Z

cake² (say **kayk**) *verb* (**caking, caked**)
to cover something with a thick or sticky substance that becomes hard when it dries: *Their hair was **caked** with dirt.* ◇ *He was **caked** in mud.*

calabash (say **kal**-uh-bash) *noun* (*plural* **calabashes**)
a type of large fruit with a hard skin and soft flesh inside that is often dried and used as a container
ORIGIN: 17th century, through French *calebasse*, from Spanish *calabaza*

calamari (say kal-uh-**maah**-ree) (*no plural*)
squid eaten as food

calamity (say ka-**lam**-i-tee) *noun* (*plural* **calamities**)
something very bad that happens and causes a lot of damage or suffering: *natural **calamities** such as earthquakes, floods and hurricanes*

calcium (say **kal**-si-uhm) *noun* (*no plural*) (symbol Ca)
a chemical element that you should have in your diet to keep your bones and teeth strong

calculate (say **kal**-kyoo-layt) *verb* (**calculating, calculated**)
to find an amount or a number by using mathematics: *Can you **calculate** how much the holiday will cost?*

calculation (say kal-kyoo-**lay**-shuhn) *noun* (*plural* **calculations**)
a way of finding an answer by using mathematics

calculator (say **kal**-kyoo-lay-tuh) *noun* (*plural* **calculators**)
a small electronic instrument that you use for calculating numbers

calculus (say **kal**-kyoo-luhss) *noun* (*no plural*)
the study in mathematics of rates of change, for example in the slope of a curve or the speed of a falling object

calendar (say **kal**-in-duh) *noun* (*plural* **calendars**)
a list of the days, weeks and months of one year

SPELLING Remember! You spell **calendar** with **-ar** at the end.

calf (say **kaaf**) *noun* (*plural* **calves**)
1 the back of your leg, below your knee
➲ See illustration at **body**
2 a young cow

calf bone *noun* (*plural* **calf bones**) (also **fibula**)
the outer bone of the two bones in the leg between the knee and the ankle ➲ See illustration at **skeleton**

calibre (say **kal**-i-buh) *noun* (*plural* **calibres**)
1 the level of a person's ability or the quality of something: *The company's employees are of a high **calibre**.*
2 the width of the inside of a tube or a gun **barrel** 2: *a small-**calibre** rifle*

call¹ (say **kawl**) *verb* (**calling, called**)
1 to give a name to a person or a thing: *They **called** the baby Lindiwe.*
2 to speak loudly and clearly: *'Lunch is ready,' she **called**.* ◇ *She **called** out the names of the winners.*
3 to telephone somebody: *I'll **call** you later.* ◇ *Who's **calling**, please?* ➲ SYNONYM **ring²** 1
4 to ask somebody to come: *He was so ill that we had to **call** the doctor.*
5 to make a short visit: *We **called** at his house but there was nobody home.*
be called to have as a name: *'What is your teacher **called**?' 'She's **called** Mrs Maharaj.'*
call somebody back to telephone somebody again: *I can't talk now – I'll **call** you back later.*
call something off to say that a planned activity or event will not happen: *The match was **called** off because of bad weather.*
➲ SYNONYM **cancel**

call² (say **kawl**) *noun* (*plural* **calls**)
1 an act of using the telephone or a conversation on the telephone: *I got a **call** from Zolani.* ◇ *I'll give you a **call** later.*
2 a loud cry or shout: *a **call** for help*
3 a short visit to somebody: *The doctor has several **calls** to make this morning.*

calligraphy (say kuh-**lig**-ruh-fee) *noun* (*no plural*)
the art of producing beautiful writing by hand

calling (say **kawl**-ing) *noun* (*plural* **callings**)
a job or profession, especially one that you believe is suitable for you or you have been specially chosen for: *a **calling** to preach*

callous (say **kal**-uhss) *adjective*
unkind and not caring about the feelings of other people: *a cruel and **callous** act*

calm¹ (say **kaam**) *adjective* (**calmer, calmest**)
1 quiet, and not excited or afraid: *Keep **calm** – there's no danger.*
2 without big waves: *a **calm** sea*

3 without much wind: ***calm*** *weather*
▸ **calm** (*noun*): *a time of* ***calm***
▸ **calmly** (*adverb*): *He spoke* ***calmly*** *about the accident.*

calm² (say **kaam**) *verb* (**calming, calmed**)
to make an animal or person less afraid or excited: *The mother* ***calmed*** *her crying baby.*
calm down to become less afraid or excited or to make somebody less afraid or excited: ***Calm down*** *and tell me what happened.*

calorie (say **kal**-uh-ree) *noun* (*plural* **calories**)
1 a unit for measuring the energy value of food: *a low-****calorie*** *drink* ◇ *Food that has a lot of* ***calories*** *in it can make you fat.*
2 (*science*) a unit for measuring a quantity of heat. A **calorie** is the amount of heat needed to increase the temperature of a gram of water by one degree Celsius. ➲ See **joule** and **kilojoule**

calves (say **kaavz**) *noun* plural of **calf**

calyx (say **kay**-likss) *noun* (*plural* **calyxes** or **calyces**) (*biology*)
the group of small leaves (called **sepals**) that surrounds and protects a flower before it opens
➲ See illustration at **flower**

cam (say **kam**) *noun* (*plural* **cams**) (*technology*)
a part in a machine that turns and changes the movement of another piece of the machine when it touches it

camaraderie (say kam-uh-**raad**-uh-ree) *noun* (*no plural*)
a feeling of friendship and trust that two or more people share: *Mawethu misses the* ***camaraderie*** *of his classmates.*

cambium (say **kam**-bi-uhm) *noun* (*plural* **cambia** or **cambiums**) (*biology*)
a layer of cells in plants that keeps on growing and makes the roots and stems of the plant thicker

camcorder (say **kam**-kawd-uh) *noun* (*plural* **camcorders**)
a camera that you can carry around and use for recording moving pictures and sound
🛈 **Camcorder** is short for 'camera' + 'recorder'.
➲ See **video**

came (say **kaym**) form of **come**

camel (say **kam**-uhl) *noun* (*plural* **camels**)
a large mammal with one or two round parts (called **humps**) on its back. **Camels** carry people and goods in hot dry places.

camel

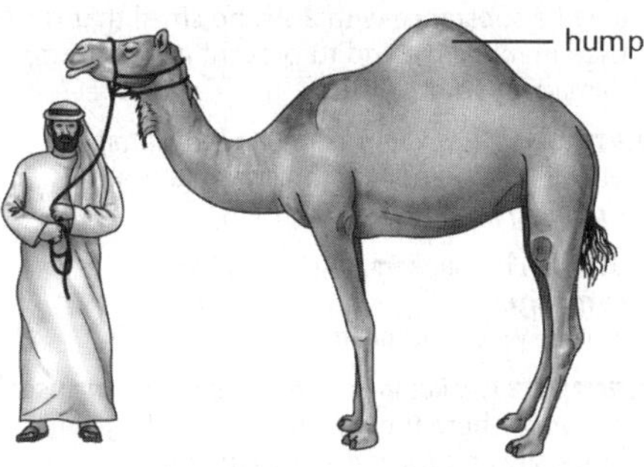

cameo (say **kam**-ee-oh) *noun* (*plural* **cameos**)
1 a small part in a film or play that is played by a famous actor
2 a piece of jewellery that has a design in one colour and a background in a different colour

camera (say **kam**-uh-ruh) *noun* (*plural* **cameras**)
a piece of equipment that you use for taking photographs or moving pictures: *a digital* ***camera***

camouflage (say **kam**-uh-flaaj) *noun* (*no plural*)
1 anything that makes soldiers or their equipment difficult for their enemy to see: ***camouflage*** *uniforms*
2 the way in which the shape and colour of an animal makes it difficult for others to see
▸ **camouflage** (*verb*): *The white fur of the polar bear* ***camouflages*** *it well in a snowy landscape.*

camp¹ (say **kamp**) *noun* (*plural* **camps**)
a place where people live in tents for a short time

camp² (say **kamp**) *verb* (**camping, camped**)
to live in a tent for a short time: *The children* ***camped*** *in the garden overnight.*

> **USAGE** It is more usual to say **go camping** when you mean that you are staying in a tent on holiday: *We* ***went camping*** *in the mountains last summer.*

campaign¹ (say kam-**payn**) *noun* (*plural* **campaigns**)
a plan to do a number of things in order to get a special result: *a* ***campaign*** *to stop people smoking*

campaign² (say kam-**payn**) *verb* (**campaigning, campaigned**)
to take part in planned activities in order to get a special result: *The school is* ***campaigning*** *for new computer equipment.*

A B C D E F G H I J K L M N O P Q R S T U V W X Y Z

camphor (say **kam**-fuh) *noun* (*no plural*)
a white substance with a strong smell that is used in medicine and to prevent insects from damaging your clothes

camping (say **kamp**-ing) *noun* (*no plural*)
sleeping or spending a holiday in a tent: *Camping is no fun when it rains.*

campsite (say **kamp**-site) *noun* (*plural* **campsites**)
a place where you can stay in a tent

campus (say **kamp**-uhss) *noun* (*plural* **campuses**)
the area where the buildings of a college or university are: *the university **campus***

can[1] (say **kan**) *modal verb* (**could**)
1 to be able to do something, or to be strong enough or clever enough to do something: *She **can** speak three languages.* ◇ ***Can** you fly a plane?*
2 to be possible or likely to happen: *It **can** be very cold in the mountains in winter.*
3 a word that you use with verbs such as 'see', 'hear', 'smell' and 'taste': *I **can** smell something burning.* ◇ *I **can't** hear the TV.*
4 to be allowed to do something: *You **can** go now.* ◇ *The doctor said she **can't** go back to school yet.*
5 a word that you use when you ask somebody to do something: ***Can** you tell me the time, please?* ➲ See **modal verb**

USAGE
- The negative form of **can** is **cannot** or **can't**: *She **can't** swim.*
- The past tense of **can** is **could**: *We **could** see the sea from our hotel room.*
- The future tense of **can** is **will be able to**: *You **will be able to** see it if you stand here.*

WHICH WORD? **Can** or **may**?
- **Can** is used to mean **able** to do something: *Can you swim?* (Do you know how to swim?)
- In formal English **may** is used to mean **allowed** to do something: ***May** we swim?* (Are we allowed to swim?)
- In informal English we often use **can I...?** to mean **am I allowed to...?**

can[2] (say **kan**) *noun* (*plural* **cans**)
a metal container for food or drink that keeps it fresh: *a **can** of lemonade* ➲ SYNONYM **tin** 2

can[3] (say **kan**) *verb* (**canning, canned**)
to put food or drink into a metal can in order to keep it fresh for a long time

canal (say kuh-**nal**) *noun* (*plural* **canals**)
1 a passage made through land and filled with water on which boats can travel: *the Suez **Canal***
2 a smaller passage for carrying water to fields and crops

canary (say kuh-**nair**-ree) *noun* (*plural* **canaries**)
a small singing bird that people often keep as a pet

cancel (say **kan**-suhl) *verb* (**cancelling, cancelled**)
to say that a planned activity or event will not happen: *The singer was ill, so the concert was **cancelled**.*

cancellation (say kan-suh-**lay**-shuhn) *noun* (*plural* **cancellations**)
a decision that a planned activity or event will not happen: *the **cancellation** of the President's visit*

cancer (say **kan**-suh) *noun* (*no plural*)
a very dangerous illness that makes some cells in the body grow too fast and kill normal cells: *Smoking can cause **cancer**.*

candela (say kan-**del**-uh or **kan**-deel-uh) *noun* (*plural* **candelas**) (*science*) (abbr. cd)
a unit used for measuring how bright a light is

candid (say **kan**-did) *adjective*
very honest and open in what you say or write ➲ SYNONYM **frank** ➲ The noun is **candour**
► **candidly** (*adverb*): *She spoke **candidly** about her personal life.*

candidate (say **kan**-di-duht) *noun* (*plural* **candidates**)
1 a person who wants to be chosen for something: *There were a lot of **candidates** for the job.* ◇ ***candidates** in an election*
2 a person who is writing an exam

candle (say **kan**-duhl) *noun* (*plural* **candles**)
a stick of wax with a piece of string in the middle (called a **wick**) that burns to give light
❶ ORIGIN: through Old English, from Latin *candere* meaning 'white or shining'

candlestick (say **kan**-duhl-stik) *noun* (*plural* **candlesticks**)
a thing that holds a candle

candour (say **kan**-duh) *noun* (*no plural*)
the quality of being honest and open in what you say or write ➲ The adjective is **candid**

cane[1] (say **kayn**) *noun* (*plural* **canes**)
1 the long, hard, smooth stem that some plants have: *sugar **cane*** ◇ *Bamboo **cane** is used for furniture.*
2 a stick used to help a person walk: *walk with a **cane***

cane[2] (say **kayn**) *verb* (**caning, caned**)
to hit somebody with a stick as punishment

canine[1] (say **kay**-nine) *noun* (*plural* **canines**) (also **canine tooth**)
one of the four pointed teeth in the front of a person's or an animal's mouth ➲ See **incisor**, **molar**

canine[2] (say **kay**-nine) *adjective* (*formal*)
relating to dogs: *The police use their* ***canine*** *unit to search for drugs.*

canister (say **kan**-iss-tuh) *noun* (*plural* **canisters**)
a small round metal container: *a gas* ***canister*** ◇ *a film* ***canister***

cannabis (say **kan**-uh-biss) *noun* (*no plural*)
a plant whose dried leaves and flowers are smoked as a drug. The drug is illegal in many countries. ➲ SYNONYMS **dagga**, **marijuana**

canned (say **kand**) *adjective*
in a can: ***canned*** *fruit*

cannibal (say **kan**-ib-l) *noun* (*plural* **cannibals**)
a person who eats other people
🛈 **ORIGIN:** 16th century, from Spanish *Canibales*, from *Caribes*, the name of a group of Caribbean people who the Spanish thought ate people.

cannon (say **kan**-uhn) *noun* (*plural* **cannons**)
1 a large simple gun used in past times to fire large stone or metal balls
2 a large automatic gun on military aircraft, vehicles or ships
🛈 **ORIGIN:** 19th century, through Spanish *cañón* meaning 'tube' from Latin *canna* meaning 'reed, cane'

cannot (say **kan**-not) form of **can**[1]

canoe (say kuh-**noo**) *noun* (*plural* **canoes**)
a light narrow boat for one or two people that you move through the water using a flat piece of wood (called a **paddle**): *We went* ***canoeing*** *on the river.*
🛈 **ORIGIN:** 16th century, through Spanish *canoa*, from Carib *canaoua*. Carib is a South American language. Spanish colonists brought the word to Europe.

canola (say kuh-**noh**-luh) *noun* (*no plural*)
a crop plant, the seeds of which are used to produce an oil for cooking: ***canola*** *oil*

canopy (say **kan**-uh-pee) *noun* (*plural* **canopies**)
something that forms a cover or covering over another thing: *a* ***canopy*** *for a bakkie* ◇ *the* ***canopies*** *of trees*
🛈 **ORIGIN:** 14th–15th century, from Latin *canopeum* meaning 'ceremonial canopy', an alteration of Latin *conopeum* meaning 'mosquito net over a bed', from Greek *kōnōpeion* meaning 'couch with mosquito curtains'

can't (say **kaant**) short for **cannot**

cantankerous (say kan-**tang**-kuh-ruhss) *adjective*
bad-tempered and prepared to argue or complain: *a* ***cantankerous*** *old man*

cantata (say kan-**taa**-tuh) *noun* (*plural* **cantatas**)
a piece of music, often on a religious subject, for singers and musical instruments: *Bach wrote many* ***cantatas****.*

canteen (say kan-**teen**) *noun* (*plural* **canteens**)
a place where people can get a meal when they are at school or work ➲ See **cafeteria**

canter (say **kan**-tuh) *verb* (**cantering**, **cantered**)
(used about a horse and its rider) to run fairly fast but not very ➲ See **gallop**, **trot**
▸ **canter** (*noun*): *She set off at a* ***canter****.*

cantilever (say **kan**-ti-lee-vuh) *noun* (*plural* **cantilevers**) (*technology*)
a long piece of metal or wood fixed to a wall that supports a bridge or other structure: *a* ***cantilever*** *bridge*

canvas (say **kan**-vuhss) *noun* (*no plural*)
a strong heavy cloth, used for making tents, bags and sails, and for painting pictures on

canvass (say **kan**-vuhss) *verb* (**canvassing**, **canvassed**)
1 to ask people to support a plan or a political party in an election: *to* ***canvass*** *for votes*
2 to find out what people think about a particular matter: *They* ***canvassed*** *opinions from local residents.*

canyon (say **kan**-yuhn) *noun* (*plural* **canyons**) (*geography*)
a deep valley with steep sides of rock

cap (say **kap**) *noun* (*plural* **caps**)
1 a soft hat with a hard curved part at the front: *a baseball* ***cap***
2 a covering that fits over the top of a bottle or tube: *Put the* ***cap*** *back on the bottle.*

capable (say **kay**-puhb-l) *adjective*
1 able to do something: *You are* ***capable*** *of passing the exam if you work harder.*
2 able to do things well: *a* ***capable*** *student*
➲ OPPOSITE **incapable**
▸ **capability** (*noun*): *These sums are beyond my* ***capabilities*** (= they are too difficult for me).

capacity (say kuh-**pass**-i-tee) *noun* (*plural* **capacities**)
1 the amount that a container or space can hold: *a tank with a* ***capacity*** *of 1 000 litres*
2 the ability to understand or do something: *She has a* ***capacity*** *for hard work.*
🛈 **ORIGIN:** 14th–15th century, through French from Latin *capere* meaning 'take or hold'

A B C D E F G H I J K L M N O P Q R S T U V W X Y Z

cape (say **kayp**) *noun* (*plural* **capes**)
1 a high part of the land that goes out into the sea: *a rocky* ***cape*** ◊ ***Cape*** *Agulhas*
2 a piece of clothing that covers your body and your arms, but does not have separate sleeves

Cape Dutch *adjective*
a style of architecture and furniture that was developed at the Cape of Good Hope in the eighteenth century

Cape Floral Kingdom *noun* (*no plural*)
a group of plant types that grow mainly in the Western and Eastern Cape, consisting mainly of **fynbos**

caper (say **kay**-puh) *noun* (*plural* **capers**)
1 (*informal*) a silly or an illegal activity: *The audience laughed at the* ***capers*** *of the clown.*
2 a playful dancing or skipping movement

capillary (say kuh-**pil**-uh-ree) *noun* (*plural* **capillaries**)
one of the many small narrow tubes that carry blood around the body ➲ See **artery**, **vein**

capital (say **kap**-it-l) *noun*
1 (*plural* **capitals**) the most important city in a country, where the government is: *Windhoek is the* ***capital*** *of Namibia.*
2 (*no plural*) (*business*) a large amount of money that you use to start a business: *When she had enough* ***capital****, she bought a shop.*
3 (*plural* **capitals**) (also **capital letter**) a big letter of the alphabet, used at the beginning of sentences, for example 'A' or 'B': *Names of people and places begin with a* ***capital*** *letter.*
➲ See Study page 16
🛈 **ORIGIN**: 13th–15th century, through Old French from Latin *caput* meaning 'head'

capitalism (say **kap**-i-tuh-liz-m) *noun* (*no plural*)
an economic system in which individuals own businesses and run them for profit, not the government

capitalist (say **kap**-i-tuh-list) *noun* (*plural* **capitalists**)
1 a person who believes that **capitalism** is the best type of economic system
2 a person who makes a lot of money for themselves through business
▸ **capitalist** (*adjective*): *We are living in a* ***capitalist*** *society.*

capitalize (say **kap**-i-tuh-lize) *verb* (**capitalizing**, **capitalized**) (also **capitalise**)
1 to write or print something with capital letters, or with a capital letter at the beginning
2 (*business*) to supply money for the development of a business or a project
3 to use something to gain an advantage: *We can* ***capitalize*** *on the mistakes of our rivals.*
▸ **capitalization** (*noun*) (also **capitalisation**)

capital punishment *noun* (*no plural*)
punishment by death for crimes such as murder, rape and **treason**

capitulate (say kuh-**pit**-shuu-layt) *verb* (**capitulating**, **capitulated**) (*formal*)
to stop fighting because you cannot win or to give in to somebody
▸ **capitulation** (*noun*): *the* ***capitulation*** *of the Japanese in 1945*

cappuccino (say kap-*uu*-**chee**-noh) *noun* (*plural* **cappuccinos**)
a cup of coffee mixed with hot milk that is frothy (= with many small white bubbles)

> **SPELLING** Remember! You spell **cappuccino** with **pp** and **cc**.

capricious (say kuh-**pree**-shuhss) *adjective*
(of a person) changing their behaviour suddenly in a way that is difficult to predict: ***capricious*** *teenager moods*

capsize (say kap-**size**) *verb* (**capsizing**, **capsized**)
(of a boat) to turn over in the water: *A big wave* ***capsized*** *the boat.*

capsule (say **kap**-syool) *noun* (*plural* **capsules**)
1 a very small container with medicine inside that you swallow
2 a container that is closed so that air or water cannot enter: *a space* ***capsule*** (= the part of a spacecraft in which people travel)

captain (say **kap**-tuhn) *noun* (*plural* **captains**)
1 the person who is in charge of a ship or an aircraft: *The* ***captain*** *landed the plane safely.*
2 the leader of a group of people: *the* ***captain*** *of the netball team*

caption (say **kap**-shuhn) *noun* (*plural* **captions**)
the words above or below a picture in a book or newspaper that explain what it is about

captivate (say **kap**-ti-vayt) *verb* (**captivating**, **captivated**)
to attract and hold somebody's attention
▸ **captivating** (*adjective*): *a* ***captivating*** *singer and performer*

captive (say **kap**-tiv) *noun* (*plural* **captives**)
a person who is not free ➲ **SYNONYM** **prisoner**

captivity (say kap-**tiv**-uh-tee) *noun* (*no plural*)
being kept in a place that you cannot leave: *Wild animals rarely do well in* ***captivity****.*

captor (say **kap**-tuh) *noun* (*plural* **captors**)
a person who keeps somebody as a prisoner

capture (say **kap**-tshuh) *verb* (**capturing, captured**)
1 to catch a person or animal and keep them somewhere so that they cannot leave: *The police* ***captured*** *the criminals.*
2 to take control of something: *The rebels* ***captured*** *the town.*
3 to successfully represent or record something in words or pictures: *The robbery was* ***captured*** *on video.*
4 to put data into a computer in a form that it can use
▶ **capture** (*noun*): *the* ***capture*** *of the escaped prisoners*

car (say **kaa**) *noun* (*plural* **cars**) (also **motor car**)
a road vehicle with an engine and four wheels that can carry a small number of passengers: *She travels to work by* ***car***.

carbohydrate (say kaa-boh-**hide**-rayt) *noun* (*plural* **carbohydrates**) (*science*)
one of the substances in certain foods, for example sugar and cereals, that gives your body energy: *Bread and rice contain* ***carbohydrates***.

carbon (say **kaa**-buhn) *noun* (*no plural*) (*science*) (symbol C)
the chemical that coal and diamonds are made of and that is in all living things

carbonated (say **kaa**-buh-nayt-uhd) *adjective*
(used about a liquid) containing **carbon dioxide** gas under pressure so that it has bubbles: ***carbonated*** *water*

carbon dioxide (say kaa-buhn dy-**okss**-ide) *noun* (*no plural*) (symbol CO_2)
a gas without colour or smell that people and animals breathe out and that is released when **carbon** burns

car

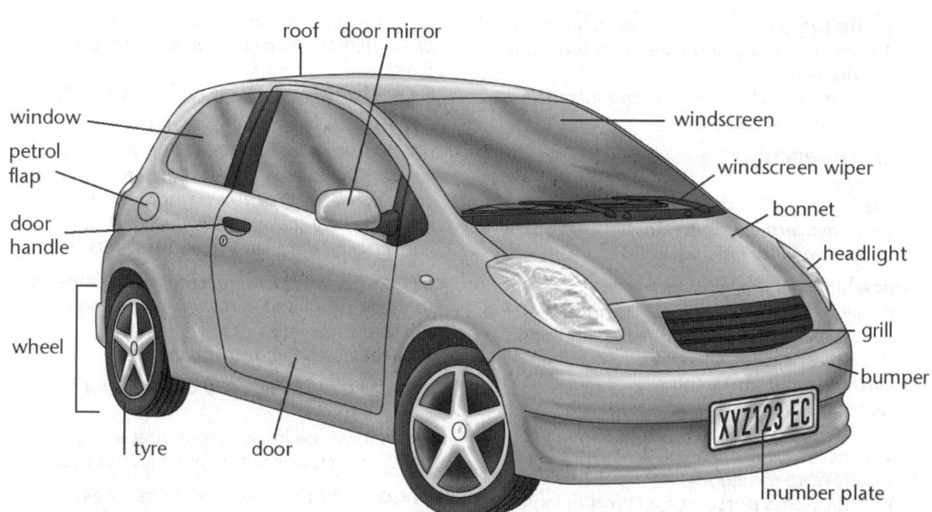

caramel (say **ka**-ruh-mel) *noun* (*no plural*)
1 a sticky sweet made from sugar, butter and milk
2 sugar that is heated until it turns brown and is used to add flavour and colour to food

carat (say **ka**-ruht) *noun* (*plural* **carats**)
1 a unit used for measuring the weight of diamonds and other precious stones
2 a unit used for measuring how pure gold is

caravan (say **ka**-ruh-van) *noun* (*plural* **caravans**)
a large **trailer** in which you can sleep, cook and live when you are travelling or on holiday

carburettor (say kaa-buh-**ret**-uh) *noun* (*plural* **carburettors**)
a device in the engine of a vehicle that mixes petrol and air

carcass (say **kaa**-kuhss) *noun* (*plural* **carcasses**)
the dead body of an animal: *A* ***carcass*** *of a whale washed up on the beach.*

card (say **kaad**) *noun* (*plural* **cards**)
1 a stiff piece of paper with writing or pictures on it: *We send birthday* ***cards*** *and* ***postcards*** *to our friends.*
2 (also **playing card**) one of a set of 52 cards (called a **pack of cards**) that you use to play

A B C D E F G H I J K L M N O P Q R S T U V W X Y Z

games: *a game of **cards** ◇ They often play **cards** in the evening.* ➲ See **credit card**, **phonecard**

cardboard (say **kaad**-bawd) *noun* (*no plural*) very thick paper that is used for making boxes

cardiac (say **kaa**-di-ak) *adjective* of or relating to the heart: ***cardiac** arrest ◇ a **cardiac** monitor*

cardigan (say **kaa**-di-guhn) *noun* (*plural* **cardigans**) a piece of clothing which fastens at the front like a jacket and is usually made of wool
🛈 **ORIGIN**: 19th century, from James Brudenell, Earl of Cardigan in Wales (1797–1868), a British army officer whose soldiers first wore cardigans

cardinal number (say kaa-din-l **num**-buh) *noun* (*plural* **cardinal numbers**) (*maths*) a whole number that shows a quantity, for example 0, 3, 8 and 10: *Four and five are **cardinal numbers** but fourth and fifth are ordinal numbers.* ➲ See Study page 20 ➲ See **ordinal number**

cardiology (say kaa-di-**ol**-uh-jee) *noun* (*no plural*) the scientific study of the heart, its functions and diseases
▶ **cardiologist** (*noun*): *The **cardiologist** treated my chest pains.*

cardiovascular (say kaa-di-oh-**vass**-kyuh-luh) *adjective* relating to the heart and blood **circulation** 1 in the body: ***cardiovascular** fitness ◇ **cardiovascular** diseases*

care[1] (say **kair**) *noun* (*no plural*) thinking about what you are doing so that you do not make a mistake or break something: *Wash these glasses with **care**!*
care of (a person) another word for **c/o**
take care
1 to be careful: *Take **care** crossing the road.*
2 (*informal*) used when you are saying 'goodbye' to somebody: *Bye now! Take **care**!*
take care of a person or **a thing** to look after a person or a thing, or to do what is necessary: *She is taking **care** of her sister's baby today.*

care[2] (say **kair**) *verb* (**caring**, **cared**) to think that somebody or something is important: *The only thing he **cares** about is sport. ◇ I don't **care** what other people think.*
care for somebody to do the things for somebody that they need: *After the accident, her parents **cared** for her until she was better.*

SPEAKING In many situations it is not polite to say **I don't care**, **Who cares?** or **I couldn't care less**. You can say **I don't mind** instead: '*Would you like tea or coffee?*' '***I don't mind** – either.*'

USAGE It is not correct to say 'I'm not cared'. Instead say '*I don't **care***' (but see the note above).

career[1] (say kuh-**reer**) *noun* (*plural* **careers**) a job that you learn to do and then do for many years: *a **career** in teaching*

career[2] (say kuh-**reer**) *verb* (**careering**, **careered**) to move quickly in a way that is not controlled and cannot be stopped easily: *The truck **careered** off the road.*

carefree (say **kair**-free) *adjective* with no worries or responsibilities: *the **carefree** days of a summer holiday*

careful (say **kair**-fuul) *adjective* thinking about what you are doing so that you do not make a mistake or have an accident: *Be **careful**! There's a car coming. ◇ He's a **careful** driver.*
▶ **carefully** (*adverb*): *Please listen **carefully**.*

careless (say **kair**-luhss) *adjective* not thinking enough about what you are doing so that you make mistakes: ***Careless** drivers can cause accidents.* ➲ **SYNONYM negligent**
▶ **carelessly** (*adverb*): *She threw her coat **carelessly** on the floor.* ▶ **carelessness** (*noun*)

caress (say kuh-**ress**) *verb* (**caressing**, **caressed**) to move your hand gently over a person or a thing to show love
▶ **caress** (*noun*): *a tender **caress***

caretaker (say **kair**-tayk-uh) *noun* (*plural* **caretakers**) a person whose job is to look after a large building such as a school or a block of flats

cargo (say **kaa**-goh) *noun* (*plural* **cargoes**) the goods that a ship, train, truck or plane carries: *a **cargo** of wheat*
🛈 **ORIGIN**: 17th century, through Spanish *cargo* from Latin *carricare* meaning 'to load'

Caribbean (say ka-ri-**bee**-uhn) *adjective* relating to the people, languages and cultures of the Caribbean Sea and its islands

caricature (say **ka**-ri-kuh-tshoor) *noun* (*plural* **caricatures**) a funny drawing or description of a person or a thing in which an important feature is made more extreme than it really is

▸ **caricature** (*verb*): *He* ***caricatures*** *famous people in his cartoons.*

carnage (say **kaa**-nij) *noun* (*no plural*) (*formal*) the violent killing of a lot of people

carnival (say **kaa**-niv-l) *noun* (*plural* **carnivals**) a public festival that takes place in the streets with music and dancing: *the Rio* ***carnival***

carnivore (say **kaan**-i-vaw) *noun* (*plural* **carnivores**) an animal that mainly eats meat ➲ See **herbivore**, **omnivore**, **insectivore**
▸ **carnivorous** (*adjective*): *Lions and eagles are* ***carnivorous.***

carol (say **ka**-ruhl) *noun* (*plural* **carols**) a Christian song that people sing at Christmas

carp (say **kaap**) *noun* (*plural* **carp**) a large fish that lives in lakes and rivers

carpel (say **kaap**-l) *noun* (*plural* **carpels**) (*biology*) the organ of a flower that contains the female sex cells ➲ See illustration at **flower**

carpenter (say **kaa**-puhn-tuh) *noun* (*plural* **carpenters**) a person whose job is to make things from wood

carpentry (say **kaa**-puhn-tree) *noun* (*no plural*) the skill or work of a carpenter

carpet (say **kaa**-puht) *noun* (*plural* **carpets**) a soft covering for a floor that is often made of wool and is usually the same size as the floor

carport (say **kaa**-pawt) *noun* (*plural* **carports**) a structure with poles and a roof under which you park your car

carriage (say **ka**-rij) *noun* (*plural* **carriages**)
1 one of the parts of a train in which people travel: *a first-class* ***carriage***
➲ SYNONYM **coach**[1] 3
2 a road vehicle, usually with four wheels, that is pulled by horses and was used in the past to carry people ➲ SYNONYM **coach**[1] 4

carriageway (say **ka**-rij-way) *noun* (*plural* **carriageways**) one of the two sides of a highway on which vehicles travel in one direction only: *The outside lane of the* ***carriageway*** *was closed for repairs.*

carried (say **ka**-reed) form of **carry**

carrier (say **ka**-ri-uh) *noun* (*plural* **carriers**)
1 a company that transports people or things from one place to another: *SAA is one of the South African* ***carriers.***
2 (also **aircraft carrier**) a very large military ship with a flat deck on which planes can take off and land
3 a person or animal that is able to pass an infectious disease on to others without suffering from it themselves

carrier bag *noun* (*plural* **carrier bags**) a bag made from plastic, paper or cloth that you use for carrying shopping

carrion (say **ka**-ri-uhn) *noun* (*no plural*) the flesh of a animal that has been dead for some time: *The vultures fed on the rotting* ***carrion.***

carrot (say **ka**-ruht) *noun* (*plural* **carrots**) a long thin orange vegetable that grows under the ground

carry (*rhymes with* **marry**) *verb* (**carrying**, **carried**)
1 to hold something and take it to another place or keep it with you: *He* ***carried*** *the suitcase to my room.* ◇ *Do the police* ***carry*** *guns?*
2 to move people or things: *Special fast trains* ***carry*** *people to the city centre.*
carry on to continue: ***Carry*** *on with your work.* ◇ ***Carry*** *on to the end of this road.*
carry out something to do or finish what you have planned: *The bridge was closed while they* ***carried*** *out the repairs.*

cart[1] (say **kaat**) *noun* (*plural* **carts**) an open wooden vehicle with two or four wheels pulled by a horse or donkey

cart[2] (say **kaat**) *verb* (**carting, carted**) (*informal*) to take or carry a heavy thing somewhere, especially with difficulty: *It is a real nuisance to* ***cart*** *around these books all day.*

Cartesian (say kaa-**tee**-zhuhn) *adjective* connected with Descartes and his ideas about **philosophy** and mathematics
🛈 **ORIGIN:** 17th century, from the name of René Descartes (1596–1650), French scientist and philosopher

Cartesian coordinate *noun* (*plural* **Cartesian coordinates**) one of two numbers, one on a vertical line and one on a horizontal line, that show the exact position of something

cartilage (say **kaa**-ti-lij) *noun* (*no plural*) the strong **flexible tissue** found in places where your bones join that prevents them from rubbing against each other. It also forms the tube of your throat and the shape of your ear.

cartography (say kaa-**tog**-ruh-fee) *noun* (*no plural*) the art or process of drawing or making maps
▸ **cartographer** (*noun*): *The* ***cartographer*** *drew the map with a scale of 1: 50 000.*

A B C D E F G H I J K L M N O P Q R S T U V W X Y Z

▸ **cartographic** (*adjective*): ***cartographic** modelling*

carton (say **kaa**-tuhn) *noun* (*plural* **cartons**)
a container made of cardboard or plastic: *a **carton** of milk*

cartoon (say kaa-**toon**) *noun* (*plural* **cartoons**)
1 a funny drawing, for example in a newspaper
2 a film that tells a story by using moving drawings instead of real people and places: *a Mickey Mouse **cartoon***

cartridge (say **kaat**-rij) *noun* (*plural* **cartridges**)
1 a container with something inside it that you put into a machine to do a particular job: *an ink **cartridge** ◇ a filter **cartridge***
2 a small metal tube with explosive powder and a bullet inside it that you put into a gun

cartwheel (say **kaat**-weel) *noun* (*plural* **cartwheels**)
a fast physical movement in which you form a circle with your body by throwing it sideways, landing on your hands and bringing your legs, one at a time, over your head
▸ **cartwheel** (*verb*): *The boys **cartwheeled** along the path.*

carve (say **kaav**) *verb* (**carving, carved**)
1 to cut wood or stone to make a picture or shape: *Her father **carved** a little horse for her.*
2 to cut meat into thin pieces after you have cooked it

cascade (say kass-**kayd**) *noun* (*plural* **cascades**)
1 water that falls from a high place to a low place
2 a large quantity of something that falls or hangs down: *a **cascade** of sparks*
▸ **cascade** (*verb*): *Water **cascaded** from the roof.*

case (say **kayss**) *noun* (*plural* **cases**)
1 a situation or an example of something: *In some **cases**, learners waited months for their exam results. ◇ Two new **cases** of the disease were reported.*
2 a crime that the police must find an answer to: *a murder **case***
3 a question that people in a court of law must decide about: *a divorce **case***
4 a container or cover for keeping something in: *a pencil **case*** ➲ See **briefcase**, **suitcase**
in any case words that you use when you give a second reason for something: *I don't want to see the film, and in any **case** I'm too busy.*
➲ SYNONYM **anyway**
in case because something might happen: *Take an umbrella in **case** it rains.*
in that case if that is the situation: *'There's no coffee.' 'Well, in that **case** we'll have tea.'*

cash¹ (say **kash**) *noun* (*no plural*)
money in coins and notes: *Are you paying in **cash** or with a credit card?* ➲ See note at **money**

cash² (say **kash**) *verb* (**cashing, cashed**)
to give somebody a **cheque** and get money for it: *Can I **cash** this cheque, please?*

cashew (say **kash**-oo) *noun* (*plural* **cashews**)
a type of nut
🛈 ORIGIN: 16th century, through Portuguese, from Tupi *cajú*. Tupi is a South American language.

cash flow *noun* (*no plural*) (*business*)
the amount of money passing into and out of a business: *If a business makes more money than it spends it has a positive **cash flow**.*

cashier (say **kash**-eer) *noun* (*plural* **cashiers**)
the person whose job is to take or give out money in a bank, shop or hotel

cashmere (say **kash**-meer) *noun* (*no plural*)
a type of wool that is very fine and soft

casino (say kuh-**see**-noh) *noun* (*plural* **casinos**)
a place where people go to try to win money by playing games that need luck

cask (say **kaask**) *noun* (*plural* **casks**)
a wooden container for storing liquids, especially alcoholic drinks ➲ See **barrel** 1

casket (say **kaas**-kit) *noun* (*plural* **caskets**)
1 a small box with a lid that you use for storing jewellery and other valuable things
2 another word for **coffin**

cassava (say kuh-**saa**-vuh) *noun* (*no plural*)
a tropical plant with thick roots that you can eat if you cook them

casserole (say **kass**-uh-rohl) *noun* (*plural* **casseroles**)
1 a dish with a lid that you use to cook food slowly in the oven
2 food that you make by cooking meat and vegetables slowly in liquid

cassette (say kuh-**set**) *noun* (*plural* **cassettes**)
a plastic box with special tape inside for recording and playing sound or pictures: *a video **cassette***

SPELLING Remember! You spell **cassette** with **ss** and **tt**.

cast¹ (say **kaast**) *verb* (**casting, cast**)
1 to choose an actor for a particular part in a film or a play: *She is always **cast** as the heroine of the play.*
2 to throw something in a certain direction: *The fishermen **cast** their net into the water.*

3 to make an object by pouring hot liquid metal into a shaped container
cast a/your vote to make your choice, for example in an election
cast a spell to use magic words that have the power to change somebody or something: *The witch **cast** a spell **on** the handsome prince.*

cast² (say **kaast**) *noun* (*plural* **casts**)
all the actors in a film or play: *The whole **cast** was excellent.*

castaway (say **kaass**-tuh-way) *noun* (*plural* **castaways**)
somebody whose ship has sunk and who is left in a place far away from where other people live

caste (say **kaast**) *noun* (*plural* **castes**)
the social class or position of a person in society, based on, for example, their family origin, how much money they have or what work they do

castigate (say **kass**-ti-gayt) *verb* (**castigating, castigated**) (*formal*)
to criticize somebody very much, especially officially or publicly: *He was **castigated** by the judge for protecting a corrupt colleague.*

castle (say **kaass**-l) *noun* (*plural* **castles**)
a large strong building with thick high walls and towers that was built in the past to keep people safe from attack: *We visited the **Castle** in Cape Town.*

PRONUNCIATION Don't pronounce the **t** in **castle.**

castor (say **kaass**-tuh) *noun* (*plural* **castors**) (also **caster**)
one of a set of small wheels that can turn in all directions and that is fixed to the bottom of a piece of furniture to make it easier to move

castrate (say kass-**trayt**) *verb* (**castrating, castrated**)
to remove part of the sexual organs of a male animal so that it cannot produce young
► **castration** (*noun*)

casual (say **kazh**-yuu-uhl) *adjective*
1 relaxed, and showing that you are not worried about something: *She gave us a **casual** wave as she passed.*
2 (used about clothes) not formal: *I like **casual** clothes such as jeans and T-shirts.*
3 (used about work) done only for a short period and not regular or permanent: *Most of the **casual** workers in the shop are students.*
► **casually** (*adverb*): *They chatted **casually** on the phone.*

casualty (say **kazh**-yuu-uhl-tee) *noun*
1 (*plural* **casualties**) a person who is hurt or killed in an accident or a war
2 (*no plural*) (also **casualty department**) the place in a hospital where you go if you have been hurt in an accident or if you have suddenly become ill: *The victims were rushed to **casualty**.*

cat (say **kat**) *noun* (*plural* **cats**)
1 a small animal with soft fur that people keep as a pet: *My **cat** purrs when she's happy.* ◇ *The **cat** had five kittens.*
2 a wild hunting animal of the **feline** family: *the big **cats**, such as tigers and lions*

cataclysm (say **kat**-uh-kliz-uhm) *noun* (*plural* **cataclysms**) (*formal*)
a terrible disaster or sudden big change
► **cataclysmic** (*adjective*): *a **cataclysmic** war*

catalogue (say **kat**-uh-log) *noun* (*plural* **catalogues**)
a complete list of all the things that you can buy or see somewhere: *a library **catalogue***

catalyst (say **kat**-uh-list) *noun* (*plural* **catalysts**)
1 a person or thing that causes change or makes it happen faster: *The Internet is a **catalyst** for change.*
2 (*science*) a substance that makes a chemical reaction happen faster without being changed itself
► **catalytic** (*adjective*): *a **catalytic** reaction* ◇ *a **catalytic** converter*

catamaran (say kat-uh-muh-**ran**) *noun* (*plural* **catamarans**)
a fast sailing boat with a **hull** on each side of its flat deck

catapult¹ (say **kat**-uh-pult) *noun* (*plural* **catapults**)
1 a Y-shaped stick with a piece of rubber tied to each side that is used for shooting small stones
2 (*history*) a machine used for shooting large rocks or other things at an enemy

catapult² (say **kat**-uh-pult) *verb* (**catapulting, catapulted**)
to throw a person or a thing suddenly and with great force: *The force of the accident **catapulted** the car into the air.* ◇ *(figurative) The success of the film **catapulted** the actress to fame.*

cataract (say **kat**-uh-rakt) *noun* (*plural* **cataracts**)
1 a medical condition in which a kind of cloud forms over the eye, making your sight less clear: ***cataract** surgery*
2 (*geography*) a large **waterfall** or a series of waterfalls

A B C D E F G H I J K L M N O P Q R S T U V W X Y Z

catastrophe (say kuh-**tass**-truh-fee) *noun* (*plural* **catastrophes**)
a sudden disaster that causes great suffering or damage: *Floods are major **catastrophes**.*

catch (say **kach**) *verb* (**catching, caught, has caught**)
1 to take and hold something that is moving: *He threw the ball and I **caught** it.*
2 to find and hold somebody or something: *They **caught** a fish in the river.* ◇ *The thief ran away but the police **caught** him.*
3 to be early enough for a bus or train that is going to leave: *I **caught** the three o'clock bus home.* ➲ OPPOSITE **miss** 3
4 to get an illness: *She **caught** a cold.*
5 to stop suddenly or be held up or hook on something: *My dress **caught** on a nail.*
catch fire to start to burn: *The house **caught** fire.*
catch up to do something quickly so that you are not behind others: *I must **catch** up the work I missed.*

catching (say **kach**-ing) *adjective* (*informal*)
(of a sickness) that is easily passed on from one person to another: *Don't worry, asthma is not catching.* ➲ SYNONYMS **contagious, infectious**

catchment area (say **kach**-muhnt air-ri-uh) *noun* (*plural* **catchment areas**)
1 (also **catchment, drainage basin**) (*geography*) the area in which surface water (in the form of rain or snow) flows into a particular lake or river
2 the area from which a school, for example, gets its students or a hospital its patients

catechism (say **kat**-uh-kiz-uhm) *noun* (*no plural*)
a set of questions and answers used for teaching people about the beliefs and principles of the Christian religion

categorical (say kat-uh-**go**-rik-l) *adjective*
very definite and clear
▸ **categorically** (*adverb*): *The Minister **categorically** denied the rumour.*

category (say **kat**-uh-guh-ree) *noun* (*plural* **categories**)
a group of people or things that are similar to each other: *We can divide foods into **categories** such as meat, fish or vegetables.*

cater (say **kay**-tuh) *verb* (**catering, catered**)
1 to provide what somebody wants or needs: *The school **caters** for children with special needs.* ◇ *The magazine **caters** to businessmen and professional people.*
2 to provide and serve food and drink at an event

caterpillar (say **kat**-uh-pil-uh) *noun* (*plural* **caterpillars**)
a small animal with a long soft body and a lot of legs that later becomes an insect with large coloured wings (called a **butterfly**).

cathedral (say kuh-**theed**-ruhl) *noun* (*plural* **cathedrals**)
the main church of a district, under the care of a **bishop**

cathode (say **kath**-ohd) *noun* (*plural* **cathodes**) (*science*)
the negative pole in an electric current system: *A **cathode** is a negatively charged electrode.* ➲ See **anode, electrode**

Catholic (say **kath**-lik) *noun* (*plural* **Catholics**) = **Roman Catholic**

catseye™ (say **kat**-sy) *noun* (*plural* **catseyes**)
a device that sends back light. They are put in a line into a road to mark where the centre or edge of the road is.

cattle (say **kat**-l) *plural noun*
cows that people keep for their milk or meat: *a herd* (= a group) *of **cattle***

catty (say **kat**-ee) *noun* (*plural* **catties**) (*informal*)
short for **catapult**[1] 1

caucus (say **kaw**-kuhss) *noun* (*plural* **caucuses**)
1 a meeting of the leaders of a political party to decide on **strategy**
2 a group of people with similar interests within a larger organization

caught (say **kawt**) form of **catch**

cauldron (say **kawl**-druhn) *noun* (*plural* **cauldrons**) (also **caldron**)
a large metal pot that is used for cooking things over a fire

cauliflower (say **kol**-i-flow-uh) *noun* (*plural* **cauliflowers**)
a large vegetable with green leaves on the outside and a round head of hard white flowers in the centre

cause[1] (say **kawz**) *noun* (*plural* **causes**)
1 a thing or person that makes something happen: *Bad driving is the **cause** of many road accidents.*
2 something that people care about and want to contribute to: *They raised funds for a good **cause** – to build a new hospital.*

cause[2] (say **kawz**) *verb* (**causing, caused**)
to be the reason why something happens: *What **caused** the accident?* ◇ *The fire was **caused** by a cigarette.*

causeway (say **kawz**-way) *noun* (*plural* **causeways**)
a road or track that is built higher than the area around it in order to cross low land or water: *Cross the **causeway** over the river.*

caustic (say **kawss**-tik) *adjective*
1 able to burn or dissolve things by chemical action: *a **caustic** substance*
2 (*formal*) very critical of a person or thing in a cruel way: ***caustic** sarcasm*

caution[1] (say **kaw**-shuhn) *noun* (*no plural*)
great care, because of possible danger: *Cross the river with **caution**.*

caution[2] (say **kaw**-shuhn) *verb* (**cautioning, cautioned**)
1 to warn somebody about possible danger and tell them what they should do: *Her father **cautioned** her against studying drama.*
2 to give somebody an official warning: *The football player was **cautioned** by the referee.*

cautious (say **kaw**-shuhss) *adjective*
careful because there may be danger: *She is very **cautious** when driving at night.*
➲ OPPOSITE **impetuous**
▶ **cautiously** (*adverb*): *He opened the door **cautiously**.*

cavalcade (say kav-uhl-**kayd**) *noun* (*plural* **cavalcades**)
a line of people walking, riding on horses, or driving in cars ➲ SYNONYM **procession**

cavalry (say **kav**-uhl-ree) *noun* (*plural* **cavalries**)
1 (*history*) the part of an army that is made up of soldiers who fight on horses
2 the part of a modern army that uses vehicles covered with metal to protect them in an attack

cave[1] (say **kayv**) *noun* (*plural* **caves**)
a large hole in the side of a mountain or under the ground: *We turned on our torches when we entered the **cave**.*

cave[2] (say **kayv**) *verb* (**caving, caved**)
cave in
1 to fall or sink down suddenly: *The roof of the tunnel had **caved** in and we could go no further.*
2 to stop arguing against something or accept something that you did not want to accept or agree to: *The city council finally **caved** in and approved the project.*

cavern (say **kav**-uhn) *noun* (*plural* **caverns**)
a large **cave**[1]
▶ **cavernous** (*adjective*): *a **cavernous** warehouse*

caviar (say **kav**-i-aa) *noun* (*no plural*) (also **caviare**)
the eggs of a large fish (called a **sturgeon**) that are eaten as a special and expensive type of food

cavity (say **kav**-i-tee) *noun* (*plural* **cavities**)
1 an empty space inside something solid: *a **cavity** between two walls*
2 a hole in a tooth: *If you don't care for your teeth you'll get **cavities**.*

cavort (say kuh-**vawt**) *verb* (**cavorting, cavorted**)
to jump around in a noisy or excited way: *The children were **cavorting** around the playground.*

cayenne (say **kay**-en) *noun* (*no plural*) (also **cayenne pepper**)
a type of red pepper with a hot taste that you put on food

CBD (say see-bee-**dee**) *noun* (*plural* **CBDs**)
the most important commercial part of a town or city ❶ ***CBD*** is short for 'central business district'.

CC (say see-**see**) *abbreviation* (*plural* **CCs**) **close corporation**

cc (say see-**see**) *abbreviation* (*plural* **cc**) (also **cm**^{3})
cubic centimetre

CD (say see-**dee**) *noun* (*plural* **CDs**) (also **disc**)
a round, flat piece of hard plastic on which you can record sound or store information ❶ **CD** is short for 'compact disc'.

CD player *noun* (*plural* **CD players**)
a machine that you use to play the music stored on a CD

CD-ROM (say see-dee-**rom**) *noun* (*plural* **CD-ROMs**)
a CD on which you can store large amounts of information, sound and pictures, to use on a computer ❶ **CD-ROM** is short for 'compact disc read-only memory'.

CE (say see-**ee**) *abbreviation*
used in dates for showing the number of years after the time when Jesus Christ was born. It is another word for **AD**: *Mapungubwe was an important centre for trade between 1220 and 1300 CE.* ❶ **CE** is short for 'Common Era' ➲ See **BCE**

cease (say **seess**) *verb* (**ceasing, ceased**) (*formal*)
to stop: *Fighting in the area has now **ceased**.*

ceasefire (say **seess**-fy-uh) *noun* (*plural* **ceasefires**)
an agreement between two groups involved in a war that they will stop fighting ➲ See **truce**

A B C D E F G H I J K L M N O P Q R S T U V W X Y Z

ceaseless (say **seess**-luhss) *adjective*
continuing for a long time without stopping
➲ SYNONYM **incessant**
▸ **ceaselessly** (*adverb*): *He complained **ceaselessly** about not having enough money.*

cedar (say **see**-duh) *noun* (*plural* **cedars**)
a type of **evergreen** tree with spreading branches

ceiling (say **see**-ling) *noun* (*plural* **ceilings**)
the top part of the inside of a room

SPELLING **ie** or **ei**? When the sound rhymes with **be**, the rule is **i before e, except after c**, so **ceiling** is spelt with **ei**.

celebrate (say **sel**-i-brayt) *verb* (**celebrating, celebrated**)
to do something to show that you are happy for a special reason or because it is a special day: *Grandma **celebrated** her 90th birthday last week.*

celebration (say sel-i-**bray**-shuhn) *noun* (*plural* **celebrations**)
a time when you enjoy yourself because you have a special reason to be happy: *birthday **celebrations***

celebrity (say suh-**leb**-ri-tee) *noun*
1 (*plural* **celebrities**) a famous person: *international **celebrities***
2 (*no plural*) the state of being famous: *glamour and **celebrity***

celery (say **sel**-uh-ree) *noun* (*no plural*)
a vegetable with long crisp green stems: *a stick of **celery***

celestial (say suh-**less**-ti-uhl) *adjective*
(*old-fashioned*) relating to the sky, outer space or heaven

celibate (say **sel**-i-buht) *adjective*
not married and not having sex, often because of religious beliefs

cell (say **sel**) *noun* (*plural* **cells**)
1 (*biology*) the smallest part of all living plants and animals: *red blood **cells*** ➲ See illustration
2 a small room for one or more prisoners in a prison or police station
3 each of the small sections that together form a larger structure, for example a **honeycomb**
4 one of the small rectangles in a table of rows and columns
5 (*technology*) a device for producing an electric current: *a solar **cell***
6 (*informal*) short for **cellphone**
🛈 ORIGIN: Old English, from Old French *celle* or Latin *cella* meaning 'storeroom'

cells (biology)

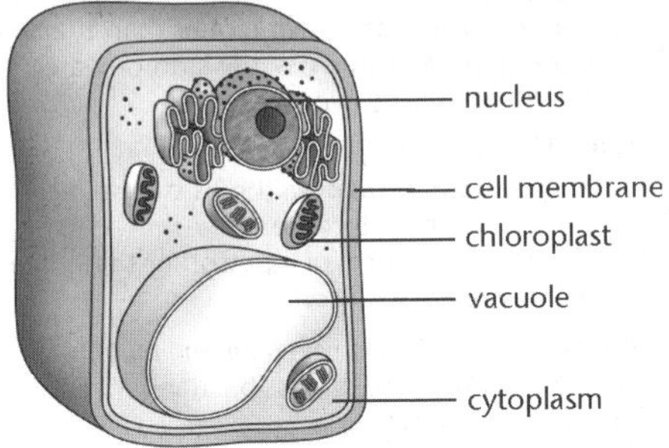

a plant cell

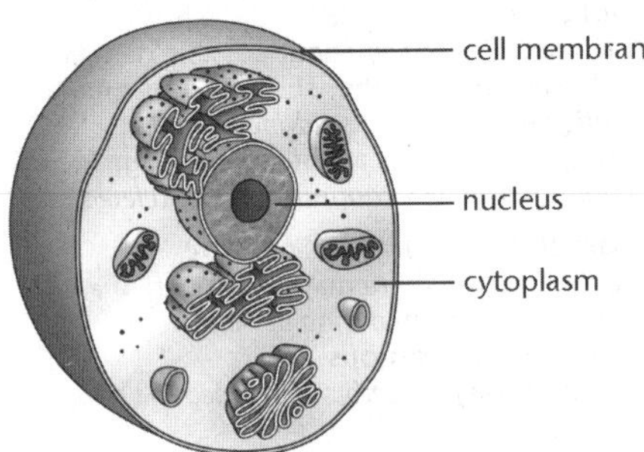

an animal cell

cellar (say **sel**-uh) *noun* (*plural* **cellars**)
a room in the part of a building that is under the ground

cello (say **chel**-oh) *noun* (*plural* **cellos**)
a large wooden musical instrument with strings which you play with a **bow**³ 2 while sitting down with the instrument between your knees

cellphone (say **sel**-fohn) *noun* (*plural* **cellphones**) (also **cell, mobile phone**)
a telephone that you can carry around with you: *I'll phone you on your **cellphone** tonight.*
🛈 **Cellphone** is short for 'cellular phone'.

cellular (say **sel**-yuu-luh) *adjective*
relating to or consisting of cells: ***cellular** tissue* ◇ ***cellular** respiration* ◇ *a **cellular** construction*

celluloid (say **sel**-yuu-loyd) *noun* (*no plural*)
a plastic substance that burns easily, once used as photographic film: *Table tennis balls are made from **celluloid**.*

cellulose (say **sel**-yuu-lohz) *noun* (*no plural*)
a natural substance that forms the cell walls of plants and is used in making plastics and paper

Celsius (say **sel**-si-uhss) *noun* (*no plural*) (also **centigrade**) (abbr. C)
a scale for measuring temperature. On this scale, water freezes at 0 degrees **Celsius** (0 °C)

and boils at 100 degrees **Celsius** (100 °C)
➲ See **Fahrenheit**
🛈 ORIGIN: from the name of Anders Celsius (1701–1744), the Swedish scientist who invented the scale

WORD BUILDING The symbol ° stands for **degree**. In writing we usually shorten **100 degrees Celsius** to **100 °C**.

Celtic (say **kel**-tik) *adjective*
relating to a group of people (the **Celts**) who lived in western and central Europe in ancient times, or to their culture and language

cement (say si-**ment**) *noun* (*no plural*)
a grey powder that becomes hard like stone when you mix it with water and leave it to dry. It is used in building for sticking bricks or stones together or for making very hard surfaces.

cemetery (say **sem**-uh-tree) *noun* (*plural* **cemeteries**)
a piece of land where dead people are buried
➲ SYNONYM **graveyard**

censor (say **sen**-suh) *verb* (**censoring**, **censored**)
to examine films, books or newspapers before they are published or shown in public to remove those parts that might offend people or are considered a threat to the country
► **censorship** (*noun*): *state* ***censorship*** *of radio and television programmes*

censure (say **sen**-shuh) *verb* (**censuring**, **censured**) (*formal*)
to tell somebody that they have done something wrong in a strong and formal way: *The company was* ***censured*** *for false advertising.*
► **censure** (*noun*): *The minister escaped* ***censure****.*

census (say **sen**-suhss) *noun* (*plural* **censuses**)
an official count of the population of a country that includes finding out about people's ages, levels of education, jobs and what type of houses they live in

cent (say **sent**) *noun* (*plural* **cents**) (abbr. c)
a small coin that people use in many countries around the world: *There are 100* ***cents*** *in a rand.*

centenary (say sen-**ten**-uh-ree) *noun* (*plural* **centenaries**)
a year that is exactly one hundred years after an important event or the beginning of something: *The school celebrated its* ***centenary*** *in 2009.*

centi- (say **sen**-ti) *prefix*
1 one hundred: ***centipede***
2 one hundredth: ***centilitre***
🛈 ORIGIN: from Latin *centum* meaning 'hundred'

centigrade (say **sen**-ti-grayd) another word for **Celsius**

centilitre (say **sen**-ti-lee-tuh) *noun* (*plural* **centilitres**) (abbr. cl or cL)
a unit for measuring the volume of a liquid: *There are 100* ***centilitres*** *in a litre.* ◇ *250* ***cl***
➲ See **millilitre**, **litre**

centimetre (say **sen**-ti-mee-tuh) *noun* (*plural* **centimetres**) (abbr. cm)
a unit for measuring length: *There are 100* ***centimetres*** *in a metre.*
🛈 ORIGIN: from Latin *centum* meaning 'hundred' + *meter* from Greek *metron* meaning 'measure'

centipede (say **sen**-ti-peed) *noun* (*plural* **centipedes**)
a small creature that has a slightly poisonous bite, with a long thin body divided into many sections, each with a pair of legs

central (say **sen**-truhl) *adjective*
in the middle part of something: ***central*** *Africa*

centralize (say **sen**-truh-lize) *verb* (**centralizing**, **centralized**) (also **centralise**)
to give control of all parts of a country or organization to a group of people in one place
► **centralization** (*noun*) (also **centralisation**): *the* ***centralization*** *of power*

centre (say **sent**-uh) *noun* (*plural* **centres**)
1 the part in the middle of something: *the city* ***centre*** ◇ *The flower has a yellow* ***centre*** *with white petals.*
2 a place where people come to do a particular activity: *a shopping* ***centre*** ◇ *Our town has a new sports* ***centre****.*
🛈 ORIGIN: 14th–15th century, from Greek *kentron* meaning 'sharp point'. To draw a circle you put the sharp point of a tool called a pair of compasses at the centre of the circle.

centrifugal (say sen-tri-**fyoo**-guhl) *adjective*
moving away from a central point: *a* ***centrifugal*** *force* ➲ See **centripetal**

centripetal (say sent-ri-**pee**-tuhl) *adjective*
moving towards a central point: *a* ***centripetal*** *force* ➲ See **centrifugal**

century (say **sen**-tshuh-ree) *noun* (*plural* **centuries**)
a period of 100 years: *People have been making wine in this area for* ***centuries****.* ◇ *We are living in the twenty-first* ***century****.*

CEO (say see-ee-**oh**) *noun* (*plural* **CEOs**)
the person with the most powerful position in a company or business 🛈 **CEO** is short for 'chief executive officer'.

A B C D E F G H I J K L M N O P Q R S T U V W X Y Z

ceramic (say suh-**ram**-ik) *adjective*
made of clay that has been heated in a very hot oven (called a **kiln**): *ceramic mugs*
▸ **ceramics** (*plural noun*): *African people have made **ceramics** for centuries.*

cereal (say **seer**-ri-uhl) *noun*
1 (*plural* **cereals**) a plant that farmers grow for its seeds (called **grain**), from which food such as bread and porridge is made: *Wheat and oats are **cereals**.*
2 (*no plural*) a food made from grain that you eat for breakfast: *a bowl of **cereal** with milk*

cerebral (say **se**-ruh-bruhl) *adjective*
relating to the brain: ***cerebral** palsy ◇ She is more **cerebral** than emotional.*

ceremonial (say se-ri-**moh**-ni-uhl) *adjective*
relating to or used for a ceremony: *The judge wore his **ceremonial** robes.*
▸ **ceremonially** (*adverb*): *The bride was **ceremonially** dressed in traditional clothes.*

ceremony (say **se**-ruh-muh-nee) *noun* (*plural* **ceremonies**)
a formal public or religious event: *the opening **ceremony** of the Olympic Games ◇ a wedding **ceremony***

certain (say **sur**-tuhn) *adjective*
1 sure about something and without any doubt: *I'm **certain** that I've seen her before. ◇ Are you **certain** about that?* ➲ OPPOSITE **uncertain**
2 used for talking about a particular thing or person without saying what or who they are: *Do we need to finish the project by a **certain** date? ◇ **Certain** people might not agree with that.*
for certain without any doubt: *I don't know for **certain** where she is.*
make certain to check something so that you are sure about it: *Please make **certain** that the window is closed before you leave.*

certainly (say **sur**-tuhn-lee) *adverb*
1 without any doubt: *She is **certainly** the best swimmer in the team.* ➲ SYNONYM **definitely**
2 (used when answering questions) of course: *'Will you open the door for me, please?' '**Certainly**.'*

certainty (say **sur**-tuhn-tee) *noun*
1 (*no plural*) the state of being completely sure about something: *We cannot say with **certainty** that there is no life on other planets.*
2 (*plural* **certainties**) something that is definitely going to happen: *I'm going to win the lotto. It is a **certainty**.*

certificate (say suh-**tif**-i-kuht) *noun* (*plural* **certificates**)
an important piece of paper that shows that something is true: *Your birth **certificate** shows when and where you were born.*

certify (say **sur**-ti-fy) *verb* (**certifying, certified**)
1 to formally say that something is true or correct: *I **certify** that the information is accurate.*
2 to show that somebody has successfully completed a course of training for a particular profession by giving them an official certificate: *a **certified** accountant*

cervix (say **sur**-vikss) *noun* (*plural* **cervixes** or **cervices**) (*biology*)
the narrow passage at the opening of the **uterus**
▸ **cervical** (*adjective*): ***cervical** cancer*

cesspit (say **sess**-pit) *noun* (*plural* **cesspits**) (also **cesspool**)
a covered hole in the ground or an underground container where liquid waste is stored

chafe (say **chayf**) *verb* (**chafing, chafed**)
to make or become sore or damaged by rubbing: *The strap **chafes** her skin.*

chaff (say **chaaf**) *noun* (*no plural*)
the dry outer coverings (called **husks**) of wheat or other grain that have been separated from the seeds using a machine or a special tool

chagrin (say **shag**-rin) *noun* (*no plural*) (*formal*)
the angry feeling that you get when you are annoyed or disappointed: *To his **chagrin**, his visa application was turned down.*
▸ **chagrin** (*verb*): (**be chagrined**)
*I was **chagrined** to find that they had left without me.*

chain¹ (say **chayn**) *noun* (*plural* **chains**)
a line of metal rings that are joined together: *a gold **chain** ◇ My bicycle **chain** is broken.*

chain

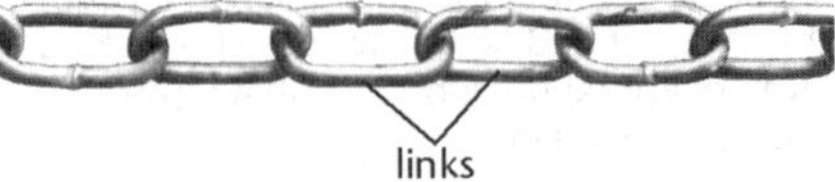

chain² (say **chayn**) *verb* (**chaining, chained**)
to fasten a person or a thing to a place with a chain: *The dog was **chained** to a tree.*

chair¹ *noun* (*plural* **chairs**)
1 a piece of furniture for one person to sit on, with four legs, a seat and a back: *a table and four **chairs***
2 short for **chairperson**

chair² (say **chair**) *verb* (**chairing, chaired**)
to be the **chairperson** of a formal meeting: *Who is **chairing** the meeting this evening?*

chairperson (say **chair**-pur-suhn) *noun* (*plural* **chairpeople**) (also **chair, chairman, chairwoman**)
a person who controls a formal meeting

chalet (say **shal**-ay) *noun* (*plural* **chalets**)
1 a type of wooden house with a steep roof, originally built in Switzerland
2 a simple house, especially one used by people on holiday

chalk (say **chawk**) *noun* (*no plural*)
1 a type of soft white rock
2 a white or coloured stick that you can write or draw with: *The teacher wrote on the chalkboard with a piece of* ***chalk****.*

chalkboard (say **chawk**-bawd) *noun* (*plural* **chalkboards**)
a dark board that a teacher writes on with chalk. ➲ See **blackboard**

challenge¹ (say **chal**-inj) *noun* (*plural* **challenges**)
1 a new or difficult thing that makes you try hard: *Climbing the mountain will be a real* ***challenge****.*
2 an invitation to fight or play a game against somebody
▸ **challenging** (*adjective*): *a* ***challenging*** *race*
🛈 **ORIGIN:** 13th–15th century, through Old French *chalenge* from Latin

challenge² (say **chal**-inj) *verb* (**challenging, challenged**)
1 to refuse to accept a set of rules or to question if something is true or right or not: *She does not like anyone* ***challenging*** *her authority.*
2 to ask somebody to play a game with you or fight with you to see who wins: *The boxer* ***challenged*** *the world champion to a fight.*

chamber (say **chaym**-buh) *noun* (*plural* **chambers**)
1 the elected group of people responsible for making the laws of a country, or the room or building where they meet: *The National Assembly is the first* ***chamber*** *of Parliament in South Africa.*
2 a group of people who work together for a special reason: *the* ***Chamber*** *of Mines*
3 an enclosed space inside the body, a machine or a plant: *the four* ***chambers*** *of the heart*
4 (*old-fashioned*) a bedroom or other room in a house: *She returned to her* ***chamber*** *and slept for a few hours.*

chameleon (say kuh-**mee**-li-uhn) *noun* (*plural* **chameleons**)
a small type of reptile that can change the colour of its skin
🛈 **ORIGIN:** 13th–15th century, through Latin *chamaeleon* from Greek *khamaileōn* meaning 'lion on the ground'

chamois (say **sham**-waa or **sham**-ee) *noun* (*plural* **chamois**) (also **chamois leather**)
a type of very soft leather, or a piece of this used for polishing and cleaning things

champagne (say sham-**payn**) *noun* (*no plural*)
a French white wine with a lot of bubbles

champion (say **cham**-pi-uhn) *noun* (*plural* **champions**)
a person who is the best at a sport or game: *a chess* ***champion*** *◇ the world* ***champion***

championship (say **cham**-pi-uhn-ship) *noun* (*plural* **championships**)
a competition to find the best player or team in a sport or game: *Our team won the* ***championship*** *this year.*

chance (say **chaanss**) *noun*
1 (*no plural*) a possibility that something may happen: *There's no* ***chance*** *that she'll come. ◇ He has a good* ***chance*** *of winning. ◇ I may lose money but I'll have to take that* ***chance****.*
2 (*plural* **chances**) a time when you can do something: *It was their last* ***chance*** *to escape. ◇ Please give her a* ***chance*** *to explain.*
➲ SYNONYM **opportunity**
3 (*no plural*) when something happens that you cannot control or that you have not planned: *Plan well and don't leave anything to* ***chance****. ◇ We met by* ***chance****.* ➲ SYNONYM **luck** 2
no chance (*informal*) used to say that there is no possibility of something happening: *'Will your mum give you the money?' 'No* ***chance****!'*

chancellor (say **chaan**-suh-luh) *noun* (*plural* **chancellors**)
1 the leader of the government in some countries, for example in Germany
2 the person with the highest position in a university or college

chandelier (say shan-duh-**leer**) *noun* (*plural* **chandeliers**)
a large frame that hangs from the ceiling with many lights or candles fitted to it

change¹ (say **chaynj**) *verb* (**changing, changed**)
1 to become different or to make something different: *She has* ***changed*** *– she looks much older. ◇ Water* ***changes*** *into steam when it gets very hot. ◇ I'm going to* ***change*** *my hairstyle.*
2 to put or take something in place of another thing: *My new watch didn't work, so I took it back to the shop and* ***changed*** *it.*
3 (also **get changed**) to put on different clothes: *I need to* ***change*** *before I go out.*

4 to get off a train or bus and get on another one: *I have to **change** trains at Bloemfontein.*

change[2] (say **chaynj**) *noun*
1 (*plural* **changes**) when something becomes different: *The government made many **changes**.* ◇ *a **change** in the weather*
2 (*no plural*) the money that you get back if you pay more than the amount something costs: *If a sweet costs R4,50 and you pay with a R5 coin, you will get 50c **change**.*
3 (*no plural*) small pieces of money or coins: *I haven't got any **change**.*
for a change because you want something different: *Today we played rounders for a **change**.*

changeable (say **chayn**-juhb-l) *adjective*
changing often or likely to change soon: *The weather is **changeable** at this time of the year.*

SPELLING Notice the spelling of **changeable**.

channel[1] (say **chan**-l) *noun* (*plural* **channels**)
1 a television station: *Which **channel** is the film on?*
2 a way or route along which news or information is sent: ***channels** of communication*
3 a passage that water can flow along: *a drainage **channel***
4 the part of a river or sea which is deep enough for boats to pass through
5 (*geography*) a passage of water that connects two areas of water, especially two seas: *the Mozambique **Channel*** (= the sea between Mozambique and Madagascar)

channel[2] (say **chan**-l) *verb* (**channelling, channelled**)
to make something pass or move along a particular route or path: *The pipe **channels** water to the fields.* ◇ *You should **channel** your energy into doing something constructive.*

chant (say **chaant**) *noun* (*plural* **chants**)
1 a word or phrase that you sing or speak loudly many times
2 a prayer or religious song with only a few notes: *The Gregorian **chant** is used in the Catholic church.*
▸ **chant** (*verb*): *They marched through the town **chanting** 'Stop the war!'*

Chanukkah (say *khu*-**nuu**-kaa) = **Hanukkah**

chaos (say **kay**-oss) *noun* (*no plural*)
a situation in which everything is confused and nothing is organized: *The kitchen was in **chaos**.*

chap *noun* (*plural* **chaps**) (*informal*)
a man or boy: *The poor little **chap** started to cry.*

chapel (say **chap**-l) *noun* (*plural* **chapels**)
a room or a small church where Christians go to pray

chapped (say **chapt**) *adjective*
(of your skin) rough and sore because it is too dry

chapter (say **chap**-tuh) *noun* (*plural* **chapters**)
one of the parts of a book: *Turn to **Chapter** 4.*

char[1] (say **chaa**) *verb* (**charring, charred**)
to burn something so that its colour changes but it is not destroyed completely: *The fire **charred** everything inside the house.*
▸ **charred** (*adjective*): *the **charred** remains of the burnt-out car*

char[2] (say **chaa**) *noun* (*plural* **chars**)
a woman whose job is to clean a house

character (say **ka**-rik-tuh) *noun*
1 (*no plural*) the qualities that make a person or a thing different from other people or things: *He has a strong **character**.* ◇ *The factory spoilt the **character** of the village.* ➲ SYNONYM **temperament**
2 (*plural* **characters**) a person in a book, play or film: *Homer Simpson is a famous cartoon **character**.*

characteristic (say ka-rik-tuh-**riss**-tik) *noun* (*plural* **characteristics**)
a typical feature or quality that a person or a thing has: *Spiciness is a **characteristic** of Indian food.* ◇ *The two groups have quite different **characteristics**.*
▸ **characteristic** (*adjective*): *Schalk shaved off his **characteristic** mop of blond hair.*

characterize (say **ka**-rik-tuh-rize) *verb* (**characterizing, characterized**) (also **characterise**) (*formal*)
1 to be a typical feature of a person or a thing: *The disease is **characterized** by fever and pain.*
2 to describe what a person or a thing is like: *The report **characterizes** the figures as a 'rough estimate'.*
▸ **characterization** (*noun*) (also **characterisation**)

charade (say shuh-**raad**) *noun* (*plural* **charades**)
1 a situation or event that is clearly false but which people pretend is pleasant or improving
2 charades (*plural noun*) a game in which people try to guess a word or phrase that one person must explain not by speaking, but only by moving their face, hands and body

charcoal (say **chaa**-kohl) *noun* (*no plural*)
a black substance that is produced from burnt wood and can be used as fuel and for drawing

charge[1] (say **chaaj**) *noun* (*plural* **charges**)
1 the money that you must pay to use something: *'What is the* ***charge*** *for parking here?' 'There is a* ***charge*** *of R10 an hour.'* ◇ *We deliver free of* ***charge***. ➲ See **price**
2 a statement from the police saying that a person has done something wrong: *a murder* ***charge***
3 (*science*) the amount of electricity that is put into a battery or carried by a substance: *a positive or negative* ***charge***
be in charge of a person or **a thing** to take care of or be responsible for a person or a thing: *He is in* ***charge*** *of his baby brother today.*

charge[2] (say **chaaj**) *verb* (**charging, charged**)
1 to ask somebody to pay a certain price for using or doing something: *The garage* ***charged*** *me R700 for the repairs.*
2 to say that somebody has done something wrong: *The police* ***charged*** *him with murder.*
3 to run quickly and with a lot of force: *The bull* ***charged***. ◇ *The dog* ***charged*** *into the room.*
4 to put electricity into something: *I* ***charged*** *the battery.*

chariot (say **cha**-ri-uht) *noun* (*plural* **chariots**) (*history*)
a vehicle with two wheels and no seats that was pulled by a horse

charisma (say kuh-**riz**-muh) *noun* (*no plural*)
the special quality that some people have to attract and influence other people

charismatic (say ka-riz-**mat**-ik) *adjective*
with special qualities that attract and influence other people: *He's an inspiring and* ***charismatic*** *leader.*

charity (say **cha**-ri-tee) *noun*
1 (*plural* **charities**) an organization that collects money to help people who need it: *The Red Cross is a* ***charity***.
2 (*no plural*) the aim of giving money, food or help to people who are in need: *They give a lot of money to* ***charity***.
3 (*no plural*) (*old-fashioned*) kindness towards other people

charlatan (say **shaa**-luh-tuhn) *noun* (*plural* **charlatans**)
a person who pretends to have knowledge or skills that they do not really have
➲ SYNONYM **fraud** 2

charm[1] (say **chaam**) *noun*
1 (*no plural*) a quality that makes people like you: *He was a man of great* ***charm***.
2 (*plural* **charms**) a small thing that you wear because you think it will bring good luck: *She wears a bracelet with a lucky* ***charm***.

charm[2] (say **chaam**) *verb* (**charming, charmed**)
to make somebody like you: *The baby* ***charmed*** *everybody with her smile.*

charming (say **chaam**-ing) *adjective*
very pleasant or attractive: *a* ***charming*** *house*

chart[1] (say **chaat**) *noun* (*plural* **charts**)
1 a drawing that shows information in the form of a diagram: *a temperature* ***chart*** ◇ *a bar* ***chart***
➲ See **graph**, **pie chart**, **flow chart**
2 a map of the sea or the sky
🛈 **ORIGIN**: 16th century, through French, through Latin *charta* meaning 'paper, papyrus leaf', from Greek *khartēs* meaning 'papyrus leaf'. Paper was first made from the leaves of the papyrus plant which grew along the Nile River in Egypt.

chart[2] (say **chaat**) *verb* (**charting, charted**)
1 to record the progress or development of something carefully and in detail: *The museum* ***charts*** *South Africa's path to democracy.*
2 to make a map of an area of the sea or the sky: ***charting*** *the Earth's oceans*

charter[1] (say **chaa**-tuh) *noun*
1 (*plural* **charters**) an official document that describes the rights, aims and functions of an organization or of a particular group of people: *the Children's* ***Charter***
2 (*no plural*) (*S. African*) short for **Freedom Charter**
3 (*no plural*) the renting of a ship, plane or other vehicle for private or special use

charter[2] (say **chaa**-tuh) *verb* (**chartering, chartered**)
to pay to use a ship, plane or other vehicle for a particular purpose or for a particular group of people

chase (say **chayss**) *verb* (**chasing, chased**)
to run behind somebody or something and try to catch them: *The dog* ***chased*** *the cat.* ◇ *The police* ***chased*** *after the thief.* ➲ SYNONYM **pursue**
▸ **chase** (*noun*): *The film includes a car* ***chase***.

chasm (say **kaz**-uhm) *noun* (*plural* **chasms**)
1 a deep opening in the ground
2 a great difference between two groups or things, for example feelings or opinions: *the* ***chasm*** *between theory and practice*

chassis (say **shass**-ee) *noun* (*plural* **chassis**) (*technology*)
the metal frame of a vehicle onto which the other parts fit

chaste (say **chayst**) *adjective* (*old-fashioned*)
1 behaving in a moral way with no thoughts about sex: *She gave him a* ***chaste*** *kiss on the cheek.*
2 not having sex with anyone, or only having

A B C D E F G H I J K L M N O P Q R S T U V W X Y Z

sex with the person you are married to
▸ **chastity** (*noun*): *a vow of* ***chastity***

chastise (say chass-**tize**) *verb* (**chastising, chastised**) (*formal*)
1 to criticize somebody for doing something wrong: *She* ***chastised*** *the child for wasting food.*
2 (*old-fashioned*) to punish somebody, especially by beating them
▸ **chastisement** (*noun*)

chat *verb* (**chatting, chatted**)
to talk in a friendly, informal way to somebody: *We* ***chatted*** *on the phone.*
▸ **chat** (*noun*): *Let's have a* ***chat*** *about it later.*

chat room *noun* (*plural* **chat rooms**)
an area on the Internet where you can join in a discussion with other people

chatter (say **chat**-uh) *verb* (**chattering, chattered**)
to talk quickly about things that are not very important: *Stop* ***chattering*** *and finish your work.*

chauffeur (say **shoh**-fuh) *noun* (*plural* **chauffeurs**)
a person whose job is to drive a car for somebody else
▸ **chauffeur** (*verb*): *He* ***chauffeured*** *the VIPs to the hotel.*

chauvinism (say **shoh**-vin-i-zuhm) *noun* (*no plural*)
1 the belief that your country and its people are better than all others: *ethnic* ***chauvinism***
2 (also **male chauvinism**) the belief that men are better than women
▸ **chauvinist** (*noun*): *an arrogant* ***chauvinist***
▸ **chauvinist** (*adjective*): *a* ***chauvinist*** *attitude to women* ▸ **chauvinistic** (*adjective*): *a* ***chauvinistic*** *society*
🛈 ORIGIN: 19th century, named after Nicolas Chauvin, a French soldier who was extremely faithful and loyal to his country and leaders in war

cheap (say **cheep**) *adjective* (**cheaper, cheapest**)
1 costing little money: *That restaurant is very good and quite* ***cheap***. ◇ *Computers are getting* ***cheaper*** *all the time.* ➲ OPPOSITE **expensive**, ➲ SYNONYM **inexpensive**
2 low in price and quality and therefore not attractive: *The clothes in that shop look* ***cheap***.

cheat (say **cheet**) *verb* (**cheating, cheated**)
to do something that is not honest or fair: *She* ***cheated*** *in the exam – she copied her friend's work.*
▸ **cheat** (*noun*): *That man's a liar and a* ***cheat***.

check¹ (say **chek**) *verb* (**checking, checked**)
to look at something to see that it is right, good or safe: *Do the sums and then* ***check*** *your answers with a calculator.* ◇ ***Check*** *that all the windows are closed.*
check in to tell the person at the desk in a hotel or an airport that you have arrived: *I have to* ***check*** *in an hour before my flight.*
check out to pay your bill and leave a hotel

check² (say **chek**) *noun* (*plural* **checks**)
1 a look to see that everything is right, good or safe: *The company does safety* ***checks*** *on all their products.* ◇ *a security* ***check***
2 a pattern of squares or one of the squares in a pattern: *a shirt with blue and red* ***checks***

checked (say **chek**-t) *adjective*
with a pattern of squares: *a* ***checked*** *shirt*

checklist (say **chek**-list) *noun* (*plural* **checklists**)
a list of things that you must do, have or think about

checkout (say **chek**-owt) *noun* (*plural* **checkouts**)
the place in a large shop where you pay for things: *a supermarket* ***checkout***

check-up (say **chek**-up) *noun* (*plural* **check-ups**)
a general examination by a doctor to make sure that you are healthy: *You should visit your dentist for a* ***check-up*** *twice a year.*

cheddar (say **ched**-uh) *noun* (*no plural*) (also **cheddar cheese**)
a type of hard yellow cheese

cheek (say **cheek**) *noun*
1 (*plural* **cheeks**) one of the two soft parts of your face below your eyes ➲ See illustration at **face¹**
2 (*no plural*) talk or behaviour that people think is annoying, rude or not showing respect: *What a* ***cheek***! *Somebody has eaten my sandwiches.*

cheeky (say **cheek**-ee) *adjective* (**cheekier, cheekiest**)
not polite and not showing respect: *Don't be so* ***cheeky***! ◇ *She was punished for being* ***cheeky*** *to a teacher.* ➲ SYNONYM **impertinent**

cheer¹ (*rhymes with* **gear**) *noun* (*plural* **cheers**)
a loud shout that shows that you are pleased: *The crowd gave a loud* ***cheer*** *as the singer came onto the stage.*

cheer² (*rhymes with* **gear**) *verb* (**cheering, cheered**)
to shout to show that you like something or to encourage somebody: *The crowd* ***cheered*** *loudly when the players ran onto the pitch.*
cheer up, cheer somebody up to become or to make somebody happier: ***Cheer*** *up! You'll feel better soon.* ◇ *We gave her some flowers to* ***cheer*** *her up.*

cheerful (say **cheer**-ful) *adjective*
happy: *a* ***cheerful*** *smile* ◇ *You don't look very* ***cheerful*** *today. What's the matter?*

cheers (say **cheerz**) *exclamation* (*informal*)
1 a word that people say to each other as they hold up their glasses to drink: *'****Cheers****,' she said, raising her glass.*
2 goodbye

cheese (say **cheez**) *noun*
1 (*no plural*) a yellow or white food made from milk **curd**: *bread and* ***cheese***
2 (*plural* **cheeses**) a type of this food: *a selection of* ***cheeses***
ⓘ **ORIGIN:** from Old English *cese*, *cyse*, related to Dutch *kaas*

cheetah (say **cheet**-uh) *noun* (*plural* **cheetahs**)
a large wild cat with black spots that can run very fast

chef (say **shef**) *noun* (*plural* **chefs**)
a professional cook, especially the head cook in a hotel or restaurant

chemical[1] (say **kem**-ik-l) *adjective*
connected with chemistry or chemicals: *a* ***chemical*** *experiment*

chemical[2] (say **kem**-ik-l) *noun* (*plural* **chemicals**)
a substance that has its own **atomic** 1 structure and that is used or prepared by chemistry

chemist (say **kem**-ist) *noun* (*plural* **chemists**)
1 a person who prepares and sells medicines ➲ **SYNONYM pharmacist**
2 a shop that sells medicines, soap and other personal goods: *I'm going to the* ***chemist*** *to get my tablets.* ➲ See **pharmacy**
3 a person who studies chemistry

chemistry (say **kem**-iss-tree) *noun* (*no plural*)
the science that studies gases, liquids and solids to find out what they are and how they behave

cheque (say **chek**) *noun* (*plural* **cheques**)
a piece of paper from a bank that you can write on and use to pay for things: *I gave him a* ***cheque*** *for R150.* ◇ *Can I pay by* ***cheque****?*

chequebook (say **chek**-buuk) *noun* (*plural* **chequebooks**)
a set of cheques in a book from which they can be removed once you have filled them in

cherish (say **che**-rish) *verb* (**cherishing, cherished**)
1 to protect and look after a person or a thing carefully
2 to keep a wish, feeling or memory in your mind because you think it is important or because it makes you feel happy

cherry (*rhymes with* **very**) *noun* (*plural* **cherries**)
a small round red or black fruit that has a large seed inside it (called a **stone**)

chess *noun* (*no plural*)
a game of **tactics** that two people play on a board with 64 black and white squares. Each player has sixteen pieces that they move around the board according to fixed rules.

chest (say **chest**) *noun* (*plural* **chests**)
1 the top part of the front of your body ➲ See illustration at **body**
2 a large strong box with a lid that you use for storing or carrying things

chestnut (say **chest**-nut) *noun* (*plural* **chestnuts**)
1 a large nut with a shiny red-brown skin
2 the colour of this nut
3 a horse that is this colour

chest of drawers *noun* (*plural* **chests of drawers**)
a large piece of furniture with deep drawers used for keeping clothes in.

chew (say **choo**) *verb* (**chewing, chewed**)
to use your teeth to break up food in your mouth when you are eating: *You should* ***chew*** *your food thoroughly.*

chic (say **shik**) *adjective*
fashionable and elegant: ***chic****, smart women who want classy clothes*

chick (say **chik**) *noun* (*plural* **chicks**)
a baby bird, especially a baby chicken: *a hen with her* ***chicks***

chicken (say **chik**-in) *noun*
1 (*plural* **chickens**) a bird that people often keep for its eggs and its meat
2 (*no plural*) the meat from this bird: *roast* ***chicken***

chickenpox (say **chik**-in-pokss) *noun* (*no plural*)
a disease, especially of children, which makes you feel very hot and gives you red spots on your skin that make you want to scratch

chief[1] (say **cheef**) *adjective*
most important: *Bad driving is one of the* ***chief*** *causes of road accidents.*

chief[2] (say **cheef**) *noun* (*plural* **chiefs**)
the leader or ruler of a group of people: *the* ***chief*** *of a tribe* ◇ *police* ***chiefs***

chiefdom (say **cheef**-duhm) *noun* (*plural* **chiefdoms**)
an area of land that is ruled by a chief

chiefly (say **cheef**-lee) *adverb*
not completely, but mostly: *His success was due* ***chiefly*** *to hard work.* ➲ **SYNONYMS largely, mainly**

A B C D E F G H I J K L M N O P Q R S T U V W X Y Z

chieftain (say **cheef**-tuhn) *noun* (*plural* **chieftains**)
the leader of a small group of people who have the same language and customs

chiffon (say **shif**-on) *noun* (*no plural*)
a thin, transparent cloth that is used for making clothes

child (say **chyld**) *noun* (*plural* **children**)
1 a young boy or girl: *Her **child** is sick.*
2 a daughter or son: *Have you got any **children**?* ◇ *One of her **children** got married.*

childbirth (say **chyld**-burth) *noun* (*no plural*)
the act of giving birth to a baby: *His wife died in **childbirth**.* ◇ *natural **childbirth***

childhood (say **chyld**-huud) *noun* (*no plural*)
the time when you are a child: *She had a happy **childhood**.*

childish (say **chyld**-ish) *adjective*
like a child: *Don't be so **childish**! It's only a game.* ➲ SYNONYM **immature**

chill¹ (say **chil**) *verb* (**chilling**, **chilled**)
1 to become or to make somebody or something colder: ***Chill** the wine before serving it.* ◇ *The cold wind **chilled** our fingers.*
2 (also **chill out**) (*informal*) to relax and not feel angry or worried about anything
3 to shock and frighten somebody: *The sound **chilled** me to the bone.*

chill² (say **chil**) *noun* (*no plural*)
an unpleasant cold feeling: *Autumn brought a **chill** to the air.* ◇ *(figurative) A **chill** of fear crept down my spine.*

chilli (say **chil**-ee) *noun* (*plural* **chillies**)
a small green or red vegetable that has a very strong hot taste: ***chilli** powder*
ⓘ ORIGIN: 17th century, through Spanish from Nahuatl *chilli*. Nahuatl is a language spoken in Mexico and Central America.

chilly (say **chil**-ee) *adjective* (**chillier**, **chilliest**)
cold: *a **chilly** morning* ➲ SYNONYM **nippy** 1

chime (*rhymes with* **time**) *verb* (**chiming**, **chimed**)
to make the sound that a bell makes: *The clock **chimed** midnight.*

chimney (say **chim**-nee) *noun* (*plural* **chimneys**)
a pipe which carries smoke or steam up and out through the roof of a building

chimpanzee (say chim-pan-**zee**) *noun* (*plural* **chimpanzees**)
a smallish very intelligent **ape** that lives in the forests of central Africa

chin *noun* (*plural* **chins**)
the part of your face below your mouth
➲ See illustration at **face¹**

china (say **chine**-uh) *noun* (*no plural*)
a hard white material made from baked clay, or objects such as plates and cups that are made from this: *a **china** cup*

chink *noun* (*plural* **chinks**)
1 a small narrow opening, or a line of light shining through such an opening: *Daylight came in through a **chink** between the curtains.*
2 the short high sound that objects made of metal or glass make when they touch each other: *the **chink** of bottles*

chintz (say **chintss**) *noun* (*no plural*)
a shiny cotton cloth with a colourful pattern that is used for making curtains or covering furniture

chip¹ (say **chip**) *noun* (*plural* **chips**)
1 a thin stick of potato cooked in hot oil and eaten hot: *We had fish and **chips** for lunch.*
2 a very thin slice of potato cooked in hot oil and eaten cold. They are sold in bags and have many different flavours: *salt and vinegar **chips***
3 the place where a small piece of wood, stone or other material has broken off a larger piece: *This dish has a **chip** in it.*
4 (also **microchip**) a small part inside a computer that carries an electronic **circuit** 2 which makes the computer work

chip² (say **chip**) *verb* (**chipping**, **chipped**)
to break a small piece off something hard: *I **chipped** a cup.*

chipboard (say **chip**-bawd) *noun* (*no plural*)
a hard board made from small pieces of wood that are pressed and stuck together

chirp (say **churp**) *verb* (**chirped**, **chirping**)
to make the short high sound typical of birds

chisel (say **chiz**-l) *noun* (*plural* **chisels**)
a tool with a sharp end that you use for cutting and shaping wood or stone
► **chisel** (*verb*): *He **chiselled** the date into the rock.*

chitin (say **ky**-tin) *noun* (*no plural*) (*biology*)
a hard horn-like substance: *The exoskeleton of a beetle is made of **chitin**.*

chivalrous (say **shiv**-uhl-ruhss) *adjective* (*formal*)
(of a man) polite and showing respect for other people, especially women
► **chivalry** (*noun*): *old-fashioned **chivalry***

chive (*rhymes with* **dive**) *noun* (*plural* **chives**)
a small plant with long green leaves that taste like onions

chloride (say **klaw**-ride) *noun* (*plural* **chlorides**) (*science*)
a compound of **chlorine** and another chemical element: *sodium **chloride***

chlorinate (say **klaw**-rin-ayt) *verb* (**chlorinating, chlorinated**)
to put **chlorine** into something, especially water: *a **chlorinated** swimming pool*

chlorine (say **klaw**-reen) *noun* (*no plural*) (*science*) (symbol Cl)
1 a yellow-green gas with a strong smell, that is used to clean drinking water
2 a white powder containing this gas, that is used to clean swimming pools

chlorophyll (say **klo**-ruh-fil) *noun* (*no plural*) (*biology*)
the green substance in plants and other organisms that takes in light from the sun and helps them to grow ➲ See illustration at **photosynthesis**

chloroplast (say **klo**-ruh-plast *or* **klo**-ruh-plaast) *noun* (*plural* **chloroplasts**) (*biology*)
the part of the cells in green plants and other organisms that contains **chlorophyll**, and where **photosynthesis** is carried out

chock-a-block (say chok-a-**blok**) *adjective* (*informal*)
(not before a noun) very full of people or things pressed close together: *Her shelves were **chock-a-block** with books.*

chock-full (say chok-**fuul**) *adjective* (*informal*)
completely full ➲ SYNONYM **packed**

chocolate (say **chok**-luht) *noun* (*plural* **chocolates**)
a dark brown sweet food that is made from seeds (called **cocoa beans**) that grow on trees in hot countries: *Do you like **chocolate**?* ◇ *a bar of **chocolate*** ◇ *Who ate all the **chocolates**?*
❶ ORIGIN: 17th century, through French and Spanish, from Nahuatl *chocolatl* meaning 'food made from cacao seeds'. Nahuatl is a language spoken in Mexico and Central America.

choice (say **choyss**) *noun*
1 (*plural* **choices**) the act of choosing between two or more people or things: *You made the right **choice**.*
2 (*no plural*) the right or chance to choose: *We have no **choice**. We have to leave.*
3 (*no plural*) the things that you can choose from: *We have a **choice** of six different films.*
➲ The verb is **choose**

choir (say **kwy**-uh) *noun* (*plural* **choirs**)
a group of people who sing together: *a school **choir***
❶ ORIGIN: 13th–15th century through Old French *quer*, through Latin *chorus* from Greek *khoros*

choke (*rhymes with* **joke**) *verb* (**choking, choked**)
to not be able to breathe because something is in your throat: *He **choked** on a fish bone.*

cholera (say **kol**-uh-ruh) *noun* (*no plural*)
a serious infectious disease that causes **diarrhoea** and vomiting and even death: *The flooding caused an outbreak* (= sudden increase) *of **cholera**.*

cholesterol (say kol-**ess**-tuh-rol) *noun* (*no plural*)
a fat-like substance that is found in the blood, muscles and other parts of the body. Too much cholesterol can cause heart disease.

choose (say **chooz**) *verb* (**choosing, chose, has chosen**)
to decide which thing or person you want: *You can **choose** whether to come home now or later.* ◇ *I had to **choose** between dancing and tennis.*
➲ The noun is **choice**

chop[1] *verb* (**chopping, chopped**)
to cut something into pieces with an **axe** or big knife: ***Chop** the meat up into small pieces.* ◇ *We **chopped** some wood for the fire.*

chop[2] *noun* (*plural* **chops**)
a thick slice of meat with a piece of bone in it: *a lamb **chop***

chopper (say **chop**-uh) *noun* (*plural* **choppers**)
1 (*informal*) short for **helicopter**
2 a machine or device used for cutting something into pieces: *a straw **chopper***

chopsticks (say **chop**-stikss) *plural noun*
a pair of thin sticks that are used for eating with, especially in some Asian countries

choral (say **kaw**-ruhl) *adjective*
relating to music that is written for, or is sung by, a group of singers (a **choir**)

chord (say **kawd**) *noun* (*plural* **chords**)
1 two or more musical notes that are played at the same time
2 (*maths*) a straight line connecting two points on a curve or circle

chordophone (say **kawd**-oh-fohn) *noun* (*plural* **chordophones**) (*music*)
a musical instrument that uses strings to produce sound, such as a guitar or a piano

chore (say **chaw**) *noun* (*plural* **chores**)
a task that is boring but that you must do: *We share the household **chores**.*

choreograph (say **ko**-ree-uh-graaf) *verb* (**choreographing, choreographed**)
to design and arrange the movements for a dance performance

▶ **choreographer** (*noun*): *She is a teacher, dancer and **choreographer**.*

choreography (say ko-ree-**og**-ruh-fee) *noun* (*no plural*)
the art of designing and arranging the movements for a dance performance
▶ **choreographic** (*adjective*): *The songs turned into **choreographic** presentations when they were played live.*

chorus (say **kaw**-ruhss) *noun* (*plural* **choruses**)
a part of a song that you repeat

chose (say **chohz**) form of **choose**

chosen (say **chohz**-uhn) form of **choose**

Christ (say **kryst**) = **Jesus Christ**

christen (say **kriss**-uhn) *verb* (**christening, christened**)
to give a name to a baby and make him or her a member of the Christian church in a special ceremony
▶ **christening** (*noun*): *The baby wore a white dress at her **christening**.*

Christian (say **kriss**-tshuhn) *noun* (*plural* **Christians**)
a person who believes in Jesus Christ and what he taught
▶ **Christian** (*adjective*): *the **Christian** church*

Christianity (say kriss-ti-**an**-i-tee) *noun* (*no plural*)
the religion that follows what Jesus Christ taught

Christmas (say **kriss**-muhss) *noun* (*no plural*)
the period of time around and including 25 December, when Christians remember the birth of Jesus Christ: *Merry **Christmas**!* ◇ *We spent **Christmas** with my grandmother.*

chromatic (say kroh-**mat**-ik) *adjective* (*music*)
used to describe a series of musical notes that rise and fall

chrome (say **krohm**) *noun* (*no plural*)
= **chromium**

chromium (say **kroh**-mi-uhm) *noun* (*no plural*) (also **chrome**) (symbol Cr)
a hard shiny metal that is used for covering other metals

chromosome (say **kroh**-muh-sohm) *noun* (*plural* **chromosomes**) (*biology*)
a thread-like structure in the core of living cells that carries **genetic** information about the sex, character, shape and other features that a person, animal or plant will have

chronic (say **kron**-ik) *adjective*
continuing for a long time or always present: *a **chronic** illness* ◇ *a **chronic** water shortage*
▶ **chronically** (*adverb*): ***chronically** ill patients*

chronicle (say **kron**-ik-l) *noun* (*plural* **chronicles**)
a written record of historical events describing them in the order in which they happened
▶ **chronicle** (*verb*): *The film **chronicles** his life story.*

chronological (say kron-oh-**loj**-ik-l) *adjective*
arranged in the order in which the events happened: *Please list your work experience in **chronological** order.*
▶ **chronologically** (*adverb*): *The exhibition is arranged **chronologically**.*

chronology (say kron-**ol**-uh-jee) *noun* (*plural* **chronologies**)
the order in which a series of events happened, or their arrangement according to this order

chrysalis (say **kriss**-uh-liss) *noun* (*plural* **chrysalises**) (*biology*)
the stage of an insect while it is changing into an adult, usually inside a hard case: *The **chrysalis** was slowly turning into a butterfly inside its cocoon.* ➲ SYNONYM **pupa** ➲ See illustration at **metamorphosis**

chrysanthemum (say kriss-**an**-thuh-muhm) *noun* (*plural* **chrysanthemums**)
a type of flower with brightly coloured petals

chubby (say **chub**-ee) *adjective* (**chubbier, chubbiest**)
slightly fat in a pleasant way: *a baby with **chubby** cheeks*

chuck (say **chuk**) *verb* (**chucking, chucked**) (*informal*)
1 to throw something in a careless way: *She **chucked** her bag into the back of the car.*
2 to get rid of something that you do not want: *You can **chuck** those old shoes.*
3 (also **chuck in**) to give something up: *He **chucked** his job because he was fed up.*
chuck somebody out of something to force somebody to leave a place: *If you don't pay your rent you will be **chucked** out of the flat.*

chuckle (say **chuk**-l) *verb* (**chuckling, chuckled**)
to laugh quietly
▶ **chuckle** (*noun*): *There was a **chuckle** from the audience.*

chuffed (say **chuft**) *adjective* (*informal*)
very pleased or happy: *She was **chuffed** with her progress.*

chunk *noun* (*plural* **chunks**)
a large piece of something: *a **chunk** of cheese*

church (say **church**) *noun* (*plural* **churches**)
a building where Christians go to **worship**

God: *They go to **church** every Sunday.*
ⓘ **ORIGIN**: from Old English *circe*, *cirice*, related to Dutch *kerk*, from Greek *kuriakon* meaning 'Lord's house'

USAGE When we talk about going to a ceremony (a **service**) in a **church**, we say **in church**, **to church** or **at church** without 'a' or 'the': *Was Mrs Dyanti at **church** today?* We use **a** or **the** to talk about the building: *the **church** where we got married.*

churn *verb* (**churning**, **churned**)
1 (also **churn up**) to move or to make a liquid or a soft solid move around violently: *The buck **churned** up the dust as they ran towards the water hole.* ◇ *The water **churned** beneath the huge ship.*
2 (your stomach) to feel sick: *Reading about the murder made my stomach **churn**.*
3 to make butter by beating cream
churn something out to produce large numbers of something very quickly: *Modern factories can **churn** out cars at an amazing speed.*

chute (say **shoot**) *noun* (*plural* **chutes**)
a long narrow passage down which you can send things such as rubbish or water

chutney (say **chut**-nee) *noun* (*no plural*)
a thick sauce with a strong taste, that you eat cold with meat dishes
ⓘ **ORIGIN**: 19th century, from Hindi *caṭnī*

cicada (say si-**kaa**-duh) *noun* (*plural* **cicadas**)
a large insect that makes a continuous high sound

cider (say **side**-uh) *noun* (*no plural*)
an alcoholic drink made from apples

cigar (say si-**gaa**) *noun* (*plural* **cigars**)
a roll made of a dried **tobacco** leaf that some people like to smoke. It is larger and thicker than a cigarette.

cigarette (say sig-uh-**ret**) *noun* (*plural* **cigarettes**)
a thin tube of white paper filled with dried **tobacco** that some people like to smoke: *a packet of **cigarettes***
ⓘ **ORIGIN**: through French *cigare* or Spanish *cigarro*, probably from Mayan *sik'ar* meaning 'smoking'. Mayan is a language spoken in Central America.

cinder (say **sin**-duh) *noun* (*plural* **cinders**)
a piece of burnt coal or wood, especially one that continues to send out heat

cinema (say **sin**-i-muh) *noun* (also **movie house**)
1 (*plural* **cinemas**) a place where you go to see a film: *Let's go to the **cinema** tonight.*
2 (*no plural*) films as art, or the film industry
➲ See **movie** 1, **film**[1] 1
ⓘ **ORIGIN**: 20th century, through French from Greek *kinema* meaning 'movement'

cinematography (say sin-uh-ma-**tog**-ruh-fee) *noun* (*no plural*)
the art or process of making films

cinnamon (say **sin**-uh-muhn) *noun* (*no plural*)
a brown powder used in cooking as a spice, especially to give flavour to sweet foods

cipher (say **sife**-uh) *noun* (*plural* **ciphers**)
a way of writing secret messages in which certain letters are put in the place of other letters according to a system ➲ See **decipher**
▸ **cipher** (*verb*): ***ciphering** a message*

circa (say **sur**-kuh) *preposition* (abbr. c or ca)
used before a date to show that the date of the event is approximately known, but not certain: *Shaka Zulu was born **circa** 1787.* ◇ *The photograph was taken **c** 1984.*

circle[1] (say **surk**-l) *noun* (*plural* **circles**)
a flat round shape or a ring: *There are 360 degrees in a **circle**.*
ⓘ **ORIGIN**: from Old English, through Old French *cercle* from Latin *circus* meaning 'ring'

circle

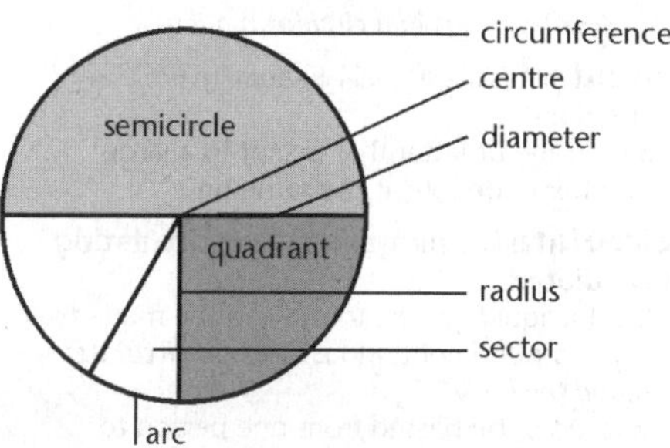

circle[2] (say **surk**-l) *verb* (**circling**, **circled**)
1 to move in a circle, or to go around something in a circle: *The lions **circled** the buck and caught it.*
2 to draw a circle around something: *Please **circle** the words in the puzzle.*

circuit (say **sur**-kit) *noun* (*plural* **circuits**)
1 a circular route, track or journey: *the Kyalami motor racing **circuit***
2 the complete path of wires and equipment along which an electric current flows: *an electrical **circuit*** ◇ *a **circuit** diagram* ➲ See illustration on next page
3 a series of sports competitions or other

organized events that the same people regularly visit: *She's one of the best players on the tennis **circuit**.*

electrical circuit

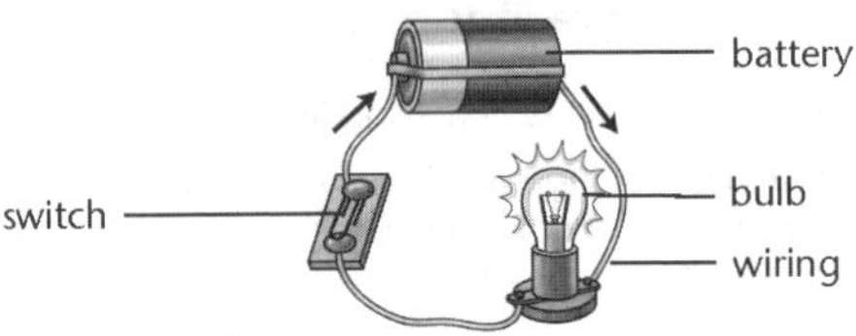

actual circuit, with switch closed and light on, showing direction of current

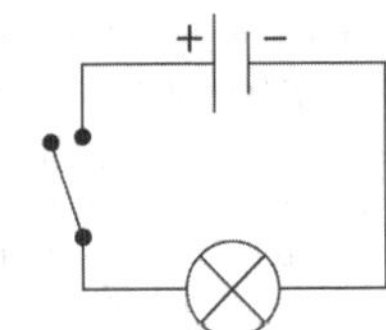

diagram of circuit, with switch open

circuitous (say sur-**kyoo**-it-uhss) *adjective* (*formal*)
not straight or direct: *They followed the **circuitous** course of the river.*

circular[1] (say **sur**-kyuu-luh) *adjective*
with the shape of a circle: *a **circular** table* ◇ *Move your legs in a **circular** motion.*

circular[2] (say **sur**-kyuu-luh) *noun* (*plural* **circulars**)
a message or letter that is sent to a large number of people at the same time

circulate (say **sur**-kyuu-layt) *verb* (**circulating, circulated**)
1 (of a liquid or gas) to move or be made to move around continuously: *Blood **circulates** round the body.*
2 to go or be passed from one person to another: *We've **circulated** a copy of the report.*

circulation (say sur-kyuu-**lay**-shuhn) *noun* (*no plural*)
1 the movement of blood around the body
2 the passing or spreading of something from one person or place to another: *the **circulation** of news or information or rumours*
3 the usual number of copies of a newspaper or magazine sold each day, week or month

circum- (say **sur**-kuhm) *prefix*
around: *The **circumpolar** region is made up of eight countries that circle the North Pole.*
ⓘ **ORIGIN:** from Latin *circum* meaning 'round'

circumcise (say **sur**-kuhm-size) *verb* (**circumcising, circumcised**)
to cut off the skin at the end of a man's sexual organ **(penis)** or to remove part of a woman's sexual organs, for religious, cultural, or (in the case of a man) medical reasons
▸ **circumcision** (*noun*)

circumference (say sur-**kum**-fuh-rinss) *noun* (*plural* **circumferences**) (*maths*)
the distance around a circle ➲ See illustration at **circle**[1]
ⓘ **ORIGIN:** 14th–15th century, from Latin *circum* meaning 'around' + *ferre* meaning 'carry'

circumnavigate (say sur-kuhm-**nav**-i-gayt) *verb* (**circumnavigating, circumnavigated**)
to move all the way around something
▸ **circumnavigation** (*noun*): *the **circumnavigation** of the world along the equator*

circumspect (say **sur**-kyhm-spekt) *adjective* (*formal*)
thinking carefully about something before you make decisions or judgements: *Be more **circumspect** about walking home alone at night.*

circumstance (say **sur**-kuhm-stanss) *noun* (*plural* **circumstances**)
a fact that is true in a particular situation
in or **under no circumstances** never, not for any reason: *Under no **circumstances** should you go out alone at night.*
in or **under the circumstances** as the result of a particular situation: *This is the best solution in the **circumstances**.*

circumvent (say sur-kuhm-**vent**) *verb* (**circumventing, circumvented**) (*formal*)
1 to find a way of avoiding a difficulty, rule or law
2 to go around something that is in your way: *The players tried to **circumvent** the puddles.*

circus (say **sur**-kuhss) *noun* (*plural* **circuses**)
a show in a big tent by entertainers, sometimes with trained animals, who perform skilful or amusing acts

cirrus (say **si**-ruhss) *noun* (*no plural*)
a type of light white cloud that forms high in the sky: ***Cirrus** clouds are composed of ice crystals.*

cistern (say **siss**-tuhn) *noun* (*plural* **cisterns**)
a container for storing water, especially one that is part of a toilet

citadel (say **sit**-uh-del) *noun* (*plural* **citadels**)
a large strong building in or near a city that was built in the past to keep people safe from attack

citation (say sy-**tay**-shuhn) *noun* (*plural* **citations**)
1 words or lines taken from a book or a speech
2 an official statement about something special that somebody has done: *a **citation** for bravery*

cite (say **site**) *verb* (**citing, cited**) (*formal*)
to mention something, such as a fact from a

book, as an example to support or help explain what you are saying

citizen (say **sit**-i-zuhn) *noun* (*plural* **citizens**)
a person who belongs to a country or a city: *She became a South African **citizen** in 1995.*

citronella (say sit-roh-**nel**-uh) *noun* (*no plural*)
a sweet-smelling oil obtained from a type of grass that is used in **perfume** and soap, and to keep **mosquitoes** away

citrus fruit (say **sit**-ruhss froot) *noun* (*plural* **citrus fruits**)
a fruit such as an orange or a lemon

city (say **sit**-ee) *noun* (*plural* **cities**)
a big and important town: *the **city** of Johannesburg* ◇ *the **city** centre*
ORIGIN: 13th–15th century, through Old French *cite* from Latin *civitas* meaning 'citizenship or city-state'

civic (say **siv**-ik) *adjective*
relating to the government and community of a town or city: ***civic** duties*

civics (say **siv**-ikss) *plural noun*
the study of the duties and rights of citizens

civil (say **siv**-uhl) *adjective*
1 (only *before* a noun) related to the people who live in a country: ***civil** disorder* (= involving groups of people within the same country)
2 (only *before* a noun) connected with the state rather than with religion or with the armed forces: *a **civil** wedding* (= not a religious one)
3 (only *before* a noun) (in law) connected with the personal legal matters of ordinary people and not criminal law: ***civil** courts*
➲ See **criminal**[1]
4 polite, but not very friendly: *They remained **civil** to each other after they broke up.*

civilian (say suh-**vil**-i-uhn) *noun* (*plural* **civilians**)
a person who does not belong to a military organization or the police

civilization (say siv-uhl-*y*-**zay**-shuhn) *noun* (*plural* **civilizations**) (also **civilisation**)
the way people live together in a society with laws, education and a government: *the ancient **civilizations** of Greece and Rome*

civilized (say **siv**-uh-lize-d) *adjective* (also **civilised**)
(used about a society) well-organized and having a high level of social and cultural development

civil rights *plural noun*
a person's legal rights to freedom and to equal treatment in society: *the **civil rights** leader Martin Luther King* ➲ See **human rights**

civil servant *noun* (*plural* **civil servants**)
a person who works in **civil service**

civil service *noun* (*no plural*)
the government departments in a country, and the people who work for them

civil war *noun* (*plural* **civil wars**)
a war between groups of people who live in the same country

cl *abbreviation* (*plural* **cl**) (also **cL**) **centilitre**

claim[1] (say **klaym**) *noun* (*plural* **claims**)
1 a statement that something is true, but which does not have any proof: *Nobody believed his **claim** that he found the money.*
2 something that you ask for because you think you have a right to it: *The workers are making a **claim** for better pay.*

claim[2] (say **klaym**) *verb* (**claiming, claimed**)
1 to say that something is true: *He **claims** that he did the work without help.*
2 to ask for something because it is yours: *If nobody **claims** the camera you found, you may keep it.*

clairvoyant (say klair-**voy**-uhnt) *noun* (*plural* **clairvoyants**)
a person who some people believe can see things that cannot be explained and who can predict what will happen in the future
▸ **clairvoyant** (*adjective*): ***clairvoyant** visions*

clam (say **klam**) *noun* (*plural* **clams**)
a type of shellfish that you can eat

clamber (say **klam**-buh) *verb* (**clambering, clambered**)
to move or climb with difficulty, usually using both your hands and feet: *You have to **clamber** over the rocks to get to the spot.*

clammy (say **klam**-ee) *adjective* (**clammier, clammiest**)
a little wet, cold and sticky in an unpleasant way: *Her clothes were wet and **clammy**.*

clamour (say **klam**-uh) *verb* (**clamouring, clamoured**)
to demand something in a noisy or angry way: *The children were **clamouring** for attention.*
▸ **clamour** (*noun*): *The **clamour** of angry voices*

clamp[1] (say **klamp**) *verb* (**clamping, clamped**)
1 to use a device to join two things together or to fasten one thing to another: ***Clamp** the wood to the table so that it doesn't move.*
2 to hold something tightly in a particular position: *Blow up the balloon and **clamp** the opening with a peg.*
3 to fit a special metal device to the wheel of a vehicle that has been parked illegally so that it cannot move

A B C D E F G H I J K L M N O P Q R S T U V W X Y Z

clamp down on something to take strong action in order to control or stop something: *The police are **clamping** down on people who drive too fast.*

clamp[2] (say **klamp**) *noun* (*plural* **clamps**)
1 a tool used to hold things tightly together, usually by means of a screw
2 a device that is fixed to the wheel of a car that has been parked illegally, so that it cannot drive away

clan (say **klan**) *noun* (*plural* **clans**)
a group of families who are related to each other: *Can you marry a member of the same **clan**?*

clandestine (say klan-**dess**-tin) *adjective* (*formal*)
done secretly, often because it is illegal: ***clandestine** operations to kill political opponents*

clang (say **klang**) *verb* (**clanging, clanged**)
to make a loud sound, such as that you hear when you hit metal with something: *The iron gates **clanged** shut.*

clap (say **klap**) *verb* (**clapping, clapped**)
1 to hit your hands together to make a noise, usually to show that you like something: *At the end of the concert the audience **clapped**.*
2 to put something onto something else quickly and firmly: *'Oh no, I shouldn't have said that,' she said, **clapping** a hand over her mouth.*

clarify (say **kla**-ri-fy) *verb* (**clarifying, clarified**)
to make something easier to understand by explaining it in a different way or in greater detail
▸ **clarification** (*noun*): *Ask for **clarification** if you don't understand a question.*

clarinet (say kla-ri-**net**) *noun* (*plural* **clarinets**)
a musical instrument of the **woodwind** group. The top end into which you blow has a reed, the body is a cylinder of dark wood, the holes have stops and the bottom end is flared.

clarity (say **kla**-ri-tee) *noun* (*no plural*)
the quality of being clear and easy to see, hear or understand

clash[1] (say **klash**) *noun* (*plural* **clashes**)
1 a fight or a serious argument: *a **clash** between police and demonstrators*
2 a loud noise made by hitting two metal objects together

clash[2] (say **klash**) *verb* (**clashing, clashed**)
1 to fight or argue about something: *Police **clashed** with demonstrators at the station.*
2 to happen at the same time: *The match **clashed** with my swimming lesson.*
3 (colours) to look ugly when put together: *That red tie **clashes** with your shirt.*

clasp[1] (say **klaasp**) *verb* (**clasping, clasped**)
to hold somebody or something tightly: *He **clasped** her hand.* ➲ SYNONYMS **clutch**[1], **grip**

clasp[2] (say **klaasp**) *noun* (*plural* **clasps**)
a metal object that fastens or holds something together: *the **clasp** on a necklace*

class (say **klaass**) *noun* (*plural* **classes**)
1 a group of children or students who learn together: *There is a new girl in my **class**.* ◇ *The whole **class** passed the exam.*
2 the time when you learn something with a teacher: ***Classes** begin at nine o'clock.* ◇ *You mustn't eat in **class*** (= during the lesson). ➲ SYNONYM **lesson**
3 a group of people or things that are the same in some way: *There are many different **classes** of animals.*
4 each of two or more levels of comfort available to travellers in a plane or train: *It costs more to travel first **class**.*

classic (say **klass**-ik) *noun* (*plural* **classics**)
a book, film or piece of music that is so good that it is still popular many years after it was written or made: *'Alice in Wonderland' is a children's **classic**.*

classical (say **klass**-ik-uhl) *adjective*
1 in a style that people have used for a long time because they think it is good: ***classical** dance* ➲ OPPOSITE **modern** ➲ See **traditional**
2 related to ancient Greece or Rome: ***classical** Greek architecture*
3 describing music that is considered serious and is written in a traditional or formal style, such as that of the **symphony** or opera: *Mozart is a well-loved composer* (= a person who writes music) *of **classical** music.*

classify (say **klass**-i-fy) *verb* (**classifying, classified**)
to put somebody or something into a group with other people or things that are the same in some way: *Most African countries are **classified** as developing nations.*
▸ **classification** (*noun*): *a **classification** system for library books*

classmate (say **klaass**-mayt) *noun* (*plural* **classmates**)
a person who is in the same class as you at school

classroom (say **klaass**-room) *noun* (*plural* **classrooms**)
a room where you have lessons in a school or college

clatter (say **klat**-uh) *verb* (**clattering, clattered**)
to make the loud noise of hard things hitting

each other: *The knives and forks* ***clattered*** *to the floor.*
▶ **clatter** (*noun*): *the* ***clatter*** *of horses' hoofs*
🛈 **ORIGIN**: from Old English. The word came from imitating the sound.

clause (say **klawz**) *noun* (*plural* **clauses**)
1 (*grammar*) a part of a sentence that has a verb in it: *The sentence 'After we had finished eating, we went out' contains two* ***clauses****.*
2 a section in a document that says something must or must not be done: *Do you understand all the* ***clauses*** *in this contract?*

claustrophobia (say klawss-truh-**foh**-bi-uh) *noun* (*no plural*)
a fear of being in a small enclosed space or being in situations which are difficult to escape from
▶ **claustrophobic** (*adjective*): *I feel* ***claustrophobic*** *when I go up in a lift.*

clavicle (say **klav**-ik-uhl) *noun* (*plural* **clavicles**)
= **collarbone**

claw (say **klaw**) *noun* (*plural* **claws**)
one of the hard pointed parts on the feet of some animals and birds: *Cats have sharp* ***claws****.*

clay (say **klay**) *noun* (*no plural*)
a type of heavy, sticky earth that becomes hard when it is baked. It is used to make things such as pots and bricks.

clean¹ (say **kleen**) *adjective* (**cleaner**, **cleanest**)
1 free from dirt, marks or stains: ***clean*** *clothes* ◇ *Are your hands* ***clean****?*
2 that does not offend or refer to sex: *Keep your jokes* ***clean****, please.* ◇ *good* ***clean*** *fun for the whole family*
3 having no record of offences or crimes: *a* ***clean*** *driving licence*

clean² (say **kleen**) *verb* (**cleaning**, **cleaned**)
to remove the dirt or marks from something or to make something clean: *We* ***cleaned*** *the kitchen.* ◇ ***Clean*** *your teeth before you go to bed.*
▶ **clean** (*noun*): *The car needs a* ***clean****.*

cleaner (say **kleen**-uh) *noun* (*plural* **cleaners**)
1 a person whose job is to clean people's houses or other buildings: *an office* ***cleaner***
2 a substance or a machine that you use to clean something: *I bought some floor* ***cleaner****.*
➲ See **vacuum cleaner**

clear¹ (say **kleer**) *adjective* (**clearer**, **clearest**)
1 easy to see, hear or understand: *She spoke in a loud,* ***clear*** *voice.* ◇ *These instructions aren't very* ***clear****.* ◇ *It's* ***clear*** *that he's not happy.*
➲ The noun is **clarity**
2 easy to see through: ***clear*** *glass*
3 free from marks: *a* ***clear*** *sky* (= without clouds) ◇ ***clear*** *skin* (= without spots)
4 with nothing blocking the way: *The pass is now* ***clear*** *of fallen rocks.*

clear² (say **kleer**) *verb* (**clearing**, **cleared**)
1 to remove things from a place because you do not want or need them there: *After the meal, please* ***clear*** *the table* (= take away the dirty plates).
2 (used about the sky, the weather or water) to become free of clouds, rain or mud: *After the rain, the sky* ***cleared****.*
clear something out to make something empty and clean by removing things or throwing things away that you do not want
clear up, **clear something up** to make a place clean and tidy: *She helped me to* ***clear*** *up after the party.* ◇ ***Clear*** *up your own mess!*
clear a person (of something) to provide proof that a person is innocent of something: *The official has finally been* ***cleared*** *of fraud* (= doing dishonest things for money).

clearly (say **kleer**-lee) *adverb*
1 in a way that is easy to see, hear or understand: *I can't hear you very* ***clearly****.* ◇ *The notes explain* ***clearly*** *what you have to do.*
2 without any doubt: *She is* ***clearly*** *very intelligent.*

clef (say **klef**) *noun* (*plural* **clefs**) (*music*)
a symbol at the beginning of the lines on which music is written that shows the range of sound that the notes are in: *the bass* ***clef*** ◇ *the treble* ***clef***

clemency (say **klem**-uhn-see) *noun* (*no plural*) (*formal*)
kindness shown to a person who has committed a crime: *The president refused to grant* ***clemency*** *to the murderer.*

clench (say **klench**) *verb* (**clenching**, **clenched**)
to close or hold tightly: *She* ***clenched*** *her lips to hold back the sobs.*
▶ **clench** (*noun*): *He tightened his* ***clench*** *on her wrist.*

clergy (say **klurj**-ee) *plural noun*
the people who have been made priests or ministers and who perform religious ceremonies: *There was a meeting of all the* ***clergy*** *of the town.*

clerical (say **kle**-rik-uhl) *adjective*
1 relating to the work of a **clerk**: *Phangela has a* ***clerical*** *job at the hospital.*
2 relating to the **clergy**

clerk (say **klaak**) *noun* (*plural* **clerks**)
a person whose job is to do written work or look after accounts in an office, a bank or a shop

A B C D E F G H I J K L M N O P Q R S T U V W X Y Z

clever (say **klev**-uh) *adjective* (**cleverer**, **cleverest**)
quick at learning and understanding things: *a **clever** student* ➲ SYNONYM **intelligent** ➲ OPPOSITE **stupid**
▸ **cleverly** (*adverb*): *The book is **cleverly** written.*

WORD BUILDING There are many words that you can use instead of **clever**, but check their exact meanings first. Examples are: **astute**, **brainy** (informal), **bright** 3, **brilliant** 2, **capable** 2, **crafty**, **creative**, **cunning**, **gifted**, **imaginative**, **ingenious**, **intellectual** 1, **intelligent**, **inventive**, **knowledgeable**, **sensible**, **sharp**[1] 4, **shrewd**, **smart** 2, **wise** and **witty**.

cliché (say **kleesh**-ay) *noun* (*plural* **clichés**)
a phrase or idea that has been used so many times that it no longer has any real meaning or effect

click[1] (say **klik**) *verb* (**clicking**, **clicked**)
1 to make a short sharp sound: *The door **clicked** shut.*
2 (*computing*) to press one of the buttons on a computer mouse: *To open a file, **click** on the menu.*
3 (*informal*) (used about people) to become friends at once or to work well together: *We met at a party and just **clicked**.*
4 (*informal*) (used about a problem) to suddenly become clear or understood: *Once I found the missing letter, it all **clicked** into place.*

click[2] (say **klik**) *noun* (*plural* **clicks**)
1 a short sharp sound: *the **click** of a switch*
2 (*computing*) the act of pressing a button on a computer mouse: *You can do this with a **click** of the mouse.*

client (say **kly**-uhnt) *noun* (*plural* **clients**)
a person who pays another person, for example a lawyer, for help or advice

cliff (say **klif**) *noun* (*plural* **cliffs**)
the high steep side of a hill or mountain
➲ See illustration at **mountain**

climate (say **klime**-uht) *noun* (*plural* **climates**)
the average weather conditions of a place: *Coffee will not grow in a cold **climate**.*
➲ See **weather**[1]

climax (say **kly**-makss) *noun* (*plural* **climaxes**)
the most important part of something or of a period of time: *Winning a medal at the Olympics was the **climax** of her career.*

climb (say **klime**) *verb* (**climbing**, **climbed**)
1 to go up towards the top of something: *She **climbed** up the stairs.*
2 (a road) to slope upwards
3 (an aircraft) to go higher in the sky
4 to move to or from a place when it is not easy to do it: *The boys **climbed** through a hole in the fence.*
▸ **climb** (*noun*): *It was a long **climb** to the top of the mountain.* ▸ **climber** (*noun*): *She's a strong mountain **climber**.*

climbing (say **klime**-ing) *noun* (*no plural*)
the sport of climbing mountains or rocks: *They usually go **climbing** in their holidays.*

clinch (say **klinch**) *verb* (**clinching**, **clinched**) (*informal*)
to finally manage to get what you want: *The team **clinched** the championship last year.* ◇ *The company failed to **clinch** a deal with the bank.*

cling (say **kling**) *verb* (**clinging**, **clung**)
to hold tightly or stick to a person or a thing: *The girl cried and **clung** to her mother.*

clinic (say **klin**-ik) *noun* (*plural* **clinics**)
1 a place where you can go to see a nurse or doctor: *If you are sick, you should go to the **clinic**.*
2 a place, usually in a hospital, where you can get special help from a doctor: *an ear, nose and throat **clinic***

clip[1] (say **klip**) *noun* (*plural* **clips**)
a small piece of metal or plastic for holding things together or in place: *a hair **clip***
➲ See **paper clip**

clip[2] (say **klip**) *verb* (**clipping**, **clipped**)
to join something to another thing with a **clip**[1]: ***Clip** the photo to the letter.* ◇ *Do your earrings **clip** on?*

clippers (say **klip**-uhz) *plural noun*
a tool with two blades that come together, which you use for cutting things, for example hair or fingernails

clique (say **kleek**) *noun* (*plural* **cliques**)
a small group of people who spend time together and do not want others to join their group

cloak (say **clohk**) *noun* (*plural* **cloaks**)
a long loose coat that does not have separate sleeves

clobber (say **klob**-uh) *verb* (**clobbering**, **clobbered**) (*informal*)
1 to hit somebody hard
2 to defeat somebody easily or heavily: *The team was expected to win, but they got **clobbered**.*

clock (say **klok**) *noun* (*plural* **clocks**)
a thing that shows you what time it is: *an alarm clock*

WORD BUILDING A small **clock** that you wear on your wrist is called a **watch**. You say that a **clock** or watch is **fast** if it shows a time that is later than the real time. You say that it is **slow** if it shows a time that is earlier than the real time.

clockwise (say **klok**-wize) *adjective, adverb*
in the direction that the hands of a clock move: *Turn the handle* ***clockwise***.
➲ OPPOSITE **anticlockwise**

clog¹ (say **klog**) *noun* (*plural* **clogs**)
a type of shoe made completely of wood or with a wooden bottom part (called a **sole**)

clog² (say **klog**) *verb* (**clogging, clogged**) (also **clog up**)
to block or become blocked: *The roads were* ***clogged*** *with traffic.* ◇ *Cats make me sneeze and then my nose* ***clogs*** *up.*

cloister (say **kloyss**-tuh) *noun* (*plural* **cloisters**)
a covered passage built against buildings that surround an open garden, especially in a place where religious people live and work

clone (*rhymes with* **stone**) *noun* (*plural* **clones**)
1 (*biology*) an exact copy of a plant or animal that has been produced artificially by scientific methods
2 (*informal*) a person or thing that is very similar to another: *IBM computer* ***clones***
▸ **clone** (*verb*): *a technique for* ***cloning*** *animals*

close¹ (say **klohz**) *verb* (**closing, closed**)
1 to shut: *Please* ***close*** *the window.* ◇ ***Close*** *your eyes!* ◇ *The door* ***closed*** *quietly.*
2 to stop being open, so that people cannot go there: *What time does the library* ***close****?*
➲ OPPOSITE **open²**
close down, close something down to stop all business at a shop or factory: *The shop* ***closed*** *down when the owner died.*

PRONUNCIATION Notice that you pronounce the verb differently from the adverb and adjective.

close² (say **klohss**) *adverb, adjective* (**closer, closest**)
1 near: *We live* ***close*** *to the station.* ◇ *Please stand* ***closer*** *together so you can all fit onto the photo.*
2 (of people) knowing each other well and liking each other very much: *I'm very* ***close*** *to my sister.* ◇ ***close*** *friends*
3 (used about a competition or race) only won by a small amount: *a* ***close*** *match*
4 careful: *Take a* ***close*** *look at this picture.*
▸ **closely** (*adverb*): *We watched her* ***closely*** (= carefully).

close corporation *noun* (*plural* **close corporations**) (abbr. CC) (*S. African*)
a small company or business that is run and managed by the people who own it

closed (say **klohz**-d) *adjective*
not open: *The shops are* ***closed*** *on Sundays.* ◇ *Keep your eyes* ***closed***. ➲ SYNONYM **shut²**

closet (say **kloz**-it) *noun* (*plural* **closets**)
a space in a wall with a door that reaches the floor, used for storing clothes and shoes: *a walk-in* ***closet***

closure (say **kloh**-*zhuh*) *noun*
1 (*plural* **closures**) the process of permanently closing down a business, shop or factory: *the* ***closure*** *of the Khayelitsha hospital*
2 (*plural* **closures**) the act of blocking the way to or into a place: *emergency road* ***closures***
3 (*no plural*) the feeling that a difficult or an unpleasant experience has come to an end: *The conviction of their daughter's murderer helped to give them* ***closure***.

clot¹ (say **klot**) *noun* (*plural* **clots**)
1 a small lump of liquid, especially blood, that has become partly solid
2 (*informal*) a silly person: *Don't be such a* ***clot****!*

clot² (say **klot**) *verb* (**clotting, clotted**)
to form or cause to form lumps that are partly solid: *a drug that stops blood from* ***clotting***

cloth (say **kloth**) *noun*
1 (*no plural*) material made of wool or cotton that you use for making clothes for example
2 (*plural* **cloths**) a piece of cloth that you use for a special job: *Do you have a* ***cloth*** *I can use to wipe the floor with?* ➲ See **tablecloth**
ⓘ ORIGIN: from Old English *clath*, related to Dutch *kleed*

clothe (say **kloh*th***) *verb* (**clothing, clothed**)
to provide somebody with clothes: *She struggled to feed and* ***clothe*** *her two children.*

clothes (say **kloh*thz***) *plural noun*
things such as trousers, shirts and coats that you wear to cover your body: *She was wearing new* ***clothes***. ◇ *Take off those wet* ***clothes***.

clothing (say **klo*th***-ing) *noun* (*no plural*)
clothes, especially a particular type of clothes: *You will need waterproof* ***clothing***.

cloud (say **klowd**) *noun* (*plural* **clouds**)
1 a white or grey shape in the sky that is made of small drops of water: *Look at those dark* ***clouds***. *It's going to rain.*

A B C D E F G H I J K L M N O P Q R S T U V W X Y Z

2 a large mass of something in the air, for example dust or smoke: ***clouds** of smoke*

cloudburst (say **klowd**-burst) *noun* (*plural* **cloudbursts**)
a sudden heavy fall of rain

cloudy (say **klowd**-ee) *adjective* (**cloudier**, **cloudiest**)
with a lot of clouds: *a **cloudy** sky ◇ **cloudy** weather*

clout (say **klowt**) *noun* (*informal*)
1 (*plural* **clouts**) a hard hit
2 (*no plural*) influence and power: *He is an important man with a lot of political **clout**.*
▸ **clout** (*verb*): *She **clouted** him over the head with her handbag.*

clove (say **klohv**) *noun* (*plural* **cloves**)
1 a small dried flower that looks like a little nail, of a tree that grows in hot countries and used as a spice in cooking.
2 one of the small separate sections of **garlic**: *Crush two **cloves** of garlic.*

cloven (say **klohv**-uhn) *adjective*
split or divided
cloven hoof an animal's foot that is divided into two parts: *A cow has a **cloven** hoof.*

clover (say **kloh**-vuh) *noun* (*no plural*)
a small plant with leaves that are divided into three parts: *Some people believe that a four-leaf **clover** brings good luck.*

clown (say **klown**) *noun* (*plural* **clowns**)
a person who wears funny clothes and a big red nose and does silly things to make people laugh
🛈 **ORIGIN**: 16th century. The origin of this word is not known.

cloying (say **kloy**-ing) *adjective* (*formal*)
1 so sweet that it is unpleasant: *the **cloying** smell of incense*
2 showing feelings that are too strong and not appropriate: *the **cloying** lyrics of a love song*

club¹ (say **klub**) *noun* (*plural* **clubs**)
1 a group of people who do something together, or the place where they meet: *I belong to the golf **club**.*
2 (also **nightclub**) a place where people, especially young people, go and listen to music, talk and dance
3 a heavy stick with one thick end, used as a weapon
4 a long thin stick that is used for hitting a ball when playing golf ➲ See note at **bat¹**
5 clubs (*plural noun*) the group of playing cards (called a **suit**) that have the shape ♣ on them: *the three of **clubs***

club² (say **klub**) *verb* (**clubbing**, **clubbed**)
to hit a person or an animal with a heavy stick or other object: *People get very upset when seal pups are **clubbed**.*
club together (a group of people) to each give an amount of money, the total of which is used to pay for something: *We all **clubbed** together to buy him a present.*

clue (say **kloo**) *noun* (*plural* **clues**)
something that helps to find the answer to a problem, or to know the truth: *The police looked for **clues** to help them find the man.*
not have a clue (*informal*) to know nothing about something: *'What's his name?' 'I haven't a **clue**.'*
🛈 **ORIGIN**: 13th–15th century, from Old English *cliwen, cleowen* meaning 'a rounded mass, a ball of thread'. The word got its modern meaning because a ball of thread can be used to guide someone out of a maze and hence solve a problem.

clump (say **klump**) *noun* (*plural* **clumps**)
1 a small group of growing things: *a **clump** of trees*
2 a mass or lump of something: *a **clump** of earth*

clumsy (say **klum**-zee) *adjective* (**clumsier**, **clumsiest**)
describing a person who often drops things or does things badly because they do not move in an easy or careful way: *I'm so **clumsy**! I've just broken a glass.*
▸ **clumsily** (*adverb*): *He **clumsily** knocked the cup off the table.*

clung (say **klung**) form of **cling**

cluster (say **kluss**-tuh) *noun* (*plural* **clusters**)
a small group of people, plants or things that stand or grow close together: *a **cluster** of buildings*
▸ **cluster** (*verb*): *The tourists **clustered** around their guide.*

clutch¹ (say **kluch**) *verb* (**clutching**, **clutched**)
to hold something tightly: *The child **clutched** his mother's hand.* ➲ **SYNONYMS** **clasp¹**, **grip**

clutch² (say **kluch**) *noun* (*plural* **clutches**)
1 (in a vehicle) the **pedal¹** you press while your hand moves the stick that changes the engine speed
2 the device that the pedal is linked to that connects or disconnects a **gear** 1 from the engine

clutter (say **klut**-uh) *noun* (*no plural*)
a lot of things, especially useless things, that lie around and make a place untidy: *The room was full of **clutter**.*

► **clutter** (*verb*): *All these files are* ***cluttering*** *up the hard disk on my computer.*
► **cluttered** (*adjective*): *a* ***cluttered*** *desk*

cm *abbreviation* (*plural* **cm**) **centimetre**

Co. *abbreviation* **company**

c/o *abbreviation*
used when writing to a person who is staying at another person's house: *Mr S Khumalo,* ***c/o*** *Mr M Mkhize* ❶ **c/o** is short for 'care of'.

co- (say **koh**) *prefix*
together with, or involving two or more people or things together: ***co-star*** ◇ ***cooperate***
❶ ORIGIN: from Latin, meaning 'with'

coach[1] (say **kohch**) *noun* (*plural* **coaches**)
1 a person who trains a person or team in a sport: *a baseball* ***coach***
2 a comfortable bus for taking people on long journeys: *It's cheaper to travel by* ***coach*** *than by plane.*
3 one of the parts of a train where people sit ➲ SYNONYM **carriage**
4 a vehicle with four wheels that is pulled by horses ➲ SYNONYM **carriage**

coach[2] (say **kohch**) *verb* (**coaching, coached**)
to teach somebody to play a sport or do something better: *She is* ***coaching*** *the team for the Olympics.*

coal (say **kohl**) *noun*
1 (*no plural*) a hard black substance that comes from under the ground and gives out heat when you burn it: *Put some more* ***coal*** *on the fire.*
2 (*plural* **coals**) burning pieces of coal

coalfield (say **kohl**-feeld) *noun* (*plural* **coalfields**)
a large area where coal is found under the ground: *the Mpumalanga* ***coalfields***

coalition (say koh-uh-**lish**-uhn) *noun* (*plural* **coalitions**)
an agreement between countries, political parties or groups of people to work together

coarse (say **kawss**) *adjective* (**coarser, coarsest**)
made of thick pieces so that it is not smooth: *coarse sand* ◇ ***coarse*** *material* ➲ OPPOSITE **fine[1]** 6

coast[1] (say **kohst**) *noun* (*plural* **coasts**)
the part of the land that is next to the sea: *Their house is near the* ***coast.*** ◇ *the south* ***coast***
► **coastal** (*adjective*): *Durban is a* ***coastal*** *city.*

coast[2] (say **kohst**) *verb* (**coasting, coasted**)
1 to continue moving in a vehicle or on a bicycle without using power ➲ SYNONYM **free-wheel**
2 to achieve something without much effort: *They* ***coasted*** *to victory.*

coastline (say **kohst**-line) *noun* (*plural* **coastlines**)
the edge of the land next to the sea: *a rocky* ***coastline***

coat[1] (say **koht**) *noun* (*plural* **coats**)
1 a piece of clothing that you wear over your other clothes when you are outside: *Put your* ***coat*** *on – it's cold today.*
2 the hair or fur that covers an animal: *a dog with a smooth* ***coat***
3 a layer of something that covers a surface: *The house needs a* ***coat*** *of paint.*
a coat of arms a design that is used as the symbol of a country or an institution like a school

coat[2] (say **koht**) *verb* (**coating, coated**)
to put a thin covering of something over another thing: *Their shoes were* ***coated*** *with mud.*

coax (say **kohkss**) *verb* (**coaxing, coaxed**)
to persuade somebody to do something by using gentle or kind words: *The shop assistant* ***coaxed*** *her into buying the expensive perfume.* ◇ *She managed to* ***coax*** *the information out of the child.*

cob (say **kob**) *noun* (*plural* **cobs**)
the hard middle part of a **mealie** to which the seeds are attached

cobble (say **kob**-l) *verb* (**cobbling, cobbled**)
cobble something together to make something or put something together quickly and without much care

cobbled (say **kob**-ld) *adjective*
(of streets and roads) having a surface that is made of **cobbles**

cobbler (say **kob**-luh) *noun* (*plural* **cobblers**)
(*old-fashioned*)
a person who repairs or makes shoes

cobbles (say **kob**-lz) *plural noun* (also **cobblestones**)
small round stones used to **pave** the surfaces of roads, especially in the past

cobra (say **koh**-bruh) *noun* (*plural* **cobras**)
a poisonous snake that can spread out the skin at the back of its neck

cobweb (say **kob**-web) *noun* (*plural* **cobwebs**)
a net that a spider makes to catch insects
➲ SYNONYM **web** 1

coca (say **koh**-kuh) *noun* (*no plural*)
a South American plant, the dried leaves of

A B C D E F G H I J K L M N O P Q R S T U V W X Y Z

which are eaten by some people as a kind of drug: *Cocaine is made from **coca**.*

cocaine (say koh-**kayn**) *noun* (*no plural*) (also **coke**)
a dangerous drug made from the **coca** plant that some people take for pleasure: *Cocaine can be very addictive.*

coccyx (say **kok**-sikss) *noun* (*plural* **coccyxes** or **coccyges**)
the small bone at the bottom of the **spine**

cochlea (say **kok**-lee-uh) *noun* (*plural* **cochleae**) (*biology*)
the part of your inner ear that is shaped like a shell and is very important for hearing
▸ **cochlear** (*adjective*): ***cochlear** implants*

cock[1] (say **kok**) *noun* (*plural* **cocks**)
an adult male chicken

cock[2] (say **kok**) *verb* (**cocking**, **cocked**)
1 to move a part of your body in a certain direction: *She **cocked** her head to one side and listened carefully.*
2 to make a gun ready to fire: *He **cocked** the gun and squeezed the trigger.*

cockerel (say **kok**-ruhl) *noun* (*plural* **cockerels**)
a young male chicken

cockney (say **kok**-nee) *noun*
1 (*plural* **cockneys**) a person who was born and grew up in the east of London
2 (*no plural*) the form of English that people from the east of London speak

cockpit (say **kok**-pit) *noun* (*plural* **cockpits**)
the part of a plane where the pilot sits

cockroach (say **kok**-rohch) *noun* (*plural* **cockroaches**)
a large brown insect that you find in houses, especially dirty ones
🛈 **ORIGIN**: 17th century, from Spanish *cucaracha*. The English spelt the unfamiliar word using two English words, *cock* and *roach*, a type of fish.

cocktail (say **kok**-tayl) *noun* (*plural* **cocktails**)
a drink usually made of alcohol and fruit juices mixed together. It can also be made without alcohol: *a **cocktail** bar*

cocky (say **kok**-ee) *adjective* (**cockier**, **cockiest**) (*informal*)
too confident and proud of yourself
➲ See **arrogant**

cocoa (say **koh**-koh) *noun* (*no plural*)
1 a dark brown powder made from the seeds (called **cocoa beans**) of a tree that grows in hot countries. It is used to make chocolate.
2 a drink of hot milk mixed with this powder: *a cup of **cocoa***
🛈 **ORIGIN**: 18th century, through Spanish from Nahuatl *cacaua*. Nahuatl is a language spoken in Mexico and Central America.

coconut (say **koh**-kuh-nut) *noun* (*plural* **coconuts**)
a large fruit that grows on trees in hot countries. They are brown and hard on the outside, and they have sweet white food and liquid inside.

cocoon (say kuh-**koon**) *noun* (*plural* **cocoons**)
a covering of thin threads that some insects make to protect themselves before they become adults: *a silkworm's **cocoon***

COD (say see-oh-**dee**) *abbreviation*
cash on delivery

cod (say **kod**) *noun* (*plural* **cod or cods**)
a large fish that lives in the North Atlantic Ocean. It is an important food fish.

code (say **kohd**) *noun* (*plural* **codes**)
1 a way of writing secret messages, using letters, numbers or special signs: *The list of names was written in **code**.*
2 a group of numbers or letters that helps you find something: *What's the **code*** (= the telephone number) *for Port Elizabeth?*
3 a set of rules for a group of people: *the Highway **Code*** (= the rules for driving on the roads)

co-ed (say **koh**-ed) *adjective* (also **co-educational**)
describing a school where boys and girls are educated together in the same classes

coefficient (say koh-uh-**fish**-uhnt) *noun* (*plural* **coefficients**)
1 (*maths*) a number which is placed before another quantity and which multiplies it: *In the term 3x, the **coefficient** of x is 3.*
2 (*science*) a number that measures a particular characteristic of a substance: *the **coefficient** of friction or expansion*

coelacanth (say **see**-luh-kanth) *noun* (*plural* **coelacanths**)
a large, bony fish from the deep waters of the Indian Ocean. Scientists thought the **coelacanth** was **extinct** until one was discovered in 1938.

coerce (say koh-**urss**) *verb* (**coercing**, **coerced**) (*formal*)
to make somebody do something that they do not want to do by using force or threats
▸ **coercion** (*noun*): *the **coercion** of workers not to join a trade union*

coexist (say **koh**-ekss-ist) *verb* (**coexisting, coexisted**)
1 to live or be together in the same place at the same time
2 to live together in peace
▶ **coexistence** (*noun*): *the* ***coexistence*** *of different religions*

coffee (say **kof**-ee) *noun*
1 (*no plural*) a brown powder made from the seeds (called **coffee beans**) of a tree that grows in hot countries
2 (*no plural*) a drink made by adding hot water to this powder: *Would you like* ***coffee*** *or tea?* ◇ *a cup of black* ***coffee*** (= coffee with no milk)
3 (*plural* **coffees**) a cup of this drink: *Two* ***coffees****, please.*
🛈 **ORIGIN:** 16th century, through Turkish *kahveh*, from Arabic *kahwa*. The word was probably brought to Europe by Dutch traders.

coffer (say **kof**-uh) *noun*
1 (*plural* **coffers**) a strong box that you use for storing money or valuable things
2 the coffers a supply of money that belongs to an organization or a government: *Money went missing from the company's* ***coffers****.*

coffin (say **kof**-in) *noun* (*plural* **coffins**)
a box that a dead person's body is put in to be buried

cog (say **kog**) *noun* (*plural* **cogs**) (*technology*)
one of a series of teeth around the edge of a wheel that fit into similar teeth on another wheel and cause it to move

cogent (say **koh**-juhnt) *adjective* (*formal*)
expressed in a logical and clear way that convinces or persuades other people: *a* ***cogent*** *reason* ◇ *a* ***cogent*** *argument*

cognition (say kog-**ni**-shuhn) *noun* (*no plural*) (*formal*)
the process by which knowledge is developed in the mind through thought, understanding and experience

coherent (say koh-**heer**-ruhnt) *adjective*
logical and easy to understand
➲ **OPPOSITE incoherent**
▶ **coherently** (*adverb*): *He was too confused to think* ***coherently****.*

coil¹ (say **koyl**) *verb* (**coiling, coiled**)
to make something into a lot of circles that are joined together: *The snake* ***coiled*** *itself round a branch.*

coil² (say **koyl**) *noun* (*plural* **coils**)
a long piece of rope or wire that goes round in circles: *a* ***coil*** *of rope*

coin¹ (say **koyn**) *noun* (*plural* **coins**)
a piece of money made of metal: *a R5* ***coin***
➲ See note at **money**

coin² (say **koyn**) *verb* (**coining, coined**)
to invent a new word or phrase: *Who was it who* ***coined*** *the phrase 'I shop, therefore I am'?*

coincidence (say koh-**in**-si-duhnss) *noun* (*plural* **coincidences**)
two or more similar things happening at the same time or in the same place by chance, in a surprising way: *What a* ***coincidence****! I was thinking about you when you phoned!*

coincidental (say koh-in-si-**den**-tuhl) *adjective*
happening by chance and not planned

coir (say **koy**-uh) *noun* (*no plural*)
the natural threads from the outside of a **coconut** that are used for making things such as ropes

coke (say **kohk**) *noun* (*no plural*)
1 a hard black substance produced from coal that is used as fuel
2 (*informal*) **cocaine**

cola (say **koh**-luh) *noun* (*no plural*)
a sweet brown drink with bubbles in it: *a glass of cola*

colander (say **kol**-uhn-duh) *noun* (*plural* **colanders**)
a metal or plastic bowl with a lot of small holes in it that is used to separate food from the water that it has been washed or boiled in

cold¹ (say **kohld**) *adjective* (**colder, coldest**)
1 not hot or warm, but with a low temperature: *Put your coat on – it's* ***cold*** *outside.* ◇ *I'm* ***cold****. Will you put the heater on?* ◇ *hot and* ***cold*** *water* ➲ **OPPOSITE hot** 1
2 not friendly or kind: *She gave him a* ***cold****, hard look.*
▶ **coldly** (*adverb*): *She looked at me* ***coldly****.*

WHICH WORD? Cool, cold or **freezing**?
- In sense 1 above, **cool** means quite cold, especially in a pleasant way: *It's hot outside but it's nice and* ***cool*** *in here.*
- **Freezing** is used informally to mean extremely cold, often in an unpleasant way: *It's absolutely* ***freezing*** *outside.*

cold² (say **kohld**) *noun*
1 (*no plural*) cold weather: *Don't go out in the* ***cold****.*
2 (*plural* **colds**) a common illness that makes it difficult to breathe through your nose and makes your throat hurt: *I've got a* ***cold****.* ◇ *Come in out of the rain, or you'll catch a* ***cold****.*

A B C D E F G H I J K L M N O P Q R S T U V W X Y Z

cold-blooded (say **kohld**-blud-uhd) *adjective*
1 relating to animals that have a blood temperature that changes if the temperature of the surroundings changes: *Reptiles are **cold-blooded**.* ➲ OPPOSITE **warm-blooded**
2 cruel or having or showing no pity: ***cold-blooded** killers*

coleslaw (say **kohl**-slaw) *noun* (*no plural*)
a dish of thin pieces of cabbage and other vegetables that have not been cooked, mixed with **mayonnaise**

colic (say **kol**-ik) *noun* (*no plural*)
very bad pain in the stomach area, which is suffered especially by babies

collaborate (say kuh-**lab**-uh-rayt) *verb* (**collaborating**, **collaborated**)
1 to work together with another person or a group of people in order to produce or create something
2 to help or support an enemy
▸ **collaboration** (*noun*): *We work in **collaboration** with several community groups.*
▸ **collaborative** (*adjective*): *a **collaborative** partnership between the government and schools*
▸ **collaborator** (*noun*): *He was a **collaborator** on her music album.*

collage (say kol-**aazh**) *noun* (*plural* **collages**)
a picture that you make by sticking pieces of coloured paper, cloth, photographs and other objects onto a surface

collagen (say **kol**-uh-juhn) *noun* (*no plural*) (*biology*)
the main **protein** found in skin, bones and many other parts of the body, and that supports and gives structure to cells

collapse (say kuh-**lapss**) *verb* (**collapsing**, **collapsed**)
to fall down suddenly: *The building **collapsed** in the earthquake.* ◇ *She **collapsed** in the road.*
▸ **collapse** (*noun*): *the **collapse** of the bridge*

collar (say **kol**-uh) *noun* (*plural* **collars**)
1 the part of your clothes that goes round your neck
2 a band that you put round the neck of a dog or cat

collarbone (say **kol**-uh-bohn) *noun* (*plural* **collarbones**) (also **clavicle**)
one of the two bones that connect your chest bones to your shoulder ➲ See illustration at **skeleton**

collate (say kuh-**layt**) *verb* (**collating**, **collated**)
1 to bring together information from different sources and examine and compare it
2 to collect pieces of paper and put them in the correct order
▸ **collation** (*noun*): *the collection and **collation** of data*

colleague (say **kol**-eeg) *noun* (*plural* **colleagues**)
a person who works with you

> PRONUNCIATION Notice how to say **colleague**.

collect (say kuh-**lekt**) *verb* (**collecting**, **collected**)
1 to take things from different people or places and put them together: *The waiter **collected** the dirty glasses.*
2 to bring together things that are the same in some way, to study or enjoy them: *My son **collects** stamps.*
3 to go and bring a person or thing from a place: *She **collects** her children from school at 3.30.*

collection (say kuh-**lek**-shuhn) *noun* (*plural* **collections**)
1 a group of similar things that somebody has brought together: *The National Gallery has a large **collection** of paintings.* ◇ *a CD **collection***
2 taking something from a place or from people: *rubbish **collections***

collective (say kuh-**lek**-tiv) *adjective*
shared by or involving everybody in a group: ***collective** duties*
▸ **collectively** (*adverb*): *We took the decision **collectively** at a meeting.*

collector (say kuh-**lek**-tuh) *noun* (*plural* **collectors**)
a person who collects things as a hobby or as a job: *a stamp **collector*** ◇ *a ticket **collector** at a railway station*

college (say **kol**-ij) *noun* (*plural* **colleges**)
1 a place where you can study after you have left school: *a teacher training **college***
2 (used in names of some schools) a high school: *Maritzburg **College***
🛈 ORIGIN: 14th–15th century, through Old French, from Latin *collegium* meaning 'partnership'

collide (say kuh-**lide**) *verb* (**colliding**, **collided**)
to move fast towards a person or thing and hit them hard: *The two trucks **collided**.* ◇ *He **collided** with his teacher.* ➲ SYNONYM **crash**[2] 1

colliery (say **kol**-i-uh-ree) *noun* (*plural* **collieries**)
a place where coal is dug from the ground as well as the buildings and equipment connected with it

collision (say kuh-**lizh**-uhn) *noun* (*plural* **collisions**)
when things or people **collide**: *The driver of the car was killed in the **collision**.* ➲ SYNONYM **crash**[1] 1

colloquial (say kuh-**loh**-kwi-uhl) *adjective*
(used about words and expressions) used when you speak or write to people you know well, not in formal speech or writing

colon (say **koh**-luhn or **koh**-lon) *noun* (*plural* **colons**)
1 the mark (:) that you use in writing, for example before a list ➲ See Study page 16
2 the lower part of your **intestine** ➲ See illustration at **alimentary canal**

colonel (say **kur**-nuhl) *noun* (*plural* **colonels**)
an officer of a high level in the army

PRONUNCIATION Notice that the sound of this word is very different from the spelling.

colonial (say kuh-**loh**-ni-uhl) *adjective*
1 relating to an area or country that is ruled by another country: *Cape Town was an important **colonial** port.*
2 relating to a powerful country that takes control of and rules another country: *Europe's **colonial** powers*

colonialism (say kuh-**loh**-ni-uh-liz-m) *noun* (*no plural*)
the policy in which a powerful country rules another nation, sends people to settle there and uses the natural and economic supplies in order to become richer

colonist (say **kol**-uh-nist) *noun* (*plural* **colonists**)
a person who settles and lives in a **colony** 1: *The island was settled by Dutch **colonists**.* ➲ SYNONYM **settler**

colonize (say **kol**-uh-nize) *verb* (**colonizing, colonized**) (also **colonise**)
1 to take control of a place or a country and rule it: *Who **colonized** Angola?*
2 (*biology*) to start or set up a new **colony** 2 of animals, insects or plants: *These plants are the first to **colonize** the dunes.*
► **colonization** (*noun*) (also **colonisation**): *the history of **colonization** in Africa* ► **colonizer** (*noun*) (also **coloniser**): *The fortress was built by Portuguese **colonizers**.*

colony (say **kol**-uh-nee) *noun* (*plural* **colonies**)
1 a country or an area that is ruled by another country: *Kenya was once a British **colony**.*
2 (*biology*) a group of the same type of animals, insects or plants living or growing in the same place: *a **colony** of ants*

colossal (say kuh-**loss**-uhl) *adjective*
extremely big ➲ SYNONYMS **enormous, gigantic**

colour[1] (say **kul**-uh) *noun* (*plural* **colours**)
the appearance that things have that results from the way in which they reflect light. Red, blue, yellow and green are all colours: *'What **colour** are your new shoes?' 'Black.'* ◇ *The leaves change **colour** in autumn.*

colour[2] (say **kul**-uh) *verb* (**colouring, coloured**)
to put colour on something, for example by painting it: *The children **coloured** their pictures with crayons.*

coloured (say **kul**-uhd) *adjective*
1 having a particular colour or different colours: *She was wearing a brightly **coloured** jersey.* ◇ ***coloured** paper*
2 (also **Coloured**) (*S. African*) describing a person whose ancestors (= the people in your family who lived a long time before you) came from various population groups, for example the Khoikhoi, Malays, whites and Africans

USAGE People have different opinions about using the word **Coloured** to refer to a person. Some people think it is rude, but others think it is acceptable.

colourful (say **kul**-uh-fuul) *adjective*
with a lot of bright colours: *The garden is very **colourful** in summer.*

colt (say **kohlt**) *noun* (*plural* **colts**)
a young male horse ➲ See **filly**

column (say **kol**-uhm) *noun* (*plural* **columns**)
1 a tall solid piece of stone that supports part of a building ➲ See picture at **arch**[1]
2 a narrow section of writing on one side or part of a page: *Each page of this dictionary has two **columns**.*
3 a list of numbers or words one under the other, sometimes written in a table: *Add up the numbers in **column** 1.*

coma (say **koh**-muh) *noun* (*plural* **comas**)
a deep unconscious state, sometimes lasting a long time, and caused by serious illness or injury: *After her accident, she was in a **coma** for many years.*

comb (*rhymes with* **home**) *noun* (*plural* **combs**)
a flat piece of metal or plastic with thin parts like teeth. You use it to make your hair tidy.
► **comb** (*verb*): *Have you **combed** your hair?*

PRONUNCIATION Don't pronounce the **b** in **comb**.

A B C D E F G H I J K L M N O P Q R S T U V W X Y Z

combat[1] (say **kom**-bat) *noun* (*no plural*)
a fight, especially between armies: *The soldiers died in **combat**.*
▸ **combat** (*adjective*): *a **combat** vehicle*

combat[2] (say **kom**-bat) *verb* (**combating** or **combatting**, **combated** or **combatted**)
to fight against something or to try to stop something: *The government has taken measures to **combat** crime.*

combi (say **kom**-bee) *noun* (*plural* **combis**)
= **kombi**

combination (say kom-bi-**nay**-shuhn) *noun* (*plural* **combinations**)
two or more things joined together: *The building is a **combination** of new and old styles.*
➲ SYNONYM **mixture**

combine (say kom-**bine**) *verb* (**combining, combined**)
to join or to mix two or more things together: *The two schools **combined** and moved to a larger building.*

combustible (say kuhm-**buss**-tib-l) *adjective*
able to burn easily: *a **combustible** material*

combustion (say kuhm-**buss**-tshuhn) *noun* (*no plural*)
the process of burning: *an internal **combustion** engine* ◇ *spontaneous **combustion***

come (say **kum**) *verb* (**coming, came, has come**)
1 to move towards the person who is speaking or the place that you are talking about: ***Come** here, please.* ◇ *The dog didn't **come** when I called him.* ◇ *She **came** back at six o'clock.* ◇ ***Come** on* (= hurry up) *or we'll be late.*
2 to arrive at or reach a place: *If you go along that road, you will **come** to the river.* ◇ *A letter **came** for you this morning.*
3 to go somewhere with the person who is speaking: *Would you like to **come** to the party?*
4 to be in a particular position: *June **comes** after May.*
how come ...? (*informal*) why or how ...?: *How **come** you're here so early?*
come across something to find something when you are not looking for it: *I **came** across these old photos yesterday.*
come down to fall or become lower: *The price of oil is **coming** down.*
come from somewhere or **something**
1 to have been born somewhere or to live somewhere: *I **come** from Zambia.* ◇ *Where do you **come** from?*
2 to be made from something or produced somewhere: *Wool **comes** from sheep.*
come out to appear: *The rain stopped and the sun **came** out.* ◇ *His book **came** out in 2005.*

comedian (say kuh-**mee**-di-uhn) *noun* (*plural* **comedians**)
a person whose job is to make people laugh

comedy (say **kom**-uh-dee) *noun* (*plural* **comedies**)
a funny play or film

comet (say **kom**-uht) *noun* (*plural* **comets**)
an object in space that moves around the sun. It looks like a bright star with a tail.

comfort[1] (say **kum**-fuht) *noun*
1 (*no plural*) having everything your body needs or being without pain or problems: *They have enough money to live in **comfort**.*
2 (*plural* **comforts**) a person or thing that helps you or makes life better: *Her children were a **comfort** to her when she was ill.* ◇ *home **comforts***

comfort[2] (say **kum**-fuht) *verb* (**comforting, comforted**)
to make somebody feel less unhappy or worried: *She **comforted** her crying child.*
➲ SYNONYM **console**[2]

comfortable (say **kumf**-tuhb-l) *adjective*
1 nice to sit in, to be in, or to wear: *This is a very **comfortable** bed.* ◇ ***comfortable** shoes*
2 physically relaxed, with no pain or worry: *Sit down and make yourself **comfortable**.*
➲ OPPOSITE **uncomfortable**
▸ **comfortably** (*adverb*): *If you're all sitting **comfortably**, I'll begin.*

comic[1] (say **kom**-ik) *adjective* (also **comical**)
funny: *a **comic** scene in a play*

comic[2] (say **kom**-ik) *noun* (*plural* **comics**)
a magazine with pictures that tell a story

comma (say **kom**-uh) *noun* (*plural* **commas**)
a mark (,) that you use in writing to separate parts of a sentence or things in a list
➲ See Study page 16

command[1] (say kuh-**maand**) *noun*
1 (*plural* **commands**) words that tell you that you must do something: *The soldiers must obey their general's **commands**.* ➲ SYNONYM **order**[1] 3
2 (*plural* **commands**) an instruction to a computer to do something: *Use the Find **command** to look for a word in the file.*
3 (*no plural*) the power to tell people what to do: *Who is in **command** of this ship?*
➲ SYNONYM **control**[1] 1

command[2] (say kuh-**maand**) *verb* (**commanding, commanded**)
to tell somebody that they must do something: *He **commanded** us to leave immediately.*
➲ SYNONYM **order**[2] 1

commandant (say kom-uhn-**dant**) *noun* (*plural* **commandants**) (*history*) (*S. African*)
an officer in charge of a **commando** 2

commandeer (say kom-uhn-**deer**) *verb* (**commandeering, commandeered**)
to take something from its owner for military or police use: *The police* ***commandeered*** *his car and followed the thief.*

commander (say kuh-**maan**-duh) *noun* (*plural* **commanders**)
a person who leads or is in charge of a group, especially a military organization

commandment (say kuh-**maand**-muhnt) *noun* (*plural* **commandments**)
a command or instruction from God: *the Ten* ***Commandments*** *given to the Jews in the Bible*

commando (say kuh-**maan**-doh) *noun* (*plural* **commandos**)
1 one of a small group of soldiers trained to carry out sudden attacks
2 (*history*) (*S. African*) a force of **Boer** soldiers, especially during the **South African War**

commemorate (say kuh-**mem**-uh-rayt) *verb* (**commemorating, commemorated**)
to help people remember a person or event, for example by holding a ceremony
▸ **commemoration** (*noun*): *activities planned in* ***commemoration*** *of the women's march of 1956* ▸ **commemorative** (*adjective*): *the Mandela 90th birthday* ***commemorative*** *coin*

commence (say kuh-**menss**) *verb* (**commencing, commenced**) (*formal*)
to begin or to start to do something: *Classes will* ***commence*** *in January.* ◇ *Workers* ***commenced*** *digging the tunnel.*
▸ **commencement** (*noun*): *the* ***commencement*** *of the academic year*

commend (say kuh-**mend**) *verb* (**commending, commended**) (*formal*)
to say officially that somebody or something is good: *The principal* ***commended*** *Peter for his excellent work.*
▸ **commendation** (*noun*): *a certificate of* ***commendation***

commendable (say kuh-**mend**-uhb-l) *adjective* (*formal*)
that people think is good: *a* ***commendable*** *initiative*

comment[1] (say **kom**-ent) *noun* (*plural* **comments**)
something that you say that shows what you think about something: *She made some interesting* ***comments*** *about the film.*

comment[2] (say **kom**-ent) *verb* (**commenting, commented**)
to say what you think about something: *A lot of people at school* ***commented*** *on my new watch.*

commentary (say **kom**-uhn-tree) *noun* (*plural* **commentaries**)
when somebody describes an event while it is happening, especially on the radio or on television: *a sports* ***commentary***

commentator (say **kom**-uhn-tay-tuh) *noun* (*plural* **commentators**)
a person who gives a **commentary** on the radio or on television

commerce (say **kom**-urss) *noun* (*no plural*)
the business of buying and selling things

commercial[1] (say kuh-**mur**-shuhl) *adjective*
connected with buying and selling things: *commercial law* ➲ SYNONYM **mercantile**

commercial[2] (say kuh-**mur**-shuhl) *noun* (*plural* **commercials**)
an advertisement on television or radio

commiserate (say kuh-**miz**-uh-rayt) *verb* (**commiserating, commiserated**) (*formal*)
to show that you understand and feel sorry for somebody when they have problems or are unhappy: *She* ***commiserated*** *with her disappointed friends.*

commission[1] (say kuh-**mish**-uhn) *noun* (*plural* **commissions**)
1 a group of people who are officially asked to do something or to find out about something: *The government set up a* ***commission*** *to investigate the causes of the disaster.*
2 money that a person, bank or company charges, usually a part of the cost of the product they sell or the service they provide
3 a request to an artist or writer to produce a piece of work: *He received a* ***commission*** *to write a play for the festival.*

commission[2] (say kuh-**mish**-uhn) *verb* (**commissioning, commissioned**)
to officially ask somebody to do something, especially an artist or writer, to produce a piece of work: *They have* ***commissioned*** *an architect to design the building.*

commissioner (say kuh-**mish**-uh-nuh) *noun* (*plural* **commissioners**)
1 a member of a **commission**[1] 1
2 the head of the police or of a government department in some countries: *the* ***Commissioner*** *of Police*

commit (say kuh-**mit**) *verb* (**committing, committed**)
1 to do something bad: *This man has **committed** a very serious crime.*
2 to make an agreement or promise to do something: *I've **committed** myself to helping in the library on Fridays.*

commitment (say kuh-**mit**-muhnt) *noun*
1 (*plural* **commitments**) a promise to do something: *When I make a **commitment**, I always stick to it.*
2 (*no plural*) being prepared to give a lot of your time and attention to something: *I admire his **commitment** to his work.*

committed (say kuh-**mit**-d) *adjective*
prepared to give a lot of your time and attention to something: *We are **committed** to raising standards in schools.*

committee (say kuh-**mit**-ee) *noun* (*plural* **committees**)
a group of people that other people choose to discuss or decide something: *She's on the planning **committee**.*

SPELLING Remember! You spell **committee** with **mm**, **tt** and **ee**.

PRONUNCIATION Notice how to say **committee**.

commodity (say kuh-**mod**-uh-tee) *noun* (*plural* **commodities**)
1 a product or material that is bought and sold: *Maize prices have fallen on the **commodities** market.*
2 something valuable or useful: *Time is now a very precious **commodity**.*

common¹ (say **kom**-uhn) *adjective*
1 happening often or found in many places: *Smith is a **common** English name.*
➲ OPPOSITE **rare** 1
2 shared by two or more people or by everybody in a group: *They share a **common** interest in photography.*

common² (say **kom**-uhn) *noun* (*plural* **commons**)
a piece of land that everybody can use: *We went for a walk on the **common**.*
have something in common to be like somebody in a certain way, or to have the same interests as somebody: *We are good friends and we have a lot in **common**.*

common sense *noun* (*no plural*)
the ability to think about things and do the right thing and not make stupid mistakes: *She's got no **common sense**. She lay in the sun all day and got sunburnt.*

Commonwealth (say **kom**-uhn-welth) *noun* (*no plural*)
(usually **the Commonwealth**) a group of countries that were part of the British Empire in the past and that now work together

commotion (say kuh-**moh**-shuhn) *noun* (*no plural*)
a lot of noise, confusion and excitement: *There was a **commotion** at the school gate.*

communal (say kuh-**myoon**-l or **kom**-yuu-nuhl) *adjective*
shared or done by a group of people: *The women started a **communal** vegetable garden.*

commune (say **kom**-yoon) *noun* (*plural* **communes**)
a group of people who live together and share their possessions and responsibilities, even though they are not members of the same family

communicate (say kuh-**myoo**-ni-kayt) *verb* (**communicating, communicated**)
to share and exchange information, ideas or feelings with somebody: *Parents often find it difficult to **communicate** with their children.*

communication (say kuh-myoo-ni-**kay**-shuhn) *noun*
1 (*no plural*) sharing or exchanging information, feelings or ideas with somebody: ***Communication** is difficult when two people don't speak the same language.*
2 communications ways of sending or receiving information, especially telephones, radio or computers: *a **communications** satellite*

communicative (say kuh-**myoo**-ni-kuh-tiv) *adjective*
likely to enjoy talking to people and sharing information and ideas: *She is friendly and **communicative**.*

communion (say kuh-**myoo**-ni-uhn) *noun* (*no plural*)
1 (*formal*) the sharing of thoughts and feelings
2 Communion (also **Holy Communion**) a Christian church ceremony in which people share bread and wine

communism (say **kom**-yuu-niz-m) *noun* (*no plural*)
an economic and political system in which the state owns and controls all industry, land and services and which aims to treat everybody equally

communist (say **kom**-yuu-nist) *noun* (*plural* **communists**)
a person who believes in or who is a member of an organization or party that supports **communism**
▶ **communist** (*adjective*): *the end of communist rule in Russia*

community (say kuh-**myoo**-nuh-tee) *noun* (*plural* **communities**)
1 all the people who live in a place and the place itself: *Life in a small fishing* ***community*** *is very different from life in a big city.*
2 a group of people who join together, for example because they have the same interests or religion: *the country's French-speaking* ***community***

commutative (say kuh-**myoo**-tuh-tiv) *adjective* (*maths*)
(of a calculation) giving the same result whatever the order in which the quantities are shown: *a x b = b x a is a* ***commutative*** *operation.*

commute (say kuh-**myoot**) *verb* (**commuting, commuted**)
to travel a long way from home to work every day: *She lives in Tshwane and* ***commutes*** *to Johannesburg.*
▶ **commuter** (*noun*): *Thousands of* ***commuters*** *take the train every day.*

compact[1] (say **kom**-pakt) *adjective*
1 small and easy to carry: *a* ***compact*** *camera*
2 closely and tightly packed together: *a* ***compact*** *schedule*

compact[2] (say kom-**pakt**) *verb* (**compacting, compacted**)
to press or join firmly together: *The cans are flattened and* ***compacted*** *into blocks.*

compact disc *noun* (*plural* **compact discs**)
➲ See **CD**

companion (say kuhm-**pan**-i-uhn) *noun* (*plural* **companions**)
a person who travels with you or spends time with you

company (say **kum**-puh-nee) *noun*
1 (*plural* **companies**) a group of people who work together to make or sell things: *an advertising* ***company*** ➲ SYNONYM **firm**[1]
2 (*no plural*) being with a person or people: *I always enjoy his* ***company*** ◇ *Please keep me* ***company*** (= be with me) *for a while.*

> USAGE With meaning 1 above **company** is written with a capital letter in names: *the Fresher Foods* ***Company***. The abbreviation is **Co.**: *The Fresher Foods* ***Co.***

comparable (say **kom**-puh-ruhb-l) *adjective*
similar in size or quality to something else: *Are teachers' salaries* ***comparable*** *to nurses' salaries?*

comparative (say kuhm-**pa**-ruh-tiv) *noun* (*plural* **comparatives**) (*grammar*)
the form of an adjective or adverb that shows more of something: *The* ***comparative*** *of 'bad' is 'worse'.* ◇ *'More intelligent', 'better' and 'faster' are all* ***comparatives.*** ➲ See Study pages 10 and 11
▶ **comparative** (*adjective*): *'Longer' is the* ***comparative*** *form of 'long'.* ➲ See **superlative**

compare (say kuhm-**pair**) *verb* (**comparing, compared**)
to think about or look at people or things together so that you can see how they are different: ***Compared*** *to the place where I grew up, this town is exciting.* ◇ ***Compare*** *your answers with your partner's.*
ℹ ORIGIN: 14th–15th century, through Old French, from Latin *compar* meaning 'alike, equal'

comparison (say kuhm-**pa**-ri-suhn) *noun* (*plural* **comparisons**)
looking at or understanding how things are different or the same: *It's hard to make* ***comparisons*** *between athletes from different sports.*
by or **in comparison with somebody** or **something** when you compare two or more people or things: *In* ***comparison*** *with many other people, they're quite rich.*

compartment (say kuhm-**paat**-muhnt) *noun* (*plural* **compartments**)
1 one of the sections which a part of a train (called a **carriage**) is divided into: *He found an empty first-class* ***compartment.***
2 a separate part inside a box, bag or other container: *The suitcase had a secret* ***compartment*** *at the back.*

compass (say **kum**-puhss) *noun* (*plural* **compasses**)
1 an instrument for finding direction, with a needle that always points north: *You need a map and a* ***compass.***
2 (also **a pair of compasses**) an instrument with two long thin parts joined together at the top that is used for drawing circles: *Use a pair of* ***compasses.***
➲ See illustrations on next page

compasses

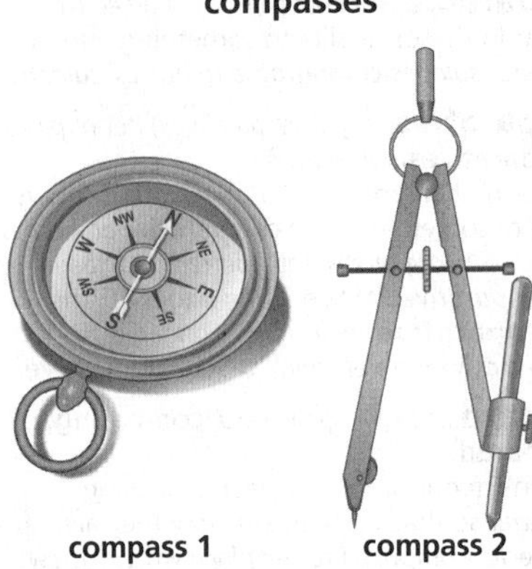

compass 1 compass 2

compassion (say kuhm-**pash**-uhn) *noun* (*no plural*)
a feeling of understanding another person's suffering and of wanting to help: *to have **compassion** for people suffering from AIDS* ➲ SYNONYM **sympathy**
► **compassionate** (*adjective*): *He's very **compassionate** towards others.*

compatible (say kuhm-**pat**-uhb-l) *adjective*
able to be used, exist or live together without problems or fighting ➲ OPPOSITE **incompatible**
► **compatibility** (*noun*): *Check the **compatibility** of the hardware and software before you start.*

compatriot (say kuhm-**pat**-ri-uht) *noun* (*plural* **compatriots**)
a person who comes from the same country as you

compel (say kuhm-**pel**) *verb* (**compelling, compelled**) (*formal*)
to force somebody to do something: *He was **compelled** to retire at the age of 70.*

compensate (say **kom**-pen-sayt) *verb* (**compensating, compensated**)
1 to remove or reduce the bad effect of something: *His willingness to work hard **compensates** for his lack of skill.*
2 to give money to somebody because you are responsible for a loss or injury they have suffered: *The company will **compensate** the owner for any damage caused.*
► **compensation** (*noun*): *The workers got **compensation** when they were injured in the accident.*

compete (say kuhm-**peet**) *verb* (**competing, competed**)
to try to win a race or a competition: *The world's best athletes **compete** in the Olympic Games.*

competent (say **kom**-pi-tuhnt) *adjective*
1 having the necessary knowledge, ability or skill to do something ➲ OPPOSITE **incompetent**
2 good enough, but not excellent
► **competence** (*noun*): *advancing to new levels of **competence*** ► **competently** (*adverb*): *We will train you so that you are able to do this **competently** on your own.*

competition (say kom-puh-**tish**-uhn) *noun*
1 (*plural* **competitions**) a game or test that people try to win: *I entered the painting **competition** and won first prize.*
2 (*no plural*) a situation where two or more people or organizations **compete** with each other for something that not everyone can have: *We were in **competition** with a team from another school.*

competitive (say kuhm-**pet**-uh-tiv) *adjective*
1 in which people or organizations **compete** against each other: ***competitive** sports*
2 wanting to win or be better than other people: *She's very **competitive**.*

competitor (say kuhm-**pet**-i-tuh) *noun* (*plural* **competitors**)
a person who is trying to win a competition

compilation (say kom-pi-**lay**-shuhn) *noun* (*plural* **compilations**)
1 a collection of pieces of music, writing or film, taken from different places and put together: *a **compilation** CD of the band's greatest hits*
2 the act of compiling something

compile (say kuhm-**pile**) *verb* (**compiling, compiled**)
1 to collect information and arrange it, for example in a list, report or book: *Let's **compile** a list of the things you have to do every day.*
2 (*computing*) to change instructions from one computer language to another using a special program
► **compiler** (*noun*)

complacent (say kuhm-**play**-suhnt) *adjective*
feeling too satisfied with yourself or with what you have done, so that you think that there is no need to do more
► **complacency** (*noun*): *Their **complacency** made them fail.* ► **complacently** (*adverb*): *She folded her hands **complacently**.*

complain (say kuhm-**playn**) *verb* (**complaining, complained**)
to say that you do not like something or that you are unhappy about something: *She is always **complaining** about not having any new clothes.* ◇ *I **complained** to the teacher that we get too much homework.*

complaint (say kuhm-**playnt**) *noun* (*plural* **complaints**)
1 a statement that you are not satisfied with something: *We made a **complaint** to the hotel manager about the dirty rooms.*
2 an illness or disease: *a heart **complaint***

complement[1] (say **kom**-pli-muhnt) *noun* (*plural* **complements**)
1 (*formal*) a thing that combines well with something else: *Ice cream is the perfect **complement** to this dessert.*
2 the number of people or things that are needed to make something complete: *Without a full **complement** of players, the team will not be able to take part in the match.*
3 (*grammar*) a word or group of words that must be used after a verb such as 'be', 'become' or 'get' to complete the meaning of the sentence: *In the sentence 'He got into trouble', 'into trouble' is the **complement**.*

complement[2] (say **kom**-pli-muhnt) *verb* (**complementing, complemented**)
to go well with, or to add to something in a way that makes it better: *Her red dress was **complemented** by a white hat and white shoes.*

> SPELLING Be careful! Don't confuse **complement** and **compliment**, which have different meanings.

complementary (say kom-pli-**men**-tree) *adjective*
1 combining well with a person or thing, or adding something that makes the other person or thing better: *Their skills are **complementary**: he is practical and she is creative.*
2 (*maths*) describing either of two angles that together add up to a right angle of 90 degrees

complete[1] (say kuhm-**pleet**) *adjective*
1 in every way: *Their visit was a **complete** surprise.* ➲ SYNONYM **total**[1] 1
2 with none of its parts missing: *I've got a **complete** set of Shakespeare's plays.* ➲ SYNONYM **whole**[1] 1 ➲ OPPOSITE **incomplete**
3 finished: *The work is **complete**.* ➲ OPPOSITE **incomplete**

complete[2] (say kuhm-**pleet**) *verb* (**completing, completed**)
to finish doing or making something: *She has not **completed** her studies yet.* ◇ *When will the new building be **completed**?*
▸ **completion** (*noun*): *the **completion** of her studies* ◇ *the **completion** of the building*

completely (say kuhm-**pleet**-lee) *adverb*
in every way: *The money has **completely** disappeared.* ◇ *I **completely** forgot that it was your birthday!* ➲ SYNONYM **totally**

complex[1] (say **kom**-plekss) *adjective*
difficult to understand because it has a lot of different parts: *a **complex** problem*
➲ SYNONYM **complicated** ➲ OPPOSITE **simple** 1

complex[2] (say **kom**-plekss) *noun* (*plural* **complexes**)
a group of buildings: *a sports **complex***

complexion (say kuhm-**plek**-shuhn) *noun* (*plural* **complexions**)
1 the natural colour or appearance of the skin on your face: *a healthy **complexion***
2 the general character of something: *Their win puts a different **complexion** on our final game.*

compliant (say kuhm-**ply**-uhnt) *adjective* (*formal*)
working in agreement with or obeying particular rules, orders or standards: *The company is fully **compliant** with the latest labour laws.* ◇ *This computer program is standards-**compliant**.* ➲ The verb is **comply**
▸ **compliance** (*noun*): *Workers must wear hard hats in **compliance** with safety regulations.*

complicate (say **kom**-pli-kayt) *verb* (**complicating, complicated**)
to make something difficult to understand or deal with

complicated (say **kom**-pli-kayt-d) *adjective*
difficult to understand because it has a lot of different parts: *I can't explain how to play the game. It's too **complicated**.*
➲ OPPOSITE **simple** 1, ➲ SYNONYM **complex**[1]

complication (say kom-pli-**kay**-shuhn) *noun* (*plural* **complications**)
something that makes a situation more difficult

compliment[1] (say **kom**-pli-muhnt) *noun* (*plural* **compliments**)
1 something nice that you say about somebody: *People often pay her **compliments** on her piano playing.*
2 compliments (*plural noun*) (*formal*) a polite greeting or a way of showing respect: ***compliments** of the season*

compliment[2] (say **kom**-pli-muhnt) *verb* (**complimenting, complimented**)
to say that you think a person or thing is very good: *The teacher **complimented** her on her good work.*

> SPELLING Be careful! Don't confuse **compliment** and **complement**. They mean different things.

comply (say kuhm-**ply**) *verb* (**complying, complied**) (*formal*)
to follow or obey an order, request, rule or law:

A B C D E F G H I J K L M N O P Q R S T U V W X Y Z

A B C D E F G H I J K L M N O P Q R S T U V W X Y Z

*The parties must **comply** with the United Nations resolution.* ➲ The adjective is **compliant**

component (say kuhm-**poh**-nuhnt) *noun* (*plural* **components**)
one of the parts that a thing such as a machine or vehicle is made of
▸ **component** (*adjective*): *the **component** parts of an engine*

compose (say kuhm-**pohz**) *verb* (**composing, composed**)
1 to write something, usually with a lot of care and thought about the arrangement of information
2 to create and arrange a work of art, for example a piece of music or a painting: *Verdi **composed** many operas.* ➲ The noun is **composition** 2
3 to be the parts that form something: *the judges that **compose** the court*
4 to become calm and quiet after being angry or upset: *The news came as such a shock that it took me a while to **compose** myself.*
🛈 ORIGIN: 15th century, through Old French from Latin *componere* meaning 'put together', from *com-* meaning 'together' + *ponere* meaning 'put'

composed (say kuhm-**pohz**-d) *adjective*
1 made or formed from different parts or people: *Water is **composed** of oxygen and hydrogen.*
2 calm and in control of your feelings: *He was very nervous, but he managed to look calm and **composed**.*

composer (say kuhm-**poh**-zuh) *noun* (*plural* **composers**)
a person who writes music: *My favourite **composer** is Mozart.*

composite (say **kom**-puh-zit) *adjective*
1 consisting of different parts or materials
2 (*biology*) describing a plant with a flower that looks like a big single flower, but that actually consists of many small flowers: *Sunflowers and daisies are **composite** flowers.*
▸ **composite** (*noun*): *A collage is a **composite** of photographs and other objects.*

composition (say kom-puh-**zi**-shuhn) *noun* (*plural* **compositions**)
1 the parts that form something, or the way in which the parts of something are arranged: *Choose some of your drawings and fit them together to form a **composition**.* ◇ *the chemical **composition** of a substance*
2 a piece of writing or music ➲ The verb is **compose** 1

compost (say **kom**-post) *noun* (*no plural*)
a mixture of dead plants, waste material from the bodies of animals and old food that is added to soil to help plants grow

compound[1] (say **kom**-pownd) *noun* (*plural* **compounds**)
1 something that is made of two or more parts: *Salt is a chemical **compound**.*
2 (*grammar*) a word that is made from two or more other words: *'Hairdryer' and 'web page' are **compounds**.*
3 an area of land with a group of buildings on it and a wall or fence around it: *The staff live in a **compound** next to the hotel.*

compound[2] (say **kom**-pownd) *adjective*
1 made from two or more parts or things: *a **compound** noun*
2 (*biology*) describing the leaf of a plant that is divided into two or more parts: ***compound** leaves*

compound[3] (say kom-**pownd**) *verb* (**compounding, compounded**)
to make something such as a problem or difficulty worse: *His uncertainty **compounded** his fear that he would fail the test.*

comprehend (say kom-pri-**hend**) *verb* (**comprehending, comprehended**) (*formal*)
to understand something or be able to imagine it: *She's too young to **comprehend** what has happened.*

comprehensible (say kom-pri-**henss**-uhb-l) *adjective*
easy to understand: *The book is written in clear, **comprehensible** language.*
➲ OPPOSITE **incomprehensible**

comprehension (say kom-pri-**hen**-shuhn) *noun* (*no plural*)
understanding something that you hear or read: *a test in listening **comprehension*** ➲ See Study page 19

comprehensive (say kom-pri-**hen**-siv) *adjective*
including everything that is necessary or connected with a particular subject: *We offer **comprehensive** instruction in dance and drama.*
▸ **comprehensively** (*adverb*): *The report deals **comprehensively** with the sources of pollution.*

compress (say kuhm-**press**) *verb* (**compressing, compressed**)
1 to become or to make something flatter or smaller so that it takes up less space: *When you **compress** air it heats up.*
2 (*computing*) to make computer files or data smaller so that they use less space
▸ **compression** (*noun*)

comprise (say kuhm-**prize**) *verb* (**comprising, comprised**)
to contain, include or consist of: *a flat*

comprising a bedroom, lounge, kitchen and bathroom

> USAGE Note that we use **comprise** in this way: *The village* ***comprises*** *three shops and ten houses.* It is not correct to use **of** with **comprise**. Don't say 'The village comprises of three shops and ten houses.'

compromise (say **kom**-pruh-mize) *noun* (*plural* **compromises**)
an agreement between people when each person gets part, but not all, of what they wanted: *After long talks, the workers and management reached a* ***compromise****.*

compulsive (say kuhm-**pul**-siv) *adjective*
1 happening because of a strong feeling that you cannot control: *a* ***compulsive*** *desire to win*
2 relating to a person who has a bad habit that they cannot control or give up: *a* ***compulsive*** *gambler*
3 so interesting or exciting that you cannot take your attention away from it: *This book makes* ***compulsive*** *reading.*
▸ **compulsively** (*adverb*): *She is* ***compulsively*** *neat.*

compulsory (say kuhm-**pul**-suh-ree) *adjective*
that must be done because of a law or a rule: *School is* ***compulsory*** *from Grade R to Grade 9.*
➲ OPPOSITE **optional**, ➲ SYNONYM **obligatory**

computer (say kom-**pyoo**-tuh) *noun* (*plural* **computers**)
a machine that can store and find information, calculate amounts and control other machines: *All the work is done by* ***computer****.* ◇ *He spends a lot of time on the* ***computer****, sending emails.* ◇ *a* ***computer*** *program* (= information that tells a computer what to do) ◇ ***computer*** *games* ➲ See **PC, personal computer, word processor**

computer

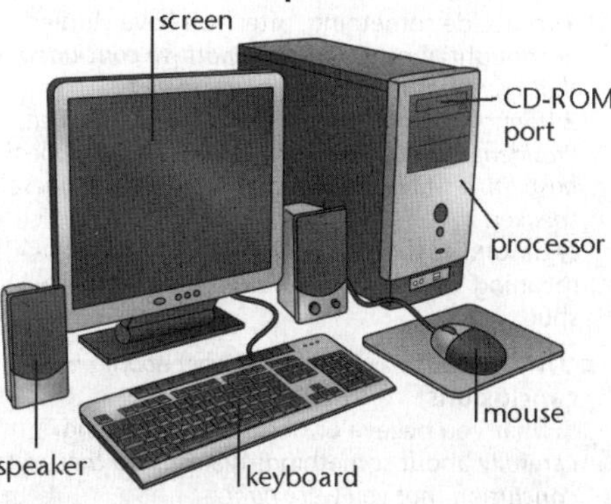

comrade (say **kom**-rayd) *noun* (*plural* **comrades**)
1 a person who spends time with you or who works with you
2 a person who is a member of the same political party or group as you, especially somebody who believes in **communism** or **socialism**
3 a person who fights on the same side as you in a war

con (say **kon**) *verb* (**conning, conned**) (*informal*)
to trick somebody, especially in order to get money: *He* ***conned*** *her into investing in a company that didn't really exist.* ◇ *The old lady was* ***conned*** *out of her savings.*
▸ **con** (*noun*): *the latest* ***con***

concave (say **kong**-kayv) *adjective*
having a surface shaped like the inside of a bowl: *a* ***concave*** *mirror* ➲ See **convex**

concave and convex

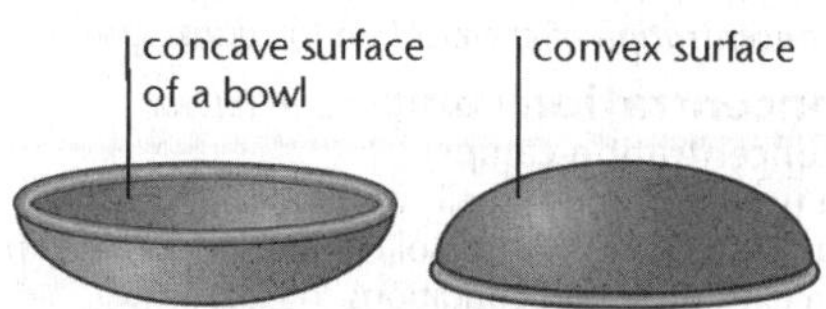

conceal (say kuhn-**seel**) *verb* (**concealing, concealed**) (*formal*)
to hide something: *They* ***concealed*** *the bomb in a suitcase.* ◇ ***conceal*** *the truth*
▸ **concealed** (*adjective*): *a* ***concealed*** *weapon*

> USAGE **Hide** is the word that we usually use. **Conceal** is quite formal.

concede (say kuhn-**seed**) *verb* (**conceding, conceded**) (*formal*)
1 to admit that something is true although you do not want to: *She finally had to* ***concede*** *that the problem was mostly her fault.*
2 to accept that you have lost: *He reluctantly* ***conceded*** *defeat.*
3 to allow somebody to have control of something that you were controlling: *They lost the war and had to* ***concede*** *territory to their enemy.* ➲ The noun is **concession** 1

conceit (say kuhn-**seet**) *noun* (*no plural*)
too much pride in yourself and your abilities
▸ **conceited** (*adjective*): *She is very* ***conceited****.*

conceive (say kuhn-**seev**) *verb* (**conceiving, conceived**)
1 to think of a plan or invent something new: *He* ***conceived*** *the idea for developing the telephone in 1874.* ➲ SYNONYM **devise**
2 (*formal*) to imagine or believe something:

A B C D E F G H I J K L M N O P Q R S T U V W X Y Z

*He started to **conceive** of the world as a dangerous place.*
3 to become pregnant with a baby

concentrate (say **kon**-suhn-trayt) *verb* (**concentrating, concentrated**)
1 to give all your attention to something: *Settle down and **concentrate** on your work.* ◇ *Be quiet and let him **concentrate**.*
2 to come together or to bring people or things together in one place: *The veld fires were **concentrated** in two main areas.*
▸ **concentrated** (*adjective*): *This is **concentrated** orange juice. You need to add water to it.*

concentration (say kon-suhn-**tray**-shuhn) *noun*
1 (*no plural*) the ability to give all your attention to something: *You need total **concentration** for this type of work.*
2 (*plural* **concentrations**) a large number of people or things in one place: *There is a high **concentration** of chemicals in the drinking water.*

concentration camp *noun* (*plural* **concentration camps**)
a type of prison (usually a number of buildings inside a fence) where political prisoners are kept in extremely bad conditions: *a Nazi **concentration camp***

concentric (say kuhn-**sen**-trik) *adjective*
having the same centre: ***concentric** polygons, **concentric** fibres*
concentric circles circles that have the same centre but a different **radius**

concept (say **kon**-sept) *noun* (*plural* **concepts**)
an idea or general principle: *We came up with a **concept** for our design.* ◇ *the **concept** of human rights*

concern[1] (say kuhn-**surn**) *noun*
1 (*no plural*) worry: *There is a lot of **concern** about this problem.*
2 (*plural* **concerns**) something that is important or interesting to somebody: *Her problems are not my **concern**.*

concern[2] (say kuhn-**surn**) *verb* (**concerning, concerned**)
1 to be important or interesting to somebody: *Please pay attention because this information **concerns** all of you.* ➲ SYNONYM **affect**
2 to be about something: *The story **concerns** a young boy and his parents.*
3 to worry somebody: *It **concerns** me that she is always late.*

concerned (say kuhn-**surnd**) *adjective*
worried about something: *They are very **concerned** about their son's health.*

concerning (say kuhn-**surn**-ing) *preposition* (*formal*)
about something: *He asked several questions **concerning** the outing to the museum.*
➲ SYNONYM **regarding**

concert (say **kon**-suht) *noun* (*plural* **concerts**)
a public performance of music: *a rock **concert***

concertina (say kon-suh-**tee**-nuh) *noun* (*plural* **concertinas**)
a small musical instrument that you hold in your hands and play by pulling the ends apart and pressing them together again while pressing buttons

concerto (say kuhn-**chur**-toh) *noun* (*plural* **concertos**)
a piece of music for an orchestra in which some passages are performed by one musical instrument

concession (say kuhn-**sesh**-uhn) *noun* (*plural* **concessions**)
1 something that you admit or agree to give to somebody in order to end an argument: *Employers have been forced to make **concessions** to the trade union.* ➲ The verb is **concede**
2 an official piece of paper that shows that you are allowed to use land that belongs to the government or to somebody else for a special purpose: *a mining **concession***
3 a lower price or a sum subtracted from a total amount, allowed for certain groups of people: *a tax **concession***

concise (say kuhn-**syss**) *adjective*
giving the most important information in a few words ➲ OPPOSITE **long-winded** ➲ SYNONYM **brief**[1]
▸ **concisely** (*adverb*): *the art of writing **concisely***

conclude (say kuhn-**klood**) *verb* (**concluding, concluded**)
1 to decide something, after you have studied or thought about it: *In our report we **concluded** that most learners eat too many sweets.*
2 (*formal*) to end or make something end: *The President **concluded** his tour with a visit to a local hospital.* ◇ *May I **conclude** by thanking our guest speaker.*
🛈 ORIGIN: 13th–15th century, from Latin *con-* meaning 'completely' + *claudere* meaning 'to shut'

conclusion (say kuhn-**kloo**-zhuhn) *noun* (*plural* **conclusions**)
1 what you believe or decide after thinking carefully about something: *We came to the **conclusion** that you were right.*
2 (*formal*) an end to something: *The peace talks reached a successful **conclusion**.*

concoct (say kuhn-**kokt**) *verb* (**concocting, concocted**)
1 to create something unusual or surprising by mixing different things together, especially in cooking
2 to tell somebody a story or plan that is not true: *They* ***concocted*** *an elaborate hoax.*
▸ **concoction** (*noun*): *a* ***concoction*** *of different herbs and spices*

concord (say **kong**-kawd) *noun*
1 (*no plural*) an agreement, or the friendly relationship that exists between people, groups or countries who live together in peace ➲ OPPOSITE **discord**
2 (*plural* **concords**) (*grammar*) the fact that words in a phrase have a particular form according to other words in the phrase

concrete[1] (say **kong**-kreet) *noun* (*no plural*)
a hard grey material used for building things: *a* ***concrete*** *wall*

concrete[2] (say **kong**-kreet) *adjective*
existing, not just imagined, but definite: *We should discuss the options and make* ***concrete*** *decisions.* ➲ SYNONYM **tangible** ➲ OPPOSITE **abstract**[1] 1

concussion (say kuhn-**kush**-uhn) *noun* (*no plural*)
a temporary injury to the brain that is caused by a hard hit on the head
▸ **concuss** (*verb*): *The child fell off her bike and was slightly* ***concussed.***

condemn (say kuhn-**dem**) *verb* (**condemning, condemned**)
1 to say strongly that a person or thing is very bad or wrong: *Many people* ***condemned*** *the government's decision.* ➲ OPPOSITE **condone**
2 to say that somebody must be punished in a certain way: *The murderer was* ***condemned*** *to death.* ➲ SYNONYM **sentence**[2]

condensation (say kon-den-**say**-shuhn) *noun* (*no plural*)
1 small drops of water that form when water **vapour** cools down
2 the process in which a gas changes into a liquid

condense (say kuhn-**denss**) *verb* (**condensing, condensed**)
1 (used about a gas) to cool down and change to a liquid ➲ See **evaporate**
2 to make a piece of writing shorter by removing words or by giving only the most important facts

condescend (say kon-di-**send**) *verb* (**condescending, condescended**)
1 to behave towards other people in a way that shows that you think you are better or more important than them ➲ SYNONYM **patronize**
2 to agree to do something although you think that it is below your level of importance: *He finally* ***condescended*** *to discuss the problem with me.*
▸ **condescending** (*adjective*): *I don't like your* ***condescending*** *smile!*

condition (say kuhn-**dish**-uhn) *noun*
1 (*no plural*) the state that a person or thing is in: *The CD player was cheap and in good* ***condition,*** *so I bought it.*
2 (*plural noun*) the situation in which people live, work or do things: *The prisoners lived in terrible* ***conditions.***
3 (*plural* **conditions**) something that must happen before another thing can happen: *You can go to the party but my* ***condition*** *is that you finish your homework first.*
on condition that ... only if: *You can go out on* ***condition*** *that you come home for supper.*

conditional (say kuhn-**dish**-uhn-l) *adjective*
1 that will only be done or will only happen if another thing is done or happens first: *a* ***conditional*** *ceasefire*
2 (*grammar*) describing a situation that must exist before something else can happen: *'If she wins the money, she will buy some new clothes' is a* ***conditional*** *sentence.*
▸ **conditionally** (*adverb*): *The licence is granted* ***conditionally*** *until final approval.*

condom (say **kon**-dom) *noun* (*plural* **condoms**)
a thin rubber covering that a man puts over his **penis** during sex. It prevents diseases from passing from one sexual partner to the other and the woman from becoming pregnant.
▸ **condomize** (*verb*) (also **condomise**) (*informal*): *Protect yourself.* ***Condomize.***

condone (say kuhn-**dohn**) *verb* (**condoning, condoned**)
to accept something that most people think is wrong or immoral ➲ OPPOSITE **condemn** 1

conduct[1] (say kuhn-**dukt**) *verb* (**conducting, conducted**)
1 to organize or do an activity: *They are going to* ***conduct*** *an experiment.*
2 to stand in front of a group of musicians and control what they do: *The orchestra was* ***conducted*** *by Peter Jones.*
3 to show somebody where to go: *She* ***conducted*** *us on a tour of the museum.*
4 (*science*) to allow heat, electricity or sound to pass along or through something: *Rubber does not* ***conduct*** *electricity.*

conduct[2] (say **kon**-dukt) *noun* (*no plural*) (*formal*)
the way somebody behaves
➲ SYNONYM **behaviour**

conduction (say kuhn-**duk**-shuhn) *noun* (*no plural*) (*science*)
the transfer of heat, electricity or sound through a material by direct contact
▸ **conductive** (*adjective*): *a* ***conductive*** *surface*

conductor (say kuhn-**duk**-tuh) *noun* (*plural* **conductors**)
1 a person who stands in front of a group of musicians and controls what they do
2 a person who sells or checks people's tickets on a bus or train
3 (*science*) a substance that allows heat or electricity to pass through or along it ➲ See **semiconductor**

cone (*rhymes with* **stone**) *noun* (*plural* **cones**)
1 a solid shape with a flat round base and a pointed end ➲ The adjective is **conical**
2 the hard fruit of some trees, for example **pine**[1] trees: *a pine* ***cone***

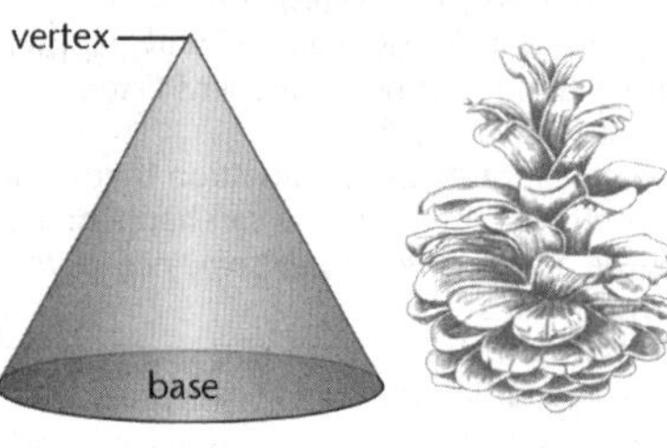

cone **pine cone**

confectionery (say kuhn-**fek**-shuhn-ree) *noun* (*no plural*)
sweets, biscuits, cakes and chocolates

confederation (say kuhn-fed-uh-**ray**-shuhn) *noun* (*plural* **confederations**)
an organization formed by a number of smaller groups: *a* ***confederation*** *of trade unions*
➲ SYNONYM **league** 2

conference (say **kon**-fuh-ruhnss) *noun* (*plural* **conferences**)
a large meeting, where many people with the same job or interests come together to discuss their views: *an international* ***conference*** *on climate change*

confess (say kuhn-**fess**) *verb* (**confessing, confessed**)
to say that you have done something wrong: *She* ***confessed*** *that she had stolen the money.* ◇ *He* ***confessed*** *to the crime.* ➲ SYNONYM **admit** 1 ➲ OPPOSITE **deny**

confession (say kuhn-**fesh**-uhn) *noun* (*plural* **confessions**)
an act of admitting that you have done something wrong: *She made a full* ***confession*** *to the police.*

confetti (say kuhn-**fet**-ee) *noun* (*no plural*)
small pieces of coloured paper that people throw over a couple who have just got married

confide (say kuhn-**fide**) *verb* (**confiding, confided**)
to tell somebody a secret: *Thandi* ***confided*** *to me that she was applying for another job.*
confide in somebody to talk to somebody that you trust about something secret or private: *He's a friend I can* ***confide*** *in.*

confidence (say **kon**-fi-duhnss) *noun* (*no plural*)
the feeling that you can do something well: *She answered the questions with* ***confidence.*** ◇ *I have great* ***confidence*** *in you.*
in confidence trusting that a person will keep information private

confident (say **kon**-fi-duhnt) *adjective*
sure that you can do something well, or that something will happen: *I'm* ***confident*** *that our team will win.*

confidential (say kon-fi-**den**-shuhl) *adjective*
(used about information) that you should keep a secret and not tell other people: ***confidential*** *information*

configure (say kuhn-**fig**-uh) *verb* (**configuring, configured**) (*formal*)
1 to set up, arrange or fit together the parts of a thing in a particular way
2 (*computing*) to connect and arrange computer equipment for a particular task
▸ **configuration** (*noun*): *the* ***configuration*** *of seats in a plane*

confine (say kuhn-**fine**) *verb* (**confining, confined**) (*formal*)
1 to prevent a person or a thing from leaving an enclosed space: *The prisoners were* ***confined*** *to their cells.*
2 to keep or stay within the limits of something: *Please* ***confine*** *your questions to the topic.*

confirm (say kuhn-**furm**) *verb* (**confirming, confirmed**)
to say that something is true or that something will happen: *Please write and* ***confirm*** *the date of your arrival.*
▸ **confirmation** (*noun*): *We are waiting for* ***confirmation*** *of the report.*

confiscate (say **kon**-fiss-kayt) *verb* (**confiscating, confiscated**)
to take something away from somebody because you have the authority to do it: *The teachers at our school are allowed to* ***confiscate*** *cellphones.*

conflict[1] (say **kon**-flikt) *noun* (*plural* **conflicts**)
a fight or an argument

conflict[2] (say kuhn-**flikt**) *verb* (**conflicting, conflicted**)
to disagree or be different: *These results* ***conflict*** *with earlier research results.*

confluence (say **kon**-fl*uu*-uhnss) *noun* (*plural* **confluences**) (*geography*)
a place where two rivers meet and join together

conform (say kuhn-**fawm**) *verb* (**conforming, conformed**)
1 to obey a rule or law, or to be in agreement with: *The computers* ***conform*** *to industry standards.*
2 to behave in the way that other people and society expect you to behave
▸ **conformity** (*noun*): ***conformity*** *to peer pressure* ◇ *in* ***conformity*** *with international regulations*

confront (say kuhn-**frunt**) *verb* (**confronting, confronted**)
1 to deal with a difficult situation: *If we don't* ***confront*** *this crisis soon, it will be too late!*
2 to make a person face of deal with something that is difficult or unpleasant: *The police* ***confronted*** *him with the evidence.*
3 to stand in front of a person and prepare to argue or fight with them: *If robbers come into your house, don't* ***confront*** *them.*
▸ **confrontation** (*noun*)

confuse (say kuhn-**fyooz**) *verb* (**confusing, confused**)
1 to mix up a person's ideas, so that they cannot think clearly or understand: *They* ***confused*** *me by asking so many questions.*
2 to think that one thing or person is another thing or person: *I often* ***confuse*** *Lee with his brother. They look so similar.*
▸ **confusing** (*adjective*): *This map is* ***confusing*** (= it is difficult to understand).

confused (say kuhn-**fyoozd**) *adjective*
not able to think clearly: *The waiter got* ***confused*** *and brought us the wrong food!*

confusion (say kuhn-**fyoo**-zhuhn) *noun* (*no plural*)
1 a state of not being able to think clearly or understand something: *He looked at me in* ***confusion*** *when I asked him a question.*
2 a state of disorder: *Their unexpected visit threw all our plans into* ***confusion.***

congeal (say kuhn-**jeel**) *verb* (**congealing, congealed**)
(a liquid) to become thick and sticky as it dries or cools

congenital (say kuhn-**jen**-i-tuhl) *adjective*
existing at birth: *a* ***congenital*** *disease* ◇ *a* ***congenital*** *heart problem*

congested (say kuhn-**jess**-tid) *adjective*
so crowded or full of something that nothing can move: *The streets are* ***congested*** *with traffic.*
▸ **congestion** (*noun*): *rush-hour* ***congestion***

conglomeration (say kuhn-glom-uh-**ray**-shuhn) *noun* (*plural* **conglomerations**)
a group of different things that have been brought together: *a* ***conglomeration*** *of buildings in different styles*

congratulate (say kuhn-**grat**-sh*uu*-layt) *verb* (**congratulating, congratulated**)
to tell a person that you are pleased about something they have done: *I* ***congratulated*** *Sue on passing her exam.*

congratulations (say kuhn-grat-sh*uu*-**lay**-shuhnz) *plural noun*
what you say to a person when you are pleased about something they have done: ***Congratulations*** *on your new job!*

congregate (say **kong**-gri-gayt) *verb* (**congregating, congregated**)
to come together in a group or a crowd: *Many spectators* ***congregated*** *to watch the game.*
➲ SYNONYM **assemble** 2

congregation (say kong-gri-**gay**-shuhn) *noun* (*plural* **congregations**)
a group of people who come together to attend a church service, or the members of a particular church

congress (say **kong**-gress) *noun*
1 (*plural* **congresses**) a large formal meeting of many people to talk about important things
2 Congress (*no plural*) a group of people who make the laws in some countries, for example in the United States of America

congruent (say **kong**-gr*uu*-uhnt) *adjective*
1 (*maths*) having exactly the same shape and size: ***congruent*** *triangles*
2 (*formal*) suitable or right for a particular situation: *We must set goals that are* ***congruent*** *with our values.*
▸ **congruence** (*noun*)

conical (say **kon**-ik-l) *adjective*
having a round base and a pointed end ➲ The noun is **cone**

conifer (say **kon**-i-fuh) *noun* (*plural* **conifers**)
an **evergreen** tree that has narrow leaves (called **needles**) and hard brown fruit (called **cones**): *Pine trees are examples of* ***conifers.***

A B C D E F G H I J K L M N O P Q R S T U V W X Y Z

conjunction (say kon-**jungk**-shuhn) *noun* (*plural* **conjunctions**) (*grammar*)
a word that joins other words, parts of sentences, and sentences: *'And', 'or' and 'but' are* ***conjunctions****.* ➲ See Study page 4

conjure (say **kun**-juh) *verb* (**conjuring, conjured**)
to do clever tricks by moving your hands quickly and skilfully
conjure something up
1 to cause a memory or an image to appear in your mind: *Hawaiian music* ***conjures*** *up images of sunshine, flowers and beaches.*
2 to create something surprising in a very short time: *She can* ***conjure*** *up a delicious meal from the simplest ingredients.*
▸ **conjuror** (*noun*): *The* ***conjuror*** *pulled a rabbit out of a hat.*

connect (say kuh-**nekt**) *verb* (**connecting, connected**)
to join one thing to another thing: *This wire* ***connects*** *the DVD player to the television.* ◇ *The two cities are* ***connected*** *by a highway.*
➲ OPPOSITE **disconnect**
❶ ORIGIN: 14th–15th century, from Latin *con-* meaning 'together' + *nectere* meaning 'join tightly, bind'

connection (say kuh-**nek**-shuhn) *noun* (*plural* **connections**)
1 the way that one thing is joined or related to another: *We had a bad* ***connection*** *on the phone so I couldn't hear him very well.* ◇ *Is there a* ***connection*** *between violence on TV and crime?*
2 a train, plane or bus that leaves a place soon after another arrives, so that people can change from one to the other: *The train was late, so I missed my* ***connection****.*
in connection with something (*formal*) about something: *A man has been arrested in* ***connection*** *with the murder of the teenager.*

connoisseur (say kon-uh-**sur**) *noun* (*plural* **connoisseurs**)
a person who knows a lot about something, such as food, art or music

connotation (say kon-uh-**tay**-shuhn) *noun* (*plural* **connotations**)
what a word makes you think of in addition to its main meaning: *Words can have negative or positive* ***connotations****.*

conquer (say **kong**-kuh) *verb* (**conquering, conquered**)
1 to defeat an enemy in war and take control of their country: *King Shaka* ***conquered*** *many nations.*
2 to succeed in controlling or dealing with a difficult thing in your life: *She's trying to* ***conquer*** *her fear of heights.*
▸ **conqueror** (*noun*)

conquest (say **kong**-kwest) *noun* (*plural* **conquests**)
1 the act of taking control of a place by force, especially in a war
2 something such as land that has been taken in a war: *the* ***conquest*** *of land by European colonizers*

conscience (say **kon**-shunss) *noun* (*plural* **consciences**)
the feeling inside you about what is right and wrong: *He has a guilty* ***conscience*** (= he feels that he has done something wrong).

conscientious (say kon-shi-**en**-shuhss) *adjective*
careful to do things correctly and well: *She's a very* ***conscientious*** *student.*

conscious (say **kon**-shuhss) *adjective*
1 knowing of something: *I was* ***conscious*** *that somebody was watching me.* ➲ SYNONYM **aware**
2 awake and able to see, hear, feel and think: *The patient was* ***conscious*** *during the operation.*
➲ OPPOSITE **unconscious** 1

consciousness (say **kon**-shuss-nuhss) *noun* (*no plural*)
the state of being able to see, hear, feel and think: *As she fell, she hit her head and lost* ***consciousness****.*

conscript (say **kon**-skript) *verb* (**conscripting, conscripted**)
to officially order somebody to join the army, navy or air force
▸ **conscription** (*noun*): ***Conscription*** *was abolished in South Africa in 1993.*

consecutive (say kuhn-**sek**-yuh-tiv) *adjective*
coming or happening one after the other: *This is the team's fourth* ***consecutive*** *win.*
▸ **consecutively** (*adverb*): *I numbered the pages* ***consecutively****.*

consensus (say kuhn-**sen**-suhss) *noun* (*no plural*)
agreement among a group of people: *He is confident that a* ***consensus*** *can be reached.*

consent[1] (say kuhn-**sent**) *noun* (*no plural*)
agreeing to let somebody do something: *Her parents gave their* ***consent*** *to the marriage.*
➲ SYNONYM **permission**

consent[2] (say kuhn-**sent**) *verb* (**consenting, consented**) (*formal*)
to agree to something: *He finally* ***consented*** *to his daughter's marriage.*

consequence (say **kon**-si-kwuhnss) *noun* (*plural* **consequences**)
a result of something that has happened: *Their actions had terrible* ***consequences***.

consequently (say **kon**-si-kwuhnt-lee) *adverb*
because of that: *He didn't do any work, and* ***consequently*** *failed the exam.* ➲ SYNONYM **therefore**

conservation (say kon-suh-**vay**-shuhn) *noun* (*no plural*)
taking good care of the world and its land, rivers, plants, and animals: *the* ***conservation*** *of the rainforests*

conservative (say kuhn-**sur**-vuh-tiv) *adjective*
not liking change or new ideas: *the* ***conservative*** *opinions of his parents*

conserve (say kuhn-**surv**) *verb* (**conserving, conserved**)
to prevent something from being wasted, damaged or changed: *She was* ***conserving*** *her energy for the next day.* ◇ *We need to* ***conserve*** *our natural and cultural heritage.* ➲ See **preserve**

consider (say kuhn-**si**-duh) *verb* (**considering, considered**)
1 to think carefully about something: *I'm* ***considering*** *going to university.*
2 to think that something is true: *I* ***consider*** *her to be a good teacher.*
3 to think about the feelings of other people when you do something: *I can't move to Australia! I have to* ***consider*** *my family.*

considerable (say kuhn-**si**-duh-ruhb-l) *adjective* (*formal*)
great or large: *The car cost a* ***considerable*** *amount of money.*
▸ **considerably** (*adverb*): *My flat is* ***considerably*** *smaller than yours.*

considerate (say kuhn-**sid**-uh-ruht) *adjective*
(used about a person) kind, and who thinks and cares about other people: *Please be* ***considerate*** *and don't play loud music late at night.* ➲ OPPOSITE **inconsiderate**

consideration (say kuhn-si-duh-**ray**-shuhn) *noun*
1 (*plural* **considerations**) (*formal*) thinking carefully about something: *After* ***consideration***, *I decided not to take the job.* ➲ SYNONYM **thought**[2].
2 (*no plural*) being kind, and caring about other people's feelings: *He shows no* ***consideration***.
take something into consideration to think carefully about something when you are deciding: *We must take the cost into* ***consideration*** *when planning our holiday.*

consignment (say kuhn-**sine**-muhnt) *noun* (*plural* **consignments**) (*formal*)
a quantity of goods that is being sent somewhere or delivered to somebody: *The government sent a* ***consignment*** *of food and tents to the disaster area.*

consist (say kuhn-**sist**) *verb* (**consisting, consisted**)
consist of something to be made from two or more things or to have such things as parts: *Jam* ***consists*** *of fruit and sugar.*

consistent (say kuhn-**siss**-tuhnt) *adjective*
always the same: *His work isn't very* ***consistent***.
➲ OPPOSITE **inconsistent**
▸ **consistently** (*adverb*): *We must try to keep a* ***consistently*** *high standard.*

consolation (say kon-suh-**lay**-shuhn) *noun* (*no plural*)
something that makes you feel better when you are upset or disappointed

console[1] (say **kon**-sohl) *noun* (*plural* **consoles**)
a piece of equipment with buttons and switches on it which you connect to a computer to play games

console[2] (say kuhn-**sohl**) *verb* (**consoling, consoled**)
to make somebody happier when they are sad or disappointed ➲ SYNONYM **comfort**[2]

consolidate (say kuhn-**sol**-i-dayt) *verb* (**consolidating, consolidated**)
1 to make your position stronger, or to become stronger and firmer: *The team's excellent performance allowed them to* ***consolidate*** *their lead.*
2 to combine or unite two or more things: *All the information is* ***consolidated*** *into one report.*
▸ **consolidation** (*noun*): *the* ***consolidation*** *of power*

consonant (say **kon**-suh-nuhnt) *noun* (*plural* **consonants**)
any letter of the alphabet except *a*, *e*, *i*, *o* and *u*: *The letters 't', 'm', 's' and 'b' are all* ***consonants***.
➲ See **vowel**

consort (say kuhn-**sawt**) *verb* (**consorting, consorted**) (*formal*)
consort with to often spend time with somebody: *She was accused of* ***consorting*** *with the rebels.*

consortium (say kuhn-**saw**-ti-uhm) *noun* (*plural* **consortiums** or **consortia**)
a group of people, companies or organizations that work together for a particular purpose: *a* ***consortium*** *of businesswomen*

conspicuous (say kuhn-**spik**-yuu-uhss) *adjective*
easily seen or attracting attention ➲ OPPOSITE **inconspicuous**
▸ **conspicuously** (*adverb*): *The bird sat **conspicuously** on top of the bush.*

conspiracy (say kuhn-**spi**-ruh-see) *noun* (*plural* **conspiracies**)
a secret plan that a group of people make to do something bad or illegal ➲ SYNONYM **plot**[1] 2

conspire (say kuhn-**spy**-uh) *verb* (**conspiring, conspired**)
1 to plan and act secretly with a group of people to do something bad or illegal: *She was charged with **conspiring** with others to kill her husband.*
2 (*formal*) (events) to seem to combine and work together against a person or thing to cause a particular result: *Circumstances **conspired** against us today.*
🛈 ORIGIN: 14th–15th century, through Old French from Latin *con-* meaning 'together with' + *spirare* meaning 'breathe'

constable (say **kon**-stuhb-l) *noun* (*plural* **constables**)
an ordinary police officer

constant (say **kon**-stuhnt) *adjective*
happening all the time: *the **constant** noise of traffic*
▸ **constantly** (*adverb*): *The situation is **constantly** changing.*

constellation (say kon-stuh-**lay**-shuhn) *noun* (*plural* **constellations**)
1 a group of parts or elements
2 a group of stars that, when seen from the Earth, form a pattern: *the **constellation** of Scorpio*

constituency (say kuhn-**sti**-tyuu-uhn-see) *noun* (*plural* **constituencies**)
the people who live in a particular district and vote there to elect their own representative to parliament

constituent (say kuhn-**sti**-tyuu-uhnt) *noun* (*plural* **constituents**)
1 one of the parts that make up something: *Cells and plasma are the **constituents** of blood.*
2 a person who lives in a **constituency**
▸ **constituent** (*adjective*): *the **constituent** elements of water*

constitute (say **kon**-sti-tyoot) *verb* (**constituting, constituted**) (*formal*)
1 to be the parts that make up or form something: *the planets and stars that **constitute** our universe*
2 to represent or be considered as something: *To deny a child love and affection **constitutes** neglect.*

constitution (say kon-sti-**tyoo**-shuhn) *noun* (*plural* **constitutions**)
the laws of a country, a state or an organization

constraint (say kuhn-**straynt**) *noun* (*plural* **constraints**)
a thing that limits your freedom to do or develop something: *There are always some financial **constraints** on a project like this.*

constrict (say kuhn-**strikt**) *verb* (**constricting, constricted**)
1 to become or make something narrower, tighter or less: *The valve **constricts** the flow of air.*
2 to limit somebody's freedom to do something: *These new laws **constrict** everybody's freedom to say what they want to say.*
▸ **constriction** (*noun*): *Headaches are caused by the **constriction** of blood vessels in your brain.*

construct (say kuhn-**strukt**) *verb* (**constructing, constructed**)
1 to build something: *The bridge was **constructed** of stone.* ◇ *Will you help me to **construct** a boat?*
2 to form something such as a sentence or a **theory** by bringing different things together: *Learn how to **construct** a logical argument.*

construction (say kuhn-**struk**-shuhn) *noun*
1 (*no plural*) building something: *the **construction** of a new airport*
2 (*plural* **constructions**) (*formal*) a thing that people have built

constructive (say kuhn-**struk**-tiv) *adjective*
useful and helpful: ***constructive** feedback*
▸ **constructively** (*adverb*): *Please contribute **constructively** to the debate.*

consul (say **kon**-suhl) *noun* (*plural* **consuls**)
an official who works in a foreign country and helps people from his or her own country who are living in or visiting the foreign country

consult (say kuhn-**sult**) *verb* (**consulting, consulted**)
1 to ask somebody for information or advice: *If the pain doesn't go away, you should **consult** a doctor.*
2 to look for information in a book or on the Internet
3 to discuss something with somebody: *Harry **consulted** with his sister before selling the family business.*

consultant (say kuhn-**sul**-tuhnt) *noun* (*plural* **consultants**)
a person who knows a lot about a subject and

gives advice to other people about it: *She is a financial **consultant**.*

consume (say kuhn-**syoom**) *verb* (**consuming, consumed**) (*formal*)
to eat, drink or use something: *This car **consumes** a lot of fuel.* ◇ *Active teenagers **consume** thousands of calories a day.*

consumer (say kuhn-**syoom**-uh) *noun* (*plural* **consumers**)
1 a person who buys things or uses services: ***Consumers** want more information about the food they buy.*
2 a person or an animal that eats or uses something: ***consumers** in a food chain* (= a series of living creatures in which each creature eats the one below it in the series)

consumption (say kuhn-**sump**-shuhn) *noun* (*no plural*)
1 the act of eating, drinking or using something: *This water is not safe for human **consumption**.*
2 the amount of fuel or material that something uses

contact[1] (say **kon**-takt) *noun*
1 (*no plural*) the act of talking or writing to somebody: *Are you in **contact** with your family in Harare?*
2 (*no plural*) the state of meeting somebody or having to deal with something: *Doctors come into **contact** with* (= meet) *a lot of people.*
3 (*no plural*) the state of touching something: *This product should not come into **contact** with food.*
4 (*plural* **contacts**) a person that you know who may be able to help you: *business **contacts***
5 (*plural* **contacts**) an electrical connection: *The switches close the **contacts** and complete the circuit.*

contact[2] (say **kon**-takt) *verb* (**contacting, contacted**)
to telephone or write to somebody, or go to see them: *If you see this man, please **contact** the police.*

contact lens *noun* (*plural* **contact lenses**)
a small round piece of thin plastic that you wear in your eye so that you can see better ➲ See **glasses**

contagious (say kuhn-**tay**-juhss) *adjective*
(of a disease) that passes from one person to another person if they touch each other ➲ See **infectious**

contain (say kuhn-**tayn**) *verb* (**containing, contained**)
to have something inside: *This box **contains** pens and pencils.* ◇ *Chocolate **contains** a lot of sugar.*
ℹ ORIGIN: 13th–15th century, through Old French from Latin *con-* meaning 'altogether' + *tenere* meaning 'to hold'

container (say kuhn-**tayn**-uh) *noun* (*plural* **containers**)
a thing such as a box, bottle or packet in which you can put other things

contaminate (say kuhn-**tam**-i-nayt) *verb* (**contaminating, contaminated**)
to spoil something or make it dirty by adding harmful substances to it
▸ **contamination** (*noun*): *the **contamination** of drinking water with poisonous chemicals*

contemplate (say **kon**-tem-playt) *verb* (**contemplating, contemplated**)
1 to think carefully about what you plan to do: *She is **contemplating** a career in marketing.*
2 (*formal*) to look carefully at a person or thing for a long time: *We sat down and silently **contemplated** the river.*
▸ **contemplation** (*noun*)

contemporary[1] (say kuhn-**tem**-pruh-ree) *adjective*
1 belonging to the same time as another person or thing: *The event was recorded by a **contemporary** reporter* (= one who lived at the time).
2 belonging to the present time: ***contemporary** art* ➲ SYNONYM **modern**

contemporary[2] (say kuhn-**tem**-pruh-ree) *noun* (*plural* **contemporaries**)
a person who lives or does something at the same time as somebody else

contempt (say kuhn-**tempt**) *noun* (*no plural*)
the feeling that a person or thing does not deserve any respect or is without value: *The teacher treated my question with **contempt**.*
➲ SYNONYM **disdain**

contemptuous (say kuhn-**temp**-tshuu-uhss) *adjective*
showing or feeling a lack of respect for somebody or something: *He is **contemptuous** of slow people.*

contend (say kuhn-**tend**) *verb* (**contending, contended**)
1 to have to deal with a problem or a difficult situation: *She had a lot of problems to **contend** with.* ➲ SYNONYMS **cope, grapple** 2
2 to compete against somebody to try to win or gain something: *Two athletes are **contending** for first place.* ➲ SYNONYM **vie**
3 (*formal*) to say that something is true,

A B C D E F G H I J K L M N O P Q R S T U V W X Y Z

especially in an argument: *He **contended** that he was innocent.*

content[1] (say kuhn-**tent**) *adjective*
happy or satisfied with what you have: *She is not **content** with the money she has – she wants more.*

content[2] (say **kon**-tent) *noun*
1 (*no plural*) the topics, ideas or questions dealt with in a book, article or television programme: *The **content** of the essay is good, but there are too many grammatical mistakes.*
2 (*no plural*) the amount of a substance that something contains: *Broccoli has a high vitamin **content**.*
3 contents (*plural noun*) the thing or things that are inside something: *I poured the **contents** of the bottle into a bowl.*
4 contents (*plural noun*) the different sections that are contained in a book: *The **contents** page of a book tells you what is in it.*
5 (*no plural*) the information or other material contained on a website or **CD-ROM**: *online **content** providers*

contented (say kuhn-**ten**-tuhd) *adjective*
happy or satisfied, especially because your life is good: *a **contented** smile*

contents (say **kon**-tentss) *plural noun* ➲ See **content[2]** 3-4

contest (say **kon**-test) *noun* (*plural* **contests**)
a game or competition that people try to win: *a boxing **contest***

contestant (say kuhn-**tess**-tuhnt) *noun* (*plural* **contestants**)
a person who tries to win a **contest**: *There are six **contestants** in the race.*

context (say **kon**-tekst) *noun* (*plural* **contexts**)
the words that come before and after another word or sentence: *Try to understand the meaning of a word by looking at its **context**.*

continent (say **kon**-ti-nuhnt) *noun* (*plural* **continents**)
one of the seven main areas of land in the world, for example Africa, Asia or Europe
▸ **continental** (*adjective*): *a **continental** climate*

continual (say kuhn-**tin**-yuu-uhl) *adjective*
happening often: *We have had **continual** problems with this machine.*
▸ **continually** (*adverb*): *He is **continually** late for work.*

continue (say kuhn-**tin**-yoo) *verb* (**continuing, continued**)
1 to not stop happening or doing something: *We **continued** working until five o'clock.* ◇ *The rain **continued** all afternoon.*
2 to go further in the same direction: *We **continued** along the path.*
3 to start again after stopping: *Let's stop now and **continue** the game after lunch.*

continuous (say kuhn-**tin**-yuu-uhss) *adjective*
not stopping: *a **continuous** line* ◇ *a **continuous** noise*
▸ **continuously** (*adverb*): *It rained **continuously** for five hours.*

contort (say kuhn-**tawt**) *verb* (**contorting, contorted**)
to change the natural shape of a thing by bending or twisting it or to become twisted or bent: *His face **contorts** as he screams.*

contour (say **kon**-toor) *noun* (*plural* **contours**)
1 the shape of the outer surface of a thing: *I could just make out the **contours** of the house in the dark.*
2 (also **contour line**) (*geography*) a line on a map joining all places of the same height above sea level

contra- (say **kon**-truh) *prefix*
against or opposite: ***contraceptive*** ◇ ***contradict***
🛈 **ORIGIN**: from Latin *contra-* meaning 'against'

contraband (say **kon**-truh-band) *noun* (*no plural*)
goods that are taken into or out of a country illegally: *They were trying to smuggle **contraband** across the border.*

contraceptive (say kon-truh-**sep**-tiv) *noun* (*plural* **contraceptives**)
a pill, device or practice that prevents a woman becoming pregnant: *oral **contraceptives***
▸ **contraception** (*noun*): *The clinic advises women on **contraception**.*

contract[1] (say **kon**-trakt) *noun* (*plural* **contracts**)
an official piece of paper that says that somebody agrees to do something: *The company signed a **contract** to build the road.*

contract[2] (say kuhn-**tract**) *verb* (**contracting, contracted**)
1 to become or to make something smaller, thinner or shorter: *We often **contract** words in English.* ◇ *Metals **contract** as they cool.*
➲ **OPPOSITE** **expand**
2 to get an illness or disease: *Joyce **contracted** a rare disease.*
3 to make a legal agreement with somebody to do work or provide goods or services
▸ **contraction** (*noun*): *'Can't' is a **contraction** of 'cannot'.* ◇ *muscle **contractions***

contradict (say kon-truh-**dikt**) *verb* (**contradicting, contradicted**)
1 to say that something that someone has said

is wrong, and that the opposite is true: *He got very angry when his friend* ***contradicted*** *everything he said.* ◇ ***contradict*** *yourself* (= say the opposite of what you said before)
2 (of statements or pieces of evidence) to be so different from each other that one of them must be wrong: *These instructions seem to* ***contradict*** *previous ones.*

contralto (say kuhn-**tral**-toh) *noun* (*music*)
1 (*no plural*) the lowest type of singing voice found in women or young boys
2 (*plural* **contraltos**) a singer with such a voice, usually a woman ➲ See **alto, soprano**

contraption (say kuhn-**trap**-shuhn) *noun* (*plural* **contraptions**) (*informal*)
a strange machine or piece of equipment that you are not sure what it is for or how it works

contrary[1] (say **kon**-truh-ree) *adjective*
contrary to something very different from something or opposite to something: *He didn't stay in bed,* ***contrary*** *to the doctor's orders.*

contrary[2] (say **kon**-truh-ree) *noun* (*no plural*)
on the contrary
1 the opposite is true
2 (*old-fashioned*) certainly not: *'You look ill.' 'On the* ***contrary****, I feel fine!'*

contrast[1] (say **kon**-traast) *noun* (*plural* **contrasts**)
a difference between things that you can see clearly: *There is a clear* ***contrast*** *between the cultures of Europe and Africa.*
ⓘ **ORIGIN:** 17th century, through French and Italian, from Latin *contra-* meaning 'against' + *stare* meaning 'stand'

contrast[2] (say kuhn-**traast**) *verb* (**contrasting, contrasted**)
to look at or think about two or more things together and see the differences between them: *The book* ***contrasts*** *life today with life 100 years ago.*

contribute (say kuhn-**trib**-yoot or **kon**-tri-byoot) *verb* (**contributing, contributed**)
1 to give a part of the total, together with others: *We* ***contributed*** *R5 each for a class party.*
2 to be one of the causes of something: *The bad weather* ***contributed*** *to the accident.*
3 to write articles for a magazine or newspaper

contribution (say kon-tri-**byoo**-shuhn) *noun* (*plural* **contributions**)
something that you give, especially money or help, or do together with other people: *I made a* ***contribution*** *to the children's fund.*

contrite (say kon-**trite**) *adjective* (*formal*)
feeling ashamed and sorry because you have done something wrong: *'Sorry,' he mumbled, looking* ***contrite****.*

contrive (say kuhn-**trive**) *verb* (**contriving, contrived**)
1 to succeed in doing something, although there are difficulties: *He somehow* ***contrived*** *to get off work early to meet with her.*
2 to make something happen by being clever or dishonest: *She* ***contrived*** *a scheme to cheat insurance companies.*

control[1] (say kuhn-**trohl**) *noun*
1 (*no plural*) the power to make people or things do what you want: *Who has* ***control*** *of the government?* ◇ *The driver lost* ***control*** *of the car.*
2 controls (*plural noun*) the parts of a machine that you press or move to make it work: *the* ***controls*** *of an aeroplane*
be or **get out of control** to be or become impossible to deal with: *The fire got out of* ***control*** *and many houses were destroyed.*
under control being dealt with successfully: *Everything's under* ***control****.*
be in control to have the power or ability to deal with something: *The police are now in* ***control*** *after last night's violence.*

control[2] (say kuhn-**trohl**) *verb* (**controlling, controlled**)
to make people or things do what you want: *He can't* ***control*** *his dog.* ◇ *This switch* ***controls*** *the heating.*
▸ **controller** (*noun*): *an air traffic* ***controller***

controversial (say kon-truh-**vur**-shuhl) *adjective*
making people argue and disagree with each other: *a* ***controversial*** *new law*

controversy (say **kon**-truh-vur-see or kuhn-**tro**-vur-see) *noun* (*plural* **controversies**)
public discussion and disagreement about something: *The government's plans caused a lot of* ***controversy****.*

conundrum (say kuh-**nun**-druhm) *noun* (*plural* **conundrums**)
1 a difficult question that has a clever or funny answer
2 a problem or question that is difficult to understand or explain

convalesce (say kon-vuh-**less**) *verb* (**convalescing, convalesced**) (*formal*)
to spend time resting and getting better again after you have been ill
▸ **convalescence** (*noun*): *He spent ten days in hospital and two months in* ***convalescence****.*
▸ **convalescent** (*adjective*): *Mpho has a job as a nurse at a* ***convalescent*** *home.*

A B C D E F G H I J K L M N O P Q R S T U V W X Y Z

convection (say kuhn-**vek**-shuhn) *noun* (*no plural*)
1 (*science*) the process in which energy, especially heat, moves through a gas or a liquid. This is caused by the movement of very small parts of the gas or liquid: *a* ***convection*** *oven*
2 the vertical movement of energy in the atmosphere: ***convection*** *currents*

convene (say kuhn-**veen**) *verb* (**convening, convened**) (*formal*)
to come together or to call people together for a formal meeting: *The United Nations* ***convened*** *a peace conference.* ◇ *Parliament* ***convened*** *to elect a new president.*

convenience (say kuhn-**vee**-ni-uhnss) *noun*
1 (*no plural*) the quality of being easy, useful or suitable for somebody: *For* ***convenience****, I usually do all my shopping in the same place.*
2 (*plural* **conveniences**) something that makes things easier, quicker or more comfortable: *houses with all the modern* ***conveniences*** (= hot water, flushing toilets, etc.)

convenient (say kuhn-**vee**-ni-uhnt) *adjective*
1 useful, easy or quick to do, and not causing problems: *Let's meet on Friday. What's the most* ***convenient*** *time for you?*
2 near to a place or easy to get to: *The house is very* ***convenient*** *for the station.* ➲ OPPOSITE **inconvenient**
▸ **conveniently** (*adverb*): *We live* ***conveniently*** *close to the shops.*

convent (say **kon**-vuhnt) *noun* (*plural* **convents**)
a building in which members of a female religious community (called **nuns**) live and work

convention (say kuhn-**ven**-shuhn) *noun* (*plural* **conventions**)
1 a traditional way of behaving or of doing something: *spelling* ***conventions***
2 a large meeting of people who share a common interest or profession: *They are attending the teachers'* ***convention*** *in Bloemfontein.* ➲ SYNONYM **conference**
3 an agreement between different groups or countries: *the UN* ***convention*** *on refugees*

conventional (say kuhn-**ven**-shuhn-l) *adjective*
following traditional customs or normal styles and methods: *The book challenges* ***conventional*** *attitudes in education.*
▸ **conventionally** (*adverb*): *We need to learn skills beyond those* ***conventionally*** *taught in schools.*

converge (say kuhn-**vurj**) *verb* (**converging, converged**)
to move towards each other from different directions and meet at the same point: *People* ***converged*** *on the stadium to watch the match.*
▸ **convergence** (*noun*): *a* ***convergence*** *of opinions* ▸ **convergent** (*adjective*): ***convergent*** *technologies*

conversation (say kon-vuh-**say**-shuhn) *noun* (*plural* **conversations**)
a talk between two or more people: *I had a long* ***conversation*** *with my friend on the phone.*

converse[1] (say kuhn-**vurss**) *verb* (**conversing, conversed**) (*formal*)
to talk to somebody or to have a conversation with somebody: *She is able to* ***converse*** *fluently in isiXhosa.*

converse[2] (say **kon**-vurss) *adjective* (*formal*)
opposite to something: *a* ***converse*** *effect*
▸ **converse** (*noun*): *In actual fact, the* ***converse*** *is true.* ▸ **conversely** (*adverb*): *In summer the sun rises at 5.30 a.m.* ***Conversely****, it only rises at 8.00 a.m. in mid-winter.*

conversion (say kuhn-**vur**-zhuhn) *noun* (*plural* **conversions**)
the act or process of changing from one form, system or use to another: *the* ***conversion*** *of rands into dollars* ◇ *a* ***conversion*** *table for kilometres and miles*

convert (say kuhn-**vurt**) *verb* (**converting, converted**)
to change something from one form, system or use to another: *They* ***converted*** *the house into two flats.* ◇ *How do you* ***convert*** *feet to metres?*
🛈 ORIGIN: 13th–15th century, through Old French, from Latin *conversus* meaning 'turned about'

convertible (say kuhn-**vu**r-tuhb-l) *adjective*
able to be changed from one form or use to another: *a* ***convertible*** *sofa-bed*

convex (say **kon**-vekss) *adjective*
having a surface shaped like the outside of a bowl: *a* ***convex*** *lens* ➲ See illustration at **concave**

convey (say kuhn-**vay**) *verb* (**conveying, conveyed**)
1 to make other people aware of your ideas, feelings or opinions: *Beads are used to* ***convey*** *special messages.*
2 (*formal*) to transport persons or things from one place to another: *The emergency supplies were* ***conveyed*** *in an aircraft.*

convict[1] (say kuhn-**vikt**) *verb* (**convicting, convicted**)
to decide in a court of law that somebody has done something wrong: *She was* ***convicted*** *of murder and sent to prison.*

convict² (say **kon**-vikt) *noun* (*plural* **convicts**)
a person who has been found guilty of a crime and who has been put in prison

conviction (say kuhn-**vik**-shuhn) *noun*
1 (*plural* **convictions**) the action of finding somebody guilty of a crime or a case of being found guilty: *He has a* ***conviction*** *for shoplifting.*
2 (*plural* **convictions**) a very strong belief or opinion: *religious* ***convictions***
3 (*no plural*) the feeling of being confident that what you say or believe is true: *'I want to finish school and get a job,' she said with* ***conviction****.*

convince (say kuhn-**vinss**) *verb* (**convincing, convinced**)
to make somebody believe something: *I couldn't* ***convince*** *him that I was right.*

convinced (say kuhn-**vinst**) *adjective*
completely sure about something: *I'm* ***convinced*** *that I have seen her before.*

convoluted (say **kon**-vuhl-oo-tuhd) *adjective*
1 too complicated to understand easily: *a* ***convoluted*** *story* ➲ SYNONYM **complex¹**
2 having many bends or folds or changing direction often: *a* ***convoluted*** *river delta*

convoy (say **kon**-voy) *noun* (*plural* **convoys**)
a group of vehicles or ships travelling together: *a* ***convoy*** *of lorries*
in convoy in a group: *The ships set off in* ***convoy****.*

convulsion (say kuhn-**vul**-shuhn) *noun* (*plural* **convulsions**)
a sudden violent movement of a part of your body that you cannot control: *Children sometimes have* ***convulsions*** *when they are ill.*

cook¹ (say **kuuk**) *verb* (**cooking, cooked**)
to make food ready to eat by heating it: *My father* ***cooked*** *the dinner.* ◇ *I am learning to* ***cook****.*
▸ **cooked** (*adjective*): ***cooked*** *chicken*

WORD BUILDING There are different ways of **cooking** food. For example, you can **bake**, **boil**, **braai**, **fry**, **grill**, **roast**, **simmer** or **steam** food.

cook² (say **kuuk**) *noun* (*plural* **cooks**)
a person who cooks: *She works as a* ***cook*** *in a big hotel.* ◇ *He is a good* ***cook****.* ➲ See **chef**

cooker (say **kuuk**-uh) *noun* (*plural* **cookers**)
1 another word for **stove**
2 a device that cooks food in a particular or special way: *a pressure* ***cooker*** ◇ *a solar* ***cooker***

cookery (say **kuuk**-uh-ree) *noun* (*no plural*)
the skill or activity of preparing and cooking food: ***cookery*** *lessons*

cookie (say **kuuk**-ee) *noun* (*plural* **cookies**)
a kind of small thin hard cake that is usually sweet ➲ SYNONYM **biscuit**
a smart or **tough cookie** (*informal*) a smart or tough person

cooking (say **kuuk**-ing) *noun* (*no plural*)
1 making food ready to eat: *Who does the* ***cooking*** *in your family?*
2 the food that you cook: *He missed his mother's* ***cooking*** *when he left home.*

cool¹ (say **kool**) *adjective* (**cooler, coolest**)
1 a little cold, but not hot or warm: ***cool*** *weather* ◇ *I'd like a glass of* ***cool*** *water.* ➲ See note at **cold¹**
2 not excited or angry ➲ SYNONYM **calm¹** 1
3 (*informal*) very good or fashionable: *Those are* ***cool*** *shoes you're wearing!*

cool² (say **kool**) *exclamation*
used to show that someone thinks something is a good idea: *'We're planning to go out for lunch tomorrow.' '****Cool****!'*

cool³ (say **kool**) *verb* (**cooling, cooled**)
to make something less hot or to become less hot: *Take the cake out of the oven and leave it to* ***cool****.*
cool down
1 to become less hot: *We swam in the river to* ***cool down*** *after our long walk.*
2 (*informal*) to become less excited or angry

cooldrink (say **kool**-drink) *noun* (*plural* **cooldrinks**) (*S. African*)
a cold sweet drink that has no alcohol in it

coop (say **koop**) *noun* (*plural* **coops**)
a cage for chickens or ducks

cooperate (say koh-**op**-uh-rayt) *verb* (**cooperating, cooperated**) (also **co-operate**)
to work together with someone else in a helpful way: *The three learners agreed to* ***cooperate*** *and do the work together.*
🛈 ORIGIN: 16th century, from Latin from *co-* meaning 'together' + *operari* meaning 'to work'

cooperation (say koh-op-uh-**ray**-shuhn) *noun* (*no plural*) (also **co-operation**)
help that you give by doing what somebody asks you to do: *The teacher thanked them for their* ***cooperation****.*

cooperative (say koh-**op**-uh-ruh-tiv) *adjective* (also **co-operative**)
helpful by doing what you are asked to do

co-opt (say koh-**opt**) *verb* (**co-opting, co-opted**)
to officially ask somebody to become a member of a group of people who work together for a particular purpose: *He was* ***co-opted*** *onto the Education Committee.*

A B C D E F G H I J K L M N O P Q R S T U V W X Y Z

coordinate[1] (say koh-**aw**-di-nuht) *noun* (*plural* **coordinates**) (also **co-ordinate**)
one of two sets of numbers and letters that you use for finding the exact position of something such as a place on a map: *GPS* ***coordinates***

coordinate[2] (say koh-**awd**-i-nayt) *verb* (**coordinating, coordinated**) (also **co-ordinate**)
1 to organize different things or people so that they work together: *It is her job to* ***coordinate*** *the various departments.*
2 to make the parts of your body move or work together in a smooth way
▸ **coordination** (*noun*): ***coordination*** *of information between the government departments ◇ hand-eye* ***coordination***

cop (say **kop**) *noun* (*plural* **cops**) (*informal*)
a **police officer**

cope (say **kohp**) *verb* (**coping, coped**)
to deal with something, although it is difficult: *He finds it difficult to* ***cope*** *with the pressure of sport, homework and tests.*

copied (say **kop**-eed) form of **copy**[2]

copier (say **kop**-i-uh) *noun* (*plural* **copiers**)
a machine or device that makes copies of something, especially a **photocopier**

copies (say **kop**-eez) form of **copy**[1]

copious (say **koh**-pi-uhss) *adjective* (*formal*)
existing in large quantities: *There were* ***copious*** *supplies of food and drink at the wedding.*
➲ SYNONYM **abundant**
▸ **copiously** (*adverb*): *Water the trees* ***copiously*** *once a month.*

copper (say **kop**-uh) *noun* (*no plural*) (symbol Cu)
a common metal with a colour between brown and red: ***copper*** *wire*

copulate (say **kop**-yuu-layt) *verb* (**copulating, copulated**) (*formal*)
(used especially about animals) to have sex
➲ SYNONYM **mate**[2]
▸ **copulation** (*noun*)

copy[1] (say **kop**-ee) *noun* (*plural* **copies**)
1 a thing that is made to look exactly like another thing: *This isn't a real painting by Van Gogh. It's only a* ***copy****. ◇ The secretary made two* ***copies*** *of the letter.*
2 one example of a book or newspaper: *Two million* ***copies*** *of this newspaper are sold every day.*

copy[2] (say **kop**-ee) *verb* (**copying, copied**)
1 to write, draw or make something exactly the same as something else: *We* ***copied*** *the list of words into our books.*
2 to do or try to do the same as somebody else: *He* ***copies*** *everything his brother does.*
➲ SYNONYM **imitate**

copyright (say **kop**-ee-rite) *noun* (*no plural*) (symbol ©)
the legal right of an artist, musician or writer who produces a piece of original work to control the use of their works

coral (say **ko**-ruhl) *noun* (*no plural*) (*biology*)
a hard red, pink or white substance that forms in the sea from the skeletons of very small sea animals

cord (say **kawd**) *noun* (*plural* **cords**)
1 strong thick string
2 a piece of wire covered with plastic, which carries electricity to electrical equipment

cordial (say **kaw**-di-uhl) *adjective*
friendly and pleasant: *a* ***cordial*** *welcome*
▸ **cordially** (*adverb*): *'Please come in,' he said* ***cordially****.*

cordon (say **kaw**-duhn) *noun* (*plural* **cordons**)
a line or ring of police officers, soldiers or guards that prevents people from entering an area

corduroy (say **kaw**-duh-roy) *noun* (*no plural*)
1 a thick cotton cloth with lines on it, used for making clothes
2 corduroys (*plural noun*) trousers made of this material

core (say **kaw**) *noun* (*plural* **cores**)
1 the part at the centre of something: *the* ***core*** *of an apple, where the seeds are ◇ the Earth's* ***core***
2 the central or most important part of something: *the* ***core*** *of the problem*

cork (say **kawk**) *noun*
1 (*no plural*) a light soft material that comes from the outside of a particular tree
2 (*plural* **corks**) a round piece of cork that you put in a bottle to close it

corkscrew (say **kawk**-skroo) *noun* (*plural* **corkscrews**)
a tool that you use to pull a **cork** out of a bottle

corm (say **kawm**) *noun* (*plural* **corms**) (*biology*)
a thick solid underground stem of a plant that is used to store food, especially for the winter: *Banana plants have* ***corms****.*

corn (say **kawn**) *noun*
1 (*no plural*) the seeds of plants that are grown for their grain, for example **wheat**
2 (*plural* **corns**) an area of hard skin on your foot

cornea (say **kaw**-ni-uh) *noun* (*plural* **corneas**) (*biology*)
the transparent layer that covers and protects the eye ➲ See illustration at **eye**

corner[1] (say **kaw**-nuh) *noun* (*plural* **corners**)
a place where two lines, walls or roads meet: *Put the lamp in the **corner** of the room.* ◇ *The shop is on the **corner** of East Avenue and Union Street.* ◇ *He walked round the **corner** and disappeared.*

corner[2] (say **kaw**-nuh) *verb* (**cornering, cornered**)
1 to get a person or an animal into a place or a situation that they cannot easily escape from: *The police **cornered** the criminals inside the building.*
2 to get control in a particular area of business so that nobody else can have any success in it: *That company has really **cornered** the market in cartoon films.*
3 to drive around a corner: *Keep your eyes on the road when **cornering**.*

cornflakes (say **kawn**-flaykss) *plural noun*
small pieces of dried crushed **maize** that you eat with milk and sugar for breakfast

cornflour (say **kawn**-flow-uh) *noun* (*no plural*)
very fine **maize** flour, used in cooking to make sauces thicker

corny (say **kaw**-nee) *adjective* (**cornier, corniest**) (*informal*)
not original and used too often to be interesting or amusing: *a **corny** joke*

corolla (say kuh-**rol**-uh) *noun* (*plural* **corollas**) (*biology*)
the group of coloured leaves (called **petals**) that forms a ring around the centre of a flower ➲ See illustration at **flower**

corona (say kuh-**roh**-nuh) *noun* (*plural* **coronae**) (*science*)
a layer of gas that surrounds the sun and other stars

coronary (say **ko**-ruh-nuh-ree) *adjective*
relating to the heart: *a **coronary** disease*

coronation (say ko-ruh-**nay**-shuhn) *noun* (*plural* **coronations**)
an official ceremony at which somebody is made a king or a queen: *the **coronation** of King Letsie III of Lesotho in 1997*

corporal (say **kawp**-uh-ruhl) *noun* (*plural* **corporals**)
a person at a low **rank**[1] 1 in the army or air force

corporal punishment *noun* (*no plural*)
the physical punishment of hitting or beating a person, especially a child by parents or teachers

corporation (say kaw-puh-**ray**-shuhn) *noun* (*plural* **corporations**)
a big company

corps (say **kaw**) *plural noun*
1 a group of soldiers who are trained to carry out special duties and tasks: *the medical **corps***
2 a group of people involved in the same activity: *the diplomatic **corps***

PRONUNCIATION Don't pronounce the **ps** in **corps**.

corpse (say **kawpss**) *noun* (*plural* **corpses**)
the body of a dead person

corpuscle (say kaw-**puss**-l) *noun* (*plural* **corpuscles**) (*biology*)
any of the white or red cells found in the blood

correct[1] (say kuh-**rekt**) *adjective*
1 right or true: *What is the **correct** time, please?*
2 with no mistakes: *All your answers were correct.* ➲ OPPOSITE **incorrect**
▸ **correctly** (*adverb*): *Have I spelt your name **correctly**?*

correct[2] (say kuh-**rekt**) *verb* (**correcting, corrected**)
to show where the mistakes are in something and make it right: *The class did the exercises and the teacher **corrected** them.* ◇ *Please **correct** me if I make a mistake.*

correction (say kuh-**rek**-shuhn) *noun* (*plural* **corrections**)
a change that makes something right or better: *The teacher made a few **corrections** to my essay.*

correlate (say **ko**-ruh-layt) *verb* (**correlating, correlated**) (*formal*)
1 to have or to show a relationship or connection between two or more things: ***Correlate** your content with your pictures.*
2 to bring together and compare or connect related things: *She **correlates** all the information once a month and writes a report.*
▸ **correlation** (*noun*): *There is a **correlation** between a person's diet and heart disease.*

correspond (say ko-ruh-**spond**) *verb* (**corresponding, corresponded**)
1 to be the same, or almost the same, as something: *Does the name on the envelope **correspond** with the name inside the letter?*
2 (*formal*) to write letters to and receive them from somebody: *I **correspond** regularly with my friend overseas.*

correspondence (say ko-ruh-**spond**-uhnss) *noun* (*no plural*)
the letters a person sends and receives: *Her secretary reads all her* ***correspondence****.*

corridor (say **ko**-ri-daw) *noun* (*plural* **corridors**)
a long narrow part inside a building with rooms on each side of it

corrode (say kuh-**rohd**) *verb* (**corroding, corroded**)
to become weak or destroyed by chemical action: *Parts of the car were* ***corroded*** *by rust.*
▸ **corrosion** (*noun*)

corrugated (say **ko**-ruh-gayt-d) *adjective*
shaped into folds that look like waves: *a roof made of* ***corrugated*** *iron* ◇ ***corrugated*** *cardboard*

corrupt (say kuh-**rupt**) *adjective*
1 doing or involving illegal or dishonest things in exchange for money or presents
2 (*computing*) describing computer data or programs that can no longer be used because they contain changes or faults
▸ **corruption** (*noun*): *There were accusations of* ***corruption*** *among senior police officers.*

cos (say **koz**) *abbreviation* **cosine**

cosine (say **koh**-sine) *noun* (*plural* **cosines**)
the **ratio** of the length of the side next to an **acute angle** in a right-angled **triangle** to the length of the longest side ➲ See **sine**, **tangent** 2

cosmetics (say koz-**met**-ikss) *plural noun*
special powders or creams that you use on your face or hair to make yourself more beautiful

cosmic (say **koz**-mik) *adjective*
relating to outer space or the whole universe

cosmopolitan (say koz-muh-**pol**-i-tuhn) *adjective*
1 containing people from different countries and cultures: *a* ***cosmopolitan*** *city*
2 showing the influence of the cultures of many countries: *a* ***cosmopolitan*** *and sophisticated young woman*

cosmos (say **koz**-moss) *noun* (*no plural*)
(usually **the cosmos**) the universe seen as a complete system

cost[1] (say **kost**) *noun*
1 (*plural* **costs**) the money that you must pay for something: *The* ***cost*** *of the repairs was very high.*
2 (*no plural*) what you lose or give to have another thing: *He saved the child at the* ***cost*** *of his own life.*
at all costs no matter what you must do to make it happen: *We must win at all* ***costs****.*

cost[2] (say **kost**) *verb* (**costing, cost**)
1 to have the price of: *This plant* ***costs*** *R40.* ◇ *How much did the book* ***cost****?*
2 to make you lose something: *One mistake* ***cost*** *him his job.*

costly (say **kost**-lee) *adjective* (**costlier, costliest**)
costing a lot of money: *The repairs will be very* ***costly****.* ➲ SYNONYM **expensive**

costume (say **koss**-tyoom) *noun* (*plural* **costumes**)
the special clothes that people wear in a country or at a certain time: *The actors wore beautiful* ***costumes****.* ◇ *the country's national* ***costume*** ➲ See **swimming costume**

cosy (say **koh**-zee) *adjective* (**cosier, cosiest**)
warm and comfortable: *a* ***cosy*** *room*
➲ SYNONYM **snug** 1

cot (say **kot**) *noun* (*plural* **cots**)
a bed with high sides for a baby ➲ See **cradle**

cottage (say **kot**-ij) *noun* (*plural* **cottages**)
a small house in an area that is away from towns and cities

cotton (say **kot**-uhn) *noun* (*no plural*)
a natural cloth or thread that is made from the soft white hairs around the seeds of a plant that grows in hot countries: *a* ***cotton*** *shirt* ◇ *a reel of* ***cotton***
🛈 **ORIGIN:** 14th–15th century, through Old French *coton*, from Arabic *kutn*

cotton wool *noun* (*no plural*)
soft light material made from cotton that you often use for cleaning your skin: *The nurse cleaned the cut with* ***cotton wool****.*

cotyledon (say kot-i-**lee**-duhn) *noun* (*plural* **cotyledons**) (*biology*)
the first leaves of a developing seed ➲ See **dicotyledon, monocotyledon**

couch[1] (say **kowch**) *noun* (*plural* **couches**)
a long comfortable seat for two or more people to sit on ➲ SYNONYM **sofa**

couch[2] (say **kowch**) *verb* (**couching, couched**) (*formal*)
to express a thought or idea using a particular style of language or choice of words: *His reply was* ***couched*** *in very polite terms.*

cough[1] (say **kof**) *verb* (**coughing, coughed**)
to send air out of your throat with a sudden loud noise: *The smoke made me* ***cough****.*

cough[2] (say **kof**) *noun* (*plural* **coughs**)
the act of sending air out of your throat with a sudden loud noise: *I've got a bad* ***cough****.* ◇ *He gave a little* ***cough*** *before he started to speak.*

could (say **kuud**) *modal verb*
1 the word for 'can' in the past: *He* ***could*** *run very fast when he was young.* ◇ *I* ***could*** *hear the birds singing.*
2 a word that you use to ask something in a polite way: ***Could*** *you open the door?* ◇ ***Could*** *I have another sweet, please?*
3 a word that shows what is or may be possible: *I don't know where Mum is. She* ***could*** *be in the kitchen.* ◇ *It* ***could*** *rain tomorrow.* ➲ See note at **modal verb**

> USAGE Be careful! Notice how **could** is used in certain tenses:
> ■ *I* ***could have*** *gone* (not 'I could of gone'). *We* ***could have*** *swum* (not 'We could of swum').

couldn't (say **kuud**-uhnt) (*informal*) short for **could not**

could've (say **kuud**-uhv) (*informal*) short for **could have**

coulomb (say **koo**-lom) *noun* (*plural* **coulombs**) (*science*) (abbr. C)
a unit for measuring electrical charge: *One* ***coulomb*** *is the amount of electrical charge transported in one second by a current of one ampere.*

council (say **kown**-sil) *noun* (*plural* **councils**)
a group of people who are chosen to work together and to make rules and decide things: *The city* ***council*** *is planning to widen the road.*

> SPELLING Be careful! Don't confuse **council** with the verb, **counsel**. They sound the same but have different meanings.

councillor (say **kown**-sil-uh) *noun* (*plural* **councillors**)
a member of a **council**

counsel (say **kown**-suhl) *verb* (**counselling, counselled**)
1 to give professional help and support to somebody in order to find a solution to their problems
2 to tell somebody what you think they should do: *Mr Dean's lawyers* ***counselled*** *him against making public statements.*
▸ **counselling** (*noun*): *training in HIV/Aids* ***counselling*** ◇ *career* ***counselling*** ▸ **counsellor** (*noun*): *a marriage* ***counsellor*** ◇ *a debt* ***counsellor***

> SPELLING Be careful! Don't confuse **counsel** with the noun, **council**. They sound the same but have different meanings.

count[1] (say **kownt**) *verb* (**counting, counted**)
1 to say numbers one after the other in the correct order: *The children are learning to* ***count*** *from one to ten.*
2 to look at people or things to see how many there are: *I have* ***counted*** *the chairs – there are 32.*
3 to include a person or thing when you are finding a total: *There were twenty people on the bus, not* ***counting*** *the driver.*
4 to be important or accepted: *Every point in this game* ***counts.*** ◇ *Your throw won't* ***count*** *if you go over the line.*
count on a person or **thing** to feel sure that a person or thing will do what you want: *Can I* ***count*** *on you to help me?*

count[2] (say **kownt**) *noun* (*plural* **counts**)
1 an act of counting or a number that you get after counting: *After an election there is a* ***count*** *of all the votes.*
2 a point that is made in a discussion or argument: *I proved him wrong on all* ***counts.***
keep count of something to know how many there are of something: *Try to keep* ***count*** *of the number of tickets you sell.*
lose count of something to not know how many there are of something

countable noun (say **kown**-tuhb-l **nown**) *noun* (*plural* **countable nouns**) (*grammar*)
a noun that you can use in the plural or with 'a' or 'an', for example *chair* and *idea* ➲ See Study page 5 ➲ OPPOSITE **uncountable noun**

countenance (say **kown**-tuh-nuhnss) *noun* (*plural* **countenances**) (*formal*)
a person's face or the look on their face that shows how they feel: *a happy* ***countenance***

counter[1] (say **kown**-tuh) *noun* (*plural* **counters**)
1 a long high table in a shop, bank or bar, that is between the people who work there and the customers: *The man behind the* ***counter*** *in the bank was very helpful.*
2 a small round thing that you use when you play some games

counter[2] (say **kown**-tuh) *verb* (**countering, countered**)
1 to reply to criticism or to say the opposite of what somebody else has said: *Their complaints were* ***countered*** *by promises to improve the service.*
2 to try to reduce or stop the effects of something: *The shop has installed security cameras to* ***counter*** *theft.*

counteract (say **kown**-tuh-akt) *verb* (**counteracting, counteracted**)
to act against something in order to reduce or cancel its effect: *The banks have taken measures to* ***counteract*** *fraud.*

counter-attack (say **kown**-tuh-uh-tak) *noun* (*plural* **counter-attacks**)
an attack made in reaction to an attack by an enemy or opponent
▸ **counter-attack** (*verb*): *The rebels did not retreat, but instead **counter-attacked**.*

counterbalance (say **kown**-tuh-bal-uhnss) *noun* (*plural* **counterbalances**)
1 a weight that exactly balances another weight
2 a person or thing that has the opposite influence or effect to that of another person or thing
▸ **counterbalance** (*verb*): *The film's dark beginning is **counterbalanced** by the happy ending.*

counterfeit (say **kown**-tuh-feet) *adjective*
not genuine, but made as a copy of a valuable thing: ***counterfeit** money*
▸ **counterfeit** (*noun*): ***Counterfeits** usually have a slightly different colour from genuine coins.*

counterfoil (say **kown**-tuh-foyl) *noun* (*plural* **counterfoils**)
the part of a cheque or ticket that you keep as a record when you give the other part to somebody else ➲ SYNONYM **stub**[1]

counterpart (say **kown**-tuh-paat) *noun* (*plural* **counterparts**)
a person or thing that has a similar position or function in a different organization or system: *Like its **counterpart** in nature, a computer virus infects files in one computer and then spreads the infection to other computers.*

countless (say **kownt**-luhss) *adjective*
very many: *I have tried to phone him **countless** times.*

country (say **kun**-tree) *noun*
1 (*plural* **countries**) an area of land with its own people and government: *Kenya, Malawi and other African **countries** ◇ The whole **country** is in a state of panic.*
2 an area of land with its own government: *Lesotho is a mountainous **country**.*
3 the country (*no plural*) open land that is away from towns and cities: *Do you live in the town or in the **country**?*

> WHICH WORD? **Country** or **nation**?
> **Country** in sense 1 above and **nation** have similar meanings. We usually use **nation** when we refer to the people of the country: *The whole **nation** watched the match on TV.*

> PRONUNCIATION Notice how to say **country**.

countryside (say **kun**-tree-side) *noun* (*no plural*)
land that is away from towns, with **veld**, forests or farms: *We have magnificent views over open countryside.*

coup (say **koo**) *noun* (*plural* **coups**)
1 (also **coup d'état**) a sudden, illegal and often violent change of government: *a military **coup** to overthrow the president*
2 an unexpected and clever success or victory: *Getting that contract was quite a **coup**.*

> PRONUNCIATION Don't pronounce the **p** in **coup**.

couple (say **kup**-l) *noun*
1 a couple (*no plural*) two or a small number of people or things: *I invited a **couple** of friends to lunch. ◇ I'll be back in a **couple** of minutes.*
2 (*plural* **couples**) two people who are married or in a romantic relationship: *A young **couple** live next door.*

couplet (say **kup**-luht) *noun* (*plural* **couplets**)
two lines of poetry of the same length that form a single unit

coupon (say **koo**-pon) *noun* (*plural* **coupons**)
a small piece of paper that you can use to buy things at a lower price, or that you can collect and use instead of money to buy things

courage (say **ku**-rij) *noun* (*no plural*)
the ability to control your fear when you do something dangerous or difficult: *She showed great **courage** in the face of danger.*
ⓘ ORIGIN: 13th–15th century, through Old French *corage*, from Latin *cor* meaning 'heart'. When the word came into English people believed that the heart was the place where emotions were based.

courageous (say kuh-**rayj**-uhss) *adjective*
brave

courgette (say koor-**zhet**) *noun* (*plural* **courgettes**)
a long vegetable that is green on the outside and white on the inside

courier (say **kuu**-ri-uh) *noun* (*plural* **couriers**)
1 a person or company that carries or delivers important papers, letters or parcels
2 a person who takes illegal things into or out of a country secretly: *a drug **courier***
▸ **courier** (*verb*): *We **couriered** the documents to you last Friday.*

course (say **kawss**) *noun*
1 (*plural* **courses**) a set of lessons on a certain subject: *He's taking a **course** in computer programming.*
2 (*no plural*) the direction that something

moves in: *the **course** of a river* ◇ *The plane changed **course** to avoid the storm.*
3 (*no plural*) the time when something is happening: *The telephone rang six times during the **course** of the evening.*
4 (*plural* **courses**) one separate part of a meal: *a three-**course** meal*
5 (*plural* **courses**) a piece of ground for some kinds of sport: *a golf **course***
of course certainly: *Of **course** I'll help you.* ◇ *'Are you angry with me?' 'Of **course** not!'*

court[1] (say **kawt**) *noun* (*plural* **courts**)
1 (also **court of law, law court**) the place where a judge or a **magistrate** decide whether a person has done something wrong, and what the punishment will be: *The man will appear in **court** tomorrow.*
2 a piece of ground where you can play certain sports: *a tennis **court*** ◇ *a basketball **court*** ➲ See note at **pitch**[1]
ⓘ **ORIGIN:** 13th–15th century, from Old French *cort* from Latin *cohors, cohort-* meaning 'yard' or 'followers or group of advisers'

court[2] (say **kawt**) *verb* (**courting, courted**)
1 to try to get somebody's support or approval by paying special attention to them: *Politicians from all parties will be **courting** voters this week.*
2 (*old-fashioned*) to try to win somebody's love, with the intention of eventually getting married
3 to do something that might have a very bad effect: *He **courted** death by refusing to take the medicines.*

courteous (say **kur**-ti-uhss) *adjective*
polite and showing respect for other people ➲ **OPPOSITE discourteous**

courtesy (say **kur**-tuh-see) *noun* (*no plural*)
polite behaviour that shows respect for other people

court of law *noun* (*plural* **courts of law**)
= court[1] 1

courtyard (say **kawt**-yaad) *noun* (*plural* **courtyards**)
an open space without a roof, inside a building or between buildings

cousin (say **kuz**-in) *noun* (*plural* **cousins**)
the child of your aunt or uncle

USAGE You use the same word for both male and female **cousins**.

cove (*rhymes with* **stove**) *noun* (*plural* **coves**)
a small area of the coast where the land goes in to form a curve, especially an area that is enclosed by cliffs

cover[1] (say **kuv**-uh) *verb* (**covering, covered**)
1 to put one thing over another thing to hide it or to keep it safe or warm: *She **covered** her head with a scarf.* ➲ **OPPOSITE uncover**
2 to be all over a person or thing: *A thick mist **covered** the city.* ◇ *The children were **covered** in mud.*

cover[2] (say **kuv**-uh) *noun* (*plural* **covers**)
1 a thing that you put over another thing, for example to keep it safe: *The computer has a plastic **cover**.*
2 the outside part of a book or magazine: *The book had a picture of a film star on the front **cover**.*

covering (say **kuv**-uh-ring) *noun* (*plural* **coverings**)
something that covers another thing: *There was a thick **covering** of dust on the floor.*

covert (say **koh**-vurt or **kuv**-urt) *adjective* (*formal*)
done secretly: *The government is accused of providing **covert** military aid to the rebels.*

covet (say **kuv**-uht) *verb* (**coveting, coveted**)
to want to have something very much, especially something that belongs to somebody else: *She never achieved the success she **coveted**.*

cow (say **kow**) *noun* (*plural* **cows**)
a large female farm animal that is kept for its milk or meat

coward (say **kow**-wuhd) *noun* (*plural* **cowards**)
a person who is afraid when there is danger or a problem

cowboy (say **kow**-boy) *noun* (*plural* **cowboys**)
a man who rides a horse and looks after cows in some parts of North America

cower (say **kow**-wuh) *verb* (**cowering, cowered**)
to move back or into a low position because you are afraid: *They **cowered** in fear when the armed robber started to shoot.*

cowrie (say **kow**-ree) *noun* (*plural* **cowries**) (also **cowry**)
a type of sea shell

coy (say **koy**) *adjective* (**coyer, coyest**)
1 pretending to be shy, embarrassed or innocent: *a coy smile* ➲ **SYNONYM bashful**
2 not wanting to tell people about yourself or your plans or give a direct answer to a question: *Don't be **coy**, tell me how much you earn.*
▸ **coyly** (*adverb*): *'I can't tell you that,' she said **coyly**.*

crab (say **krab**) *noun* (*plural* **crabs**)
an animal that lives in and near the sea or rivers. It has a broad hard shell, four pairs of

A B C D E F G H I J K L M N O P Q R S T U V W X Y Z

legs and a pair of curved and pointed arms for catching and holding things (called **claws**). ➲ See **crustacean**

crack[1] (say **krak**) *verb* (**cracking, cracked**)
1 to break, but not into separate pieces: *The glass will **crack** if you pour boiling water into it.* ◇ *This cup is **cracked**.*
2 to make a sudden loud noise
crack down on somebody or something to become stricter when dealing with bad or illegal behaviour: *The police are **cracking** down on drug dealers.*

crack[2] (say **krak**) *noun* (*plural* **cracks**)
1 a thin line on something where it has broken, but not into separate pieces: *There's a **crack** in this glass.*
2 a narrow space between two things or two parts of something: *a **crack** in the curtains*
3 a sudden loud noise: *a **crack** of thunder*

cracker (say **krak**-uh) *noun* (*plural* **crackers**)
1 a thin dry biscuit that you can eat with cheese
2 a cardboard tube with a small toy inside that makes a loud noise when people pull it apart at Christmas parties

crackle (say **krak**-l) *verb* (**crackling, crackled**)
to make a lot of short sharp sounds: *Dry wood **crackles** when you burn it.*

cradle (say **krayd**-l) *noun* (*plural* **cradles**)
a small bed for a baby which can be moved from side to side ➲ See **cot**

craft (say **kraaft**) *noun* (*plural* **crafts**)
a job or activity for which you need skill with your hands: *Pottery is a traditional **craft**.*

craftsman (say **kraaftss**-muhn) *noun* (*plural* **craftsmen**)
a person who is good at making things with their hands

crafty (say **kraaf**-tee) *adjective* (**craftier, craftiest**)
clever at getting what you want in a way that is not completely honest

crag (say **krag**) *noun* (*plural* **crags**)
a steep rough area of rock on the side of a hill or mountain

cram (say **kram**) *verb* (**cramming, crammed**)
to push too many people or things into a small space: *She **crammed** her clothes into a bag.*

cramp[1] (say **kramp**) *verb* (**cramping, cramped**)
1 to prevent something from developing or to make it happen more slowly: *to **cramp** somebody's creative talent*
2 to experience a **cramp**[2]: *I squatted down for too long and my legs **cramped** up.*

cramp[2] (say **kramp**) *noun* (*plural* **cramps**)
a sudden pain that you get in a muscle, for example in your leg, which makes it difficult to move: *'Ow! I've got **cramp**!'* ◇ *tummy **cramps***

crane (say **krayn**) *noun* (*plural* **cranes**)
1 a big machine with a long metal arm for lifting heavy things
2 a large bird with long legs and a long neck

cranium (say **krayn**-i-uhm) *noun* (*plural* **craniums** or **crania**) (*biology*)
the bone inside your head that surrounds the brain ➲ See illustration at **skeleton**
▸ **cranial** (*adjective*): ***cranial** nerves*

crank (say **krangk**) *noun* (*plural* **cranks**)
1 a piece of equipment consisting of an L-shaped bar or handle that you connect to a machine and turn to make something move
2 (*informal*) a person who has unusual ideas or who behaves in a strange way

cranny (say **kran**-ee) *noun* (*plural* **crannies**)
a small, narrow opening, especially in a rock or wall ➲ SYNONYM **crevice**

crash[1] (say **krash**) *noun* (*plural* **crashes**)
1 an accident when a thing that is moving hits another thing: *He was killed in a car **crash**.* ◇ *a plane **crash*** ➲ SYNONYM **collision**
2 a loud noise when a thing falls or hits another thing: *I heard a **crash** as the tree fell.*
🛈 **ORIGIN:** 13th–15th century. The word came from imitating the sound.

crash[2] (say **krash**) *verb* (**crashing, crashed**)
1 to have an accident in a car or other vehicle and hit something: *The bus **crashed** into a tree.* ◇ *I **crashed** my father's car.*
2 to fall or hit something with a loud noise: *The tree **crashed** to the ground.*
3 (a computer) to suddenly stop working

crate (say **krayt**) *noun* (*plural* **crates**)
a big box for carrying bottles or other things

crater (say **krayt**-uh) *noun* (*plural* **craters**)
1 a large hole in the ground: *The bomb left a large **crater**.* ◇ ***craters** on the moon*
2 the hole in the top of a **volcano** ➲ See illustration at **volcano**

crave (say **krayv**) *verb* (**craving, craved**)
to want and need to have something very much: *He's a sociable person and **craves** contact with other people.*
▸ **craving** (*noun*): *When she was pregnant she had a **craving** for junk food.*

crawl[1] (say **krawl**) *verb* (**crawling, crawled**)
to move slowly on your hands and knees or with your body close to the ground: *Babies*

crawl before they can walk. ◇ *A spider **crawled** across the floor.*

crawl² (say **krawl**) *noun* (*no plural*)
a fast way of swimming on your front by moving one arm over your head, and then the other, while kicking with your feet ➲ See **backstroke**, **breaststroke**

crayfish (say **kray**-fish) *noun* (*plural* **crayfish**)
1 (*S. African*) a sea animal that is a type of **lobster** that you can eat
2 an animal like a small **lobster**, that lives in rivers and lakes and that people eat ➲ See **crustacean**

crayfish

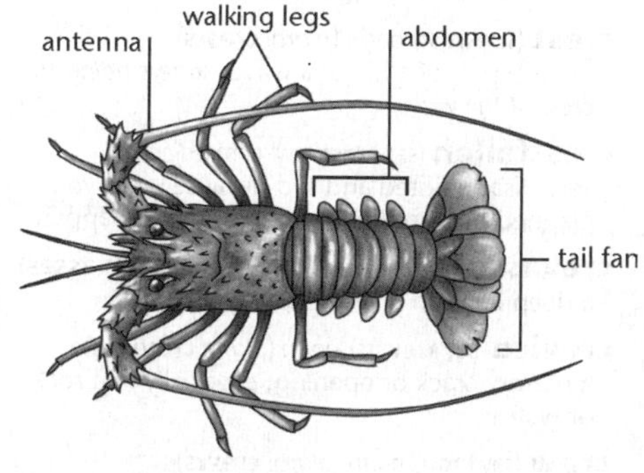

crayon (say **kray**-uhn) *noun* (*plural* **crayons**)
a soft, thick coloured pencil: *The children were drawing pictures with **crayons**.*

craze (say **krayz**) *noun* (*plural* **crazes**)
something that is very popular or fashionable for a short time: *There was a **craze** for that kind of music last year.* ➲ SYNONYM **fad**

crazy (say **kray**-zee) *adjective* (**crazier**, **craziest**) (*informal*)
1 stupid and not sensible: *You must be **crazy** to ride a bike at night with no lights.*
2 very angry: *My mum will go **crazy** if I get home late.*
to be crazy about a person or thing to like a person or thing very much: *She's **crazy** about football.*

creak (say **kreek**) *verb* (**creaking**, **creaked**)
to make a noise like a door that needs oil, or like an old wooden floor when you walk on it
▸ **creak** (*noun*): *The door opened with a **creak**.*

cream¹ (say **kreem**) *noun*
1 (*no plural*) the thick liquid on the top of milk
2 (*plural* **creams**) a thick liquid that you put on your skin, for example to keep it soft: *hand **cream***

cream² (say **kreem**) *adjective*
with a colour between white and yellow: *She was wearing a **cream** dress.*

crease (say **kreess**) *verb* (**creasing**, **creased**)
to get or to make a thing get untidy lines or folds: *Don't sit on my jacket – you'll **crease** it.*
▸ **crease** (*noun*): *My jacket was full of **creases**.*

create (say kree-**ayt**) *verb* (**creating**, **created**)
to make something happen or exist: *Do you believe that God **created** the world?* ◇ *We need to **create** more jobs.* ◇ ***Create** a poster to advertise your product.*

creation (say kree-**ay**-shuhn) *noun*
1 (*no plural*) the act or process of making a new thing, or of causing a thing to exist that did not exist before: *the **creation** of the world*
2 (*plural* **creations**) a new thing that somebody has made: *Mickey Mouse was the **creation** of Walt Disney.*

creationism (say kree-**ay**-shuh-niz-m) *noun* (*no plural*)
the belief that God created the universe, life, and everything on Earth
▸ **creationist** (*adjective*): *the **creationist** debate*

creative (say kree-**ay**-tiv) *adjective*
describing a person who has a lot of new ideas or is good at making new things: *She's a very good painter – she's so **creative**.*
▸ **creativity** (*noun*): *Her **creativity** is obvious in her work.*

creator (say kree-**ay**-tuh) *noun* (*plural* **creators**)
a person who makes something new: *Walt Disney was the **creator** of Mickey Mouse.*

creature (say **kree**-tshuh) *noun* (*plural* **creatures**)
any living thing that is not a plant: *birds, fish and other **creatures*** ◇ *This story is about **creatures** from another planet.*

crèche (say **kraysh**) *noun* (*plural* **crèches**)
a place where young children are looked after while their parents are at work ➲ See **nursery** 1

credentials (say kri-**den**-shuhlz) *plural noun*
1 the qualities, past experience and training that make somebody suitable for something: *He has the perfect **credentials** for the job.*
2 documents that show who you are, or prove that you have the authority, training or education to do something

credible (say **kred**-ib-l) *adjective*
1 that you can believe or trust: *The judge said that she was a **credible** and reliable witness.* ➲ SYNONYM **believable**
2 that seems possible: *We need to find a **credible** alternative to nuclear energy.*

A B C D E F G H I J K L M N O P Q R S T U V W X Y Z

credit[1] (say **kred**-it) *noun*
1 (*no plural*) a way of buying something and not paying for it until later: *I bought the television on* ***credit****.*
2 (*plural* **credits**) an amount of money that is put into a bank account: *Yesterday there was a* ***credit*** *of R200 in my account* ➲ OPPOSITE **debit**[1] 1
3 (*no plural*) saying that somebody has done something well: *I did the work but she got the* ***credit*** *for it!*

credit[2] (say **kred**-it) *verb* (**crediting, credited**)
1 to add money to someone's bank account: *R500 has been* ***credited*** *to your account.* ➲ OPPOSITE **debit**[2]
2 to believe or say that a person has done something well: *Palesa was* ***credited*** *with the good planning.*

credit card *noun* (*plural* **credit cards**)
a plastic card from a bank that you can use to buy something and pay for it later: *Can I pay by* ***credit card****?*

creditor (say **kred**-i-tuh) *noun* (*plural* **creditors**)
a person or company to whom money is owed: *He was unable to pay his* ***creditors****.* ➲ OPPOSITE **debtor**

creed (say **kreed**) *noun* (*plural* **creeds**)
a set of principles or beliefs, especially religious beliefs: *Everybody has the right to work, regardless of their gender, race or* ***creed****.*

creek (say **kreek**) *noun* (*plural* **creeks**)
1 a small river
2 a narrow area of water where the sea flows into the land

creep (say **kreep**) *verb* (**creeping, crept**)
to move quietly and carefully so that nobody hears or sees you: *The cat* ***crept*** *towards the bird.*

creepy (say **kreep**-ee) *adjective* (**creepier, creepiest**) (*informal*)
making you feel nervous or afraid: *a* ***creepy*** *ghost story* ➲ SYNONYM **scary**

cremate (say kri-**mayt**) *verb* (**cremating, cremated**)
to burn a dead person's body instead of burying it
► **cremation** (*noun*): *The funeral service will be followed by a private* ***cremation****.*

crept (say **krept**) form of **creep**

crescendo (say kruh-**shen**-doh) *noun* (*plural* **crescendos**)
a noise or piece of music that gets louder and louder

crescent (say **kress**-uhnt) *noun* (*plural* **crescents**)
1 the shape of the moon when it is less than half a circle
2 a street or line of houses with a curved shape: *I live at 34 Elgin* ***Crescent****.*

crescent

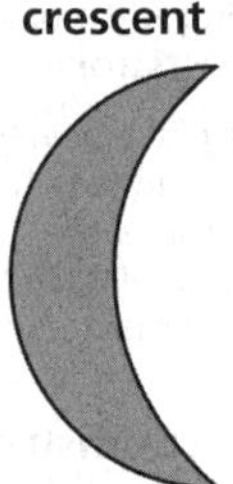

crest (say **krest**) *noun* (*plural* **crests**)
the top part of a hill or a wave: *surfers riding the* ***crest*** *of the wave*

crestfallen (say **krest**-fawl-uhn) *adjective*
very disappointed and sad because what you planned or wanted to happen did not happen

crevasse (say kruh-**vass**) *noun* (*plural* **crevasses**)
a deep crack in a very thick layer of ice

crevice (say **krev**-iss) *noun* (*plural* **crevices**)
a narrow crack or opening, especially in a rock or wall

crew (say **kroo**) *noun* (*plural* **crews**)
all the people who work on a ship or a plane

crib (say **krib**) *verb* (**cribbing, cribbed**) (*informal*)
to copy somebody else's work and pretend it is your own ➲ SYNONYM **plagiarize**

cricket (say **krik**-uht) *noun*
1 (*no plural*) a game for two teams of eleven players who try to hit a small hard ball with a piece of wood (called a **bat**) on a large field (their **pitch**): *We watched a* ***cricket*** *match.*
➲ See note at **bat**[1]
2 (*plural* **crickets**) a small brown insect that jumps and makes a loud high noise by rubbing its wings together
► **cricketer** (*noun*): *He is a famous South African* ***cricketer****.*

cried (say **kride**) form of **cry**[1]

cries (say **krize**) form of **cry**[1]

crime (say **krime**) *noun* (*plural* **crimes**)
something that somebody does that is against the law: *Murder and robbery are serious* ***crimes****.* ◊ *They had committed a* ***crime****.*

criminal[1] (say **krim**-in-l) *adjective*
connected with crime: *Damaging public property is a* ***criminal*** *offence.*

criminal² (say **krim**-in-l) *noun* (*plural* **criminals**) a person who does something that is against the law

crimson (say **krim**-zuhn) *adjective* with a dark red colour, like blood

crinkle (say **krink**-l) *verb* (**crinkling, crinkled**) to have, or to make something have, fine lines or folds in it: *Her nose **crinkles** up when she smiles.*
▸ **crinkly** (*adjective*): *a leaf with a **crinkly** edge*

cripple (say **krip**-l) *verb* (**crippling, crippled**) to damage somebody's body so that they cannot walk or move normally: *She was **crippled** in an accident.*
▸ **cripple** (*noun*) (*old-fashioned*): *She's a **cripple** with one leg.*

> USAGE Many people think the noun, **cripple**, is offensive. It is better to say **a disabled person**.

crisis (say **kry**-siss) *noun* (*plural* **crises**) a time when something very dangerous or serious happens: *a political **crisis***

crisp¹ (say **krisp**) *adjective* (**crisper, crispest**)
1 hard and dry: *If you keep the biscuits in a tin, they will stay **crisp**.*
2 fresh and not soft: ***crisp** apples*

crisp² (say **krisp**) *noun* (*plural* **crisps**) another word for **chip¹** 2

criterion (say kry-**teer**-ri-uhn) *noun* (*plural* **criteria**)
a standard that you use when you make a decision or judgement about something: *There are several **criteria** for deciding who will get into the team.* ◇ *What is the most important **criterion**?*

> USAGE Be careful! Remember that **criteria** is the plural. You say **one criterion** and **three criteria**.

critic (say **krit**-ik) *noun* (*plural* **critics**)
1 a person who says that somebody or something is wrong or bad: ***critics** of the government*
2 a person who writes about a book, film or play and says if they like it or not: *The **critics** loved his new film.*

critical (say **krit**-ik-l) *adjective*
1 saying that somebody or something is wrong or bad: *They were very **critical** of my work.*
2 making fair and careful judgements about the good and bad qualities of something: *Develop good **critical** thinking skills.*
3 very important: *The peace talks are at a **critical** stage.* ➲ SYNONYM **crucial**
4 very serious or dangerous: *The patient is in a **critical** condition.*
▸ **critically** (*adverb*)

criticism (say **krit**-i-siz-uhm) *noun* (*plural* **criticisms**)
1 what you think is bad about somebody or something: *I listened to his **criticisms** of my plan.*
2 the work of making fair, careful judgements about the good and bad qualities of something

criticize (say **krit**-i-size) *verb* (**criticizing, criticized**) (also **criticise**)
1 to say that somebody or something is wrong or bad: *She was **criticized** for not following orders.*
2 to judge the good and bad qualities of something carefully, and to express your judgement: *Learn how to **criticize** poetry and fiction well.*

critique (say krit-**eek**) *noun* (*plural* **critiques**) a piece of writing that describes the good and bad points of somebody or something: *a **critique** of the Freedom Charter*

croak (*rhymes with* **broke**) *verb* (**croaking, croaked**)
1 to make the low rough sound that a frog makes: *the sound of frogs **croaking** in the river*
2 to speak in a low rough voice: *'My throat's really sore,' he **croaked**.*
▸ **croak** (*noun*): *the loud **croaks** of a frog*
ⓘ ORIGIN: 13th–15th century. The word came from imitating the sound.

crochet (say **kroh**-shay) *noun* (*no plural*) a way of making things from thread or wool with a needle that has a small hook at one end
▸ **crochet** (*verb*): *My granny **crocheted** this bedspread for me.*

crockery (say **krok**-uh-ree) *noun* (*no plural*) plates, cups and dishes

crocodile (say **krok**-uh-dile) *noun* (*plural* **crocodiles**)
a large reptile with a long tail and a big mouth with sharp teeth. They live in rivers in hot countries: ***Crocodiles** are very dangerous.*
ⓘ ORIGIN: 13th–15th century, through Old French and Latin, from Greek *krokodilos* meaning 'worm of the stones', from the crocodile's habit of lying on the stones near the water's edge

croissant (say **krwuss**-ong or **krwuss**-ont) *noun* (*plural* **croissants**)
a type of bread roll with a curved shape that is often eaten for breakfast

crook (say **kruuk**) *noun* (*plural* **crooks**)
1 (*informal*) a person who cheats, steals something or does something illegal

A B C D E F G H I J K L M N O P Q R S T U V W X Y Z

➲ SYNONYM **criminal**[2]
2 a bend in something, especially the curve inside your elbow when you bend your arm

crooked (say **kruuk**-uhd) *adjective*
not straight: *She has **crooked** teeth.*

crop[1] (say **krop**) *noun* (*plural* **crops**)
all the plants of one kind that a farmer grows at one time: *There was a good **crop** of potatoes last year.* ◇ *Rain is good for the **crops**.*
ℹ ORIGIN: from Old English *crop*

crop[2] (say **krop**) *verb* (**cropping**, **cropped**)
1 to cut something short or to cut it off, for example hair or grass: *The prisoners have their hair **cropped** short.*
2 to cut off or hide the parts of a photograph or a print that you do not want
crop up (*informal*) to occur or appear suddenly and unexpectedly: *We should have finished this work yesterday, but some problems **cropped** up.*

cross[1] (say **kross**) *noun* (*plural* **crosses**)
1 a mark like X or ×: *The **cross** on the map shows where I live.*
2 something with the shape X or †: *She wears a **cross*** (= a symbol of the Christian religion) *around her neck.*

cross[2] (say **kross**) *verb* (**crossing**, **crossed**)
1 to go from one side of something to the other: *Be careful when you **cross** the road.*
2 to put one thing over another thing: *She sat down and **crossed** her legs.*
cross something out to draw a line through a word or words, for example because you have made a mistake: *I **crossed** the word out and wrote it again.*

cross[3] (say **kross**) *adjective*
angry: *I was **cross** with her because she was late.*
➲ SYNONYM **annoyed**

cross- (say **kross**) *prefix*
1 from one side to the other side of something: ***crossbar***
2 done or given by each of two sides or people to the other: ***cross-question***

crossbar (say **kross**-baa) *noun* (*plural* **crossbars**)
a horizontal bar, line or stripe: *He didn't score a goal because the ball hit the **crossbar**.*

crossbow (say **kross**-boh) *noun* (*plural* **crossbows**)
a weapon which consists of a **bow**[3] 1 that is fixed onto a larger piece of wood, and that shoots short heavy arrows (called **bolts**)

crossing (say **kross**-ing) *noun* (*plural* **crossings**)
a place where you can cross over something, for example a road or a river

cross-question (say **kross**-kwess-tshuhn) *verb* (**cross-questioning**, **cross-questioned**) (also **cross-examine**)
to ask somebody a lot of detailed questions in a court of law to find out the truth about something

cross-reference (say **kross**-ref-ruhnss) *noun* (*plural* **cross-references**)
a note in a book or document that tells you to look in another place in the book or document for more information

crossroad (say **kross**-rohd) *noun* (*plural* **crossroads**) (also **crossroads**)
a place where two roads meet and cross each other: *We came to a **crossroad**.*

cross section (say **kross**-sek-shuhn) *noun* (*plural* **cross sections**)
1 a picture of what the inside of something would look like if you cut through it: *a **cross section** of the brain*
2 a number of people that come from the different parts of a group, and so are considered to represent the whole group: *This is a **cross section** of Durban's population.*

cross sections of an apple

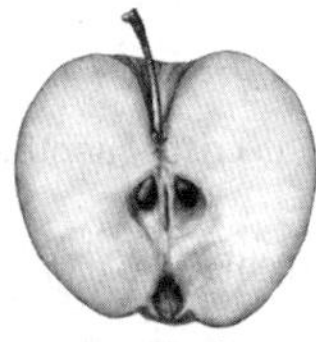
vertical cross section

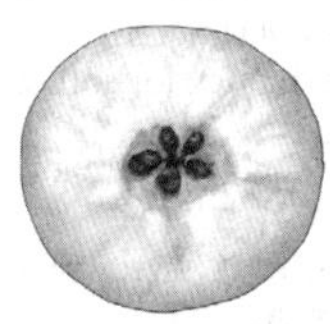
horizontal cross section

crossword (say **kross**-wurd) *noun* (*plural* **crosswords**) (also **crossword puzzle**)
a game in which you have to write the answers to questions (called **clues**) in square spaces across and down a page

crotch (say **kroch**) *noun* (*plural* **crotches**)
the place where your legs, or a pair of trousers, join at the top

crotchet (say **kroch**-it) *noun* (*plural* **crotchets**) (*music*)
a musical note that lasts a quarter of the time of a whole note (called a **semibreve**)

crouch (say **krowch**) *verb* (**crouching**, **crouched**)
to bend your legs and back so that your body is close to the ground: *I **crouched** under the table to hide.*

crow[1] (say **kroh**) *noun* (*plural* **crows**)
a large black bird that makes a loud noise

crow² (say **kroh**) *verb* (**crowing, crowed**)
1 to make a loud noise like a male chicken (called a **cock**) makes
2 to talk in a way that shows you are very proud of something: *'This is a nice trophy,' he **crowed** in triumph.*

crowbar (say **kroh**-baa) *noun* (*plural* **crowbars**)
a metal bar with one sharp end, used for lifting something heavy or for opening something

crowd¹ (say **krowd**) *noun* (*plural* **crowds**)
a lot of people together: *There was a large **crowd** at the concert.*

crowd² (say **krowd**) *verb* (**crowding, crowded**)
to come together in a big group: *The journalists **crowded** round the film star.*

crowded (say **krowd**-id) *adjective*
full of people: *The streets were very **crowded**.* ◇ *a **crowded** bus*

crown¹ (say **krown**) *noun* (*plural* **crowns**)
a circle made of valuable metal and stones (called **jewels**) that a king or queen wears on his or her head

crown² (say **krown**) *verb* (**crowning, crowned**)
to put a **crown¹** on the head of a new king or queen, as a sign that he or she is the new ruler: *Queen Elizabeth II was **crowned** in 1953.*

crucial (say **kroo**-shuhl) *adjective*
very important: *a **crucial** moment* ➲ SYNONYM **critical** 2

crucifix (say **kroo**-si-fikss) *noun* (*plural* **crucifixes**)
a model of a cross with a figure of Jesus Christ on it, used as a symbol of the Christian religion

crucify (say **kroo**-si-fy) *verb* (**crucifying, crucified**)
1 to kill somebody by fastening them to an upright cross and leaving them until they die
2 to criticize somebody in a cruel way: *She was **crucified** by the critics for her performance.*
▸ **crucifixion** (*noun*): ***Crucifixion** was used in ancient times to execute prisoners.*

crude (say **krood**) *adjective* (**cruder, crudest**)
1 simple and not showing much skill or care: *The method was **crude** but effective.*
2 rude in a way that many people do not like: ***crude** jokes*

cruel (say **kroo**-uhl) *adjective* (**crueller, cruellest**)
describing a person who is unkind and likes to hurt other people or animals: *I think it's **cruel** to keep animals in cages.*
▸ **cruelly** (*adverb*): *He was **cruelly** treated when he was a child.*

cruelty (say **kroo**-uhl-tee) *noun* (*no plural*)
behaviour that is unkind and hurts other people or animals

cruise¹ (say **krooz**) *noun* (*plural* **cruises**)
a holiday when you travel on a ship and visit different places: *They went on a world **cruise**.*

cruise² (say **krooz**) *verb* (**cruising, cruised**)
1 to move along at a steady speed in a car, boat, etc.: *He **cruised** down the road on his bike.*
2 to travel on a ship as a holiday, visiting different places

crumb (say **krum**) *noun* (*plural* **crumbs**)
a very small piece of bread, cake or biscuit

PRONUNCIATION Don't pronounce the **b** in **crumb**.

crumble (say **krumb**-l) *verb* (**crumbling, crumbled**)
to break into very small pieces: *The old building is **crumbling**.*

crumple (say **krump**-l) *verb* (**crumpling, crumpled**)
to be pressed or to press something into an untidy shape: *She **crumpled** the paper into a ball and threw it away.*

crunch (say **krunch**) *verb* (**crunching, crunched**)
1 to make a loud noise when you eat something that is hard: *She **crunched** her apple noisily.*
2 to make a noise like the sound of something being crushed: *The broken glass **crunched** under our shoes.*

crusade (say kroo-**sayd**) *noun* (*plural* **crusades**)
1 a set of actions organized by a person or a group of people who feel strongly about a particular cause
2 Crusade one of the wars fought in Palestine by European Christians against Muslims in the Middle Ages
▸ **crusader** (*noun*): *a **crusader** for justice*

crush (say **krush**) *verb* (**crushing, crushed**)
to press something very hard so that you break or damage it: *She sat on my hat and **crushed** it.*

crust (say **krust**) *noun* (*plural* **crusts**)
1 the hard layer on the outside of something: *the Earth's **crust***
2 the hard part on the outside of bread

crustacean (say kruss-**tay**-shuhn) *noun* (*plural* **crustaceans**)
a class of animals with a hard outer shell and a body divided into sections, often living in water: *Crayfish and crabs are **crustaceans**.*

crutch (say **kruch**) *noun* (*plural* **crutches**)
a long stick that you put under your arm to help you walk when you have hurt your leg: *He broke his leg and now he's on* ***crutches****.*

cry[1] (say **kry**) *verb* (**crying, cried**)
1 to have drops of water falling from your eyes because you are unhappy or hurt: *The baby* ***cries*** *a lot.* ➲ SYNONYM **weep**
2 to shout or make a loud noise: *'Help!' he* ***cried****.* ◇ *She* ***cried*** *out in pain.*

cry[2] (say **kry**) *noun* (*plural* **cries**)
a loud noise that you make to show strong feelings such as pain, fear or excitement: *He gave a* ***cry*** *of pain.* ◇ *We heard her* ***cries*** *and ran to help.*

cryptic (say **krip**-tik) *adjective*
with a meaning that is hidden and not easy to understand
▸ **cryptically** (*adverb*): *She smiled* ***cryptically*** *and said nothing.*

crystal (say **kriss**-tuhl) *noun*
1 (*plural* **crystals**) a shape that some substances make when they become solid: *salt* ***crystals***
2 (*no plural*) a kind of rock that looks like glass

crystallize (say **kriss**-tuh-lize) *verb* (**crystallizing, crystallized**) (also **crystallise**)
1 to form or make something form into crystals
2 (thoughts, plans or beliefs) to become clear and fixed or to make thoughts or beliefs clear and fixed: *Our ideas* ***crystallized*** *into a plan.*

cub (say **kub**) *noun* (*plural* **cubs**)
1 a young of an animal such as a lion, a bear or a **tiger**
2 the Cubs (*plural noun*) the part of the **Scout** organization that is for younger boys
3 Cub (also **Cub Scout**) a boy who is a member of the Cubs

cube[1] (say **kyoob**) *noun* (*plural* **cubes**)
1 a solid shape like a box with six square sides all the same size
2 the number that you get if you multiply a number by itself twice: *The* ***cube*** *of 5 is 125* (5 x 5 x 5 = 125)

a cube

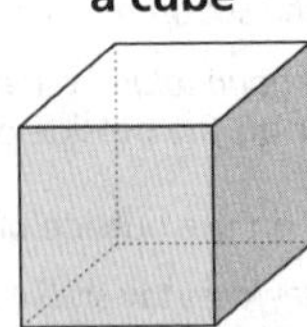

WORD BUILDING You can also write **the cube of 5** like this: **5³**.

cube[2] *verb* (**cubing, cubed**) (*maths*)
to multiply a number by itself twice: *3* ***cubed*** *is 27 (3 x 3 x 3).*

cubic (say **kyoo**-bik) *adjective*
relating to a measurement of volume that is expressed as a **cube**[1]: *If a box is 4 cm long, 4 cm wide and 4 cm high, its volume is 64* ***cubic*** *centimetres.* ◇ *The lake holds over a million* ***cubic*** *metres of water.*

cubicle (say **kyoo**-bik-l) *noun* (*plural* **cubicles**)
a small room that is made by separating off part of a larger room: *a shower* ***cubicle***

cubit (say **kyoo**-bit) *noun* (*plural* **cubits**) (*history*)
a measurement of length, about 45 cm or the length from the elbow to the end of the fingers

cuboid (say **kyoob**-oyd) *noun* (*plural* **cuboids**) (*maths*)
a solid object which has six rectangular sides at right angles to each other

cuckoo (say **kuu**-koo) *noun* (*plural* **cuckoos**)
a bird that makes a sound like its name

cucumber (say **kyoo**-kum-buh) *noun* (*plural* **cucumbers**)
a long vegetable with a green skin, that we often eat in salads

cuddle (say **kud**-l) *verb* (**cuddling, cuddled**)
to hold a person, pet or toy in your arms to show love: *He* ***cuddled*** *his baby.* ➲ SYNONYM **hug**
▸ **cuddle** (*noun*): *I gave her a* ***cuddle****.*

cue (say **kyoo**) *noun* (*plural* **cues**)
1 something said or done that is the signal for somebody else to say or do something, especially in a play: *When Julia puts the tray on the table, that's your* ***cue*** *to come on stage.*
2 something that causes or reminds you to behave in a particular way: *I'm not sure how to behave at a Japanese wedding, so I'll take my* ***cue*** *from the hosts.*
3 a long stick used hit the ball in games such as **snooker**
on cue at exactly the moment expected: *Just as I was starting to worry about Sam, he phoned right on* ***cue****.*

cuff[1] (say **kuf**) *noun* (*plural* **cuffs**)
the end part of a sleeve, near your hand

cuff[2] (say **kuf**) *verb* (**cuffing, cuffed**)
1 to hit somebody with an open hand, especially on the head: *His father* ***cuffed*** *him across the side of his head.*
2 (*informal*) to put handcuffs (= two metal rings

with a chain that the police put on a prisoner's arms) on somebody: *The policeman arrested him and **cuffed** his hands behind his back.*

cuisine (say kwi-**zeen**) *noun* (*plural* **cuisines**) (*formal*)
a typical style of cooking, especially of a particular country, region or restaurant: *Italian **cuisine***

cul-de-sac (say **kul**-duh-sak) *noun* (*plural* **cul-de-sacs** or **culs-de-sac**)
a street that is closed at one end

culinary (say **kul**-in-uh-ree) *adjective* (*formal*)
relating to food or the activity of preparing and cooking food: ***culinary** herbs*

cull (say **kul**) *verb* (**culling, culled**)
1 to remove a person or a thing from a group: *The party **culled** thirty people from its list of election candidates.*
2 to kill an animal that is sick or weak or to kill a group of animals to reduce their numbers
3 (*formal*) to choose and collect information from different sources: *The program **culls** information from around the Web.*
▸ **cull** (*noun*): *the annual baby seal **cull** in Namibia*

culminate (say **kul**-mi-nayt) *verb* (**culminating, culminated**) (*formal*) to reach a final result or point of highest development: *The team's efforts **culminated** in victory in the championships.*
▸ **culmination** (*noun*): *The joint space mission was the **culmination** of years of research.*

culpable (say **kul**-puhb-l) *adjective* (*formal*) being responsible for something bad that has happened and deserving to be blamed or punished for it

culprit (say **kul**-prit) *noun* (*plural* **culprits**)
a person who is responsible for something bad that has happened or is guilty of a crime

cult (say **kult**) *noun* (*plural* **cults**)
1 a type of religion or a religious group, especially one that is considered unusual by other people
2 a person or thing that has become popular among a particular group of people: *'Buffy' became a bit of a **cult** in South Africa.*

cultivate (say **kul**-ti-vayt) *verb* (**cultivating, cultivated**)
1 to use land for growing plants: *Only a small area of the island was **cultivated**.*
2 to keep and care for plants
▸ **cultivation** (*noun*): ***cultivation** of the land*

cultural (say **kul**-tshuh-ruhl) *adjective*
1 connected with the ideas, customs and way of life of a group of people or a country: *There are many **cultural** differences between our two countries.* ➲ See **multicultural**
2 connected with art, music or literature

culture (say **kul**-tshuh) *noun*
1 (*plural* **cultures**) the customs, ideas and way of life of a group of people or a country: *the language and **culture** of the Aztecs*
2 (*no plural*) art, music, literature and the theatre: *The city is a centre of **culture**.*
❶ ORIGIN: 13th–15th century, from Latin *colere* meaning 'take care of and prepare (land and crops)'. In the 19th century the word came to mean 'taking care of the mind, senses and behaviour'.

cumbersome (say **kum**-buh-suhm) *adjective*
1 large or heavy and difficult to carry, use, wear or handle ➲ SYNONYM **unwieldy**
2 slow and complicated: *Getting a passport is a **cumbersome** process that takes weeks.*

cumulative (say **kyoo**-muh-luh-tiv) *adjective*
increasing steadily in amount, quantity or degree because new parts or things are continuously added: *Sun damage to your skin is **cumulative** over time.*

cumulonimbus (say kyoom-yuh-loh-**nim**-buhss) *noun* (*no plural*)
a high mass of thick cloud with a flat base, often seen during a **thunderstorm**

cumulus (say **kyoom**-yuh-luss) *noun* (*no plural*)
a type of thick white cloud

cuneiform (say **kyoo**-ni-fawm) *adjective*
relating to a style of writing used in ancient Southwest Asia in which signs or letters were formed by making small triangles in soft clay

cunning (say **kun**-ing) *adjective*
clever, especially at making people believe something that is not true: *Their plan was quite **cunning**.* ➲ SYNONYMS **crafty, sly**

cup (say **kup**) *noun* (*plural* **cups**)
1 a small round container with a handle, that you can drink from: *a **cup** and saucer*
2 a metal container shaped like a cup that you get for winning in a sport

cupboard (say **kub**-uhd) *noun* (*plural* **cupboards**)
a piece of furniture with shelves and doors, where you store food or clothes

curator (say kyoo-**ray**-tuh) *noun* (*plural* **curators**)
a person who is in charge of the things that are kept in a museum or library

curb (say **kurb**) *verb* (**curbing, curbed**)
to control or limit something, especially something bad: *He should **curb** his temper.*

A B C D E F G H I J K L M N O P Q R S T U V W X Y Z

A B C D E F G H I J K L M N O P Q R S T U V W X Y Z

curd (say **kurd**) *noun*
1 (*no plural*) a thick soft substance that forms when milk goes sour
2 curds (*plural noun*) a quantity of **curd**: *When you make cheese, you separate the milk into **curds** and whey.* ➲ See **whey**

curdle (say **kurd**-l) *verb* (**curdling, curdled**)
(milk or another liquid) to go sour or form lumps: *Do not boil cream or else it will **curdle**.*

cure (say **kyoor**) *verb* (**curing, cured**)
1 to make a sick person well again: *The doctors can't **cure** her.*
2 to make an illness go away: *Can this disease be **cured**?*
▸ **cure** (*noun*): *a **cure** for cancer*

curfew (say **kur**-fyoo) *noun* (*plural* **curfews**)
1 times between which people are not allowed to go outside their homes, for example during a war: *a dusk-to-dawn **curfew***
2 a time by which children must be home in the evening: *She has a ten o'clock **curfew**.*
🛈 **ORIGIN:** 13th–15th century, from Old French *cuevrefeu* from *cuvrir* meaning 'to cover' and *feu* meaning 'fire'. This referred to a rule that people had to put out their fires at a certain time in the evening.

curio (say **kyoo**-ri-oh) *noun* (*plural* **curios**)
an unusual item or object of art, especially one bought by tourists to remember a place

curiosity (say kyoo-ri-**oss**-uh-tee) *noun*
1 (*no plural*) a strong desire to know about things: *I was full of **curiosity** about the letter.*
2 (*plural* **curiosities**) an unusual and interesting thing: *The museum is full of historical **curiosities**.*

curious (say **kyoo**-ri-uhss) *adjective*
1 having a strong desire to know about something: *They were very **curious** about the people who lived upstairs.*
2 strange or unusual: *There was a **curious** mixture of people in the audience.*
▸ **curiously** (*adverb*): *'Where are you going?' she asked **curiously**.*

curl¹ (say **kurl**) *verb* (**curling, curled**)
to form or make something form into a round or curved shape: *Does your hair **curl** naturally?*
curl up to put your arms, legs and head close to your body: *The cat lay **curled** up.*

curl² (say **kurl**) *noun* (*plural* **curls**)
a piece of hair in a round shape
▸ **curly** (*adjective*): *He's got **curly** hair.*

currant (say **ku**-ruhnt) *noun* (*plural* **currants**)
a very small black dried grape that is used in cooking

currency (say **ku**-ruhn-see) *noun* (*plural* **currencies**)
the money that a country uses: *South Africa's **currency** is the rand.*

current¹ (say **ku**-rint) *adjective*
happening or used now: ***current** fashions*
▸ **currently** (*adverb*): *He is **currently*** (= now) *working overseas.*

current² (say **ku**-rint) *noun*
1 (*plural* **currents**) air or water that is moving: *It is dangerous to swim here because of the strong **current**.*
2 (*no plural*) the flow of electricity through a **conductor** 3

curriculum (say kuh-**rik**-yuh-luhm) *noun* (*plural* **curricula** or **curriculums**)
all the subjects that you study in a school or at a university: *Latin is not in our **curriculum**.* ➲ See **syllabus**

curriculum vitae (say kuh-rik-yuh-luhm **vee**-ty) *noun* (*plural* **curriculum vitaes**) = **CV**

curry (say **ku**-ree) *noun* (*plural* **curries**)
an Indian dish of meat or vegetables cooked with spices: *a chicken **curry***
🛈 **ORIGIN:** 16th century, from Tamil, a language spoken in India and Sri Lanka. Colonists and traders brought the word to Europe.

curse (say **kurss**) *noun* (*plural* **curses**)
1 a rude word that some people use when they are angry ➲ **SYNONYM swear word**
2 a word or phrase that people think has a magic power to make something bad happen: *The family seemed to be under a **curse*** (= lots of bad things happened to them).
▸ **curse** (*verb*): *He hit his head and **cursed** loudly.* ◇ *She believed she had been **cursed**.*

cursor (say **kur**-suh) *noun* (*plural* **cursors**)
(*computing*)
a small ticking stripe on a computer screen that shows where on the screen you are working

curt (say **kurt**) *adjective*
using few words and not polite
▸ **curtly** (*adverb*): *'I'm not interested,' he replied **curtly**.* ▸ **curtness** (*noun*): *She ignored the **curtness** in his voice.*

curtail (say kur-**tayl**) *verb* (**curtailing, curtailed**)
(*formal*)
to make something shorter or less: *We had to **curtail** our holiday because my mother-in-law became ill.*
▸ **curtailment** (*noun*): *the **curtailment** of inflation*

curtain (say **kur**-tuhn) *noun* (*plural* **curtains**)
a piece of cloth that you can move to cover a

window: *Could you draw the **curtains*** (= open or close the curtains), *please?*

curve¹ (say **kurv**) *noun* (*plural* **curves**)
1 a line that is not straight
2 a bend

curve² (say **kurv**) *verb* (**curving, curved**)
to make a round shape or to bend: *The road **curves** to the right.*
▸ **curved** (*adjective*): *a table with **curved** legs* ◇ *a **curved** line*

cushion (say **kuu**-shuhn) *noun* (*plural* **cushions**)
a cloth bag filled with something soft, which you put on a chair
▸ **cushion** (*verb*): *The grass **cushioned** his fall.*

custard (say **kuss**-tuhd) *noun* (*no plural*)
a sweet yellow sauce made with milk. You eat it with fruit or other sweet dishes.

custody (say **kuss**-tuh-dee) *noun* (*no plural*)
1 the legal right or duty to take care of somebody or something: *After the divorce, the mother had **custody** of the children.*
2 the condition of being held by the police or of being kept in prison: *The man was taken into **custody** on suspicion of murder.*

custom (say **kuss**-tuhm) *noun*
1 (*plural* **customs**) a way of behaving or doing things that a particular group or society has had for a long time: *the **custom** of lighting lamps at Diwali*
2 (*plural* **customs**) (*formal*) the way a person always behaves: *It was her **custom** to get up early.*
3 (*no plural*) (*business*) the practice of people buying things regularly from a particular shop: *The local shop lost a lot of **custom** when the new supermarket opened.*

customer (say **kuss**-tuh-muh) *noun* (*plural* **customers**)
a person who buys goods or services from a shop or restaurant

customs (say **kuss**-tuhmz) *plural noun*
the place at an airport or a port where you must show what you have brought with you from another country: *a **customs** officer*

cut¹ (say **kut**) *verb* (**cutting, cut**)
1 to break or damage something with something sharp, for example a knife or scissors: *I **cut** the string with the scissors.* ◇ *I **cut** the apple in half* (= into two parts). ◇ *She **cut** her finger on a knife.* ◇ *He **cut** down the tree.*
2 to take one piece from something bigger using a knife or scissors: *Can you **cut** me a piece of cake, please?*
3 to make something shorter with a knife or scissors: *Have you had your hair **cut**?*
be cut off to be kept alone, away from other people: *Our house was **cut** off from the town by the flood.*
cut something off to stop the supply of something: *The workmen **cut** off the electricity.*

cut² (say **kut**) *noun* (*plural* **cuts**)
1 an injury on the skin, made by something sharp like a knife: *He had a deep **cut** on his leg.*
2 a hole or opening in something, made with something sharp: *Make a small **cut** in the material.*
3 a reduction in amount, size or supply: *a **cut** in spending* ◇ *job **cuts***

cute (say **kyoot**) *adjective* (**cuter, cutest**)
pretty and attractive: *What a **cute** little puppy!*
➲ SYNONYM **sweet¹** 3

cutlass (say **kut**-luhss) *noun* (*plural* **cutlasses**)
a short curved **sword**

cutlery (say **kut**-luh-ree) *noun* (*no plural*)
knives, forks and spoons that you use for eating

CV (say see-**vee**) *noun* (*plural* **CVs**)
a written list of your education and work experience that you send when you are trying to get a new job: *Send a full **CV** with your job application.* ℹ **CV** is short for the Latin words 'curriculum vitae' meaning 'course of life'.

cyanide (say **sy**-uh-nide) *noun* (*no plural*)
a highly poisonous chemical

cyberspace (say **sibe**-uh-spayss) *noun* (*no plural*)
a place that is not real where emails go when you send them from one computer to another

cycad (say **sike**-ad) *noun* (*plural* **cycads**)
a palm-like plant that grows in hot wet places and that has existed since the time of the dinosaurs (= large reptiles that lived a long time ago)

cycle¹ (say **sike**-uhl) *noun* (*plural* **cycles**)
(usually in combinations) a bicycle: *We went for a **cycle** ride at the weekend.* ◇ *a **cycle** shop*
➲ SYNONYM **bike**
ℹ ORIGIN: 14th–15th century, through Middle English, from Greek *kuklos* meaning 'circle'

cycle² (say **sike**-uhl) *verb* (**cycling, cycled**)
to ride a bicycle: *I **cycle** to school every day.*

cycling (say **sike**-ling) *noun* (*no plural*)
the sport or activity of riding a bicycle: *We go **cycling** most weekends.*

cyclist (say **sike**-list) *noun* (*plural* **cyclists**)
a person who rides a bicycle: *He's a keen **cyclist*** (= he likes cycling).

cyclone (say **sike**-lohn) *noun* (*plural* **cyclones**)
(*geography*)
an area of low pressure with winds that move in

A B C D E F G H I J K L M N O P Q R S T U V W X Y Z

a circle towards the centre, sometimes causing storms ➲ See **anticyclone**

cylinder (say **sil**-in-duh) *noun* (*plural* **cylinders**)
long round shape, like a tube or a tin of food
▸ **cylindrical** (*adjective*): *a* ***cylindrical*** *shape*

cylinder

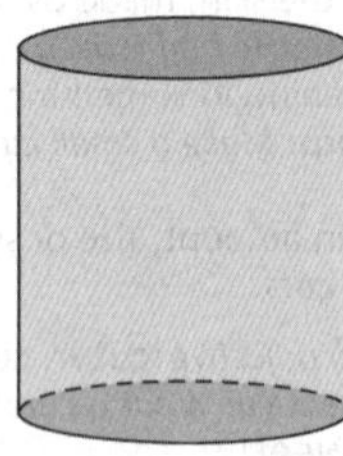

cymbal (say **simb**-l) *noun* (*plural* **cymbals**)
a musical instrument that consists of a round metal plate. You play it by hitting it with special sticks or by hitting two of them together.

cynic (say **sin**-ik) *noun* (*plural* **cynics**)
a person who believes that people only do things for themselves, rather than to help others
▸ **cynical** (*adjective*): *There is a* ***cynical*** *belief that all politicians are corrupt.* ▸ **cynically** (*adverb*): *'Oh really?' he asked* ***cynically****.*
▸ **cynicism** (*noun*): *Is there a difference between* ***cynicism*** *and realism?*

cyst (say **sist**) *noun* (*plural* **cysts**)
a swelling or a lump filled with liquid in the body or under the skin

cytoplasm (say **site**-oh-plaz-uhm) *noun* (*no plural*) (*biology*)
all the living material in a cell, except for the **nucleus** ➲ See illustration at **cell**

czar (say **zaa**) *noun* (*plural* **czars**) = **tsar**

Dd

dab *verb* (**dabbing, dabbed**)
to touch something lightly and quickly: *She **dabbed** the cut with cotton wool.*

dachshund (say **dukss**-huund) *noun* (*plural* **dachshunds**)
a small type of dog with a long body and short legs

dad *noun* (*plural* **dads**) (*informal*)
father: *Hello, **Dad**.* ◇ *This is my **dad**.*

daddy (say **dad**-ee) *noun* (*plural* **daddies**)
a word for 'father' that children use

daffodil (say **daf**-oh-dil) *noun* (*plural* **daffodils**)
a yellow flower that grows in spring

daft (say **daaft**) *adjective* (**dafter, daftest**) (*informal*)
silly: *You're **daft** to work for nothing!*

dagga (say **du*kh***-uh) *noun* (*no plural*) (*S. African*)
another word for **cannabis**
ℹ **ORIGIN:** 17th century, through Afrikaans and South African Dutch, from Khoikhoi *dachab*

PRONUNCIATION Pronounce the **gg** in this word like the **g** in the Afrikaans word **lag**.

dagger (say **dag**-uh) *noun* (*plural* **daggers**)
a short pointed knife that people use as a weapon ➲ See **sword**

dagha (say **dug**-uh) *noun* (*no plural*) (*S. African*)
a mixture of sand, water and mud or cement that is used in building
ℹ **ORIGIN:** through Afrikaans from isiXhosa and isiZulu *udaka* meaning 'clay, mud'

daily (say **day**-lee) *adjective, adverb*
happening or coming every day or once a day: *a **daily** newspaper* ◇ *The museum is open **daily** from 9 a.m. to 5 p.m.*

dainty (say **dayn**-tee) *adjective* (**daintier, daintiest**)
small and pretty: *a **dainty** little girl*

dairy (say **dair**-ree) *noun* (*plural* **dairies**)
a place where milk is kept or where milk products such as butter and cheese are made
▶ **dairy** (*adjective*): ***dairy** products* (= milk, butter and cheese)

SPELLING Be careful! Don't confuse **dairy** and **diary**.

daisy (say **day**-zee) *noun* (*plural* **daisies**)
a small flower with a yellow centre

dam *noun* (*plural* **dams**)
a wall that is built across a river to hold the water back and store it

damage¹ (say **dam**-ij) *noun* (*no plural*)
harm or injury that is caused when something is broken or spoiled: *The fire caused a lot of **damage**.*

damage² (say **dam**-ij) *verb* (**damaging, damaged**)
to break or harm something: *The house was badly **damaged** by fire.*
▶ **damaging** (*adjective*): *Cars have a **damaging** effect on the environment.*

damn (say **dam**) *exclamation*
a rude word that people sometimes use when they are angry: ***Damn**! I've lost my key!*

damp *adjective* (**damper, dampest**)
a little wet: *a cold **damp** house*

dance¹ (say **daanss**) *verb* (**dancing, danced**)
to move your body to music: *Ian **dances** well.*
▶ **dancing** (*noun*): *Will there be **dancing** at the party?*

dance² (say **daanss**) *noun* (*plural* **dances**)
1 movements that you do to music
2 a party where people dance: *My parents met at a **dance**.*

dancer (say **daan**-suh) *noun* (*plural* **dancers**)
a person who dances: *I'm a good **dancer**.*

dandelion (say **dan**-di-ly-uhn) *noun* (*plural* **dandelions**)
a small, yellow wild flower

dandruff (say **dan**-druf) *noun* (*no plural*)
small pieces of dead skin in a person's hair

danger (say **dayn**-juh) *noun*
1 (*no plural*) the possibility that something bad may happen: *You may be in **danger** if you travel alone late at night.*
2 (*plural* **dangers**) a person or thing that may bring harm or trouble: *Smoking is a **danger** to health.*

dangerous (say **dayn**-juh-ruhss) *adjective*
describing a person or thing that may hurt you: *a **dangerous** illness*
▶ **dangerously** (*adverb*): *She drives **dangerously**.*

dangle (say **dang**-guhl) *verb* (**dangling, dangled**)
to hang loosely: *She sat on the fence with her*

A
B
C
D
E
F
G
H
I
J
K
L
M
N
O
P
Q
R
S
T
U
V
W
X
Y
Z

*legs **dangling**. ◇ The Christmas decorations **dangled** from the tree.*

dapper (say **dap**-uh) *adjective*
dressed in a tidy and elegant way: *He looks very **dapper** in his new jacket.*

dappled (say **dap**-uhld) *adjective*
marked with spots or shapes of a different colour: ***dappled** sunlight under a tree*

dare (say **dair**) *verb* (**daring**, **dared**)
dare do something to be brave enough to do something: *I didn't **dare** ask for more money.* ◇ *I **daren't** go home late.*
dare somebody to do something to ask somebody to do something dangerous or silly to see if they are brave enough: *I **dare** you to jump off that wall!*
▸ **daring** (*adjective*): *a **daring*** (= brave) *attack*

USAGE The negative is **daren't** or **don't dare** or **doesn't dare**: *They **daren't** ask her for money. He **doesn't dare** go home late.* In the past tense it is **didn't dare**.

daredevil (say **dair**-dev-il) *noun* (*plural* **daredevils**)
a person who likes to do exciting, dangerous things: *James Bond is a **daredevil** who likes taking risks.*

dark[1] (say **daak**) *adjective* (**darker**, **darkest**)
1 with no light, or not much light: *It was so **dark** that I couldn't see anything.*
2 describing a colour that is nearer to black than to white: *a **dark** green skirt* ◇ ***dark** brown eyes* ➲ OPPOSITE **pale** 2
3 describing a person who has brown or black hair or skin: *a thin, **dark** woman*
🛈 ORIGIN: from Old English *deorc*

dark[2] (say **daak**) *noun* (*no plural*)
(usually **the dark**) the state of having no light, especially because it is night: *Cats can see in the **dark**.* ◇ *Are you afraid of the **dark**?*
after dark after the sun goes down in the evening
before dark before the sun goes down in the evening: *I got home before **dark**.*

darkness (say **daak**-nuhss) *noun* (*no plural*)
the state of being dark, without any light: *The whole house was in **darkness**.*

darling (say **daa**-ling) *noun* (*plural* **darlings**)
a name that you call somebody that you love: *Are you all right, **darling**?*

darn (say **daan**) *verb* (**darning**, **darned**)
to repair a hole in clothes by making stitches across it in one direction and then in the other
▸ **darn** (*noun*): *His socks were full of **darns**.*

dart[1] (say **daat**) *verb* (**darting**, **darted**)
to move quickly and suddenly: *He **darted** across the road.*

dart[2] (say **daat**) *noun* (*plural* **darts**)
a small pointed metal arrow that you use in the game of **darts**

darts (say **daatss**) *plural noun*
a game in which you throw a small metal arrow (called a **dart**) at a round board with numbers on it (called a **dartboard**)

dash[1] *noun* (*plural* **dashes**)
1 a sudden short run somewhere: *The robber made a **dash** for the door.*
2 a mark (–) that you use in writing

dash[2] *verb* (**dashing**, **dashed**)
to run quickly somewhere: *I **dashed** into a shop when it started to rain.*

dashboard (say **dash**-bawd) *noun* (*plural* **dashboards**)
the part of a car in front of the driver where most of the switches and controls are

dassie (say **duss**-ee) *noun* (*plural* **dassies**)
(*S. African*)
a small wild mammal with brown fur and short legs: ***Dassies** often live in rocky places.*
🛈 ORIGIN: 18th century, through Afrikaans from South African Dutch *das* meaning 'badger' because these animals reminded settlers of European badgers

data (say **daa**-tuh) *plural noun*
facts or information: *We are studying the **data** that we have collected.*

USAGE **Data** can be treated as a singular or plural noun: *Is the **data** accurate?* ◇ *Are the **data** accurate?*

database (say **daa**-tuh-bayss) *noun* (*plural* **databases**)
information that is stored in a computer in an organized system that lets you look at it and use it in different ways: *Information about every car is stored in the police **database**.*

date[1] (say **dayt**) *noun* (*plural* **dates**)
1 the number of the day, the month and sometimes the year: *'What's the **date** today?' 'The first of February.'* ◇ *Today's **date** is 11 December 2009.* ◇ *What is your **date** of birth?*
2 a romantic meeting when two people go out somewhere: *He's asked her out on a **date**.*
3 a small sweet brown fruit that comes from a tree which grows in hot countries
out of date
1 not modern: *The machinery they use is completely out of **date**.*

2 too old, so that you cannot use it: *This ticket is out of **date**.*
up to date
1 modern: *The new kitchen will be right up to **date**, with all the latest gadgets.*
2 with the newest information: *Is this list of names up to **date**?*

date² (say **dayt**) *verb* (**dating, dated**)
1 to write the day's date on something: *The letter was **dated** 21 January 2009.*
2 to say or guess how old something is: *Scientists used a machine to **date** the bones.*
3 to go out with a person with whom you are, or want to be, in a romantic relationship

dated (say **dayt**-uhd) *adjective*
old-fashioned: *This sort of jacket looks rather **dated** now.*

daughter (say **daw**-tuh) *noun* (*plural* **daughters**)
a girl or woman who is somebody's child: *They have two **daughters** and a son.*
ⓘ **ORIGIN:** from Old English *dohtor*, related to Dutch *dochter*

daughter-in-law (say **daw**-tuh-in-law) *noun* (*plural* **daughters-in-law**)
the wife of your son

dawdle (say **dawd**-l) *verb* (**dawdling, dawdled**)
to waste time by going somewhere slowly or doing something in a lazy way

dawn *noun* (*plural* **dawns**)
the time in the early morning when the sun comes up ➲ **SYNONYM sunrise**

day *noun* (*plural* **days**)
1 a time of 24 hours from midnight to the next midnight: *There are seven **days** in a week.* ◇ *'What **day** is it today?' 'Tuesday.'*
2 the time when it is light outside: *Most people work during the **day**.*
3 a time in the past: *In my grandparents' **day**, not many people had cars.*
one day
1 at a certain point in the past: *One **day**, a letter arrived.*
2 (also **some day**) at some time in the future: *I hope to become a doctor one **day**.*
the day after tomorrow not tomorrow, but the next day
the day before yesterday not yesterday, but the day before
the other day a short while ago: *I went to town the other **day**.*

WORD BUILDING The days of the week are: **Monday**, **Tuesday**, **Wednesday**, **Thursday**, **Friday**, **Saturday**, **Sunday**.

daybreak (say **day**-brayk) *noun* (*no plural*)
the time of day when light first appears

daydream (say **day**-dreem) *noun* (*plural* **daydreams**)
happy thoughts that make you forget about what you should be doing now: *She stared out of the window, lost in a **daydream**.*
▸ **daydream** (*verb*): *He **daydreamed** about being rich.*

daylight (say **day**-lite) *noun* (*no plural*)
the light from the sun during the day: *These colours look different in **daylight**.*

daytime (say **day**-time) *noun* (*no plural*)
the time when it is day and not night: *I study in the **daytime** and go to bed early.* ➲ **OPPOSITE night-time**

dazed (say **dayzd**) *adjective*
confused and unable to think clearly: *He had a **dazed** look on his face after the accident.*

dazzle (say **daz**-l) *verb* (**dazzling, dazzled**)
(a light) to shine brightly in your eyes so that you cannot see for a short time: *I was **dazzled** by the car's lights.*

DC (say dee-**see**) *noun*
a flow of electricity that goes in one direction only ⓘ **DC** is short for 'direct current'. ➲ See **AC**

DDT (say dee-dee-**tee**) *noun* (*no plural*)
a poisonous chemical used especially in the past for killing harmful insects ⓘ **DDT** is short for 'dichlorodiphenyltrichloroethane'.

dead¹ (say **ded**) *adjective*
1 not alive now: *All my grandparents are **dead**.* ◇ *Survivors helped to bury the **dead*** (= the ***dead** people).*
2 (*informal*) very quiet: *This town is **dead** at night: everywhere is closed after ten.*

dead² (say **ded**) *adverb* (*informal*)
completely or very: *I'm **dead** tired.*

deadline (say **ded**-line) *noun* (*plural* **deadlines**)
a day or time before which you must do something: *The **deadline** for finishing this essay is next Tuesday.*

deadlock (say **ded**-lok) *noun* (*no plural*)
a situation in which two sides cannot reach an agreement: *The parties tried to break the **deadlock**.*
▸ **deadlock** (*verb*)

deadly¹ (say **ded**-lee) *adjective* (**deadlier, deadliest**)
describing something that may kill people or other living things: *a **deadly** weapon*
➲ **SYNONYM lethal**

A B C D E F G H I J K L M N O P Q R S T U V W X Y Z

A B C D E F G H I J K L M N O P Q R S T U V W X Y Z

deadly[2] (say **ded**-lee) *adverb* (*informal*)
extremely: *I'm **deadly** serious.*

deaf (say **def**) *adjective* (**deafer, deafest**)
not able to hear anything or not able to hear very well: *My grandma's starting to go **deaf**.* ◇ *a TV programme for the **deaf*** (= people who cannot hear)
▸ **deafness** (*noun*): *In old age she was troubled by **deafness**.*

deafen (say **def**-uhn) *verb* (**deafening, deafened**)
to make a such a loud noise that people are unable to hear: *We were **deafened** by the loud music.*
▸ **deafening** (*adjective*): *The music at the club was **deafening**.*

deal[1] (say **deel**) *verb* (**dealing, dealt**)
1 to give cards to players in a game of cards: *Start by **dealing** seven cards to each player.*
2 to buy and sell something in business: *Our company **deals** with customers all over the world.*
deal out to give something to a number of people: *She **dealt** out the sweets.*
deal with something
1 to take action in a situation in order to solve a problem or do a particular job: *I am too busy to **deal** with this problem now.*
2 to be about a special subject: *The first chapter of the book **deals** with letter writing.*

deal[2] (say **deel**) *noun* (*plural* **deals**)
an agreement, usually about buying, selling or working: *Let's make a **deal** – I'll help you today if you help me tomorrow.*
a good deal or **a great deal** a lot: *I've spent a great **deal** of time on this essay.*

dealer (say **deel**-uh) *noun* (*plural* **dealers**)
a person who buys and sells things: *a car **dealer***

dealt (say **delt**) form of **deal**[1]

dear (say **deer**) *adjective* (**dearer, dearest**)
1 Dear a word that you use before a person's name at the beginning of a letter: ***Dear** Mr Muleya, …* ◇ ***Dear** Sir or Madam, …*
2 that you love very much: *a **dear** friend*

death (say **deth**) *noun* (*plural* **deaths**)
the end of somebody's life: *There are thousands of **deaths** in car accidents every year.*

deathly (say **deth**-lee) *adjective* (**deathlier, deathliest**)
like death: *There was a **deathly** silence.*

debate (say di-**bayt**) *noun* (*plural* **debates**)
a discussion at a public meeting or a formal argument
▸ **debate** (*verb*): *They **debated** ways to make our roads safer.*

debit[1] (say **deb**-it) *noun* (*plural* **debits**)
1 an amount of money taken out of a bank account: *Please explain this **debit** of R200 from my account.* ➲ OPPOSITE **credit**[1] 2
2 a record showing how much money a person owes for something they bought

debit[2] (say **deb**-it) *verb* (**debiting, debited**)
to take money out of someone's bank account: *I agreed that my account could be **debited** with R400.* ➲ OPPOSITE **credit**[2] 1

debit card *noun* (*plural* **debit cards**)
a plastic card that you can use to pay for things directly from your bank account: *Can I pay by **debit card**?*

debris (say **deb**-ree) *noun* (*no plural*)
what is left when something has been destroyed or broken: *The **debris** of the accident lay all over the street.*

debt (say **det**) *noun* (*plural* **debts**)
money that you must pay to somebody: *The company has **debts** because it borrowed money and bought expensive machinery.*
to be in debt to have to pay money to somebody

debtor (say **det**-uh) *noun* (*plural* **debtors**)
a person who owes money: *The lawyer sold the **debtor's** property to pay the people who were owed money.* ➲ OPPOSITE **creditor**

debut (say **day**-byoo) *noun* (*plural* **debuts**)
a first appearance in public of an actor, a musician or a performer: *She made her **debut** as a singer in 2001.*

deca- (say **dek**-uh) *prefix*
ten, or having ten: ***decathlon*** (= a sports event in which people compete in ten different sports)
ⓘ ORIGIN: from Greek *deka* meaning 'ten'

decade (say **dek**-ayd) *noun* (*plural* **decades**)
a period of ten years: *The country has become richer in the past **decade**.*

decadent (say **dek**-uh-duhnt) *adjective*
becoming less good or less pure: *We live in a **decadent** society that accepts low standards of discipline.*
▸ **decadence** (*noun*): *moral **decadence***

decaffeinated (say dee-**kaf**-i-nay-tid) *adjective*
(used about coffee or tea) with all or most of the **caffeine** taken out: *I drink only **decaffeinated** coffee in the evenings.*

decagon (say **dek**-uh-guhn) *noun* (*plural* **decagons**) (*maths*)
a flat closed shape with ten straight sides

decahedron (say dek-uh-**hee**-druhn) *noun* (*plural* **decahedra** or **decahedrons**) (*maths*)
a solid shape with ten flat surfaces

decapitate (say di-**kap**-i-tayt) *verb* (**decapitating, decapitated**)
to cut off a person's head: *He was* ***decapitated*** *by a falling metal sheet.*

decay (say di-**kay**) *verb* (**decaying, decayed**)
to become bad or be slowly destroyed: *If you don't clean your teeth, they will* ***decay****.*
▶ **decay** (*noun*): *tooth* ***decay***

deceased (say di-**seest**) *adjective* (*formal*) having died recently: *He married his* ***deceased*** *brother's wife.*
▶ **the deceased** (*noun*): *Are you related to the* ***deceased****?*

deceit (say di-**seet**) *noun* (*no plural*)
dishonest behaviour, such as making somebody believe something that is not true: *lies and* ***deceit***

deceive (say di-**seev**) *verb* (**deceiving, deceived**)
to deliberately make somebody believe something that is not true: *She* ***deceived*** *me into thinking she was a police officer.*

> **SPELLING** **ie** or **ei**? When the sound rhymes with **be**, the rule is **i before e, except after c**, so **deceive** is spelt with **ei**.

December (say di-**sem**-buh) *noun*
the twelfth month of the year
ORIGIN: 13th–15th century, from Latin *decem* meaning 'ten'. December was the tenth month of the Roman year.

decent (say **dee**-suhnt) *adjective*
1 good enough or right: *You should buy some* ***decent*** *clothes for your job interview.*
2 honest and good: ***decent*** *people*

deception (say di-**sep**-shuhn) *noun* (*no plural*)
something you do or say to deliberately make somebody believe things that are not true

decibel (say **dess**-i-bel) *noun* (*plural* **decibels**)
a unit used for measuring how loud a sound is
ORIGIN: 20th century, from *deci-* meaning 'ten' + *bel* from the name of Alexander Graham Bell (1847–1922), a teacher and scientist who studied sound and invented the telephone

decide (say di-**side**) *verb* (**deciding, decided**)
to choose something after thinking about the possibilities: *I* ***decided*** *to tell the truth about what happened.* ◇ *I can't* ***decide*** *which book to read.*

deciduous (say di-**sid**-yuu-uhss) *adjective*
referring to a tree or bush that loses its leaves every year: *Some* ***deciduous*** *plants lose their leaves during the dry season.*

> **WORD BUILDING** Compare **deciduous** with **evergreen.**

decimal[1] (say **dess**-im-l) *noun* (*plural* **decimals**)
part of a number that is written after a comma (in South Africa) or after a small round mark (called a **decimal point**) in other parts of the world: *Three-quarters written as a* ***decimal*** *is 0,75.*

> **SPEAKING** We say **0,75** as **nought comma seven five**. We say **0.75** as **nought point seven five.**

decimal[2] (say **dess**-im-l) *adjective* (*maths*)
relating to a number system that uses ten as its base: *a* ***decimal*** *system*

decipher (say di-**sife**-uh) *verb* (**deciphering, deciphered**)
to succeed in reading or working out something that is not easy to see or understand

decision (say di-**sizh**-uhn) *noun* (*plural* **decisions**)
a choice or judgement that you make after thinking about various possibilities: *I must make a* ***decision*** *about what I'm going to do when I leave school.*

decisive (say di-**sise**-iv) *adjective*
1 very important and having a definite result: *a* ***decisive*** *victory* ➲ **SYNONYM crucial**
2 able to make decisions quickly: *Now is the time for* ***decisive*** *action!* ➲ **OPPOSITE indecisive**
▶ **decisively** (*adverb*): *The team was beaten* ***decisively*** *in the final game.* ▶ **decisiveness** (*noun*): *He always thinks clearly and acts with* ***decisiveness****.*

deck (say **dek**) *noun* (*plural* **decks**)
1 the top outside floor of a ship or boat ➲ See illustration at **ship**
2 one of the floors of a ship, plane or bus: *the lower* ***deck*** *of the bus*
3 a wooden floor built outside a home: *They built a* ***deck*** *round their pool.*

deckchair (say **dek**-chair) *noun* (*plural* **deckchairs**)
a chair that you use outside and that you can fold up and carry

A B C D E F G H I J K L M N O P Q R S T U V W X Y Z

declare (say di-**klair**) *verb* (**declaring, declared**)
1 to say very clearly what you think or what you will do, often to a lot of people: *He **declared** that he was not a thief.* ◇ *The country **declared** war on its enemy.*
2 to give information about money you have earned, on which you must pay tax: *I **declared** my income on the form.*
▸ **declaration** (*noun*): *a **declaration** of independence*

decline (say di-**kline**) *verb* (**declining, declined**)
1 to become smaller, weaker or less good: *The quality of the soil is **declining** and farming is becoming more difficult.* ◇ *His health has **declined** recently.*
2 to politely say 'no' when somebody asks you to do or to have something: *We had to **decline** her offer of a lift.* ➲ SYNONYM **refuse**[1]
▸ **decline** (*noun*): *The country is in **decline**.*

decode (say dee-**kohd**) *verb* (**decoding, decoded**)
to find the meaning of a secret message (called a **code**)

decompose (say **dee**-kuhm-pohz) *verb* (**decomposing, decomposed**)
to be destroyed by natural chemical processes: *All living things **decompose** after they die.*
➲ SYNONYMS **decay, rot**
▸ **decomposed** (*adjective*): *a badly **decomposed** body* ▸ **decomposer** (*noun*): *the role of **decomposers** in ecosystems*
▸ **decomposition** (*noun*): *Bacteria help with the **decomposition** of organic matter.*

decor (say **day**-kaw) *noun* (*no plural*)
the style in which the inside of a house or building is decorated

decorate (say **dek**-uh-rayt) *verb* (**decorating, decorated**)
1 to make something look nicer by adding beautiful things to it: *We **decorated** the room with flowers.*
2 to put paint or paper on the walls of a room: *I am **decorating** the kitchen.*
▸ **decorator** (*noun*): *Who was the **decorator** of this lovely room?*

decoration (say dek-uh-**ray**-shuhn) *noun* (*plural* **decorations**)
a beautiful thing that you add to something to make it look nicer: *Christmas **decorations***

decoy (say **dee**-koy) *noun* (*plural* **decoys**)
a person or object that you use to trick somebody or to catch something: *She acted as a **decoy** and took the guard's attention away from the gate.*

decrease[1] (say di-**kreess**) *verb* (**decreasing, decreased**)
to become or to make something smaller or less: *The number of people in the village has **decreased** from 200 to 100.* ➲ OPPOSITE **increase**[1]
🛈 ORIGIN: 14th–15th century, through Old French from Latin *decrescere* from *de-* meaning 'down' + *crescere* meaning 'grow'

PRONUNCIATION Notice that you pronounce the noun and the verb differently.

decrease[2] (say **dee**-kreess) *noun* (*plural* **decreases**)
the process of reducing something or the amount that something is reduced by: *There was a **decrease** in the number of accidents on our roads.* ➲ OPPOSITE **increase**[2]

decree (say di-**kree**) *noun* (*plural* **decrees**)
an official order given by a government or ruler which says what people may or may not do
▸ **decree** (*verb*): *The king **decreed** that all first-born boys should be killed.*

decrepit (say di-**krep**-it) *adjective*
old and in very bad condition or poor health: *They bought a **decrepit** hotel and renovated it.*

dedicate (say **ded**-i-kayt) *verb* (**dedicating, dedicated**)
1 to give all your energy or time to something because you believe it is important ➲ SYNONYM **devote**
2 to say that something is specially for somebody: *I **dedicate** this book to my parents, who always encouraged me to write.*
▸ **dedication** (*noun*): *The doctor won a prize for her **dedication** to her work.*

deduce (say di-**dyooss**) *verb* (**deducing, deduced**)
to work something out using the facts you already know: *The detective examined the body and **deduced** that the man had died during the night.* ➲ SYNONYM **infer**

deduct (say di-**dukt**) *verb* (**deducting, deducted**)
to take something such as money or points away from a total amount: *Your bank will **deduct** the payment automatically.*

deduction (say di-**duk**-shuhn) *noun* (*plural* **deductions**)
1 something that you work out using the facts that you already know: *an intelligent **deduction***
2 the action of taking something away from a total amount: *There are point **deductions** if one player fouls another player.*

3 a sum subtracted from a total amount: *monthly **deductions** for tax and insurance*

deed *noun* (*plural* **deeds**) (*formal*)
a thing that somebody does that is usually very good or very bad: *Doing the shopping for her grandmother was a good **deed**.*

deep *adjective* (**deeper**, **deepest**)
1 describing something that goes down a long way: *Be careful: the water is very **deep**.* ◇ *There were **deep** cuts in his face.* ➲ OPPOSITE **shallow**
2 saying or asking how far something is from the top to the bottom: *The hole was about six metres **deep** and three metres wide.* ➲ The noun is **depth**
3 describing a sound that is low and strong: *He has a **deep** voice.* ➲ OPPOSITE **high**[1] 5
4 describing a colour that is strong and dark: *She has **deep** blue eyes.* ➲ OPPOSITE **pale** 2
5 describing a sleep from which it is difficult for somebody to wake you up
6 describing feelings that are very strong: ***deep** sadness*

Deepavali (say dee-puh-**vaa**-li) *noun* (*no plural*) (also **Divali**, **Diwali**)
a Hindu festival at which people light lamps as a sign of the victory of good over evil
ⓘ ORIGIN: through Hindi, from Sanskrit *dipavali* meaning 'row of lights'. Sanskrit is an ancient language of India.

deeply (say **deep**-lee) *adverb*
strongly or completely: *He is sleeping very **deeply**.*

deer (*rhymes with* **gear**) *noun* (*plural* **deer**)
a wild mammal similar to an **antelope**, that lives in America and Europe.
ⓘ ORIGIN: from Old English *deor*, related to Dutch *dier*. This word originally meant any four-legged animal.

deface (say di-**fayss**) *verb* (**defacing**, **defaced**)
to spoil the way something looks by deliberately writing on or marking its surface

defame (say di-**faym**) *verb* (**defaming**, **defamed**)
to say or write something about a person, that could be harmful to them: *You've **defamed** me and ruined my good reputation!*
▸ **defamation** (*noun*)

default (say di-**fawlt**) *verb* (**defaulting**, **defaulted**)
1 to not do something that you should do by law: *He **defaulted** on the rent payments for three months and had to move out.*
2 (*computing*) to use a particular instruction when no other command is given: *The computer **defaults** to this option automatically.*
▸ **default** (*noun*): *We won by **default** because the other team didn't arrive.*

defeat (say di-**feet**) *verb* (**defeating**, **defeated**)
to win a fight or game against a person or group of people: *The army **defeated** the rebels.*
▸ **defeat** (*noun*): *It was another **defeat** for the team.*

defecate (say **def**-uh-kayt) *verb* (**defecating**, **defecated**) (*formal*)
to get rid of your body's solid waste (called **faeces**) by going to the toilet: *Don't let your dog **defecate** on the pavement!*
▸ **defecation** (*noun*)

defect[1] (say **dee**-fekt) *noun* (*plural* **defects**)
a fault or physical problem in a machine, structure, system or person: *a birth **defect*** ◇ ***defects** in the education system*
▸ **defective** (*adjective*): *Send us the **defective** equipment and we will repair it.*

defect[2] (say di-**fekt**) *verb* (**defecting**, **defected**)
to leave your country or a political party and join one that is considered to be the enemy
▸ **defection** (*noun*) ▸ **defector** (*noun*)

defence (say di-**fenss**) *noun* (*no plural*)
fighting against people who attack, or keeping away dangerous people or things: *They fought the war in **defence** of their country.*

defend (say di-**fend**) *verb* (**defending**, **defended**)
1 to fight to keep away people or things that attack: *They **defended** the city against the enemy.*
2 to say that somebody has not done something wrong: *My sister **defended** me when my father said I was lazy.* ◇ *He had a lawyer to **defend** him in court.*
3 to say or write something in support of something, especially if it has been criticized: ***Defend** your point of view, using examples from your research.*
4 to try to stop another person or team scoring goals or points in a game

defensive (say di-**fen**-siv) *adjective*
1 designed to protect people or things from attack: ***defensive** weapons* ➲ OPPOSITE **offensive**[1] 2
2 showing that you think that somebody is criticizing you: *She got **defensive** and accused me of insulting her.*
3 preventing another person or team from scoring goals or points in a game: ***defensive** play in basketball* ➲ OPPOSITE **offensive**[1] 3

defer (say di-**fur**) *verb* (**deferring**, **deferred**) (*formal*)
1 to not do something until a later time: *Let's **defer** our discussion till tomorrow.*

2 to accept somebody's opinion and give way to their wishes: *He* ***deferred*** *to his wife in everything.*

defiant (say di-**fy**-uhnt) *adjective*
refusing to do what somebody tells you: *She was* ***defiant*** *as a teenager.* ➲ The verb is **defy**

deficiency (say di-**fish**-uhn-see) *noun* (*plural* **deficiencies**)
1 the state of not having enough of something: *a protein* ***deficiency*** ➲ SYNONYM **shortage**
2 a fault or a weakness: *The problems were caused by* ***deficiencies*** *in the design.*

deficient (say di-**fish**-uhnt) *adjective*
1 not having enough of something, especially something that is essential: *Their diet is* ***deficient*** *in vitamin C.*
2 not good enough or not complete: ***Deficient*** *sports equipment can cause injuries.*

deficit (say **def**-i-sit) *noun* (*plural* **deficits**)
the amount by which something, especially a sum of money, is smaller than what is needed: *a budget* ***deficit*** ➲ OPPOSITE **surplus**

define (say di-**fine**) *verb* (**defining, defined**)
to say what a word means: *How do you* ***define*** *'rich'?*

definite (say **def**-i-nuht) *adjective*
describing something that is clear, fixed and unlikely to change: *I want a* ***definite*** *answer, 'yes' or 'no'.* ◇ *There is a* ***definite*** *change in the weather.* ➲ SYNONYM **certain**

definite article *noun* (*plural* **definite articles**) (*grammar*)
in English grammar, the word 'the' ➲ See **indefinite article**

definitely (say **def**-i-nuht-lee) *adverb*
certainly: *I'll* ***definitely*** *think about what you said.* ➲SYNONYM **certainly** 1

definition (say def-i-**nish**-uhn) *noun* (*plural* **definitions**)
a group of words that tell you what another word means

deflate (say dee-**flayt**) *verb* (**deflating, deflated**)
1 to become smaller or to make something smaller by letting the air or gas out of it: *The balloon slowly* ***deflated.*** ➲ OPPOSITE **inflate**
2 to make you feel disappointed and less confident or proud of yourself: *I felt really* ***deflated*** *when I got my exam results.*

deflation (say dee-**flay**-shuhn) *noun* (*no plural*) (*economics*)
a reduction in the amount of money in a country's economy so that prices fall or remain the same ➲ OPPOSITE **inflation**

deflect (say di-**flekt**) *verb* (**deflecting, deflected**)
1 to change direction or to make a thing change direction because of hitting something: *The ball* ***deflected*** *off the bat and onto the pitch.*
2 to take somebody's attention away from something: *Nothing could* ***deflect*** *her from her aim.* ➲ SYNONYM **sidetrack**
▸ **deflection** (*noun*): *the* ***deflection*** *of light rays*

defoliate (say dee-**foh**-li-ayt) *verb* (**defoliating, defoliated**)
to destroy the leaves of trees or plants: *The insects* ***defoliated*** *the trees very quickly.*
▸ **defoliation** (*noun*): *chemical* ***defoliation***

deforest (say dee-**fo**-ruhst) *verb* (**deforesting, deforested**)
to cut down and remove trees from a large area: *They are* ***deforesting*** *the area and selling the wood for timber.*
▸ **deforestation** (*noun*): ***Deforestation*** *often results in soil erosion.*

deform (say di-**fawm**) *verb* (**deforming, deformed**)
to make something change so that its shape or form is different from what is normal and natural
▸ **deformed** (*adjective*): *Rosie has a* ***deformed*** *foot.*

defraud (say di-**frawd**) *verb* (**defrauding, defrauded**)
to get money or something somebody has a right to in a dishonest way: *He* ***defrauded*** *the company of millions.* ➲ See **fraud** 1

defrost (say dee-**frost**) *verb* (**defrosting, defrosted**)
1 to let food that has been frozen reach a normal temperature so that it is suitable for eating or cooking
2 to allow ice formed inside or on something to melt: *to* ***defrost*** *a freezer*

deft *adjective*
very quick and skilful at doing something: *The player's* ***deft*** *footwork led to the goal.*
▸ **deftly** (*adverb*): *He* ***deftly*** *untied the knots and opened the parcel.*

defuse (say dee-**fyooz**) *verb* (**defusing, defused**)
1 to remove part of a bomb so that it cannot explode
2 to make a dangerous or tense situation calmer: *The African Union* ***defused*** *the political crisis just before the elections.*

defy (say di-**fy**) *verb* (**defying, defied**)
to refuse to obey somebody in authority or a

law or a rule: *She **defied** her parents and stayed out all night.* ➲ The adjective is **defiant**

degenerate (say di-**jen**-uh-rayt) *verb* (**degenerating, degenerated**)
to get worse or become lower in quality: *CDs don't **degenerate** as quickly as videotapes.*
▸ **degeneration** (*noun*): *the **degeneration** of brain cells*

degree (say di-**gree**) *noun* (*plural* **degrees**)
1 a measurement of temperature: *Water boils at 100 **degrees** Celsius (100 °C).*
2 a measurement of angles: *There are 90 **degrees** (90°) in a right angle.*
3 the amount or level of something: *There is always a **degree** of risk involved in extreme sports.* ◇ *I agree with you to a certain **degree**.*
4 an official document that a university gives to students who have completed special courses there: *She has a **degree** in Mathematics.*

dehydrate (say dee-hy-**drayt**) *verb* (**dehydrating, dehydrated**)
1 to lose too much water from your body: *Children become **dehydrated** when they have diarrhoea.*
2 to remove all the water from something: *Food is often **dehydrated** to preserve it.*
▸ **dehydrated** (*adjective*): ***Dehydrated** vegetables can be stored for months.*
▸ **dehydration** (*noun*): *What are the signs of **dehydration**?*

deity (say **day**-uh-tee) *noun* (*plural* **deities**) (*formal*)
a god: *Apollo is a well-known **deity** in Greek myths.*

dejected (say di-**jek**-tuhd) *adjective*
feeling sad and unhappy because what you wanted did not happen
▸ **dejectedly** (*adverb*): *She gazed **dejectedly** out of the window.* ▸ **dejection** (*noun*): *She was in a state of **dejection** about her exam results.*

delay¹ (say di-**lay**) *noun* (*plural* **delays**)
a period of time by which somebody or something is late: *There was a long **delay** at the airport.* ◇ *Do it without **delay*** (= immediately).

delay² (say di-**lay**) *verb* (**delaying, delayed**)
1 to make somebody or something late: *My train was **delayed** because of bad weather.*
2 to not do something until a later time: *Can we **delay** our meeting until next week?*
➲ SYNONYM **postpone**

delegate¹ (say **del**-i-guht) *noun* (*plural* **delegates**)
a person who has been chosen to represent a group of people, especially at a meeting: *The **delegates** arrived late.*

delegate² (say **del**-i-gayt) *verb* (**delegating, delegated**)
1 to make somebody responsible for doing something: *I **delegated** the task to Anna.*
2 to ask somebody to represent a group of people: *The board of directors **delegated** Bongi to go to the conference.*
▸ **delegation** (*noun*): *The party sent a **delegation** to Britain for talks.* ◇ *the **delegation** of duties*

delete (say di-**leet**) *verb* (**deleting, deleted**)
to remove something that is written or that is stored on a computer: *I **deleted** some important files on my computer by accident.*

deliberate (say di-**lib**-uh-ruht) *adjective*
describing something that is planned and not done by mistake: *Was it an accident or was it **deliberate**?* ➲ SYNONYM **intentional**
▸ **deliberately** (*adverb*): *The police think that somebody started the fire **deliberately**.*

delicacy (say **del**-i-kuh-see) *noun*
1 (*no plural*) the quality of being easy to damage or break: *the **delicacy** of lace*
2 (*plural* **delicacies**) a type of food that is considered particularly good to eat, rare or expensive: *a local **delicacy***
3 (*no plural*) the fact that a situation requires you to understand other people's feelings and be careful about them: *Be tactful! It's a matter of extreme **delicacy**.*

delicate (say **del**-i-kuht) *adjective*
1 describing something that can very easily be broken or damaged: *I've got **delicate** skin, so I use special soap.*
2 light and pleasant but not strong: ***delicate** colours like pale pink and pale blue* ◇ *The food had a **delicate** flavour.*

delicatessen (say del-i-kuh-**tess**-uhn) *noun* (*plural* **delicatessens**)
a shop that sells special, unusual or foreign food, especially cold cooked meat and cheeses

delicious (say di-**lish**-uhss) *adjective*
very good to eat: *This soup is **delicious**.*

delight¹ (say di-**lite**) *noun* (*no plural*)
great happiness: *The children shrieked with **delight**.* ➲ SYNONYM **joy 1**
▸ **delighted** (*adjective*): *I'm **delighted*** (= very happy) *to meet you.*

delight² (say di-**lite**) *verb* (**delighting, delighted**)
to make somebody very pleased or happy

delighted (say di-**lite**-uhd) *adjective*
very pleased or happy: *I'm **delighted** to meet you.*

delightful (say di-**lite**-fuhl) *adjective*
very pleasant or attractive: *We stayed in a **delightful** little hotel.* ➲ SYNONYM **lovely**

delinquent (say di-**ling**-kwuhnt) *adjective* (*formal*)
behaving badly and often breaking the law: *Some **delinquent** youngsters broke into the tuckshop.*
▸ **delinquent** (*noun*): *juvenile **delinquents***

delirious (say di-**li**-ree-uhss) *adjective*
1 speaking or thinking in a confused way, often because of illness
2 (*informal*) extremely happy or excited
▸ **deliriously** (*adverb*): *He's in love and **deliriously** happy.*

deliver (say di-**liv**-uh) *verb* (**delivering, delivered**)
to take something to the place where it must go: *The postman **delivered** two letters this morning.*
▸ **delivery** (*noun*): *We are waiting for a **delivery** of bread.*

delta (say **del**-tuh) *noun* (*plural* **deltas**) (*geography*)
an area of flat land at the mouth of a river where it splits into smaller rivers before entering into a large body of water, usually the sea

delude (say di-**lood**) *verb* (**deluding, deluded**)
to make somebody believe something that is not true: *We are **deluding** ourselves if we think that the world is a peaceful place.* ➲ The noun is **delusion**

deluge (say **del**-yooj) *noun* (*plural* **deluges**)
1 a sudden heavy fall of rain or a large flood
2 a great number of things that happen or arrive at the same time: *There was a **deluge** of entries for the competition.*
▸ **deluge** (*verb*): *They were **deluged** with applications for the job.*

delusion (say di-**loo**-zhuhn) *noun* (*plural* **delusions**)
a false belief: *He seems to be under the **delusion** that he's popular.* ➲ The verb is **delude**

demand[1] (say di-**maand**) *noun*
1 (*plural* **demands**) a very firm request for something: *a **demand** for higher pay*
2 demands (*plural noun*) things that a person or thing makes you do, especially things that are difficult or make you tired or worried: *Running a marathon makes huge **demands** on the body.*
3 (*no plural*) the desire or need of customers for goods or services which they want to buy or use: *We no longer sell that product because there is no **demand** for it.*
in demand wanted by a lot of people: *Good teachers are always in **demand**.*

demand[2] (say di-**maand**) *verb* (**demanding, demanded**)
1 to ask for something in a very firm way: *The workers are **demanding** more money.* ◇ *She **demanded** to see the manager.*
2 to need something in order to be done successfully: *a sport that **demands** both speed and strength*

demeanour (say di-**meen**-uh) *noun* (*no plural*)
behaviour that shows what type of personality you have or what mood you are in: *Desmond's relaxed **demeanour** made her feel at ease.*

demented (say di-**men**-tuhd) *adjective*
1 having a decrease of brain function, especially of memory: *She became **demented** in her old age.*
2 (*informal*) behaving in a crazy way because you are extremely upset or worried: *She was **demented** with worry.*

dementia (say di-**men**-shuh) *noun* (*no plural*)
a medical term for a serious mental disorder caused by brain disease or injury, that affects the ability to think, remember and behave normally

demise (say di-**mize**) *noun* (*no plural*) (*formal*)
1 the end or failure of something: *the **demise** of the plan to build another library*
2 a person's death

demo (say **dem**-oh) *noun* (*plural* **demos**) short for **demonstration**

democracy (say di-**mok**-ruh-see) *noun* (*plural* **democracies**)
1 a system of government where the people choose their leader by voting
2 a country with such a system
ⓘ ORIGIN: 16th century, from Greek *demos* meaning 'the people' + *-kratia* meaning 'power, rule'

democrat (say **dem**-oh-krat) *noun* (*plural* **democrats**)
a person who wants **democracy**

democratic (say dem-uh-**krat**-ik) *adjective*
describing a country or organization whose people can all choose its leaders or decide about the way it is organized

demography (say di-**mog**-ruh-fee) *noun* (*no plural*) (*geography*)
the study of the characteristics of a **population** over a period of time, using information about changing numbers of births, deaths and cases of disease

▸ **demographic** (*adjective*): *The report focuses on **demographic** changes in the population of the country.* ▸ **demographics** (*noun*): *Because of racial discrimination in the past the workplace does not reflect the **demographics** of the country.*

demolish (say di-**mol**-ish) *verb* (**demolishing, demolished**)
to break a building so that it falls down: *The old building was **demolished** last year.*
▸ **demolition** (*noun*): *The **demolition** of the factory will make room for more houses.*

demon (say **dee**-muhn) *noun* (*plural* **demons**)
an evil spirit: *In the story, the **demon** tries to kill the prince.*

demonstrate (say **dem**-uhn-strayt) *verb* (**demonstrating, demonstrated**)
1 to show something clearly: *He **demonstrated** how to operate the machine.*
2 to walk or stand in public with a group of people to show that you have strong feelings about something: *Thousands of people **demonstrated** against the war.* ➲ SYNONYM **protest**[2]

demonstration (say dem-uhn-**stray**-shuhn) *noun* (*plural* **demonstrations**)
1 a group of people walking or standing together in public to show that they have strong feelings about something: *anti-government **demonstrations***
2 showing how to do something, or how something works: *He gave us a cookery **demonstration**.*

demoralize (say di-**mo**-ruh-lize) *verb* (**demoralizing, demoralized**) (also **demoralise**)
to make somebody lose confidence and hope
▸ **demoralization** (*noun*) (also **demoralisation**): *The **demoralization** of teachers resulted in anti-government demonstrations.*
▸ **demoralized** (*adjective*) (also **demoralised**): *He felt **demoralized** after losing his job.*

demote (say dee-**moht**) *verb* (**demoting, demoted**)
to move somebody to a lower position or level, often as a punishment ➲ OPPOSITE **promote** 2
▸ **demotion** (*noun*): *A string of bad losses led to the **demotion** of the coach.*

demure (say di-**myoor**) *adjective*
describing a girl or young woman who is shy, quiet and polite

den *noun* (*plural* **dens**)
the place where a wild animal lives ➲ SYNONYM **lair**

denial (say di-**ny**-uhl) *noun*
1 (*plural* **denials**) a statement that says that something is not true: *The mayor issued a **denial** that he was involved in the scandal.* ➲ The verb is **deny**
2 (*plural* **denials**) a refusal to allow somebody to do or have something: *the **denial** of medical benefits*
3 (*no plural*) not accepting that something unpleasant or painful has happened: *She has been in **denial** ever since the accident.*

denied, denies forms of **deny**

denim (say **den**-im) *noun* (*no plural*)
strong cotton material that is used for making jeans and other clothes. The material is usually blue: *a **denim** jacket*
🛈 ORIGIN: 17th century, from French *serge de Nîmes*, which means 'serge from the town of Nîmes'. Serge is a type of strong cloth. The name came into English as *serge denim* and was later shortened to *denim*.

denominator (say di-**nom**-i-nay-tuh) *noun* (*plural* **denominators**) (*maths*)
the number that is below the line in a fraction: *In the fraction $\frac{1}{4}$, 4 is the **denominator**.* ➲ See **numerator**

denote (say di-**noht**) *verb* (**denoting, denoted**)
1 to mean something: *The colour red often **denotes** danger.*
2 to be a short way of saying or writing something: *In algebra x **denotes** an unknown quantity.*

denouement (say day-**noo**-maa) *noun* (*plural* **denouements**)
the final part of a play, film or story, where everything is explained or settled: *a dramatic **denouement***

denounce (say di-**nownss**) *verb* (**denouncing, denounced**)
to say publicly that somebody or something is very bad or wrong: *The government **denounced** the terrorist attacks.* ➲ The noun is **denunciation**

dense (say **denss**) *adjective* (**denser, densest**)
1 with a lot of things or people close together: ***dense** bush*
2 thick and difficult to see through: *The fire created a lot of **dense** smoke.*

density (say **den**-si-tee) *noun* (*plural* **densities**)
1 the number of people or things in a place in relation to its area: *Write a sentence to explain the link between population **density** and dry climates.*
2 the relation between the mass of a substance and its **volume**: *Some hormones can increase the **density** of red blood cells that carry oxygen around the body.*

A B C D E F G H I J K L M N O P Q R S T U V W X Y Z

dent *noun* (*plural* **dents**)
a place where a flat surface, especially metal, has been hit and pushed in but not broken: *There's a big **dent** in the side of my car.*
▸ **dent** (*verb*): *I dropped the tin and **dented** it.*

dental (say **den**-tuhl) *adjective*
connected with teeth: ***dental** care*

dentist (say **den**-tist) *noun* (*plural* **dentists**)
a person whose job is to look after your teeth: *I have to go to the **dentist** today.* ➲ See note at **tooth**

denture (say **den**-tshuh) *noun* (*plural* **dentures**)
a set of artificial teeth, worn by somebody who has lost their natural teeth

USAGE It is more usual to say **dentures** than **denture**.

denunciation (say di-nun-see-**ay**-shuhn) *noun* (*plural* **denunciations**)
an expression of strong disapproval in public
➲ The verb is **denounce**

deny (say di-**ny**) *verb* (**denying, denied**)
to say that something is not true: *He **denied** that he had stolen the car.* ➲ The noun is **denial**,
➲ OPPOSITE **admit** 1

deodorant (say di-**oh**-duh-ruhnt) *noun* (*plural* **deodorants**)
a liquid that you put on your body to hide bad smells

depart (say di-**paat**) *verb* (**departing, departed**) (*formal*)
to leave a place: *The next train to Bellville **departs** from platform 23.* ➲ OPPOSITE **arrive** 1

USAGE **Leave** is the word that we usually use. **Depart** is quite formal.

department (say di-**paat**-muhnt) *noun* (*plural* **departments**)
one of the parts of a university, school, government, shop or big company: *The book **department** is on the second floor.* ◇ *the English **department***
ⓘ ORIGIN: 14th–15th century, through Old French *departement* from Latin *dispertire* meaning 'to divide'

departure (say di-**paa**-tshuh) *noun* (*plural* **departures**)
leaving a place: *We must be at the airport an hour before the plane's **departure**.* ➲ OPPOSITE **arrival**

depend (say di-**pend**) *verb* (**depending, depended**)
it depends, that depends words that you use to show that something is not certain: *I don't know whether I'll go to the beach or not. It **depends** on the weather.*
depend on somebody or something
1 to need somebody or something: *She still **depends** on her parents for money because she hasn't got a job.*
2 to trust somebody or to feel sure that somebody or something will do what you want: *I can **depend** on my friends to help me.*

dependant (say di-**pen**-duhnt) *noun* (*plural* **dependants**)
a person, especially a child, who depends on another person for a home, food or money

SPELLING Be careful! Don't confuse the noun, **dependant**, with the adjective, **dependent**.

dependent (say di-**pen**-duhnt) *adjective*
needing a person or thing to support you: *A baby is completely **dependent** on its parents.*
➲ OPPOSITE **independent**

depict (say di-**pikt**) *verb* (**depicting, depicted**)
1 to show something or somebody in a painting, drawing or photograph: *a photo **depicting** a human figure*
2 to describe somebody or something in words: *The novel **depicts** life in rural South Africa.*
➲ SYNONYM **portray**
▸ **depiction** (*noun*): *Her **depiction** of people is interesting.*

deplete (say di-**pleet**) *verb* (**depleting, depleted**)
to reduce the amount of something so that there is not much left: *Oil resources will eventually be **depleted**.*
▸ **depletion** (*noun*): *a **depletion** in oxygen levels*

deplore (say di-**plaw**) *verb* (**deploring, deplored**) (*formal*)
to say or think that something is very bad, wrong or shocking: *The organization **deplores** the cruel treatment of animals.*
▸ **deplorable** (*adjective*): *The roads are in **deplorable** condition.*

deport (say di-**pawt**) *verb* (**deporting, deported**)
to force a foreign person to leave a country because they have no legal right to be there
▸ **deportation** (*noun*): *The government has stopped the **deportation** of illegal immigrants.*

depose (say di-**pohz**) *verb* (**deposing, deposed**)
to remove a ruler or leader from power by force: *There was a revolution and the dictator was **deposed**.*

deposit[1] (say di-**poz**-it) *noun* (*plural* **deposits**)
1 money that you pay to show that you want

something and that you will pay the rest later: *We paid a **deposit** on the house.*
2 extra money that you pay when you rent something. You get it back if you do not damage or lose what you have rented: *If you damage the car they will keep your **deposit**.*
3 money that you pay into a bank: *I'd like to make a **deposit**, please.*
4 (*geography*) a layer of a substance that has formed naturally underground or has been left somewhere by a river or flood: *mineral **deposits***

deposit² (say di-**poz**-it) *verb* (**depositing, deposited**)
to put something somewhere to keep it safe: *The money was **deposited** in the bank.*

depot (say **dep**-oh) *noun* (*plural* **depots**)
a place where a lot of goods or vehicles are stored

depraved (say di-**prayvd**) *adjective*
showing behaviour that is morally bad: ***depraved** and wicked criminals*
▸ **depravity** (*noun*): *a life of poverty and **depravity***

depreciate (say di-**pree**-shi-ayt) *verb* (**depreciating, depreciated**)
to become less valuable over a period of time: *New cars start **depreciating** as soon as they are being driven.* ➲ OPPOSITE **appreciate** 4
▸ **depreciation** (*noun*): *the **depreciation** of the Rand*

depress (say di-**press**) *verb* (**depressing, depressed**)
1 to make somebody feel sad: *This wet weather really **depresses** me.*
2 (*economics*) to make trade and business less active: *The drop in tourism has **depressed** local trade.*
3 (*formal*) to press or push something down, especially part of a machine: ***depress** the clutch pedal* (= when driving)

depressed (say di-**prest**) *adjective*
very unhappy for a long period of time: *He's been very **depressed** since he lost his job.*

depressing (say di-**press**-ing) *adjective*
describing something that makes you feel very unhappy: *That film about the war was very **depressing**.*

depression (say di-**presh**-uhn) *noun* (*no plural*)
a feeling of unhappiness that lasts for a long time: *She often suffers from **depression**.*

deprive (say di-**prive**) *verb* (**depriving, deprived**)
to prevent somebody from having or using something: *If you **deprive** somebody of food, they will starve in the end.*
▸ **deprivation** (*noun*): *sleep **deprivation***

depth (say **depth**) *noun* (*plural* **depths**)
how deep something is, or how far it is from the top of it to the bottom: *What is the **depth** of the swimming pool?* ◇ *The hole was two metres in **depth**.* ➲ The adjective is **deep**

deputy (say **dep**-yuu-tee) *noun* (*plural* **deputies**)
the person in a company or school who does the work of the leader when they are not there: *the school's **deputy** principal* ➲ SYNONYM **vice-**

derail (say di-**rayl**) *verb* (**derailing, derailed**)
1 to cause a train to come off the railway tracks
2 to come or bring to a sudden stop: *Don't let anybody **derail** your career plans!*
▸ **derailment** (*noun*): *We don't know what caused the **derailment**.*

derelict (say **de**-ruh-likt) *adjective*
no longer used and in bad condition: *a **derelict** house*

deride (say di-**ride**) *verb* (**deriding, derided**)
to make rude remarks about somebody and laugh at them in an unkind way
▸ **derision** (*noun*): *He looked at her with **derision** and she felt embarrassed.* ▸ **derisive** (*adjective*): ***derisive** laughter.*

derivative (say di-**riv**-uh-tiv) *noun* (*plural* **derivatives**)
a thing that is made or developed from another thing: *The word 'sadness' is a **derivative** of 'sad'.* ◇ *Find out if tar is a **derivative** of coal.*

derive (say di-**rive**) *verb* (**deriving, derived**)
1 to get a feeling or an advantage from something: *I **derive** great satisfaction from my work.*
2 to come or develop from something: *The name 'Zambia' **derives** from the Zambezi River.*

dermatology (say dur-muh-**tol**-uh-jee) *noun* (*no plural*)
the study of the skin and the diseases affecting it
▸ **dermatologist** (*noun*): *Ask a **dermatologist** about a good treatment for your skin problem.*

dermis (say **durm**-iss) *noun* (*no plural*) (*biology*)
the inner layer of the skin below the **epidermis**: *The **dermis** contains glands, blood vessels and nerve endings.*

derogatory (say di-**rog**-uh-tree) *adjective*
showing a lack of respect or a low opinion of something: ***derogatory** remarks about the police*

desalinate (say dee-**sal**-i-nayt) *verb* (**desalinating, desalinated**)
to remove the salt from sea water so that it can

be used for drinking, watering crops or in factories
▸ **desalination** (*noun*): *a* ***desalination*** *plant*

descend (say di-**send**) *verb* (**descending, descended**) (*formal*) to go down: *The plane started to* ***descend.*** ➲ OPPOSITE **ascend**
be descended from somebody to be related to a person who lived a long time ago
▸ **descent** (*noun*): *The plane began its* ***descent*** *to the airport.*
ⓘ ORIGIN: 13th–15th century, through Old French from Latin *de-* meaning 'down' + *scandere* meaning 'to climb'

descendant (say di-**sen**-duhnt) *noun* (*plural* **descendants**)
your children, your children's children (called **grandchildren**) and everybody in your family who lives after you: *This bird is a* ***descendant*** *of the dinosaurs.*

describe (say di-**skribe**) *verb* (**describing, described**)
to say what a person or thing is like or what happened: *Can you* ***describe*** *the man you saw?* ◇ *She* ***described*** *the accident to the police.*

description (say di-**skrip**-shuhn) *noun* (*plural* **descriptions**)
words that tell what a person or thing is like or what happened: *She wrote a beautiful* ***description*** *of her village.*

descriptor (say di-**skrip**-tuh) *noun* (*plural* **descriptors**)
a word or group of words that you use to describe or identify something

desert[1] (say di-**zurt**) *verb* (**deserting, deserted**)
1 to leave a person without help or support: *He* ***deserted*** *his wife and children.*
2 to go away from a place and leave it empty: *The owl has* ***deserted*** *its nest.*
3 (used especially about a person in the armed forces) to leave without permission

desert[2] (say **dez**-uht) *noun* (*plural* **deserts**)
a large, dry area of land with very few plants: *the Sahara* ***Desert***

SPELLING Be careful! Don't confuse **desert** and **dessert**. These words sound different and have different meanings.

deserted (say di-**zur**-tuhd) *adjective*
empty, because all the people have left: *At night the streets are* ***deserted.***

deserve (say di-**zurv**) *verb* (**deserving, deserved**)
to be good or bad enough to have something: *You have worked very hard and you* ***deserve*** *a rest.* ◇ *They stole money from old people, so they* ***deserve*** *to go to prison.*

desiccated (say dess-i-**kay**-tid) *adjective*
1 (used about food) dried so that you can keep it for a long time: ***desiccated*** *coconut*
2 completely dry: ***desiccated*** *soil*

design[1] (say di-**zine**) *noun* (*plural* **designs**)
1 a drawing that shows how to make something or how it will look once built: *Have you seen the* ***designs*** *for the new shopping centre?*
2 a pattern of lines, shapes and colours on something: *The wallpaper has a* ***design*** *of blue and green squares on it.*

PRONUNCIATION Don't pronounce the **g** in **design**.

design[2] (say di-**zine**) *verb* (**designing, designed**)
to decide how something will look or work, especially by drawing plans: *The building was* ***designed*** *by a German architect.*

designate[1] (say **dez**-ig-nayt) *verb* (**designating, designated**)
1 to give something a legal or official position which shows that it has a particular purpose: *This area has been* ***designated*** *as a reserve.*
2 to give somebody a particular position: *He was* ***designated*** *as her deputy.*
3 to mark something: *These arrows* ***designate*** *the emergency exit.*

designate[2] (say **dez**-ig-nayt) *adjective* (*formal*)
(only *after* a noun) appointed to a job but not yet doing it: *the manager* ***designate***

designer (say di-**zine**-uh) *noun* (*plural* **designers**)
a person whose job is to make drawings that show how something will be made: *a fashion* ***designer***

desirable (say di-**zy**-ruhb-l) *adjective*
1 wanted, often by many people, and worth having: *Experience is* ***desirable*** *but not essential for this job.*
2 sexually attractive ➲ OPPOSITE **undesirable**

desire[1] (say di-**zy**-uh) *noun* (*plural* **desires**)
a feeling of wanting something very much: *a* ***desire*** *for peace*

desire[2] (say di-**zy**-uh) *verb* (**desiring, desired**) (*formal*)
to want something very much or wish for it: *You can't have everything you* ***desire.***

desk (say **desk**) *noun* (*plural* **desks**)
1 a type of table, often with drawers, that you

sit at to write or work: *The pupils worked at their **desks**.*
2 a table or place in a building where somebody gives information or receives visitors: *Ask at the information **desk**.*

desktop (say **desk**-top) *noun* (*plural* **desktops**)
1 the top of a desk
2 (also **desktop computer**) a computer that you can put on a desk ➲ See **laptop**, **PC**
3 the computer screen where you can see pictures (called **icons**) that you can use to start a program or open a file

desolate (say **dess**-uh-luht) *adjective*
1 empty and not pleasant to live in: *a **desolate** town*
2 very unhappy and lonely: *She felt a **desolate** sense of loss when her friend died.*
▸ **desolation** (*noun*): *images of **desolation** and despair* ◇ *the **desolation** of the Antarctic*

despair (say diss-**pair**) *noun* (*no plural*)
a feeling of not having hope: *He was in **despair** because he had no money.*
▸ **despair** (*verb*): *We began to **despair** of ever finding somewhere to live.*

despatch (say diss-**pach**) *verb* (**despatching**, **despatched**) = **dispatch**[1]

desperate (say **dess**-puh-ruht) *adjective*
1 having little hope but ready to do anything to get what you want: *She is so **desperate** for a job that she will work anywhere.*
2 very serious: *a **desperate** need for food*
▸ **desperately** (*adverb*): *He is **desperately** unhappy.*

desperation (say dess-puh-**ray**-shuhn) *noun* (*no plural*)
the feeling of having little hope, that makes you do anything to get what you want: *In **desperation**, she studied all night.*

despise (say di-**spize**) *verb* (**despising**, **despised**)
to hate somebody or something: *I **despise** people who tell lies.*

despite (say di-**spite**) *preposition*
without being affected by the thing mentioned: *We decided to go out **despite** the bad weather.*

despondent (say di-**spon**-duhnt) *adjective*
feeling a lack of hope and expecting no improvement: *She was becoming **despondent** about her future.*
▸ **despondency** (*noun*): *He was filled with uncertainty and **despondency**.*
▸ **despondently** (*adverb*): *'I'll try harder,' she sighed **despondently**.*

despot (say **dess**-pot) *noun* (*plural* **despots**)
a person with a lot of power who uses it in a cruel way: *The country was ruled by a **despot**.* ➲ SYNONYM **tyrant**
▸ **despotic** (*adjective*): *the **despotic** regime of Idi Amin*

dessert (say di-**zurt**) *noun* (*plural* **desserts**)
something sweet that you eat at the end of a meal: *We had ice cream for **dessert**.* ➲ SYNONYM **pudding**

> SPELLING Be careful! Don't confuse **dessert** and **desert**. These words sound different and have very different meanings.

dessertspoon (say di-**zurt**-spoon) *noun* (*plural* **dessertspoons**)
1 a spoon that you use for eating desserts
2 the amount a dessertspoon can hold, about 12 ml, as used in cooking

destination (say dess-ti-**nay**-shuhn) *noun* (*plural* **destinations**)
the place where somebody or something is going: *They were very tired when they reached their **destination**.*

destitute (say **dess**-ti-tyoot) *adjective*
having no money, possessions or a home: *There are many **destitute** people living in this city.*
▸ **destitution** (*noun*): *a government programme to reduce **destitution** and hunger*

destroy (say di-**stroy**) *verb* (**destroying**, **destroyed**)
to break something completely so that you cannot use it again or so that it is gone: *The house was **destroyed** by fire.*

destruction (say di-**struk**-shuhn) *noun* (*no plural*)
breaking something completely so that you cannot use it again or so that it is gone: *the **destruction** of the city by bombs*

detach (say di-**tach**) *verb* (**detaching**, **detached**)
to separate something from another thing that it is joined to: *Please complete and **detach** the form below.* ➲ OPPOSITE **attach**

detached (say di-**tacht**) *adjective*
1 describing a house that stands alone and is not joined to any other house.
2 not being or not feeling involved in something: *We struggle to remain emotionally **detached** when we see a sad situation.*

detail (say **dee**-tayl) *noun* (*plural* **details**)
1 one of the very small parts that make the whole of something: *Tell me the main news – I don't want to know all the **details**.*

A B C D E F G H I J K L M N O P Q R S T U V W X Y Z

2 details (*plural noun*) information about something: *For more **details**, please telephone this number.*
in detail with all the small parts: *Tell me about your plan in **detail**.*

detailed (say **dee**-tayld) *adjective*
giving a lot of information: *a **detailed** description*

detain (say di-**tayn**) *verb* (**detaining, detained**)
1 to make somebody late by holding them up: *Don't let me **detain** you if you are busy.*
2 to stop somebody from leaving a place: *They were **detained** for several hours at the police station.* ➲ The noun is **detention** 1

detect (say di-**tekt**) *verb* (**detecting, detected**)
to discover or notice something that is difficult to see: *I think I **detected** tears in his eyes.*

detective (say di-**tek**-tiv) *noun* (*plural* **detectives**)
a person whose job is to find out who did a crime. They are usually police officers: *Sherlock Holmes is a famous **detective** in stories.*

detention (say di-**ten**-shuhn) *noun*
1 (*no plural*) the state of being kept in a place, especially a prison, and prevented from leaving
2 (*plural* **detentions**) the punishment of being kept at school after the other children have gone home: *They can't give me a **detention** for this.* ➲ The verb is **detain**

detention centre *noun* (*plural* **detention centres**)
1 a place like a prison where young people who have broken the law are kept
2 a place like a prison where people, especially if they have entered a country illegally, are kept for a short time

deter (say di-**tur**) *verb* (**deterring, deterred**)
to prevent something from happening or to make somebody decide not to do something: *The alarm will **deter** burglars from breaking into the house.* ➲ SYNONYM **dissuade** ➲ The noun is **deterrent**

detergent (say di-**tur**-juhnt) *noun* (*plural* **detergents**)
a powder or liquid that you use for washing things

deteriorate (say di-**teer**-ri-uh-rayt) *verb* (**deteriorating, deteriorated**)
to get worse: *Her health **deteriorated** as she got older.*

determination (say di-turm-i-**nay**-shuhn) *noun* (*no plural*)
the quality that makes you continue trying to do something even if it is difficult: *She has shown great **determination** to succeed.*

determine (say di-**tur**-min) *verb* (**determining, determined**) (*formal*)
1 to discover the facts about something: *We need to **determine** the cause of the accident.*
2 to make something happen in a particular way or be of a particular type: *The results of the tests will **determine** what treatment you need.*
3 to decide something officially: *The government has **determined** that voting day will be a public holiday.*

determined (say di-**turm**-ind) *adjective*
very certain that you want to do something: *She is **determined** to win the match.*

determiner (say di-**tur**-min-uh) *noun* (*plural* **determiners**) (*grammar*)
a word that comes before a noun to show how the noun is being used: *'Her', 'most' and 'those' are all **determiners**.*

deterrent (say di-**te**-ruhnt) *noun* (*plural* **deterrents**)
a thing that makes somebody less likely to do something: *Their punishment will be a **deterrent** to others.* ➲ The verb is **deter**

detest (say di-**test**) *verb* (**detesting, detested**)
to hate a person or thing: *They have always **detested** each other.*

detonate (say **det**-uh-nayt) *verb* (**detonating, detonated**)
to explode or to make something such as a bomb explode
▸ **detonation** (*noun*): *the **detonation** of the atomic bomb in 1945*

detour (say **dee**-toor) *noun* (*plural* **detours**)
a longer way to a place when you cannot go by the usual way: *The bridge was closed so we had to make a **detour**.*

detract (say di-**trakt**) *verb* (**detracting, detracted**)
to make something seem less good and therefore less impressive: *These criticisms in no way **detract** from his achievements.*

detrimental (say det-ri-**men**-tuhl) *adjective*
describing something that has a harmful effect on something else: *Smoking is **detrimental** to your health.*

deuce (say **dyooss**) *noun* (*no plural*)
a score of 40 points for both players in a game of tennis. One player must then get two points one after the other to win the game.

devalue (say dee-**val**-yoo) *verb* (**devaluing, devalued**)
1 to lower the value of the money of one

country in relation to the value of the money of other countries: *The government **devalued** the currency by 15%.*
2 to reduce the value or quality of something: *When top players refused to take part, it **devalued** the competition.*
▸ **devaluation** (*noun*): *the **devaluation** of the Rand against other major currencies*

devastate (say **dev**-uhss-tayt) *verb* (**devastating, devastated**)
1 to destroy something or damage it very badly: *War **devastated** the country.*
2 to make somebody extremely upset and shocked: *This tragedy has **devastated** the community.*
▸ **devastating** (*adjective*): *The storm had a **devastating** effect on the island.*
▸ **devastation** (*noun*): *The storm left a path of **devastation**.*

develop (say di-**vel**-uhp) *verb* (**developing, developed**)
1 to grow slowly, increase, or change into something else or to make a person or thing do this: *Children **develop** into adults.*
2 to think of or produce a new idea or product and make it successful: *Scientists are **developing** new treatments for TB.*
3 to begin to have a problem or disease: *She **developed** the disease at the age of 27.*
4 to use special chemicals on film so that the photograph becomes clear

developing country *noun* (*plural* **developing countries**)
a country that is poor and is just starting to have modern industries

development (say di-**vel**-uhp-muhnt) *noun*
1 (*no plural*) the process of growing bigger or becoming more complete: *We studied the **development** of babies in their first year of life.*
2 (*plural* **developments**) something new that happens: *There are new **developments** in science almost every day.*

device (say di-**vise**) *noun* (*plural* **devices**)
a tool or piece of equipment that you use for doing a special job: *a **device** for opening tins*

devil (say **dev**-il) *noun* (*plural* **devils**)
1 an evil spirit or demon
2 the Devil (in the Christian, Jewish and Muslim religions) the most powerful evil being
ORIGIN: from Old English *deofol*, through Latin from Greek *diaballein* meaning 'to speak badly of someone'

devious (say **dee**-vi-uhss) *adjective*
achieving things in a clever but secret and dishonest way
▸ **deviously** (*adverb*): *Their plan was **deviously** cunning.* ▸ **deviousness** (*noun*): *He used **deviousness** to get what he wanted.*

devise (say di-**vize**) *verb* (**devising, devised**)
to think of a new way of doing something
➲ SYNONYMS **conceive** 1, **invent** 1

devoid (say di-**voyd**) *adjective*
not having a particular quality or completely free from something: *His voice was **devoid** of hope.* ◇ *The river is polluted and **devoid** of fish.*

devote (say di-**voht**) *verb* (**devoting, devoted**)
to give a lot of time or energy to somebody or something: *She **devoted** her life to helping the poor.* ➲ SYNONYM **dedicate** 1

devoted (say di-**voht**-uhd) *adjective*
giving all your love or your time and resources to somebody or something: *He is **devoted** to his wife and children.*

devour (say di-**vow**-uh) *verb* (**devouring, devoured**)
1 to eat or swallow something quickly: *She's so greedy – she **devoured** all the ice cream!*
2 (*informal*) to enjoy reading a book so much that you finish it quickly
3 to destroy something quickly and completely: *The houses were **devoured** by fire.*

devout (say di-**vowt**) *adjective*
believing in something strongly and giving a lot of your time and attention to it
▸ **devoutly** (*adverb*): *My parents are **devoutly** religious.*

dew (say **dyoo**) *noun* (*no plural*)
small drops of water that form on plants and grass in the night: *In the morning, the grass was wet with **dew**.*

diabetes (say dy-uh-**bee**-tiz) *noun* (*no plural*)
a disease that makes it difficult for your body to control the level of sugar in your blood
▸ **diabetic** (*adjective*): *His mother is **diabetic**.*

diabolical (say dy-uh-**bol**-ik-l) *adjective*
clever but evil: *a **diabolical** plot to kill the president*

diagnose (say dy-uhg-**nohz**) *verb* (**diagnosing, diagnosed**)
to find out what disease a person has or to identify the cause of a problem
▸ **diagnosis** (*noun*): *The doctor used the symptoms of her illness to make the **diagnosis**.*
▸ **diagnostic** (*adjective*): *Teachers use **diagnostic** processes to identify learning problems.*

diagonal (say dy-**ag**-nuhl) *adjective*
1 lying at an angle: *a **diagonal** pattern on my shirt.*
2 (*maths*) relating to a straight line that joins

two corners of a shape that are not next to each other: *a **diagonal** line.*
▸ **diagonal** (*noun*): *The line is a **diagonal**.*
▸ **diagonally** (*adverb*): *Walk **diagonally** across the field to the far corner.*

diagonal line

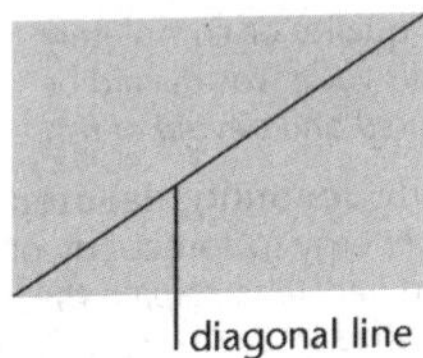

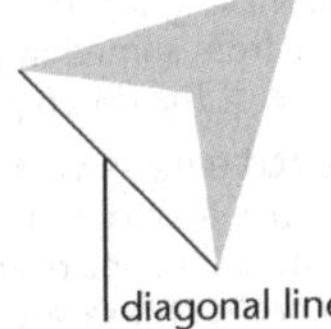

diagram (say **dy**-uh-gram) *noun* (*plural* **diagrams**)
a picture that explains something: *This **diagram** shows all the parts of an engine.*

dial[1] (say **dy**-uhl) *verb* (**dialling, dialled**)
to use a telephone by pushing buttons or turning the dial to call a number: *You have **dialled** the wrong number.*

dial[2] (say **dy**-uhl) *noun* (*plural* **dials**)
a round part of a clock or other piece of equipment with numbers or letters on it which shows the time, speed or temperature: *Check the **dial** of the fuel tank.*

dialect (say **dy**-uh-lekt) *noun* (*plural* **dialects**)
the form of a language that people speak in one part of a country: *a local **dialect***

dialogue (say **dy**-uh-log) *noun* (*plural* **dialogues**)
1 words that two or more people say to each other in a book, play or film ➲ See **monologue**
2 a discussion between people who have different opinions: *a **dialogue** between the major political parties*

diameter (say dy-**am**-i-tuh) *noun* (*plural* **diameters**)
a straight line that goes from one side of a circle to the other, through the centre ➲ See illustration at **circle**[1]

diamond (say **dy**-uh-muhnd) *noun* (*plural* **diamonds**)
1 a hard stone that looks like clear glass and is very expensive: *The ring has a large **diamond** in it.* ◇ *a **diamond** necklace*
2 the shape ♦
3 diamonds (*plural noun*) the set of playing cards that have red ♦ shapes on them: *the eight of **diamonds***
🛈 **ORIGIN:** 13th–15th century, from Old French *diamant* from Latin *diamas, diamant-*

diaphragm (say **dy**-uh-fram) *noun* (*plural* **diaphragms**)
1 the muscle that separates your lungs from your stomach and that helps you to breathe
➲ See illustration at **lung**
2 a thin piece of rubber that a woman puts inside her **vagina** before having sex to stop her from becoming pregnant

diarrhoea (say dy-uh-**ree**-uh) *noun* (*no plural*)
an illness that causes you to get rid of waste matter (called **faeces**) from your body much more frequently than normal, and in liquid form: *an attack of **diarrhoea***

diary (say **dy**-uh-ree) *noun* (*plural* **diaries**)
1 a book with spaces for each day of the year in which you write down things that you have to do or remember: *I'll look in my **diary** to see if I'm free tomorrow.*
2 a book in which you write down what you have done each day: *Do you keep a **diary*** (= write in a ***diary** every day*) *?* ➲ See **journal** 1

SPELLING Be careful! Don't confuse **diary** and **dairy**.

dice[1] (say **dise**) *noun* (*plural* **dice**)
a small piece of wood or plastic in the shape of a cube with dots on the sides for playing games: *Throw the **dice**.*

dice[2] (say **dise**) *verb* (**dicing, diced**)
1 to cut food such as vegetables or meat into small shapes all the same size
2 (*informal, S. African*) to race against another driver: *We **diced** each other at the traffic lights.*
▸ **diced** (*adjective*): ***diced** pumpkin*

dicotyledon (say **dy**-kot-i-leed-n) *noun* (*plural* **dicotyledons**) (*biology*)
a flowering plant with two seed leaves when it begins to grow: *Beans, daisies and oak trees are **dicotyledons**.* ➲ See **monocotyledon**

dictate (say dik-**tayt**) *verb* (**dictating, dictated**)
to say words so that another person can write them: *She **dictated** a letter to her secretary.*

dictation (say dik-**tay**-shuhn) *noun* (*plural* **dictations**)
words that you say or read so that another person can write them down: *We had **dictation** in English today* (= a test when we wrote down what the teacher said).

dictator (say dik-**tay**-tuh) *noun* (*plural* **dictators**)
a person who has complete control of a country, especially one who got that control by force

dictionary (say **dik**-shuhn-ree) *noun* (*plural* **dictionaries**)
a book that gives words from A to Z and explains what each word means: *Look up the words in your* ***dictionary****.*

did form of **do**[2]

didn't (say **did**-uhnt) short for **did not**

die (*rhymes with* **my**) *verb* (**dying, died**)
to stop living: *People, animals and plants* ***die*** *if they don't have water.* ◇ *She* ***died*** *of cancer.*
die down to slowly become less strong: *The storm* ***died*** *down.*
ORIGIN: 13th–15th century, from Old Norse *deyja* meaning 'die'

diesel (say **dee**-zuhl) *noun*
1 (*no plural*) a type of heavy oil that is used in some engines instead of petrol: *a* ***diesel*** *engine* ◇ *a taxi that runs on* ***diesel***
2 (*plural* **diesels**) a vehicle that uses such fuel: *My new car's a* ***diesel****.*
ORIGIN: 19th century, named after Rudolf Diesel (1858–1913), the German inventor of this engine

Die Stem (say di **stem**) *noun* (also **Die Stem van Suid-Afrika**)
the former national song of South Africa, a part of which has been included in the national song that is used now ➲ See **Nkosi sikelel' iAfrika**
ORIGIN: 20th century, from Afrikaans, short for *Die Stem van Suid-Afrika* meaning 'The Voice of South Africa'

diet (say **dy**-uht) *noun* (*plural* **diets**)
1 the food that you usually eat: *It is important to have a healthy* ***diet****.*
2 special foods that you eat when you are ill or when you want to get thinner: *You need to go on a* ***diet*** *if you want to lose weight.*

Difaqane (say **di**-fuh-kaa-ne) *noun* (*no plural*)
another word for **Mfecane**
ORIGIN: from Sesotho, meaning 'time of disaster, mass migration of people'

difference (say **dif**-ruhnss) *noun* (*plural* **differences**)
the way that one thing is not the same as another thing: *What's the* ***difference*** *in price between these bikes?* ◇ *She looks exactly like her sister – I can't tell the* ***difference*** *between them.* ➲ **OPPOSITE similarity**
make a difference to change or have an effect on somebody or something: *Doing sport made a big* ***difference*** *to her life.*

different (say **dif**-ruhnt) *adjective*
1 not the same: *These two shoes are* ***different*** *sizes!* ◇ *Cricket is* ***different*** *from baseball.*
2 many and not the same: *They sell 30* ***different*** *sorts of ice cream.*
▸ **differently** (*adverb*): *He's quiet at home but he behaves* ***differently*** *at school.*

differentiate (say dif-uh-**ren**-shi-ayt) *verb* (**differentiating, differentiated**)
1 to see or show how things are different: *Sometimes it is hard to* ***differentiate*** *between black and blue.* ◇ *You have been taught to* ***differentiate*** *right from wrong.* ➲ **SYNONYM distinguish**
2 to make or appear different: *The coloured feathers* ***differentiate*** *the male bird from the plain brown female.*
3 to treat one person or group of people differently from another ➲ **SYNONYM discriminate**
▸ **differentiation** (*noun*)

difficult (say **dif**-i-kuhlt) *adjective*
1 not easy to do or understand: *a* ***difficult*** *problem* ◇ *The exam was very* ***difficult****.* ◇ *It's* ***difficult*** *to learn a new language.* ➲ **OPPOSITE easy**
2 describing a person who is not easy to please or who will not do what you want: *She's a very* ***difficult*** *child.*

difficulty (say **dif**-i-kuhl-tee) *noun*
1 (*plural* **difficulties**) a problem: *children with learning* ***difficulties*** ◇ *We've run into a* ***difficulty*** *with the new project.*
2 (*no plural*) something that is not easy to do or understand: *I have* ***difficulty*** *understanding isiZulu.* ◇ *to walk with* ***difficulty***

dig *verb* (**digging, dug**)
to move earth and make a hole in the ground: ***Dig*** *the garden, then plant the seeds.* ◇ *They* ***dug*** *a tunnel through the mountain.* ◇ *They* ***dug*** *up the potatoes.*

digest (say dy-**jest**) *verb* (**digesting, digested**)
When you **digest** food, it is changed into substances that your body can use: *You* ***digest*** *food in your alimentary canal.*
▸ **digestion** (*noun*): *Vegetables are usually cooked to help* ***digestion****.*

digit (say **dij**-it) *noun* (*plural* **digits**)
1 the ten figures 0 to 9: *Don't forget to add the three-****digit*** *area code when you dial a number.* ◇ *double-****digit*** *earnings*
2 (*formal*) a finger or toe

digital (say **dij**-it-l) *adjective*
1 using an electronic system that changes sounds or pictures into numbers before it stores or sends them: *a* ***digital*** *camera*
2 (used about a clock or watch) showing the time in numbers

A B C D E F G H I J K L M N O P Q R S T U V W X Y Z

dignified (say **dig**-ni-fide) *adjective* behaving in a calm, serious way that makes other people respect you

dignity (say **dig**-nuh-tee) *noun* (*no plural*) calm and serious behaviour that makes other people respect you: *to behave with* ***dignity***

digress (say dy-**gress**) *verb* (**digressing**, **digressed**) to stop talking or writing about the main subject and deal with something else for a short time
▶ **digression** (*noun*): *I have to make a* ***digression*** *from the story to explain something.*

dike *noun* (*plural* **dikes**) = **dyke**

dilapidated (say di-**lap**-i-day-tuhd) *adjective* old and falling to pieces ➲ SYNONYM **ramshackle**
▶ **dilapidation** (*noun*): *After many years of* ***dilapidation*** *the palace has been restored.*

dilate (say dy-**layt**) *verb* (**dilating**, **dilated**) to become or to make something wider, larger or more open
▶ **dilation** (*noun*): *This camera measures the* ***dilation*** *of the pupil of the eye.*

dilemma (say di-**lem**-uh) *noun* (*plural* **dilemmas**) a situation when you have to make a difficult choice between two things: *to be in a* ***dilemma***

diligent (say **dil**-i-juhnt) *adjective* careful to do your work or duties correctly and well: *She's a very* ***diligent*** *learner.* ➲ OPPOSITE **lax**
▶ **diligence** (*noun*): *He fulfils his duties with* ***diligence***. ▶ **diligently** (*adverb*): *Scientists work* ***diligently*** *in the hope of finding a cure.*

dilute (say dy-**lyoot**) *verb* (**diluting**, **diluted**) to make a liquid weaker by adding water or another liquid to it: *You need to* ***dilute*** *this paint before you use it.*
🛈 ORIGIN: 16th century, from Latin *dilut-* meaning 'washed away, dissolved'

dim *adjective* (**dimmer**, **dimmest**)
1 not bright or clear: *The light was so* ***dim*** *that we couldn't see anything.*
2 (*informal*) not clever: *She's really* ***dim!***
▶ **dimly** (*adverb*): *The room was* ***dimly*** *lit and full of smoke.*

dimension (say dy-**men**-shuhn) *noun* (*plural* **dimensions**)
1 a measurement of the length, width or height of something: *The* ***dimensions*** *of the box are 50 cm long by 30 cm wide by 25 cm high.*
2 dimensions (*plural noun*) how big something is: *the huge* ***dimensions*** *of the new aeroplane* ◇ *The full* ***dimensions*** *of this problem are only now being recognized.*
3 a thing or feature that influences a situation and the way you think about it: *The information adds a new* ***dimension*** *to the discussion.*
▶ **-dimensional** (*adjective*): *a three-****dimensional*** *work of art* ➲ See **three-dimensional**, **two-dimensional**

diminish (say di-**min**-ish) *verb* (**diminishing**, **diminished**) to become or to make something smaller or less ➲ SYNONYM **lessen**

diminutive (say di-**min**-yuh-tiv) *adjective* much smaller than usual

din *noun* (*no plural*) a very loud, unpleasant noise: *Stop making that terrible* ***din!***

dinghy (say **ding**-gee) *noun* (*plural* **dinghies**) a small open boat

dingy (say **din**-jee) *adjective* (**dingier**, **dingiest**) dirty, dark and not nice to look at
▶ **dinginess** (*noun*): *the unpleasant* ***dinginess*** *of the room*

dining room (say **dine**-ing ruum) *noun* (*plural* **dining rooms**) a room where people eat

dinner (say **din**-uh) *noun* (*plural* **dinners**) the largest meal of the day, that you have either in the evening or in the middle of the day: *What time do you usually have* ***dinner?*** ◇ *What's for* ***dinner?***
🛈 ORIGIN: 13th–15th century, from Old French *disner* meaning 'eat dinner'

dinosaur (say **dy**-nuh-saw) *noun* (*plural* **dinosaurs**) a type of land reptile that disappeared from the Earth **(became extinct)** millions of years ago. Some grew to enormous sizes, and some were very aggressive.

dip[1] *verb* (**dipping**, **dipped**)
1 to put something into a liquid for a short time and then take it out again: ***Dip*** *your hand in the water to see how hot it is.*
2 to go down to a lower level: *The temperature* ***dipped*** *to three degrees below zero last night.*
3 to make a downward movement: *The road* ***dips*** *down to the river.*
4 to wash an animal with a liquid that cleans it and kills harmful insects such as fleas

dip[2] *noun* (*plural* **dips**)
1 a fall to a lower level, especially for a short time: *a* ***dip*** *in prices*
2 an area of lower ground: *a* ***dip*** *in the road*

3 a quick swim: *We went for a short **dip** before lunch.*
4 a thick sauce into which you **dip**[1] 1 food such as biscuits before eating them: *an onion **dip***
5 a mixture of chemicals that you use to **dip**[1] 4 animals

diploma (say di-**ploh**-muh) *noun* (*plural* **diplomas**)
a piece of paper that shows you have passed an exam or finished special studies: *a teaching **diploma***

diplomat (say **dip**-luh-mat) *noun* (*plural* **diplomats**)
an official whose job is to speak and do things for their country in another country

diplomatic (say dip-luh-**mat**-ik) *adjective*
1 connected with managing relations between countries: ***diplomatic** talks*
2 careful not to say or do things that may make people unhappy or angry: *a **diplomatic** answer*
➲ SYNONYM **tactful**

dire (say **dy**-uh) *adjective* (**direr**, **direst**) (*formal*)
very bad or serious: ***dire** warnings*

direct[1] (say dy-**rekt**) *adjective, adverb*
1 as straight as possible, without turning or stopping: *Which is the most **direct** route to town from here?* ◇ *We flew **direct** to Perth.*
2 from one person or thing to another person or thing with nobody or nothing between them: *This plant needs **direct** sunlight.* ◇ *They are in **direct** contact with the hijackers.* ➲ OPPOSITE **indirect**

direct[2] (say dy-**rekt**) *verb* (**directing**, **directed**)
1 to manage or control somebody or something: *A policeman was in the middle of the road, **directing** the traffic.*
2 to be in charge of actors in a play or a film: *The movie was **directed** by Quentin Tarantino.*
3 to tell somebody how to get to a place: *Can you **direct** me to the station, please?*

direction (say dy-**rek**-shuhn) *noun*
1 (*plural* **directions**) where a person or thing is going or looking: *They got lost because they went in the wrong **direction**.*
2 directions (*plural noun*) words that tell you how to get to a place or how to do something: *Let's stop and ask for **directions**.* ◇ *Simple **directions** for building the model are printed on the box.*

directly (say dy-**rekt**-lee) *adverb*
in a direct line or way: *The supermarket is **directly** opposite the bank.* ◇ *Lung cancer is **directly** related to smoking.*

direct object *noun* (*plural* **direct objects**) (*grammar*)
the person or thing that is directly affected by the action of a verb: *In 'I met him in town', the word 'him' is the **direct object**.* ➲ See **indirect object**

director (say dy-**rek**-tuh) *noun* (*plural* **directors**)
1 a person who controls a business or a group of people
2 a person in charge of a film or play who tells the actors what to do

directory (say dy-**rek**-tuh-ree) *noun* (*plural* **directories**)
1 a book or list of people's addresses and telephone numbers: *a telephone **directory***
2 (*computing*) a file containing a group of other files or programs in a computer ➲ See **folder**

direct speech *noun* (*no plural*) (*grammar*)
the actual words that a person says, as in 'I will come later'. ➲ See **reported speech** and **indirect speech**

dirt (say **durt**) *noun* (*no plural*)
a substance that is not clean, for example mud or dust: *The children came in from the garden covered in **dirt**.*

dirty (say **dur**-tee) *adjective* (**dirtier**, **dirtiest**)
not clean: *My hands are **dirty**.*

dis- (say **diss**) *prefix*
(in adjectives, adverbs, nouns and verbs) used to make the meaning of a word negative or to express the opposite meaning: ***disagree*** ◇ ***dishonest***
ⓘ ORIGIN: from Latin

disability (say diss-uh-**bil**-uh-tee) *noun* (*plural* **disabilities**)
a physical or mental condition that means you cannot use a part of your body completely or easily, or that you cannot learn easily: *people with severe learning **disabilities***

disabled (say diss-**ay**-buhld) *adjective*
not able to use a part of your body well: *Peter is **disabled** – he lost a leg in an accident.* ◇ *The hotel has improved facilities for **disabled** people.*

disadvantage (say diss-uhd-**vaan**-tij) *noun* (*plural* **disadvantages**)
1 a problem that makes something difficult or less good: *One **disadvantage** of living out of town is the lack of public transport.*
2 something that may make you less successful than other people: *Your lack of experience is a **disadvantage**.* ➲ OPPOSITE **advantage**

disagree (say diss-uh-**gree**) *verb* (**disagreeing**, **disagreed**)
to have a different opinion from somebody

A B C D E F G H I J K L M N O P Q R S T U V W X Y Z

else: *I said it was a good film, but Tapello **disagreed** with me.* ◇ *My sister and I **disagree** about everything!* ➲ OPPOSITE **agree 1**

disagreement (say diss-uh-**gree**-muhnt) *noun* (*plural* **disagreements**)
a situation where people have different opinions about something and often argue: *My parents sometimes have **disagreements** about money.* ➲ OPPOSITE **agreement 1**

disappear (say diss-uh-**peer**) *verb* (**disappearing, disappeared**)
1 to become impossible to see: *The sun **disappeared** behind the clouds.* ➲ OPPOSITE **appear**
2 to stop existing: *Plant and animal species are **disappearing** at an alarming rate.*
3 to be lost or impossible to find: *My wallet seems to have **disappeared**.* ➲ SYNONYM **vanish**
▸ **disappearance** (*noun*): *the child's **disappearance***

SPELLING Remember! You spell **disappear** with one **s** and **pp**.

disappoint (say diss-uh-**poynt**) *verb* (**disappointing, disappointed**)
to make you sad because what you wanted did not happen: *I'm sorry to **disappoint** you, but I can't come to your party.*

disappointed *adjective*
feeling sad because what you wanted did not happen: *Sue was **disappointed** when she didn't win the prize.*

SPELLING Remember! You spell **disappointed** with one **s** and **pp**.

disappointing (say diss-uh-**poynt**-ing) *adjective*
making you feel sad because something is not as good as you hoped: ***disappointing** exam results*

disappointment (say diss-uh-**poynt**-muhnt) *noun*
1 (*no plural*) a feeling of sadness because what you wanted did not happen: *She hid her **disappointment** at losing the match.*
2 (*plural* **disappointments**) something that makes you sad because it is not what you hoped: *Her party was a **disappointment** – only six people came.*

disapproval (say diss-uh-**proov**-l) *noun* (*no plural*)
a feeling that something is bad or that somebody is behaving badly: *She shook her head in **disapproval**.* ➲ OPPOSITE **approval**

disapprove (say diss-uh-**proov**) *verb* (**disapproving, disapproved**)
to think that somebody or something is bad: *Mandla's parents **disapproved** of his new girlfriend.* ➲ OPPOSITE **approve**

disaster (say di-**zaass**-tuh) *noun* (*plural* **disasters**)
1 something very bad that happens and that may hurt a lot of people: *Floods and earthquakes are natural **disasters**.*
2 a very bad situation or event: *Our holiday was a **disaster**! It rained all week!*

disastrous (say di-**zaass**-truhss) *adjective*
describing something very bad that causes great trouble: *The heavy rain brought **disastrous** floods.*

disbelief (say diss-buh-**leef**) *noun* (*no plural*)
the state of not believing that something is real or true: *He shook his head in **disbelief**.*

disc (say **disk**) *noun* (*plural* **discs**)
1 a round flat object: *The dog has an identity **disc** on his collar.*
2 a **CD**: *This recording is available on **disc** or cassette.*
3 one of the pieces of thin strong material (called **cartilage**) between the bones in your back: *a slipped **disc***

discard (say diss-**kaad**) *verb* (**discarding, discarded**)
to throw something away because you do not want it or do not need it

discerning (say di-**surn**-ing) *adjective*
able to recognize the quality of things and people: *The **discerning** tourist will appreciate the museums and art galleries.*

discharge[1] (say diss-**chaaj**) *verb* (**discharging, discharged**)
1 to give somebody official permission to leave: *He was **discharged** from hospital.*
2 to send something out, for example gas or smoke: *a device for **discharging** steam*
3 (*formal*) to do something that you have to do: *He **discharged** his duties successfully.*

discharge[2] (say **diss**-chaaj) *noun*
1 (*no plural*) the act of allowing somebody to leave, especially a hospital
2 (*plural* **discharges**) a substance that flows out of or from something: *a sticky **discharge** from the eye*
3 (*plural* **discharges**) the process of sending something out: *the **discharge** of water from a dam*
4 (*no plural*) (*formal*) the act of performing a task or a duty

disciple (say di-**sipe**-uhl) *noun* (*plural* **disciples**)
a person who believes in and supports a teacher or leader, especially a religious one

discipline (say **diss**-uh-plin) *noun* (*no plural*)
the practice of teaching yourself to control your actions and follow rules: *Children learn* ***discipline*** *at school.*
▸ **discipline** (*verb*): *You must* ***discipline*** *yourself to work harder.*

PRONUNCIATION Don't pronounce the **c** in **discipline**.

disc jockey *noun* (*plural* **disc jockeys**) (abbr. DJ)
a person whose job is to introduce and play popular recorded music, on radio or at a club

disclose (say diss-**klohz**) *verb* (**disclosing, disclosed**)
to tell somebody something they do not know or to make something known publicly
➲ SYNONYMS **reveal, divulge**
▸ **disclosure** (*noun*): *The newspaper published the latest* ***disclosures*** *about the scandal.*

disco (say **diss**-koh) *noun* (*plural* **discos**) (*old-fashioned*)
a place where people dance and listen to pop music

disconnect (say diss-kuh-**nekt**) *verb* (**disconnecting, disconnected**)
to stop a supply of water, gas or electricity going to a piece of equipment or a building: *Your phone will be* ***disconnected*** *if you don't pay the bill.* ➲ OPPOSITE **connect**

discontinue (say diss-kuhn-**tin**-yoo) *verb* (**discontinuing, discontinued**)
to stop doing, making or providing something: *The bus service has been* ***discontinued.***

discord (say **diss**-kawd) *noun* (*no plural*) (*formal*) a situation in which people have different opinions about something and argue with one another ➲ OPPOSITE **concord** 1

discount (say **diss**-kownt) *noun* (*plural* **discounts**)
an amount of money that is taken off the usual price of something to make it cheaper: *I got a* ***discount*** *for paying cash.*

discourage (say diss-**ku**-rij) *verb* (**discouraging, discouraged**)
1 to make somebody not want to do something: *Her parents tried to* ***discourage*** *her from leaving school.*
2 to make somebody feel less confident about something: *I was* ***discouraged*** *by my poor results.* ➲ OPPOSITE **encourage**
▸ **discouraging** (*adjective*): *a* ***discouraging*** *result*

discourteous (say diss-**kur**-ti-uhss) *adjective*
rude and not thinking or caring about other people ➲ OPPOSITE **courteous**
▸ **discourtesy** (*noun*): *I did not respond to your enquiry. I apologize for my* ***discourtesy.***

discover (say diss-**kuv**-uh) *verb* (**discovering, discovered**)
to find or learn something for the first time: *Who* ***discovered*** *Australia?* ◇ *I was in the shop when I* ***discovered*** *that I had no money.*
▸ **discovery** (*noun*): *the* ***discovery*** *of gold* ◇ *scientific* ***discoveries***

WHICH WORD? **Discover** or **invent**?
- When you **discover** something, you find something that already exists.
- When you **invent** something, you make it for the first time. *Gold was* ***discovered*** *and the bicycle was* ***invented.***

discredit (say diss-**kred**-it) *verb* (**discrediting, discredited**)
to stop people thinking well of a person or thing because they can no longer trust them

discreet (say diss-**kreet**) *adjective*
1 careful in what you say or do so as not to cause embarrassment or trouble for somebody ➲ OPPOSITE **indiscreet** ➲ The noun is **discretion**
2 not attracting attention: *The fabric is a* ***discreet*** *beige colour.*
▸ **discreetly** (*adverb*): *I* ***discreetly*** *explained my awkward situation.*

SPELLING Be careful! Don't confuse **discreet** and **discrete**. They sound the same but have different meanings.

discrepancy (say diss-**krep**-uhn-see) *noun* (*plural* **discrepancies**)
a difference between things that should be the same or ought to match: *There are a few errors and* ***discrepancies*** *in the report.*

discrete (say diss-**kreet**) *adjective* (*formal*)
separate or clearly different: *a large number of* ***discrete*** *items*

SPELLING Be careful! Don't confuse **discrete** and **discreet**. They sound the same but have different meanings.

discretion (say diss-**kresh**-uhn) *noun* (*no plural*)
1 the quality of being careful in what you say or do so as not to cause embarrassment or trouble for somebody ➲ The adjective is **discreet** 1
2 the freedom to decide what you should do in

A B C D E F G H I J K L M N O P Q R S T U V W X Y Z

a particular situation: *You must decide what is best. Use your **discretion**.*

discriminate (say diss-**krim**-i-nayt) *verb* (**discriminating, discriminated**)
1 to treat one person or a group in a worse way than others: *This company **discriminates** against women – it pays them less than men for doing the same work.*
2 to recognize that there is a difference between people or things: *When do babies learn to **discriminate** between different people's voices?*
▸ **discrimination** (*noun*): *religious **discrimination*** (= treating somebody in an unfair way because their religion is not the same as yours)

discuss (say diss-**kuss**) *verb* (**discussing, discussed**)
1 to talk about something: *I **discussed** the problem with my parents.*
2 to write or talk about something in detail, showing the different ideas about it: *This topic is **discussed** in the next chapter.*

discussion (say diss-**kush**-uhn) *noun* (*plural* **discussions**)
talking about something seriously or deeply: *We had a **discussion** about politics.*

disdain (say diss-**dayn**) *noun* (*no plural*)
the feeling that somebody or something is not good enough or important enough to be respected: *She felt that her boss always treated her ideas with **disdain**.*
▸ **disdainful** (*adjective*): *a **disdainful** remark*
▸ **disdainfully** (*adverb*): *They stared **disdainfully** at him.*

disease (say di-**zeez**) *noun* (*plural* **diseases**)
an illness, especially one that you can catch from another person: *Malaria and measles are **diseases**.*
ℹ ORIGIN: 13th–15th century, from Old French *desaise* meaning 'lack of ease, inconvenience'

disembark (say diss-em-**baak**) *verb* (**disembarking, disembarked**) (*formal*)
to get off an aircraft, a ship or a train
➲ OPPOSITE **embark**
▸ **disembarkation** (*noun*): *You have to fill in the **disembarkation** card before leaving the plane.*

disempower (say diss-em-**pow**-uh) *verb* (**disempowering, disempowered**)
to make a person or thing less powerful or take away their confidence to do something
➲ OPPOSITE **empower**
▸ **disempowerment** (*noun*): *the **disempowerment** of women in many developing countries*

disfigure (say diss-**fig**-uh) *verb* (**disfiguring, disfigured**)
to spoil the appearance of a person or thing: *He was attacked by a dog and now his arm is **disfigured**.*
▸ **disfigurement** (*noun*): *a facial **disfigurement***

disgrace (say diss-**grayss**) *noun* (*no plural*)
when other people stop thinking well of you, because you have done something bad: *He's in **disgrace** because he stole money from his brother.*

disgraceful (say diss-**grayss**-fuhl) *adjective*
very bad, making other people feel sorry and embarrassed: *The way the other team behaved was **disgraceful**.*

disgruntled (say diss-**grun**-tuhld) *adjective*
not pleased with something and annoyed: *The **disgruntled** customer complained to the manager.*

disguise¹ (say diss-**gize**) *verb* (**disguising, disguised**)
to change the appearance of a person or thing so that people will not know who or what they are: *They **disguised** themselves as guards and escaped from the prison.*

disguise² (say diss-**gize**) *noun* (*plural* **disguises**)
things that you wear so that people do not know who you are: *She is so famous that she has to go shopping in **disguise**.*

disgust (say diss-**gust**) *noun* (*no plural*)
a strong feeling of not liking something: *They left the restaurant in **disgust** because the food was so bad.*
▸ **disgust** (*verb*): *The violence in the film **disgusted** me.* ▸ **disgusted** (*adjective*): *He was **disgusted** to find a fly in his soup.*

disgusting (say diss-**guss**-ting) *adjective*
very unpleasant: *What a **disgusting** smell!*
➲ SYNONYM **revolting**

dish *noun* (*plural* **dishes**)
1 a container that you can use to cook food in an oven, or to put food on the table
2 the dishes (*plural noun*) all the plates, bowls and cups that you must wash after a meal: *I'll wash the **dishes**.*
3 a part of a meal: *We had a fish **dish** and a vegetarian **dish**.*

dishcloth (say **dish**-kloth) *noun* (*plural* **dishcloths**)
a cloth used for washing dirty dishes

dishevelled (say di-**shev**-uhld) *adjective*
very untidy or not well cared for: *Her hair was **dishevelled** by the wind.* ➲ SYNONYM **unkempt**

dishonest (say diss-**on**-uhst) *adjective*
describing a person who says things that are not true, or steals or cheats ➲ OPPOSITE **honest**

dishwasher (say **dish**-wosh-uh) *noun* (*plural* **dishwashers**)
a machine that washes things such as plates, glasses, knives and forks

disillusion (say diss-i-**loo**-zhuhn) *verb* (**disillusioning, disillusioned**)
to destroy somebody's good opinion of something they approved of or believed in
▸ **disillusion** (*noun*): *growing* ***disillusion*** *and pessimism* ▸ **disillusioned** (*adjective*): *She's* ***disillusioned*** *with her job.* ▸ **disillusionment** (*noun*): *signs of* ***disillusionment*** *with democracy*

disincentive (say diss-in-**sen**-tiv) *noun* (*plural* **disincentives**)
something that makes you feel less confident about taking action: *Crime is a major* ***disincentive*** *to companies that want to invest in Nigeria.* ➲ OPPOSITE **incentive**

disinfect (say diss-in-**feft**) *verb* (**disinfecting, disinfected**)
to clean something using a **disinfectant**

disinfectant (say diss-in-**fek**-tuhnt) *noun* (*plural* **disinfectants**)
a cleaning liquid that kills harmful bacteria and other small living things that can make you ill: *Vinegar is a natural* ***disinfectant.***
▸ **disinfectant** (*adjective*): *a* ***disinfectant*** *spray*

disintegrate (say diss-**in**-tuh-grayt) *verb* (**disintegrating, disintegrated**)
1 to break into a lot of small pieces: *The rocket* ***disintegrated*** *on lift-off.*
2 to become weaker or fall apart: *The team's confidence* ***disintegrated*** *after they lost the game.*
▸ **disintegration** (*noun*): *Who is responsible for the* ***disintegration*** *of their marriage?*

disinterested (say diss-**in**-truhss-tuhd) *adjective*
1 not personally connected with something or not involved in a situation, and therefore able to be fair: *He made an objective and* ***disinterested*** *judgment.*
2 (*informal*) not interested

> USAGE In formal English, only the first meaning given above is accepted as correct. However, many people do use **disinterested** to mean 'not interested'.

disinvest (say diss-in-**vest**) *verb* (**disinvesting, disinvested**)
to reduce or take away money that you gave to a project, business or bank earlier: *Many companies* ***disinvested*** *from South Africa during the 1980s.*
▸ **disinvestment** (*noun*): *sanctions and* ***disinvestment***

disjointed (say diss-**joyn**-tuhd) *adjective*
not logical or clearly connected and therefore difficult to follow: *She gave the police a* ***disjointed*** *account of what had happened.*
➲ OPPOSITE **coherent**

disk *noun* (*plural* **disks**) (*computing*)
a flat piece of plastic that stores information for use by a computer ➲ See **hard drive**

disk drive *noun* (*plural* **disk drives**) (*computing*)
a piece of electrical equipment that passes information to or from a computer disk

dislike¹ (say diss-**like**) *verb* (**disliking, disliked**) (*formal*)
to not like somebody or something: *I* ***dislike*** *getting up early.*

dislike² (say diss-**like**) *noun* (*no plural*)
1 the feeling of not liking a person or thing: *I have a strong* ***dislike*** *of hospitals.*
2 dislikes (*plural noun*) things you do not like: *Make a list of your likes and* ***dislikes.***
take a dislike to a person or **thing** to start hating or not liking a person or thing: *He took an immediate* ***dislike*** *to his new science teacher.*

dislocate (say **diss**-loh-kayt) *verb* (**dislocating, dislocated**)
to pull a bone out of the joint into which it fits: *She* ***dislocated*** *her shoulder when she fell off the horse.*
▸ **dislocation** (*noun*): ***dislocation*** *of the hip*

disloyal (say diss-**loy**-uhl) *adjective*
not supporting your friends, family or country: *He was accused of being* ***disloyal*** *to the government.* ➲ OPPOSITE **loyal**

dismal (say **diz**-muhl) *adjective*
very bad and making you feel sad: *It was a wet,* ***dismal*** *day.*

dismay (say diss-**may**) *noun* (*no plural*)
a strong feeling of worry and sadness after you have received an unpleasant surprise: *She had a look of* ***dismay*** *when she heard the bad news.*
▸ **dismayed** (*adjective*): *I was* ***dismayed*** *when somebody stole my bike.*

dismiss (say diss-**miss**) *verb* (**dismissing, dismissed**)
1 (*formal*) to make somebody leave their job: *He was* ***dismissed*** *for stealing from the company.*
➲ SYNONYMS **sack², fire²** 2
2 to allow somebody to leave a place: *At the end of the lesson the teacher* ***dismissed*** *us.*

disobedient (say diss-uh-**bee**-di-uhnt) *adjective*
not doing what somebody tells you to do: *a*

A B C D E F G H I J K L M N O P Q R S T U V W X Y Z

disobedient child ➲ OPPOSITE **obedient**
▸ **disobedience** (*noun*)

disobey (say diss-uh-**bay**) *verb* (**disobeying, disobeyed**)
to not do what somebody tells you to do: *She **disobeyed** her parents and went to the party.*
➲ OPPOSITE **obey**

disorder (say diss-**aw**-duh) *noun*
1 (*no plural*) a confused, untidy or badly organized state: *The children left the room in terrible **disorder**.* ➲ OPPOSITE **order**[1] 2
2 (*no plural*) violent behaviour by a large number of people: *There were a number of incidents of public **disorder**.*
3 (*plural* **disorders**) an illness in which the mind or part of the body is not working properly: *Acne is a type of skin **disorder**.*

disorganized (say diss-**aw**-guh-nize-d) *adjective* (also **disorganised**)
badly planned or not tidy: *The meeting was very **disorganized**.* ➲ OPPOSITE **organized**

disown (say diss-**ohn**) *verb* (**disowning, disowned**)
to formally say that you no longer want to be connected with or be responsible for somebody or something: *They publicly **disowned** their son for marrying a foreigner.*

disparity (say diss-**pa**-ruh-tee) *noun* (*plural* **disparities**) (*formal*)
a big difference, especially one that is caused by unfair treatment: ***disparities** between rich people and poor people*

dispatch[1] (say diss-**pach**) *verb* (**dispatching, dispatched**) (also **despatch**)
1 to send a person or thing to a place: *A rescue team was **dispatched** to look for the missing man.* ◇ *Your order will be **dispatched** within seven days.*
2 to kill a person or thing: ***Dispatch** weeds while they are small.*

dispatch[2] (say diss-**pach**) *noun* (*plural* **dispatches**) (also **despatch**)
1 the act of sending a person or thing somewhere: *All orders must be paid before the **dispatch** of any goods.*
2 an official report, especially one sent by a military officer, or a report sent by a journalist working in a foreign country

dispel (say diss-**pel**) *verb* (**dispelling, dispelled**)
to make something, especially a feeling or belief, go away or disappear: *His words **dispelled** all her fears.*

dispensary (say diss-**pen**-suhrry) *noun* (*plural* **dispensaries**)
a place in a hospital or shop where medicines are prepared for patients

dispense (say diss-**penss**) *verb* (**dispensing, dispensed**) (*formal*)
1 to give or provide people with something: *This machine **dispenses** hot and cold drinks.*
2 to prepare and give medicines to people: *The pharmacist **dispensed** the pills.*
dispense with a person or **thing** to get rid of or manage without a person or thing: *His leg got better and he could **dispense** with the walking stick.*

dispenser (say diss-**pen**-suh) *noun* (*plural* **dispensers**)
a machine or container from which you can get something such as money or drinks: *a cash **dispenser** at a bank* ◇ *a soap **dispenser***

disperse (say diss-**purss**) *verb* (**dispersing, dispersed**)
to separate and go in different directions or be spread over a wide area, or to make a person or thing do this: *Police ordered the crowd to **disperse**.*
▸ **dispersal** (*noun*): *Wind and water help in the **dispersal** of seeds.*

displace (say diss-**playss**) *verb* (**displacing, displaced**)
1 to take the place or position of a person or thing: *Computers have **displaced** typewriters.*
2 to force a person or thing to move from the usual or correct place: *A half a million people were **displaced** by the tsunami.*
▸ **displaced** (*adjective*): ***displaced** civilians*

display[1] (say diss-**play**) *verb* (**displaying, displayed**)
to show something so that people can see it: *Many toys were **displayed** in the window.* ◇ ***Display** your work attractively.* ◇ ***Display** the data using a graph or a pie chart.*

display[2] (say diss-**play**) *noun* (*plural* **displays**)
1 something that people look at: *an artwork **display*** ◇ *The paintings are on **display** in the museum.*
2 behaviour that shows a particular feeling or quality: *a **display** of courage*

disposable (say diss-**pohz**-uhb-l) *adjective*
designed to be thrown away after you have used it once or for a short time: ***disposable** nappies*

dispose (say diss-**pohz**) *verb* (**disposing, disposed**)
dispose of something to throw something away or give something away because you do not want it: *Where can I **dispose** of this rubbish?*
▸ **disposal** (*noun*): *the **disposal** of nuclear waste*

dispossess (say diss-puh-**zess**) *verb* (**dispossessing, dispossessed**)
to take away land or property from somebody: *Many families were **dispossessed** of their land.*
▸ **dispossession** (*noun*): *the **dispossession** of property*

dispute (say **diss**-pyoot or diss-**pyoot**) *noun* (*plural* **disputes**)
an argument or disagreement between people with different ideas: *There was a **dispute** about which driver caused the accident.*

disqualify (say diss-**kwol**-i-fy) *verb* (**disqualifying, disqualified**)
to officially forbid somebody from doing something or taking part in something, usually because they have broken a rule or law: *The athlete was **disqualified** for taking drugs.*
▸ **disqualification** (*noun*): *Failure to obey this rule will result in immediate **disqualification**.*

disregard (say diss-ri-**gaad**) *verb* (**disregarding, disregarded**)
to not pay attention to a person or thing or to ignore them deliberately
▸ **disregard** (*noun*): *The driver showed total **disregard** for the cyclists.*

disrepair (say diss-ri-**pair**) *noun* (*no plural*)
the state of being in bad condition and needing to be repaired: *The road had fallen into **disrepair** and could no longer be used.*

disreputable (say diss-**rep**-yuu-tuhb-l) *adjective*
1 known for being bad and dishonest and not to be trusted: *Even the most **disreputable** person has the right to a fair trial.* ➲ OPPOSITE **reputable**
2 looking untidy and dirty because it has been used a lot

disrespect (say diss-ri-**spekt**) *noun* (*no plural*)
a lack of respect for a person or thing that is shown in what you do or say: ***disrespect** for the law* ➲ OPPOSITE **respect**[1]
▸ **disrespectful** (*adjective*): *Your behaviour was **disrespectful** and you need to apologize.*

disrupt (say diss-**rupt**) *verb* (**disrupting, disrupted**)
to stop something happening or being done for a time
▸ **disruption** (*noun*): *The bad weather caused the **disruption** of telephone services.*
▸ **disruptive** (*adjective*): *Noisy and **disruptive** behaviour will not be tolerated.*

dissatisfied (say diss-**sat**-iss-fide) *adjective*
not pleased with something: *I am very **dissatisfied** with your work* ➲ OPPOSITE **satisfied**

dissect (say diss-**sekt** or **dy**-sekt) *verb* (**dissecting, dissected**)
to cut up a plant or a dead body of a person or animal in order to examine it
▸ **dissection** (*noun*): *the **dissection** of a sheep's heart*

dissent (say diss-**sent**) *noun* (*no plural*) (*formal*)
disagreement with an accepted opinion or official decision: *The **dissent** over the Cabinet's decision led to discord among the members.*
➲ OPPOSITE **assent**
▸ **dissent** (*verb*): *He **dissents** from the common view concerning AIDS.* ▸ **dissenting** (*adjective*): ***dissenting** opinions*

dissident (say **diss**-i-duhnt) *noun* (*plural* **dissidents**)
a person who strongly disagrees with and criticizes their government or an organization they belong to
▸ **dissident** (*adjective*): *The rebels are led by a **dissident** army chief.*

dissipate (say **diss**-i-payt) *verb* (**dissipating, dissipated**) (*formal*)
1 to disappear or to make something do this: *The fog began to **dissipate** as the sun rose.*
2 to waste money or energy: *He **dissipated** his father's fortune.*

dissolve (say di-**zolv**) *verb* (**dissolving, dissolved**)
(a solid) to become part of a liquid: *Sugar **dissolves** in water.* ➲ See **solution**

dissuade (say diss-**swayd**) *verb* (**dissuading, dissuaded**)
to make somebody decide not to do something: *I tried to **dissuade** her from spending the money, but she insisted.* ➲ OPPOSITE **persuade** ➲ SYNONYM **deter**

distance (say **diss**-tuhnss) *noun*
1 (*plural* **distances**) how far it is from one place to another place: *It's a short **distance** to the station.* ◇ *We usually measure **distance** in kilometres.*
2 (*no plural*) a place that is far from somebody or something: *I saw a light in the **distance**.*

distant (say **diss**-tuhnt) *adjective*
1 far away in space or time: ***distant** countries*
2 (used about a relative) not closely related to you: *a **distant** cousin*

distasteful (say diss-**tayst**-fuhl) *adjective*
unpleasant or causing offence: *The film is **distasteful** and upsetting.*

distend (say diss-**tend**) *verb* (**distending, distended**) (*science*)
to become or make bigger than normal because of pressure from inside

A B C D E F G H I J K L M N O P Q R S T U V W X Y Z

▶ **distended** (*adjective*): *malnourished children with **distended** bellies*

distil (say diss-**til**) *verb* (**distilling, distilled**) (*science*)
to make a liquid pure by heating it until it turns into a gas and then cooling the gas so that it becomes a liquid again
▶ **distillation** (*noun*): *You can use **distillation** to extract oil from plants.*

distinct (say diss-**tinkt**) *adjective*
1 clear and easy to hear, see or smell: *There is a **distinct** smell of burning in this room.*
2 clearly different: *isiXhosa and Sesotho are two **distinct** languages.*
▶ **distinctly** (*adverb*): *I **distinctly*** (= clearly and easily) *smelt burning.*

distinction (say diss-**tink**-shuhn) *noun* (*plural* **distinctions**)
1 a clear or important difference between people or things: *There is a **distinction** between the feeling of shame and that of embarrassment.*
2 very good in quality or in what somebody has achieved: *a musician of **distinction***
3 a special mark or grade that is given to a person, especially a student, for excellent work: *Naomi got a **distinction** in Maths.*

distinguish (say diss-**ting**-gwish) *verb* (**distinguishing, distinguished**)
to see or hear the difference between two things or people: *Some people can't **distinguish** between me and my twin sister.* ➲ SYNONYM **differentiate**

distinguished (say diss-**ting**-gwisht) *adjective*
famous or important: *a **distinguished** actor*

distort (say diss-**tawt**) *verb* (**distorting, distorted**)
1 to change the shape or sound of something so that it seems strange or is not clear: *Her face was **distorted** with grief.*
2 to give a false account or description of something: *A lie **distorts** the truth.*
▶ **distortion** (*noun*): *the **distortion** of sound*

distract (say diss-**trakt**) *verb* (**distracting, distracted**)
to take a person's attention away from what they are trying to do: *The noise **distracted** me from my homework.*
▶ **distraction** (*noun*)

distraught (say diss-**trawt**) *adjective*
very upset and worried: *The **distraught** parents feared for the safety of their child.*

distress (say diss-**tress**) *noun* (*no plural*)
1 a strong feeling of pain or sadness
2 being in danger and needing help: *a ship in **distress***
▶ **distress** (*verb*): *It **distressed** her to see her mother crying.*

distressing (say diss-**tress**-ing) *adjective*
making you feel sad or upset: *The news of her death was extremely **distressing**.*

distribute (say diss-**trib**-yoot) *verb* (**distributing, distributed**)
1 to give or send things to each person: *New books are **distributed** on the first day of school.*
2 to spread something over an area: *Stand on both feet so that your weight is evenly **distributed**.*
▶ **distribution** (*noun*): *a map to show the **distribution** of rainfall in Africa ◇ the **distribution** of newspapers*

district (say **diss**-trikt) *noun* (*plural* **districts**)
a part of a country or town: *Johannesburg's financial **district** ◇ magisterial **districts***

distrust (say diss-**trust**) *noun* (*no plural*)
a lack of trust or a suspicion that you cannot believe somebody or something ➲ See **mistrust**
▶ **distrust** (*verb*): *She **distrusts** him because he lied to her once before.*

disturb (say diss-**turb**) *verb* (**disturbing, disturbed**)
1 to stop somebody doing something, for example thinking, working or sleeping: *I'm sorry to **disturb** you, but you have a phone call. ◇ Do not **disturb*** (= a notice on a door).
2 to worry somebody: *We were **disturbed** by the news that Nyeleti was ill.*
▶ **disturbing** (*adjective*): *The news was very **disturbing**.*

disturbance (say di-**sturb**-uhnss) *noun* (*plural* **disturbances**)
1 a thing that stops you doing something, for example thinking, working or sleeping
2 when a group of people fight or make a lot of noise and trouble: *The music from the club caused a **disturbance** in the area.*

disuse (say diss-**yooss**) *noun* (*no plural*) (*formal*)
the state of not being used or followed any more: *The water pipes are rusted after years of **disuse**. ◇ Some of the old customs have fallen into **disuse**.*

disused (say diss-**yoozd**) *adjective*
not used any more: *a **disused** railway line*

ditch[1] (say **dich**) *noun* (*plural* **ditches**)
a long narrow **channel**[1] 3 at the side of a road or field that carries away water

ditch[2] (say **dich**) *verb* (**ditching, ditched**) (*informal*)
to get rid of or leave a person or thing: *She **ditched** her boyfriend.*

ditto (say **dit**-oh) *noun* (*plural* **dittoes**) (abbr. do. or ″)
a word used especially in a list to show that the word or figure written directly above it is the same and is being repeated
▸ **ditto** (*adverb*): *'I'm starving.' '**Ditto**.'* (= me too)

diurnal (say dy-**ur**-nuhl) *adjective*
1 active at day or relating to the day: *Many flowers are **diurnal**. They open during the day and they close at night.* ➲ OPPOSITE **nocturnal**
2 every day: *the **diurnal** rotation of the Earth*

Divali (say di-**waa**-li) = **Deepavali**

dive (*rhymes with* **drive**) *verb* (**diving, dived**)
1 to jump into water with your arms and head first: *She **dived** into the pool.*
2 to swim underwater wearing breathing equipment: *He wanted to go **diving** in Durban.*
3 to go to a deeper level underwater: *The birds were **diving** for fish.*
▸ **diver** (*noun*): *Mcebisi works as a police **diver**.*
▸ **diving** (*noun*): *I love **diving**.*
🛈 ORIGIN: from Old English *dufan* meaning 'dive, sink' and *dyfan* meaning 'put under water'

diverse (say dy-**vurss**) *adjective*
1 very different from each other: *South Africa's **diverse** cultures*
2 including a lot of different things: *My interests are very **diverse**.*

diversify (say dy-**vur**-si-fy) *verb* (**diversifying, diversified**)
to increase or develop the number or types of something: *The company is keen to **diversify** into tourism.*
▸ **diversification** (*noun*): ***diversification** of the economy*

diversion (say dy-**vurzh**-uhn) *noun* (*plural* **diversions**)
1 the act of changing the direction of something or what it is used for, especially to solve or avoid a problem: *the **diversion** of the river to prevent flooding* ◇ *the **diversion** of funds to areas where the need is greatest*
2 something that takes your attention away from something: *Some prisoners created a **diversion** while others escaped.*
3 a **detour**

diversity (say dy-**vur**-sit-ee) *noun* (*no plural*)
the wide variety of something: *cultural and ethnic **diversity***

divert (say dy-**vurt**) *verb* (**diverting, diverted**)
to make something go a different way: *Our flight was **diverted** to another airport because of the bad weather.*

divide (say di-**vide**) *verb* (**dividing, divided**)
1 to share or cut something into smaller parts: *The teacher **divided** the class into groups of three.* ◇ *The book is **divided** into ten chapters.*
2 to go into parts: *When the road **divides**, go left.*
3 (*maths*) to find out how many times one number goes into a bigger number: *36 **divided** by 4 is 9.*

dividend (say **div**-i-dend) *noun* (*plural* **dividends**)
1 a sum of money that is divided among a number of people, especially a part of a company's profits that is paid to the people who own shares in it
2 (*maths*) a number that is divided by another number into equal parts: *In the sum 15 ÷ 3 = 5, 15 is the **dividend**.* ➲ See **divisor**

divine (say di-**vine**) *adjective*
1 of, like or from God or a god: *a **divine** message*
2 (*informal*) wonderful or beautiful: *She has the most **divine** smile.*

diving board (say **dive**-ing bawd) *noun* (*plural* **diving boards**)
a board at the side of a swimming pool that you use to jump or dive into the water

division (say di-**vizh**-uhn) *noun*
1 (*no plural*) sharing or cutting something into parts: *the **division** of Africa among European powers*
2 (*no plural*) (*maths*) finding out how many times one number goes into a bigger number
3 (*plural* **divisions**) one of the parts of a big company: *She works in the sales **division**.*

divisor (say di-**vize**-uh) *noun* (*plural* **divisors**) (*maths*)
a number by which another number is divided: *In the sum 15 ÷ 3 = 5, 3 is the **divisor** of 15.*
➲ See **dividend 2**

divorce (say di-**vawss**) *noun* (*plural* **divorces**)
the end of a marriage by law: *They are getting a **divorce**.*
▸ **divorce** (*verb*): *He **divorced** his wife.*
▸ **divorced** (*adjective*): *I'm not married – I'm **divorced**.*

USAGE It is common to say **get divorced**: *They got **divorced** last year.*

divulge (say di-**vulj**) *verb* (**divulging, divulged**) (*formal*)
to tell people about something that is secret: *Never **divulge** your computer password to anyone.* ➲ SYNONYM **disclose**

Diwali (say di-**waa**-li) = **Deepavali**

A B C **D** E F G H I J K L M N O P Q R S T U V W X Y Z

DIY (say dee-y-**wy**) *noun* (*no plural*)
making, painting or repairing things in your house yourself: *a **DIY** store* (= where you can buy materials for DIY) ℹ **DIY** is short for 'do-it-yourself'.

dizzy (say **diz**-ee) *adjective* (**dizzier, dizziest**)
feeling that everything is turning round and round and that you are going to fall: *The room was very hot and I started to feel **dizzy**.*
➲ SYNONYM **giddy**

DJ (say dee-**jay**) *noun* (*plural* **DJs**) abbreviation
disc jockey

DNA (say dee-en-**ay**) *noun* (*no plural*) (*science*)
a substance in the centre of a cell (called the **nucleus**) that includes the information that controls what a person, animal or plant will be like ℹ **DNA** is short for 'deoxyribonucleic acid'.

do[1] (say **doo**) *verb* (**doing, did, has done**)
1 a word that you use with another verb to make a question: ***Do** you want an apple?*
2 a word that you use with another verb when you are saying 'not': *I like football but I **don't*** (= do not) *like tennis.*
3 a word that you use in place of saying something again: *She **doesn't** speak English, but I **do*** (= I speak English). ◇ *'I like football.' 'So **do** I.'* ◇ *'I **don't** speak Chinese.' 'Neither **do** I.'*
4 a word that you use before another verb to make it stronger: *You **do** look nice!*

do[2] (say **doo**) *verb* (**doing, did, has done**)
1 to carry out an action: *What are you **doing**?* ◇ *He **did** the cooking.* ◇ *What **did** you **do** with my key?* (= where did you put it?)
2 to have a job or study something: *'What **do** you **do**?' 'I'm a doctor.'* ◇ *She's **doing** matric this year.*
3 to finish something or to find the answer: *I have **done** my homework.* ◇ *I can't **do** this sum – it's too difficult.*
be or **have to do with a person or thing** to be connected with a person or thing: *I think his job has something to **do** with computers.*
do something up to fasten something: ***Do** up the buttons on your shirt.* ➲ OPPOSITE **undo**

USAGE We use the verb **do** for many of the jobs we **do** at home. We **do the shopping**, **do the cleaning**, **do the washing** and **do the ironing**. We use **make** for beds: ***Make** your bed after breakfast.*

docile (say **doh**-sile) *adjective*
describing a person or animal that obeys you and is easy to control: *The horses stood still and **docile**.*

dock (say **dok**) *noun* (*plural* **docks**)
a place by the sea or a river where ships go so that people can move things on and off them or repair them
▸ **dock** (*verb*): *The ship had **docked*** (= stopped at the dock) *at Durban.*

doctor (say **dok**-tuh) *noun* (*plural* **doctors**) (abbr. Dr)
1 a person whose job is to make sick people well again: *The **doctor** sees patients every morning.*
2 a person who has the highest degree from a university

USAGE When we talk about visiting the doctor, we say **go to the doctor**: *If you're feeling ill, you should go to the **doctor**.*

doctrine (say **dok**-trin) *noun* (*plural* **doctrines**)
a set of beliefs and rules about how we should live that is taught by a religious or other group: *the **doctrine** of salvation*
▸ **doctrinal** (*adjective*): ***doctrinal** differences among Christians*

document (say **dok**-yuu-muhnt) *noun* (*plural* **documents**)
1 an official paper with important information on it: *a legal **document***
2 (*computing*) a computer file that contains writing

documentary (say dok-yuu-**men**-tree) *noun* (*plural* **documentaries**)
a film about true things: *I watched an interesting **documentary** about Japan on TV last night.*

dodecagon (say doh-**dek**-uh-guhn) *noun* (*plural* **dodecagons**) (*maths*)
a flat closed shape with twelve straight sides

dodecahedron (say doh-dek-uh-**hee**-druhn) *noun* (*plural* **dodecahedra** or **dodecahedrons**) (*maths*)
a solid shape with twelve flat surfaces all the same size. In a regular **dodecahedron** each surface is a **pentagon**.

dodge (say **doj**) *verb* (**dodging, dodged**)
to move quickly to avoid a person or thing: *He ran across the busy road, **dodging** the cars.*

doe (*rhymes with* **go**) *noun* (*plural* **does**)
the adult female of certain animals

WORD BUILDING You use **doe** for the females of deer, hares, kangaroos, rabbits and rats. The male of these animals is called a **buck**.

does (say **duz**) form of **do**[2]

doesn't (say **duz**-uhnt) short for **does not**

A B C D E F G H I J K L M N O P Q R S T U V W X Y Z

dog *noun* (*plural* **dogs**)
an animal that many people keep as a pet or train to do work, for example on farms or to hunt or to guard buildings

dogged (say **dog**-uhd) *adjective*
determined to continue doing something even when it is difficult
▸ **doggedly** (*adverb*): *She was **doggedly** determined to be at the line first.*

dogma (say **dog**-muh) *noun* (*plural* **dogmas**)
a set of beliefs or a rule that a group of people who are in a position of power declare is true and must be accepted

dogmatic (say dog-**mat**-ik) *adjective*
being certain that your ideas or beliefs are right and not considering other opinions
▸ **dogmatically** (*adverb*): *We cannot **dogmatically** impose our views on the younger generation.*

dole (*rhymes with* **hole**) *verb* (**doling, doled**)
dole something out to give things such as food or money in small amounts to a number of people

doll (say **dol**) *noun* (*plural* **dolls**)
a toy that looks like a very small person or a baby

dollar (say **dol**-uh) *noun* (*plural* **dollars**) (symbol $)
a unit of money that people use in the USA, Canada, Australia and some other countries. There are 100 cents in a **dollar**: *You will be paid in American **dollars**.*

SPELLING Remember! You spell **dollar** with **-ar** at the end.

dolphin (say **dol**-fin) *noun* (*plural* **dolphins**)
a sea mammal that looks like a big fish. It has a beak-like mouth and a curved **dorsal** fin and is known for its intelligence.

dome (*rhymes with* **home**) *noun* (*plural* **domes**)
the round roof of a building

dome

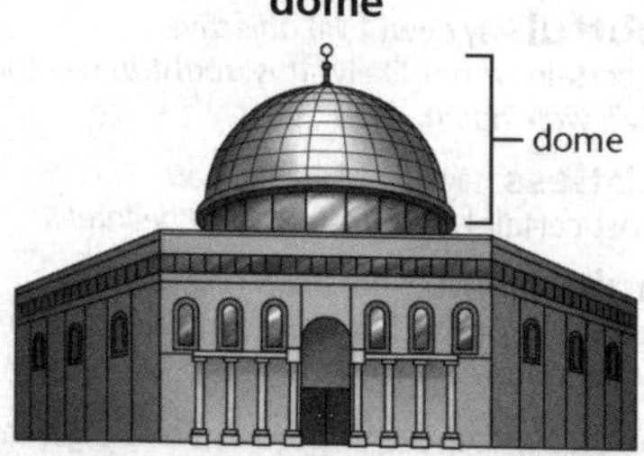

domestic (say duh-**mess**-tik) *adjective*
1 only inside one country, not international: *a **domestic** flight* (= to a place in the same country) **2** connected with the home or family: *Cooking and cleaning are **domestic** jobs.* ◇ *a **domestic** worker* ◇ *Many cats and dogs are **domestic** animals* (= animals that live in your home with you).

dominate (say **dom**-i-nayt) *verb* (**dominating, dominated**)
to control somebody or something because you are stronger or more important: *Our first team **dominated** in the second half of the game.*

dominee (say **door**-muh-nee) *noun* (*plural* **dominees**) (*S. African*)
a minister in some **Afrikaans** Christian churches
ⓘ ORIGIN: from Dutch *dominee* meaning 'priest', from Latin *domine* meaning 'master'

domino (say **dom**-i-noh) *noun* (*plural* **dominoes**)
one of a set of small flat pieces of wood or plastic, used to play a game (called **dominoes**)

donate (say doh-**nayt**) *verb* (**donating, donated**)
to give something, especially money, to people who need it: *They **donated** R10 000 to the hospital.*
▸ **donation** (*noun*): *He made a **donation** to the hospital.*

done (say **dun**) form of **do**²

donga (say **dong**-guh) *noun* (*plural* **dongas**) (*S. African*)
a deep narrow hole in the ground with steep sides where the water has washed away the soil
ⓘ ORIGIN: 19th century, from isiXhosa and isiZulu *udonga*

donkey (say **dong**-kee) *noun* (*plural* **donkeys**)
an animal like a small horse with long ears

donor (say **doh**-nuh) *noun* (*plural* **donors**)
somebody who gives something to help a person or an organization

don't (say **dohnt**) short for **do not**

doodle (say **dood**-l) *verb* (**doodling, doodled**)
to make small drawings, especially when you are bored or thinking about something else

doom (*rhymes with* **loom**) *noun* (*no plural*)
death or a terrible event in the future that you cannot avoid

door (say **daw**) *noun* (*plural* **doors**)
a piece of wood, glass or metal that you use to open and close the way in to a building, room, cupboard or car: *Can you close the **door**, please?* ◇ *She knocked on the **door**. 'Come in,' Peter said.* ◇ *There is somebody at the **door**.*
next door in the next house, room or building:

A B C D E F G H I J K L M N O P Q R S T U V W X Y Z

*Swazi lives next **door** to us.*
out of doors outside and not in a building: *Farmers spend a lot of time out of **doors**.*

doorbell (say **daw**-bel) *noun* (*plural* **doorbells**)
a bell outside a house that you ring to tell people inside that you are there

doorknob (say **daw**-nob) *noun* (*plural* **doorknobs**)
a round object on a door that you use to open and close it

doormat (say **daw**-mat) *noun* (*plural* **doormats**)
a piece of material on the floor in front of a door for cleaning your shoes on

doorway (say **daw**-way) *noun* (*plural* **doorways**)
an opening for going into a building or room: *He was standing in the **doorway**.*

dope (*rhymes with* **hope**) *noun* (*informal*)
1 (*no plural*) a drug, especially one that is taken or given illegally: *They were caught smoking **dope**.* ◇ *The winning horse failed a **dope** test.*
2 (*plural* **dopes**) a stupid person
▸ **dope** (*verb*): *There were rumours that the athlete was **doped**.*

dormant (say **daw**-muhnt) *adjective*
not active or growing for some time: *The seeds can lie **dormant** for ten years.* ◇ *a **dormant** volcano*

dormitory (say **daw**-muh-tree) *noun* (*plural* **dormitories**)
a big bedroom for a lot of people, usually in a school

dorp (say **dawp**) *noun* (*plural* **dorps**) (*S. African*)
a small town or village in the country
🛈 **ORIGIN:** 19th century, from Dutch *dorp* meaning 'village'

dorsal (say **daw**-suhl) *adjective* (*biology*)
on or relating to the back of an animal: *Sharks usually have large **dorsal** fins.* ➲ See illustration at **fish**[1] ➲ See **ventral**

dose (say **dohss**) *noun* (*plural* **doses**)
an amount of medicine that you take at one time: *Take a **dose** of medicine before you go.*

dot *noun* (*plural* **dots**)
a small round mark: *The letter 'i' has a **dot** over it.*
on the dot at exactly the right time: *Please be here at nine o'clock on the **dot**.*

> **SPEAKING** We use **dot** when we say a person's email address. For the address **taliep@davids.co.za** we say: '*Taliep at davids **dot** co **dot** za*'.

dote (*rhymes with* **goat**) *verb* (**doting, doted**)
to have a lot of love for somebody, especially so much that you cannot see their faults: *She **dotes** on her only son and will do anything for him.*
▸ **doting** (*adjective*): *They are loving and **doting** parents.*

double[1] (say **dub**-l) *verb* (**doubling, doubled**)
to become, or make something become, twice as much or as many: *The price of petrol has almost **doubled** in two years.*

double[2] (say **dub**-l) *adjective*
1 two times as much or as many: *a **double** portion of chips*
2 with two parts that are the same: ***double** doors* ◇ *Does 'necessary' have a **double** 's'?* ◇ *My phone number is **double** four nine five one* (= 44951).
3 made for two people or things: *a **double** bed* ◇ *a **double** room* ➲ See **single**[1]

double bass *noun* (*plural* **double basses**)
the largest musical instrument with strings, that you usually play standing up

double-click (say **dub**-l-klik) *verb* (**double-clicking, double-clicked**)
to quickly press a button twice on a computer control (called a **mouse**): *To start the program, just **double-click** on the icon.*

double-decker (say **dub**-l-dek-uh) *noun* (*plural* **double-deckers**)
a bus with two levels

doubt[1] (say **dowt**) *noun* (*plural* **doubts**)
a feeling that you are not sure about something: *She says the story is true but I have my **doubts** about it.* ◇ *If you are in **doubt**, ask your teacher.*

> **PRONUNCIATION** Don't pronounce the **b** in **doubt**.

doubt[2] (say **dowt**) *verb* (**doubting, doubted**)
to not feel sure about something or to think that something is probably not true or probably will not happen: *I **doubt** if he will come.*

doubtful (say **dowt**-fuhl) *adjective*
not certain or not likely: *It is **doubtful** whether he will walk again.*

doubtless (say **dowt**-luhss) *adverb*
almost certainly: ***Doubtless** she'll be late!*

dough (*rhymes with* **go**) *noun* (*no plural*)
flour, water and other things mixed together, for making bread

> **PRONUNCIATION** Don't pronounce the **gh** in **dough**.

doughnut (say **doh**-nut) *noun* (*plural* **doughnuts**)
a small round cake that is cooked in oil

dour (say **dow**-uh) *adjective* (*formal*)
serious and unfriendly: *He's such a **dour** man – he never makes a joke.*

dove (say **duv**) *noun* (*plural* **doves**)
a bird of the **pigeon** family that is often used as a sign of peace

dovetail (say **duv**-tayl) *verb* (**dovetailing, dovetailed**)
to fit together easily and with everything in the right place: *Our goals **dovetail** neatly with theirs.*

dowel (say **dow**-uhl) *noun* (*plural* **dowels**)
a thin piece of wood or metal that you use for joining together two bigger pieces of wood or metal. You make holes in the bigger pieces and push each end of the **dowel** into the holes.

down[1] (*rhymes with* **town**) *adverb, preposition*
1 in or to a lower place, but not up: *The sun goes **down** in the evening.* ◇ *We ran **down** the hill.* ◇ *Put that box **down** on the floor.*
2 from standing to sitting or lying: *Sit **down**.*
3 at or to a lower level: *Turn that music **down**!* (= so that it is not so loud) ➲ OPPOSITE **up** 4
4 along: *He lives just **down** the street.* ◇ *Go **down** the road till you reach the traffic lights.*
5 on paper or on a list: *Write these words **down**.*

down[2] (*rhymes with* **town**) *adjective*
1 lower than before: *Unemployment figures are **down** on last month.*
2 sad and unhappy: *You're looking a bit **down** today.*
3 not working: *The computer system is **down** and cannot be used.*

down[3] (*rhymes with* **town**) *noun* (*no plural*)
very soft feathers: *a duvet* (= a thick warm cover for a bed) *filled with duck **down***

downcast (say **down**-kaast) *adjective*
1 feeling very sad and thinking that bad things will happen: *Rainy weather always makes her **downcast**.*
2 looking down at the ground: ***downcast** eyes*

downfall (say **down**-fawl) *noun* (*no plural*)
something that happens that causes somebody to lose their powerful and successful position: *the **downfall** of apartheid* ◇ *Greed was her **downfall**.*

downhill (say down-**hil**) *adverb*
down, towards the bottom of a hill: *My bicycle can go fast **downhill**.* ➲ OPPOSITE **uphill**

download (say **down**-lohd) *verb* (**downloading, downloaded**) (*computing*)
to make a copy on your own computer of a computer program or information from the Internet: *I **downloaded** some music files.*

downpour (say **down**-paw) *noun* (*plural* **downpours**)
a sudden heavy fall of rain

downstairs (say down-**stairz**) *adverb*
to or on a lower floor of a building: *I went **downstairs** to make breakfast.* ➲ OPPOSITE **upstairs**
▸ **downstairs** (*adjective*): *She lives in the **downstairs** flat.*

downwards (say **down**-wuhdz) *adverb* (also **downward**)
towards the ground or towards a lower level: *She was lying face **downwards** on the grass.* ➲ OPPOSITE **upwards**

dowry (say **dow**-ree) *noun* (*plural* **dowries**)
money or property that, in some countries, a woman's family gives to the man she marries ➲ See **lobola**

doze (*rhymes with* **nose**) *verb* (**dozing, dozed**)
to sleep lightly for a short time: *My grandfather was **dozing** in his armchair.* ◇ *I **dozed** off in front of the television.*
▸ **doze** (*noun*): *She had a **doze** after lunch.*

dozen (say **duz**-uhn) *noun* (*plural* **dozen**)
twelve: *a **dozen** red roses* ◇ *two **dozen** boxes* ◇ *half a **dozen** eggs*
dozens of (*informal*) a lot of: *They've invited **dozens** of people to the party.*

Dr *abbreviation* (*plural* **Drs**) **doctor**

drab *adjective* (**drabber, drabbest**)
not interesting or attractive, without any variety and therefore very boring: *a **drab** grey office building* ◇ *a **drab** voice* ➲ SYNONYM **dreary**

draft (say **draaft**) *noun* (*plural* **drafts**)
1 a piece of writing that is not exactly correct and that will be improved with changes: *Write a rough **draft** of your essay and then edit it.*
2 a written order to a bank for the payment of money
▸ **draft** (*verb*): *I'll **draft** a letter and show it to you before I type it.*

drag[1] *verb* (**dragging, dragged**)
1 to pull something along the ground slowly, often because it is heavy: *He couldn't lift the sack, so he **dragged** it outside.*
2 (a class, a workday) to seem to go slowly

A B C D E F G H I J K L M N O P Q R S T U V W X Y Z

because it is not interesting: *Time **drags** when you're waiting for a bus.*

drag² (say **drag**) *noun*
1 (*no plural*) (*informal*) a person or thing that is boring or annoying
2 (*no plural*) women's clothes worn by a man: *men in **drag***
3 (*plural* **drags**) an act of sucking in air through a cigarette
4 (*no plural*) (*science*) the force of the air that acts against the movement of an aircraft or other vehicle

dragon (say **drag**-uhn) *noun* (*plural* **dragons**)
a big, dangerous animal with fire in its mouth, that you only find in stories

dragonfly (say **drag**-uhn-fly) *noun* (*plural* **dragonflies**)
an insect that often flies near water and that has two pairs of large wings and a long, thin body

drain¹ (say **drayn**) *verb* (**draining, drained**)
1 to let liquid flow away from something, so that it becomes dry: ***Drain** and rinse the pasta.*
2 to become dry because liquid is flowing away: *Leave the dishes to **drain**.*
3 to flow away: *The water **drained** away slowly.*
▸ **drainage** (*noun*)

drain² (say **drayn**) *noun* (*plural* **drains**)
a pipe that carries away dirty water from a building: *The **drain** is blocked.*

drainpipe (say **drayn**-pipe) *noun* (*plural* **drainpipes**)
a pipe that takes water from the roof of a building to a **drain²** when it rains

drake (say **drayk**) *noun* (*plural* **drakes**)
a male duck

drama (say **draa**-muh) *noun*
1 (*plural* **dramas**) a story that you watch in the theatre or on television, or listen to on the radio: *a TV **drama***
2 (*no plural*) the study of plays and acting: *She went to **drama** school.*
3 (*plural* **dramas**) an exciting thing that happens: *There was a big **drama** at school when one of the teachers fell in the swimming pool!*

dramatic (say druh-**mat**-ik) *adjective*
1 sudden, great or exciting: *The finish of the race was very **dramatic**.*
2 of plays or the theatre: *a **dramatic** society*
▸ **dramatically** (*adverb*): *Prices went up **dramatically**.*

dramatist (say **dram**-uh-tist) *noun* (*plural* **dramatists**)
a person who writes plays

drank (say **drangk**) form of **drink¹**

drape (say **drayp**) *verb* (**draping, draped**)
1 to arrange a piece of material or clothing loosely on or round something: *They **draped** a blanket over the parrot's cage.*
2 to cover with or wrap somebody or something in cloth: *The furniture was **draped** in sheets.*

drapery (say **drayp**-uh-ree) *noun* (*plural* **draperies**)
cloth, curtains or clothing hanging in loose folds

drastic (say **drass**-tik) *adjective*
extreme and having a very strong effect or great influence on a lot of other things
▸ **drastically** (*adverb*): *Shops are selling their goods at **drastically** reduced prices.*

draught (say **draaft**) *noun* (*plural* **draughts**)
cold air that comes into a room: *Can you shut the window? I can feel a **draught**.*
▸ **draughty** (*adjective*): *a **draughty** old house*

draughts (say **draaftss**) *plural noun*
a game that two people play with round flat pieces on a board that has black and white squares on it: *a game of **draughts***

draughtsman (say **draaftss**-muhn) *noun* (*plural* **draughtsmen**)
a person whose job is to do technical drawings: *He worked as a **draughtsman** for an engineering firm.*

draw¹ *verb* (**drawing, drew, has drawn**)
1 to make a picture with a pen or a pencil: *She **drew** a picture of a horse. ◇ My sister **draws** well.*
2 to pull or take something from a place: *He **drew** a knife from his pocket.*
3 to pull something to make it move: *The carriage was **drawn** by two horses.*
4 to open or close curtains: *I switched on the light and **drew** the curtains.*
5 to move or come: *The train **drew** into the station. ◇ A taxi **drew** up outside the house.*
6 to end a game with the same number of points for both players or teams: *South Africa and Australia **drew** in the rugby match.*
draw something out to take money out of a bank: *I **drew** out R150 before I went shopping.*
draw something up to write something: *They **drew** up a list of people who they wanted to invite.*

draw² *noun* (*plural* **draws**)
the result of a game when both players or teams have the same number of points: *The football match ended in a 1–1 **draw**.*

drawback (say **draw**-bak) *noun* (*plural* **drawbacks**)
a disadvantage or problem that makes something a less attractive idea

drawer (say **draw**(-uh)) *noun* (*plural* **drawers**)
a thing like a box that you can pull out from a cupboard or a desk: *There's some paper in the top **drawer** of my desk.*

drawing (say **draw**-ing) *noun*
1 (*plural* **drawings**) a picture made with a pen or a pencil, but not paint: *He did a **drawing** of the old farmhouse.*
2 (*no plural*) the art or skill of making pictures or plans using a pen or pencil: *She is very good at **drawing**.*

drawing pin *noun* (*plural* **drawing pins**)
a short pin with a flat round top, that you use for fastening paper to a wall or a board: *I put the poster up with **drawing pins**.*

drawl *verb* (**drawling, drawled**)
to speak in a slow, lazy-sounding way, making the vowel sounds very long
▸ **drawl** (*noun*): *to speak with a **drawl***

drawn (*rhymes with* **born**) form of **draw**[1]

DRC (say dee-aar-**see**) *abbreviation*
1 Democratic Republic of the Congo
2 Dutch Reformed Church

dread (say **dred**) *verb* (**dreading, dreaded**)
to be very afraid of something that is going to happen: *I'm **dreading** the exams.*

dreadful (say **dred**-fuhl) *adjective*
very bad: *I had a **dreadful** journey – my train was two hours late!*

dream[1] (say **dreem**) *noun* (*plural* **dreams**)
1 pictures or events which happen in your mind when you are asleep: *I had a **dream** about school last night.*
2 something nice that you hope for: *His **dream** was to give up his job and live in the country.*
➲ SYNONYM **fantasy**

WORD BUILDING A bad or frightening **dream** that you have when you are asleep is called a **nightmare**.

dream[2] (say **dreem**) *verb* (**dreaming, dreamt** or **dreamed, has dreamt** or **has dreamed**)
1 to have a picture or idea in your mind when you are asleep: *I **dreamt** about you last night.* ◇ *I **dreamt** that I was flying.*
2 to hope for something nice in the future: *She **dreams** of becoming a famous actress.*

dreary (say **dreer**-ree) *adjective* (**drearier, dreariest**)
not at all interesting or attractive: *His voice is so **dreary** that it sends me to sleep.* ➲ SYNONYM **drab**

dredge (say **drej**) *verb* (**dredging, dredged**)
to remove something such as mud or sand from the bottom of a river, a canal or the sea, using a special machine
▸ **dredger** (*noun*): *They are using **dredgers** to make the harbour wider and deeper.*

dregs (say **dregz**) *plural noun*
1 the last drops and solid bits that are left at the bottom of a container of liquid: *coffee **dregs***
2 the worst and most useless part of something: *These people were regarded as the **dregs** of society.*

drench *verb* (**drenching, drenched**)
1 to make a person or thing completely wet
2 to cover with large amounts of something: *The room was **drenched** with sunlight.*
▸ **drenched** (*adjective*): *rain-**drenched** spectators*

dress[1] *noun*
1 (*plural* **dresses**) a piece of clothing with a top part and a skirt, that a woman or girl wears
2 (*no plural*) clothes: *The group of dancers wore Bulgarian national **dress**.*

dress[2] (say **dress**) *verb* (**dressing, dressed**)
1 to put clothes on yourself or another person: *I got **dressed**.* ◇ *She **dressed** quickly and went out.* ◇ *He **dressed** the baby.* ➲ OPPOSITE **undress**
2 to wear a particular style, type or colour of clothes: *She **dresses** like a film star.* ◇ *He was **dressed** in black.*

dress up
1 to put on your best clothes: *They **dressed** up to go to the theatre.*
2 to put on special clothes for fun, so that you look like another person or a thing: *The children **dressed** up as ghosts.*

dressing (say **dress**-ing) *noun* (*plural* **dressings**)
1 a covering for part of your body that is hurt: *You should put a **dressing** on that cut.*
2 a sauce for food, especially for salads

dressing gown *noun* (*plural* **dressing gowns**)
a piece of clothing like a loose coat with a belt, which you wear before or after a bath or before you get dressed in the morning: *She got up and put on her **dressing gown**.*

drew (say **droo**) form of **draw**[1]

dribble (say **drib**-l) *verb* (**dribbling, dribbled**)
1 to fall slowly in small drops or in a thin flow, or to make a liquid move in this way: *The paint **dribbled** down the side of the pot.* ➲ SYNONYM **trickle**

2 to allow liquid to run from the mouth: *Babies often **dribble**.*
3 to take a ball forward with short kicks or hits: *He **dribbled** past four opponents and scored a goal.*
▶ **dribble** (*noun*)

dried (say **dride**) form of **dry**[2]

drier[1] (say **dry**-uh) form of **dry**[1]

drier[2] (say **dry**-uh) *noun* (*plural* **driers**)
a machine that you use for drying something: *a **hairdrier***

dries (say **drize**) form of **dry**[2]

driest (say **dry**-uhst) form of **dry**[1]

drift[1] *verb* (**drifting, drifted**)
1 to move slowly in the air or on water: *The empty boat **drifted** out to sea.* ◇ *The balloon **drifted** away.*
2 (used about a person) to move somewhere gradually or without any particular purpose: *People **drifted** into the cafeteria in small groups.*

drift[2] *noun* (*plural* **drifts**)
1 (*no plural*) a continuous slow movement: *continental **drift***
2 (*plural* **drifts**) (*S. African*) a shallow place in a river where people or vehicles can go across
3 (*no plural*) the general meaning of something: *I don't understand all the details of the discussion but I get the **drift**.*
4 (*plural* **drifts**) a pile of snow or sand created by wind or water: *The car got stuck in a sand **drift**.*

drill (say **dril**) *noun* (*plural* **drills**)
a tool that you use for making holes: *an electric **drill*** ◇ *a dentist's **drill***
▶ **drill** (*verb*): ***Drill** two holes in the wall.*

drink[1] (say **dringk**) *verb* (**drinking, drank, has drunk**)
1 to take in liquid, for example water, milk or coffee, through your mouth: *What do you want to **drink**?* ◇ *She was **drinking** a cup of tea.*
2 to drink alcohol: *'Would you like some wine?' 'No, thank you. I don't **drink**.'*

drink[2] (say **dringk**) *noun*
1 (*plural* **drinks**) liquid, for example water, milk or coffee, that you take in through your mouth: *Would you like a **drink**?* ◇ *Can I have a **drink** of water?*
2 (*no plural*) drink with alcohol in it, for example beer or wine: *There was lots of food and **drink** at the party.*

drip *verb* (**dripping, dripped**)
1 to fall slowly in small drops: *Water was **dripping** through the roof.*
2 to produce small drops of liquid: *The tap is **dripping**.*

drive[1] *verb* (**driving, drove, has driven**)
1 to control a car or bus and make it go where you want to go: *Can you **drive**?* ◇ *She usually **drives** to work.*
2 to take somebody to a place in a car: *My parents **drove** me to the airport.*
▶ **driver** (*noun*): *She is a good **driver**.* ◇ *a taxi **driver***

drive[2] *noun* (*plural* **drives**)
1 a journey in a car: *It's a long **drive** from Johannesburg to Durban.* ◇ *We went for a **drive**.*
2 (*computing*) the part of a computer that reads and stores information: *I saved my work on the C: **drive**.*
3 a wide hard path or private road that goes from the street to one house: *You can park your car in the **drive**.*

driven (say **driv**-uhn) form of **drive**[1]

driving (say **drive**-ing) *noun* (*no plural*)
controlling a car or a bus: ***Driving** in the rain can be dangerous.*

drizzle (say **driz**-l) *verb* (**drizzling, drizzled**)
1 to rain lightly
2 to put a small amount of liquid over food in a thin flow: *Melt the chocolate and **drizzle** it over the strawberries.*
▶ **drizzle** (*noun*): *The rain turned into a mild **drizzle**.*

drone[1] (say **drohn**) *verb* (**droning, droned**)
to make a continuous low sound: *A plane **drones** overhead.*
drone on to talk for a long time in a boring way: *We had to listen to the chairman **drone** on for an hour.*

drone[2] (say **drohn**) *noun* (*plural* **drones**)
1 a low continuous sound: *the **drone** of traffic*
2 a male bee: ***Drones** do not work but can fertilize a queen bee.*

droop (*rhymes with* **group**) *verb* (**drooping, drooped**)
to bend or hang down: *Flowers **droop** if you don't put them in water.*

drop[1] *verb* (**dropping, dropped**)
1 to let something fall: *I **dropped** my watch and it broke.*
2 to fall: *The glass **dropped** from her hands.*
3 to become lower or less: *The temperature has **dropped**.*
4 (also **drop somebody off**) to stop your car and let somebody get out: *Could you **drop** me at the station?*

5 to stop doing something: *I'm going to **drop** art* (= stop studying it) *at school.* ◇ *I **dropped** out of the team.*
drop in to visit somebody who does not know that you are coming: *We were in the area so we thought we'd **drop** in.*
drop off to fall asleep: *She **dropped** off in front of the TV.*

drop² *noun*
1 (*plural* **drops**) a very small amount of liquid: ***drops** of rain* ◇ *a **drop** of blood*
2 (*no plural*) a fall in the amount or level of something: *a **drop** in temperature* ◇ *a **drop** in prices*

droplet (say **drop**-lit) *noun* (*plural* **droplets**)
a very small amount of a liquid that forms a round shape: *small **droplets** of blood*

droppings (say **drop**-ingz) *plural noun*
the waste material from the bodies of animals: *bird **droppings***

drought (say **drowt**) *noun* (*plural* **droughts**)
a long time when there is not enough rain: *Thousands of people died in the **drought**.*
ORIGIN: from Old English *drugath* meaning 'dryness'

drove (*rhymes with* **stove**) form of **drive¹**

drown *verb* (**drowning, drowned**)
to die under water because you cannot breathe or to make somebody die in this way: *The boy fell in the river and **drowned**.* ◇ *Twenty people were **drowned** in the floods.*

drowsy (say **drow**-zee) *adjective* (**drowsier, drowsiest**)
feeling tired and wanting to sleep: *The heat made him very **drowsy**.*

drug *noun* (*plural* **drugs**)
1 an illegal chemical substance that people take because it makes them feel happy or excited: *He doesn't take **drugs**.* ◇ *She is on **drugs*** (= regularly using illegal drugs). ◇ *a dangerous **drug***
2 a chemical substance used as a medicine, that you take when you are ill to make you better: ***drug** companies* ◇ *Some **drugs** you can only get with a prescription from a doctor.*

drug addict *noun* (*plural* **drug addicts**)
a person who is unable to stop taking harmful drugs

drum *noun* (*plural* **drums**)
1 a musical instrument that you hit with special sticks (called **drumsticks**) or with your hands: *He plays the **drums** in a band.*
2 a big round container for oil: *an oil **drum***

drummer (say **drum**-uh) *noun* (*plural* **drummers**)
a person who plays a drum

drunk¹ (say **drungk**) form of **drink¹**

drunk² (say **drungk**) *adjective*
having drunk so much alcohol that you cannot think or speak clearly: *He gets **drunk** every Friday night.*

drunk³ (say **drungk**) *noun* (*plural* **drunks**)
a person who has drunk too much alcohol or somebody who often drinks too much alcohol: *There were two **drunks** asleep under the bridge.*

drunkard (say **drung**-kuhd) *noun* (*plural* **drunkards**)
a person who often drinks too much alcohol

dry¹ (*rhymes with* **cry**) *adjective* (**drier, driest**)
1 with no water or liquid in it or on it: *The washing isn't **dry** yet.* ➲ OPPOSITE **wet** 1
2 with no rain: ***dry** weather* ➲ OPPOSITE **wet** 2
3 not sweet: ***dry** white wine*

dry² (*rhymes with* **cry**) *verb* (**drying, dried**)
to become or make something dry: *Our clothes were **drying** in the sun.* ◇ *There was no rain for several months and all the rivers **dried** up* (= became completely dry). ◇ *If I wash the dishes, could you **dry** up?*

dry-clean (say **dry**-kleen) *verb* (**dry-cleaning, dry-cleaned**)
to make clothes clean by using chemicals, not water: *I had my suit **dry-cleaned**.*

dual (say **dyoo**-uhl) *adjective*
having two parts or qualities: ***Dual**-purpose cattle breeds produce milk and meat.*

dual carriageway *noun* (*plural* **dual carriageways**)
a wide road with a narrow piece of land or a fence between the two lines of traffic

duchess (say **duch**-ess) *noun* (*plural* **duchesses**)
(in England) a woman who has a very high position in society or who is married to a **duke**: *the **Duchess** of York*

duck¹ (say **duk**) *noun* (*plural* **ducks**)
a bird that lives on and near water

duck² (say **duk**) *verb* (**ducking, ducked**)
to move your head down quickly, so that something does not hit you or so that somebody does not see you: *He saw the ball coming towards him and **ducked**.*

duckling (say **duk**-ling) *noun* (*plural* **ducklings**)
a young **duck¹**

A B C D E F G H I J K L M N O P Q R S T U V W X Y Z

duct (say **dukt**) *noun* (*plural* **ducts**)
a tube or pipe through which a substance or material can pass: *a tear* ***duct*** ◇ *an electric cable* ***duct***

due (say **dyoo**) *adjective*
1 because of something or caused by something: *The accident was* ***due*** *to bad driving.*
2 planned or expected to happen or come at a certain time: *When's the baby* ***due***? ◇ *Our essay is* ***due*** *on Monday.*
3 (of an amount of money) that you must pay immediately: *My rent is* ***due*** *at the beginning of the month.*
4 ready for something: *My car is* ***due*** *for a service.*

duet (say dyoo-**et**) *noun* (*plural* **duets**)
music for two people to sing or play on musical instruments: *Pule and Mpho sang a* ***duet***.

dug form of **dig**

duiker (say **day**-kuh) *noun* (*plural* **duikers**)
a small African antelope that hides quickly when somebody disturbs it
🛈 **ORIGIN:** 18th century, through South African Dutch, from Dutch *duiker* meaning 'diver'. This animal got its name because of the way it disappears into bushes when it is chased.

duke (say **dyook**) *noun* (*plural* **dukes**)
(in England and some parts of Europe) a man who has a very high position in society in some parts of Europe ➲ See **duchess**

dull (say **dul**) *adjective* (**duller**, **dullest**)
1 not interesting or exciting: *Life is never* ***dull*** *in a big city.* ➲ **SYNONYMS boring**, **humdrum**
2 not bright: *It was a* ***dull****, cloudy day.*
3 not strong or loud: *a* ***dull*** *pain*

dumb (say **dum**) *adjective* (**dumber**, **dumbest**)
1 (*old fashioned*) not able to speak: *She was born deaf and* ***dumb***.
2 (*informal*) not intelligent but stupid: *That was a* ***dumb*** *thing to do!*

PRONUNCIATION Don't pronounce the **b** in **dumb**.

USAGE Many people think it is offensive to use **dumb** in sense 1. It is better to say that someone is **speech impaired**.

dumbfound (say dum-**fownd**) *verb* (**dumbfounding**, **dumbfounded**)
to surprise or shock you so much that you are not able to speak
▸ **dumbfounded** (*adjective*): *They looked at each other,* ***dumbfounded***.

dummy (say **dum**-ee) *noun* (*plural* **dummies**)
a small rubber object that you put in a baby's mouth to stop it crying

dump *verb* (**dumping**, **dumped**)
1 to take something to a place and leave it there because you do not want it: *They* ***dumped*** *their rubbish by the side of the road.*
2 to put something down without being careful: *Don't* ***dump*** *your clothes on the floor!*
▸ **dump** (*noun*): *Take these old things to the rubbish* ***dump***.

dune (say **dyoon**) *noun* (*plural* **dunes**)
a small hill of sand near the sea or in a desert

dung *noun* (*no plural*)
the waste material from the bodies of animals, especially large animals such as cows and elephants

dungarees (say dung-guh-**reez**) *plural noun*
trousers with a part that covers the top of your body: *a new pair of* ***dungarees***
🛈 **ORIGIN:** 17th century, from Hindi *dungri*

dungeon (say **dun**-juhn) *noun* (*plural* **dungeons**)
a prison under the ground, for example in a castle

duodecimal (say dyoo-oh-**dess**-im-l) *adjective* (*maths*)
relating to a number system that uses twelve as its base: *a* ***duodecimal*** *system* ➲ See **decimal²**

duplicate¹ (say **dyoo**-pli-kayt) *verb* (**duplicating**, **duplicated**)
1 to make an exact copy of something one or more times: *The experiment can be* ***duplicated*** *many times.*
2 to do something that has already been done: *We don't want to* ***duplicate*** *the work of other departments.*
▸ **duplication** (*noun*): *the unnecessary* ***duplication*** *of work*

duplicate² (say **dyoo**-pli-kuht) *noun* (*plural* **duplicates**)
something that is exactly the same as something else: *Keep a set of* ***duplicates*** *away from the originals.*
in duplicate with the purpose of creating two exact versions of something: *The form must be completed in* ***duplicate***.
▸ **duplicate** (*adjective*): *a* ***duplicate*** *birth certificate*

durable (say **dyoo**-ruhb-l) *adjective*
able to last for a long time without breaking or getting weaker
▸ **durability** (*noun*): *clothing of the highest quality and* ***durability***

duration (say dyoo-**ray**-shuhn) *noun* (*no plural*)
the period of time something lasts or takes: *They rented a car for the **duration** of their stay.*

during (say **dyoo**-ring) *preposition*
1 all the time that something is happening: *The sun gives us light **during** the day.*
2 at some time while something else is happening: *She died **during** the night.* ◇ *I fell asleep **during** the film.*

dusk *noun* (*no plural*)
the time in the evening when it is nearly dark

dust[1] *noun* (*no plural*)
dry dirt that is like powder: *The old table was covered in **dust**.*

dust[2] (say **dust**) *verb* (**dusting, dusted**)
to take dust off something with a cloth: *I **dusted** the furniture.*

dustbin (say **dust**-bin) *noun* (*plural* **dustbins**)
a large container for rubbish that you keep outside your house

duster (say **duss**-tuh) *noun* (*plural* **dusters**)
a cloth that you use for taking the dust off furniture

dustpan (say **dust**-pan) *noun* (*plural* **dustpans**)
a flat container with a handle that you use for getting dust or rubbish off the floor: *Have you got a **dustpan** and brush?*

dusty (say **duss**-tee) *adjective* (**dustier**, **dustiest**)
covered with dust: *The furniture was very **dusty**.*

Dutch *noun* (*no plural*)
the language spoken in the Netherlands. Afrikaans developed from **Dutch**.

duty (say **dyoo**-tee) *noun* (*plural* **duties**)
1 something that you must do because it is part of your job or because you think it is right: *It's your **duty** to look after your parents when they get older.*
2 money (called **tax**) that you pay to the government when you bring things into a country from another country
off duty not working: *The police officer was off **duty**.*
on duty working: *Some nurses at the hospital are on **duty** all night.*

duvet (say **doo**-vay) *noun* (*plural* **duvets**)
a thick warm cover for a bed. They are often filled with feathers.

DVD (say dee-vee-**dee**) *noun* (*plural* **DVDs**)
a small plastic disk that you record films and music on. You can play a it on a computer or a machine (called a **DVD player**): *Is the film available on **DVD**?*

dwarf (say **dwawf**) *noun* (*plural* **dwarfs** or **dwarves**)
1 a person, animal or plant that is much smaller than the usual size
2 (in children's stories) a very small person: *Snow White and the Seven **Dwarfs***

dwelling (say **dwel**-ing) *noun* (*plural* **dwellings**) (also **dwelling place**) (*formal*)
a house or other place where a person or a family lives

dye (*rhymes with* **my**) *verb* (**dyeing, dyed**)
to change the colour of something by using a special liquid or substance: *She **dyed** her hair blonde.*
▸ **dye** (*noun*): *She used purple hair **dye**.*

dying (say **dy**-ing) form of **die**

dyke (say **dike**) *noun* (*plural* **dykes**) (also **dike**)
1 a long wall of stone or earth that people build to prevent the sea or a river from flooding low land
2 a **ditch**[1] dug to carry a stream of water
3 (*geography*) a long narrow section of rock that enters into a space in surrounding rock

dynamic (say dy-**nam**-ik) *adjective*
1 describing a person who is full of energy and enthusiasm and is good at getting things done.
2 experiencing activity and development all the time: *a **dynamic** and successful economy*
3 (*science*) relating to energy and forces that produce movement ➲ OPPOSITE **static**

dynamite (say **dy**-nuh-mite) *noun* (*no plural*)
a powerful substance that can explode: *a stick of **dynamite***

dynamo (say **dy**-nuh-moh) *noun* (*plural* **dynamos**)
a machine that uses the movement of something such as wind or water to make electricity

dynasty (say **din**-uhss-tee) *noun* (*plural* **dynasties**)
a series of rulers or powerful people that come from the same family: *the Ming **dynasty** in China*

dysentery (say **diss**-uhn-tree) *noun* (*no plural*)
an infection of your gut that causes severe **diarrhoea** with loss of blood: *Diseases such as **dysentery** spread rapidly.*

dyslexia (say diss-**lekss**-i-uh) *noun* (*no plural*)
a difficulty that some people have with reading and writing
▸ **dyslexic** (*adjective*): *special educational programmes for **dyslexic** children*

A B C D E F G H I J K L M N O P Q R S T U V W X Y Z

Ee

A
B
C
D
E
F
G
H
I
J
K
L
M
N
O
P
Q
R
S
T
U
V
W
X
Y
Z

E *abbreviation* **east** or **eastern**

each (say **eech**) *adjective, pronoun*
every person or thing in a group: *He gave a present to* ***each*** *child.* ◇ *These T-shirts are R50* ***each****.*

each other *pronoun*
used for saying that somebody does the same thing as another person: *Gary and Susy looked at* ***each other*** (= Gary looked at Susy and Susy looked at Gary).

eager (say **ee**-guh) *adjective*
wanting to do something very much: *She's* ***eager*** *to help with the party.* ➲ SYNONYM **keen** 1
▸ **eagerly** (*adverb*): *The children waited* ***eagerly*** *for the film to begin.* ▸ **eagerness** (*noun*): *I couldn't hide my* ***eagerness*** *to get home.*

eagle (say **eeg**-l) *noun* (*plural* **eagles**)
a very large bird with a sharp curved beak and very good sight. It catches and eats small animals. ➲ See **bird of prey**

ear (say **eer**) *noun* (*plural* **ears**)
one of the two parts of your body that you use to hear with: *Elephants have big* ***ears****.* ➲ See illustration at **face**[1]

earache (say **eer**-ayk) *noun* (*no plural*)
pain inside your ear: *I've got* ***earache****.*

eardrum (say **eer**-drum) *noun* (*plural* **eardrums**)
a thin piece of skin inside your ear that is tightly stretched and that allows you to hear sounds

early (say **ur**-lee) *adjective, adverb* (**earlier, earliest**)
1 near the beginning of a period of time: *I have to get up* ***early*** *tomorrow.* ◇ *She was in her* ***early*** *twenties* (= aged between 20 and about 23 or 24). ➲ OPPOSITE **late** 1
2 before the usual or right time: *The train arrived ten minutes* ***early****.* ◇ *I was* ***early*** *for the lesson.* ◇ *I'm tired, I think I'll have an* ***early*** *night* (= go to bed earlier than usual). ➲ OPPOSITE **late** 2

earn (say **urn**) *verb* (**earning, earned**)
1 to get money by working: *How much do teachers* ***earn****?* ◇ *She* ***earns*** *about R4 500 a month.*
2 to get something because you have worked well or done something good: *You've* ***earned*** *a holiday!*

earnest (say **ur**-nuhst) *adjective*
very serious or determined: *We had an* ***earnest*** *discussion about the environment.*
in earnest happening in a serious way: *The builders will work on the stadium in* ***earnest*** *next month.*
▸ **earnestly** (*adverb*)

earnings (say **ur**-ningz) *plural noun*
money that you earn by working

earphones (say **eer**-fohnz) *plural noun* = **headphones**

earring (say **eer**-ring) *noun* (*plural* **earrings**)
a piece of jewellery that you wear on your ear: *a pair of silver* ***earrings***

earshot (say **eer**-shot) *noun* (*no plural*)
to be within earshot to be close enough to hear something
to be out of earshot to be too far way to hear something

earth[1] (say **urth**) *noun* (*no plural*)
1 (usually **the earth**, **the Earth**) this world, the planet that we live on: *The moon travels round the* ***Earth****.* ◇ *They live in one of the hottest places on* ***Earth****.*
2 the substance that plants grow in: *Cover the seeds with* ***earth****.* ➲ SYNONYM **soil**[1]
how, who, what, where, etc. on earth? (*informal*) used in questions when you are very surprised or want to say something very strongly: *What on* ***earth*** *are you doing?* ◇ *Where on* ***earth*** *is Paul? He's two hours late!*

the Earth

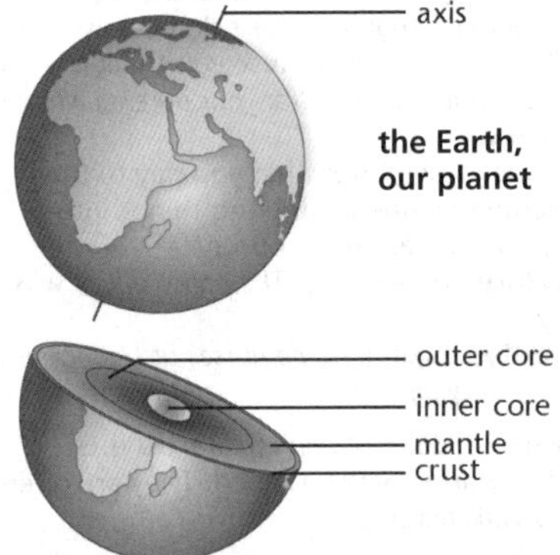

cross section of the Earth showing its structure

earth² (say **urth**) *verb* (**earthing, earthed**) (*technology*)
to make a piece of electric equipment safe by connecting it to the ground with a wire

earthquake (say **urth**-kwayk) *noun* (*plural* **earthquakes**)
a sudden strong shaking of the ground

earthworm (say **urth**-wurm) *noun* (*plural* **earthworms**)
a small long creature that lives in the soil

ease¹ (say **eez**) *noun* (*no plural*)
be or **feel at ease** to be or feel comfortable and relaxed: *Everyone was so friendly that I felt completely at **ease**.*
with ease with no difficulty: *She answered the questions with **ease**.* ➲ SYNONYM **easily**

ease² (say **eez**) *verb* (**easing, eased**)
to become or to make something less painful or serious: *Take this tablet to **ease** the pain.*

easel (say **eez**-l) *noun* (*plural* **easels**)
a frame that an artist uses to hold a picture while it is being painted
ⓘ ORIGIN: 16th century, from Dutch *ezel* meaning 'ass, donkey'. The word was used because a painter's easel carries a load, as a donkey does.

easily (say **ee**-zuh-lee) *adverb*
with no difficulty: *I can **easily** ring and check the time of the film.* ◇ *He passed the test **easily**.*
➲ The adjective is **easy**

east (say **eest**) *noun* (*no plural*) (abbr. E)
1 the direction you look in to see the sun come up in the morning: *Which way is **east**?* ◇ *There was a cold wind from the **east**.*
2 the East the countries of Asia, for example China and Japan
▸ **east** (*adjective, adverb*): *They live on the **east** coast.* ◇ *an **east** wind* (= that comes from the east) ◇ *We travelled **east**.*

Easter (say **eess**-tuh) *noun* (*no plural*)
a Sunday in March or April, and the days around it, when Christians celebrate Jesus Christ coming back to life: *I'm going on holiday at **Easter**.*
ⓘ ORIGIN: from Old English *ēastre*. The name possibly came from *Ēastre*, the name of an ancient goddess related to spring.

eastern (say **eess**-tuhn) *adjective*
in, of or from the east of a place: *the **Eastern** Cape*

easy (say **ee**-zee) *adjective* (**easier, easiest**)
1 not difficult to do or understand: *The homework was very **easy**.* ◇ *English isn't an **easy** language to learn.* ➲ OPPOSITE **difficult** 1
2 without problems or pain: *He has had an **easy** life.* ➲ OPPOSITE **hard¹** 3
take it easy, take things easy to relax and not worry or work too much: *After my exams I'm going to take it **easy** for a few days.*

eat (say **eet**) *verb* (**eating, ate, has eaten**)
1 to put food in your mouth and swallow it: *Have you **eaten** all the chocolate?* ◇ *Do you want something to **eat**?*
2 to have a meal: *What time shall we **eat**?* ◇ *We don't **eat** out* (= eat in a restaurant) *very often.*

eaves (say **eevz**) *plural noun*
the edges of a roof that stick out over the walls

ebb (say **eb**) *verb* (**ebbing, ebbed**)
1 (used about the sea) to flow away from the land, which happens twice a day ➲ See **tide**
2 to get weaker: *Our enthusiasm **ebbed** as we became tired.*

ebony (say **eb**-uh-nee) *noun* (*no plural*)
a type of hard black wood: *The box is made of **ebony**.*

eccentric (say ik-**sen**-trik) *adjective*
behaving in a strange or unusual way: *Some people say she is crazy but I think she is just a bit **eccentric**.*
▸ **eccentric** (*noun*): *She is an **eccentric**.*
▸ **eccentricity** (*noun*)

echo (say **ek**-oh) *noun* (*plural* **echoes**)
a sound that a surface such as a wall sends back so that you hear it again
▸ **echo** (*verb*): *His footsteps **echoed** in the empty hall.*

echolocation (say ek-oh-luh-**kay**-shuhn) *noun* (*no plural*)
the process of finding the position of an object by sending out a sound and listening to the **reflection** of that sound from the object: *Dolphins and bats find their way by means of **echolocation**.*

eclipse (say i-**klipss**) *noun* (*plural* **eclipses**)
1 a time when the moon comes between the Earth and the sun so that we cannot see the sun's light: *There will be a solar **eclipse*** (= an eclipse of the sun) *today.*
2 a time when the Earth comes between the sun and the moon so that we cannot see the moon's light: *There was a lunar **eclipse*** (= an eclipse of the moon) *last night.*
ⓘ ORIGIN: 13th–15th century, through Old French and Latin, from Greek *ekleipsis*, from *ekleipein* meaning 'not appearing, fail to appear'

ecology (say i-**kol**-uh-jee) *noun* (*no plural*)
1 the relationship between living things and everything around them

2 the study of this subject
▶ **ecological** (*adjective*): *an* ***ecological*** *disaster*
▶ **ecologist** (*noun*): ***Ecologists*** *are studying the effects of commercial fishing on sea birds.*

economic (say ee-kuh-**nom**-ik) *adjective*
connected with the way that people and countries spend money and make, buy and sell things: *The country has serious* ***economic*** *problems.*

> WHICH WORD? **Economic** or **economical**?
> Be careful! **Economical** has a different meaning.

economical (say ee-kuh-**nom**-ik-l) *adjective*
costing or using less time or money than usual: *This car is very* ***economical*** *to run* (= it does not use a lot of petrol).
▶ **economically** (*adverb*): *The company could be run more* ***economically***.

economics (say ee-kuh-**nom**-ikss) (*no plural*)
the study of the way that people and countries spend money and make, buy and sell things

economist (say i-**kon**-uh-mist) *noun* (*plural* **economists**)
a person who studies or knows a lot about **economics**

economy (say i-**kon**-uh-mee) *noun* (*plural* **economies**)
1 the way that a country spends its money and makes, buys and sells things: *the* ***economies*** *of Japan and Germany*
2 using money or things well and carefully: *We need to make some* ***economies*** *in this family!*

ecosystem (say **ee**-koh-siss-tuhm) *noun* (*plural* **ecosystems**)
a system made up of the community of all living organisms and their physical environment: *Large developments along our beaches have an impact on coastal* ***ecosystems***.

ecotourism (say ee-koh-**toor**-ri-zuhm) *noun* (*no plural*)
travel that involves learning about the nature in that area and avoiding harm to the environment: ***Ecotourism*** *helps to protect the wildlife.*
▶ **ecotourist** (*noun*)

ecstasy (say **ek**-stuh-see) *noun* (*no plural*)
1 a feeling of great happiness: *She had a look of* ***ecstasy*** *on her face as she listened to the music.*
2 an illegal drug

ecstatic (say ik-**stat**-ik) *adjective*
extremely happy: *The winner was* ***ecstatic***.

eczema (say **ekss**-muh or **ekss**-uh-muh) *noun* (*no plural*)
a disease that makes the skin red and dry so that you want to scratch it

edge (say **ej**) *noun* (*plural* **edges**)
1 the part along the end or side of something: *She stood at the water's* ***edge***. ◇ *the* ***edge*** *of the table*
2 the sharp part of a knife or tool
be on edge to be nervous or worried

edible (say **ed**-ib-l) *adjective*
good or safe to eat: *This type of mushroom is* ***edible****, but those ones are poisonous.*

edit (say **ed**-it) *verb* (**editing, edited**)
1 to check and correct a piece of writing to make sure it has no mistakes
2 to arrange and cut material in a film, radio or television programme
3 to be in charge of a magazine or newspaper
▶ **editor** (*noun*): *The* ***editor*** *will check the text before it is printed.*

edition (say i-**dish**-uhn) *noun* (*plural* **editions**)
1 one of a number of books, magazines or newspapers that appear at the same time: *the morning* ***edition*** *of the newspaper*
2 the form in which a book is published: *a paperback or hardback* ***edition*** ◇ *the electronic* ***edition*** *of the Mail & Guardian* (= available on the Internet)

editorial (say ed-i-**taw**-ri-uhl) *noun* (*plural* **editorials**)
an article in a newspaper which gives an opinion about an important event

educate (say **ed**-yuu-kayt) *verb* (**educating, educated**)
1 to teach somebody at a school or college: *Where was she* ***educated****?*
2 to give people information about something: *We must* ***educate*** *young people about the dangers of smoking.*
ORIGIN: 14th–15th century, from Latin *educat-* meaning 'led out'

education (say ed-yuu-**kay**-shuhn) *noun* (*no plural*)
teaching somebody at a school or college: *He had a good* ***education***. ◇ ***Education*** *is extremely important.*
▶ **educational** (*adjective*): *an* ***educational*** *video*

eel *noun* (*plural* **eels**)
a long fish that looks like a snake

eerie (say **eer**-ree) *adjective* (**eerier, eeriest**)
strange and frightening: *an* ***eerie*** *noise*

effect (say i-**fekt**) *noun* (*plural* **effects**)
1 a change that happens because of something: *We are studying the* ***effects*** *of heat on different metals.* ◇ *Her shouting had little* ***effect*** *on him.* ◇ *Climate change has many negative* (= harmful) ***effects***.
2 a particular look, sound or feeling that an artist or writer wants to create: *He created a 3D* (= three-dimensional) ***effect*** *in the painting.*

effective (say i-**fek**-tiv) *adjective*
(used about a method, medicine, etc.) that works well: *Cycling is an* ***effective*** *way of keeping fit.*

effectively (say i-**fek**-tiv-lee) *adverb*
in a way that gets the result you wanted: *She dealt with the situation* ***effectively***.

efficient (say i-**fish**-uhnt) *adjective*
working well without making mistakes or wasting energy: *Our secretary is very* ***efficient***. ◇ *an* ***efficient*** *way of working* ➲ OPPOSITE **inefficient**
▸ **efficiency** (*noun*): *ways of increasing* ***efficiency*** *at the factory* ▸ **efficiently** (*adverb*): *Try to use your time more* ***efficiently***.

effigy (say **ef**-i-jee) *noun* (*plural* **effigies**)
a statue or other image of a famous person: *The people burned an* ***effigy*** *of the unpopular president.*

effort (say **ef**-uht) *noun* (*plural* **efforts**)
the physical or mental energy that you need to do something: *Thank you for all your* ***efforts***. ◇ *He made an* ***effort*** *to arrive on time.*

effortless (say **ef**-uht-luhss) *adjective*
something which needs little or no effort: *He danced with* ***effortless*** *skill.*
▸ **effortlessly** (*adverb*)

e.g. (say ee-**jee**) *abbreviation*
for example: *popular sports,* ***e.g.*** *football, tennis and swimming* ⓘ **E.g.** is short for the Latin phrase 'exempli gratia'. ➲ See **example**

egalitarian (say i-gal-i-**tair**-ri-uhn) *adjective*
following the principle that everyone should have equal rights: *an* ***egalitarian*** *community*

egg (say **eg**) *noun* (*plural* **eggs**)
1 a round or **oval** object that has a baby bird, fish, insect or snake inside it: *The hen has laid an* ***egg***.
2 a bird's egg, especially one from a chicken, that is eaten as food: *a boiled* ***egg***
ⓘ ORIGIN: 13th–15th century, from Old Norse

ego (say **ee**-goh) *noun* (*plural* **egos**)
the good opinion that you have of yourself: *She has a huge* ***ego***. (= she thinks she is very good or special) ◇ *It was a blow to my* ***ego*** *when I failed the test.*

egotist (say **eg**-oh-tist) *noun* (*plural* **egotists**) (also **egoist**)
a person who thinks they are better or more important than other people
▸ **egotism** (also **egoism**) (*noun*)

Eid (say **eed**) *noun* (*no plural*)
the name of two Muslim festivals, especially the festival to celebrate the end of the **Ramadan** fast
ⓘ ORIGIN: from Arabic *īd* meaning 'feast'

eight (say **ayt**) *number*
8

eighteen (say ay-**teen**) *number*
18
▸ **eighteenth** (*adjective, adverb*): *He had a party on his* ***eighteenth*** *birthday.*

eighth (say **ayt**-th) *adjective, adverb, noun*
1 8th: *It's his* ***eighth*** *birthday today.*
2 one of eight equal parts of something, $\frac{1}{8}$

eighty (say **ay**-tee) *number*
1 80
2 the eighties (*plural noun*) the numbers 80 to 89 or the years 1980 to 1989: *She was born in the* ***eighties*** (= in the 1980s).
in your eighties between the ages of 80 and 89
▸ **eightieth** (*adjective, adverb*): *my grandpa's* ***eightieth*** *birthday.*

either[1] (say ***y***-thuh or **ee**-thuh) *adjective, pronoun*
1 one of two things or people: *There is cake and ice cream. You can have* ***either***. ◇ ***Either*** *of us will help you.*
2 each: *There are trees along* ***either*** *side of the street.*

either[2] (say ***y***-thuh or **ee**-thuh) *adverb*
(used in sentences with 'not') also: *Sadiq can't swim and I can't* ***either***.
either ... or words that show two different things or people that you can choose: *You can have* ***either*** *tea or coffee.* ◇ *You can* ***either*** *come now or later.*

ejaculate (say i-**jak**-yuu-layt) *verb* (**ejaculating, ejaculated**)
(of a man or male animal) to send out a liquid called **semen** from the **penis**
▸ **ejaculation** (*noun*)

eject (say i-**jekt**) *verb* (**ejecting, ejected**)
1 to push or send a person or thing out of a place
2 to remove a disk or a tape from a machine: *How do I* ***eject*** *this CD?*
▸ **ejection** (*noun*)

A B C D **E** F G H I J K L M N O P Q R S T U V W X Y Z

elaborate[1] (say i-**lab**-uh-ruht) *adjective*
not simple, but with a lot of different parts: *The carpet has a very **elaborate** pattern.* ➲ SYNONYM **complicated**
▶ **elaborately** (*adverb*): *The rooms were **elaborately** decorated.*

elaborate[2] (say i-**lab**-uh-rayt) *verb* (**elaborating, elaborated**)
to give more information or details about something: *He didn't want to **elaborate** on his plans.*

eland (say **eer**-lunt) *noun* (*plural* **eland** or **elands**)
the largest African antelope
ⓘ ORIGIN: 18th century, through South African Dutch, from Dutch *eland* meaning 'elk', which is a type of large deer found in Europe and Asia

elapse (say i-**lapss**) *verb* (**elapsing, elapsed**)
(used to talk about time) to pass: *A year has **elapsed** since the President was elected.*

elastic (say i-**lass**-tik) *noun* (*no plural*)
material that becomes longer when you pull it and then goes back to its usual size: *This skirt needs some new **elastic** in the waist.*
▶ **elastic** (*adjective*): ***elastic** material*

elated (say i-**layt**-uhd) *adjective*
very happy and excited: *I was **elated** at the good news.*

elbow (say **el**-boh) *noun* (*plural* **elbows**)
the part in the middle of your arm where it bends: *She fell and broke her **elbow**.* ➲ See illustration at **body**

elder (say **el**-duh) *adjective*
older, especially of two members of the same family: *My **elder** brother lives in France.*

elderly (say **el**-duh-lee) *adjective*
(used about people) a polite way of saying 'old': *an **elderly** lady*

eldest (say **el**-dist) *adjective*
oldest of three or more people, especially members of the same family: *Their **eldest** son is at university.*

elect (say i-**lekt**) *verb* (**electing, elected**)
to choose somebody to be a leader by voting for him or her: *The new president was **elected**.*

election (say i-**lek**-shuhn) *noun* (*plural* **elections**)
a time when people choose somebody to be a leader by voting for him or her: *The **election** will be held on Wednesday.*

electric (say i-**lek**-trik) *adjective*
using or providing electricity: *an **electric** stove* ◇ *an **electric** socket*
ⓘ ORIGIN: 17th century, from Latin *electrum* meaning 'amber', from Greek *ēlektron*, so named because rubbing amber creates a type of weak electric current

electrical (say i-**lek**-trik-l) *adjective*
of or using electricity: *an **electrical** appliance* ◇ *an **electrical** engineer*

electrician (say i-lek-**trish**-uhn) *noun* (*plural* **electricians**)
a person whose job is to make and repair electrical systems and equipment: *Danie's an **electrician**. He'll be able to mend your light.*

electricity (say i-lek-**triss**-uh-tee) *noun* (*no plural*)
a type of energy that we use to make heat, light and power to work machines: *Turn the light off. We don't want to waste **electricity**.*

electric shock *noun* (*plural* **electric shocks**)
a sudden painful feeling that you get if electricity goes through your body

electrocute (say i-**lek**-truh-kyoot) *verb* (**electrocuting, electrocuted**)
to kill someone with electricity that goes through their body
▶ **electrocution** (*noun*): *He was put to death by **electrocution**.*

electrode *noun* (*plural* **electrodes**) (*science*)
any material that you put into a substance to allow an electric current to pass through: *Batteries have positive and negative **electrodes**.*

electromagnet (say i-**lek**-troh-mag-nuht) *noun* (*plural* **electromagnets**)
a type of **magnet** that works when an electric current passes through it
▶ **electromagnetic** (*adjective*): *an **electromagnetic** field* ▶ **electromagnetism** (*noun*)

electron (say el-**ek**-tron) *noun* (*plural* **electrons**) (*science*)
one of the three types of **particles** that form all atoms. Electrons have a negative electric charge. ➲ See **neutron**, **proton**

electronic (say i-lek-**tron**-ik) *adjective*
(of devices such as computers and televisions) that use electricity and very small electrical parts (called **microchips** and **transistors**) to make them work: *an **electronic** calculator*

electronics (say i-lek-**tron**-ikss) *noun* (*no plural*)
the technology that is used to make devices such as computers and televisions: *the **electronics** industry*

elegant (say **el**-i-guhnt) *adjective*
with a beautiful style or shape: *She looked very **elegant** in her new black dress.* ➲ OPPOSITE **inelegant**
▶ **elegance** (*noun*): *a simple **elegance***

element (say **el**-i-muhnt) *noun* (*plural* **elements**)
1 an important part of something: *Cost was an important* ***element*** *in our decision.*
2 a pure substance made up of only one type of **atom**, for example iron or gold: *Water is made of the* ***elements*** *hydrogen and oxygen.*

elementary (say el-i-**men**-tree) *adjective*
1 connected with the early stages of learning: *an* ***elementary*** *dictionary*
2 not difficult: ***elementary*** *maths*

elephant (say **el**-i-fuhnt) *noun* (*plural* **elephants**)
a very large grey mammal from Africa and Asia, with big ears, two long curved teeth (called **tusks**) and a long nose (called a **trunk**) that hangs down

elevate (say **el**-i-vayt) *verb* (**elevating, elevated**)
to move something to a higher place: *an* ***elevated*** *stage*

elevation (say el-uh-**vay**-shuhn) *noun* (*no plural*)
1 the process of moving to a higher place
2 (*geography*) the height of a place above the level of the sea

elevator (say **el**-i-vay-tuh) *noun* (*plural* **elevators**) another word for **lift**[2] 1

eleven (say i-**lev**-uhn) *number*
11
▸ **eleventh** (*adjective, adverb*): *It's her* ***eleventh*** *birthday today.*

elf *noun* (*plural* **elves**)
a very small person in stories who has pointed ears and magic powers

eligible (say **el**-i-juhb-l) *adjective*
having the right to do something or to have something: *In South Africa you are* ***eligible*** *to vote when you are eighteen years old.* ◇ *Only club members are* ***eligible*** *for election.* ➲ OPPOSITE **ineligible**

eliminate (say i-**lim**-i-nayt) *verb* (**eliminating, eliminated**)
to remove something that is not needed or wanted: *We must try to* ***eliminate*** *waste.*
▸ **elimination** (*noun*): ***elimination*** *of waste*

elite (say ay-**leet**) *noun* (*plural* **elites**)
a social group that we think is important because it is rich, powerful or the best: *a member of the* ***elite***
▸ **elite** (*adjective*): *an* ***elite*** *group of artists*

Elizabethan (say i-liz-uh-**bee**-thuhn) *adjective*
relating to the time of Queen Elizabeth I of England: *Shakespeare wrote plays during* ***Elizabethan*** *times.*

ellipse (say i-**lipss**) *noun* (*plural* **ellipses**)
a regular **oval**, like a circle that has been pressed in from two sides

elongate (say **ee**-long-gayt) *verb* (**elongating, elongated**)
to become longer or to make something longer and thinner
▸ **elongated** (*adjective*): *an* ***elongated*** *body*
▸ **elongation** (*noun*)

eloquent (say **el**-uh-kwuhnt) *adjective*
able to use language and express your opinions well, especially when you speak in public: *She is an* ***eloquent*** *speaker.*
▸ **eloquence** (*noun*) ▸ **eloquently** (*adverb*)

else (say **elss**) *adverb*
1 more or extra: *What* ***else*** *would you like?* ◇ *Is anyone* ***else*** *coming to the party?*
2 different: *This cafe's full, let's go somewhere* ***else.*** ◇ *It's not mine – it must be somebody* ***else's.*** ◇ *There was nothing* ***else*** *to eat so we had eggs again.*
or else if not, then: *Go now, or* ***else*** *you'll be late.* ➲ SYNONYM **otherwise**[2]

USAGE You use **else** after words such as **anybody**, **nothing** and **somewhere**, and after question words such as **where** and **who**.

elsewhere (say **elss**-wair) *adverb*
in or to another place: *He can't find a job near home so he's looking* ***elsewhere.***

elves (say **elvz**) plural of **elf**

emaciated (say i-**may**-shi-ayt-uhd) *adjective*
very thin and weak because of illness or not eating enough food

email (say **ee**-mayl) *noun* (also **e-mail**)
1 (*no plural*) a system for sending messages from one computer to another: *to send a message by* ***email*** ◇ *What's your* ***email*** *address?*
2 (*plural* **emails**) a message that is written on one computer and sent to another: *I'll send you an* ***email.*** ❶ **email** is short for 'electronic mail'.
▸ **email** (also **e-mail**) (*verb*): ***Email*** *me when you arrive.* ◇ *I'll* ***email*** *the form to her.*

emancipate (say i-**man**-si-payt) *verb* (**emancipating, emancipated**)
to give people the same social, political and legal rights as other people: *When were slaves* ***emancipated?***
▸ **emancipation** (*noun*): *the* ***emancipation*** *of women*

embargo (say im-**baa**-goh) *noun* (*plural* **embargoes**)
an official order to stop doing business with another country: *an arms **embargo*** ◇ *The government lifted* (= stopped) *the trade **embargo**.*

embark (say im-**baak**) *verb* (**embarking, embarked**)
to get on a ship: *When will the passengers **embark**?* ➲ OPPOSITE **disembark**
to embark on to start something new: *He **embarked** on a new career.*
▸ **embarkation** (*noun*)

embarrass (say im-**ba**-ruhss) *verb* (**embarrassing, embarrassed**)
to make somebody feel shy or worried about what other people think of them: *Please don't **embarrass** me in front of my friends.*
▸ **embarrassing** (*adjective*): *I couldn't remember her name – it was so **embarrassing**!*

embarrassed (say im-**ba**-ruhst) *adjective*
feeling shy or worried about what other people think of you: *He felt **embarrassed** at being the centre of attention.* ◇ *I'm **embarrassed**!*

SPELLING Remember! You spell **embarrassed** with **rr** and **ss**.

embarrassment (say im-**ba**-ruhss-muhnt) *noun* (*no plural*)
shy, awkward or guilty feelings: *His face was red with **embarrassment**.*

embassy (say **em**-buh-see) *noun* (*plural* **embassies**)
a group of people whose job is to speak and act for their government in another country, or the building where they work: *To get a visa, you should apply to the American **embassy**.*

embellish (say im-**bel**-ish) *verb* (**embellishing, embellished**)
to make something more beautiful or interesting: *The plate was **embellished** with gold.* ◇ *She **embellished** the story with information that was not quite true.*

ember (say **em**-buh) *noun* (*plural* **embers**)
a piece of wood or coal that is not burning, but is still hot and red

embezzle (say im-**bez**-l) *verb* (**embezzling, embezzled**)
to steal money that belongs to your employer: *She **embezzled** money from the business.*
▸ **embezzlement** (*noun*)

emblem (say **em**-bluhm) *noun* (*plural* **emblems**)
an object that represents something: *The protea is a national **emblem** of South Africa.*

embody (say im-**bod**-ee) *verb* (**embodying, embodied**)
1 to be a good example of something: *She **embodies** the best qualities of leadership.*
2 (*formal*) to include or contain something: *This model **embodies** many new features.*
▸ **embodiment** (*noun*)

embrace (say im-**brayss**) *verb* (**embracing, embraced**) (*formal*)
to put your arms around a person to show that you love them: *She **embraced** each member of her family in turn.* ➲ SYNONYM **hug**

embroider (say im-**broy**-duh) *verb* (**embroidering, embroidered**)
to decorate cloth by sewing patterns on it
▸ **embroidered** (*adjective*): *an **embroidered** blouse*

embroidery (say im-**broy**-duh-ree) *noun* (*no plural*)
patterns that are sewn onto cloth to decorate it

embryo (say **em**-bri-oh) *noun* (*plural* **embryos**) (*biology*)
a living thing at an early stage of development, just after the egg or seed has been fertilized

emerald (say **em**-uh-ruhld) *noun* (*plural* **emeralds**)
1 a bright green precious stone (called a **jewel**): *an **emerald** ring*
2 (also **emerald green**) bright green, the colour of an emerald

emerge (say i-**murj**) *verb* (**emerging, emerged**)
to come out from a place: *The moon **emerged** from behind the clouds.*

emergency (say i-**mur**-juhn-see) *noun* (*plural* **emergencies**)
a sudden dangerous situation, when people need help quickly: *Come quickly, doctor! It's an **emergency**!* ◇ *an **emergency** exit* (= a way out of a building when there is a fire or other threat)

emigrant (say **em**-i-gruhnt) *noun* (*plural* **emigrants**)
a person who leaves their country to live in another

emigrate (say **em**-i-grayt) *verb* (**emigrating, emigrated**)
to leave your country and go to live in another country: *They **emigrated** to Australia in the 1990s.*

▸ **emigration** (*noun*): ***emigration** by people in search of work*

WHICH WORD? **Emigrate** or **immigrate**?
■ To **emigrate** means to leave a country to live somewhere else, and to **immigrate** means to come to a country to live.

eminent (say **em**-i-nuhnt) *adjective*
famous or important: *an **eminent** musician*

emission (say i-**mish**-uhn) *noun*
1 (*plural* **emissions**) something that is sent out into the air, such as gas, heat or light: *Carbon dioxide **emissions** harm the planet.*
2 (*no plural*) (*formal*) the production or sending out of something such as light, heat or gas

emit (say i-**mit**) *verb* (**emitting, emitted**)
to send out something, for example light, sound, heat, smoke, a smell: *The sun **emits** radiation.*

emoticon (say i-**moh**-ti-kon) *noun* (*plural* **emoticons**) (*informal*)
a symbol formed from punctuation marks or letters to show feelings ➲ See Study page 21

emotion (say i-**moh**-shuhn) *noun* (*plural* **emotions**)
a strong feeling, for example love or anger: *She was overcome with **emotion** and she broke down and cried.*

emotional (say i-**moh**-shuhn-l) *adjective*
1 connected with feelings: ***emotional** problems*
2 showing strong feelings, sometimes by crying: *He got very **emotional** when we said goodbye.*

emotive (say i-**moh**-tiv) *adjective*
making people feel strong emotions: *War is an **emotive** issue.* ◇ *The poet used **emotive** language.*

empathy (say **em**-puh-thee) *noun* (*no plural*)
the ability to understand how other people feel

emperor (say **em**-puh-ruh) *noun* (*plural* **emperors**)
a man who rules a group of countries (called an **empire**): *the **Emperor** Napoleon*

emphasis (say **em**-fuh-siss) *noun* (*plural* **emphases**)
special importance that is given to something: *Our school places a lot of **emphasis** on science.* ➲ SYNONYM **stress**[1] 2

emphasize (say **em**-fuh-size) *verb* (**emphasizing, emphasized**) (also **emphasise**)
to say something strongly to show that it is important: *She **emphasized** the importance of hard work.* ➲ SYNONYM **stress**[2]

empire (say **em**-py-uh) *noun* (*plural* **empires**)
1 a group of countries that is controlled by one ruler or government: *the Roman **Empire***
2 a group of commercial organizations controlled by one person or company: *a business **empire***
🛈 ORIGIN: 13th–15th century, through Old French from Latin *imperium*, related to *imperare* meaning 'to command'

employ (say im-**ploy**) *verb* (**employing, employed**)
1 to pay somebody to do work for you: *The factory **employs** 800 workers.* ◇ *She is **employed** in a factory.*
2 to use something such as a skill or method: *He **employed** several techniques.*

employee (say im-**ploy**-ee) *noun* (*plural* **employees**)
a person who works for somebody: *This company treats its **employees** very well.*

employer (say im-**ploy**-uh) *noun* (*plural* **employers**)
a person or company that pays other people to do work

employment (say im-**ploy**-muhnt) *noun* (*no plural*)
having a job that you are paid to do: *It can be hard for young people to find **employment**.* ➲ See **unemployment**

empower (say im-**pow**-uh) *verb* (**empowering, empowered**)
to give someone the power, authority or confidence to do something: *Education **empowers** people to lead better lives.* ➲ OPPOSITE **disempower**
▸ **empowerment** (*noun*): *the **empowerment** of rural women* (= who live far from towns or cities)

empress (say **em**-pruhss) *noun* (*plural* **empresses**)
a woman who rules an empire, or the wife of an **emperor**

empty[1] (say **emp**-tee) *adjective*
with nothing or nobody inside or on it: *The hall was almost **empty**.* ◇ *an **empty** box*

empty[2] (say **emp**-tee) *verb* (**emptying, emptied**)
1 to take everything out of something: *The cleaner **emptied** the rubbish bins.*
2 to become unfilled of what was in it or **vacant** of the people in it: *After assembly, the hall started to **empty**.*

emulsion (say i-**mul**-shuhn) *noun* (*plural* **emulsions**)
1 (*science*) a mixture of liquids that do not

normally combine well: *an **emulsion** of oil and water*
2 a substance on the surface of photographic film that makes it sensitive to light

enable (say en-**ayb**-l) *verb* (**enabling, enabled**) (*formal*)
to make it possible for somebody to do something: *Your help **enabled** me to finish.*

enamel (say i-**nam**-l) *noun* (*no plural*)
1 a hard, shiny substance used for protecting and decorating: *an **enamel** bowl ◇ **enamel** paint*
2 the hard white outer covering of a tooth

encase (say en-**kayss**) *verb* (**encasing, encased**) (*formal*)
to put something inside a box or case so that it is completely covered

enchanted (say en-**chaan**-tuhd) *adjective*
1 something which is affected by magic: *an **enchanted** garden*
2 very pleased with something: *The children were **enchanted** by the story.*
▸ **enchanting** (*adjective*): *an **enchanting** evening*

enclose (say in-**kloze**) *verb* (**enclosing, enclosed**)
1 to put something inside a letter or package: *I **enclosed** a photo.*
2 to put something, for example a wall or fence, around a place on all sides: *The school is **enclosed** by a high fence.*

enclosure (say in-**kloh**-zhuh) *noun* (*plural* **enclosures**)
1 a piece of land inside a wall or fence: *an **enclosure** for animals*
2 something that you put with a letter or a package

encore (say **ong**-kaw) *noun* (*plural* **encores**)
a short, extra performance at the end of a concert: *The audience clapped and shouted for an **encore** at the end of the show.*

encounter (say in-**kown**-tuh) *verb* (**encountering, encountered**)
to experience something unexpected or difficult: *They **encountered** many problems on the journey.*
▸ **encounter** (*noun*): *an **encounter** with a lion*

encourage (say in-**ku**-rij) *verb* (**encouraging, encouraged**)
to give somebody hope or help so that they do something or continue doing something: *We **encouraged** him to write a book about his adventures.* ➲ OPPOSITE **discourage** 1
▸ **encouragement** (*noun*): *Kim's parents have always given her a lot of **encouragement**.*
▸ **encouraging** (*adjective*): *Ann's school report is very **encouraging**.*

encroach (say in-**krohch**) *verb* (**encroaching, encroached**) (*formal*)
to use more of something than you should: *My work began to **encroach** on my free time.*

encyclopedia (say en-sike-loh-**pee**-di-uh) *noun* (*plural* **encyclopedias**)
a book or CD that gives information about a lot of different things: *an **encyclopedia** of world history*

end[1] *noun* (*plural* **ends**)
the furthest or last part of something: *It's at the **end** of the street. ◇ They were at the other **end** of the room. ◇ at the **end** of June* ➲ OPPOSITE **beginning**
in the end finally, at last: *In the **end** we got home at midnight.*
put an end to something to stop something happening: *We must put an **end** to this terrible war.*
make ends meet to have enough money for your needs: *I can't make **ends** meet.*

end[2] *verb* (**ending, ended**)
to stop or to finish something: *What time does the film **end**? ◇ The road **ends** here. ◇ Most adverbs in English **end** in '-ly'.* ➲ OPPOSITES **begin, start**[1] 2
end up to finally be in a place or doing something when you did not plan it: *I **ended** up doing all the work myself.*

endanger (say in-**dayn**-juh) *verb* (**endangering, endangered**)
to cause danger to something: *Drinking and driving **endangers** lives.*

endangered (say in-**dayn**-juhd) *adjective*
(used about animals or plants) in danger of disappearing from the world **(becoming extinct)**: *The oystercatcher is an **endangered** South African bird.*

endeavour (say in-**dev**-uh) *verb* (**endeavouring, endeavoured**) (*formal*)
to try hard to do something: *I will **endeavour** to finish the job this week.* ➲ SYNONYM **attempt, try**[1] 1
▸ **endeavour** (*noun*): *a great human **endeavour***

endemic (say en-**dem**-ik) *adjective*
1 natural or limited to a certain region: *South Africa has many **endemic** plant species, not existing naturally anywhere else in the world.*
2 (used about a disease or problem) regularly found in a particular place or among a particular group of people: *Malaria is **endemic***

in many hot countries. ➲ See **epidemic**, **pandemic**

ending (say **en**-ding) *noun* (*plural* **endings**)
the last part of something, for example a word, story or film: *The film has a happy **ending**.*

endless (say **end**-luhss) *adjective*
never stopping or finishing and very long: *The journey seemed **endless**.*
▸ **endlessly** (*adverb*): *He talks **endlessly** about nothing.*

endoskeleton (say **en**-doh-skel-uh-tuhn) *noun* (*plural* **endoskeletons**) (*biology*)
the bones inside the body of an animal that give it shape and support ➲ See **exoskeleton**

endure (say in-**dyoor**) *verb* (**enduring**, **endured**) (*formal*)
to suffer something that is painful or uncomfortable, usually without complaining: *The pain was almost too great to **endure**.*
➲ SYNONYM **bear[1] 1**

enemy (say **en**-uh-mee) *noun*
1 (*plural* **enemies**) a person who hates you: *He has made a lot of **enemies**.*
2 the enemy (*no plural*) the army or country that your country is fighting against in a war: *The **enemy** is attacking from the north.*

energetic (say en-uh-**jet**-ik) *adjective*
full of energy so that you can do a lot of things

energy (say **en**-uh-jee) *noun* (*no plural*)
1 the ability to be active without getting tired: *Children are usually full of **energy**.*
2 the power from electricity, gas, coal or other sources that is used to make machines work and to make heat and light: *It is important to try to save **energy**.* ◇ *atomic **energy** and solar **energy***
3 (*science*) the ability of something to do work
➲ See **potential energy**

enforce (say in-**fawss**) *verb* (**enforcing**, **enforced**)
to make people obey a rule or law: *The police **enforce** the law.*
▸ **enforcement** (*noun*): *law **enforcement***

engage (say in-**gayj**) *verb* (**engaging**, **engaged**)
1 to interest someone in something and keep them interested: *A good speaker **engages** the audience.*
2 to give someone a job: *The company **engaged** new staff.*
engage in something to take part in something: *I try not to **engage** in gossip!*

engaged (say in-**gayjd**) *adjective*
1 (used about two people) having agreed to get married: *She is **engaged** to Michael.* ◇ *They got **engaged** last year.* ➲ SYNONYM **betrothed**
2 (used about a telephone) being used: *I tried to phone him but his number was **engaged**.*
➲ SYNONYM **busy 3**

engagement (say in-**gayj**-muhnt) *noun* (*plural* **engagements**)
an agreement to marry somebody

engine (say **en**-jin) *noun* (*plural* **engines**)
1 a machine that makes things move: *a car engine*
2 the front part of a train which pulls the rest.
ℹ ORIGIN: 13th–15th century, through Old French *engin*, from Latin *ingenium* meaning 'talent' and 'device'

engineer (say en-ji-**neer**) *noun* (*plural* **engineers**)
a person whose job is to plan, make or repair things such as machines, roads or bridges: *My brother is an electrical **engineer**.*

engineering (say en-ji-**neer**-ring) *noun* (*no plural*)
(the study of) planning and making things such as machines, roads or bridges: *She's studying mechanical **engineering**.*

English (say **ing**-glish) *noun* (*no plural*)
the language that is spoken in Britain and many other countries, including the USA, Canada, Australia and South Africa: *Do you speak English?*

engrave (say in-**grayv**) *verb* (**engraving**, **engraved**)
to cut words or pictures into a surface: *Her name was **engraved** on the pen.* ◇ *The cup was **engraved** with the name of the winner.*

engraving (say in-**grayv**-ing) *noun* (*plural* **engravings**)
a design that is cut into a surface

engrossed (say in-**grohst**) *adjective*
very interested in something and giving it all your attention: *He was so **engrossed** in his book that he didn't hear the phone.*

enhance (say in-**haanss**) *verb* (**enhancing**, **enhanced**)
to improve something or make it look better: *Can you **enhance** the photograph?*
▸ **enhanced** (*adjective*): *an **enhanced** recording*

enigma (say i-**nig**-muh) *noun* (*plural* **enigmas**)
a person, thing or situation that is difficult to understand ➲ SYNONYM **mystery**

enjoy (say in-**joy**) *verb* (**enjoying**, **enjoyed**)
to like something very much: *I **enjoy** swimming.* ◇ *Did you **enjoy** your dinner?* ◇ *I **enjoyed** myself* (= had a good time) *at the party.*

A B C D E F G H I J K L M N O P Q R S T U V W X Y Z

enjoyable (say in-**joy**-uhb-l) *adjective*
describing something that makes you happy: *a very **enjoyable** evening*

enjoyment (say in-**joy**-muhnt) *noun* (*no plural*)
pleasure or a thing which gives you pleasure: *I get a lot of **enjoyment** from travelling.*
➲ SYNONYM **pleasure**

enlarge (say in-**laaj**) *verb* (**enlarging, enlarged**)
1 to make something bigger: *Reading will **enlarge** your vocabulary.*
2 to say or write more about something: ***Enlarge** on this description by adding illustrations and more facts.*
▸ **enlargement** (*noun*): *an **enlargement** of a photograph*

enlighten (say in-**lite**-uhn) *verb* (**enlightening, enlightened**)
to give somebody information so that they understand something better

enlightened (say in-**lite**-uhnd) *adjective*
having modern ideas: *an **enlightened** attitude*

enlist (say in-**list**) *verb* (**enlisting, enlisted**)
1 to get help or support: *They **enlisted** some help.*
2 to join the army, navy or air force: *She **enlisted** in the air force.*

enormity (say i-**naw**-mi-tee) *noun* (*plural* **enormities**)
how serious, difficult or big something is: *I hadn't realized the **enormity** of the problem!*

enormous (say i-**naw**-muhss) *adjective*
very big: *an **enormous** dog* ➲ SYNONYMS **gigantic, huge, massive**

enormously (say i-**naw**-muhss-lee) *adverb*
very or very much: *The film was **enormously** successful.*

enough (say i-**nuff**) *adjective, pronoun, adverb*
as much or as many as you need: *There isn't **enough** food for us all.* ◇ *You don't eat **enough**.* ◇ *Is she old **enough** to drive?* ➲ SYNONYM **sufficient**

> USAGE If you have **enough** of something you have the right amount: *There's **enough** cake for everyone.*

enquire (say en-**kwy**-uh) *verb* (**enquiring, enquired**) (also **inquire**) (*formal*)
to ask for information about something: *Could you **enquire** about train times?* ◇ *Journalists have been **enquiring** into* (= finding out about) *his past.* ➲ SYNONYM **ask 1**

enquiry (say en-**kwy**-uh-ree) *noun* (*plural* **enquiries**) (also **inquiry**) (*formal*)
a question that you ask to get information about something: *I'll make some **enquiries** about dance classes.*

enrage (say in-**rayj**) *verb* (**enraging, enraged**)
to make somebody very angry: *People were **enraged** by the news.*

enrich (say en-**rich**) *verb* (**enriching, enriched**)
1 to improve the quality of a thing by adding something to it: *The milk is **enriched** with vitamins.*
2 to make someone rich ➲ OPPOSITE **impoverish**
▸ **enrichment** (*noun*)

enrol (say in-**rohl**) *verb* (**enrolling, enrolled**)
to join a group, for example a school, college, course or club. You usually pay money (called a **fee**) when you do so: *I've **enrolled** in an art course.*

ensemble (say on-**somb**-l) *noun* (*plural* **ensembles**)
1 a small group of actors, dancers or musicians who often perform together
2 a set of clothes that you wear together

ensure (say en-**shoor**) *verb* (**ensuring, ensured**) (*formal*)
to make certain that something happens: *Please **ensure** that the lights are off when you leave.*

entail (say in-**tayl**) *verb* (**entailing, entailed**)
to involve something: *What does this work **entail**?*

enter (say **en**-tuh) *verb* (**entering, entered**)
1 (*formal*)
to come or go into a place: *They stopped talking when she **entered** the room.*
2 to put your name on the list for an exam, a race or a competition: *I **entered** a competition.*
3 to put information on paper or in a computer: *I've **entered** the data onto the computer.*

> USAGE **Go in** or **come in** are the words that we usually use for sense 1 above. **Enter** is quite formal.

enterprise (say **en**-tuh-prize) *noun* (*plural* **enterprises**)
a new plan, project or business: *a business **enterprise***

enterprising (say **en**-tuh-prize-ing) *adjective*
doing something in a new, enthusiastic and successful way: *The concert was organized by an **enterprising** group of students.*

entertain (say en-tuh-**tayn**) *verb* (**entertaining, entertained**)
1 to say or do things that other people find interesting or funny: *She* ***entertained*** *us all with her funny stories.*
2 to give food and drink to visitors in your house: *We're* ***entertaining*** *friends this evening.*

entertainer (say en-tuh-**tayn**-uh) *noun* (*plural* **entertainers**)
a person whose job is to help people have a good time, for example by singing, dancing or telling jokes

entertaining (say en-tuh-**tayn**-ing) *adjective*
funny and interesting: *The talk was informative and* ***entertaining****.*

entertainment (say en-tuh-**tayn**-muhnt) *noun* (*no plural*)
anything that entertains people, for example films, concerts or television: *There isn't much* ***entertainment*** *in this town.*

enthusiasm (say en-**thoo**-zi-az-uhm) *noun* (*no plural*)
a strong feeling of wanting to do something or liking something: *The pupils showed great* ***enthusiasm*** *for the new project.*

enthusiastic (say en-**thoo**-zi-ass-tik) *adjective*
full of enthusiasm: *The children are very* ***enthusiastic*** *about sport.*

entice (say en-**tise**) *verb* (**enticing, enticed**)
to persuade somebody to do something by offering something nice: *The low price will* ***entice*** *many people to buy this product.* ➲ SYNONYM **tempt**
► **enticement** (*noun*) ► **enticing** (*adjective*): *an* ***enticing*** *idea*

entire (say en-**ty**-uh) *adjective*
whole or complete: *We spent the* ***entire*** *day on the beach.*

entirely (say en-**ty**-uh-lee) *adverb*
completely: *That is an* ***entirely*** *different question.* ◇ *I* ***entirely*** *agree with you.*

entitle *verb* (**entitling, entitled**)
to give somebody the right to do or have something: *I am* ***entitled*** *to take a holiday every year.*

entitled (say in-**tite**-uhld) *adjective*
with the name or title: *The book is* ***entitled*** *'Adventures'.*

entrails (say **en**-traylz) *plural noun*
the internal organs of your body, especially those in the stomach area ➲ SYNONYM **viscera**

entrance (say **en**-truhnss) *noun*
1 (*plural* **entrances**) the door, gate or opening through which you go into a place: *I'll meet you at the* ***entrance*** *to the museum.*
2 (*plural* **entrances**) coming or going into a place: *He made his* ***entrance*** *onto the stage.*
3 (*no plural*) the right to go into a place: *They were refused* ***entrance*** *to the club.*

entrant (say **en**-truhnt) *noun* (*plural* **entrants**)
a person who enters a competition, an exam, a college or a university

entreat (say in-**treet**) *verb* (**entreating, entreated**) (*formal*)
to ask somebody to do something in a serious and often emotional way ➲ SYNONYM **beg** 1

entrenched (say in-**trencht**) *adjective*
something that has existed for a long time and cannot be changed: *an* ***entrenched*** *idea*

entrepreneur (say on-truh-pruh-**nur**) *noun* (*plural* **entrepreneurs**)
a person who makes money by starting and running businesses
► **entrepreneurial** (*adjective*)
► **entrepreneurship** (*noun*)

entrust (say in-**trust**) *verb* (**entrusting, entrusted**) (*formal*)
to make a person responsible for something: *He was* ***entrusted*** *with the care of his younger brother.*

entry (say **en**-tree) *noun*
1 (*no plural*) the act of going into a place: *The thieves gained* ***entry*** (= got in) *through a window.*
2 (*no plural*) the right to go into a place: *There's a sign that says 'No* ***Entry****'.* ◇ *They were refused* ***entry*** *into the country.*
3 (*plural* **entries**) a person or thing that is entered in a competition: *The standard of the* ***entries*** *was very high.*
4 (*plural* **entries**) an item that is written down in a list, account book, index, etc.
5 (*plural* **entries**) a word in a dictionary and all the information that relates to it: *You will find the* ***entries*** *for 'entrust' and 'entrepreneur' just before this* ***entry****.*

enumerate (say i-**nyoo**-muh-rayt) *verb* (**enumerating, enumerated**)
to name or count things one by one

envelop (say in-**vel**-uhp) *verb* (**enveloping, enveloped**)
to cover or surround something completely: *The mountain was* ***enveloped*** *in cloud.*

envelope (say **on**-vuh-lohp or **en**-vuh-lohp) *noun* (*plural* **envelopes**)
a paper cover for a letter: *Have you written his address on the* ***envelope****?*

envied, envies forms of **envy**

A B C D E F G H I J K L M N O P Q R S T U V W X Y Z

envious (say **en**-vi-uhss) *adjective*
wanting what somebody else has: *She's **envious** of her sister's success.* ➲ The noun and verb are both **envy**

environment (say in-**vy**-ruhn-muhnt) *noun*
1 (*plural* **environments**) everything around you: *Children need a happy home **environment**.*
2 the environment (*no plural*) the air, water, land, animals and plants around us: *We must do more to protect the **environment**.*
▸ **environmental** (*adjective*): *pollution and other **environmental** problems*

PRONUNCIATION Make sure you pronounce the **n** before the **m** in **environment**.

environmentalist (say in-vy-ruhn-**men**-tuh-list) *noun* (*plural* **environmentalists**)
a person who tries to protect the **environment**

environmentally friendly *adjective* (also **environment-friendly**)
(used about things you buy) not harming the **environment**: ***environmentally friendly** packaging*

envisage (say in-**viz**-ij) *verb* (**envisaging, envisaged**)
to think that something might happen in the future: *We don't **envisage** any problems.*

envy (say **en**-vee) *noun* (*no plural*)
a sad or angry feeling of wanting what another person has: *I couldn't hide my **envy** of her success.* ◇ *a look of **envy***
▸ **envy** (*verb*): *I **envy** you! You seem so happy!*

enzyme (say **en**-zime) *noun* (*plural* **enzymes**) (*biology*)
a substance, produced by living cells, which helps a chemical change to happen more quickly, without being changed itself: *Some **enzymes** help with the digestion of food.*

epic (say **ep**-ik) *noun* (*plural* **epics**)
a long film or book that contains a lot of action: *His latest film is a historical **epic**.*

epicentre (say **ep**-i-sen-tuh) *noun* (*plural* **epicentres**)
1 the point on the Earth's surface where the effects of an **earthquake** are felt most strongly
2 the central point of a difficulty or problem: *the **epicentre** of the war*

epidemic (say ep-i-**dem**-ik) *noun* (*plural* **epidemics**)
a disease that many people in a place have at the same time: *a flu **epidemic*** ➲ See **endemic** 2, **pandemic**

epidermis (say ep-i-**der**-miss) *noun* (*no plural*)
the outer layer of the skin ➲ See **dermis**
▸ **epidermal** (*adjective*)

epilepsy (say ep-i-**lep**-see) *noun* (*no plural*)
a medical condition of the brain that can cause a person to become unconscious, often with strong movements that they cannot control
▸ **epileptic** (*adjective*)

epilogue (say **ep**-i-log) *noun* (*plural* **epilogues**)
a speech at the end of a play or a section at the end of a book ➲ See **prologue**

episode (say **ep**-i-sohd) *noun* (*plural* **episodes**)
a programme on radio or television that is part of a longer story: *You can see the final **episode** of the series on Monday.*

epitaph (say **ep**-i-taaf) *noun* (*plural* **epitaphs**)
words you write about a dead person: *Have you read the **epitaph** on the tombstone?*

epithet (say **ep**-i-thet) *noun* (*plural* **epithets**)
a word or words you use to say something about the character of a person or a thing: *We often use the **epithet** 'great' to describe leaders, e.g. Catherine the Great.*

epoch (say **ee**-pok) *noun* (*plural* **epochs**)
a period of time in history that is important

equal[1] (say **ee**-kwuhl) *adjective*
the same in size, amount, value or level as another person or thing: *Women want **equal** pay for **equal** work.* ◇ *two **equal** pieces*

equal[2] (say **ee**-kwuhl) *verb* (**equalling, equalled**)
1 to be exactly the same amount as something: *Two plus two **equals** four (2 + 2 = 4).*
2 to be as good as another person or thing: *She **equalled** the Olympic record.*

equal[3] (say **ee**-kwuhl) *noun* (*plural* **equals**)
a person who has the same ability or rights as somebody else: *She treats everyone as her **equal**.*

equality (say ee-**kwo**l-uh-tee) *noun* (*no plural*)
being the same or having the same rights: *People are still fighting for racial **equality**.*
➲ OPPOSITE **inequality**

equalize (say **ee**-kwuh-lize) *verb* (**equalizing, equalized**) (also **equalise**)
to reach the same number of points as an opponent in a game or sport: *The team **equalized** with a goal before half-time.*

equally (say **ee**-kwuh-lee) *adverb*
1 in the same way: *Diet and exercise are **equally** important.*
2 in equal parts or amounts: *The money was divided **equally** among her four children.*

equate (say i-**kwayt**) *verb* (**equating, equated**)
1 to make equal: *One inch* ***equates*** *to approximately 25 millimetres.*
2 to consider one thing to be the same as something else: *You can't always* ***equate*** *money with happiness.*

equation (say i-**kway**-zhuhn) *noun* (*plural* **equations**) (*maths*)
a statement that two quantities are equal: *2x + 5 = 11 is an* ***equation****.*

equator (say i-**kway**-tuh) *noun* (*no plural*)
the line on maps around the middle of the world. Countries near this line are very hot.
➲ See illustration at **globe**
ⓘ **ORIGIN**: 14th–15th century, from Latin *aequator* meaning 'make equal', from a Latin phrase meaning 'circle making day and night equal'

equatorial (say ek-wuh-**taw**-ri-uhl) *adjective*
relating to or near the imaginary line round the centre of the Earth (the **equator**): *equatorial rainforests*

equestrian (say i-**kwess**-tri-uhn) *adjective*
relating to horse riding: *an* ***equestrian*** *show*

equi- (say **ek**-wi) *prefix*
equal or the same as

equidistant (say eek-wi-**diss**-tuhnt) *adjective*
equally far from two or more places

equilateral (say ee-kwi-**lat**-uh-ruhl) *adjective*
having all sides the same length: *an* ***equilateral*** *triangle* ◇ *an* ***equilateral*** *polygon*

equilibrium (say ee-kwi-**lib**-ri-uhm) *noun* (*no plural*)
a state of balance, especially between forces or influences that are working in opposite ways: *a chemical* ***equilibrium***

equine (say **ek**-wine) *adjective*
relating to or similar to horses: ***equine*** *influenza*

equinox (say **ek**-wi-nokss) *noun* (*plural* **equinoxes**)
either of the two times of the year when the sun is above the **equator** and day and night are of equal length: *the spring and autumn* ***equinoxes***

equip (say i-**kwip**) *verb* (**equipping, equipped**)
to get or have all the things that are needed for doing something: ***Equip*** *yourself with a map.*

equipment (say i-**kwip**-muhnt) *noun* (*no plural*)
special things that you need for doing something: *sports* ***equipment***

> **USAGE** **Equipment** does not have a plural. If you are talking about one item, you say **a piece of equipment**.

equity (say **ek**-wi-tee) *noun* (*no plural*)
fair and equal treatment of people: *Is there employment* ***equity*** *in the business?*

equivalence (say i-**kwiv**-uh-luhnss) *noun* (*no plural*)
the condition of being equal in value, amount, meaning or importance: *There was an* ***equivalence*** *between the two teams.*

equivalent (say i-**kwiv**-uh-luhnt) *adjective*
equal in value, amount, meaning or importance: *two* ***equivalent*** *arguments* ◇ *It is roughly* ***equivalent*** *to the size of a brick.*
▸ **equivalent** (*noun*): *She is the female* ***equivalent*** *of Ben.*
ⓘ **ORIGIN**: 14th–15th century, through Old French from Latin *aequivalent* from *aequi-* meaning 'equally' + *valere* meaning 'be worth'

era (say **eer**-ruh) *noun* (*plural* **eras**)
a period of time in history that is special for some reason: *We live in a technological* ***era****.*

eradicate (say i-**rad**-i-kayt) *verb* (**eradicating, eradicated**)
to destroy or get rid of something completely: *Scientists have almost* ***eradicated*** *diseases like polio and smallpox.*
▸ **eradication** (*noun*)

erase (say i-**rayz**) *verb* (**erasing, erased**)
to remove marks, or pictures, music or information: ***Erase*** *the pencil marks.* ◇ *I* ***erased*** *all the files from the computer.*

> **USAGE** We usually say **rub out** when we talk about removing a pencil mark.

eraser (say i-**rayz**-uh) *noun* (*plural* **erasers**)
a small piece of rubber that you use to remove pencil marks from paper ➲ **SYNONYM** **rubber** 2

erect[1] (say i-**rekt**) *adjective* (*formal*)
standing or pointing straight up: *He stood with his head* ***erect****.*

erect[2] (say i-**rekt**) *verb* (**erecting, erected**) (*formal*)
to build something or to make something stand up straight: *The police* ***erected*** *barriers to keep the crowds back.*

erode (say i-**rohd**) *verb* (**eroding, eroded**)
1 (*geography*) to pick up and carry soil, rocks, earth and other particles away: *The sea cliff has been* ***eroded*** *by the waves.*
2 to wear away or destroy something gradually: *My self-esteem was* ***eroded*** *after the injury.*
▸ **erosion** (*noun*): *soil* ***erosion***

A B C D E F G H I J K L M N O P Q R S T U V W X Y Z

A B C D E F G H I J K L M N O P Q R S T U V W X Y Z

erotic (say i-**rot**-ik) *adjective*
causing sexual excitement: *an **erotic** film*

err (say **ur**) *verb* (**erring, erred**) (*formal*)
to make a mistake or do something wrong

errand (say e-**ruhnd**) *noun* (*plural* **errands**)
a short journey to do something for somebody, for example to buy something from a shop: *I've got to run a few **errands** for my mum.*

erratic (say i-**rat**-ik) *adjective*
changing without reason or in a way that is not regular: *Susan's behaviour has been **erratic** recently.*
▶ **erratically** (*adverb*): *He often loses because he plays **erratically**.*

error (say **e**-ruh) *noun* (*plural* **errors**) (*formal*)
something that is done wrong: *The letter was sent to the wrong address because of a computer **error**.* ◇ *I made an **error**.* ➲ SYNONYM **mistake**[1]

erupt (say i-**rupt**) *verb* (**erupting, erupted**)
(used about a **volcano**) to explode and throw out fire, rock that has melted (called **lava**) and smoke: *When Mount Vesuvius **erupted**, it buried the city of Pompeii.*
▶ **eruption** (*noun*): *a volcanic **eruption***

escalate (say **ess**-kuh-layt) *verb* (**escalating, escalated**)
1 to increase or become stronger or bigger: *The cost of living has **escalated** in the last few years.*
2 to become worse or more serious: *The protest march **escalated** into a violent riot.*
▶ **escalation** (*noun*): *a rapid price **escalation***

escalator (say **ess**-kuh-lay-tuh) *noun* (*plural* **escalators**)
moving stairs that carry people up and down

escape[1] (say i-**skayp**) *verb* (**escaping, escaped**)
1 to get free from somebody or something: *Two prisoners **escaped**, but were later caught.*
2 to manage to avoid something dangerous or unpleasant: *The pilot **escaped** death.*

escape[2] (say i-**skayp**) *noun* (*plural* **escapes**)
the act or a method of getting free from a person or place or avoiding an unpleasant or dangerous situation: *When it got dark, she made her **escape**.* ◇ *She had a lucky **escape*** (= something bad almost happened to her) *when her car crashed.*

escarpment (say i-**skaap**-muhnt) *noun* (*plural* **escarpments**) (*geography*)
a long steep slope or cliff that separates an area of high ground from an area of low ground: *the Great **Escarpment***

escort[1] (say **ess**-kawt) *noun* (*plural* **escorts**)
one or more people or vehicles that go with somebody to protect them: *The President always travels with an armed **escort**.*

escort[2] (say i-**skawt**) *verb* (**escorting, escorted**)
to go with somebody, for example to protect them or to make sure that they arrive somewhere: *The police **escorted** him out of the building.*

especially (say i-**spesh**-uh-lee) *adverb*
1 more than usual or more than others: *I hate getting up early, **especially** in winter.* ◇ *She loves animals, **especially** horses.*
2 for a particular person or thing: *I bought these flowers **especially** for you.*

espionage (say **ess**-pi-uh-naazh) *noun* (*no plural*)
the act of finding out secret information about another country or organization ➲ See **spy**[2]

essay (say **ess**-ay) *noun* (*plural* **essays**)
a short piece of writing about a particular subject: *I wrote an **essay** called 'Dreams'.*

essence (say **ess**-uhnss) *noun*
1 (*no plural*) the basic or most important idea or quality of something: *What is the **essence** of the problem?*
2 (*plural* **essences**) a substance from a plant or other matter that has a strong smell or taste: *vanilla **essence***

essential (say i-**sen**-shuhl) *adjective*
describing something that is completely necessary and that you must have or do: *It is **essential** that you work hard for this exam.*

essentially (say i-**sen**-shuh-lee) *adverb*
when you consider the basic or most important part of something: *The problem is **essentially** one of money.*

establish (say i-**stab**-lish) *verb* (**establishing, established**)
to start something new: *The school was **established** in 1904.*

establishment (say i-**stab**-lish-muhnt) *noun*
1 (*plural* **establishments**) an organization or business: *an educational **establishment***
2 (*plural* **establishments**) when you start an organization or business: *The government provided money for the **establishment** of new schools.*
3 the Establishment the organizations and people in a country that have power and do not usually support change

estate (say i-**stayt**) *noun* (*plural* **estates**)
1 a large piece of land away from towns and

cities that one person or family owns
2 land with a lot of houses or factories on it: *a wine **estate** ◇ an industrial **estate*** (= where there are a lot of factories)
3 all the money and property that a person owns, especially everything that is left when they die

esteem (say i-**steem**) *noun* (*no plural*)
great respect and admiration for somebody: *Many people hold her in high **esteem**.*

estimate[1] (say **ess**-ti-muht) *noun* (*plural* **estimates**)
a guess about the size or cost of something before you have all the facts and figures: *Can you give me a rough **estimate** of how many people will be there?*

estimate[2] (say **ess**-ti-mayt) *verb* (**estimating, estimated**)
to say how much you think something will cost, how big something is, or how long it will take to do something: *The builders **estimated** that it would take a week to repair the roof.*

estuary (say **ess**-tyuu-uh-ree) *noun* (*plural* **estuaries**)
the wide part of a river where it goes into the sea: *the St Lucia **Estuary***

etc. (say et-**set**-ruh) *abbreviation* used at the end of a list to show that there are other things but you are not going to name them all: *Remember to take some paper, a pen, **etc.*** ❶ **Etc.** is short for the Latin words 'et cetera', which mean 'and the rest'.

etch (say **ech**) *verb* (**etching, etched**)
to cut words or pictures into a hard surface: *Their initials were **etched** on the rock.*

eternal (say i-**turn**-l) *adjective*
existing or continuing for ever: *They believe in **eternal** life* (= life after death).

ethical (say **eth**-ik-l) *adjective*
1 relating to beliefs about what is right or wrong: *an **ethical** problem*
2 morally correct and good: *His behaviour was not **ethical**.*

ethics (say **eth**-ikss) *plural noun*
ideas and beliefs about what is morally right and wrong: *Health care professionals have a code of **ethics**.*

ethnic (say **eth**-nik) *adjective*
connected with or belonging to a group of people who share a cultural tradition: *South Africa is home to many different **ethnic** groups.* ◇ ***ethnic** food* ◇ ***ethnic** violence* (= between people who belong to different cultural or religious or language groups)

etiquette (say **et**-i-ket) *noun* (*no plural*)
rules about polite and correct behaviour

etymology (say et-i-**mol**-uh-jee) *noun*
1 (*no plural*) the study of the origins and history of words and their meanings
2 (*plural* **etymologies**) the origin and history of a particular word

eucalyptus (say yoo-kuh-**lip**-tuhss) *noun* (*plural* **eucalyptuses** or **eucalypti**)
a tall straight tree that comes mainly from Australia. Its leaves produce an oil with a strong smell, that is used in medicine.

euphemism (say **yoo**-fuh-miz-uhm) *noun* (*plural* **euphemisms**)
words or phrases that you use instead of other words that may be embarrassing or unpleasant: *'To pass away' is a **euphemism** for 'to die'.*
▸ **euphemistic** (*adjective*)
▸ **euphemistically** (*adverb*)

euphoria (say yoo-**faw**-ri-uh) *noun* (*no plural*)
a very strong feeling of happiness
▸ **euphoric** (*adjective*): *a **euphoric** mood*

euro (say **yoo**-roh) *noun* (*plural* **euros**) (symbol €)
the unit of money that is used in many countries of the European Union: *All prices are in **euros**.*

Eurocentric (say **yoor**-roh-sen-trik) *adjective*
using European ideas to judge or view things: *A **Eurocentric** view*

European (say **yoor**-ruh-**pee**-uhn) *adjective*
from or connected with Europe: ***European** languages*
▸ **European** (*noun*): *Many **Europeans*** (= people from Europe) *settled here in the nineteenth century.*

European Union *noun* (*no plural*) (abbr. EU)
an organization of European countries that encourages **trade[1]** between its members

euthanasia (say yoo-thuh-**nay**-zhuh) *noun* (*no plural*)
the practice of killing a person or animal without pain, usually because they are suffering from a disease that cannot be cured

evacuate (say i-**vak**-yuu-ayt) *verb* (**evacuating, evacuated**)
to take people away from a dangerous place to a safer place: *The area near the factory was **evacuated** after the explosion.*
▸ **evacuation** (*noun*): *the **evacuation** of cities during a war*

evade (say i-**vayd**) *verb* (**evading, evaded**)
1 to escape from something or avoid meeting someone: *The robbers managed to **evade** the police.*

A B C D E F G H I J K L M N O P Q R S T U V W X Y Z

2 to avoid dealing with something: *Politicians often **evade** questions!*
▸ **evasion** (*noun*)

evaluate (say i-**val**-yuu-ayt) *verb* (**evaluating, evaluated**)
to study something and assess it or form an opinion about it: *The engineers **evaluated** the project.* ◇ *You need to **evaluate** this story critically.*
▸ **evaluation** (*noun*): *We need an **evaluation** of each learner's work* ➲ See Study page 19

evangelical (say i-van-**jel**-ik-l) *adjective*
of or belonging to a Christian group that believes that religious ceremony is not as important as belief in Jesus Christ and study of the Bible

evangelist (say i-**van**-juh-list) *noun* (*plural* **evangelists**)
a person who enthusiastically tries to make other people believe in Christianity

evaporate (say i-**vap**-uh-rayt) *verb* (**evaporating, evaporated**)
(used about a liquid) to change into a gas: *Water **evaporates** when you heat it.*
➲ See **condense** 1

eve (say **eev**) *noun* (*no plural*)
the day before a special day: *24 December is Christmas **Eve**.* ◇ *I went to a party on New Year's **Eve*** (= 31 December).

even[1] (say **eev**-uhn) *adverb*
1 a word that you use to say that something is surprising: *The game is so easy that **even** a child can play it.* ◇ *He didn't laugh – he didn't **even** smile.*
2 a word that you use to make another word stronger: *Their house is **even** smaller than ours.*
even if it does not change anything if: ***Even** if you run, you won't catch the bus.*
even so although that is true: *I didn't have any lunch, but **even** so I'm not hungry.*
even though although: *I went to the party, **even** though I was tired.*

even[2] (say **eev**-uhn) *adjective*
1 flat and smooth: *The game must be played on an **even** surface.* ➲ OPPOSITE **uneven**
2 the same or equal: *She won the first game and I won the second, so we're **even**.*
3 (*maths*) describing numbers that can be divided exactly by two: *4, 6 and 8 are **even** numbers.* ➲ OPPOSITE **odd** 2

evening (say **eev**-ning) *noun* (*plural* **evenings**)
the part of the day between the afternoon and when you go to bed: *What are you doing this **evening**?* ◇ *Most people watch television in the **evening**?* ◇ *John came on Monday **evening**.*

event (say i-**vent**) *noun* (*plural* **events**)
1 something important that happens: *My sister's wedding was a big **event** for our family.*
2 a race or competition: *The next **event** will be the high jump.*

eventuality (say i-ven-tshuu-**al**-i-tee) *noun* (*plural* **eventualities**)
something that may happen: *You should be prepared for all **eventualities**.*

eventually (say i-**ven**-tshuu-uh-lee) *adverb*
after a long time: *The bus **eventually** arrived two hours late.*

ever (say **ev**-uh) *adverb*
at any time: *'Have you **ever** been to London?' 'No, I haven't.'* ◇ *I hardly **ever*** (= almost never) *see Andile any more.*
ever since in all the time since: *I have known Dimako **ever** since we were children.*
for ever always, for all time: *I will love you for **ever**.*
ⓘ ORIGIN: from Old English *ǣfre*

evergreen (say **ev**-uh-green) *noun* (*plural* **evergreens**)
a tree or bush that has green leaves throughout the year
▸ **evergreen** (*adjective*): ***evergreen** trees*

everlasting (say ev-uh-**laass**-ting) *adjective*
continuing for ever or for a very long time: ***everlasting** love*

every *adjective*
1 all of the people or things in a group: *She knows **every** student in the school.*
2 used for saying how often something happens: *He phones **every** evening.* ◇ *I see Robert **every** now and then* (= sometimes, but not often). ◇ *She comes **every** other day* (= for example on Monday, Wednesday and Friday but not on Tuesday or Thursday).

everybody (say **ev**-ri-bod-ee) *pronoun*
each person or all people: ***Everybody** knows Lerato.* ◇ ***Everybody** has a chance to win.*
➲ SYNONYM **everyone**

everyday (say **ev**-ri-day) *adjective*
not special, but normal: *Computers are now part of **everyday** life.*

everyone (say **ev**-ri-wun) *pronoun*
each person or all people: *If **everyone** is here, then we can start.*

everything (say **ev**-ri-thing) *pronoun*
each thing or all things: *He lost **everything** in the fire.*

everywhere (say **ev**-ri-wair) *adverb*
in all places or to all places: *I've looked **everywhere** for my pen, but I can't find it.*

evict (say i-**vikt**) *verb* (**evicting, evicted**)
to force somebody to leave a place that they are renting: *They were **evicted** because they did not pay the rent.*
▸ **eviction** (*noun*)

evidence (say **ev**-i-duhnss) *noun* (*no plural*)
the facts, signs or objects that make you believe that something is true: *The police searched for **evidence**.* ◇ *There is **evidence** of a link between smoking and cancer.*
give evidence to say what you know about a person or thing in a court of law: *The man who saw the accident will give **evidence** in court.*

evident (say **ev**-i-duhnt) *adjective*
easy to see or understand: *It was **evident** that the damage was very serious.* ➲ SYNONYM **obvious**

evidently (say **ev**-i-duhnt-lee) *adverb*
clearly, obviously: *She was **evidently** very upset.*

evil (say **eev**-il) *adjective*
morally bad and cruel: *an **evil** person*
➲ SYNONYM **wicked** 1
▸ **evil** (*noun*): *a terrible **evil***

evoke (say i-**vohk**) *verb* (**evoking, evoked**)
to make a person feel an emotion or remember something: *That music always **evokes** memories of my childhood.*
▸ **evocative** (*adjective*): *an **evocative** piece of writing*

evolution (say ee-vuh-**loo**-shuhn) *noun* (*no plural*)
1 (*biology*) the change or development of populations of living organisms over many thousands of years: *Darwin's theory of **evolution***
2 the gradual process of change or development of something: *the **evolution** of a city*

evolve (say i-**volv**) *verb* (**evolving, evolved**)
1 (*biology*) (used about populations of living organisms) to change and develop over many thousands of years
2 to gradually change and develop: *His style of painting has **evolved** over the past twenty years.*

ewe (say **yoo**) *noun* (*plural* **ewes**)
a female sheep ➲ See **ram**[1]

ex- (say **ekss**) *prefix*
used to be, former: *She never sees her **ex-husband**.* ◇ *the **ex-president***
ℹ ORIGIN: from Greek *ex* meaning 'out of'

exact (say ig-**zakt**) *adjective*
completely correct: *We need to know the **exact** time the incident occurred.*

exactly (say ig-**zakt**-lee) *adverb*
1 used when you are asking for or giving information that is completely correct: *Can you tell me **exactly** what happened?* ◇ *It cost **exactly** R10.* ➲ SYNONYM **precisely**
2 in every way or detail: *This shirt is **exactly** what I wanted.* ➲ SYNONYM **just**[1] 1
3 used to agree with somebody: *'So you mean somebody in this room must be the murderer?' '**Exactly**.'*

exaggerate (say ig-**zaj**-uh-rayt) *verb* (**exaggerating, exaggerated**)
to say that something is bigger, better or worse than it really is: *Don't **exaggerate**! I was only two minutes late, not twenty.*
▸ **exaggeration** (*noun*): *It's a bit of an **exaggeration** to say she can't speak English!*

SPELLING Remember! You spell **exaggerate** with **gg**.

exam (say ig-**zam**) *noun* (*plural* **exams**)
a test of what you know or can do: *We've got an English **exam** next week.* ℹ **Exam** is short for 'examination'.

WORD BUILDING You **write** an exam or **take** an exam. If you do well, you **pass**, and if you do badly, you **fail**.

examination (say ig-zam-i-**nay**-shuhn) *noun* (*plural* **examinations**)
1 an act of looking carefully at a person or thing: *a medical **examination***
2 (*formal*) a test of what you know or can do
➲ SYNONYM **exam**

examine (say ig-**zam**-in) *verb* (**examining, examined**)
1 to look carefully at a person or thing: *The doctor **examined** her but found nothing wrong.*
2 (*formal*) to ask questions to find out what somebody knows or what they can do: *You will be **examined** on this year's work.*

example (say ig-**zaam**-puhl) *noun* (*plural* **examples**)
something that shows what other things of the same kind are like: *This dictionary gives many **examples** of how we use words.*
for example used for giving an example: *Do you speak any other languages, for **example** French or German?* ℹ The short way of writing 'for example' is **e.g.**

exasperate (say ig-**zass**-puh-rayt) *verb* (**exasperating, exasperated**)
to make somebody very angry or annoyed
▸ **exasperating** (*adjective*): *What an **exasperating** experience!* ▸ **exasperation** (*noun*): *She threw the book down in **exasperation**.* ▸ **exasperated** (*adjective*): *They were **exasperated** by all the delays.*

A B C D E F G H I J K L M N O P Q R S T U V W X Y Z

A B C D E F G H I J K L M N O P Q R S T U V W X Y Z

excavate (say **ekss**-kuh-vayt) *verb* (**excavating, excavated**)
to dig in the ground, for example to look for old objects or buildings: *Bones and spears were **excavated** from the site of the battle.*
▸ **excavation** (*noun*): *The archaeology students helped with the **excavation** of the temple.*

exceed (say ik-**seed**) *verb* (**exceeding, exceeded**)
to be more than a particular number or amount: *The weight must not **exceed** 20 kilograms.* ➲ SYNONYM **surpass**
➲ The noun is **excess**

exceedingly (say ik-**see**-ding-lee) *adverb*
very: *It is an **exceedingly** difficult problem.*

excel (say ek-**sel**) *verb* (**excelling, excelled**)
to be very good at something: *She **excelled** at mathematics.*
to excel yourself to do something better than you usually do: *You really **excelled** yourself this time!*

excellent (say **ek**-suh-luhnt) *adjective*
very good: *She speaks **excellent** Sesotho.*

> SPELLING Remember! You spell **excellent** with a **c** and **ll**.

> WORD BUILDING See the note at **good**.

except (say ik-**sept**) *preposition*
not including a person or thing: *The restaurant is open every day **except** Sunday.* ◇ *Everyone went to the party **except** me.*
except that apart from the fact that: *I don't know what he looks like, **except** that he's very tall.*

> SPELLING Be careful! Don't confuse **except** and **accept**, which sound similar but have different spellings and different meanings.

exception (say ik-**sep**-shuhn) *noun* (*plural* **exceptions**)
a person or thing that is not the same as the others: *Most of his films are good but this one is an **exception**.*
with the exception of a person or **thing** except or apart from: *I like all vegetables with the **exception** of cabbage.*

exceptional (say ik-**sep**-shuhn-l) *adjective*
very good: *She is an **exceptional** pianist.*
▸ **exceptionally** (*adverb*): *He was an **exceptionally** bright student.*

excess (say ik-**sess**) *noun* (*no plural*)
more than is necessary or usual: *An **excess** of stress can make you ill.* ➲ The verb is **exceed**
▸ **excess** (*adjective*): *Cut any **excess** fat off the meat.* ▸ **excessive** (*adjective*): *an **excessive** amount of fat* ◇ ***excessive** spending*

> WHICH WORD? **In excess of** or **more than**? In sentences such as these, it is simpler and clearer to say **more than** or **over**: *More than 300 people came.* ◇ *He earned **over** R9 000.*

exchange¹ (say ikss-**chaynj**) *noun* (*plural* **exchanges**)
giving or receiving something in return for something else: *I'll give you my jacket in **exchange** for your jeans.* ➲ See **stock exchange**

exchange² (say ikss-**chaynj**) *verb* (**exchanging, exchanged**)
to give one thing and get another thing for it: *Can I **exchange** this skirt for a bigger size?* ◇ *We **exchanged** phone numbers.*

exchange rate *noun* (*plural* **exchange rates**)
how much money from one country you can buy with money from another country: *The **exchange rate** is R14,54 to the pound.*

excise (say **ek**-size) *noun* (*no plural*)
a government tax on certain goods such as cigarettes and alcohol

excite (say ik-**site**) *verb* (**exciting, excited**)
to make a person feel very happy or enthusiastic so that they are not calm: *Please don't **excite** the children too much.*
▸ **excitement** (*noun*): *There was great **excitement** about the party.*

excited (say ik-**site**-uhd) *adjective*
not calm, for example because you are happy about something that is going to happen: *He's **excited** about his holiday.*

exciting (say ik-**site**-ing) *adjective*
describing something that makes you have strong feelings of happiness and enthusiasm: *an **exciting** film* ◇ *Her new job sounds very **exciting**.*

exclaim (say ikss-**klaym**) *verb* (**exclaiming, exclaimed**)
to say something suddenly and loudly because you are surprised or angry: *'I don't believe it!' she **exclaimed**.*

exclamation (say ekss-kluh-**may**-shuhn) *noun* (*plural* **exclamations**)
a short sound, word or phrase that you say suddenly because of a strong feeling, pain, etc.: *'Ouch!' is an **exclamation**.*

exclamation mark *noun* (*plural* **exclamation marks**)
a mark (**!**) that you use in writing to show loud or strong words, or surprise
➲ See Study page 16

exclude (say ikss-**klood**) *verb* (**excluding, excluded**)
1 to deliberately not include something: *The bill **excludes** a tip.* ➲ OPPOSITE **include**
2 to not allow a person to enter a place or do an activity: *Students were **excluded** from the meeting.*
ℹ ORIGIN: 14th–15th century, from Latin *excludere* meaning 'to shut out' from *ex-* meaning 'out' + *claudere* meaning 'to shut'

excluding (say ikss-**kloo**-ding) *preposition*
without: *The meal cost R45, **excluding** drinks.* ➲ OPPOSITE **including**

exclusive (say ikss-**kloo**-siv) *adjective*
1 something which is not to be shared with another person or group: *The musician gave an **exclusive** interview.*
2 expensive and only for people who are rich or important: *an **exclusive** club*
exclusive of (*formal*) not including something: *The price of the ticket is **exclusive** of tax.*

excommunicate (say ekss-kuh-**myoon**-i-kayt) *verb* (**excommunicating, excommunicated**)
to remove somebody from being a member of a Christian church

excrement (say **ekss**-kri-muhnt) *noun* (*no plural*) (*formal*)
the solid waste material that you get rid of when you go to the toilet

excrete (say ik-**skreet**) *verb* (**excreting, excreted**) (*biology*)
to get rid of waste material from the body
▸ **excretion** (*noun*)

excursion (say ik-**skur**-shuhn) *noun* (*plural* **excursions**)
a short journey to see something interesting or to enjoy yourself: *We're going on an **excursion** to the beach.* ➲ SYNONYMS **outing, trip**[1]

excuse[1] (say ik-**skyooss**) *noun* (*plural* **excuses**)
words you say or write to explain why you have done something wrong: *What's your **excuse**?* ◇ *There's no **excuse** for rudeness.*

> **PRONUNCIATION** Notice that you pronounce the noun and the verb differently.

excuse[2] (say ik-**skyooz**) *verb* (**excusing, excused**)
used when you are saying sorry for something that is not very bad: *Please **excuse** us for being late – we missed the bus.*
excuse me Used when you want to stop a person who is speaking, or when you want to speak to a person you do not know: ***Excuse** me, could you tell me the time?*

execute (say **ek**-si-kyoot) *verb* (**executing, executed**)
to kill a person as a legal punishment: *He was **executed** for murder.*
▸ **execution** (*noun*): *the **execution** of prisoners*

executive[1] (say ig-**zek**-yuh-tiv) *noun* (*plural* **executives**)
a person who has an important position in a business or organization

executive[2] (say ig-**zek**-yuh-tiv) *adjective*
1 relating to managing a business and making decisions: *She is an **executive** director of the bank.*
2 something designed for important business people: *an **executive** briefcase*

exemplar (say ig-**zem**-plaa) *noun* (*plural* **exemplars**)
a typical or very good example of something

exempt (say ig-**zempt**) *verb* (**exempting, exempted**)
to say officially that a person does not have to do something or pay something: *You are **exempted** from paying tax if you earn a very low salary.*
▸ **exempt** (*adjective*): *Fresh fruit is **exempt** from VAT.* ▸ **exemption** (*noun*): *a tax **exemption***

exercise[1] (say **ek**-suh-size) *noun*
1 (*no plural*) moving your body to keep it strong and well: *Swimming is very good **exercise**.*
2 (*plural* **exercises**) a special movement that you do to keep your body strong and well: *This **exercise** is good for your back.*
3 (*plural* **exercises**) a piece of work that you do to learn something: *Please do **exercises** 1 and 2 for homework.*

exercise[2] (say **ek**-suh-size) *verb* (**exercising, exercised**)
to move your body to keep it strong and well: *They **exercise** in the park every morning.*

exercise book *noun* (*plural* **exercise books**)
a book that you use at school for writing in

exhale (say ekss-**hayl**) *verb* (**exhaling, exhaled**)
to breathe out ➲ OPPOSITE **inhale**
▸ **exhalation** (*noun*)

exhaust[1] (say ig-**zawst**) *noun*
1 (*no plural*) the waste gas that comes out of a vehicle, an engine or a machine: *car **exhaust** fumes*
2 (*plural* **exhausts**) (also **exhaust pipe**) a pipe through which waste gases come out, for example on a car

A B C D E F G H I J K L M N O P Q R S T U V W X Y Z

exhaust[2] (say ig-**zawst**) *verb* (**exhausting, exhausted**)
to make you feel very tired: *The long journey **exhausted** us.*
▸ **exhausted** (*adjective*): *I'm **exhausted** – I think I'll go to bed.*

exhausting (say ig-**zawss**-ting) *adjective*
making you feel very tired: *Teaching young children can be **exhausting**.*

exhibit[1] (say ig-**zib**-it) *verb* (**exhibiting, exhibited**)
to show something in a public place for people to look at: *Her photographs have been **exhibited** all over the world.*

exhibit[2] (say ig-**zib**-it) *noun* (*plural* **exhibits**)
an object or group of objects shown in a museum, art gallery or fair
▸ **exhibitor** (*noun*): *Were there many **exhibitors** at the agricultural fair?*

exhibition (say ek-si-**bish**-uhn) *noun* (*plural* **exhibitions**)
a group of things that are arranged in a place so that people can look at them: *an **exhibition** of paintings by Monet*

exhilarate (say ig-**zil**-uh-rayt) *verb* (**exhilarating, exhilarated**)
to make somebody feel excited or happy: *We were **exhilarated** by the music!*
▸ **exhilarating** (*adjective*): *an **exhilarating** experience* ▸ **exhilaration** (*noun*)

exile (say **ek**-sile) *noun*
1 (*no plural*) having to live away from your own country, especially for political reasons or as a punishment: *Napoleon spent the last years of his life in **exile**.*
2 (*plural* **exiles**) a person who has to live away from their own country

exist (say ig-**zist**) *verb* (**existing, existed**)
to live, or to be real: *Does life **exist** on other planets?* ◇ *You can't **exist** on water alone.*

existence (say ig-**ziss**-tuhnss) *noun* (*no plural*)
the state of existing or being real: *The company came into **existence*** (= started up) *in 2003.*

exit (say **ek**-sit) *noun* (*plural* **exits**)
a way out of a building: *Where is the **exit**?* ◇ *an emergency **exit***

exorbitant (say ig-**zaw**-bi-tuhnt) *adjective*
something that is more expensive than it should be: *an **exorbitant** price*

exorcize (say **ek**-saw-size) *verb* (**exorcizing, exorcized**) (also **exorcise**)
to try to make evil spirits leave a person or a place
▸ **exorcism** (*noun*): ***exorcism** of ghosts*
▸ **exorcist** (*noun*): *He's an **exorcist**.*

exoskeleton (say **ek**-soh-skel-uh-tuhn) *noun* (*plural* **exoskeletons**) (*biology*)
a hard outer covering that protects the bodies of certain animals, such as insects ➲ See **endoskeleton**

exotic (say ig-**zot**-ik) *adjective*
1 from another country, especially a tropical one: *Some **exotic** plants take resources from indigenous plants.* ◇ ***exotic** fruits* ➲ See **alien**[1] 1
2 exciting and unusual because it is connected with foreign countries

expand (say ik-**spand**) *verb* (**expanding, expanded**)
to become bigger or to make something bigger: *Metals **expand** when they are heated.* ◇ *We hope to **expand** the business this year.*
➲ OPPOSITE **contract**[2] 1
▸ **expansion** (*noun*): *the city's rapid **expansion***

expanse (say ik-**spanss**) *noun* (*plural* **expanses**)
a large open area of land or sea or sky

expect (say ik-**spekt**) *verb* (**expecting, expected**)
1 to think that somebody or something will come or that something will happen: *I'm **expecting** a letter.* ◇ *We **expected** the weather to be cold, but it was quite hot.*
2 (*informal*) to think that something will happen or is probably true: *I **expect** she'll be late. She usually is.*
be expected to do something to have to do something: *I am **expected** to work every Saturday.*

expectation (say ek-spek-**tay**-shuhn) *noun* (*plural* **expectations**)
a belief that something will happen: *Against all **expectations**, we enjoyed ourselves.*

expedite (say **ekss**-puh-dite) *verb* (**expediting, expedited**)
to make something happen more quickly: *What can we do to **expedite** the process?*

expedition (say ekss-puh-**dish**-uhn) *noun* (*plural* **expeditions**)
a journey to find or do something special: *an **expedition** to the South Pole*

expel (say ik-**spel**) *verb* (**expelling, expelled**)
to send somebody away from a school, a club or a country: *The boys were **expelled** from school for smoking.*

expense (say ik-**spenss**) *noun*
1 (*plural* **expenses**) the cost of something: *Having a car is a big **expense**.*
2 expenses (*plural noun*) money that you

spend on a certain thing: *When you start a business, there are many **expenses**.*

expensive (say ik-**spen**-siv) *adjective* describing something that costs a lot of money: ***expensive** clothes* ◇ *The meal was very **expensive**.* ➲ OPPOSITE **cheap** 1 ➲ SYNONYM **costly**

experience[1] (say ik-**speer**-ri-uhnss) *noun* **1** (*no plural*) knowing about something because you have seen it or done it: *She has four years' teaching **experience**.* ◇ *Do you have much **experience** of working with children?* ➲ OPPOSITE **inexperience**
2 (*plural* **experiences**) something that has happened to you: *He wrote a book about his **experiences** in Africa.*

experience[2] (say ik-**speer**-ri-uhnss) *verb* (**experiencing, experienced**) to have something happen to you: *Everyone **experiences** failure at some time in their lives.*

experienced (say ik-**speer**-ri-uhnst) *adjective* knowing about something because you have done it many times before: *She's an **experienced** driver.* ➲ OPPOSITE **inexperienced**

experiment (say ik-**spe**-ri-muhnt) *noun* (*plural* **experiments**) a scientific test that you do to find out what will happen or to see if something is true: *They have to do **experiments** to find out if the drug is safe for humans.*
▸ **experiment** (*verb*): *I don't think it's right to **experiment** on animals.* ▸ **experimental** (*adjective*)

expert (say **ekss**-purt) *noun* (*plural* **experts**) a person who knows a lot about something: *He's an **expert** on Shakespeare.* ◇ *a computer **expert***

expire (say ik-**spy**-uh) *verb* (**expiring, expired**) to come to the end of the time when you can use something: *I need to renew my licence before it **expires**.*

expiry (say ik-**spy**-ree) *noun* (*no plural*) the end of a period when you can use something: *The **expiry** date on this yoghurt was 20 November.*

explain (say ik-**splayn**) *verb* (**explaining, explained**)
1 to tell somebody about something so that they understand it: *The teacher usually **explains** the new words to us.* ◇ *He **explained** how to use the machine.*
2 to give a reason for something: *I **explained** why we needed the money.*

explanation (say ekss-pluh-**nay**-shuhn) *noun* (*plural* **explanations**) something that helps somebody understand something, or a reason for something: *The teacher gave a long **explanation**.*

explicit (say ik-**spliss**-it) *adjective*
1 very clear and exact: *She gave us **explicit** instructions.*
2 not hiding anything: *The film has an age restriction because the sex and violence in it are **explicit**.*

explode (say ik-**splohd**) *verb* (**exploding, exploded**) to burst suddenly with a very loud noise: *A bomb **exploded** in the city centre, killing two people.* ➲ The noun is **explosion**

exploit (say ik-**sployt**) *verb* (**exploiting, exploited**) to treat somebody badly to get what you want: *Some employers **exploit** foreign workers, making them work long hours for low pay.*

explore (say ik-**splaw**) *verb* (**exploring, explored**)
1 to travel around a new place to learn about it: *They **explored** the area on foot.*
2 to examine something carefully in order to find out more about it: ***Explore** the history of the amaXhosa before 1820.*
▸ **exploration** (*noun*): *the **exploration** of space*

explorer (say ik-**splaw**-ruh) *noun* (*plural* **explorers**) a person who travels around a new place to learn about it: *The first European **explorers** arrived in America in the 15th century.*

explosion (say ik-**sploh**-zhuhn) *noun* (*plural* **explosions**) the sudden bursting and loud noise of something such as a bomb going off: *There was an **explosion** and pieces of glass flew everywhere.* ➲ The verb is **explode**

explosive (say ik-**sploh**-siv) *adjective*
1 describing something that can cause an explosion: *an **explosive** gas*
2 causing strong feelings or having dangerous effects: *The leader of the protest gave an **explosive** speech.*
▸ **explosive** (*noun*): *Gunpowder is an **explosive**.*

expo (say **ekss**-poh) *noun* (*plural* **expos**) a big exhibition ❶ **Expo** is short for 'exposition'.

export[1] (say ek-**spawt**) *verb* (**exporting, exported**) to sell things to another country: *Japan **exports** cars to Britain.* ➲ See **import[1]**

A B C D E F G H I J K L M N O P Q R S T U V W X Y Z

A B C D E F G H I J K L M N O P Q R S T U V W X Y Z

▸ **exporter** (*noun*): *the world's biggest* ***exporter*** *of oil*

PRONUNCIATION Notice that you pronounce the verb and the noun differently.

export² (say **ek**-spawt) *noun*
1 (*no plural*) the process of selling things to another country: *These cars are made for* ***export****.*
2 (*plural* **exports**) something that you sell to another country: *The country's main* ***exports*** *are tea and cotton.* ➲ See **import²**

expose (say ik-**spohz**) *verb* (**exposing, exposed**)
1 to show something that is usually covered or hidden: *The angry dog* ***exposed*** *its teeth.* ◇ *The newspaper* ***exposed*** *his terrible secret.*
2 to put yourself or another person or thing in a situation that could be difficult or dangerous: *The factory workers were* ***exposed*** *to dangerous chemicals.*

express¹ (say ik-**spress**) *verb* (**expressing, expressed**)
to say or show how you think or feel: *She* ***expressed*** *her ideas well.*

express² (say ik-**spress**) *adjective*
that goes or is sent very quickly: *an* ***express*** *letter* ◇ *an* ***express*** *coach*
▸ **express** (*adverb*): *I sent the parcel* ***express****.*

express³ (say ik-**spress**) *noun* (*plural* **expresses**) (also **express train**)
a fast train that does not stop at all stations

expression (say ik-**spresh**-uhn) *noun* (*plural* **expressions**)
1 the look on your face that shows how you feel: *an* ***expression*** *of surprise*
2 a word or group of words, or a way of saying something: *The* ***expression*** *'to drop off' means 'to fall asleep'.*

exquisite (say ek-**skwiz**-it) *adjective*
extremely beautiful: *She has an* ***exquisite*** *face.*

extend (say ik-**stend**) *verb* (**extending, extended**)
1 to make something longer or bigger: *I'm* ***extending*** *my holiday for another week.*
2 to reach or stretch over an area: *The park* ***extends*** *as far as the river.*

extension (say ik-**sten**-shuhn) *noun* (*plural* **extensions**)
1 a part that you add to something to make it bigger: *They've built an* ***extension*** *on the back of the house.*
2 one of the telephones in a building that is connected to the main telephone: *Can I have* ***extension*** *4110, please?*

extensive (say ik-**sten**-siv) *adjective*
large in area or amount: *The floods caused* ***extensive*** *damage.*

extent (say ik-**stent**) *noun* (*no plural*)
how big something is: *I had no idea of the full* ***extent*** *of the problem* (= how big it was).
to a certain extent, to some extent used to show that you do not think something is completely true: *I agree with you to a certain* ***extent****.*

exterior (say ik-**steer**-ri-uh) *noun* (*plural* **exteriors**)
the outside part of something, especially a building: *We painted the* ***exterior*** *of the house white.* ➲ OPPOSITE **interior**
▸ **exterior** (*adjective*): *an* ***exterior*** *door*

external (say ik-**stur**-nuhl) *adjective*
on, of or from the outside: ***external*** *walls*
➲ OPPOSITE **internal**

extinct (say ik-**stinkt**) *adjective*
(used about a type of animal or plant) that does not exist now: *Dinosaurs became* ***extinct*** *millions of years ago.*

extinguish (say ik-**sting**-gwish) *verb* (**extinguishing, extinguished**) (*formal*)
to make something stop burning: *The fire engines* ***extinguished*** *the fire.*

extort (say ik-**stawt**) *verb* (**extorting, extorted**)
to get something by using threats or violence: *The gang* ***extorted*** *money from local businesses.*
▸ **extortion** (*noun*)

extra¹ (say **ek**-struh) *adjective, adverb*
more than what is usual: *I've put an* ***extra*** *blanket on your bed because it's cold tonight.*
ⓘ ORIGIN: from Latin *extra* meaning 'outside'

extra² (say **ek**-struh) *noun* (*plural* **extras**)
1 something that costs more or that is not included: *Air-conditioning is an optional* ***extra*** *on this car.*
2 a person in a film who has a small part

extra- (say **ek**-struh) *prefix*
1 outside, beyond: ***extraterrestrial*** *life*
2 very, more than usual: *an* ***extra-special*** *gift*

extract¹ (say ik-**strakt**) *verb* (**extracting, extracted**) (*formal*)
1 to take something out, often with difficulty: *The dentist had to* ***extract*** *the tooth.*
2 to get something that you want from a person: *I wasn't able to* ***extract*** *the information from him.*

PRONUNCIATION Notice that you pronounce the noun and the verb differently.

extract[2] (say **ek**-strakt) *noun* (*plural* **extracts**)
1 a part of a book or poem or a piece of music that you choose: *The author read an* ***extract*** *from her new book.*
2 a substance you take from other substances: *vegetable* ***extract***

extramural (say ek-struh-**myoo**-ruhl) *adjective*
about things that you do in addition to school or work: ***extramural*** *activities*

extraordinarily (say ik-**straw**-duhn-ruh-lee) *adverb*
extremely: *She's* ***extraordinarily*** *clever.*

extraordinary (say ik-**straw**-duhn-ree) *adjective*
very unusual or strange: *What an* ***extraordinary*** *thing to say!*

extravagant (say ik-**strav**-uh-guhnt) *adjective*
spending or costing too much money: *He's terribly* ***extravagant*** *– he goes everywhere by taxi.*
▸ **extravagance** (*noun*): *His* ***extravagance*** *is well-known.*

extreme (say ik-**streem**) *adjective*
1 very great or strong: *the* ***extreme*** *cold of the Arctic*
2 much stronger than what most people would consider to be normal, reasonable or acceptable: ***extreme*** *views on foreigners* (= people from other countries)
3 as far away as possible: *They came from the* ***extreme*** *north of the country.*

extremely (say ik-**streem**-lee) *adverb*
very: *He's* ***extremely*** *good-looking.*

extremist (say ik-**streem**-ist) *noun* (*plural* **extremists**)
a person who has extreme opinions

exuberant (say ig-**zyoo**-buh-ruhnt) *adjective*
full of energy, happiness and excitement: ***exuberant*** *behaviour*

eye (*rhymes with* **my**) *noun* (*plural* **eyes**)
one of the two organs in your head that you see with: *blue* ***eyes*** ◇ *Open your* ***eyes!***
keep an eye on a person or **thing** to look after or watch a person or thing: *Please keep an* ***eye*** *on the baby.*
see eye to eye with somebody to agree with somebody: *He doesn't always see* ***eye*** *to* ***eye*** *with his neighbours.*

eye

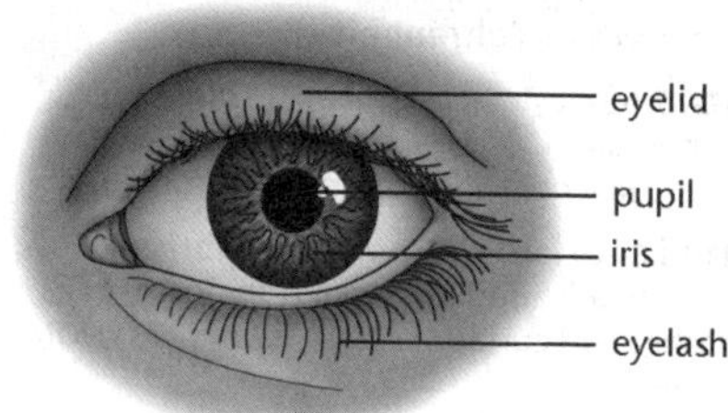

front view of the eye

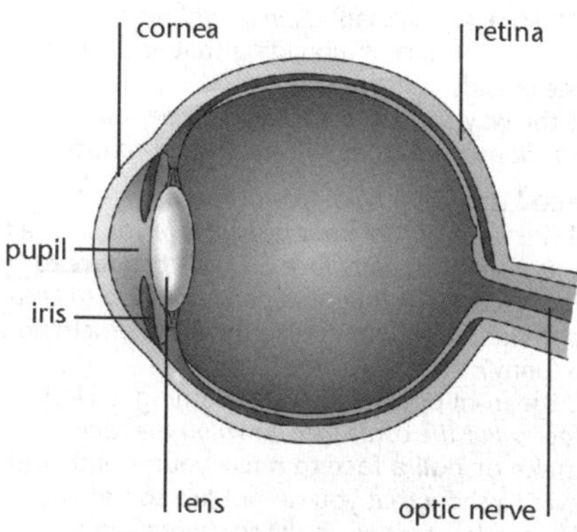

cross section of the eye

eyeball (say *y*-bawl) *noun* (*plural* **eyeballs**)
the ball of the eye (including the part that is hidden inside your head)

eyebrow (say *y*-brow) *noun* (*plural* **eyebrows**)
one of the two lines of hair above your eyes

eyelash (say *y*-lash) *noun* (*plural* **eyelashes**) (*also* **lash**)
one of the hairs that grow in a line on your **eyelid**: *She's got beautiful long* ***eyelashes.***

eyelid (say *y*-lid) *noun* (*plural* **eyelids**)
the piece of skin that can move to close your eye

eyesight (say *y*-site) *noun* (*no plural*)
the ability to see: *Your* ***eyesight*** *is very good.*

Ff

F *abbreviation* **Fahrenheit**

fable (say **fayb**-l) *noun* (*plural* **fables**)
a short story, usually about animals, that teaches people a lesson (called a **moral**)

fabric (say **fab**-rik) *noun* (*plural* **fabrics**)
cloth that is used for making things such as clothes and curtains: *cotton* ***fabrics*** ➲ SYNONYM **material**[1] 1

fabulous (say **fab**-yuu-luhss) *adjective*
very good: *The food smells* ***fabulous****!*
➲ SYNONYM **wonderful**

facade (say fuh-**saad**) *noun* (*plural* **facades**)
1 the front part of a building that you see from the outside
2 the way something appears to be, but is not: *She appears to be happy but it is only a* ***facade****.*

face[1] (say **fayss**) *noun* (*plural* **faces**)
1 the front part of your head: *Have you washed your* ***face****?* ◇ *a pretty* ***face*** ◇ *They stood* ***face*** *to* ***face*** (= looking straight at each other). ◇ *to keep a straight* ***face*** (= to not laugh when something is funny)
2 the front or one side of something: *a clock* ***face*** ◇ *Put the cards* ***face*** *down on the table.*
make or pull a face to move your mouth and eyes to show that you do not like something: *She made a* ***face*** *when she saw what was for dinner.*

face

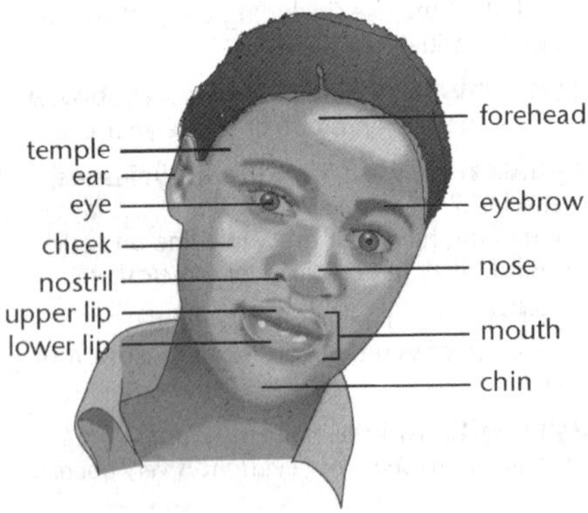

face[2] (say **fayss**) *verb* (**facing, faced**)
1 to have your face or front towards something: *Please* ***face*** *the front of the class.* ◇ *My bedroom* ***faces*** *the garden.*
2 to deal with an unfriendly person or a difficult situation: *I can't* ***face*** *going to work.*
let's face it (*informal*) we must agree that it is true: *Let's* ***face*** *it – you're not very good at maths.*

Facebook™ (say **fayss**-buuk) *noun* (*no plural*)
the name of a **website** that people join and use to send messages to friends and give other people their news

facetious (say fuh-**see**-shuhss) *adjective*
trying to make jokes or be clever about something at a time and in a way that annoys other people: *She always makes* ***facetious*** *comments while listening to the news.*

facial (say **fay**-shuhl) *adjective*
of or on a person's face: ***facial*** *hair* ◇ *a* ***facial*** *expression*

facilitate (say fuh-**sil**-i-tayt) *verb* (**facilitating, facilitated**)
to make something possible or easier: *The new bus and train services will* ***facilitate*** *transport in the area.*
▸ **facilitator** (*noun*)

facilities (say fuh-**sil**-i-teez) *plural noun*
a service, building or piece of equipment that makes it possible to do something: *Our school has very good sports* ***facilities****.*

facsimile (say fak-**sim**-i-lee) *noun* (*plural* **facsimiles**)
an exact copy of a picture or piece of writing
➲ See **fax**

fact (say **fakt**) *noun* (*plural* **facts**)
something that you know has happened or is true: *It's a* ***fact*** *that the Earth travels around the sun.*
in fact, in actual fact used to show that something is true or really so: *I thought she was from Namibia, but in actual* ***fact*** *she's from Botswana.*

faction (say **fak**-shuhn) *noun* (*plural* **factions**)
a small group of people who are part of a larger group but who have different ideas to the larger group: *There are left-wing and right-wing* ***factions*** *within the political party.*

factor (say **fak**-tuh) *noun* (*plural* **factors**)
1 something that has an effect on a decision or a situation: *A low salary was a* ***factor*** *in my decision to look for a new job.*
2 (*maths*) any of the two or more values that form a product when multiplied together: *2, 3, 4 and 6 are* ***factors*** *of 12.*

factorize (say **fak**-tuh-rize) *verb* (**factorizing, factorized**) (also **factorise**) (*maths*)
to divide or separate a quantity into **factors**: *In maths class today we **factorized** polynomials.*

factory (say **fak**-tree) *noun* (*plural* **factories**)
a place where people make things, usually with machines: *He works at the car **factory**.*

factual (say **fak**-tshuu-uhl) *adjective*
based on or containing things that are true or real: *a **factual** account of events*

faculty (say **fak**-uhl-tee) *noun* (*plural* **faculties**)
1 one of the natural abilities of a person's body or mind: *the **faculty** of speech/sight/hearing* ◇ *The old woman has lost some of her **faculties**.*
2 (also **Faculty**) a department in a university or college: *the Law **faculty*** ◇ *the **Faculty** of Medicine*

fad *noun* (*plural* **fads**)
a fashionable idea that will probably not last very long: *a diet **fad***

fade (say **fayd**) *verb* (**fading, faded**)
to become lighter in colour or less strong: *Will this shirt **fade** when I wash it?* ◇ *The cheers of the crowd **faded** away.*

faeces (say **fee**-seez) *plural noun*
the solid waste material that you get rid of when you go to the toilet

fag *noun* (*plural* **fags**) (*informal*) a cigarette

Fahrenheit (say **fa**-ruhn-hite) *noun* (*no plural*) (abbr. F)
a scale for measuring temperature. On this scale, water freezes at 32 degrees **Fahrenheit** (32 °F) and boils at 212 degrees **Fahrenheit** (212 °F): *110 °F* (= We say 'a hundred and ten degrees Fahrenheit'.) ➲ See **Celsius**
❶ **ORIGIN**: 18th century, named after Gabriel Daniel Fahrenheit (1686–1736), a German scientist

fail (say **fayl**) *verb* (**failing, failed**)
1 to not pass an exam or test: *How many learners **failed** the test?* ➲ OPPOSITE **pass**[1] 6
2 to try to do something but not be able to do it: *He played quite well but **failed** to win the match.* ➲ OPPOSITE **succeed**
3 to not do something that you should do: *The driver **failed** to stop at a red light.*

failure (say **fayl**-yuh) *noun*
1 (*no plural*) lack of success: *The search for the missing children ended in **failure**.*
2 (*plural* **failures**) a person or thing that does not do well: *I felt that I was a **failure** because I didn't have a job.* ➲ OPPOSITE **success**

faint[1] (say **faynt**) *adjective* (**fainter, faintest**)
1 not clear or strong: *We could hear the **faint** sound of music in the distance.*
2 feeling that you are going to fall, for example because you are ill or tired

faint[2] (say **faynt**) *verb* (**fainting, fainted**)
to suddenly become unconscious for a short time, for example because you are weak, ill or shocked: *She **faints** at the sight of blood.*

fair[1] *adjective* (**fairer, fairest**)
1 treating people equally or in the right way: *They didn't get a **fair** trial.* ◇ *It's not **fair**! I have to go to bed before my sister!* ➲ OPPOSITE **unfair**
2 quite good or quite large: *They have a **fair** chance of winning.* ◇ *They've invited a **fair** number of people to their party.*
3 (used about a person's skin or hair) light in colour: *He's got **fair** hair.*
4 (used about the weather) bright and not raining

fair[2] *noun* (*plural* **fairs**)
1 (also **funfair**) a place outdoors where you can ride on big machines and play games to win prizes
2 a large event where people and businesses show and sell the things they make: *a book **fair*** ◇ *a world trade **fair***

fairly (say **fair**-lee) *adverb*
1 quite, or not very: *She speaks English **fairly** well.* ◇ *I'm **fairly** certain it was him.*
2 in a way that is right and honest: *This company treats its workers **fairly**.*

fairy (say **fair**-ree) *noun* (*plural* **fairies**)
a very small person in stories. They have wings and can do magic.

fairy tale *noun* (*plural* **fairy tales**) (also **fairy story**)
a story for children that is about magic

faith (say **fayth**) *noun*
1 (*no plural*) feeling sure that somebody or something is good, right or honest: *I've got great **faith** in your ability to do the job* (= I'm sure that you can do it).
2 (*plural* **faiths**) a religion: *the Muslim **faith***

faithful (say **fayth**-fuhl) *adjective*
always ready to help your friends and to do what you have promised to do: *a **faithful** friend*

faithfully (say **fayth**-fuh-lee) *adverb*
Yours faithfully words that you write at the end of a formal letter, before your name

fake[1] (say **fayk**) *noun* (*plural* **fakes**)
a copy of something that seems real but is not: *This painting is not really by Van Gogh – it's a fake.*
▸ **fake** (*adjective*): *a **fake** passport*

fake² (say **fayk**) *verb* (**faking, faked**)
1 to copy something in order to make people believe it is the real thing: *He **faked** his father's signature.*
2 to pretend that you are feeling something: *Are you really ill or are you just **faking**?*

falcon (say **fal**-kuhn) *noun* (*plural* **falcons**)
a bird with long pointed wings that kills and eats other animals. They can be trained to hunt.: *A **falcon** is a bird of prey.*

fall¹ (say **fawl**) *verb* (**falling, fell, has fallen**)
1 to go down quickly towards the ground: *The book **fell** off the table.* ◇ *She **fell** down the stairs and broke her arm.*
2 (also **fall over**) to suddenly stop standing: *He slipped and **fell**.* ◇ *I **fell** over and hurt my leg.*
3 to become lower or less: *In the desert the temperature **falls** quickly at night.* ◇ *Prices have **fallen** again.* ➲ OPPOSITE **rise¹** 1
fall in love with somebody to begin to love somebody: *He **fell** in love with Anna the first time they met.*
fall asleep to start sleeping: *She **fell** asleep in the armchair.*
fall apart to break into pieces: *The chair **fell** apart when I sat on it.*
fall behind to become slower than others, or not do something when you should do it: *She's **falling** behind with her school work.*
fall through If a plan **falls through**, it does not happen.

fall² (say **fawl**) *noun* (*plural* **falls**)
1 a sudden drop from a higher place to a lower place: *He had a **fall** from his horse.*
2 becoming lower or less: *a **fall** in the price of oil*

fallacy (say **fal**-uh-see) *noun* (*plural* **fallacies**)
a belief or idea that is not true: *It's a **fallacy** to believe that all rich people are happy.*

fallen (say **fawl**-uhn) form of **fall¹**

Fallopian tubes (say fuh-**loh**-pi-uhn tyoobz) *plural noun* (*biology*)
the two tubes in the body of a woman or female animal along which eggs pass from the place where they are produced (the ovaries) to the place where a baby is formed (the uterus)
ℹ **ORIGIN:** 18th century, from the name of Gabriello Fallopio (1523–1562), who first described the Fallopian tube

fallow (say **fal**-oh) *adjective*
(used about land) not used for growing crops so that the soil will improve: *The field lay **fallow** for two years.*

falls (say **fawlz**) *plural noun*
a waterfall: *the Victoria **Falls***

false (say **foss**) *adjective*
1 wrong, or not true: *She gave a **false** name to the police.* ◇ *A spider has eight legs – true or **false**?*
2 not real or not natural: *He has **false** teeth* (= teeth that are made of plastic).
false alarm a warning about something bad that does not happen: *Everyone thought there was a fire, but it was a **false** alarm.*

falsetto (say fol-**set**-oh) *noun* (*plural* **falsettos**)
a man's voice singing higher notes than normal

falter (say **fol**-tuh) *verb* (**faltering, faltered**)
to speak or move in a way that is not steady: *Her voice **faltered** as she tried to speak.* ◇ *The engine started to **falter** and then it stopped.*

fame (say **faym**) *noun* (*no plural*)
being known by many people ➲ The adjective is **famous**

familiar (say fuh-**mil**-i-uh) *adjective*
that you know well: *I heard a **familiar** voice in the next room.* ◇ *I'm not **familiar** with this computer.* ➲ OPPOSITE **unfamiliar**

family (say **fam**-uh-lee) *noun* (*plural* **families**)
1 parents and children: *How many people are there in your **family**?* ◇ *My **family** have all got red hair.* ◇ *His **family** lives on a farm.*
2 a group of plants or animals: *Lions belong to the cat **family**.*

family tree *noun* (*plural* **family trees**)
a plan or diagram that shows all the people in a family

famine (say **fam**-uhn) *noun* (*no plural*)
a lack of food during a long period of time in a region: *The long drought* (= a long time without rain) *caused a **famine**.*

famished (say **fam**-isht) *adjective* (*informal*)
very hungry: *I'm **famished**!*

famous (say **fay**-muhss) *adjective*
known by many people: *South Africa is **famous** for its wildlife.* ◇ *a **famous** actress* ➲ The noun is **fame**

fan¹ *noun* (*plural* **fans**)
1 a person who likes a person or thing, for example a singer or a sport, very much: *She was a big **fan** of the Beatles.*
2 a thing that moves the air to make you cooler: *an electric **fan***

fan² *verb* (**fanning, fanned**)
to make a person or thing cooler by moving the air: *I **fanned** my face with the newspaper.*

Fanagalo (say fun-uh-guh-**law**) *noun* (*no plural*) (*S. African*)
a simple language based on Nguni languages,

English and Afrikaans, used by people working on mines: ***Fanagalo** is a language of instructions, and many people find it offensive.*
ⓘ ORIGIN: 20th century, from Nguni *fana ka lo*, an incorrect way of saying 'like this'

fanatic (say fuh-**nat**-ik) *noun* (*plural* **fanatics**)
a person who is very enthusiastic about something and may have extreme or dangerous opinions: *a religious **fanatic***

fancy[1] (say **fan**-see) *verb* (**fancying, fancied**) (*informal*)
to feel that you would like something: *Do you **fancy** a drink?* ◇ *I don't **fancy** going.*

fancy[2] (say **fan**-see) *adjective* (**fancier, fanciest**)
not simple or ordinary: *a **fancy** restaurant*

fancy dress *noun* (*no plural*)
clothes that you wear at a party so that you look like a different person or an animal: *We went to the party in **fancy dress**.*

fang *noun* (*plural* **fangs**)
a very long sharp tooth: *a snake's **fang***

fanlight (say **fan**-lite) *noun* (*plural* **fanlights**)
a small window above a door or other window

fantasize (say **fan**-tuh-size) *verb* (**fantasizing, fantasized**) (also **fantasise**)
to imagine something that you would like to happen: *I often **fantasize** about becoming a famous actor!*

fantastic (say fan-**tass**-tik) *adjective* (*informal*)
very good or wonderful: *We had a **fantastic** holiday.* ➲ SYNONYMS **great** 4, **brilliant** 3

fantasy (say **fan**-tuh-see) *noun* (*plural* **fantasies**)
something nice that you think about and that you hope will happen, although it is very unlikely: *It was just a **fantasy**.* ◇ *a **fantasy** world*
➲ SYNONYM **dream[1]** 2

FAQ (say ef-ay-**kyoo**) *abbreviation* (*plural* **FAQs**)
frequently asked question

far[1] (say **faa**) *adverb* (**farther** or **further, farthest** or **furthest**)
1 a long way from somewhere: *The river is **far** away.* ◇ *My house isn't **far** from the station.* ◇ *It's too **far** to drive in one day.* ◇ *I walked **further** than you.*
2 a word you use to ask about the distance from one place to another place: *How **far** is it to the coast from here?*
3 very much: *He's **far** taller than his brother.*
as far as ... to a place: *We walked as **far** as the village and then came back.*
as far as I know used when you think something is true, but you are not certain: *As **far** as I know, she's coming.*
so far until now: *So **far** the work has been easy.*

far[2] (say **faa**) *adjective* (**farther** or **further, farthest** or **furthest**)
1 a long way away: *Let's walk – it's not **far**.*
➲ OPPOSITE **near**
2 a long way from the centre in the direction mentioned: *Who's that on the **far** left of the photo?*

> USAGE Notice how to use this word when you talk about a place that is far away. It is not correct to say 'That place is far.' Say: *That place is **far away**.* It is not correct to say 'That's a far place.' Say: *That is a **faraway** place.*

faraway (say **faa**-ruh-way) *adjective*
a great distance away: *He lives in a **faraway** town.*

farce (say **faass**) *noun* (*plural* **farces**)
1 a play for the theatre in which a lot of funny things happen
2 something important or serious that is not well organized and becomes ridiculous: *The meeting turned into a complete **farce**.*

fare[1] (say **fair**) *noun* (*plural* **fares**)
the money that you pay to travel by bus, train or plane: *My bus **fare** has gone up.*

fare[2] (say **fair**) *verb* (**faring, fared**)
to perform in a certain situation: *Did they **fare** well or badly in the exams?*

farewell (say fair-**wel**) *noun* (*plural* **farewells**) (*formal*)
goodbye: *a **farewell** party*

farm[1] (say **faam**) *noun* (*plural* **farms**)
land and buildings where people keep animals and grow crops: *They work on a **farm**.* ◇ ***farm** animals*

farm[2] (say **faam**) *verb* (**farming, farmed**)
to grow crops or keep animals in order to earn money: *He **farms** in the Eastern Cape.*

farmer (say **faam**-uh) *noun* (*plural* **farmers**)
a person who owns or looks after a farm

farmhouse (say **faam**-howss) *noun* (*plural* **farmhouses**)
the main house on a farm

farming (say **faam**-ing) *noun* (*no plural*)
managing a farm or working on it: ***farming** methods*

farmyard (say **faam**-yaad) *noun* (*plural* **farmyards**)
the area beside the main house on a farm, with buildings or walls around it

farther form of **far[1]** 1

farthest form of **far[1]** 1

A B C D E **F** G H I J K L M N O P Q R S T U V W X Y Z

A B C D E **F** G H I J K L M N O P Q R S T U V W X Y Z

fascinate (say **fass**-i-nayt) *verb* (**fascinating**, **fascinated**)
to attract or interest somebody very much: *China has always **fascinated** me.* ◇ *I've always been **fascinated** by his ideas.*
▶ **fascination** (*noun*): *The girls listened in **fascination**.*

fascinating (say **fass**-i-nayt-ing) *adjective*
very interesting: *She told us **fascinating** stories about her life.*

Fascism (say **fash**-iz-uhm) *noun* (*no plural*)
(also **fascism**) an extreme political system which is in favour of a strong central government and which does not allow any criticism (called **opposition**)
▶ **Fascist** (also **fascist**) (*noun*): *a **Fascist** government*

fashion (say **fash**-uhn) *noun* (*no plural*)
a way of dressing or doing something that people like and try to copy for a time: *Bright colours are back in **fashion**.* ◇ *a **fashion** show*
🛈 **ORIGIN**: 13th–15th century, through Old French from Latin *factio(n-)*, from *facere* meaning 'do, make'

fashionable (say **fash**-nuhb-l) *adjective*
popular or in a popular style at the time: *She was wearing a **fashionable** black hat.*
➲ **OPPOSITE** **unfashionable**
▶ **fashionably** (*adverb*): *He was always **fashionably** dressed.*

fast¹ (say **faast**) *adjective* (**faster**, **fastest**)
1 moving, happening or doing something very quickly: *the **fastest** rate of increase for many years* ◇ *a **fast** learner*
2 (about a clock or watch) showing a time that is later than the real time: *My watch is five minutes **fast**.* ➲ **OPPOSITE** **slow¹**

> **WHICH WORD?** **Fast** or **quick**?
> - We say **fast** with meaning 1 above for a person or thing that moves at great speed: *a **fast** car* ◇ *a **fast** train.*
> - We say **quick** for something that is done in a short time: *a **quick** visit* ◇ *a **quick** meal.*

fast² (say **faast**) *adverb* (**faster**, **fastest**)
1 quickly: *Don't drive so **fast**!* ◇ *I can't go any **faster**.*
2 firmly or deeply: *The baby was **fast** asleep.* ◇ *The car was stuck **fast** in the mud.*

fast³ (say **faast**) *verb* (**fasting**, **fasted**)
to not eat food for a certain time: *Muslims **fast** during Ramadan.*

fasten (say **faa**-suhn) *verb* (**fastening**, **fastened**)
1 to join or close something so that it will not come open: *Please **fasten** your seat belts.* ◇ *Can you **fasten** this suitcase for me?*
2 to fix or tie one thing to another thing: ***Fasten** this badge to your jacket.* ➲ **OPPOSITE** **unfasten**

> **PRONUNCIATION** Don't pronounce the **t** in **fasten**.

fastener (say **faass**-nuh) *noun* (*plural* **fasteners**)
a thing that joins together two parts of something: *The **fastener** on my skirt has just broken.*

fast food *noun* (*no plural*)
hot food that is served very quickly in special restaurants, and often taken away to be eaten in the street

fat¹ *adjective* (**fatter**, **fattest**)
weighing too much: *You'll get **fat** if you eat so much.* ➲ **OPPOSITES** **slim¹**, **thin** 2

> **WORD BUILDING** It is not polite to say somebody is **fat**. It is better to say **large** or **plump**: *She's a rather **large** lady.* ◇ *He's a bit **plump**.* You can say **chubby** to describe babies and children: *a **chubby** little girl.*

fat² *noun*
1 (*no plural*) the soft white substance under the skins of animals and people: *Cut the **fat** off the meat.*
2 (*plural* **fats**) the substance containing oil that we get from animals, plants, or seeds and use for cooking: *foods which are low in **fat*** ◇ *Heat some **fat** in a frying pan.*

fatal (say **fay**-tuhl) *adjective*
1 causing death: *a **fatal** car accident*
2 having very bad results: *It was a **fatal** mistake not to learn for the Maths test.*
▶ **fatally** (*adverb*): *She was **fatally** injured in the crash.*

fatalist (say **fay**-tuh-list) *noun* (*plural* **fatalists**)
a person who accepts things that happen and believes that we cannot change events
▶ **fatalism** (*noun*): *There was a mood of **fatalism** before the war.*

fatality (say fuh-**tal**-i-tee) *noun* (*plural* **fatalities**)
the death of a person caused by an accident, war or disease: *Many people were injured in the crash but there were no **fatalities**.*

fate (say **fayt**) *noun*
1 (*plural* **fates**) the things, especially bad things, that will happen or have happened to somebody or something: *What will be the **fate** of the prisoners?*
2 (*no plural*) the power that some people believe controls everything that happens: *It was*

fate that brought them together again after twenty years.

father (say **faa**-*th*uh) *noun* (*plural* **fathers**)
a man who has a child: *Where do your mother and **father** live?* ➲ See **dad, daddy**
ℹ ORIGIN: from Old English *fæder*, related to Dutch *vader* and to Latin *pater*

Father Christmas *noun* (*no plural*)
an old man with a red coat and a long white beard. Children believe that he brings presents at Christmas. ➲ SYNONYM **Santa Claus**

fatherhood (say **faa**-*th*uh-huud) *noun* (*no plural*)
being a father

father-in-law (say **faa**-*th*uh-in-law) *noun* (*plural* **fathers-in-law**)
the father of your husband or wife

fathom¹ (say **fa*th***-uhm) *verb* (**fathoming, fathomed**)
to understand what something means: *I can't **fathom** what she means.*

fathom² (say **fa*th***-uhm) *noun* (*plural* **fathoms**)
a measure of the depth of water (1 fathom = 1,8 metres)

fatigue (say fuh-**teeg**) *noun* (*no plural*)
1 the feeling of being very tired: *He is suffering from mental and physical **fatigue**.*
2 (*technology*) weakness in metal caused by repeated bending or stretching: *The plane crash was caused by metal **fatigue** in the wing.*

fatten (say **fat**-uhn) *verb* (**fattening, fattened**)
to make an animal fatter
fatten up : *The farmers **fatten** up the sheep before they take them to the market.*

fatty (say **fat**-ee) *adjective* (**fattier, fattiest**)
containing a lot of fat: *Some foods are very **fatty**.*

fault (say **fawlt**) *noun*
1 (*no plural*) responsibility for a mistake: *It's her **fault** that we are late.* ◇ *It's my **fault** for being careless.*
2 (*plural* **faults**) something that is wrong or bad in a person or thing: *There is a serious **fault** in the machine.*

faultless (say **fawlt**-luhss) *adjective*
without any mistakes: *a **faultless** performance*
➲ SYNONYM **perfect** 1

faulty (say **fawl**-tee) *adjective* (**faultier, faultiest**)
not working well: *This light doesn't work – the switch is **faulty**.*

fauna (say **faw**-nuh) *noun* (*no plural*)
all the animals of an area or a period of time: *the flora and **fauna** of South Africa* ➲ See **flora**

favour (say **fay**-vuh) *noun* (*plural* **favours**)
something that you do to help somebody: *Would you do me a **favour** and open the door?* ◇ *Could I ask you a **favour**?*
be in favour of something to like or agree with something: *Are you in **favour** of the new school uniform?*

favourable (say **fayv**-uh-ruhb-l) *adjective*
good, suitable, or acceptable: *She made a **favourable** impression on his parents.*

favourite¹ (say **fayv**-uh-rit) *adjective*
liked more than others of the same kind: *What's your **favourite** food?*

favourite² (say **fayv**-uh-rit) *noun* (*plural* **favourites**)
a person or thing that you like more than any other: *I like all chocolates but these are my **favourites**.*

fawn *noun*
1 (*no plural*) a light yellow-brown colour
2 (*plural* **fawns**) a young deer ➲ See **deer**

fax (say **fakss**) *noun* (*plural* **faxes**)
a copy of a letter or document that you send by telephone lines using a special machine (called a **fax machine**): *They need an answer today so I'll send a **fax**.* ℹ **Fax** is short for 'facsimile'.
▶ **fax** (*verb*): *Can you **fax** the drawings to me?*

fear¹ (say **feer**) *noun* (*plural* **fears**)
the feeling that you have when you think that something bad might happen: *I have a terrible **fear** of dogs.* ◇ *He was shaking with **fear**.*

fear² (say **feer**) *verb* (**fearing, feared**)
1 to be afraid of a person or thing: *We all **fear** illness and death.*
2 (*formal*) to feel that something bad might happen: *I **fear** we will be late.*

> USAGE **Be afraid of** or **be frightened of** are the words we usually use instead of **fear** for sense 1 above.

fearful (say **feer**-fuhl) *adjective* (*formal*)
afraid or worried about something: *They were **fearful** that they would miss the plane.*

fearless (say **feer**-luhss) *adjective*
not afraid of anything

feasible (say **feez**-uhb-l) *adjective*
possible to do: *Is this plan **feasible**?*

feast (say **feest**) *noun* (*plural* **feasts**)
a large special meal for a lot of people: *a wedding **feast***

feat (say **feet**) *noun* (*plural* **feats**)
something you do that is clever, difficult or

A B C D E F G H I J K L M N O P Q R S T U V W X Y Z

dangerous: *Climbing Mount Everest was an amazing **feat**.*

feather (say ***feth**-uh*) *noun* (*plural* **feathers**)
one of the light, soft things that grow in a bird's skin and cover its body

feature[1] (say **fee**-tshuh) *noun* (*plural* **features**)
1 an important part of something: *Pictures are a **feature** of this dictionary.*
2 one of the parts of your face, for example your eyes, nose or mouth: *Her eyes are her best **feature**.*
3 a newspaper or magazine article or television programme about something: *The magazine has a special **feature** on education.*

feature[2] (say **fee**-tshuh) *verb* (**featuring, featured**)
to include a person or thing as an important part: *The film **features** many South African actors.*
feature in something to form a part of something: *Does the work of this artist **feature** in the collection?*

February (say **feb**-yuu-ree *or* **feb**-ruu-ree) *noun*
the second month of the year
ⓘ **ORIGIN:** 13th–15th century, from *feverer*, through Old French from Latin *februa*, which was the name of an ancient Roman festival held in February

fête (say **fayt**) *noun* (*plural* **fêtes**)
an event where you can buy things and play games, often organized to get money for a particular purpose: *the school **fête***

fed form of **feed[1]**

federal (say **fed**-uh-ruhl) *adjective*
used for describing a political system in which a group of states or countries are joined together under a central government, but also have their own governments: *a **federal** system of rule* ◇ *the **Federal** Government of the United States*

fed up *adjective* (*informal*)
bored or unhappy, especially with a situation that has continued for too long: *I'm **fed up** with waiting – let's go.*

fee *noun* (*plural* **fees**)
1 the money you pay for professional advice or service from private doctors, lawyers, schools, universities, etc.: *We can't afford private school **fees**.* ◇ *a large **fee***
2 the money that you pay to do something, for example to join a club or visit a museum: *There is no entrance **fee** to the gallery.*

feeble (say **feeb**-l) *adjective* (**feebler, feeblest**)
not strong: *a **feeble** old man* ➲ SYNONYM **weak**

feed[1] *verb* (**feeding, fed**)
1 to give food to a person or an animal: *The baby's crying – I'll go and **feed** her.*
2 (used about animals or babies) to eat: *Mosquitoes **feed** at night.*
3 to supply something to somebody or to a machine for example: *The TV **feeds** us with news about the election.* ◇ *The stream **feeds** into the river.* ◇ *The rubber is **fed** into the machine by hand.*

feed[2] *noun* (*plural* **feeds**)
1 a meal for a baby or an animal
2 food for farm animals: *chicken **feed***

feedback (say **feed**-bak) *noun* (*no plural*)
advice or information about how well or badly you have done something: *The teacher will give you **feedback** on the test.*

feel *verb* (**feeling, felt**)
1 to know something because your body tells you: *How do you **feel**?* ◇ *I don't **feel** well.* ◇ *I'm **feeling** tired.* ◇ *He **felt** somebody touch his arm.*
2 used for saying how something seems when you touch it or experience it: *The water **felt** cold.* ◇ *This towel **feels** wet – can I have a dry one?*
3 to touch something in order to find out what it is like: ***Feel** this wool – it's really soft.*
4 to have an opinion about something: *I **feel** that we should talk about this.* ➲ SYNONYM **believe** 2
5 to try to find something with your hands instead of your eyes: *She **felt** in her pocket for some matches.*
feel like something to want something: *Do you **feel** like going for a walk?*

feeler (say **feel**-uh) *noun* (*plural* **feelers**)
either of the two long thin parts on the heads of some animals that they use to touch, smell and taste things: *Crustaceans and insects have **feelers**.* ➲ SYNONYM **antenna**

feeling (say **feel**-ing) *noun*
1 (*plural* **feelings**) something that you feel inside yourself, such as happiness or anger: *a **feeling** of sadness* ◇ *Don't tell him you don't like his shirt – you'll hurt his **feelings*** (= make him feel sad).
2 (*no plural*) the ability to feel in your body: *I was so cold that I had no **feeling** in my feet.*
3 (*plural* **feelings**) an idea that you are not certain about: *I have a **feeling** that she isn't telling the truth.*

feet plural of **foot**

feline (say **fee**-line) *noun* (*plural* **felines**)
an animal of the cat family: *Lions and cheetahs are **felines**.*
▸ **feline** (*adjective*): *a **feline** characteristic*

fell (say **fel**) form of **fall[1]**

fellow[1] (say **fel**-oh) *noun* (*plural* **fellows**) (*informal*)
a man: *What is that* ***fellow*** *doing?*

fellow[2] (say **fel**-oh) *adjective*
used for saying that somebody is the same as you in some way: *her* ***fellow*** *students*

felon (say **fel**-uhn) *noun* (*plural* **felons**)
a person who commits a very serious crime, like a murder

felt[1] form of **feel**

felt[2] *noun* (*no plural*)
a type of soft thick cloth

felt-tip pen *noun* (*plural* **felt-tip pens**)
➲ SYNONYM **koki™**

female[1] (say **fee**-mayl) *adjective*
1 (used about animals) belonging to the sex that can produce eggs or give birth to babies: ***female*** *students*
2 (used about plants) able to produce fruit or seeds ➲ See **male**

female[2] (say **fee**-mayl) *noun* (*plural* **females**)
1 an animal that can produce eggs or babies: *Cows are* ***females*** *and bulls are males.*
2 a woman or a girl

feminine (say **fem**-i-nuhn) *adjective*
typical of a woman or right for a woman: ***feminine*** *clothes*

feminist (say **fem**-i-nist) *noun* (*plural* **feminists**)
a person who believes that women should have the same rights and opportunities as men
▸ **feminist** (*adjective*): ***feminist*** *literature*
▸ **feminism** (*noun*)

femur (say **fee**-muh) *noun* (*plural* **femurs** or **femora**) (also **thigh bone**)
the large thick bone in the top part of the leg above the knee ➲ See illustration at **skeleton**

fence[1] (say **fenss**) *noun* (*plural* **fences**)
a thing like a wall that is made of pieces of wood or metal. They are put round gardens and fields.
to sit on the fence to avoid making a decision or choice

fence[2] (say **fenss**) *verb* (**fencing, fenced**)
to put a fence around something
to fence something in
1 *They* ***fenced*** *in the vegetable garden.*
2 to limit somebody's freedom: *Too many rules can make you feel* ***fenced*** *in.*
to fence something off: *The grazing land has been* ***fenced*** *off from the rest of the farm*

ferment[1] (say fuh-**ment**) *verb* (**fermenting, fermented**)
to change chemically, or make the chemistry of something change, often sugar into alcohol: *The wine is* ***fermenting*** *in wooden barrels.*

ferment[2] (say **fur**-ment) *noun* (*no plural*)
a state of political or social excitement and change: *The country is in* ***ferment.***

fern (say **furn**) *noun* (*plural* **ferns**)
a plant with long thin leaves and no flowers that grows in wet areas

ferocious (say fuh-**roh**-shuss) *adjective*
violent and aggressive: *a* ***ferocious*** *wild animal*
➲ SYNONYM **fierce** 1

ferocity (say fuh-**ross**-i-tee) *noun* (*no plural*)
violent, aggressive behaviour

ferret (say **fe**-ruht) *noun* (*plural* **ferrets**)
a small aggressive mammal that is often used for hunting rats and rabbits

ferry (*rhymes with* **very**) *noun* (*plural* **ferries**)
a boat that takes people or goods on short journeys across a river or sea: *We went by* ***ferry.***

fertile (say **fur**-tile) *adjective*
1 (used about soil) in which plants grow well
2 (used about a female animal) able to have babies ➲ OPPOSITE **infertile**

fertilize (say **fur**-ti-lize) *verb* (**fertilizing, fertilized**) (also **fertilise**)
1 (*biology*) to join a male sex cell with a female sex cell to produce a new organism
2 to put natural or artificial substances in soil in order to make plants grow better

fertilizer (say **fur**-ti-lize-uh) *noun* (*plural* **fertilizers**) (also **fertiliser**)
food for plants

fervent (say **fur**-vuhnt) *adjective*
having or showing very strong feelings about something: *He is a* ***fervent*** *believer in animal rights.*

fester (say **fess**-tuh) *verb* (**festering, festered**)
1 (used about a wound) to become infected: *The cut on my finger* ***festered.***
2 (used about a problem) to become worse or more unpleasant because you have not dealt with it

festival (say **fess**-ti-vuhl) *noun* (*plural* **festivals**)
1 a series of public events, for example concerts and shows, in one place: *an international jazz* ***festival***
2 a time when people celebrate something, especially a religious event: *Christmas is an important Christian* ***festival.***

FET (say ef-ee-**tee**) *abbreviation* (*S. African*) **Further Education and Training**

A B C D E F G H I J K L M N O P Q R S T U V W X Y Z

FETC (say ef-ee-tee-**see**) *abbreviation* (*plural* **FETCs**)
Further Education and Training College

fetch (say **fech**) *verb* (**fetching, fetched**)
to go and bring back a person or thing: *Can you **fetch** me my bag?*

fetus (say **fee**-tuhss) *noun* (*plural* **fetuses**) (also **foetus**)
a young human or animal that is still growing inside its mother's body

feud (say **fyood**) *noun* (*plural* **feuds**)
a serious argument between two people or groups of people that lasts a long time: *There is a **feud** over who owns the land.* ◇ *a family **feud***

feudal (say **fyoo**-duhl) *adjective*
relating to **feudalism**

feudalism (say **fyoo**-duh-liz-m) *noun* (*no plural*)
the social system that existed in the Middle Ages in Europe, in which people worked and fought for a person who owned land and received land and protection from him in return

fever (say **fee**-vuh) *noun* (*plural* **fevers**)
a condition of the body when it is too hot because you are ill ➲ See **temperature**
▸ **feverish** (*adjective*): *I feel **feverish**.*

few (say **fyoo**) *adjective, pronoun* (**fewer, fewest**)
not many: ***Few** people live to the age of 100.* ◇ *There are **fewer** buses in the evenings.* ➲ See note at **less**[1]
a few some, but not many: *a **few** people* ◇ *I have read a **few** of her books.*
quite a few quite a lot: *It's been quite a **few** years since I saw him last.*

fewer form of **few** ➲ See note at **less**[1]

fez (say **fez**) *noun* (*plural* **fezzes**)
a flat, red hat which men in some Muslim countries wear

fiancé (say fi-**on**-say) *noun* (*plural* **fiancés**)
the man a woman has promised to marry

fiancée (say fi-**on**-say) *noun* (*plural* **fiancées**)
the woman a man has promised to marry

fiasco (say fi-**ass**-koh) *noun* (*plural* **fiascos**)
an event which does not succeed: *The meeting was a complete **fiasco**!*

fib *noun* (*plural* **fibs**) (*informal*)
a small lie, or something you say that you know is not true: *Don't tell **fibs**!*
▸ **fib** (*verb*) (*informal*): *I was **fibbing** when I said I liked her hat.*

Fibonacci series (say fee-buh-**naa**-chi seer-reez) *noun* (*maths*)
a series of numbers in which each number is equal to the two numbers before it added together. The simplest is the series 1, 1, 2, 3, 5, 8, etc.
🛈 ORIGIN: from the name of Leonardo Fibonacci, an Italian mathematician who lived in the 12th to 13th centuries

fibre (say **fibe**-uh) *noun*
1 (*no plural*) the part of your food that helps to move other food through your body and keep you healthy: *Dried fruits are high in **fibre**.*
➲ SYNONYM **roughage**
2 (*plural* **fibres**) one of the many thin threads that form a material: *cotton **fibres***

fibreglass (say **fibe**-uh-glaass) *noun* (*no plural*)
a material made from small threads of glass, used for making things such as small boats, parts of cars and roofs

fibula (say **fib**-yuh-luh) *noun* (*plural* **fibulae** or **fibulas**) (also **calf bone**)
the outer and thinner of the two bones of your leg between your knee and foot

fickle (say **fik**-l) *adjective*
always changing your mind or your feelings: *a **fickle** crowd*

fiction (say **fik**-shuhn) *noun* (*no plural*)
stories and novels that describe events and people that are not real: *I enjoy reading **fiction**.*
➲ OPPOSITE **non-fiction**

fictitious (say fik-**tish**-uhss) *adjective*
something that is invented, not real or true: *a **fictitious** name*

fiddle[1] (say **fid**-l) *verb* (**fiddling, fiddled**)
1 to touch something a lot with your fingers, because you are bored or nervous: *Stop **fiddling** with your pen and do some work!*
2 (*informal*) to change the details or figures of something in order to get money dishonestly: *to **fiddle** the accounts*

fiddle[2] (say **fid**-l) *noun* (*plural* **fiddles**) (*informal*)
a violin

fidelity (say fi-**del**-i-itee) *noun* (*no plural*)
the quality of being faithful or loyal to a partner
➲ OPPOSITE **infidelity**

fidget (say **fij**-uht) *verb* (**fidgeting, fidgeted**)
to keep moving your body, hands, or feet because you are nervous, excited, or bored: *Sit still and stop **fidgeting**!*

field[1] (say **feeld**) *noun* (*plural* **fields**)
1 a piece of land used for animals or for growing crops, usually surrounded by a fence or trees
2 an area of study or knowledge: *Dr Marumo is an expert in her **field**.*

3 a piece of land used for something special: *a sports **field***
4 (*science*) an area in which a particular force has an effect: *a magnetic **field*** ◇ *the Earth's gravitational **field***

field² (say **feeld**) *verb* (**fielding, fielded**)
1 to be ready to catch and throw back the ball in a game such as cricket: *Our team will **field** and the other team will bat first.*
2 to choose a team for a sports game: *The club **fielded** a strong team for the match.*
to field questions to answer questions

fiend (say **fee**-uhnd) *noun* (*plural* **fiends**)
1 a very cruel person
2 (*informal*) a person who is very interested in one particular thing: *a health **fiend***
▸ **fiendish** (*adjective*): *a **fiendish** criminal*

fierce (say **feerss**) *adjective* (**fiercer, fiercest**)
1 angry and wild: *a **fierce** dog* ➲ SYNONYM **ferocious**
2 very strong: *the **fierce** heat of the sun*
▸ **fiercely** (*adverb*): *The dog **fiercely** defended its owner.*

fiery (say **fy**-uh-ree) *adjective* (**fierier, fieriest**)
1 quick to become angry: *She has a **fiery** temper.*
2 looking like fire: ***fiery** red hair* ◇ *a **fiery** sunset*

fifteen (say fif-**teen**) *number*
15
▸ **fifteenth** (*adjective, adverb*): *I pay the bill on the **fifteenth*** (= the 15th day) *of the month.*

fifth (say **fifth**) *adjective, adverb, noun*
1 5th: *She came **fifth** in the race.*
2 one of five equal parts of something, $\frac{1}{5}$

fifty (say **fif**-tee) *number*
1 50
2 the fifties (*plural noun*) the numbers 50 to 59 or the years 1950 to 1959: *He was born in the **fifties*** (= in the 1950s).
in your fifties between the ages of 50 and 59: *Her husband died when she was in her **fifties**.*
▸ **fiftieth** (*adjective, adverb*): *It is her **fiftieth*** (= 50th) *birthday today.*

fig *noun* (*plural* **figs**)
a soft sweet fruit that is full of small seeds

fight¹ (say **fite**) *verb* (**fighting, fought**)
1 to use physical strength, guns or other weapons against a person or thing: *He **fought** in the war.* ◇ *My brothers are always **fighting**.*
2 to try very hard to stop something: *He **fought** against the illness for two years.*
3 to try very hard to do or get something: *The workers are **fighting** for better pay.*
4 to argue: *It's not worth **fighting** about this.*

fight² (say **fite**) *noun* (*plural* **fights**)
the act of using physical force against a person or thing: *Don't get into a **fight**.*

fighter (say **fite**-uh) *noun* (*plural* **fighters**)
1 a person who fights
2 (also **fighter plane**) a fast plane that shoots at other planes during a war

figurative (say **fig**-uh-ruh-tiv) *adjective*
words or expressions having an imaginative rather than an exact meaning: *We often use **figurative** language in poetry.* ➲ OPPOSITE **literal** 1 ➲ See **metaphor**

figure¹ (say **fig**-uh) *noun* (*plural* **figures**)
1 one of the symbols (0–9) that we use to show numbers: *Shall I write the numbers in words or **figures**?*
2 an amount or price: *unemployment **figures*** (= the number of people who are unemployed)
3 the shape of a person's body: *She's got a good **figure**.*
4 a shape of a person that you cannot see clearly: *I saw a tall **figure** outside the window.*
5 figures (*plural noun*) (*informal*) the area of mathematics that deals with adding, subtracting, multiplying or dividing numbers: *I'm not very good at **figures**.* ➲ SYNONYM **arithmetic**
6 (*maths*) a diagram: *a three-dimensional **figure*** ◇ ***figure** ABCD*

figure² (say **fig**-uh) *verb* (**figuring, figured**)
1 to be a part of something: *Men don't **figure** much in her books.*
2 (*informal*) to think or to guess: *I **figured** you were away.*
figure a person or thing out to think about a person or thing until you understand them or it: *I haven't **figured** her out yet!* ◇ *Have you **figured** out where we are?*

figure of speech *noun* (*plural* **figures of speech**)
a word or phrase used in a different way from its usual meaning to create a particular effect: *I didn't really mean that she was mad – it was just a **figure of speech**.* ➲ See Study page 17

filament (say **fil**-uh-muhnt) *noun* (*plural* **filaments**)
1 a thin wire in a **light bulb** that produces light when electricity is passed through it
2 (*technology*) a long thin piece of something that looks like a thread: *glass **filaments***
3 (*biology*) in a flower, the part of the **stamen** that supports the **anther** ➲ See illustration at **flower**

file¹ *noun* (*plural* **files**)
1 a box or cover for keeping papers in
2 a collection of information that is stored in a

computer and that has a particular name: *Did you save your **file**? ◇ You can delete that **file** now.*
3 a tool with rough sides that you use for making things smooth: *a nail **file***
in single file in a line with each person following the one in front: *The children walked into the hall in single **file**.*

file² *verb* (**filing**, **filed**)
1 to put papers in their correct place, for example in a cover or drawer: *Can you **file** these letters, please?*
2 to walk in a line, one behind the other: *The learners **filed** into the classroom.*
3 to make something smooth using a tool with rough sides: *She **filed** her nails.*

filing cabinet *noun* (*plural* **filing cabinets**)
a piece of office furniture with large drawers, in which you keep documents

fill (say **fil**) *verb* (**filling**, **filled**)
1 to make something full: *Can you **fill** this glass with water, please?*
2 to become full: *His eyes **filled** with tears.*
fill something in, **fill something out** to write facts or answers in the spaces that have been left for them: *She gave me a form and told me to **fill** it in.*
fill up, **fill something up** to become full or to make something completely full: *The room soon **filled** up. ◇ He **filled** up the tank with petrol.*

fillet (say **fil**-uht) *noun* (*plural* **fillets**)
a piece of meat or fish with the bones taken out

filling (say **fil**-ing) *noun* (*plural* **fillings**)
1 the substance that a dentist uses to fill a hole in your tooth: *I've got three **fillings** in my teeth.*
2 the food that is put inside a sandwich or cake: *a choice of sandwich **fillings***

filly (say **fil**-ee) *noun* (*plural* **fillies**)
a young female horse ➲ See **colt**

film¹ (say **film**) *noun* (*plural* **films**)
1 a story shown in moving pictures that you see on television or at the cinema: *Let's go and see a **film**. ◇ the **film** industry* ➲ SYNONYM **movie** 1
2 the thin plastic that you use in a camera for taking photographs: *I bought a roll of black and white **film**.*
3 a thin layer of a substance or material: *Can you see the **film** of oil on the surface of the water?*

film² (say **film**) *verb* (**filming**, **filmed**)
to use a camera to make moving pictures of a story or news: *That show was **filmed** for TV.*

film star *noun* (*plural* **film stars**)
an actor or actress who is famous for being in films

filter (say **fil**-tuh) *noun* (*plural* **filters**)
a device used for holding back the solid parts in a liquid or gas: *a coffee **filter***
▸ **filter** (*verb*): ***Filter** the water before you drink it.*

filthy (say **filth**-ee) *adjective* (**filthier**, **filthiest**)
very dirty: *Wash your hands. You're **filthy**!*

fin *noun* (*plural* **fins**)
one of the thin flat parts on a fish that help it to swim and balance ➲ See illustration at **fish¹**

final¹ (say **fine**-uhl) *adjective*
not followed by any others: *This will be our **final** lesson.* ➲ SYNONYM **last¹** 1

final² (say **fine**-uhl) *noun* (*plural* **finals**)
1 the last game or race in a competition, for the winners of the earlier games or races: *We've got through to the **final**.*
2 finals (*plural noun*) the exams in your last year at school or university

finalist (say **fine**-uh-list) *noun* (*plural* **finalists**)
a person who is in the last parts of a competition

finalize (say **fine**-uh-lize) *verb* (**finalizing**, **finalized**) (also **finalise**)
to make final decisions about something: *We haven't **finalized** our plans yet.*

finally (say **fine**-uh-lee) *adverb*
1 after a long time: *After a long wait the bus **finally** arrived.*
2 used before saying the last thing in a list: *And **finally**, I would like to thank my parents for all their help.*

finance¹ (say **fy**-nanss) *noun*
1 (*no plural*) money, or the activity of managing money: *an expert in **finance** ◇ the Minister of **Finance***
2 finances (*plural noun*) the money that you have and that you can spend: *You need to sort out your **finances**.*

finance² (say **fy**-nanss) *verb* (**financing**, **financed**)
to give the money that is needed to pay for something: *The building was **financed** by the government.*

financial (say fi-**nan**-shuhl) *adjective*
connected with money: ***financial** problems*

find *verb* (**finding**, **found**)
1 to see or get something after looking or trying: *I can't **find** my glasses. ◇ Has anybody **found** the answer to this question?*
2 to see or get something that you did not expect: *I **found** some money in the street. ◇ I woke up and **found** myself in hospital.*
3 used for talking about your opinion or

experience: *I didn't* ***find*** *that book very interesting.* ◇ *He* ***finds*** *it difficult to sleep.*
find something out to get information about something: *Can you* ***find*** *out what time the train leaves?*

fine[1] *adjective* (**finer**, **finest**)
1 beautiful or of good quality: *a* ***fine*** *view* ◇ *This is one of her* ***finest*** *paintings.*
2 well or happy: *'How are you?'* ***'Fine,*** *thanks.'*
3 used for saying that something is good or acceptable: *'Let's meet on Monday.'* ***'Fine.'*** ➲ SYNONYM **OK**[1]
4 not raining: *I hope it stays* ***fine*** *for our picnic.* ➲ SYNONYM **sunny**
5 (used about hair, string etc.) very thin: *I've got very* ***fine*** *hair.* ➲ OPPOSITE **thick** 3
6 made of very small pieces: *Salt is* ***finer*** *than sugar.* ➲ OPPOSITE **coarse**

fine[2] *noun* (*plural* **fines**)
money that you must pay because you have done something wrong: *You'll get a* ***fine*** *if you park your car there.*
▶ **fine** (*verb*): *I was* ***fined*** *R250 for parking there.*

finger (say **fing**-guh) *noun* (*plural* **fingers**)
one of the five parts at the end of your hand
➲ See illustration at **hand**[1]
keep your fingers crossed to hope that somebody or something will be successful: *I'll keep my* ***fingers*** *crossed for you in your exams.*

fingernail (say **fing**-guh-nayl) *noun* (*plural* **fingernails**)
the thin hard part at the end of your finger
➲ See illustration at **hand**[1]

fingerprint (say **fing**-guh-print) *noun* (*plural* **fingerprints**)
the mark that a finger makes when it touches something: *The police found his* ***fingerprints*** *on the gun.*

fingertip (say **fing**-guh-tip) *noun* (*plural* **fingertips**)
the end of your finger

finicky (say **fin**-i-kee) *adjective*
fussy about needs and details: *a* ***finicky*** *eater*

finish[1] (say **fin**-ish) *verb* (**finishing**, **finished**)
1 to stop doing something: *I* ***finish*** *school at half past two.* ◇ *Have you* ***finished*** *cleaning your room?*
2 to stop happening: *School* ***finishes*** *at four o'clock.* ➲ OPPOSITES **begin** 1, **start**[1]
finish something off to do or eat the last part of something: *He* ***finished*** *off the bread.*
finish with something to stop needing or using something: *Have you* ***finished*** *with that book?*

finish[2] (say **fin**-ish) *noun* (*plural* **finishes**)
the last part or the end of something: *There was a dramatic* ***finish*** *to the race.* ➲ OPPOSITE **start**[2]

finite (say **fine**-ite) *adjective*
having an end, a definite limit or a fixed size: *The world's coal resources are* ***finite.*** ➲ OPPOSITE **infinite**

fiord (say fee-**awd**) *noun* (*plural* **fiords**) = **fjord**

fir (say **fur**) *noun* (*plural* **firs**) (also **fir tree**)
a tall tree with thin sharp leaves (called **needles**) that do not fall off in winter

fire[1] (say **fy**-uh) *noun*
1 (*no plural*) the heat and bright light that comes from burning things: *Many animals are afraid of* ***fire.*** ◇ *There was a big* ***fire*** *at the factory last night.* ◇ *She dropped her cigarette and the chair caught* ***fire*** (= started to burn). ◇ *My house is on* ***fire*** (= burning)! ◇ *Somebody set the house on* ***fire*** (= made it start to burn). ◇ *We put out the* ***fire*** *with buckets of water.*
2 (*plural* **fires**) burning wood, coal or gas that you use for keeping a place warm or for cooking: *They lit a* ***fire*** *to keep warm.*
🛈 **ORIGIN:** from Old English *fyr* meaning 'fire', related to Dutch *vuur*

fire[2] (say **fy**-uh) *verb* (**firing**, **fired**)
1 to shoot with a gun: *The soldiers* ***fired*** *at the enemy.*
2 to tell somebody to leave their job: *He was* ***fired*** *because he was always late for work.*
➲ SYNONYM **dismiss**, **sack**[2]

fire alarm *noun* (*plural* **fire alarms**)
a bell that rings to tell people that there is a fire

firearm (say **fy**-uh-raam) *noun* (*plural* **firearms**)
a gun that you can carry

fire brigade *noun* (*plural* **fire brigades**)
an organization of people trained to deal with fires: *Call the* ***fire brigade!***

fire engine *noun* (*plural* **fire engines**)
a vehicle that takes people and equipment to stop fires

fire escape *noun* (*plural* **fire escapes**)
stairs on the outside of a building that people can go down if there is a fire

fire extinguisher *noun* (*plural* **fire extinguishers**)
a metal container with water or chemicals inside for stopping small fires

firefighter (say **fy**-uh-fite-uh) *noun* (*plural* **firefighters**)
a person whose job is to stop fires

fireman (say **fy**-uh-muhn) *noun* (*plural* **firemen**)
a man whose job is to stop fires

fireplace (say **fy**-uh-playss) *noun* (*plural* **fireplaces**)
the place in a room where you light a fire

fire station *noun* (*plural* **fire stations**)
a building where fire engines are kept

firework (say **fy**-uh-wurk) *noun* (*plural* **fireworks**)
a thing that explodes with coloured lights and loud noises, used for entertainment: *We watched a **fireworks** display in the park.*

firm^{1} (say **furm**) *noun* (*plural* **firms**)
a group of people working together in a business: *My father works for a building **firm**.*
➲ SYNONYM **company** 1

firm^{2} (say **furm**) *adjective* (**firmer, firmest**)
1 quite hard or not moving easily: *Wait until the glue is **firm**.* ◇ *The shelf isn't very **firm**, so don't put too many books on it.*
2 showing that you will not change your ideas: *She's very **firm** with her children* (= she makes them do what she wants). ◇ *a **firm** promise*
▸ **firmly** (*adverb*): *Nail the pieces of wood together **firmly**.* ◇ *'No,' she said **firmly**.*

first^{1} (say **furst**) *adjective*
before all the others, 1st: *January is the **first** month of the year.* ◇ *You've won **first** prize!*
➲ OPPOSITE **last^{1}** 1

first^{2} (say **furst**) *adverb*
1 before all the others, 1st: *I arrived at the house **first**.* ◇ *She came **first*** (= she won) *in the competition.*
2 for the first time: *I **first** met him in 2006.*
3 at the start, before doing anything else: *At **first** she was afraid of the water, but she soon learned to swim.* ◇ ***First** fry the onions, then add the potatoes.*
first and foremost more than anything else, most importantly ➲ See **foremost**

first^{3} (say **furst**) *noun, pronoun* (*no plural*)
the first a person or thing that comes earliest or before all others, 1st: *I was the **first** to arrive at the party.*

first aid *noun* (*no plural*)
medical help that you give to somebody who is hurt, before a doctor comes

first class *noun* (*no plural*)
the part of a train, plane or ship that it is more expensive to travel in: *I got a seat in **first class**.*
➲ See **second class**
▸ **first class** (*adverb*): *How much is it to travel **first class**?*

first-class *adjective*
1 excellent: *a **first-class** player* ◇ *I know a place where the food is **first-class**.*
2 related to the best and most expensive way of travelling on a train, plane or ship: *a **first-class** cabin*

first floor *noun*
the first floor the floor of a building above the floor that is level with the street: *I live in a flat on the **first floor**.*

firstly (say **furst**-lee) *adverb*
used when you are giving the first thing in a list: *We were angry **firstly** because he didn't come, and secondly because he didn't phone.*

first name *noun* (*plural* **first names**)
the first of your names that come before your family name: *'What is Mrs Mlaudzi's **first name**?' 'Ronewa.'* ➲ See note at **name^{2}**

fiscal (say **fiss**-kuhl) *adjective*
relating to government money and taxes

fish^{1} *noun* (*plural* **fish** or **fishes**)
an animal that lives and breathes in water, and has thin flat parts (called **fins**) that help it to swim: *I caught a big **fish**.* ◇ *We had **fish** and chips for dinner.* ◇ *Goldfish, salmon, sardines, hake and sharks are all types of **fish**.*

fish

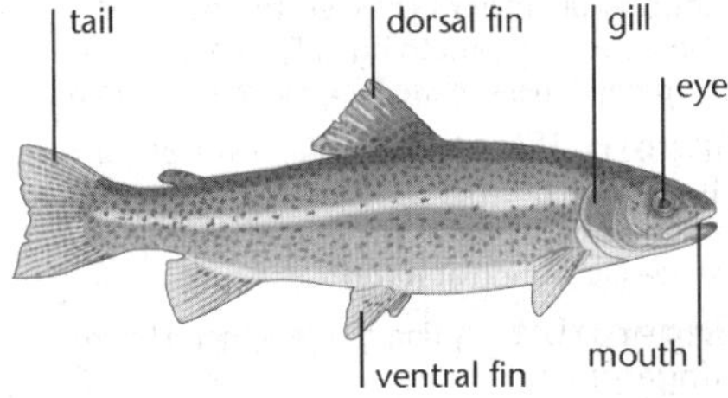

fish^{2} *verb* (**fishing, fished**)
to try to catch fish
to fish for
1 to try to catch fish: *You can **fish** for trout in this stream.*
2 to try to get something you want in an indirect way: *to **fish** for information*
to fish out
1 to take or pull a person of thing out of a place: *The police **fished** the car out of the river.*
2 to catch all the fish in a particular part of the ocean: *The Mediterranean Sea has largely been **fished** out* (= there is hardly any fish left in it).
▸ **fishing** (*noun*): ***Fishing** is an important industry.*

> USAGE When you talk about spending time fishing as a sport, you often say **go fishing**: *I **go fishing** at weekends.*

fisherman (say **fish**-uh-muhn) *noun* (*plural* **fishermen**)
a person who catches fish as a job or sport

fishing rod *noun* (*plural* **fishing rods**)
a long thin stick with a thin thread (called a **line**) and a hook, used for catching fish

fishmoth (say **fish**-moth) *noun* (*plural* **fishmoths**)
a small silvery insect with no wings that eats paper

fishy (say **fish**-ee) *adjective* (**fishier**, **fishiest**)
1 tasting or smelling like fish: *What's that **fishy** smell?*
2 something that seems suspicious: *There's something **fishy** about his story.*

fissure (say **fish**-uh) *noun* (*plural* **fissures**)
a long deep crack in something, especially in a rock

fist *noun* (*plural* **fists**)
a hand with the fingers closed tightly: *She banged on the door with her **fist**.*

fit¹ *verb* (**fitting**, **fitted**)
1 to be the right size or shape for somebody or something: *I tried the dress on, but it didn't **fit**.* ◇ *This key doesn't **fit** the lock.*
2 to put or fix something somewhere: *They **fitted** new glass in the broken window.* ◇ *She **fitted** the pieces of the puzzle together.* ◇ *We can't **fit** in here* (= there is not enough space for us).

fit² *adjective* (**fitter**, **fittest**)
1 healthy and strong: *I keep **fit** by jogging every day.*
2 good enough: *This food isn't **fit** to eat.* ◇ *Do you think she's **fit** for the job?* ➲ SYNONYM **suitable** ➲ OPPOSITE **unfit**

fit³ *noun* (*plural* **fits**)
1 a sudden illness in which somebody becomes unconscious and may make violent movements
2 when you cannot stop laughing, coughing, or feeling angry: *We were in **fits** of laughter.* ◇ *a **fit** of anger*

fitness (say **fit**-nuhss) *noun* (*no plural*)
being healthy and strong

fitting¹ (say **fit**-ing) *adjective*
1 right or suitable: *This is a **fitting** award for all the hard work you have done.*
2 how something fits around somebody or something: *She wore a tight-**fitting** dress.*

fitting² (say **fit**-ing) *noun* (*plural* **fittings**)
1 (usually **fittings**) something in a room or on a piece of furniture that can be moved or changed: *We bought new **fittings** for the bathroom.*
2 trying on clothing that somebody is making for you: *I need to go for a second **fitting**.*

five *number*
5 ➲ The adjective is **fifth**
ⓘ ORIGIN: from Old English *fif*, related to Dutch *vijf*

fix¹ (say **fikss**) *verb* (**fixing**, **fixed**)
1 to put something in a place so that it will not move: *We **fixed** the shelf to the wall.*
2 to decide a date or an amount for something: *They've **fixed** a date for the wedding.* ➲ SYNONYM **set² 1**
3 to repair something: *The light isn't working – can you **fix** it?* ➲ SYNONYM **mend**

fix² (say **fikss**) *noun* (*plural* **fixes**)
1 an easy solution to a problem: *There is no quick **fix** to this problem.*
2 a difficult situation: *I was in quite a **fix** because I had no money on me.*
3 (*informal*) something that you need regularly: *She says she needs her **fix** of coffee every day.*

fixative (say **fikss**-uh-tiv) *noun* (*plural* **fixatives**)
1 a substance that is used to stick things together or keep them in position
2 a substance that is used to prevent colours or smells from changing or becoming weaker, for example in art or the making of **perfume**

fixed (say **fikst**) *adjective*
1 already decided: *a **fixed** price*
2 not changing: *He has such **fixed** ideas that you can't discuss anything with him.*

fizz (say **fiz**) *noun* (*no plural*)
bubbles of gas in a liquid and the sound that they make: *The cooldrink has lost its **fizz**.*
► **fizz** (*verb*): *The cooldrink was **fizzing** in the glass.*

fizzle (say **fiz**-l) *verb* (**fizzling**, **fizzled**)
to end in a weak or disappointing way: *The party **fizzled** out and people started to leave.*

fizzy (say **fiz**-ee) *adjective* (**fizzier**, **fizziest**)
(used about a drink) containing many small bubbles of gas: *Do you like **fizzy** drinks?*

fjord (say fee-**awd**) *noun* (*plural* **fjords**) (also **fiord**) (*geography*)
a long narrow piece of sea between cliffs, common in Norway

flabbergasted (say **flab**-uh-gaass-tuhd) *adjective*
extremely surprised or shocked

flabby (say **flab**-ee) *adjective* (**flabbier**, **flabbiest**)
having too much soft fat on your body: *a **flabby** stomach*

flag[1] *noun* (*plural* **flags**)
a piece of cloth with a pattern on it which is joined to a pole. It is used as a symbol of a country or organization, or as a signal: *The **flag** is flying outside Parliament.*

flag[2] *verb* (**flagging, flagged**)
1 to put a special mark next to information that you think is important
2 to become tired or less strong: *After the long day the children began to **flag**.*
to flag down to wave to the driver of a vehicle to make them stop: *The police **flagged** down the truck.*

flagrant (say **flay**-gruhnt) *adjective*
shocking because it is done in an obvious way and is wrong: *a **flagrant** disregard for the rules*

flagship (say **flag**-ship) *noun* (*plural* **flagships**)
1 a ship in a group (called a **fleet**) that carries the commanding officer (called an **admiral**).
2 the best or most important product, service or shop that an organization has

flair *noun* (*no plural*)
1 a natural ability to do something well: *He has a **flair** for drawing.*
2 the quality of having style and being interesting: *She dresses with such **flair**.*

flake[1] (say **flayk**) *noun* (*plural* **flakes**)
a small thin piece of something: ***Flakes** of old paint fell off the wall.*

flake[2] (say **flayk**) *verb* (**flaking, flaked**)
to come off in small pieces (called flakes): *The paint is starting to **flake** off.*
▸ **flaky** (*adjective*): *dry, **flaky** skin*

flamboyant (say flam-**boy**-uhnt) *adjective*
1 acting in a loud, confident way that makes people look at you: *a **flamboyant** pop singer*
2 bright and easily noticed: ***flamboyant** colours*
▸ **flamboyance** (*noun*) ▸ **flamboyantly** (*adverb*)

flame[1] (say **flaym**) *noun* (*plural* **flames**)
a hot bright pointed piece of fire: *The house was in **flames*** (= burning). ◇ *The paper burst into **flames*** (= began to burn).
to go up in flames to be destroyed by fire: *The factory went up in **flames**.*

flame[2] (say **flaym**) *verb* (**flaming, flamed**)
1 to burn and produce flames
2 to become red with embarrassment: *Her cheeks **flamed** when they called out her name.*

flamenco (say fluh-**meng**-koh) *noun* (*plural* **flamencos**)
a traditional type of dancing and music from Spain

flamingo (say fluh-**ming**-go) *noun* (*plural* **flamingoes** or **flamingos**)
a large pink bird that has long legs and lives near water

flammable (say **flam**-uhb-l) *adjective*
able to burn easily: *a **flammable** liquid*
➲ SYNONYM **inflammable**

> WHICH WORD? **Flammable** or **inflammable**?
> These words mean the same thing, though they look like opposites.

flan *noun* (*plural* **flans**)
a round open pie filled with fruit, cheese or vegetables ➲ See **quiche, tart**

flank[1] *noun* (*plural* **flanks**)
1 the side of an animal's body
2 in a battle, the parts of an army at the sides

flank[2] *verb* (**flanking, flanked**)
to be on the side or sides of something: *The road was **flanked** by trees.*

flap[1] *noun* (*plural* **flaps**)
a piece of material or paper that is fixed to something at one side only, often covering an opening: *the **flap** of the envelope*

flap[2] *verb* (**flapping, flapped**)
to move or to make something move up and down or from side to side: *The bird **flapped** its wings.*

flare[1] (say **flair**) *verb* (**flaring, flared**)
flare up
1 to suddenly burn more strongly
2 to suddenly start or get worse: *The pain **flared** up again.*

flare[2] (say **flair**) *noun* (*plural* **flares**)
a thing that produces a bright light or flame, used especially as a signal

flash[1] *verb* (**flashing, flashed**)
1 to send out a bright light that comes and goes quickly or to make something do this: *The light kept **flashing** on and off.* ◇ *She **flashed** her torch.*
2 to appear and disappear very quickly, or to make something do this: *I saw something **flash** past the window.*

flash[2] *noun* (*plural* **flashes**)
1 a bright light that comes and goes quickly: *a **flash** of lightning*
2 a bright light that you use with a camera for taking photographs
in a flash very quickly: *The weekend was over in a **flash**.*

flashback (say **flash**-bak) *noun* (*plural* **flashbacks**)
part of a film or book that shows what happened before the main story began

flask (say **flaask**) *noun* (*plural* **flasks**)
a container for keeping a liquid hot or cold: *a flask of coffee*

flat[1] *adjective* (**flatter**, **flattest**)
1 smooth, with no parts that are higher or lower than the rest: *You need a **flat** surface to play this game.*
2 (about a tyre) that does not have enough air inside it

flat[2] *adverb*
with no parts that are higher or lower than the rest: *He lay **flat** on his back on the floor.*

flat[3] *noun* (*plural* **flats**)
a group of rooms for living in, usually in a big building: *I live in a large block of **flats**.*
➲ SYNONYM **apartment**

flatten (say **flat**-uhn) *verb* (**flattening**, **flattened**)
to make something flat: *I sat on the box and **flattened** it.*

flatter (say **flat**-uh) *verb* (**flattering**, **flattered**)
to say nice things about somebody, because you want them to do something
be or **feel flattered** to be pleased because somebody has made you feel important or special: *I'm **flattered** that she wants my advice.*

flattering (say **flat**-uh-ring) *adjective*
making somebody look or sound more attractive or important than they really are: ***flattering** remarks*

flattery (say **flat**-uh-ree) *noun* (*no plural*)
nice things that somebody says when they want you to do something

flaunt (say **flawnt**) *verb* (**flaunting**, **flaunted**)
to show something in an obvious way so that other people can admire you: *She **flaunts** her wealth by wearing very expensive clothes.*

flavour (say **flay**-vuh) *noun* (*plural* **flavours**)
the taste of food: *They sell 20 different **flavours** of ice cream.*
▸ **flavour** (*verb*): *chocolate-**flavoured** milk*

flaw (*rhymes with* **more**) *noun* (*plural* **flaws**)
1 a mistake in something that makes it not good enough: *There are some **flaws** in your argument.*
2 a weakness in somebody's character: *We all have our **flaws**!*
▸ **flawed** (*adjective*): *a **flawed** plan*
▸ **flawless** (*adjective*): *The performance of the champion (= a person who is the best at a sport or game) was **flawless**.*

flax (say **flakss**) *noun* (*no plural*)
1 a plant with blue flowers, grown for its stem that is used to make thread
2 the threads from this plant, used to make **linen**

flea (say **flee**) *noun* (*plural* **fleas**)
a very small insect without wings that can jump and that lives on and bites animals and people: *Our cat has got **fleas**.*
ⓘ ORIGIN: from Old English *flea*, *fleah*

fleck (say **flek**) *noun* (*plural* **flecks**)
a very small piece of something: *You have some **flecks** of paint in your hair.*

fledgling (say **flej**-ling) *noun* (*plural* **fledglings**) (also **fledgeling**)
1 a young bird that has just learnt to fly
2 a person or organization with no experience: *a **fledgling** democracy*

flee *verb* (**fleeing**, **fled**)
to run away from something bad or dangerous: *During the war, thousands of people **fled** the country.*

fleece (say **fleess**) *noun*
1 (*plural* **fleeces**) the wool coat of a sheep
2 (*no plural*) a type of soft warm cloth that feels like sheep's wool, or a jacket made from this cloth

fleet *noun* (*plural* **fleets**)
a big group of ships

fleeting (say **fleet**-ing) *adjective*
something that lasts for only a short time: *I caught a **fleeting** glimpse of the girl in the crowd.*

flesh *noun* (*no plural*)
the soft part of your body under your skin

> WORD BUILDING The **flesh** of an animal that we eat is called **meat**.

flew (say **floo**) form of **fly[1]**

flex (say **flekss**) *noun* (*plural* **flexes**) another word for **cord** 2

flexible (say **flek**-sib-l) *adjective*
1 able to change easily: *We can start earlier if you like – I can be **flexible**.* ◇ ***flexible** working hours*
2 able to bend easily without breaking
▸ **flexibility** (*noun*)

flick (say **flik**) *verb* (**flicking**, **flicked**)
1 to hit something lightly and quickly with your fingers: *I **flicked** the dust off my jacket.*
2 to move or to make something move with a

quick sudden movement: *She **flicked** the switch and the lights went off.*
flick through something: *He **flicked** through the magazine quickly.*
▸ **flick** (*noun*): *with a **flick** of the wrist*

flicker¹ (say **flik**-uh) *verb* (**flickering, flickered**)
1 (used about a light or flame) to keep going on and off: *The light **flickered** and went out.*
2 to appear for a short time: *A smile **flickered** across her face.*
3 to move lightly and quickly up and down: *Her eyelids **flickered** for a moment.*

flicker² (say **flik**-uh) *noun* (*plural* **flickers**)
1 a light that shines on and off quickly: *I saw a **flicker** in the window.*
2 a feeling of something that only lasts for a short time: *a **flicker** of hope*
3 a small sudden movement of a part of the body

flies (say **flize**) form of **fly²**

flight (say **flite**) *noun*
1 (*no plural*) flying: *Have you ever seen an eagle in **flight**?*
2 (*plural* **flights**) a journey in a plane: *Our **flight** leaves at 10 a.m.* ◇ *a direct **flight***
3 (*plural* **flights**) a group of steps: *a **flight** of stairs*
4 (*plural* **flights**) the act of running away from a bad situation: *the **flight** of the refugees*

flimsy (say **flim**-zee) *adjective* (**flimsier, flimsiest**)
1 not strong, easy to break or tear: *a **flimsy** strap*
2 difficult to believe: *He gave a **flimsy** excuse for being late.*

fling *verb* (**flinging, flung**)
to throw something carelessly or with great force: *She **flung** her coat on the chair.*

flip *verb* (**flipping, flipped**)
1 to turn over with a quick movement: *I **flipped** the book open.*
2 to throw something up into the air.: *Let's **flip** a coin to see who starts.*
3 (*informal*) to become very angry or excited: *My mum will **flip** if she sees this mess!*
flip through something: *I **flipped** through the notes quickly.*

flip-flop *noun* (*plural* **flip-flops**) (*S. African*) (also **slip-slop**)
a simple type of **sandal** with a thin strap that goes between your big toe and the toe next to it

flippant (say **flip**-uhnt) *adjective*
not serious about important things: *a **flippant** answer*

flipper (say **flip**-uh) *noun* (*plural* **flippers**)
1 a flat part of the body of some sea animals which they use for swimming: *Seals have **flippers***
2 a flat rubber shoe that you wear to help you swim fast underwater

flirt (say **flurt**) *verb* (**flirting, flirted**)
to behave as if you like somebody in a sexual way: *She was **flirting** with him at the party.*

flit *verb* (**flitting, flitted**)
to move quickly from one place to another place: *The birds **flitted** about from tree to tree.*

float¹ (say **floht**) *verb* (**floating, floated**)
1 to stay on top of a liquid: *Wood **floats** on water.* ➲ OPPOSITE **sink¹**
2 to move slowly in the air: *Clouds were **floating** across the sky.*

float² (say **floht**) *noun* (*plural* **floats**)
1 a decorated vehicle that travels down streets during celebrations
2 an object that floats on water, used in swimming and fishing

flock¹ (say **flok**) *verb* (**flocking, flocked**)
to go in large numbers to see something: *People are **flocking** to the exhibition.*

flock² (say **flok**) *noun* (*plural* **flocks**)
a group of sheep or birds: *a **flock** of geese* ➲ See **herd¹**

floe (*rhymes with* **go**) *noun* (*plural* **floes**) (also **ice floe**)
a large mass of ice floating in the sea

flog *verb* (**flogging, flogged**)
1 to hit somebody hard several times with a stick or a whip as punishment: *The prisoner was **flogged**.*
2 (*informal*) to sell something: *I had to **flog** my car.*

flood¹ (say **flud**) *noun* (*plural* **floods**)
1 a lot of water that has spread from a river or the sea, covering an area of land that should be dry: *Many homes were destroyed in the **flood**.*
2 a lot of something: *The child was in **floods** of tears* (= crying a lot).
ℹ ORIGIN: from Old English *flod*, related to Dutch *vloed*

flood² (say **flud**) *verb* (**flooding, flooded**)
to fill a place with water, or to be filled or covered with water: *A pipe burst and **flooded** the kitchen.*

floodlight (say **flud**-lite) *noun* (*plural* **floodlights**)
a powerful light that is used outside, for example near a building or for sports

floor (say **flaw**) *noun* (*plural* **floors**)
1 the part of a room that you walk on: *There weren't any chairs so we sat on the **floor**.*
2 all the rooms at the same height in a building: *I live on the ground **floor**.* ◇ *Our hotel room was on the sixth **floor**.*

floorboard (say **flaw**-bawd) *noun* (*plural* **floorboards**)
a long flat piece of wood in a wooden floor

flop¹ *verb* (**flopping, flopped**)
1 to sit or lie down in a sudden or relaxed way because you are tired: *I **flopped** down onto the bed after work.*
2 to move around without control or hang loosely: *Her hair always **flops** in her face.*
3 (used about a film, play, party) to be unsuccessful: *The play **flopped**.*

flop² *noun* (*plural* **flops**)
(used about a film, play, party) something that is not successful: *a box office **flop***

floppy (say **flop**-ee) *adjective* (**floppier, floppiest**)
soft and hanging downwards: *a **floppy** hat* ◇ ***floppy** ears*

flora (say **flaw**-ruh) *noun* (*no plural*)
all the plants growing in an area or in a period of time: *the **flora** and fauna of a million years ago* ➲ See **fauna**

floral (say **flaw**-ruhl) *adjective*
made from or decorated with flowers: *a **floral** design*

florist (say **flo**-rist) *noun* (*plural* **florists**)
a person who owns or works in a shop that sells flowers

flounce (say **flownss**) *verb* (**flouncing, flounced**)
to go or move in an angry or impatient manner: *She **flounced** out of the room.*

flounder (*rhymes with* **rounder**) *verb* (**floundering, floundered**)
1 to move with difficulty, making wild movements in order to get out of something: *They **floundered** about in the water until they were rescued.*
2 to find it difficult to speak or act: *She **floundered** during the interview.*
3 to have many problems and to begin to fail: *The business is **floundering** because of the economic crisis.*

flour (say **flow**-uh) *noun* (*no plural*)
a soft white or brown powder that is made from grain such as wheat and that we use to make bread and cakes

flourish (say **flu**-rish) *verb* (**flourishing, flourished**)
to develop or grow successfully: *The plant **flourished**.* ◇ *Their business is **flourishing**.*

flow¹ (*rhymes with* **go**) *noun* (*plural* **flows**)
a steady, continuous movement of something in one direction: *I used a handkerchief to stop the **flow** of blood.*

flow² (*rhymes with* **go**) *verb* (**flowing, flowed**)
to move in a steady, continuous way in one direction: *This river **flows** into the Atlantic Ocean.*

flow chart (say **floh** chaat) *noun* (*plural* **flow charts**) (*also* **flow diagram**)
a diagram that shows the connections between different stages of a process or parts of a system

flower (*rhymes with* **power**) *noun* (*plural* **flowers**)
the brightly coloured part of a plant that comes before the seeds or fruit: *She gave me a bunch of **flowers**.* ◇ *Roses, lilies and daisies are types of **flowers**.*

flower

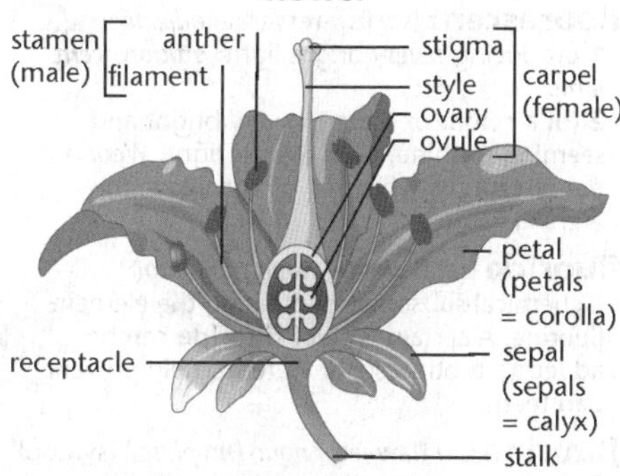

cross section of a flower

flown (*rhymes with* **bone**) *form of* **fly¹**

flu (say **floo**) *noun* (*no plural*)
an illness like a very bad cold that makes your body sore and hot: *I think I've got **flu**.*

fluctuate (say **fluk**-tyuu-ayt) *verb* (**fluctuating, fluctuated**)
to change frequently from one thing to another: *The number **fluctuates** between 50 and 60.*
▸ **fluctuation** (*noun*)

flue (say **floo**) *noun* (*plural* **flues**)
a pipe or tube that takes smoke, gas or hot air away from a fire or oven

fluent (say **floo**-uhnt) *adjective*
1 able to speak easily and correctly: *He is **fluent** in English and isiXhosa.*

A B C D E F G H I J K L M N O P Q R S T U V W X Y Z

2 spoken easily and correctly: *She speaks **fluent** Arabic.*
► **fluently** (*adverb*): *She speaks five languages **fluently**.*

fluff (say **fluf**) *noun* (*no plural*)
very light, soft pieces of wool, cotton or fur or very light and soft new feathers

fluffy (say **fluf**-ee) *adjective* (**fluffier, fluffiest**)
feeling or looking very light and soft: *a **fluffy** kitten* ◇ ***fluffy** clouds*

fluid[1] (say **floo**-id) *noun* (*plural* **fluids**)
a substance that can flow, such as a liquid: *The doctor told her to drink plenty of **fluids**.*

fluid[2] (say **floo**-id) *adjective*
1 able to flow smoothly, like a liquid: *His style of running is very **fluid**.*
2 able or likely to change: *a **fluid** situation*

fluke (say **flook**) *noun* (*plural* **flukes**) (*informal*)
something that happens because of good luck and not because you were skilful or clever

flung form of **fling**

fluorescent (say flaw-**ress**-uhnt) *adjective*
1 producing a very bright light: *a **fluorescent** lamp*
2 (of a colour or material) very bright and seeming to shine, even in little light: *Wear a **fluorescent** top when you go running in the evening.*

fluoride (say **flaw**-ride) *noun* (*no plural*)
a chemical substance containing the element fluorine. A certain type of **fluoride** can be added to toothpaste or water to help prevent bad teeth.

fluorine (say **flaw**-reen) *noun* (*no plural*) (symbol F)
a poisonous pale yellow gas

flurry (*rhymes with* **hurry**) *noun* (*plural* **flurries**)
a short time in which there is suddenly a lot of activity: *a **flurry** of excitement*

flush[1] *verb* (**flushing, flushed**)
1 to clean a toilet by pressing or pulling a handle that sends water through it: *Remember to **flush** the toilet.*
2 (about your face) to go red because you are embarrassed or angry: *He **flushed** with anger.*

flush[2] *noun* (*plural* **flushes**)
1 a red colour or hot feeling on your face: *The excitement brought a **flush** to my cheeks.*
2 the action of cleaning a toilet with water

flustered (say **fluss**-tuhd) *adjective*
being nervous and confused: *I get **flustered** when everyone shouts at me!*

flute (say **floot**) *noun* (*plural* **flutes**)
a musical instrument like a pipe that you hold out to the side and play by blowing over a hole at one side

flutter (say **flut**-uh) *verb* (**fluttering, fluttered**)
to make a quick, light movement through the air: *Flags **fluttered** in the breeze.*

flux (say **flukss**) *noun* (*no plural*)
1 a state of change or movement: *The country is in a state of **flux** because of the political changes.*
2 (*science*) a flow or an act of flowing: *a **flux** of neutrons* ◇ *magnetic **flux***

fly[1] (*rhymes with* **my**) *verb* (**flying, flew, has flown**)
1 to move through the air: *In autumn some birds **fly** to warmer countries.*
2 to make an aircraft move through the air: *A pilot is a person who **flies** an aircraft.*
3 to travel in a plane: *I'm **flying** to Abu Dhabi tomorrow.*
4 to move quickly: *The door suddenly **flew** open and John came in.*

fly[2] (*rhymes with* **my**) *noun* (*plural* **flies**)
1 a small insect with two wings
2 (also **flies**) the part where you fasten a pair of trousers at the front: *Your **fly** is undone!*

flying (say **fly**-ing) *adjective*
able to fly: ***flying** insects*
with flying colours very well, and with great success: *They all passed the exam with **flying** colours.*

flyover (say **fly**-oh-vuh) *noun* (*plural* **flyovers**)
a bridge that carries a road over other roads

foal (say **fohl**) *noun* (*plural* **foals**)
a young horse

foam (say **fohm**) *noun* (*no plural*)
a lot of very small white bubbles that you see when you move liquid quickly

focal (say **foh**-kuhl) *adjective*
1 central, very important: *The girl's face is the **focal** point in this painting.*
2 (*science*) connected with or providing a focus: ***focal** length*

focus[1] (say **foh**-kuhss) *verb* (**focusing, focused**)
1 to give all your attention to something: *to **focus** on a problem*
2 (used about a camera or your eyes) to change or be changed so that things can be seen clearly

focus[2] (say **foh**-kuhss) *noun* (*no plural*)
special attention that is given to a person or thing: *It was the main **focus** of attention at the meeting.*
in focus, out of focus (used about a

photograph) clear or not clear: *This picture is so badly out of* ***focus*** *that you can't recognize anyone.*

fodder (say **fod**-uh) *noun* (*no plural*)
food for farm animals

foe (*rhymes with* **go**) *noun* (*plural* **foes**)
(*old-fashioned*) an enemy

foetus (say **fee**-tuhss) *noun* (*plural* **foetuses**) = **fetus**

fog *noun* (*no plural*)
thick cloud that forms close to the ground, and that is difficult to see through: *The* ***fog*** *will clear by late morning.*
▸ **foggy** (*adjective*): *a* ***foggy*** *day* ◇ *It was very* ***foggy*** *this morning.*

foil[1] (say **foyl**) *noun* (*no plural*)
thin metal paper that is used for covering food: *Wrap the meat in* ***foil*** *and put it in the oven.*

foil[2] (say **foyl**) *verb* (**foiling, foiled**)
to stop a plan from succeeding: *The police* ***foiled*** *the plot to kill the president.*

fold[1] (*rhymes with* **sold**) *verb* (**folding, folded**) (also **fold up**)
1 to bend something so that one part is on top of another part: *I* ***folded*** *the letter and put it in the envelope.* ◇ ***Fold*** *up your clothes.* ➲ OPPOSITE **unfold**
2 to be able to be made smaller in order to be carried or stored more easily: *a* ***folding*** *chair* ◇ *This table* ***folds*** *up flat.*
fold your arms to cross your arms in front of your chest: *She* ***folded*** *her arms and waited.*

fold[2] (*rhymes with* **sold**) *noun* (*plural* **folds**)
a line that is made when you bend cloth or paper

folder (say **fohl**-duh) *noun* (*plural* **folders**)
1 a cover made of cardboard or plastic for keeping papers in
2 a collection of information or files on one subject that is stored in a computer or on a disk

foliage (say **foh**-li-uhj) *noun* (*no plural*)
the leaves of a plant: *autumn* ***foliage***

folk (say **fohk**) *plural noun*
people: *A lot of old* ***folk*** *live in this village.*
ℹ ORIGIN: from Old English *folc*, related to Dutch *volk*

PRONUNCIATION Don't pronounce the **l** in **folk**.

folk dance *noun* (*plural* **folk dances**)
a traditional dance: *the* ***folk dances*** *of Turkey*

folklore (say **fohk**-law) *noun* (*no plural*)
traditional stories and beliefs

folk song *noun* (*plural* **folk songs**)
a traditional song

follow (say **fol**-oh) *verb* (**following, followed**)
1 to come or go after a person or thing: *I think that car is* ***following*** *us!* ◇ *The film will be* ***followed*** *by the news.*
2 to go along a road or a path: ***Follow*** *this road for about a kilometre.*
3 to do what somebody says you should do: *Please* ***follow*** *the instructions carefully.*
4 to understand something: *Has everyone* ***followed*** *the lesson so far?*
as follows as you will now hear or read: *The dates of the meetings will be as* ***follows****: 21 March, 3 April, 19 April.*

following (say **fol**-oh-ing) *adjective*
next: *I saw him the* ***following*** *day.*

folly (say **fol**-ee) *noun* (*plural* **follies**)
a foolish act

fond *adjective* (**fonder, fondest**)
be fond of a person or **thing** to like a person or thing a lot: *They are very* ***fond*** *of their uncle.*

fondle (say **fond**-l) *verb* (**fondling, fondled**)
to touch in a loving or sexual way

font (say **font**) *noun* (*plural* **fonts**)
1 the size and style of letters used in printing and on a computer: *Use a big* ***font*** *for the words on the poster.*
2 a container in a church which holds water for a baptism

food (*rhymes with* **mood**) *noun* (*no plural*)
things that people or animals eat: *Let's go and get some* ***food*** *– I'm hungry.* ◇ *They gave the horses* ***food*** *and water.*
ℹ ORIGIN: from Old English *foda*. This word is related to English *fodder*, meaning 'food for farm animals'.

food chain *noun* (*plural* **food chains**) (*biology*)
a series of living creatures in which each type of creature feeds on the one below it in the series

food web *noun* (*plural* **food webs**) (*biology*)
a system of **food chains** that are related to each other and depend on each other

fool[1] (*rhymes with* **pool**) *noun* (*plural* **fools**)
a person who is silly or who does something silly: *You* ***fool****! You forgot to lock the door!*
make a fool of yourself to do something that makes you look silly in front of other people: *He always makes a* ***fool*** *of himself at parties.*

fool[2] (*rhymes with* **pool**) *verb* (**fooling, fooled**)
to make somebody believe something that is not true: *You can't* ***fool*** *me! I know you're lying!*
➲ SYNONYM **trick**[2]

A B C D E **F** G H I J K L M N O P Q R S T U V W X Y Z

fool about, **fool around** to do silly things: *Stop **fooling** about with that knife.*

foolish (say **fool**-ish) *adjective*
stupid or silly: *a **foolish** mistake*
▸ **foolishly** (*adverb*): *I **foolishly** forgot to bring a coat.*

foolproof (say **fool**-proof) *adjective*
not capable of going wrong or being used wrongly: *Our method is **foolproof**.*

foot (say **fuut**) *noun*
1 (*plural* **feet**) the part of your leg that you stand on: *I've been walking all day and my **feet** hurt.* ◇ *Shall we go by car or on **foot*** (= walk)*?*
2 (*plural* **foot** or **feet**) a measure of length (= 30,48 centimetres) used in some countries: *There are twelve inches in a **foot**.* ◇ *'How tall are you?' 'Five **foot** six* (= five feet and six inches).*'*
➲ See **inch**
3 (*no plural*) the lowest part of something: *She was standing at the **foot** of the stairs.*
➲ SYNONYM **bottom** 1
🛈 ORIGIN: from Old English *fot*, related to Dutch *voet*

foot

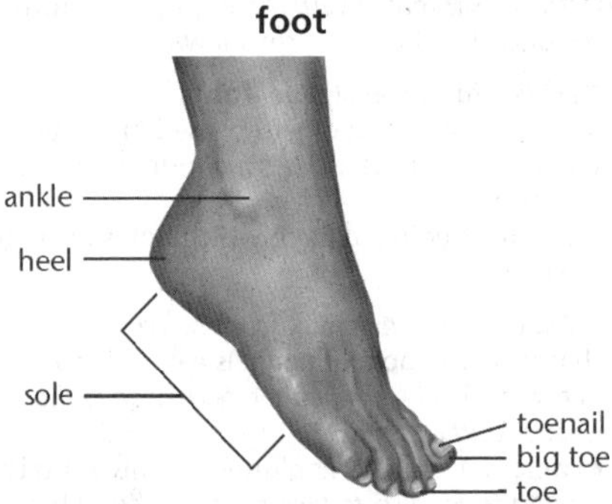

football (say **fuut**-bawl) *noun*
1 (*no plural*) a game for two teams of eleven players who try to kick a round ball into the other team's goal on a field (called a **football pitch**): *I'm playing in a **football** match tomorrow.*
➲ SYNONYM **soccer**
2 (*plural* **footballs**) a ball for playing this game
▸ **footballer** (*noun*): *He's a professional **footballer**.*

foothill (say **fuut**-hil) *noun* (*plural* **foothills**)
(usually **foothills**) a hill at the base of a mountain: *We have a farm in the **foothills**.*

foothold (say **fuut**-hohld) *noun* (*plural* **footholds**)
1 a place where you can safely put your foot when you are climbing
2 a place from which you can work and make progress: *The business is trying to get a **foothold** in the Asian market.*

footnote (say **fuut**-noht) *noun* (*plural* **footnotes**)
an extra piece of information that you add to the bottom of a page in a book

footpath (say **fuut**-paath) *noun* (*plural* **footpaths**)
a path for people to walk on in areas away from towns and cities

footprint (say **fuut**-print) *noun* (*plural* **footprints**)
a mark that your foot or shoe makes on the ground

footstep (say **fuut**-step) *noun* (*plural* **footsteps**)
the sound of a person walking: *I heard **footsteps**, and then a knock on the door.*

for[1] (say **faw**) *preposition*
1 a word that shows who will get or have something: *These flowers are **for** you.*
2 a word that shows how something is used or why something is done: *We had fish and chips **for** dinner.* ◇ *Take this medicine **for** your cold.* ◇ *He was sent to prison **for** murder.*
3 a word that shows how long something has been happening: *She has lived here **for** 20 years.*
➲ See note at **since**
4 a word that shows how far somebody or something goes: *We walked **for** miles* (= a very long way).
5 a word that shows where a person or thing is going: *Is this the train **for** Umlazi?*
6 a word that shows the person or thing you are talking about: *It's time **for** us to go.*
7 a word that shows how much something is: *I bought this book **for** R90.*
8 a word that shows that you like an idea: *Some people were **for** the strike and others were against it.* ➲ OPPOSITE **against** 2
9 on the side of somebody or something: *He plays tennis **for** Brazil.*
10 with the meaning of: *What is the word **for** 'table' in Afrikaans?*

for[2] (say **faw**) *conjunction* (*formal*) because: *She was crying, **for** she knew they could never meet again.*

USAGE **Because** and **as** are the words that we usually use. **For** is quite formal or old-fashioned.

forage[1] (say **fo**-rij) *noun* (*no plural*)
plants that we grow as food for animals

forage[2] (say **fo**-rij) *verb* (**foraging, foraged**)
(used about animals) to move around and search for food

forbid (say fuh-**bid**) *verb* (**forbidding, forbade, has forbidden**)
to order somebody not to do something: *My parents have* **forbidden** *me to see him again.* ◇ *Smoking is* **forbidden** (= not allowed) *inside the building.* ➲ OPPOSITE **allow** ➲ SYNONYM **prohibit**

force[1] (say **fawss**) *noun*
1 (*no plural*) power or strength: *He was killed by the* **force** *of the explosion.* ◇ *I lost the key so I had to open the door by* **force**.
2 (*plural* **forces**) a group of people, for example police or soldiers, who do a special job: *the police* **force**
3 (*plural* **forces**) (*science*) a pushing or pulling action that changes the movement or shape of an object. It is measured in newtons (N): *the* **force** *of gravity* ◇ *magnetic* **force** ➲ See illustration at **lever**

force[2] (say **fawss**) *verb* (**forcing, forced**)
1 to make somebody do something that they do not want to do: *They* **forced** *him to give them the money.*
2 to do something by using a lot of strength: *The thief* **forced** *the window open.*

forceful (say **fawss**-fuhl) *adjective*
having the power to persuade people and to demand action: *She has a* **forceful** *personality.*
▸ **forcefully** (*adverb*): *He argued the point* **forcefully**.

ford (say **fawd**) *noun* (*plural* **fords**)
a place in a river where you can walk or drive across because the water is not deep
▸ **ford** (*verb*): *We* **forded** *the river where it's shallow.*

fore- (say **faw**) *prefix*
1 before or in advance: **foretell** ◇ **foreword** ➲ See **foretell** ➲ See **foreword**
2 in front of: **foreground** ➲ See **foreground**
ℹ ORIGIN: from Old English

forearm (say **faw**-aam) *noun* (*plural* **forearms**)
the part of your arm between your elbow and your hand ➲ See illustration at **body**

forebear (say **faw**-bair) *noun* (*plural* **forebears**)
somebody in your family who lived a long time before you ➲ SYNONYM **ancestor**

foreboding (say faw-**bohd**-ing) *noun* (*no plural*)
a strong feeling that danger or trouble is coming: *I was suddenly filled with a sense of* **foreboding**.

forecast[1] (say **faw**-kaast) *noun* (*plural* **forecasts**)
what somebody thinks will happen, based on the information that is available: *The weather* **forecast** *said that it would rain today.*

forecast[2] (say **faw**-kaast) *verb* (**forecasting, forecast**)
to say what you think will happen, based on the information that is available: *They've* **forecast** *rain.* ➲ SYNONYM **predict**
▸ **forecaster** (*noun*): *She's a weather* **forecaster** *on TV.*

forefather (say **faw**-faath-uh) *noun* (*plural* **forefathers**)
somebody in your family who lived before you ➲ SYNONYM **ancestor**

forefinger (say **faw**-fing-guh) *noun* (*plural* **forefingers**) (also **index finger**)
the finger next to the thumb ➲ See illustration at **hand[1]**

foreground (say **faw**-grownd) *noun* (*no plural*)
the part of a picture that seems nearest to you: *The man in the* **foreground** *is my father.* ➲ OPPOSITE **background** 1

forehand (say **faw**-hand) *noun* (*plural* **forehands**)
(in sports such as tennis) a way of hitting the ball that is made with the **palm** of the hand facing forward ➲ See **backhand**

forehead (say **fo**-ruhd) *noun* (*plural* **foreheads**)
the part of your face above your eyes ➲ SYNONYM **brow** ➲ See illustration at **face[1]**

foreign (say **fo**-ruhn) *adjective*
belonging to or connected with a country that is not your own: *a* **foreign** *language*
ℹ ORIGIN: 13th–15th century, through Old French from Latin *foras*, *foris* meaning 'outside', from *fores* meaning 'door'

foreigner (say **fo**-ruhn-uh) *noun* (*plural* **foreigners**)
a person from another country

foreman (say **faw**-muhn) *noun* (*plural* **foremen**)
a worker who leads other workers: *He's a* **foreman** *at the factory.*

foremost (say **faw**-mohst) *adjective*
most famous or important, best: *She is one of South Africa's* **foremost** *scientists.*

foresee (say faw-**see**) *verb* (**foreseeing, foresaw, has foreseen**)
to know or guess what will happen in the future: *Nobody could have* **foreseen** *what would happen.* ➲ SYNONYM **predict**

foreshorten (say faw-**shawt**-uhn) *verb* (**foreshortening, foreshortened**)
to show an object in a drawing or photograph so that it looks closer than it really is

foresight (say **faw**-site) *noun* (*no plural*)
the ability to see what will probably happen in

A B C D E F G H I J K L M N O P Q R S T U V W X Y Z

the future and to use this knowledge to make good plans: *They had the **foresight** to save money for their children's education.* ➲ See **hindsight**

foreskin (say **faw**-skin) *noun* (*plural* **foreskins**)
the piece of skin that covers the end of a boy's or a man's **penis**: *When a boy is circumcised, his **foreskin** is cut and removed.*

forest (say **fo**-rist) *noun* (*plural* **forests**)
a large area of land covered with trees: *We went for a walk in the **forest**.*

forestry (say **fo**-riss-tree) *noun* (*no plural*)
the science of planting and taking care of trees in a forest

foretell (say faw-**tel**) *verb* (**foretelling, foretold**)
to say what is going to happen in the future: *She **foretold** that many people would die in a war.*

WHICH WORD? **Foretell**, **predict** or **forecast**?
We use the words **predict** or **forecast** to talk about what the weather will be in the future – not **foretell**.

forever (say fuh-**rev**-uh) *adverb* (also **for ever**)
1 for all time: *I will love you **forever**.* ➲ SYNONYM **always** 2
2 (*informal*) very often: *I can't read because she is **forever** asking me questions!*

foreword (say **faw**-wurd) *noun* (*plural* **forewords**)
a piece of writing at the beginning of a book that introduces the book or the author

forfeit (say **faw**-fit) *verb* (**forfeiting, forfeited**)
to lose something or have something taken away from you because you have done something wrong: *You have **forfeited** the right to swim here because you didn't obey the rules.*
▸ **forfeit** (*noun*)

forgave (say fuh-**gayv**) form of **forgive**

forge (say **fawj**) *verb* (**forging, forged**)
to make an illegal copy of something in order to cheat people: *The passport had been **forged**.*
forge somebody's signature to sign another person's name, pretending to be that person

forgery (say **faw**-juh-ree) *noun*
1 (*no plural*) the crime of making an illegal copy of something in order to cheat people
2 (*plural* **forgeries**) something that has been copied in order to cheat people: *This painting is not really by Picasso – it's a **forgery**.*

forget (say fuh-**get**) *verb* (**forgetting, forgot, has forgotten**)
1 to not remember something: *I've **forgotten** her name.* ◇ *Don't **forget** to do your homework!*
2 to not bring something with you: *I had **forgotten** my glasses.*
3 to stop thinking about something: ***Forget** about your exams and enjoy yourself!* ➲ OPPOSITE **remember**

forgetful (say fuh-**get**-fuhl) *adjective*
often forgetting things: *My grandmother had become rather **forgetful**.*
➲ SYNONYM **absent-minded**

forgive (say fuh-**giv**) *verb* (**forgiving, forgave, has forgiven**)
to stop being angry with somebody for a bad thing that they did: *I can't **forgive** him for behaving like that.*
▸ **forgiveness** (*noun*): *He begged for **forgiveness**.* ▸ **forgiving** (*adjective*): *She has a kind and **forgiving** nature*

forgot, forgotten forms of **forget**

fork (say **fawk**) *noun* (*plural* **forks**)
1 a metal object with long points at one end, that you use for putting food in your mouth
2 a large tool with points at one end, that you use for digging the ground
3 a place where a road or river divides into two parts: *When you get to the **fork** in the road, go left.*

forlorn (say fuh-**lawn**) *adjective*
lonely and unhappy: *Why does she look so **forlorn**?*

form[1] (say **fawm**) *noun* (*plural* **forms**)
1 a type of something: *Cars, trains and buses are all **forms** of transport.*
2 a piece of paper with spaces for you to answer questions: *You need to fill in this **form** to get a new passport.*
3 the shape of a person or thing: *a cake in the **form** of a car*
4 one of the ways you write or say a word: *'Forgot' is a **form** of 'forget'.*
5 (in some countries) a class in a school: *I'm in the sixth **form**.*

form[2] (say **fawm**) *verb* (**forming, formed**)
1 to make something or to give a shape to something: *We **formed** a line outside the classroom.* ◇ *In English we usually **form** the past tense by adding 'ed'.*
2 to grow or take shape: *Ice **forms** when water freezes.*
3 to start a group or an organization: *The club was **formed** last year.*

formal (say **fawm**-l) *adjective*
(about language or behaviour) used at important or serious times and with people you do not know very well: *'Yours faithfully' is a*

formal ending to a letter. ◇ *I wore a suit and tie to the* ***formal*** *dinner.* ➲ OPPOSITE **informal**
▸ **formally** (*adverb*): *'How do you do?' she said* ***formally***.

USAGE Some words and expressions in this dictionary are labelled **formal**. They are used mainly in writing, and especially in reports and official letters and documents. Examples of formal words are **acquire**, **impertinent**, **misconduct**, **permissible**, **rectify**, and **residence**. Often it is better to use a simpler word that other people understand.

format¹ (say **faw**-mat) *noun* (*plural* **formats**)
1 the shape or size of something or the way it is arranged or presented: *It's the same book but the* ***format*** *has changed.*
2 (*computing*) the structure in which you store or process data on a computer: *What is the* ***format*** *of this file?*

format² (say **faw**-mat) *verb* (**formatting, formatted**)
1 (*computing*) to prepare a computer disk so that you can store data on it: *You need to* ***format*** *the disk before you can use it.*
2 to arrange text on a page or on a screen

formation (say faw-**may**-shuhn) *noun*
1 (*no plural*) the act of making or developing something: *the* ***formation*** *of a new government*
2 (*plural* **formations**) a number of people or things in a particular shape or pattern: *The planes flew in* ***formation***. ◇ *rock* ***formations***

formative (say **fawm**-uh-tiv) *adjective*
having an important influence on a person's character and opinions or on the way they perform a task: *Our most* ***formative*** *years are those of our childhood.* ◇ ***formative*** *assessment* (= checks whether a learner can perform a task or not)

former (say **fawm**-uh) *noun* (*no plural*)
the former the first of two things or people: *He had to choose between losing his job and losing his family. He chose the* ***former***. ➲ See **latter**
▸ **former** (*adjective*): *the* ***former*** *Prime Minister*

formerly (say **fawm**-uh-lee) *adverb*
before this time: *Tanzania was* ***formerly*** *called Tanganyika.*

formidable (say **fawm**-i-duhb-l) *adjective*
1 (about a person) strong and a little frightening: *Her mother is a* ***formidable*** *woman.*
2 (about a thing) difficult and needing a lot of effort: *a* ***formidable*** *task*

formula (say **fawm**-yuu-luh) *noun* (*plural* **formulae** or **formulas**)
1 a group of letters, numbers or symbols that show a rule in mathematics or science: *The* ***formula*** *for finding the area of a circle is* πr^2.
2 a list of the substances that you need to make something: *The* ***formula*** *for the new drug has not yet been made public.*

formulate (say **fawm**-yuu-layt) *verb* (**formulating, formulated**)
1 to prepare and organize a plan for doing something: *We* ***formulated*** *a plan for dealing with the problem.*
2 to say something in a clear and exact way: *I tried to* ***formulate*** *an answer to the question.*

forsake (say faw-**sayk**) *verb* (**forsaking, forsook, has forsaken**)
to leave a person or thing when you should stay

fort (say **fawt**) *noun* (*plural* **forts**)
a strong building that was made to protect a place against its enemies

forthcoming (say **fawth**-kum-ing) *adjective*
1 going to happen soon, in the near future: *a* ***forthcoming*** *election*
2 offered or given: *If no money is* ***forthcoming***, *we will not be able to complete the project.*
3 ready to be helpful

forthright (say **fawth**-rite) *adjective*
saying exactly what you think in a clear and direct way: *a* ***forthright*** *manner*

fortieth (say **faw**-ti-uth) *adjective, adverb*
40th: *I had a party on my* ***fortieth*** *birthday.*

fortify (say **fawt**-i-fy) *verb* (**fortifying, fortified**)
to make a place stronger to protect it against an attack: *The city was* ***fortified***.
ℹ ORIGIN: 14th–15th century, through French *fortifier*, from Latin *fortificare*, from Latin *fortis* meaning 'strong'

fortnight (say **fawt**-nite) *noun* (*no plural*)
a period of two weeks: *I'm going on holiday for a* ***fortnight***.
▸ **fortnightly** (*adjective, adverb*): *We have* ***fortnightly*** *meetings.* ◇ *We meet* ***fortnightly***.

fortress (say **faw**-truhss) *noun* (*plural* **fortresses**)
a large strong building that was made to protect a place against its enemies

fortunate (say **faw**-tshuh-nuht) *adjective*
lucky: *I was very* ***fortunate*** *to get the job.*
➲ OPPOSITE **unfortunate**
▸ **fortunately** (*adverb*): ***Fortunately*** (= luckily) *nobody was hurt in the accident.*

A B C D E F G H I J K L M N O P Q R S T U V W X Y Z

fortune (say **faw**-tshoon) *noun*
1 (*no plural*) things that happen that you cannot control: *I had the good **fortune** to get the job.* ➲ SYNONYM **luck**
2 (*plural* **fortunes**) a lot of money: *He made a **fortune** selling old cars.*
tell somebody's fortune to say what will happen to somebody in the future: *She told my **fortune** by looking at my hand.*

forty (say **faw**-tee) *number*
1 40
2 the forties (*plural noun*) the numbers 40 to 49 or the years 1940 to1949: *She grew up in the **forties*** (= in the 1940s).
in your forties between the ages of 40 and 49: *I think my teacher must be in his **forties**.*
▸ **fortieth** (*adjective, adverb, pronoun*): *my **fortieth*** (= 40th) *birthday party*

SPELLING Remember! There is a **u** in **four**, but no **u** in **forty**.

forum (say **faw**-ruhm) *noun* (*plural* **forums**)
a place or meeting where people can discuss and exchange ideas

forward¹ (say **faw**-wuhd) *adverb* (also **forwards**)
in the direction that is in front of you: *Move **forwards** to the front of the train.* ➲ OPPOSITE **backwards** 1
look forward to something to wait for something with pleasure: *We're looking **forward** to seeing you again.*

forward² (say **faw**-wuhd) *verb* (**forwarding, forwarded**)
to send a letter that you receive at one address to another address: *Could you **forward** all my post to me while I'm away?*

forward³ (say **faw**-wuhd) *noun* (*plural* **forwards**)
a player in a game such as football who plays in the front row and tries to score goals

fossil (say **foss**-uhl) *noun* (*plural* **fossils**)
part of a dead plant or an animal that has been in the ground for a very long time and has turned into rock

fossil fuel *noun* (*plural* **fossil fuels**)
fuel such as coal or oil, that was formed millions of years ago from the remains of animals or plants

foster (say **foss**-tuh) *verb* (**fostering, fostered**)
1 (*formal*) to let a good feeling or situation develop: *The aim is to **foster** good relations between the two countries.*
2 to look after another person's child in your home for a time, without becoming their legal parent ➲ See **adopt**
▸ **foster** (*adjective*): *her **foster** parents ◇ their **foster** child*

fought (say **fawt**) form of **fight¹**

foul¹ (say **fowl**) *adjective*
1 dirty, or with a bad smell or taste: *What a **foul** smell!*
2 very bad: *We had **foul** weather all week.*

foul² (say **fowl**) *verb* (**fouling, fouled**)
(in sport) to do something to another player that is not allowed: *Johnson was **fouled** twice.*
▸ **foul** (*noun*): *He was sent off for a **foul** on the goalkeeper.*

found¹ (say **fownd**) form of **find**

found² (say **fownd**) *verb* (**founding, founded**)
to start a new organization: *This school was **founded** in 1865.*
▸ **founder** (*noun*): *the school's **founder*** (= the person who started it)

foundation (say fown-**day**-shuhn) *noun*
1 (*plural* **foundations**) the bricks or stones that form the solid base of a building, under the ground
2 (*plural* **foundations**) the idea, principle or fact on which something is based: *You need a solid **foundation** in maths.*
3 (*plural* **foundations**) an organization that provides money for a special purpose: *the Heart **Foundation***
4 (*no plural*) the act of starting a new organization

Foundation Phase *noun* (*no plural*)
(*S. African*)
Grades R,1, 2 and 3 at school

foundry (say **fown**-dree) *noun* (*plural* **foundries**)
a place where metal or glass is melted and made into objects

fountain (say **fown**-tuhn) *noun* (*plural* **fountains**)
water that shoots up into the air and then falls down again. **Fountains** are often used for decoration in gardens and parks.

fountain pen *noun* (*plural* **fountain pens**)
a pen that you fill with ink

four (say **faw**) *number*
4
on all fours with your hands and knees on the ground: *We went through the tunnel on all **fours**.*
▸ **fourth** (*adjective, adverb*): *He came **fourth*** (= 4th) *in the race.*

fourteen (say faw-**teen**) *number*
14
▸ **fourteenth** (*adjective, adverb*): *What day is it today? It's the **fourteenth*** (= the 14th day of the month).

fowl (*rhymes with* **owl**) *noun* (*plural* **fowl** or **fowls**)
a bird that is kept for its meat and eggs, for example a chicken

fox (say **fokss**) *noun* (*plural* **foxes**)
a wild animal like a small dog with a pointed nose, a long thick tail and, especially in Europe and North America, red fur

foyer (say **foy**-uh) *noun* (*plural* **foyers**)
an entrance hall in a building where people can meet: *the hotel **foyer***

fraction (say **frak**-shuhn) *noun* (*plural* **fractions**)
1 an exact part of a number: $\frac{1}{4}$ (= a quarter) *and* $\frac{1}{3}$ (= a third) *are **fractions**.*
2 a small part of something: *She won by a **fraction** of a second.*

fracture (say **frak**-tshuh) *noun* (*plural* **fractures**)
a break in one of your bones: *She had a **fracture** of the arm.*
► **fracture** (*verb*): *She fell and **fractured** her ankle.*

fragile (say **fraj**-ile) *adjective*
describing something that can break easily: *Be careful with those glasses. They're very **fragile**.*

fragment (say **frag**-muhnt) *noun* (*plural* **fragments**)
a very small piece that has broken off something: *a **fragment** of broken glass*

fragrance (say **fray**-gruhnss) *noun* (*plural* **fragrances**)
a pleasant smell: *The flowers are chosen for their delicate **fragrance**.*

fragrant (say **fray**-gruhnt) *adjective*
having a pleasant smell: *The air was **fragrant**.*

frail (say **frayl**) *adjective* (**frailer**, **frailest**)
not strong or healthy: *a **frail** old woman*
➲ SYNONYM **weak** 1

frame[1] (say **fraym**) *noun* (*plural* **frames**)
1 a thin piece of wood or metal round the edge of a picture, window or mirror
2 strong pieces of wood or metal that give something its shape: *the **frame** of the bicycle*
3 the metal or plastic round the edge of a pair of glasses
frame of mind the way that you feel at a particular time: *I'm not in the right **frame** of mind for a party.* ➲ SYNONYM **mood**

frame[2] (say **fraym**) *verb* (**framing**, **framed**)
to put a picture in a frame: *Let's have this photograph **framed**.*

framework (say **fraym**-wurk) *noun* (*plural* **frameworks**)
the strong part of something that gives it shape: *The bridge has a steel **framework**.*

franchise (say **fran**-chize) *noun*
1 (*plural* **franchises**) the right to sell a company's goods or services in a particular area using the company's name: *a restaurant franchise*
2 (*no plural*) (*formal*) the right to vote in elections

frank *adjective* (**franker**, **frankest**)
saying exactly what you think: *To be **frank**, I don't like your shirt.* ➲ SYNONYMS **candid**, **honest**, **truthful**
► **frankly** (*adverb*): *Tell me **frankly** what you think of my work.*

frantic (say **fran**-tik) *adjective*
1 very worried or frightened: *We heard the **frantic** cries for help.* ◇ *I went **frantic** when I couldn't find my sister.*
2 very busy or done in a hurry: *We made a **frantic** dash for the airport.* ◇ *Things get quite **frantic** towards the end of the year.*
► **frantically** (*adverb*): *We searched **frantically** for the keys.*

fraternal (say fruh-**turn**-l) *adjective*
like a brother or relating to the relationship with a brother: ***fraternal** love*

fraternity (say fruh-**turn**-i-tee) *noun*
1 (*no plural*) the feeling of friendship and support between people in the same group
2 (*plural* **fraternities**) a group of people who share the same work or interests: *the medical **fraternity***

fraud (say **frawd**) *noun*
1 (*no plural*) doing things that are not honest to get money: *Her father was sent to prison for **fraud**.*
2 (*plural* **frauds**) a person or thing that is not what they seem to be: *He said he was a police officer but I knew he was a **fraud**.*

fraught (say **frawt**) *adjective*
1 filled with something that is dangerous or not pleasant: *The trip was **fraught** with difficulties.*
2 causing people to become nervous and worried: *Things were quite **fraught** at work last week.*

fray *verb* (**fraying**, **frayed**)
(about the threads of cloth) to become loose at the edges: ***frayed** trousers*

freak (say **freek**) *noun* (*plural* **freaks**)
1 a person who looks strange or behaves in a very strange way

2 (*informal*) a person with a very strong interest in something: *a health **freak*** ◇ *a computer **freak***

freckle (say **frek**-uhl) *noun* (*plural* **freckles**)
a small, light brown spot on a person's skin: *A lot of people with red hair have **freckles**.*

free¹ *verb* (**freeing**, **freed**)
to make somebody or something free: *He was **freed** after ten years in prison.*

free² *adjective*, *adverb*
1 able to go where you want and do what you want: *After ten years in prison she was finally **free**.* ◇ *We set the bird **free*** (= let it go).
2 for which you do not have to pay: *We've got **free** tickets for the concert.* ◇ *Children under five travel **free**.*
3 not busy: *Are you **free** this afternoon?* ◇ *I don't have much **free** time.*
4 not being used: *Excuse me, is this seat **free**?*
free from something, **free of something** without something bad: *She was finally **free** from pain.*

Free Burgher *noun* (*plural* **Free Burghers**) (*history*)
a white male at the Cape in the 17th century who did not work for the Dutch East India Company

freedom (say **free**-duhm) *noun* (*no plural*)
the state of being free: *They gave their children too much **freedom**.*
freedom fighter a name used to describe a person who uses violence to try to remove a government from power, by people who support this ➲ See **guerrilla**

Freedom Charter *noun* (*no plural*) (*history*)
a document written in 1955 that set out the principles for introducing **human rights** and **democracy** in South Africa. It was written by the Congress of the People, which included the African National Congress and its allies.

freelance (say **free**-laanss) *adjective*
earning money by selling your work or services to different organizations rather than being employed by a single company: *a **freelance** journalist*

freely (say **free**-lee) *adverb*
1 in a way that is not controlled or limited: *He is the country's first **freely** elected president for 40 years.*
2 in an honest way without trying to avoid the truth, even though it might be embarrassing: *I **freely** admit that I made a mistake.*

free-range (say free-**raynj**) *adjective*
(about farm animals, especially farm birds) kept in natural conditions and able to move around freely: ***free-range** chickens*

freestyle (say **free**-stile) *noun* (*no plural*)
a competition in which a competitor can use any style: *a **freestyle** swimming event*

freeway (say **free**-way) *noun* (*plural* **freeways**)
a wide road that is specially built for fast traffic in and near cities

free-wheel (say **free**-weel) *verb* (**free-wheeling**, **free-wheeled**)
to ride a bicycle and not push on the pedals with your feet

freeze (say **freez**) *verb* (**freezing**, **froze**, **has frozen**)
1 to become hard because of extreme cold: *Water **freezes** and becomes ice at 0 degrees Celsius.*
2 to make food very cold so that it stays fresh for a long time: ***frozen** vegetables*
3 to stop suddenly and stay very still: *The cat **froze** when it saw the bird.*
freeze to death to be so cold that you die

freezer (say **freez**-uh) *noun* (*plural* **freezers**)
an electric container that freezes food so that it stays fresh for a long time ➲ See **fridge**

freezing (say **freez**-ing) *adjective*
very cold: *Can you close the window? I'm **freezing**!*

freezing point *noun* (*no plural*)
the temperature at which a liquid freezes: *Water has a **freezing point** of 0 degrees Celsius.*

freight (say **frayt**) *noun* (*no plural*)
goods that lorries, ships, trains and planes carry from one place to another: *a **freight** train*

freighter (say **frayt**-uh) *noun* (*plural* **freighters**)
a ship or an aircraft that carries only goods and not passengers

French *noun* (*no plural*)
the language spoken in France and some other countries: *I can speak **French**.*

frenzy (say **fren**-zee) *noun* (*plural* **frenzies**)
a state of great emotion or activity that is not under control

frequency (say **free**-kwuhn-see) *noun*
1 (*no plural*) the number of times something happens in a particular period: *Fatal road accidents have decreased in **frequency** over recent years.*
2 (*no plural*) the fact that something happens often: *the alarming **frequency** of computer errors*
3 (*plural* **frequencies**) (*science*) the rate at which a sound wave or radio wave moves up and down **(vibrates)**

frequent (say **free**-kwuhnt) *adjective*
happening often: *Her visits became less **frequent**.*

▸ **frequently** (*adverb*): *Simon is **frequently** late for school.* ➲ OPPOSITE **infrequent** ➲ SYNONYM **often**

fresco (say **fress**-koh) *noun* (*plural* **frescos** or **frescoes**)
a picture that is painted on a wall while the **plaster**[1] is still wet

fresh (say **fresh**) *adjective* (**fresher**, **freshest**)
1 (used especially about food) made or picked not long ago, or not frozen or in a tin: *I'll make some **fresh** coffee.* ◇ *Eat plenty of **fresh** fruit and vegetables.*
2 new or different: ***fresh** ideas*
3 clean and cool: *Open the window and let some **fresh** air in.*
4 (used about water) not containing salt, or not from the sea
▸ **freshly** (*adverb*): ***freshly** baked bread*

freshwater (say **fresh**-waw-tuh) *adjective*
1 living in water that is not the sea and is not salty: ***freshwater** fish*
2 having water that is not salty: ***freshwater** lakes*

fret[1] *verb* (**fretting**, **fretted**)
to worry or be unhappy about something

fret[2] *noun* (*plural* **frets**)
the bar or place on a guitar where you put your finger to make a particular sound

friction (say **frik**-shuhn) *noun* (*no plural*)
1 the action of one object or surface rubbing against another: *Oil in an engine reduces **friction** between the moving parts.*
2 disagreement between people: *There is a lot of **friction** between the children and the parents in this home.*

Friday (say **fry**-day) *noun*
the day of the week after Thursday and before Saturday ➲ See note at **day**

fridge (say **frij**) *noun* (*plural* **fridges**)
a metal container, usually electric, that keeps food cold, but not frozen: *Can you put the milk in the **fridge**?* ➲ See **freezer** ❶ **Fridge** is short for 'refrigerator'.

fried (say **fride**) form of **fry**

friend (say **frend**) *noun* (*plural* **friends**)
a person that you like and know very well: *She's my best **friend**.* ◇ *We are good **friends**.* ◇ *I made **friends** with* (= became a friend of) *a boy in my class.*

friendly (say **frend**-lee) *adjective* (**friendlier**, **friendliest**)
kind and helpful: *My neighbours are very **friendly**.* ➲ OPPOSITE **unfriendly**
be friendly with somebody to be somebody's friend: *Jan is **friendly** with their daughter.*

friendship (say **frend**-ship) *noun* (*plural* **friendships**)
the state of being friends with somebody: *a close **friendship*** ◇ *Your **friendship** is very important to me.*

fries (say **frize**) form of **fry**

frieze (say **freez**) *noun* (*plural* **friezes**)
1 a border that goes around the top of a room or building with painted pictures or pictures cut into stone **(carvings)** on it
2 a long narrow picture, usually put up in a school, that children have made

fright (say **frite**) *noun* (*plural* **frights**)
a sudden feeling of fear: *I hope I didn't give you a **fright** when I shouted.*

frighten (say **frite**-uhn) *verb* (**frightening**, **frightened**)
to make somebody feel afraid: *Did I **frighten** you?* ➲ SYNONYM **scare**[1]

frightened (say **frite**-uhnd) *adjective*
afraid: *He's **frightened** of spiders.* ◇ *I'm **frightened**!* ➲ SYNONYM **scared**

> USAGE Notice that we say **frightened of**, not 'frightened for': *Are you **frightened of** dogs?*

frightening (say **frite**-ning) *adjective*
making you feel afraid: *That was the most **frightening** film I have ever seen.*

frigid (say **frij**-uhd) *adjective*
1 very cold: ***frigid** air*
2 not showing any feelings of friendship or kindness: *There was a **frigid** atmosphere in the room.*

frill (say **fril**) *noun* (*plural* **frills**)
a narrow piece of cloth with a lot of folds which decorates the edge of a shirt or dress: *a white blouse with **frills** at the cuffs*
▸ **frilly** (*adjective*): *a **frilly** skirt*

fringe (say **frinj**) *noun* (*plural* **fringes**)
1 the short hair that hangs down above your eyes
2 a line of loose threads that decorate the edge of a piece of cloth or carpet

frisk *verb* (**frisking**, **frisked**)
1 to pass your hands over a person's body to find out if they are hiding something: *The security guards **frisked** everyone for weapons.*
2 to play and jump about happily and with energy: *The lambs **frisked** in the grass.*

fritter[1] (say **frit**-uh) *noun* (*plural* **fritters**)
pieces of meat, fruit and vegetables that you

put in a flour, egg and water mixture (called **batter**) and fry in a pan

fritter[2] (say **frit**-uh) *verb* (**frittering, frittered**)
to waste time or money gradually on things that are not important: *She **frittered** away her money instead of saving it.*

frivolous (say **friv**-uh-luhss) *adjective*
not serious, silly

frizzy (say **friz**-ee) *adjective* (**frizzier, frizziest**)
(used about hair) with a lot of small tight curls

fro (*rhymes with* **go**) *adverb*
to and fro first one way and then the other way, many times: *She rocked the baby to and fro.*

frock (say **frok**) *noun* (*plural* **frocks**)
(*old-fashioned*) a dress: *a party **frock***

frog *noun* (*plural* **frogs**)
a small animal with a smooth skin, that lives both on land and in water. **Frogs** have very long back legs for jumping. ➲ See illustration at **life cycle**

frogman (say **frog**-muhn) *noun* (*plural* **frogmen**)
a person whose job is to work under the water, wearing special clothes and equipment for breathing: *The **frogmen** searched the sunken boat.*

frolic (say **frol**-ik) *verb* (**frolicking, frolicked**)
to play or move about in a happy and excited way: *The children **frolicked** in the sea.*
➲ SYNONYM **romp**

from *preposition*
1 a word that shows where somebody or something starts: *We travelled **from** Mafikeng to Vryburg.* ◇ *She began to walk away **from** him.* ◇ *The tickets cost **from** R50 to R150.*
2 a word that shows when something starts: *The shop is open **from** 9.30 until 5.30.*
3 a word that shows who gave or sent something: *I had a letter **from** Mseni.* ◇ *I borrowed a dress **from** my sister.*
4 a word that shows where somebody lives or was born: *I come **from** Harare.*
5 a word that shows what is used to make something: *Paper is made **from** wood.*
6 a word that shows how far away something is: *My house is 2 km **from** town.*
7 a word that shows how something changes: *The sky changed **from** blue to grey.*
8 a word that shows why: *Children are dying **from** this disease.*
9 a word that shows difference: *My book is different **from** yours.*

frond *noun* (*plural* **fronds**)
a long leaf of a plant or tree: *the **fronds** of a palm tree*

front (say **frunt**) *noun* (*plural* **fronts**)
the side or part of something that faces forwards and that you usually see first: *a book with a picture on the **front*** ◇ *Thabang and I sat in the **front** of the car.*
in front of a person or **thing**
1 further forward than another person or thing: *She sat in **front** of her son on the bus.*
2 when other people are there: *Please don't talk about it in **front** of my parents.*
► **front** (*adjective*): *the **front** door* ◇ *the **front** seat of a car*

frontier (say **frun**-teer) *noun* (*plural* **frontiers**)
the line where one country joins another country

frost *noun* (*no plural*)
ice like white powder that covers the ground when the weather is very cold: *There was a **frost** last night.*
► **frosty** (*adjective*): *a **frosty** morning*

frost-bite (say **frost**-bite) *noun* (*no plural*)
a serious medical condition in which parts of the body, such as the fingers, toes and ears, are damaged by being in very cold temperatures for too long

froth *verb* (**frothing, frothed**)
to have or make many small white bubbles: *She used a machine to **froth** the milk.* ◇ *The mad dog **frothed** at the mouth.*
► **froth** (*noun*): *the **froth** on a milkshake*
► **frothy** (*adjective*): *a **frothy** cappuccino*

frown (*rhymes with* **brown**) *verb* (**frowning, frowned**)
to show feelings of anger or worry by making tight folds appear on the skin of your forehead: *John **frowned** at me when I came in. 'You're late,' he said.*
► **frown** (*noun*): *She looked at me with a **frown**.*

froze (say **frohz**) form of **freeze**

frozen[1] (say **froh**-zuhn) form of **freeze**

frozen[2] (say **froh**-zuhn) *adjective*
1 (used about food) kept at a very cold temperature so that it stays fresh for a long time: ***frozen** peas*
2 (*informal*) (used about people) very cold: *I'm **frozen** stiff.*

frugal (say **froo**-guhl) *adjective*
1 using only as much money or eating as much food as necessary

2 (used about meals) small and not expensive: *a **frugal** meal*
▸ **frugally** (*adverb*): *to live **frugally***

fruit (say **froot**) *noun* (*plural* **fruits**)
The part of a plant or tree that holds the seeds. Examples are oranges and apples: *'Would you like a piece of **fruit**?' 'Yes please – I'll have a pear.'* ◇ *'Have some **fruit**. We have bananas, dates, mangoes and strawberries.'* ➲ See illustration at **plant**[1]
🛈 **ORIGIN:** 13th–15th century, through Old French from Latin *fructus* meaning 'enjoyment of produce, harvest'

frustrate (say fruss-**trayt**) *verb* (**frustrating, frustrated**)
to make a person feel annoyed or impatient because they cannot achieve or do what they want to: *Traffic jams **frustrate** most people!*
▸ **frustrated** (*adjective*): *He was **frustrated** by the delays at the station.* ▸ **frustration** (*noun*): *Her **frustration** at not being able to walk fast was plain to see.*

frustrating (say fruss-**tray**-ting) *adjective*
making you angry because you cannot do what you want to do: *It's **frustrating** when you can't say what you mean in another language.*

fry (*rhymes with* **my**) *verb* (**frying, fried**)
to cook something in hot oil: *Fry the onions in butter.* ◇ ***fried** eggs*

frying pan (say **fry**-ing pan) *noun* (*plural* **frying pans**)
a flat metal container with a long handle that you use for frying food

fudge (say **fuj**) *noun* (*no plural*)
a soft sweet: *My sister showed me how to make **fudge**.*

fuel[1] (say **fyoo**-uhl) *noun* (*no plural*)
anything that you burn to make heat or power. Examples are wood, coal and oil.

fuel[2] (say **fyoo**-uhl) *verb* (**fuelling, fuelled**)
1 to supply something with material that can be burnt to produce heat or power
2 to fill up a vehicle with fuel such as petrol: *The car was **fuelled** up and ready for the trip.*
3 to increase something: *Magazine articles **fuelled** our fears about eating meat.*

fugitive (say **fyoo**-juh-tiv) *noun* (*plural* **fugitives**)
a person who is running away or escaping from the police or from a dangerous situation ➲ See **refugee**

fulfil (say fuul-**fil**) *verb* (**fulfilling, fulfilled**)
to do what you have planned or promised to do: *She **fulfilled** her dream of going to India.*

full (say **fuul**) *adjective*
1 with a lot of people or things in it, so that there is no more space: *My glass is **full**.* ◇ *The bus was **full** so we waited for the next one.*
2 having had enough to eat: *'Would you like anything else to eat?' 'No thank you, I'm **full**.'*
3 complete, with nothing missing: *Please tell me the **full** story.* ◇ *Please write your name in **full**.*
4 (only before a noun) to the highest level or greatest amount possible: *The train was travelling at **full** speed.*

full moon *noun* (*plural* **full moons**)
the moon when it appears as a complete circle

full stop *noun* (*plural* **full stops**)
a mark (**.**) that you use in writing to show the end of a sentence, or in some abbreviations
➲ See Study page 16

full-time (say **fuul**-time) *adjective, adverb*
for all the normal working hours of the day or week: *My mother has a **full-time** job.* ◇ *Do you work **full-time**?* ➲ See **part-time**

fully (say **fuul**-ee) *adverb*
completely or totally: *The hotel was **fully** booked.*

fumble (say **fumb**-l) *verb* (**fumbling, fumbled**)
to try to hold or find something with your hands in a nervous way or with difficulty: *I **fumbled** in my bag for a pen.*

fume (say **fyoom**) *verb* (**fuming, fumed**)
to be very angry about something: *She is still **fuming** about what happened this morning.*

fumes (say **fyoomz**) *plural noun*
smoke or gases that smell unpleasant and that can be dangerous to breathe in: *petrol **fumes***

fumigate (say **fyoom**-i-gayt) *verb* (**fumigating, fumigated**)
to use chemical gases to destroy harmful organisms in a place: *I **fumigated** my house because there were so many cockroaches.*

fun *noun* (*no plural*)
pleasure and enjoyment: *Tennis is good **fun**.* ◇ *Have **fun*** (= enjoy yourself)*!*
make fun of somebody to laugh about somebody in an unkind way: *The children make **fun** of him because he wears glasses.*

function[1] (say **fungk**-shuhn) *noun* (*plural* **functions**)
1 the special work that a person or thing does: *The **function** of the heart is to send blood round the body.*
2 an important social event or ceremony

function[2] (say **fungk**-shuhn) *verb* (**functioning, functioned**)
to work: *The car engine will not **function** without oil.*

functional (say **fungk**-shuhn-l) *adjective*
1 designed to be practical and useful rather than attractive: ***functional** clothes*
2 working, or being used: *The new bus services are not yet fully **functional**.*

fund (say **fund**) *noun* (*plural* **funds**)
money that will be used for something special: *a **fund** to help homeless people ◊ The school wants to raise **funds** for new computers.*

fundamental (say fun-duh-**men**-tuhl) *adjective*
most important, and from which everything else develops: *There is a **fundamental** difference between the two points of view.* ➲ SYNONYM **basic** 1
▸ **fundamentally** (*adverb*): *The government's policy has changed **fundamentally**.*

fundamentalist (say fun-duh-**men**-tuh-list) *noun* (*plural* **fundamentalists**)
a person who follows the rules of a religion exactly

fund-raising (say **fund**-rayz-ing) *noun* (*no plural*)
the activity of collecting money for a particular use: ***fund-raising** activities at school*

funeral (say **fyoo**-nuh-ruhl) *noun* (*plural* **funerals**)
the time when a dead person is buried or burned **(cremated)**

funfair (say **fun**-fair) *noun* (*plural* **funfairs**) (also **fair**)
a place outdoors where you can ride on big machines and play games to win prizes

fungus (say **fung**-guhss) *noun* (*plural* **fungi** or **funguses**)
a type of organism that is neither a plant nor an animal, and that lives on **organic** matter. **Mushrooms** and **moulds** are fungi.

funnel (say **fun**-l) *noun* (*plural* **funnels**)
1 a tube that is wide at the top to help you pour a liquid or powder into a bottle
2 a metal **chimney**, for example on a ship or an engine, through which smoke comes out

funny (say **fun**-ee) *adjective* (**funnier, funniest**)
1 making you laugh or smile: *a **funny** story ◊ He's so **funny**!* ➲ SYNONYMS **amusing, humorous**
2 strange or surprising: *There's a **funny** smell in this room.*

fur *noun* (*no plural*)
the soft thick hair that covers the bodies of some animals
▸ **furry** (*adjective*): *a **furry** animal*

furious (say **fyoo**-ri-uhss) *adjective*
very angry: *My parents were **furious** with me.*
➲ The noun is **fury**
▸ **furiously** (*adverb*): *He shouted **furiously**.*

furnace (say **fur**-nuhss) *noun* (*plural* **furnaces**)
a very hot fire in a closed place, used for heating metals or making glass

furnish (say **furn**-ish) *verb* (**furnishing, furnished**)
to put furniture into a room or house
▸ **furnished** (*adjective*): *a **furnished** flat*

furnishings (say **furn**-ish-ingz) *plural noun*
the furniture, curtains, carpets and other decorations in a room

furniture (say **furn**-i-tshuh) *noun* (*no plural*)
tables, chairs, beds, etc.: *They've bought some **furniture** for their new house. ◊ I'm cleaning all the **furniture** in our flat.*

USAGE **Furniture** does not have a plural. If you are talking about one item, you say **a piece of furniture**.

furrow (say **fu**-roh) *noun* (*plural* **furrows**)
1 a line in a field (made by a tool called a **plough**) in which you can plant seeds
2 a deep line in the skin on a person's face, especially on the forehead

furry (say **fur**-ree) *adjective* (**furrier, furriest**)
having fur: *A cat is a **furry** animal.*

further[1] (say **fur**-thuh) *adjective, adverb*
1 at or to a greater distance: *The hospital is **further** down the road.* ➲ SYNONYM **farther**
2 more or extra: *Are there any **further** questions?*

further[2] (say **fur**-thuh) *verb* (**furthering, furthered**) (*formal*)
to help something to develop or be successful: *I hope to **further** my education later.*

further education *noun* (*no plural*) (abbr. FE)
education for people who have left school but who are not at university ➲ See **higher education**

Further Education and Training *noun* (*no plural*) (abbr. FET) (*S. African*)
education in Grades 10-12 in schools and colleges

furthest (say **fur**-thuhst) form of **far**[1]

furtive (say **fur**-tiv) *adjective* (*formal*)
secret, acting as though you are trying to hide something: *a **furtive** glance*
▸ **furtively** (*adverb*)

fury (say **fyoo**-ree) *noun* (*no plural*) (*formal*)
very strong anger: *She was filled with* ***fury****.*
➲ The adjective is **furious**

fuse¹ (say **fyooz**) *noun* (*plural* **fuses**)
a small wire inside a piece of electrical equipment that stops it from working if too much electricity goes through it

fuse² (say **fyooz**) *verb* (**fusing, fused**)
1 (used about two things) join or be joined to become one: *As they heal, the bones will* ***fuse*** *together.* ◇ *The two companies have been* ***fused*** *into a single organization.*
2 to stop working because a **fuse¹** has melted: *The lights have* ***fused****.*

fusion (say **fyoo**-zhuhn) *noun* (*no plural*)
1 the process or result of joining two things together: *the* ***fusion*** *of two political parties*
2 (*science*) the act or process of combining the nuclei (plural of **nucleus**) of atoms to form a heavier nucleus, with energy being released

fuss *noun* (*no plural*)
a lot of excitement or worry about small things that are not important: *He makes a* ***fuss*** *when I'm five minutes late.*
▶ **fuss** (*verb*): *Stop* ***fussing****!*

fussy (say **fuss**-ee) *adjective* (**fussier, fussiest**)
caring a lot about small things that are not important, and difficult to please: *Rod is* ***fussy*** *about his food* (= there are many things that he will not eat).

futile (say **fyoo**-tile) *adjective*
having no success: *We made a last* ***futile*** *attempt to get the car started.*
▶ **futility** (*noun*): *the* ***futility*** *of the situation*

future¹ (say **fyoo**-tshuh) *adjective*
happening or existing in the time that will come: *Have you met Tshedi's* ***future*** *husband?*

future² (say **fyoo**-tshuh) *noun*
1 the future (*no plural*) the time that will come: *Nobody knows what will happen in the* ***future****.*
2 (*plural* **futures**) what will happen to a person or thing in the time that will come: *Our children's* ***futures*** *depend on a good education.* ◇ *The company's* ***future*** *is uncertain.*
3 the future (*no plural*) (also **the future tense**) (*grammar*) the form of a verb that shows what will happen after now ➲ See **past²**, **present²** 2-3
in future from now on: *You must work harder in* ***future****.*

future perfect tense *noun* (*no plural*) (*grammar*)
the form of a verb which expresses an action in the future that will be finished before the time mentioned, for example 'will have been married' in this sentence: 'We will have been married for ten years next month'.
➲ See Study pages 6 and 7

future tense *noun* (*no plural*) (*grammar*)
the form of a verb that shows what will happen after now: *'She will sing' is in the* ***future tense****.*
➲ See Study pages 6 and 7

fuzzy (say **fuz**-ee) *adjective* (**fuzzier, fuzziest**)
1 not clear: *The picture on the TV screen went all* ***fuzzy****.*
2 covered in soft hair: *a* ***fuzzy*** *teddy bear*

fynbos (say **fayn**-bawss) *noun* (*no plural*)
a type of wild **vegetation** that grows mainly in the Western Cape, and that includes **proteas**, **daisies**, and many other types of plant: ***Fynbos*** *is famous for its beauty and its diversity.*
🛈 **ORIGIN**: 19th century, from Afrikaans *fynbos*, meaning 'fine bush'. Many fynbos plants have small, fine leaves.

Gg

A B C D E F **G** H I J K L M N O P Q R S T U V W X Y Z

g *abbreviation* (*plural* **g**) **gram**

gable (say **gayb**-l) *noun* (*plural* **gables**)
the pointed or curved part at the top of an outside wall of a house, between two parts of the roof

gadget (say **gaj**-uht) *noun* (*plural* **gadgets**)
a small machine or useful tool: *Their kitchen is full of electrical* ***gadgets****.*

gag *noun* (*plural* **gags**)
1 a piece of cloth that is put in or tied over a person's mouth to stop them talking
2 (*informal*) a joke: *We played a* ***gag*** *on our teacher.*
▸ **gag** (*verb*): *He was tied up and* ***gagged****.*

gain (say **gayn**) *verb* (**gaining, gained**)
1 to get something that you want or need: *I* ***gained*** *useful experience from that job.*
2 to get more of something: *I have* ***gained*** *weight recently.*

gala (say **gaa**-luh) *noun* (*plural* **galas**)
a special social or sporting event: *a swimming* ***gala*** ◇ *They held the* ***gala*** *dinner at the hotel.*

galaxy (say **gal**-uhk-see) *noun* (*plural* **galaxies**)
a very large group of stars and planets
🛈 **ORIGIN:** 14th–15th century, through Old French and Latin, from Greek *galaxias* meaning 'milky'. This word was originally used to describe the Milky Way, the band of light across the night sky, made up of stars that are part of our galaxy.

gale (say **gayl**) *noun* (*plural* **gales**)
a very strong wind: *The trees were blown down in the* ***gale****.*

galjoen (say *khul*-**yuun**) *noun* (*plural* **galjoen** or **galjoens**)
a sea fish that is found only along the coast of South Africa. It is our national fish.
🛈 **ORIGIN:** 19th century, through Afrikaans from Dutch *galjoen* meaning 'galleon'. The fish possibly got this name because its shape is similar.

gallant (say **gal**-uhnt or guh-**lant**) *adjective* (*formal*)
1 brave: *She made a* ***gallant*** *effort.*
2 polite behaviour towards women: *He is a* ***gallant*** *gentleman.*
▸ **gallantly** (*adverb*) ▸ **gallantry** (*noun*): *He showed great* ***gallantry*** *when he saved the child.*

galleon (say **gal**-i-uhn) *noun* (*plural* **galleons**)
a large Spanish sailing ship used from the 15th to the 18th centuries

gallery (say **gal**-uh-ree) *noun* (*plural* **galleries**)
a place where people can look at or buy art: *an art* ***gallery***

galley (say **gal**-ee) *noun* (*plural* **galleys**)
1 a long flat ship with sails, especially one used by ancient Greeks or Romans in war
2 the kitchen on a ship or a plane

gallon (say **gal**-uhn) *noun* (*plural* **gallons**)
a unit for measuring the volume of liquids (= 4,55 litres), used in Britain. ➲ See **pint**

gallop (say **gal**-uhp) *verb* (**galloping, galloped**)
(used about a horse or a rider) to go at the fastest speed: *The horses* ***galloped*** *round the field.*

gallows (say **gal**-ohz) *noun* (*plural* **gallows**)
a wooden frame that was used in the past for hanging people

galvanize (say **gal**-vuh-nize) *verb* (**galvanizing, galvanized**) (also **galvanise**)
1 to cover iron or steel with **zinc** to protect it from being damaged by water: *The corrugated iron roof sheets were* ***galvanized*** *so that they didn't rust.*
2 to make a person take action by shocking them or by making them excited: *The urgency of his voice* ***galvanized*** *them into action.*
▸ **galvanized** (*adjective*) (also **galvanised**): *galvanized iron*

gamble (say **gamb**-l) *verb* (**gambling, gambled**)
1 to try to win money by playing games that need luck: *He* ***gambled*** *a lot of money on the last race.*
2 to take a risk, hoping that something will happen: *We* ***gambled*** *on the weather staying fine.*
▸ **gamble** (*noun*): *We took a* ***gamble****, and it paid off* (= was successful). ▸ **gambling** (*noun*): *He had heavy* ***gambling*** *debts.*

gambler (say **gamb**-luh) *noun* (*plural* **gamblers**)
a person who tries to win money by playing games that need luck

gambol (say **gamb**-l) *verb* (**gambolling, gambolled**) (*old-fashioned*)
to run and jump and play: *The lambs were* ***gambolling*** *in the field.*

game (say **gaym**) *noun*
1 (*plural* **games**) something you play that has rules: *Shall we have a **game** of football?* ◇ *Let's play a **game**!* ◇ *computer **games***
2 (*no plural*) wild animals or birds that people kill for sport or food

game show *noun* (*plural* **game shows**)
a television programme in which people play games or answer questions to win prizes

gammon (say **gam**-uhn) *noun* (*no plural*)
smoked meat from the leg of a pig

gander (say **gan**-duh) *noun* (*plural* **ganders**)
a male **goose**

gang[1] *noun* (*plural* **gangs**)
1 an organized group of criminals: *a **gang** of criminals*
2 a group of young people who spend a lot of time together and often cause trouble or fight against other groups: *street **gangs***
3 (*informal*) a group of friends: *The whole **gang** is coming tonight.*

gang[2] *verb* (**ganging, ganged**)
gang up on or **against somebody** to join together in a group to hurt or frighten somebody: *At school the older boys **ganged** up on him and called him names.*

gangplank (say **gang**-plank) *noun* (*plural* **gangplanks**)
a board for people to walk on between the side of a boat and land

gangrene (say **gang**-green) *noun* (*no plural*)
the infection and death of a part of the body because of a lack of blood supply: *After the motorbike accident, his leg developed **gangrene** and had to be amputated.*
▸ **gangrenous** (*adjective*)

gangster (say **gang**-stuh) *noun* (*plural* **gangsters**)
a member of a group of criminals

gangway (say **gang**-way) *noun* (*plural* **gangways**)
a bridge that you use for getting on or off a ship

gaol (say **jay**-uhl) *noun* (*plural* **gaols**) another word for **jail**

gap *noun* (*plural* **gaps**)
a space in something or between two things, or a space where something should be: *The goats got out through a **gap** in the fence.* ◇ *Fill in the **gaps** in the text.*

gape (say **gayp**) *verb* (**gaping, gaped**)
to look at a person or thing with your mouth open because you are surprised: *She **gaped** at me in astonishment.*

gaping (say **gayp**-ing) *adjective*
wide open: *a **gaping** hole in a fence*

garage (say **ga**-raaj) *noun* (*plural* **garages**)
1 a building in which you keep your car
2 a place where vehicles are repaired and where you can buy petrol and oil

garbage (say **gar**-bij) *noun* (*no plural*)
things that you throw away because you do not want them any more ➲ SYNONYMS **refuse**[2], **rubbish** 1, **trash**

garden (say **gaa**-duhn) *noun* (*plural* **gardens**)
1 a piece of land by your house where you can grow flowers, fruit, and vegetables: *Let's have lunch in the **garden**.*
2 gardens (*plural noun*) a public park: *the Company **Gardens***
▸ **garden** (*verb*): *My mother **gardened*** (= worked in the garden) *all weekend.*
▸ **gardening** (*noun*): *She loves **gardening**.*

gardener (say **gaad**-nuh) *noun* (*plural* **gardeners**)
a person who works in a garden

gargle (say **gaag**-l) *verb* (**gargling, gargled**)
to wash your mouth and throat by moving liquid around your mouth without swallowing

gargoyle (say **gaa**-goyl) *noun* (*plural* **gargoyles**)
a stone figure of an ugly person or animal through which water is carried away from the roof of a building, especially a church

garland (say **gaa**-luhnd) *noun* (*plural* **garlands**)
a ring made of flowers and leaves that you can wear on your head or around your neck

garlic (say **gaa**-lik) *noun* (*no plural*)
a plant like a small onion with a strong taste and smell, that you use in cooking
ⓘ ORIGIN: from Old English *garleac* from *gar* meaning 'spear' + *leac* meaning 'leek'. A clove of garlic has the same shape as the pointed head of a spear.

garment (say **gaa**-muhnt) *noun* (*plural* **garments**) (*formal*)
a piece of clothing

garnish (say **gaa**-nish) *verb* (**garnishing, garnished**)
to decorate food using a small amount of another food: *I **garnished** the soup with parsley.*
▸ **garnish** (*noun*): *A slice of tomato was used as a **garnish**.*

garrison (say **ga**-ri-suhn) *noun* (*plural* **garrisons**)
a group of soldiers who live in and guard a town or city

garter (say **gaa**-tuh) *noun* (*plural* **garters**)
a band that you wear around your leg to keep your sock or stocking up

gas (say **gass**) *noun*
1 (*plural* **gases**) a substance like air that is not a solid or a liquid: *Hydrogen and oxygen are* ***gases****.*
2 (*no plural*) a particular type of gas or mixture of gases used as fuel for heating and cooking: *Do you use electricity or* ***gas*** *for cooking?* ◇ *a* ***gas*** *cylinder*

gash *noun* (*plural* **gashes**)
a long deep cut: *That's a nasty* ***gash*** *on your leg.*

gasp (say **gaasp**) *verb* (**gasping, gasped**)
to breathe in quickly and noisily through your mouth: *She* ***gasped*** *in surprise.* ◇ *He came out of the water* ***gasping*** *for air.*
▸ **gasp** (*noun*): *a* ***gasp*** *of surprise*

gastric (say **gass**-trik) *adjective*
of the stomach: *a* ***gastric*** *ulcer* ◇ ***gastric*** *juices*

gate (say **gayt**) *noun* (*plural* **gates**)
1 a thing like a door in a fence or wall, that opens so that you can go through: *Please close the* ***gate****.*
2 a door in an airport that you go through to reach the plane: *Please go to* ***gate*** *15.*

gatecrash (say **gayt**-krash) *verb* (**gatecrashing, gatecrashed**)
to go to a party that you have not been invited to: *Other learners* ***gatecrashed*** *our class party.*

gateway (say **gayt**-way) *noun* (*plural* **gateways**)
a way in or out of a place

gather (say **ga*th***-uh) *verb* (**gathering, gathered**)
1 to come together in a group: *We all* ***gathered*** *round to listen to the teacher.*
2 to bring together things that are in different places: *Can you* ***gather*** *up all the books and papers?*
3 to believe or understand something: *I* ***gather*** *that you know my sister.*

gathering (say **ga*th***-uh-ring) *noun* (*plural* **gatherings**)
a meeting, or a time when people come together: *a family* ***gathering***

gauge[1] (say **gayj**) *noun* (*plural* **gauges**)
an instrument that measures how much of something there is: *the petrol* ***gauge*** *in a car*

gauge[2] (say **gayj**) *verb* (**gauging, gauged**)
to judge, calculate, or guess something: *It was hard to* ***gauge*** *the mood of the audience.*

gaunt (say **gawnt**) *adjective*
(used about a person) very thin because of hunger or illness: *He is looking* ***gaunt*** *after his illness.*

gauze (say **gawz**) *noun* (*no plural*)
a thin material like a net that you use to cover an area of skin that has been hurt: *Put some* ***gauze*** *on your cut so it keeps clean.*

gave (say **gayv**) form of **give**

gay *adjective*
1 attracted to people of the same sex ➲ SYNONYM **homosexual** ➲ See **lesbian**
2 (*old-fashioned*) happy and full of fun

gaze (say **gayz**) *verb* (**gazing, gazed**)
to look at a person or thing for a long time: *She sat and* ***gazed*** *out of the window.* ➲ See note at **stare**

gazelle (say guh-**zel**) *noun* (*plural* **gazelle** or **gazelles**)
a small antelope that lives in Africa and Asia

gazette (say guh-**zet**) *noun* (*plural* **gazettes**)
a newspaper, especially the official one of an organization: *The government* ***gazette*** *has information about new laws.*

GDP (say jee-dee-**pee**) *noun* (*plural* **GDPs**)
the total value of all the goods and services produced in a country in one year ℹ **GDP** is short for 'Gross Domestic Product'. ➲ See **GNP**

GEAR (say **geer**) *noun* (*no plural*)
a plan of the South African government to make the economy stronger, so that more people can share in it, especially those who have not had the chance to do so ℹ **GEAR** is short for 'Growth, Employment and Redistribution'.

gear (say **geer**) *noun*
1 (*plural* **gears**) the parts in a machine, for example a car or a bicycle, that control how fast the wheels turn round: *You need to change* ***gear*** *to get up the hill in this car.*
2 (*no plural*) special clothes or equipment that you need for a job or sport: *camping* ***gear***

gecko (say **gek**-oh) *noun* (*plural* **geckos** or **geckoes**)
a small reptile like a **lizard** with sticky ends on its fingers that lives in warm countries
ℹ ORIGIN: 18th century, from Malay *geko*, from the sound that some types of gecko make

geek *noun* (*plural* **geeks**) (*informal*)
a person who spends a lot of time on a particular interest and who is not popular or fashionable: *a computer* ***geek*** ➲ SYNONYM **nerd**

geese (say **geess**) plural of **goose**

gel (say **jel**) *noun* (*no plural*)
1 a thick liquid that you put on your hair to

keep it in shape: *hair gel*
2 a thick liquid that you can use instead of soap to wash your body with: *shower gel*

gelatine (say **jel**-uh-teen) *noun* (*no plural*)
a clear substance without any taste that is made from boiling animal bones and other animal parts and is used to make liquid food set (= become hard)

gelding (say **gel**-ding) *noun* (*plural* **geldings**)
a male horse that has been castrated (= has had its testicles removed)

gem (say **jem**) *noun* (*plural* **gems**)
a stone that is very valuable and can be made into jewellery ➲ SYNONYM **jewel**

gemsbok (say ***kh*emss**-bawk) *noun* (*plural* **gemsbok** or **gemsboks**)
a large African antelope with very long straight horns with black and white marks on its face
➲ See illustration at **antelope**

gem squash *noun* (*plural* **gem squashes**)
a round vegetable with a hard green skin and yellow flesh that you need to cook before you can eat it

gender (say **jen**-duh) *noun* (*plural* **genders**)
the fact of being male or female

gene (say **jeen**) *noun* (*plural* **genes**) (*biology*)
a unit of information inside a cell that is passed from parents to children and that controls what a living thing will be like: *The colour of your eyes is decided by your **genes**.* ➲ See **genetic**

general[1] (say **jen**-ruhl) *adjective*
1 of, by or for most people or things: *Is this car park for **general** use?*
2 not in detail: *Can you give me a **general** idea of what the book is about?*
in general usually: *I don't eat much meat in **general**.*

general[2] (say **jen**-ruhl) *noun* (*plural* **generals**)
the highest officer in an army

General Education and Training *noun* (abbr. GET)
the stage at school between Grade 1 and Grade 9, that includes the Foundation Phase, Intermediate Phase and Senior Phase

General Education and Training Certificate *noun* (abbr. GETC)
a certificate that you receive when you have finished Grade 9

general election *noun* (*plural* **general elections**)
a process by which people choose a new government: *Did you vote in the last **general election**?*

generalize (say **jen**-ruh-lize) *verb* (**generalizing, generalized**) (also **generalise**)
to form an opinion or make a statement about something without knowing all the details: *The new teacher **generalized** when she said children were noisy.*

general knowledge *noun* (*no plural*)
what you know about a lot of different things

generally (say **jen**-ruh-lee) *adverb*
usually, or mostly: *I **generally** get up at about eight o'clock.*

generate (say **jen**-uh-rayt) *verb* (**generating, generated**)
to produce or create something: *Power stations **generate** electricity.* ◇ *We need someone to **generate** new ideas.*

generation (say jen-uh-**ray**-shuhn) *noun* (*plural* **generations**)
all the people in a family, group or country who were born at about the same time: *This photo shows three **generations** of my family.* ◇ *the younger **generation***

generator (say **jen**-uh-ray-tuh) *noun* (*plural* **generators**)
a machine that produces electricity

generosity (say jen-uh-**ross**-i-tee) *noun* (*no plural*)
liking to give things to other people

generous (say **jen**-uh-ruhss) *adjective*
always ready to give people things or to spend money: *a **generous** gift* ◇ *It was **generous** of your parents to pay for the meal.* ➲ OPPOSITE **mean**[2] 1
▶ **generously** (*adverb*): *Please give **generously**.*

genetic (say juh-**net**-ik) *adjective*
connected with the parts in the cells of living things (called **genes**) that control what a person, animal or plant will be like: *The disease has a **genetic** origin.*

genetics (say juh-**net**-ikss) *noun* (*no plural*)
the scientific study of the way that the development of living things is controlled by qualities that have been passed on from parents to children ➲ See **gene**

genial (say **jeen**-i-uhl) *adjective*
(used about a person) pleasant and friendly: *We had a **genial** waiter.*

genie (say **jee**-ni) *noun* (*plural* **genies**)
a spirit with magic powers, especially one that lives in a bottle or a lamp

genitals (say **jen**-i-tuhlz) *plural noun* (also **genitalia**)
the parts of your sex organs that are outside

A B C D E F G H I J K L M N O P Q R S T U V W X Y Z

your body: ***Genitals*** *include the penis and the vulva.*
▸ **genital** (*adjective*): *the* ***genital*** *area*

genius (say **jeen**-i-uhss) *noun* (*plural* **geniuses**)
a very clever person: *Einstein was a* ***genius****.*

genocide (say **jen**-uh-side) *noun* (*no plural*)
the murder of all the people who belong to a certain race or religious group

genre (say ***zh*****aan**-ruh) *noun* (*plural* **genres**)
a particular type of art, literature, film or music that you can recognize because of its characteristics: *We study different* ***genres*** *of film, such as comedy and drama.*

gentile (say **jen**-tile) *noun* (*plural* **gentiles**)
a person who is not a **Jew**

gentle (say **jen**-tuhl) *adjective* (**gentler**, **gentlest**)
1 quiet and kind: *Be* ***gentle*** *with the baby.* ◇ *a* ***gentle*** *voice*
2 not strong or unpleasant: *It was a hot day, but there was a* ***gentle*** *breeze* (= a soft wind).
▸ **gently** (*adverb*): *She stroked the kitten very* ***gently****.*

gentleman (say **jen**-tuhl-muhn) *noun* (*plural* **gentlemen**)
1 a man who is polite and kind to other people: *He's a real* ***gentleman****.*
2 (*formal*) a polite way of saying 'man': *There is a* ***gentleman*** *here to see you.* ◇ *Ladies and* ***gentlemen*** *…* (= at the beginning of a speech)
➲ See **lady**

genuine (say **jen**-yuu-in) *adjective*
real and true: *The painting was found to be* ***genuine****.* ➲ See **fake**[1]
▸ **genuinely** (*adverb*) really: *Do you think he's* ***genuinely*** *sorry?*

geography (say jee-**og**-ruh-fee) *noun* (*no plural*)
the study of the Earth and everything on it, such as mountains, rivers, land and people
▸ **geographical** (*adjective*): *There is a list of* ***geographical*** *names* (= names of countries, seas, etc.) *at the back of this dictionary.*

geology (say jee-**ol**-uh-jee) *noun* (*no plural*)
the study of rocks and soil and how they were made
▸ **geologist** (*noun*): *She is a* ***geologist****.*

geometry (say jee-**om**-uh-tree) *noun* (*no plural*)
the study in mathematics of lines, shapes and angles
🛈 **ORIGIN:** 13th–15th century, from Old French through Latin *geometria*, from Greek *geometres* meaning 'land-measurer'. The Greek word came from *ge* meaning 'earth' + *metrēs* meaning 'measurer'.

geothermal (say jee-oh-**thurm**-l) *adjective* (*science*)
relating to the natural heat of the Earth deep below the ground surface: ***geothermal*** *energy*

germ (say **jurm**) *noun* (*plural* **germs**)
a very small living thing that can make you ill: *flu* ***germs***

German (say **jur**-muhn) *noun* (*no plural*)
the language spoken in Germany

German measles *noun* (*no plural*)
a disease that causes red spots all over the body: *She's got* ***German measles****.*

German shepherd = **Alsatian**

germinate (say **jurm**-i-nayt) *verb* (**germinating**, **germinated**)
to start to grow and develop: *The sunflower seed* ***germinated*** *a week after I planted it.*
▸ **germination** (*noun*): *Seeds need water before* ***germination*** *can occur.*

gesture[1] (say **jess**-tshuh) *noun* (*plural* **gestures**)
a movement of your head or hand to show how you feel or what you want: *The boy made a rude* ***gesture*** *before running off.*

gesture[2] (say **jess**-tshuh) *verb* (**gesturing**, **gestured**)
to point at something or make a sign to somebody: *She asked me to sit down and* ***gestured*** *towards a chair.*

GET (say jee-ee-**tee**) *abbreviation* **General Education and Training**

get *verb* (**getting**, **got**)
1 to buy, take or receive something: *Will you* ***get*** *some bread when you go shopping?* ◇ *I* ***got*** *a lot of presents for my birthday.* ◇ *She* ***got*** *a pen out of her bag.*
2 to go and bring back a person or thing: *She will* ***get*** *the children from school.* ➲ SYNONYM **fetch**
3 to become: *He is* ***getting*** *fat.* ◇ *Mum* ***got*** *angry.* ◇ *It's* ***getting*** *cold.*
4 to climb into or out of something such as a train or car: *When Tom* ***got*** *into the car, I* ***got*** *out.* ◇ *Where did you* ***get*** *off the bus?* ◇ *I* ***got*** *on the train.*
5 to arrive somewhere or to return: *We* ***got*** *to town at ten o'clock.* ◇ *When did you* ***get*** *back from your holiday?* ◇ *My train* ***got*** *in at 7.15.* ◇ *I've* ***got*** (= read) *to page 180.*
6 to start to have an illness: *I think I'm* ***getting*** *a cold.*
7 to understand or hear something: *I don't* ***get*** *the joke.*
get away with something to do something bad and not be punished for it: *He lied but he* ***got*** *away with it.*

get on with somebody to live or work in a friendly way with somebody: *We **get** on well with our neighbours.*
get over something to become well or happy again after you have been ill or sad: *He still hasn't **got** over his wife's death.*
get through to be able to speak to somebody on the telephone: *I tried to ring her but I couldn't **get** through.*
get up
1 to stand up: *She **got** up to let an elderly lady sit down.*
2 to rise from your bed: *What time do you usually **get** up?*

GETC (say jee-ee-tee-**see**) *abbreviation* **General Education and Training Certificate**

geyser (say **geez**-uh) *noun* (*plural* **geysers**)
1 (*geography*) a place where naturally hot water comes out of the ground
2 a machine that heats water for a house or building
ORIGIN: 18th century, from Icelandic *Geysir*, from the name of a particular spring in Iceland that shoots out hot water

ghastly (say **gaast**-lee) *adjective* (**ghastlier**, **ghastliest**)
extremely unpleasant, bad or ugly: *a **ghastly** accident* ➲ SYNONYM **horrific**

ghetto (say **get**-oh) *noun* (*plural* **ghettos** or **ghettoes**)
an area of a city where many people of the same race or background live in crowded, poor conditions

ghost (*rhymes with* **toast**) *noun* (*plural* **ghosts**)
the form of a dead person that a living person thinks they see: *Do you believe in **ghosts**?*
➲ SYNONYM **phantom**
▶ **ghostly** (*adjective*): ***ghostly** noises*

GHz *abbreviation* **gigahertz**

giant¹ (say **jy**-uhnt) *noun* (*plural* **giants**)
1 (in stories) a very large strong person who is often cruel and stupid
2 an unusually tall or large person, animal or plant: *The little tree I planted has grown into a **giant**.*
3 a very large company or organization: *the multinational oil **giants***

giant² (say **jy**-uhnt) *adjective*
very big: *a **giant** insect*

gibberish (say **jib**-uh-rish) *noun* (*no plural*)
words that have no meaning or are impossible to understand: *My baby sister speaks **gibberish**.*

gibbous (say **gib**-uhss) *adjective*
(used about the moon) with the bright part bigger than half and smaller than full moon

giddy (say **gid**-ee) *adjective* (**giddier**, **giddiest**)
having the feeling that everything is going round and round and you are going to fall: *I feel **giddy** after spinning round.*
➲ SYNONYM **dizzy**

gift *noun* (*plural* **gifts**)
1 something that you give to or get from somebody: *This magazine comes with a free **gift**.*
➲ SYNONYM **present²** 1
2 the natural ability to do something well: *She has a **gift** for languages.*

gifted (say **gift**-uhd) *adjective*
having great natural ability or being very intelligent: *a **gifted** athlete* ◇ *a **gifted** student*

gig *noun* (*plural* **gigs**)
1 (*informal*) an event where musicians perform for money: *Our band has a **gig** this weekend.*
2 short for **gigabyte**

gigabyte (say **gig**-uh-bite) *noun* (*plural* **gigabytes**) (abbr. GB)
a unit for measuring computer memory or how much information a computer can store. One gigabyte is equal to one billion bytes.: *Jack has a 250 **gigabyte** hard drive for his computer.*

gigahertz (say **gig**-uh-hurtss) *noun* (*plural* **gigahertz**) (abbr. GHz)
a unit for measuring **frequency** 3. A **gigahertz** is equal to one billion **hertz**. ➲ See **hertz**

gigantic (say jy-**gan**-tik) *adjective*
very big: ***gigantic** trees* ➲ SYNONYMS **enormous, huge, massive**

giggle (say **gig**-l) *verb* (**giggling**, **giggled**)
to laugh in a silly way: *The children couldn't stop **giggling**.*
▶ **giggle** (*noun*): *There was a **giggle** from the back of the class.*

gild *verb* (**gilding**, **gilded**)
to cover something with a layer of gold or with something that looks like gold: ***Gild** the leaves and leave them to dry.*
▶ **gilt** (*adjective*): *I got a **gilt** photo frame for my birthday.*

gill (say **gil**) *noun* (*plural* **gills**)
the part on each side of a fish that it breathes through ➲ See illustration at **fish¹**

gimmick (say **gim**-ik) *noun* (*plural* **gimmicks**)
something that attracts people to buy something: *It is a **gimmick** to call bottled water fat free.*

A B C D E F **G** H I J K L M N O P Q R S T U V W X Y Z

A B C D E F G H I J K L M N O P Q R S T U V W X Y Z

gin (say **jin**) *noun* (*no plural*)
a strong, colourless alcoholic drink

ginger[1] (say **jin**-juh) *noun* (*no plural*)
the root of a plant with a hot strong taste, that is used in cooking: *a **ginger** biscuit*

ginger[2] (say **jin**-juh) *adjective*
with a colour between brown and orange: *My brother has got **ginger** hair.*

gipsy (say **jip**-see) *noun* (*plural* **gipsies**) = **gypsy**

giraffe (say ji-**raaf**) *noun* (*plural* **giraffe** or **giraffes**)
a large animal from Africa with a very long neck and legs and big dark spots on its skin

girl (say **gurl**) *noun* (*plural* **girls**)
a female child or a young woman: *They have three children, two **girls** and a boy.*

girlfriend (say **gurl**-frend) *noun* (*plural* **girlfriends**)
a girl or woman who somebody has a romantic relationship with: *Have you got a **girlfriend**?*

Girl Guide *noun* (*plural* **Girl Guides**)
(*old-fashioned*) ➲ See **Guide[1]** 4

girth (say **gurth**) *noun* (*plural* **girths**)
1 the measurement around the middle of something, especially a person's waist
2 a band that is strapped around a horse's stomach to keep the saddle (= seat) in place

gist (say **jist**) *noun* (*no plural*)
the general meaning of something, rather than the details: *I got the **gist** of the article.*

give (say **giv**) *verb* (**giving, gave, has given**)
1 to let somebody have something: *She **gave** me a watch for my birthday.* ◇ *I **gave** my ticket to the man at the door.* ◇ ***Give** me the keys, please.* ◇ *Can you **give** me back that book I lent you?* ◇ *I've **given** all my old clothes away.* ◇ *We have to **give** our essays in* (= hand them to the teacher) *today.* ◇ *Could you **give** out these books* (= hand a book to each learner), *please?*
2 to make a sound or movement: *He **gave** me an angry look.* ◇ *He **gave** a shout.*
3 to make somebody have or feel something: *That noise is **giving** me a headache.* ◇ *Whatever **gave** you that idea?*
give in to accept or agree to something that you did not want to accept or agree to: *My parents finally **gave** in and said I could go to the party.*
give up to stop trying to do something: *I **give** up – what's the answer?*
give something up to stop doing or having something: *He's trying to **give** up smoking.*

gizzard (say **giz**-uhd) *noun* (*plural* **gizzards**)
the part of the stomach in many birds, reptiles and other animals, which crushes food into smaller pieces

glacier (say **glay**-si-uh) *noun* (*plural* **glaciers**)
a mass of ice that moves slowly down a valley

glad *adjective*
happy about something: *He was **glad** to see us.*
➲ SYNONYM **pleased**
▸ **gladly** (*adverb*): *I'll **gladly*** (= happily) *help you.*

WHICH WORD? **Glad** or **happy**?
- You usually use **glad** for a particular event or situation: *I'm **glad** that you came.* ◇ *We're **glad** that you passed your exam.*
- You use **happy** to describe a state of mind: *I always feel **happy** when the sun's shining.* You also use it before a noun: *a **happy** child.*

WORD BUILDING See the Word Building note at **happy**.

glade (say **glayd**) *noun* (*plural* **glades**)
an open space in a forest or wood where there are no trees

gladiator (say **glad**-i-ay-tuh) *noun* (*plural* **gladiators**)
(in Ancient Rome) a man who fought against another man or a wild animal in a public show

glamorous (say **glam**-uh-ruhss) *adjective*
attractive in an exciting way: *a **glamorous** model* ◇ *Making films is less **glamorous** than people think.*

glamour (say **glam**-uh) *noun* (*no plural*)
the quality of seeming to be more exciting and attractive than ordinary things and people: *Young people are attracted by the **glamour** of city life.*

glance[1] (say **glaanss**) *verb* (**glancing, glanced**)
to look quickly at a person or thing: *She **glanced** at her watch.*

glance[2] (say **glaanss**) *noun* (*plural* **glances**)
a quick look: *a **glance** at the newspaper*
at a glance immediately, with only a quick look: *I could see at a **glance** that he was ill.*

gland *noun* (*plural* **glands**)
a group of cells in your body that produce substances for your body to use: *sweat **glands***
▸ **glandular** (*adjective*): ***glandular** fever*

glare[1] (say **glair**) *verb* (**glaring, glared**)
1 to look at somebody in an angry way: *He **glared** at the children.*
2 to shine with a bright light that hurts your eyes: *The sun **glared** down.*

glare[2] (say **glair**) *noun*
1 (*no plural*) strong light that hurts your eyes: *the **glare** of the car's headlights*
2 (*plural* **glares**) a long, angry look: *I tried to say something, but he gave me a **glare**.*

glaring (say **glair**-ring) *adjective*
1 very bad and easy to notice: *The article was full of **glaring** mistakes.*
2 (about a light) very bright and hurting your eyes: *a **glaring** white light*

glass (say **glaass**) *noun*
1 (*no plural*) hard material that you can see through, used for bottles and windows: *I cut myself on some broken **glass**.* ◇ *a **glass** jar*
2 (*plural* **glasses**) a container made of glass that you drink from: *Could I have a **glass** of milk, please?* ◇ *a wine **glass***

glasses (say **glaa**-suhz) *plural noun*
two pieces of glass or plastic (called **lenses**) in a frame that people wear over their eyes to help them see better: *Does she wear **glasses**?* ◇ *I have two pairs of **glasses**.* ➲ SYNONYM **spectacles**
➲ See **sunglasses**

USAGE Be careful! You cannot say 'a glasses'. You can say **a pair of glasses**: *I need a new **pair of glasses*** or *I need some new **glasses**.*

glaze (say **glayz**) *verb* (**glazing, glazed**)
1 to put a shiny transparent surface on a brick or clay pot or some food: *We **glazed** the pots we made.* ◇ *a **glazed** ham*
2 lose brightness: *Her eyes **glazed** over when she heard the story again.*
▸ **glaze** (*noun*): *These pots have a **glaze**.*

gleam (say **gleem**) *verb* (**gleaming, gleamed**)
to shine with a soft light: *The moonlight **gleamed** on the lake.*
▸ **gleam** (*noun*): *I could see a **gleam** of light through the trees.*

glean (say **gleen**) *verb* (**gleaning, gleaned**)
to get information from different sources, sometimes with difficulty: *He **gleaned** the information from different articles.*

glee *noun* (*no plural*)
a feeling of happiness, especially when something bad happens to somebody else: *She couldn't hide her **glee** when her rival came last.*

glide (*rhymes with* **side**) *verb* (**gliding, glided**)
1 to move smoothly and quietly: *The dancers **glided** across the floor.*
2 to fly in a **glider**: *I always wanted to go **gliding**.*

glider (say **glide**-uh) *noun* (*plural* **gliders**)
a light plane without an engine that flies on air currents

glimmer (say **glim**-uh) *noun* (*plural* **glimmers**)
1 a small, weak light
2 a small sign of something: *There's still a **glimmer** of hope.*
▸ **glimmer** (*verb*): *A light **glimmered** in the distance.*

glimpse (say **glimpss**) *noun* (*plural* **glimpses**)
a view of a person or thing that is quick and not clear: *I caught a **glimpse** of myself in the mirror.*
▸ **glimpse** (*verb*): *I just **glimpsed** him in the crowd.*

glint *verb* (**glinting, glinted**)
to shine with small bright flashes of light: *Her eyes **glinted** with happiness.*
▸ **glint** (*noun*): *There was a **glint** of gold under the leaves.*

glisten (say **gliss**-uhn) *verb* (**glistening, glistened**)
(used about wet surfaces) to shine: *His eyes **glistened** with tears.*

glitter (say **glit**-uh) *verb* (**glittering, glittered**)
to shine brightly with a lot of small flashes of light: *The broken glass **glittered** in the sun.*
▸ **glitter** (*noun*): *the **glitter** of jewels*

glittering (say **glit**-uh-ring) *adjective*
1 very impressive or successful: *a **glittering** career*
2 shining with a lot of small flashes of light

global (say **glohb**-l) *adjective*
of or about the whole world: *Pollution is a **global** problem.*

globalize (say **gloh**-buh-lize) *verb* (**globalizing, globalized**) (also **globalise**)
(used about business) to operate all over the world: *Our company is doing so well, we're going to **globalize**.* ➲ See **multinational**
▸ **globalization** (*noun*) (also **globalisation**): *the **globalization** of the economy*

global warming *noun* (*no plural*)
the increase in the temperature of the Earth's atmosphere, that is caused by the increase of particular gases, especially **carbon dioxide**.
➲ See illustration at **greenhouse effect**

A B C D E F G H I J K L M N O P Q R S T U V W X Y Z

globe (*rhymes with* **robe**) *noun*
1 (*plural* **globes**) an object in the shape of a ball with a map of the world on it
2 any object shaped like a ball
3 the globe (*no plural*) the world: *She's travelled all over the **globe**.*

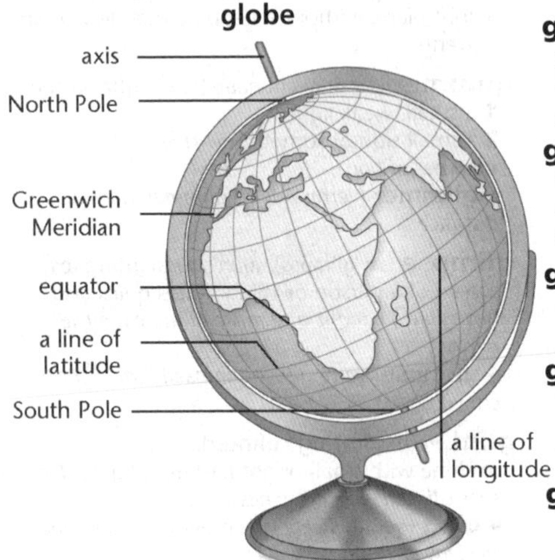

globule (say **glob**-yool) *noun* (*plural* **globules**)
a small drop of liquid: *A **globule** of wax dropped onto the table.*

gloomy (say **gloom**-ee) *adjective* (**gloomier**, **gloomiest**)
1 dark: *What a **gloomy** day!*
2 sad and without hope: *He's feeling very **gloomy** because he can't get a job.*
▸ **gloomily** (*adverb*): *She looked **gloomily** out of the window at the rain.*

glorify (say **glaw**-ri-fy) *verb* (**glorifying**, **glorified**)
1 to make something seem better or more important than it really is: *That war movie does little more than **glorify** violence.*
2 (*formal*) to praise and worship God

glorious (say **glaw**-ri-uhss) *adjective*
1 (*formal*) famous and full of **glory**: *a **glorious** history*
2 wonderful or beautiful: *The weather was **glorious**.*

glory (say **glaw**-ree) *noun* (*no plural*)
1 fame and respect that you get when you do great things: *The winner returned covered in **glory**.*
2 great beauty: *Spring is the best time to see the flowers in all their **glory**.*

glossary (say **gloss**-uh-ree) *noun* (*plural* **glossaries**)
a list of difficult words and their meanings, especially at the end of a book

glossy (say **gloss**) *adjective* (**glossier**, **glossiest**)
smooth and shiny: ***glossy** hair*

glove (say **gluv**) *noun* (*plural* **gloves**)
a piece of clothing that covers your hand and keeps it warm or safe: *I need a new pair of **gloves**.* ◇ *rubber **gloves***

glow (say **gloh**) *verb* (**glowing**, **glowed**)
to send out soft light or heat without flames or smoke: *His cigarette **glowed** in the dark.*
▸ **glow** (*noun*): *the **glow** of the sky at sunset*

glowing (say **gloh**-ing) *adjective*
saying that a person or thing is very good: *His teacher wrote a **glowing** report about his work.*

glucose (say **gloo**-kohss) *noun* (*no plural*)
a type of sugar in your blood that gives you energy. It is found in fruit, vegetables and other foods. ➲ See **sucrose**

glue[1] (say **gloo**) *noun* (*no plural*)
a thick liquid that you use for sticking things together

glue[2] (say **gloo**) *verb* (**gluing**, **glued**)
to stick one thing to another thing with glue: ***Glue** the two pieces of wood together.*

glum *adjective* (**glummer**, **glummest**)
sad and quiet: *Why are you looking so **glum**?*
▸ **glumly** (*adverb*)

gluten (say **gloo**-tuhn) *noun* (*no plural*)
a sticky substance (called a **protein**) found in grains such as wheat

glutton (say **glut**-uhn) *noun* (*plural* **gluttons**)
1 a person who eats too much
2 (*informal*) a person who enjoys doing something unpleasant or difficult: *He's a **glutton** for hard work.*

glycerine (say **gliss**-uh-reen) *noun* (*no plural*)
a thick, sweet colourless liquid made from fats and oils and used in food, medicines and beauty products

GM (say jee-**em**) *adjective*
(used about food and plants) grown from cells whose genes (= units of information that control what a living thing will be like) have been changed: *GM crops* ❶ **GM** is short for 'genetically modified'.

GMT (say jee-em-**tee**) *abbreviation* **Greenwich Mean Time**

gnarled (say **naald**) *adjective*
rough and having grown into a strange shape

because of old age or hard work: *a **gnarled** tree* ◇ ***gnarled** fingers*

gnash (say **nash**) *verb* (**gnashing, gnashed**)
gnash your teeth to feel very angry about something: *He was **gnashing** his teeth after he was tricked.*

gnat (say **nat**) *noun* (*plural* **gnats**)
a type of very small fly that bites

gnaw (say **naw**) *verb* (**gnawing, gnawed**)
to bite something for a long time: *The dog was **gnawing** a bone.*

gnome (say **nohm**) *noun* (*plural* **gnomes**)
(in children's stories) a little old man with a pointed hat and a beard

GNP (say jee-en-**pee**) *noun* (*plural* **GNPs**)
the total value of all the goods and services produced in a country in one year, including the total amount of money that comes from foreign countries ❶ **GNP** is short for 'Gross National Product'. ➲ See **GDP**

WORD BUILDING
GNP = GDP + net foreign income

go¹ (say **goh**) *verb* (**going, went, has gone**)
1 to move from one place to another: *She **goes** very fast on her bike.* ◇ *I'll **go** and make some coffee.*
2 to travel to a place to do something: *He has **gone** shopping.* ◇ *Are you **going** to Clarence's party?* ◇ *They have **gone** away for the weekend.* ◇ *I **went** to work by train.*
3 to leave a place: *I must **go** now – it's four o'clock.* ◇ *What time does the train **go**?* ◇ ***Go** away! I'm doing my homework.*
4 to become: *Her hair has **gone** grey.*
5 to have as its place: *'Where do these plates **go**?' 'In that cupboard.'*
6 to lead to a place: *Does this road **go** to the station?*
7 (used about a machine, etc.) to work: *The car won't **go**.*
8 to happen in a certain way: *How is your new job **going**?* ◇ *The week **went** very quickly.*
9 to disappear: *My headache has **gone**.*
10 to be or look good with something else: *Does this jumper **go** with my skirt?* ➲ SYNONYM **match²** 2
be going to
1 words that show what you plan to do in the future: *I'm **going** to cook the dinner.*
2 words that you use when you are sure that something will happen in the future: *It's **going** to rain.*
go by to pass: *The holidays **went** by quickly.*
go off
1 to explode: *A bomb **went** off in the station.*
2 (about food or drink) become too old to eat or drink: *This milk has **gone** off – it smells horrible.*
go on
1 to happen: *What's **going** on?*
2 to continue: *I **went** on working.*
go out
1 to leave the place where you live or work for a short time, returning on the same day: *I **went** out for a walk.* ◇ *We're **going** out tonight.*
2 to stop shining or burning: *The fire has **gone** out.*
go out with somebody to have somebody as a boyfriend or girlfriend: *She's **going** out with a boy at school.*
go through something
1 (also **go over something**) to look at or explain something carefully from the beginning to the end: *The teacher **went** through our homework.*
2 to have a bad experience: *She **went** through a difficult time when she was ill.*
go up to become higher or more ➲ SYNONYM **rise¹** 1: *The price of petrol has **gone** up again.*
➲ See **been**

go² (say **goh**) *noun* (*plural* **goes**)
the time when a person should move or play in a game or an activity: *Get off the bike – it's my **go**!* ➲ SYNONYM **turn²** 3
in one go (*informal*) all together at one time: *They ate the biscuits all in one **go**.*

goal (say **gohl**) *noun* (*plural* **goals**)
1 the place where the ball must go to win a point in a game such as football: *He kicked the ball into the **goal**.*
2 a point that a team wins in a game such as football when the ball goes into the goal: *Swallows won by three **goals** to two.*
3 something that you want to do very much: *She has finally achieved her **goal** of taking part in the Olympics.*

goalkeeper (say **gohl**-keep-uh) *noun* (*plural* **goalkeepers**)
a player in a game such as football who tries to stop the ball from going into the goal

goat (say **goht**) *noun* (*plural* **goats**)
an animal with horns and a coat of hair, that lives wild in mountain areas or that people keep on farms for its milk or meat

gobble (say **gob**-l) *verb* (**gobbling, gobbled**) (*informal*)
to eat quickly and noisily: *The children **gobbled** up the cake.*

goblin (say **gob**-lin) *noun* (*plural* **goblins**)
(in children's stories) an ugly little creature who tricks people

A B C D E F G H I J K L M N O P Q R S T U V W X Y Z

god (say **god**) *noun*
1 God (*no plural*) the one great spirit that Christians, Jews and Muslims believe made the world: *Do you believe in **God**?*
2 (*plural* **gods**) a spirit or force that people believe has power over them and nature: *Mars was the Roman **god** of war.*

goddess (say **god**-ess) *noun* (*plural* **goddesses**)
a female god: *Venus was the Roman **goddess** of love.*

godparent (say **god**-pair-ruhnt) *noun* (*plural* **godparents**) (also **godfather**, **godmother**)
a person that parents choose to help their child and teach them about the Christian religion

goes (say **gohz**) form of **go**[1]

gogga (say ***kh*aw**-khuh) *noun* (*plural* **goggas**) (*S. African*)
an insect or other small creature: *There are **goggas** in the kitchen.*
ⓘ ORIGIN: through Afrikaans, from Khoikhoi *xo-xon* meaning 'creeping things'

> PRONUNCIATION Pronounce the **g** sounds in **gogga** like the **g** in the Afrikaans word **lag**.

goggles (say **gog**-uhlz) *plural noun*
big glasses that you wear so that water, dust, or wind cannot get in your eyes: *I always wear **goggles** when I swim.*

going (say **goh**-ing) form of **go**[1]

gold (say **gohld**) *noun* (*no plural*) (symbol Au)
a yellow metal that is very valuable: *Is your ring made of **gold**?* ◇ *a **gold** watch*
▸ **gold** (*adjective*): ***gold** paint* (= paint with the colour of gold)

golden (say **gohl**-duhn) *adjective*
1 made of gold: *a **golden** crown*
2 with the colour of gold: ***golden** hair*

goldfield (say **gohld**-feeld) *noun* (*plural* **goldfields**)
an area where gold can be found as a mineral

goldfish (say **gohld**-fish) *noun* (*plural* **goldfish**)
a small orange fish that people keep as a pet

gold mine (say **gohld** mine) *noun* (*plural* **gold mines**)
1 a place where gold is taken from the ground
2 a place, person or thing that provides a lot of information, value or profit: *This magazine is a **gold mine** of information.* ◇ *This shop is a **gold mine** for gifts.*

goldsmith (say **gohld**-smith) *noun* (*plural* **goldsmiths**)
a person who makes things with gold

golf *noun* (*no plural*)
a game played over a large area of grass using specially shaped sticks (called **golf clubs**) to hit a small hard ball into a series of holes (usually 18), using as few strokes as possible: *My mother plays **golf** on Sundays.*
▸ **golfer** (*noun*): *He's a keen **golfer**.*

gondola (say **gon**-duh-luh) *noun* (*plural* **gondolas**)
a light, flat-bottomed boat that people use on canals in Venice

gone (say **gon**) form of **go**[1]

gong *noun* (*plural* **gongs**)
a large metal disc that people hit to make a loud, deep sound: *We heard the dinner **gong**.*

gonorrhoea (say gon-uh-**ree**-uh) *noun* (*no plural*)
a disease that causes pain of the sexual organs, which is passed from one person to another by sexual contact

good[1] (say **guud**) *adjective* (**better**, **best**)
1 done or made very well: *It's a **good** knife – it cuts very well.* ◇ *The film was really **good**.*
2 pleasant or enjoyable: *Did you have a **good** time?* ◇ *The weather was very **good**.*
➲ SYNONYMS **nice**, **lovely**
3 able to do something well: *She's a **good** driver.* ◇ *James is very **good** at tennis.*
4 kind, or doing the right thing: *It's **good** of you to help.* ◇ *The children were very **good** while you were out.*
5 right or suitable: *This is a **good** place for a picnic.*
6 having a useful or helpful effect: *Fresh fruit and vegetables are **good** for you.*
7 a word that you use when you are pleased: *Is everyone here? **Good**. Now let's begin.* ➲ The adverb is **well**[1]

> WORD BUILDING There are many words that you can use instead of 'very good', but check their exact meanings first. Examples are: **awesome** (informal), **brilliant** 3 (informal), **excellent**, **fantastic** (informal), **fine**[1] 1, **great** 4 and 5 (informal), **lovely**, **outstanding**, **superb**, **terrific** (informal) and **wonderful**. See the Word Building note at **nice** also.

good[2] (say **guud**) *noun* (*no plural*)
something that is right or helpful: *They know the difference between **good** and bad.*
be no good, **not be any good** to not be useful: *This jumper isn't any **good**. It's too small.* ◇ *It's no **good** asking Mum for money – she hasn't got any.*
do somebody good to make somebody well

or happy: *It will do you **good** to go to bed early tonight.*
for good for ever: *She has left home for **good**.*

good afternoon *exclamation* (*formal*) words that you say when you see or speak to somebody in the afternoon

SPEAKING **Hello** or **Hi** are the words that we usually use when we see friends. **Good afternoon** is formal.

goodbye (say guud-**by**) *exclamation*
a word that you say when somebody goes away, or when you go away: ***Goodbye**! See you tomorrow.*

SPEAKING We sometimes just say **Bye**: '***Bye**, Raylene. See you tomorrow.*'

good evening *exclamation* (*formal*) words that you say when you see or speak to somebody in the evening

SPEAKING **Hello** or **Hi** are the words that we usually use when we see friends. **Good evening** is formal.

good-looking (say guud-**luuk**-ing) *adjective*
(used about people) nice to look at: *He's a **good-looking** boy.* ➲ SYNONYM **attractive** 1
➲ See note at **beautiful**

good morning *exclamation* (*formal*)
words that you say when you see or speak to somebody in the morning

SPEAKING **Hello** or **Hi** are the words that we usually use when we see friends. **Good morning** is formal.

goodness (say **guud**-nuhss) *noun* (*no plural*)
1 being good or kind
2 something in food that is good for your health: *Fruit has a lot of **goodness** in it.*
for goodness' sake words that show anger: *For **goodness**' sake, hurry up!*
goodness, goodness me words that show surprise: ***Goodness**! What a big cake!*
thank goodness words that show you are happy because a problem or danger has gone away: *Thank **goodness** it's stopped raining.*

goodnight (say guud-**nite**) *exclamation*
words that you say when you leave somebody in the evening or when somebody is going to bed: '***Goodnight**, Raeesa. Sleep well.*' '***Night*** (= short for ***goodnight***).'

goods (say **guudz**) *plural noun*
1 things that you buy or sell: *That shop sells electrical **goods**.*
2 things that a train or lorry carries: *a **goods** train*

goodwill (say guud-**wil**) *noun* (*no plural*)
friendly, helpful feelings towards other people: *There was a feeling of **goodwill** over the festive season.*

goose (say **gooss**) *noun* (*plural* **geese**)
a bird like a large duck with a long neck. They either live wild or people keep them on farms for their meat and feathers.

gooseberry (say **guuz**-buh-ree) *noun* (*plural* **gooseberries**)
a small green or orange fruit with a sharp taste

gooseflesh (say **gooss**-flesh) *noun* (*no plural*)
small lumps on your skin which appear when you are cold or frightened

gore (say **gaw**) *verb* (**goring, gored**)
(used about an animal) to wound with its horn or horns: *She was **gored** by a bull.*

gorge (say **gawj**) *noun* (*plural* **gorges**)
a deep valley with steep sides and a river running through it ➲ See illustration at **mountain**

gorgeous (say **gaw**-juhss) *adjective* (*informal*)
very good or attractive: *The weather was **gorgeous**!* ◇ *What a **gorgeous** dress!*
➲ SYNONYMS **lovely, beautiful**

gorilla (say guh-**ril**-uh) *noun* (*plural* **gorillas**)
a very large powerful **ape** covered with black or brown hair that lives in the forests of central Africa

gory (say **gaw**-ree) *adjective* (**gorier, goriest**)
full of violence and blood: *It's the **goriest** film I've ever seen.* ➲ SYNONYM **bloody**

gosh *exclamation*
a word that shows surprise: ***Gosh**! What a big house!*

gosling (say **goz**-ling) *noun* (*plural* **goslings**)
a young **goose**

gospel (say **goss**-puhl) *noun*
1 Gospel (*plural* **Gospels**) one of the four books in the Bible that describe the life and teachings of Jesus Christ
2 (*no plural*) (also **gospel music**) a style of religious music: *I listen to **gospel**.*
ⓘ ORIGIN: through Old English *gōdspel*, from *gōd* meaning 'good' + *spel* meaning 'news, a story'

A B C D E F G H I J K L M N O P Q R S T U V W X Y Z

A B C D E F G H I J K L M N O P Q R S T U V W X Y Z

gossamer (say **goss**-uh-muh) *noun* (*no plural*)
1 a light, thin, smooth substance that spiders make
2 very light, thin material

gossip (say **goss**-ip) *noun* (*no plural*)
talk about other people that is often unkind or not true: *Have you heard the latest **gossip** about her?*
▸ **gossip** (*verb*): *They were **gossiping** about their friends.*

got form of **get**

USAGE In formal writing and schoolwork, use **got to** and **got a**, never 'gotta': *I have **got to** go now.* ◇ *We have **got a** dog.*

WHICH WORD? **Got** or **gotten**?
Gotten is used (usually informally) in American English, but it is not seen as correct in South African and British English. We recommend that you do not use **gotten** in schoolwork.

Gothic (say **goth**-ik) *adjective*
relating to a style of western European architecture of the 12th to 16th centuries

gotten (say **got**-uhn) (*Am. Eng.*) form of **get**

gouge (say **gowj**) *verb* (**gouging, gouged**)
to make a hole in a surface by using a sharp object in a rough way

gourd (say **goord**) *noun* (*plural* **gourds**)
a type of large fruit with a hard skin that is dried to make a container

gourmet (say **goor**-may) *noun* (*plural* **gourmets**)
a person who enjoys food and knows a lot about it

govern (say **guv**-uhn) *verb* (**governing, governed**)
to officially rule or control a country or part of a country: *The country is **governed** by Parliament.*
ⓘ ORIGIN: 13th–15th century, from Old French *governer* through Latin from Greek *kubernan* meaning 'to steer'

government (say **guv**-uhn-muhnt) *noun* (*plural* **governments**)
(often **the Government**) the group of people who officially rule or control a country: *Leaders of the African **governments** met today.*

USAGE **Government** can be used with a singular or a plural verb: *The **government** has failed to act.* ◇ *The **government** have discussed the problem.*

governor (say **guv**-uh-nuh) *noun* (*plural* **governors**)
1 a person who rules or controls part of a country (especially in the USA): *the **Governor** of California*
2 the head of a public institution: *the **Governor** of the Reserve Bank*

gown (*rhymes with* **town**) *noun* (*plural* **gowns**)
1 a long dress that a woman wears at a special time: *a ball **gown***
2 a long loose piece of clothing that judges and sometimes members of universities wear over their other clothes: *a graduation **gown***

GP (say jee-**pee**) *noun* (*plural* **GPs**)
a medical doctor who treats many different types of illnesses and works in a town or village, not in a hospital. A **GP** is also called a family doctor. ⓘ **GP** is short for 'General Practitioner'.

GPS (say jee-pee-**ess**) *noun* (*no plural*)
the system that uses devices that receive signals from satellites (= electronic equipment that travels around Earth in space) to tell you your exact position anywhere on Earth ⓘ **GPS** is short for 'Global Positioning System'.

grab *verb* (**grabbing, grabbed**)
to take something in a rough and sudden way: *The thief **grabbed** her bag and ran away.*
➲ SYNONYMS **seize, snatch**

grace (say **grayss**) *noun* (*no plural*)
1 a beautiful way of moving: *She dances with **grace**.*
2 thanks to God that people say before or after they eat: *Let's say **grace**.*

graceful (say **grayss**-fuhl) *adjective*
(about a person or thing) moving in a smooth and beautiful way: *a **graceful** dancer*
▸ **gracefully** (*adverb*): *He moves very **gracefully**.*

gracious (say **gray**-shuhss) *adjective*
(used about people's behaviour) kind and polite: *a **gracious** smile*
▸ **graciously** (*adverb*): *She accepted the invitation **graciously**.*

grade[1] (say **grayd**) *noun* (*plural* **grades**)
1 a class in a school where all the children are about the same age: *My sister is in **Grade** 5.*
2 the level or quality of something: *We use only high-**grade** materials.*
3 a number or letter that a teacher gives for your work to show how good it is: *She got very good **grades** in all her exams.* ➲ SYNONYM **mark**[2] 3

grade[2] (say **grayd**) *verb* (**grading, graded**)
to sort things or people into sizes or kinds: *The eggs are **graded** by size.*

gradient (say **grayd**-i-uhnt) *noun* (*plural* **gradients**)
1 a measure to describe how steep a line or surface is: *a steep* ***gradient*** ◇ *The road has a* ***gradient*** *of 9°.* ◇ *The* ***gradient*** *of that mountain is 1:4.*
2 a measure of change in a physical quality over space or time: *a pressure* ***gradient***

gradual (say **grad**-yuu-uhl) *adjective*
happening slowly: *There has been a* ***gradual*** *increase in prices.* ➲ OPPOSITE **sudden**

gradually (say **grad**-yuu-uh-lee) *adverb*
slowly, over a long period of time: *Life* ***gradually*** *returned to normal.*

graduate[1] (say **grad**-yuu-uht) *noun* (*plural* **graduates**)
a person who has passed their exams at a university or college and who has a **degree**: *a university* ***graduate***
▸ **graduate** (*adjective*): *a* ***graduate*** *school of business*

graduate[2] (say **grad**-yuu-ayt) *verb* (**graduating, graduated**)
to finish a course of studies at a university or college and get a **degree**: *I* ***graduated*** *from Rhodes University.*

graffiti (say gruh-**fee**-ti) *plural noun*
words or pictures that people write or draw on walls: *The walls were covered with* ***graffiti***.

graft[1] (say **graaft**) *noun*
1 (*plural* **grafts**) a piece of a living plant that is fixed onto another plant where it grows to become one plant
2 (*plural* **grafts**) a piece of living skin or bone that is fixed onto a damaged part of the body in an operation: *a skin* ***graft***
3 (*no plural*) (*informal*) hard work: *Their success was the result of years of hard* ***graft***.

graft[2] (say **graaft**) *verb* (**grafting, grafted**)
1 to attach part of a living plant to another plant so that it will grow
2 to attach a piece of living skin or bone to a damaged part of the body in a medical operation

grain (say **grayn**) *noun*
1 (*no plural*) the seeds of a plant that we eat, for example rice or **wheat**: *The animals are fed on* ***grain***.
2 (*plural* **grains**) a very small hard piece of something: *a* ***grain*** *of sand* ◇ ***grains*** *of rice*

gram *noun* (*plural* **grams**) (also **gramme**) (abbr. g)
the basic unit for measuring mass. There are 1 000 grams in a kilogram: *30 g of butter*

grammar (say **gram**-uh) *noun* (*no plural*)
the rules that tell you how to put words together when you speak or write

> SPELLING Remember! You spell **grammar** with **-ar** at the end.

grammatical (say gruh-**mat**-ik-l) *adjective*
1 connected with grammar: *What is the* ***grammatical*** *rule for making plurals in English?*
2 correct because it follows the rules of grammar: *The sentence 'They is happy' is not* ***grammatical***.
▸ **grammatically** (*adverb*): *The sentence is* ***grammatically*** *correct.*

gran *noun* (*plural* **grans**) (*informal*) short for **grandmother**

granadilla (say gran-uh-**dil**-uh) *noun* (*plural* **granadillas**) (also **passion-fruit**)
a round purple or yellow fruit that has juicy orange flesh and grows on vines

granary (say **gran**-uh-ree) *noun* (*plural* **granaries**)
a storehouse for grain

grand *adjective* (**grander, grandest**)
very big, important or rich: *The wealthy businessman built a* ***grand*** *house.* ◇ *a* ***grand*** *ceremony* ➲ The noun is **grandeur**
➲ SYNONYMS **magnificent, splendid**
ⓘ ORIGIN: 13th–15th century, through Old French *grand*, from Latin *grandis* meaning 'fully-grown, big, great'

grandad (say **gran**-dad) *noun* (*plural* **grandads**) (*informal*) = **grandfather**

grandchild (say **gran**-chyld) *noun* (*plural* **grandchildren**)
the child of your son or daughter

granddaughter (say **gran**-daw-tuh) *noun* (*plural* **granddaughters**)
the daughter of your son or daughter

grandeur (say **grand**-yuh) *noun* (*no plural*) (*formal*)
1 the quality of being large and impressive: *the* ***grandeur*** *of the mountains*
2 a feeling of being important ➲ SYNONYM **splendour**

grandfather (say **grand**-faath-uh) *noun* (*plural* **grandfathers**)
the father of your mother or father

grandma (say **gran**-maa) *noun* (*plural* **grandmas**) (*informal*) = **grandmother**

grandmother (say **grand**-muth-uh) *noun* (*plural* **grandmothers**)
the mother of your mother or father

grandpa (say **gran**-paa) *noun* (*plural* **grandpas**) (*informal*) = **grandfather**

grandparent (say **grand**-pair-uhnt) *noun* (*plural* **grandparents**)
the mother or father of your mother or father

grandson (say **grand**-sun) *noun* (*plural* **grandsons**)
the son of your son or daughter

grandstand (say **grand**-stand) *noun* (*plural* **grandstands**)
a large covered structure with rows of seats for people to watch sports events: *The* ***grandstand*** *was packed with spectators* (= people who watch an event) *for the final of the competition.*

granite (say **gran**-it) *noun* (*no plural*)
a hard type of rock, often used as a building stone: *a* ***granite*** *tombstone*

granny (say **gran**-ee) *noun* (*plural* **grannies**) (also **grannie**) (*informal*) = **grandmother**

grant[1] (say **graant**) *verb* (**granting, granted**) (*formal*)
to give somebody what they have asked for: *They* ***granted*** *him a visa to enter the country.*
take a person or **thing for granted** to be so used to a person or thing that you forget you are lucky to have them: *He takes his comfortable life for* ***granted****.*

grant[2] (say **graant**) *noun* (*plural* **grants**)
money that you are given for a special reason: *a student* ***grant*** (= to help pay for study at university)

granular (say **gran**-yuu-luh) *adjective*
made of small hard pieces or grains: ***granular*** *sugar*

granule (say **gran**-yool) *noun* (*plural* **granules**)
a small grain or small piece of something: *sand* ***granules*** ◇ *a* ***granule*** *of sugar*

grape (say **grayp**) *noun* (*plural* **grapes**)
a small green or purple fruit that we eat or make into wine: *a bunch of* ***grapes***

grapefruit (say **grayp**-froot) *noun* (*plural* **grapefruit** or **grapefruits**)
a fruit that looks like a big orange, but is yellow or pink

grapevine (say **grayp**-vine) *noun* (*plural* **grapevines**)
the plant that grapes grow on
through the grapevine (*informal*) the way that news passes from one person to another: *I heard it through the* ***grapevine****.*

graph (say **graaf**) *noun* (*plural* **graphs**)
a diagram in which a line, curve or shape shows the relationship between two quantities or measurements: *a* ***graph*** *showing the relationship between volume and heat* ◇ *a bar* ***graph*** *of the number of cars sold each month* ➲ See **chart[1]** 1, **pie chart**, **ordinate**
🛈 **ORIGIN:** 17th century, through Latin from Greek *graphikos*, from *graphē* meaning 'writing, drawing'

graphs

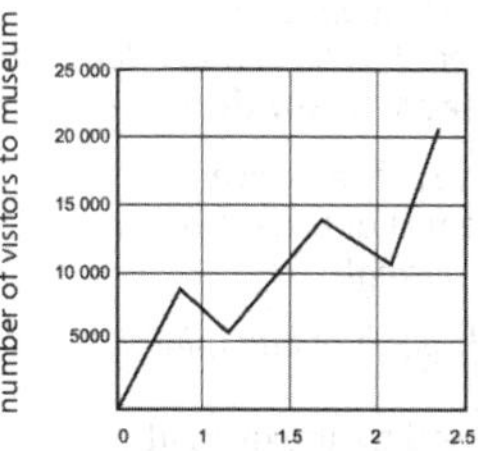

line graph

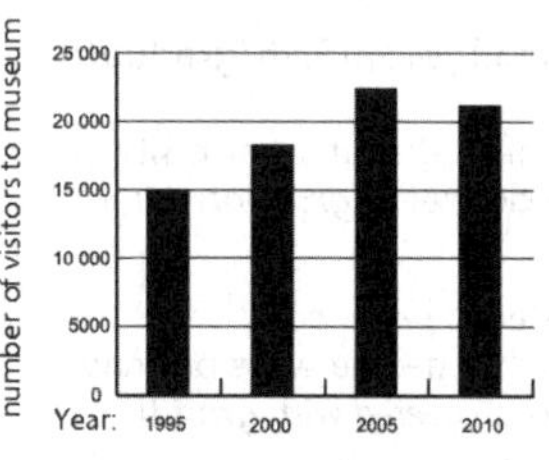

bar graph

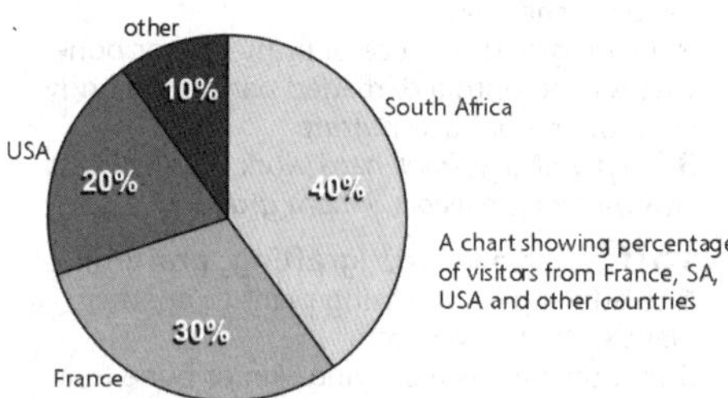

pie chart

graphic (say **graf**-ik) *adjective*
1 relating to drawings, diagrams and art: *I'm going to study* ***graphic*** *design.*
2 very detailed, usually about something unpleasant: *He gave a* ***graphic*** *description of the murder scene.*
▸ **graphically** (*adverb*): *The photo showed the accident very* ***graphically****.*

graphics (say **graf**-ikss) *plural noun*
drawings, pictures and diagrams, especially those produced on a computer

graphite (say **graf**-ite) *noun* (*no plural*)
a soft black substance (a type of **carbon**) used in pencils

grapple (say **grap**-l) *verb* (**grappling, grappled**)
1 to fight with someone: *They **grappled** on the grass.*
2 to try very hard to do something that is not easy: *I **grappled** with my maths homework.*

grasp (say **graasp**) *verb* (**grasping, grasped**)
1 to hold something tightly: *The child **grasped** his mother's hand.*
2 to understand something: *He couldn't **grasp** what I was saying.*
▶ **grasp** (*noun*): *The ball fell from my **grasp**.*

grass (say **graass**) *noun* (*no plural*)
a common plant with thin green leaves that grows in the **veld**, on farms and in gardens. Cows and many other animals eat it: *Dad cuts the **grass** twice a month.*
▶ **grassy** (*adjective*): *a **grassy** hill*
ⓘ ORIGIN: from Old English *graes*, related to Dutch *gras* and to English *green* and *grow*

grasshopper (say **graass**-hop-uh) *noun* (*plural* **grasshoppers**)
an insect with long back legs with which it can jump high in the air and make short, high sounds

grate (say **grayt**) *verb* (**grating, grated**)
to rub food over a metal tool (called a **grater**) so that it is in very small pieces: *Can you **grate** some cheese?* ◇ ***grated** carrot*

grateful (say **grayt**-fuhl) *adjective*
feeling or showing thanks (to a person): *We are **grateful** to you for the help you have given us.*
➲ The noun is **gratitude** ➲ OPPOSITE **ungrateful**

grater (say **grayt**-uh) *noun* (*plural* **graters**)
a kitchen tool with holes in it that you use to cut food into very small pieces by rubbing it across its surface

gratitude (say **grat**-i-tyood) *noun* (*no plural*)
the feeling of wanting to thank a person for something: *We gave her a present to show our **gratitude** for all her help.*

gratuitous (say gruh-**tyoo**-i-tuhss) *adjective*
done without good reason: *The movie had too much **gratuitous** violence.*
▶ **gratuitously** (*adverb*)

grave¹ (say **grayv**) *noun* (*plural* **graves**)
a hole in the ground where a dead person's body is buried: *We put flowers on the **grave**.*
➲ See **tomb**

grave² (say **grayv**) *adjective* (**graver, gravest**) (*formal*)
very bad or serious: *The children were in **grave** danger.*

gravel (say **grav**-uhl) *noun* (*no plural*)
very small stones that are used for making paths and roads

gravestone (say **grayv**-stohn) *noun* (*plural* **gravestones**)
a piece of stone on a **grave¹** that shows the name of the dead person

graveyard (say **grayv**-yaad) *noun* (*plural* **graveyards**)
a piece of land where dead people are buried: *The **graveyard** is next to a small mosque* (= a building where Muslims pray). ➲ SYNONYM **cemetery**

gravitate (say **grav**-i-tayt) *verb* (**gravitating, gravitated**)
to move towards something or be attracted to something: *At break, the learners **gravitate** towards the tuckshop.*

gravity (say **grav**-i-tee) *noun* (*no plural*)
the force that pulls everything towards the Earth
▶ **gravitational** (*adjective*): *The Earth's **gravitational** pull*

gravy (say **gray**-vee) *noun* (*no plural*)
a hot brown sauce that you eat with meat

graze (say **grayz**) *verb* (**grazing, grazed**)
1 to eat grass: *The sheep were **grazing** in the fields.*
2 to hurt your skin by rubbing it against something rough: *He fell and **grazed** his arm.*
▶ **graze** (*noun*): *She's got a **graze** on her knee.*

grease (say **greess**) *noun* (*no plural*)
fat from animals, or any thick substance that is like oil: *Use hot water to get the **grease** off these plates.*

greasy (say **greess**-ee) *adjective* (**greasier, greasiest**)
covered with or containing a lot of **grease**: ***greasy** hair* ◇ ***Greasy** food is not good for you.*

great (say **grayt**) *adjective* (**greater, greatest**)
1 very large: *a **great** river* ◇ *It's a **great** pleasure to meet you.*
2 important or special: *Einstein was a **great** scientist.*
3 (*informal*) very: *There's a **great** big dog in the garden!*
4 (*informal*) very good: *They are **great** friends.*
5 (*informal*) very nice or enjoyable: *I had a **great** weekend.* ➲ SYNONYM **wonderful**

A B C D E F G H I J K L M N O P Q R S T U V W X Y Z

great- (say **grayt**) *prefix*
a word that you put before words for family members to show the next older or younger **generation**. For example, your **great-grandmother** is the mother of your grandmother or grandfather, and your **great-grandson** is the son of your grandson or granddaughter.

greatly (say **grayt**-lee) *adverb*
very much: *I wasn't **greatly** surprised to see her there.*

greed *noun* (*no plural*)
the feeling that you want more of something than you need

greedy (say **greed**-ee) *adjective* (**greedier**, **greediest**)
wanting or taking more of something than you need: *She's so **greedy** – she's eaten all the chocolates!*

Greek *noun* (*no plural*)
the language of the people who live in Greece

green[1] *adjective* (**greener**, **greenest**)
1 with the colour of leaves and grass: *My brother has **green** eyes.* ◇ *a dark **green** shirt*
2 covered with grass or other plants: ***green** fields*
3 connected with protecting the environment or the natural world: ***green** products* (= that do not damage the environment)

green[2] *noun*
1 (*plural* **greens**) the colour of leaves and grass: *She was dressed in **green**.*
2 greens (*plural noun*) green vegetables: *Eat up your **greens**.*

greengrocer (say **green**-groh-suh) *noun* (*plural* **greengrocers**)
a person who sells fruit and vegetables in a shop

greenhouse (say **green**-howss) *noun* (*plural* **greenhouses**)
a building made of glass in which plants can be grown protected from cold weather

greenhouse effect *noun* (*no plural*)
the problem of the warming of the Earth's atmosphere, caused by an increase in certain gases such as **carbon dioxide**. These gases trap the heat of the sun: *Emissions from cars and smoke from factories add to the **greenhouse effect**.* ➲ See **global warming**

greenhouse effect

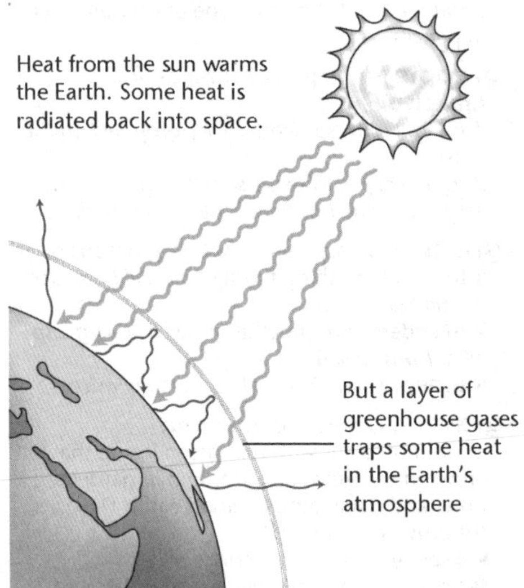

greenhouse gas *noun* (*plural* **greenhouse gases**)
one of the harmful gases that is making the Earth's atmosphere get warmer: *vehicles stuck in traffic pouring out **greenhouse gases*** ➲ See **carbon dioxide**

Greenwich Mean Time (say **gren**-ich meen time) *noun* (abbr. GMT)
the local time at Greenwich, England. It is used as a standard for calculating time in other parts of the world: *South Africa's time zone is **GMT**+2. We are two hours ahead of England.* ➲ See **meridian**

greet *verb* (**greeting**, **greeted**)
to say words such as 'hello' or 'good evening' when you meet somebody: *He **greeted** me with a smile.*

greeting (say **greet**-ing) *noun* (*plural* **greetings**)
friendly words that you say when you meet somebody: *'Hello' and 'Good morning' are **greetings**.*

gregarious (say gri-**gair**-ri-uhss) *adjective*
liking to be with other people: *a **gregarious** girl who loves parties*

gremlin (say **grem**-lin) *noun* (*plural* **gremlins**) (*informal*)
a creature that is not real, that people blame for things that go wrong in machines: *There's a **gremlin** in the printer and I can't print anything.*

grenade (say gruh-**nayd**) *noun* (*plural* **grenades**)
a small bomb that is thrown by hand

grew (say **groo**) form of **grow**

grey (say **gray**) *adjective* (**greyer**, **greyest**)
with a colour like black and white mixed together: *a **grey** skirt* ◇ *The sky was **grey**.* ◇ *He's starting to go **grey*** (= to have ***grey** hair*).
▶ **grey** (*noun*): *He was dressed in **grey**.*

grid *noun* (*plural* **grids**)
lines that cross each other to make squares, for example on a map

grief (say **greef**) *noun* (*no plural*)
great sadness, especially because somebody has died

grievance (say **gree**-vuhnss) *noun* (*plural* **grievances**)
something that you think is unfair and you want to complain or protest about: *The staff told their employer about their **grievances**.*

grieve (say **greev**) *verb* (**grieving**, **grieved**)
to feel great sadness, especially because somebody has died: *She is **grieving** for her dead son.*

grill[1] *noun* (*plural* **grills**)
1 the part of a stove where food is cooked from above
2 a metal frame that you put food on to cook over an open fire

grill[2] *verb* (**grilling**, **grilled**)
to cook food such as meat and fish on metal bars under or over heat: *Let's **grill** the steak.*

grim *adjective* (**grimmer**, **grimmest**)
1 (used about a person) very serious and not smiling: *a **grim** expression*
2 (used about a situation) very bad and making you feel worried: *The news is **grim**.*

grimace (say **gri**-muhss) *noun* (*plural* **grimaces**)
an ugly expression on your face that shows you are angry, disgusted or in pain: *He gave a **grimace** of disgust.*
▶ **grimace** (*verb*): *She **grimaced** in pain.*

grime (*rhymes with* **time**) *noun* (*no plural*)
a thick layer of dirt
▶ **grimy** (*adjective*): *My hands were **grimy** after I changed the tyre.*

grin *verb* (**grinning**, **grinned**)
to give a broad smile that shows your teeth: *She **grinned** at me.*
▶ **grin** (*noun*): *He had a big **grin** on his face.*

grind (*rhymes with* **find**) *verb* (**grinding**, **ground**)
to make something into very small pieces or powder by crushing it: *They **ground** the wheat into flour.* ◇ ***ground** coffee*

grip *verb* (**gripping**, **gripped**)
to hold something tightly: *Marie **gripped** my hand as we crossed the road.*
▶ **grip** (*noun*): *He kept a tight **grip** on the rope.*

gripping (say **grip**-ing) *adjective*
very exciting, in a way that holds your attention: *a **gripping** adventure film*

grisly (say **griz**-lee) *adjective* (**grislier**, **grisliest**)
(usually connected with death and violence) **horrible** and extremely frightening: *The town was shocked by the **grisly** murder.* ➲ SYNONYM **gruesome**

gristle (say **griss**-l) *noun* (*no plural*)
a hard substance in a piece of meat that is unpleasant to eat: *This meat is full of **gristle**!*

grit[1] *noun* (*no plural*)
very small pieces of stone

grit[2] *verb* (**gritting**, **gritted**)
grit your teeth to bite your teeth together: *He **gritted** his teeth when he got the injection.*

grizzled (say **griz**-uhld) *adjective*
having hair that is grey or partly grey: *a **grizzled** old man*

groan *verb* (**groaning**, **groaned**)
to make a deep sad sound, for example because you are unhappy or in pain: *'I've got a headache,' he **groaned**.*
▶ **groan** (*noun*): *She gave a **groan**, then lay still.*

grocer (say **groh**-suh) *noun* (*plural* **grocers**)
a person who has a shop that sells food and other articles for the home

groceries (say **groh**-suh-reez) *plural noun*
food and other articles for the home that you buy regularly: *We buy **groceries** from the supermarket.*

groggy (say **grog**-ee) *adjective* (**groggier**, **groggiest**)
unsteady and sleepy, from being ill or too tired or from medicine or drugs: *These pills have made me feel very **groggy**.*

groin (say **groyn**) *noun* (*plural* **groins**)
the front part of your body where it joins your legs

groom[1] (*rhymes with* **doom**) *noun* (*plural* **grooms**)
1 a person whose job is to look after horses
2 a man on the day of his wedding
➲ SYNONYM **bridegroom**

groom[2] (*rhymes with* **doom**) *verb* (**grooming**, **groomed**)
1 to clean or look after an animal: *Please **groom** the horses.*
2 to prepare somebody for a particular job: *She's being **groomed** as the next president.*
▶ **groomed** (*adjective*): *She always looks well **groomed** at work.*

groove (say **groov**) *noun* (*plural* **grooves**)
a long thin cut in the surface of something hard

grope (say **grohp**) *verb* (**groping, groped**)
1 to try to find something by using your hands, when you cannot see: *He **groped** around for the light switch.*
2 (*informal*) to touch a person sexually, especially when they do not want you to

gross (say **grohss**) *adjective*
1 (used about money received and profit) before anything such as costs or taxes are taken away: ***Gross** income is income before tax.*
2 (*formal*) very bad or serious: ***gross** misconduct*
3 very rude and unpleasant: *Eat your food properly, don't be **gross**!*
4 very fat and ugly

grotesque (say groh-**tesk**) *adjective*
strange or ugly in a way that offends or frightens: *He wore a **grotesque** mask.*

grotto (say **grot**-oh) *noun* (*plural* **grottos** or **grottoes**)
a small cave, often artificial and pretty

ground[1] (*rhymes with* **found**) form of **grind**

ground[2] (*rhymes with* **found**) *noun*
1 (*no plural*) the surface of the Earth: *We sat on the **ground** to eat our picnic.* ◇ *The **ground** was too dry for the plants to grow.*
2 (*plural* **grounds**) a piece of land that is used for something special: *a sports **ground*** ◇ *a **playground***
3 grounds (*plural noun*) the land around a large building: *the **grounds** of the hospital*
4 (*no plural*) an area of interest or study: *Research into AIDS covers new **ground**.*
5 grounds (*plural noun*) a reason for doing or believing something: *She retired on medical **grounds**.*
ORIGIN: from Old English *grund*, related to Dutch *grond*

ground floor *noun* (*plural* **ground floors**)
the part of a building that is at the same level as the street: *My office is on the **ground floor**.*

grounding (say **grownd**-ing) *noun* (*no plural*)
the teaching and learning of the basic facts or principles of a subject: *To study science you need a good **grounding** in maths.*

groundnut (say **grownd**-nut) *noun* (*plural* **groundnuts**) another word for **peanut**

grounds (say **growndz**) *plural noun*
a reason for doing or believing something: *Your bad behaviour is **grounds** for detention!*

groundwater (say **grownd**-waw-tuh) *noun* (*no plural*)
water that is found under the ground in soil and in spaces between rocks: *The windpump on his farm pumps up **groundwater** for his cattle to drink.*

groundwork (say **grownd**-wurk) *noun* (*no plural*)
work that is done to prepare you for further work or study: *The talks will lay the **groundwork** for a new agreement.*

group[1] (say **groop**) *noun* (*plural* **groups**)
1 a number of people or things that are together or that are related in some way: *A **group** of people were standing outside the shop.* ◇ *Proteins are a **group** of foods that build your body.*
2 a number of people who play music together ➲ SYNONYM **band** 1

group[2] (say **groop**) *verb* (**grouping, grouped**)
to form one or more groups: ***Group** these words into nouns and adjectives.*

grouse (say **growss**) *verb* (**grousing, groused**) (*informal*)
to complain about something that is not serious: *He **groused** about the dirt.*
▸ **grouse** (*noun*)

grove (*rhymes with* **stove**) *noun* (*plural* **groves**)
a small group of trees, especially of one particular type: *a **grove** of apple trees*

grovel (say **grov**-l) *verb* (**grovelling, grovelled**)
1 to try too hard to please someone who is more important than you or who can give you something: *He **grovelled** for forgiveness.* ◇ *She **grovels** for attention.*
2 to move around on your hands and knees while looking for something: *He **grovelled** in the dirt looking for his glasses.*

grow (*rhymes with* **go**) *verb* (**growing, grew, has grown**)
1 to become bigger: *Children **grow** very quickly.* ◇ *She's **grown** out of* (= got too big for) *her shoes.*
2 (used about plants) to occur or do well in a particular place: *Oranges **grow** in warm countries.*
3 to plant something in the ground and look after it: *We **grow** vegetables in our garden.*
4 to allow your hair or nails to grow: *He has **grown** a beard.*
5 to become: *It was **growing** dark.* ➲ SYNONYM **get** 3
grow into something to get bigger and become something: *Kittens **grow** into cats.*
grow up to change from a child to a man or

woman, or to become an adult: *I want to be a doctor when I **grow** up.*

growl (*rhymes with* **howl**) *verb* (**growling, growled**)
(used about a dog) to make a low angry sound: *The dog **growled** at the stranger.*
▸ **growl** (*noun*): *The dog gave a low **growl**.*
🛈 ORIGIN: 17th century. The word probably came from imitating the sound.

grown-up (say **grohn**-up) *noun* (*plural* **grown-ups**)
a man or woman, not a child: *Ask a **grown-up** to help you.* ➲ SYNONYM **adult**
▸ **grown-up** (*adjective*): *She has a **grown-up** son.*

growth (*rhymes with* **both**) *noun* (*no plural*)
the process of getting bigger: *A good diet is important for children's **growth**.* ◇ *population **growth***

grub *noun*
1 (*plural* **grubs**) a young insect when it comes out of the egg ➲ SYNONYM **larva**
2 (*no plural*) (*informal*) food

grubby (say **grub**-ee) *adjective* (**grubbier, grubbier**) (*informal*)
dirty: ***grubby** hands*

grudge (say **gruj**) *noun* (*plural* **grudges**)
a feeling of anger towards somebody, because of something bad that they have done to you in the past: *I don't bear him a **grudge** about what happened.*

gruelling (say **groo**-uh-ling) *adjective*
very tiring and long: *It was a **gruelling** race.*

gruesome (say **groo**-suhm) *adjective*
very unpleasant and shocking: *a **gruesome** murder*

gruff (say **gruf**) *adjective*
(used about a person or voice) rough and unfriendly: *'Who's there?' he asked in a **gruff** voice.*

grumble (say **grumb**-l) *verb* (**grumbling, grumbled**)
to say many times that you do not like something: *She's always **grumbling** about her boss.*

grumpy (say **grum**-pee) *adjective* (**grumpier, grumpiest**) (*informal*)
a little angry: *She gets **grumpy** when she's tired.* ➲ SYNONYM **bad-tempered**

grunt *verb* (**grunting, grunted**)
to make a short rough sound, like a pig makes
▸ **grunt** (*noun*): *He gave a **grunt** of pain.*

guano (say **gwaa**-noh) *noun* (*no plural*)
the waste substance passed from the bodies of birds and bats, which you use to make plants grow well

guarantee[1] (say ga-ruhn-**tee**) *noun* (*plural* **guarantees**)
1 a promise that something will happen: *I want a **guarantee** that you will do the work today.*
2 a written promise by a company that it will repair a product you have bought, or give you a new one, if it breaks or becomes faulty: *a two-year **guarantee*** ◇ *The computer is still under **guarantee**.*

guarantee[2] (say ga-ruhn-**tee**) *verb* (**guaranteeing, guaranteed**)
1 to promise that something will be done or will happen: *I can't **guarantee** that I will be able to help you, but I'll try.*
2 to say that you will repair a product that somebody buys, or give them a new one, if it breaks or becomes faulty: *The television is **guaranteed** for three years.*

guard[1] (say **gaad**) *noun* (*plural* **guards**)
a person who keeps somebody or something safe from other people, or who stops somebody from escaping: *There are security **guards** outside the bank.* ◇ *The soldiers were on **guard** outside the palace* (= guarding the palace).
be on your guard to be ready if something bad happens

guard[2] (say **gaad**) *verb* (**guarding, guarded**)
to keep somebody or something safe from other people, or to stop somebody from escaping: *The house was **guarded** by dogs.*

guardian (say **gaad**-i-uhn) *noun* (*plural* **guardians**)
a person who looks after a child with no parents

guava (say **gwaa**-vuh) *noun* (*plural* **guavas**)
a round yellow fruit with pink flesh inside
🛈 ORIGIN: 16th century, from Spanish *guayaba*, probably from Taino, a language that used to be spoken in the Caribbean

guerrilla (say guh-**ril**-uh) *noun* (*plural* **guerrillas**) (*also* **guerilla**)
a member of a small military group who are not part of an official army but make surprise attacks against them, usually to try to change a government
🛈 ORIGIN: 19th century, from Spanish *guerilla* meaning 'small war'

guess (say **gess**) *verb* (**guessing, guessed**)
to give an answer when you do not know if it is right: *Can you **guess** how old he is?*
▸ **guess** (*noun*): *Have a **guess**!*

A B C D E F G H I J K L M N O P Q R S T U V W X Y Z

guest (say **gest**) *noun* (*plural* **guests**)
1 a person that you invite to your home or to a party or special event: *There were 200* ***guests*** *at the wedding.*
2 a person who is staying in a hotel

guffaw (say **guf**-aw) *noun* (*plural* **guffaws**)
a loud laugh
▸ **guffaw** (*verb*): *The whole class* ***guffawed*** *when I told a joke.*

guidance (say **gide**-uhnss) *noun* (*no plural*)
help and advice: *I want some* ***guidance*** *on how to find a job.*

guide[1] (say **gide**) *noun* (*plural* **guides**)
1 a book that tells you about something, or how to do something: *a* ***guide*** *to birdwatching*
2 (also **guidebook**) a book that tells you about a place you are visiting: *a* ***guide*** *to Bangkok*
3 a person who shows other people where to go and tells them about a place: *The* ***guide*** *took us round the castle.*
4 Guide a member of a special club for girls (called the **Guides Association**) which trains girls in practical skills and does a lot of activities with them, for example camping

guide[2] (say **gide**) *verb* (**guiding, guided**)
to show somebody where to go or what to do: *He* ***guided*** *us through the busy streets to our hotel.*

guidelines (say **gide**-line-z) *plural noun*
general advice about how something should be done: *Just follow the* ***guidelines*** *and you'll get it right.*

guild (say **gild**) *noun* (*plural* **guilds**)
an organization of people who do the same job: *the Screen Actors'* ***Guild*** ◇ *a car manufacturers'* ***guild***

guillotine (say **gil**-uh-teen) *noun* (*plural* **guillotines**)
1 a machine used for cutting paper
2 a machine that was used in France in the past for cutting people's heads off

guilt (say **gilt**) *noun* (*no plural*)
1 the feeling you have when you know that you have done something wrong: *She felt terrible* ***guilt*** *after stealing the money.*
2 the fact of having broken the law: *The police could not prove his* ***guilt****.*

guilty (say **gil**-tee) *adjective* (**guiltier, guiltiest**)
1 feeling ashamed because you have done something that you know is wrong: *I feel* ***guilty*** *about lying to her.*
2 having done something illegal: *He is* ***guilty*** *of murder.* ➲ OPPOSITE **innocent**

guineafowl (say **gin**-ee-fowl) *noun* (*plural* **guineafowl**)
a large dark grey bird with white spots and a loud call that spends most of its time on the ground. It is common in South Africa.

guinea pig (say **gin**-ee-pig) *noun* (*plural* **guinea pigs**)
1 a small animal with short ears and no tail, that people sometimes keep as a pet
2 a person who is used in an experiment

guitar (say gi-**taa**) *noun* (*plural* **guitars**)
a musical instrument with strings: *I play the* ***guitar*** *in a band.*
▸ **guitarist** (*noun*): *I'm the lead* ***guitarist*** *in the band.*
🛈 ORIGIN: 17th century, through Spanish *guitarra*, from Greek *kithara*

gulf *noun* (*plural* **gulfs**)
a large part of the sea that has land almost all the way around it: *the* ***Gulf*** *of Mexico*

gull *noun* (*plural* **gulls**) (also **seagull**)
a large grey or white bird that lives by the sea

gullet (say **gul**-uht) *noun* (*plural* **gullets**)
the tube that carries food from your mouth to your stomach ➲ SYNONYM **oesophagus**

gullible (say **gul**-ib-l) *adjective*
(used about a person) trusting and believing people too easily, and therefore easily tricked: *Des is so* ***gullible*** *– he'll believe anything!*

gully (say **gul**-ee) *noun* (*plural* **gullies**)
a small narrow passage or valley formed by running water

gulp *verb* (**gulping, gulped**)
to eat or drink something quickly: *He* ***gulped*** *down a cup of tea and left.*
▸ **gulp** (*noun*): *She took a* ***gulp*** *of coffee.*

gum *noun*
1 (*plural* **gums**) the hard pink parts of your mouth that hold the teeth
2 (*no plural*) thick liquid that you use for sticking pieces of paper together ➲ SYNONYM **glue**[1]

gumboot (say **gum**-boot) *noun* (*plural* **gumboots**)
a long rubber boot: ***Gumboots*** *are best for walking in the mud.* ➲ SYNONYM **wellington**

gum tree *noun* (*plural* **gum trees**)
a tall fast-growing tree that uses up a lot of water and is not originally from South Africa
➲ See **eucalyptus**

gun *noun* (*plural* **guns**)
a weapon that shoots out pieces of metal (called **bullets**) to kill or hurt people or animals: *He aimed the* ***gun*** *at the bird and fired.*

gunman (say **gun**-muhn) *noun* (*plural* **gunmen**)
a man who uses a gun to rob or kill people

gunpowder (say **gun**-pow-duh) *noun* (*no plural*)
an explosive powder that is used in guns and other weapons

gurgle (say **gur**-guhl) *verb* (**gurgling**, **gurgled**)
to make a sound like water flowing quickly through a narrow space: *The stream* ***gurgles*** *over the rocks.* ◇ *The baby* ***gurgles*** *and giggles.*

guru (say **guu**-roo) *noun* (*plural* **gurus**)
1 a spiritual teacher in the Hindu religion
2 (*informal*) somebody whose opinions you admire, and whose ideas you follow: *a health* ***guru*** ◇ *an investment* ***guru***

gush (*rhymes with* **rush**) *verb* (**gushing**, **gushed**)
to flow out suddenly and strongly: *Blood was* ***gushing*** *from the cut in her leg.*

gust *noun* (*plural* **gusts**)
a sudden strong wind: *A* ***gust*** *of wind blew his hat off.*

gusto (say **guss**-toh) *noun* (*no plural*)
great enthusiasm: *She tackled the project with great* ***gusto.*** ➲ SYNONYM **enthusiasm**

gut *noun*
1 (*plural* **guts**) the tube in your body that food passes through when it leaves your stomach ➲ SYNONYM **intestine**
2 guts the stomach and the organs around it, especially of an animal: *I could see the* ***guts*** *of the dog that was run over.*

guts *plural noun* (*informal*)
the courage to do something difficult or unpleasant: *It takes* ***guts*** *to admit you're wrong.*

gutter (say **gut**-uh) *noun* (*plural* **gutters**)
1 a pipe under the edge of a roof to carry away water when it rains
2 the lower part at the edge of a road where water is carried away when it rains

guy (say **gy**) *noun*
1 (*plural* **guys**) (*informal*) a man: *He's a nice* ***guy!***
2 guys (*plural noun*) (*informal*) used when speaking to a group of men and women or boys and girls: *Come on* ***guys,*** *let's go.*

guzzle (say **guz**-l) *verb* (**guzzling**, **guzzled**) (*informal*)
1 to eat or drink too quickly and too much: *He always* ***guzzles*** *his food during break.*
2 to use something very fast: *This car* ***guzzles*** *more petrol than my old one.* ◇ *A geyser* ***guzzles*** *lots of electricity.*

gym (say **jim**) *noun*
1 (*plural* **gyms**) (also *formal* **gymnasium**) a room or building with equipment for doing physical exercise
2 (*no plural*) (also **gymnastics**) exercises for your body: *a* ***gym*** *class*

gymkhana (say jim-**kaa**-nuh) *noun* (*plural* **gymkhanas**)
an event in which people, especially children, take part in horse-riding competitions

gymnastics (say jim-**nass**-tikss) (*plural noun*) (also **gym**)
exercises for your body: *a* ***gymnastics*** *competition*
► **gymnast** (*noun*): *She's an Olympic* ***gymnast.***

gymnosperm (say **jim**-noh-spurm) *noun* (*plural* **gymnosperms**) (*biology*)
a plant whose seeds are not contained in a fruit, for example a pine tree or a cycad
➲ See **angiosperm**

gypsy (say **jip**-see) *noun* (*plural* **gypsies**) (also **gipsy**)
a member of a people, originally from Asia, who travel around in Europe and traditionally live in homes with wheels (called **caravans**). Many prefer to use the name **Romany**.

gyrate (say jy-**rayt**) *verb* (**gyrating**, **gyrated**)
to move around in circles: *They were* ***gyrating*** *their hips on the dance floor.*

Hh

A B C D E F G **H** I J K L M N O P Q R S T U V W X Y Z

ha *abbreviation* (*plural* **ha**) **hectare**

habit (say **hab**-it) *noun* (*plural* **habits**)
something that you do very often: *Smoking is a bad* ***habit***. ◇ *She's got a* ***habit*** *of phoning me when I'm in bed.*

habitat (say **hab**-i-tat) *noun* (*plural* **habitats**)
the natural place where a plant or an animal lives: *Scientists studied polar bears in their natural* ***habitat***.

habitation (say hab-i-**tay**-shuhn) *noun* (*no plural*)
living in a place: *That block of flats is not fit for human* ***habitation***.

hack (say **hak**) *verb* (**hacking, hacked**)
1 to cut something or somebody in a rough and violent way: *I* ***hacked*** *the dead branches off the tree.*
2 to use a computer to get into somebody else's computer in order to damage it or get secret information: *He* ***hacked*** *into the bank's computer system.*

hackneyed (say **hak**-need) *adjective*
(used about a phrase or idea) used so often that it is no longer interesting: *a* ***hackneyed*** *expression*

hacksaw (say **hak**-saw) *noun* (*plural* **hacksaws**)
a tool with a narrow cutting edge in a frame, used for cutting metal

had form of **have**[1]

haddock (say **had**-uhk) *noun* (*plural* **haddock**)
a type of sea fish that you can eat

hadeda (say **haa**-di-daa) *noun* (*plural* **hadedas**)
a large brown bird with a long curved beak that has a loud harsh call
🛈 **ORIGIN:** from the sound of its call

hadn't (say **had**-uhnt) short for **had not**

haemoglobin (say hee-moh-**gloh**-bin) *noun* (*no plural*)
a substance in your red blood cells that contains iron and that carries the gas we need to live **(oxygen)**

haemorrhage (say **hem**-uh-rij) *noun* (*no plural*)
heavy bleeding: *a brain* ***haemorrhage***
▸ **haemorrhage** (*verb*): *He was* ***haemorrhaging*** *badly from the wounds to his body.*

hag *noun* (*plural* **hags**)
an ugly old woman

haggard (say **hag**-uhd) *adjective*
(used about a person) looking tired or worried

haggle (say **hag**-l) *verb* (**haggling, haggled**)
to argue with somebody until you agree about the price of something: *Tourists were* ***haggling*** *over the price of a carpet.*

haiku (say **hy**-koo) *noun* (*plural* **haiku** or **haikus**)
a poem that has three lines and seventeen syllables
🛈 **ORIGIN:** from Japanese *haikai no ku* meaning 'light verse'

hail (say **hayl**) *noun* (*no plural*)
frozen rain that falls in small hard balls (called **hailstones)**
▸ **hail** (*verb*): *It's* ***hailing***.

hair *noun*
1 (*plural* **hairs**) one of the long thin things that grow on the skin of people and animals
2 (*no plural*) all the hairs on a person's head: *She's got long black* ***hair***.

hairbrush (say **hair**-brush) *noun* (*plural* **hairbrushes**)
a brush that you use to make your hair tidy

haircut (say **hair**-kut) *noun* (*plural* **haircuts**)
1 the act of somebody cutting your hair: *I need a* ***haircut***.
2 the way that your hair is cut: *I like your new* ***haircut***.

hairdresser (say **hair**-dress-uh) *noun* (*plural* **hairdressers**)
a person who washes, cuts and arranges people's hair or a shop where you can go to have this done: *I'm going to the* ***hairdresser***.
➲ See **barber**

hairdryer (say **hair**-dry-uh) *noun* (*plural* **hairdryers**) (also **hairdrier**)
a machine that dries your hair by blowing hot air on it

hair-raising (say **hair**-rayz-ing) *adjective*
frightening: *It was a* ***hair-raising*** *experience.*

hairstyle (say **hair**-stile) *noun* (*plural* **hairstyles**)
the way that your hair is cut and arranged

hairy (say **hair**-ree) *adjective* (**hairier, hairiest**)
covered with a lot of hair: *He has got* ***hairy*** *legs.*

Haji (say **huj**-ee) *noun* (*plural* **Hajis**) (also **Hajji**)
a Muslim who has been to Mecca
🛈 **ORIGIN:** through Persian and Turkish, from Arabic *ḥajj* meaning 'pilgrimage'

Hajj (say **huj**) *noun* (*plural* **Hajjes**)
the religious journey (called a **pilgrimage**) to Mecca that many Muslims make
ℹ ORIGIN: from Arabic *ḥajj* meaning 'pilgrimage'

hake (say **hayk**) *noun* (*plural* **hake**)
one of a variety of sea fish, popular for its soft white flesh

halaal (say hul-**aal**) *adjective* (also **halal**)
(about meat and other food) prepared according to Muslim law
ℹ ORIGIN: 19th century, from Arabic *halal* meaning 'according to religious law'

half¹ (say **haaf**) *noun* (*plural* **halves**)
one of two equal parts of something, $\frac{1}{2}$: ***Half** of six is three.* ◇ *I lived there for two and a **half** years.* ◇ *The journey takes an hour and a **half**.* ◇ *I've been here more than **half** an hour.* ◇ *She gave me **half** of her apple.* ➲ The verb is **halve**
in half so that there are two equal parts: *Cut the cake in **half**.*
▸ **half** (*adjective, adverb*): ***half** raw* ◇ *a **half**-baked pie*

half² (say **haaf**) *adverb*
1 not completely: *The bottle is **half** empty.*
2 to the amount of half, 50%: *He's **half** German* (= one of his parents is German).
half past 30 minutes after an hour on the clock: *It's **half** past nine.*

half-brother (say **haaf**-bru*th*-uh) *noun* (*plural* **half-brothers**)
a brother with whom you share one parent: *My father's son with his new wife is my **half-brother**.*

half-hearted (say haaf-**haat**-uhd) *adjective*
without interest or enthusiasm
▸ **half-heartedly** (*adverb*): *He ate his spinach **half-heartedly**.*

half-price (say **haaf**-prise) *adjective, adverb*
for half the usual price: *You can get **half-price** tickets one hour before the show.*

half-sister (say **haaf**-siss-tuh) *noun* (*plural* **half-sisters**)
a sister with whom you share one parent: *My **half-sister** sometimes lives with us and sometimes with her mother.*

half-time (say haaf-**time**) *noun* (*no plural*)
a short time in the middle of a game such as football, when play stops

halfway (say haaf-**way**) *adverb*
in the middle: *They live **halfway** between Bhisho and Mthatha.* ◇ *She went out **halfway** through the lesson.* ➲ SYNONYM **midway**

hall (say **hawl**) *noun* (*plural* **halls**)
1 a big room or building where a lot of people meet: *a concert **hall*** ◇ *We wrote our exams in the school **hall**.*
2 the room in a house that is near the front door and has doors to other rooms: *You can leave your coat in the **hall**.*

hallmark (say **hawl**-maak) *noun* (*plural* **hallmarks**)
1 a characteristic that is typical of a person: *Patience is the **hallmark** of a good babysitter.*
2 a mark that is made on valuable metals to give information about the quality of the metal, and where and when the object was made

Halloween (say hal-oh-**een**) *noun* (*no plural*) (also **Hallowe'en**)
the night of 31 October, traditionally when many children dress up as devils, ghosts and other characters

hallucination (say huh-**loo**-si-nay-shuhn) *noun* (*plural* **hallucinations**)
something you think you can see, hear or feel that is not really there
▸ **hallucinate** (*verb*): *Some drugs can cause you to **hallucinate**.*

halo (say **hay**-loh) *noun* (*plural* **haloes** or **halos**)
1 the circle of light that is drawn around or above the head of an important religious person in pictures
2 a circle of white or coloured light around the sun or moon

halt (say **hawlt**) *noun* (*no plural*)
come to a halt to stop: *The car came to a **halt** in front of the school.*
▸ **halt** (*verb*): *She **halted** outside the gate.*

halter (say **hawl**-tuh) *noun* (*plural* **halters**)
a rope or leather strap that you put around the head of a horse to lead it

halve (say **haav**) *verb* (**halving, halved**)
to divide something into two parts that are the same: *There were two of us, so I **halved** the orange.* ➲ The noun is **half¹**

halves (say **haavz**) plural of **half¹**

ham *noun* (*no plural*)
meat from a pig's leg that you can keep for a long time because it was prepared with salt or smoke ➲ See note at **pig**

hamburger (say **ham**-bur-guh) *noun* (*plural* **hamburgers**) (also **burger**)
meat cut into very small pieces and made into a flat round shape. You often eat it in a round piece of bread (called a **roll**): *I'd like a **hamburger** and chips, please.*

hamlet (say **ham**-luht) *noun* (*plural* **hamlets**)
a very small village

hammer[1] (say **ham**-uh) *noun* (*plural* **hammers**)
a tool with a handle and a heavy metal part, that you use for hitting nails into things

hammer[2] (say **ham**-uh) *verb* (**hammering, hammered**)
1 to hit something with a hammer: *I **hammered** the nail into the wood.*
2 to hit something hard: *He **hammered** loudly on the door.*

hammock (say **ham**-uhk) *noun* (*plural* **hammocks**)
a bed made of cloth or rope that you hang up at the two ends
🛈 **ORIGIN:** 16th century, through Spanish from Taino *hamaka*. Taino was a language that used to be spoken in the Caribbean.

hamper[1] (say **ham**-puh) *noun* (*plural* **hampers**)
1 a large basket with a lid for carrying food: *a picnic **hamper***
2 a box or package of food: *I gave my teacher a **hamper** of fruit.*

hamper[2] (say **ham**-puh) *verb* (**hampering, hampered**)
to make something difficult: *The building of the house was **hampered** by the rain.*

hamster (say **ham**-stuh) *noun* (*plural* **hamsters**)
a small animal that people keep as a pet

hand[1] *noun*
1 (*plural* **hands**) the part at the end of your arm that has four **fingers** and a **thumb**: *She held the letter in her **hand**.* ◊ *The young couple were holding **hands**.* ◊ *The curtains were made by **hand**.* ◊ *Put your **hand** up if you can answer the question.*
2 a hand (*no plural*) (*informal*) some help: *Could you give me a **hand** with my homework?*
3 (*plural* **hands**) one of the parts of a clock or watch that move to show the time
get out of hand to become difficult to control: *The party got out of **hand**.*
in good hands well looked after: *Don't worry – your son is in good **hands**.*
on hand near and ready to help: *There is a doctor on **hand** all day.*
on the one hand … on the other hand words that show the good and bad things about something: *On the one **hand** cars are very useful; on the other **hand** they cause a lot of pollution.*

hands

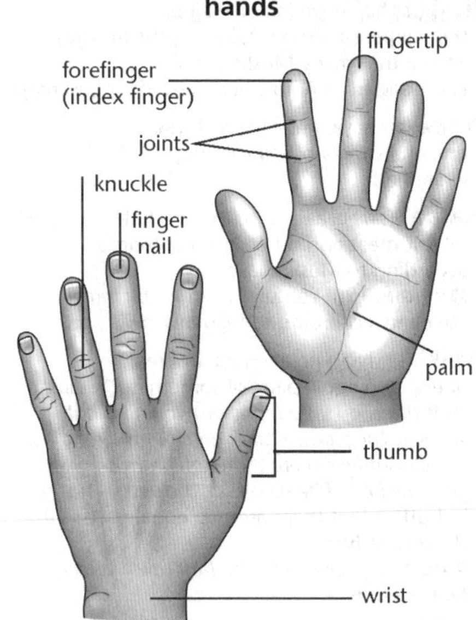

hand[2] *verb* (**handing, handed**)
to put something into somebody's hand: *Can you **hand** me the scissors, please?* ◊ *I **handed** the money to the shop assistant.* ◊ *The teacher asked us to **hand** in our homework.* ◊ *Please **hand** out these books.* ◊ ***Hand** over your weapons!*
hand something down to pass something from an older person to a younger one: *He **handed** his clothes down to his younger brother.*

handbag (say **hand**-bag) *noun* (*plural* **handbags**)
a small bag that a woman uses for carrying things like money and keys

handcuffs (say **hand**-kufss) *plural noun*
two metal rings with a chain that the police put on a prisoner's arms so that they cannot use their hands

handful (say **hand**-fuul) *noun* (*plural* **handfuls**)
1 as much as you can hold in one hand: *a **handful** of stones*
2 a small number: *Only a **handful** of people came to the meeting.*

handicap (say **hand**-i-kap) *noun* (*plural* **handicaps**)
something that makes it more difficult for you to do something: *Not being able to drive is a bit of a **handicap**.*
► **handicap** (*verb*): *They were **handicapped** by their lack of education.*

handkerchief (say **hang**-kuh-chif) *noun* (*plural* **handkerchiefs** or **handkerchieves**)
a square piece of cloth or paper that you use for clearing **(blowing)** your nose

handle[1] (say **hand**-l) *noun* (*plural* **handles**)
the part of a thing that you hold in your hand: *I turned the **handle** and opened the door.* ◇ *Hold that knife by the **handle**.*

handle[2] (say **hand**-l) *verb* (**handling, handled**)
1 to touch something with your hands: *Always wash your hands before you **handle** food.*
2 to control or deal with a person or thing: *He's not very good at **handling** problems.*

handlebars (say **hand**-uhl-baaz) *plural noun*
the part at the front of a bicycle or motorbike that you hold when you are riding it

handmade (say hand-**mayd**) *adjective*
made by a person, not by a machine: ***handmade** chocolates*

handsome (say **han**-suhm) *adjective*
attractive: *a **handsome** man* ➲ SYNONYM **good-looking** ➲ See note at **beautiful**

hands-on (say **handz**-on) *adjective*
doing something yourself, rather than watching somebody else do it: *She needs some **hands-on** experience.*

handstand (say **hand**-stand) *noun* (*plural* **handstands**)
a movement in which you stand on your hands with your legs in the air: *We had a **handstand** competition in gym.*

handwriting (say **hand**-rite-ing) *noun* (*no plural*)
the way you write: *Her **handwriting** is difficult to read.*

handy (say **hand**-ee) *adjective* (**handier, handiest**)
1 useful: *This bag will be **handy** for carrying my books.*
2 near and easy to find or reach: *Have you got a pen **handy**?*
come in handy to be useful: *Don't throw that box away – it might come in **handy**.*

handyman (say **hand**-ee-man) *noun* (*plural* **handymen**)
a person who is clever at making or fixing things, especially around the house

hang *verb*
1 (**hanging, hung**) to fix something, or to be fixed at the top so that the lower part is free: ***Hang** your coat up in the hall.* ◇ *I **hung** the washing on the line to dry.*
2 (**hanging, hanged**) to kill yourself or another person by putting a rope around the neck and allowing the body to drop downwards: *She was **hanged** for murder.*
hang about, hang around (*informal*) to stay somewhere with nothing special to do: *My bus was late so I **hung** about waiting.*
hang on (*informal*) to wait for a short time: *Hang on – I'm not ready.*
hang on to a person or **thing** to hold a person or thing firmly: ***Hang** on to your purse.*
hang up to end a telephone call by putting the telephone down

hangar (say **hang**-uh) *noun* (*plural* **hangars**)
a big building where planes are kept

hanger (say **hang**-uh) *noun* (*plural* **hangers**) (also **coat hanger**)
a piece of metal, wood or plastic with a hook. You use it for hanging clothes on.

hang-glider (say **hang**-glide-uh) *noun* (*plural* **hang-gliders**)
1 a very large piece of material on a frame, which you hang from and fly down from a mountain
2 a person who uses a hang-glider (in the meaning above) for sport
▸ **hang-gliding** (*noun*): *I'd love to try **hang-gliding**.*

hanky (say **hang**-kee) *noun* (*plural* **hankies**) (also **hankie**) (*informal*) short for **handkerchief**

Hanukkah (say *khu*-**nuu**-kaa) *noun* (*no plural*) (also **Chanukkah**)
a Jewish festival in December

> PRONUNCIATION Pronounce the first **h** in **Hannukah** like the **g** in the Afrikaans word **lag**.

haphazard (say hap-**haz**-uhd) *adjective*
with no particular order or plan
▸ **haphazardly** (*adverb*): *She chose books **haphazardly**.*

happen (say **hap**-uhn) *verb* (**happening, happened**)
to take place, usually without being planned first: *How did the accident **happen**?* ◇ *Did you hear what **happened** to me yesterday?*
happen to do something to do something by chance: *I **happened** to meet Mpho yesterday.*

happily (say **hap**-i-lee) *adverb*
1 in a happy way: *Everyone was smiling **happily**.*
2 it is lucky that, fortunately: ***Happily**, the accident was not serious.*

happiness (say **hap**-i-nuhss) *noun* (*no plural*)
the feeling of being happy

happy (say **hap**-ee) *adjective* (**happier, happiest**)
1 feeling pleased or showing that you are

A B C D E F G H I J K L M N O P Q R S T U V W X Y Z

pleased: *She looks very **happy**.* ◇ *That was one of the **happiest** days of my life.* ➲ OPPOSITES **unhappy**, **sad** ➲ See note at **glad**
2 a word that you use to say that you hope somebody will enjoy a special time: ***Happy** New Year!* ◇ ***Happy** Christmas!* ◇ ***Happy** Birthday!*

WORD BUILDING There are many words that you can use instead of **happy**, but check their exact meanings first. Examples are: **blissful**, **cheerful**, **chuffed** (informal), **content**, **contented**, **delighted**, **ecstatic**, **elated**, **excited**, **exhilarated**, **glad**, **jolly**, **jovial**, **joyful**, **jubilant**, **light-hearted**, **merry**, **overjoyed**, **pleased**, **proud** 1, **satisfied** and **thrilled**.

haraam (say huh-**raam**) *adjective* (also **haram**)
not allowed by Muslim law: *Eating pork is **haraam**.*
🛈 ORIGIN: from Arabic *haram* meaning 'not allowed'

harass (say **ha**-ruhss or huh-**rass**) *verb* (**harassing**, **harassed**)
to annoy or worry somebody by doing unpleasant things to them, often over a long time: *Stop **harassing** me while I'm working!*
➲ SYNONYM **pester**
▸ **harassment** (*noun*): *sexual **harassment***

harbour[1] (say **haa**-buh) *noun* (*plural* **harbours**)
a place on the coast where ships can be tied up (**moored**) and protected from the sea and bad weather
🛈 ORIGIN: from Old English *herebeorg* meaning 'shelter, safe place'. This word is related to Dutch *herberge* meaning 'inn, place to stay'.

harbour[2] (say **haa**-buh) *verb* (**harbouring**, **harboured**)
1 to keep feelings or thoughts secret in your mind for a long time: *He **harbours** feelings for her.*
2 to hide or protect a person or thing: *They have been **harbouring** fugitives.*

hard[1] (say **haad**) *adjective* (**harder**, **hardest**)
1 not soft: *These apples are very **hard**.* ◇ *I couldn't sleep because the bed was too **hard**.*
2 difficult to do or understand: *The exam was very **hard**.* ◇ ***hard** work* ➲ OPPOSITE **easy** 1
3 full of problems: *He's had a **hard** life.*
➲ OPPOSITE **easy** 2
4 not kind or gentle: *She is very **hard** on her children.* ➲ OPPOSITE **soft** 5

hard[2] (say **haad**) *adverb*
1 a lot: *She works very **hard**.* ◇ *You must try **harder**!*
2 strongly: *It's raining **hard**.* ◇ *She hit him **hard**.*

hardback (say **haad**-bak) *noun* (*plural* **hardbacks**)
a book with a hard cover ➲ See **paperback**

hardboard (say **haad**-bawd) *noun* (*no plural*)
a type of wooden board made by pressing very small pieces of wood together into thin sheets

hard drive *noun* (*plural* **hard drives**) (also **hard disk**) (*computing*)
a piece of equipment inside a computer that stores information (called **data**) and programs

harden (say **haad**-uhn) *verb* (**hardening**, **hardened**)
to become harder or to make something harder: *Wait for the cement to **harden**.*
➲ OPPOSITE **soften**

hard-hearted (say hard-**haat**-uhd) *adjective*
not kind to other people and not thinking about their feelings

hardly (say **haad**-lee) *adverb*
almost not and only just: *She spoke so quietly that I could **hardly** hear her.* ◇ *There's **hardly** any* (= almost no) *coffee left.* ➲ SYNONYM **scarcely**

hardware (say **haad**-wair) *noun* (*no plural*)
1 tools and equipment that we use in the house and garden: *I bought a spade at the **hardware** shop.*
2 the electronic parts of a computer system, not the programs that work on it ➲ See **software**

hardy (say **haad**-ee) *adjective* (**hardier**, **hardiest**)
strong and able to survive difficult conditions and bad weather: *Plant something **hardy** in your garden.*

hare (say **hair**) *noun* (*plural* **hares**)
an animal like a rabbit, but bigger and with longer ears. It can run very fast.

harem (say haa-**reem**) *noun* (*plural* **harems**)
a number of women living with one man, especially in Muslim societies

harm[1] (say **haam**) *noun* (*no plural*)
hurt or damage: *Make sure the children don't come to any **harm**.* ◇ *There's no **harm** in asking for help.*

harm[2] (say **haam**) *verb* (**harming**, **harmed**)
to hurt or damage a person or thing: *These chemicals **harm** the environment.*

harmful (say **haam**-fuhl) *adjective*
that can hurt or damage people or things: *Traffic fumes are **harmful** to the environment.*

harmless (say **haam**-luhss) *adjective*
not dangerous: *Don't be frightened – these insects are **harmless**.*

A B C D E F G H I J K L M N O P Q R S T U V W X Y Z

harmonica (say haa-**mon**-i-kuh) *noun* (*plural* **harmonicas**) (also **mouth organ**)
a small musical instrument that you play by moving it across your mouth while you are blowing air into it or drawing air out of it

harmonious (say haa-**moh**-ni-uhss) *adjective*
1 friendly or peaceful: *We live in a* ***harmonious*** *environment in my block of flats.*
2 (used about musical notes, colour and such things) producing a pleasant effect when heard or seen together
▸ **harmoniously** (*adverb*): *These colours work together* ***harmoniously***.

harmony (say **haa**-muh-nee) *noun*
1 (*no plural*) a state of agreement or of living together in peace: *The different races live together in* ***harmony***.
2 (*plural* **harmonies**) musical notes that sound good together: *They sang in* ***harmony***.

harness (say **haa**-nuhss) *noun* (*plural* **harnesses**)
1 a set of leather straps that is put around a horse's head and neck so that it can pull something
2 a set of straps for fastening something, such as a rope, to a person's body: *a climbing harness*
▸ **harness** (*verb*): *The pony was* ***harnessed*** *to the cart.*

harp[1] (say **haap**) *noun* (*plural* **harps**)
a large musical instrument that has many strings stretching from the top to the bottom of a frame. You pluck the strings with your fingers.

harp[2] (say **haap**) *verb* (**harping, harped**)
to harp on to keep talking about something in a way that makes it boring for other people: *She* ***harped*** *on about the weather all day.*

harpoon (say haa-**poon**) *noun* (*plural* **harpoons**)
a long thin weapon with a sharp pointed end and a rope tied to it that is used to catch large sea animals **(whales)**

harpsichord (say **haap**-si-kawd) *noun* (*plural* **harpsichords**) (*music*)
an early type of musical instrument similar to a piano, but with strings that are plucked **(pulled)**, not hit

harsh (say **haash**) *adjective* (**harsher, harshest**)
1 not kind, but cruel: *a* ***harsh*** *punishment*
2 rough and unpleasant to see or hear: *a* ***harsh*** *voice*
▸ **harshly** (*adverb*): *He laughed* ***harshly***.
▸ **harshness** (*noun*): *Her voice had a surprising* ***harshness***.

hartebeest (say **haa**-tuh-bee-uhst) *noun* (*plural* **hartebeest** or **hartebeests**)
a large African antelope with a long head, horns that curve backwards and a red-brown coat
🛈 **ORIGIN**: 18th century, through South African Dutch, from Dutch *hert* meaning 'a male buck' + *beest* meaning 'animal, beast'

harvest (say **haav**-uhst) *noun* (*plural* **harvests**)
1 the time when grain, fruit, or vegetables are ready to cut or pick: *The apple* ***harvest*** *is in autumn.*
2 all the grain, fruit, or vegetables that are cut or picked: *We had a good* ***harvest*** *this year.*
▸ **harvest** (*verb*): *When do they* ***harvest*** *the wheat?*

has (say **haz**) form of **have[1]**

hash *noun*
1 (*plural* **hashes**) the symbol **(#)** that means 'number' and that is one of the keys on your phone and computer
2 (*no plural*) another word for **hashish**

hashish (say hash-**eesh**) *noun* (*no plural*) (also **hash**)
a drug made from the oil produced by the flowers and leaves of a plant (called **cannabis**) which is illegal in many countries

hasn't (say **haz**-uhnt) short for **has not**

hassle[1] (say **hass**-l) *noun* (*plural* **hassles**) (*informal*)
something that annoys you because it takes time or effort: *Waiting for a bus is a* ***hassle***.

hassle[2] (say **hass**-l) *verb* (**hassling, hassled**) (*informal*)
to annoy somebody by asking them many times to do something: *I wish he'd stop* ***hassling*** *me about that essay!*

haste (say **hayst**) *noun* (*no plural*) (*formal*)
speed in doing something, especially because you do not have enough time: *The letter was written in* ***haste*** (= quickly).

hasty (say **hayst**-ee) *adjective* (**hastier, hastiest**)
said or done quickly, sometimes too quickly: *We ate a* ***hasty*** *lunch, then left.* ◇ *Don't be too* ***hasty***. *This is a very important decision.*
▸ **hastily** (*adverb*): *He* ***hastily*** *changed the subject.*

hat *noun* (*plural* **hats**)
a thing that you wear on your head: *She's wearing a* ***hat***.

hatch[1] (say **hach**) *verb* (**hatching, hatched**)
(used about baby birds, insects or fish) to come out of an egg

hatch[2] (say **hach**) *noun* (*plural* **hatches**)
1 an opening in the floor of a ship that cargo can be passed through

2 an opening in the wall between a kitchen and another room that food can be passed through
3 the door of an aeroplane or spacecraft

hate[1] (say **hayt**) *verb* (**hating, hated**)
to have a very strong feeling of not liking a person or thing: *Most cats **hate** water.* ◇ *I **hate** waiting for buses.* ➲ OPPOSITE **love[2]**

hate[2] (say **hayt**) *noun* (*no plural*)
a very strong feeling of not liking a person or thing: *Her love for him had turned to **hate**.*
➲ SYNONYM **hatred** ➲ OPPOSITE **love[1] 1**

hatred (say **hayt**-rid) *noun* (*no plural*)
a very strong feeling of not liking a person or thing: *He had a deep **hatred** of injustice.*
➲ SYNONYM **hate[2]**

haughty (say **hawt**-ee) *adjective* (**haughtier, haughtiest**)
proud and thinking that you are better than other people: *The new girl seems **haughty**.*
➲ SYNONYM **supercilious**

haul (say **hawl**) *verb* (**hauling, hauled**)
to pull something heavy: *They **hauled** the boat out of the river.*

haunch (say **hawnch**) *noun* (*plural* **haunches**)
the back of your legs between your knees and your bottom: *We sat on our **haunches**.*

haunt (say **hawnt**) *verb* (**haunting, haunted**)
1 (used about a ghost of a dead person) to appear in a place regularly: *The house is said to be **haunted**.*
2 (used about something sad or unpleasant) to be often in your mind: *Her unhappy face still **haunts** me.*
▸ **haunted** (*adjective*): *a **haunted** house*

have[1] (say **hav**) *verb* (**having, had**)
a word that you use with parts of other verbs to show that something happened or started in the past: ***We've** been in Gauteng for six months.* ◇ *I **haven't** seen that film.* ◇ ***Have** you been to Malawi?* ➲ See Study page 6

have[2] (say **hav**) *verb* (**having, had**)
1 to own or keep something: *She **has** blue eyes.* ◇ ***They've*** (= They have) *got a big car.* ◇ *Do you **have** any brothers and sisters?* ◇ ***Have** you got time to help me?*
2 a word that you use with many nouns to talk about doing something: *Let's **have** breakfast.* ◇ ***Have** you had a shower?* ◇ *Lebo and I **have** had a fight.* ◇ ***Have** fun!* ◇ *He has **had** an accident.*
3 (also **have got**) to be ill with something: ***She's*** (= She has) *got a headache.* ◇ *I **have** flu.*
have something done to let somebody do something for you: *I **had** my hair cut yesterday.* ◇ *Have you **had** your car mended?*

haven (say **hay**-vuhn) *noun* (*plural* **havens**)
a place where people can be safe and can rest: *This is a **haven** for injured animals.* ◇ *a tax **haven***
🛈 ORIGIN: through Old English *hæfen* meaning 'haven', from Old Norse *hǫfn*. The word is related to Dutch *haven* meaning 'harbour'.

haven't (say **hav**-uhnt) short for **have not**

have to *modal verb* (also **have got to**)
used for saying that somebody must do something or that something must happen: *I **have to** go to school on Saturday.* ◇ *We don't **have to** get up early tomorrow.* ◇ ***Have** we **got to** pay for this now?* ◇ *We **had to** do lots of boring exercises.*

havoc (say **hav**-uhk) *noun* (*no plural*)
a situation in which there is a lot of damage or confusion: *There was **havoc** in the classroom when the teacher left.* ◇ *That puppy will cause **havoc** in the garden!*

hawk (*rhymes with* **fork**) *noun* (*plural* **hawks**)
a big bird that catches and eats other birds and small animals

hawker (say **hawk**-uh) *noun* (*plural* **hawkers**)
a person who goes from place to place selling things: *A **hawker** came to our door selling brooms.*

hay *noun* (*no plural*)
dry grass that is used as food for farm animals

hay fever *noun* (*no plural*)
an illness like a cold that is caused by the powder (called **pollen**) from grass and other plants

hazard (say **haz**-uhd) *noun* (*plural* **hazards**)
a danger: *Muddy roads are a **hazard** for drivers.* ◇ *a fire **hazard***

hazardous (say **haz**-uh-duhss) *adjective*
dangerous: *Motor racing is a **hazardous** sport.*

haze (say **hayz**) *noun* (*no plural*)
air that is difficult to see through because of heat, dust or smoke

hazel (say **hay**-zuhl) *noun*
1 (*plural* **hazels**) a small tree or bush that produces nuts
2 (*no plural*) a light brown colour

hazy (say **hay**-zee) *adjective* (**hazier, haziest**)
1 not clear, especially because of heat: *When it isn't **hazy** we can see the mountains.*
2 difficult to remember or understand clearly: *My memory of that day is **hazy**.*
3 (used about a person) uncertain, not expressing things clearly: *We're **hazy** about the details.*

H-bomb (say **aych**-bom) *noun* (*plural* **H-bombs**)
a nuclear weapon that gets its energy from **hydrogen** reactions ℹ **H-bomb** is short for 'hydrogen bomb'.

HCF (say aych-see-**ef**) *noun* (*plural* **HCFs**) (*maths*)
the largest number that divides into two different numbers exactly: *The **HCF** of 36 and 48 is 12.* ℹ **HCF** is short for 'highest common factor'.

HDI (say aych-dee-***y***) *noun* (*plural* **HDIs**)
a measurement used to compare living standards in different countries ℹ **HDI** is short for 'Human Development Index'.

he (say **hee**) *pronoun* (*plural* **they**)
the man or boy that the sentence is about: *I saw Thabang when **he** arrived.* ◇ *'Where's Monde?' '**He's** (= he is) at home.'*

head[1] (say **hed**) *noun* (*plural* **heads**)
1 the part of your body above your neck: *She turned her **head** to look at me.* ◇ *She jumped into the water **head** first.* ➲ See illustration at **body**
2 your mind or brain: *A strange thought came into his **head**.* ◇ *Use your **head** (= think)!*
3 the top, front or most important part: *She sat at the **head** of the table.*
4 the most important person: *The Pope is the **head** of the Catholic church.*
5 (usually **Head**) the person who is in charge of a school or college: *I've been called in to see the Head.* ➲ SYNONYMS **principal[2]**, **headmaster**, **headmistress**
6 heads (*plural noun*) the side of a coin that has the head of a leader or the symbol of the country (called **the coat of arms**) on it
➲ See **tail** 3
a head, per head for one person: *The meal cost R50 a **head**.*
go to your head to make you too pleased with yourself: *Stop telling him how clever he is, it will go to his **head**!*

> WORD BUILDING You say **Heads or tails?** with sense 6 above when you are throwing a coin in the air to decide something, for example who will start a game.

head[2] (say **hed**) *verb* (**heading, headed**)
1 to move in the direction mentioned: *Let's **head** for home.* ◇ *Where are you **heading**?*
2 to be at the front or top of a group: *Her name **heads** the list.*
3 to hit a ball with your head

headache (say **hed**-ayk) *noun* (*plural* **headaches**)
a pain in your head: *I've got a **headache**.*

heading (say **hed**-ing) *noun* (*plural* **headings**)
the words at the top of a piece of writing to show what it is about

headland (say **hed**-luhnd) *noun* (*plural* **headlands**)
a narrow piece of land that sticks out into the sea

headlight (say **hed**-lite) *noun* (*plural* **headlights**) (also **headlamp**)
one of the two big bright lights on the front of a car ➲ See illustration at **car**

headline (say **hed**-line) *noun*
1 (*plural* **headlines**) the words in big letters at the top of a newspaper story
2 the headlines (*plural noun*) the most important news on radio or television: *Here are the news **headlines**.*

headmaster (say hed-**maass**-tuh) *noun* (*plural* **headmasters**)
a man who is in charge of a school

headmistress (say hed-**miss**-truhss) *noun* (*plural* **headmistresses**)
a woman who is in charge of a school

headphones (say **hed**-fohnz) *plural noun* (also **earphones**)
things that you put over your head and ears so that you can listen to music without other people hearing it

headquarters (say hed-**kawt**-uhz) *plural noun* (abbr. HQ)
the main offices where the leaders of an organization work: *The company's **headquarters** are in Tshwane.*

head teacher *noun* (*plural* **head teachers**) (also **Head**)
a person who is in charge of a school
➲ SYNONYM **principal[2]**

headway (say **hed**-way) *noun* (*no plural*)
make headway to go forward or make progress: *We haven't made much **headway** with our project.*

heal (say **heel**) *verb* (**healing, healed**)
to become well again or to make something well again: *The cut on his leg **healed** slowly.*
ℹ ORIGIN: from Old English *hǣlen* meaning 'make healthy again'. This word is related to Dutch *heelen* and English *whole*.

healer (say **heel**-uh) *noun* (*plural* **healers**)
a person who cures people of illness and disease by using natural powers rather than medicine

A B C D E F G **H** I J K L M N O P Q R S T U V W X Y Z

health (say **helth**) *noun* (*no plural*)
the condition of your body: *Smoking is bad for your* ***health****.*

healthcare (say **helth**-kair) *noun* (*no plural*)
the care of mental and physical health by preventing, treating or managing illness: *a* ***healthcare*** *provider*

healthy (say **hel**-thee) *adjective* (**healthier, healthiest**)
1 well and not often ill: ***healthy*** *children*
2 helping to make or keep you well: ***healthy*** *food* ➲ OPPOSITE **unhealthy**

heap[1] (say **heep**) *noun*
1 (*plural* **heaps**) a lot of things on top of one another in an untidy way: *She left her clothes in a* ***heap*** *on the floor.*
2 heaps (*plural noun*) (*informal*) a lot: *We've got* ***heaps*** *of time.*

heap[2] (say **heep**) *verb* (**heaping, heaped**)
to put a lot of things on top of one another: *She* ***heaped*** *food onto my plate.*

hear (say **heer**) *verb* (**hearing, heard**)
1 to notice sounds with your ears: *Can you* ***hear*** *that noise?* ◇ *I* ***heard*** *somebody laughing in the next room.*
2 to be told about something: *Have you* ***heard*** *the news?*
hear from somebody to get a letter or a phone call from somebody: *Have you* ***heard*** *from your sister?*
hear of a person or thing to know about a person or thing: *Who is he? I've never* ***heard*** *of him.*
will not hear of something will not agree to something: *My father wouldn't* ***hear*** *of me paying for the meal.*

WHICH WORD? **Hear** or **listen**?
Hear with sense 1 above and **listen** are used in different ways.
- When you **hear** something, sounds come to your ears: *I* ***heard*** *the door close.*
- When you **listen to** something, you are trying to hear it: *I* ***listen*** *to the radio every morning.*

SPELLING Be careful! Don't confuse **hear** with **here**, which has a different meaning.

hearing (say **heer**-ring) *noun* (*no plural*)
the ability to hear: *Speak louder – her* ***hearing*** *isn't very good.*

hearing aid *noun* (*plural* **hearing aids**)
a small machine that fits inside the ear and helps people to hear better

hearse (say **hurss**) *noun* (*plural* **hearses**)
a large car used for carrying a dead person's body to their funeral

heart (say **haat**) *noun*
1 (*plural* **hearts**) the organ in the chest that sends blood around the body: *Your* ***heart*** *beats faster when you run.* ➲ See illustration at **organ**
2 (*plural* **hearts**) your feelings: *She has a kind* ***heart*** (= she is kind). ◇ *It broke his* ***heart*** *when his wife died.* ◇ *My* ***heart*** *sank when I saw my report.*
3 (*no plural*) the centre or middle part: *They live in the* ***heart*** *of Johannesburg.*
4 (*plural* **hearts**) the shape ♥
5 hearts (*plural noun*) the group of playing cards (called a **suit**) that have red shapes like hearts on them: *the six of* ***hearts***
by heart so that you know every word: *I have learned the poem by* ***heart****.*
lose heart to stop hoping: *Don't lose* ***heart*** *– keep trying.*

heart

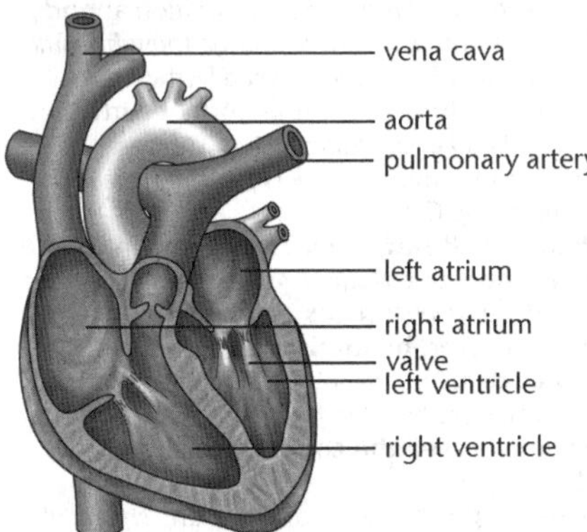

the human heart

heartache (say **haat**-ayk) *noun* (*no plural*)
a strong feeling of sadness

heart attack *noun* (*plural* **heart attacks**)
a sudden dangerous illness, when your heart stops working properly: *She had a* ***heart attack*** *and died.*

heartbeat (say **haat**-beet) *noun* (*plural* **heartbeats**)
the movement or sound of your heart as it pushes blood around your body

heartbroken (say **haat**-broh-kuhn) *adjective*
extremely sad because of something that has happened: *Bongi was* ***heartbroken*** *when her dog died.*

heartless (say **haat**-luhss) *adjective*
not kind but cruel

hearty (say **haa**-tee) *adjective* (**heartier, heartiest**)
1 showing warm and friendly feelings: *a **hearty** welcome*
2 loud, happy and full of energy: *He gave a **hearty** laugh.*
3 large, that makes you feel full: *We ate a **hearty** breakfast.*
▶ **heartily** (*adverb*): *He sang **heartily**.*

heat[1] (say **heet**) *noun*
1 (*no plural*) the feeling of something hot: *the **heat** of the sun*
2 (*no plural*) hot weather: *I love the **heat**.* ➲ OPPOSITE **cold**[2] 1
3 (*plural* **heats**) one of the first parts of a race or competition

heat[2] (say **heet**) *verb* (**heating, heated**) (also **heat up**)
to make something hot or to become hot: *I **heated** some milk in a saucepan.* ◇ *Let the oven **heat** up before you put the food in.*

heater (say **heet**-uh) *noun* (*plural* **heaters**)
a thing that makes a place warm: *Switch on the **heater** if you feel cold.*

heathen (say **hee*th***-uhn) *noun* (*plural* **heathens**) (*old-fashioned*)
a person who does not belong to one of the world's main religions
ℹ ORIGIN: from Old English *hǣthen*, based on an older word meaning 'living in open country (not in a town)'. The word probably changed in meaning because rural people living far away from towns were converted to Christianity later than people in towns.

heating (say **heet**-ing) *noun* (*no plural*)
a way of making a room or a building warm: *We use gas for **heating**.*

heatstroke (say **heet**-strohk) *noun* (*no plural*)
a serious medical condition that you can get if you are in a hot place for too long: *The hikers suffered from **heatstroke** and had to be taken to hospital.*

heave[1] (say **heev**) *verb* (**heaving, heaved**)
to lift or pull something heavy: *We **heaved** the suitcase up the stairs.*

heave[2] (say **heev**) *noun* (*plural* **heaves**)
a strong push, pull or lift: *Okay, one more **heave** should get the car going.*

heaven (say **hev**-uhn) *noun* (*no plural*)
1 the place where many people believe God lives and where good people go to when they die ➲ See **hell**
2 a place or a thing that makes you very happy: *Our holiday was **heaven**!*
the heavens the sky
▶ **heavenly** (*adjective*): *a **heavenly** day*

heavy (say **hev**-ee) *adjective* (**heavier, heaviest**)
1 weighing a lot and difficult to lift or move: *I can't carry this bag – it's too **heavy**.* ➲ OPPOSITE **light**[1] 3
2 larger, stronger or more than usual: ***heavy** rain* ◇ *The traffic was very **heavy** this morning.* ➲ OPPOSITE **light**[1] 4
▶ **heavily** (*adverb*): *It was raining **heavily**.*

heavy metal *noun* (*no plural*)
a kind of very loud rock music

Hebrew (say **hee**-broo) *noun* (*no plural*)
the language of the people who live in Israel and the religious language of Jewish people generally

heckle (say **hek**-l) *verb* (**heckling, heckled**)
to interrupt a speaker at a public meeting with difficult questions or rude comments: *People were **heckling** the speaker.*
▶ **heckler** (*noun*): *There were **hecklers** in the audience.*

hectare (say **hek**-tair) *noun* (*plural* **hectares**) (abbr. ha)
a measure of land, equal to 10 000 square metres

hectic (say **hek**-tik) *adjective*
very busy: *I had a **hectic** day at work.*

hecto- (say **hek**-toh) *prefix*
one hundred: *A **hectolitre** is one hundred litres.*

he'd (say **heed**) short for **he had; he would**

hedge (say **hej**) *noun* (*plural* **hedges**)
a line of small trees planted around the edge of a garden or park

hedgehog (say **hej**-hog) *noun* (*plural* **hedgehogs**)
a small animal covered with hard sharp hairs (called **prickles**)

heed *verb* (**heeding, heeded**)
to pay attention to something: *I **heeded** your advice.*
▶ **heed** (*noun*): *Take **heed** of your principal's advice.*

heel *noun* (*plural* **heels**)
1 the back part of your foot ➲ See illustration at **foot**
2 the back part of a shoe under the **heel** of your foot
3 the part of a sock that covers the **heel** of your foot

height (say **hite**) *noun*
1 (*plural* **heights**) how far it is from the bottom to the top of a person or thing: *What is the*

A B C D E F G H I J K L M N O P Q R S T U V W X Y Z

height of this mountain? ◇ *The wall is two metres in* ***height****.* ➲ See illustration at **length**
2 (*plural* **heights**) a high place: *I'm afraid of* ***heights****.*
3 (*no plural*) the strongest or most important part of something: *the* ***height*** *of summer*

heighten (say **hite**-uhn) *verb* (**heightening, heightened**)
to become or to make something stronger or bigger: *My sense of hearing was* ***heightened*** *when I was at home alone.*
▸ **heightened** (*adjective*): *Dogs have a* ***heightened*** *sense of smell.*

heir (say **air**) *noun* (*plural* **heirs**)
a person who gets money or property when another person dies: *He's the* ***heir*** *to a large fortune.*

heiress (say **air**-ess) *noun* (*plural* **heiresses**)
an **heir** who is a woman

heirloom (say **air**-loom) *noun* (*plural* **heirlooms**)
something valuable that has belonged to the same family for a long time: *This jewellery is a family* ***heirloom****.*

held form of **hold**[2]

helicopter (say **hel**-i-kop-tuh) *noun* (*plural* **helicopters**)
an aircraft without wings that has large blades (called **rotors**) on top that go round. It can fly straight up from the ground and stay in one position in the air.

helium (say **heel**-i-uhm) *noun* (*no plural*) (symbol He)
a very light colourless gas that does not burn: ***helium*** *balloons*

helix (say **heel**-ikss) *noun* (*plural* **helices**)
a curve like a **spiral** (= a line that moves round and round away from a central point) or a spring: *A* ***helix*** *can look like a wire wound round a cylinder, or like a wire wound round a cone.*

hell (say **hel**) *noun* (*no plural*)
the place where some people believe that bad people go when they die ➲ See **heaven**

he'll (say **hee**-uhl) short for **he will**

hello (say **hel**-oh) *exclamation*
a word that you say when you meet somebody or when you answer the telephone ➲ See note at **good morning**

helm (say **helm**) *noun* (*plural* **helms**)
the part of a boat or ship that guides it. The helm can be a handle or a wheel

helmet (say **hel**-mit) *noun* (*plural* **helmets**)
a hard hat that keeps your head safe

help[1] (say **help**) *verb* (**helping, helped**)
1 to do something useful for somebody or to make somebody's work easier: *Will you* ***help*** *me with the washing-up?* ◇ *She* ***helped*** *me to carry the box.*
2 a word that you shout when you are in danger: ***Help!*** *I can't swim!*
can't help to not be able to stop yourself from doing something: *It was so funny that I couldn't* ***help*** *laughing.*
help yourself to take something that you want: ***Help*** *yourself to a biscuit.*

help[2] (say **help**) *noun* (*no plural*)
1 the act of helping somebody: *Thank you for all your* ***help****.* ◇ *Do you need any* ***help****?*
2 a person or thing that helps: *He was a great* ***help*** *to me when I was ill.*

helpful (say **help**-fuhl) *adjective*
1 able to improve a situation: ***helpful*** *advice* ➲ SYNONYM **useful**
2 (about a person) wanting to help you: *The waiter was very* ***helpful****.* ➲ OPPOSITE **unhelpful**
▸ **helpfully** (*adverb*): *She* ***helpfully*** *carried my bags.*

helping (say **help**-ing) *noun* (*plural* **helpings**)
the amount of food on your plate: *I had a big* ***helping*** *of pie.*

helpless (say **help**-luhss) *adjective*
not able to do things without help: *Babies are totally* ***helpless****.*

hem *noun* (*plural* **hems**)
the bottom edge of something such as a skirt or trousers, that is folded and sewn

hemisphere (say **hem**-iss-feer) *noun* (*plural* **hemispheres**) (*geography*)
one half of the Earth, especially the half above or below the **equator**: *the northern* ***hemisphere***
ⓘ ORIGIN: 14th–15th century, through Old French and Latin from Greek *hēmisphairion*, from *hēmi-* meaning 'half' + *sphaira* meaning 'sphere'

hemp (say **hemp**) *noun* (*no plural*)
the **cannabis** plant, especially when grown to make rope and rough cloth from

hen *noun* (*plural* **hens**)
a female bird, especially a chicken, that people keep on farms for its eggs ➲ See **chicken**

hence (say **henss**) *adverb*
1 (*formal*) for this reason: *Less fog means more sunshine and* ***hence*** *higher temperatures.*
2 from this time: *We don't know what will happen five years* ***hence****.*

henry (say **hen**-ree) *noun* (*plural* **henries** or **henrys**) (abbr. H)
a measure of inductance (= electricity moving with magnets)

hepatitis (say hep-uh-**tite**-uhss) *noun* (*no plural*)
a serious disease of one of the body's main organs (called the **liver**)

hepta- (say **hep**-tuh) *prefix*
seven: *A **heptagon** has seven sides.*

heptagon (say **hep**-tuh-guhn) *noun* (*plural* **heptagons**) (*maths*)
a flat closed shape with seven straight sides
▸ **heptagonal** (*adjective*)

heptahedron (say hep-tuh-**hee**-druhn) (*plural* **heptahedra** or **heptahedrons**) (*maths*)
a solid shape with seven flat surfaces

her[1] (say **hur**) *pronoun* (*plural* **them**)
a word that shows the woman or girl that you have just talked about: *Tell Jane that I'll see **her** tonight.* ◇ *I wrote to **her** yesterday.*

her[2] (say **hur**) *adjective*
of or belonging to the woman or girl that you have just talked about: *That's **her** book.* ◇ *Aisha has hurt **her** leg.*

herald (say **he**-ruhld) *verb* (**heralding, heralded**)
to be a sign that something is going to happen soon: *This news could **herald** a change in the economy.*
▸ **herald** (*noun*): *Jacaranda flowers are a **herald** of summer.*

herb (say **hurb**) *noun* (*plural* **herbs**)
a plant whose leaves, seeds or roots are used in medicine or in cooking ➲ See **spice**

herbalist (say **hurb**-uh-list) *noun* (*plural* **herbalists**)
a person who uses special plants (called **herbs**) as medicine
▸ **herbalism** (*noun*)

herbicide (say **hurb**-i-side) *noun* (*plural* **herbicides**)
a chemical substance you use to kill plants that you do not want

herbivore (say **hurb**-i-vaw) *noun* (*plural* **herbivores**)
an animal that only eats grass and other plants
➲ See **carnivore, insectivore, omnivore**
▸ **herbivorous** (*adjective*): *A cow is a **herbivorous** mammal.*

herd[1] (say **hurd**) *noun* (*plural* **herds**)
a big group of animals of the same kind: *a **herd** of cows* ➲ See **flock**[2]

herd[2] (say **hurd**) *verb* (**herding, herded**)
to move people or animals somewhere together in a group: *Can you **herd** those sheep through the gate?*

herder (say **hurd**-uh) *noun* (*plural* **herders**)
a person who looks after a group of animals such as cows or goats

here (say **heer**) *adverb*
in, at or to this place: *Your books are **here**.* ◇ *Come **here**, please.* ◇ ***Here's** my pen.* ◇ ***Here** comes the bus.* ➲ See **there** 2
here and there in different places: *There were groups of people **here** and there along the beach.*
here goes (*informal*) words that you say before you do something exciting or dangerous: *'**Here** goes,' said Dudu, and jumped into the river.*
here you are words that you say when you give a person something: *'Can I borrow a pen, please?' 'Yes, **here** you are.'*

> SPELLING Be careful! Don't confuse **here** with **hear**, which has a different meaning.

hereditary (say huh-**red**-i-tree) *adjective*
referring to a characteristic passed on from parent to child: ***hereditary** diseases* ◇ *a **hereditary** monarchy*

heredity (say huh-**red**-i-tee) *noun* (*no plural*)
the process by which physical or mental qualities pass from parent to child

heretic (say **he**-ruh-tik) *noun* (*plural* **heretics**)
a person whose religious beliefs are thought to be wrong or evil

heritage (say **he**-ri-tij) *noun* (*no plural*)
the traditions, qualities and culture of a country that have existed for a long time and have great importance for the country: *Are you proud of your **heritage**?*
🛈 ORIGIN: 13th–15th century, from Old French *heritage*, from *heriter* meaning 'inherit'

Heritage Site *noun* (*plural* **Heritage Sites**)
a place of historical, environmental or cultural importance: *St Lucia became a World **Heritage Site** .*

hermaphrodite (say hur-**maf**-ruh-dite) *noun* (*plural* **hermaphrodites**)
an animal or a plant that has both male and female sexual organs or characteristics

hermit (say **hur**-mit) *noun* (*plural* **hermits**)
a person who prefers to live alone, without contact with other people

hero (say **heer**-roh) *noun* (*plural* **heroes**)
1 a person, especially a man, who has done something brave or good: *Anele was a **hero** when he saved his sister from the fire.*

2 the most important man or boy in a book, play or film ➲ See **heroine**
▸ **heroic** (*adjective*): *a **heroic** act*

heroin (say **he**-roh-in) *noun* (*no plural*)
a very strong illegal drug

heroine (say **he**-roh-in) *noun* (*plural* **heroines**)
1 a woman who has done something brave or good
2 the most important woman or girl in a book, play or film: *The **heroine** of the story is a brave little girl.*

heron (say **he**-ruhn) *noun* (*plural* **herons**)
a large bird with a long neck and long legs that lives near water

herring (say **he**-ring) *noun* (*plural* **herring** or **herrings**)
a small silver fish that swims in the sea in a large group (a **shoal**) and is used for food

hers (say **hurz**) *pronoun*
something that belongs to her: *Gcina says this book is **hers**.* ◇ *Are these keys **hers**?*

herself (say hur-**self**) *pronoun* (*plural* **themselves**)
1 a word that shows the same woman or girl that you have just talked about: *She fell and hurt **herself**.*
2 a word that makes 'she' stronger: *'Who told you that Deneo was married?' 'She told me **herself**.'*
by herself
1 without other people: *She lives by **herself**.* ➲ SYNONYM **alone** 1
2 without help: *She can carry the box by **herself**.*

hertz (say **hurtss**) *noun* (*plural* **hertz**) (abbr. Hz)
a unit for measuring **frequency** 3: *The average person can hear sounds between 20 and 20 000 **hertz**.*
❶ ORIGIN: 19th century, named after Heinrich Hertz (1857–1894), a German scientist

he's (say **heez**) short for **he is; he has**

WHICH WORD? **He's** or **his**?
Be careful! Don't confuse these words. They should be pronounced differently, and they have different meanings: ***He's** going now!* ◇ *Max brought **his** sister.*

hesitant (say **hez**-i-tuhnt) *adjective*
slow to speak or act because you are not sure whether you should or not: *I was **hesitant** to sign the contract.* ➲ SYNONYM **tentative** 2
▸ **hesitancy** (*noun*) ▸ **hesitantly** (*adverb*)

hesitate (say **hez**-i-tayt) *verb* (**hesitating, hesitated**)
to stop for a moment before you do or say something because you are not sure about it: *He **hesitated** before answering the question.*
▸ **hesitation** (*noun*): *They agreed without **hesitation**.*

hessian (say **hess**-i-uhn) *noun* (*no plural*)
a strong rough brown cloth that is used especially for making large bags (called **sacks**)

heterosexual (say het-roh-**sek**-shuul) *adjective*
attracted to someone of the opposite sex ➲ See **homosexual**
▸ **heterosexual** (*noun*)

hexa- (say **hekss**-uh) *prefix*
six: *A **hexagon** has six sides.*

hexadecimal (say hekss-uh-**dess**-i-muhl) *adjective* (*maths*)
relating to a number system that uses 16 as its base

hexagon (say **hekss**-uh-guhn) *noun* (*plural* **hexagons**) (*maths*)
a flat closed shape with six straight sides
▸ **hexagonal** (*adjective*): *a **hexagonal** box*

hexahedron (say hekss-uh-**hee**-druhn) *noun* (*plural* **hexahedra** or **hexahedrons**) (*maths*)
a solid shape with six flat surfaces

hey (say **hay**) *exclamation* (*informal*)
a word that you say to make somebody listen to you, or when you are surprised: ***Hey**! Where are you going?*

hi (say **hy**) *exclamation* (*informal*)
a word that you say when you meet somebody: *Hi Tony! How are you?* ➲ SYNONYM **hello**

hibernate (say **hibe**-uh-nayt) *verb* (**hibernating, hibernated**)
(used about animals in very cold areas) to go to sleep for the winter

hiccup (say **hik**-up) *noun* (*plural* **hiccups**) (also **hiccough**)
a sudden noise that you make in your throat, for example when you have eaten or drunk too quickly.

hide[1] (*rhymes with* **side**) *verb* (**hiding, hid, has hidden**)
1 to put something where people cannot find it: *I **hid** the money under the bed.*
2 to be or get in a place where people cannot see or find you: *Somebody was **hiding** behind the door.*
3 to not tell or show something to somebody: *She tried to **hide** her feelings.*

hide[2] (*rhymes with* **side**) *noun* (*plural* **hides**)
1 the skin of an animal, used for making leather: *a zebra **hide** mat.*

2 a place from which you can watch birds or animals without them seeing you: *a bird **hide***

hide-and-seek (say hide-uhn-**seek**) *noun* (*no plural*)
a children's game in which one player covers his or her eyes while the other players hide, and then tries to find them

hideous (say **hid**-i-uhss) *adjective*
very ugly: *That shirt is **hideous!***

hiding (say **hide**-ing) *noun* (*no plural*)
be in hiding, **go into hiding** to be in, or to go into a place where people will not find you: *The police believe that the escaped prisoners are in **hiding**.*

hierarchy (say **hy**-raa-kee) *noun* (*plural* **hierarchies**)
a system or organization that has many levels from the lowest to the highest: *You can move up the **hierarchy**.*
▸ **hierarchical** (*adjective*): *This company has a **hierarchical** structure.*

hieroglyphics (say hy-ruh-**glif**-ikss) *plural noun*
the system of writing that was used in ancient Egypt in which a small picture represents a word or sound

hi-fi (say **hy**-fy) *noun* (*plural* **hi-fis**)
a machine for playing CDs, tapes and records

high¹ (say **hy**) *adjective* (**higher**, **highest**)
1 having a long distance between the top and the bottom: *a **high** wall ◇ Mount Everest is the **highest** mountain in the world.*
2 the word you use to say or ask how far something is from the bottom to the top: *The table is 80 cm **high**.*
3 far from the ground: *a **high** shelf*
4 more than the usual level or amount: *The car was travelling at **high** speed. ◇ **high** temperatures*
5 (about a sound) not deep: *I heard the **high** voice of a child.* ➲ The noun is **height**
➲ OPPOSITE **low**

> WHICH WORD? **Tall** or **high**?
> - We use **high** to describe things that are high above the ground: *a **high** branch ◇ **high** clouds ◇ a **high** fence ◇ a **high** mountain ◇ a **high** table ◇ a **high** wall.*
> - **Tall** describes things that have a certain shape. They are usually high above the ground also: *a **tall** giraffe ◇ a **tall** person.*
> - We can use both **tall** and **high** for some things: *a **high** building ◇ a **tall** building ◇ a **high** tree ◇ a **tall** tree.*

high² (say **hy**) *adverb* (**higher**, **highest**)
a long way above the ground: *The plane flew high above the clouds.* ➲ OPPOSITE **low** 1
high and low everywhere: *I've looked **high** and low, but I can't find my keys.*

higher education *noun* (*no plural*)
education at a university, or a university of technology after the age of 18 ➲ See **tertiary**

high jump *noun* (*no plural*)
a sport where people jump over a high bar

highlight¹ (say **hy**-lite) *noun* (*plural* **highlights**)
the best or most exciting part of something: *The **highlight** of our holiday was a visit to the palace.*

highlight² (say **hy**-lite) *verb* (**highlighting**, **highlighted**)
1 to emphasize something so that people give it special attention: *This report **highlights** the needs of the poor.*
2 to mark part of a text with a different colour so that people give it more attention: ***Highlight** the lines you're going to read.*

highly (say **hy**-lee) *adverb*
1 very or very much: *Their children are **highly** intelligent. ◇ She has a **highly** paid job.*
2 very well: *I think very **highly** of your work* (= I think it is very good).

Highness (say **hy**-nuhss) *noun* (*plural* **Highnesses**)
a word that you use when speaking to or about a royal person: *Yes, Your **Highness**.*

high school *noun* (*plural* **high schools**) (*also* **secondary school**)
a school for young people in Grades 8 to 12

high-tech (say hy-**tek**) *adjective* (*also* **hi-tech**) (*informal*)
using the most modern methods and machines, especially electronic ones: *The country's future is in **high-tech** industries.*

highveld (say **hy**-felt) *noun* (*no plural*)
the highveld the high-lying flat land in the inner region of South Africa: *Gauteng is on the **highveld**.*
ⓘ ORIGIN: 19th century, from Afrikaans *hoëveld* meaning 'high land'

highway (say **hy**-way) *noun* (*plural* **highways**)
a wide main road that connects one town to another

hijack (say **hy**-jak) *verb* (**hijacking**, **hijacked**)
to take control of a plane or a car and make the pilot or driver take you somewhere or give you something against your wishes
▸ **hijacker** (*noun*): *The **hijackers** threatened to blow up the plane.*

hike (*rhymes with* **bike**) *noun* (*plural* **hikes**)
a long walk in the country: *We're going for a*

A B C D E F G H I J K L M N O P Q R S T U V W X Y Z

hike in the mountains. ➲ SYNONYM **trek**
▸ **hike** (*verb*): *They went* ***hiking*** *in Malawi.*

hilarious (say hi-**lair**-ri-uhss) *adjective*
very funny: *That movie was* ***hilarious!***
▸ **hilariously** (*adverb*) ▸ **hilarity** (*noun*): *There was great* ***hilarity*** *at the party.*

hill (say **hil**) *noun* (*plural* **hills**)
a high piece of land that is not as high as a mountain: *I pushed my bike up the* ***hill.*** ◇ *Their house is at the top of the* ***hill.*** ➲ See **downhill**, **uphill**
▸ **hilly** (*adjective*): *The land is very* ***hilly*** *in this area*

him *pronoun* (*plural* **them**)
a word that shows a man or boy: *Where's Andile? I can't see* ***him.*** ◇ *I spoke to* ***him*** *yesterday.*

himself (say him-**self**) *pronoun* (*plural* **themselves**)
1 a word that shows the same man or boy that you have just talked about: *Sfiso looked at* ***himself*** *in the mirror.*
2 a word that makes 'he' stronger: *Did he make this cake* ***himself?***
by himself
1 without other people: *Dad went shopping by* ***himself.*** ➲ SYNONYM **alone** 1
2 without help: *He did it by* ***himself.***

hind (say **hynd**) *adjective*
(used about an animal's body) at the back: ***hind*** *legs*

hinder (say **hin**-duh) *verb* (**hindering, hindered**)
to make it more difficult to do something: *Teachers are* ***hindered*** *by a lack of resources.*

Hindi (say **hin**-dee) *noun* (*no plural*)
one of the languages of the people who live in India

hindsight (say **hynd**-site) *noun* (*no plural*)
the understanding that you have of a situation only after it has happened: *In* ***hindsight*** *that was a silly thing to do.* ◇ *With* ***hindsight*** *I wouldn't have lent him those books.* ➲ See **foresight**

Hindu (say **hin**-doo or hin-**doo**) *noun* (*plural* **Hindus**)
a person who follows the religion of **Hinduism**

Hinduism (say **hin**-doo-iz-uhm) *noun* (*no plural*)
the main religion of India which includes the worship of one or more gods and the belief that after death, people return in a different form (called **reincarnation**)

hinge[1] (say **hinj**) *noun* (*plural* **hinges**)
a piece of metal that joins a lid to a box or a door to a frame so that you can open and close it

hinge[2] (say **hinj**) *verb* (**hinging, hinged**)
to depend on something: *Everything* ***hinges*** *on today's meeting.*

hint[1] *noun* (*plural* **hints**)
1 something that you say, but not in a direct way: *He keeps dropping* ***hints*** (= making hints) *about wanting a bike for his birthday.*
2 a piece of advice or information: *helpful* ***hints***
3 a small amount of something: *There's a* ***hint*** *of garlic in the soup.*

hint[2] *verb* (**hinting, hinted**)
to say something, but not in a direct way: *She* ***hinted*** *that she was unhappy.*

hinterland (say **hin**-tuh-land) *noun* (*no plural*)
the areas of a country that are away from the coast, a large river or the main cities

hip (*rhymes with* **lip**) *noun* (*plural* **hips**)
the place where your leg joins the side of your body ➲ See illustration at **body** ➲ See illustration at **skeleton**

hippie (say **hip**-ee) *noun* (*plural* **hippies**) (also **hippy**)
a person who refuses to accept the Western way of life. They often had long hair, wore brightly coloured clothes and took illegal drugs. Their movement was most popular in the 1960s in America.

hippo (say **hip**-oh) *noun* (*plural* **hippos**) (*informal*)
a **hippopotamus**

hippopotamus (say hip-uh-**pot**-uh-muhss) *noun* (*plural* **hippopotamuses** or **hippopotami**)
a large African animal with a thick skin that lives in or near water

hire (say **hy**-uh) *verb* (**hiring, hired**)
1 to pay to use something for a short time: *We* ***hired*** *a car when we were on holiday.* ➲ See **rent**[2] 1
2 to pay somebody to do a job for you: *We* ***hired*** *somebody to mend the roof.*
hire something out to let somebody use something for a short time, in return for money: *They* ***hire*** *out bicycles.* ➲ See **rent**[2] 2
▸ **hire** (*noun*): *Have you got any boats for* ***hire?***
▸ **hired** (*adjective*): *a* ***hired*** *car*

his[1] (say **hiz**) *adjective*
of or belonging to the man or boy that you

have just talked about: *Piet came with **his** sister.* ◇ *He has hurt **his** arm.*

WHICH WORD? **His** or **he's**?
- Be careful! Don't confuse these words. They should be pronounced differently, and they have different meanings.
- **He's** is short for **he is** or **he has**: ***He's** coming now!*

his² (say **hiz**) *pronoun*
something that belongs to him: *Are these books yours or **his**?*

hiss (*rhymes with* **kiss**) *verb* (**hissing, hissed**)
to make a noise like a very long **s**: *The snake **hissed** at me.*
▸ **hiss** (*noun*): *the **hiss** of steam*

histogram (say **hiss**-tuh-gram) *noun* (*plural* **histograms**)
a diagram showing amounts as vertical bars, which can be of different heights and of different widths: *The **histogram** showed the monthly rainfall figures in our village.* ➲ See **graph**

historian (say hiss-**taw**-ri-uhn) *noun* (*plural* **historians**)
a person who studies or writes about history, or is an expert in history

historic (say hiss-**to**-rik) *adjective*
important in history: *It was a **historic** moment when a person first walked on the moon.*

historical (say hiss-**to**-rik-l) *adjective*
1 connected with real people or events in the past: *She writes **historical** novels.*
2 connected with the study of history: ***historical** records*

history (say **hiss**-tree) *noun* (*no plural*)
1 all the things that happened in the past: *It was an important moment in **history**.*
2 the study of things that happened in the past: ***History** is my favourite subject.*

hit¹ *verb* (**hitting, hit, has hit**)
to touch a person or thing hard: *He **hit** me on the head with a book.* ◇ *The car **hit** a wall.* ◇ *I **hit** my knee on the chair.*

hit² *noun* (*plural* **hits**)
1 the act of touching a person or thing hard: *That was a good **hit**!* (= in a game of cricket or baseball, for example)
2 a person or a thing that a lot of people like: *This song was a **hit** last year.*
3 (*computing*) a result of a search on a computer, especially on the Internet

hitch¹ (say **hich**) *verb* (**hitching, hitched**)
1 hitchhike
2 to fasten one thing to another: *We **hitched** the trailer to the car.*
3 to raise or pull something up with a quick movement: *She **hitched** up her skirt to climb the tree.*

hitch² (say **hich**) *noun* (*plural* **hitches**)
a small problem or difficulty: *There was a technical **hitch** before the show.*

hitchhike (say **hich**-hike) *verb* (**hitchhiking, hitchhiked**) (also **hitch**)
to travel by asking for free rides in cars and trucks: *We **hitchhiked** across Europe.*
▸ **hitchhiker** (*noun*): *We gave a **hitchhiker** a lift.*

HIV (say aych-y-**vee**) *noun* (*no plural*)
the **virus** that can cause AIDS ❶ **HIV** is short for 'human immunodeficiency virus'.
be HIV-positive to have HIV
be HIV-negative not to have HIV ➲ See **AIDS**

hive (*rhymes with* **five**) *noun* (*plural* **hives**) (also **beehive**)
a box where bees live

hoard (say **hawd**) *noun* (*plural* **hoards**)
a secret store of something, for example food or money: *a **hoard** of gold*
▸ **hoard** (*verb*): *The old man **hoarded** the money under his bed.*

SPELLING Be careful! Don't confuse **hoard** with **horde**, which has a different meaning.

hoarse (say **hawss**) *adjective*
(used about your voice) rough and quiet, for example because you have a cold: *He spoke in a **hoarse** whisper.*

hoax (say **hohkss**) *noun* (*plural* **hoaxes**)
a trick that makes somebody believe something that is not true: *There was no bomb in the station – it was a **hoax**.*

hob *noun* (*plural* **hobs**)
the heating surface at the top of a stove, used for frying and boiling things

hobble (say **hob**-l) *verb* (**hobbling, hobbled**)
1 to walk with difficulty because your feet or ankles are hurt: *I **hobbled** home after the race.*
2 to tie an animal's legs together so it cannot run away: *The farmer **hobbled** the injured sheep.*

hobby (say **hob**-ee) *noun* (*plural* **hobbies**)
something that you like doing in your free time: *My **hobbies** are reading and swimming.*
➲ SYNONYM **pastime**

hockey (say **hok**-ee) *noun* (*no plural*)
a game for two teams of eleven players who hit

A B C D E F G H I J K L M N O P Q R S T U V W X Y Z

a small hard ball with long curved sticks on a field (called a **pitch**)

hocus-pocus (say hoh-kuhss-**poh**-kuhss) *noun* (*no plural*)
talk or behaviour that is nonsense and meant to confuse people: *This new diet looks like **hocus-pocus** to me.*

hoe (*rhymes with* **go**) *noun* (*plural* **hoes**)
a garden tool with a long handle that you use for turning the soil and removing plants that you do not want
▸ **hoe** (*verb*): *Were you **hoeing** the vegetable patch this morning?*

hog *noun* (*plural* **hogs**)
a male pig kept for its meat

hoist (say **hoyst**) *verb* (**hoisting, hoisted**)
to lift or pull something up, usually using ropes: *The injured whale was **hoisted** onto the ship.*

hold[1] (say **hohld**) *noun* (*no plural*)
the part of a ship or plane where goods are kept
get hold of somebody to find somebody so that you can speak to them: *I'm trying to get **hold** of Peter but he's not at home.*
get hold of something
1 (also **take hold of something**) to take something in your hands: *Get **hold** of the rope!*
2 to find something: *I can't get **hold** of the book I need.*

hold[2] (say **hohld**) *verb* (**holding, held**)
1 to have something in your hand or arms: *She was **holding** a gun. ◇ He **held** the baby in his arms.*
2 to keep something in a certain way: ***Hold** your hand up. ◇ Try to **hold** the camera still.*
3 to support the weight of a person or thing: *Are you sure that branch will **hold** you?*
4 to have space for a certain number or amount: *The car **holds** five people.*
5 to make something happen: *The meeting was **held** in the town hall.*
Hold it! (*informal*) Wait! Don't move!
hold a person or **thing back** to stop a person or thing from moving forwards: *The police **held** back the crowd.*
hold on
1 (*informal*) to wait: ***Hold** on, I'm coming.*
2 to keep holding something tightly: *The child **held** on to her mother's hand.*
hold a person or **thing up**
1 to make a person or thing late: *The plane was **held** up for 40 minutes.*
2 to try to steal from a place, using a gun: *Two men **held** up a bank in Gauteng today.*

hold-up (say **hohld**-up) *noun* (*plural* **hold-ups**)
1 something that makes you wait: *There was a long **hold-up** on the highway.* ➲ SYNONYM **delay**[1]
2 when somebody tries to rob somebody using a gun: *There's been a **hold-up** at the local supermarket.* ➲ SYNONYM **robbery**

hole (say **hohl**) *noun* (*plural* **holes**)
an empty space or opening in something: *I'm going to dig a **hole** in the garden. ◇ My socks are full of **holes**.*

holiday (say **hol**-i-day) *noun* (*plural* **holidays**)
1 a time when you do not go to work or school, and often travel and stay away from home: *The school **holidays** start next week. ◇ a summer **holiday** ◇ Mrs Smith is away on **holiday**.*
2 a day when most people do not go to work or school, especially because of a religious or national celebration: *Next Monday is a **holiday**.*

hollow (say **hol**-oh) *adjective*
with an empty space inside: *A drum is **hollow**.*

holly (say **hol**-ee) *noun* (*no plural*)
a plant that has leaves with a lot of sharp points, and red berries

holocaust (say **hol**-uh-kawst) *noun*
1 (*plural* **holocausts**) a situation where a large number of things are destroyed and people killed: *a nuclear **holocaust***
2 the Holocaust (*no plural*) the murder of millions of Jews in Germany between 1941 and 1945
🛈 ORIGIN: 13th–15th century, through Old French and Latin from Greek *holokauston*, from *holos* meaning 'whole' + *kaustos* meaning 'burnt'

holster (say **hohl**-stuh) *noun* (*plural* **holsters**)
a leather case for a gun that a person wears on a belt or under their arm

holy (say **hoh**-lee) *adjective* (**holier, holiest**)
1 very special because it is about God or a god: *The Bible is the **holy** book of Christians.*
2 (about a person) living a good and religious life

Holy Communion ➲ See **communion** 2

homage (say **hom**-ij) *noun* (*no plural*)
something that is said or done to show public respect for somebody: *The band paid **homage** to great singers.*

home[1] (say **hohm**) *noun* (*plural* **homes**)
1 the place where you live: *He left **home*** (= stopped living in his parents' house) *at the age of 18.*
2 a place where they look after people, for example children who have no parents, or old people: *My grandmother lives in a retirement **home**.*

at home in your house or flat: *I stayed at* ***home*** *yesterday.* ◇ *Is your aunt at* ***home****?*

home[2] (say **hohm**) *adverb*
to the place where you live

USAGE Be careful! We do not use **to** before **home** in sentences like these: *Let's go* ***home****. What time did you get* ***home*** *last night?*

home[3] (say **hohm**) *adjective*
connected with your **home[1]** 1 or your country: *What is your* ***home*** *address?* ◇ ***home*** *cooking*
▸ **homely** (*adjective*): *a* ***homely*** *atmosphere*

homeland (say **hohm**-luhnd) *noun* (*plural* **homelands**)
1 the country where you or your parents were born
2 (*history*) an area that was meant for black people during apartheid: *The Transkei was a* ***homeland*** *until 1993.*

homeless (say **hohm**-luhss) *adjective*
not having anywhere to live: *The floods made many people* ***homeless****.*

home-made (say **hohm**-mayd) *adjective*
made in your house, not bought in a shop: ***home-made*** *bread*

home page *noun* (*plural* **home pages**)
the first of a number of pages of information on the Internet that belongs to a person or an organization. This page contains connections to other pages of information.

homesick (say **hohm**-sik) *adjective*
sad because you are away from home

homeward (say **hohm**-wuhd) *adjective, adverb*
going towards home: *a* ***homeward*** *direction* ◇ *Let's go* ***homeward*** *and stop along the way.*

homework (say **hohm**-wurk) *noun* (*no plural*)
work that a teacher gives to you to do at home: *Have you done your English* ***homework****?*

homicide (say **hom**-i-side) *noun* (*no plural*)
the illegal killing of one person by another
➲ SYNONYM **murder[1]**

hominid (say **hom**-uh-nid) *noun* (*plural* **hominids**)
a member of the family which includes all forms of humans, both living and **extinct**: *Homo sapiens and Australopithecus belong to the* ***hominid*** *family.*

homo- (say **hom**-oh or **hoh**-moh) *prefix*
the same: *A* ***homophone*** *is a word that sounds the same as another word.*
ⓘ ORIGIN: from Greek *homos* meaning 'same'

homogeneous (say hoh-muh-**jeen**-i-uhss) *adjective*
made up of parts that are of the same type: *Our country is not* ***homogeneous*** *– it is made up of many different groups of people.*

homonym (say **hom**-uh-nim) *noun* (*plural* **homonyms**)
a word that is spelt and pronounced like another word that has a different meaning: *A bank where you keep your money and a bank on the side of a river are* ***homonyms****.*
ⓘ ORIGIN: 17th century, through Latin from Greek *homōnumon* meaning ' with the same name'

homophone (say **hom**-uh-fohn) *noun* (*plural* **homophones**)
a word that is pronounced the same as another word that is spelt differently: *Sell and cell are* ***homophones****.*

Homo sapiens (say hoh-moh **sap**-i-uhnz) *noun* (*no plural*) (*science*)
the scientific name for modern humans: ***Homo sapiens*** *is the only surviving species of the hominids.*
ⓘ ORIGIN: 18th century, from Latin, meaning 'wise man'. The name was given by Carolus Linnaeus (1707–1778), a Swedish botanist, who created the first modern system for grouping and naming living things.

homosexual (say hoh-muh-**sek**-sh*uu*-uhl) *adjective*
attracted to people of the same sex ➲ See **heterosexual**
▸ **homosexual** (*noun*)

honest (say **on**-uhst) *adjective*
describing a person who says what is true and does not steal, lie or cheat: *She's a very* ***honest*** *person.* ◇ *Be* ***honest*** *– do you really like this dress?*
➲ OPPOSITE **dishonest**
▸ **honestly** (*adverb*): *Try to answer the questions* ***honestly****.* ▸ **honesty** (*noun*): *I have doubts about his* ***honesty****.*

honey (say **hun**-ee) *noun* (*no plural*)
the sweet food that is made by bees

honey badger (say **hun**-ee **bad**-juh) *noun* (*plural* **honey badgers**)
a wild African mammal with grey and black fur that eats other small animals and honey

honeycomb (say **hun**-ee-kohm) *noun* (*no plural*)
a structure of holes (called **cells**) with six sides in which bees keep their eggs and honey

honeymoon (say **hun**-ee-moon) *noun* (*plural* **honeymoons**)
a holiday for two people who have just got married

A B C D E F G H I J K L M N O P Q R S T U V W X Y Z

honour[1] (say **on**-uh) *verb* (**honouring, honoured**)
1 to show great public respect for somebody, or to make them proud and pleased: *We can **honour** our beautiful country.*
2 to do what you have promised: *I will **honour** my promise to wash my mom's car.*

honour[2] (say **on**-uh) *noun* (*no plural*)
1 respect from other people for something good that you have done: *The principal was the guest of **honour**.*
2 something that makes you proud and pleased: *It was a great **honour** to meet Mr Mandela.*
in honour of a person or **thing** to show that you respect a person or thing: *There is a party tonight in **honour** of our visitors.*

hood (say **huud**) *noun* (*plural* **hoods**)
the part of a coat or jacket that covers your head and neck

hoof *noun* (*plural* **hoofs** or **hooves**)
the hard part of the foot of horses and some other animals

hook (say **huuk**) *noun* (*plural* **hooks**)
a curved piece of metal or plastic for hanging things on, or for catching fish with: *Hang your coat on that **hook**. ◇ a fish **hook***
off the hook (used about a telephone) not having the part that you speak into (called the **receiver**) in place so that it cannot ring
▸ **hook** (*verb*): *He **hooked** a large fish.*

hooked (say **huukt**) *adjective* (*informal*)
unable to stop wanting something: *He was **hooked** on drugs.*

hooligan (say **hool**-i-guhn) *noun* (*plural* **hooligans**)
a young person who behaves in a noisy way and fights other people: *football **hooligans***
ORIGIN: 19th century, possibly from *Hooligan*, the name of a noisy Irish family in a popular song of the 1890s

hoop *noun* (*plural* **hoops**)
a large metal or plastic ring

hooray (say huu-**ray**) *exclamation* (also **hurray**) (also **hurrah**)
a word that you shout when you are very pleased about something: ***Hooray**! She's won!*

hoot *noun* (*plural* **hoots**)
the sound that a car's horn or an **owl** makes
▸ **hoot** (*verb*): *The driver **hooted** at the dog.*

hooves (say **hoovz**) plural of **hoof**

hop *verb* (**hopping, hopped**)
1 (used about a person) to jump on one foot
2 (used about an animal or bird) to jump with two or all feet together: *The frog **hopped** onto the stone.*
▸ **hop** (*noun*): *a small **hop***

hope[1] (*rhymes with* **rope**) *verb* (**hoping, hoped**)
to want something to happen or be true: *I **hope** that you have a nice holiday. ◇ I **hope** to see you soon. ◇ She's **hoping** for a bike for her birthday. ◇ 'Do you think it will rain?' 'I **hope** not.' ◇ 'Will you be at the party?' 'I'm not sure – I **hope** so.'*

hope[2] (*rhymes with* **rope**) *noun*
1 (*plural* **hopes**) a feeling of wanting something to happen and thinking that it will: *There's little **hope** of finding survivors. ◇ Don't give up **hope**; you may still pass.*
2 (*no plural*) a person or thing that gives you hope: *Can you help me? You're my only **hope**.*

hopeful (say **hohp**-fuhl) *adjective*
thinking that something that you want will happen: *I'm **hopeful** about getting a job.*

hopefully (say **hohp**-fuh-lee) *adverb*
1 (*informal*) I or we hope: ***Hopefully** he won't be late.*
2 hoping that what you want will happen: *The cat looked **hopefully** at our plates.*

hopeless (say **hohp**-luhss) *adjective*
1 with no hope of success: *a **hopeless** situation ◇ It's **hopeless** trying to work with all this noise!*
2 (*informal*) very bad: *I'm **hopeless** at tennis.*
▸ **hopelessly** (*adverb*): *We got **hopelessly** lost in the forest.*

hopscotch (say **hop**-skoch) *noun* (*no plural*)
a children's game where you jump on squares marked on the ground

horde (say **hawd**) *noun* (*plural* **hordes**)
a very large number of people: *A **horde** of guests arrived at the same time.* ➲ SYNONYMS **crowd[1]**, **mob[1]**

SPELLING Be careful! Don't confuse **horde** with **hoard**, which has a different meaning.

horizon (say huh-**rize**-uhn) *noun*
1 (*no plural*) the line between the earth or sea and the sky: *The sun dropped below the **horizon**.*
2 horizons (*plural noun*) the limits of your knowledge or experience: *Travelling is a good way to broaden your **horizons**.*
on the horizon likely to happen soon: *There are exciting changes on the **horizon**.*

horizontal (say ho-ri-**zon**-tuhl) *adjective*
going from side to side, not up and down: *a **horizontal** line* ➲ See **vertical**

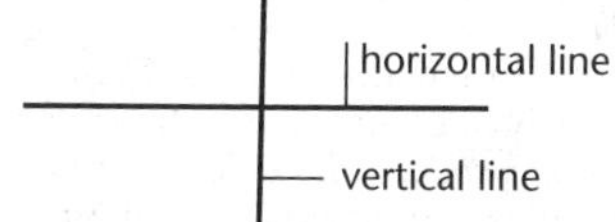

hormone (say **haw**-mohn) *noun* (*plural* **hormones**)
a substance in your body that influences the way you grow and develop or how your body functions

horn (say **hawn**) *noun* (*plural* **horns**)
1 one of the hard pointed things that some animals have on their heads
2 a thing in a car or other vehicle that makes a loud sound to warn people: *Don't sound your **horn** late at night.*
3 a musical instrument with a curved metal tube that you blow into

hornet (say **hawn**-it) *noun* (*plural* **hornets**)
a black and yellow flying insect that has a powerful sting

horoscope (say **ho**-ruh-skohp) *noun* (*plural* **horoscopes**)
something that tells you what will happen, using the planets and your date of birth: *Have you read* (= in a newspaper, for example) *your **horoscope** today?*

horrendous (say ho-**ren**-duhss) *adjective*
(*informal*) very bad or unpleasant ➲ SYNONYMS **awful**, **terrible**
▸ **horrendously** (*adverb*)

horrible (say **ho**-rib-l) *adjective* (*informal*)
very bad or unpleasant: *What **horrible** weather!* ◇ *I had a **horrible** dream.*

WORD BUILDING There are many words that you can use instead of **horrible**, but check their exact meanings first. Examples are: **abominable**, **atrocious**, **awful**, **bad**, **cruel**, **disgusting**, **dreadful**, **evil**, **ghastly**, **gruesome**, **horrid** (informal), **horrific**, **lousy** (informal), **mean**[2]2, **nasty**, **obnoxious**, **offensive**[1]1, **repulsive**, **revolting**, **rude**1, **shocking**, **terrible**, **ugly**, **unkind**, **unpleasant**, **vicious** and **vile**.

horrid (say **ho**-rid) *adjective* (*informal*)
very bad or unpleasant: *Don't be so **horrid**!*
➲ SYNONYM **horrible**

horrific (say ho-**rif**-ik) *adjective*
very shocking or frightening: *a **horrific** accident*
➲ SYNONYM **ghastly**

horrify (say **ho**-ri-fy) *verb* (**horrifying**, **horrified**)
to shock and frighten somebody: *Everyone was **horrified** by the murders.*

horror (say **ho**-ruh) *noun* (*no plural*)
a feeling of fear or shock: *They watched in **horror** as the child ran in front of the bus.*
horror film, **horror story** a film or a story which tries to frighten or shock you for entertainment

horse (say **hawss**) *noun* (*plural* **horses**)
a big animal that can carry people and pull heavy things: *Can you ride a **horse**?*

horse

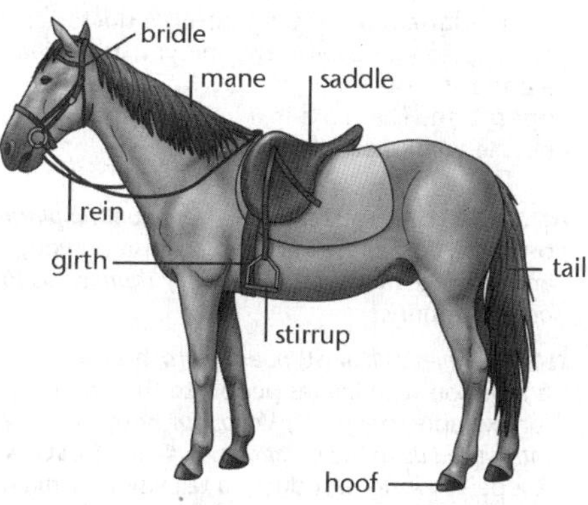

horseback (say **hawss**-bak) *noun*
on horseback sitting on a horse: *We saw a lot of police officers on **horseback**.*

horsepower (say **hawss**-pow-uh) *noun* (*no plural*) (abbr. hp)
in the past, a unit for measuring the power of an engine: *My grandfather said his car produced 300 **horsepower**.*

USAGE The power of an engine is now measured in **kilowatts** (1 hp = 0,746 kW). **Horsepower** is still used in some countries.

horseshoe (say **hawss**-shoo) *noun* (*plural* **horseshoes**)
a piece of metal like a U that a horse wears on its hoof

horticulture (say **haw**-ti-kul-tshuh) *noun* (*no plural*)
the study or practice of growing plants in gardens
▸ **horticultural** (*adjective*): *Ben belongs to a **horticultural** society.* ▸ **horticulturist** (*noun*)

A B C D E F G **H** I J K L M N O P Q R S T U V W X Y Z

hose (say **hohz**) *noun* (*plural* **hoses**) (also **hosepipe**)
a long soft tube that you use to bring water, for example in the garden or when there is a fire

hospitable (say hoss-**pit**-uhb-l) *adjective*
friendly and kind to visitors ➲ OPPOSITE **inhospitable** 1

hospital (say **hoss**-pit-uhl) *noun* (*plural* **hospitals**)
a place where doctors and nurses look after people who are ill or hurt: *My brother is in **hospital** – he's broken his leg.* ◇ *The ambulance took her to **hospital**.*

WORD BUILDING If you are very ill or you **have an accident** you go **to hospital**. A doctor or nurse gives you **treatment** and you are called a **patient**. You might need to **have an operation**. The room in a hospital where people sleep is called a **ward**.

hospitality (say hoss-pi-**tal**-i-tee) *noun* (*no plural*)
being friendly to people who are visiting you, and looking after them well: *They thanked us for our **hospitality**.*

host (*rhymes with* **most**) *noun* (*plural* **hosts**)
1 a person who invites people to their house, for example to a party: *Vuyo, our **host**, introduced us to the other guests.* ➲ See **hostess**
2 a person who introduces a television or radio show and talks to the guests

hostage (say **hoss**-tij) *noun* (*plural* **hostages**)
a prisoner that you keep until people give you what you want: *Several passengers were taken **hostage**.* ◇ *They held his daughter **hostage** until he paid them the money.*

hostel (say **hoss**-tuhl) *noun* (*plural* **hostels**)
a place like a cheap hotel where people can stay: *a youth **hostel***

hostess (say **hohss**-tess) *noun* (*plural* **hostesses**)
a woman who invites people to her house, for example to a party ➲ See **host** 1

hostile (say **hoss**-tile) *adjective*
very unfriendly: *a **hostile** crowd*
▸ **hostility** (*noun*): *She said nothing but I could sense her **hostility**.*

hot *adjective* (**hotter**, **hottest**)
1 having a high temperature: *I'm **hot**. Can you open the window?* ◇ *It's **hot** today, isn't it?* ◇ ***hot** water* ➲ OPPOSITE **cold**[1] 1
2 (used about food) having a strong, burning taste: *a **hot** spicy curry* ➲ OPPOSITE **bland** 2
3 getting easily excited: *a **hot** temper* ➲ The noun is **heat**[1]

WHICH WORD? **Warm**, **hot** or **boiling**?
- **Warm** means slightly hot, especially in a pleasant way: *Sit by the fire. You'll soon be warm.*
- **Boiling** is used informally to mean extremely hot, often in an unpleasant way: *Open the window – it's **boiling** in here!*
- **Hot** is between **warm** and **boiling**.

hot-air balloon *noun* (*plural* **hot-air balloons**) = **balloon** 2

hot dog *noun* (*plural* **hot dogs**)
a hot sausage that you eat in a long bread roll

hotel (say hoh-**tel**) *noun* (*plural* **hotels**)
a place where you pay to sleep and eat: *I stayed at a **hotel** near the airport.*

hotline (say **hot**-line) *noun* (*plural* **hotlines**)
a special telephone line that people can call to get advice or information

hotplate (say **hot**-playt) *noun* (*plural* **hotplates**)
a heated surface for cooking food or keeping it warm

hound[1] (say **hownd**) *noun* (*plural* **hounds**)
a type of dog that is used for hunting or racing: ***greyhound** racing*

hound[2] (say **hownd**) *verb* (**hounding**, **hounded**)
to follow and disturb somebody: *He **hounded** me for answers all week.*

hour (say **ow**-uh) *noun*
1 (*plural* **hours**) a measure of time. There are 60 minutes in an hour: *The journey took two **hours**.* ◇ *I've been waiting for an **hour**.* ◇ *half an **hour***
2 hours (*plural noun*) the time when somebody is working, or when a shop or office is open: *Our office **hours** are 9 a.m. to 5 p.m.*
3 the hour (*no plural*) the time when a new hour starts (= 1 o'clock, 2 o'clock, and so on): *Buses leave on the **hour** and at twenty past the **hour**.*
for hours (*informal*) for a long time: *I've been waiting for **hours**.*

hourly (say **ow**-uh-lee) *adjective, adverb*
happening or coming once an hour: *There is an **hourly** bus to the airport.* ◇ *Trains run **hourly**.*

house[1] (say **howss**) *noun* (*plural* **houses**)
1 a building where a person or a family lives: *We're going to Lindi's **house** now.*
2 a building that has a special use: *an opera **house***

house[2] (say **howz**) *verb* (**housing**, **housed**)
1 to give somebody a place to live: *The students are **housed** in residences.*

2 to contain or keep something: *Factories were built to **house** the machines.*

household (say **howss**-hohld) *noun* (*plural* **households**)
all the people who live in a house and the money, organization and work that is needed to look after them: *Members of our **household** take turns doing chores.* ◇ ***household** insurance*

housekeeping (say **howss**-keep-ing) *noun* (*no plural*)
1 the work involved in looking after a house: *We need to do some **housekeeping**.*
2 the money that you need to manage a house: *Have you paid your **housekeeping** this month?*

housewife (say **howss**-wife) *noun* (*plural* **housewives**)
a woman who stays at home and looks after her family

housework (say **howss**-wurk) *noun* (*no plural*)
work that you do in your house, for example cleaning and washing

WHICH WORD? **Housework** or **homework**?
Be careful! Work that a teacher gives you to do at home is called **homework**.

housing (say **howz**-ing) *noun* (*no plural*)
flats and houses for people to live in: *We need more **housing**.*

housing estate *noun* (*plural* **housing estates**)
a big group of houses that were built at the same time: *We live on a **housing estate**.*

hovel (say **hov**-uhl) *noun* (*plural* **hovels**)
a house or room that is very dirty or in a very bad condition: *I can't live in this **hovel**!*

hover (say **hov**-uh) *verb* (**hovering, hovered**)
to stay in the air in one place: *A helicopter **hovered** above the building.*

hovercraft (say **hov**-uh-kraaft) *noun* (*plural* **hovercraft**)
a kind of boat that moves over the top of water on a cushion of air

how (*rhymes with* **now**) *adverb*
1 in what way: ***How** does this machine work?* ◇ *She told me **how** to get to the station.*
2 a word that you use to ask if somebody is well: *'**How** is your sister?' 'She's well, thank you.'*
3 a word that you use to ask if something is good: ***How** was the film?*
4 a word that you use to ask questions about things like age, amount or time: ***How** old are you?* ◇ ***How** many brothers and sisters have you got?* ◇ ***How** much does this cost?*
5 a word that shows surprise or strong feeling: ***How** terrible!*
how about ...? words that you use when you suggest something: ***How** about some tea?*
how do you do? polite words that you say when you meet somebody for the first time

WHICH WORD? **How** or **like**?
- You use **how** with meaning 2 above only when you are asking about somebody's health: *'**How** are you?' 'I've got flu.'*
- Don't use **how** when you ask somebody to describe another person or a thing. Use **what ... like**?: *'**What** is your sister **like**?' 'She's tall with brown hair.' '**What** is her house **like**?'*

SPEAKING If someone says **How do you do**? you answer **How do you do**? and you shake hands. This is a formal way of greeting people, and nowadays many people say **Pleased to meet you** instead when they meet.

however (say how-**ev**-uh) *adverb*
1 it does not matter how: *I never win, **however** hard I try.*
2 but: *She's very intelligent. **However**, she's quite lazy.*

howl (*rhymes with* **fowl**) *verb* (**howling, howled**)
to make a long, loud sound, like a dog makes: *The dogs **howled** all night.* ◇ *The wind **howled** around the house.*
▸ **howl** (*noun*): *He let out a **howl** of anger.*

HQ (say aych-**kyoo**) abbreviation **headquarters**

hub *noun* (*plural* **hubs**)
1 the central and most important part of a place or activity: *This is the entertainment **hub** of the city.*
2 the central part of a wheel ➲ See illustration at **wheel**[1]

huddle (say **hud**-l) *verb* (**huddling, huddled**)
to get close to other people because you are cold or frightened: *We **huddled** together for warmth.*

hue (say **hyoo**) *noun* (*plural* **hues**)
a colour, or a particular shade of a colour: *The water was a strange green-blue **hue**.*
hue and cry strong public protest about something: *There was a **hue** and cry from the community about the school closing.*

hug *verb* (**hugging, hugged**)
to put your arms around somebody to show that you love them: *She **hugged** her parents and said goodbye.* ➲ SYNONYM **embrace**
▸ **hug** (*noun*): *Come and give me a **hug**.*

A B C D E F G H I J K L M N O P Q R S T U V W X Y Z

huge (say **hyooj**) *adjective*
very big: *They live in a **huge** house.* ➲ SYNONYM **enormous**

WORD BUILDING See the Word Building note at **big**.

Huguenot (say **hyoo**-guh-noh) *noun* (*plural* **Huguenots**)
a French Protestant of the 16th and 17th centuries. After they were severely treated by the Catholic majority, many left France: *French **Huguenots** settled in South Africa.*

hull (say **hul**) *noun* (*plural* **hulls**)
the body of a ship ➲ See illustration at **ship**

hum *verb* (**humming, hummed**)
1 to sing with your lips closed: *You can **hum** the tune if you don't know the words.*
2 to make a low continuous sound: *The overhead wires **hummed** with power.*
▸ **hum** (*noun*): *The computer was making a low **hum**.*
ⓘ ORIGIN: 14th–15th century. The word came from imitating the sound.

human¹ (say **hyoo**-muhn) *adjective*
related to people, not animals or machines: *the **human** body*

human² (say **hyoo**-muhn) *noun* (*plural* **humans**) (also **human being**)
a person: *Dogs can hear much better than **humans**.*

humane (say hyoo-**mayn**) *adjective*
having or showing kindness and understanding, especially to a person or animal that is suffering: *Farm animals need to be kept in **humane** conditions.* ➲ OPPOSITE **inhumane**
▸ **humanely** (*adverb*): *Did they kill it **humanely**?*

humanity (say hyoo-**man**-i-tee) *noun* (*no plural*)
1 all of the people in the world, thought of as a group: *crimes against **humanity***
2 the quality of being kind and understanding: *He showed **humanity** and compassion.*

humankind (say **hyoo**-muhn-kynd) *noun* (*no plural*)
people in general

human race *noun* (*no plural*)
all the people in the world

human rights *plural noun*
the basic freedoms that all people should have: *The Constitution protects our **human rights**.*

humble (say **humb**-l) *adjective* (**humbler, humblest**)
1 not thinking you are better or more important than other people: *Despite her success she is still very **humble**.*
2 simple or poor: *a **humble** home* ➲ The noun is **humility**

humdrum (say **hum**-drum) *adjective*
boring ➲ SYNONYM **dull** 1

humid (say **hyoo**-mid) *adjective*
(used about the weather or climate) warm and wet: *The island is hot and **humid**.* ➲ SYNONYM **muggy**
▸ **humidity** (*noun*): *high levels of **humidity***

humiliate (say hyoo-**mil**-i-ayt) *verb* (**humiliating, humiliated**)
to make a person feel very embarrassed: *I was **humiliated** when the class laughed at me.* ➲ SYNONYM **mortify**
▸ **humiliation** (*noun*)

humility *noun* (*no plural*)
the quality of not thinking that you are better than other people ➲ The adjective is **humble**

humorous (say **hyoo**-muh-ruhss) *adjective*
making you smile or laugh: *a **humorous** story* ➲ SYNONYM **funny** 1

SPELLING Be careful! **Humorous** is spelt with **-or-** and **humour** is spelt with **-our**.

humour (say **hyoo**-muh) *noun* (*no plural*)
1 the quality of being funny or amusing: *a story full of **humour***
2 the ability to laugh and know that something is funny: *She has a good sense of **humour**.*

hump *noun* (*plural* **humps**)
a round lump on an animal's or a person's back: *A camel has a **hump** on its back.*

humus (say **hyoo**-muhss) *noun* (*no plural*)
the dark substance in soil formed by the breaking down of dead plant and animal matter: *The soil in my garden has a high **humus** content and is very fertile.*

hunch *verb* (**hunching, hunched**)
to bend your back and shoulders into a round shape: ***Hunch** your shoulders.*

hundred (say **hun**-druhd) *number*
1 100: *We invited a **hundred** people to the party.* ◇ *two **hundred** rand* ◇ *four **hundred** and twenty*
2 hundreds (*informal*) a lot: *I've got **hundreds** of things to do today.*
▸ **hundredth** (*adjective, adverb, noun*): *Today is the **hundredth*** (= 100th) *day of the race.* ◇ *She beat the record by one **hundredth*** (= fraction $\frac{1}{100}$) *of a second.*

hung form of **hang** 1

hunger (say **hung**-guh) *noun* (*no plural*)
the feeling that you want or need to eat ➲ See **thirst**
🛈 ORIGIN: from Old English *hungor*, related to Dutch *honger*

hungry (say **hung**-gree) *adjective* (**hungrier**, **hungriest**)
wanting to eat: *Let's eat soon – I'm* ***hungry****!*
➲ See **thirsty**

hunk (say **hungk**) *noun* (*plural* **hunks**)
1 a large piece of something: *a* ***hunk*** *of cheese*
2 (*informal*) a man who is big, strong and attractive

hunt *verb* (**hunting**, **hunted**)
to chase and kill animals as a sport or for food: *They went* ***hunting*** *last weekend.* ◇ *Young lions must learn how to* ***hunt****.*
hunt for something to try to find something: *I've* ***hunted*** *everywhere for my watch but I can't find it.*
▸ **hunt** (*noun*): *a kudu* ***hunt*** ◇ *a* ***hunt*** *for the missing child* ▸ **hunting** (*noun*): ***Hunting*** *is illegal in some places.*

hunter (say **hun**-tuh) *noun* (*plural* **hunters**)
a person who hunts wild animals

hunter-gatherer (say hun-tuh-**ga*th***-uh-ruh) *noun* (*plural* **hunter-gatherers**)
a member of a group of people who do not live in one place but move around hunting, fishing and collecting plants for food

hurdle (say **hurd**-l) *noun* (*plural* **hurdles**)
1 a type of light fence that people or horses jump over in a race: *Don't kick the* ***hurdle*** *when you jump over it.*
2 hurdles a race in which people or horses jump over hurdles: *The next race is the* ***hurdles****.*
3 a problem or difficulty that you must solve or deal with before you can achieve something: *Not having an Internet connection is a* ***hurdle*** *for a small business.*

hurl *verb* (**hurling**, **hurled**)
to throw something very strongly: *She* ***hurled*** *the book across the room.*

hurrah, hurray (say huh-**raa** huh-**ray**)
= **hooray**

hurricane (say **hu**-ri-kuhn) *noun* (*plural* **hurricanes**)
a storm with very strong winds: ***Hurricane*** *Katrina caused much damage in the city of New Orleans.* ➲ See note at **storm**[1]

hurry[1] (*rhymes with* **curry**) *verb* (**hurrying**, **hurried**)
to move or do something quickly: *We* ***hurried*** *home after school.*
hurry up to move or do something more quickly because there is not much time: ***Hurry*** *up or we'll be late!*
▸ **hurried** (*adjective*): *a* ***hurried*** *conversation*

hurry[2] (*rhymes with* **curry**) *noun*
in a hurry needing or wanting to do something quickly: *I can't talk to you now – I'm in a* ***hurry****.*

hurt[1] *verb* (**hurting**, **hurt**)
1 to make somebody or something feel pain: *I fell and* ***hurt*** *my leg.* ◇ *Did you* ***hurt*** *yourself?*
➲ SYNONYM **injure**
2 to feel pain: *My leg* ***hurts****.*
3 to make somebody unhappy: *I never meant to* ***hurt*** *your feelings.*

hurt[2] (say **hurt**) *adjective*
1 physically harmed or injured: *Was anyone* ***hurt*** *in the accident?*
2 upset: *I was very* ***hurt*** *by what you said.*

> WHICH WORD? **Hurt** or **injured**?
> These words are similar in meaning. We usually use **injured** when someone has been **hurt** in a car accident or during sport.

hurtful (say **hurt**-fuhl) *adjective*
making somebody feel upset: ***hurtful*** *remarks*
➲ SYNONYM **unkind**

hurtle (say **hurt**-l) *verb* (**hurtling**, **hurtled**)
to move with great speed, perhaps causing danger: *The truck* ***hurtled*** *down the hill.* ◇ *The cat* ***hurtled*** *out the bushes.*

husband (say **huz**-buhnd) *noun* (*plural* **husbands**)
the man that a woman is married to ➲ See **wife**
🛈 ORIGIN: through Old English, from Old Norse *húsbóndi* meaning 'master of a house', from *hús* meaning 'house' + *bóndi* meaning 'person who occupies the land and tills the soil'. When the word first came into English it meant 'male head of a household' and 'manager'.

hush[1] *noun* (*no plural*)
a situation in which it is completely quiet: *A* ***hush*** *fell over the room.* ➲ SYNONYM **silence** 1

hush[2] *verb* (**hushing**, **hushed**)
(spoken) used to tell somebody to be quiet, to stop talking or crying: ***Hush*** *now, and go to sleep.*

husk *noun* (*plural* **husks**)
the dry outside layer of nuts, fruits and seeds, and especially of grain

husky (say **husk**-ee) *adjective* (**huskier**, **huskiest**)
(used about a person's voice) sounding rough as though your throat is dry

hut *noun* (*plural* **huts**)
a small simple building with one room

hutch (say **huch**) *noun* (*plural* **hutches**)
a wooden box with a front made of wire, that is used for keeping rabbits or other small pets

hybrid (say **hy**-brid) *noun* (*plural* **hybrids**)
an animal or plant that has parents of two different types **(species)**: *A mule is a **hybrid** of a horse and a donkey.*

hydraulic (say hy-**drol**-ik) *adjective*
(used about equipment) worked by liquid moving under pressure: ***hydraulic** brakes*

hydrochloric acid (say hy-droh-klaw-rik **ass**-id) *noun* (*no plural*)
a very strong acid made from hydrogen and chlorine

hydroelectric (say hy-droh-i-**lek**-trik) *adjective*
using the power of water to produce electricity: ***hydroelectric** power*

hydrogen (say **hy**-druh-jin) *noun* (*no plural*) (symbol H)
a light gas that you cannot see or smell: *Water is made of **hydrogen** and oxygen.*

hydroponics (say hy-droh-**pon**-ikss) *noun* (*no plural*)
the study or practice of growing plants in mineral solutions rather than in soil
► **hydroponic** (*adjective*): ***hydroponic** tomatoes* ► **hydroponically** (*adverb*): *Mike grow all his vegetables **hydroponically**.*

hyena (say hy-**een**-uh) *noun* (*plural* **hyenas**)
a large African mammal that is similar to a dog, and that scavenges (= eats animals that are already dead) but also hunts very well in packs

hygiene (say **hy**-jeen) *noun* (*no plural*)
keeping yourself and things around you clean: *Good **hygiene** is very important when you are preparing food.*
► **hygienic** (*adjective*): ***hygienic** conditions*

hymn (say **him**) *noun* (*plural* **hymns**)
a song that Christians sing in church

hype (say **hipe**) *noun* (*no plural*) (*informal*)
advertisements that make you think something is better than it really is: *Don't believe the **hype** – the film's rubbish!*

hyper- (say **hy**-puh) *prefix*
too much, or more than normal: ***hyperactive** children*
ⓘ **ORIGIN**: from Greek *huper* meaning 'over, beyond'

hyperbole (say hy-**pur**-buh-lee) *noun* (*no plural*)
a way of speaking or writing that makes something sound better, bigger, more exciting or dangerous than it really is: *He always talks in **hyperbole**; you never know which stories to believe.* ➲ See Study page 17 ➲ See **exaggerate**

hypermarket (say **hy**-puh-maak-uht) *noun* (*plural* **hypermarkets**)
a very large shop that sells food and things for your home: *A **hypermarket** is bigger than a supermarket.*
ⓘ **ORIGIN**: 20th century, through French from Greek *hyper-* meaning 'beyond, more than' + French *marché* meaning 'market'

hyphen (say **hy**-fuhn) *noun* (*plural* **hyphens**)
a mark (-) that you use in writing. It joins words together (for example '*left-handed*') or shows that a word continues on the next line.
➲ See Study page 16

hypnosis (say hip-**noh**-siss) (*no plural*)
a kind of deep sleep in which you can still see and hear but your mind and actions can be controlled by another person to follow commands or answer questions: *She spoke about the attack under **hypnosis**.*
► **hypnotize** (also **hypnotise**) (*verb*): *Do you know how to **hypnotize** a person?*

hypocrite (say **hip**-uh-krit) *noun* (*plural* **hypocrites**)
a person who pretends to have moral beliefs that they do not really have
► **hypocrisy** (*noun*): *He says one thing and does another. It's **hypocrisy**!*

hypotenuse (say hy-**pot**-uh-nyooz) *noun* (*plural* **hypotenuses**) (*maths*)
the side opposite the right angle of a right-angled triangle ➲ See illustration at **triangle**

hypothermia (say hy-poh-**thurm**-i-uh) *noun* (*no plural*)
a dangerous medical condition in which your body temperature is much lower than normal

hypothesis (say hy-**poth**-uh-siss) *noun* (*plural* **hypotheses**)
an idea that is suggested as the possible explanation for something but has not yet been proved to be true or correct
► **hypothesize** (*verb*) (also **hypothesise**): *Some scientists **hypothesize** that the universe began 20 billion years ago.* ► **hypothetical** (*adjective*): *a **hypothetical** question ◇ a **hypothetical** situation*
► **hypothetically** (*adverb*): ***Hypothetically** speaking, if I was a billionaire, I would still live in my village.*

hysterical (say hiss-**te**-rik-l) *adjective*
so excited or upset that you cannot control yourself: ***hysterical** laughter*

Hz *abbreviation* (*plural* **Hz**) **hertz**

Ii

I (*rhymes with* **my**) *pronoun* (*plural* **we**)
the person who is speaking or writing: ***I** phoned and said **I** was busy.* ◇ ***I'll*** (= I will) *see you tomorrow.* ◇ ***I'm** not going to fall, am **I**?*

ibis (say **ibe**-iss) *noun* (*plural* **ibises**)
a bird that has long legs and a curved beak and lives near water

ice (say **ise**) *noun* (*no plural*)
water that has become hard because it is frozen: *Do you want **ice** in your juice?*

iceberg (say **ise**-burg) *noun* (*plural* **icebergs**)
a very large piece of ice that floats in the sea

ice cream *noun* (*plural* **ice creams**)
frozen sweet food made from milk: *Do you like **ice cream**?* ◇ *Two chocolate **ice creams**, please.*

ice cube *noun* (*plural* **ice cubes**)
a small piece of ice that you put in a drink to make it cold

ice rink *noun* (*plural* **ice rinks**) (also **rink**)
a special place where you can **ice-skate**

ice-skate (say **ise**-kayt) *verb* (**ice-skating**, **ice-skated**) (also **skate**)
to move on ice in special boots (called **ice skates**) that have long sharp pieces of metal on the bottom

icicle (say **ise**-ik-l) *noun* (*plural* **icicles**)
a long piece of ice that hangs down from something

icing (say **ise**-ing) *noun* (*no plural*)
a sweet substance that you use for covering cakes: *a cake with pink **icing***

icon (say **ike**-uhn or **ike**-on) *noun* (*plural* **icons**)
1 a person or a thing that people feel is a symbol of something: *Mr Mandela is an **icon** of freedom.*
2 (*computing*) a small picture on a computer screen that you can use to start a program or open a file: *Double-click on the **icon**.*

icosagon (say y-**koss**-uh-guhn) *noun* (*plural* **icosagons**) (*maths*)
a flat closed shape with twenty straight sides

icosahedron (say y-koss-uh-**hee**-druhn) *noun* (*plural* **icosahedra** or **icosahedrons**) (*maths*)
a solid shape with twenty flat surfaces

ICU (say y-see-**yoo**) *noun* (*plural* **ICUs**)
a department in a hospital that cares for patients who are very ill or badly injured
ⓘ **ICU** is short for 'intensive care unit'.

icy (say **ise**-ee) *adjective* (**icier**, **iciest**)
1 very cold: *an **icy** wind*
2 covered with ice: ***icy** roads*

ID (say y-**dee**) *noun* (*plural* **IDs**) (*informal*) a document with your name, photograph, etc. in it, which proves who you are: *an **ID** book* ◇ *Do you have any **ID**?* ⓘ **ID** is short for 'identity' or 'identification'.

I'd (say **ide**) short for **I had; I would**

idea (say y-**deer**) *noun* (*plural* **ideas**)
1 a plan or new thought: *It was a good **idea** to give Mandla a pen for his birthday.* ◇ *I've got an **idea**. Let's have a party!*
2 a picture in your mind: *The film gives you a good **idea** of what Iceland is like.* ◇ *I've got no **idea*** (= I do not know) *where she is.*

ideal[1] (say y-**deel**) *adjective*
the best or exactly right: *This is an **ideal** place for a picnic.* ➲ SYNONYM **perfect** 1

ideal[2] (say y-**deel**) *noun* (*plural* **ideals**)
an idea or a standard that seems perfect and worth trying to achieve: *He's a politician with high **ideals**.*
▸ **idealistic** (*adjective*): *Her goals are **idealistic**, but are they realistic?* ▸ **idealism** (*noun*): *the **idealism** of young activists*

identical (say y-**den**-tik-l) *adjective*
exactly the same: ***identical** twins* ◇ *These two cameras are **identical**.*

identification (say y-den-tuh-fi-**kay**-shuhn) *noun*
1 (*no plural*) the process of showing or finding out who somebody or something is: *The **identification** of bodies after the accident was difficult.*
2 (*plural* **identifications**) (abbr. ID) a document that shows who you are: *Do you have any **identification**?*

identify (say y-**den**-ti-fy) *verb* (**identifying**, **identified**)
to say or know who somebody is or what something is: *The police have not **identified** the dead man yet.* ◇ ***Identify** the mammals in the illustration and list them.*

identity (say y-**den**-tuh-tee) *noun* (*plural* **identities**)
who or what a person or thing is: *The **identity** of the killer is not known.*

A B C D E F G H I J K L M N O P Q R S T U V W X Y Z

identity book *noun* (*plural* **identity books**) (also **ID book**)
a small book that shows who you are

ideology (say y-dee-**ol**-uh-jee) *noun* (*plural* **ideologies**)
a set of ideas and beliefs that form the basis for a political, social or economic system
▸ **ideological** (*adjective*): *There are major* ***ideological*** *differences between the parties.*

idiom (say **id**-i-uhm) *noun* (*plural* **idioms**)
a group of words with a special meaning: *The* ***idiom*** *'break somebody's heart' means 'make somebody very unhappy'.*

idiomatic (say id-i-uh-**mat**-ik) *adjective*
using language that contains natural expressions: *She speaks fluent and* ***idiomatic*** *English.*

idiot (say **id**-i-uht) *noun* (*plural* **idiots**)
a person who is stupid or does something silly: *I was an* ***idiot*** *to forget my key.* ➲ SYNONYM **moron**
▸ **idiotic** (*adjective*): *an* ***idiotic*** *mistake*

idle (say **ide**-uhl) *adjective*
1 lazy and not wanting to work: *an* ***idle*** *student*
2 not busy: *She can't bear to be* ***idle****.*
3 not working, operating or being used: ***idle*** *machines*
4 not to be taken seriously because it is unlikely to have any value, use, purpose or effect: ***idle*** *talk* ◇ ***idle*** *threats*
▸ **idleness** (*noun*): ***Idleness*** *leads to boredom.*
▸ **idly** (*adverb*): *to sit around* ***idly*** *doing nothing*

idol (say **ide**-uhl) *noun* (*plural* **idols**)
1 a famous person that people love and admire: *He was the pop* ***idol*** *of millions of teenagers.*
2 an object that people treat as a god

idolize (say **ide**-uh-lize) *verb* (**idolizing, idolized**) (also **idolise**)
to love or admire somebody very much, especially so much that you forget that they also have faults and weaknesses ➲ SYNONYM **worship** 2

idyllic (say i-**dil**-ik) *adjective*
1 pleasant and peaceful: *an* ***idyllic*** *island*
2 happy and free from difficulty: *an* ***idyllic*** *childhood*

i.e. (say y-**ee**) *abbreviation*
used in writing to mean 'that is' or 'in other words': *You can buy hot drinks,* ***i.e.*** *tea and coffee, on the train.* ❶ **i.e.** is short for the Latin phrase 'id est'.

if (say **if**) *conjunction*
1 a word that you use to say what is possible or true when another thing happens or is true: ***If*** *you see her, give her this letter.* ◇ ***If*** *your feet were smaller, you could wear my shoes.* ◇ ***If*** *I had a million rand, I would buy a big house.* ◇ *I may see you tomorrow.* ***If*** *not, I'll see you next week.*
2 a word that shows a question: *She asked me* ***if*** *I wanted a sweet.* ➲ SYNONYM **whether** 2
3 every time: ***If*** *I try to phone her she just hangs up.* ➲ SYNONYM **whenever** 2
as if in a way that makes you think something: *She looks as* ***if*** *she has been on holiday.*
if only a phrase that shows that you want something very much: ***If*** *only I could drive!*

igloo (say **ig**-loo) *noun* (*plural* **igloos**)
a small house that is made out of blocks of hard snow

igneous (say **ig**-ni-uhss) *adjective*
relating to rocks that are formed when **magma** (= melted or liquid material from below the Earth's surface) becomes solid: *Granite is an* ***igneous*** *rock.* ➲ See **metamorphic** 1, **sedimentary**

ignite (say ig-**nite**) *verb* (**igniting, ignited**) (*formal*)
to start burning or to make something start burning: *The gas* ***ignited*** *and caused an explosion.*

ignorance (say **ig**-nuh-ruhnss) *noun* (*no plural*)
not knowing about something: *Her* ***ignorance*** *surprised me.*

ignorant (say **ig**-nuh-ruhnt) *adjective*
not knowing about something: *I'm very* ***ignorant*** *about computers.*

ignore (say ig-**naw**) *verb* (**ignoring, ignored**)
to know about somebody or something, but to not do anything about it: *He completely* ***ignored*** *his doctor's advice.* ◇ *I said hello to her, but she* ***ignored*** *me!*

iguana (say ig-yuu-**aa**-nuh) *noun* (*plural* **iguanas**)
a type of very large **lizard** that lives in hot places

il- (say **il**) *prefix*
You can add **il-** to the beginning of some words to give them the opposite meaning, for example '*illegal*' (= not legal).
❶ ORIGIN: from Latin

I'll (say **ile**) short for **I shall; I will**

ill (say **il**) *adjective*
not well or not in good health: *Abdul is in bed because he is* ***ill****.* ◇ *I feel too* ***ill*** *to go to school.*
➲ SYNONYM **sick** ➲ OPPOSITE **well**[2]

illegal (say il-**leeg**-l) *adjective*
not allowed by law: *It's **illegal** to drive without a licence.* ➲ OPPOSITE **legal** 2
▶ **illegally** (*adverb*)

illegible (say il-**lej**-uhb-l) *adjective*
difficult or impossible to read: *Your handwriting is completely **illegible**.* ➲ OPPOSITE **legible**

illegitimate (say il-uh-**jit**-uh-muht) *adjective*
1 not allowed by or in agreement with the law or rules: *The African Union declared the elections **illegitimate**.*
2 (used about a child) having parents who are not married to each other ➲ OPPOSITE **legitimate**
▶ **illegitimacy** (*noun*)
▶ **illegitimately** (*adverb*)

illiterate (say il-**lit**-uh-ruht) *adjective*
1 not able to read or write
2 not experienced in a particular field or not having a good understanding of a particular subject: *computer **illiterate*** ➲ OPPOSITE **literate**

illness (say **il**-nuhss) *noun*
1 (*no plural*) being ill: *I missed a lot of school because of **illness** last year.*
2 (*plural* **illnesses**) a type or period of illness: *She died after a long **illness**.*

illogical (say il-**loj**-ik-l) *adjective*
not logical
▶ **illogically** (*adverb*): *arguing **illogically***

ill-treat (say il-**treet**) *verb* (**ill-treating, ill-treated**)
to do cruel things to a person or an animal: *This dog has been **ill-treated**.*

illuminate (say il-**loo**-mi-nayt) *verb* (**illuminating, illuminated**)
1 to shine a light or lights on somebody or something: *The light **illuminates** the dials when it is dark.*
2 to decorate something with lights, especially for a celebration: *The palace was **illuminated** by spotlights.*
3 (*formal*) to explain something or make it easier to understand ➲ SYNONYM **clarify**

illusion (say il-**loo**-zhuhn) *noun* (*plural* **illusions**)
a false idea or belief: *I have no **illusions** about the situation – I know it's serious.*

illustrate (say **il**-uh-strayt) *verb* (**illustrating, illustrated**)
1 to add pictures to a book or magazine: *The book is **illustrated** with colour photographs.*
2 to explain or make something clear by adding examples or pictures

illustration (say il-uh-**stray**-shuhn) *noun* (*plural* **illustrations**)
1 a picture in a book or magazine: *This dictionary has many **illustrations**.*
2 an example that makes a point or an idea clear: *Can you give me an **illustration** of what you mean?*

I'm (say **ime**) short for **I am**

im- *prefix*
You can add **im-** to the beginning of some words to give them the opposite meaning, for example '*impatient*' (= not patient).
ⓘ ORIGIN: from Latin

image (say **im**-ij) *noun* (*plural* **images**)
1 a picture or description that appears in a book, film, painting, etc.: ***images** of the war in Sudan*
2 a copy or picture of somebody or something seen in a mirror, through a camera, on television, computer, etc.: *The lens projected an **image** onto the wall.*
3 a picture in people's minds of somebody or something: *Many people have an **image** of South Africa as hot and dry.* ◇ *He's very different from his public **image**.*

imagery (say **im**-ij--uh-ree) *noun* (*no plural*)
1 language that produces pictures in the minds of the people reading or listening, used in poetry, plays, etc.: *a poem filled with frightening **imagery*** ◇ *What **imagery** does this writer use to create a sense of peace?*
2 pictures, photographs, etc.: *computer-generated **imagery***

imaginary (say i-**maj**-uhn-ree) *adjective*
1 that exists only in your mind: *an **imaginary** friend*
2 not real: *The film is about an **imaginary** country.*

imagination (say i-maj-uh-**nay**-shuhn) *noun* (*no plural*)
the ability to think of new ideas or make pictures in your mind: *He has a lively **imagination**.* ◇ *You didn't really see a ghost – it was just your **imagination**.*
▶ **imaginative** (*adjective*): *an **imaginative** suggestion*

imagine (say i-**maj**-uhn) *verb* (**imagining, imagined**)
1 to make a picture of something in your mind: *I lay down and **imagined** I was on a beach.* ◇ *Can you **imagine** life without cars?*
2 to see, hear, or think something that is not true: *I never said that, you're **imagining** things.*
▶ **imaginary** (*adjective*): *an **imaginary** character*

A B C D E F G H I J K L M N O P Q R S T U V W X Y Z

imam (say im-**aam**) *noun* (*plural* **imams**)
a man who leads Muslims in their prayers
ORIGIN: from Arabic *imām* meaning 'leader', from *amma* meaning 'lead the way'

imbalance (say im-**bal**-uhnss) *noun* (*plural* **imbalances**)
a difference or lack of balance between two or more people or things: *symptoms of hormone **imbalances*** ◇ *There is an **imbalance** of power between adults and children.*

imbongi (say im-**bong**-gi) *noun* (*plural* **iimbongi** or **imbongis**) (also **praise singer**) (*S. African*)
a person who sings specially created songs at public ceremonies, which say what a leader or important person has achieved
ORIGIN: from isiXhosa and isiZulu *imbongi*, meaning 'praise poet'

imitate (say **im**-i-tayt) *verb* (**imitating**, **imitated**)
to copy somebody or something: *Children learn by **imitating** adults.*

imitation (say im-i-**tay**-shuhn) *noun* (*plural* **imitations**)
something that you make to look like another thing: ***imitation** leather* ◇ *It's not a real diamond, it's only an **imitation**.* ➲ See **copy**[1]

immaculate (say i-**mak**-yuh-luht) *adjective*
1 absolutely clean and tidy: ***immaculate** white shirts*
2 perfectly correct and free from mistakes: *His performance was **immaculate**.*

immature (say im-uh-**tyoor**) *adjective*
behaving in a way that is not sensible and is typical of younger people: *He's very **immature** for his age.* ➲ SYNONYM **childish** ➲ OPPOSITE **mature**

immediate (say i-**mee**-di-uht) *adjective*
happening now or very soon: *I can't wait – I need an **immediate** answer.*

immediately (say i-**mee**-di-uht-lee) *adverb*
without delay: *Come to my office **immediately**!*

> SPELLING Remember! You spell **immediate** and **immediately** with **mm**.

immense (say i-**menss**) *adjective*
very big or great: *an **immense** house* ◇ *I have **immense** problems.* ◇ *The gift gave us **immense** pleasure.*

immensely (say i-**menss**-lee) *adverb*
very or very much: *an **immensely** difficult sum* ◇ *We enjoyed the party **immensely**.*

immerse (say i-**murss**) *verb* (**immersing**, **immersed**)
1 to put something into a liquid so that it is completely covered: *Make sure the spaghetti is completely **immersed** in the boiling water.*
2 to involve yourself completely in something, giving all your attention, time and energy to it: *Rachel was so **immersed** in her work that she did not hear what Marco said.*
▸ **immersion** (*noun*)

immigrant (say **im**-i-gruhnt) *noun* (*plural* **immigrants**)
a person who comes to another country to live there permanently or for a long time: *South Africa has many **immigrants** from other African countries.*

immigrate (say **im**-i-grayt) *verb* (**immigrating**, **immigrated**)
to come to another country to live there permanently or for a long time: *They **immigrated** to South Africa last year.*
▸ **immigration** (*noun*): *The government is trying to control **immigration**.*

> WHICH WORD? **Immigrate** or **emigrate**?
> ■ To **immigrate** means to come to a country to live, and to **emigrate** means to leave a country to live somewhere else.

imminent (say **im**-i-nuhnt) *adjective*
likely to happen very soon or threatening to happen: *These plants are in **imminent** danger of becoming extinct.*
▸ **imminently** (*adverb*): *We expect construction to begin **imminently**.*

immobile (say i-**moh**-bile) *adjective*
not able to move or be moved, or without moving: *A wall is an **immobile** structure.* ◇ *She stood **immobile**, staring ahead of her.*
➲ OPPOSITE **mobile**[1]
▸ **immobility** (*noun*)

immobilize (say i-**moh**-buh-lize) *verb* (**immobilizing**, **immobilized**) (also **immobilise**)
to prevent somebody or something from moving or working normally
▸ **immobilization** (*noun*) (also **immobilisation**): *The injury will require two weeks of **immobilization**.*

immoral (say i-**mo**-ruhl) *adjective*
(used about people and their behaviour) not honest or good: *It's **immoral** to steal.*
➲ OPPOSITE **moral**[1]
▸ **immorality** (*noun*): *acts of **immorality***

immortal (say i-**maw**-tuhl) *adjective*
living or lasting for ever ➲ OPPOSITE **mortal**
▸ **immortality** (*noun*): *a belief in **immortality***

immune (say i-**myoon**) *adjective*
If you are **immune** to a disease, you cannot get

it: *You're **immune** to measles if you've had it before.*
▸ **immunity** (*noun*): ***immunity** to diseases*

immunize (say **im**-yuu-nize) *verb* (**immunizing, immunized**) (also **immunise**)
to make someone **immune** to a disease, for example by putting a substance called a **vaccine** into their blood
▸ **immunization** (*noun*) (also **immunisation**): *an **immunization** programme*

immunodeficiency (say i-myoo-noh-di-**fish**-uhn-see) *noun* (*no plural*)
a decrease in your body's ability to fight disease or illness: *acquired **immunodeficiency** syndrome (AIDS)*

imp *noun* (*plural* **imps**)
a small **naughty** creature in stories

impact (say **im**-pakt) *noun* (*plural* **impacts**)
1 the effect that something has: *Pollution from factories has a negative **impact** on the environment.*
2 the action or force of one object hitting another: *The **impact** of the crash threw the passengers out of their seats.*

impair (say im-**pair**) *verb* (**impairing, impaired**)
to damage something or make it weaker, worse or less
▸ **impairment** (*noun*): *A person with a visual **impairment** cannot see properly.*

impala (say im-**paa**-luh) *noun* (*plural* **impala** or **impalas**)
a light brown medium-sized African antelope
🛈 **ORIGIN:** 19th century, from isiZulu *impala*

impale (say im-**payl**) *verb* (**impaling, impaled**)
to push a sharp pointed object through somebody or something: *The earthworms were **impaled** on the hook.*

impart (say im-**paat**) *verb* (**imparting, imparted**) (*formal*)
1 to pass information or knowledge to other people: *The project is helping to **impart** skills to young people.*
2 to give something a particular quality: *The low lighting **imparted** a romantic atmosphere to the room.*

impartial (say im-**paa**-shuhl) *adjective*
not supporting one person, group or side more than another ➲ SYNONYMS **neutral**[1] 1, **unbiased**
▸ **impartiality** (*noun*): *The player questioned the **impartiality** of the umpire.*

impatient (say im-**pay**-shuhnt) *adjective*
not wanting to wait for something: *Don't be so **impatient**! The bus will be here soon.* ➲ OPPOSITE **patient**[1]
▸ **impatience** (*noun*): *He couldn't hide his **impatience**.* ▸ **impatiently** (*adverb*): *'Hurry up!' she said **impatiently**.*

impeccable (say im-**pek**-uhb-l) *adjective*
without any mistakes or faults
▸ **impeccably** (*adverb*): ***impeccably** high standards*

impede (say im-**peed**) *verb* (**impeding, impeded**) (*formal*)
to make it difficult or impossible for a person or thing to move, develop or progress
➲ SYNONYM **hinder**

impediment (say im-**ped**-i-muhnt) *noun* (*plural* **impediments**) (*formal*)
1 something that makes it difficult for a person or thing to move or progress: *Her gender has never been an **impediment** to her career.*
2 A person who has a speech **impediment** cannot say certain sounds properly.

impending (say im-**pen**-ding) *adjective*
(usually used about something dangerous or bad) about to happen: *rumours of an **impending** coup*

impenetrable (say im-**pen**-i-truhb-l) *adjective*
1 impossible to go through or into: *The jungle was **impenetrable**.*
2 impossible to understand: *an **impenetrable** mystery* ➲ SYNONYM **incomprehensible**

imperative[1] (say im-**pe**-ruh-tiv) *adjective*
very important or urgent: *It's **imperative** that you see a doctor immediately.*

imperative[2] (say im-**pe**-ruh-tiv) *noun* (*plural* **imperatives**) (*grammar*)
the form of a verb that you use for telling somebody to do something: *'Listen!' and 'Go away!' are in the **imperative**.*

imperfect *adjective*
with mistakes or faults: *an **imperfect** world*
➲ OPPOSITE **perfect** 1
▸ **imperfection** (*noun*): *They learnt to live with each other's **imperfections**.*

imperfect tense (say im-**pur**-fikt) *noun* (*no plural*) (*grammar*)
the form of the verb that is used to talk about an action in the past that is not finished or that lasted for a long time: *In the sentence 'I was having a bath', the verb is in the **imperfect tense**.*

imperial (say im-**peer**-ri-uhl) *adjective*
1 relating to an empire or its ruler: *Britain's **imperial** history*
2 using the system of measures and weights that includes the **foot**, **pound**[1] 2, **pint**, etc.

imperialism (say im-**peer**-ri-uh-liz-m) *noun* (*no plural*)
a political system in which an empire or a powerful country takes control of and rules other less powerful countries (called **colonies**), often by force
▸ **imperialist** (*noun*): *the British **imperialist**, Cecil John Rhodes* ▸ **imperialist** (*adjective*): ***imperialist** ideology*

impersonate (say im-**pur**-suh-nayt) *verb* (**impersonating**, **impersonated**)
1 to copy the behaviour, voice and appearance of another person, especially as a way of entertaining other people: *The comedian can **impersonate** many different politicians.*
2 to pretend to be a different person, especially in order to trick other people: *He was in trouble because he **impersonated** a police officer.*

impertinent (say im-**pur**-ti-nuhnt) *adjective* (*formal*)
rude and not showing respect: *Don't be **impertinent**!* ➲ SYNONYM **cheeky**

impervious (say im-**pur**-vi-uhss) *adjective*
1 not affected or influenced by something: *She was **impervious** to criticism.*
2 not allowing water, etc. to pass through: *a layer of **impervious** rock*

impetuous (say im-**pet**-sh*uu*-uhss) *adjective*
doing things quickly and without thinking carefully: *His **impetuous** behaviour often got him into trouble.* ➲ OPPOSITE **cautious**

impetus (say **im**-puh-tuhss) *noun* (*no plural*)
something that makes you do something or encourages something new or different to happen: *I need fresh **impetus** to start working on this essay again.*

impi (say **im**-pee) *noun* (*plural* **impis**) (*S. African*)
a group of Zulu soldiers or a group of armed men involved in a fight
🛈 ORIGIN: 19th century, from isiZulu *impi* meaning 'group of armed men, soldiers'

implement¹ (say **im**-pluh-muhnt) *verb* (**implementing**, **implemented**)
to do or start using something that you have planned
▸ **implementation** (*noun*): *The government is monitoring the **implementation** of the new curriculum.*

implement² (say **im**-pluh-ment) *noun* (*plural* **implements**)
a tool or instrument that is designed to do a particular task: *farm **implements***

implicate (say **im**-pli-kayt) *verb* (**implicating**, **implicated**)
to show that somebody is involved in or connected with something unpleasant such as a crime: *Several politicians have been **implicated** in the fraud case.*

implication (say im-pli-**kay**-shuhn) *noun* (*plural* **implications**)
1 what is said indirectly or made known by something that somebody does or says: *The **implication** of what she said was that we had made a bad mistake.* ➲ The verb is **imply**
2 the effect that something will have on something else in the future: *the wider **implications** of a decision*
3 the action of showing that somebody is involved in something unpleasant or the fact of being involved, especially in a crime: *her **implication** in the scandal* ➲ The verb is **implicate**

implicit (say im-**pliss**-it) *adjective*
1 not said in a direct way but understood by the people involved ➲ See **explicit** 1
2 complete: *I have **implicit** faith in your ability to do the job.*
▸ **implicitly** (*adverb*): *He is a friend and I trust him **implicitly**.*

implore (say im-**plaw**) *verb* (**imploring**, **implored**) (*formal*)
to ask somebody in an anxious way to do something or to stop doing something: *She **implored** him not to leave her alone.*

imply (say im-**ply**) *verb* (**implying**, **implied**)
to suggest something in an indirect way or without actually saying it: *He asked if I had any work to do. He was **implying** that I was lazy.*

impolite (say im-puh-**lite**) *adjective*
rude: *It was **impolite** of her to ask you to leave.* ➲ OPPOSITE **polite**

import¹ (say im-**pawt**) *verb* (**importing**, **imported**)
to buy things from another country and bring them into your country: *South Africa **imports** computers from Japan.* ➲ See **export¹**
▸ **importer** (*noun*): *an **importer** of gold*

> PRONUNCIATION Notice that you pronounce the verb and noun differently.

import² (say **im**-pawt) *noun*
1 (*no plural*) the process of buying things from another country: *the **import** of clothing from China*
2 (*plural* **imports**) something that you buy from another country: *These shoes are **imports** from Brazil.* ➲ See **export²**

importance (say im-**paw**-tuhnss) *noun* (*no plural*)
the quality of being important: *Oil is of great **importance** to industry.*

important (say im-**paw**-tuhnt) *adjective*
1 If something is **important**, you must do, have or think about it: *It is **important** to sleep well the night before an exam.* ◇ *I think that happiness is more **important** than money.*
2 powerful or special: *The president is a very **important** person.*

impose (say im-**pohz**) *verb* (**imposing, imposed**)
1 to use your power or authority to make people obey a law or rule, or to make them accept or agree to something
2 to ask or expect somebody to do something that may cause extra work or trouble: *I hate to **impose** on you, but can you lend me some money?*
▸ **imposition** (*noun*): *the **imposition** of sanctions* ◇ *I know it's an **imposition**, but could you babysit tonight?*

imposing (say im-**pohz**-ing) *adjective*
very big, important or impressive: *We visited the **imposing** Union Buildings in Pretoria.*

impossible (say im-**poss**-ib-l) *adjective*
If something is **impossible**, you cannot do it, or it cannot happen: *It's **impossible** for me to finish this work by five o'clock.* ◇ *The house was **impossible** to find.* ➲ OPPOSITE **possible**

impostor (say im-**poss**-tuh) *noun* (*plural* **impostors**) (also **imposter**)
a person who dishonestly pretends to be somebody else in order to trick people

impotent (say **im**-puh-tuhnt) *adjective*
1 not having the power to influence a situation or succeed in doing something
2 (used about men) not capable of having sex

impoverish (say im-**pov**-uh-rish) *verb* (**impoverishing, impoverished**) (*formal*)
to cause somebody or something to be poorer or lower in quality than before ➲ OPPOSITE **enrich**
▸ **impoverishment** (*noun*): *malnutrition and **impoverishment***

impractical (say im-**prak**-tik-l) *adjective*
not sensible or realistic: *It would be **impractical** to take our bikes on the train.* ➲ OPPOSITE **practical** 2

impregnate (say **im**-preg-nayt) *verb* (**impregnating, impregnated**)
to make a woman or female animal pregnant

impress (say im-**press**) *verb* (**impressing, impressed**)
to make somebody admire and respect you: *We were very **impressed** by your work.*

impression (say im-**presh**-uhn) *noun* (*plural* **impressions**)
feelings or thoughts you have about somebody or something: *What was your first **impression** of the city?* ◇ *I get the **impression** that she's not very happy.* ◇ *He made a good **impression** on his first day at work.*

impressionism (say im-**presh**-uh-niz-m) *noun* (*no plural*) (*art*)
a style of painting that does not include details but concentrates on the general effect of the person or thing that is being painted
▸ **impressionist** (*noun*): *Claude Monet is one of the most famous **impressionists**.*
▸ **impressionist** (*adjective*): *French **impressionist** paintings*

impressive (say im-**press**-uhv) *adjective*
If somebody or something is **impressive**, you admire them: *an **impressive** building* ◇ *Your work is very **impressive**.*

imprison (say im-**priz**-uhn) *verb* (**imprisoning, imprisoned**)
to put somebody in prison: *He was **imprisoned** for killing his wife.*
▸ **imprisonment** (*noun*): *two years' **imprisonment***

improbable (say im-**prob**-uhb-l) *adjective*
not likely to be true or to happen: *an **improbable** explanation* ➲ OPPOSITE **probable**

impromptu (say im-**promp**-tyoo) *adjective*
done or happening without being prepared, organized or planned in advance: *an **impromptu** party* ➲ SYNONYM **spontaneous**

improper (say im-**prop**-uh) *adjective*
illegal, dishonest or morally wrong: *The accountant was charged with **improper** conduct and fined.*
▸ **improperly** (*adverb*)

improve (say im-**proov**) *verb* (**improving, improved**)
to become better or to make something better: *Your English has **improved** a lot this year.* ◇ *You must **improve** your spelling.*

improvement (say im-**proov**-muhnt) *noun* (*plural* **improvements**)
a change that makes something better than it was before: *There has been a big **improvement** in Sam's work.*

A B C D E F G H I J K L M N O P Q R S T U V W X Y Z

improvise (say **im**-pruh-vize) *verb* (**improvising, improvised**)
1 to make, do or manage something with whatever is available: *If you don't have all the ingredients for the cake, you'll have to **improvise**.*
2 to perform something as you think of it, without having prepared it in advance
➲ SYNONYM **ad lib**
▸ **improvisation** (*noun*): *modern **improvisations** of old songs*

impudent (say **imp**-yuh-duhnt) *adjective* (*formal*)
rude and not showing respect
▸ **impudence** (*noun*): *They were punished for their **impudence**.* ▸ **impudently** (*adverb*): *He stared **impudently** at her.*

impulse (say **im**-puls) *noun* (*plural* **impulses**)
a sudden strong wish to do something: *She felt an **impulse** to run away.*

impulsive (say im-**pul**-siv) *adjective*
doing things suddenly and without thinking carefully: *It was an **impulsive** decision.*

impure (say im-**pyoor**) *adjective*
1 not pure or clean, or mixed with things that are harmful or spoil the quality of something: ***impure** water*
2 (used about people and their behaviour) morally wrong: ***impure** thoughts*
▸ **impurity** (*noun*): *dissolved **impurities** in water*

in[1] (say **in**) *preposition*
1 a word that shows where somebody or something is or when something happens: *The fish swam **in** the water.* ◇ *She was **in** bed.* ◇ *It's cold **in** June.*
2 making all or part of something: *There are 100 centimetres **in** a metre.*
3 a word that shows how long something takes: *I'll be ready **in** ten minutes.*
4 a word that shows how somebody or something is or should be: *This room is **in** a mess.* ◇ *She was **in** tears* (= she was crying). ◇ *Write **in** capital letters.* ◇ *He was dressed **in** a suit.*
5 a word that shows somebody's job: *He's **in** the army.*
ℹ ORIGIN: from Latin

in[2] (say **in**) *adverb*
1 to a place, from outside: *I opened the door and went **in**.*
2 at home or at work: *Nobody was **in** when we called.*

in- (say **in**) *prefix*
You can add **in-** to the beginning of some words to give them the opposite meaning, for example '*incomplete*' (= not complete).

inability (say in-uh-**bil**-uh-tee) *noun* (*no plural*)
not being able to do something: *He has an **inability** to talk about his problems.*
➲ The adjective is **unable**

inaccessible (say in-ak-**sess**-uhb-l) *adjective*
1 difficult or impossible to reach, get or contact: *The beach is **inaccessible** by car.*
2 difficult or impossible to understand: *This book is **inaccessible** to readers because there are too many difficult words in it.* ➲ OPPOSITE **accessible**
▸ **inaccessibility** (*noun*)

inaccurate (say in-**ak**-yuh-ruht) *adjective*
not correct or with mistakes in it: *The report in the newspaper was **inaccurate**.* ➲ OPPOSITE **accurate**

inactive (say in-**ak**-tuhv) *adjective*
not active, busy or working
▸ **inactivity** (*noun*): *The mine resumed production after three months of **inactivity**.*

inadequate (say in-**ad**-i-kwuht) *adjective*
not enough, or not good enough: *These shoes are **inadequate** for wet weather.* ➲ OPPOSITE **adequate**

inanimate (say in-**an**-i-muht) *adjective*
not alive in the way that people, animals and plants are: *an **inanimate** object* ➲ OPPOSITE **animate**

inappropriate (say in-uh-**proh**-pri-uht) *adjective*
not suitable: *This dress is **inappropriate** for a formal dinner.* ➲ OPPOSITE **appropriate**

inarticulate (say in-aa-**tik**-yuh-luht) *adjective*
1 not able to choose the right words to express what you want to say ➲ OPPOSITE **articulate**[1]
2 (used about speech) not clear or capable of being understood: *an **inarticulate** grunt*

inaudible (say in-**aw**-dib-l) *adjective*
not loud enough to be heard: *Her words were almost **inaudible**.* ➲ OPPOSITE **audible**

inaugurate (say in-**awg**-yuh-rayt) *verb* (**inaugurating, inaugurated**)
1 to formally put somebody such as a new leader in an official position at a special ceremony
2 to start, introduce or open something new and important, especially with a formal ceremony
▸ **inaugural** (*adjective*): *the President's **inaugural** speech* ▸ **inauguration** (*noun*): *We attended the **inauguration** of the new museum.*

inborn (say **in**-bawn) *adjective*
that you are born with: ***inborn** characteristics*

inbox (say **in**-bokss) *noun* (*plural* **inboxes**)
the part of an email system where messages that people have sent to you are stored

incalculable (say in-**kal**-kyuh-luhb-l) *adjective*
1 too great to calculate or too many to be counted: *an* ***incalculable*** *number of stars*
2 that cannot be known or planned for in advance: *an* ***incalculable*** *risk*

incapable (say in-**kay**-puhb-l) *adjective*
not able to do something: *He's* ***incapable*** *of lying.* ➲ OPPOSITE **capable** 1

incarcerate (say in-**kaa**-suh-rayt) *verb* (**incarcerating, incarcerated**) (*formal*)
to put somebody in prison or in another place from which they cannot escape
▸ **incarceration** (*noun*): *The investigation led to his arrest and* ***incarceration****.*

incendiary (say in-**sen**-di-uh-ree) *adjective*
designed to cause or start a fire easily: *A petrol bomb is an* ***incendiary*** *device.*

incense[1] (say **in**-senss) *noun* (*no plural*)
a substance that produces a sweet smell when you burn it and is used in some religious ceremonies

incense[2] (say in-**senss**) *verb* (**incensing, incensed**)
to make somebody extremely angry
➲ SYNONYM **infuriate**

incentive (say in-**sen**-tuhv) *noun* (*plural* **incentives**)
something that makes you want to do something: *People need* ***incentives*** *to save money.* ➲ OPPOSITE **disincentive**

incessant (say in-**sess**-uhnt) *adjective*
continuing for a long time without stopping: ***incessant*** *noise* ➲ SYNONYM **ceaseless**
▸ **incessantly** (*adverb*): *The rain poured down* ***incessantly****.*

incest (say **in**-sest) *noun* (*no plural*)
the crime of having sex with a person who is a close relative, for example a brother or sister

inch *noun* (*plural* **inches**)
a measure of length (= 2,54 centimetres) used in some countries: *a twelve-****inch*** *ruler*

incidence (say **in**-si-duhnss) *noun* (*no plural*)
how often something happens or occurs, or the rate of something: *a high* ***incidence*** *of crime*

incident (say **in**-si-duhnt) *noun* (*plural* **incidents**)
something that happens, especially something bad or unusual: *an unpleasant* ***incident***

incidentally (say in-si-**dent**-lee) *adverb*
a word that you say when you are going to talk about something different: ***Incidentally****, have you seen that new movie yet?*

incinerate (say in-**sin**-uh-rayt) *verb* (**incinerating, incinerated**)
to destroy something completely by burning
▸ **incineration** (*noun*): *the* ***incineration*** *of waste products*

incisor (say in-**size**-uh) *noun* (*plural* **incisors**)
one of the teeth at the front of the mouth that is used for biting ➲ See **canine**[1], **molar**

incite (say in-**site**) *verb* (**inciting, incited**)
to encourage somebody to do something by making them very angry or excited
▸ **incitement** (*noun*): *His comments were an* ***incitement*** *to violence.*

incline (say **in**-kline) *noun* (*plural* **inclines**)
a piece of ground that has one end higher than the other: *The train made its way up a steep* ***incline****.*
▸ **incline** (*verb*): *The road* ***inclines*** *slightly.*

inclined (say in-**kline**-d) *adjective*
1 wanting to do something: *I'm* ***inclined*** *to agree with you.*
2 likely to do something: *She's* ***inclined*** *to change her mind a lot.*

include (say in-**klood**) *verb* (**including, included**)
1 to have somebody or something as one part of the whole: *The price* ***includes*** *breakfast.*
2 to make somebody or something part of a group: *Did you* ***include*** *the new girl in the list?*
➲ OPPOSITE **exclude**
🛈 ORIGIN: 14th–15th century, from Latin *includere*, from *in-* meaning 'into' + *claudere* meaning 'to shut'. When the word first came into English, it also meant 'to shut inside'.

including (say in-**klood**-ing) *preposition*
with or if you count: *There were five people in the car,* ***including*** *the driver.* ➲ OPPOSITE **excluding**

inclusive (say in-**kloo**-siv) *adjective*
including everything or the thing mentioned: *The hotel price is* ***inclusive*** *of meals.*

incognito (say in-kog-**nee**-toh) *adverb, adjective*
hiding your real identity, for example by using a false name or changing your appearance: *The film star was travelling* ***incognito****.* ◇ *He made an* ***incognito*** *visit to South Africa.*

incoherent (say in-koh-**heer**-ruhnt) *adjective*
(of speaking or writing) not clear or logical and therefore difficult to understand: ***incoherent*** *speech* ➲ OPPOSITE **coherent**
▸ **incoherence** (*noun*)
▸ **incoherently** (*adverb*)

A B C D E F G H I J K L M N O P Q R S T U V W X Y Z

income (say **in**-kum) *noun* (*plural* **incomes**)
all the money that you receive as payment for your work, as interest on money that you have saved, etc.: *It's difficult for a family to live on one person's* ***income****.*

income tax *noun* (*no plural*)
the money that you pay to the government from the money that you earn

incomparable (say in-**kom**-pruhb-l) *adjective*
so good or great that it does not have an equal: ***incomparable*** *beauty*

incompatible (say in-kom-**pat**-ib-l) *adjective*
People and things that are **incompatible** are so different from each other that they cannot live, exist or function together. ➲ OPPOSITE **compatible**
▸ **incompatibility** (*noun*): *The problem was caused by an* ***incompatibility*** *between the software and the computer.*

incompetent (say in-**kom**-puh-tuhnt) *adjective*
not having the necessary knowledge, ability or skill to do something well ➲ OPPOSITE **competent** 1
▸ **incompetence** (*noun*): *allegations of* ***incompetence*** ▸ **incompetently** (*adverb*)

incomplete (say in-kom-**pleet**) *adjective*
not finished or with parts missing: *This list is* ***incomplete****.* ➲ OPPOSITE **complete**[1]

incomprehensible (say in-kom-pree-**hen**-sib-l) *adjective*
very difficult or impossible to understand: *Her attitude is* ***incomprehensible*** *to the rest of the committee.* ➲ OPPOSITE **comprehensible**
▸ **incomprehension** (*noun*): *a look of complete* ***incomprehension***

inconclusive (say in-kuhn-**kloo**-siv) *adjective*
not producing a definite decision or result
▸ **inconclusively** (*adverb*): *The meeting ended* ***inconclusively*** *due to disagreements.*

inconsiderate (say in-kuhn-**sid**-uh-ruht) *adjective*
(used about a person) not thinking or caring about other people and their feelings: *It's* ***inconsiderate*** *of you to make so much noise.*
➲ OPPOSITE **considerate**

inconsistent (say in-kuhn-**siss**-tuhnt) *adjective*
not always the same: *She's so* ***inconsistent*** *– sometimes she's really friendly and sometimes she's not.* ➲ OPPOSITE **consistent**

inconspicuous (say in-kuhn-**spik**-yuu-uhss) *adjective*
not easily noticed, usually because you are trying to avoid attracting attention ➲ OPPOSITE **conspicuous**
▸ **inconspicuously** (*adverb*): *He nodded* ***inconspicuously*** *in the direction of the teacher.*

inconvenient (say in-kuhn-**vee**-ni-uhnt) *adjective*
causing you problems or difficulty: *Is this an* ***inconvenient*** *time to talk? I can phone later.*
➲ OPPOSITE **convenient**
▸ **inconvenience** (*noun*): *We apologize for any* ***inconvenience****.*

incorporate (say in-**kaw**-puh-rayt) *verb* (**incorporating**, **incorporated**)
to include something as a part of something else or to have something as a part
▸ **incorporation** (*noun*): *the* ***incorporation*** *of the college with the university*

incorrect (say in-kuh-**rekt**) *adjective*
not right or true: *There were several* ***incorrect*** *answers.* ➲ OPPOSITE **correct**[1]
▸ **incorrectly** (*adverb*): *Her name was spelled* ***incorrectly****.*

increase[1] (say in-**kreess**) *verb* (**increasing**, **increased**)
1 to make something bigger or more: *I'm going to* ***increase*** *your pocket money to R10.*
➲ SYNONYM **raise** 2 ➲ OPPOSITE **reduce**
2 to become bigger or more: *The number of women who go out to work has* ***increased****.*
➲ SYNONYM **rise**[1] 1 ➲ OPPOSITE **decrease**[1]

PRONUNCIATION Notice that you pronounce the noun and the verb differently.

increase[2] (say **in**-kreess) *noun* (*plural* **increases**)
a rise in the amount, number or value of something: *a price* ***increase***

increasingly (say in-**kree**-sing-lee) *adverb*
more and more: *This city is becoming* ***increasingly*** *dangerous.*

incredible (say in-**kred**-ib-l) *adjective*
1 impossible or very difficult to believe: *I found the story completely* ***incredible****.*
➲ SYNONYMS **amazing**, **unbelievable**
2 (*informal*) very large or very good: *She earns an* ***incredible*** *amount of money.* ◇ *The hotel was* ***incredible****.*
▸ **incredibly** (*adverb*) (*informal*): *He's* ***incredibly*** *clever.*

incredulous (say in-**kred**-yuu-luhss) *adjective*
not able or prepared to believe something or showing that you do not believe something: *They were* ***incredulous*** *that anyone could be so cruel.* ◇ *an* ***incredulous*** *frown*
▸ **incredulity** (*noun*)
▸ **incredulously** (*adverb*)

increment (say **in**-kruh-muhnt) *noun* (*plural* **increments**)
an increase in the amount or size of something, especially one of a series of regular or planned increases: *a salary with annual* ***increments***
▸ **incremental** (*adjective*): ***incremental*** *costs*
▸ **incrementally** (*adverb*): *The project will have to be done* ***incrementally***.

incubate (say **in**-kyuu-bayt) *verb* (**incubating, incubated**)
1 to provide a warm environment for an egg so that the young animal can develop and **hatch**[1] (= come out of the egg)
2 to develop an infection or a disease over a period of time without showing signs, or to carry a disease without showing signs of illness: *Malaria* ***incubates*** *in your body for one to two weeks.*
▸ **incubation** (*noun*)

incubator (say **in**-kyuu-bay-tuh) *noun* (*plural* **incubators**)
a special machine that hospitals use to keep small or weak babies alive

incur (say in-**kur**) *verb* (**incurring, incurred**) (*formal*)
to suffer something unpleasant as a result of something you've done: *Motorists who have* ***incurred*** *traffic fines have twenty days to pay.*

incurable (say in-**kyoor**-ruhb-l) *adjective*
that cannot be cured or made better: *an* ***incurable*** *disease*
▸ **incurably** (*adverb*): ***incurably*** *ill*

indaba (say in-**daa**-buh) *noun* (*plural* **indabas**) (*S. African*)
1 a large meeting or discussion: *a peace* ***indaba***
2 (*informal*) a problem or worry: *Her problems are not my* ***indaba***.
ⓘ **ORIGIN**: 19th century, from isiXhosa and isiZulu *indaba* meaning 'matter, business'

indebted (say in-**det**-uhd) *adjective*
very grateful: *I am* ***indebted*** *to my family for all their help and support.*

indecent (say in-**dee**-suhnt) *adjective*
shocking or rude, especially because something involves sex or the body: ***indecent*** *behaviour*
▸ **indecency** (*noun*) ▸ **indecently** (*adverb*): *The victim had been* ***indecently*** *assaulted.*

indecisive (say in-di-**sise**-iv) *adjective*
not able to make decisions easily ➲ **OPPOSITE** **decisive** 2
▸ **indecision** (*noun*): *my* ***indecision*** *about the future* ▸ **indecisiveness** (*noun*): *Her* ***indecisiveness*** *irritates us.*

indeed (say in-**deed**) *adverb*
1 a word that makes a positive statement or answer stronger: *'Did you have a good holiday?' 'I did* ***indeed****.'* ➲ **SYNONYM** **certainly** 1
2 a word that makes 'very' stronger: *Thank you very much* ***indeed****.* ◇ *She's very happy* ***indeed****.*

indefensible (say in-di-**fen**-suhb-l) *adjective*
too bad or wrong to be defended or excused: *War crimes are* ***indefensible****.*

indefinable (say in-di-**fine**-uhb-l) *adjective*
difficult or impossible to be described exactly: *the* ***indefinable*** *smell of rain*
▸ **indefinably** (*adverb*)

indefinite (say in-**def**-i-nuht) *adjective*
not clear or certain: *Our plans are still rather* ***indefinite****.*

indefinite article *noun* (*plural* **indefinite articles**) (*grammar*)
the name for the words 'a' and 'an'
➲ See **definite article**

indefinitely (say in-**def**-i-nuht-lee) *adverb*
for a long time, perhaps for ever: *The trial was postponed* ***indefinitely****.*

indent (say in-**dent**) *verb* (**indenting, indented**)
1 to start a line of writing or a row of printed text further from the side than the main part of the text
2 to make a mark in the surface of something by hitting it, pushing it in or cutting away a small part of it
▸ **indentation** (*noun*)

independence (say in-di-**pen**-duhnss) *noun* (*no plural*)
being free from another person, thing or country: *America declared its* ***independence*** *from Britain in 1776.*

independent (say in-di-**pen**-duhnt) *adjective*
1 not controlled by another person, thing or country: *Mozambique became* ***independent*** *in 1975.*
2 not needing or wanting help: *She lives alone now and she is very* ***independent****.* ➲ **OPPOSITE** **dependent**

> **SPELLING** Remember! You spell **independent** with three **e**'s.

indestructible (say in-di-**struk**-tuhb-l) *adjective*
impossible or very difficult to be destroyed or damaged
▸ **indestructibility** (*noun*)

indeterminate (say in-di-**turm**-i-nuht) *adjective*
not exactly known or decided, or not definite or clear: *The strike will continue for an* ***indeterminate*** *period of time.*

index (say **in**-dekss) *noun*
1 (*plural* **indexes**) a list of words from A to Z at

A B C D E F G H I J K L M N O P Q R S T U V W X Y Z

the end of a book. It tells you what things are in the book and where you can find them.
2 (*plural* **indexes** or **indices**) a system that shows the level of prices, wages etc. so that they can be compared with those of a previous date
3 (*plural* **indices**) a sign or measure that something else can be judged by: *House prices are an **index** of the state of the economy.*
4 (*plural* **indices**) (*maths*) the small number written above a larger number to show how many times that number must be multiplied by itself. In the **equation** $4^2 = 16$ the number ^{2} is an index.

index finger *noun* (*plural* **index fingers**)
the finger next to your thumb ➲ See illustration at **hand**[1]

indicate (say **in**-di-kayt) *verb* (**indicating, indicated**)
1 to show that something is true, exists or will happen: *The arrows on the map **indicate** one-way streets.* ◇ *Black clouds **indicate** that it's going to rain.*
2 to make somebody notice something, especially by pointing to it: *The receptionist **indicated** the place where I should sign.*
3 to show that your car is going to turn by using a light: *You should **indicate** left now.*

indication (say in-di-**kay**-shuhn) *noun* (*plural* **indications**)
something that shows something: *He gave no **indication** that he was angry.* ➲ SYNONYM **sign**[1]

indicative (say in-**dik**-uh-tiv) *adjective*
1 (*formal*) being a sign of something: *Is the unusual weather **indicative** of changes in the climate?*
2 (*grammar*) relating to the form of a verb that is used in a simple statement such as 'I love you', and that is not a command or a question

indicator (say **in**-di-kay-tuh) *noun* (*plural* **indicators**)
1 something that gives information or shows something: *Growth is an **indicator** of good health in children.*
2 a light on a car that shows that it is going to turn left or right

indifferent (say in-**dif**-ruhnt) *adjective*
not interested in or caring about somebody or something: *He seemed completely **indifferent** to my feelings.*

indigenous (say in-**dij**-uh-nuhss) *adjective*
(used about people, animals or plants) living or growing in the place where they are from originally: ***indigenous** knowledge* ◇ *Giraffes are **indigenous** to Africa.* ◇ *It is a good idea to plant **indigenous** trees in your garden* ➲ See **alien**[1], **exotic** 1

indigestion (say in-dy-**jess**-tshuhn) *noun* (*no plural*)
pain in your stomach caused by something you have eaten: *Onions give me **indigestion**.*

indignant (say in-**dig**-nuhnt) *adjective*
shocked or angry because somebody has done, written or said something that you do not like or agree with: *She was **indignant** when I said she was lazy.*
▸ **indignantly** (*adverb*) ▸ **indignation** (*noun*)

indignity (say in-**dig**-nuh-tee) *noun* (*plural* **indignities**)
a situation that makes you feel embarrassed because you are not treated with respect, or an act that causes these feelings: *The sportswoman had to suffer the **indignity** of being disqualified.*

indigo (say **in**-di-goh) *adjective*
with a very dark blue colour: *an **indigo** linen suit*
▸ **indigo** (*noun*): ***Indigo** is my favourite colour.*

indirect (say **in**-dy-rekt) *adjective*
1 happening not as the main aim, cause or result of an action, but in addition to it: *These problems are an **indirect** result of the war.*
➲ OPPOSITE **direct**[1]
2 not saying or writing something in a clear and obvious way: ***indirect** answers*
3 not moving or going in a straight line: *We came by an **indirect** route.*
▸ **indirectly** (*adverb*)

indirect object *noun* (*plural* **indirect objects**) (*grammar*)
a person or thing that an action is done to or for: *In the sentence 'I sent him a letter', 'him' is the **indirect object**.* ➲ See **direct object**

indirect speech *noun* (*no plural*) = **reported speech**

indiscreet (say in-di-**skreet**) *adjective*
not careful or polite in what you say or do: *an **indiscreet** comment* ➲ OPPOSITE **discreet** 1
▸ **indiscreetly** (*adverb*)

indiscriminate (say in-di-**skrim**-i-nuht) *adjective*
done or acting without careful judgement or without caring about possible harmful effects: *The **indiscriminate** use of water has made it a scarce resource.*
▸ **indiscriminately** (*adverb*)

indispensable (say in-di-**spen**-suhb-l) *adjective*
very important or useful, so that it is not possible to be without it: *This book is an **indispensable** guide for anyone interested in gardening.* ➲ SYNONYM **essential**

indistinct (say in-di-**stinkt**) *adjective*
not clear: ***indistinct** sounds* ◇ ***indistinct** memories*
➲ OPPOSITE **distinct** 1
▸ **indistinctly** (*adverb*)

individual[1] (say in-di-**vid**-yuu-uhl) *adjective*
1 considered separately and not as part of a group: *Each **individual** student gets their own study plan.*
2 for only one person or thing: *an **individual** portion of cheese*
▸ **individually** (*adverb*)

individual[2] (say in-di-**vid**-yuu-uhl) *noun* (*plural* **individuals**)
one person: *Teachers must treat each child as an **individual**.*

indivisible (say in-di-**viz**-uhb-l) *adjective*
not able to be divided or split into smaller pieces

indoctrinate (say in-**dok**-tri-nayt) *verb* (**indoctrinating, indoctrinated**)
to persuade somebody to accept particular beliefs or ideas, so that they refuse to accept any others ➲ SYNONYM **brainwash**
▸ **indoctrination** (*noun*): *the political **indoctrination** of children*

indoor (say **in**-daw) *adjective*
done or used inside a building: *an **indoor** swimming pool* ◇ ***indoor** games* ➲ OPPOSITE **outdoor**

indoors (say in-**dawz**) *adverb*
in or into a building: *Let's go **indoors**. I'm cold.*
➲ OPPOSITE **outdoors**

induce (say in-**dyooss**) *verb* (**inducing, induced**) (*formal*)
1 to persuade or influence somebody to do or think something: *Nothing could **induce** him to change his mind.*
2 to cause a particular state or feeling: *drugs that **induce** sleep*
3 to make a woman start giving birth to her baby before it happens naturally, usually by giving her special drugs

induct (say in-**dukt**) *verb* (**inducting, inducted**)
to introduce a person to a new school, organization, job, etc. and explain what is expected of them

induction (say in-**duk**-shuhn) *noun*
1 (*plural* **inductions**) the process of introducing a person to a new school, organization, job etc.: *an **induction** day for new students*
2 (*no plural*) (*technology*) the process by which electricity or **magnetism** passes from one object to another without them touching

indulge (say in-**dulj**) *verb* (**indulging, indulged**)
1 to allow yourself to have or experience something enjoyable: *I'm going to **indulge** myself and go shopping for some new clothes.*
2 to allow somebody to have or do what they want: ***Indulging** that child could make him very selfish.*

industrial (say in-**duss**-tri-uhl) *adjective*
1 connected with making things in factories: ***industrial** machines*
2 with a lot of factories: *an **industrial** area*

industrialist (say in-**duss**-tri-uh-list) *noun* (*plural* **industrialists**)
a person who owns or manages a large industrial company

industrialized (say in-**duss**-tri-uh-lize-d) *adjective* (also **industrialised**)
(used about a country or region) having a lot of modern industries ➲ See **developing country**

industrious (say in-**duss**-tri-uhss) *adjective*
always working hard: *Our English teacher is enthusiastic and **industrious**.*
▸ **industriously** (*adverb*)
▸ **industriousness** (*noun*): *the **industriousness** of ants*

industry (say **in**-duhss-tree) *noun*
1 (*no plural*) the work of making things in factories: *Is there much **industry** in your country?*
2 (*plural* **industries**) all the companies that make the same thing: *Japan has a big car **industry**.*

inebriated (say i-**nee**-bri-ay-tid) *adjective* (*formal*)
very drunk

inedible (say in-**ed**-ib-l) *adjective*
not good or safe to eat: ***inedible** mushrooms*
➲ OPPOSITE **edible**

inefficient (say in-i-**fish**-uhnt) *adjective*
not working or producing results in the best way, so that time or money is wasted: *This washing machine is very old and **inefficient**.*
➲ OPPOSITE **efficient**
▸ **inefficiency** (*noun*)

inelegant (say in-**el**-i-guhnt) *adjective*
not attractive, or not moving smoothly
➲ OPPOSITE **elegant**

ineligible (say in-**el**-i-juhb-l) *adjective*
not having the legal right or the necessary certificates to do, be or get something: *The player was **ineligible** for selection because he had been suspended.* ➲ OPPOSITE **eligible**

inept (say in-**ept**) *adjective*
not having the necessary ability or skill to do

A B C D E F G H I J K L M N O P Q R S T U V W X Y Z

something well: *She is totally **inept** at dealing with people.*

inequality (say in-i-**kwol**-uh-tee) *noun* (*plural* **inequalities**)
a big difference between people or groups in society, especially an unfair difference in how they are treated or what they have: *social **inequalities*** ➲ OPPOSITE **equality**

inert (say i-**nurt**) *adjective*
1 not moving or not able to move or act: *He stood **inert** for a moment.*
2 (*science*) (used about chemical elements) that do not react quickly or easily with other chemicals: *Helium, argon, krypton and neon are **inert** gases.*

inertia (say i-**nur**-shuh) *noun* (*no plural*)
1 the inability to move or act, or a feeling of not being enthusiastic about something: *Overcome the **inertia** and do your work.*
2 (*science*) the physical force that keeps things still or, if they are moving, keeps them moving in a straight line, unless they are affected by some outside force

inescapable (say in-i-**skay**-puhb-l) *adjective* (*formal*)
that cannot be avoided or that must be accepted as true or real: *an **inescapable** responsibility* ◇ ***inescapable** consequences*

inevitable (say in-**ev**-i-tuhb-l) *adjective*
that will certainly happen: *The accident was **inevitable** – he was driving too fast.*
▸ **inevitably** (*adverb*)

inexcusable (say in-ikss-**kyoo**-zuhb-l) *adjective*
too bad, rude or wrong to be forgiven or allowed: *Racism is **inexcusable**.*

inexpensive (say in-ikss-**pen**-siv) *adjective*
not expensive ➲ SYNONYM **cheap** 1

inexperience (say in-ikss-**peer**-ri-uhnss) *noun* (*no plural*)
a position in which you do not know how to do something because you have not done it before: *The mistakes were all due to **inexperience**.* ➲ OPPOSITE **experience**[1] 1

inexperienced (say in-ik-**speer**-ri-uhnst) *adjective*
not knowing how to do something because you have not done it many times before: *a young **inexperienced** driver* ➲ OPPOSITE **experienced**

inexplicable (say in-ik-**splik**-uhb-l) *adjective*
that cannot be explained or understood: *I found his behaviour **inexplicable**.*

infancy (say **in**-fuhn-see) *noun* (*no plural*)
1 the time when you are a baby or a very young child
2 an early stage of development or existence: *Research in this field is still in its **infancy**.*

infant (say **in**-fuhnt) *noun* (*plural* **infants**) (*formal*)
a baby or very young child

infantry (say **in**-fuhn-tree) *noun* (*no plural*)
the part of an army that is made up of soldiers who fight on foot rather than on horses or in vehicles

infatuated (say in-**fat**-yuu-ay-tid) *adjective*
having a very strong feeling of love or attraction for a person or thing that usually does not last long: *She became **infatuated** with the handsome actor.*
▸ **infatuation** (*noun*): *teenage **infatuation***

infect (say in-**fekt**) *verb* (**infecting, infected**)
to pass a disease on to somebody or something: *Thousands of people have been **infected** with the virus.*

infected (say in-**fek**-tid) *adjective*
full of small living things (called **germs**) that can make you ill: *Clean that cut or it could become **infected**.*

infection (say in-**fek**-shuhn) *noun* (*plural* **infections**)
a disease or an illness that affects one part of the body: *I have an ear **infection**.*

infectious (say in-**fek**-shuhss) *adjective*
(about a disease, an illness, etc.) that can be easily passed on from one living being to another. ➲ See **contagious** ➲ SYNONYM **catching**

infer (say in-**fur**) *verb* (**inferring, inferred**)
to come to a conclusion or form an opinion using the facts you have: *I **inferred** from our conversation that he was unhappy at school.* ➲ SYNONYM **deduce**
▸ **inference** (*noun*): *sensible **inferences***

inferior (say in-**feer**-ri-uh) *adjective, adverb*
not as good or important as another person or thing: *fruit of **inferior quality*** ◇ *Lisa's so clever that she always makes me feel **inferior**.* ➲ OPPOSITE **superior** 1
▸ **inferiority** (*noun*): *a sense of **inferiority***

inferno (say in-**fur**-noh) *noun* (*plural* **infernos**)
a large fire that is out of control, or a place that is on fire and being destroyed by it: *The **inferno** destroyed 500 houses.*

infertile (say in-**fur**-tile) *adjective*
1 not able to have babies or produce young animals ➲ SYNONYM **sterile** 1

2 not able to produce good crops ➲ OPPOSITE **fertile**
▸ **infertility** (*noun*): *male **infertility***

infest (say in-**fest**) *verb* (**infesting, infested**)
to live or exist in or on something in large numbers: *worms that **infest** livestock*
▸ **infestation** (*noun*): *an **infestation** of lice*
▸ **infested** (*adjective*): *a rat-**infested** building*

infidel (say **in**-fi-duhl) *noun* (*plural* **infidels**) (*old-fashioned*)
a disapproving way of referring to a person who does not believe in what the speaker considers to be the true religion
➲ SYNONYM **heathen**

infidelity (say in-fi-**del**-uh-tee) *noun* (*plural* **infidelities**)
the action or state of not being faithful to your partner by having a sexual relationship with somebody else: *past **infidelities*** ➲ OPPOSITE **fidelity**

infiltrate (say **in**-fil-trayt) *verb* (**infiltrating, infiltrated**)
to join an organization or enter a place secretly so that you can collect information or influence events: *The police managed to **infiltrate** the gang.*
▸ **infiltration** (*noun*): *the **infiltration** of rebel forces* ▸ **infiltrator** (*noun*): *a successful **infiltrator** and spy*

infinite (say **in**-fi-nuht) *adjective*
with no end, or too much or too many to count or measure: *There is an **infinite** number of stars in the sky.* ➲ OPPOSITE **finite**
ⓘ ORIGIN: 14th–15th century, from Latin *infinitus*, from *in-* meaning 'not' + *finitus* meaning 'finished, having limits'

infinitely (say **in**-fi-nuht-lee) *adverb*
very much: *DVDs are **infinitely** better than videos.*

infinitive (say in-**fin**-uh-tiv) *noun* (*plural* **infinitives**) (*grammar*)
the basic form of a verb, which can be used either by itself or with the word 'to' before it: *'Eat', 'go' and 'play' are all **infinitives**.*

infinity (say in-**fin**-i-tee) *noun* (*no plural*)
space or time without end

infirm (say in-**furm**) *adjective*
very weak, especially because of being ill or old
▸ **infirmity** (*noun*): *She continued to work despite her **infirmity**.*

inflame (say in-**flaym**) *verb* (**inflaming, inflamed**)
1 to make a feeling such as anger become stronger, or to cause strong feelings such as anger in somebody
2 to become, or to make a part of your body become, red and sore because of an infection or injury
▸ **inflamed** (*adjective*): *an **inflamed** mob* ◇ ***inflamed** eyes* ▸ **inflammatory** (*adjective*): *anti-**inflammatory** drugs* ◇ ***inflammatory** remarks*

inflammable (say in-**flam**-uhb-l) *adjective*
that burns easily: *Petrol is highly **inflammable**.*
➲ SYNONYM **flammable**

> WHICH WORD? **Inflammable** or **flammable**?
> ■ These words mean the same thing, though they look like opposites.

inflammation (say in-fluh-**may**-shuhn) *noun* (*plural* **inflammations**)
a condition in which a part of your body becomes red and sore because of an infection or injury: ***inflammation** of the liver*

inflatable (say in-**flay**-tuhb-l) *adjective*
that can or must be filled with air or gas to make it ready for use: *an **inflatable** mattress*
▸ **inflatable** (*noun*): *The **inflatable** disappeared beneath the waves.*

inflate (say in-**flayt**) *verb* (**inflating, inflated**) (*formal*)
to fill something with air or gas: *He **inflated** the tyre.* ➲ OPPOSITE **deflate** 1

> SPEAKING We usually say **blow up** or **pump up**: *I **pumped up** my bicycle tyres.*

inflation (say in-**flay**-shuhn) *noun* (*no plural*)
a general rise in prices in a country: *The government is trying to control **inflation**.*
➲ OPPOSITE **deflation**

inflect (say in-**flekt**) *verb* (**inflecting, inflected**)
1 (*grammar*) to change the basic form of a word in a way that shows its relationship with other words in the same sentence
2 to change the way your voice sounds as you speak, especially to express how you feel at a particular time
▸ **inflected** (*adjective*): *The **inflected** form of the noun 'child' is 'children'.* ▸ **inflection** (*noun*): *He spoke without **inflection**.*

inflexible (say in-**flek**-sib-l) *adjective*
1 that cannot be changed or made more suitable for a particular situation: *an **inflexible** rule*
2 not wanting to change your opinions or plans: ***inflexible** attitudes*
3 not able to bend or be bent easily: *an **inflexible** solid steel bar* ➲ OPPOSITE **flexible** 2
▸ **inflexibility** (*noun*)

inflict (say in-**flikt**) *verb* (**inflicting, inflicted**)
to force somebody to experience something unpleasant or harmful: *The team **inflicted** a third defeat on their rivals.*
▸ **infliction** (*noun*): *the **infliction** of pain*

inflow (say **in**-floh) *noun* (*no plural*)
1 the movement of a lot of money, people or things into a place: *the **inflow** of tourists from West Africa*
2 the movement of a liquid or of air into a place: *an increased **inflow** of water into the river*

influence[1] (say **in**-fluu-uhnss) *noun*
1 (*no plural*) the power to change what somebody believes or does: *Television has a strong **influence** on people.*
2 (*plural* **influences**) a person or thing that can change somebody or something: *Danie's new girlfriend is a good **influence** on him.*

influence[2] (say **in**-fluu-uhnss) *verb* (**influencing, influenced**)
to change the way that somebody thinks or the way that something happens: *She is easily **influenced** by her friends.*

influential (say in-fluu-**en**-shuhl) *adjective*
having power or influence: *Her father's very **influential**.*

influenza (say in-fluu-**en**-zuh) *noun* (*no plural*)
= **flu**

influx (say **in**-flukss) *noun* (*no plural*)
large numbers of people or things arriving or appearing suddenly: *The company expects an **influx** of customers.*

inform (say in-**fawm**) *verb* (**informing, informed**) (*formal*)
to tell somebody something: *You should **inform** the police of the accident.*

informal (say in-**fawm**-l) *adjective*
relaxed and friendly, or suitable for a relaxed occasion: *I wear **informal** clothes, such as jeans and T-shirts, at weekends.* ◇ *an **informal** letter*
➲ OPPOSITE **formal**
▸ **informally** (*adverb*): *We have discussed the matter **informally**.*

> SPEAKING Some words and expressions in this dictionary are labelled **informal**. You use them when speaking and writing to people you know well, but not in serious writing or official letters. Examples of informal words are **bloke**, **clout**, **gogga**, **lousy** and **OK**.

information (say in-fuh-**may**-shuhn) *noun* (*no plural*)
facts about people or things: *Can you give me some **information** about trains to Soweto?*

> USAGE Be careful! You cannot say 'an information'. You say **some information** or a **piece of information**. *She gave me an interesting **piece of information**.*

informative (say in-**faw**-muh-tiv) *adjective*
that gives useful information: *The talk was very **informative**.*

informed (say in-**fawm**-d) *adjective*
1 having information or knowledge about something: *Voters should be well **informed** about the elections.*
2 using the understanding you have of a situation to make a judgement or decision: *This guide will help you to make **informed** decisions about your career.*

infrastructure (say **in**-fruh-struk-tshuh) *noun* (*no plural*)
the necessary services and systems that make it possible for a country or an organization to function properly, including buildings, electricity and water supplies, roads and schools
▸ **infrastructural** (*adjective*): ***infrastructural** facilities*

infrequent (say in-**free**-kwuhnt) *adjective*
not frequent
▸ **infrequently** (*adverb*): *We see each other **infrequently**.*

infringe (say in-**frinj**) *verb* (**infringing, infringed**)
1 to break a rule, law or agreement: *The penalty for **infringing** this regulation is a fine of up to R100.*
2 to reduce or limit somebody's rights, freedom, etc.: *She refused to answer questions that **infringed** on her private affairs.*
▸ **infringement** (*noun*): *copyright **infringements***

infuriate (say in-**fyoo**-ri-ayt) *verb* (**infuriating, infuriated**)
to make somebody extremely angry
➲ SYNONYMS **enrage, incense[2]**
▸ **infuriating** (*adjective*): *an **infuriating** habit*
▸ **infuriatingly** (*adverb*): *The queue was **infuriatingly** slow.*

infuse (say in-**fyooz**) *verb* (**infusing, infused**)
1 (*formal*) to make somebody or something have a particular quality: *Her novels are **infused** with sadness.*
2 (*formal*) to spread through or be present in every part of something: *Politics **infuses** all aspects of our lives.*
3 to put the leaves of a plant in a liquid so that the flavour or other qualities pass into the liquid: *To make tea, **infuse** one teaspoon of the*

dried leaves in a cup of hot water.
▶ **infusion** (*noun*)

ingenious (say in-**jee**-ni-uhss) *adjective*
1 clever at inventing things or at finding solutions to problems: *an **ingenious** cook*
2 clever, original and working well: *an **ingenious** plan*
▶ **ingeniously** (*adverb*) ▶ **ingenuity** (*noun*): *the **ingenuity** of people*

ingrained (say in-**graynd**) *adjective*
1 firmly fixed in somebody's mind and therefore difficult to change: ***ingrained** prejudices*
2 (used about dirt) that has become stuck in or on something and is difficult to remove: ***ingrained** carpet dirt*

ingratiate (say in-**gray**-shi-ayt) *verb* (**ingratiating, ingratiated**) (*formal*)
to try to make friends with somebody by doing or saying things that will please them, especially because their friendship might be useful to you: *He was always trying to **ingratiate** himself with his teachers.*
▶ **ingratiating** (*adjective*): ***ingratiating** charm*

ingredient (say in-**gree**-di-uhnt) *noun* (*plural* **ingredients**)
one of the things that you put in when you make something to eat: *The **ingredients** for this cake are flour, butter, sugar and eggs.*

inhabit (say in-**hab**-it) *verb* (**inhabiting, inhabited**)
to live in a place: *Is the island **inhabited*** (= does anybody live there)? ◇ *The Antarctic is **inhabited** by penguins.*

inhabitant (say in-**hab**-i-tuhnt) *noun* (*plural* **inhabitants**)
a person or an animal that lives in a place: *The town has 30 000 **inhabitants**.*

inhale (say in-**hayl**) *verb* (**inhaling, inhaled**) (*formal*)
to take air, smoke, etc. into your body by breathing: *Be careful not to **inhale** the fumes from the paint.* ➲ OPPOSITE **exhale**

inherent (say in-**heer**-ruhnt) *adjective*
that is a permanent part, quality or feature of somebody or something and that cannot be changed or removed
▶ **inherently** (*adverb*): *War is **inherently** violent.*

inherit (say in-**he**-rit) *verb* (**inheriting, inherited**)
to get money or things from somebody who has died: *She **inherited** some money from her grandmother.*
▶ **inheritance** (*noun*): *She spent her **inheritance** in one year.*

inhibit (say in-**hib**-it) *verb* (**inhibiting, inhibited**)
1 to stop something from developing or continuing, or to slow it down: *a drug to **inhibit** the growth of tumours*
2 to prevent somebody from behaving or speaking in an open and relaxed way
▶ **inhibited** (*adjective*) ▶ **inhibition** (*noun*)

inhospitable (say in-hoss-**pit**-uhb-l) *adjective*
1 not friendly or kind to visitors ➲ OPPOSITE **hospitable**
2 not pleasant to live or work in, especially because of the weather: *an **inhospitable** desert*

inhuman (say in-**hyoo**-muhn) *adjective*
1 very cruel and without pity: *the **inhuman** treatment of innocent creatures*
2 not seeming to be human: *an **inhuman** noise*
▶ **inhumanity** (*noun*): *the **inhumanities** endured by slaves*

inhumane (say in-hyoo-**mayn**) *adjective*
not caring if people or animals suffer, or causing suffering: *the **inhumane** way in which seals are killed* ➲ OPPOSITE **humane**

iniquitous (say i-**nik**-wi-tuhss) *adjective*
very unfair, wrong or immoral: *This law is **iniquitous**.* ➲ SYNONYM **unjust**
▶ **iniquity** (*noun*): *society's **iniquities***

initial[1] (say i-**nish**-uhl) *adjective*
first: *My **initial** reaction was to refuse, but I later changed my mind.*
▶ **initially** (*adverb*)

initial[2] (say i-**nish**-uhl) *noun* (*plural* **initials**)
the first letter of a person's name: *John Moloi's **initials** are J.M.*

initiate (say i-**nish**-i-ayt) *verb* (**initiating, initiated**)
1 to cause something to begin, especially an important process or event: *to **initiate** peace talks*
2 to allow somebody to become a member of a group, organization or society, especially with a secret or special ceremony
3 to make somebody experience something for the first time or to teach them how to do something new: *Years ago I was **initiated** to the joys of fishing.*
▶ **initiate** (*noun*): *Experienced elders advise the **initiates**.* ▶ **initiation** (*noun*): *an **initiation** ritual*

initiative (say i-**nish**-i-uh-tiv) *noun*
1 (*plural* **initiatives**) official action that is taken to deal with a particular problem or improve a

A B C D E F G H I J K L M N O P Q R S T U V W X Y Z

situation: *a government **initiative** to help people start small businesses*
2 (*no plural*) the ability to think and do what is necessary without waiting for somebody to tell you what to do: *Are you capable of working on your own **initiative** without constant supervision?*

inject (say in-**jekt**) *verb* (**injecting, injected**)
to put a medicine or a drug into a person's body using a special needle (called a **syringe**)
▸ **injection** (*noun*): *The doctor gave the baby an **injection**.*

injure (say **in**-juh) *verb* (**injuring, injured**)
to hurt yourself or somebody else, especially in an accident: *She **injured** her arm when she was playing tennis. ◇ He was **injured** in a car accident.* ➲ SYNONYM **hurt**[1] 1
▸ **injured** (*adjective*): *The **injured** woman was taken to hospital.*

injury (say **in**-juh-ree) *noun* (*plural* **injuries**)
harm done to the body of a person or an animal, especially in an accident: *He had serious head **injuries**.*

injustice (say in-**juss**-tiss) *noun*
1 (*no plural*) the fact of a situation not being fair or right: *the struggle against **injustice*** ➲ OPPOSITE **justice** 1
2 (*plural* **injustices**) an unfair act or an example of unfair treatment: *the **injustices** suffered by poor people*

ink (say **ingk**) *noun* (*no plural*)
coloured liquid for writing and printing: *Please write in black or blue **ink**.*

inkosi (say ing-**kaw**-si) *noun* (*S. African*)
1 (*plural* **amakhosi** or **amakosi**) the leader of a group of people or a member of a council: *Inkosi Albert Luthuli* ➲ SYNONYM **chief**[2]
2 Inkosi (*no plural*) God or Jesus Christ
ⓘ ORIGIN: 19th century, from isiXhosa and isiZulu *inkosi*

inkosikazi (say ing-kaw-si-**kaa**-zi) *noun* (also **nkosikazi**) (*S. African*)
1 (*plural* **amakhosikazi**) a married woman or a wife
2 (*no plural*) a word that you use before the name of a woman who is married or who is the leader of a group of people: ***Inkosikazi** Maphumulo*
ⓘ ORIGIN: 19th century, from isiXhosa and isiZulu *inkosi* meaning 'chief' + *kazi* (used for a woman)

inland (say **in**-land) *adjective*
in the middle of a country, not on the coast: *an **inland** lake*
▸ **inland** (*adverb*): *The town lies a few kilometres **inland**.*

inlet (say **in**-luht) *noun* (*plural* **inlets**)
a narrow area of water that stretches into the land from the sea or a lake

inmate (say **in**-mayt) *noun* (*plural* **inmates**)
a person living with others in a prison or in a hospital for mentally ill people

inn (say **in**) *noun* (*plural* **inns**)
a small hotel, usually in the country

inner (say **in**-uh) *adjective*
inside, or towards or close to the centre: *the **inner** ear* ➲ OPPOSITE **outer**

innings (say **in**-ingz) *noun* (*plural* **innings**)
the period of a cricket game when it is the turn of one particular player or team to hit the ball (= to **bat**[2]): *He hit four sixes during his **innings**.*

innocent (say **in**-uh-suhnt) *adjective*
If you are **innocent**, you have not done anything wrong: *She claims she's **innocent** of the crime.* ➲ OPPOSITE **guilty**
▸ **innocence** (*noun*): *The prisoner's family are convinced of his **innocence**.*

innocuous (say i-**nok**-yuu-uhss) *adjective* (*formal*)
not meant to upset or offend anybody, or not dangerous: *an **innocuous** remark ◇ an **innocuous** chemical* ➲ SYNONYM **harmless**

innovation (say in-uh-**vay**-shuhn) *noun*
1 (*no plural*) the process or act of creating new things, ideas or ways of doing something: *We encourage **innovation** among our employees.*
2 (*plural* **innovations**) a new thing, idea or way of doing something: *major **innovations** in higher education*
▸ **innovative** (*adjective*): ***innovative** ideas*
▸ **innovator** (*noun*): *She won the young **innovator** award.*

innuendo (say in-yuu-**en**-doh) *noun* (*plural* **innuendos** or **innuendoes**)
an indirect remark or way of talking about somebody that usually suggests something rude or unpleasant: *gossip and **innuendo** ◇ subtle **innuendos***

innumerable (say i-**nyoo**-muh-ruhb-l) *adjective*
very many or too many to be counted: *There are **innumerable** pages of information on the Internet.*

inoculate (say i-**nok**-yuu-layt) *verb* (**inoculating, inoculated**)
to put a substance into the body of a person or an animal in order to protect them against a particular disease ➲ SYNONYM **vaccinate**
▸ **inoculation** (*noun*): *an **inoculation** against rabies*

inoffensive (say in-uh-**fen**-siv) *adjective* not likely to offend or harm somebody or something ➲ OPPOSITE **offensive**[1] 1

inordinate (say in-**aw**-di-nuht) *adjective* (*formal*) much greater than usual, expected or reasonable: *They spent an **inordinate** amount of time trying to settle the argument.*
▸ **inordinately** (*adverb*)

inorganic (say in-aw-**gan**-ik) *adjective* being or coming from something that has never been alive: *Metal is an **inorganic** substance.* ➲ OPPOSITE **organic** 1

input (say **in**-puut) *noun*
1 (*no plural*) time, ideas or work that you put into something to make it successful: *Her **input** to the discussions was very useful.*
2 (*plural* **inputs**) work, money, material etc. that are put into a project: *Compare the **inputs** with the outputs and work out if you have made a profit.*

inquest (say **ing**-kwest) *noun* (*plural* **inquests**)
1 an official process to find out how somebody died: *An **inquest** was held to discover the cause of death.*
2 a discussion to find out why something bad happened: *An **inquest** was held on the cricket team's poor performance.*

inquire, inquiry (say ing-**kwy**-uh, ing-**kwy**-uh-ree) other words for **enquire, enquiry**

inquisitive (say in-**kwiz**-i-tiv) *adjective* wanting to find out as much as possible about things: *Don't be so **inquisitive** – it's none of your business!*

insane (say in-**sayn**) *adjective* seriously mentally ill: *The prisoners were slowly going **insane**.* ➲ SYNONYM **mad** 1
➲ OPPOSITE **sane**

insatiable (say in-**say**-shuhb-l) *adjective* that is impossible to satisfy: *an **insatiable** desire for knowledge*
▸ **insatiably** (*adverb*)

inscribe (say in-**skribe**) *verb* (**inscribing, inscribed**)
1 to write, print or cut words, letters or symbols on a surface: *His name is **inscribed** on the trophy.*
➲ SYNONYM **engrave**
2 to write a special message to somebody in a book: *The book was **inscribed** 'To Susan with best wishes'.*
▸ **inscription** (*noun*): *an **inscription** on a tombstone*

inscrutable (say in-**skroo**-tuhb-l) *adjective* (*formal*) difficult to understand or explain: *His face was **inscrutable**.*

insect (say **in**-sekt) *noun* (*plural* **insects**) a very small animal that has six legs and a body that is divided into three parts: *Ants, flies, butterflies and beetles are all **insects**.*
ⓘ ORIGIN: 17th century, from Latin *insectum* meaning 'divided into parts', from *insecare* meaning 'cut up, cut into'

insect

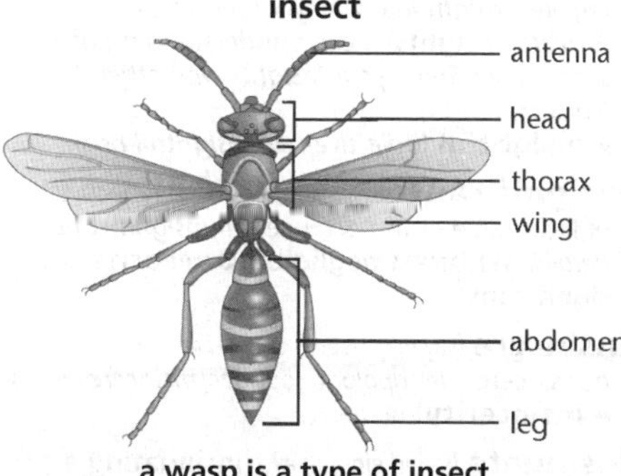

a wasp is a type of insect

insecticide (say in-**sek**-ti-side) *noun* (*plural* **insecticides**) a chemical substance you use to kill insects that you do not want

insectivore (say in-**sek**-ti-vaw) *noun* (*plural* **insectivores**) an animal that eats mainly insects
➲ See **carnivore, herbivore, omnivore**
▸ **insectivorous** (*adjective*): *Many birds are **insectivorous**.*

insecure (say in-si-**kyoor**) *adjective*
1 worried and not sure about yourself: *Many teenagers feel **insecure** about their appearance.*
2 not safe or firm: *This ladder looks a bit **insecure**.* ➲ OPPOSITE **secure** 2
▸ **insecurity** (*noun*): *She had feelings of **insecurity**.*

insensitive (say in-**sen**-suh-tiv) *adjective* not knowing or caring how another person feels: *That was a very **insensitive** remark.* ◇ *She's completely **insensitive** to my feelings.* ➲ OPPOSITE **sensitive** 1

insert (say in-**surt**) *verb* (**inserting, inserted**) (*formal*) to put something into something or between two things: ***Insert** the CD into the computer.*

inside[1] (say in-**side**) *preposition, adverb, adjective* in, on or to the inner part of something: *What's **inside** the box?* ◇ *It's raining – let's go **inside***

(= into the building). ◇ *the **inside** pocket of a jacket* ➲ OPPOSITE **outside**[3]

inside[2] (say in-**side**) *noun* (*plural* **insides**)
the part near the middle of something: *The door was locked from the **inside**.* ◇ *There's a label somewhere on the **inside**.* ➲ See **outside**[1]
inside out with the wrong side on the outside: *You've got your shirt on **inside** out.*

insight (say **in**-site) *noun*
1 (*no plural*) the ability to understand clearly what somebody or something is like: *Marketing requires **insight** into who your market is.*
2 (*plural* **insights**) a clear understanding of something: *Share your **insights** with other learners.*
▸ **insightful** (*adjective*): *an **insightful** book*

insignificant (say in-sig-**nif**-i-kuhnt) *adjective*
of little value or importance: *an **insignificant** detail* ➲ SYNONYM **negligible** ➲ OPPOSITE **significant**

insincere (say in-sin-**seer**) *adjective*
not sincere: *Her apology sounded **insincere**.*
▸ **insincerity** (*noun*)

insinuate (say in-**sin**-yuu-ayt) (**insinuating, insinuated**)
to suggest that something unpleasant is true, without saying it directly: *She **insinuated** that we'd been stupid.*
▸ **insinuation** (*noun*): *unfair **insinuations***

insipid (say in-**sip**-id) *adjective*
1 not interesting or exciting: *The team put on an **insipid** performance against the opposition.*
2 having too little taste, flavour or colour: *This is the most **insipid** meal I have ever eaten.*
➲ SYNONYM **bland** 1

insist (say in-**sist**) *verb* (**insisting, insisted**)
1 to say very strongly that something must happen or be done: *She **insisted** on driving me to the station.*
2 to say very strongly that something is true, when somebody does not believe you: *He **insists** that he didn't take the money.*

insolation (say in-sol-**ay**-shuhn) *noun* (*no plural*) (*science*)
1 the amount of energy the sun sends out that reaches the Earth or another planet
2 the act or process of putting something in sunlight

insolent (say **in**-suh-luhnt) *adjective* (*formal*)
not showing respect: *She gave him an **insolent** stare.* ➲ SYNONYM **rude** 1
▸ **insolence** (*noun*)

insoluble (say in-**sol**-yuhb-uhl) *adjective*
1 (*science*) referring to a substance that cannot dissolve in another particular substance: *Enamel paint is **insoluble** in water.* ➲ OPPOSITE **soluble** 1
2 (of a problem or difficulty) not able to be solved: *This puzzle is **insoluble**.* ➲ OPPOSITE **soluble** 2

insolvent (say in-**sol**-vuhnt) *adjective*
not able to continue in business because you cannot pay the money that you owe: *Her company has been declared **insolvent**.*
➲ SYNONYM **bankrupt**
▸ **insolvency** (*noun*)

insomnia (say in-**som**-ni-uh) *noun* (*no plural*)
the inability to sleep: *I suffer from **insomnia**, so I had very little sleep this week.*
▸ **insomniac** (*noun*): *The **insomniac** found it difficult to sleep.*

inspect (say in-**spekt**) *verb* (**inspecting, inspected**)
to look at something carefully: *I **inspected** the car before I bought it.*
▸ **inspection** (*noun*): *The police made an **inspection** of the house.*

inspector (say in-**spek**-tuh) *noun* (*plural* **inspectors**)
1 a person whose job is to see that things are done correctly: *a factory **inspector***
2 a police officer

inspiration (say in-spuh-**ray**-shuhn) *noun* (*no plural*)
a person or thing that makes you want to do something or gives you good ideas: *The beauty of the sea is an **inspiration** to many artists.*

inspire (say in-**spy**-uh) *verb* (**inspiring, inspired**)
1 to make somebody want to do something: *His wife **inspired** him to write this poem.*
2 to make somebody feel or think something: *Her words **inspired** us all with hope.*
▸ **inspiring** (*adjective*): *an **inspiring** teacher*
ⓘ ORIGIN: 13th–15th century, through Old French, from Latin *inspirare* meaning 'breathe or blow into'. The word was originally used about the ability of a god to 'give a truth or idea to someone'.

instability (say in-stuh-**bil**-uh-tee) *noun* (*no plural*)
the state of being likely to change or the condition of being likely to move or fall: *The **instability** of this ladder is dangerous.* ◇ *The country's political and economic **instability** made people nervous.* ➲ The adjective is **unstable**
➲ OPPOSITE **stability**

install (say in-**stawl**) *verb* (**installing, installed**)
to put a new thing in its place so it is ready to use: *They have **installed** a new computer system.*

instalment (say in-**stawl**-muhnt) *noun* (*plural* **instalments**)
1 a regular payment that you make for something: *She's paying for her new car in monthly* ***instalments.***
2 one part of a story on radio or television, or in a magazine: *Don't miss next week's exciting* ***instalment.***

instance (say **in**-stuhnss) *noun* (*plural* **instances**)
an example or case of something: *Police have uncovered several* ***instances*** *of fraud in the company.*
for instance as an example: *There are several interesting places to visit around here – the museum, for* ***instance.***

instant[1] (say **in**-stuhnt) *adjective*
1 happening very quickly: *The film was an* ***instant*** *success.*
2 (used about food) quick and easy to prepare: ***instant*** *coffee ◇ an* ***instant*** *meal*
▶ **instantly** (*adverb*): *The driver was killed* ***instantly.***

instant[2] (say **in**-stuhnt) *noun* (*no plural*)
a very short time: *She thought for an* ***instant*** *before she answered.* ➲ SYNONYM **moment**

instead (say in-**sted**) *adverb, preposition*
in the place of somebody or something: *There's no coffee. Would you like tea* ***instead?*** *◇ He's been playing football all afternoon* ***instead*** *of studying.*

instigate (say **in**-sti-gayt) *verb* (**instigating, instigated**) (*formal*)
to make something start to happen or to try to make somebody do something: *to* ***instigate*** *changes in the living conditions of poor people.* ◇ *Who* ***instigated*** *the violent demonstrations?*
▶ **instigation** (*noun*)

instil (say in-**stil**) *verb* (**instilling, instilled**) (also **instill**)
to influence the way that somebody thinks or feels: *Parents should try to* ***instil*** *a sense of responsibility into their children.*

instinct (say **in**-stingkt) *noun* (*plural* **instincts**)
something that makes people and animals do certain things without thinking or learning about them: *Birds build their nests by* ***instinct.***
▶ **instinctive** (*adjective*): *Animals have an* ***instinctive*** *fear of fire.*

institute (say **in**-sti-tyoot) *noun* (*plural* **institutes**)
a group of people who meet to study or talk about a special thing, or the building where they meet: *the* ***Institute*** *of Science*

institution (say in-sti-**tyoo**-shuhn) *noun* (*plural* **institutions**)
1 a large, important organization that has a particular purpose, such as a bank, hospital, prison or school: *Hospitals are large* ***institutions*** *that employ many people.*
2 a building where certain people with special needs live and are looked after: *a mental* ***institution*** (= a hospital for the mentally ill)
▶ **institutional** (*adjective*)

instruct (say in-**strukt**) *verb* (**instructing, instructed**)
1 to tell somebody what they must do: *He* ***instructed*** *the driver to wait.*
2 (*formal*) to teach somebody something: *Children must be* ***instructed*** *in road safety.*

instruction (say in-**struk**-shuhn) *noun* (*plural* **instructions**)
words that tell you what you must do or how to do something: *Read the* ***instructions*** *carefully.* ◇ *You should always follow the* ***instructions.***

instructor (say in-**struk**-tuh) *noun* (*plural* **instructors**)
a person who teaches you how to do something: *a driving* ***instructor***

instrument (say **in**-struh-muhnt) *noun* (*plural* **instruments**)
1 a thing that you use for doing a special job: *surgical* ***instruments*** (= used by doctors)
2 a thing that you use for playing music: *Violins and trumpets are musical* ***instruments.*** ◇ *What* ***instrument*** *do you play?*

insubordinate (say in-suh-**baw**-di-nuht) *adjective* (*formal*)
refusing to obey rules or orders from a person in authority: ***insubordinate*** *employees*
▶ **insubordination** (*noun*): *He was dismissed from the army for* ***insubordination.***

insufficient (say in-suh-**fish**-uhnt) *adjective*
not enough: *Johannesburg has* ***insufficient*** *water for its large population.* ➲ OPPOSITE **sufficient**
▶ **insufficiently** (*adverb*): ***insufficiently*** *developed reading skills*

insulate (say **in**-syuu-layt) *verb* (**insulating, insulated**)
1 to cover or protect something to prevent heat, cold, electricity or sound from passing through: *The walls are* ***insulated*** *against noise.* ◇ ***Insulating*** *your house can save you a lot of money in electricity.*
2 to keep a person or thing separate: *We were* ***insulated*** *from what was happening in the rest of the world by living on an isolated farm.*
▶ **insulation** (*noun*): *electrical* ***insulation*** ◇ ***insulation*** *tape*

insulator (say **in**-syuu-lay-tuh) *noun* (*plural* **insulators**)
a material or device that prevents electricity,

A B C D E F G H I J K L M N O P Q R S T U V W X Y Z

sound or heat from passing through: *Glass and plastic are good electrical* ***insulators****.*

insulin (say **in**-syuh-luhn) *noun* (*no plural*)
a substance, normally produced by the body, which controls the amount of sugar in the blood: *Some diabetics need* ***insulin*** *injections.*

insult[1] (say in-**sult**) *verb* (**insulting, insulted**)
to be deliberately rude to somebody: *She* ***insulted*** *my brother by saying he was fat.*
▸ **insulting** (*adjective*): *an* ***insulting*** *remark*

insult[2] (say **in**-sult) *noun* (*plural* **insults**)
something that is said or done in order to offend somebody: *The boys shouted* ***insults*** *at each other.*

insurance (say in-**shoor**-ruhnss) *noun* (*no plural*)
an agreement where you pay money to a company so that it will give you a lot of money if something bad happens: *When I crashed my car, the* ***insurance*** *paid for the repairs.*

insure (say in-**shoor**) *verb* (**insuring, insured**)
to pay money to a company, so that it will give you money if something bad happens: *Have you* ***insured*** *your house against fire?*

intact (say in-**takt**) *adjective, adverb*
complete, or not broken, damaged or harmed: *an almost* ***intact*** *collection of comics* ◇ *Very few of the buildings remain* ***intact*** *following the earthquake.*

intake (say **in**-tayk) *noun* (*plural* **intakes**)
1 an amount or quantity of something that is taken in: *Reduce your coffee* ***intake****.* ◇ *There are two* ***intakes*** *of 50 students each year.*
2 the act or process of taking something in: *an* ***intake*** *of air*

intangible (say in-**tan**-jib-l) *adjective* (*formal*)
difficult to describe, measure or understand: *the* ***intangible*** *rewards of parenthood* ➲ OPPOSITE **tangible**

integer (say **in**-ti-jur) *noun* (*plural* **integers**) (*maths*)
a number, including zero, that does not contain a fraction or **decimal**[1]: *3 and –3 are* ***integers****, but not* $\frac{1}{3}$ *or 3,4.*

integral (say **in**-ti-gruhl) *adjective*
1 necessary in order to make something complete: *Ceremonies are an* ***integral*** *part of every society.*
2 included as part of a whole: *an* ***integral*** *design*

integrate (say **in**-ti-grayt) *verb* (**integrating, integrated**)
1 to join two or more things together so that they work together or become one thing: *The two small schools were* ***integrated*** *into one large one.* ◇ ***Integrate*** *the climate data with your map.*
2 to join in and become part of a group or community and its activities, or to help somebody do this: ***integrating*** *children with special needs into general school classes*
▸ **integrated** (*adjective*): *an* ***integrated*** *circuit* ◇ *an* ***integrated*** *approach to teaching*
▸ **integration** (*noun*): ***integration*** *with other projects* ◇ *racial* ***integration***

integrity (say in-**teg**-ruh-tee) *noun* (*no plural*)
the quality of being honest and having strong moral principles: *a person of great* ***integrity*** *who can be relied on to tell the truth*

intellect (say **in**-tuh-lekt) *noun*
1 (*no plural*) the ability to think, learn and understand: *a woman of considerable* ***intellect***
2 (*plural* **intellects**) a very intelligent person who knows a lot: *one of the outstanding* ***intellects*** *of the world*

intellectual (say in-tuh-**lek**-tshuu-uhl) *adjective*
1 connected with a person's ability to think in a logical way and understand things: *a child's* ***intellectual*** *development*
2 (of a person) enjoying activities in which you have to think deeply about things

intelligence (say in-**tel**-i-juhnss) *noun* (*no plural*)
the ability to think, learn and understand quickly and well: *He is a man of great* ***intelligence****.* ◇ *an* ***intelligence*** *test*

intelligent (say in-**tel**-i-juhnt) *adjective*
1 (of a person) able to think, learn and understand quickly and well: *Their daughter is very* ***intelligent****.* ➲ SYNONYM **clever**
2 that shows that somebody is able to think, learn and understand quickly and well: *an* ***intelligent*** *question*
▸ **intelligently** (*adverb*)

> **WORD BUILDING** See the Word Building note at **clever**.

intend (say in-**tend**) *verb* (**intending, intended**)
to plan to do something: *When do you* ***intend*** *to go to Harare?* ➲ SYNONYM **mean**[1] 3 ➲ The noun is **intention**
be intended for somebody or **something** to be planned or made for a particular person or reason: *This dictionary is* ***intended*** *for learners in schools.*

intense (say in-**tenss**) *adjective*
very great or strong: ***intense*** *pain* ◇ *The heat from the fire was* ***intense****.*
▸ **intensely** (*adverb*)

intensive (say in-**ten**-siv) *adjective*
involving a lot of work in a short time: *an **intensive** cooking course*

intent (say in-**tent**) *noun* (*no plural*) (*formal*) what somebody plans to do or has decided to do: *peaceful **intent***

intention (say in-**ten**-shuhn) *noun* (*plural* **intentions**)
what you plan to do: *They have no **intention** of getting married.* ➲ The verb is **intend**

intentional (say in-**ten**-shuhn-l) *adjective*
done on purpose, not by mistake: *I'm sorry I upset you – it wasn't **intentional**!* ➲ SYNONYM **deliberate**
▸ **intentionally** (*adverb*)

inter- (say in-tur) *prefix*
between, or involving two or more different things: ***interact*** ◇ ***international*** ◇ ***Internet***
🛈 ORIGIN: from Old French *entre-* or Latin *inter* meaning 'between, among'

interact (say in-tuh-**rakt**) *verb* (**interacting, interacted**)
1 to communicate and be with somebody else, especially while you work or play: *People have the need to **interact** with other human beings.*
2 to have an effect on somebody or something else or on one another: *In the natural environment, plants and animals **interact** and depend on each other.*
▸ **interaction** (*noun*): *my **interaction** with fellow students*

interactive (say in-tuh-**rak**-tiv) *adjective*
1 that involves people working together and having an influence on one another: ***interactive** language-learning techniques*
2 (*computing*) involving direct communication both ways, between the computer and the person using it: ***interactive** computer games*

intercept (say in-tuh-**sept**) *verb* (**intercepting, intercepted**)
to stop or catch somebody or something that is moving from one place to another: *The thieves were **intercepted** at the airport.*
▸ **interception** (*noun*): *The boat managed to avoid **interception** by the patrol.*

interchange (say **in**-tuh-chaynj) *verb* (**interchanging, interchanged**)
1 to share or exchange ideas, information, etc.
2 to put each of two things in the place of the other: *Steps one and two of the process can be **interchanged**.*
▸ **interchange** (*noun*): *an **interchange** of ideas*
▸ **interchangeable** (*adjective*): *an **interchangeable** razor blade*

intercom (say **in**-tuh-kom) *noun* (*plural* **intercoms**)
a system or device that makes it possible for people in different parts of a building, plane or ship to speak to each other

interdependent (say in-tuh-di-**pen**-duhnt) *adjective*
that depend or rely on each other: *Countries have become more **interdependent** economically.*
▸ **interdependence** (*noun*): *the **interdependence** between people and nature*

interest[1] (say **in**-truhst) *noun*
1 (*no plural*) wanting to know or learn about somebody or something: *She read the story with **interest**.* ◇ *He takes no **interest** in politics.*
2 (*plural* **interests**) something that you like doing or learning about: *Her main **interest** is computers.*
3 (*no plural*) the extra money that you receive if you put money in a bank or that you pay back if you borrow money: *The **interest** rate is 10%.*

interest[2] (say **in**-truhst) *verb* (**interesting, interested**)
to make somebody want to know more: *Religion doesn't **interest** her.*

interested (say **in**-truhss-tid) *adjective*
wanting to know more about somebody or something: *Are you **interested** in cars?*

interesting (say **in**-truhss-ting) *adjective*
A person or thing that is **interesting** makes you want to know more about them: *This book is very **interesting**.* ◇ *That's an **interesting** idea!* ➲ OPPOSITE **boring**

interfere (say in-tuh-**feer**) *verb* (**interfering, interfered**)
1 to try to do something with or for somebody, when they do not want your help: *Don't **interfere**! Let her decide what she wants to do.*
2 to stop something from being done well: *His interest in football often **interferes** with his studies.*
▸ **interference** (*noun*): *I don't want any **interference** in my work!*

interior (say in-**teer**-ri-uh) *noun* (*plural* **interiors**)
the inside part: *We painted the **interior** of the house white.* ➲ OPPOSITE **exterior**
▸ **interior** (*adjective*): ***interior** walls* ◇ *Measure the **interior** angles of this shape.*

interject (say in-tuh-**jekt**) *verb* (**interjecting, interjected**)
to say something while somebody else is speaking, especially in a way that interrupts what is being discussed: *'Give me a moment, please!' I **interjected**.*
▸ **interjection** (*noun*)

interlock (say in-tuh-**lok**) *verb* (**interlocking, interlocked**)
to connect or be connected by using parts that fit into each other or fasten together closely: *When you close a zip, the small parts **interlock**.*

interlude (say **in**-tuh-lood) *noun* (*plural* **interludes**)
a short period of time between two longer periods, during which something different happens: *They took photographs during the **interlude** between the wedding ceremony and the reception.*

intermediate (say in-tuh-**mee**-di-uht) *adjective*
coming between two things or levels: *She's in an **intermediate** class.*

Intermediate Phase *noun* (*no plural*) (*S. African*)
Grades 4, 5 and 6 at school

intermission (say in-tuh-**mish**-uhn) *noun* (*plural* **intermissions**)
a short period of time separating the parts of a film, play or other performance: *a five-minute **intermission** between halves* ➲ SYNONYM **interval**

intermittent (say in-tuh-**mit**-uhnt) *adjective*
stopping for a short time and then starting again several times: *Tomorrow will be cloudy, with **intermittent** showers.*
▶ **intermittently** (*adverb*)

intern (say **in**-turn) *noun* (*plural* **interns**)
somebody who has finished studying at a university or college and who is working to gain practical experience in their job
▶ **internship** (*noun*): *an **internship** programme for young researchers*

internal (say in-**tur**-nuhl) *adjective*
1 of or on the inside: *He has **internal** injuries* (= inside his body). ➲ OPPOSITE **external**
2 that happens or exists inside an organization, country, etc.: *an **internal** police inquiry* ◇ *a country's **internal** affairs*
▶ **internally** (*adverb*): *The school dealt with the problem **internally**.*

international (say in-tuh-**nash**-nuhl) *adjective*
between different countries: *an **international** football match* ◇ *an **international** flight*
▶ **internationally** (*adverb*)

Internet (say **in**-tuh-net) *noun* (*no plural*) (also *informal* **the Net**) (*computing*)
the international system of computers that makes it possible for you to see information from all around the world on your computer and to send information to other computers: *You can find out almost anything on the **Internet**.* ◇ *Do you have **Internet** access?*

interpret (say in-**tur**-pruht) *verb* (**interpreting, interpreted**)
1 to say in one language what somebody has said in another language: *I can't speak Italian – can you **interpret** for me?*
2 to explain the meaning of something: *You have to **interpret** the facts, not just repeat them.*

interpretation (say in-tur-pri-**tay**-shuhn) *noun* (*plural* **interpretations**)
1 an explanation of something: *What's your **interpretation** of this poem?*
2 the way an actor or musician chooses to perform or understand a character or piece of music: *a modern **interpretation** of Hamlet*

interpreter (say in-**tur**-prit-uh) *noun* (*plural* **interpreters**)
a person whose job is to translate what somebody is saying into another language

interrogate (say in-**te**-ruh-gayt) *verb* (**interrogating, interrogated**)
to ask somebody a lot of questions over a long period of time, often in an aggressive way
▶ **interrogation** (*noun*): *The prisoner broke down under **interrogation** and confessed.*
▶ **interrogator** (*noun*): *a police **interrogator***

interrupt (say in-tuh-**rupt**) *verb* (**interrupting, interrupted**)
1 to stop somebody speaking or doing something by saying or doing something yourself: *Please don't **interrupt** me when I'm speaking.*
2 to stop something for a time: *The game was **interrupted** by rain.*
▶ **interruption** (*noun*): *I can't do my homework here. There are too many **interruptions**.*

intersect (say in-tuh-**sekt**) *verb* (**intersecting, intersected**)
to meet or cross each other: *The lines **intersect** at right angles.*
ⓘ ORIGIN: 17th century, from Latin *intersecare* meaning 'to cut, divide into sections' from *inter-* meaning 'between' + *secare* meaning 'to cut'

intersection (say in-tuh-**sek**-shuhn) *noun* (*plural* **intersections**)
a place where two or more roads, lines, etc. meet or cross each other: *the **intersection** of a circle and a rectangle* ◇ *There is a stop sign at the busy **intersection**.*

interval (say **in**-tuh-vuhl) *noun* (*plural* **intervals**)
1 a period of time between two events: *There was an **interval** of several weeks between the attacks.*
2 a short time between two parts of a play or concert ➲ SYNONYM **intermission**

intervene (say in-tuh-**veen**) *verb* (**intervening, intervened**)
1 to deliberately act in a way that influences the result of something or stops something from happening: *They asked the government to **intervene** to save the textile industry.*
2 to interrupt somebody who is speaking in order to say something
3 to happen in a way that stops or delays something from happening or being done: *We will have to cancel the match if wet weather **intervenes**.*
▸ **intervention** (*noun*): ***interventions** aimed at supporting small businesses*

interview¹ (say **in**-tuh-vyoo) *noun* (*plural* **interviews**)
1 a meeting when somebody asks you questions to decide if you will get a job: *I've got a job **interview** tomorrow.*
2 a meeting when somebody answers questions for a newspaper or for a television or radio programme: *There was an **interview** with the President on TV last night.*

interview² (say **in**-tuh-vyoo) *verb* (**interviewing, interviewed**)
to ask somebody questions in an **interview**: *They **interviewed** six people for the job.*
▸ **interviewer** (*noun*): *The **interviewer** asked me why I wanted the job.*

intestine (say in-**tess**-tin) *noun* (*plural* **intestines**) (also **intestines**)
the tube in your body that carries food away from your stomach to the place where it leaves your body ➲ SYNONYM **bowel** ➲ See illustration at **alimentary canal**, **organ**

intimate (say **in**-ti-muht) *adjective*
(used about people) having a close relationship: *They're **intimate** friends.*
▸ **intimacy** (*noun*): *a relationship based on **intimacy***

intimidate (say in-**tim**-i-dayt) *verb* (**intimidating, intimidated**)
1 to make somebody do something or not do something by using threats ➲ SYNONYM **coerce**
2 to make somebody feel worried and prevent them from behaving in an open and relaxed way
▸ **intimidating** (*adjective*): *an **intimidating** manner* ▸ **intimidation** (*noun*): *The bully controlled the other learners by **intimidation**.*

into (say **in**-too) *preposition*
1 to the middle or the inside of something: *Come **into** the house.* ◇ *I went **into** town.*
➲ OPPOSITE **out of 1**
2 in the direction of something: *Look **into** my eyes.*
3 against something: *The car crashed **into** a tree.*
4 a word that shows how somebody or something changes: *When it is very cold, water changes **into** ice.*
5 a word that you use when you divide a number: *Four goes **into** twelve three times.*
be into something (*informal*) to like something or to be interested in something: *What sort of music are you **into**?*

intolerable (say in-**tol**-uh-ruhb-l) *adjective*
so bad or difficult that you cannot accept it: *The situation was **intolerable**.* ➲ SYNONYM **unbearable**

intolerant (say in-**tol**-uh-ruhnt) *adjective*
1 not able to accept beliefs, opinions or behaviour that are different from your own: *He is rude and **intolerant** towards foreigners.*
2 finding somebody or something too unpleasant to bear or accept: *She's very **intolerant** of young children.* ➲ OPPOSITE **tolerant**
▸ **intolerance** (*noun*)

intonation (say in-tuh-**nay**-shuhn) *noun* (*no plural*)
the way your voice goes up and down and becomes higher or lower while you are speaking

intoxicated (say in-**tokss**-i-kay-tuhd) *adjective* (*formal*)
1 having had too much alcohol to drink
2 very excited and happy
▸ **intoxicating** (*adjective*): *It is prohibited to sell **intoxicating** liquor to children.*
▸ **intoxication** (*noun*): *the harmful effects of narcotic **intoxication***

intranet (say **in**-truh-net) *noun* (*plural* **intranets**) (*computing*)
a system of computers inside an organization that makes it possible for people to share information ➲ See **Internet**

intransitive (say in-**traan**-suh-tiv) *adjective* (*grammar*)
An **intransitive** verb does not have an object: *In the sentence 'The sun shone brightly', 'shone' is an **intransitive** verb.* ➲ See **transitive**

intravenous (say in-truh-**vee**-nuhss) *adjective*
going into a **vein** (= a tube in your body that carries blood): *an **intravenous** injection*

intrepid (say in-**trep**-id) *adjective* (*formal*)
brave and not afraid: *an **intrepid** explorer*

intricate (say **in**-tri-kuht) *adjective*
having many details or small parts that are put together in a complicated way
▸ **intricacy** (*noun*): *Please explain the*

intricacies of cricket to me. ▸ **intricately** (*adverb*): *an **intricately** built bird's nest*

intrigue (say in-**treeg**) *verb* (**intriguing, intrigued**)
to make somebody very interested: *His story **intrigued** me.*

intrinsic (say in-**trin**-sik) *adjective*
belonging to something as a basic part of its nature: *Minibus taxis are an **intrinsic** part of the lives of many South Africans.*

introduce (say in-truh-**dyooss**) *verb* (**introducing, introduced**)
1 to bring people together for the first time and tell each of them the name of the other: *Let me **introduce** you – Jane, this is Bob. Bob, this is Jane.* ◇ *He **introduced** himself to me* (= told me his name).
2 to bring in something new: *This law was **introduced** in 2002.*

introduction (say in-truh-**duk**-shuhn) *noun*
1 (*no plural*) bringing in something new: *the **introduction** of computers into schools*
2 (*plural* **introductions**) the act of bringing people together to meet each other
3 (*plural* **introductions**) a piece of writing at the beginning of a book that tells you about the book

introspective (say in-truh-s**pek**-tiv) *adjective*
carefully examining your own feelings and reasons for doing things: *She was thoughtful and **introspective**.*
▸ **introspection** (*noun*): *His book is full of **introspection** and sincerity.*

introvert (say **in**-truh-vurt) *noun* (*plural* **introverts**)
a quiet, shy person who does not mix easily with other people

intrude (say in-**trood**) *verb* (**intruding, intruded**)
to enter a place or situation without permission or when you are not invited or wanted
▸ **intrusion** (*noun*)

intruder (say in-**trood**-uh) *noun* (*plural* **intruders**)
a person who enters a place without permission: *Police say the **intruder** was not armed.*

intuition (say in-tyoo-**ish**-uhn) *noun* (*no plural*)
the ability to understand something immediately without having any definite knowledge or proof of it.
▸ **intuitive** (*adjective*): *The controls are simple and **intuitive** to operate* (= easy to use and understand). ▸ **intuitively** (*adverb*): ***Intuitively**, she knew that he was lying.*

Inuit (say **in**-yuu-it) *noun* (*no plural*)
the language that is spoken by a group of people living in northern Canada and parts of Alaska and Greenland

inundate (say **in**-un-dayt) *verb* (**inundating, inundated**)
1 to give or send somebody so many things that they cannot deal with them all: *We are **inundated** with applications for the job*
2 (*formal*) to flood a place with water, or to be covered or filled with water: *The flood waters blocked roads and **inundated** homes.*
▸ **inundation** (*noun*)

invade (say in-**vayd**) *verb* (**invading, invaded**)
to go into another country to attack it: *They **invaded** the country with tanks and guns.*
➲ See **invasion**
▸ **invader** (*noun*): *The **invaders** marched across the country.*

invalid[1] (say in-**val**-id) *adjective*
not legally or officially acceptable: *Without your photograph your passport is **invalid**.* ➲ OPPOSITE **valid**

invalid[2] (say **in**-vuh-lid) *noun* (*plural* **invalids**)
a person who has been very ill for a long time and needs another person to look after them

invaluable (say in-**val**-yoo-uhb-l) *adjective*
very useful: *Your help was **invaluable**.*

WHICH WORD? **Invaluable** or **worthless**?
- Be careful! **Invaluable** is not the opposite of **valuable**. The opposite of **valuable** is **worthless**.

invariable (say in-**vair**-ri-uhb-l) *adjective*
never changing: *an **invariable** rule*

invariably (say in-**vair**-ri-uhb-lee) *adverb*
always or almost always: *He **invariably** arrives late.*

invasion (say in-**vay**-zhuhn) *noun* (*plural* **invasions**)
a time when an army from one country goes into another country to attack it: *Germany's **invasion** of Poland in 1939* ➲ The verb is **invade**

invent (say in-**vent**) *verb* (**inventing, invented**)
1 to make or think of something for the first time: *Who **invented** the bicycle?*
2 to say something that is not true: *I realized that he had **invented** the whole story.*
▸ **inventor** (*noun*): *Marconi was the **inventor** of the radio.* ▸ **inventive** (*adjective*): *an **inventive** mind*

invention (say in-**ven**-shuhn) *noun*
1 (*plural* **inventions**) a thing that somebody has made for the first time

2 (*no plural*) inventing something: *The **invention** of the telephone changed the world.*

inventory (say **in**-vuhn-tree) *noun*
1 (*plural* **inventories**) a detailed list of things such as goods or the contents of a building: *The landlord is coming to make an **inventory** of the contents of the flat.*
2 (*no plural*) (*business*) the things that a shop or company keeps ready to sell: *Will the company buy back **inventory** that is not sold?*

inverse (say **in**-vurss) *noun* (*no plural*)
1 the exact opposite of something
2 (*maths*) the opposite action that is done on a value: *The **inverse** of 6 is –6.*
▸ **inverse** (*adjective*): ***inverse** proportions*

invert (say in-**vurt**) *verb* (**inverting, inverted**)
to change the normal position of something, especially by turning it upside down or by arranging it in the opposite order: ***Invert** the bowl so that the water drains out.* ◇ *I **inverted** the colours of a picture on my computer.*
▸ **inversion** (*noun*): *the **inversion** of the order of numbers.*

invertebrate (say in-**vur**-ti-bruht) *noun* (*plural* **invertebrates**)
an animal without a line of bones going down its back (called a **spine**): *Insects, snails and jellyfish are **invertebrates**.* ➲ See **vertebrate**

inverted commas (say in-vur-tid **kom**-uhz) *plural noun*
the signs " " or ' ' that you use in writing before and after words that somebody said ➲ See Study page 16 ➲ SYNONYM **quotation marks**

invest (say in-**vest**) *verb* (**investing, invested**)
to give money to a business or bank so that you will get more money back: *He **invested** all his money in the company.*
▸ **investment** (*noun*): *an **investment** of R10 000* ▸ **investor** (*noun*): *He is an **investor** in my business.*

investigate (say in-**vess**-ti-gayt) *verb* (**investigating, investigated**)
to research or study a subject or a problem to find out facts and information: *We **investigated** the problem of litter in our school.* ◇ *The police are **investigating** the murder.*
▸ **investigation** (*noun*): *They carried out an **investigation** into the fire.*

invigilate (say in-**vij**-i-layt) *verb* (**invigilating, invigilated**)
to watch people who are writing an exam and make sure that nobody cheats

invigorate (say in-**vig**-uh-rayt) *verb* (**invigorating, invigorated**)
to make somebody feel healthy, fresh and full of energy
▸ **invigorating** (*adjective*): *I had an **invigorating** shower to cool down.*

invincible (say in-**vin**-sib-l) *adjective*
too strong, powerful or skilful to be defeated

invisible (say in-**viz**-uhb-l) *adjective*
that you cannot see: *Wind is **invisible**.*
➲ OPPOSITE **visible**

invitation (say in-vi-**tay**-shuhn) *noun* (*plural* **invitations**)
1 the act of inviting somebody or being invited by somebody
2 a written or spoken request to go somewhere or do something: *He sent me an **invitation** to his party.*

invite (say in-**vite**) *verb* (**inviting, invited**)
to ask somebody to come somewhere or do something: *She **invited** me to her party.* ◇ *Let's **invite** them to our house for dinner.*

invoice (say **in**-voyss) *noun* (*plural* **invoices**)
a list that shows how much you must pay for things that somebody has sold you, or for work that somebody has done for you

invoke (say in-**vohk**) *verb* (**invoking, invoked**) (*formal*)
1 to ask God or a god for help, advice or support: *They **invoked** the goddess of peace.*
2 to use something such as a law as a reason or explanation, or for support: *to **invoke** the protection of the court*

> PRONUNCIATION The second part of this word rhymes with **broke**.

involuntary (say in-**vol**-uhn-tree) *adjective*
done without wanting or meaning to, or not deliberate: *He gave an **involuntary** gasp of pain when the doctor inserted the needle.* ➲ OPPOSITE **voluntary** 1
▸ **involuntarily** (*adverb*): *She shivered **involuntarily**.*

involve (say in-**volv**) *verb* (**involving, involved**)
1 to have something as a necessary part: *The job **involves** using a computer.*
2 to make somebody take part in something: *I want to **involve** more people in the concert.*

involved (say in-**volv**-d) *adjective*
taking part in something, or being part of something or connected with something: *I'm very **involved** in local politics.* ◇ *We need to interview the people **involved**.*

A B C D E F G H I J K L M N O P Q R S T U V W X Y Z

inward (say **in**-wuhd) *adjective*
1 existing inside your mind, or mental or spiritual: *my **inward** feelings*
2 travelling or moving towards the inside or centre of something: *an **inward** movement of water* ➲ OPPOSITE **outward**
▸ **inwardly** (*adverb*)

inwards (say **in**-wuhdz) *adverb*
towards the inside or centre: *The doors open **inwards**.* ➲ OPPOSITE **outwards**

iodine (say **y**-uh-deen) *noun* (*no plural*) (symbol I)
a dark-coloured substance that is found in sea water and in animals and plants living in the sea. It is often used in medicine.

ion (say **y**-uhn) *noun* (*plural* **ions**) (*science*)
an atom or a group of atoms having an electrical charge. The charge is a result of the gain or loss of one or more of its parts (**electrons**): *The atom Na becomes the positively charge **ion** Na^{+}.*
▸ **ionic** (*adjective*): *an **ionic** bond*
▸ **ionization** (*noun*) (also **ionisation**): ***ionization** energy* ▸ **ionize** (*verb*) (also **ionise**): *Salt **ionizes** when it is dissolved in water.*

ionosphere (say *y*-**on**-uhss-feer) *noun*
the layer of the Earth's atmosphere that has many charged particles (called **ions**) ➲ See illustration at **atmosphere** ➲ See **mesosphere**, **stratosphere**, **thermosphere**, **troposphere**

IOU (say *y*-oh-**yoo**) *noun* (*plural* **IOUs**) (*informal*)
a piece of paper that shows that you promise to pay somebody the money you owe them
ℹ **IOU** is short for 'I owe you'.

IQ (say *y*-**kyoo**) *noun* (*plural* **IQs**)
a way of measuring how intelligent somebody is: *She has an **IQ** of 128.* ℹ **IQ** is short for 'intelligence quotient'.

ir- *prefix*
You can add **ir-** to the beginning of some words to give them the opposite meaning, for example *irregular* (= not regular).
ℹ ORIGIN: from Latin

irate (say *y*-**rayt**) *adjective* (*formal*)
very angry: *How do you deal with **irate** clients?*
➲ SYNONYM **furious**

iridescent (say i-ri-**dess**-uhnt) *adjective*
having many bright colours that seem to change in different lights

iris (say **y**-riss) *noun* (*plural* **irises**)
1 the coloured part of your eye ➲ See illustration at **eye**
2 a plant with long narrow leaves and flowers that come in a variety of colours

iron¹ (say **y**-uhn) *noun*
1 (*no plural*) (symbol Fe) a strong hard metal: *an **iron** bar* ◇ *The gates are made of **iron**.*
2 (*plural* **irons**) a device with a flat base that you heat and use for making clothes smooth: *an electric **iron***

iron² (say **y**-uhn) *verb* (**ironing**, **ironed**)
to make clothes smooth using an iron: *Would you please **iron** this shirt for me?*
▸ **ironing** (*noun*): *I've finished the **ironing**.*

ironic (say *y*-**ron**-ik) *adjective*
If you are **ironic**, you say the opposite of what you mean because you want to make people laugh or show them you are annoyed: *When I said it was a beautiful day, I was being **ironic**.*

irony (say **y**-ruh-nee) *noun*
1 (*no plural*) humour that is based on saying the opposite of what you mean: *'You're in a good mood,' he said with heavy **irony**.* ➲ See Study page 17
2 (*plural* **ironies**) an unusual or unexpected part of a situation, etc. that seems strange or amusing: *The **irony** was that I tripped while telling someone else to be careful.*

irradiate (say i-ray-di-**ayt**) *verb* (**irradiating**, **irradiated**)
to send out or receive energy waves, especially to treat food by exposing it to these waves: ***Irradiated** food lasts longer, but some people think it isn't safe.*
▸ **irradiation** (*noun*): *food **irradiation***

irrational (say i-**rash**-uh-nuhl) *adjective*
not logical or reasonable: *an **irrational** fear of spiders* ➲ OPPOSITE **rational**
▸ **irrationality** (*noun*): *the **irrationality** of superstition* ▸ **irrationally** (*adverb*): *She became **irrationally** jealous of her husband's ex-wife.*

irrational number *noun* (*plural* **irrational numbers**)
a number that you cannot write as a simple fraction: *Pi is an **irrational number**.*

irregular (say i-**reg**-yuu-luh) *adjective*
1 happening or being without a fixed pattern or shape: *an **irregular** shape*
2 happening at different times: *Their visits were **irregular**.* ➲ OPPOSITE **regular** 1
3 (*grammar*) A word that is **irregular** does not have the usual verb forms or plural: *'Catch' is an **irregular** verb.* ➲ OPPOSITE **regular** 4
ℹ ORIGIN: 14th–15th century, through Old French from Latin *irregularis*, from *in-* meaning 'not' + *regula* meaning 'rule'

irrelevant (say i-**rel**-uh-vuhnt) *adjective*
not connected with something and not

important: *Don't include anything **irrelevant** in your report.* ➲ OPPOSITE **relevant**

irresistible (say i-ri-**ziss**-tuhb-l) *adjective*
1 so strong that it cannot be stopped or prevented: *I had an **irresistible** urge to laugh.*
2 very attractive: *He is apparently **irresistible** to women.*
▶ **irresistibly** (*adverb*): *an **irresistibly** funny comedy*

irresponsible (say i-ri-**spon**-suhb-l) *adjective*
not thinking about the effects your actions will have ➲ OPPOSITE **responsible**
▶ **irresponsibility** (*noun*): *Freedom does not mean **irresponsibility**.* ▶ **irresponsibly** (*adverb*): *to behave **irresponsibly***

irreverent (say i-**rev**-uh-ruhnt) *adjective*
not feeling or showing respect for somebody or something: *an **irreverent** student* ➲ OPPOSITE **reverent**
▶ **irreverence** (*noun*): *an **irreverence** towards social conventions* ▶ **irreverently** (*adverb*)

irrevocable (say i-**rev**-uh-kuhb-l) *adjective*
that cannot be changed: *They made an **irrevocable** commitment to fight corruption.*
▶ **irrevocably** (*adverb*): *Mbuli's life changed **irrevocably** after the accident.*

irrigate (say **i**-ri-gayt) *verb* (**irrigating, irrigated**)
to make water flow onto a piece of land, especially in order to help crops to grow
▶ **irrigation** (*noun*): ***irrigation** pipes*

irritable (say **i**-ri-tuhb-l) *adjective*
becoming angry or very annoyed easily: *He's very **irritable** in the mornings.*

irritate (say **i**-ri-tayt) *verb* (**irritating, irritated**)
1 to make somebody quite angry or very annoyed: *She **irritates** me when she asks so many questions.*
2 to make a part of your body hurt a little: *Cigarette smoke **irritates** my eyes.*
▶ **irritation** (*noun*): *This plant can cause **irritation** to your skin.*

is (say **iz**) form of **be**

Isicamtho *noun* (*no plural*) (*S. African*)
an informal language that is spoken in the main cities of South Africa. **Isicamtho** uses words from isiZulu, isiXhosa, Afrikaans and other languages.
ℹ ORIGIN: the name in Isicamtho, probably from isiZulu *qamutha* or *qamunda* meaning 'speak a lot'

PRONUNCIATION The **c** in **Isicamtho** is pronounced as a click. Listen to a speaker of Isicamtho saying it.

isiNdebele (say iss-i-ndeh-**beh**-leh) *noun* (*no plural*) (also **Ndebele**)
the language of the Ndebele people

isiXhosa (say iss-i-**kaw**-zuh) *noun* (*no plural*) (also **Xhosa**)
the language of the Xhosa people

PRONUNCIATION The **Xh** in **isiXhosa** is pronounced as a click. Listen to a speaker of isiXhosa saying it.

isiZulu (say iss-i-**zoo**-loo) *noun* (*no plural*) (also **Zulu**)
the language of the Zulu people

Islam (say **iz**-laam) *noun* (*no plural*)
the religion of Muslim people. **Islam** teaches that there is only one God and that Muhammad is his **prophet** (= the person that God has chosen to give his message to people).
▶ **Islamic** (*adjective*): ***Islamic** law*

island (say **ile**-uhnd) *noun* (*plural* **islands**)
a piece of land with water all around it: *Robben Island*
▶ **islander** (*noun*): *Most of the **islanders** have boats.*

isle (say **ile**) *noun* (*plural* **Isles**)
an island: *the British **Isles***

isn't (say **iz**-uhnt) short for **is not**

iso- (say *y*-soh) *prefix*
equal: ***isosceles*** (= having two sides of equal length)

isobar (say *y*-suh-baa) *noun* (*plural* **isobars**) (*geography*)
a line on a weather map that joins places that have the same air pressure

isolate (say *y*-suh-layt) *verb* (**isolating, isolated**)
to put or keep somebody or something away from other people or things: *We need to **isolate** all the animals with the disease so that the others don't catch it.*

isolated (say *y*-suh-layt-uhd) *adjective*
far from other people or things: *an **isolated** house in the mountains*

isolation (say *y*-suh-**lay**-shuhn) *noun* (*no plural*)
being away from other people or things: *The old man lived alone, in complete **isolation**.*

A B C D E F G H I J K L M N O P Q R S T U V W X Y Z

A B C D E F G H I J K L M N O P Q R S T U V W X Y Z

isometric (say y-suh-**met**-rik) *adjective* (*technology*)
having the same measurement: *an **isometric** drawing* ◇ ***isometric** projection*

isosceles (say y-**soss**-uh-leez) *adjective* (*maths*)
having two sides of the same length: *an **isosceles** triangle*

issue[1] (say **ish**-oo) *noun* (*plural* **issues**)
1 an important problem that people talk, think or write about: *Pollution is a serious **issue**.*
2 a magazine or newspaper of a particular day, week, or month: *Have you read this week's **issue**?*

issue[2] (say **ish**-oo) *verb* (**issuing, issued**)
to give or say something officially: *The soldiers were **issued** with uniforms.* ◇ *The police have **issued** a statement.*

isthmus (say **iss**-muhss) *noun* (*plural* **isthmuses**) (*geography*)
a narrow piece of land, with water on both sides, that joins two larger pieces of land

IT (say y-**tee**) *noun* (*no plural*)
the study or use of computers and other electronic equipment to store and send information ❶ **IT** is short for 'Information Technology'.

it *pronoun* (*plural* **they** or **them**)
1 a word that shows a thing or animal: *Where's the coffee? I can't find **it**.* ◇ ***They** have gone.* ◇ *Have you found **them**?*
2 a word that points to an idea that follows: ***It's** difficult to learn Japanese.*
3 a word that shows who somebody is: *'Who's on the telephone?' '**It's** Jo.'*
4 a word at the beginning of a sentence about time, the weather or distance: ***It's** six o'clock.* ◇ ***It's** hot today.*

Italian (say i-**tal**-i-uhn) *noun* (*no plural*)
the language that is spoken in Italy and parts of Switzerland

italics (say i-**tal**-ikss or y-**tal**-ikss) *plural noun*
a type of writing or printing in which the letters do not stand straight up: *This sentence is in **italics**.*
▸ **italic** (*adjective*): ***italic** writing*

itch (say **ich**) *verb* (**itching, itched**)
to have a feeling on your skin that makes you want to rub or scratch it: *My nose **itches**.* ◇ *This jersey makes me **itch**.*
▸ **itch** (*noun*): *I've got an **itch**.* ▸ **itchy** (*adjective*): ***itchy** skin*

it'd (say **it**-uhd) short for **it had; it would**

item (say **ite**-uhm) *noun* (*plural* **items**)
1 one thing in a list or group of things: *an **item** of clothing* ◇ *She had the most expensive **item** on the menu.*
2 a piece of news: *There was an interesting news **item** about Namibia.*

itinerary (say y-**tin**-uh-ruh-ree) *noun* (*plural* **itineraries**)
a plan for a journey or trip that lists the route and the places that you will visit in the order in which they are to be visited

it'll (say **it**-uhl) short for **it will**

its (say **itss**) *adjective*
of the thing or animal that you have just talked about: *The dog has hurt **its** leg.* ◇ *The company has **its** factory in Tshwane.*

WHICH WORD? **Its** or **it's**?
- Be careful! **Its** means **belonging to it**: *The bird has broken **its** wing.*
- **It's** is a short way of saying **it is** or **it has**: ***It's*** (= it is) cold today. ◇ ***It's*** (= it has) been raining.

it's (say **itss**) short for **it is; it has**

itself (say it-**self**) *pronoun* (*plural* **themselves**)
1 a word that shows the same thing or animal that you have just talked about: *The cat was washing **itself**.* ◇ *The dogs are scratching **themselves**.*
2 a word that makes 'it' stronger: *The hotel **itself** was nice but I didn't like the town.*
by itself
1 alone: *The house stands by **itself** in the forest.*
2 without being controlled by a person: *The machine will start by **itself**.*

I've (say **ive**) short for **I have**

ivory (say **ive**-uh-ree) *noun* (*no plural*)
the hard white substance that makes up the long teeth (called **tusks**) of an elephant

ivy (say **ive**-ee) *noun* (*no plural*)
a plant with dark green leaves, which climbs up walls or trees

Jj

jab *verb* (**jabbing**, **jabbed**)
to push at somebody with a sudden rough movement: *She **jabbed** me in the stomach with her elbow.*
▸ **jab** (*noun*): *I felt a **jab** in my ribs.*

jacaranda (say jak-uh-**ran**-duh) *noun* (*plural* **jacarandas**)
a large tropical tree with purple flowers

jack (say **jak**) *noun* (*plural* **jacks**)
1 a piece of equipment for lifting a car, etc. off the ground, for example to change its wheel
2 the playing card that has a picture of a young man on it: *the **jack** of hearts*

jackal (say **jak**-uhl) *noun* (*plural* **jackals**)
a wild animal, related to dogs, that lives in Africa and Asia. Jackals hunt small animals and eat animals that are already dead.

jacket (say **jak**-uht) *noun* (*plural* **jackets**)
a short coat with sleeves
🛈 **ORIGIN**: 14th–15th century, from Old French *jaquet*

jackknife (say **jak**-nife) *verb* (**jackknifing**, **jackknifed**)
If a lorry that is in two parts **jackknifes**, it goes out of control and bends into a V-shape.

jackpot (say **jak**-pot) *noun* (*plural* **jackpots**)
(usually **the jackpot**) the largest money prize that you can win in a game or competition
hit the jackpot to win a lot of money or have great or unexpected success: *He thought he'd hit the **jackpot** when he inherited the house.*

jade (say **jayd**) *noun* (*no plural*)
1 a stone that is usually green and is used for making jewellery and objects of art
2 a light and usually bright green colour
▸ **jade** (*adjective*): *She wore a **jade** dress.*

jaded (say **jayd**-uhd) *adjective*
tired and bored, often because of having done the same thing for a long time: *a **jaded** musician* ➲ **SYNONYM weary**

jagged (say **jag**-uhd) *adjective*
rough and with sharp points: ***jagged** rocks*

jaguar (say **jag**-yuu-uh) *noun* (*plural* **jaguars**)
a large wild cat with black spots that lives in Central and South America

jail (say **jayl**) *noun* (*plural* **jails**) (also **gaol**)
a prison: *She was sent to **jail** for two years.*
▸ **jail** (*verb*): *He was **jailed** for killing his wife.*

jam¹ *noun*
1 (*no plural*) sweet food made from fruit and sugar. You eat **jam** on bread: *a jar of strawberry **jam***
2 (*plural* **jams**) a situation in which you cannot move because there are too many people or vehicles: *a traffic **jam***

jam² *verb* (**jamming**, **jammed**)
1 to push something into a place where there is not much space: *She **jammed** all her clothes into a suitcase.*
2 to fix something or to become fixed so that you cannot move it: *I can't open the window. It's **jammed**.*

January (say **jan**-yuu-uh-ree) *noun*
the first month of the year
🛈 **ORIGIN**: through Old English, from Latin *Januarius mensis* meaning 'month of Janus'. Janus was an ancient Roman god who guarded doors and gates and watched over new beginnings.

Japanese (say jap-uh-**neez**) *noun* (*no plural*)
the language of the Japanese people

jar¹ (say **jaa**) *noun* (*plural* **jars**)
1 a container with a lid, usually made of glass and used for keeping food, etc. in it: *a jam **jar***
2 the food a jar contains: *a **jar** of coffee*

jar² (say **jaa**) *verb* (**jarring**, **jarred**)
1 to move or to make somebody or something move in a sudden rough way that may hurt or damage them: *The impact **jarred** his arm.*
2 to have an unpleasant or annoying effect: *The dripping tap **jarred** on my nerves.*
▸ **jarring** (*adjective*): *a **jarring** punch on the chin* ◇ *a **jarring** note*

jargon (say **jaa**-guhn) *noun* (*no plural*)
special or technical words that are used by people who take part in a particular activity, job or profession and that other people do not understand: *medical **jargon***

jaundice (say **jawn**-diss) *noun* (*no plural*)
a medical condition in which the skin and white parts of the eye become yellow

jaunt (say **jawnt**) *noun* (*plural* **jaunts**)
a short trip, especially for pleasure: *a weekend **jaunt** to Durban*

javelin (say **jav**-lin) *noun* (*plural* **javelins**)
a long pointed stick that people throw as a sport

jaw *noun* (*plural* **jaws**)
one of the two bones in the head of a person or animal that hold the teeth

jazz (say **jaz**) *noun* (*no plural*)
a kind of music with a strong rhythm, in which the players often **improvise** 2 (= make up the music as they are playing): *a **jazz** band*

jealous (say **jel**-uhss) *adjective*
1 angry or sad because you think that somebody you like or love is showing interest in somebody else: *Sarah's boyfriend gets **jealous** if she speaks to other boys.*
2 angry or sad because you want to be like somebody else or because you want what another person has: *Neo was **jealous** of his brother's new car.* ➲ SYNONYM **envious**
▸ **jealousy** (*noun*): *He felt sick with **jealousy**.*

jeans (say **jeenz**) *plural noun*
trousers made of strong cotton material (called **denim**). **Jeans** are usually blue: *a pair of **jeans** ◇ He wore **jeans** and a T-shirt.*

> USAGE It is not standard English to say 'a jeans' or 'a jean'. You say a **pair of jeans**: *I need **a pair of jeans**. ◇ I own three **pairs of jeans**.*

Jeep™ *noun* (*plural* **Jeeps**)
a strong, small to medium-sized vehicle that can go well over rough ground

jeer (*rhymes with* **peer**) *verb* (**jeering, jeered**)
to laugh or shout at someone in an unkind way that shows you do not respect them: *The crowd **jeered** at him.*

jelly (say **jel**-ee) *noun* (*plural* **jellies**)
a soft food made from fruit juice and sugar, that shakes when you move it

jellyfish (say **jel**-ee-fish) *noun* (*plural* **jellyfish** or **jellyfishes**)
a sea animal with a body like jelly and long thin parts (called **tentacles**) that can sting you

jeopardize (say jep-**uh**-dize) *verb* (**jeopardizing, jeopardized**) (also **jeopardise**)
to do something that puts a person or thing in danger of being harmed, destroyed or lost: *He would never do anything to **jeopardize** his career.*

jerk (say **jurk**) *verb* (**jerking, jerked**)
to move quickly or suddenly, or to pull or make something move like this: *The car **jerked** forward. ◇ She **jerked** the door open.*
▸ **jerk** (*noun*): *The bus started with a **jerk**.*
▸ **jerky** (*adjective*): *a **jerky** movement*

jersey (say **jur**-zee) *noun* (*plural* **jerseys**)
a warm piece of clothing with sleeves, which you wear on the top part of your body. **Jerseys** are often made of wool.

jest *noun*
a joke or an amusing remark
in jest as a joke: *Don't say that! Not even in **jest**.*

Jesus Christ (say jee-zuhss **kry**st) *noun*
the man who Christians believe is the son of God and whose teachings the Christian religion is based on

jet¹ *noun* (*plural* **jets**)
1 a type of fast modern plane: *a passenger **jet***
2 liquid or gas that comes very fast out of a small hole: *a **jet** of gas ◇ **jets** of water*

jet² *verb* (**jetting, jetted**)
1 (*informal*) to travel in a plane: *She is always **jetting** off to a conference or workshop somewhere in the world.*
2 to come or to make something come very fast out of a small hole: *Steam **jetted** out of the nozzle.*

jet lag *noun* (*no plural*)
the feeling of being very tired after a long plane journey

jetty (say **jet**-ee) *noun* (*plural* **jetties**)
a platform at the edge of a river, a dam or the sea where people get on and off boats

Jew (say **joo**) *noun* (*plural* **Jews**)
a person who follows the religion of Judaism
▸ **Jewish** (*adjective*): *She is **Jewish**.*

jewel (say **joo**-uhl) *noun* (*plural* **jewels**)
a beautiful stone that is very valuable: *Diamonds, emeralds and rubies are all **jewels**.*
➲ SYNONYM **gem**
ℹ ORIGIN: 13th–15th century, through Old French *joel*, from *jeu* meaning 'game, play' from Latin *jocus* meaning 'jest, something that is said or done for amusement'

jeweller (say **joo**-uh-luh) *noun* (*plural* **jewellers**)
a person who sells, makes or repairs jewellery and watches

jewellery (say **joo**-uhl-ree) *noun* (*no plural*)
objects that people wear to decorate parts of their body such as their fingers, ears and arms: *a piece of gold **jewellery***

jiggle (say **jig**-l) *verb* (**jiggling, jiggled**)
to move quickly from side to side or up and down, or to make something do this
▸ **jiggle** (*noun*): *If the door sticks, give it a little **jiggle** and it should open.*

jigsaw (say **jig**-saw) *noun* (*plural* **jigsaws**) (also **jigsaw puzzle**)
a picture in many pieces that you put together

jihad (say **ji**-haad) *noun* (*plural* **jihads**)
a religious war that is fought by some Muslims against people, organizations or countries that are considered to be enemies of Islam

jingle[1] (say **jing**-guhl) *verb* (**jingling, jingled**)
to make a pleasant sound like small bells or to cause something to make this sound: *She* ***jingled*** *the coins in her pocket.*

jingle[2] (say **jing**-guhl) *noun* (*plural* **jingles**)
1 a sound like that of small bells or metal objects gently hitting each other: *the* ***jingle*** *of coins*
2 a short simple tune or song that is easy to remember: *an advertising* ***jingle***

jitters (say **jit**-uhz) *plural noun* (*informal*)
(usually **the jitters**) feelings of worry and fear: *Just thinking about the exams gives me the* ***jitters.***

job *noun* (*plural* **jobs**)
1 the work that you do for money: *She got a* ***job*** *as a waitress.* ◇ *He has just lost his* ***job.*** ◇ *Are you going to apply for a* ***job****?*
2 something that you must do: *I have a lot of* ***jobs*** *to do in the house.*
make a good job of something to do something well: *You made a good* ***job*** *of the painting.*
out of a job without paid work ➲ SYNONYM **unemployed**

jockey (say **jok**-ee) *noun* (*plural* **jockeys**)
a person who rides horses in races

jog *verb* (**jogging, jogged**)
1 to run slowly for exercise: *I* ***jogged*** *round the park.* ◇ *I go* ***jogging*** *every morning.*
2 to push or touch something a little, so that it moves: *She* ***jogged*** *my arm and I spilled my drink.*
▶ **jog** (*noun*): *She goes for a three-kilometre* ***jog*** *every day.* ◇ *He gave my arm a* ***jog.***

join (say **joyn**) *verb* (**joining, joined**)
1 to bring or fix one thing to another thing: *The bridge* ***joins*** *one half of the town to the other.* ◇ ***Join*** *the two pieces of wood together.*
2 to come together with somebody or something: *Will you* ***join*** *us for dinner?* ◇ *This road* ***joins*** *the highway soon.*
3 to become a member of a group: *He* ***joined*** *the army.* ◇ *I've* ***joined*** *an aerobics class.*
join in to do something with other people: *Everyone started singing but Khaya refused to* ***join in.***

joint[1] (say **joynt**) *adjective*
involving two or more people together: *The report was a* ***joint*** *effort* (= we worked on it together). ◇ *My wife and I have a* ***joint*** *account* (= a shared bank account).

joint[2] (say **joynt**) *noun* (*plural* **joints**)
1 a part of your body where bones come together, for example your elbow or your knee ➲ See illustration at **finger**
2 a place where two parts of something join together: *the* ***joints*** *of the pipe*

joke[1] *noun* (*plural* **jokes**)
something that you say or do to make people laugh, for example a funny story that you tell: *She told us a* ***joke.*** ◇ *I didn't get the* ***joke*** (= understand it).

joke[2] *verb* (**joking, joked**)
1 to tell funny stories: *They were laughing and* ***joking*** *together.*
2 to say things that are funny but not true: *I didn't mean what I said – I was only* ***joking.***

joker (say **johk**-uh) *noun* (*plural* **jokers**)
1 a person who likes to tell jokes or play tricks
2 an extra card that can be used instead of any other one in some card games

jolly (say **jol**-ee) *adjective* (**jollier, jolliest**)
happy and full of fun ➲ SYNONYM **jovial**

jolt (say **johl**-t) *verb* (**jolting, jolted**)
to move or to make somebody or something move in a sudden rough way: *The bus* ***jolted*** *to a stop.* ◇ *The crash* ***jolted*** *us forwards.*
➲ SYNONYM **jerk**
▶ **jolt** (*noun*): *The train stopped with a* ***jolt.***

jostle (say **joss**-l) *verb* (**jostling, jostled**)
1 to push hard against somebody in a crowd: *People* ***jostled*** *each other to catch a glimpse of their hero.*
2 to compete against other people or things to try to win or gain something: *children* ***jostling*** *for attention*

jot *verb* (**jotting, jotted**)
jot something down to write something quickly: *I* ***jotted*** *down his phone number.*

joule (say **jool**) *noun* (*plural* **joules**) (abbr. J)
a unit for measuring energy or work
➲ See **kilojoule**

journal (say **jurn**-uhl) *noun* (*plural* **journals**)
1 a written account of your thoughts and ideas or what you have done each day ➲ See **diary** 1
2 a magazine about one particular thing: *a medical* ***journal***
3 a record that a company keeps of the business that it does every day

journalism (say **jurn**-uh-liz-uhm) *noun* (*no plural*)
the work of collecting and reporting news for newspapers, magazines, television and radio

journalist (say **jurn**-uh-list) *noun* (*plural* **journalists**)
a person whose job is to collect and report

news for newspapers, television and radio ➲ See **reporter**

journey (say **jur**-nee) *noun* (*plural* **journeys**)
the act of travelling from one place to another: *Did you have a good **journey**?*

jovial (say **joh**-vi-uhl) *adjective*
(used about a person) happy and friendly ➲ SYNONYM **jolly**
▸ **jovially:** *'Are you enjoying yourselves?' he asked **jovially**.*

joy (*rhymes with* **boy**) *noun*
1 (*no plural*) a very happy feeling: *Their children give them so much **joy**.*
2 (*plural* **joys**) a person or thing that makes you very happy: *the **joys** of a beach in summer*
➲ SYNONYMS **pleasure** 1, **delight**[1] ➲ OPPOSITE **sorrow**
▸ **joyful** (*adjective*): *a **joyful** occasion*

joystick (say **joy**-stik) *noun* (*plural* **joysticks**)
a handle that is usually in the shape of a stick and that you move to control something, for example a computer game

jubilant (say **joo**-bi-luhnt) *adjective* (*formal*)
very happy because you have won or succeeded at something
▸ **jubilantly** (*adverb*)

jubilee (say **joo**-bi-lee) *noun* (*plural* **jubilees**)
a special anniversary of an important event, especially one celebrating twenty-five years (silver **jubilee**) or fifty years (golden **jubilee**) of something

Judaism (say **joo**-day-iz-uhm) *noun* (*no plural*)
the religion of the Jewish people

judge[1] (say **juj**) *noun* (*plural* **judges**)
1 the person in certain courts of law who decides how to punish somebody: *The **judge** sent him to prison for 20 years.*
2 a person who chooses the winner of a competition
🛈 ORIGIN: 13th–15th century, through Old French *juge*, from Latin *jus* meaning 'law' + *dicere* meaning 'to say'

judge[2] (say **juj**) *verb* (**judging, judged**)
1 to have or to form an opinion about somebody or something: *It's difficult to **judge** how long the project will take.*
2 to decide who or what wins a competition: *The principal **judged** the painting competition.*

judgement (say **juj**-muhnt) *noun* (also **judgment**)
1 (*no plural*) your ability to form opinions or make sensible decisions: *Use your **judgement*** (= you decide). ◇ *In my **judgement**, she will do the job very well.*
2 (*plural* **judgements**) the decision of a judge in a court of law

judicial (say juu-**dish**-uhl) *adjective*
relating to a court of law, a judge or a judgement in a court: *We have confidence in South Africa's **judicial** system.*

judicious (say juu-**dish**-uhss) *adjective*
sensible and showing good judgement: *the **judicious** use of resources*
▸ **judiciously** (*adverb*)

judo (say **joo**-doh) *noun* (*no plural*)
an Asian sport where two people fight and try to throw each other onto the floor
🛈 ORIGIN: 19th century, from Japanese, from *jū* meaning 'gentle' + *dō* meaning 'way'

jug *noun* (*plural* **jugs**)
a container with a handle, which you use for holding or pouring liquids: *a milk **jug*** ◇ *a **jug** of water*

juggle (say **jug**-l) *verb* (**juggling, juggled**)
1 to keep two or more things in the air by throwing and catching them quickly
2 to try to deal with two or more important jobs or activities at the same time
▸ **juggler** (*noun*): *Sandile is a **juggler** in the circus.*

jugular (say **jug**-yuu-luh) *adjective*
of or in the throat or neck: ***jugular** veins*

juice (say **jooss**) *noun* (*no plural*)
the liquid from fruit and vegetables: *a glass of orange **juice***

juicy (say **jooss**-ee) *adjective* (**juicier, juiciest**)
1 full of juice: *big **juicy** tomatoes*
2 (*informal*) (used about information) interesting because it is shocking: ***juicy** gossip*

jukebox (say **jook**-bokss) *noun* (*plural* **jukeboxes**) (*old-fashioned*)
a machine in a bar or a cafe that plays music when you put money in it

July (say juu-**ly**) *noun*
the seventh month of the year
🛈 ORIGIN: 13th–15th century, from Latin *Julius mensis* meaning 'month of July', named after Julius Caesar (100–44 BC), a Roman general and political leader

jumble[1] (say **jumb**-l) *noun* (*no plural*)
a lot of things that are mixed together in an untidy way: *a **jumble** of old clothes and books*

jumble[2] (say **jumb**-l) *verb* (**jumbling, jumbled**)
jumble something up to mix things so that they are untidy or in the wrong place: *His clothes were all **jumbled** up in the cupboard.*

jumble sale *noun* (*plural* **jumble sales**)
a sale of things that people do not want any more. Clubs, churches and schools often have **jumble sales** to make money.

jumbo (say **jum**-boh) *adjective* (*informal*)
very large: ***jumbo** eggs*

jumbo jet *noun* (*plural* **jumbo jets**)
a very big jet plane that can carry a lot of people

jump *verb* (**jumping, jumped**)
1 to move quickly off the ground, using your legs to push you up: *The cat **jumped** onto the table.* ◇ *The horse **jumped** over the wall.*
2 to move quickly: *He **jumped** into the car and drove away.*
3 to move suddenly because you are surprised or frightened: *A loud noise made me **jump**.*
jump at something to accept an opportunity or an offer with enthusiasm: *I **jumped** at the chance to work in New York for a year.*
▶ **jump** (*noun*): *With a huge **jump** the horse cleared the fence.*

jumper (say **jump**-uh) *noun* (*plural* **jumpers**)
a warm piece of clothing with long sleeves and no buttons, which you wear on the top part of your body. **Jumpers** are often made of wool.

jumper cable *noun* (*plural* **jumper cables**)
one of a set of two cables with clips on both ends, which you use to start a car when its battery has gone flat

junction (say **junk**-shuhn) *noun* (*plural* **junctions**)
a place where roads or railway lines meet: *Turn right at the next **junction**.*

June (say **joon**) *noun*
the sixth month of the year
🛈 **ORIGIN**: 13th–15th century, through Old French *juin* from Latin *Junius mensis* meaning 'month of June'. The month was named after Juno, the most important of the ancient Roman goddesses.

jungle (say **jung**-guhl) *noun* (*plural* **jungles**)
a thick forest in a hot part of the world: *the **jungles** of South America and Africa*
🛈 **ORIGIN**: 18th century, through Hindi, from Sanskrit *jangala* meaning 'rough and dry (land)'. Sanskrit is an ancient language of India. Over time the word changed to mean an area overgrown with large trees.

junior (say **joo**-ni-uh) *adjective*
1 having a lower position in an organization: *a **junior** doctor*
2 of or for children below a particular age: *the **junior** athletics championships* ➲ **OPPOSITE senior**

junior school (*plural* **junior schools**)
= primary school

junk (say **jungk**) *noun* (*no plural*)
things that are old or useless: *The cupboard is full of **junk**.*

junk food *noun* (*no plural*) (*informal*)
food that is ready to eat or quick and easy to make and eat, but that is bad for your health

jurisdiction (say joor-riss-**dik**-shuhn) *noun*
1 (*no plural*) the power or authority to make legal decisions: *The farm is on state land and is under the **jurisdiction** of the Ministry of Agriculture.*
2 (*plural* **jurisdictions**) the area in which the power or authority to make legal decisions can be used

juror (say **joor**-ruhr) *noun* (*plural* **jurors**)
a member of a **jury**

jury (say **joor**-ree) *noun* (*plural* **juries**)
a group of people in a court of law in some countries who decide whether somebody has done something wrong or not: *The **jury** decided that the woman was guilty of killing her husband.*

just[1] *adverb*
1 exactly: *This jacket is **just** my size.* ◇ *You're **just** in time.* ◇ *She looks **just** like her mother.*
2 a very short time before: *I've **just** heard the news.* ◇ *Jim isn't here – he's **just** gone out.*
3 now or very soon, or at this or that moment: *I'm **just** going to make some coffee.*
4 by a small amount: *I got here **just** after nine.* ◇ *I only **just** caught the train.*
5 a word that makes what you say stronger: ***Just** look at that funny little dog!*
6 only: *It's **just** a small present.*
just about (*informal*) almost or very nearly: *I've met **just** about everyone.*
just a minute, just a moment used for asking somebody to wait for a short time: ***Just** a minute – there's someone at the door.*
just now
1 soon or very soon: *Wait a minute – I'm coming **just** now.*
2 at this moment: *I can't talk to you **just** now. I'm busy.*
3 a short time before: *Where's Liz? She was here **just** now.*

just[2] *adjective*
fair and right: *a **just** punishment* ➲ **OPPOSITE unjust**

justice (say **juss**-tiss) *noun* (*no plural*)
1 treatment of people in a fair way: *the struggle for **justice*** ➲ **OPPOSITE injustice** 1
2 the law: *the criminal **justice** system*

A B C D E F G H I **J** K L M N O P Q R S T U V W X Y Z

justify (say **juss**-ti-fy) *verb* (**justifying, justified**)
to give or be a good reason for something: *Can you **justify** what you did?* ◇ *Use information from your research to **justify** your point of view.*
▸ **justifiable** (*adjective*): *a **justifiable** action*
▸ **justification** (*noun*): *Do you have any **justification** for what you did?*

jut *verb* (**jutting, jutted**)
to stick out from or continue beyond the surface or edge of something, or to make something do this: *Her lower lip **jutted** out and she looked like she was going to cry.*

juvenile (say **joo**-vuh-nile) *adjective* (*formal*)
1 relating to or intended for young people who are not yet adults: ***juvenile** crime*
2 behaving like somebody of a younger age: *He's twenty-three but he's still quite **juvenile**.*
➲ SYNONYM **immature**
▸ **juvenile** (*noun*): ***Juveniles** should not be put in the same prisons as adults.*

juxtapose (say jukss-tuh-**pohz**) *verb* (**juxtaposing, juxtaposed**) (*formal*)
to put things close together, often in order to show the differences between them: *The artist achieves a special effect by **juxtaposing** light and dark.*
▸ **juxtaposition** (*noun*): *the **juxtaposition** of old and new buildings*

Kk

kaleidoscope (say kuh-**lide**-uh-skohp) *noun* (*plural* **kaleidoscopes**)
1 a toy that consists of a tube with mirrors and coloured pieces of glass or paper inside it. When you look into one end of the tube and turn it, you see changing patterns of colour.
2 a set of different things or events that change all the time: *a **kaleidoscope** of dance and music*

kalimba (say kuh-**lim**-buh) *noun* (*plural* **kalimbas**)
a small musical instrument consisting of a wooden box that has thin pieces of metal fastened to it and that you play by moving your fingers across the metal bars

kangaroo (say kang-guh-**roo**) *noun* (*plural* **kangaroos**)
an Australian mammal that jumps on its strong back legs and carries its babies in a pocket (called a **pouch**) on its front ➲ See **wallaby**
🛈 **ORIGIN**: 18th century, from an extinct Aboriginal language of Australia

kangaroo

kaolin (say **kay**-uh-lin) *noun* (*no plural*)
a type of fine white clay that is used in some medicines and for making things such as cups, plates, paper, powder and cloth

karakul (say **ka**-ruh-kuul) *noun*
1 (*plural* **karakuls**) a type of sheep that has curly black wool when it is very young
2 (*no plural*) the wool from this sheep

karaoke (say ka-ri-**oh**-kee) *noun* (*no plural*)
a type of entertainment in which people sing the words of well-known songs while a machine plays the music

karate (say kuh-**raa**-tee) *noun* (*no plural*)
a Japanese sport where people fight with their hands and feet
🛈 **ORIGIN**: from Japanese *karate* meaning 'empty hand'

karma (say **kaa**-muh) *noun* (*plural* **karmas**)
all of somebody's good and bad actions in their present and previous lives, which some religious people believe will influence the quality of their next life: *Buddhists and Hindus believe in **karma**.*

kayak (say **ky**-ak) *noun* (*plural* **kayaks**)
a light narrow boat that you move through the water using a flat piece of wood (called a **paddle**) ➲ See **canoe**
🛈 **ORIGIN**: 18th century, from Inuit *qayaq*. Inuit is a language spoken by a people who live in northern Canada, Greenland and Alaska.

kazoo (say kuh-**zoo**) *noun* (*plural* **kazoos**)
a simple musical instrument that consists of a tube with a hole in it that is covered by a thin layer of material. A **kazoo** makes a sound like a bee when you sing into the tube.

kb *abbreviation* (*plural* **kb**) **kilobyte**

kebab (say ki-**bab**) *noun* (*plural* **kebabs**)
small pieces of meat and vegetables that are cooked on a thin stick ➲ **SYNONYM sosatie**
🛈 **ORIGIN**: 17th century, from Arabic *kabāb*

keel[1] *noun* (*plural* **keels**)
a long piece of wood or metal on the bottom of a boat that stops it falling over sideways in the water ➲ See illustration at **ship**
🛈 **ORIGIN**: 13th–15th century, from Old Norse *kjǫlr* meaning 'keel'

keel[2] *verb* (**keeling, keeled**)
keel over
1 (used about a boat or ship) to fall over sideways in the water ➲ **SYNONYM capsize**
2 (*informal*) to fall over suddenly: *He **keeled** over and fell on his back.*

keen *adjective* (**keener, keenest**)
1 wanting to do something or interested in something: *She is a **keen** swimmer.* ◇ *He was **keen** to go out but I wanted to stay at home.*
➲ **SYNONYM eager**
2 very good or strong: ***keen** eyesight*
be keen on somebody or **something** (*informal*) to like somebody or something very much: *Tom's very **keen** on Anna.*

keep *verb* (**keeping, kept**)
1 to stay in a particular state or condition: *We **kept** warm by the fire.*
2 to make somebody or something stay in a

particular state or condition: ***Keep** this door closed.* ◇ *I'm sorry to **keep** you waiting.* ◇ ***Keep** away from the river.* ◇ ***Keep** still* (= don't move).
3 to continue to have something: *You can **keep** that book – I don't need it.*
4 to put or store something in a particular place: *Where do you **keep** the coffee?*
5 to look after and buy food and other things for a person or an animal: *They **keep** sheep and pigs on their farm.*
6 to stay fresh: *Will this fish **keep** until tomorrow?*
keep somebody from doing something to stop somebody from doing something: *You can't **keep** me from going out!*
keep going to continue: *I was very tired but I **kept** going to the end of the race.*
keep off something to not go on something: ***Keep** off the grass!*
keep on doing something to continue doing something or to do something many times: *We **kept** on driving all night!*
keep out to stay outside: *The sign on the door said 'Danger. **Keep** out!'*
keep something out to force something to stay outside: *We put a fence round the garden to **keep** the sheep out.*
keep up with somebody or **something** to go as fast as another person or thing so that you are together: *Slow down – I can't **keep** up with you.*

keg *noun* (*plural* **kegs**)
a small metal or wooden container with round sides and flat ends, used for storing liquids, especially beer ➲ See **barrel** 1

kelp *noun* (*no plural*)
a large brown **seaweed**

kelvin (say **kel**-vin) *noun* (*plural* **kelvins**) (*science*) (abbr. K)
a unit for measuring temperature ➲ See **Celsius**

WORD BUILDING An interval of 1K is equal to 1 °C. Zero kelvin is called **absolute zero**. Ice melts at 273K and water boils at 373K.

kennel (say **ken**-l) *noun* (*plural* **kennels**)
a small house where a dog sleeps

kept form of **keep**

kernel (say **kurn**-l) *noun* (*plural* **kernels**)
the softer part inside a nut, seed or the stone of some types of fruit

kerosene (say **ke**-ruh-zeen) *noun* (*no plural*)
= **paraffin**

ketchup (say **kech**-up) = **tomato sauce**
ORIGIN: 17th century, perhaps from Chinese *k'ē chap* meaning 'tomato juice'

kettle (say **ket**-uhl) *noun* (*plural* **kettles**)
a container with a handle, for boiling water: *an electric **kettle*** ◇ *I'll go and put the **kettle** on* (= fill it with water and make it start to get hot).

key¹ (say **kee**) *noun*
1 (*plural* **keys**) a piece of metal that opens or closes a lock: *He turned the **key** and opened the door.*
2 (*plural* **keys**) one of the parts of a computer, a calculator, a piano or other musical instrument that you press with your fingers: *Pianos have black and white **keys**.*
3 (*plural* **keys**) answers to questions: *Check your answers with the **key** at the back of the book.*
4 (*plural* **keys**) a list of the symbols and signs used in a map or book, showing what they mean: *If you don't understand the symbols in the map, look at the **key**.*
5 the key (to something) (*no plural*) something that helps you to achieve or understand something: *A good education is the **key** to success.*
6 (*plural* **keys**) a set of musical notes that is based on one note: *This song is in the **key** of A minor.*

key² (say **kee**) *verb* (**keying**, **keyed**)
key something in to put words or numbers into a computer or calculator by pressing the keys: ***Key** in your password.*

keyboard (say **kee**-bawd) *noun* (*plural* **keyboards**)
1 all the keys on a computer or a piano ➲ See illustration at **computer**
2 a musical instrument like a small electrical piano: *a **keyboard** player*

keyhole (say **kee**-hohl) *noun* (*plural* **keyholes**)
a hole in a lock where you put a key

keynote (say **kee**-noht) *noun* (*plural* **keynotes**)
the most important idea of a book, a speech, etc.: *The president made the **keynote** speech.*

kg (say kay-**jee**) *abbreviation* (*plural* **kg**) **kilogram**

khaki (say **kaa**-ki) *adjective*
having the pale brown-green or brown-yellow colour of a soldier's uniform: ***khaki** uniforms*
▸ **khaki** (*noun*)
ORIGIN: 19th century, from Urdu *kaki* meaning 'dust-coloured', from Persian *kak* meaning 'dust'. Urdu is a language spoken by many people in Pakistan and India.

Khoikhoi (say **koy**-koy) *noun* (also **Khoi**)
1 (*plural* **Khoikhoi**) a member of a group of people from southern Africa who, in the past, moved about from place to place, and lived by herding cattle, hunting, and gathering wild plants: *His family are descendants of the **Khoikhoi**.*
2 (*no plural*) one of the group of languages spoken by these people
ORIGIN: 18th century, from Khoikhoi *khoe-khoen* meaning 'the Khoikhoi people', from *khoe* meaning 'person' + *khoen* meaning 'people'

Khoisan (say **koy**-san) *plural noun*
1 a word used for the **Khoikhoi** people and the **San** people together: *The **Khoisan** lived on this coast for hundreds of years.*
2 the group of languages spoken by these people

kick[1] (say **kik**) *verb* (**kicking, kicked**)
1 to hit somebody or something with your foot: *I **kicked** the ball to Tina.*
2 to move your foot or feet up and down quickly: *The child was **kicking** and screaming.*
kick off to start a game of football
kick somebody out (*informal*) to make somebody leave a place: *The boys were **kicked** out of class because they were noisy.*

kick[2] (say **kik**) *noun* (*plural* **kicks**)
1 a movement with your foot or your leg, usually to hit something with your foot: *If the door won't open, give it a **kick**.*
2 (*informal*) a feeling of excitement: *He gets a **kick** out of driving fast cars.*

kid[1] *noun* (*plural* **kids**)
1 (*informal*) a child: *How old are your **kids**?*
2 a young goat

kid[2] *verb* (**kidding, kidded**) (*informal*)
to say something that is not true as a joke: *I didn't mean it – I was only **kidding**.*

kidnap (say **kid**-nap) *verb* (**kidnapping, kidnapped**)
to take somebody away and hide them, usually so that their family or friends will pay money to free them ➲ **SYNONYM abduct**
▸ **kidnapper** (*noun*): *The **kidnappers** are demanding a ransom of R1 million.*

kidney (say **kid**-nee) *noun* (*plural* **kidneys**)
either of the two **organs** inside your body that separate waste liquid from your blood ➲ See illustration at **organ**

kif *adjective* (*informal, S. African*)
nice, very good or fashionable: *My new cellphone is **kif**!* ➲ **SYNONYM cool**[1] 3
ORIGIN: 19th century, from Arabic *kayf* meaning 'enjoyment, pleasure'

kill (say **kil**) *verb* (**killing, killed**)
to make somebody or something die: *The police do not know who **killed** the old man.* ◇ *Three people were **killed** in the accident.*
▸ **killer** (*noun*): *The police tracked down the **killer**.*

kiln (say **kiln**) *noun* (*plural* **kilns**)
a large oven, used for baking clay and bricks and for drying materials such as wood

kilo (say **kee**-loh) *noun* (*plural* **kilos**) short for **kilogram**
ORIGIN: through French from Greek *khilioi* meaning 'thousand'

kilo- (say **kil**-oh) *prefix*
one thousand: ***kilometre*** (= a measure of length equal to 1 000 metres)

kilobyte (say **kil**-uh-bite) *noun* (*plural* **kilobytes**) (abbr. KB, Kb)
a measure of computer memory or information. There are 1 024 **bytes** in a **kilobyte**.

> **USAGE** Usually **kilo-** stands for 1 000. However, because computer memory or information is divided into sizes that are a power of two, a **kilobyte** is 2^{10} or 1 024 bytes.

kilogram (say **kil**-uh-gram) *noun* (*plural* **kilograms**) (also **kilo**) (abbr. kg)
a unit for measuring mass. There are 1 000 **grams** in a **kilogram**: *I bought two **kilograms** of potatoes.* ◇ *1 **kg** of bananas*

kilojoule (say **kil**-uh-jool) *noun* (*plural* **kilojoules**) (abbr. kJ)
1 000 **joules**. **Kilojoule** is a unit for measuring energy that you get from food.: *Boys aged twelve need to consume about 9 000 **kilojoules** a day.*

kilolitre (say **kil**-uh-lee-tuh) *noun* (*plural* **kilolitres**) (abbr. kl or kL)
a unit for measuring the volume of liquids. There are 1 000 **litres** in a kilolitre. ➲ See **litre**

kilometre (say **kil**-uh-mee-tuh) *noun* (*plural* **kilometres**) (abbr. km)
a unit for measuring length. There are 1 000 **metres** in a **kilometre**: *They live 100 **km** from here.*
ORIGIN: 18th century, through French *kilomètre* from Greek *khilioi* meaning 'thousand' + *metron* meaning 'measure'

kilowatt (say **kil**-uh-wot) *noun* (*plural* **kilowatts**) (abbr. kW)
a unit for measuring electrical power. There are 1 000 **watts** in a kilowatt.

kilowatt-hour *noun* (*plural* **kilowatt-hours**) (abbr. kWh)
a unit for measuring electric energy. One **kilowatt-hour** is equal to using one kilowatt of electricity in one hour.

kilt (say **kilt**) *noun* (*plural* **kilts**)
a skirt that men in Scotland sometimes wear

kimono (say ki-**moh**-noh) *noun* (*plural* **kimonos**)
a long loose piece of clothing with wide sleeves, originally worn by Japanese men and women on formal occasions
ORIGIN: 17th century, from Japanese *ki* meaning 'wearing' and *mono* meaning 'thing'

kin *noun* (*no plural*) (*formal*)
the people in your family: *Who is your next of **kin*** (= your closest relative)*?*

kind[1] (say **kynd**) *noun* (*plural* **kinds**)
a group of things or people that are the same in some way: *What **kind** of music do you like?* ◇ *The shop sells ten different **kinds** of bread.* ➲ SYNONYMS **sort**[1], **type**[1] 1
kind of (*informal*) words that you use when you are not sure about something: *He looks **kind** of tired.*

kind[2] (say **kynd**) *adjective* (**kinder**, **kindest**)
friendly and good to other people and animals: *'Thanks! It was **kind** of you to help.'* ◇ *Be **kind** to animals.* ➲ SYNONYM **considerate** ➲ OPPOSITE **unkind**

kind-hearted (say kynd-**haat**-uhd) *adjective*
kind and generous to other people

kindle (say **kind**-l) *verb* (**kindling**, **kindled**)
1 to make something start to burn: *He taught me how to **kindle** a fire.*
2 to catch fire: *The fire slowly **kindled**.*
3 (*formal*) to become or make something stronger: *The book **kindled** my interest in science.*

kindly (say **kynd**-lee) *adverb*
in a kind way: *She **kindly** drove me to the station.*

kindness (say **kynd**-nuhss) *noun* (*no plural*)
the quality of being kind: *Thank you for your **kindness**.*

kinetic (say ki-**net**-ik) *adjective*
of or produced by movement: ***kinetic** energy*
► **kinesis** (*noun*) ► **kinetics** (*noun*)

king *noun* (*plural* **kings**)
1 a man from a royal family who rules a country: ***King** Sobhuza II* ➲ See **queen**
2 one of the four playing cards in a pack, which has a picture of a king on it: *the **king** of spades*

kingdom (say **king**-duhm) *noun* (*plural* **kingdoms**)
a country where a king or queen rules: *the United **Kingdom***

kingfisher (say **king**-fish-uh) *noun* (*plural* **kingfishers**)
a small colourful bird that has a large head and feeds on fish

kingklip (say **king**-kluhp) *noun* (*plural* **kingklip** or **kingklips**)
a fish that is found in southern oceans and is caught for food

kink (*rhymes with* **sink**) *noun* (*plural* **kinks**)
a bend or turn in something that should be straight, for example a rope or wire

kiosk (say **kee**-osk) *noun* (*plural* **kiosks**)
a small shop in a street or at a station where you can buy things like sweets and newspapers through a window

kiss (say **kiss**) *verb* (**kissing**, **kissed**)
to touch somebody with your lips to show love or to say hello or goodbye: *She **kissed** me on the cheek.* ◇ *They **kissed**, and then he left.*
► **kiss** (*noun*): *Give me a **kiss**!*

kist *noun* (*plural* **kists**) (*S. African*)
a large strong box with a lid that you use for storing things ➲ SYNONYM **chest** 2

kit *noun* (*plural* **kits**)
1 a set of tools, equipment or clothes that you need for a particular purpose, sport or activity: *Where's my football **kit**?* ◇ *There's a hammer in the tool **kit**.*
2 a set of small pieces that you put together to make something: *a **kit** for making a model aeroplane*

kitchen (say **kich**-uhn) *noun* (*plural* **kitchens**)
a room where you prepare and cook food

kite (*rhymes with* **site**) *noun* (*plural* **kites**)
a toy that you fly in the wind on a long piece of string

kitten (say **kit**-uhn) *noun* (*plural* **kittens**)
a young cat

kiwi fruit (say kee-wi **froot**) *noun* (*no plural*) (also **kiwi**)
a small green fruit with black seeds and rough brown skin

kl *abbreviation* (*plural* **kl**) (also **kL**) **kilolitre**

kleptomania (say klep-tuh-**may**-ni-uh) *noun* (*no plural*)
a mental illness that makes a person unable to stop stealing things
▸ **kleptomaniac** (*noun*): *Robert is a* ***kleptomaniac****. He even steals things he cannot use.*

kloof (say **kloo**-uhf) *noun* (*plural* **kloofs**)
a small and narrow valley
ℹ ORIGIN: 18th century, through Afrikaans and South African Dutch, from Dutch *clove* meaning 'a split, a deep hollow'

km (say kay-**em**) *abbreviation* (*plural* **km**)
kilometre

km/h *abbreviation* **kilometres per hour**

knack (say **nak**) *noun* (*no plural*)
the ability to do something skilfully, that you have naturally or that you can learn: *She had the* ***knack*** *of making people feel special.* ➲ See **talent**

knead (say **need**) *verb* (**kneading, kneaded**)
to press and stretch a mixture of flour and water (called **dough**) to make bread

PRONUNCIATION Don't pronounce the **k** in words that start with **kn**.

knee (say **nee**) *noun* (*plural* **knees**)
the part in the middle of your leg where it bends: *I fell and cut my* ***knee****.* ➲ See illustration at **body**

kneecap (say **nee**-kap) *noun* (*plural* **kneecaps**) (also **patella**)
the bone that covers the front of your knee
➲ See illustration at **skeleton**

kneel (say **neel**) *verb* (**kneeling, knelt** or **kneeled**)
to bend your legs and rest on one or both of your knees: *He* ***knelt*** *down to pray.* ◇ *Jane was* ***kneeling*** *on the floor.*

knew (say **nyoo**) form of **know**

knickers (say **nik**-uhz) *plural noun* = **panties**

knife (say **nife**) *noun* (*plural* **knives**)
a sharp metal thing with a handle, which you use to cut things or to fight with: *a* ***knife*** *and fork*
ℹ ORIGIN: through Old English *cnīf* meaning 'knife', from Old Norse *knífr*

knight (say **nite**) *noun* (*plural* **knights**)
1 in the past, a soldier of a high level who rode a horse and fought for his king
2 a man who has been given a title of honour by a king or queen for good work he has done and who can use *Sir* before his name: *Sir David Beckham was made a* ***knight*** *for his services to soccer and his community work.*
3 (in the game of chess) a piece that is usually shaped like a horse's head

knit (say **nit**) *verb* (**knitting, knitted**)
to make clothes from wool using two long sticks (called **knitting needles**): *My grandmother* ***knitted*** *this hat for me.*
▸ **knitting** (*noun*): *I usually do some* ***knitting*** *while I'm watching television.*

knitting needle *noun* (*plural* **knitting needles**)
one of two metal or plastic sticks that you use for making clothes from wool

knives (say **nive**-z) plural of **knife**

knob (say **nob**) *noun* (*plural* **knobs**)
1 a round thing that you turn to control part of a machine: *the volume control* ***knob***
2 a round handle on a door or drawer

knock[1] (say **nok**) *verb* (**knocking, knocked**)
1 to hit something and make a noise: *I* ***knocked*** *on the door, but nobody answered.*
2 to hit something hard, usually by accident: *I* ***knocked*** *my head on the door.* ◇ *She* ***knocked*** *a glass off the table.*
knock somebody down, knock somebody over to hit somebody so that they fall onto the ground: *The boy was* ***knocked*** *down by a car.*
knock something down to break a building so that it falls down ➲ SYNONYM **demolish**: *They're* ***knocking*** *down the old houses.*
knock somebody out to make somebody fall asleep or become unconscious: *The blow* ***knocked*** *him out.*
knock something over to hit something so that it falls over: *I* ***knocked*** *over a vase of flowers.*

knock[2] (say **nok**) *noun* (*plural* **knocks**)
the action of hitting something or the sound that this makes: *I heard a* ***knock*** *at the door.*

knot[1] (say **not**) *noun* (*plural* **knots**)
a place where you have tied two pieces of rope, string or thread tightly together: *I tied a* ***knot*** *in the rope.* ◇ *Can you undo this* ***knot*** (= make it loose)*?*

knot[2] (say **not**) *verb* (**knotting, knotted**)
to tie a **knot** in something: *He* ***knotted*** *the ends of the rope together.*

know (say **noh**) *verb* (**knowing, knew, has known**)
1 to have information in your head: *I don't* ***know*** *her name.* ◇ *He* ***knows*** *a lot about cars.* ◇ *Do you* ***know*** *how to use this machine?* ◇ *Did you* ***know*** *that she's going to live abroad?*
2 to be familiar with a person or place: *I have*

A B C D E F G H I J **K** L M N O P Q R S T U V W X Y Z

known him for six years. ◇ *I* ***know*** *Durban quite well.* ◇ *I liked him when I got to* ***know*** *him* (= started to know him).
I know (*informal*) used to agree with something somebody has just said: *'What a ridiculous situation!' 'I know.'*
let somebody know to tell somebody about something: *Let me* ***know*** *if you need any help.*

know-all (say **noh**-awl) *noun* (*plural* **know-alls**) an annoying person who behaves as if they know everything

knowledge (say **nol**-ij) *noun* (*no plural*) what you know and understand about something: *She has a good* ***knowledge*** *of history.* ◇ *He did it without my* ***knowledge*** (= I did not know) ➲ See Study page 19

knowledgeable (say **nol**-ij-uhb-l) *adjective* knowing a lot: *She's very* ***knowledgeable*** *about history.*

known (say **nohn**) form of **know**

knuckle (say **nuk**-l) *noun* (*plural* **knuckles**) one of the parts where your fingers bend or where they join your hand ➲ See illustration at **hand**[1]

koala (say koh-**aa**-luh) *noun* (*plural* **koalas**) an Australian animal that has large ears and thick grey fur and lives in trees

koeksister (say **kuuk**-suhss-tuh) *noun* (*plural* **koeksisters**) (*S. African*) a small cake that you fry in oil and then put into a thick sweet liquid for a short time

koki™ (say **koh**-kee) *noun* (*plural* **kokis**) (also **koki pen**) a coloured pen with a soft point: *Use paper, a pencil and* ***kokis*** *to create your art work.* ➲ SYNONYM **felt-tip pen**

kombi (say **kom**-bee) *noun* (*plural* **kombis**) (also **combi**) (*S. African*) a large car like a van, especially one used for carrying people ➲ SYNONYM **minibus**
🛈 ORIGIN: 20th century, German, from the Volkswagen company's name *Kombi*, short for *Kombiwagen* meaning 'combination car'. The vehicle can carry both people and goods.

koppie (say **kaw**-pi) *noun* (*plural* **koppies**) (*S. African*) a small hill
🛈 ORIGIN: 19th century, through Afrikaans, from Dutch *kopje* meaning 'small head'

kora (say **kaw**-raa) *noun* (*plural* **koras**) a West African musical instrument with strings that is played with the fingers

Koran (say kuh-**raan**) *noun* (*no plural*) (also **Qur'an**)
the Koran the most important book of the Islamic religion
🛈 ORIGIN: from Arabic *kur'ān* meaning 'reciting'

kosher (say **koh**-shuh) *adjective* prepared according to the Jewish laws about food: ***Kosher*** *meals are available by arrangement.*
🛈 ORIGIN: 19th century, from Hebrew *kāšēr* meaning 'proper'

kraal *noun* (*plural* **kraals**) (*S. African*)
1 a village of traditional African homes, sometimes with a fence around it
2 a small area of land with a fence around it for keeping farm animals such as cattle
🛈 ORIGIN: 18th century, through Dutch from Portuguese *curral* meaning 'enclosure'

kramat (say kruh-**mut**) *noun* (*plural* **kramats**) a small building where a Muslim person who lived a religious life is buried: *the* ***kramat*** *of Sheikh Yusuf in Cape Town*
🛈 ORIGIN: from Malay *keramat* meaning 'holy person' or 'holy place', from Arabic

krans (say **kraanss**) *noun* (*plural* **kranses** or **kranse**) (*S. African*) a cliff
🛈 ORIGIN: through South African Dutch *krantz*, from Dutch *crans* meaning 'small crown'

krill (say **kril**) *noun* (*plural* **krill**) a tiny shellfish that lives in large groups in the sea near the South Pole and is eaten by large sea animals **(whales)**

krypton (say **krip**-ton) *noun* (*no plural*) (symbol Kr) a heavy colourless gas that does not react with other chemicals

kudu (say **kuu**-duu) *noun* (*plural* **kudu** or **kudus**) a large African antelope with white stripes on its body and curved horns
🛈 ORIGIN: 18th century, through Afrikaans *koedoe* from isiXhosa *iqudu*

kung fu (say kung **foo**) *noun* (*no plural*) a Chinese style of fighting in which people use their hands and feet as weapons

kW *abbreviation* (*plural* **kW**) **kilowatt**

kwaito (say **kwy**-toh) *noun* (*no plural*) (*S. African*) a type of dance music with a strong beat and words that are repeated in a regular way
🛈 ORIGIN: named after the Amakwaito, a group of 1950s gangsters in Sophiatown, from Afrikaans *kwaai* meaning 'angry, dangerous'

A B C D E F G H I J K L M N O P Q R S T U V W X Y Z

kwasa kwasa (say kwaa-suh-**kwaa**-suh) *noun* (*no plural*) (*S. African*)
1 a kind of dance that is full of life and energy, originally from central and west Africa
2 the style of music to which this dance is performed

kwashiorkor (say kwaa-shi-**aw**-kaw) *noun* (*no plural*)
a disease that children can get from a poor diet. These children are often very thin but have large stomachs.
🛈 **ORIGIN:** 20th century, from a local word in Ghana

kwela (say **kwair**-luh) *noun* (*no plural*) (*S. African*)
a kind of music in which the main musical instrument is a straight metal tube (called a **penny whistle**) that you play by blowing
🛈 **ORIGIN:** 20th century, from isiXhosa and isiZulu *khwela* meaning 'climb on'. The word also meant 'get going' or 'join in' with the music and dancing.

kWh *abbreviation* (*plural* **kWh**) **kilowatt-hour**

Ll

l *abbreviation* (*plural* **l**) (also **L**) **litre**

laager (say **laa**-guh) *noun* (*plural* **laagers**) (*history*) (*S. African*)
a camp formed by bringing together wagons (= a vehicle with four wheels that a horse pulls) in a circle in order to keep away and fight people that attack: *They formed a* ***laager*** *for protection.*
▸ **laager** (*verb*): *They* ***laagered*** *for the night.*
🛈 **ORIGIN:** 19th century, through South African Dutch, from Dutch *lager* meaning 'camp'

lab (*plural* **labs**) (*informal*) short for **laboratory**

Labarang (say luh-**buh**-rung) *noun* (*no plural*)
= **Eid**

label[1] (say **layb**-l) *noun* (*plural* **labels**)
1 a piece of paper or material on something that tells you about it: *The* ***label*** *on the bottle says 'Made in Kenya'.*
2 a word next to a diagram that tells you the name of something in the diagram: *Look at the illustration of a skeleton and read the* ***labels***.

label[2] (say **layb**-l) *verb* (**labelling, labelled**)
1 to put a label on something: *I* ***labelled*** *all the boxes with my name and address.*
2 When you label a diagram you write the names of its different parts next to it: *Draw a flower and* ***label*** *its parts.*

laboratory (say luh-**bo**-ruh-tree) *noun* (*plural* **laboratories**) (also *informal* **lab**)
a special room or building where people do scientific testing or research or teach about science: *a science* ***laboratory***

laborious (say luh-**baw**-ri-uhss) *adjective*
needing a lot of hard work, effort or time
➲ **OPPOSITE effortless**
▸ **laboriously** (*adverb*)

labour[1] (say **lay**-buh) *noun* (*no plural*)
hard work that you do with your hands and body: *manual* ***labour*** (= work using your hands)

labour[2] (say **lay**-buh) *verb* (**labouring, laboured**)
1 to work hard, especially with your hands: *We* ***laboured*** *from dawn till dusk.*
2 to try very hard to do something that is not easy to do or to move somewhere with great effort: *She spent an hour* ***labouring*** *over the problem.* ◇ *The lorries* ***laboured*** *up the hill.*

labourer (say **lay**-buh-ruh) *noun* (*plural* **labourers**)
a person who does hard work with their hands and body: *a farm* ***labourer***

Labrador (say **lab**-ruh-daw) *noun* (*plural* **Labradors**)
a large type of dog with a yellow or black coat
🛈 **ORIGIN:** 20th century, named after the area in eastern Canada where this type of dog was developed

labyrinth (say **lab**-uh-rinth) *noun* (*plural* **labyrinths**)
a place with a lot of paths and passages, which it is difficult to find your way out of ➲ **SYNONYM maze**

lace (say **layss**) *noun*
1 (*no plural*) very thin cloth with holes that form a pretty pattern: ***lace*** *curtains* ◇ *a handkerchief with* ***lace*** *round the edge*
2 (*plural* **laces**) a string that you use for tying your shoe: *Do up your shoe* ***laces***.

lack[1] (say **lak**) *noun* (*no plural*)
the state of not having something or of not having enough of something: *There is a* ***lack*** *of good teachers.*

lack[2] (say **lak**) *verb* (**lacking, lacked**)
to have none or not enough of something: *He* ***lacked*** *confidence.*

lacquer (say **lak**-uh) *noun* (*no plural*)
a transparent paint that you put on wood, metal, etc. to give it a hard, shiny covering
▸ **lacquer** (*verb*): *You should* ***lacquer*** *the shelves for protection.*

lad *noun* (*plural* **lads**) (*informal*)
a boy or young man

ladder (say **lad**-uh) *noun* (*plural* **ladders**)
a thing that you climb up when you want to reach a high place. A **ladder** is made of two tall pieces of metal or wood with shorter pieces between them (called **rungs**) .

laden (say **layd**-n) *adjective*
carrying a heavy load or having a lot of something: *The trees were* ***laden*** *with fruit.*

ladle (say **layd**-l) *noun* (*plural* **ladles**)
a spoon in the shape of a cup with a long handle, used for serving soup

lady (say **lay**-dee) *noun*
1 (*plural* **ladies**) a polite way of saying 'woman': *an old* ***lady*** ➲ See **gentleman**
2 Lady (*no plural*) (in Britain) a title given to a woman with a high social position: ***Lady*** *Diana Spencer* ➲ See **lord**

ladybird (say **lay**-dee-burd) *noun* (*plural* **ladybirds**)
a small red or yellow insect with black spots

lag *verb* (**lagging, lagged**)
to move, develop or progress more slowly than somebody or something similar and fall behind: *His feet were sore and he **lagged** behind the group.*

lagoon (say luh-**goon**) *noun* (*plural* **lagoons**)
a lake of salt water that is separated from the sea by sand or rock

laid (say **layd**) form of **lay**[1]

laid-back (say **layd**-bak) *adjective* (*informal*) calm and relaxed or not worried

lain (say **layn**) form of **lie**[1]

lair (*rhymes with* **care**) *noun* (*plural* **lairs**)
a safe place where a wild animal rests or lives
➲ SYNONYM **den**

lake (say **layk**) *noun* (*plural* **lakes**)
a big area of water with land all around it: ***Lake** Victoria* ◇ *We went swimming in the **lake**.*

lamb (say **lam**) *noun*
1 (*plural* **lambs**) a young sheep
2 (*no plural*) meat from a **lamb**: *We had roast **lamb** for lunch.*

PRONUNCIATION Don't pronounce the **b** in **lamb**.

lame (say **laym**) *adjective* (**lamer, lamest**)
not able to walk properly: *My horse is **lame**.*

lament (say luh-**ment**) *noun* (*plural* **laments**) (*formal*)
a song, poem or statement that shows that you feel sad or disappointed about something: *a **lament** for those who died in battle*
► **lament** (*verb*): *She was **lamenting** the lack of romance in her life.*

laminated (say **lam**-i-nay-tid) *adjective*
1 covered with a layer of thin transparent material for protection: *a **laminated** map*
2 made by sticking several sheets or layers together: ***laminated** safety glass*

lamp *noun* (*plural* **lamps**)
a device that uses electricity, gas or oil to produce light: *It was dark, so I lit the **lamp**.*

lamp post *noun* (*plural* **lamp posts**)
a tall pole in the street with a light on the top: *The car skidded and hit a **lamp post**.*

lampshade (say **lamp**-shayd) *noun* (*plural* **lampshades**)
a cover for a lamp that makes it look more attractive and makes the light softer

lance (say **laanss**) *noun* (*plural* **lances**)
a long stick with a sharp point at one end, used for fighting or hunting

land[1] *noun*
1 (*no plural*) the part of the Earth that is not the sea: *After two weeks in a boat, we were happy to be back on **land**.*
2 (*no plural*) a piece of ground: *They bought a piece of **land** and built a house on it.* ◇ *farming **land***
3 (*plural* **lands**) (*formal*) a country: *the **land** where I was born*

land[2] *verb* (**landing, landed**)
1 to come down from the air or to bring something down to the ground: *The bird **landed** on the roof.* ◇ *The plane **landed** at OR Tambo airport.* ◇ *The pilot **landed** the plane safely.*
2 to go onto **land** or to put something onto **land** from a ship: *They **landed** the cargo in Durban.*

landfill (say **land**-fil) *noun* (*plural* **landfills**)
a place where you bury waste material under layers of soil: *The council takes the rubbish from our city to a **landfill** site.*

landform (say **land**-fawm) *noun* (*plural* **landforms**)
any physical feature on the Earth's surface, such as a valley, mountain or sea cliff

landing (say **land**-ing) *noun* (*plural* **landings**)
1 the area at the top of stairs in a building: *There's a telephone on the **landing**.*
2 coming down onto the ground in a plane: *The plane made an emergency **landing** in a field.*
➲ OPPOSITE **take-off**

landlady (say **land**-lay-dee) *noun* (*plural* **landladies**)
a woman who rents a house or room to people for money

landline (say **land**-line) *noun* (*plural* **landlines**)
1 a wire for a telephone connection that is laid across land
2 a traditional telephone that is not a cellphone: ***Landlines** are being replaced by wireless phones.*

landlord (say **land**-lawd) *noun* (*plural* **landlords**)
a man who rents a house or room to people for money

landmark (say **land**-maak) *noun* (*plural* **landmarks**)
a big building or another thing that you can see easily from far away: *Table Mountain is one of Cape Town's most famous **landmarks**.*

A B C D E F G H I J K L M N O P Q R S T U V W X Y Z

landmass (say **land**-mass) *noun* (*plural* **landmasses**)
a very large continuous area of land: *Asia and Europe form one large **landmass**.*

landmine (say **land**-mine) *noun* (*plural* **landmines**)
a type of bomb that is hidden on or in the ground, which explodes when vehicles or people move over it

Landsat (say **land**-sat) *noun* (*plural* **Landsats**)
a system of **satellites** (= large electronic devices that travel around the Earth) that produces images of the Earth

landscape (say **land**-skayp) *noun* (*plural* **landscapes**)
everything you can see in an area of land: *The **landscape** is very beautiful.*

landslide (say **land**-slide) *noun* (*plural* **landslides**)
1 a sudden fall of a large mass of soil and rocks sliding down the side of a mountain
2 a great victory for a person or a political party in an election

lane (say **layn**) *noun* (*plural* **lanes**)
1 a narrow road
2 one part of a wide road: *We were driving in the middle **lane** of the highway.*

language (say **lang**-gwij) *noun*
1 (*plural* **languages**) words that people from a particular country say and write: *How many **languages** do you speak?*
2 (*no plural*) words that people use to speak and write: *This word is not often used in spoken **language**.*
3 (*no plural*) any system of signs, symbols, movements, etc. that is used to express something: *sign **language***
4 (*plural* **languages**) (*computing*) a system of symbols and rules that is used to operate a computer or run a program on a computer: *a programming **language***
ORIGIN: 13th–15th century, through Old French *langage*, based on Latin *lingua* meaning 'tongue'

languish (say **lang**-gwish) *verb* (**languishing, languished**) (*formal*)
to lose your strength or energy, usually because of a difficult experience or from having to stay in an unpleasant place: *Sandile **languished** in prison for two years.*

lank (say **langk**) *adjective*
1 (used about hair) long, straight and hanging down
2 (*informal, S. African*) very much or very many: *I'm **lank** tired.* ◇ *There were **lank** people around.*

lanky (say **lang**-kee) *adjective* (**lankier, lankiest**)
very tall and thin and not able to move your body in an elegant way

lantern (say **lan**-tuhn) *noun* (*plural* **lanterns**)
a light in a container made of glass or paper, which usually has a handle so you can carry it

lap¹ *noun* (*plural* **laps**)
1 the flat part at the top of your legs when you are sitting: *The child was sitting on his mother's lap.*
2 one journey around a track in a race: *There are three more **laps** to go in the race.*

lap² *verb* (**lapping, lapped**)
1 to flow against something with gentle sounds: *The waves **lapped** against the rocks.*
2 An animal **laps** or **laps up** a liquid when it drinks it using its tongue.
3 to go past another competitor who is still on the previous **lap¹** 2 in a race: *She **lapped** the runner who was in last place.*
lap up (*informal*) to accept or enjoy something with great enthusiasm, especially without stopping to think if it is good or true

lapa (say **laa**-puh) *noun* (*plural* **lapas**) (*S. African*)
an enclosed area that is surrounded by a wall and often has a roof made of dried grass: *a thatched braai **lapa***
ORIGIN: 20th century, from Sesotho *lelapha* meaning 'courtyard'

lapel (say luh-**pel**) *noun* (*plural* **lapels**)
one of the two sections of the front of a coat or jacket that is folded back against your chest

lapse¹ (say **lapss**) *noun* (*plural* **lapses**)
1 a short time when you cannot remember something or stop giving your attention to something: *a temporary **lapse** in concentration*
2 an example of bad behaviour from somebody who normally behaves well: *He admitted to driving over the speed limit and apologized for the lapse.*
3 an amount of time that has passed or a period of time when you stop doing something: *She returned to work after a **lapse** of ten years.*

lapse² (say **lapss**) *verb* (**lapsing, lapsed**)
1 to finish or stop, or to not be able to use something any more: *My membership has **lapsed** because I forgot to renew it.*
2 to pass gradually into a different, often weaker or worse, state or condition: *to **lapse** into bad habits* ◇ *to **lapse** into a coma*

laptop (say **lap**-top) *noun* (*plural* **laptops**)
a small computer that is easy to carry

lard (say **laad**) *noun* (*no plural*)
a soft white food that is made from melted fat from pigs and used in cooking

large (say **laaj**) *adjective* (**larger**, **largest**)
greater in size, amount, etc. than the usual: *a **large** house* ◇ *She has a **large** family.* ◇ *Have you got this shirt in a **larger** size?* ➲ SYNONYM **big** 1 ➲ OPPOSITE **small**

WORD BUILDING See the note at **big**.

largely (say **laaj**-lee) *adverb*
mostly: *The room is **largely** used for meetings.* ➲ SYNONYM **mainly**

larva (say **laa**-vuh) *noun* (*plural* **larvae**)
a stage of development in many insects and other animals where it has just come out of an egg and has a short fat body with no legs ➲ SYNONYM **grub** 1 ➲ See illustration at **metamorphosis**
▶ **larval** (*adjective*): *Caterpillars and tadpoles are at the **larval** stage of their metamorphosis.*

laryngitis (say la-rin-**jy**-tiss) *noun* (*no plural*)
a mild illness of the throat that makes it difficult for you to speak

larynx (say **la**-rinkss) *noun* (*plural* **larynxes**)
an organ in the throat that you use for talking, swallowing and breathing

lasagne (say luh-**zan**-yuh) *noun* (*no plural*)
broad flat pieces of pasta (= a food made from flour, water and sometimes eggs) or a dish consisting of layers of this baked with meat or vegetables and covered with a cheese sauce

laser (say **lay**-zuh) *noun* (*plural* **lasers**)
an instrument that makes a very strong line of light (called a **laser beam**). Some **lasers** are used to cut metal and others are used by doctors in operations.

lash[1] *verb* (**lashing**, **lashed**)
1 to hit something with great force: *The rain **lashed** against the windows.*
2 to hit somebody with a long piece of rope, leather, etc.
to lash something or **somebody to something else** to tie two things together firmly with rope, etc.
to lash out at somebody or **something** to suddenly attack somebody or something: *The actor **lashed** out at the photographer outside his house.*

lash[2] *noun* (*plural* **lashes**)
1 short for **eyelash**
2 a hit with a long piece of rope, leather, etc.: *He received three **lashes** as punishment.*
▶ **lashing** (*noun*): *to get a **lashing***

lass *noun* (*plural* **lasses**) (also **lassie**) (*informal*)
a girl or young woman

USAGE **Lass** is most commonly used in Scotland and the north of England.

lasso (say la-**soo**) *noun* (*plural* **lassos** or **lassoes**)
a long rope tied in a circle at one end that is used for catching cows and horses
▶ **lasso** (*verb*): *The cowboy **lassoed** the wild horse.*
ⓘ ORIGIN: 18th century, from Spanish *lazo*

last[1] (say **laast**) *adjective*
1 after all the others: *December is the **last** month of the year.* ➲ SYNONYM **final**[1] ➲ OPPOSITE **first**[1]
2 just before now or most recent: *It's June now, so **last** month was May.* ◇ *I was at school **last** week, but this week I'm on holiday.* ◇ *Did you go out **last** (= yesterday) night?*
3 The **last** person or thing is the only one left: *Who wants the **last** cookie?*
▶ **lastly** (*adverb*): ***Lastly**, I want to thank my parents for all their help.*

last[2] (say **laast**) *adverb*
1 after all the others: *He finished **last** in the race.*
2 at a time that is nearest to now: *I **last** saw her in 2007.*

last[3] (say **laast**) *noun* (*no plural*)
the last a person or thing that comes after all the others, or what comes at the end: *I was the **last** to arrive at the party.*
at last in the end; after some time: *She waited all week, and at **last** the letter arrived.* ➲ SYNONYM **finally** 1

last[4] (say **laast**) *verb* (**lasting**, **lasted**)
1 to continue for a time: *The film **lasted** for three hours.* ◇ *How long did the game **last**?*
2 to be enough for a certain time: *We have enough food to **last** us till next week.*

lasting (say **laass**-ting) *adjective*
continuing for a long time: *Their trip to India made a **lasting** impression on them.*

latch (say **lach**) *noun* (*plural* **latches**)
1 a device for fastening a door or gate that consists of a small bar that you can move up and down
2 a type of lock for a door that can be opened from the inside by a handle but from the outside can only be opened with a key
▶ **latch** (*verb*): ***Latch** the door, please.*

late (say **layt**) *adjective*, *adverb* (**later**, **latest**)
1 near the end of a time: *They arrived in the **late** afternoon.* ◇ *She's in her **late** twenties* (= between

A B C D E F G H I J K L M N O P Q R S T U V W X Y Z

the age of 25 and 29). ➲ OPPOSITE **early** 1
2 after the usual or right time: *I went to bed **late** last night.* ◇ *I was **late** for school today* (= I arrived late). ◇ *My train was **late**.* ➲ OPPOSITE **early**
3 no longer alive: *Her **late** husband was a doctor.*
a late night an evening when you go to bed later than usual
at the latest no later than a time or a date: *Please be here by twelve o'clock at the **latest**.*

USAGE It is not standard English to say 'My father is late' when you mean that he has died. Instead say: '*My father is dead*' or '*My father has died*' or '*My father has passed away*'. It is correct to say '*my **late** father*' to mean the same as '*my dead father*'.

lately (say **layt**-lee) *adverb*
recently: *Have you seen Palisa **lately**?* ◇ *The weather has been very bad **lately**.*

later[1] (say **lay**-tuh) *adverb*
at a time in the future or after the time you are talking about: *See you **later**.* ◇ *His father died **later** that year.*
later on (*informal*) at a time in the future or after the time you are talking about: *I'm going out **later** on.*

later[2] (say **lay**-tuh) *adjective*
1 coming after something else or at a time in the future: *The match has been postponed to a **later** date.*
2 near the end of a period of time: *the **later** part of the twentieth century*

lateral (say **lat**-uh-ruhl) *adjective*
1 on or relating to the side of something: *the **lateral** branches of a tree*
2 with movement to the side
▸ **laterally** (*adverb*): *Move **laterally** to your next position.*

latest (say **lay**-tuhst) *adjective*
the newest or most recent: *the **latest** fashions*

latex (say **lay**-tekss) *noun* (*no plural*)
a thick white liquid that can be natural or artificial and is used to make paint, **glue[1]** and material. Natural latex is produced by many different plants, but especially rubber trees.

lathe (say **lay*th***) *noun* (*plural* **lathes**)
a machine that shapes pieces of metal or wood by holding and turning them against the edge of a cutting tool

lather (say **laa*th***-uh) *noun* (*no plural*)
a lot of small white bubbles that are produced when you mix soap with water
▸ **lather** (*verb*): *He **lathered** his face before shaving.*

Latin (say **lat**-in) *noun* (*no plural*)
the language that people used a long time ago in ancient Rome: *Do you study **Latin** at school?*
▸ **Latin** (*adjective*): *Spanish, Italian and other **Latin** languages* (= that developed from Latin)

latitude (say **lat**-i-tyood) *noun* (*no plural*) (abbr. lat.)
the distance of a place north or south of the line around the middle of the Earth (called the **equator**). **Latitude** is measured in degrees.
➲ See illustration at **globe** ➲ See **longitude**

latter (say **lat**-uh) *noun* (*no plural*)
the latter the second of two things or people: *I studied both French and Arabic, but I preferred the **latter**.* ➲ See **former**
▸ **latter** (*adjective*): *the **latter** question*

laugh[1] (say **laaf**) *verb* (**laughing, laughed**)
to make sounds to show that you are happy or that you think something is funny: *His jokes always make me **laugh**.*
laugh at somebody or something to **laugh** to show that you think somebody or something is funny or silly: *The children **laughed** at the clown.* ◇ *He **laughed** at me when I said I was afraid of dogs.*

laugh[2] (say **laaf**) *noun* (*plural* **laughs**)
the sound you make when you are happy or when you think something is funny: *My brother has a loud **laugh**.* ◇ *She told us a joke and we all had a good **laugh*** (= laughed a lot).
for a laugh as a joke or for fun: *The boys put a spider in her bed for a **laugh**.*

laughable (say **laaf**-uhb-l) *adjective*
so bad or silly that it deserves to be laughed at: *This matter would be **laughable** if it were not so serious.* ➲ SYNONYM **ridiculous**

laughter (say **laaf**-tuh) *noun* (*no plural*)
the sound of laughing: *I could hear **laughter** in the next room.*

launch[1] (say **lawnch**) *verb* (**launching, launched**)
1 to start something new: *The magazine was **launched** last year.*
2 to put a ship into the water or a spacecraft into the sky: *This ship was **launched** in 2005.*

launch[2] (say **lawnch**) *noun* (*plural* **launches**)
1 the event at which something such as a ship is put into the water or a spacecraft is sent into the sky
2 the event at which a new product is presented
3 a large boat that has a motor

launder (say **lawn**-duh) *verb* (**laundering, laundered**)
1 (*formal*) to wash and iron dirty clothes, sheets and towels
2 (*informal*) to move money that somebody has got illegally through a legal business or bank account in order to hide where it came from

launderette (say lawn-**dret**) *noun* (*plural* **launderettes**) (also **laundrette**)
a shop where you pay to wash and dry your clothes in machines

laundry (say **lawn**-dree) *noun* (*no plural*)
clothes and sheets that you must wash or that you have washed: *a pile of dirty **laundry***
➲ SYNONYM **washing**

lava (say **laa**-vuh) *noun* (*no plural*)
hot liquid rock that comes out of a mountain with an opening at the top (called a **volcano**)
➲ See illustration at **volcano**

lavatory (say **lav**-uh-tree) *noun* (*plural* **lavatories**) (*formal*)
an old-fashioned word for a toilet: *Where's the **lavatory**, please?*

lavender (say **lav**-uhn-duh) *noun* (*no plural*)
1 a garden plant with purple flowers that smell pleasant
2 a light purple colour

lavish (say **lav**-ish) *adjective*
1 giving or spending money generously: *She was always very **lavish** with her presents.*
2 large in amount, especially larger than is necessary: *a **lavish** meal*
▸ **lavishly** (*adverb*)

law (*rhymes with* **for**) *noun*
1 the law (*no plural*) all the rules of a country: *Stealing is against the **law*** (= illegal). ◇ *You're breaking the **law*** (= doing something illegal).
2 (*plural* **laws**) a rule of a country that says what people may or may not do: *There is a **law** against carrying guns.*

law court (*plural* **law courts**) = **court of law**

lawful (say **law**-fuhl) *adjective* (*formal*)
allowed or accepted by law
▸ **lawfully** (*adverb*): *He is the **lawfully** elected president of the country.*

lawless (say **law**-luhss) *adjective* (*formal*)
breaking the law or having no laws: ***lawless** conduct* ◇ *a **lawless** community.*
▸ **lawlessness** (*noun*): *acts of violence and **lawlessness***

lawn (*rhymes with* **born**) *noun* (*plural* **lawns**)
an area of short grass in a garden or park: *They were sitting on the **lawn**.*

lawnmower (say **lawn**-moh-uh) *noun* (*plural* **lawnmowers**)
a machine that you use to cut grass in a garden or park

lawyer (say **law**-yuh) *noun* (*plural* **lawyers**)
a person who has studied the law and who helps people or talks for them in a court of law

lax (say **lakss**) *adjective*
not careful or strict enough: *a **lax** police force*

laxative (say **lakks**-uh-tiv) *noun* (*plural* **laxatives**)
a medicine or food that helps you get rid of solid waste from your body more easily

lay[1] *verb* (**laying, laid**)
1 to put somebody or something carefully on another thing: *I **laid** the papers on the desk.*
2 to make an egg: *Birds and insects **lay** eggs.*
lay the table to put knives, forks, plates and other things on the table before you eat

WHICH WORD? **Lay** or **lie**?
Lay with meaning 1 above and **lie** have similar meanings.
- **Lay** has an object: *He is **laying** a carpet in our new house.* The past simple tense is **laid**: *She **laid** the baby down gently on the bed.*
- **Lie** does not have an object: *He is **lying** on the beach.* The past simple tense is **lay**: *She was tired so she **lay** on the bed.*

lay[2] form of **lie**[1]

layer (say **lay**-uh) *noun* (*plural* **layers**)
something flat that lies on another thing or that is between other things: *The table was covered with a thin **layer** of dust.* ◇ *The cake has a **layer** of jam in the middle.*

layout (say **lay**-owt) *noun* (*plural* **layouts**)
the way that something is arranged or organized according to a plan: *Make sure that you use the correct **layout** when you write your CV.*

layperson (say **lay**-pur-suhn) *noun* (*plural* **laypersons** or **laypeople**)
a person who does not have special training in or professional knowledge of a particular subject

lazy (say **lay**-zee) *adjective* (**lazier, laziest**)
A person who is **lazy** does not want to work: *Don't be so **lazy** – come and help me!* ◇ *My teacher said I was **lazy**.*
▸ **laziness** (*noun*)

LCD (say el-see-**dee**) *noun* (*plural* **LCDs**)
1 a way of showing pictures and other information on the screen of electronic equipment, such as cameras, computers,

watches and televisions ⓘ **LCD** is an abbreviation of 'liquid crystal display'.
2 (*maths*) the smallest number that the bottom numbers of a group of fractions can be divided into exactly: *The **LCD** of $\frac{1}{3}$ and $\frac{1}{4}$ is 12. Both 4 and 3 can be divided into 12 exactly.* ⓘ **LCD** is short for 'lowest common denominator'.

LCM (say el-see-**em**) *noun* (*plural* **LCMs**) (*maths*)
the smallest number that two different numbers can be divided into exactly: *The **LCM** of 6 and 9 is 18.* ⓘ **LCM** is short for 'lowest common multiple'.

lead[1] (say **leed**) *verb* (**leading, led**)
1 to take a person or an animal somewhere by going with them or in front of them: *He **led** me to the classroom.*
2 to go to a place: *This path **leads** to the river.*
3 to make something happen: *Smoking can **lead** to heart disease.*
4 to have a particular type of life: *They **lead** a very busy life.*
5 to be the first or the best, for example in a race or game: *Who's **leading** in the race?*
6 to control a group of people: *The team was **led** by Themba.*

lead[2] (say **led**) *noun*
1 (*no plural*) (symbol Pb) a soft grey metal that is very heavy
2 (*plural* **leads**) the grey part inside a pencil

lead[3] (say **leed**) *noun*
1 (*no plural*) the first place or position in front of other people: *The Kenyan runner has gone into the **lead**.* ◇ *Who is in the **lead*** (= winning)*?*
2 (*plural* **leads**) (also **leash**) a long piece of leather or a chain that you tie to a dog's neck so that it walks with you: *All dogs must be kept on a **lead**.*
3 (*plural* **leads**) a long piece of wire that brings electricity to things like lamps and machines

leader (say **leed**-uh) *noun* (*plural* **leaders**)
1 a person who controls a group of people: *They chose a new **leader**.*
2 a person or thing that is the first or the best: *The **leader** is ten metres in front of the other runners.*

leadership (say **leed**-uh-ship) *noun* (*no plural*)
the state or position of being the person who controls a group of people: *The country is under new **leadership*** (= has new leaders).

leading (say **leed**-ing) *adjective*
best or most important: *He's one of the **leading** experts in this field.*

leaf (say **leef**) *noun* (*plural* **leaves**)
one of the flat green parts that grow on a plant or tree: ***Leaves** fall from the trees in autumn.*
➲ See illustration at **plant**[1]

leaflet (say **leef**-luht) *noun* (*plural* **leaflets**)
a piece of paper with writing on it that gives information about something: *I picked up a **leaflet** on museums and art galleries.*

league (say **leeg**) *noun* (*plural* **leagues**)
1 a group of teams that play against each other in a sport: *the football **league***
2 a group of people or countries that work together to do something: *the **League** of Nations*

leak[1] (say **leek**) *verb* (**leaking, leaked**)
1 to have a small hole or crack that liquid or gas can go through: *The roof of our house **leaks** when it rains.* ◇ *The boat is **leaking**.*
2 (used about liquid or gas) to go out through a hole: *Water is **leaking** from the pipe.*

leak[2] (say **leek**) *noun* (*plural* **leaks**)
a small hole or crack that liquid or gas can get through: *There's a **leak** in the pipe.*
▸ **leaky** (*adjective*): *a **leaky** roof*

lean[1] (say **leen**) *verb* (**leaning, leant** or **leaned**)
1 to not be straight, or to bend forwards, backwards or to the side: *She **leaned** out of the window and waved.*
2 to put your body or a thing against another thing: ***Lean** your bike against the wall.*

lean[2] (say **leen**) *adjective* (**leaner, leanest**)
1 thin and healthy: *He is tall and **lean**.*
2 Lean meat does not have very much fat.

leant (say **lent**) form of **lean**[1]

leap (say **leep**) *verb* (**leaping, leapt** or **leaped**)
to jump high or a long way: *The cat **leapt** onto the table.*
▸ **leap** (*noun*): *With one **leap**, he was over the top of the wall.*

leapt (say **lept**) form of **leap**

leap year *noun* (*plural* **leap years**)
a year when February has 29 days. **Leap years** happen every four years.

learn (say **lurn**) *verb* (**learning, learnt** or **learned**)
1 to find out something, or how to do something, by studying or by doing it often: *When did you **learn** to swim?* ◇ *I **learnt** English at school.* ◇ ***Learn** this list of words for homework* (= so you can remember them).
2 to hear about something: *I was sorry to **learn** of your father's death.*

learner (say **lurn**-uh) *noun* (*plural* **learners**)
a person who is learning: *This dictionary is for learners of English.*

learnership (say **lurn**-uh-ship) *noun* (*plural* **learnerships**) (*S. African*)
a job that includes training as part of the work you do so that you can learn new skills while working

learnt (say **lurnt**) form of **learn**

lease (say **leess**) *noun* (*plural* **leases**)
a legal contract that allows you to use somebody's property for a fixed period of time in return for payment
▶ **lease** (*verb*): *They* ***lease*** *the land from a local farmer.*

least (say **leest**) *adjective, adverb, pronoun*
1 smallest in size, amount, etc.: *Sue has some money; Jane has less, and Kate has the* ***least*** *money.* ➲ OPPOSITE **most[1]**
2 less than all others: *I bought the* ***least*** *expensive tickets.* ◇ *We seldom run, but Jo runs* ***least***. ◇ *I used the* ***least***. ➲ OPPOSITE **most[1]**
at least
1 not less than: *It will cost at* ***least*** *R150.*
2 even though other things are bad: *We're not rich, but at* ***least*** *we're happy.*
not in the least not at all: *'Are you angry?' 'Not in the* ***least****!'*

leather (say **le*th***-uh) *noun* (*no plural*)
the skin of an animal, which is used to make things like shoes, jackets or bags: *a* ***leather*** *jacket*
🛈 ORIGIN: from Old English *lether*, related to Dutch *leer*

leave[1] (say **leev**) *verb* (**leaving, left**)
1 to go away from a place or a person: *The train* ***leaves*** *at 8.40.* ◇ *At what age do most people* ***leave*** *school in your country?* ◇ *We are* ***leaving*** *for Durban tomorrow.*
2 to let somebody or something stay in the same place or in the same way: ***Leave*** *the door open, please.*
3 to forget to bring something with you: *I* ***left*** *my books at home.* ◇ *I can't find my glasses. Maybe I* ***left*** *them behind at work.*
4 to not use something: ***Leave*** *some cake for me!*
5 to give something to somebody when you die: *She* ***left*** *all her money to her two sons.*
6 to give the responsibility for something to another person: *I'll* ***leave*** *it to you to organize the food.*
be left to still be there after everything else has gone: *There is only one piece of cake* ***left***.
leave somebody or **something alone** to not touch, annoy or speak to somebody or something: ***Leave*** *me alone – I'm busy!* ◇ ***Leave*** *that bag alone – it's mine!*
leave somebody out to not include somebody or something: *The other children* ***left*** *him out of the game.*
leave something out to not put in or do something: *I* ***left*** *out question 3 in the exam – it was too difficult.*

leave[2] (say **leev**) *noun* (*no plural*)
a period of time when you are allowed to be away from work for a holiday or for a special reason: *I have 25 days'* ***leave*** *each year.* ◇ *She's not working – she's on sick* ***leave***.

leaves (say **leevz**) plural of **leaf**

lecture (say **lek**-tshuh) *noun* (*plural* **lectures**)
a talk to a group of people to teach them about something: *She gave a fascinating* ***lecture*** *on Spanish history.*
▶ **lecture** (*verb*): *Professor Sims* ***lectures*** *in Modern Art.*

lecturer (say **lek**-tshuh-ruh) *noun* (*plural* **lecturers**)
a person who gives talks to teach people about a subject, especially as a job in a university: *He is a university* ***lecturer***.

LED (say el-ee-**dee**) *noun* (*plural* **LEDs**)
an electronic device that lights up when an electric current passes through it, producing very little heat: *My digital clock has an* ***LED*** *display.* 🛈 **LED** is short for 'light emitting diode'.

led form of **lead[1]**

ledge (say **lej**) *noun* (*plural* **ledges**)
a long narrow flat place, for example under a window or on the side of a mountain: *a window* ***ledge***

ledger (say **lej**-uh) *noun* (*plural* **ledgers**)
a record of all the money that a business has received and paid

leek *noun* (*plural* **leeks**)
a vegetable like a long onion that is white at one end and green at the other: ***leek*** *and potato soup*

leer (*rhymes with* **gear**) *verb* (**leering, leered**)
to look or smile at somebody in a way that shows sexual interest or bad intentions
▶ **leer** (*noun*): *a* ***leer*** *of desire*

left[1] (say **left**) form of **leave[1]**

left[2] (say **left**) *adjective, adverb*
on the side where your heart is in the body: *I've broken my* ***left*** *arm.* ◇ *Turn* ***left*** *at the shop.*
➲ OPPOSITE **right[1]** 4

left[3] (say **left**) *noun* (*no plural*)
the **left** side or direction: *In South Africa we*

A B C D E F G H I J K L M N O P Q R S T U V W X Y Z

*drive on the **left**.* ◇ *The house is on your **left**.* ➲ OPPOSITE **right**[3] 3

left-hand (say **left**-hand) *adjective*
of or on the left: *Your heart is on the **left-hand** side of your body.* ➲ OPPOSITE **right-hand**

left-handed (say left-**hand**-uhd) *adjective, adverb*
using your left hand more easily than your right hand, for example when you write: *Are you **left-handed**?* ◇ *I can't write **left-handed**.* ➲ OPPOSITE **right-handed**

leg *noun* (*plural* **legs**)
1 one of the long parts of the body of a person or an animal that is used for walking and standing: *A spider has eight **legs**.* ◇ *She sat down and crossed her **legs**.*
2 one of the parts of a pair of trousers that covers your leg: *a trouser **leg***
3 one of the long parts that a table or chair stands on: *a table **leg***

legacy (say **leg**-uh-see) *noun* (*plural* **legacies**)
1 money or things that you get from somebody when they die because they left it to you in their will
2 a situation that exists now because of something that happened in the past: *Future generations could be left with a **legacy** of pollution.*

legal (say **leeg**-l) *adjective*
1 using or connected with the law: ***legal** advice*
2 allowed by the law: *In some countries it is **legal** to carry a gun.* ➲ OPPOSITE **illegal**
► **legally** (*adverb*)

legalize (say **leeg**-uh-lize) *verb* (**legalizing, legalized**) (also **legalise**)
to change or introduce a law to make something legal
► **legalization** (*noun*) (also **legalisation**): *the **legalization** of gambling*

legend (say **lej**-uhnd) *noun* (*plural* **legends**)
1 an old story that is perhaps not true: *the **legend** of Robin Hood*
2 a very famous person or event: *He was a **legend** in the world of music.*
► **legendary** (*adjective*): *a **legendary** hero*

legible (say **lej**-uhb-l) *adjective*
clear enough to read or read easily: ***legible** writing* ➲ OPPOSITE **illegible**

legion (say **lee**-juhn) *noun* (*plural* **legions**)
1 a large group of soldiers: ***legions** of Roman soldiers*
2 a large number of people or things, usually of one type: *There was a **legion** of journalists at the news conference.*

legislate (say **lej**-iss-layt) *verb* (**legislating, legislated**) (*formal*)
to make a law or laws: *The government has decided to **legislate** for children in need of care and protection.*

legitimate (say li-**jit**-i-muht) *adjective*
1 allowed by or in agreement with the law or rules: ***legitimate** tax deductions*
2 acceptable or reasonable: *a **legitimate** excuse*
3 (used about a child) having parents who are married to each other ➲ OPPOSITE **illegitimate**
► **legitimacy** (*noun*) ► **legitimately** (*adverb*)

legume (say **leg**-yoom) *noun* (*plural* **legumes**)
a plant that has seeds in long pods (= seed containers) that we use for food: *Peas, beans and lentils are all **legumes**.*

leisure (say **lezh**-uh) *noun* (*no plural*)
the time when you are not working and can do what you want: ***leisure** activities* ➲ SYNONYM **recreation**

lekgotla (say le-***khawt***-luh) *noun* (*plural* **lekgotlas**) (*S. African*)
a meeting where people discuss important issues, try to find answers to problems and plan what to do in the future: *This was one of the decisions taken at the recent government **lekgotla**.*
ⓘ ORIGIN: 19th century, from Sesotho and Setswana *kgotla* meaning 'courtyard, meeting place'

> PRONUNCIATION Pronounce the **g** in **lekgotla** like the **g** in the Afrikaans word **lag**.

lemon (say **lem**-uhn) *noun* (*plural* **lemons**)
a yellow fruit with sour juice that is used for giving flavour to food and drink: ***lemon** juice*

lemonade (say lem-uh-**nayd**) *noun* (*no plural*)
1 a sweet clear drink with bubbles in it: *a glass of **lemonade***
2 a drink that is made from fresh lemon juice, sugar and water

lemur (say **lee**-muh) *noun* (*plural* **lemurs**)
an animal like a monkey with thick fur and a long tail, which lives in trees in Madagascar. There are many different types of lemurs.

lend *verb* (**lending, lent**)
to give something to somebody for a short time: *I **lent** the book to Jo.* ◇ *Rick **lent** me his car for an hour.* ➲ See note at **borrow** ➲ SYNONYM **loan**[2]

length (say **leng**-th) *noun* (*no plural*)
how long something is: *The table is two metres in **length**.* ◇ *We measured the **length** of the garden.* ➲ The adjective is **long**[1]

length, width and height

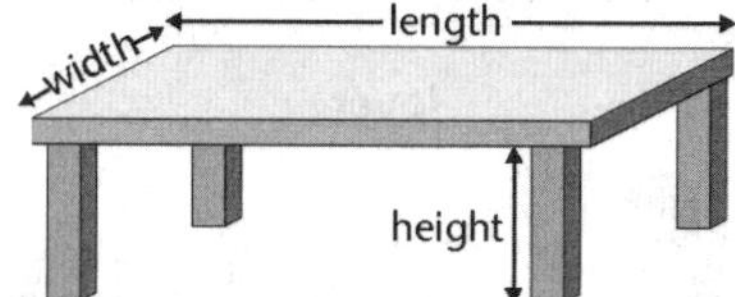

lengthen (say **leng**-thuhn) *verb* (**lengthening, lengthened**)
to become or to make something longer: *I need to **lengthen** this skirt.* ➲ OPPOSITE **shorten**

lengthways (say **length**-wayz) *adverb* (also **lengthwise**)
in a direction along the longest part of something: *Fold the paper **lengthways**.*

lengthy (say **leng**-thee) *adjective* (**lengthier, lengthiest**)
very long: *a **lengthy** meeting*

lenient (say **lee**-ni-uhnt) *adjective*
not as strict or harsh as a punishment or a person who punishes somebody could have been ➲ OPPOSITE **severe** 1
► **leniency** (*noun*): *She appealed to the judge for **leniency**.* ► **leniently** (*adverb*): *Fraud should not be treated **leniently**.*

lens (say **lenz**) *noun* (*plural* **lenses**)
1 a special piece of glass in things such as cameras, **microscopes** or glasses. It makes things look bigger, smaller or clearer when you look through it.
2 the transparent part of the eye, behind the round hole in the middle of the eye (called the **pupil**) that changes shape in order to direct light so that you can see clearly
➲ See illustration at **eye**

lent form of **lend**

lentil (say **lent**-l) *noun* (*plural* **lentils**)
a small round dried seed. You cook **lentils** in water before you eat them: ***lentil** soup*

leopard (say **lep**-uhd) *noun* (*plural* **leopards**)
a wild animal like a big cat with yellow fur and dark spots. **Leopards** live in Africa and southern Asia.

leotard (say **lee**-uh-taad) *noun* (*plural* **leotards**)
a piece of clothing that fits the body tightly from the neck to the tops of the legs, worn by dancers or by women doing some sports
❶ ORIGIN: 20th century, named after Jules Léotard (1839–1870), a French circus performer

leper (say **lep**-uh) *noun* (*plural* **lepers**)
a person who has **leprosy**

leprosy (say **lep**-ruh-see) *noun* (*no plural*)
a serious infectious disease that mainly affects the skin and nerves and can cause parts of the body to fall off

lesbian (say **lez**-bi-uhn) *noun* (*plural* **lesbians**)
a woman who is sexually attracted to other women ➲ See **homosexual**
► **lesbian** (*adjective*): *a **lesbian** relationship*

less[1] *adjective, adverb, pronoun*
a smaller amount of something: *A poor person has **less** money than a rich person.* ◇ *The doctor advised him to drink **less** beer.* ➲ OPPOSITE **more**[1]

WHICH WORD? **Less** or **fewer**?
- We use **less** when we talk about something that has no plural, such as **fat**: *You should eat **less** fat.*
- We use **fewer** when we talk about things that have a plural, such as **sweets**: *You should eat **fewer** sweets.*

less[2] *adverb*
not so much: *It rains **less** in summer.* ◇ *He's **less** intelligent than his sister.* ➲ OPPOSITE **more**[1]
➲ See **least**

lessen (say **less**-uhn) *verb* (**lessening, lessened**)
to become or to make something less: *This medicine will **lessen** the pain.* ➲ SYNONYMS **diminish, reduce**

lesson (say **less**-uhn) *noun* (*plural* **lessons**)
a time when you learn something with a teacher: *We have a Maths **lesson** after lunch.* ◇ *She gives piano **lessons**.* ◇ *I'm taking driving **lessons**.* ➲ SYNONYM **class** 2

let *verb* (**letting, let**)
1 to allow somebody or something to do something: *Her parents won't **let** her stay out late.* ◇ ***Let** the dog in* (= let it come in). ◇ ***Let** go of my hand!*
2 let's (short for **let us**) used for making suggestions about what you and other people can do: ***Let's** watch a film.*
3 to allow somebody to use your house or land if they pay you: *We have a room to **let**.*
let somebody down to not do something that you promised to do for somebody: *She **let** me down. She didn't come to my party.*

A B C D E F G H I J K L M N O P Q R S T U V W X Y Z

let somebody off to not punish somebody: *He didn't go to prison – the judge **let** him **off**.*

> USAGE You cannot use **let** with meaning 1 above in the passive. You must use **allow** and **to**: *They **let** him take the exam again. He **was allowed to** take the exam again.*

> USAGE The negative of **let's** in meaning 2 above is **let's not**: ***Let's not** go out this evening.*

lethal (say **leeth**-l) *adjective*
Something that is **lethal** can cause a lot of damage or death: *a **lethal** weapon* ➲ SYNONYM **deadly**[1]

lethargy (say **leth**-uh-jee) *noun* (*no plural*)
the feeling of being very tired and not having any energy
▸ **lethargic** (*adjective*)

letter (say **let**-uh) *noun* (*plural* **letters**)
1 a piece of writing that one person sends to another person: *He got a **letter** from his cousin.* ◊ *a thank-you **letter***
2 a sign in writing that represents a sound in a language: *Z is the last **letter** in the English alphabet.*

> WORD BUILDING A, B and C are **capital** letters (also called **upper case** letters), and a, b, and c are **small** letters (also called **lower case** letters).

letter box *noun* (*plural* **letter boxes**)
1 (also **mail box**) a private box outside a house or a building, or a hole in a door for putting letters through
2 (also **postbox**) a metal box in the street where you put letters that you want to send

lettuce (say **let**-iss) *noun* (*plural* **lettuces**)
a plant with big green leaves that you eat cold in salads

leukaemia (say loo-**keem**-i-uh) *noun* (*no plural*)
a serious disease **(cancer)** of the blood

level[1] (say **lev**-l) *noun* (*plural* **levels**)
1 the amount, size or number of something: *a low **level** of unemployment*
2 the height, position, standard, etc. of something: *The town is 500 metres above sea **level**.* ◊ *a beginners-**level** isiZulu class*

level[2] (say **lev**-l) *adjective*
1 with no part higher than another part: *We need **level** ground to play football on.* ◊ *This shelf isn't **level**.* ➲ SYNONYM **flat**[1] 1
2 at the same height, standard or position: *The teams are **level** with 40 points each.* ◊ *His head is **level** with her shoulder.*

lever (say **lee**-vuh) *noun* (*plural* **levers**)
1 a handle that you pull or push to make a machine work: *Pull this **lever**.*
2 a bar for lifting something heavy or opening something. You put one end under the thing you want to lift or open and push the other end down.

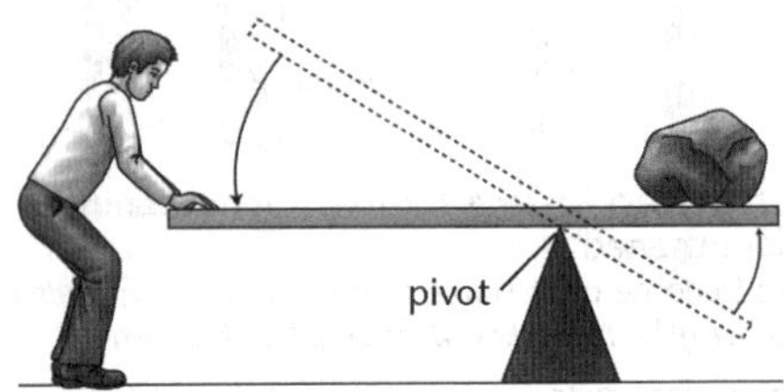

how a lever works

leverage (say **lee**-vuh-rij) *noun* (*no plural*)
1 the action of using a **lever** to lift or open something; the force that is produced when you do this
2 power or influence over other people that allows somebody to get or do what they want: *political **leverage***

levy (say **lev**-ee) *verb* (**levying, levied**)
to officially demand and collect money: *to **levy** a tax*
▸ **levy** (*noun*): *fuel **levies***

lexicography (say lek-si-**kog**-ruh-fee) *noun* (*no plural*)
the process of writing and creating dictionaries
▸ **lexicographer** (*noun*): *Dr Samuel Johnson was a famous English **lexicographer**.*

liability (say ly-uh-**bil**-uh-tee) *noun*
1 (*no plural*) the state of being legally responsible for something
2 (*plural* **liabilities**) a person or thing that can cause you a lot of problems
3 (*plural* **liabilities**) the amount of money that a person or company owes

liable (say **ly**-uhb-l) *adjective*
be liable to do something to be likely to do something: *We're all **liable** to have accidents when we are very tired.*

liaise (say lee-**ayz**) *verb* (**liaising, liaised**)
to share and exchange information with a person, group or organization so that everybody can work together well

liaison (say lee-**ayz**-uhn) *noun*
1 (*no plural*) communication between two or more people or groups that work together
2 (*plural* **liaisons**) a person who regularly shares information with two or more people or

groups: *She acted as the chief **liaison** between the customers and the management of the store.*
3 (*plural* **liaisons**) a secret sexual relationship

liar (say **ly**-uh) *noun* (*plural* **liars**)
a person who says or writes things that are not true (called **lies**): *I don't believe her – she's a **liar**.*
➲ The verb is **lie³**

libel (say **libe**-uhl) *noun* (*no plural*)
the act of writing and publishing a false statement about a person or organization that would give people a bad opinion of them
➲ See **slander**
▸ **libel** (*verb*): *The actor says he was **libelled** by the magazine article.* ▸ **libellous** (*adjective*): ***libellous** content on a website*

liberal (say **lib**-uh-ruhl) *adjective*
a person who is **liberal** lets other people do and think what they want: *Her parents are very **liberal**, but mine are quite strict.*

liberate (say **lib**-uh-rayt) *verb* (**liberating, liberated**)
to make somebody or something free: *The city was **liberated** by the advancing army.*
▸ **liberation** (*noun*): ***liberation** from oppression*

liberty (say **lib**-uh-tee) *noun* (*no plural*)
being free to go where you want and do what you want ➲ See **freedom**
🛈 **ORIGIN:** 14th–15th century, through Old French *liberte*, from Latin *liber* meaning 'free'

librarian (say libe-**rair**-ri-uhn) *noun* (*plural* **librarians**)
a person who works in a library

library (say **libe**-ruh-ree) *noun* (*plural* **libraries**)
a room or building where you go to borrow or read books
🛈 **ORIGIN:** 14th–15th century, through Old French from Latin *libraria* meaning 'bookshop', from *liber* meaning 'book'

libretto (say lib-**ret**-oh) *noun* (*plural* **librettos** or **libretti**) (*music*)
the words of an opera or other musical play, including both the spoken and sung parts

lice (say **lise**) form of **louse**

licence (say **lise**-uhnss) *noun* (*plural* **licences**)
an official document that shows you are allowed to do or have something: *Do you have a driver's **licence**?*

license (say **lise**-uhnss) *verb* (**licensing, licensed**)
to give somebody official permission to do or have something: *This shop is **licensed** to sell guns.*

lichen (say **like**-uhn) *noun* (*no plural*)
a very small organism that spreads over the surface of rocks, walls and trees: ***Lichen** is a combination of a fungus and an alga.*

lick (say **lik**) *verb* (**licking, licked**)
to move your tongue over something: *The child **licked** the spoon clean.*
▸ **lick** (*noun*)

lid *noun* (*plural* **lids**)
the top part of a box, pot or other container that covers it and that you can take off

lie¹ (say **ly**) *verb* (**lying, lay, has lain**)
1 to put your body flat on something so that you are not sitting or standing: *He **lay** on the bed.* ➲ See note at **lay¹**
2 to have your body flat on something: *The baby was **lying** on its back.*
3 to be or stay in a position or state: *The hills **lie** to the north of the town.*
lie down to put or have your body flat so that you can rest: *She **lay** down on the bed.*

lie² (say **ly**) *verb* (**lying, lied, has lied**)
to say something that you know is not true: *He **lied** about his age. He said he was 16 but really he's 14.* ◇ *Don't ever **lie** to me again!*

WORD BUILDING A person who lies is a **liar**.

lie³ (say **ly**) *noun* (*plural* **lies**)
something you say that you know is not true: *She told me a **lie**.* ➲ See **liar**

lieutenant (say lef-**ten**-uhnt) *noun* (*plural* **lieutenants**)
an officer at a middle level in the army or navy

life (*rhymes with* **wife**) *noun*
1 (*no plural*) People, animals and plants have **life** while they are alive, but things like stone, metal and water do not: *Do you believe there is **life** after death?* ◇ *Is there **life** on other planets?*
2 (*plural* **lives**) the state of being alive: *Many people lost their **lives*** (= died) *in the fire.* ◇ *The doctor saved her **life*** (= stopped her from dying).
3 (*plural* **lives**) the time that somebody is alive: *He has **lived** here all his life.*
4 (*plural* **lives**) the way that you live or the experiences that you have when you are alive: *They were very happy throughout their married **life**.* ◇ *They lead a busy **life**.*
5 (*no plural*) energy or being busy and interested: *Young children are full of **life**.*

lifebelt (say **life**-belt) *noun* (*plural* **lifebelts**)
a large ring made from light material that floats. A **lifebelt** is thrown to a person who has fallen into water to stop them from sinking.

lifeboat (say **life**-boht) *noun* (*plural* **lifeboats**)
1 a small boat that is carried on a large ship and that is used to escape from the ship if it is in danger of sinking
2 a boat that goes to help people who are in danger at sea

life cycle *noun* (*plural* **life cycles**)
the series of forms into which a living thing changes as it develops: *the **life cycle** of a frog* ◇ *During its **life cycle** this insect changes from a caterpillar into a butterfly.* ➲ See **metamorphosis**

life cycle

life cycle of a frog

lifeguard (say **life**-gaad) *noun* (*plural* **lifeguards**)
a person at a beach or a swimming pool whose job is to help people who are in danger in the water

life jacket *noun* (*plural* **life jackets**)
a special jacket with no sleeves that can be filled with air. You wear it to help you float if you fall in the water.

lifeless (say **life**-luhss) *adjective*
1 dead or appearing to be dead
2 not able to support life or without living things: *Water pollution caused the river to become **lifeless**.*
3 without excitement, energy or interest: *a **lifeless** performance*

lifelike (say **life**-like) *adjective*
looking like a real person or thing, or very similar to real life: *The flowers are made of silk but they are very **lifelike**.*

lifelong (say **life**-long) *adjective*
lasting or continuing for all of your life: *a **lifelong** friend*

lifesaver (say **life**-say-vuh) *noun* (*plural* **lifesavers**)
1 = **lifeguard**
2 (*informal*) a person or thing that helps you in a crisis or emergency: *Thank you for all your help. You're a **lifesaver**!*

life skill *noun* (*plural* **life skills**)
a skill that makes it possible for you to deal with situations that happen during normal life: *Learning to communicate with the people you work with is an important **life skill**.*

lifespan (say **life**-span) *noun* (*plural* **lifespans**)
the length of time that a living thing or an object can be expected to live, work or last

lifestyle (say **life**-stile) *noun* (*plural* **lifestyles**)
the way that you live: *They have a healthy **lifestyle**.*

lifetime (say **life**-time) *noun* (*plural* **lifetimes**)
all the time that you are alive: *There have been a lot of changes in my grandma's **lifetime**.*

lift¹ *verb* (**lifting**, **lifted**)
to move somebody or something to a higher position: *I can't **lift** this box. It's too heavy.* ◇ ***Lift** your arm up.*

lift² *noun* (*plural* **lifts**) (also **elevator**)
1 a machine that takes people and things up and down in a high building: *Shall we use the stairs or take the **lift**?*
2 a free journey in another person's car: *Can you give me a **lift** to the station?*

ligament (say **lig**-uh-muhnt) *noun* (*plural* **ligaments**)
a strong band in a person's or animal's body that connects bones together and supports joints

light¹ (say **lite**) *adjective* (**lighter**, **lightest**)
1 full of natural light: *In summer it's **light** until late.* ◇ *The room has a lot of windows so it's very **light**.* ➲ OPPOSITE **dark¹** 1
2 with a pale colour: *a **light** blue shirt* ➲ OPPOSITE **dark¹** 2
3 easy to lift or move: *Will you carry this bag for me? It's very **light**.* ➲ OPPOSITE **heavy** 1
4 not very much or not very strong: ***light** rain* ◇ *I had a **light** breakfast.* ➲ OPPOSITE **heavy** 2
▸ **lightly** (*adverb*)

light² (say **lite**) *noun*
1 (*no plural*) the energy from the sun, a lamp or another light source that allows us to see things: *Strong **sunlight** is bad for the eyes.* ◇ *The **light** was not very good so it was difficult to read.*

2 (*plural* **lights**) a thing that gives light, for example an electric lamp
3 (*plural* **lights**) something, for example a match, that you use to start a cigarette burning: *Do you have a* ***light****?*

WORD BUILDING A light can be **on** or **off**. You can **put**, **turn** or **switch** a light **on**: *Switch the* ***light*** *on.*
You can **put**, **turn** or **switch** a light **off**: *Turn the* ***lights*** *off.* ◇ *Shall I put the* ***light*** *off?*

light³ (say **lite**) *verb* (**lighting, lit** or **lighted**)
1 to make something start to burn: *Will you* ***light*** *the fire?* ◇ *She* ***lit*** *a candle.*
2 to give **light** to something: *The room is* ***lit*** *by two big lamps.*

light bulb *noun* (*plural* **light bulbs**)
the glass part of an electric lamp that gives light

lighten (say **lite**-uhn) *verb* (**lightening, lightened**)
to become lighter or to make something lighter in colour or weight
lighten up (*informal*) to become happier or less worried about something

lighter (say **lite**-uh) *noun* (*plural* **lighters**)
a thing for lighting cigarettes

lighthouse (say **lite**-howss) *noun* (*plural* **lighthouses**)
a tall building by or in the sea, with a strong light to show ships that there are rocks

lighting (say **lite**-ing) *noun* (*no plural*)
the quality or type of lights used in a room, building, etc.: *electric* ***lighting***

lightning (say **lite**-ning) *noun* (*no plural*)
a sudden bright light in the sky when there is a storm: *He was struck* (= hit) *by* ***lightning.*** ➲ See **thunder¹**

light year *noun* (*plural* **light years**)
the distance that light travels in one year (about $9,5 \times 10^{12}$ kilometres): *The nearest star to our sun is 4* ***light years*** *away.*

like¹ *verb* (**liking, liked**)
1 to feel that somebody or something is good or nice, or to enjoy something: *Do you* ***like*** *your new teacher?* ◇ *I don't* ***like*** *carrots.* ◇ *I* ***like*** *playing tennis.* ➲ OPPOSITE **dislike¹**
2 to want: *Do what you* ***like.*** *I don't care.* ◇ *We can go whenever you* ***like.***
if you like used to agree with somebody or to suggest something: *'Shall we go out tonight?' 'Yes, if you* ***like.****'*

WORD BUILDING There are many words that you can use instead of **like**1, but check their exact meanings first. Examples are: **admire, adore, enjoy, be fond of, idolize, love²**, and **worship**2 (informal).

WHICH WORD? **Would like** or **want**?
Would like is a more polite way of saying **want**. *Would you* ***like*** *some coffee? I'd* ***like*** *to speak to the manager.*

like² *preposition, conjunction*
1 the same as or similar to somebody or something: *She is wearing a dress* ***like*** *mine.* ◇ *John looks* ***like*** *his father.* ➲ OPPOSITE **unlike**
2 in the same way as somebody or something: *She acted* ***like*** *a child.*
3 for example: *I bought a lot of things* ***like*** *books and clothes.*
what is ... like? words that you say when you want to know more about somebody or something: *'What's that book* ***like****?' 'It's very interesting.'*

likeable (say **like**-uhb-l) *adjective*
If a person is **likeable**, they are friendly and easy to like.

likelihood (say **like**-lee-huud) *noun* (*no plural*)
the chance of something happening: *There is very little* ***likelihood*** *of you passing this exam* (= it is very unlikely that you will pass).

likely (say **like**-lee) *adjective* (**likelier, likeliest**)
If something is **likely**, it will probably happen: *It's* ***likely*** *that she will agree.* ◇ *They are* ***likely*** *to be late.* ➲ OPPOSITE **unlikely**

likeness (say **like**-nuhss) *noun* (*no plural*)
being or looking the same: *There's a strong* ***likeness*** *between her and her sister.*

likewise (say **like**-wize) *adverb* (*formal*)
the same: *I sat down and he did* ***likewise.***

liking (say **like**-ing) *noun* (*no plural*)
the feeling that you like somebody or something: *She has a* ***liking*** *for spicy food.*

lilac (say **lile**-uhk) *noun*
1 (*plural* **lilacs**) a bush or small tree with sweet-smelling white or purple flowers
2 (*no plural*) a pale purple colour
► **lilac** (*adjective*): *She wore a grey dress and a* ***lilac*** *hat.*

lily (say **lil**-ee) *noun* (*plural* **lilies**)
a plant with big white or coloured flowers

limb (say **lim**) *noun* (*plural* **limbs**)
1 an arm or a leg
2 one of the main branches of a tree

limbo (say **lim**-boh) *noun*
in limbo a period of time when you are kept waiting and not sure about what is going to happen next: *The applicants ended up in **limbo** for months, waiting for an answer.*

lime *noun* (*plural* **limes**)
a small green fruit like a lemon

limelight (say **lime**-lite) *noun* (*no plural*)
the limelight special attention that is given to somebody by the public, either because they are famous or because they have done something unusual

limerick (say **lim**-uh-rik) *noun* (*plural* **limericks**)
a funny poem with five lines and a characteristic rhythm

limestone (say **lime**-stohn) *noun* (*no plural*)
a hard white rock that is used in building and for making cement: ***Limestone** is a sedimentary rock.*

limit[1] (say **lim**-it) *noun* (*plural* **limits**)
the most that is possible or allowed: *There is a **limit** to the amount of pain we can bear.* ◇ *What is the speed **limit*** (= how fast are you allowed to go)*?*

limit[2] (say **lim**-it) *verb* (**limiting, limited**)
to do or have no more than a certain amount or number: *There are only 100 seats, so we must **limit** the number of tickets we sell.*

limousine (say lim-uh-**zeen**) *noun* (*plural* **limousines**) (also *informal* **limo**)
a large, expensive and comfortable car that is usually driven by a chauffeur (= a person whose job is to drive a car for somebody else)

limp[1] (say **limp**) *adjective*
not firm or strong: *Her whole body went **limp** and she fell to the ground.*

limp[2] (say **limp**) *verb* (**limping, limped**)
to walk with difficulty because you have hurt your foot or leg
▸ **limp** (*noun*): *He walks with a **limp**.*

line[1] (say **line**) *noun* (*plural* **lines**)
1 a long thin mark like this ____: *Draw a straight **line**.* ◇ *The ball went over the **line**.*
2 people or things beside each other or one after the other: *There was a long **line** of people in the bank.* ➲ SYNONYM **queue**[1]
3 all the words that are beside each other on a page: *the first **line** of a poem* ◇ *How many **lines** are there on this page?*
4 a long piece of string or rope: *Hang the washing on the **line**.*
5 a very long wire for telephones or electricity: *I tried to phone her but the **line** was busy.*
6 a section of railway track that a train moves along: *The accident was caused by a cow on the **line**.*

line[2] *verb* (**lining, lined**)
1 to cover the inside of something with a different material: *The boots are **lined** with fur.*
2 to stand or be in lines along something: *People **lined** the streets to watch the race.*
line up to stand in a **line** or make a line: *We **lined** up to buy tickets.*

linear (say **lin**-i-uh) *adjective*
of, in or relating to a line or length: ***linear** measurement* ◇ *a **linear** equation* ◇ ***linear** development* ◇ *She thinks in a very **linear** way.*

linen (say **lin**-uhn) *noun* (*no plural*)
1 a kind of strong cloth: *a white **linen** jacket*
2 sheets and other things made of cloth that you use in the home: *bed **linen***

liner (say **line**-uh) *noun* (*plural* **liners**)
1 a big ship that carries people a long way
2 a bag that you put inside something to keep it clean: *a dustbin **liner***

linesman (say **line**-z-muhn) *noun* (*plural* **linesmen**)
a sports official who watches if the ball has gone over the line in some games that are played on a field or court

linger (say **ling**-guh) *verb* (**lingering, lingered**)
to stay somewhere for a long time: *The smell of her perfume **lingered** in the room.*

lingerie (say **laan**-juh-ree) *noun* (*no plural*)
women's underwear and clothes they wear in bed

linguist (say **ling**-gwist) *noun* (*plural* **linguists**)
1 a person who knows several foreign languages well
2 a person who studies languages or who is an expert on the structures, development and use of language in general

lining (say **line**-ing) *noun* (*plural* **linings**)
material that covers the inside of something: *My coat has a thick **lining** so it's very warm.*

link[1] (say **lingk**) *noun* (*plural* **links**)
1 something that joins things or people together: *There's a **link** between smoking and heart disease.*
2 (*computing*) a place where one electronic document on the Internet is connected to another one: *To visit our other website, click on this **link**.*
3 one of the round parts in a chain ➲ See illustration at **chain**[1]

link² (say **lingk**) *verb* (**linking, linked**)
to join one person or thing to another: *The computers are* ***linked*** *together in a network.*

linocut (say **line**-oh-kut) *noun* (*plural* **linocuts**)
a picture made by cutting a pattern of lines and shapes into the surface of a piece of **linoleum**, covering it with paint and pressing it onto paper or cloth

linoleum (say line-**oh**-li-uhm) *noun* (*no plural*) (also *informal* **lino**)
a hard, shiny material used for covering floors

lintel (say **lin**-tuhl) *noun* (*plural* **lintels**)
a horizontal piece of wood or stone that supports the wall above a door or window

lion (say **ly**-uhn) *noun* (*plural* **lions**)
a large animal of the cat family that lives in parts of Africa and Asia. **Lions** have yellow fur, and the males have a lot of hair around their head and neck (called a **mane**).

WORD BUILDING A female lion is called a **lioness** and a young lion is called a **cub**.

lip *noun* (*plural* **lips**)
one of the two soft edges above and below your mouth: *to kiss somebody on the* ***lips*** ➲ See illustration at **face¹**

lip-read (say **lip**-reed) *verb* (**lip-reading, lip-read**)
to understand what somebody is saying by watching the movements of their lips
► **lip-reading** (*noun*)

lipstick (say **lip**-stik) *noun*
1 (*no plural*) a substance made into a small stick and used for colouring the lips: *She put on some* ***lipstick.***
2 (*plural* **lipsticks**) a small stick of a substance used for colouring the lips: *I found my* ***lipstick*** *in my bag.*

liquefy (say **lik**-wi-fy) *verb* (**liquefying, liquefied**)
1 to become liquid: *Gases can* ***liquefy*** *when temperature decreases or pressure increases.*
2 to change a solid or a gas to a liquid, or to cause such a change

liquid (say **lik**-wid) *noun* (*plural* **liquids**)
anything that is not a solid or a gas. Water, oil and milk are **liquids**.
► **liquid** (*adjective*): ***liquid*** *soap*
ⓘ ORIGIN: 14th–15th century, from Latin *liquidus* meaning 'liquid'

liquidate (say **lik**-wi-dayt) *verb* (**liquidating, liquidated**)
1 (*business*) to close down a business and sell its property in order to pay its debts
2 to get rid of somebody or something, usually by killing or destroying them
► **liquidation** (*noun*): *If the company does not receive a big order soon, it will have to go into* ***liquidation.***

liquidity (say lik-**wid**-i-tee) *noun* (*no plural*) (*business*)
the state of owning things that are worth a lot of money and that can be exchanged for cash

liquidize (say **lik**-wi-dize) *verb* (**liquidizing, liquidized**) (also **liquidise**)
to make something solid become liquid: *Chop and* ***liquidize*** *the tomatoes in a liquidizer* (= a machine that is used for making food into liquid).

liquor (say **lik**-uh) *noun* (*no plural*)
strong alcoholic drink: *a selection of wine, beer and* ***liquor*** ➲ SYNONYM **spirits** 2

liquorice (say **lik**-uh-rish) *noun* (*no plural*)
a black substance, made from the root of a plant, that has a strong flavour and is used in some sweets

lisp (say **lisp**) *noun* (*plural* **lisps**)
a speech difficulty in which 's' and 'z' are pronounced as 'th'
► **lisp** (*verb*): *Ntombi* ***lisps*** *a little.*

list¹ (say **list**) *noun* (*plural* **lists**)
a lot of names or other things that you write or say, one after another: *a shopping* ***list*** (= of things that you must buy)

list² (say **list**) *verb* (**listing, listed**)
to write or say things in a list: *Please* ***list*** *the items in alphabetical order.*

listen (say **liss**-uhn) *verb* (**listening, listened**)
1 to pay attention to something or somebody in order to hear it or them: *I was* ***listening*** *to the radio.* ◇ ***Listen!*** *I want to tell you something.*
2 take notice of or believe what somebody says: *You should* ***listen*** *to what the doctor says.*

listless (say **list**-luhss) *adjective*
very tired, not interested and not prepared to make an effort
► **listlessly** (*adverb*) ► **listlessness** (*noun*): *The symptoms include fever and* ***listlessness.***

lit form of **light³**

litchi (say **lee**-chee) *noun* (*plural* **litchis**) (also **lychee**)
a small round fruit with a hard red-brown skin and juicy white flesh

literacy (say **lit**-uh-ruh-see) *noun* (*no plural*)
1 the ability to read and write: *basic* ***literacy*** *skills*

A B C D E F G H I J K M N O P Q R S T U V W X Y Z

2 a good understanding of a particular subject: *computer **literacy*** ➲ The adjective is **literate**

literal (say **lit**-uh-ruhl) *adjective*
1 The **literal** sense of a word or phrase is its usual or basic meaning. ➲ See **figurative**
2 following the words of an original text exactly: *The **literal** translation of the proverb is 'to lead somebody by the nose', but in English we would say 'to pull someone's leg'.*
▸ **literally** (*adverb*)

literary (say **lit**-uh-ruh-ree) *adjective*
relating to the writing or study of literature: *a **literary** masterpiece*

literate (say **lit**-uh-ruht) *adjective*
1 able to read and write
2 experienced in a particular field or having a good understanding of a particular subject: *computer-**literate*** ➲ OPPOSITE **illiterate**

literature (say **lit**-ri-tshuh) *noun* (*no plural*)
books, plays and poetry that people consider works of art: *He is studying English **literature**.*

litigation (say lit-i-**gay**-shuhn) *noun* (*no plural*)
the process of taking legal action or fighting a case in a court of law

litmus (say **lit**-muhss) *noun* (*no plural*)
a substance that turns red when it touches an acid and blue when it touches an **alkali** or base: *a **litmus** test*
litmus paper (*noun*) paper covered in litmus: *I used **litmus** paper to check whether my soil was acidic or alkaline.*

litre (say **lee**-tuh) *noun* (*plural* **litres**) (abbr. l or L)
the basic unit for measuring the volume of liquids: *three **litres** of water* ◇ *20 l*
➲ See **millilitre**, **centilitre**, **kilolitre**

SPELLING **Litre** is the correct British and South African spelling. **Liter** is used in American spelling.

litter¹ (say **lit**-uh) *noun*
1 (*no plural*) pieces of paper and other rubbish that people leave in a public place: *The park was full of **litter** after the concert.*
2 (*plural* **litters**) all the baby animals that are born to the same mother at the same time: *Our dog had a **litter** of six puppies.*

litter² (say **lit**-uh) *verb* (**littering**, **littered**)
to be or to make something untidy with **litter**: *My desk was **littered** with papers.*

little¹ (say **lit**-l) *adjective*
1 not big: *a **little** table* ➲ SYNONYM **small**
2 young: *a **little** girl* ◇ *my **little*** (= younger) *brother*
3 (used about distance or time) short: *Do you mind waiting a **little** while?*

WORD BUILDING See the Word Building note at **small**.

little² (say **lit**-l) *pronoun, adjective*
not much: *I did very **little** today.* ◇ *We have very **little** money.*
a little a small amount of something: *I've got some ice cream. Would you like a **little**?* ◇ *I speak a **little** Afrikaans.*
little by little slowly: ***Little** by **little** she started to feel better.*

little³ (say **lit**-l) *adverb*
not much: *I'm tired – I slept very **little** last night.*
➲ See **bit**
a little rather or to a small degree: *This skirt is a **little** too short for me.*

live¹ (say **liv**) *verb* (**living**, **lived**)
1 to have your home somewhere: *Where do you **live**?* ◇ *She still **lives** with her parents.*
2 to be or stay alive: *You can't **live** without water.* ◇ *He **lived** to the age of 93.*
3 to spend your life in a certain way: *They **live** a busy life in the city.*
live on something
1 to eat something as your only food: *Cows **live** on grass.*
2 to have enough money to buy what you need to live: *They **live** on R400 a week.*

live² (say **live**) *adjective*
1 not dead: *Have you ever touched a real **live** snake?*
2 If a radio or television programme is **live**, you see or hear it at the same time as it happens: *The match is going out **live** on TV.*
3 with electricity passing through it: *Don't touch that wire – it's **live**!*

lively (say **live**-lee) *adjective* (**livelier**, **liveliest**)
full of life, or always moving or doing things: *The children are very **lively**.*

liver (say **liv**-uh) *noun*
1 (*plural* **livers**) the **organ** inside your body that cleans the blood ➲ See illustration at **organ**
2 (*no plural*) the **liver** of an animal that you can cook and eat as food

lives (say **live**-z) plural of **life**

livestock (say **live**-stok) *noun* (*no plural*)
animals such as cows, goats and sheep that are kept on a farm

livid (say **liv**-id) *adjective*
1 extremely angry: *She was **livid** when she found out what had happened.*

2 with a dark purple, blue or red colour: *The skin around the scar was **livid**.*

living¹ (say **liv**-ing) *adjective*
not dead: *Some people say he is the greatest **living** writer.*

living² (say **liv**-ing) *noun* (*no plural*)
1 money to buy the things you need in life: *How did he earn a **living**?*
2 the way that you live: *The cost of **living** has risen in recent years.*

living room *noun* (*plural* **living rooms**) (also **sitting room**)
a room in a house where people sit together and talk, watch television, etc. ➲ SYNONYM **lounge¹**

lizard (say **liz**-uhd) *noun* (*plural* **lizards**)
a small reptile that has four short legs, a long tail and rough skin

lizard

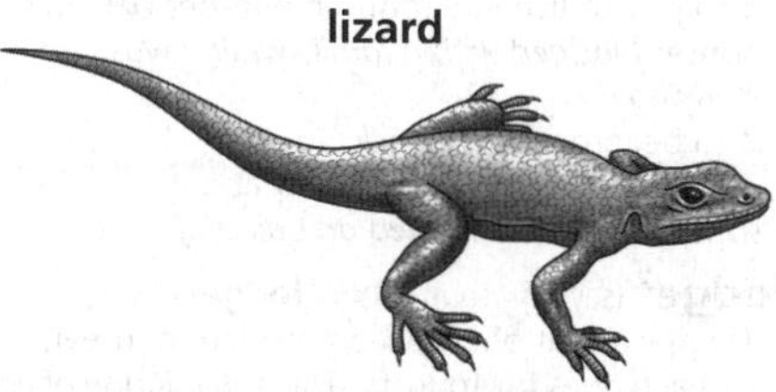

llama (say **laa**-muh) *noun* (*plural* **llamas**)
a South American animal that is kept for its soft wool or to carry loads

load¹ (*rhymes with* **road**) *noun*
1 (*plural* **loads**) something that is carried: *The truck brought another **load** of wood.*
2 loads (*plural noun*) (*informal*) a lot: *We've got **loads** of time.*

load² (say **lohd**) *verb* (**loading, loaded**)
1 to put a lot of things into or onto something or someone: *They're **loading** the plane now.* ◇ *Two men **loaded** the furniture into the van.* ➲ OPPOSITE **unload**
2 to put bullets in a gun or film in a camera
3 (*computing*) to put data or a program into the memory of a computer, or to put a disk into a computer

loaf¹ (say **lohf**) *noun* (*plural* **loaves**)
bread that has been baked in one piece: *a **loaf** of bread*
❶ ORIGIN: from Old English *hlaf*

loaf² (say **lohf**) *verb* (**loafing, loafed**) (*informal*)
to pass time doing nothing and being lazy: *They spent the day **loafing** in the sun.*

loam (*rhymes with* **home**) *noun* (*no plural*)
a kind of good quality soil consisting of clay, sand and dead plant material
► **loamy** (*adjective*): *Vegetables grow best in fertile **loamy** soils.*

loan¹ (say **lohn**) *noun* (*plural* **loans**)
money that somebody or a bank, company, etc. lends you: *to take out a bank **loan***

loan² (say **lohn**) *verb* (**loaning, loaned**)
to give something to somebody for a period of time: *A friend **loaned** me R1 000.* ➲ SYNONYM **lend**

loathe (say **loh*th***) *verb* (**loathing, loathed**)
to hate somebody or something: *I **loathe** modern art.*

loaves (say **lohvz**) plural of **loaf¹**

lob *verb* (**lobbing, lobbed**)
to throw, kick or hit a ball high into the air, so that it lands behind your opponent
► **lob** (*noun*): *The tennis player won the point when he sent a **lob** to the back of the court.*

lobby¹ (say **lob**-ee) *noun* (*plural* **lobbies**)
1 an area just inside a big building, where people can meet and wait: *a hotel **lobby***
2 a group of people who try to influence the government to do something: *an anti-smoking **lobby***

lobby² (say **lob**-ee) *verb* (**lobbying, lobbied**)
to try to influence a politician or member of the government on a particular issue

lobe (say **lohb**) *noun* (*plural* **lobes**)
1 a round, fairly flat part of an organ in your body (such as in the ear, brain, lungs and heart): *My ear **lobes** were sore after I had them pierced.*
2 a round part of a leaf that sticks out

lobola (say law-**baw**-luh) *noun* (*no plural*) (*S. African*)
money or cattle that a man or his family gives to the parents of the woman he marries ➲ See **dowry**
❶ ORIGIN: 19th century, from isiXhosa and isiZulu *lobola*

lobster (say **lob**-stuh) *noun* (*plural* **lobsters**)
a medium-sized sea animal with a hard shell, a long body divided into sections, eight legs and two large **claws**. **Lobsters** are sometimes called **crayfish**.

local (say **loh**-kuhl) *adjective*
of a place near you: *Her children go to the **local** school.* ◇ *a **local** newspaper* ◇ ***local** government*
► **locally** (*adverb*)

locality (say loh-**kal**-i-tee) *noun* (*plural* **localities**) (*formal*)
a particular place or area: *The exact **locality** of the treasure was kept secret.*

locate (say loh-**kayt**) *verb* (**locating, located**)
1 to find the exact place or position of somebody or something: *The dogs are trained to **locate** earthquake victims.*
2 to put or build something in a particular place: *The company decided to **locate** the supermarket near the station.*

located (say loh-**kayt**-d) *adjective*
in a place: *The factory is **located** near Musina.*

location (say loh-**kay**-shuhn) *noun* (*plural* **locations**)
1 a place: *The house is in a quiet **location** on top of a hill.*
2 (*S. African*) a part of a town or city that was set aside for black people to live in during the time of apartheid ➲ SYNONYM **township**

loch (say lo*kh*) *noun* (*plural* **lochs**)
a Scottish word for a lake: *the **Loch** Ness Monster*

PRONUNCIATION Pronounce the **ch** in **loch** like the **g** in the Afrikaans word **lag**.

lock¹ (say **lok**) *verb* (**locking, locked**)
to close something in such a way that it can only be opened with a key or code: *Don't forget to **lock** the door when you leave.* ➲ OPPOSITE **unlock** 1
lock something away to put something in a place that can only be opened with a key or code: *The paintings are **locked** away at night.*
lock somebody in to **lock** a door so that somebody cannot get out: *The prisoners are **locked** in.*
lock somebody out to **lock** a door so that somebody cannot get in
lock up to **lock** all the doors and windows of a building: *Make sure you **lock** up before you leave.*

lock² (say **lok**) *noun* (*plural* **locks**)
a metal thing that keeps a door, gate or box closed so that you need a key or a code to open it again: *I heard the key turn in the **lock**.*

locker (say **lok**-uh) *noun* (*plural* **lockers**)
a small cupboard with a lock for keeping things in, for example in a school or at a sports centre

locket (say **lok**-uht) *noun* (*plural* **lockets**)
a piece of jewellery in the form of a small metal case with a photograph or a piece of hair inside, that you wear on a chain round your neck

locomotion (say loh-kuh-**moh**-shuhn) *noun* (*no plural*) (*formal*)
movement or the ability to move from one place to another: *Fish use their fins for **locomotion**.*

locomotive¹ (say loh-kuh-**moh**-tiv) *noun* (*plural* **locomotives**)
a railway engine that pulls or pushes a train ➲ SYNONYM **engine** 2

locomotive² (say loh-kuh-**moh**-tiv) *adjective* (*formal*)
relating to movement or the ability to move from one place to another

locust (say **loh**-kuhst) *noun* (*plural* **locusts**)
a large insect that lives in hot countries and flies in very large groups, eating all the plants. A **locust** is a type of large **grasshopper**.

lodestone (say **lohd**-stohn) *noun* (*plural* **lodestones**)
a type of rock that contains minerals which make it **magnetic** (= having the ability to attract metal objects)

lodge¹ (say **loj**) *verb* (**lodging, lodged**)
1 to pay to live in a room in another person's house: *I **lodged** with a family when I was studying.*
2 to become firmly stuck
3 to make a formal complaint about something: *They **lodged** an objection.*

lodge² (say **loj**) *noun* (*plural* **lodges**)
1 a place that offers accommodation, meals and activities for tourists: *The game **lodge** offers guests a unique bushveld experience.*
2 a small house in the country where people live for a short time: *There is a small **lodge** at the top of the mountain where walkers can sleep.*

loft *noun* (*plural* **lofts**)
the room or space under the roof of a house, often used for storing things and sometimes used as a room: *My old books are in a box in the loft.* ➲ See **attic**

log¹ *noun* (*plural* **logs**)
1 a thick round piece of wood from a tree: *Put another **log** on the fire.*
2 (also **logbook**) the official written record of a ship's or an aircraft's journey: *to keep a **log***

log² *verb* (**logging, logged**)
to keep an official record of things that happen: *to **log** somebody's phone calls* ➲ SYNONYM **record²** 1
log in, log on to type your name or words so that you can start using a computer or program: *You need a password to **log** on.*
log off, log out to stop using a computer or program: *Please **log** out before you switch off the computer.*

logarithm (say **log**-uh-ri*th*-uhm) *noun* (*plural* **logarithms**) (*maths*) (abbr. log)
the **exponent** to which a given base must be raised in order to produce a number. It allows

you to solve problems in mathematics by adding or subtracting numbers instead of multiplying and dividing.: *The **logarithm** of 10 000 with a base of 10 is 4 (10 x 10 x 10 x 10).* ◇ *The **logarithm** of 64 with a base of 2 is 6 (2 x 2 x 2 x 2 x 2 x 2).*

loggerheads (say **log**-uh-hedz) *noun*
at loggerheads You are at **loggerheads** with somebody if you argue or strongly disagree with them.

logic (say **loj**-ik) *noun* (*no plural*)
1 a sensible reason or way of thinking: *There is no **logic** in what you are saying.*
2 a formal system using reason: ***Logic** involves statements and arguments.* ◇ *mathematical **logic***

logical (say **loj**-ik-uhl) *adjective*
seeming natural or sensible: *There is only one **logical** conclusion.* ➲ OPPOSITE **illogical**

logo (say **loh**-goh) *noun* (*plural* **logos**)
a picture or a design that a company or an organization uses as its special sign: *You will find the company **logo** on all our products.*

loiter (say **loy**-tuh) *verb* (**loitering, loitered**)
to stand or walk around somewhere without any obvious purpose

lollipop (say **lol**-i-pop) *noun* (*plural* **lollipops**) (also *informal* **lolly**)
a big sweet on a stick

lone (*rhymes with* **bone**) *adjective*
1 without other people: *a **lone** rider* ➲ SYNONYM **solitary**
2 only: *For many years she was the **lone** representative of the opposition party in parliament.*

lonely (say **lohn**-lee) *adjective* (**lonelier, loneliest**)
1 unhappy because you are not with other people: *She felt very **lonely** when she first went to live in the city.*
2 far from other places: *a **lonely** house in the hills* ➲ See **alone**
▸ **loneliness** (*noun*)

long[1] *adjective* (**longer, longest**)
1 far from one end to the other: *the **longest** river* ◇ *She has **long** hair.* ◇ *Cape Town is a **long** way from London.* ➲ OPPOSITE **short** 1 ➲ See note at **far**[1]
2 You use **long** to ask or talk about how far something is from one end to the other: *How **long** is the table?* ◇ *The wall is 5 m **long**.* ➲ The noun is **length**
3 continuing for a lot of time: *a **long** film* ◇ *He's lived here for a **long** time.* ➲ OPPOSITE **short** 3
4 You use **long** to ask or talk about the time from the beginning to the end of something: *How **long** is the lesson?*

long[2] *adverb* (**longer, longest**)
for a lot of time: *I can't stay **long**.* ◇ *How **long** have you been waiting?* ◇ *My grandfather died **long** before I was born.* ◇ *She went out, but not for **long**.* ◇ *You'll have to wait **longer**.*
as long as, so long as only if: *You can borrow the book as **long** as you return it.*
long ago many years in the past: ***Long** ago there were no cars.*
no longer, not any longer not now, or not as before: *She doesn't live here any **longer**.*

long[3] *verb* (**longing, longed**) (*formal*)
to want something very much, especially if this does not seem likely: *I **long** to see my family again.* ◇ *She's **longing** for a letter from her boyfriend.*

long-distance (say long-**diss**-tuhnss) *adjective*
travelling or communicating between places that are far from each other: *a **long-distance** phone call*

longevity (say lon-**jev**-uh-tee) *noun* (*no plural*) (*formal*)
long life or the state of lasting a long time: *You can improve the **longevity** of flowers by cutting their stems underwater.*

long-haul (say **long**-hawl) *adjective*
travelling between places that are a long way from each other: *a **long-haul** trip*

longing (say **long**-ing) *noun* (*no plural*) (*formal*)
a strong feeling of wanting something: *a **longing** for peace* ➲ SYNONYM **desire**[1]

longitude (say **long**-gi-tyood) *noun* (*no plural*) (abbr. long.)
the position of a place east or west of the Greenwich Meridian (a line from the North Pole to the South Pole that passes through Greenwich in London). **Longitude** is measured in degrees. ➲ See illustration at **globe** ➲ See **latitude**

long jump *noun* (*no plural*)
a sport where you try to jump as far as you can

long-winded (say long-**win**-did) *adjective*
A piece of writing or a speech that is **long-winded** is boring because it is too long. ➲ OPPOSITE **concise**

loo *noun* (*plural* **loos**) (*informal*)
toilet: *I need to go to the **loo**.* ➲ See note at **toilet**
ⓘ **ORIGIN:** 20th century. The origin of this word is not known, although there have been many theories. One was that the name came from

Waterloo, the trade name of a toilet cistern at the beginning of the century.

look¹ (say **luuk**) *noun* (*plural* **looks**)
1 turning your eyes towards somebody or something: *Have a **look** at this article.* ◇ *Do you want to take a **look** around?*
2 trying to find somebody or something: *I've had a **look** for your pen, but I can't find it.*
3 the way somebody or something seems: *I don't like the **look** of the sky. It's going to rain.*
4 looks (*plural noun*) a person's appearance: *He has his father's good **looks**.*

look² (say **luuk**) *verb* (**looking, looked**)
1 to turn your eyes towards somebody or something and try to see them: ***Look** at this picture.* ◇ ***Look** both ways before you cross the road.* ◇ *I'm **looking** for my keys.* ➲ See note at **see**
2 to seem to be: *You **look** tired.* ◇ *It **looks** as if it's going to rain.*
look after somebody or something to take care of somebody or something: *Can you **look** after my cat when I'm on holiday?*
look forward to something to wait for something with pleasure: *I'm **looking** forward to seeing you tomorrow.*
look like somebody or something
1 to seem to be something: *That **looks** like a good film.*
2 words that you use to ask about somebody's appearance: *'What does he **look** like?'*
3 to have the same appearance as somebody or something: *She **looks** like her mother.*
look something up to try to find information in a book: *I **looked** the word up in my dictionary.*

loom¹ (say **loom**) *noun* (*plural* **looms**)
a machine that is used for making cloth by passing pieces of thread across and under other pieces (called **weaving**)

loom² (say **loom**) *verb* (**looming, loomed**)
1 to appear as a shape that is not clear and that may be frightening: *The buildings **loomed** up out of the fog.*
2 to be about to happen or arrive, often in a way that seems frightening: *The exams are **looming**.*

loony (say **loo**-nee) *adjective* (**loonier, looniest**) (*informal*)
silly or crazy: *a **loony** idea*
▸ **loony** (*noun*): *He's a bit of a **loony**.*

loop *noun* (*plural* **loops**)
a round shape made by something like string or rope

loose (say **looss**) *adjective* (**looser, loosest**)
1 not tied or fixed: *The horse managed to get **loose** and escape.* ◇ *One of his teeth is **loose**.*
2 not fitting closely: *a **loose** white shirt*
➲ OPPOSITE **tight** 1
▸ **loosely** (*adverb*): *The rope was tied **loosely** round a tree.*

SPELLING Be careful! Don't confuse **loose** with **lose**, which is a verb. They sound different and they have different meanings.

loosen (say **loo**-suhn) *verb* (**loosening, loosened**)
to become looser or to make something looser: *Can you **loosen** this knot? It's too tight.*
➲ OPPOSITE **tighten**

loot *noun* (*no plural*)
1 money or valuable objects taken from an enemy in war
2 money or goods that have been stolen by thieves or obtained illegally
▸ **loot** (*verb*)

lope (*rhymes with* **hope**) *verb* (**loping, loped**)
to run in a relaxed and easy way with long steps: *The giraffe **loped** across the road.*

lopsided (say lop-**side**-id) *adjective*
not balanced, or with one side lower or smaller than the other: *a **lopsided** smile*

lord (say **lawd**) *noun*
1 (*plural* **lords**) (*history*) in the **Middle Ages**, a powerful man who owned a lot of land
2 (*plural* **lords**) (also **Lord**) (in Britain) a man who has a high position in society, and the title that you use when you speak to him: *princes, **lords**, and other aristocrats* ◇ *Good morning, **Lord** Fraser.* ➲ See **lady**
3 the Lord (*no plural*) God or Jesus Christ
ⓘ ORIGIN: from Old English *hlaford*, from *hlafweard* meaning 'bread-keeper' or 'the person who guards the bread'. The lord was the master of the household and responsible for making sure there was food.

lorry (say **lo**-ree) *noun* (*plural* **lorries**)
a big vehicle for carrying heavy things
➲ SYNONYM **truck**

lose (say **looz**) *verb* (**losing, lost**)
1 to not be able to find something: *I can't open the door because I've **lost** my key.*
2 to not have somebody or something that you had before: *I **lost** my job at the factory.*
3 to not win: *Our team **lost** the match.*

loser (say **looz**-uh) *noun* (*plural* **losers**)
a person who does not win a game, race or competition ➲ OPPOSITE **winner**

loss *noun* (*plural* **losses**)
1 losing something: *Has she told the police*

about the ***loss*** *of her car?* ◇ *job* ***losses***
2 how much money a business loses: *The company made a* ***loss*** *of R5 million.* ➲ OPPOSITE **profit**[1]
at a loss If you are **at a loss**, you do not know what to do or say.

lost[1] form of **lose**

lost[2] *adjective*
1 If you are **lost**, you do not know where you are: *I took the wrong road and now I'm* ***lost.*** ◇ *Take this map so you don't get* ***lost!***
2 If something is **lost**, you cannot find it.

lost property *noun* (*no plural*)
things that people have lost or left in a public place: *I left my bag on the train, so I went to the* ***lost property*** *office at the station.*

lot[1] *pronoun*
a lot (also *informal* **lots**) very much, or a large amount or number of things or people: *We ate a* ***lot.***
a lot of, **lots of** a large number or amount of things or people: *She's got a* ***lot*** *of friends.* ◇ ***Lots*** *of love from Jan* (= words at the end of a letter).

> SPELLING Be careful! Remember that **a lot** is two words: *I used* ***a lot*** *of paper.* Don't write 'alot'. There is no such word!

lot[2] *adverb*
a lot very much or often: *Your flat is a* ***lot*** *bigger than mine.* ◇ *I go to the library a* ***lot.***

lotion (say **loh**-shuhn) *noun* (*plural* **lotions**)
liquid that you put on your skin: *suntan* ***lotion***

lottery (say **lot**-uh-ree) *noun* (*plural* **lotteries**)
a game in which you buy a ticket with numbers on it. You win money if your numbers are chosen.

lotto (say **lot**-oh) *noun* (*no plural*)
1 a **lottery**
2 a children's game in which each player has a card with numbers on it, which they must match with numbers that they take out of a container

lotus (say **loh**-tuss) *noun* (*plural* **lotuses**)
a water plant with a large flower

loud (say **lowd**) *adjective, adverb* (**louder, loudest**)
making a lot of noise: ***loud*** *voices* ◇ *Please turn down the music. It's too* ***loud.*** ◇ *Please speak a bit* ***louder*** *– I can't hear you.* ➲ OPPOSITE **quiet**[1] 1
out loud so that other people can hear it: *I read the story out* ***loud.***
▸ **loudly** (*adverb*): *She laughed* ***loudly.***

loudspeaker (say **lowd**-speek-uh) *noun* (*plural* **loudspeakers**)
a piece of equipment that makes sounds or voices louder: *Music was coming from the* ***loudspeakers.***

lounge[1] (say **lownj**) *noun* (*plural* **lounges**)
a room in a house where people sit together and talk, watch television, etc. ➲ SYNONYMS **living room, sitting room**

lounge[2] (say **lownj**) *verb* (**lounging, lounged**)
to sit, stand or lie in a relaxed or lazy way: *We* ***lounged*** *around on the beach all day.*

louse (say **lowss**) *noun* (*plural* **lice**)
a small insect that lives on the bodies and in the hair of people and animals

lousy (say **lowz**-ee) *adjective* (**lousier, lousiest**) (*informal*)
very bad: *The weather was* ***lousy.*** ➲ SYNONYM **awful**

lovable (say **luv**-uhb-l) *adjective*
easy to love: *a* ***lovable*** *little boy*

love[1] (say **luv**) *noun*
1 (*no plural*) the strong warm feeling you have when you like somebody or something very much: *Their* ***love*** *for each other was very strong.*
2 (*plural* **loves**) a person, a thing or an activity that you love: *Who was your first* ***love?***
3 (*no plural*) a word in the game of tennis that means zero: *The score is 15-****love.***
be in love with somebody to love somebody very much, usually a person who you are sexually attracted to: *He says he is in* ***love*** *with her.*
fall in love with somebody to begin to love somebody very strongly, usually a person who you are sexually attracted to: *She fell in* ***love*** *with him the first time they met.*
love, love from (*informal*) a way of ending a letter to somebody that you know well: *See you soon.* ***Love,*** *Dan.*

> WORD BUILDING See the Word Building note at **like**1.

love[2] (say **luv**) *verb* (**loving, loved**)
1 to have a very strong warm feeling for somebody: *I* ***love*** *him very much.* ◇ *She* ***loves*** *her parents.*
2 to like something very much: *I* ***love*** *reading.* ◇ *I would* ***love*** *to go to America.* ➲ OPPOSITE **hate**[1]

love affair *noun* (*plural* **love affairs**)
a romantic or sexual relationship between two people who love each other but who are not married

A B C D E F G H I J K **L** M N O P Q R S T U V W X Y Z

lovely (say **luv**-lee) *adjective* (**lovelier**, **loveliest**)
beautiful or very nice: *That's a **lovely** dress.* ◇ *It's **lovely** to see you again.*

lover (say **luv**-uh) *noun* (*plural* **lovers**)
1 If two people are **lovers**, they have a sexual relationship but they are not married.
2 a person who likes something very much: *a music **lover***

loving (say **luv**-ing) *adjective*
feeling or showing love: ***loving** parents*

low (*rhymes with* **go**) *adjective* (**lower**, **lowest**)
1 near the ground: *a **low** bridge* ◇ *There was a **low** wall round the garden.* ➲ OPPOSITE **high**[1] 1
2 less than usual: ***low** temperatures* ◇ ***low** pay* ➲ OPPOSITE **high**[1] 4
3 deep or quiet: *a **low** sound* ◇ *I heard **low** voices in the next room.*
▸ **low** (*adverb*): *The plane flew **low** over the trees.*

lower[1] (say **loh**-uh) *adjective*
that is under something or at the bottom of something: *She bit her **lower** lip.* ➲ OPPOSITE **upper**

lower[2] (say **loh**-uh) *verb* (**lowering**, **lowered**)
1 to move somebody or something down: *They **lowered** the boat into the water.*
2 to make something less: *Please **lower** your voice* (= speak more quietly). ➲ OPPOSITE **raise** 1

lower case *noun* (*no plural*)
the small form of letters, for example a, b, c (not A, B, C): *john@cell.com is all in **lower case**.* ➲ OPPOSITE **upper case**

lowveld (say **loh**-felt) *noun* (*no plural*)
the lowveld the subtropical low-lying area in the north and north-east of South Africa
ⓘ ORIGIN: 19th century, from Afrikaans *laeveld* from *lae* meaning 'low' and *veld* meaning 'open countryside'

loyal (say **loy**-uhl) *adjective*
not changing your friends or beliefs easily: *a **loyal** friend* ◇ *He is **loyal** to his classmates.* ➲ OPPOSITE **disloyal**
▸ **loyalty** (*noun*): ***loyalty** between friends*

Ltd (say **lim**-it-id) *abbreviation*
(used after the name of a company or business) **Limited**: *Pierce and Co. **Ltd***

lubricate (say **loo**-bri-kayt) *verb* (**lubricating**, **lubricated**)
to put a substance such as oil onto or into something to make it work smoothly

lucerne (say luu-**surn**) *noun* (*no plural*)
a plant with small green leaves that is grown as food for farm animals ➲ SYNONYM **alfalfa**

lucid (say **loo**-sid) *adjective* (*formal*)
1 clear and easy to understand: *She gave a **lucid** explanation of the concept.*
2 able to think clearly, especially after a period of mental confusion or illness: *The patient became **lucid** and could speak again.*
▸ **lucidity** (*noun*): *mental **lucidity*** ▸ **lucidly** (*adverb*): *a **lucidly** written guide*

luck (say **luk**) *noun* (*no plural*)
1 good things that happen to you that you cannot control: *I wish you **luck** in the job.* ◇ *I was in **luck** – the shop had the book I wanted.*
2 things that happen to you that you cannot control or have not planned: *to have good **luck***
bad luck, **hard luck** words that you say to somebody when you are sorry that they did not have good luck
good luck words that you say to somebody when you hope that they will do well: *Good **luck**! I'm sure you'll get the job.*

lucky (say **luk**-ee) *adjective* (**luckier**, **luckiest**)
1 having good luck: *She is **lucky** to be alive after the accident.*
2 bringing success or good luck: *My **lucky** number is 3.* ➲ OPPOSITE **unlucky**
▸ **luckily** (*adverb*): *I was late, but **luckily** they waited for me.*

lucrative (say **loo**-kruh-tiv) *adjective* (*formal*)
allowing somebody to earn a lot of money: *a **lucrative** business deal* ➲ SYNONYM **profitable**

ludicrous (say **loo**-di-kruhss) *adjective*
very silly or unreasonable: *What a **ludicrous** idea!*
▸ **ludicrously** (*adverb*): ***ludicrously** expensive clothes*

lug *verb* (**lugging**, **lugged**) (*informal*)
to carry or pull something that is heavy with great effort: *He **lugged** the suitcase up the stairs.*

luggage (say **lug**-ij) *noun* (*no plural*)
bags and suitcases that you take with you when you travel: *'How much **luggage** do you have?' 'Only one suitcase.'* ➲ SYNONYM **baggage**

lukewarm (say look-**wawm**) *adjective*
If a liquid is **lukewarm**, it is only slightly warm: *I had to have a **lukewarm** shower.*

lull[1] (say **lul**) *noun* (*plural* **lulls**)
a short period when there is no noise or less activity: *She waited for a **lull** in the traffic and then crossed the road.*

lull² (say **lul**) *verb* (**lulling, lulled**)
1 to make calm or relaxed: *We were **lulled** to sleep by the gentle sound of the waves.*
2 to cause somebody to feel safe so that an unpleasant situation takes them by surprise: *Our first success **lulled** us into a false sense of security.*

lullaby (say **lul**-uh-by) *noun* (*plural* **lullabies**)
a gentle song that you sing to help a child fall asleep

lumber¹ (say **lum**-buh) *noun* (*no plural*) = **timber**

lumber² (say **lum**-buh) *verb* (**lumbering, lumbered**)
1 to move in a slow, heavy way: *A group of elephants **lumbered** past.*
2 (*informal*) to be given a responsibility or task that you do not want: *He got **lumbered** with organizing the conference dinner.*

luminous (say **loom**-i-nuhss) *adjective*
shining brightly: *My watch has **luminous** hands, so I can see the time even when it is dark.*
► **luminosity** (*noun*)

lump *noun* (*plural* **lumps**)
1 a hard piece of something: *a **lump** of coal*
2 a part in or on your body which has become hard and bigger: *I've got a **lump** on my head where I hit it.*

lumpy (say **lump**-ee) *adjective* (**lumpier, lumpiest**)
full of or covered with lumps: *The sauce is rather **lumpy**.* ➲ OPPOSITE **smooth** 2

lunar (say **loon**-uh) *adjective*
of the moon: ***lunar** eclipse* ◇ ***lunar** landscape* ◇ ***lunar** calendar*

lunatic (say **loon**-uh-tik) *noun* (*plural* **lunatics**) (*informal*)
a person who does stupid and often dangerous things

lunch *noun* (*plural* **lunches**)
a meal that you eat in the middle of the day: *What would you like for **lunch**?* ◇ *When do you have **lunch**?*

lunchtime (say **lunch**-time) *noun* (*plural* **lunchtimes**)
the time when you eat lunch: *I'll meet you at **lunchtime**.*

lung *noun* (*plural* **lungs**)
one of the two organs inside your body that you use for breathing ➲ See illustration in the next column and at **organ**

human lungs

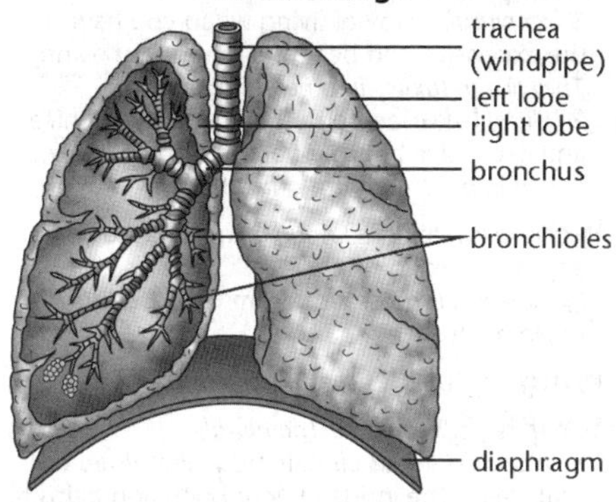

lurch (*rhymes with* **church**) *verb* (**lurching, lurched**)
1 to lean or move suddenly forward or to one side: *The car skidded and **lurched** forward.*
2 to walk as if you are going to fall
► **lurch** (*noun*)

lure (say **lyoor**) *verb* (**luring, lured**)
to persuade or trick somebody to go somewhere or do something, usually by offering them something nice: *He **lured** her to Johannesburg with the promise of a job.*

lurid (say **loor**-rid) *adjective*
1 having colours that are too bright, in a way that is not attractive: *a **lurid** purple outfit*
2 shocking or unpleasant, especially because of violent or disgusting detail: *a **lurid** news story*
► **luridly** (*adverb*)

lurk (*rhymes with* **work**) *verb* (**lurking, lurked**)
to wait somewhere secretly, especially because you are going to do something bad: *I saw somebody **lurking** among the trees.*

luscious (say **lush**-uhss) *adjective*
sweet, juicy and tasting very good: ***luscious** fruit*

lush (*rhymes with* **brush**) *adjective*
growing very thickly and well, or covered with grass or other plants that are healthy and growing well: *a **lush** green river valley*

lust (*rhymes with* **must**) *noun* (*no plural*)
1 strong sexual desire
2 a strong desire or feeling of enthusiasm for something: *a **lust** for power* ◇ *a **lust** for life*

lusty (say **luss**-tee) *adjective* (**lustier, lustiest**)
strong, healthy and full of energy: *a **lusty** yell*
► **lustily** (*adverb*): *They were cheering and singing **lustily**.*

luxurious (say luk-**shoor**-ri-uhss) *adjective*
very comfortable and expensive: *a **luxurious** hotel*

A B C D E F G H I J K L M N O P Q R S T U V W X Y Z

A B C D E F G H I J K L M N O P Q R S T U V W X Y Z

luxury (say **luk**-shuh-ree) *noun*
1 (*no plural*) a way of living when you have all the expensive and beautiful things you want: *They live in* ***luxury*** *in a beautiful house.*
2 (*plural* **luxuries**) something that is very nice and expensive but that you do not really need: *Eating in a restaurant is a* ***luxury****.*

lychee (say **lee**-chee) *noun* (*plural* **lychees**)
another word for **litchi**
ORIGIN: 16th century, from Chinese *lìzhī* meaning 'lychee'

lying (say **ly**-ing) form of **lie**[1]

lymph (say **limf**) *noun* (*no plural*)
a colourless liquid containing white blood cells that cleans the inside of your body and helps to prevent infections from spreading: ***lymph*** *node*
▸ **lymphatic** (*adjective*): ***lymphatic*** *system*

lynch (say **linch**) *verb* (**lynching, lynched**)
to join in with other people to attack and kill a person who is believed to be guilty of a crime
ORIGIN: 19th century, named after Captain William Lynch, who with his community, set up his own law court in the USA

lynx (say **linkss**) *noun* (*plural* **lynx** or **lynxes**)
a medium-sized type of wild cat with thick fur and very sharp sight, living in the northern parts of the world

lyre (say **ly**-uh) *noun* (*plural* **lyres**)
a small musical instrument that has strings stretching from a horizontal bar at the top of a U-shaped frame to the bottom of it

lyrics (say **li**-rikss) *plural noun*
the words of a song

Contents

Study pages

The history of English

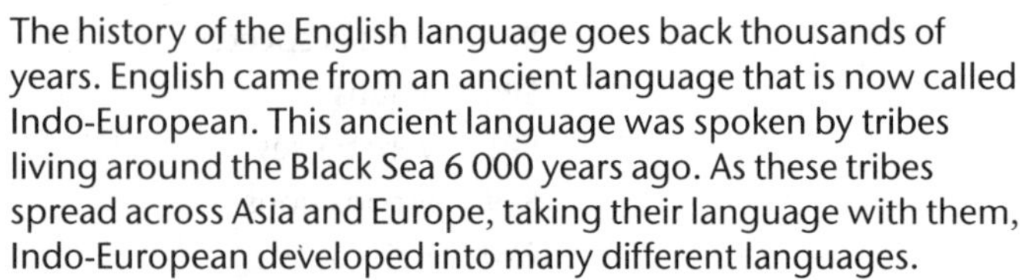

The history of the English language goes back thousands of years. English came from an ancient language that is now called Indo-European. This ancient language was spoken by tribes living around the Black Sea 6 000 years ago. As these tribes spread across Asia and Europe, taking their language with them, Indo-European developed into many different languages.

By the fifth century AD, some of the descendants of these tribes were living in northern Europe. The languages they spoke were the beginnings of German, Dutch and English.

Old English

In about AD 450, large groups of these northern European people invaded England. They pushed aside the local people (the Celts) and settled, living mainly as farmers and hunters. By AD 500, their language was the main language of England. It is known as Old English. It was very different from the English spoken today, but many of the words that are used now were in the language then. Examples are *apple, bread, brother, cheese, daughter, drought, flood, foot, milk, mother* and *swim.*

If you translate these words into Afrikaans, you will find that most are similar. This is because Afrikaans grew from Dutch, which came from the same languages that Old English came from.

The influence of Latin on Old English

In AD 597, the Pope sent a group of Roman missionaries to England to bring Christianity to more people. They spoke Latin, and they brought Latin words into English. Most of these words were related to Christianity, for example *angel* and *apostle.*

The influence of Old Norse on Old English

Viking warriors from Scandinavia invaded England in 787. Their invasions continued for over 200 years. Many of these people settled in England and made it their home. Many words from their language (which we now call Old Norse) were absorbed into English. The words *bull, die, egg, husband, knife, mistake, scare, skin* and *sky* are just some of the English words that came from Old Norse.

The influence of Old French on Old English

England was attacked yet again in 1066 when William of Normandy, a French duke, invaded the country with his

army and became king. In England, he and his court spoke an old-fashioned form of French (Old French). For over 200 years French was the language used in parliament, churches and law courts in England. Thousands of Old French words came into English. Many are related to government and law, for example *city*, *court*, *department*, *judge*, *liberty*, *mayor* and *parliament*. Others are related to religion, for example *choir* and *pray*. Many words for food, for example *beef*, *dinner*, *fruit*, *mutton*, *salad*, *sausage* and *spice* are from Old French, and so are many words related to fashion, such as *diamond*, *jacket*, *jewel* and *fashion* itself.

At the same time, English continued to be the language that most ordinary people spoke.

Middle English: English from 1200 to 1400

In the thirteenth century, English people once again started to feel proud of their culture and their language. They began to speak English again in parliament, the law courts and churches. But English was now very different from the Old English spoken before 1066; thousands of new words had been added to it, mainly from Old French, and English grammar had changed. Words from Arabic, Persian, Latin, and other languages also enriched English during this time.

Modern English: English from 1400 to the present

From the fourteenth to the sixteenth century, people in Europe and England took a passionate interest in the culture of the ancient Greeks and Romans and in new scientific discoveries. This period is called the Renaissance, which means rebirth. But English did not have the words to describe the new scientific knowledge of the time. So old Greek and Latin words were borrowed; examples are *eclipse*, *hemisphere*, *millipede* and *minimum*. And new words were made to name inventions, mainly from Greek and Latin words. If you look up *astronaut*, *photograph*, *television* and *thermometer* in the dictionary, for example, you can find out more about their origins.

As people from England and Europe travelled across the world, discovering new continents for the first time, and colonizing other places and trading, many new words came into English. And from South African languages, English now has words such as *bakkie*, *donga*, *gogga*, *impala*, *veld*, *vlei*, and many more.

English never stops changing and growing!

If you look up these words, you can learn when they came into the language, and where they came from:

avocado	*kangaroo*
bamboo	*kayak*
banana	*ketchup*
boomerang	*mango*
cannibal	*naartjie*
canoe	*potato*
chilli	*tattoo*
chocolate	*tea*
cocoa	*yacht*

Parts of speech

Parts of speech are the names of the different kinds of words in the English language.

Part of speech	Use	Examples
Nouns	name people, animals, places, ideas and things	▸ *This is the **kitchen**.*
Common nouns	name most of the things around us, like animals, plants and places	*giraffe, hill, leaf, pencil sharpener, tourists*
Proper nouns	name specific people, places, or things, which begin with capital letters	*Mthatha, Telkom, Vusi*
Collective nouns	name groups of people or things	▸ *a **flock** of birds* ▸ *a **crowd** of people*
Abstract nouns	describe things that you cannot see, hear, touch, smell or taste	▸ ***Honesty** is the best policy.* ▸ *They have a lot of **freedom**.*
Pronouns	replace or stand for nouns	▸ *Meet Jo. **She** is my sister.*
Personal pronouns	refer to people – there are subject, object, possessive and reflexive pronouns	*I, they, him, us, yours, hers, myself, themselves*
Relative pronouns	connect or relate one part of a sentence to another part	▸ *the girl **who** sits next to me* ▸ *a place **that** she knows*
Interrogative pronouns	help to ask questions	▸ ***Whose** bag is this?* ▸ ***Which** day of the week is it?*
Demonstrative pronouns	describe or point out a specific person or thing	▸ ***This** is my goat.* ▸ ***That** is my house.*
Indefinite pronouns	describe approximate quantities	▸ ***some** milk and a **few** oranges*
Verbs	describe actions	▸ *The cat **drinks** milk.*
Modal verbs	are used with other verbs to talk about something you *need* to do, *must* do or *may possibly do*	*must, shall, will, should, would, can, could, may, might*
Auxiliary verbs	help to make questions and tenses with other verbs	*be, have, do*
Adjectives	tell us more about nouns and pronouns	▸ *My cat is **black**.* ▸ *Thabo is **big** and **strong**.*
Adverbs	tell us more about verbs	▸ *The girls sang **loudly**.*
Articles	tell us if a noun is definite or indefinite; *the* tells us that a noun is definite, and *a* or *an* tell us it is indefinite	▸ ***The** girl owns **a** dog.* ▸ ***An** elephant escaped from **the** zoo.*
Prepositions	tell us how, when, or where something happens	▸ *I'll go **to** school **at** eight o'clock.*
Conjunctions	link or join parts of sentences	▸ *I want apples **and** plums.*
Exclamations	express surprise, joy or pain	▸ ***Ouch**! That's sore!*

Nouns

- Nouns name people, things and places.
- They can be singular or plural.
- Nouns can be **countable** or **uncountable** or both.
- Some nouns only have a plural form, for example: *cattle*, *clothes* and *trousers*.
- Sometimes you make **compound nouns** by using two nouns together, such as: *gum tree* and *pencil sharpener*.

Spelling the plurals of nouns

Your dictionary gives the plural form of each noun and tells you if there is no plural form. Here are some rules to help you spell plural nouns.

Rule for spelling plurals	Singular	Plural
For most nouns, add *-s*.	*spider* *table*	*spiders* *tables*
If a noun ends in *-ch*, *-sh*, *-ss* or *-x*, add *-es*.	*church* *wish* *mass* *box*	*church**es*** *wish**es*** *mass**es*** *box**es***
If a noun ends in a consonant and *-y*, change the *-y* to *-i* and add *-es*.	*baby* *family*	*bab**ies*** *famil**ies***
Some nouns that end in *o* take *-s* in the plural, some take *-es*, and a few can take either *-s* or *-es*. Look them up in your dictionary if you are not sure.	*photo* *potato* *volcano*	*photo**s*** *potato**es*** *volcano**es**/* *volcano**s***

Some plural forms are irregular. You have to learn these and check in your dictionary if you are not sure. Here are some irregular plurals.

Singular	Plural
child	*children*
foot	*feet*
larva	*larvae*
man	*men*

Singular	Plural
mouse	*mice*
nucleus	*nuclei*
vertebra	*vertebrae*
woman	*women*

Countable and uncountable nouns

Your dictionary will say *no plural* if a noun is uncountable.

Countable nouns	Uncountable nouns
■ can be singular or plural ■ can have *a* or *an* before them examples: *envelope, key, pen* ▶ *I put a **pen**, an **envelope** and three **keys** in the bag.*	■ can only be used in the singular ■ cannot have *a* or *an* before them examples: *information, woodwork, bread* ▶ *There is **information** on **woodwork** in the library.*

Verb tenses

Tenses are forms of verbs that show the time when actions happened: in the **present**, **past**, or **future**. The tenses can be **simple, progressive** (continuous) or **perfect**.

We use verb **participles** to form some tenses. The **present participle** ends in *-ing* and in most verbs the **past participle** ends in *-ed*. Some verbs have irregular forms.

Look at these entries from your dictionary.

present participle | simple past tense | past participle

eat (say **eet**) *verb* **(eating, ate, has eaten)**
1 to put food in your mouth and swallow it: *Have you* ***eaten*** *all the chocolate?* ◇ *Do you want something to* ***eat****?*
2 to have a meal: *What time shall we* ***eat****?* ◇ *We don't* ***eat*** *out (= eat in a restaurant) very often.*

present participle | simple past tense

decide (say di-**side**) *verb* **(deciding, decided)**
to choose something after thinking about the possibilities: *I* ***decided*** *to tell the truth about what happened.* ◇ *I can't* ***decide*** *which book to read.*

present participle | simple past tense

paint[2] (say **paynt**) *verb* **(painting, painted)**
1 to put **paint** on something to change the colour: *We* ***painted*** *the walls grey.*
2 to make a picture of somebody or something using **paints**: *Can I* ***paint*** *a picture of you?* ◇ *My sister* ***paints*** *well.*

The following table shows the main verb tenses in English.

	Simple	Progressive	Perfect
Present	*I work.* *You work.* *He/She/It works.* *We work.* *They work.*	*I* ***am*** *working.* *You* ***are*** *working.* *He/She/It* ***is*** *working.* *We* ***are*** *working.* *They* ***are*** *working.*	*I* ***have*** *worked.* *You* ***have*** *worked.* *He/She/It* ***has*** *worked.* *We* ***have*** *worked.* *They* ***have*** *worked.*
Past	*I worked.* *You worked.* *He/She/It worked.* *We worked.* *They worked.*	*I* ***was*** *working.* *You* ***were*** *working.* *He/She/It* ***was*** *working.* *We* ***were*** *working.* *They* ***were*** *working.*	*I* ***had*** *worked.* *You* ***had*** *worked.* *He/She/It* ***had*** *worked.* *We* ***had*** *worked.* *They* ***had*** *worked.*
Future	*I* ***will*** *work.* *You* ***will*** *work.* *He/She/It* ***will*** *work.* *We* ***will*** *work.* *They* ***will*** *work.*	*I* ***will be*** *working.* *You* ***will be*** *working.* *He/She/It will be working.* *We* ***will be*** *working.* *They* ***will be*** *working.*	*I* ***will have*** *worked.* *You* ***will have*** *worked.* *He/She/It* ***will have*** *worked.* *We* ***will have*** *worked.* *They* ***will have*** *worked.*

NOTE

You can also use *shall* instead of *will* with *I* and *we* in the future tense.

How to form verb tenses

Present simple tense

When the subject of a sentence is a name or *he*, *she* or *it*, you have to match the verb to the subject. We call this the *third person*:

- For most verbs, you add *-s* to the verb for the third person:
  - ▸ *work* → *He/She/It work***s**.
  - ▸ *love* → *He/She/It loves chocolate.*
- For verbs that end in *-ch*, *-o*, *-sh*, *-ss* and *-x*, you add *-es* to the verb:
  - ▸ ***teach*** → *He/She/It teach***es**.
  - ▸ ***do*** → *He/She/It do***es**.
  - ▸ ***rush*** → *He/She/It rush***es**.
- For verbs that end in *-y*, you change the *-y* to *-ies*:
  - ▸ ***fly*** → *He/She/It fl***ies**.

Past simple tense

In the past simple tense, we do not have to match the verb for the third person. Add *-ed* or *-d* to all the verbs:

- When the verb ends in a consonant, add *-ed* to the verb:
  - ▸ *plant* → *I plant***ed**.
    *You plant***ed**.
    *He/She/It plant***ed**.
    *We plant***ed**.
    *They plant***ed**.
- When the verb ends in *-e*, add *-d*:
  - ▸ *live* → *I live***d**.
    *He/She/It live***d**.
    *We live***d**.
    *They live***d**.
- For verbs that end in *-y*, you change the *-y* to *-ied*:
  - ▸ *try* → *I tr***ied**.
    *He/She/It tr***ied**.
    *We tr***ied**.
    *They tr***ied**.

NOTE

Some verbs have **irregular** past tense forms. You have to look these up in your dictionary if you are not sure of them. Here are examples:

- ▸ *swim* → *I* ***swam*** *yesterday.*
- ▸ *buy* → *They* ***bought*** *some fish.*
- ▸ *drink* → *He* ***drank*** *a litre of water.*
- ▸ *see* → *We* ***saw*** *a lion at the zoo.*

Progressive tenses

We use the present participle (for example *swimming*) to form progressive tenses.

Present progressive tense

Use the verb *to be* (*am*, *is* or *are*) + the verb + *-ing* (present participle):

▸ *play* → *I* ***am*** *play***ing**.

Past progressive tense

Use the simple past tense of the verb *to be* (*was* or *were*) + the verb + *-ing* (present participle):

▸ *listen* → *You* ***were*** *listen***ing**.

Future progressive tense

Use the future tense of the verb *to be* (*will be* or *shall be*) + the verb + *-ing* (present participle):

▸ *listen* → *He* ***will be*** *listen***ing**.

NOTE

If the verb ends with an *-e*, take the *-e* out and add *-ing*:

- ▸ *dance* → *We* ***are/were/will*** *be danc***ing**.
- ▸ *bake* → *She* ***is/was/will*** *be bak***ing** *scones.*

Future tenses

You can form the future tense in two ways.

The future tense with *will* or *shall*

Use the auxiliary words *shall* or *will* + the verb:

▸ *swim* → *I* ***shall/will swim.***

NOTE

These days most people say:
I ***will swim.****/We* ***will swim.***

The future tense with *going to*

Use the present simple tense of the verb *to be* + *going to* + the verb:

▸ *visit* → *You* ***are going to visit*** *your friends.*

▸ *sing* → *She* ***is going to sing*** *at the wedding.*

▸ *sail* → *They* ***are going to sail*** *in the race around the world.*

Perfect tenses

The past participle (for example *danced*, *grown*) is used to form perfect tenses:

The present perfect tense

Use *have* or *has* + the past participle (*-ed* form), for example: *He* ***has*** *danc****ed.*** Remember that past participle forms of irregular verbs do not end in *-ed*, for example: *She* ***has grown*** (*grow* is an irregular verb).

The past perfect tense

Use *had* + the past participle (*-ed* form):

▸ *walk* → *You* ***had*** *walk****ed.***

The future perfect tense

Use *shall* or *will* + *have* + the past participle (*-ed* form):

▸ *watch* → *He/She/It* ***will have*** *watch****ed.***

The verb *to be*

The verb *to be* is very common but it is not regular. Here is a table which shows how the verb works.

Present	Past	Future
I ***am*** *tired.*	*I* ***was*** *tired.*	*I* ***will/shall be*** *tired.*
You ***are*** *tired.*	*You* ***were*** *tired.*	*You* ***will be*** *tired.*
He/She/It ***is*** *tired.*	*He/She/It* ***was*** *tired.*	*He/She/It* ***will be*** *tired.*
We ***are*** *tired.*	*We* ***were*** *tired.*	*We* ***will/shall be*** *tired.*
They ***are*** *tired.*	*They* ***were*** *tired.*	*They* ***will be*** *tired.*

NOTE

- *This verb is often contracted or shortened:*
  *You'****re*** *tired.*
  *She'****s*** *tired.*
  We ***are****n't tired.*
  They ***were****n't tired.*
  *We'****ll be*** *tired.*
- Note that you can use *shall* or *will* with *I* and *we* in the future tense.

Prepositions

Prepositions are important because they tell us when or where things are, or where they happen. If you use an incorrect preposition, the meaning of what you say or write may be completely wrong.

These prepositions describe where things are.

- *The light is **above** the table.*
- *The apple is **on** the table.*
- *The cat is **under** the table.*

- *Vusi sits **near** (or **by**) the door.*
- *Anne sits **opposite** Vusi.*

- *The bus is **behind** the bicycle.*
- *The car is **in front of** the bicycle.*
- *The bicycle is **between** the bus and the car.*

- *The cat is **in** (or **inside**) the box.*
- *The box is **among** the ducks.*

- *The bank is **next to** the shop.*
- *The man is **outside** the bank.*
- *The boy is **inside** the shop.*

- *The ladder is **against** the wall.*
- *The bird is **on top of** the wall.*

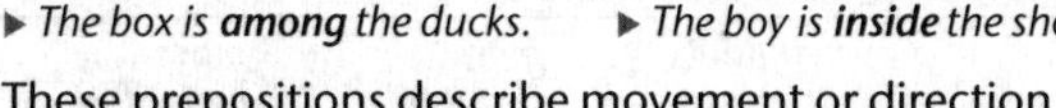

These prepositions describe movement or direction.

- *The helicopter is flying **over** the sea.*
- *It is flying **into** some clouds.*

- *She is walking **through** the field, **past** some trees, **towards** the house.*

- *The goat is going **from** the gate **to** the mealie plant.*

Prepositions show directions, like this:

- *Go **round** the corner.*
- *Go **up** this road.*
- *Go **down** the road and turn left.*
- *The house is **on** the left (or **on** the right).*
- *The shop is **opposite*** (or ***next to***, or ***across** the road **from**) the bank.*
- *It's **between** the garage and the office.*

Adjectives

Adjectives tell us more about nouns and pronouns. To compare two things you use the **comparative** form of an adjective. To compare three or more things you use a **superlative** form.

*a **small** cat*

*a **smaller** cat*

*the **smallest** cat*

- *This cat is **small**.*
- *This cat is **smaller** than that cat.*
- *This cat is the **smallest** cat of all.*

Spelling comparatives and superlatives

Your dictionary gives the comparative and superlative forms of adjectives that take them. Here are some rules to help you spell comparative and superlative forms.

Spelling rule	Example	Comparative form	Superlative form
short adjectives: add *-er* and *-est*	*hard*	*hard**er***	*hard**est***
adjectives that end in *-e*: add *-r* and *-st*	*nice*	*nice**r***	*nice**st***
adjectives that end in *-y*: drop the *-y*, add *-ier* and *-iest*	*dry*	*dr**ier***	*dr**iest***
adjectives with a short vowel before consonant: repeat consonant and add *-er* and *-est*	*big*	*big**ger***	*big**gest***
adjectives with two syllables that end in *-y*: add *-ier* and *-iest*	*busy*	*bus**ier***	*bus**iest***
longer adjectives (adjectives with two or more syllables) that do not end in *-y*: use *more* or *most*	*beautiful*	***more*** *beautiful*	***most*** *beautiful*

Some comparative and superlative forms are irregular, which means that their rules are different. Here are some irregular forms you may use quite often.

	Comparative form	Superlative form
bad	*worse*	*worst*
far	*farther/further*	*farthest/furthest*
good	*better*	*best*
little	*less*	*least*
many	*more*	*most*
much	*more*	*most*

Adverbs and pronouns

Adverbs

Adverbs tell us more about verbs. Adverbs tell us when, where, how, how often and why things happen.

In English, most adverbs end with *-ly*. Some adverbs also have comparative and superlative forms. They follow the same spelling rules as adjectives. This dictionary gives the comparative and superlative forms of adverbs.

Some adverbs also have irregular forms, for example:

	Comparative form	Superlative form
well	*better*	*best*
badly	*worse*	*worst*
far	*farther/further*	*farthest/furthest*

▶ *Sue runs* ***fast****.*

▶ *Bongi runs* ***faster*** *than Sue.*

▶ *Lindi runs the* ***fastest****!*

Pronouns

Pronouns replace nouns. They can be singular or plural and used as either the subject or the object in a sentence. Pronouns can show that something belongs to someone. They can also refer back to the person who is the subject of a sentence.

	Singular	Plural	Examples
These pronouns are the **subjects** in sentences.	*I, you, he, she, it*	*we, you, they*	▶ ***She*** *is going to the beach.* ▶ ***We*** *had lots of fun.*
These pronouns are the **objects** in sentences.	*me, you, him, her, it*	*us, you, them*	▶ *My dad took* ***me*** *home.* ▶ *Look at* ***us****!*
These pronouns show that something belongs to someone (**possessive pronouns**).	*mine, yours, his, hers*	*ours, yours, theirs*	▶ *These books are* ***mine****, but those magazines are* ***yours****.*
These pronouns refer back to a noun or to another pronoun (**reflexive pronouns**).	*myself, yourself, himself, herself, itself*	*ourselves, yourselves, themselves*	▶ *I wash* ***myself*** *with soap and water.* ▶ *The children fed* ***themselves****.*

Building words with prefixes and suffixes

Prefixes and suffixes are like building blocks that make words. They can help you to work out the meaning of a word. You can find many prefixes in the A–Z section of this dictionary and in the list below.

You can use prefixes and suffixes to change the meanings of some words, or to make new words. Look at some of the words you can build from *happy*, using prefixes and suffixes:

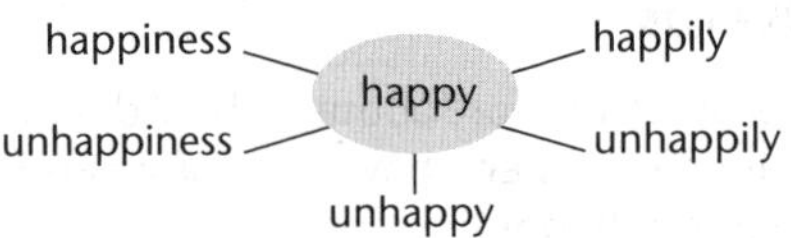

Prefixes

A prefix is used at the beginning of a word. Knowing the meaning of a prefix will help you to understand the meaning of the whole word. Most prefixes in English come from other older languages.

Prefix	Meaning	Examples of words
ab-	away from, not	*abandon, absent*
aero-	from the air, of the air	*aerobics, aeroplane*
Afro-	African	*Afro-American*
Anglo-	relating to England or Britain	*Anglo-Boer War*
anti-	against, not	*antibiotic, anticlockwise, anti-smoking*
arch-	most important, most extreme	*archbishop, arch-enemy*
auto-	self, by yourself or by itself	*autobiography, autograph, automatic*
bi-	two, twice, double	*bicycle, bilingual, binoculars*
bio-	relating to life and living things	*biodegradable, biography, biology*
cent-/centi-	one hundred, one hundredth	*centenary, centimetre, centipede*
circum-	around	*circumference, circumstance*
com-/con-/co-	with, together, involving two or more people	*combine, companion, conspire, cooperate*
contra-	against, opposite	*contraband, contraceptive*
cross-	from one side to the other, done by two sides	*crossbar, cross-question*
de-	to take away, remove, to do the opposite	*deforestation, depose*
deca-	ten	*decade, decagon*
deci-	one tenth	*decimal*
dia-	across	*diagonal, diagram, diameter*
dis-	not, the opposite of	*disagree, dislike, disobey*
e-	electronic	*email*
electr-	using electricity	*electric, electrical, electricity*
en-/em-	to put into a situation or condition	*endanger, empower*
equi-	equal or the same as	*equilateral, equilibrium*
ex-	out, away; in the past, from before	*exit, expel, explode, export; ex-wife*
extra-	outside, beyond	*extraordinary, extra-special*
fore-	before, in advance; in front of	*forecast; forehead*
geo-	earth	*geography*

Prefix	Meaning	Examples of words
giga-	indicating a factor of 10^9	*gigabyte*
great-	the next older generation	*great-grandmother*
hecto-	one hundred	*hectolitre*
hepta-	seven	*heptagon*
hexa-	six	*hexagon*
homo-	the same	*homophone*
hyper-	too much, more than normal	*hyperactive, hypermarket*
il-/im-/in-/ir-	not, the opposite of	*illogical, impatient, incorrect, irrelevant*
in-	in, into	*income, indoors, inflate*
iso-	equal	*isosceles*
inter-	between, involving two or more different things	*interactive, international, interview*
kilo-	one thousand	*kilometre, kilogram*
mal-	bad, badly, not correct, not correctly	*malnutrition, maltreat*
mega-	one million; very big, great	*megabytes; megastore*
micro-	very small	*microchip, microscope*
mid-	in the middle of	*midday, mid-twenties*
milli-	a thousand; a thousandth	*millipede; millilitre*
mini-	very small	*miniature, minibus, minimum*
mis-	badly, wrongly	*misbehave, misfortune, mislead*
mono-	one, single	*monogamy*
multi-	many, more than one	*multicoloured, multiply*
nano-	one billionth	*nanosecond*
non-	not, the opposite of	*non-fiction, nonsense, non-stop*
octa-/octo-	eight	*octagon, octopus*
omni-	all, all things	*omnivore*
out-	away from	*outcome, outdoors, outside*
over-	too much; more than is usual, extra; above	*over-eat; overflow, overtime; overhead*
pan-	including all, connected to whole	*pan-American*
penta-	five, having five	*pentagon*
peri-	round, about	*perimeter, periphery*
plat-	flat	*plateau, platform*
poly-	many	*polygamy, polymer*
post-	after, later than	*post-apartheid, postgraduate*
pre-	before, earlier than	*predict, prehistoric, premature*
pro-	supporting, in favour of; onwards, forwards	*pro-government; proceed, progress*
pseudo-	false, pretending	*pseudonym*
quadri-	four, having four	*quadrilateral*
re-	again	*refund, repay, replace, reproduce*
self-	by yourself, for yourself	*self-employed, self-service*
semi-	partly, half	*semicircle, semicolon, semi-final*
step-	related because mother or father have married again	*stepmother, stepbrother*
sub-	under, beneath, below; less important; a smaller part of something	*submarine, sub-standard; subordinate; sub-plot*

Prefix	Meaning	Examples of words
super-	over, above; better, more important than	*superior, supersonic; superhuman, superpower*
tele-	far, at a distance; by telephone	*telescope, television; telesales*
tetra-	four, having four	*tetragon*
thermo-	relating to heat	*thermometer*
trans-	across into another place or state; through	*translate, transport; transparent*
tri-	three, having three	*triangle, tricycle*
un-	not, the opposite of	*unable, uncertain, unfair*
under-	below; not enough	*underground; undernourished*
uni-	one, single	*uniform, unit*
up-	upwards	*uphill, upright, upwards*
vice-	second in position or importance	*vice-captain*

Suffixes

A suffix is added to the end of a word.

Suffix	Use or meaning	Examples of words
-able	forms adjectives	*inflatable, reliable, valuable*
-al	forms adjectives; forms nouns	*cultural, musical; approval*
-an/-ian/ -arian	showing that you belong to a group	*Christian, comedian, guardian, librarian, vegetarian*
-ence/-ance	forms nouns	*independence, performance*
-ary	forms adjectives; forms nouns	*imaginary, secondary, solitary; burglary, commentary, summary*
-ate	forms adjectives; forms verbs	*approximate, considerate; celebrate, educate, evaporate*
-ation	forms nouns, often from verbs	*abbreviation, calculation, information*
-crat/-cracy	forms nouns, means 'ruling'	*autocrat, democracy*
-dom	forms nouns	*freedom, kingdom*
-ed	forms an adjective or past participle of a verb	*disappointed, excited, tired*
-en	forms adjectives that tell you what something is made of or looks like	*golden, wooden, woollen*
-ee	forms nouns showing a person's situation	*employee, refugee*
-er/-ier	forms the comparative of short adjectives and adverbs	*crazier, fancier, faster, higher, taller*
-er/-ar/-or	forms nouns that show what a person does	*farmer, liar, sailor*
-ess	forms nouns indicating females	*actress, lioness, waitress*
-est/-iest	forms the superlative of short adjectives and adverbs	*filthiest, highest*
-ful	forms adjectives meaning 'full of something'	*beautiful, joyful, powerful*
-ful	forms nouns showing amount	*handful, spoonful*
-fy	forms verbs meaning 'make' or 'cause'	*disqualify, satisfy, terrify*

Suffix	Use or meaning	Examples of words
-gon	forms nouns meaning 'with a certain number of angles'	*hexagon, octagon, pentagon*
-gram	forms nouns meaning 'written' or 'drawn'	*diagram, program*
-graph	forms nouns meaning 'something written', 'drawn', or 'recorded'	*autograph, paragraph, photograph*
-hood	forms nouns that describe a condition or state	*fatherhood, childhood*
-ic	forms adjectives	*athletic, dramatic, scientific*
-ical	forms adjectives	*alphabetical, magical, musical*
-ician	forms nouns that describe what a person does	*electrician, magician, musician*
-ification	forms nouns from verbs that end in *-fy*	*disqualification, qualification*
-ing	forms nouns and adjectives from verbs	*building, devastating, feeling, greeting, writing*
-tion/-sion	forms nouns from verbs and adjectives	*action, collision*
-ish	forms adjectives that show the nature of someone	*foolish, selfish*
-ish	changes adjectives to mean 'rather' or 'not exactly'	*brownish, greenish, smallish*
-ism	forms nouns	*baptism, Hinduism, Judaism*
-ist	forms nouns that show what someone does	*artist, chemist, journalist*
-itis	forms nouns that name an infection	*bronchitis, tonsillitis*
-ive	forms adjectives	*active, attractive, explosive*
-ize/-ise	forms verbs	*apologize, advise*
-less	forms adjectives meaning 'without'	*careless, hopeless, spotless, useless*
-ology	forms nouns that name the study of something	*biology, ecology, technology*
-ly	forms adverbs from adjectives; forms adjectives	*carefully, quickly, slowly; deadly, friendly, lovely*
-ness	forms nouns from adjectives	*happiness, kindness, sadness*
-ous	forms adjectives that describe a certain quality	*dangerous, envious, mischievous*
-ship	forms nouns	*friendship*
-some	forms adjectives	*awesome, gruesome, handsome*
-teen	means ten (in numbers)	*eighteen, fifteen*
-ward/ -wards	forms adjectives and adverbs, usually showing direction	*backward, outwards, towards*
-wise	forms adverbs and adjectives	*clockwise*
-y	forms nouns, usually showing feelings	*jealousy, sympathy*
-y/-ie	forms informal diminutives; forms informal names	*auntie, birdie, doggy; daddy, mummy, Tommy*

Punctuation

Punctuation helps us to make meaning clear when writing and reading.

T Capital letter

- the first letter in a sentence
  - ▶ *He plays soccer.*
- names and titles of people
  - ▶ *Professor Tom Ndlela*
- names of countries, towns, rivers, mountains, dams and roads
  - ▶ *Lesotho, Mthatha, the Orange River, Table Mountain, Hennop Dam, First Avenue*
- days and months
  - ▶ *It is Tuesday, the 1st of April.*
- names of businesses and institutions
  - ▶ *Musi's Chicken, Durban High School*
- some abbreviations and acronyms
  - ▶ ***HIV, SMS, COSATU***
- important events
  - ▶ *First World War*
- titles of books and films
  - ▶ *Tsotsi, Twilight*
- personal pronoun *I*
  - ▶ *Do you know where **I** live?*

. Full stop

- to show the end of a sentence
  - ▶ *HIV/Aids is a problem.*
- in some abbreviations
  - ▶ *No. 24, e.g., etc.*

, Comma

- to separate items in a list
  - ▶ *I need paper, ink, paint and glue.*
- to separate clauses
  - ▶ *After the match, they went home.*
- before question tags
  - ▶ *You do know Morné, don't you?*
- before or after *said* in conversations
  - ▶ *'I like meat,' he said, 'and I eat a lot.'*
- to show decimal fractions
  - ▶ *34,6 litres of petrol*

? Question mark

- at the end of a direct question
  - ▶ *Who is that?*

! Exclamation mark

- at the end of a word/phrase/sentence to show surprise, anger or pain
  - ▶ *Wow!*

- Hyphen

- to join words and some prefixes to make compound words
  - ▶ *co-operate, multiple-choice*
- to show that a word has been divided from one line to the next
  - ▶ *I went home and watch-
ed television.*
- in some numbers
  - ▶ *twenty-five; a hundred and fifty-six*

: Colon

- to introduce a list of things
  - ▶ *To make the cake you will need: flour, sugar, eggs and milk.*

; Semicolon

- to separate two parts of a sentence when there is no conjunction
  - ▶ *The party ended at midnight; everyone went home.*

' Apostrophe

- to show missing letters in contractions
  - ▶ *let's, they'll*
- to show possession (that something belongs to someone)
  - ▶ *one boy's clothes (singular)*
  - ▶ *three boys' clothes (plural)*

' ' " " Quotation marks (inverted commas)

These can be double or single and are used:

- to show words that someone has spoken
  - ▶ *'What is the time?' he asked.*
- to emphasize a slang expression or words used by another person
  - ▶ *He told me that I should "get my act together" and complete my work.*

() [] Brackets

- to separate words or numbers in a sentence
  - ▶ *The Nile River (6 690 km) is the longest river in Africa.*
- for cross-references
  - ▶ *you will learn about ozone later (in Chapter 7).*
- to give extra information
  - ▶ *Drive down Cross Road (past the zoo) until you see the college ahead.*

Figures of speech and sound effects

A figure of speech is a word or phrase that is used in a different way from its usual meaning. Figures of speech and sounds are used to create particular effects in writing. Here is a list of the most common ones:

Figure of speech or sound effect	Meaning	Examples
alliteration	using the same letter or sound at the beginning of words that are close together	▶ *Betty baked some butter buns.*
anticlimax	a disappointing end to something that you expected would be exciting	▶ *You have won the competition! Come and collect your **R5** prize.*
assonance	when two or more words that are close together have the same vowel sounds but different consonants	▶ *And so, all the **night**-tide, I **lie** down by the **side** Of my darling, my darling, my life and my bride.*
hyperbole	when something is exaggerated to create humour or to emphasize something	▶ *I'm **drowning** in work!*
irony	when you say something that is the opposite of what you mean, often to create humour, or when something is the opposite of what it should be	▶ *When he screamed at me, I said, 'You are in a good mood!'*
metaphor	a word or phrase used to compare something to something else that has similar qualities	▶ *We had a **blazing** row!* ▶ *My blood was **boiling**.*
metonymy	when something associated with a person or thing is used to represent it. (Here, the White House represents the USA President.)	▶ *There was a statement from the **White House**.*
onomatopoeia	when words sound like the things they name; they are often made-up words	▶ ***splat**, **sploshing**, in the mud*
oxymoron	when two words that are opposite in meaning are placed together	▶ *There was a **deafening silence**.*
paradox	statements or situations that seem contradictory or strange together	▶ *An **ashtray** with a **'no smoking'** sign on it ...*
personification	a comparison in which an object is given human qualities	▶ *The car **coughed** and **spluttered** and came to a halt.*
pun	a clever play on words that have more than one meaning or words that sound the same	▶ *Trust your **calculator.** It's something you can **count** on.*
repetition	when words are repeated to create a rhythm or to add emphasis	▶ ***Row**, **row**, **row** your boat ...*
rhyme	when the ends of words at the ends of lines in a poem *sound* the same	▶ *The little **mouse** Crept quietly into the **house**.*
sarcasm	when you want to hurt someone and you say one thing but mean the opposite	▶ *You are so **clever**, aren't you!*
simile	a comparison in which the words *like* or *as* are used to make a direct comparison	▶ *He rode **like** the wind.*

Plain English

It is not necessary to use complicated words to explain something clearly. It is better to use language that most people understand. Here are some words and phrases that are often used unnecessarily. Next to each one is a less complicated alternative.

Words

Complicated	Clear and simple
acquire	get
ascertain	find out
assist	help
commence	start/begin
concerning	about
endeavour	try
enquire	ask
inform	tell
magnitude	size
notify	tell
numerous	many
obtain	get
participate	join in
peruse	read
proprietor	owner
purchase	buy
regarding	about
request	ask for
require	need
residence	home/house
terminate	end
utilize	use
vicinity	area

Phrases

Complicated	Clear and simple
at the present time	now
at this moment in time	now
because of the fact that	because
despite the fact that	although
during which time	while
each and every one	every one
in due course	soon
in excess of	more than
in order to	to
in respect of	about
in the amount of	for
in the event of	if
in the proximity of	close to
in view of the fact that	because
prior to	before
refrain from	stop

Instruction words

In exams it is very important to read instructions carefully. This table, based on Bloom's Taxonomy, shows the categories of questions that you can expect in tests and exams. Make sure you know exactly what these instruction words mean. This will help you to answer the question that is asked.

Look up the key verbs in your dictionary if you are not sure what they mean.

	Answer expected of you	Key verbs in instructions			
Level 1 simplest level	**Knowledge** ■ These instructions ask you to recall or remember information and show what facts you know, for example: *Who are the main characters in this story?*	*collect* *complete* *count* *define* *describe* *draw*	*examine* *fill in* *find* *give* *identify* *label*	*list* *match* *name* *quote* *recall* *relate*	*show* *state* *tabulate* *tell* *write*
Level 2	**Comprehension** ■ These instructions ask you to show that you understand something, for example: *Explain why John and his sister were living in the house.*	*classify* *describe* *discuss* *explain* *identify* *illustrate*	*indicate* *interpret* *locate* *mention* *paraphrase* *predict*	*provide* *recognize* *report* *restate* *review* *select*	*state* *summarize* *translate*
Level 3	**Application** ■ These instructions ask you to use your knowledge or information in some way, for example: *Dramatize the argument between John and his sister in a role-play.*	*apply* *arrange* *calculate* *change* *choose* *combine* *connect*	*construct* *demonstrate* *discuss* *critically* *dramatize* *employ* *examine*	*enlarge* *formulate* *illustrate* *integrate* *interpret* *operate* *predict*	*schedule* *show* *sketch* *solve* *suggest* *use*
Level 4	**Analysis** ■ These instructions ask you to think about information in a critical way, for example: *Compare John's reaction to winning the lotto with his sister's reaction to it.*	*appraise* *analyze* *categorize* *compare* *contrast* *consider*	*criticize* *deduce* *distinguish* *differentiate* *discriminate* *examine*	*experiment* *explain* *illustrate* *indicate* *investigate* *question*	*test*
Level 5	**Synthesis** ■ These instructions ask you to use information to create something new, for example: *What do you think would have happened if John had not told his sister about the winning ticket? Rewrite the end of the story.*	*assemble* *compose* *construct* *combine*	*create* *design* *develop* *discover*	*formulate* *integrate* *modify* *plan*	*produce* *propose* *rewrite*
Level 6	**Evaluation** ■ These instructions ask you to pull together several ideas and to be critical and creative, for example: *Do you think it's a good idea to buy lotto tickets? Explore this, and use examples from the story to justify your response.*	*appraise* *argue* *assess* *compose* *conclude*	*compile* *criticize* *defend* *evaluate* *explore*	*decide* *justify* *judge* *measure* *select*	*support* *value* *verify*

Numbers

Cardinal and ordinal numbers

	Cardinal numbers		Ordinal numbers
0	zero		
1	one	1st	first
2	two	2nd	second
3	three	3rd	third
4	four	4th	fourth
5	five	5th	fifth
6	six	6th	sixth
7	seven	7th	seventh
8	eight	8th	eighth
9	nine	9th	ninth
10	ten	10th	tenth
11	eleven	11th	eleventh
12	twelve	12th	twelfth
13	thirteen	13th	thirteenth
14	fourteen	14th	fourteenth
15	fifteen	15th	fifteenth
16	sixteen	16th	sixteenth
17	seventeen	17th	seventeenth
18	eighteen	18th	eighteenth
19	nineteen	19th	nineteenth
20	twenty	20th	twentieth
21	twenty-one	21st	twenty-first
22	twenty-two	22nd	twenty-second
30	thirty	30th	thirtieth
40	forty	40th	fortieth
50	fifty	50th	fiftieth
60	sixty	60th	sixtieth
70	seventy	70th	seventieth
80	eighty	80th	eightieth
90	ninety	90th	ninetieth
100	a hundred	100th	hundredth
101	a/one hundred and one	101st	one hundred and first

Arabic and Roman numbers

We use Arabic numbers (for example *1*, *6* and *9*) in maths, but Roman numbers (for example *V* and *XII*) are also used often, for example on some watches, and to number the first pages of many books.

1	I	17	XVII
2	II	18	XVIII
3	III	19	XIX
4	IV	20	XX
5	V	22	XXII
6	VI	30	XXX
7	VII	40	XL
8	VIII	50	L
9	IX	60	LX
10	X	70	LXX
11	XI	80	LXXX
12	XII	90	XC
13	XIII	100	C
14	XIV	500	D
15	XV	1 000	M
16	XVI	2 000	MM

Roman numbers are combined in this way to form other numbers:

XXXIX	39
LVIII	58
CCCXXII	322

SMS language

In cellphone text messages words are often shortened. You do not use these short cuts in other types of writing. Here are some examples.

Words

Full form	Short SMS form
anyone	ne1
ate	8
be	b
before	b4
easy	ez
excellent	xlnt
for	4
forward	fwd
good	gd
great	gr8
hate	h8
have	hv
hello	lo
kisses	xx
know	knw
late	l8
love	luv
message	msg
no one	no1
people	ppl
phone	fone
please	pls
someone	sum1
speak	spk
text	txt
thanks	thx
to, too	2
today	2day
tomorrow	2moro
tonight	2nite
very	v
weekend	wknd
without	w/o
you	u
your	yr/ur

Phrases

Full form	Short SMS form
all the best	atb
are you okay?	r u ok
as soon as possible	asap
be back late	bbl
bye for now	b4n
does not	dsnt
get a life	gal
laugh out loud	lol
lots of love	lol
mind your own business	myob
please call me	pcm
see you	cu
see you later	cul8r
want to	wan2
what's up?	wu

Emoticons

Emoticons are symbols formed from punctuation marks (and sometimes letters) to show feelings. They are only used in personal or informal SMS messages.

happy (a smiley)	☺ or :-)
sad	☹ or :-(
laughing	:-D
crying	:'(
I don't understand	:-Q
bored	😐 or :-|
kiss	:-*
surprised	:-O
I won't tell anyone	:-X
wink	;-)
being cheeky	:-p

Activities for the classroom

Lesson 1: Getting to know your dictionary

1 Work in groups. Each group takes a list of words (1, 2 or 3). Write the words down in alphabetical order. Time yourselves to see which group finishes first.

1 gambler pie aunt
vase reality deposit
laboratory fairy scarecrow

2 fake daffodil salami
team galleon upgrade
philosopher recipe varnish

3 July outside December
moment soccer urgent
fancy pizza sixteen

2 Work alone. Write these lists of words in alphabetical order. When the first letter of the words is the same, look at the second letter. If the second letter is the same, look at the third letter.

1 dancer blue egg acid cable
2 real sour epic just mean
3 jazz jeep joke juice jam
4 month Monday monkey mine miserable
5 untidy undo unworthy unload unloved

---

3 Work alone. Look at the guide words in the left column of the table. Which words in the right column can be found on the page that has these guide words?

Guide words	Entries on page
1 **avocado → Aztec**	average aware awkward axis
2 **fireplace → fish**	fireman firework fiscal fixed
3 **pea → peel**	pawn peacock peck peep

4 Work in pairs. Read these pronunciation guides aloud. What is the correct spelling of each word? Check your spelling in the dictionary, and use the guide on page vi to help you.

Pronunciation	Correct spelling
fayz	
hoo	*who*
kay-oss	
kween	
ji-**raaf**	
rek	

5 Find these words in your dictionary.

1 **injury**
- What part of speech is it?
- What is the plural?

2 **galaxy**
- Which language does the word come from?
- Does it have a plural form?

3 **meditate**
- What is the simple past tense?
- Which noun is derived from this word?

4 **nevertheless**
- What part of speech is it?
- What is another word you can use instead of it?

5 **near**
- What word means the opposite?
- Complete this sentence with a form of the word: Where is the ____________ ATM?

6 **chemist**
- How do you say the word?
- What is a synonym for this word?

7 **ghastly**
- What part of speech is it?
- What word has the same meaning?

8 **him**
- What part of speech is it?
- What is the plural?

9 **bear**
- How many meanings does this word have in this dictionary?
- What does it mean if you can't **bear** someone?

10 **MHz**
- What is this short for?
- Where should you look in the dictionary for more information?

11 **multi-**
- What does this prefix mean?
- Give an example of a word which has this prefix.

12 **-ism**

This is a suffix. Read the section on suffixes in the Study pages.
- What words could you make with this suffix?

---

6 Work in pairs. Look at the entry for **elbow**.

> **elbow** (say **el**-boh) *noun* (*plural* **elbows**) the part in the middle of your arm where it bends: *She fell and broke her* ***elbow***. ➲ See illustration at **body**

- Write your own entry for the word **shoulder**.
- Compare your entry with the dictionary's entry.

7 Work alone. Under which other word in your dictionary can you find out more about each of these words? The first one has been done for you.

1 arose *arise*
2 amakhosi
3 fugitive
4 sci-fi
5 attractive
6 femur

Lesson 2: Vocabulary

1 Work in pairs. Which word in each list is the odd one out? Say why.

	Odd one out	Why?
1 kangaroo impala aardvark		
2 rectangle polymer hexagon		
3 democrat despot tyrant		

2 In pairs, decide if these statements are true or false. Correct the false statements. Check your answers in the dictionary.

1 You will find a **regiment** in a business.
2 **Spaghetti** is a type of **paste**.
3 If you are **multilingual** you are able to speak more than two languages.
4 A **global** problem is a problem in your own country.

---

3 Think of a synonym for each of these words. Then check your answers in the dictionary.

	Your synonym	Dictionary's synonym
1 abduct		
2 eager		
3 call off		
4 eraser		

4 Think of an opposite (or antonym) for each of these words. Then check your answers in the dictionary.

	Your opposite	Dictionary's opposite
1 accurate		
2 deny		
3 worse		
4 forget		

5 Think of what the plural of each of these words is. Then find the plurals in your dictionary to check your answers.

	Your plural	Dictionary's plural
1 library		
2 wife		
3 nucleus		
4 photo		

6 Look up both the words in brackets in your dictionary. The words sound the same but their meanings are different. What is the correct word in each sentence?

1 She ate the (**whole**/**hole**) apple, including the core!
2 Long ago, ships used (**sales**/**sails**) to move through the water.
3 The helicopter changed (**course**/**coarse**) to avoid the storm.
4 How many kilos does this chicken (**way**/**weigh**)?
5 Where is your electricity (**metre**/**meter**)?
6 I need paper, pens, and other (**stationery**/**stationary**).

7 Look up both the words in brackets in your dictionary. These words are often mixed up. What is the correct word for each sentence?

1 What is the (**amount**/**number**) of money that I owe?
2 Did you (**accept**/**except**) the new job?
3 Please can you (**borrow**/**lend**) me R10?
4 She is wearing a (**lose**/**loose**) dress.

8 What are the dictionary meanings of the bold words, as they are used in these sentences?

1 Don't **squash** my hat!
2 I don't like **abstract** paintings very much.
3 The Premier will **address** Parliament tomorrow.
4 How will the company **market** their new product?

9 What is the meaning of each prefix? Give an example of each. Look at the list of prefixes on pages SP12–SP14 and at the entries in your dictionary. The first one has been done for you.

Prefix	Meaning	Example
1 micro-	*very small*	*microphone*
2 post-		
3 omni-		
4 bio-		
5 ultra-		
6 un-		

10 Look at the list of prefixes on pages SP12–SP14. How many sides does each of these shapes have?

1 quadrilateral
2 polygon
3 triangle
4 tetrahedron
5 pentagon
6 decagon

11 Use suffixes to make new words. Check your answers in the dictionary. Look at the derivatives or at the headwords close to these entries. The first one has been done for you.

	New word	Suffix used
1 Make an adjective from **value**.	*valuable*	*-able*
2 Make a noun from **perform**.		
3 Make an adjective from **wool**.		
4 Make a noun from **collect**.		
5 Make an adverb from **surprising**.		

12 Look up the words in bold print in your dictionary to help you complete these sentences.

1 Be careful on the train. Someone may ______________ your **pocket**.
2 She was always late for work so she ______________ the **sack**.
3 I've ______________ **touch** with my old primary school friend.
4 Please ______________ every one **welcome** at the party tonight.

Lesson 3: Grammar

1 Find the different parts of speech for each word in the table. The first one has been done for you.

Verb	Noun	Adjective	Adverb
complete	*completion*	*complete*	*completely*
	caution		
help			
			comfortably

2 Which derivative of the word in brackets do you need in each sentence? Look up the word in brackets and then write the sentences correctly.

1 There's a lot of (**excite**) about their holiday.
2 The new job is a (**promote**) for me.
3 Cars and trucks have a (**damage**) effect on the environment.
4 That is a (**racism**) comment!
5 It is cold and (**mist**) this morning.

3 Use each of these words in a sentence. Look the word up and check which part of speech it is before you begin.

1 practise
2 medal
3 breath
4 affect

---

4 What is the correct tense for the verb **sing** in each sentence?

1 He ____________ very well last night.
2 The birds ____________ ____________ yesterday morning.
3 Do you often ____________ in the shower?
4 She has never ____________ in a competition before.

> **sing** *verb* (**singing**, **sang**, **has sung**)
> to make music with your voice: *She **sang** a song.* ◇ *The birds were **singing**.*

5 Which is the correct form of the verb in each sentence? Study the rules for the present simple tense on page SP7. Then look up each verb in your dictionary and read the example sentences carefully.

1 My mum (**teach/teaches**) maths at this school.
2 They (**live/lives**) in this house.
3 I (**understand/understands**) isiXhosa.
4 He (**make/makes**) a lot of money from selling hamburgers.

6 Complete this table on verb tenses.
The first row has been done for you.

Simple present	Simple past	Present perfect	Past progressive
He misses me.	*He missed me.*	*He has missed me.*	*He was missing me.*
I break the glass.			
Jane fries eggs.			
The girls skip.			
They write poetry.			

7 What are the correct forms of the verbs in these sentences? Check the entries in the dictionary and the notes about verbs on pages SP6–SP8.

1 If I am (**offend**) you, please tell me. (present progressive tense)
2 Yesterday I (**lie**) on my bed and (**read**) a book. (past simple tense)
3 Have you ever (**see**) Table Mountain? (present perfect tense)
4 He always (**hurry**) home after school to have lunch. (present simple tense)
5 Next week they (**climb**) Mount Kilimanjaro. (simple future tense with *will*)

8 Look up the words in brackets in your dictionary. Then write each sentence with the correct word.

1 **Who's/Whose** coming home with me?
2 My father gave me useful (**advise**/**advice**).
3 We should eat (**fewer**/**less**) sweets!
4 Please (**borrow**/**lend**) me your bike.

9 Write the correct form of the word in brackets. (See SP10 for help.)

1 This is the (**easy**) test I have ever written!
2 The weather is (**good**) today than it was yesterday.
3 What is the (**creepy**) film you have ever watched?
4 Who can jump (**high**) – Neo or Jo?

---

10 Complete the expressions.
Then match them to the meanings.
(If you need help, look up the words in bold.)

Expression	Meaning
1 to **put** ________ ________ something	■ to not do something you promised to do
2 to **let** somebody ________	■ to stop something from moving forwards
3 to **try** something ________	■ to have pain or problems without complaining
4 to **hold** something ________	■ to put on a piece of clothing to see if you like it, and if it fits you

Lesson 4: Editing

1 Some of the words in each of these sentences are spelt incorrectly. Working in pairs, identify these words and use your dictionary to find the correct spelling. See page vi at the beginning of the dictionary if you need help.

1 I hurt my nee at jym.
2 She is so ecsited! She saw the kween!
3 He doesn't now how to rite an email.
4 My frend foned to say she was going to be an our late.

2 These paragraphs are difficult to read. Rewrite the paragraphs and add punctuation to make the meaning clear. See SP16 if you need help.

1 the most popular programmes on tv besides the sports programmes are the soap operas all the tv stations in south africa show at least one soapie the most popular soaps are isidingo the bold and the beautiful generations egoli and scandal

2 yesterday i went shopping with my mother and my aunt we wanted to buy some new clothes for summer
dont be a slave to fashion my aunt said
my mother said look for something comfortable
what do they know

3 Choose a more interesting option for the words in bold from the words in brackets. Check the meanings of the words in the dictionary if you are not sure!

1 This is a **nice** garden. I wish my garden looked like this! (fragrant, pretty, flamboyant, abundant, green, lush, fertile, arid)
2 We went for a **good** walk on the beach yesterday. (long, excellent, short, fascinating, tiring)
3 She **talks** on the phone all day. (chatters, mumbles, chirps, ponders, whispers)
4 I felt **happy** when I heard my exam results. (delighted, ecstatic, elated, satisfied)

4 Write the text in the speech bubbles in more formal language. Look up the bold words in your dictionary if you need help.

5 Some of the words in these sentences are unnecessarily complicated. Working in pairs, look at the list on SP18 and identify the words that need to be changed. Then rewrite the sentences in plain English.

1 When can you commence work?
2 I need to speak to you regarding this project.
3 Where are you at the present time?

Lesson 5: Using your dictionary for research

The Study pages (SP2–SP21) provide useful information that you can use when you are working on a project.

1 Work in pairs. Make a list of the different types of information you can find in the Study pages.

2 Consult the information in the Study pages to answer these questions.

1 Why are many English and Afrikaans words similar (such as *milk* and *melk*)? Look for the answer in the section, 'The history of English'.
2 What does a **preposition** do?
3 What is the spelling rule for the plural forms of nouns that end with **-y**?
4 What is a **conjunction** used for?
5 What are **apostrophes** used for?
6 What does the prefix **semi**- mean?
7 Give an example of the figure of speech called an **oxymoron**.
8 Read this question in an exam paper:

> What do you think would have happened if ... ?

What type of answer do you need to give?
– a short answer
– a longer answer, in which you use information that you have, to create a new idea.

9 What is the ordinal number for **twenty-two**?
10 Write this SMS message in a full sentence:

> CU 2moro. b4n. luv

3 Numbers

If you don't know the answer, look up the key words. Try to do this puzzle in less than ten minutes! Then check all your answers in the dictionary.

1 How many sides does a **hexagon** have?
2 How many centimetres are in a **metre**?
3 How many lines are in a **sonnet**?
4 How do you write the number **46** in Roman numbers?
5 How many books are in a **trilogy**?
6 How many 1 000s are in a **billion**?
7 How many players are in a **hockey** team?
8 How many kilograms are in a **metric ton**?
9 How many bytes are in a **gigabyte**?

4 Make up your own quiz

Work in groups. Make up ten quiz questions to ask other groups. You must be able to look up all the answers in your dictionary.

5 Use the illustrations

1 Explain briefly how a **windpump** works.
2 What do you need in order to build a simple electrical **circuit**?

Lesson 6: Word origins

Many words that are used in English today go back thousands of years. Read more about the etymology of words (or where English words come from) on pages SP2–SP3.

1 Which language does each of these words come from?

avocado	chutney	democracy	equator
gogga	jacket	judo	kebab
malaria	mango	month	pyjamas
rectangle	Renaissance	vlei	window

2 What is similar about the origins of these groups of words?

1 ampere cardigan diesel sandwich saxophone

2 centimetre circumference graph polygon

3 Work in pairs. Try to guess the origins of these words. Then check your answers in the dictionary.

Word	Origin (your guess)	Origin (dictionary)
boerewors		
breakfast		
Celsius		
impala		

4 Which modern English word comes from each of these words? Choose the correct word.

1 **amma:** imam/mother
2 **babuin:** baby/baboon
3 **dohter:** daughter/doctor
4 **gebed:** bead/bed

5 The Greek word **bios**, which means *life*, gives us English words like *biology* and *biosphere*. Find English words in your dictionary that were formed from these words.

1 **astron** (Greek word meaning *star*)
2 **demos** (Greek word meaning *people*)
3 **graphe** (Greek word meaning *writing or drawing*)
4 **super** (Latin word meaning *above*)
5 **therme** (Greek word meaning *heat*)
6 **transmittere** (Latin word meaning *to send across*)

6 Match the modern English words in Box 1 with two words from other languages that they are related to in Box 2.

Try to do this on your own, and then look up the origins in your dictionary.

Box 1

ten
church
shadow
leather
milk

Box 2

milc	melk
circe	kerk
decem	tien
lether	leer
sceaduwe	skotos

7 These words have interesting origins. What did they mean originally?

1 algorithm
2 assassin
3 berserk
4 clue
5 denim
6 karate
7 maverick
8 papier mâché
9 prima donna
10 sinister

Lesson 7: Exam questions

1 Study these dictionary entries and answer the questions that follow.

special (say **spesh**-uhl) *adjective*
1 not usual or ordinary, or important for a reason: *It's my birthday today so we are having a **special** dinner.*
2 for a particular person or thing: *He goes to a **special** school for deaf children.*
▸ **speciality** (*noun*): *This food is the chef's **speciality** (= a very good food that the chef is famous for).*

specialist (say **spesh**-uh-list) *noun* (*plural* **specialists**)
a person who knows a lot about something: *She's a **specialist** in Chinese art.*

specialize (say **spesh**-uh-lize) *verb* (**specializing, specialized**) (also **specialise**)
specialize in something to study or know a lot about one special thing: *He **specialized** in criminal law.*

specially (say **spesh**-uh-lee) *adverb* (also **especially**)
1 for a particular person or thing: *I made this cake **specially** for you.*
2 more than usual or more than others: *The food was not **specially** good.* ➲ SYNONYM **particularly**

1 What part of speech is **speciality**?
2 What do you call a person who knows a lot about something?
3 Give a synonym for **specially**.
4 What is another way of spelling **specialize**?

2 Study these entries in your dictionary and use the most suitable word in each sentence.

everyday
everyone
everything
everywhere

1 I have ____________ I need in this bag.
2 Cellphones are part of our ____________ life now.
3 ____________ will have some tea and biscuits.
4 They looked ____________ but they couldn't find the book.

---

3 Study these entries in your dictionary and use the most suitable word in each sentence.

account¹
accounting
account²
accountant
accountable

1 She is going to open a new bank ____________.
2 Sales to supermarkets ____________ for most of the farmer's production.
3 You will be ____________ if anything goes missing from this room.
4 The business employs an ____________.
5 My brother is studying ____________ at university.

For fun!

1 Word origins

Score one point for each correct answer. Look up the key words in bold to find the answers.

1 What did the name the **Mediterranean** (Sea) mean originally?
2 After which ancient god is the month of **March** named?
3 After which city is the fruit **tangerine** named?
4 What has **garlic** got to do with spears?
5 Which Greek god caused people to **panic** when he made strange sounds in the woods?
6 Why did the word **plumber** originally mean a person who works with lead?
7 What material were **sandals** originally made of?
8 What is the connection between the words **salad** and **salary**?
9 Are **guerillas** named after a type of ape or a type of war?

2 A grammar crossword puzzle

Clues across

1 The singular of **women**.
3 The simple past tense of **put**.
5 The plural of **mouse**.
7 An adjective derived from **access**.
8 The short form of **you would**.

Clues down

1 An adjective derived from **wash**.
2 A noun derived from **necessary**.
4 The simple past tense of **target**.
5 This noun is in the same word family as **machinery**.
6 The simple present tense of **sang**.

3 How many words can you make?

Make as many words as you can with the letters below.
Look up each word to see if it is in the dictionary.
Write your answers in a table like this.

E	C	H
T	C	O
A	L	O

Your words	Correct?	Checked in dictionary

Mm

m *abbreviation* (*plural* **m**) **metre**

macabre (say muh-**kaab**) *adjective*
unpleasant or frightening because it is connected with death: *a **macabre** story*

macaroni (say mak-uh-**roh**-nee) *noun* (*no plural*)
a type of food made from flour and water (called **pasta**) that looks like short tubes: *Macaroni with cheese is my favourite meal.*

Mach (say **mak**, **ma*kh*** or **maak**) *noun* (*no plural*)
a measurement of speed, used especially for aircraft. **Mach 1** is the speed of sound.
ℹ **ORIGIN:** from the name of Ernst Mach (1838–1916), an Austrian scientist

machete (say muh-**shet**-ee) *noun* (*plural* **machetes**)
a broad heavy knife, used as a cutting tool and a weapon ➲ **SYNONYM panga**

Machiavellian (say mak-i-uh-**vel**-i-uhn) *adjective*
(used in politics or business) dishonest and not caring what happens to other people: *He manages his company in a **Machiavellian** way.*
ℹ **ORIGIN:** from the name of Niccolò Machiavelli (1469–1527), an Italian leader who promoted this style of leadership

machine (say muh-**sheen**) *noun* (*plural* **machines**)
a piece of equipment with moving parts that is made to do a job: *a washing **machine*** ◇ *This **machine** does not work.*

machine gun *noun* (*plural* **machine guns**)
a gun that can fire a lot of bullets very quickly

machinery (say muh-**sheen**-uh-ree) *noun* (*no plural*)
1 machines in general, especially large ones: *industrial **machinery***
2 the moving parts of a machine

macho (say **mach**-oh) *adjective*
(used about a man or his behaviour) using qualities like strength in an aggressive way: *a **macho** man* ◇ ***macho** behaviour*

mackerel (say **mak**-ruhl) *noun* (*plural* **mackerels** or **mackerel**)
a sea fish you can eat, with blue-green bands on its body

macrocosm (say **mak**-roh-koz-m) *noun* (*plural* **macrocosms**)
1 the universe
2 a large complete structure containing smaller structures ➲ See **microcosm**

mad *adjective* (**madder**, **maddest**)
1 ill in your mind: *He went **mad** and killed himself.* ➲ **SYNONYM insane**
2 (*informal*) very stupid: *I think you're **mad** to work so hard!* ➲ **SYNONYM crazy** 1
3 (*informal*) very angry: *She was **mad** at me for being late.* ◇ *This noise is driving me **mad**!*
➲ **SYNONYM crazy** 2
be mad about a person or **thing** (*informal*) to like a person or thing very much: *Mina is **mad** about computer games.* ◇ *He's **mad** about her.*
like mad (*informal*) very hard or fast or much: *I had to run like **mad** to catch the bus.*

madam (say **mad**-uhm) *noun* (*no plural*)
1 (*formal*) a polite way of speaking to a woman: *'Can I help you, **madam**?' asked the shop assistant.*
2 Madam a word that you can use at the beginning of a formal letter to a woman: *Dear **Madam** ...* ➲ See **sir**

made (say **mayd**) form of **make[1]**

madly (say **mad**-lee) *adverb*
1 in a wild way: *They were rushing around **madly**.*
2 (*informal*) very much: *Thabo and Karabo are **madly** in love.*

madness (say **mad**-nuhss) *noun* (*no plural*)
stupid behaviour that could be dangerous: *It would be **madness** to take a boat out in this terrible weather.*

magazine (say mag-uh-**zeen**) *noun* (*plural* **magazines**)
a type of thin book with a paper cover that you can buy every week or every month. It has a lot of different stories and pictures in it.

magenta (say muh-**jen**-tuh) *adjective*
with a red-purple colour: ***magenta** curtains*
► **magenta** (*noun*): ***Magenta** is my favourite colour.*

maggot (say **mag**-uht) *noun* (*plural* **maggots**)
a fly in the early stage of its development before it grows wings and legs: ***Maggots** are fly larvae that eat rotting food.*

magic (say **maj**-ik) *noun* (*no plural*)
1 a special power that can make strange or impossible things happen: *He suddenly appeared as if by **magic**.*

2 clever tricks that somebody can do to entertain people
▸ **magic** (*adjective*): ***magic** tricks*

magical (say **maj**-ik-l) *adjective*
1 seeming to have special powers: *a herb with **magical** powers to cure disease*
2 (*informal*) wonderful and exciting: *We spent a **magical** week in Paris.*

magician (say muh-**ji**-shuhn) *noun* (*plural* **magicians**)
1 a person who does clever tricks to entertain people ➲ See **conjure**
2 (in stories) a man who has strange, unusual powers

magistrate (say **maj**-i-strayt) *noun* (*plural* **magistrates**)
a type of judge in a court of law who decides how to punish people for certain crimes

magma (say **mag**-muh) *noun* (*no plural*)
very hot liquid rock found below the Earth's surface ➲ See illustration at **volcano**

magnate (say **mag**-nayt) *noun* (*plural* **magnates**)
a person who is rich, powerful and successful, especially in business: *a mining **magnate*** ◇ *a property **magnate*** ➲ SYNONYM **tycoon**

magnesium (say mag-**nee**-zi-uhm) *noun* (*no plural*) (symbol Mg)
a light silver-white metal that burns with a bright white flame

magnet (say **mag**-nuht) *noun* (*plural* **magnets**)
a piece of metal, rock or other substance that can make metal objects move towards it

magnetic (say mag-**net**-ik) *adjective*
having the ability to attract metal objects: *Is this metal **magnetic**?*
magnetic field an area around a **magnet** or around materials that behave like a magnet. There is a force in this field that will attract some metals.

magnetism (say **mag**-nuht-iz-m) *noun* (*no plural*)
a characteristic that some metals such as iron have that causes forces between objects, either pulling them towards each other or pushing them apart
▸ **magnetize** (*verb*) (also **magnetise**): *We **magnetized** some nails with a magnet.*

magnificent (say mag-**nif**-i-suhnt) *adjective*
very good or beautiful: *The Taj Mahal is a **magnificent** building.*

> WORD BUILDING There are many words that you can use instead of **magnificent**, but check their exact meanings first. Examples are: **breathtaking**, **gorgeous**, **grand**, **impressive**, **majestic**, **spectacular**, **splendid** and **wonderful**.

magnify (say **mag**-ni-fy) *verb* (**magnifying**, **magnified**)
to make something look bigger than it really is: *We **magnified** the insect under a microscope.*
▸ **magnification** (*noun*): *the **magnification** of an image*

magnifying glass *noun* (*plural* **magnifying glasses**)
a circle of glass, usually with a handle, that makes things look bigger than they are when you look through it

magnitude (say **mag**-ni-tyood) *noun* (*plural* **magnitudes**) (*formal*)
the size or importance of something: *The scientist predicted the **magnitude** of the earthquake.* ◇ *The forces were of different **magnitudes**.* ◇ *Her decision was one of great **magnitude**.*

maharajah (say maa-huh-**raa**-juh) *noun* (*plural* **maharajahs**)
an Indian prince who ruled over one of the states of India in the past

mahogany (say muh-**hog**-uh-nee) *noun* (*no plural*)
a hard dark red-brown wood that you can use to make furniture

maid (say **mayd**) *noun* (*plural* **maids**)
a woman whose job is to clean in a hotel, house or flat ➲ See **char**[2]

> USAGE Many people prefer the term **domestic worker**.

maiden (say **may**-duhn) *adjective*
the first of its kind or in a series: *a **maiden** voyage* ◇ *a **maiden** speech* (= the first speech of a member of parliament)

maiden name *noun* (*plural* **maiden names**)
a woman's family name before she is married

mail (say **mayl**) *noun* (*no plural*) (also **post**)
1 the way of sending and receiving letters and packages: *to send a letter by **mail*** ➲ See **email**
2 letters and packages that you send or receive: *Is there any **mail** for me?*
▸ **mail** (*verb*): *I'll **mail** the parcel to you.*

mailbox (say **mayl**-bokss) *noun* (*plural* **mailboxes**)
1 (also **letter box**) a private box outside a house

or a building, or a hole in a door for putting letters through
2 (also **postbox**) a box in the street where you put letters that you want to send
3 (*computing*) a computer program that receives and stores email

maim (say **maym**) *verb* (**maiming, maimed**)
to injure a person or animal so badly that part of their body can no longer be used: *He was **maimed** in the accident.*

main (say **mayn**) *adjective*
most important: *My **main** reason for learning English is to get a better job.* ◇ *There are many shops along the **main** road.*

mainland (say **mayn**-land) *noun* (*plural* **mainlands**)
the main part of a country or continent, not the islands around it: *the Greek **mainland***

mainly (say **mayn**-lee) *adverb*
mostly: *She eats **mainly** vegetables.* ◇ *The books that I read are **mainly** from the library.*
➲ SYNONYMS **chiefly, largely**

mains (say **maynz**) *noun* (*no plural*)
the main supply of electricity or water to buildings: *Turn off the power at the **mains**.*

maintain (say mayn-**tayn**) *verb* (**maintaining, maintained**)
1 to make something continue at the same level: *If he can **maintain** this speed, he'll win the race.*
2 to keep something working well: *The roads are well **maintained**.*

maintenance (say **mayn**-tuh-nuhnss) *noun* (*no plural*)
keeping something in good condition: *car **maintenance*** ◇ ***maintenance** of the building*

maize (say **mayz**) *noun* (*no plural*)
a tall plant with big yellow or white seeds on a **cob** that people and farm animals can eat
➲ See **mealie, sweetcorn**
🛈 ORIGIN: 16th century, through Spanish *maíz*, from Taino *mahiz*. Taino is a language that used to be spoken in the Caribbean.

majestic (say muh-**jess**-tik) *adjective*
impressive because of its size or beauty: *a **majestic** mountain view*

majesty (say **maj**-uhss-tee) *noun*
1 (*plural* **Majesties**) (also **Majesty**) a word that you use to talk to or about a king or queen: *Her Majesty the Queen*
2 (*no plural*) the impressive and attractive quality that something has: *the splendour and **majesty** of the palace grounds*

major¹ (say **may**-juh) *adjective*
very large, important or serious: *There are airports in all the **major** cities.* ◇ ***major** problems*
➲ OPPOSITE **minor¹**

major² (say **may**-juh) *noun* (*plural* **majors**)
an officer in the army

majority (say muh-**jo**-ri-tee) *noun* (*plural* **majorities**)
most things or people in a group: *The **majority** of people agreed with the new law.*
➲ OPPOSITE **minority**

make¹ (say **mayk**) *verb* (**making, made**)
1 to produce or create something: *They **make** cars here.* ◇ *She is **making** a box out of wood.* ◇ *This shirt is **made** of cotton.* ◇ *I **made** the bedroom into an office.*
2 to cause something to be or to happen: *Stop **making** that noise!* ◇ *My father **made** me stay at home.* ◇ *Chocolate **makes** you fat.* ◇ *I **made** a mistake.*
3 to choose somebody to do a job: *They **made** him President.*
4 a word that you use with money, numbers and time: *She **makes** (= earns) a lot of money.* ◇ *Five and seven **make** twelve.*
make something up to tell somebody something that is not true: *I don't believe that story – he **made** it **up**!* ➲ SYNONYM **invent** 2
make up to become friends again after an argument: *They had an argument but they've **made up** now.*
make a bed to put sheets, blankets, etc. tidily on a bed, ready for someone to sleep in it: *I have to **make** my bed every morning.*

make² (say **mayk**) *noun* (*plural* **makes**)
the name of the company that made something: *'What **make** is your car?' 'It's a Ford.'*

maker (say **mayk**-uh) *noun* (*plural* **makers**)
a person, company or machine that makes something: *a film **maker***

make-up (say **mayk**-up) *noun* (*no plural*)
special powders and creams that you put on your face to make yourself more beautiful, or that actors wear when they are acting: *She put on her **make-up**.*

mal- *prefix*
bad or badly, or not correct or correctly: ***malnutrition*** ◇ ***malfunction*** ◇ *The animals have been **maltreated**.*
🛈 ORIGIN: through French *mal* from Latin *male* meaning 'badly'

malady (say **mal**-uh-dee) *noun* (*plural* **maladies**)
a disease

A B C D E F G H I J K L M N O P Q R S T U V W X Y Z

malapropism (say **mal**-uh-prop-iz-m) *noun* (*plural* **malapropisms**)
a mistake in which you use the wrong word, usually with a funny result: *Saying 'tangle dancers' instead of 'tango dancers' is a **malapropism**.*

malaria (say muh-**lair**-ri-uh) *noun* (*no plural*)
a serious disease that you get in hot countries from the bite of a small flying insect (called a **mosquito**)
ℹ ORIGIN: 18th century, from Italian *mal'aria* meaning 'bad air'. People used to believe that bad air was the cause of malaria.

Malay (say muh-**lay**) *noun* (*no plural*)
the language of the people who live in Malaysia and Indonesia

male (say **mayl**) *adjective*
belonging to the sex that does not give birth to babies nor produce eggs: *A ram is a **male** sheep.*
▸ **male** (*noun*): *The **males** of this species are bigger than the females.* ➲ See **female**[1]

malformed (say mal-**fawm**-d) *adjective*
not correctly formed

malfunction (say mal-**funk**-shuhn) *verb* (**malfunctioning**, **malfunctioned**)
to not work properly: *The machine **malfunctioned**.*

malice (say **mal**-iss) *noun* (*no plural*)
a wish to hurt other people: *She attacked him with **malice**.*
▸ **malicious** (*adjective*): *It was a **malicious** thing to do.* ▸ **maliciously** (*adverb*)

malign (say muh-**line**) *verb* (**maligning**, **maligned**)
to speak about someone in a cruel and critical way: *Don't **malign** my friend.*
▸ **malign** (*adjective*): *his **malign** influence*

malignant (say muh-**lig**-nuhnt) *adjective*
(used about a disease) dangerous, and likely to cause death if not controlled: *His tumour is **malignant**.* ➲ OPPOSITE **benign** 2

mall (say **mal** or **mawl**) *noun* (*plural* **malls**) (also **shopping mall**)
a large building that has a lot of shops and restaurants inside it

malleable (say **mal**-i-uhb-l) *adjective*
1 (used about metals) that can be hit or pressed into shape without breaking: *Lead is a **malleable** metal.*
2 (about people, opinions or ideas) easily influenced or changed
▸ **malleability** (*noun*)

mallet (say **mal**-it) *noun* (*plural* **mallets**)
a heavy wooden hammer

malnourished (say mal-**nu**-risht) *adjective*
not having enough food or the right kind of food: *The children were **malnourished** from never eating fresh fruit or vegetables.*

malnutrition (say mal-nyoo-**trish**-n) *noun* (*no plural*)
bad health as a result of not having enough food or the right kind of food: ***Malnutrition** is often associated with poverty.*

malombo (say muh-**lom**-boh) *noun* (*no plural*)
a style of music that combines traditional Venda drumming and other types of music
ℹ ORIGIN: 20th century, from *Malombo*, the group who created this style of music in the 1960s. Their name came from a traditional Venda ceremony.

malt (say **mawlt** or **molt**) *noun* (*no plural*)
a grain such as **barley** or **sorghum** that is used to make beer and other alcoholic drinks

maltreat (say mal **treet**) *verb* (**maltreating**, **maltreated**)
to treat a person or animal in a cruel or unkind way
▸ **maltreatment** (*noun*)

mama (say **mum**-uh) *noun* (*informal*)
1 (*plural* **mamas**) mother
2 (*no plural*) (*S. African*) a friendly form of address for an older woman: *How are you, **mama**?*

mamba (say **mum**-buh) *noun* (*plural* **mambas**)
a fast-moving and poisonous African snake
ℹ ORIGIN: from isiZulu *imamba*

mammal (say **mam**-l) *noun* (*plural* **mammals**)
any animal that gives birth to live babies, not eggs, and feeds its young on milk. They all have warm blood and most have hair on their bodies: *Dogs, whales and people are all **mammals**.*

mammoth (say **mam**-uth) *noun* (*plural* **mammoths**)
a very large animal, similar to an elephant, that no longer exists
ℹ ORIGIN: 18th century, from Russian *mamo(n)t*

man[1] *noun*
1 (*plural* **men**) an adult male person: *I saw a tall **man** with dark hair.*
2 (*no plural*) (*old-fashioned*) all humans or people: *the damage **man** has caused to the environment* ➲ See **humankind**, **mankind**
3 (*plural* **men**) (*old-fashioned*) any person: *All **men** are equal.*

WORD BUILDING Many people do not like using the word **man** to talk about all people as in meanings 2 and 3 above, and prefer to use **people** or **humans**.

man² *verb* (**manning, manned**)
to operate something, or to provide people to operate something: *The telephones were* ***manned*** *all day.*

manage (say **man**-ij) *verb* (**managing, managed**)
1 to be able to do something that is difficult: *The box was heavy but she* ***managed*** *to carry it to the car.*
2 to control somebody or something: *She* ***manages*** *a department of 30 people.*

management (say **man**-ij-muhnt) *noun* (*no plural*)
1 the control of something, for example a business, and the people who work in it: *Teachers must show good classroom* ***management***.
2 all the people who control a business: *The hotel is now under new* ***management***.

manager (say **man**-i-juh) *noun* (*plural* **managers**)
a person who controls an organization, a business or a shop: *He is the* ***manager*** *of a shoe shop.* ◇ *a bank* ***manager***

managing director *noun* (*plural* **managing directors**)
the person who controls a big business or company

mandarin (say **man**-duh-rin) *noun* (*plural* **mandarins**)
a type of small orange, similar to a **naartjie**

mandate (say **man**-dayt) *noun* (*plural* **mandates**)
the responsibility and the power to do a job, that is given to someone: *The finance ministry's* ***mandate*** *is to create a stable economic environment.*

mandible (say **man**-dib-l) *noun* (*plural* **mandibles**)
1 the lower of the two bones in your face that contain your teeth
2 the part of an animal's mouth (especially of an insect or bird), used for biting and crushing food ➲ See **maxilla**

Mandrax™ (say **man**-drakss) *noun* (*no plural*)
a dangerous and illegal drug, originally used legally as a sedative (= medicine that makes you feel calm or want to sleep)

mane (say **mayn**) *noun* (*plural* **manes**)
the long hair on the neck of some animals, for example horses and lions ➲ See illustration at **horse**

manganese (say **mang**-guh-neez) *noun* (*no plural*) (symbol Mn)
a type of hard grey metal used in making steel

manger (say **mayn**-juh) *noun* (*plural* **mangers**)
a large open container for farm animals to eat from

mangle (say **mang**-guhl) *verb* (**mangling, mangled**)
to damage something so badly that you cannot see what it looked like before: *The cars were* ***mangled*** *in the accident.*

mango (say **mang**-goh) *noun* (*plural* **mangoes**)
a fruit that grows in hot countries and that is yellow or red on the outside and yellow on the inside
🛈 **ORIGIN**: 16th century, through Portuguese *manga* from Dravidian, a language spoken in India

mangrove (say **mang**-grohv) *noun* (*plural* **mangroves**)
a tropical tree or smaller plant that grows in wet ground along the coast or on the edge of rivers near the sea: *a* ***mangrove*** *swamp*

manhole (say **man**-hohl) *noun* (*plural* **manholes**)
a hole in the road with a lid over it through which somebody can enter to check underground pipes and wires

manhood (say **man**-huud) *noun* (*no plural*)
1 the state of being a man rather than a boy
2 the qualities we think of as connected to men, such as strength and bravery: *They proved their* ***manhood*** *by fighting.*

mania (say **mayn**-i-uh) *noun* (*plural* **manias**)
1 (*informal*) a great enthusiasm for something: *World Cup* ***mania***
2 a serious mental illness that may make a person very excited or violent

maniac (say **mayn**-i-ak) *noun* (*plural* **maniacs**)
1 a person who behaves in a wild and stupid way: *He drives like a* ***maniac***.
2 a person who has a stronger love of something than is normal: *a cricket* ***maniac***

manic (say **man**-ik) *adjective* (*informal*)
full of activity and excitement: *Things are* ***manic*** *in the office at the moment.*

manicure (say **man**-i-kyoor) *noun* (*plural* **manicures**)
a treatment to make your hands and fingernails look attractive
▸ **manicure** (*verb*)

manifest (say **man**-i-fest) *verb* (**manifesting, manifested**)
to show something or be shown clearly:

A B C D E F G H I J K L M N O P Q R S T U V W X Y Z

*The disease **manifests** as a rash.*
▸ **manifestation** (*noun*)

manifesto (say man-i-**fess**-toh) *noun* (*plural* **manifestos**)
a written statement by a political party that explains what it hopes to do if it becomes the government

manioc (say **man**-i-ok) *noun* (*no plural*)
= **cassava**

manipulate (say muh-**nip**-yuu-layt) *verb* (**manipulating, manipulated**)
to influence somebody so that they do or think what you want: *Some politicians know how to **manipulate** people's opinions.*

mankind (say **man**-kynd) *noun* (*no plural*) (*old-fashioned*)
all the people in the world
➲ See **humankind**

WORD BUILDING Many people do not like the use of the word **mankind** to talk about all people, and prefer to use **humankind**.

man-made (say man-**mayd**) *adjective*
made by people, not formed in a natural way: ***man-made** materials* ➲ SYNONYM **artificial**

manner (say **man**-uh) *noun*
1 (*no plural*) the way that you do something or the way that something happens: *Don't get angry. Let's try to talk in a calm **manner**.*
2 manners (*plural noun*) the way you behave when you are with other people: *It's bad **manners** to talk with your mouth full.*

manoeuvre (say muh-**noo**-vuh) *noun* (*plural* **manoeuvres**)
1 a movement that needs care or skill: *Getting into that parking space will need a clever **manoeuvre**.*
2 something clever that you do to win something or trick somebody: *a clever political **manoeuvre***
3 manoeuvres (*plural noun*) a way of training a large group of soldiers to fight in battles: *They were on **manoeuvres**.*
▸ **manoeuvre** (*verb*): ***Manoeuvre** the car into this space.*

manor (say **man**-uh) *noun* (*plural* **manors**)
a large house in the country that has land around it

manpower (say **man**-pow-uh) *noun* (*no plural*)
the people that you need to do a certain job: *Is there enough **manpower** to complete the building in time?*

mansion (say **man**-shuhn) *noun* (*plural* **mansions**)
a very big house

manslaughter (say **man**-slaw-tuh) *noun* (*no plural*)
the crime of killing a person, but without meaning to: *She was charged with **manslaughter** but not murder.*

mantelpiece (say **man**-tuhl-peess) *noun* (*plural* **mantelpieces**)
a narrow shelf above the place where a fire is in a room (called the **fireplace**): *She has photographs of her children on the **mantelpiece**.*

mantis (say **man**-tiss) *noun* (*plural* **mantises**) (also **praying mantis**)
an insect with a long body and strong front legs with **barbs** that eats other living insects: *We saw a praying **mantis** catch and eat a bee.*

mantle (say **mant**-l) *noun* (*plural* **mantles**)
1 a layer of something that covers other things: *a **mantle** of snow*
2 the layer of the Earth between the surface and the centre ➲ See illustration at **earth**[1] 1

manual[1] (say **man**-yuu-uhl) *adjective*
using your hands: *Do you prefer **manual** work or office work?*
▸ **manually** (*adverb*): *This machine is operated **manually**.*

manual[2] (say **man**-yuu-uhl) *noun* (*plural* **manuals**)
a book that tells you how to do something: *Where is the instruction **manual** for the DVD player?*

manufacture (say man-yuu-**fak**-tshuh) *verb* (**manufacturing, manufactured**)
to make things in a factory using machines: *The company **manufactures** radios.*
▸ **manufacture** (*noun*): *the **manufacture** of cars*

manufacturer (say man-yuu-**fak**-tshuh-ruh) *noun* (*plural* **manufacturers**)
a person or company that makes something: *If it doesn't work, you must send it back to the **manufacturers**.*

manufacturing (say man-yuu-**fak**-tshuh-ring) *noun* (*no plural*)
the business of making things in a factory using machines: *the role of **manufacturing** in the economy*

manure (say muh-**nyoor**) *noun* (*no plural*)
the waste matter from animals that is put on the ground to help plants grow better

manuscript (say **man**-yuu-skript) *noun* (*plural* **manuscripts**)
1 a copy of a book before it has been printed
2 a very old book or document that was written by hand

many (say **men**-ee) *adjective, pronoun* (**more**, **most**)
a large number of people or things: ***Many** people in this country are very poor.* ◇ *There aren't **many** students in my class.* ◇ ***Many** of these books are very old.* ◇ *There are too **many** mistakes in your homework.* ◇ *Take as **many** cakes as you want.* ➲ See **much**[1]
how many? what number of?: *How **many** brothers and sisters do you have?*

WHICH WORD? **How many** or **how much**?
- We use **how many** to ask about things that have a plural, such as **books**: *How **many** books have you read?*
- We use **how much** to ask about things that have no plural, such as **sand**: *How **much** sand do we need?*

map *noun* (*plural* **maps**)
a drawing of a town, a country or the world that shows things such as mountains, rivers and roads: *Can you find Durban on the **map**?* ◇ *a street **map** of the town*

WORD BUILDING A book of maps is called an **atlas**.

maple (say **mayp**-l) *noun* (*plural* **maples**)
a large tree that grows in the northern parts of the world and produces a very sweet liquid that you can eat: ***maple** syrup*

marabi (say muh-**raa**-bee) *noun* (*no plural*) (*S. African*)
a style of dance music with a strong beat that was popular in **township** dance halls in the 1920s to 1940s
🛈 ORIGIN: 20th century, possibly from Sesotho *marabi* meaning 'gangsters' or from Marabastad, the name of a former township

maraca (say muh-**rak**-uh) *noun* (*plural* **maracas**)
a musical instrument that is made from a fruit that has been dried and emptied to make a container (called a **gourd**) that is filled with small beans or stones and shaken

marathon (say **ma**-ruh-thuhn) *noun* (*plural* **marathons**)
a very long road race when people run about 42 kilometres

marauding (say muh-**rawd**-ing) *adjective*
going about looking for people to attack or things to steal: *a **marauding** gang of thieves*
▸ **marauder** (*noun*)

marble (say **maab**-l) *noun*
1 (*no plural*) a hard attractive stone that is used to make statues and parts of buildings: ***Marble** is always cold when you touch it.*
2 (*plural* **marbles**) a small glass ball that you use in a children's game: *The children are playing **marbles**.*

March (say **maach**) *noun*
the third month of the year
🛈 ORIGIN: 13th–15th century, through Old French *marz* from Latin *Martius mensis* meaning 'month of Mars'. Mars was the ancient Roman god of war.

march[1] (say **maach**) *verb* (**marching**, **marched**)
1 to walk like a soldier: *The soldiers **marched** along the road.*
2 to walk somewhere quickly in a determined way: *She **marched** up to the manager and asked for her money back.*
3 to walk through the streets in a large group to show that you do not agree with something: *They **marched** through the town shouting 'Stop the war!'*

march[2] (say **maach**) *noun* (*plural* **marches**)
1 a journey made by soldiers walking together: *The soldiers were tired after the long **march**.*
2 an organized walk by a large group of people who want to show that they do not agree with something: *a peace **march***
➲ See **demonstration** 1

mare (say **mair**) *noun* (*plural* **mares**)
a female horse

margarine (say maa-juh-**reen**) *noun* (*no plural*)
soft yellow food that looks like butter, but is not made of milk. You put it on bread or use it in cooking.

margin (say **maa**-jin) *noun* (*plural* **margins**)
the space at the side of a page that has no writing or pictures in it

marginal (say **maa**-jin-l) *adjective*
small in size or importance: *We only made **marginal** changes.*
▸ **marginalize** (*verb*) (also **marginalise**): *We were **marginalized*** (= made to feel as if we are not important) *at the competition.*
▸ **marginally** (*adverb*): *She's feeling **marginally** better.*

marijuana (say ma-ruh-**waa**-nuh) *noun* (*no plural*)
a drug made from the dried flowers and leaves of a plant (called **cannabis**) ➲ SYNONYM **dagga**

marimba (say muh-**rim**-buh) *noun* (*plural* **marimbas**)
an African musical instrument with bars that

A B C D E F G H I J K L M N O P Q R S T U V W X Y Z

A B C D E F G H I J K L M N O P Q R S T U V W X Y Z

you hit to make different sounds
➲ See **xylophone**

marine[1] (say muh-**reen**) *adjective*
1 of or relating to the sea: ***marine** biology*
2 relating to ships or sailing: ***marine** insurance*

marine[2] (say muh-**reen**) *noun* (*plural* **marines**)
a soldier who is trained to serve on land or at sea

marionette (say ma-ri-uh-**net**) *noun* (*plural* **marionettes**)
a small model of a person or animal that you move by pulling strings ➲ See **puppet**

marital (say **ma**-rit-l) *adjective*
connected with marriage: *I'm looking for **marital** advice.*
marital status whether you are married, single or divorced: *What is your **marital** status?*

mark[1] (say **maak**) *verb* (**marking, marked**)
1 to put a sign on something by writing or drawing on it: *The price is **marked** on the bottom of the box.*
2 to show where something is: *This cross **marks** the place where he died.*
3 to look at school work to see how good it is: *The teacher **marked** all my answers wrong.*

mark[2] (say **maak**) *noun* (*plural* **marks**)
1 a spot or line that spoils the appearance of something: *There's a dirty **mark** on your shirt.*
2 a shape or special sign on something: *This **mark** shows that the ring is made of silver.* ◇ *punctuation **marks***
3 a number or letter that a teacher gives for your work to show how good it is: *She got very good **marks** in the exam.* ➲ SYNONYM **grade**[1] 3

market[1] (say **maa**-kit) *noun* (*plural* **markets**)
1 a place where people go to buy and sell things, usually outside: *There is a fruit and vegetable **market** in the town.*
2 the people who want to buy something: *There is a big **market** for computers.*

market[2] (say **maa**-kit) *verb* (**marketing, marketed**)
to sell something using advertisements: *Companies spend millions **marketing** their products.*

marketing (say **maa**-kit-ing) *noun* (*no plural*)
using advertisements to help a company sell its products: *Sales can be improved by good **marketing**.*

marmalade (say **maa**-muh-layd) *noun* (*no plural*)
a type of jam made from oranges or lemons: *We had toast and **marmalade** for breakfast.*

maroon[1] (say muh-**roon**) *adjective, noun*
(having) a colour between brown and purple

maroon[2] (say muh-**roon**) *verb* (**marooning, marooned**)
to leave a person alone in a place that they cannot get away from: *The sailor was **marooned** on an island.*

marquee (say maa-**kee**) *noun* (*plural* **marquees**)
a very large tent that is used for functions such as parties and weddings

marriage (say **ma**-rij) *noun* (*plural* **marriages**)
1 the state of two people being together as husband and wife: *They had a long and happy **marriage**.*
2 the ceremony in which two people become husband and wife: *The **marriage** will take place in church.* ➲ SYNONYM **wedding**

married (say **ma**-rid) *adjective*
having a husband or a wife: *He is **married** to Helen.* ➲ OPPOSITES **single**[1] 3, **unmarried**
get married to take somebody as your husband or wife: *They got **married** last year.*

marry (*rhymes with* **carry**) *verb* (**marrying, married**)
to take somebody as your husband or wife: *Will you **marry** me?* ◇ *They **married** when they were young.* ◇ *They got **married** last year*

> USAGE It is more usual to say **get married**: *They'll **get married** next year. They **got married** yesterday.*

marsh (say **maash**) *noun* (*plural* **marshes**)
soft wet ground

marshal (say **maash**) *noun* (*plural* **marshals**)
a person who helps to organize and control a large public event: ***Marshals** directed the cyclists in the race.*
▸ **marshal** (*verb*): *He **marshalled** the troops.*

marshmallow (say maash-**mal**-oh) *noun* (*plural* **marshmallows**)
a soft sweet that is usually pink or white

marsupial (say maa-**soop**-i-uhl) *noun* (*plural* **marsupials**)
any mammal that carries its baby in a pocket of skin **(pouch)** on the mother's stomach. There are many different types in Australia: *Kangaroos are **marsupials**.*

martial (say **maa**-shuhl) *adjective* (*formal*) relating to war ➲ SYNONYM **military**

martial art *noun* (*plural* **martial arts**)
a fighting sport such as **karate** in which you use your hands and feet as weapons

martyr (say **maa**-tuh) *noun* (*plural* **martyrs**)
1 a person who is killed because of what they

believe: *He was a **martyr** who died for his people's freedom.*
2 a person who tries to make people feel sorry for them: *Don't be such a **martyr**!*
▶ **martyr** (*verb*): *She was **martyred** for her beliefs.* ▶ **martyrdom** (*noun*)

marula (say muh-**ruu**-luh) *noun* (*plural* **marulas**)
a large African tree with yellow fruit that you can eat
ORIGIN: 19th century, from Afrikaans *maroela*, from Sesotho sa Leboa *morula*

marvel (say **maa**-vuhl) *noun* (*plural* **marvels**)
a person or thing that is wonderful or that surprises you: *He was a **marvel** to watch on the field.*
▶ **marvel** (*verb*): *They **marvelled** at all their presents.*

marvellous (say **maa**-vuh-luhss) *adjective*
very good: *I had a **marvellous** holiday.*
➲ SYNONYMS **wonderful, fantastic**

Marxism (say **maak**-siz-m) *noun* (*no plural*)
the political and economic **ideology** of Karl Marx ➲ See **communism, socialism, capitalism**
▶ **Marxist** (*adjective*): ***Marxist** ideas*

masala (say muh-**saa**-luh) *noun* (*no plural*)
a mixture of spices used in Indian cooking
ORIGIN: through Urdu *masālah*, from Arabic *maṣāliḥ* meaning 'ingredients, materials'. Urdu is a language spoken by many people in Pakistan and India.

mascara (say muh-**skaa**-ruh) *noun* (*no plural*)
a beauty product that you use to make the hairs around your eyes (called **eyelashes**) dark and attractive

mascot (say **mass**-kot) *noun* (*plural* **mascots**)
a person, animal or thing that people think brings them good luck, especially one linked to a particular organization or event: *The **mascot** for the 2010 World Cup is a little leopard with green hair called Zakumi.*

masculine (say **mass**-kyuu-lin) *adjective*
typical of a man or right for a man: *a **masculine** voice* ➲ See **feminine**

mash *verb* (**mashing, mashed**)
to press and mix food to make it soft: ***mashed** potatoes*

mask¹ (say **maask**) *noun* (*plural* **masks**)
a thing that you wear over your face to hide or protect it: *The children made animal **masks** for the play.* ◇ *The doctors and nurses wore **masks**.*

mask² (say **maask**) *verb* (**masking, masked**)
1 to cover or hide your face with a mask
2 to hide something such as a feeling, smell or fact with something else: *He **masked** his fear with a smile.* ➲ SYNONYM **obscure²**

mason (say **may**-suhn) *noun* (*plural* **masons**)
a person who builds or works with stone
▶ **masonry** (*noun*): *After the building collapsed there were piles of **masonry** across the road.*

masquerade (say mass-kuh-**rayd**) *noun* (*plural* **masquerades**)
a way of behaving that hides the truth or your true feelings: *His smile was a **masquerade** hiding his fear.*
▶ **masquerade** (*verb*): *They **masqueraded** as lawyers to get into court.*

Mass (say **mass**) *noun* (*plural* **Masses**)
an important religious ceremony, especially in the Roman Catholic Church: *She goes to **Mass** every Sunday.*

mass (say **mass**) *noun*
1 (*plural* **masses**) a large amount or quantity of something without a clear shape: *a **mass** of rock* ◇ ***masses** of clouds*
2 (*no plural*) (*science*) the quantity of matter in an object: ***Mass** is measured in grams.*
3 masses (*plural noun*) (*informal*) a large amount or number of something: *I've got **masses** of work to do.* ➲ See **lot¹**

> WHICH WORD? **Mass** or **weight**?
> Be careful! In science, **mass** (with meaning 2 above) and **weight** are not the same. **Mass** is the amount of matter in an object, whereas the **weight** of an object is the force of gravity acting on it. Your **weight** can change if the force of gravity changes (for example, if you are on the moon) but your **mass** always stays the same, wherever you are.

massacre (say **mass**-uh-kuh) *noun* (*plural* **massacres**)
the cruel killing of a lot of people
▶ **massacre** (*verb*): *The army **massacred** hundreds of women and children.*

massage (say muh-**saaj** or **mass**-aaj) *noun* (*plural* **massages**)
the act of rubbing somebody's body to get rid of pain or help them relax: *Do you want me to give you a **massage**?*
▶ **massage** (*verb*): *She **massaged** my back.*

massive (say **mass**-iv) *adjective*
very big: *The house is **massive** – it has sixteen bedrooms!* ➲ SYNONYM **huge**

mast (say **maast**) *noun* (*plural* **masts**)
1 a tall piece of wood or metal that holds the sails on a boat ➲ See illustration at **yacht**
2 a very tall metal pole that sends out sounds

or pictures for radio or television, or cellphone signals

master[1] (say **maa**-stuh) *noun* (*plural* **masters**)
1 a man who has people or animals in his control: *The dog ran to its **master**.*
2 a man who is very good at something: *paintings by the Italian **masters***

master[2] (say **maa**-stuh) *verb* (**mastering, mastered**)
to learn how to do something well: *It takes a long time to **master** a foreign language.*

masterpiece (say **maa**-stuh-peess) *noun* (*plural* **masterpieces**)
a very good painting, book, film or play: *'War and Peace' was Tolstoy's **masterpiece**.*

masturbate (say **mass**-tuh-bayt) *verb* (**masturbating, masturbated**)
to make yourself or somebody else sexually excited by touching and rubbing the sex organs
▸ **masturbation** (*noun*)

mat *noun* (*plural* **mats**)
1 a small carpet that covers a part of the floor: *Wipe your feet on the **mat** before you go in.*
➲ See **rug** 1
2 a small thing that you put under something on a table: *a table **mat*** (= that you put plates and dishes on)

matador (say **mat**-uh-daw) *noun* (*plural* **matadors**)
a person who fights with a bull to entertain a crowd of spectators (= people watching an event)

match[1] (say **mach**) *noun* (*plural* **matches**)
1 a short thin piece of wood that you use to light a fire or a cigarette: *He struck a **match** and lit his cigarette.* ◇ *a box of **matches***
2 a game between two people or teams: *a football **match*** ◇ *a boxing **match***
3 something that looks good with something else, for example because it has the same colour, shape or pattern: *Your shoes and dress are a good **match**.*

match[2] (say **mach**) *verb* (**matching, matched**)
1 to find something that is like another thing or that you can put with it: ***Match** the word with the right picture.*
2 to have the same colour, shape or pattern as something else, or to look good with something else: *That scarf doesn't **match** your dress.*
▸ **matching** (*adjective*): *She was wearing a blue skirt and **matching** jacket.*

matchbox (say **mach**-bokss) *noun* (*plural* **matchboxes**)
a small box for matches

mate[1] (say **mayt**) *noun* (*plural* **mates**)
1 (*informal*) a friend: *He went out with his **mates** last night.*
2 a person who lives, works or studies with you: *André is one of my **classmates**.* ◇ *a **flatmate***
3 one of two animals that come together to make young animals: *In spring the birds look for **mates**.*

mate[2] (say **mayt**) *verb* (**mating, mated**)
(used about animals) to have sex in order to produce young animals: *The cow and the bull have **mated**.*

material[1] (say muh-**teer**-ri-uhl) *noun*
1 (*no plural*) cloth that you use for making clothes and other things such as curtains: *I don't have enough **material** to make a dress.*
➲ SYNONYM **fabric**
2 (*plural* **materials**) what you use for making or doing something: *Wood and stone are building **materials**.* ◇ *writing **materials*** (= pens, pencils and paper, for example)

material[2] (say muh-**teer**-ri-uhl) *adjective*
relating to real or physical things rather than the spirit or emotions: ***material** needs and wants*
➲ SYNONYM **tangible**
▸ **materialism** (*noun*) *the **materialism** of modern society*
▸ **materialist** (*noun*) *Tom is spiritual, but Max is a **materialist**.*
▸ **materialistic** (*adjective*): *He's so **materialistic**: he respects only wealthy people.*

materialize (say muh-**teer**-ri-uh-lize) *verb* (**materializing, materialized**) (also **materialise**)
to become real or to happen: *The money they promised never **materialized**.*

maternal (say muh-**turn**-l) *adjective*
1 behaving like a mother: *She's not very **maternal**.* ◇ ***maternal** love*
2 (used about relations) from your mother's side of the family: *my **maternal** grandfather*
➲ See **paternal**

maternity (say muh-**tur**-ni-tee) *adjective*
relating to women who are going to have or have just had a baby: ***maternity** leave* ◇ ***maternity** clothes*

mathematician (say math-uh-muh-**tish**-uhn) *noun* (*plural* **mathematicians**)
a person who is an expert at mathematics

mathematics (say math-uh-**mat**-ikss) (*no plural*) (also **maths**)
the study of numbers, measurements and

shapes: *Maths is my favourite subject.*
▸ **mathematical** (*adjective*): *a **mathematical** problem*

maths (say **maths**s) (*informal*) **mathematics**

matriarch (say **may**-tri-aak) *noun* (*plural* **matriarchs**)
a woman or female animal who is the head of a family or social group ➲ See **patriarch**
▸ **matriarchal** (*adjective*): *a **matriarchal** society* ▸ **matriarchy** (*noun*)

matric (say muh-**trik**) *noun*
1 (*no plural*) a national examination written at the end of Grade 12 in South Africa: *When are you writing **matric**?*
2 (*plural* **matrics**) a learner in Grade 12: *The **matrics** are writing exams.*
3 (*no plural*) Grade 12: *I am in **matric**.*
▸ **matriculant** (*noun*): *My sisters are both **matriculants**: one's in Grade 12 now and one passed **matric** last year.*

matriculate (say muh-**trik**-yuu-layt) *verb* (**matriculating, matriculated**)
to pass the examination at the end of Grade 12: *I **matriculated** in 2001.*

matriculation (say muh-trik-yuu-**lay**-shuhn) *noun* (*no plural*) = **matric 1**

matrimony (say **mat**-ri-muh-nee) *noun* (*no plural*)
the state of being married: *joined in **matrimony***
▸ **matrimonial** (*adjective*): ***matrimonial** bliss*

matrix (say **may**-trikss) *noun* (*plural* **matrices**)
1 (*maths*) an arrangement of numbers or symbols in rows and columns, treated as a single quantity
2 (*formal*) a system of lines and roads that cross each other, forming a series of shapes or squares in between: *a **matrix** of roads*
➲ SYNONYMS **grid, network**
3 (*formal*) the social, political and economic situation from which a society or person grows and develops: *the cultural **matrix***
4 a container into which a liquid is poured to make a shape ➲ SYNONYM **mould**[1] **1**
5 a mass of rock in which minerals and precious stones are found in the ground

matron (say **may**-truhn) *noun* (*plural* **matrons**)
1 (*old-fashioned*) a woman who is in charge of other nurses in a hospital
2 a woman who is in charge of the living arrangements in a school where learners live (called a **boarding school**)
▸ **matronly** (*adjective*)

matt (say **mat**) *adjective*
(used about a colour or surface) not shiny: *Do you want **matt** or shiny paint?*

matted (say **mat**-id) *adjective*
(used about hair) forming a thick mass, especially because it is wet or dirty: *The dog's coat is **matted**.*

matter[1] (say **mat**-uh) *verb* (**mattering, mattered**)
to be important: *It doesn't **matter** if you're late – we'll wait for you.*

matter[2] (say **mat**-uh) *noun*
1 (*plural* **matters**) something that you must talk about or do: *Let's discuss this **matter**.*
2 (*no plural*) the physical substances that all things are made of, such as rocks, air, water, plants and animals: *In Science we study the properties of **matter**.*
the matter with a person or **thing** the reason for problems or unhappiness, for example: *What's the **matter** with him? Why is he crying?*
as a matter of fact words that you use when you say something true, important or interesting: *I like Munir a lot. As a **matter** of fact, he's my best friend.*
no matter how, what, when, who words that you use to say that something is always true: *No **matter** how hard I try, I can't get 100% for Maths!*

mattress (say **mat**-ruhss) *noun* (*plural* **mattresses**)
the thick soft part of a bed

mature (say muh-**tyoor**) *adjective*
1 behaving in a sensible way like an adult
2 fully grown or fully developed ➲ OPPOSITE **immature**
▸ **mature** (*verb*): *He has **matured** a lot since he left school.* ▸ **maturity** (*noun*)

maul (say **mawl**) *verb* (**mauling, mauled**)
to attack and injure very badly: *The hyena **mauled** the tourist.*

mausoleum (say maw-suh-**lee**-uhm) *noun* (*plural* **mausoleums**)
a building containing the bodies of important people who have died

mauve (*rhymes with* **stove**) *adjective*
pale purple

maverick (say **mav**-uh-rik) *noun* (*plural* **mavericks**)
a person who does not behave or think like everyone else, but who has independent, unusual opinions
❶ ORIGIN: 19th century, after Samuel Maverick (1803–1870), a farmer in the USA. He did not mark his cows and they became known as *mavericks*. The word came to mean 'not belonging to any group, independent'.

maxilla (say mak-**sil**-uh) *noun* (*plural* **maxillae**)
1 the upper of the two bones in your face that contain your teeth
2 the mouth part of an insect that lies behind the **mandibles** (= biting and crushing mouth parts) used for swallowing food

maximum (say **mak**-si-muhm) *noun* (*plural* **maximums** or **maxima**)
the biggest possible size, amount or number: *This plane can carry a **maximum** of 150 people.*
➲ OPPOSITE **minimum**
▸ **maximum** (*adjective*): *We drove at a **maximum** speed of 120 kilometres per hour.*

May *noun*
the fifth month of the year
ℹ ORIGIN: from Old English, through Old French *mai*, from Latin *Maius mensis* meaning 'month of the goddess Maia'. Maia was a goddess of the ancient Romans.

may (say **may**) *modal verb*
1 a word that shows what will perhaps happen or what is possible: *I **may** go to Spain next year.* ◇ *He **may** not be here.*
2 (*formal*) to be allowed to do something: *May I open the window?* ◇ *You **may** go now.*

WHICH WORD? **May** or **can**?
- **Can** is used to mean **able** to do something: *Can you swim?* (Do you know how to swim?)
- In formal English **may** is used to mean **allowed** to do something: *May we swim?* (Are we allowed to swim?)
- In informal English we often use **can I** …? to mean **am I allowed to** …?

maybe (say **may**-bee) *adverb*
a word that shows that something may happen or may be true: ***Maybe** you should phone him.* ◇ *'Are you going out tonight?' '**Maybe**.'*
➲ SYNONYM **perhaps**

mayonnaise (say may-uh-**nayz**) *noun* (*no plural*)
a cold thick sauce made with eggs and oil

mayor (say **may**-uh) *noun* (*plural* **mayors**)
the leader of a group of people who control a town or city (called a **council**)
ℹ ORIGIN: 13th–15th century, through Old French *maire*, from Latin *major* meaning 'greater'

maze (say **mayz**) *noun* (*plural* **mazes**)
1 a system of paths that is designed to confuse you so that it is difficult to find your way out
2 any confusing network of paths: *a **maze** of winding roads* ➲ SYNONYM **labyrinth**

MB *abbreviation* (*plural* **MB**) (also **Mb**)
megabyte

mbaqanga (say m-buh-**kung**-guh) *noun* (*no plural*) (*S. African*)
a style of popular music developed in the 1950s that contains a mixture of different types of music
ℹ ORIGIN: 20th century, from isiZulu *umbaqanga* meaning 'traditional maize bread', because the music was the musician's own style as well as a way to earn a living.

PRONUNCIATION The **q** in **mbaqanga** is pronounced as a click. Listen to a speaker of isiZulu or isiXhosa saying it.

mbira (say m-**bee**-ruh) *noun* (*plural* **mbiras**)
a traditional African musical instrument that you play with your thumbs
ℹ ORIGIN: 19th century, from Shona, probably from *rimba* meaning 'a musical note'. Shona is a language spoken in Zimbabwe.

MD (say em-**dee**) *abbreviation* (*plural* **MDs**)
1 Doctor of Medicine
2 Managing Director

me (say **mee**) *pronoun* (*plural* **us**)
the person who is speaking: *He telephoned **me** yesterday.* ◇ *Give it to **me**.* ◇ *Hello, it's **me**.*

meadow (say **med**-oh) *noun* (*plural* **meadows**)
a field of grass

meagre (say **mee**-guh) *adjective*
too small in amount: *my **meagre** earnings*
➲ SYNONYM **scanty**

SPELLING Note that this word is spelt **-re**, not **-er**.

meal (say **meel**) *noun* (*plural* **meals**)
food that you eat at a certain time of the day: *What's your favourite **meal** of the day?* ◇ *We had a nice **meal** in that restaurant.*

mealie (say **mee**-lee) *noun* (*plural* **mealies**) (also **mielie**) (*S. African*)
a South African word for **maize**
ℹ ORIGIN: 19th century, through Afrikaans *mielie* from Portuguese *milho* meaning 'maize, millet'

mealiemeal (say mee-lee-**meel**) *noun* (*no plural*) (*S. African*)
a powder made from crushed dry mealie seeds that people use for making **porridge**: *basic foods like **mealiemeal**, rice, salt, sugar and cooking oil*

mean[1] (say **meen**) *verb* (**meaning**, **meant**)
1 to have as a meaning: *What does 'medicine' **mean**?* ◇ *The red light **means** that you have to stop here.*

2 to plan or want to say something: *She said 'yes' but she really* ***meant*** *'no'.* ◇ *I don't understand what you* ***mean****.*
3 to plan or want to do something: *I didn't* ***mean*** *to hurt you.* ◇ *I* ***meant*** *to phone you, but I forgot.* ➲ SYNONYM **intend**
4 to make something happen: *This rain* ***means*** *there will be no sport today.*
5 to be important to somebody: *My family* ***means*** *a lot to me.*
be meant to to be supposed to (do something): *He's not* ***meant*** *to smoke here.*

mean² (say **meen**) *adjective* (**meaner, meanest**)
1 not liking to give things or to spend money: *Jim is very* ***mean*** *– he never shares his sweets.*
➲ OPPOSITE **generous**
2 unkind: *It was* ***mean*** *of you to say that Peter was fat.*

mean³ (say **meen**) *noun* (*plural* **means**)
1 (also **arithmetic mean**) the average of two or more quantities ➲ SYNONYM **average¹** 1
2 a point or number in the middle between two other numbers
► **mean** (*adjective*): *Our class has a* ***mean*** *age of fourteen.*

meander (say mi-**an**-duh) *verb* (**meandering, meandered**)
1 (used about a road, river or path) to have a lot of curves and bends: *The river* ***meandered*** *through the valley.*
2 (used about a person or animal) to walk or travel slowly without any definite direction: *They* ***meandered*** *through the market.*
➲ SYNONYM **wander** 1

meaning (say **meen**-ing) *noun* (*plural* **meanings**)
what something means or shows: *This word has two different* ***meanings****.*

means (say **meenz**) *noun* (*plural noun*)
a way of doing something, or a way of going somewhere: *Do you have any* ***means*** *of transport* (= a car, a bicycle, a motorbike) *?*
by means of something by using something: *We crossed the river by* ***means*** *of a small bridge.*

> USAGE **Means** can be treated as a singular or plural noun: *My* ***means*** *of transport is a bike.* ◇ *My* ***means*** *of transport are my bike and my car.*

meant (say **ment**) form of **mean¹**

meantime (say **meen**-time) *noun* (*no plural*)
in the meantime in the time between two things happening: *Our house isn't ready, so we're living here in the* ***meantime****.*

meanwhile (say **meen**-wile) *adverb*
at the same time as another thing is happening or in the time between two things happening: *I'm going to buy a bed soon, but* ***meanwhile*** *I'm sleeping on the floor.*

measles (say **meez**-uhlz) *noun* (*no plural*)
an illness that makes small red spots appear on your skin: *My little brother has got* ***measles****.* ◇ ***Measles*** *is a dangerous illness.*

measure¹ (say **me*zh***-uh) *verb* (**measuring, measured**)
1 to find the size, weight or amount of somebody or something: *Could you* ***measure*** *the window for me?*
2 to be a certain size or amount: *This room* ***measures*** *six metres across.*
ⓘ ORIGIN: 13th–15th century, through Old French from Latin *mensura* from *metiri* meaning 'to measure'

measure² (say **me*zh***-uh) *noun* (*plural* **measures**)
1 a way of showing the size or amount of something: *A metre is a* ***measure*** *of length.*
2 an action that somebody does in order to achieve something: *The government has taken* ***measures*** *to solve the problem.*

measurement (say **me*zh***-uh-muhnt) *noun* (*plural* **measurements**)
the size of something that is found by measuring it: *What are the* ***measurements*** *of the kitchen* (= how long and wide is it)*?*

meat (say **meet**) *noun* (*no plural*)
the parts of an animal or bird that you can eat: *You can buy* ***meat*** *at a butcher's.* ◇ *I don't eat* ***meat****.*

mechanic (say muh-**kan**-ik) *noun* (*plural* **mechanics**)
a person whose job is to repair or work with machines: *a car* ***mechanic***

mechanical (say muh-**kan**-ik-l) *adjective*
moved, done or made by a machine: *a* ***mechanical*** *toy*
► **mechanically** (*adverb*): *The pump is operated* ***mechanically****.*

mechanics (say muh-**kan**-ikss) *noun* (*no plural*)
the study of how machines work

mechanism (say **mek**-uh-niz-m) *noun* (*plural* **mechanisms**)
1 a set of moving parts in a machine that does a certain task: *The locking* ***mechanism*** *is broken.*
2 the way in which something works or is done: *There is a* ***mechanism*** *in place for changing your address.*

A B C D E F G H I J K L **M** N O P Q R S T U V W X Y Z

mechanize (say **mek**-uh-nize) *verb* (**mechanizing, mechanized**) (also **mechanise**) to use machines instead of people to do work: *We are **mechanizing** the process.*
▸ **mechanized** (*adjective*) (also **mechanised**): *We rely on a **mechanized** system.*
▸ **mechanization** (*noun*) (also **mechanisation**): *We rely on **mechanization**.*

medal (say **med**-l) *noun* (*plural* **medals**) a piece of metal with words and pictures on it that you get for doing something very good: *She won a gold **medal** in the Olympic Games.*

meddle (say **med**-l) *verb* (**meddling, meddled**) to take too much interest in people's private lives, or to touch something that you should not touch: *Stop **meddling** in my private life!* ◇ *He **meddled** with my kite and broke it.*
➲ SYNONYM **interfere** 1
▸ **meddler** (*noun*) ▸ **meddlesome** (*adjective*): *He's a **meddlesome** politician.*

media[1] plural of **medium**[2] 1

media[2] (say **mee**-di-uhm) *adjective* (say **mee**-di-uh) *plural noun* television, radio and newspapers used as a means of communication: *The reports in the **media** have been exaggerated.* ◇ *The **media** is responsible for this panic.* ◇ *The **media** are responsible for this panic.*

> USAGE **Media** is used as a singular and plural noun. Look carefully at the examples above.

mediaeval (say med-i-**eev**-l) = **medieval**

median[1] (say **mee**-di-uhn) *noun* (*plural* **medians**) (*maths*)
1 the middle value of a set of values arranged in order of size: *In the sequence of numbers 2, 4, 4, 6, 7, 8, 10, the **median** is 6.*
2 a straight line passing from a point of a triangle to the centre of the opposite side

median[2] (say **mee**-di-uhn) *adjective*
1 having a value in the middle of a series of values: *the **median** age*
2 located in or passing through the middle: *a **median** line*

mediate (say **mee**-di-ayt) *verb* (**mediating, mediated**) to try to end a disagreement between two or more people or groups: *He **mediated** for his colleagues.*
▸ **mediation** (*noun*) ▸ **mediator** (*noun*): *The **mediator** managed the meeting.*

medical (say **med**-ik-l) *adjective* connected with medicine, hospitals or doctors: *a **medical** student* ◇ ***medical** treatment*

medication (say med-i-**kay**-shuhn) *noun* (*plural* **medications**) medicine that the doctor has given you: *What **medication** are you taking?*

medicine (say **med**-suhn) *noun*
1 (*no plural*) the science of understanding illnesses and making sick people well again: *She's studying **medicine**.*
2 (*plural* **medicines**) special liquids or pills that help you to get better when you are ill: *Take this **medicine** every morning.*
ⓘ ORIGIN: 13th–15th century, through Old French from Latin *medicina*, from *medicus* meaning 'medical doctor'

medieval (say med-i-**eev**-l) *adjective* (also **mediaeval**) connected with the years between about 1100 and 1500 in Europe: *a **medieval** castle* ➲ See **Middle Ages**

mediocre (say mee-di-**oh**-kuh) *adjective* of not very high quality: *a **mediocre** essay*
▸ **mediocrity** (*noun*): *Don't settle for **mediocrity**.*

meditate (say **med**-i-tayt) *verb* (**meditating, meditated**) to think carefully and deeply, especially for spiritual reasons, or to keep your mind calm: *I **meditate** every day.* ◇ *I've **meditated** about what you said.*
▸ **meditation** (*noun*)

Mediterranean (say med-i-tuh-**ray**-ni-uhn) *adjective* relating to the Mediterranean Sea which lies between Europe and Africa, or the countries around it: *our **Mediterranean** holiday*
ⓘ ORIGIN: 16th century, from Latin *medius* meaning 'middle' + *terra* meaning 'land'. Originally the name meant '(sea) in the middle of the Earth'.

medium[1] (say **mee**-di-uhm) *adjective* not big and not small: *Would you like a small, **medium** or large drink?* ◇ *He is of **medium** height.*

medium[2] (say **mee**-di-uhm) *noun*
1 (*plural* **media** or **mediums**) a means you can use to express or communicate something: *English is the **medium** of instruction at my school.*
➲ See **media**
2 (*plural* **mediums**) a person who says that they can speak to spirits of dead people: *My dad wanted to speak to my gran through a **medium**.*
3 (*plural* **mediums**) a substance that something exists or grows in or travels through: *Soil is the best **medium** to grow seeds in.*

medley (say **med**-lee) *noun* (*plural* **medleys**)
1 a piece of music consisting of several songs or pieces of music played one after the other without a break
2 a mixture of different things: *a* ***medley*** *of flavours*
3 a swimming race in which you swim different sections in a different style: *the individual* ***medley***

meek *adjective* (**meeker**, **meekest**)
(used about people) quiet and doing what other people tell you to do: *She was* ***meek*** *and shy.* ➲ SYNONYM **docile**
▸ **meek** (*noun*): *The* ***meek*** *shall inherit the Earth.*
▸ **meekly** (*adverb*): *He* ***meekly*** *followed her lead.* ▸ **meekness** (*noun*)

meerkat (say **meer**-kut) *noun* (*plural* **meerkats**)
a small southern African mammal (a type of **mongoose**) with black marks around its eyes
🛈 ORIGIN: 18th century, through South African Dutch, from Dutch *meer* meaning 'sea' and *kat* meaning 'cat'. Earlier, the Dutch called a type of monkey a meerkat, and the South African animal probably looked similar.

meet *verb* (**meeting**, **met**)
1 to come together by chance or because you have planned it: *I* ***met*** *her in the library.* ◇ *Let's* ***meet*** *there at eight o'clock.*
2 to see and speak to somebody for the first time: *Have you* ***met*** *Anne?*
3 to go to a place and wait for somebody to arrive: *Can you* ***meet*** *me at the airport?*
4 to join together with something: *The two rivers* ***meet*** *in Mpumalanga.*

meeting (say **meet**-ing) *noun* (*plural* **meetings**)
1 a time when people come together for a special reason, usually to talk about something: *We had a* ***meeting*** *to talk about our plans.*
2 a time when two or more people come together: *Do you remember your first* ***meeting*** *with your husband?*

mega- (say **meg**-uh) *prefix*
1 (*informal*) large or great: *a computer* ***megastore***
2 (used in measurements) one million: *a* ***megawatt***
🛈 ORIGIN: from Greek *megas* meaning 'great'

megabyte (say **meg**-uh-bite) *noun* (*plural* **megabytes**) (*computing*) (abbr. MB or Mb)
a unit for measuring the size of information that is stored on a computer. 1 megabyte = 1 024 kilobytes. ➲ See note at **kilobyte**

megahertz (say **meg**-uh-hurtss) *noun* (*plural* **megahertz**) (abbr. MHz)
a unit for measuring **frequency** 3. One megahertz is equal to a million hertz.
➲ See **hertz**

melancholy (say **mel**-uhn-kuh-lee) *noun* (*no plural*)
a feeling of sadness which lasts for a long time
➲ SYNONYMS **sad**, **depressed**
▸ **melancholic** (*adjective*): *He's a* ***melancholic*** *man.*

melanin (say **mel**-uh-nin) *noun* (*no plural*)
a dark substance that gives colour to parts of our body (such as the skin, hair and eyes). Animals and plants have melanin too.

mellow (say **mel**-oh) *adjective* (**mellower**, **mellowist**)
1 (used about colours, flavours or sounds) soft and pleasant: *We need a* ***mellow*** *colour for the lounge walls.* ◇ ***mellow*** *jazz*
2 (used about people) calm and relaxed: *Our new teacher is* ***mellower*** *than last year's.*
▸ **mellow** (*verb*): *You've* ***mellowed*** *out a lot.*

melodrama (say **mel**-uh-draa-muh) *noun* (*plural* **melodramas**)
a story, play or film in which much happens and people's emotions are stronger than in real life.
▸ **melodramatic** (*adjective*): *Don't be so* ***melodramatic*** *– it's only a story!*

melody (say **mel**-uh-dee) *noun* (*plural* **melodies**)
a group of musical notes that make a nice sound when you play or sing them together: *This song has a lovely* ***melody***. ➲ SYNONYM **tune**[1]

melon (say **mel**-uhn) *noun* (*plural* **melons**)
a big round yellow or green fruit with a lot of seeds inside

melt *verb* (**melting**, **melted**)
to warm something so that it becomes liquid, or to get warmer so that it becomes liquid: ***Melt*** *the butter in a saucepan.* ◇ *The ice* ***melted*** *in the sunshine.*

member (say **mem**-buh) *noun* (*plural* **members**)
a person who is in a group: *I'm a* ***member*** *of the school football team.*

Member of Parliament *noun* (*plural* **Members of Parliament**) (abbr. MP)
a person who the people of a country or a province choose to speak for them in political matters, especially in **parliament**

membership (say **mem**-buh-ship) *noun* (*no plural*)
being in a group or an organization: ***Membership*** *of the club costs R80 a year.*

membrane (say **mem**-brayn) *noun* (*plural* **membranes**)
a thin skin or material covering a surface or separating cells or organs of plants and animals: *mucous **membranes** ◇ a cell **membrane** ◇ He applied a damp-proof **membrane** on his roof to stop the leak when it rained.*

membranophone (say mem-**bran**-uh-fohn) *noun* (*plural* **membranophones**)
a musical instrument such as a drum in which the sound is made by a thin stretched skin (called a **membrane**)

memo (say **mem**-oh) *noun* (*plural* **memos**)
a note that you write to a person who works with you: *I sent you a **memo** about the meeting on Friday.*

memoir (say **mem**-waa) *noun* (*plural* **memoirs**) (also **memoirs**)
a story of your life and experiences: *I'm reading Brenda Fassie's **memoirs**.* ➲ SYNONYM **autobiography**

memorable (say **mem**-uh-ruhb-l) *adjective*
easy to remember because it is special in some way: *Their wedding was a very **memorable** day.*

memorandum (say mem-uh-**ran**-duhm) *noun* (*plural* **memoranda**) = **memo**

memorial (say muh-**maw**-ri-uhl) *noun* (*plural* **memorials**)
something that people build or do to help us remember somebody, or something that happened: *The statue is a **memorial** to all the soldiers who died in the war.*

memorize (say **mem**-uh-rize) *verb* (**memorizing, memorized**) (also **memorise**)
to learn something so that you can remember it exactly: *We have to **memorize** a poem for homework.*

memory (say **mem**-uh-ree) *noun*
1 (*plural* **memories**) the ability to remember things: *I've got a good **memory** – I never forget names.*
2 (*plural* **memories**) something that you remember: *I have very happy **memories** of that holiday.*
3 (*no plural*) the part of a computer that holds information

men plural of **man**[1]

menace (say **men**-uhss) *noun*
1 (*plural* **menaces**) a danger or threat: *Drunk drivers are a **menace** on our roads.*
2 (*no plural*) a quality or feeling that is threatening or frightening: *There was **menace** in her warning.*
3 (*plural* **menaces**) a person or thing that causes trouble: *Your dog is a **menace** in the street.*
▶ **menace** (*verb*): *Our natural coastline is being **menaced** by more and more luxury holiday homes.* ▶ **menacing** (*adjective*)

menagerie (say muh-**naj**-uh-ree) *noun* (*plural* **menageries**)
1 (*old-fashioned*) a collection of wild animals kept in a place for other people to see
2 (*informal*) several different animals kept as pets: *They have a **menagerie** with two cats, two dogs, a hamster and a rabbit.*

mend *verb* (**mending, mended**)
to make something that is broken or damaged good again: *Can you **mend** this chair?*

menial (say **mee**-ni-uhl) *adjective*
(used about work) not skilled or important: ***menial** labour*

meningitis (say men-in-**jite**-uhss) *noun* (*no plural*)
an infection of the **membranes** covering the brain and the spinal cord (= the mass of nerves inside the length of your backbone)

menopause (say **men**-uh-pawz) *noun* (*no plural*)
the time of life when a woman stops **menstruating** and so can no longer have children
▶ **menopausal** (*adjective*): ***menopausal** symptoms*

menstruate (say **men**-struu-ayt) *verb* (**menstruating, menstruated**)
(used about a woman) to lose blood every month from the **uterus** (= the organ in a woman's body where a baby would develop)
▶ **menstrual** (*adjective*): *the **menstrual** cycle ◇ **menstrual** blood*
▶ **menstruation** (*noun*)

mental (say **men**-tuhl) *adjective*
of or in your mind: ***mental** illness ◇ **mental** arithmetic* (= done in your head)
▶ **mentally** (*adverb*): *He is **mentally** ill.*

mention (say **men**-shuhn) *verb* (**mentioning, mentioned**)
to speak or write about something without giving much information: *She **mentioned** that she was going to buy a new car. ◇ He didn't **mention** Anna in his letter.*
▶ **mention** (*noun*): *There was no **mention** of the accident in the newspaper.*

mentor (say **men**-tuh) *noun* (*plural* **mentors**)
an experienced person who advises and helps a person with less experience over a period of time: *My **mentor** showed me how to do the job.*
▶ **mentor** (*verb*): *Will you **mentor** me?*
ℹ ORIGIN: 18th century, from *Mentor*, an

adviser in the ancient Greek story of Odysseus written by Homer in the eighth century BC

menu (say **men**-yoo) *noun* (*plural* **menus**)
1 a list of the food that you can choose in a restaurant: *What's on the **menu** tonight?*
2 (*computing*) a list on the screen of a computer that shows what you can do: *Pull down the **menu** and click on New.*

mercantile (say **mur**-kuhn-tile) *adjective*
relating to buying and selling things
➲ SYNONYM **commercial**[1]

Mercator projection (say mur-**kay**-tuh pruh-jek-shuhn) *noun* (*no plural*) (*geography*)
a system of drawing maps so that lines of longitude and latitude are straight and the same length as the equator. This makes land at the top and bottom of the map appear much bigger than it is.
ℹ ORIGIN: named after Gerardus Mercator (1512–1594), who invented the system

mercenary[1] (say **mur**-suh-nuh-ree) *noun* (*plural* **mercenaries**)
a soldier who fights for any group or country that will pay them

mercenary[2] (say **mur**-suh-nuh-ree) *adjective*
interested only in making money: *She's a **mercenary** businesswoman.*

merchandise (say **mur**-chuhn-dise) *noun* (*no plural*)
goods that are for sale: *a range of **merchandise***
➲ SYNONYM **stock**[1]
▸ **merchandise** (*verb*): *You can **merchandise** your invention.* ▸ **merchandising** (*noun*): *They will earn money from **merchandising**.*

merchant (say **mur**-chuhnt) *noun* (*plural* **merchants**)
a person who buys and sells goods in large amounts

mercury (say **mur**-kyuh-ree) *noun* (*no plural*) (symbol Hg)
a heavy metal that is usually in liquid form. It is used in instruments that measure temperature (called **thermometers**)

mercy (say **mur**-see) *noun* (*no plural*)
kindness shown by a person who is in a position of power: *The prisoners begged for **mercy**.*
be at the mercy of a person or **thing** to have no power against a person or thing that is strong: *Farmers are at the **mercy** of the weather.*

mere (say **meer**) *adjective*
only or not more than: *She was a **mere** child when her parents died.*

merely (say **meer**-lee) *adverb*
only: *I don't want to buy the book – I **merely** asked the price.* ➲ SYNONYM **just**[1] 6

merge (say **murj**) *verb* (**merging, merged**)
to join together with something else: *Three small companies **merged** into one large one.*

meridian (say muh-**rid**-i-uhn) *noun* (*plural* **meridians**)
a line that we imagine on the surface of the Earth that joins the North Pole to the South Pole: *The Greenwich **Meridian** is a line of 0° longitude* ➲ See illustration at **globe**
➲ See **longitude**

meringue (say muh-**rang**) *noun* (*plural* **meringues**)
a white mixture made from egg whites and sugar, baked in the oven until crisp and used to make cakes

merino (say muh-**ree**-noh) *noun* (*plural* **merinos**)
a kind of sheep with very soft wool

merit[1] (say **me**-rit) *noun* (*plural* **merits**)
1 the thing or things that are good about somebody or something: *What are the **merits** of this plan?*
2 the quality of being excellent and deserving praise: *She got a **merit** for her performance.*

merit[2] (say **me**-rit) *verb* (**meriting, merited**)
(*formal*) to be good enough for something: *This suggestion **merits** further discussion.*
➲ SYNONYM **deserve**

mermaid (say **mur**-mayd) *noun* (*plural* **mermaids**)
(in stories) a woman who has the tail of a fish and lives in the sea

merry (*rhymes with* **very**) *adjective* (**merrier, merriest**)
happy and cheerful: ***Merry** Christmas!*

merry-go-round (say **me**-ree-goh-rownd) *noun* (*plural* **merry-go-rounds**) (also **roundabout**)
a big round machine with models of animals or cars on it. Children can ride on it as it turns.

mesembryanthemum (say mi-zem-bree-**an**-thi-muhm) *noun* (*plural* **mesembryanthemums**)
a plant with thick leaves and bright flowers that open in the sun ➲ SYNONYM **vygie**

mesh[1] *noun* (*no plural*)
a material that is like a net: *a wire **mesh** fence*

mesh[2] *verb* (**meshing, meshed**)
(of parts of a machine) to fit together as they move

A B C D E F G H I J K L M N O P Q R S T U V W X Y Z

mesmerize (say **mez**-muh-rize) *verb* (**mesmerizing**, **mesmerized**) (also **mesmerise**) to hold a person's attention completely: *We were **mesmerized** by the acrobats.*
➲ SYNONYM **fascinate**
ⓘ ORIGIN: from the name of Franz Mesmer (1734–1815), a doctor who treated his patients using hypnosis (a state similar to sleep)

mesosphere (say **mess**-uh-sfeer *or* **meess**-oh-sfeer) *noun* (*no plural*)
the mesosphere the cold middle layer of the Earth's atmosphere ➲ See illustration at **atmosphere** ➲ See **ionosphere**, **stratosphere**, **thermosphere**, **troposphere**

mess¹ *noun* (*no plural*)
1 a lot of untidy or dirty things all in the wrong place: *Your bedroom is in a **mess**.* ◇ *Don't make a **mess** in the kitchen.*
2 a person or thing that is untidy or dirty: *My hair is a **mess**!*
3 a difficult situation: *She's in a **mess** – she's got no money and nowhere to live.*

mess² *verb* (**messing**, **messed**)
mess about, **mess around** to behave in a silly way: *Stop **messing** around and finish your work!*
mess something up
1 to do something badly or make something go wrong: *The bad weather **messed** up our plans for the weekend.*
2 to make something untidy or dirty: *Don't **mess** my hair up!*

message (say **mess**-ij) *noun* (*plural* **messages**) words that one person sends to another: *Could you give a **message** to Jane, please?* ◇ *Mr Modise is not here at the moment. Can I take a **message**?*

messenger (say **mess**-in-juh) *noun* (*plural* **messengers**)
a person who brings a message

Messiah (say muh-**sy**-uh) *noun*
a person, for example Jesus Christ, who is expected to come and save the world

messy (say **mess**-ee) *adjective* (**messier**, **messiest**)
1 untidy or dirty: *a **messy** kitchen*
2 making you untidy or dirty: *Painting is a **messy** job.*

met form of **meet**

metabolism (say muh-**tab**-uh-liz-m) *noun* (*no plural*)
the chemical reactions and energy changes that happen within the cells of plants and animals: *We rely on our **metabolism** of food to provide the energy we need.*
▸ **metabolic** (*adjective*): ***metabolic** rate*
▸ **metabolize** (*verb*) (also **metabolise**): *We **metabolize** our body's fat stores more quickly by doing exercise.*

metal (say **met**-l) *noun* (*plural* **metals**)
a solid substance that is usually hard and shiny, such as iron, tin or gold: *This chair is made of **metal**.* ◇ *a **metal** box*

metallic (say muh-**tal**-ik) *adjective*
looking like metal or making a noise like one piece of metal hitting another: ***metallic** paint*

metamorphic (say met-uh-**maw**-fik) *adjective*
1 relating to rocks that have been changed by chemical reactions or extreme heat or pressure: *Slate is a **metamorphic** rock.* ➲ See **igneous**, **sedimentary**
2 relating to a change in physical form

metamorphosis (say met-uh-**maw**-fuh-siss) *noun* (*plural* **metamorphoses**) (*biology*)
a distinct change of form during development: *In its **metamorphosis**, a tadpole changes from being a small animal that lives only in water, breathes using gills, and has no legs, to being a frog with lungs and four legs.*

metamorphosis

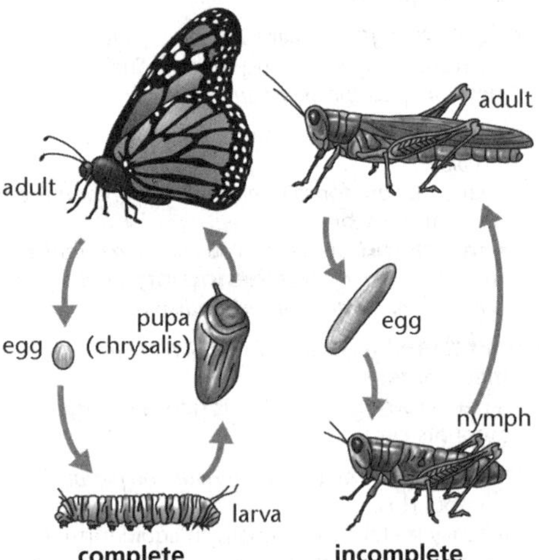

metaphor (say **met**-uh-fuh) *noun* (*plural* **metaphors**)
a word or phrase that is used in an imaginative way to show that a person or thing has the same qualities as another thing: *'My sister's a tiger when she gets angry' is a **metaphor**.* ➲ See Study page 17 ➲ See **simile**
▸ **metaphorical** (*adjective*)
▸ **metaphorically** (*adverb*)

meteor (say **mee**-ti-aw) *noun* (*plural* **meteors**)
a small piece of rock or metal from space that

enters the Earth's atmosphere and makes a bright line in the night sky. It is also called a shooting star.

meteorite (say **mee**-ti-uh-rite) *noun* (*plural* **meteorites**)
a **meteor** that has landed on the Earth

meter (say **mee**-tuh) *noun* (*plural* **meters**)
a machine that measures or counts something: *an electricity* ***meter***

SPELLING Be careful! Don't confuse **meter** with **metre**. They sound the same but they have different meanings. See the note at **metre**.

methamphetamine (say meth-am-**fet**-uh-meen) *noun* (*plural* **methamphetamines**)
a strong and dangerous illegal drug that increases your energy, prevents sleep and makes you not want to eat ➲ See **tik**

methane (say **mee**-thayn) *noun* (*no plural*)
a colourless gas with no smell that burns easily and that we can use to produce heat: ***Methane*** *is made from carbon and hydrogen.*

method (say **meth**-uhd) *noun* (*plural* **methods**)
a way of doing something: *What is the best* ***method*** *of cooking beef?*

methodical (say muh-**thod**-ik-l) *adjective*
having or using a well-organized and careful way of doing something: *A bookkeeper has to be* ***methodical*** *and neat.* ➲ SYNONYMS **organized**, **systematic**
▸ **methodically** (*adverb*): *Keep records* ***methodically*** *and accurately.*

meths (say **methss**) *noun* (*no plural*) (*informal*)
methylated spirit

methylated spirit (say meth-uh-lay-tuhd **spi**-rit) *noun* (*no plural*) (also **methylated spirits** or **meths**)
a fuel made from alcohol used for lighting, heating and cleaning

meticulous (say muh-**tik**-yuu-luhsss) *adjective*
giving or showing great attention to detail and being very careful: *She's* ***meticulous*** *about her homework.*
▸ **meticulously** (*adverb*): *He washes his car* ***meticulously***.

metonymy (say muh-**ton**-uh-mee) *noun* (*no plural*)
the act of referring to something by the name of something else that is closely connected with it, for example saying 'the White House' when you mean the USA President: *'The White House announced tax cuts' is an example of* ***metonymy***.
➲ See Study page 17

metre (say **mee**-tuh) *noun* (*plural* **metres**) (abbr. m)
the basic unit for measuring length. There are 100 centimetres in a metre: *The wall is eight* ***metres*** *long.* ➲ See **centimetre**, **millimetre**, **kilometre**

WHICH WORD? **Metre** or **meter**?
Be careful! Don't confuse **meter** and **metre**, which sound the same but have different spellings and different meanings: *three* ***metres*** *of string, a parking* ***meter***

SPELLING **Metre** is the correct British and South African spelling for **metre**, meaning a unit of length. **Meter** is used in American spelling for a unit of length.

metric system (say **met**-rik sis-tuhm) *noun* (*no plural*)
the metric system the system of measurement that uses the metre, the kilogram and the litre as basic units

metric ton *noun* (*plural* **metric tons**) (also **metric tonne**) (abbr. t)
a measure of mass. There are 1 000 kilograms in a metric ton. ➲ See note at **ton**

metropole (say **met**-ruh-pohl) *noun* (*plural* **metropoles**) (*S. African*)
a large area where towns have grown and joined together, often around a city

metropolis (say muh-**trop**-uh-liss) *noun* (*plural* **metropolises**)
a very large city
▸ **metropolitan** (*adjective*): *the Durban* ***metropolitan*** *area*

Mfecane (say m-fi-**kaa**-nee) *noun* (*no plural*) (*history*)
a series of wars and movements of many Nguni people across southern Africa in the nineteenth century
ℹ ORIGIN: from isiXhosa *imfecane*, meaning 'marauder, a person who attacks and steals'

mg *abbreviation* (*plural* **mg**) milligram

MHz *abbreviation* (*plural* **MHz**) **megahertz**

miaow (say **myow**) *noun* (*plural* **miaows**)
a sound that a cat makes
▸ **miaow** (*verb*): *Why is the cat* ***miaowing***?

mica (say **mike**-uh) *noun* (*no plural*)
a shiny mineral substance consisting of thin transparent layers: ***Mica*** *is a mineral found in granite.*

A B C D E F G H I J K L M N O P Q R S T U V W X Y Z

A B C D E F G H I J K L M N O P Q R S T U V W X Y Z

mice (say **mise**) plural of **mouse**

micro- (say **mike**-roh) *prefix*
very small: *A **microcomputer** is a tiny computer.*
ORIGIN: from Greek *mikros* meaning 'small'

microbe (say **mike**-rohb) *noun* (*plural* **microbes**)
an extremely small living thing that often causes disease: *Bacteria and viruses are **microbes**.*

microbiology (say mike-roh-by-**ol**-uh-jee) *noun* (*no plural*)
the scientific study of very small living things
▸ **microbiologist** (*noun*): *A **microbiologist** studies micro-organisms.*

microchip (say **mike**-roh-chip) *noun* (*plural* **microchips**)
a small part inside a computer that carries an electronic **circuit** 2 which makes the computer work

microcosm (say **mike**-roh-koz-m) *noun* (*plural* **microcosms**)
a small version or example of something larger: *Our village is a **microcosm** of society as a whole.*
➲ See **macrocosm**

micro-organism (say mike-roh-**aw**-guh-niz-m) *noun* (*plural* **micro-organisms**)
an extremely small living thing that you can only see with a special instrument (a **microscope**)

microphone (say **mike**-ruh-fohn) *noun* (*plural* **microphones**)
a piece of electrical equipment that makes sounds louder or records them so you can listen to them later

microscope (say **mike**-ruh-skohp) *noun* (*plural* **microscopes**)
a piece of equipment with special glass in it, that makes very small things look much bigger: *We looked at the hair under a **microscope**.*

microscope

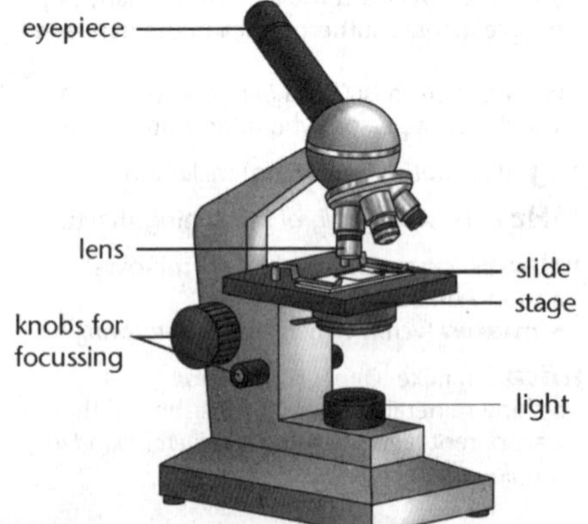

microscopic (say mike-ruh-**skop**-ik) *adjective*
too small to be seen without a **microscope**: *a **microscopic** organism ◇ a **microscopic** examination*

microwave (say **mike**-roh-wayv) *noun* (*plural* **microwaves**)
1 a type of wave that has electrical and magnetic characteristics
2 (also **microwave oven**) a type of oven that cooks or heats food very quickly using **microwaves**

mid- *prefix*
in the middle of: *My mother's in her **mid-thirties**.* ◇ ***mid-morning** coffee*

midday (say mid-**day**) *noun* (*no plural*)
twelve o'clock in the day: *We met at **midday**.*
➲ See **midnight**, ➲ SYNONYM **noon**

midden (say **mid**-uhn) *noun* (*plural* **middens**)
a pile of waste from earlier times: *We found a prehistoric **midden** in the cave.*

middle (say **mid**-l) *noun*
1 (*no plural*) the part that is the same distance from the sides, edges or ends of something: *A peach has a stone in the **middle**.*
2 (*no plural*) the time after the beginning and before the end: *The phone rang in the **middle** of the night.*
3 (*plural* **middles**) (*informal*) your waist: *He had a towel around his **middle**.*
be in the middle of doing something to be busy doing something: *I can't speak to you now – I'm in the **middle** of cooking dinner.*
▸ **middle** (*adjective*): *There are three houses and ours is the **middle** one.*

middle-aged (say mid-l-**ayj**-d) *adjective*
not old and not young, between the ages of about 40 and 60: *a **middle-aged** man*

Middle Ages *plural noun* (*history*)
the years between about 1100 and 1500 in Europe ➲ See **medieval**

midget (say **mij**-uht) *noun* (*plural* **midgets**)
a very small person

USAGE Note that some people feel that this word is offensive.

midnight (say **mid**-nite) *noun* (*no plural*)
twelve o'clock at night: *We left the party at **midnight**.* ➲ See **midday**

midst (say **midst**) *noun* (*no plural*) (*formal*)
the middle of something, or among a group of people or things: *He stood quietly in our **midst**.*
in the midst of to be in the middle of something: *The country is in the **midst** of a recession.*

midway (say mid-**way**) *adverb*
in the middle: *The village is **midway** between Welkom and Kgotsong.* ➲ SYNONYM **halfway**

midwife (say **mid**-wife) *noun* (*plural* **midwives**)
a person whose job is to help women give birth to babies

might¹ (say **mite**) *modal verb*
1 used as the form of 'may' when you repeat later what somebody has said: *He said he **might** be late* (= his words were 'I may be late'), *but he was early.*
2 a word that shows what will perhaps happen or what is possible: *Don't run because you **might** fall.* ◇ *'Where's Anne?' 'I don't know – she **might** be in the kitchen.'*
3 (*formal*) a word that you use to ask something in a very polite way: ***Might** I say something?*

might² (say **mite**) *noun* (*no plural*)
great strength or power: *the **might** of words.*
➲ SYNONYMS **power** 1, **strength**
with all your might using all your strength: *I pushed the car with all my **might**.*

mighty (say **mite**-ee) *adjective* (**mightier, mightiest**) (*formal*)
very great, strong or powerful: *He hit him with a **mighty** blow across his shoulder.*

migraine (say **mee**-grayn) *noun* (*plural* **migraines**)
a very bad pain in your head that makes you feel sick: *I develop a **migraine** when I eat too much chocolate.*

migrant (say **my**-gruhnt) *noun* (*plural* **migrants**)
1 a person who moves from one place to another to find work
2 an animal that moves from one place to another in different seasons
▸ **migrant** (*adjective*): ***migrant** workers*

migrate (say my-**grayt**) *verb* (**migrating, migrated**)
1 (used about animals and birds) to move from one part of the world to another every year
2 (used about large numbers of people) to go to live and work in another place
▸ **migration** (*noun*): *the annual **migration** of wildebeest*

mild (*rhymes with* **child**) *adjective* (**milder, mildest**)
1 not strong: *This cheese has a **mild** taste.*
2 not too hot and not too cold: *a **mild** winter*

mile (*rhymes with* **file**) *noun* (*plural* **miles**)
a measure of length that is used in Britain and the USA (= 1,6 kilometres): *We live three **miles** from the sea.*

milestone (say **mile**-stohn) *noun* (*plural* **milestones**)
an important event: *The 1994 election was a **milestone** in South African history.*

militant (say **mil**-i-tuhnt) *adjective*
ready to use force or strong pressure to get what you want: *She is a **militant** leader.*
▸ **militant** (*noun*): *He is a **militant**.*
▸ **militancy** (*noun*)

military (say **mil**-i-tuh-ree) *adjective*
connected with soldiers or the army, navy or air force: *a **military** camp* ◇ ***military** action*

militia (say muh-**lish**-uh) *noun* (*plural* **militias**)
a group of people who are not professional soldiers but have had military training

milk¹ *noun* (*no plural*)
1 the white liquid produced by cows, goats and some other animals that that we use as a drink and in food: *Do you want **milk** in your coffee?*
2 the white liquid that women and female mammals produce to feed their babies
🛈 ORIGIN: from Old English *milc*, related to Dutch *melk*

milk² *verb* (**milking, milked**)
to take **milk¹** 1 from a cow or another animal

milkshake (say **milk**-shayk) *noun* (*plural* **milkshakes**)
a drink made of milk with the flavour of chocolate or fruit added to it: *a strawberry **milkshake***

mill (say **mil**) *noun* (*plural* **mills**)
1 a building where a machine makes flour from grain ➲ See **windmill**
2 a factory where one material is made, for example cloth or paper: *a paper **mill***

millennium (say mi-**len**-i-uhm) *noun* (*plural* **millennia** or **millenniums**)
a period of a thousand years

> SPELLING Remember! You spell **millennium** with **ll** and **nn**.

millet (say **mil**-uht) *noun* (*no plural*)
a grain with many small seeds that is used as food for people and animals

milli- (say **mil**-i) *prefix*
one thousandth: *A **millilitre** is a thousandth of a litre.*
🛈 ORIGIN: from Latin *mille* meaning 'thousand'

milligram (say **mil**-i-gram) *noun* (*plural* **milligrams**) (abbr. mg)
a unit for measuring mass. There are 1 000 milligrams in a gram.

A B C D E F G H I J K L M N O P Q R S T U V W X Y Z

millilitre (say **mil**-i-lee-tuh) *noun* (*plural* **millilitres**) (abbr. ml or mL)
a unit for measuring the volume of a liquid. There are 1 000 millilitres in a litre: *a 250 millilitre bottle of cooldrink* ➲ See **centilitre, litre**

millimetre (say **mil**-i-mee-tuh) *noun* (*plural* **millimetres**) (abbr. mm)
a unit for measuring length. There are ten millimetres in a centimetre: *sixty **millimetres*** ◇ *60 mm*

million (say **mil**-i-uhn) *number* (*plural* **millions**)
1 1 000 000 or one thousand thousand: *About 48 **million** people live in this country.* ◇ ***millions** of rands* ◇ *six **million** people*
2 millions (*informal*) a lot: *I have **millions** of things to do.*

USAGE We say **six million** people (without **s**), but **millions of** people.

millionaire (say **mil**-i-uh-nair) *noun* (*plural* **millionaires**)
a very rich person who has more than a million pounds, dollars or rands

millionth (say **mil**-i-uhnth) *adjective, pronoun, noun*
1 000 000th: *Our **millionth** customer will receive a prize.* ◇ *three **millionths** of a second*

millipede (say **mil**-i-peed) *noun* (*plural* **millipedes**)
a small creature with a long thin body divided into many sections, each with two pairs of legs
🛈 ORIGIN: 17th century, from Latin *millepeda*, from *mille* meaning 'thousand' + *ped-* meaning 'foot'

mime *noun* (*no plural*)
a way of telling a story or telling somebody something by moving your face, hands and body, without speaking: *The show is a combination of dance and **mime**.*
▸ **mime** (*verb*): *He **mimed** that he was hungry.*

mimic (say **mim**-ik) *verb* (**mimicking, mimicked**)
to copy the way somebody moves and speaks in an amusing way
▸ **mimic** (*noun*): *She's a brilliant **mimic**.*

minaret (say min-uh-**ret**) *noun* (*plural* **minarets**)
a tall thin tower that usually forms part of a building where Muslims meet and pray (called a **mosque**)
🛈 ORIGIN: 17th century, through French and Turkish from Arabic *manār(a)* meaning 'lighthouse' or 'minaret'

mince (say **minss**) *noun* (*no plural*)
meat that has been cut into very small pieces
▸ **mince** (*verb*): ***Mince** the beef finely.*

mind[1] (say **mynd**) *noun* (*plural* **minds**)
the part of you that thinks and remembers: *He has a very quick **mind**.* ◇ *I've got a lot on my **mind** at the moment.*
be or **go out of your mind** (*informal*) to be or become mad or very worried: *Where were you? I was going out of my **mind** with worry.*
change your mind to have an idea, then decide to do something different: *I wanted a cat but I changed my **mind** and got a dog.*
make up your mind to decide something: *Shall I buy the blue shirt or the red one? I can't make up my **mind**.*

mind[2] (say **mynd**) *verb* (**minding, minded**)
1 to feel unhappy or angry about something: *Do you **mind** if I smoke?* ◇ *I don't **mind** the heat at all.*
2 to look out for or be careful of a thing: ***Mind** the step!*
do you mind ...?, would you mind ...? please could you ...?: *It's cold – would you **mind** closing the window?*
I don't mind it is not important to me which thing: *'Do you want tea or coffee?' 'I don't **mind**.'*
never mind don't worry, it doesn't matter: *'I forgot your book.' 'Never **mind**, I don't need it today.'*

mindmap (say **mynd**-map) *noun* (*plural* **mindmaps**) (also **mind map**)
a diagram to organize your thoughts or ideas with the main topic in the centre and related ideas linked by lines: *Draw a **mindmap** of the topics you should cover in your essay.*

mine[1] *pronoun*
something that belongs to me: *That bike is **mine**.* ◇ *Are those books **mine** or yours?*

mine[2] *noun* (*plural* **mines**)
1 a very big hole in the ground where people work to get minerals such as coal, gold or diamonds: *a coal **mine***
2 a bomb that is hidden under the ground or under water
▸ **mine** (*verb*): *Diamonds are **mined** in South Africa.*

minefield (say **mine**-feeld) *noun* (*plural* **minefields**)
1 an area of land or sea where bombs (called **mines**) have been hidden
2 a situation that is full of hidden dangers or difficulties: *The religious debate was a **minefield**.*

miner (say **mine**-uh) *noun* (*plural* **miners**)
a person who works in a mine, taking out coal, gold, etc.

mineral (say **min**-uh-ruhl) *noun* (*plural* **minerals**)
a solid **inorganic** substance such as gold, salt or iron that occurs naturally in the earth. Some minerals are also present in food and drink and are very important for good health: *a country rich in **minerals** ◇ the recommended daily intake of vitamins and **minerals***

mingle (say **ming**-guhl) *verb* (**mingling, mingled**)
to mix with other things or people: *The colours **mingled** together to make purple. ◇ The performers **mingled** with the crowd.*

mini- (say **min**-i) *prefix*
very small: *The school has a **minibus** that can carry twelve people.*

miniature (say **min**-i-tyoor) *adjective*
very small, or much smaller than usual: *a **miniature** railway*

minibus (say **min**-i-buss) *noun* (*plural* **minibuses**)
1 a small bus
2 (also **minibus taxi**) a small bus that transports passengers along a fixed route for a set fare
➲ See **taxi**

minim (say **min**-im) *noun* (*plural* **minims**) (*music*)
a type of note twice as long as a **crotchet**

minimal (say **min**-i-muhl) *adjective*
very small in amount, size or level, or as little as possible: ***minimal** effort ◇ **minimal** damage*
▸ **minimally** (*adverb*)

minimize (say **min**-i-mize) *verb* (**minimizing, minimized**) (also **minimise**)
to make something as small as possible: *During a fire, the police try to **minimize** the risk to the public.*

minimum (say **min**-i-muhm) *noun* (*plural* **minimums** or **minima**)
the smallest size, amount or number that is possible: *We need a **minimum** of six people to play this game.* ➲ OPPOSITE **maximum**
▸ **minimum** (*adjective*): *What is the **minimum** age for leaving school?*
ℹ ORIGIN: 17th century, from Latin *minimus* meaning 'least'

miniskirt (say **min**-i-skurt) *noun* (*plural* **miniskirts**)
a very short skirt

minister (say **min**-iss-tuh) *noun* (*plural* **ministers**)
1 one of the most important people in a government: *the **Minister** of Education* ➲ See **president, prime minister**
2 a priest in some Christian churches

ministry (say **min**-iss-tree) *noun* (*plural* **ministries**)
a part of the government that controls one special thing: *the **Ministry** of Defence*

mink *noun* (*plural* **mink** or **minks**)
a small animal that is kept for its fur. The fur is used to make expensive coats.

minor[1] (say **mine**-uh) *adjective*
not very big or important: *Don't worry – it's only a **minor** problem. ◇ a **minor** road* ➲ OPPOSITE **major**[1]

minor[2] (say **mine**-uh) *noun* (*plural* **minors**)
(used in law) a person who is not legally an adult

minority (say mi-**no**-ri-tee) *noun* (*plural* **minorities**)
the smaller part of a group: *Only a **minority** of the learners speak English at home. ◇ Chinese people are an ethnic **minority** in South Africa.*
➲ OPPOSITE **majority**

minstrel (say **min**-struhl) *noun* (*plural* **minstrels**)
a travelling singer or musician in the **Middle Ages**

mint *noun*
1 (*no plural*) a small plant with a strong fresh taste and smell, that you put in food and drinks: ***mint** sauce*
2 (*plural* **mints**) a sweet made from this
3 (*plural* **mints**) the place where a country's money is made
4 (*no plural*) (*informal*) a large amount of money: *He made a **mint** in the holidays!*

minuend (say **min**-yuu-end) *noun* (*plural* **minuends**) (*maths*)
the amount from which another amount is taken away: *In the equation 9 – 6 = 3, the **minuend** is 9.* ➲ See **subtrahend**

minus[1] (say **mine**-uhss) *preposition*
1 (*maths*) (used in sums) less or subtract or take away: *Six **minus** two is four (6 – 2 = 4).*
➲ See **plus**
2 (used about a number) below zero: *The temperature will fall to **minus** ten degrees.*

minus[2] (say **mine**-uhss) *adjective* (*maths*)
lower than zero: *a **minus** number*

minute[1] (say **min**-uht) *noun* (*plural* **minutes**)
1 a measure of time. There are 60 seconds in a minute and 60 minutes in an hour: *It's nine **minutes** past six. ◇ The train leaves in ten **minutes**.*
2 a short time: *Wait a **minute** – I'll get my coat.*
➲ SYNONYM **moment**
in a minute very soon: *I'll be ready in a **minute**.*

A B C D E F G H I J K L M N O P Q R S T U V W X Y Z

A B C D E F G H I J K L M N O P Q R S T U V W X Y Z

the minute as soon as: *Phone me the **minute** you arrive.*

minute² (say my-**nyoot**) *adjective*
very small: *I can't read his writing – it's **minute**.* ➲ SYNONYM **tiny**

miracle (say **mi**-rik-l) *noun* (*plural* **miracles**)
a wonderful and surprising thing that happens and that you cannot explain: *It's a **miracle** that he wasn't killed.*

miraculous (say muh-**rak**-yuu-luhss) *adjective*
wonderful and surprising: *a **miraculous** escape*
▸ **miraculously** (*adverb*): ***Miraculously**, no one was hurt.*

mirage (say mi-**raaj**) *noun* (*plural* **mirages**)
something that you think you see in very hot weather, such as water that does not really exist in a desert

mirror¹ (say **mi**-ruh) *noun* (*plural* **mirrors**)
a piece of special glass where you can see yourself: *Look in the **mirror**.*

mirror² (say **mi**-ruh) *verb* (**mirroring, mirrored**)
1 to show something in the surface of something shiny: *The still water **mirrors** the sky.*
2 to be the same as something else: *Violence in schools **mirrors** violence in society.*

mirror image *noun* (*plural* **mirror images**)
an image or object which is identical to another, but with the structure reversed, as in a mirror

mirth (say **murth**) *noun* (*no plural*)
laughter or amusement: *His joke caused much **mirth**.*

mis- (say **miss**) *prefix*
added to the beginning of some words to show that something is done wrong or badly: ***misunderstand*** (= not understand correctly)
🛈 ORIGIN: from Old English and Old French

misbehave (say miss-bi-**hayv**) *verb* (**misbehaving, misbehaved**)
to behave badly: *Children who **misbehaved** were punished.* ➲ OPPOSITE **behave**
▸ **misbehaviour** (*noun*)

miscalculate (say miss-**kal**-kyuu-layt) *verb* (**miscalculating, miscalculated**)
to make a mistake in calculating an amount or judging a situation: *She **miscalculated** the distance.*
▸ **miscalculation** (*noun*): *We made a **miscalculation**.*

miscarriage (say **miss**-ka-rij) *noun* (*plural* **miscarriages**)
the birth of a baby before it is ready to be born, with the result that it dies: *She had a **miscarriage**.* ➲ See **abortion**

miscellaneous (say miss-uh-**layn**-i-uhss) *adjective* (abbr. misc)
consisting of many different items: *a pile of **miscellaneous** documents* ➲ SYNONYMS **assorted**, **sundry**, **various**

mischief (say **miss**-chif) *noun* (*no plural*)
bad behaviour that is not very serious: *Don't get into **mischief** while I'm out!*

mischievous (say **miss**-chi-vuhss) *adjective*
(usually used about children) enjoying playing tricks and annoying people: *He gave a **mischievous** grin.* ➲ SYNONYM **naughty**

PRONUNCIATION Notice how to say this word.

misconception (say miss-kon-**sep**-shuhn) *noun* (*plural* **misconceptions**)
a wrong idea or understanding of something: *There's a common **misconception** about school fees.*

misconduct (say miss-**kon**-dukt) *noun* (*no plural*) (*formal*)
unacceptable or wrong behaviour, especially by a professional person: *She was fired for **misconduct** in the office.*

miser (say **mize**-uh) *noun* (*plural* **misers**)
a person who likes having a lot of money but does not like to spend it
▸ **miserly** (*adjective*): *He's a **miserly** old man.*

miserable (say **miz**-uh-ruhb-l) *adjective*
1 feeling very sad: *I waited in the rain for an hour, feeling cold, wet and **miserable**.* ➲ SYNONYM **unhappy**
2 making you feel sad: ***miserable** weather*

misery (say **miz**-uh-ree) *noun* (*plural* **miseries**)
great unhappiness: *the **misery** caused by war*

misfire (say miss-**fy**-uh) *verb* (**misfiring, misfired**)
to fail to work correctly: *The engine **misfired**.* ◇ *Our plans **misfired**.*

misfit (say **miss**-fit) *noun* (*plural* **misfits**)
a person who is not accepted by other people, especially because their ideas or behaviour are different: *She's a **misfit** in her new school.*

misfortune (say miss-**faw**-tyoon) *noun* (*plural* **misfortunes**) (*formal*)
something bad that happens, or bad luck: *He has known great **misfortune**.*

misguided (say miss-**gide**-uhd) *adjective*
wrong because you have understood a situation badly: *They had a **misguided** belief that they were right.*

mishap (say **miss**-hap) *noun* (*plural* **mishaps**)
a small accident that does not have serious results: *We had a few **mishaps** on our holiday.*

misinterpret (say miss-in-**tur**-pruht) *verb* (**misinterpreting, misinterpreted**)
to understand or **interpret** something wrongly: *He **misinterpreted** the situation.*
▸ **misinterpretation** (*noun*)

mislay (say miss-**lay**) *verb* (**mislaying, mislaid**)
to lose something because you cannot remember where you put it: *I've **mislaid** my glasses.* ➲ SYNONYMS **lose** 1, **misplace**

mislead (say miss-**leed**) *verb* (**misleading, misled**)
to make somebody believe something that is not true: *You **misled** me when you said you could give me a job.*

misleading (say miss-**leed**-ing) *adjective*
giving the wrong idea: *Her speech was **misleading**.*

misogynist (say muh-**soj**-i-nuhst) *noun* (*plural* **misogynists**)
a man who hates women
▸ **misogyny** (*noun*)

misplace (say miss-**playss**) *verb* (**misplacing, misplaced**)
to lose something because it has been put in the wrong place: *The keys have been **misplaced**.*
➲ SYNONYM **mislay**

misplaced (say miss-**playst**) *adjective*
1 not suitable for or correct in the situation: ***misplaced** optimism*
2 (of love, trust, etc.) given to a person who does not deserve or return those feelings: ***misplaced** loyalty*

misprint (say **miss**-print) *noun* (*plural* **misprints**)
a mistake in printing or typing: *There was a **misprint** in the newspaper.*

misquote (say miss-**kwoht**) *verb* (**misquoting, misquoted**)
to say that somebody said something when they did not: *The article **misquoted** the doctor.*
➲ OPPOSITE **quote**

misread (say miss-**reed**) *verb* (**misreading, misread**)
to read or understand something incorrectly: *She **misread** the email.* ◇ *He **misread** my silence as anger.*

Miss (say **miss**) *noun*
a word that you use before the name of a girl or woman who is not married: *Dear **Miss** Smith, …*

miss (say **miss**) *verb* (**missing, missed**)
1 to not hit or catch something: *I tried to hit the ball but I **missed**.*
2 to not see or hear something: *You **missed** a good programme on TV last night.* ◇ *Our house is the one on the corner – you can't **miss** it.*
3 to be too late for a train, bus, plane or boat: *I just **missed** my bus.* ➲ OPPOSITE **catch** 3
4 to feel sad about a person or thing that has gone: *I'll **miss** you when you leave.*
miss something out to not put in or do something, or to not include something: *I didn't finish the exam – I **missed** out two questions.*
▸ **miss** (*noun*): *After several **misses**, he hit the ball.*

missile (say **miss**-ile) *noun* (*plural* **missiles**)
1 a powerful weapon that can be sent long distances through the air and then explodes: *nuclear **missiles***
2 a thing that you throw at somebody to hurt them

missing (say **miss**-ing) *adjective*
lost, or not in the usual place: *The police are looking for the **missing** child.* ◇ *My purse is **missing**. Have you seen it?*

mission (say **mish**-uhn) *noun* (*plural* **missions**)
a journey to do a special job: *They were sent on a **mission** to the moon.*

missionary (say **mish**-uhn-ree) *noun* (*plural* **missionaries**)
a person sent on a religious mission, especially to encourage Christianity in a foreign country

mist *noun* (*plural* **mists**)
thin cloud near the ground, that is difficult to see through: *Early in the morning, the river was covered in **mist**.*
▸ **misty** (*adjective*): *a **misty** morning*

mistake[1] (say miss-**tayk**) *noun* (*plural* **mistakes**)
something that you think or do that is wrong: *a spelling **mistake*** ◇ *It was a **mistake** to go by bus – the journey took two hours!* ◇ *Sorry, I took your book by **mistake*** (= by accident). ➲ SYNONYM **error**
ORIGIN: 14th–15th century, from Old Norse *mistaka* meaning 'take by mistake'

mistake[2] (say miss-**tayk**) *verb* (**mistaking, mistook, has mistaken**)
to think that somebody or something is a different person or thing: *I'm sorry – I **mistook** you for my cousin.*

mistaken (say miss-**tayk**-n) *adjective*
wrong: *I said the exam was today but I was **mistaken** – it's tomorrow.* ◇ *a case of **mistaken** identity* (= when people think that a person is somebody else)

A B C D E F G H I J K L M N O P Q R S T U V W X Y Z

A B C D E F G H I J K L **M** N O P Q R S T U V W X Y Z

mistress (say **miss**-truhss) *noun* (*plural* **mistresses**)
1 a woman in a position of authority or control
2 (*old-fashioned*) a woman who a married man has a sexual relationship with but who is not his wife

mistrust (say miss-**trust**) *verb* (**mistrusting, mistrusted**)
to not trust a person: *I **mistrust** politicians.*
➲ OPPOSITE **trust²** ➲ See **distrust**
▸ **mistrust** (*noun*): *I have a **mistrust** of salespeople.*

misunderstand (say miss-un-duh-**stand**) *verb* (**misunderstanding, misunderstood**)
to not understand something correctly: *I'm sorry, I **misunderstood** what you said.*

misunderstanding (say miss-un-duh-**stand**-ing) *noun* (*plural* **misunderstandings**)
a situation in which somebody does not understand something correctly: *I think there's been a **misunderstanding**. I ordered two tickets, not four.*

mite (*rhymes with* **bite**) *noun* (*plural* **mites**)
a tiny creature that looks like a spider and lives on plants and animals and in our homes

mitre (say **mite**-uh) *noun* (*plural* **mitres**) (*technology*)
a joint between two pieces of wood or other material at an angle of 90°
▸ **mitre** (*verb*)

mitten (say **mit**-uhn) *noun* (*plural* **mittens**)
a glove that has one part for your thumb and another part for your other fingers. ➲ See **glove**

mix¹ (say **mikss**) *verb* (**mixing, mixed**)
1 to put different things together to make something new: ***Mix** yellow and blue paint together to make green.*
2 to join together to make something new: *Oil and water don't **mix**.*
3 to be with and talk to other people: *In my job, I **mix** with a lot of different people.*
mix a person or **thing up** to think that one person or thing is a different person or thing: *People often **mix** Mark **up** with his brother.*
mix something up to make things untidy: *Don't **mix up** my papers!*

mix² (say **mikss**) *noun* (*plural* **mixes**)
1 a group of different types of people or things: *We need a **mix** of boys and girls.* ◇ *a tomato and onion **mix***
2 a special powder that you add to water or other liquid to make something: *cake **mix*** ➲ See **mixture**

mixed (say **mikst**) *adjective*
containing different kinds of people or things: *a **mixed** salad* ◇ *Is their school **mixed*** (= with boys and girls together)*?*

mixer (say **mikss**-uh) *noun* (*plural* **mixers**)
a machine that mixes things together: *a food **mixer*** ◇ *a cement **mixer***

mixture (say **mikss**-tshuh) *noun* (*plural* **mixtures**)
something that you make by mixing different things together: *Air is a **mixture** of gases.* ◇ *a cake **mixture***

MK (say em-**kay**) *abbreviation* **Umkhonto we Sizwe**

ml *abbreviation* (*plural* **ml**) (also **mL**) **millilitre**

mm *abbreviation* (*plural* **mm**) **millimetre**

mnemonic (say ni-**mon**-ik) *noun* (*plural* **mnemonics**)
a saying or pattern that helps you to remember something: *Make up a **mnemonic** to help you remember the names of the planets.*

moan *verb* (**moaning, moaned**)
1 to make a long sad sound when you are hurt or very unhappy: *I **moaned** in pain.*
2 (*informal*) to talk a lot about something in a way that annoys other people: *He's always **moaning** about the weather.*
➲ SYNONYM **complain**
▸ **moan** (*noun*): *I heard a loud **moan**.*

moat (say **moht**) *noun* (*plural* **moats**)
a deep wide **ditch¹** around a castle that was filled with water to make it difficult for enemies to attack the castle

mob¹ *noun* (*plural* **mobs**)
a big noisy group of people who are shouting or fighting

mob² *verb* (**mobbing, mobbed**)
to form a large crowd around a person or thing: *We **mobbed** the singer.*

mobile¹ (say **moh**-bile) *adjective*
able to move easily from place to place: *A **mobile** library visits every week.* ◇ *a **mobile** phone* (= cellphone)

mobile² (say **moh**-bile) *noun* (*plural* **mobiles**)
a decoration that you hang from the roof or over a baby's bed, that moves in the air

mobile phone *noun* (*plural* **mobile phones**) = **cellphone**

mobilize (say **moh**-buh-lize) *verb* (**mobilizing, mobilized**) (also **mobilise**)
1 to organize people or things to do

something: ***Mobilize** your community to pick up litter.*
2 to get ready for war
▸ **mobilization** (*noun*) (also **mobilisation**)

moccasin (say **mok**-uh-sin) *noun* (*plural* **moccasins**)
a soft leather shoe

mock (say **mok**) *verb* (**mocking, mocked**)
to laugh at somebody or something in an unkind way: *The other children **mocked** her old-fashioned clothes.*
▸ **mocking** (*adjective*): *a **mocking** laugh*
▸ **mockery** (*noun*)

modal verb (say moh-duhl **vurb**) *noun* (*plural* **modal verbs**)
a verb, for example 'might', 'can' or 'must', that you use with another verb ➲ See Study page 4

mode (say **mohd**) *noun* (*plural* **modes**)
1 a kind of thing or a way of doing something: ***mode** of transport*
2 one of the ways in which a machine can work: *My cellphone is on silent **mode**.*
3 (*maths*) the most frequent number in a group of numbers

model[1] (say **mod**-l) *noun* (*plural* **models**)
1 a small copy of something: *a **model** of the Taj Mahal ◇ a **model** aeroplane*
2 one of the cars, machines or products that a certain company makes: *Have you seen their latest **model**?*
3 a person who wears clothes at a special show or for photographs, so that people will see them and buy them
4 a person who sits or stands so that an artist can draw, paint or photograph them

model[2] (say **mod**-l) *verb* (**modelling, modelled**)
1 to make a copy of something, usually with your hands: *I used clay to **model** a cat.*
2 to wear and show clothes as a model: *He **modelled** a suit at the fashion show.*

modem (say **moh**-duhm) *noun* (*plural* **modems**)
a piece of equipment that uses a telephone line to connect two computers

moderate[1] (say **mod**-uh-rayt) *verb* (**moderating, moderated**)
1 to become or to make something less strong or extreme: ***Moderate** your language.*
2 to check a group of exam or test results and make sure that they are being marked fairly and in the same way: *He **moderates** matric exam papers.*
▸ **moderator** (*noun*)

moderate[2] (say **mod**-uh-ruht) *adjective*
not too much and not too little: *Cook the vegetables over a **moderate** heat.*
▸ **moderation** (*noun*): *Alcohol should be taken in **moderation*** (= in small quantities).

modern (say **mod**-uhn) *adjective*
of the present time, or of the kind that is usual now: ***modern** art ◇ The airport is very **modern**.*
➲ SYNONYM **contemporary[1]** 2

modest (say **mod**-uhst) *adjective*
not talking much about good things that you have done or about things that you can do well: *You didn't tell me you could sing so well – you're very **modest**!*
▸ **modestly** (*adverb*): *He spoke quietly and **modestly** about his success.* ▸ **modesty** (*noun*): *She accepted the prize with her usual **modesty**.*

modify (say **mod**-i-fy) *verb* (**modifying, modified**)
to change something slightly: *We **modified** the plans before building the house.*
➲ SYNONYM **change[1]** 1
▸ **modification** (*noun*): *There were a few **modifications** to the script.*

module (say **mod**-yool) *noun* (*plural* **modules**)
a unit that forms part of something bigger: *Each chapter has two **modules**.*

mohair (say **moh**-hair) *noun* (*no plural*)
very soft wool that comes from the hair of a goat: *a **mohair** blanket*

moist (say **moyst**) *adjective*
a little wet: *Keep the earth **moist** or the plant will die.*
▸ **moisten** (*verb*): ***Moisten** the cloth.*

moisture (say **moyss**-tshuh) *noun* (*no plural*)
small drops of water on something or in the air

moisturize (say **moyss**-tshuh-rize) *verb* (**moisturizing, moisturized**) (also **moisturise**)
to put special cream on your skin to make it less dry

molar (say **moh**-luh) *noun* (*plural* **molars**)
one of the large teeth at the back of your mouth that you use to break food down into smaller pieces ➲ See **canine[1]**, **incisor**

molasses (say mo-**lass**-uhz) *noun* (*no plural*)
a thick, dark, sticky liquid that is made from sugar ➲ SYNONYM **treacle**

mole (*rhymes with* **hole**) *noun* (*plural* **moles**)
1 a small grey or brown animal that lives under the ground and makes tunnels
2 a small dark spot on a person's skin

molecule (say **mol**-i-kyool) *noun* (*plural* **molecules**)
the smallest part into which a substance can be

A B C D E F G H I J K L M N O P Q R S T U V W X Y Z

divided without changing its chemical nature ➲ See **atom**

molest (say mo-**lest**) *verb* (**molesting, molested**)
to attack somebody, especially a child, in a sexual way
▸ **molestation** (*noun*) ▸ **molester** (*noun*): *a child **molester***

mollusc (say **mol**-usk) *noun* (*plural* **molluscs**)
a creature with a soft body, usually having a hard outer shell: *Snails, slugs and oysters are all **molluscs**.*

molten (say **mohl**-tuhn) *adjective*
relating to metal, rocks or other substances that have melted into a liquid state: *Lava is a mass of **molten** rock that comes out of a volcano.*

mom (say **mom**) *noun* (*plural* **moms**) (*informal*)
mother: *This is my **mom**.* ◇ *Happy Birthday, **Mom***

moment (say **moh**-muhnt) *noun* (*plural* **moments**)
a very short time: *She thought for a **moment** before she answered.* ◇ *Can you wait a **moment**?* ◇ *He'll be here in a **moment**.*
➲ SYNONYM **minute**[1] 2
at the moment now: *She's on holiday at the **moment**, but she'll be back next week.*
the moment as soon as: *Tell him to phone me the **moment** he arrives.*

momentous (say muh-**men**-tuhss) *adjective*
very important: *This is a **momentous** occasion.*
➲ SYNONYMS **crucial**, **important** 1, **significant**
▸ **momentously** (*adverb*)

momentum (say muh-**men**-tuhm) *noun* (*no plural*)
1 (*science*) the quantity of movement that an object has. Momentum is the product of an object's **mass** and its **velocity**: *A car has greater **momentum** than a bicycle.*
2 the ability to keep increasing or developing: *The World Cup excitement is gaining **momentum**.*

mommy (say **mom**-ee) *noun* (*plural* **mommies**)
(*informal*) (used by or to a child) mother: *'I want my **mommy**!' he cried.*

monarch (say **mon**-uhk) *noun* (*plural* **monarchs**)
a king or queen ➲ SYNONYM **sovereign**[1]

monarchy (say **mon**-uh-kee) *noun* (*plural* **monarchies**)
a country that has a king or queen

monastery (say **mon**-uhss-tree) *noun* (*plural* **monasteries**)
a place where religious men (called **monks**) live together

Monday (say **mun**-day) *noun*
the day of the week after Sunday and before Tuesday, the first day of the working week
➲ See note at **day**

monetary (say **mun**-i-tree) *adjective*
relating to money: *a **monetary** policy*

money (say **mun**-ee) *noun* (*no plural*)
what you use when you buy or sell something: *How much **money** did you spend?* ◇ *This jacket cost a lot of **money**.* ◇ *The film made a lot of **money**.*

WORD BUILDING Money consists of **coins** (small round metal things) and **notes** (pieces of paper). This is called **cash**. The coins that you have in your purse are called **change**. The **money** somebody gives you in a shop if you pay too much is also called **change**.

mongoose (say **mong**-gooss) *noun* (*plural* **mongooses**)
a small mammal with short legs, a long tail and a lot of fur, that can kill snakes and rats
ⓘ ORIGIN: 17th century, from Marathi *maṅgūs*. Marathi is a language spoken in India.

mongrel (say **mung**-gruhl) *noun* (*plural* **mongrels**)
a dog that has parents of different types (**breeds**)

monitor[1] (say **mon**-i-tuh) *noun* (*plural* **monitors**)
1 a machine for watching or testing how something is working
2 a learner who is given a special responsibility in a school: *a playground **monitor***
3 a machine that shows pictures or information on a screen like a television: *a computer with a 17-inch colour **monitor***

monitor[2] (say **mon**-i-tuh) *verb* (**monitoring, monitored**)
to check, record or test something regularly for a period of time: ***Monitor** the seed as it grows.*

monk (say **mungk**) *noun* (*plural* **monks**)
a religious man who lives with other religious men in a special building (called a **monastery**)
➲ See **nun**
ⓘ ORIGIN: from Old English *munuc* from Greek *monos* meaning 'alone'

monkey (say **mung**-kee) *noun* (*plural* **monkeys**)
an animal with a long tail that lives in hot countries and can climb trees

mono- (say **mon**-oh) *prefix*
one or single: *A **monolingual** person can speak one language.*
ⓘ ORIGIN: from Greek *monos* meaning 'alone'

monochrome (say **mon**-oh-krohm) *adjective*
produced in one colour or in shades of one colour: *the artist's **monochrome** painting in shades of blue* ◇ *a **monochrome** computer monitor*
▸ **monochromatic** (*adjective*): *monochromatic light*

monocotyledon (say **mon**-oh-kot-i-leed-n) *noun* (*plural* **monocotyledons**) (*biology*)
a flowering plant with only one seed leaf when it begins to grow: *Grass, wheat and maize are **monocotyledons**.* ➲ See **dicotyledon**

monoculture (say **mon**-oh-kul-tshuh) *noun* (*no plural*)
1 the practice of growing a single crop in an area of land: *There are environmental dangers in **monoculture**.*
2 a system where there is little variety: *Some people think that mass media is leading to a global **monoculture**.*

monogamy (say muh-**nog**-uh-mee) *noun* (*no plural*)
the practice of being married to one person at a time ➲ See **bigamy**, **polygamy**
▸ **monogamous** (*adjective*): *a **monogamous** relationship*

monologue (say **mon**-oh-log) *noun* (*plural* **monologues**)
a long speech by one person, especially in a play
🛈 **ORIGIN**: 17th century, through French, from Greek *monologos* meaning 'speaking alone'

monomial (say muh-**noh**-mi-uhl) *noun* (*plural* **monomials**) (*maths*)
an expression with a single term: *The term 3y is a **monomial**.* ➲ See **polynomial**

monopoly (say muh-**nop**-uh-lee) *noun* (*plural* **monopolies**)
1 the control of an industry or service by only one company, and the goods or service that are controlled in this way: *The airline has a **monopoly** on flights to Limpopo.*
2 the complete control, possession or use of something by one person or group
▸ **monopolize** (*verb*) (also **monopolise**): *Don't **monopolize** the conversation.*

monotone (say **mon**-uh-tohn) *noun* (*plural* **monotones**)
a sound, especially of a person's voice, that does not change: *He spoke in a **monotone**.*

monotonous (say muh-**not**-uh-nuhss) *adjective*
always the same and therefore very boring: *It's a very **monotonous** job.*

monoxide (say muh-**nok**-side) *noun* (*no plural*) (*science*)
a chemical compound containing one atom of **oxygen**: *CO is the symbol for carbon **monoxide**.*

monsoon (say mon-**soon**) *noun* (*plural* **monsoons**)
1 the season when very heavy rain falls in southern Asia
2 a wind in southern Asia that blows from the south-west in summer bringing rain, and the north-east in winter

monster (say **mon**-stuh) *noun* (*plural* **monsters**)
an animal in stories that is big, ugly and frightening

monstrous (say **mon**-struhss) *adjective*
1 very large and frightening: *It was a **monstrous** cockroach.*
2 that people think is shocking and unacceptable because it is wrong or unfair: *a **monstrous** act of abuse.* ➲ **SYNONYM atrocious**
▸ **monstrosity** (*noun*): *The building is a **monstrosity**.*

month (say **munth**) *noun* (*plural* **months**)
1 one of the twelve parts of a year: *December is the last **month** of the year.* ◇ *We went on holiday last **month**.*
2 about four weeks: *She was in hospital for a **month**.*
🛈 **ORIGIN**: from Old English *monath*, related to Dutch *maand* and to English *moon*. In the past, many people, including the ancient Greeks and Romans, calculated time using the changes of the moon's cycle.

> **WORD BUILDING** The months of the year are: **January**, **February**, **March**, **April**, **May**, **June**, **July**, **August**, **September**, **October**, **November**, **December**.

monthly (say **munth**-lee) *adjective*, *adverb*
happening or coming every month or once a month: *a **monthly** magazine* ◇ *I am paid **monthly**.*

monument (say **mon**-yuu-muhnt) *noun* (*plural* **monuments**)
a thing that is built to help people remember a person or something that happened: *This is a **monument** to Queen Victoria.*

monumental (say mon-yuu-**ment**-l) *adjective*
very large, great or important: *I made a **monumental** mistake.* ◇ *It was a **monumental** achievement.*

moo *noun* (*plural* **moos**)
the sound that a cow makes
▸ **moo** (*verb*): *Cows were **mooing** in the barn.*

mood (*rhymes with* **food**) *noun* (*plural* **moods**)
the way that you feel at a particular time: *Dad is in a bad* ***mood*** *because he's lost his glasses.* ◇ *in a good* ***mood*** ◇ *I'm not in the* ***mood*** *for a party.*

moody (say **mood**-ee) *adjective* (**moodier, moodiest**)
often changing and becoming angry or unhappy without warning: *Teenagers can be very* ***moody***.

moon (*rhymes with* **spoon**) *noun*
1 the moon (*no plural*) the big object that shines in the sky at night and moves around the Earth every 28 days: *When was the first landing on the* ***moon****?*
2 (*plural* **moons**) an object like the moon that moves around another planet: *How many* ***moons*** *does Neptune have?*
ORIGIN: from Old English *mona*, related to Latin *mensis* meaning 'month' and *metiri* meaning 'measure', because the moon was used to measure time

moonlight (say **moon**-lite) *noun* (*no plural*)
the light from the moon

moor[1] (*rhymes with* **poor**) *noun* (*plural* **moors**)
wild land on hills in Britain that has grass and low plants, but not many trees

moor[2] (*rhymes with* **poor**) *verb* (**mooring, moored**)
to tie a boat or ship to something so that it will stay in one place

mop *noun* (*plural* **mops**)
a tool with a long handle and thick strings, pieces of cloth or a **sponge** on the end that you use to wash floors
▸ **mop** (*verb*): *I* ***mopped*** *the floor.*

mopane (say muh-**paa**-nee) *noun* (*plural* **mopanes**)
a tree with hard wood that grows only in the hot, dry regions of southern Africa
mopane worm a creature that you can eat that lives on the leaves of the mopane tree
ORIGIN: 19th century, from Setswana *mopane*

mope (*rhymes with* **hope**) *verb* (**moping, moped**)
to feel sorry for yourself and not do anything because you are unhappy: *Cheer up and stop* ***moping*** *around.*

moped (say **moh**-ped) *noun* (*plural* **mopeds**)
a vehicle like a bicycle with a small engine

moraine (say muh-**rayn**) *noun* (*no plural*) (*geography*)
a collection of rocks and earth that have been carried and left behind by a mass of ice (a **glacier**)

moral[1] (say **mo**-ruhl) *adjective*
connected with what people think is right or wrong: *Some people do not eat meat for* ***moral*** *reasons.* ◇ *a* ***moral*** *problem* ➲ See **amoral, immoral**
▸ **morally** (*adverb*): *It's* ***morally*** *wrong to tell lies.*

moral[2] (say **mo**-ruhl) *noun*
1 morals (*plural noun*) ideas about what is right and wrong: *These people have no* ***morals***.
2 (*plural* **morals**) a lesson about what is right and wrong that you can learn from a story or from something that happens: *The* ***moral*** *of the story is that we should be kind to animals.*
▸ **morality** (*noun*): *a good sense of* ***morality***

morale (say muh-**raal**) *noun* (*no plural*)
how a group of people feels at a certain time: *Their* ***morale*** *was low.* ◇ *Try to improve the team's* ***morale***.

morbid (say **maw**-bid) *adjective*
showing interest in unpleasant things, such as disease or death: *He has a* ***morbid*** *fascination with accidents.*
▸ **morbidly** (*adverb*)

more[1] (say **maw**) *adjective, pronoun*
a bigger amount or number of something: *You've got* ***more*** *money than I have.* ◇ *Can I have some* ***more*** *sugar in my tea?* ◇ *We need two* ***more*** *chairs.* ◇ *There aren't any* ***more***.
➲ **OPPOSITES** **less**[1], **fewer** ➲ See **most**[1]

more[2] (say **maw**) *adverb*
1 a word that makes an adjective or adverb stronger: *Your book was* ***more*** *expensive than mine.* ◇ *Please speak* ***more*** *slowly.* ➲ **OPPOSITE** **less**[2]
2 to a greater degree than usual, or to a greater degree than something else: *I like Anna* ***more*** *than her brother.* ➲ **OPPOSITE** **less**[1] ➲ See **most**[1]
more or less almost, but not exactly: *We are* ***more*** *or less the same age.* ➲ **SYNONYM** **roughly**
not any more not any longer: *They don't live here any* ***more***.
once more (*formal*) again: *Spring will soon be here once* ***more***.

> **USAGE** We use **more** with meaning 1 above with adjectives and adverbs that have two or more syllables: ***more*** *exciting*, ***more*** *expensive*, ***more*** *helpful*.
> - Adjectives and adverbs with one syllable and some with two syllables take **-er**: *hotter*, *happier*, *funnier*. See Study page 10.

moreover (say maw-**roh**-vuh) *adverb*
(used for adding another fact) also: *Our costs are up.* ***Moreover****, our sales are down.*

morning (say **mawn**-ing) *noun* (*plural* **mornings**)
the first part of the day, between the time when the sun comes up and the middle of the day **(midday)**: *I went swimming this **morning**.* ◇ *I felt ill all **morning**.* ◇ *I'm going away on Tuesday **morning**.*
in the morning tomorrow during the morning: *I'll see you in the **morning**.*

morogo (say maw-**raw**-*khaw*) *noun* (*no plural*) (*S. African*)
any of several leafy green plants that can be cooked and eaten as a vegetable
ORIGIN: from Sesotho and Setswana *morogo* meaning 'wild spinach' and 'vegetables'

PRONUNCIATION Pronounce the **g** in this word like the **g** in the Afrikaans word **lag**.

moron (say **maw**-ron) *noun* (*plural* **morons**) (*informal*)
a rude way of referring to a person who you think is stupid: *What is that **moron** doing in the traffic?* ➲ **SYNONYM idiot**
▸ **moronic** (*adjective*) *He's **moronic**!*

Morse code (say mawss **kohd**) *noun* (*no plural*)
an alphabet in which the letters are dots and short lines, or short and long sounds: *SMS is '… – – …' in **Morse code**.* ➲ See **code** 1
ORIGIN: 19th century, named after Samuel Morse (1791–1872), who invented this alphabet

morsel (say **mawss**-l) *noun* (*plural* **morsels**)
a very small piece of something, usually food: *I'll taste a **morsel**.*

mortal (say **mawt**-l) *adjective*
1 that cannot live forever: *We are **mortal**.* ➲ **OPPOSITE immortal**
2 that will result in death: *a **mortal** wound* ➲ **SYNONYM fatal** 1
3 very great or extreme: ***mortal** danger*
▸ **mortally** (*adverb*): *He was **mortally** wounded.* ▸ **mortal** (*noun*): *People are **mortals**.*

mortality (say maw-**tal**-i-tee) *noun* (*no plural*)
1 the fact that nobody can live for ever: *I think about my own **mortality**.*
2 the number of deaths in one place or period of time: *Infant **mortality** has decreased.*

mortar (say **maw**-tuh) *noun*
1 (*no plural*) a mixture of cement, sand and water used in building
2 (*plural* **mortars**) a type of gun that fires a bomb high into the sky: *They were under **mortar** attack.*
3 (*plural* **mortars**) a heavy bowl that is used with a special instrument (called a **pestle**) to crush food such as spices

mortgage (say **maw**-gij) *noun* (*plural* **mortgages**)
money that you borrow to buy a house

PRONUNCIATION Don't pronounce the **t** in **mortgage**.

mortify (say **maw**-ti-fy) *verb* (**mortifying, mortified**)
to make somebody feel very embarrassed: *I was **mortified** to hear the truth.* ➲ **SYNONYM humiliate**
▸ **mortification** (*noun*) ▸ **mortifying** (*adjective*): *It was **mortifying**.*

USAGE We usually use this word in the passive form: *We were **mortified**.*

mortuary (say **maw**-tshuh-ree) *noun* (*plural* **mortuaries**)
a room, usually in a hospital, where dead bodies are kept before they are buried or burned

mosaic (say moh-**zay**-ik) *noun* (*plural* **mosaics**)
a picture or pattern that you make by placing small coloured glass or stones together

Moslem (say **moz**-lim) = **Muslim**

mosque (say **mosk**) *noun* (*plural* **mosques**)
a building where Muslims go to say their prayers

mosquito (say muh-**skee**-toh) *noun* (*plural* **mosquitoes**)
a small flying insect that bites people and animals and drinks their blood. A certain type cause a serious disease **(called malaria)**.
ORIGIN: 16th century, from Spanish and Portuguese *mosquito* meaning 'little fly', from Latin *musca* meaning 'fly'

moss *noun* (*no plural*)
a soft green plant that grows like a carpet on trees, rocks and soil

most[1] (*rhymes with* **boast**) *adjective, pronoun*
greatest in number or amount: *We all did a lot of work, but I did the **most**.* ◇ *He was ill for **most** of last week.* ➲ **OPPOSITE least** ➲ See **more[1]**
make the most of something to use something in the best way: *We have only one free day, so let's make the **most** of it.*

most[2] (*rhymes with* **boast**) *adverb*
more than all others: *Which part of your holiday did you enjoy **most**?* ➲ **OPPOSITE least**

mostly (say **mohst**-lee) *adverb*
almost all: *Our learners are **mostly** South African.*

A B C D E F G H I J K L M N O P Q R S T U V W X Y Z

motel (say moh-**tel**) *noun* (*plural* **motels**)
a hotel for people who are travelling by car, with space for parking cars near the rooms
ORIGIN: 20th century, from a combination of the words *motor* and *hotel*

moth (*rhymes with* **cloth**) *noun* (*plural* **moths**)
an insect with big wings that flies at night

mother (say **mu*th***-uh) *noun* (*plural* **mothers**)
a woman who has a child: *My **mother** is a doctor.* ➲ See **mom, mommy**
ORIGIN: from Old English *modor*, related to Dutch *moeder* and to Latin *mater*

motherhood (say **mu*th***-uh-huud) *noun* (*no plural*)
the state of being a mother

mother-in-law (say **mu*th***-uh-in-law) *noun* (*plural* **mothers-in-law**)
the mother of your husband or wife

motif (say moh-**teef**) *noun* (*plural* **motifs**)
a picture or pattern on something: *I painted a floral **motif** on my bag.*

motion (say **moh**-shuhn) *noun* (*no plural*)
movement: *The **motion** of the boat made her feel sick.* ◇ *Please remain seated while the bus is in **motion*** (= moving).

motivate (say **moh**-ti-vayt) *verb* (**motivating, motivated**)
to make somebody want to do something: *The best teachers know how to **motivate** children to learn.*
▸ **motivation** (*noun*): *the need for **motivation***

motive (say **moh**-tiv) *noun* (*plural* **motives**)
a reason for doing something: *Was there a **motive** for the murder?*

motley (say **mot**-lee) *adjective*
made up of various sorts: *a **motley** crew of scholars*

motor[1] (say **moh**-tuh) *noun* (*plural* **motors**)
the part inside a machine that makes it move or work: *an electric **motor*** ◇ *The washing machine doesn't work. It needs a new **motor**.*

WORD BUILDING We usually use **engine**, not **motor**, when we are talking about cars and motorbikes.

motor[2] (say **moh**-tuh) *adjective*
1 having or using the power of an engine or motor: *a **motor** car* ◇ *a **motor** boat*
2 relating to vehicles that have engines: *the **motor** industry*

motorbike (say **moh**-tuh-bike) *noun* (*plural* **motorbikes**) (also *formal* **motorcycle**)
a vehicle with two wheels and an engine

motor car *noun* (*plural* **motor cars**) (*formal*) = **car**

motorcyclist (say **moh**-tuh-sike-list) *noun* (*plural* **motorcyclists**)
a person who rides a motorbike

motorist (say **moh**-tuh-rist) *noun* (*plural* **motorists**)
a person who drives a car

mottled (say **mot**-uhld) *adjective*
marked with shapes of different colours without a regular pattern: *The bird has a **mottled** brown chest.*

motto (say **mot**-oh) *noun* (*plural* **mottoes** or **mottos**)
a short sentence or phrase that expresses the beliefs of a person or group: *The South African **motto** means 'People who are different join together'.*

mould[1] (*rhymes with* **gold**) *noun*
1 (*plural* **moulds**) a container that you pour liquid into. The liquid then becomes hard **(sets)** and takes the shape of the container: *They poured the chocolate into a heart-shaped **mould**.*
2 (*no plural*) a soft green, grey or blue substance (called a **fungus**) that grows on food that is too old
▸ **mouldy** (*adjective*): *I threw away the **mouldy** cheese.*

mould[2] (*rhymes with* **gold**) *verb* (**moulding, moulded**)
to make something soft into a certain shape: *The children **moulded** animals out of clay.*

moult (*rhymes with* **bolt**) *verb* (**moulting, moulted**)
(used about an animal or a bird) to lose hairs or feathers before growing new ones: *Penguin feathers aren't waterproof while the penguins are **moulting**.*

mound (say **mownd**) *noun* (*plural* **mounds**)
1 a small hill, or a large pile of earth
2 a pile of things: *a **mound** of newspapers*

Mount (say **mownt**) *noun* (*plural* **Mounts**) (abbr. Mt)
used before the name of a mountain: ***Mount** Everest* ◇ ***Mt** Etna* ◇ ***Mounts** Everest and Etna*

mount (say **mownt**) *verb* (**mounting, mounted**)
1 (also **mount up**) to increase: *Tension in the area is **mounting**.* ◇ *My debts were **mounting** up.*
2 to get on a horse or a bicycle: *Can you **mount** the horse?*

mountains

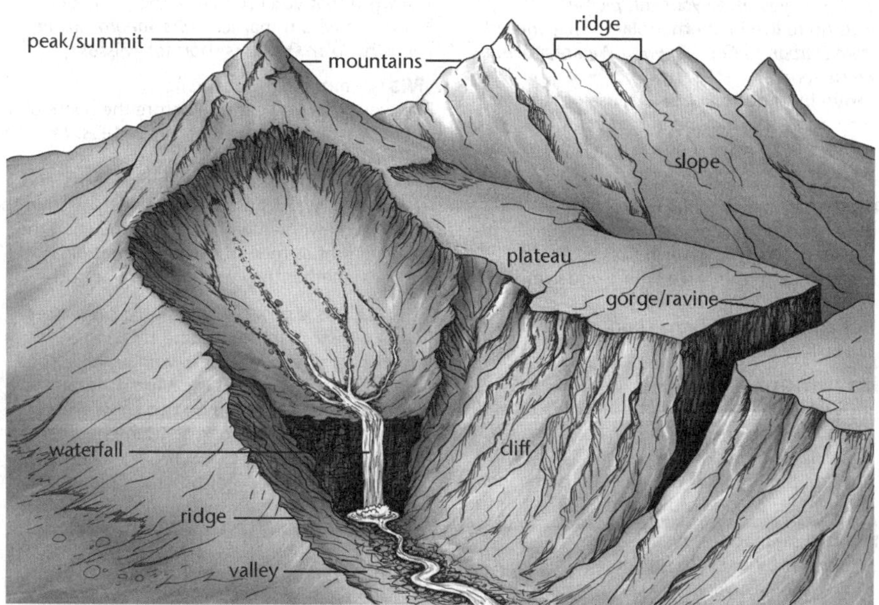

mountain (say **mown**-tuhn) *noun* (*plural* **mountains**)
a very high hill: *Everest is the highest* ***mountain*** *in the world.* ◇ *We climbed the* ***mountain****.*

mouse (say **mowss**) *noun*
1 (*plural* **mice**) a small mammal with a long tail: *Our cat caught a* ***mouse****.*
2 (*plural* **mice** or **mouses**) a small device that is moved by hand across a surface to control the movement of the **cursor** on a computer screen
➲ See illustration at **computer**

mousse (say **mooss**) *noun*
1 (*plural* **mousses**) a type of food that is made by mixing cream, egg whites and a flavour together: *chocolate* ***mousse***
2 (*no plural*) a light substance that you use in your hair to keep its style

mountain bike *noun* (*plural* **mountain bikes**)
a bicycle with a strong frame and wide tyres that you can use to ride over rough ground

mountaineer (say mown-tuh-**neer**) *noun* (*plural* **mountaineers**)
a person who climbs mountains
▸ **mountaineering** (*noun*): *He took up* ***mountaineering*** *when he was young.*

mourn (say **mawn**) *verb* (**mourning, mourned**)
to feel very sad, usually because somebody has died: *She is still* ***mourning*** *for her husband.*
▸ **mourning** (*noun*): *They are in* ***mourning*** *for their son.*

moustache (say muh-**staash**) *noun* (*plural* **moustaches**)
the hair above a man's mouth, below his nose: *He has a* ***moustache****.*

mouth (say **mowth**) *noun* (*plural* **mouths**)
1 the part of your face below your nose that you use for eating and speaking: *Open your* ***mouth****, please!* ➲ See illustration at **face**[1]
2 the place where a river goes into the sea: *the* ***mouth*** *of the Orange River*

mouthful (say **mowth**-fuul) *noun* (*plural* **mouthfuls**)
the amount of food or drink that you can put in your mouth at one time: *She only had a* ***mouthful*** *of cake.*

mouth-organ (say **mowth**-aw-guhn) *noun* (*plural* **mouth-organs**) = **harmonica**

movable (say **moo**-vuhb-l) *adjective*
that can be moved: ***movable*** *assets*

move[1] (say **moov**) *verb* (**moving, moved**)
1 to change the way you are standing or sitting: *Don't* ***move****!*
2 to go from one place to another: *Don't get off the bus while it's* ***moving****.* ◇ *We* ***moved*** *to the front of the bus.*

A B C D E F G H I J K L M N O P Q R S T U V W X Y Z

3 to put something in another place or another way: *Can you* ***move*** *your car, please?*
4 to go to live in another place: *They* ***moved*** *from Durban to Cape Town.* ◇ *We are* ***moving*** *house soon.*
move in to go to live in a house or flat: *I've got a new flat – I'm* ***moving*** *in next week.*
move out to leave a house or flat where you were living

move[2] (say **moov**) *noun* (*plural* **moves**)
1 a change of place or position: *The police are watching every* ***move*** *she makes.*
2 a change in the place where you live: *We need a big truck for the* ***move****.*
get a move on (*informal*) hurry: *Get a* ***move*** *on or you'll be late for work!*

movement (say **moov**-muhnt) *noun* (*plural* **movements**)
1 moving or being moved: *The old man's* ***movements*** *were slow and painful.*
2 a group of people who have the same ideas or beliefs: *a political* ***movement***

movie (say **moov**-ee) *noun*
1 (*plural* **movies**) (also **film**) a film that you see at the cinema: *Would you like to see a* ***movie****?*
2 the movies (*plural noun*) (also **the cinema**) the place where you go to watch a film: *We went to the* ***movies*** *last night.* ❶ **Movie** is short for 'moving picture'.

moving (say **moov**ing) *adjective*
making you feel something strongly, especially sadness: *It's a very* ***moving*** *story.* ➲ SYNONYM **touching**

mow (*rhymes with* **go**) *verb* (**mowing, mowed, has mown**)
to cut grass with a machine: *She is* ***mowing*** *the grass.*

MP (say em-**pee**) *abbreviation* (*plural* **MPs**) **Member of Parliament**

MP3 (say em-pee-**three**) *noun* (*plural* **MP3s**) (also **MP3 file**)
a type of computer file which holds music

MP3 player *noun* (*plural* **MP3 players**)
a piece of computer equipment that can play **MP3** files

Mr (say **miss**-tuh) *noun* (*no plural*)
a word that you use before the name of a man: *Mr Richard Ndamase* ◇ ***Mr*** *Landsman* ❶ **Mr** is short for 'Mister'.

> USAGE **Miss, Mrs, Ms** and **Mr** are all titles that we use before somebody's family name: *Is there a Mrs Mabena here?*

Mrs (say **miss**-uhz) *noun* (*no plural*)
a word that you use before the name of a woman who is married: ***Mrs*** *Sandra Garcia* ◇ ***Mrs*** *Nolan* ❶ **Mrs** is short for 'Missus'.

Ms (say **miz**) *noun* (*no plural*)
a word that you can use before the name of a girl or woman, instead of Mrs or Miss: ***Ms*** *Fiona Green* ◇ ***Ms*** *Zondi*
❶ ORIGIN: 1950s, from combining 'Miss' and 'Mrs'. The word started to be widely used in the 1970s by women who believed they had the same right as men to use a title that did not show whether they were married or not.

> USAGE **Ms** is now widely used in businesses and other organizations and by people generally as the title for a woman, unless she says that she wants to use **Miss** or **Mrs**. It is polite to use **Ms** if you do not know whether a woman is married or not. Many people prefer the title **Ms**, especially in situations when it is irrelevant for other people to know whether they are married or not.

MSG (say em-ess-**jee**) *noun* (*no plural*)
a chemical substance that is sometimes added to food to improve its flavour ❶ **MSG** is short for 'monosodium glutamate'.

Mt *abbreviation* **Mount**

much[1] *adjective, pronoun* (**more, most**)
a big amount of something, or a lot of something: *I haven't got* ***much*** *money.* ◇ *There's too* ***much*** *jam on the bread.* ◇ *There was so* ***much*** *food that we couldn't eat it all.* ◇ *Eat as* ***much*** *as you can.* ◇ *I bought too* ***much****.*
how much? what amount of? what amount of money?: *How* ***much*** *paper do you want?* ◇ *How* ***much*** *does this shirt cost?*

> USAGE We usually use **much** only in negative sentences, in questions, and after 'too', 'so', 'as' and 'how'. In other sentences we use **a lot (of)**: *She's got a lot of money.*

much[2] *adverb*
a lot: *I don't like him very* ***much****.* ◇ *Your flat is* ***much*** *bigger than mine.* ◇ *'Do you like it?' 'No, not* ***much****.'*

muck[1] (say **muk**) *verb* (**mucking, mucked**)
muck about, muck around (*informal*) to behave in a silly way: *Stop* ***mucking*** *about and come and help me!*

muck[2] (say **muk**) *noun* (*no plural*) (*informal*)
dirt or mud: *Don't bring that* ***muck*** *into the house!*

mucus (say **myoo**-kuhss) *noun* (*no plural*)
a thick sticky substance that is produced by groups of cells in the body (called **glands**) to clean and protect parts of the body such as the nose and lungs
▸ **mucous** (*adjective*): ***mucous** glands* ◇ ***mucous** membrane*

> SPELLING Be careful! The noun and the adjective sound the same but they are spelt differently.

mud *noun* (*no plural*)
soft wet earth: *He came home from the football match covered in **mud**.*

muddle (say **mud**-l) *verb* (**muddling, muddled**)
1 (also **muddle something up**) to put things in the wrong order or mix them up: *Their letters were all **muddled** up together in a drawer.*
2 (also **muddle somebody up**) (*informal*) to confuse a person: *Don't ask so many questions – you're **muddling** me.* ➲ SYNONYM **confuse** 1
▸ **muddle** (*noun*): *I was in such a **muddle** that I couldn't find anything.*

muddy (say **mud**-ee) *adjective* (**muddier, muddiest**)
covered with mud: *When it rains, the roads get very **muddy**.*

mudguard (say **mud**-gaad) *noun* (*plural* **mudguards**)
a curved cover over the wheel of a bicycle or motorbike

muesli (say **myooz**-lee or **mooz**-lee) *noun* (*no plural*)
food made from grain, fruit and nuts that you eat with milk for breakfast

muezzin (say moo-**ez**-in) *noun* (*plural* **muezzins**)
a man who calls Muslims to prayer

muffin (say **muf**-in) *noun* (*plural* **muffins**)
a small cake that often contains fruit or chocolate: *a bran **muffin***

muffle (say **muf**-l) *verb* (**muffling, muffled**)
to make a sound quieter: *She put her hand over her mouth to **muffle** her laughter.*
▸ **muffled** (*adjective*): *I heard a **muffled** giggle.*

mug[1] *noun* (*plural* **mugs**)
a big cup, usually with straight sides: *a **mug** of tea*

mug[2] *verb* (**mugging, mugged**)
to attack somebody in the street and take their money
▸ **mugger** (*noun*): *Watch out for **muggers**, especially at night.*

muggy (say **mug**-ee) *adjective* (**muggier, muggiest**)
(used about the weather) warm and slightly wet: *It was hot and **muggy** today.*
➲ SYNONYM **humid**

mulberry (say **mul**-buh-ree) *noun* (*plural* **mulberries**)
a dark red berry that grows on a tree and that you can eat

mulch (say **mulch**) *noun* (*no plural*)
material, for example dead leaves and grass, that you put around the base of a plant to control the temperature and improve the quality of the soil. It also helps to keep water in the soil and stops unwanted plants from growing.
▸ **mulch** (*verb*): *I **mulched** the garden with compost so that I wouldn't have to water the plants so often.*

mule (say **myool**) *noun* (*plural* **mules**)
an animal that is used for carrying heavy loads and whose parents are a horse and a **donkey**

multi- (say **mul**-ti) *prefix*
more than one or many: *a **multicoloured** scarf*
ℹ ORIGIN: from Latin *multus* meaning 'much, many'

multicultural (say mul-ti-**kul**-tshuh-ruhl) *adjective*
for or including people from many different cultures: *We live in a **multicultural** society.*

multilingual (say mul-ti-**ling**-gwuhl) *adjective*
1 (about a person) able to speak more than two languages
2 written in or using many languages: *a **multilingual** dictionary* ◇ *a **multilingual** classroom* ➲ See **bilingual**
▸ **multilingualism** (*noun*)

multimedia (say mul-ti-**mee**-di-uh) *adjective*
using sound, pictures and film as well as words on a screen: *The company makes **multimedia** software* (= computer programs) *for schools.*
▸ **multimedia** (*noun*): *the use of **multimedia** in the classroom*

multimeter (say **mul**-ti-mee-tuh) *noun* (*plural* **multimeters**)
an electronic instrument that can measure different things, particularly different electric measures: *This **multimeter** measures voltage, current and resistance.*

multimillionaire (say mul-ti-mil-yuh-**nair**) *noun* (*plural* **multimillionaires**)
a person who has money and possessions worth several million pounds, dollars or rands
➲ See **millionaire**

A B C D E F G H I J K L M N O P Q R S T U V W X Y Z

multinational (say mul-ti-**nash**-nuhl) *adjective*
existing in or involving many countries: *a **multinational** company*
▸ **multinational** (*noun*): *I work for a **multinational**.*

multiple[1] (say **mul**-tip-l) *noun* (*plural* **multiples**)
a number that contains another number an exact number of times: *28 is a **multiple** of seven, four, two and fourteen.*

multiple[2] (say **mul**-tip-l) *adjective*
involving many people or things or having many parts: ***multiple** copies of documents* ◇ *a **multiple** pile-up* (= a crash involving many vehicles)

multiple-choice (say mul-ti-puhl-**choyss**) *adjective*
(about an exam or question) giving you three or four different answers from which you have to choose the correct one

multiplicand (say mul-ti-pli-**kand**) *noun* (*plural* **multiplicands**) (*maths*)
the number that is multiplied: *In the equation 6 x 4 = 24, the **multiplicand** is 6.*

multiplicative (say mul-ti-**plik**-uh-tiv) *adjective* (*maths*)
having the ability to increase or multiply in number: *a **multiplicative** function*

multiply (say **mul**-ti-ply) *verb* (**multiplying, multiplied**)
to make a number bigger by a certain number of times: *Two **multiplied** by three is six* (= (2 x 3 = 6)). ◇ ***Multiply** three and seven.*
➲ See **divide** 3
▸ **multiplication** (*noun*): *Today we did **multiplication** and division.*

multiracial (say mul-ti-**ray**-shuhl) *adjective*
made up of or relating to people of many different races: *a survey of **multiracial** communities*

multi-storey (say mul-ti-**staw**-ree) *adjective*
with many floors: *a **multi-storey** car park*

multitude (say **mul**-ti-tyood) *noun* (*plural* **multitudes**)
a very large number of people or things: *Alcohol causes a **multitude** of problems.*

mum *noun* (*plural* **mums**) (also **mom**) (*informal*)
mother: *Hello **Mum**!* ◇ *Ask your **mum** if we can go.*

mumble (say **mumb**-l) *verb* (**mumbling, mumbled**)
to speak quietly in a way that is not clear, so that people cannot hear you well: *She **mumbled** something that I couldn't hear.*

mummy (say **mum**-ee) *noun* (*plural* **mummies**)
1 the dead body of a person or animal that has been kept by treating it with special oils and wrapping it in cloth: *an Egyptian **mummy***
2 (*informal*) = **mommy**

mumps (say **mumpss**) *noun* (*no plural*)
an illness that children get which makes their neck swell

munch (*rhymes with* **lunch**) *verb* (**munching, munched**)
to bite or eat something noisily: *I **munched** on an apple.*

mundane (say mun-**dayn**) *adjective*
not interesting or exciting but ordinary: *She had a **mundane** job.* ➲ SYNONYMS **banal, boring**

municipal (say myoo-**niss**-ip-l) *adjective*
relating to a town or city that has its own local government: ***municipal** buildings* ◇ ***municipal** workers*

municipality (say myoo-ni-si-**pal**-i-tee) *noun* (*plural* **municipalities**)
a town or district that has its own government and services: *We pay the **municipality** for our water.*

mural (say **myoo**-ruhl) *noun* (*plural* **murals**)
a large picture painted on a wall: *Let's paint a **mural** on the school wall.*

murder[1] (say **mur**-duh) *noun* (*plural* **murders**)
the crime of killing somebody deliberately: *He was sent to prison for the **murder** of a child.*
➲ SYNONYM **homicide**

murder[2] (say **mur**-duh) *verb* (**murdering, murdered**)
to kill somebody deliberately: *She was **murdered** with a knife.*
▸ **murderer** (*noun*): *The police have caught the **murderer**.*

murky (say **murk**-ee) *adjective* (**murkier, murkiest**)
(usually used about water or air) dark and unpleasant or dirty: *The water was deep and **murky** so we didn't swim.* ➲ SYNONYMS **cloudy, gloomy** 1
▸ **murkiness** (*noun*)

murmur (say **mur**-muh) *verb* (**murmuring, murmured**)
to speak in a low quiet voice: *'I love you,' she **murmured**.*
▸ **murmur** (*noun*): *the **murmur** of voices*

muscle (say **muss**-l) *noun* (*plural* **muscles**)
one of the parts inside your body that are connected to the bones and which you make tight or relax in order to move: *Riding a bicycle is good for developing the leg **muscles**.*

muscular (say **muss**-kyuh-luh) *adjective*
1 relating to muscles: ***muscular** pain* ◇ ***muscular** tissue*
2 having large strong muscles: *a **muscular** boxer*

museum (say myuu-**zee**-uhm) *noun* (*plural* **museums**)
a building where people can look at old or interesting things: *a **museum** of modern art* ◇ *a science **museum***

mushroom¹ (say **mush**-ruum) *noun* (*plural* **mushrooms**)
a type of **fungus** with a thick stalk and a fairly flat or round top. Some **mushrooms** can be eaten as a vegetable.

mushrooms

mushroom² (say **mush**-ruum) *verb* (**mushrooming, mushroomed**)
to increase, spread or develop quickly: *CD sales have **mushroomed** this year.*

music (say **myoo**-zik) *noun* (*no plural*)
1 the sounds that you make by singing, or by playing instruments: *What sort of **music** do you like?* ◇ *Classical, heavy metal, jazz, opera, reggae and rock are types of **music**.*
2 signs on paper to show people what to sing or play: *Can you read **music**?*

musical¹ (say **myoo**-zik-l) *adjective*
1 connected with music: ***musical** instruments (the piano, the guitar or the trumpet, for example)*
2 good at making music: *She's very **musical**.*

musical² (say **myoo**-zik-l) *noun* (*plural* **musicals**)
a play or film that has singing and dancing in it: *We went to see the **musical** 'Chicago'.*

musician (say myoo-**zish**-uhn) *noun* (*plural* **musicians**)
a person who writes music or plays a musical instrument

Muslim (say **muuz**-lim or **muz**-lim) *noun* (*plural* **Muslims**) (also **Moslem**)
a person who follows the religion of Islam
► **Muslim** (*adjective*): *the **Muslim** way of life*

muslin (say **muz**-lin) *noun* (*no plural*)
thin cotton cloth that is almost transparent

mussel (say **muss**-l) *noun* (*plural* **mussels**)
a sea or fresh water shellfish with two shells: ***Mussels** and crayfish are my favourite shellfish to eat.*

must (*rhymes with* **just**) *modal verb*
1 a word that you use to tell somebody what to do or what is necessary: *You **must** look before you cross the road.*
2 a word that shows that you are sure something is true: *You **must** be tired after your long journey.* ◇ *I can't find my keys. I **must** have left them at home.* ➲ See **modal verb**

USAGE In meaning 1 above, you use **must not** or the short form **mustn't** (*say* **muss**-uhnt) to tell people **not** to do something: *You **mustn't** be late.* When you want to say that somebody can do something if they want to, but that it is not necessary, you use **don't have to**: *You **don't have to** do your homework today* (= you can do it today if you want to, but it is not necessary).

mustard (say **muss**-tuhd) *noun* (*no plural*)
a thick yellow sauce with a very strong taste, that you eat with meat

mustn't (say **muss**-uhnt) short for **must not**

musty (say **muss**-tee) *adjective* (**mustier, mustiest**)
having an unpleasant old or wet smell because of a lack of fresh air: *The room is dark and musty.* ➲ SYNONYM **stale**

mutate (say myoo-**tayt**) *verb* (**mutating, mutated**)
to develop or make something develop a new form or structure: *The virus **mutated** into a new form.* ◇ *The TV show **mutated** into a comedy.*
► **mutation** (*noun*): *genetic **mutation***

mute (say **myoot**) *adjective*
not able to speak: *He was struck **mute** by her comments.* ◇ ***Mute** people can make phone calls with this instrument.*
► **mute** (*verb*): *I'll **mute** the sound while we speak.* ► **mutely** (*adverb*) ► **muteness** (*noun*)

A B C D E F G H I J K L **M** N O P Q R S T U V W X Y Z

muti (say **moo**-tee) *noun* (*no plural*) (*S. African*)
1 traditional medicine, especially one that uses plants or parts of animals
2 (*informal*) any medicine: *Put some **muti** on your cut.*
ORIGIN: isiZulu *umuthi* meaning 'plant, tree, medicine'

mutilate (say **myoo**-ti-layt) *verb* (**mutilating**, **mutilated**)
to damage a person or animal's body very badly, often by cutting off parts: *The body had been **mutilated**.* ➲ SYNONYM **maim**
▶ **mutilation** (*noun*)

mutiny (say **myoo**-ti-nee) *noun* (*plural* **mutinies**)
an act of a group of people, especially sailors, refusing to obey the people in command: *There was a **mutiny** on the ship.*
▶ **mutiny** (*verb*) ▶ **mutineer** (*noun*): *There were four **mutineers** on the ship.*

mutter (say **mut**-uh) *verb* (**muttering**, **muttered**)
to speak in a low quiet voice that is difficult to hear: *She **muttered** something about going home, and left the room.*

mutton (say **mut**-uhn) *noun* (*no plural*)
meat from a sheep: ***mutton** stew*
ORIGIN: 13th–15th century, through Old French *moton* meaning 'sheep', from Latin

mutual (say **myoo**-tshuu-uhl) *adjective*
1 (used about a feeling or an action) felt or done equally by both people involved: *The feeling is **mutual**.* ◇ *They shared a **mutual** distrust.*
2 shared by two or more people: *Jo is a **mutual** friend of ours.*
▶ **mutually** (*adverb*): *They have **mutually** agreed to stop arguing.*

muzzle (say **muz**-l) *noun* (*plural* **muzzles**)
1 the nose and mouth of some animals such as dogs
2 a leather or wire cover for an animal's mouth to stop it biting
3 the open end of a gun where the bullets come out
▶ **muzzle** (*verb*): *It's time to **muzzle** the dog.*

my *adjective*
of or belonging to me: *Where is **my** watch?* ◇ *These are **my** books, not yours.* ◇ *I've hurt **my** arm.*

mycelium (say my-**see**-li-uhm) *noun* (*plural* **mycelia**) (*biology*)
the mass of threads that make up the body of a fungus

myriad (say **mi**-ri-uhd) *noun* (*plural* **myriads**)
an extremely large number: *We saw **myriads** of birds in the game park.*
▶ **myriad** (*adjective*): *He faces **myriad** problems.*

myriapod (say **mi**-ri-uh-pod) *noun* (*plural* **myriapods**)
a small crawling animal with many legs and a body made up of sections: *Centipedes and millipedes are **myriapods**.*

myself (say my-**self**) *pronoun* (*plural* **ourselves**)
1 a word that shows the same person as the one who is speaking: *I hurt **myself**.* ◇ *I bought **myself** a new shirt.*
2 a word that makes 'I' stronger: *'Did you buy this cake?' 'No, I made it **myself**.'*
by myself
1 without other people: *I live by **myself**.* ➲ SYNONYM **alone** 1
2 without help: *I made dinner by **myself**.*

mysterious (say miss-**teer**-ri-uhss) *adjective*
strange, or what you do not know about or understand: *Several people said they had seen **mysterious** lights in the sky.*
▶ **mysteriously** (*adverb*): *The plane disappeared **mysteriously**.*

mystery (say **miss**-tree) *noun* (*plural* **mysteries**)
something strange that you cannot understand or explain: *The police say that the man's death is still a **mystery**.*

mystic (say **miss**-tik) *noun* (*plural* **mystics**)
a person who spends their life developing their spirit and communicating with a god: *A **mystic** helped me to find answers.*
▶ **mystical** (*adjective*)

mystify (say **miss**-ti-fy) *verb* (**mystifying**, **mystified**)
to make a person confused because they do not understand something: *These numbers **mystify** me.* ➲ SYNONYMS **bewilder**, **puzzle**[2]

myth (say **mith**) *noun* (*plural* **myths**)
1 a very old story: *Greek **myths***
2 a story or belief that is not true: *It's a **myth** that money makes you happy.*

mythical (say **mith**-ik-l) *adjective*
1 existing only in myths: ***mythical** heroes*
2 not real or true and existing only in your imagination: *It was a **mythical** holiday, I'm afraid.*

mythology (say mith-**ol**-uh-jee) *noun* (*no plural*)
very old stories and the beliefs contained in them: *stories from African and Indian **mythology***

Nn

N *abbreviation* **north** or **northern**

naartjie (say **naa**-chee) *noun* (*plural* **naartjies**)
a fruit like an orange, but smaller and sweeter
🛈 ORIGIN: 18th century, through Afrikaans and South African Dutch, from Tamil *nārattai* meaning 'citrus'. Tamil is a language spoken in India and Sri Lanka.

nag *verb* (**nagging, nagged**)
to keep asking somebody to do something: *My parents often* ***nag*** *me to work harder.*

nail (say **nayl**) *noun* (*plural* **nails**)
1 the hard part at the end of a finger or toe: ***toenails*** ◇ ***fingernails***
2 a small thin piece of metal with one sharp end which you hammer into wood to fix things together
▸ **nail** (*verb*): *I* ***nailed*** *the pieces of wood together.*

naive (say ny-**eev**) *adjective*
without enough experience of life and too ready to trust other people: *The* ***naive*** *girl was tricked by the salesman.*
▸ **naively** (*adverb*): *He* ***naively*** *agreed to the bet.* ▸ **naivety** (*noun*)

naked (say **nay**-kuhd) *adjective*
not wearing any clothes. ➲ SYNONYM **nude**

name[1] (say **naym**) *verb* (**naming, named**)
1 to give a name to a person or thing: *They* ***named*** *their baby Mariaan.* ◇ *They* ***named*** *him Thabiso after his grandfather* (= gave him the same ***name*** *as his grandfather*).
2 to know and say the name of a person or thing: *The headmaster could* ***name*** *every one of his 600 pupils.* ◇ ***Name*** *all the parts of a flower.*

name[2] (say **naym**) *noun* (*plural* **names**)
a word or words that you use to call or talk about a person or thing: *My* ***name*** *is Palisa Mokoena.* ◇ *What's your* ***name****?* ◇ *Do you know the* ***name*** *of this flower?*

WORD BUILDING Your **first name** is the name that you were given when you were born. Your **surname** or **last name** or **family name** is the name that everybody in your family has. Your **full name** is all your names: your **first name**, your **second** or **middle name** (if you have one) and your **surname**. Usually you don't include nicknames in your **full name**. A **nickname** is a name that your friends or family sometimes call you instead of your real name.

namely (say **naym**-lee) *adverb*
used when you are going to name a person or thing that you have just said something about: *Only two students were late,* ***namely*** *David and Msizi.*

namesake (say **naym**-sayk) *noun* (*plural* **namesakes**)
a person who has the same name as someone else

nanny (say **nan**-ee) *noun* (*plural* **nannies**)
a woman whose job is to look after the children of a family

nanny goat (say **nan**-ee goht) *noun* (*plural* **nanny goats**)
a female goat ➲ See **billy goat**

nano- (say **nan**-oh) *prefix*
(used in nouns and adjectives, especially in units of measurement) one billionth: ***nanosecond***

nap *noun* (*plural* **naps**)
a short sleep that you have during the day: *I had a* ***nap*** *after lunch.*

napkin (say **nap**-kin) *noun* (*plural* **napkins**)
a piece of cloth or paper that you use when you are eating to clean your mouth and hands and to keep your clothes clean
➲ SYNONYM **serviette**

nappy (say **nap**-ee) *noun* (*plural* **nappies**)
a piece of cloth or strong paper that a baby wears around its bottom and between its legs: *Does his* ***nappy*** *need changing?*

narcotic (say naa-**kot**-ik) *adjective*
causing sleep and stopping pain: *a* ***narcotic*** *substance*
▸ **narcotic** (*noun*): *Opium and mandrax are* ***narcotics****.*

narrate (say nuh-**rayt**) *verb* (**narrating, narrated**)
to tell a story: *She* ***narrated*** *the story.*
▸ **narration** (*noun*) ▸ **narrator** (*noun*): *I am the* ***narrator*** *of this story.*

narrative (say **na**-ruh-tiv) *noun* (*plural* **narratives**)
the description of the events in a story: *I enjoyed the* ***narrative*** *of her journey to China.*
➲ SYNONYM **story**

narrow (*rhymes with* **barrow**) *adjective* (**narrower, narrowest**)
1 not far from one side to the other: *The bridge*

A B C D E F G H I J K L M N O P Q R S T U V W X Y Z

A B C D E F G H I J K L M N O P Q R S T U V W X Y Z

*was very **narrow**. ◇ a **narrow** ribbon*
➲ OPPOSITES **broad**, **wide**[1] 1
2 by a small amount: *We had a **narrow** escape – the car nearly hit a tree. ◇ a **narrow** defeat*

narrowly (say **na**-roh-lee) *adverb*
only by a small amount: *They **narrowly** escaped injury.*

narrow-minded (say na-roh-**mine**-did) *adjective*
not wanting to accept ideas or opinions that are different from your own: *The people in this town are very **narrow-minded**.*
➲ OPPOSITE **broad-minded**

NASA (say **nass**-uh) *noun* (*no plural*)
a USA government organization that does research into space and is responsible for space travel ❶ **NASA** is short for 'National Aeronautics and Space Administration'.

nasal (say **nay**-suhl) *adjective*
1 of or for the nose: ***nasal** cavity ◇ **nasal** passages*
2 produced partly through the nose: *a **nasal** voice ◇ a **nasal** consonant*

nasty (say **naass**-tee) *adjective* (**nastier**, **nastiest**)
not nice, but bad: *There's a **nasty** smell in this room. ◇ Don't be so **nasty**!* ➲ SYNONYM **horrible**

WORD BUILDING See the Word Building note at **horrible**.

nation (say **nay**-shuhn) *noun* (*plural* **nations**)
a country and all the people who live in it
➲ See note at **country**

national (say **nash**-uhn-l) *adjective*
connected with all of a country or typical of a country: *She wore Swazi **national** costume.*
*◇ **national** newspapers*

national anthem *noun* (*plural* **national anthems**)
the official song of a country

nationality (say nash-uh-**nal**-i-tee) *noun* (*plural* **nationalities**)
the state of belonging to a certain country: *'What **nationality** are you?' 'I'm Australian.'*

nationalize (say **nash**-nuh-lize) *verb* (**nationalizing**, **nationalized**) (also **nationalise**)
to put a company or organization under the control of the government ➲ OPPOSITE **privatize**
▸ **nationalization** (*noun*) (also **nationalisation**)

national park *noun* (*plural* **national parks**)
a large area of beautiful land that is protected by the government so that people can enjoy it

native[1] (say **nay**-tiv) *adjective*
connected with the place where you were born: *I returned to my **native** country. ◇ My **native** language is French.*

native[2] (say **nay**-tiv) *noun* (*plural* **natives**)
a person who was born in a place: *She's a **native** of London.*

nativity (say nuh-**tiv**-uh-tee) *noun*
1 (*plural* **nativities**) (*formal*) a person's birth: *celebrate your **nativity***
2 the Nativity the birth of Jesus Christ
nativity play a play about the birth of Jesus Christ ➲ SYNONYM **birth**

natural (say **nat**-yuu-ruhl) *adjective*
1 made by nature, not by people: *Mpumalanga has some areas of great **natural** beauty.*
*◇ Earthquakes and floods are **natural** disasters.*
*◇ Our **natural** resources include coal, gold and diamonds.*
2 normal or usual: *It's **natural** for parents to feel sad when their children leave home.* ➲ OPPOSITE **unnatural**

naturally (say **nat**-yuu-ruh-lee) *adverb*
1 in a normal way: *Try to stand **naturally** while I take a photo.*
2 in a way that is not made or caused by people: *Is your hair **naturally** curly?*

natural science *noun* (*plural* **natural sciences**)
a part of science that deals with the physical world, for example **biology**, **geology**, **physics**, and **chemistry**

nature (say **nay**-tshuh) *noun*
1 (*no plural*) all the plants and animals in the world and all the things that happen in it that are not made or caused by people: *the beauty of **nature***
2 (*plural* **natures**) the way a person or thing is: *Our cat has a very friendly **nature**.*

naughty (say **naw**-tee) *adjective* (**naughtier**, **naughtiest**)
(used about a child) doing bad things or not doing what you ask them to do: *She's the **naughtiest** child in the class.*

nausea (say **naw**-si-uh) *noun* (*no plural*)
1 the feeling that you are going to vomit
2 a feeling of being sick or disgusted
▸ **nauseate** (*verb*): *The way you complain the whole time **nauseates** me.* ▸ **nauseous** (*adjective*): *I'm feeling a bit **nauseous** after eating that meal.*

nautical (say **naw**-tik-l) *adjective*
relating to the sea and sailing
❶ ORIGIN: 16th century, through French or

Latin from Greek *nautikos*, from *nautēs* meaning 'sailor', from *naus* meaning 'ship'

naval (say **nay**-vuhl) *adjective*
connected with a navy: *a* ***naval*** *officer*

navel (say **nay**-vuhl) *noun* (*plural* **navels**) (also *informal* **belly button**)
the small hole or lump in the middle of your stomach ➲ See illustration at **body**

navigable (say **nav**-i-guhb-l) *adjective*
(used about a river or narrow area of sea) wide and deep enough for ships and boats to sail on

navigate (say **nav**-i-gayt) *verb* (**navigating, navigated**)
to use a map or some other method to find which way a ship, a plane or a car should go: *Long ago, explorers used the stars to* ***navigate****.*
▸ **navigation** (*noun*): ***navigation*** *skills*
▸ **navigator** (*noun*): *Dad's usually the* ***navigator*** *when we go somewhere in the car.*

navy (say **nay**-vee) *noun* (*plural* **navies**)
the ships that a country uses when there is a war, and the people who work on them: *Mark is in the* ***navy****.*
🛈 **ORIGIN**: 14th–15th century, through Old French *navie* meaning 'ship, fleet', from Latin *navis* meaning 'ship'

navy blue *adjective* (also **navy**)
dark blue

Nazi (say **naat**-si) *noun* (*plural* **Nazis**)
1 (*history*) a member of the National Socialist Party which controlled Germany from 1933 to 1945
2 (*informal*) a person who uses their power in a cruel way or a person with extreme and unreasonable views about race
▸ **Nazi** (*adjective*) ▸ **Nazism** (*noun*)

NB (say en-**bee**) *abbreviation*
take note of something: ***NB****, don't be late.*
🛈 **NB** is short for the Latin words 'nota bene', which mean 'note well'.

NCS (say en-se-**ess**) *abbreviation*
National Curriculum Statement

Ndebele (say nduh-**bair**-lee or nduh-**bair**-lair) *noun*
= **isiNdebele**

NE *abbreviation* **north-east**

neap (say **neep**) *noun* (*plural* **neaps**)
a smaller than average **tide** that happens at the first and third quarters of the moon: *at* ***neap*** *tide*

near (say **neer**) *adjective, adverb, preposition* (**nearer, nearest**)
not far away but close to a person or thing: *My house is quite* ***near****.* ◇ *Where's the* ***nearest*** *hospital?* ◇ *My parents live quite* ***near****.* ◇ *I live* ***near*** *the city centre.* ➲ **OPPOSITE far²**

nearby (say **neer**-by) *adjective*
not far away but close: *We took her to a* ***nearby*** *hospital.*
▸ **nearby** (*adverb*): *Let's go and see Tim – he lives* ***nearby****.*

nearly (say **neer**-lee) *adverb*
almost but not quite: *I'm* ***nearly*** *twelve – it's my birthday next week.* ◇ *She was so ill that she* ***nearly*** *died.*
not nearly not at all: *The book wasn't* ***nearly*** *as good as the film.*

neat (say **neet**) *adjective* (**neater, neatest**)
with everything in the right place and done carefully: *Keep your room* ***neat*** *and tidy.* ◇ *She has very* ***neat*** *handwriting.* ➲ **SYNONYM tidy¹ 1**
▸ **neatly** (*adverb*): *Write your name* ***neatly****.*

necessarily (say **ness**-uh-suh-ri-lee) *adverb*
not necessarily not always: *Big men aren't* ***necessarily*** *strong.*

necessary (say **ness**-uh-suh-ree) *adjective*
that you must have or must do: *Warm clothes are* ***necessary*** *in winter.* ➲ **OPPOSITE unnecessary**

necessity (say nuh-**sess**-i-tee) *noun* (*plural* **necessities**)
something that you must have: *Food and clothes are* ***necessities*** *of life.*

neck (say **nek**) *noun* (*plural* **necks**)
1 the part of your body between your shoulders and your head: *Helen wore a thick scarf round her* ***neck****.*
2 the part of a piece of clothing that goes round your neck: *The* ***neck*** *is too tight.*
3 the thin part at the top of a bottle

necklace (say **nek**-luhss) *noun* (*plural* **necklaces**)
a piece of jewellery that you wear round your neck: *a diamond* ***necklace***

nectar (say **nek**-tuh) *noun* (*no plural*)
the sweet liquid in flowers that bees and other insects collect

nectarine (say nek-tuh-**reen**) *noun* (*plural* **nectarines**)
a sweet round fruit with red and orange skin and a large hard seed in the middle

need¹ *verb* (**needing, needed**)
1 to must have something: *All plants and animals* ***need*** *water.* ◇ *You don't* ***need*** *your coat – it's not cold.*
2 to must do something: *James is very ill. He* ***needs*** *to go to hospital.* ◇ *'Do we* ***need*** *to pay now?' 'No, you don't* ***need*** *to pay now.'*

A B C D E F G H I J K L M **N** O P Q R S T U V W X Y Z

need² (say **need**) *noun* (*plural* **needs**)
a situation in which you must have something or do something: *the growing* ***need*** *for new books and equipment* ◇ *There's no* ***need*** *for you to come.* ◇ *She's in* ***need*** *of a rest.*

needle (say **need**-l) *noun* (*plural* **needles**)
1 a small thin piece of metal that you use for sewing cloth: *Put the thread through the eye (= hole) of the* ***needle****.*
2 a small thin piece of metal that forms part of an instrument: *The compass* ***needle*** *points north.* ◇ *a hypodermic* ***needle*** (= for taking blood or giving a medicine)
3 a very thin pointed leaf on a tree that stays green all year: *pine* ***needles***

needless (say **need**-luhss) *adjective*
not necessary or able to be avoided: ***needless*** *suffering* ◇ *The problem is the cost,* ***needless*** *to say* (= it is not necessary to say this, because it is obvious).
▸ **needlessly** (*adverb*): *Many people died* ***needlessly****.*

needlework (say **need**-uhl-wurk) *noun* (*no plural*)
something that you sew by hand, especially for decoration: *She is famous for her* ***needlework****.*
➲ See **embroidery**

needn't (say **need**-uhnt) short for **need not:** *You* ***needn't*** *go if you don't want to.*

needy (say **need**-ee) *adjective* (**needier, neediest**)
(used about people) not having enough money, food or clothes

negate (say ni-**gayt**) *verb* (**negating, negated**) (*formal*)
to make something not work: *Alcohol can* ***negate*** *the effects of some medication.*
▸ **negation** (*noun*)

negative¹ (say **neg**-uh-tiv) *adjective*
1 bad or harmful: *The whole experience was definitely more positive than* ***negative****.*
➲ OPPOSITE **positive** 2
2 only thinking about the bad qualities of somebody or something: *If you go into the match with a* ***negative*** *attitude, you'll never win.*
➲ OPPOSITE **positive** 1
3 using words like 'no', 'not' and 'never': *'I don't like meat' is a* ***negative*** *sentence.*
4 (used about a number) less than zero: *a* ***negative*** *number* ➲ OPPOSITE **positive** 4
5 (used about a medical or scientific test) showing that something has not happened or has not been found: *The results of the pregnancy test were* ***negative****.* ➲ OPPOSITE **positive** 5

negative² (say **neg**-uh-tiv) *noun* (*plural* **negatives**)
a piece of film that we use to make a photograph. On it dark things are light and light things are dark.

neglect (say nig-**lekt**) *verb* (**neglecting, neglected**)
to not take care of a person or thing: *The dog was dirty and thin because its owner had* ***neglected*** *it.*
▸ **neglect** (*noun*): *The house was in a state of* ***neglect****.* ▸ **neglected** (*adjective*): ***neglected*** *children*

negligent (say **neg**-li-juhnt) *adjective*
not taking proper care of a person or thing
➲ SYNONYM **careless**
▸ **negligence** (*noun*): *The fire was a result of* ***negligence****.*

negligible (say **neg**-li-jib-l) *adjective*
very small and not important: *The risks are* ***negligible****.* ➲ SYNONYM **insignificant**

negotiate (say ni-**goh**-shi-ayt) *verb* (**negotiating, negotiated**)
to reach an agreement by talking with other people: *We have* ***negotiated*** *a deal.* ◇ *The unions were* ***negotiating*** *with the management over pay.*

Negro (say **nee**-groh) *noun* (*plural* **Negroes**)
(*old-fashioned*) a member of a group of peoples with dark skin who originally came from Africa

neigh (say **nay**) *verb* (**neighing, neighed**)
(used about a horse) to make a long high sound
▸ **neigh** (*noun*)

neighbour (say **nay**-buh) *noun* (*plural* **neighbours**)
a person who lives near you: *Don't make so much noise or you'll wake the* ***neighbours****.* ◇ *our next-door* ***neighbour***

neighbourhood (say **nay**-buh-huud) *noun* (*plural* **neighbourhoods**)
a part of a town and the people who live there: *They live in a friendly* ***neighbourhood****.* ◇ *He shouted so loudly that the whole* ***neighbourhood*** *could hear him.* ➲ See **community** 1

neighbouring (say **nay**-buh-ring) *adjective*
near or next to: *people from* ***neighbouring*** *villages*

neither¹ (say **ny**-*thuh* or **nee**-*thuh*) *adjective, pronoun*
not one and not the other of two things or people: ***Neither*** *book is very interesting.*

◇ ***Neither** of the boys was there.* ◇ ***Neither** of the boys were there.*

> USAGE Notice that you can use **neither of** with a singular or a plural verb. Look at the example sentences above.

neither² (say **ny**-thuh or **nee**-thuh) *adverb*
also not: *She can't swim and **neither** can I.* ◇ *'I don't like rice.' '**Neither** do I.'*
neither … nor not … and not: ***Neither** Paul **nor** I went to the party.*

nek (say **nek**) *noun* (*plural* **neks**) (*geography*) (*S. African*)
the lowest point of a ridge between two mountains: *The road crosses the mountain range at the **nek**.* ➲ See illustration at **mountain**
ⓘ ORIGIN: 19th century, from South African Dutch

neon (say **nee**-on) *noun* (*no plural*) (symbol Ne)
a type of gas that is used in bright lights and signs

nephew (say **nef**-yoo) *noun* (*plural* **nephews**)
the son of your brother or sister

nepotism (say **nep**-uh-tiz-m) *noun* (*no plural*)
using your power or influence to give an unfair advantage to your family, especially by giving them jobs: *The director was accused of **nepotism**.*

nerd (say **nurd**) *noun* (*plural* **nerds**) (*informal*) a person who spends a lot of time on a particular interest and who is not popular or fashionable
➲ SYNONYM **geek**

nerve (say **nurv**) *noun*
1 (*plural* **nerves**) one of the long thin thread-like things inside your body that carry feelings and messages to and from your brain
2 nerves (*plural noun*) a feeling of worry or fear: *She breathed deeply to calm her **nerves**.*
3 (*no plural*) the state of being brave or calm when there is danger: *You need a lot of **nerve** to be a racing driver.*
get on somebody's nerves (*informal*) to annoy somebody: *Stop making that noise – you're getting on my **nerves**!*

nerve-racking (say **nurv**-rak-ing) *adjective*
making you very nervous or worried: *It was a **nerve-racking** drive up the mountain.*

nervous (say **nurv**-uhss) *adjective*
1 worried or afraid: *I'm quite **nervous** about starting my new job.*
2 connected with the nerves in your body: *the **nervous** system*
▸ **nervously** (*adverb*): *He laughed **nervously**, not knowing what to say.* ▸ **nervousness** (*noun*): *She tried to hide her **nervousness**.*

nest¹ *noun* (*plural* **nests**)
a place where a bird, a snake or an insect keeps its eggs or its babies: *a bird's **nest***

nest² *verb* (**nesting, nested**)
to make and live in a **nest¹**: *The ducks are **nesting** by the river.*

nestle (say **ness**-l) *verb* (**nestling, nestled**)
to make yourself comfortable, protected or hidden: *He **nestled** in his mother's arms.*

net¹ *noun*
1 (*plural* **nets**) material that has very large spaces between the threads, or a piece of this material that we use for a particular purpose: *a fishing **net*** ◇ *a tennis **net*** ◇ *He kicked the ball into the back of the **net**.*
2 the Net (*no plural*) (*informal*) = **Internet**
3 (*plural* **nets**) (*maths*) a diagram of a solid object that shows how the faces of the object are arranged: *Draw the **net** of a cube.*

nets

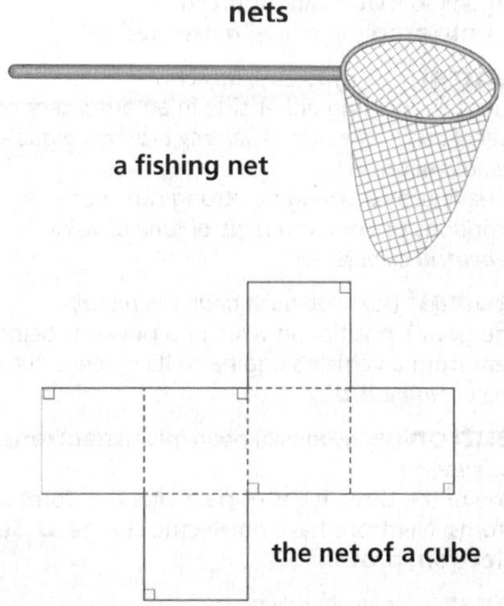

net² *adjective* (also **nett**)
(used about a number or an amount) from which nothing more needs to or can be taken away: *a salary of R7 000 **net*** (= after tax and other deductions have been paid) ◇ *The **net** mass of the jam is 350 g* (= not including the jar). ◇ *a **net** profit*

netball (say **net**-bawl) *noun* (*no plural*)
a game where two teams of seven players, usually women, try to throw a ball through a high round net

nettle (say **net**-l) *noun* (*plural* **nettles**)
a wild plant covered with hairs that can hurt you if you touch them

A B C D E F G H I J K L M N O P Q R S T U V W X Y Z

network (say **net**-wurk) *noun* (*plural* **networks**)
a number of things or people that form a single system or that are closely connected: *the rail* ***network*** ◇ *computer* ***networks*** ◇ *a* ***network*** *of friends*

neurology (say nyoo-**rol**-uh-jee) *noun* (*no plural*)
the study of the nerves and brain and their diseases
▸ **neurological** (*adjective*): *a* ***neurological*** *examination* ▸ **neurologist** (*noun*): *The* ***neurologist*** *told me that I could not move my arm because I had damaged the nerves.*

neurotic (say nyoo-**rot**-ik) *adjective*
always very worried about something: *Edward is* ***neurotic****, because he constantly worries that he is suffering from a life-threatening illness.*

neuter (say **nyoo**-tuh) *verb* (**neutering, neutered**)
(used about an animal) to remove some sexual organs so that it cannot breed
▸ **neutered** (*adjective*): *a* ***neutered*** *cat*

neutral[1] (say **nyoo**-truhl) *adjective*
1 not supporting either side in an argument or war: *I don't take sides when my brothers argue – I remain* ***neutral****.*
2 having or showing no strong qualities, emotions or colour: *a* ***neutral*** *tone of voice* ◇ ***neutral*** *colours*

neutral[2] (say **nyoo**-truhl) *noun* (*no plural*)
the **gear** 1 position in which no power is being sent from a vehicle's engine to its wheels: *Put the car in* ***neutral****.*

neutron (say **nyoo**-tron) *noun* (*plural* **neutrons**) (*science*)
one of the three types of **particles** that form all atoms. Neutrons have no electric charge. ➲ See **electron**, **proton**

never (say **nev**-uh) *adverb*
not at any time or ever: *She* ***never*** *works on Saturdays.* ◇ *I've* ***never*** *been to America.* ◇ *I will* ***never*** *forget you.*

nevertheless (say nev-uh-*thuh*-**less**) *adverb*
(*formal*) but: *They played very well.* ***Nevertheless****, they didn't win.* ➲ SYNONYM **however** 2

Nevirapine (say nuh-**vy**-ruh-peen) *noun* (*no plural*)
a medicine that is used to prevent and treat illnesses caused by **HIV**

new (say **nyoo**) *adjective* (**newer, newest**)
1 not existing before: *Have you seen his* ***new*** *film?* ◇ *a* ***new*** *pair of shoes* ➲ OPPOSITE **old** 2
2 different from before: *Our* ***new*** *flat is much bigger than our old one.* ◇ *The teacher usually explains the* ***new*** *words to us.* ➲ OPPOSITE **old** 4
3 doing something for the first time: ***New*** *parents* (= who have just had a baby) *are often tired.* ◇ *He's* ***new*** *to the job and still needs help.*

newcomer (say **nyoo**-kum-uh) *noun* (*plural* **newcomers**)
a person who has just come to a place

newly (say **nyoo**-lee) *adverb*
not long ago: *Our school is* ***newly*** *built.*
➲ SYNONYM **recently**

news (say **nyooz**) *noun* (*no plural*)
1 information about things that have just happened: *Have you heard my* ***news****? I'm getting married.* ◇ *I've got some good* ***news****.*
2 the news a programme on television or radio that tells people about important things that have just happened: *We heard about the plane crash on the* ***news****.*
break the news to be the first person to tell somebody about something important: *Have you broken the* ***news*** *to your wife?*

> USAGE Be careful! In meaning 1 above, you cannot say 'a news'. To talk about a single item, you can say **some news** or **a piece of news**: *I've got* ***some news*** *for you!*

newspaper (say **nyooss**-pay-puh) *noun*
1 (*plural* **newspapers**) large pieces of paper with news, advertisements and other things printed on them: *a daily* ***newspaper***
2 (*no plural*) paper taken from old newspapers: *We wrapped the plates in* ***newspaper*** *before packing them.*

newsprint (say **nyooz**-print) *noun* (*no plural*)
the type of paper that newspapers are printed on

newt (say **nyoot**) *noun* (*plural* **newts**)
a small **amphibian** with short legs and a long tail that lives near or in water

newton (say **nyoo**-tuhn) *noun* (*plural* **newtons**) (abbr. N)
a unit for measuring force: *On the Earth's surface a mass of 1 kilogram exerts a force of about 10* ***newtons****.*
🛈 ORIGIN: 20th century, named after Sir Isaac Newton (1642–1727), an English mathematician and scientist

new year *noun* (*no plural*) (also **New Year**)
the beginning of the year: *Happy* ***New Year****!* ◇ *We will get in touch in the* ***new year****.*

> WORD BUILDING 1 January is called **New Year's Day** and 31 December is called **New Year's Eve**.

next¹ (say **nekst**) *adjective*
1 coming after this one: *I'm going on holiday **next** week.* ◊ *Take the **next** road on the right.*
2 nearest to this one: *I live in the **next** village.*
next to a person or **thing** at the side of somebody or something: *The bank is **next** to the post office.* ➲ SYNONYM **beside**

next² (say **nekst**) *adverb*
straight after this: *I've finished this work. What shall I do **next**?*

next³ (say **nekst**) *noun* (*no plural*)
the person or thing that comes after this one: *She came first and he was the **next** to arrive.*

next door *adverb*
in or to the nearest house: *Who lives **next door**?*
▶ **next-door** (*adjective*): *They're my **next-door** neighbours.*

NGO (say en-jee-**oh**) *noun* (*plural* **NGOs**)
an organization, usually a charity, that is not run by the government ❶ **NGO** is short for 'non-governmental organization'.

Nguni (say **ngoo**-ni) *adjective*
1 relating to a group of southern African languages which includes isiNdebele, isiXhosa, isiZulu, and Siswati: ***Nguni** languages*
➲ See **Sotho**
2 (used about certain animals) belonging to Nguni-speaking people: ***Nguni** cattle* ◊ ***Nguni** sheep*

nib *noun* (*plural* **nibs**)
the metal point of a pen, where the coloured liquid (called **ink**) comes out

nibble (say **nib**-l) *verb* (**nibbling, nibbled**)
to eat something in very small bites: *The mouse **nibbled** the cheese.*

nice (say **nise**) *adjective* (**nicer, nicest**)
pleasant, good or kind: *Did you have a **nice** holiday?* ◊ *I met a **nice** boy at the party.* ◊ *It's **nice** to see you.* ◊ *It's **nice** and warm by the fire.*
▶ **nicely** (*adverb*): *You can have a cake if you ask **nicely*** (= in a polite way).

WORD BUILDING There are many words that you can use instead of **nice**, but check their exact meanings first. Examples are: **attractive**, **cool¹**3 (informal), **delicious**, **enjoyable**, **fantastic** (informal), **friendly**, **good¹**, **great**5 (informal), **kind²**, **likeable**, **lovely**, **pleasant**, and **wonderful**. See the Word Building note at **good¹** also.

niche (say **neesh**) *noun* (*plural* **niches**)
1 a position or job that is perfect for you: *I've found my **niche**.*
2 a place in a wall that is set further back where a statue or decoration can be put
3 (in business) an opportunity to sell a particular product to a particular group of people: *a **niche** market*
4 (*biology*) the conditions of its environment within which a particular animal or plant lives successfully

nick¹ (say **nik**) *noun* (*plural* **nicks**)
a very small cut in something: *Is that a **nick** on your face?*

nick² (say **nik**) *verb* (**nicking, nicked**)
1 to make a small cut: *He **nicked** himself while shaving.*
2 (*informal*) to steal: *My bike was **nicked**!*

nickel (say **nik**-l) *noun*
1 (*no plural*) (symbol Ni) a hard silver-white metal that is often mixed with other metals
2 (*plural* **nickels**) an American and Canadian coin worth five cents

nickname (say **nik**-naym) *noun* (*plural* **nicknames**)
a name that your friends or family sometimes call you instead of your real name
▶ **nickname** (*verb*): *He was **nicknamed** 'Spiderman'.*

nicotine (say **nik**-uh-teen) *noun* (*no plural*)
a poisonous chemical in cigarettes that makes it difficult to stop smoking
❶ ORIGIN: 19th century, from Latin *nicotiana* meaning 'tobacco plant', named after Jean Nicot, a French diplomat who introduced tobacco to France in 1560

niece (say **neess**) *noun* (*plural* **nieces**)
the daughter of your brother or sister
➲ See **nephew**

niggle (say **nig**-l) *verb* (**niggling, niggled**)
1 to annoy or worry somebody: *Those habits **niggle** me!*
2 to complain about something that is not important: *Everybody was **niggling** about the heat.*
▶ **niggling** (*adjective*) ▶ **niggly** (*adjective*): *The baby is **niggly** today.*

night (say **nite**) *noun* (*plural* **nights**)
1 the part of the day when it is dark and most people sleep: *These animals come out at **night**.* ◊ *The baby cried all **night**.* ◊ *She stayed at my house last **night**.* ◊ *He stayed for two **nights**.*
2 the part of the day between the afternoon and when you go to bed: *We went to a party on Saturday **night**.* ◊ *He doesn't get home until 8 o'clock at **night**.* ➲ See **tonight**

A B C D E F G H I J K L M N O P Q R S T U V W X Y Z

A B C D E F G H I J K L M **N** O P Q R S T U V W X Y Z

nightclub (say **nite**-klub) *noun* (*plural* **nightclubs**)
a place where you can go late in the evening to drink and dance ➲ SYNONYM **club**[1] 2

nightdress (say **nite**-dress) *noun* (*plural* **nightdresses**) (also **nightie**)
a loose dress that a woman or girl wears in bed

nightfall (say **nite**-fawl) *noun* (*no plural*)
the start of the night ➲ SYNONYM **dusk** ➲ OPPOSITE **dawn**

nightlife (say **nite**-life) *noun* (*no plural*)
things to do in the evenings in a particular area, such as dancing or going to bars: *What's the **nightlife** like round here?*

nightly (say **nite**-lee) *adjective, adverb*
happening or coming every night: *a **nightly** TV show* ◇ *Owls hunt for food **nightly**.*

nightmare (say **nite**-mair) *noun* (*plural* **nightmares**)
1 a dream that frightens you: *I had a **nightmare** last night.*
2 something that is very bad or frightening: *Travelling through the storm was a **nightmare**.*

night-time (say **nite**-time) *noun* (*no plural*)
the time when it is dark: *She is afraid to go out at **night-time**.* ➲ OPPOSITE **daytime**

nil *noun* (*no plural*)
the number 0, especially when it is the score in games such as football: *Our team won the match by two goals to **nil**.*

nimble (say **nimb**-l) *adjective* (**nimbler**, **nimblest**)
able to move quickly and lightly ➲ SYNONYM **agile**
▸ **nimbly** (*adverb*): *He **nimbly** got out of the way.*

nimbus (say **nim**-buhss) *noun* (*no plural*)
a large grey rain cloud ➲ See **cumulonimbus**

nine *number*
9
▸ **ninth** (*adjective, adverb*): *He was the **ninth*** (= 9th) *runner to come in.*

nineteen (say nine-**teen**) *number*
19
▸ **nineteenth** (*adjective, adverb*): *She had a party on her **nineteenth*** (= 19th) *birthday.*

ninety (say **nine**-tee) *number*
1 90
2 the nineties (*plural noun*) the numbers between 90 and 99 or the years between 1990 and 1999: *She was born in the **nineties*** (= in the 1990s).
in your nineties between the ages of 90 and 99: *My grandmother is in her **nineties**.*
▸ **ninetieth** (*adjective, adverb*): *It's his **ninetieth*** (= 90th) *birthday.*

nip *verb* (**nipping**, **nipped**)
1 to give somebody a quick painful bite: *The dog **nipped** his leg.*
2 (*informal*) to go somewhere quickly: *I'm just **nipping** to the shops.*

nipple (say **nip**-l) *noun* (*plural* **nipples**)
one of the two small dark circles on either side of your chest. A baby sucks milk from its mother's breasts through them.
➲ SYNONYM **teat** 2

nippy (say **nip**-ee) *adjective* (**nippier**, **nippiest**) (*informal*)
1 quite cold ➲ SYNONYM **chilly**
2 able to move quickly: *a **nippy** car*

Nirvana (say nur-**vaa**-nuh) *noun* (*no plural*)
(in the religion of Buddhism) the state of peace and happiness that a person achieves after giving up all personal desires

nit *noun* (*plural* **nits**)
the egg or young form of a louse (= a small insect that lives in human hair)

nitrate (say **nite**-rayt) *noun* (*plural* **nitrates**)
a chemical compound containing **nitrogen**, often used to improve the quality of the soil: *The farmer used **nitrates** to increase his soil fertility.*

nitric acid (say nite-trik **ass**-id) *noun* (*no plural*)
a powerful acid that is used to make explosive substances and other chemical products

nitrogen (say **nite**-ruh-juhn) *noun* (*no plural*) (symbol N)
the gas that makes up about 80% of the air

nitwit (say **nit**-wit) *noun* (*plural* **nitwits**) (*informal*) a silly or stupid person

nkosi (say **nkaw**-si) ➲ See **inkosi**

nkosikazi (say **nkaw**-si-kaa-zi) ➲ See **inkosikazi**

Nkosi sikelel' iAfrika (say **nkaw**-si sik-uh-**le**-li-**uf**-ri-kuh) *noun*
South Africa's national song (called an **anthem**): ***Nkosi sikelel' iAfrika** means God bless Africa.*
ℹ ORIGIN: from isiXhosa, meaning 'Lord, bless Africa'

No. *abbreviation* (*plural* **Nos.**) (also **no.**)
number[1] 1

no[1] (*rhymes with* **go**) *exclamation*
1 used for giving a negative reply or statement: *'Do you want a drink?' '**No**, thank you.'* ◇ *'He's*

Italian.' 'No, he isn't.' ➲ OPPOSITE **yes**
2 something that you say when something bad happens or to show you are surprised or shocked: *Oh **no**! I've broken my watch!*

no² (*rhymes with* **go**) *adjective*
1 not one or not any: *I have **no** money – my purse is empty.* ◇ ***No** visitors may enter without a ticket.*
2 used for saying that something is not allowed: *The sign said '**No** Smoking'.*

no³ (say **noh**) *adverb*
not any: *My flat is **no** bigger than yours.*

nobility (say noh-**bil**-uh-tee) *noun* (*no plural*)
1 being good, honest, and brave
2 the nobility the social class that **nobles** belong to: *The **nobility** were expected to defend the king.*

noble¹ (say **noh**-buhl) *adjective* (**nobler**, **noblest**)
1 good, honest, brave and caring about other people: ***noble** thoughts*
2 belonging to the highest social class: *a man of **noble** birth*

noble² (say **noh**-buhl) *noun* (*plural* **nobles**) (also **nobleman**, **noblewoman**)
(especially in the past) in Europe, a person who belongs to a high and powerful social class: *In the Middle Ages, **nobles** lived in castles and ruled the peasants.*

nobody (say **noh**-bod-ee) *pronoun*
no person or not anybody: ***Nobody** in our class speaks French.* ◇ *There was **nobody** at home.*
➲ SYNONYM **no one**

nocturnal (say nok-**turn**-l) *adjective*
active at night or relating to the night: *Most owls are **nocturnal**. They are awake at night and sleep during the day.* ➲ OPPOSITE **diurnal** 1

nocturne (say **nok**-turn) *noun* (*plural* **nocturnes**)
a short piece of music in a romantic style, especially for the piano

nod *verb* (**nodding, nodded**)
to move your head down and up again quickly as a way of saying 'yes' or 'hello' to somebody: *'Do you understand?' asked the teacher, and everybody **nodded**.*
nod off to go to sleep: *Grandma **nodded** off in her chair.*
▶ **nod** (*noun*): *He gave me a **nod** when I arrived.*

node (*rhymes with* **road**) *noun* (*plural* **nodes**)
1 (*biology*) the place on the long thin part of the plant (called a **stem**) from which a branch or leaf grows
2 (*maths*) a point at which two lines meet or cross
3 a small lump or mass: *a lymph **node***

noise (say **noyz**) *noun* (*plural* **noises**)
a sound, especially one that is loud or unpleasant: *I heard a **noise** upstairs.* ◇ *Don't make so much **noise**!*

noisy (say **noyz**-ee) *adjective* (**noisier**, **noisiest**)
making a lot of noise, or full of noise: *The children are very **noisy**.* ◇ *The restaurant was too **noisy**.* ➲ OPPOSITE **quiet¹** 1
▶ **noisily** (*adverb*): *He ate his dinner **noisily**.*

nomad (say **noh**-mad) *noun* (*plural* **nomads**)
a member of a group of people who move from place to place with their animals
▶ **nomadic** (*adjective*): *a **nomadic** people*

nominate (say **nom**-i-nayt) *verb* (**nominating, nominated**)
to **propose** 1 that a person or thing is given something such as a job or a prize: *I **nominate** Billy for class rep.* ◇ *This film has been **nominated** for an award.*
▶ **nomination** (*noun*)

non- (say **non**) *prefix*
added to the beginning of some words to give them the opposite meaning, for example: ***non-alcoholic** drinks* (= drinks containing no alcohol) ◇ *a **non-smoker*** (= a person who does not smoke) ◇ *This train is **non-stop*** (= does not stop before the end of the journey).
🛈 ORIGIN: from Latin *non* meaning 'not'

nonagon (say **non**-uh-guhn) *noun* (*plural* **nonagons**) (*maths*)
a flat closed shape with nine straight sides

nonchalant (say **non**-shuh-luhnt) *adjective*
not feeling or showing interest or excitement about something: *He was **nonchalant** about winning the prize.*
▶ **nonchalantly** (*adverb*): *She walked past **nonchalantly**.* ▶ **nonchalance** (*noun*)

non-committal (say non-kuh-**mit**-l) *adjective*
not saying or showing what your opinion is: *They were **non-committal** about the art.*

nondescript (say **non**-duh-skript) *adjective*
not having any interesting or unusual qualities: *It was a **nondescript** house.* ➲ SYNONYM **ordinary**

none (say **nun**) *pronoun*
not any, or not one: *She ate all the sweets – there are **none** left.* ◇ *I went to four shops, but*

none of them had the book I wanted. ◇ ***None** of the girls is hungry.*

> USAGE Note that with **none of** you can use the verb in the plural or the singular: ***None** of the boys **want** to come.* ◇ ***None** of the boys **wants** to come.*

non-fiction (say non-**fik**-shuhn) *noun* (*no plural*)
writing that is about real people, events and facts: *I enjoy reading **non-fiction**.*
➲ OPPOSITE **fiction**

nonsense (say **non**-suhnss) *noun* (*no plural*)
words or ideas that have no meaning or that are not true: *It's **nonsense** to say that she is lazy.*

noodles (say **nood**-uhlz) *plural noun*
long thin lines of food made from flour, eggs and water (called **pasta**), which are used especially in Chinese and Italian cooking: *Would you prefer rice or **noodles**?*

nook (say **nuuk**) *noun* (*plural* **nooks**)
a small quiet place or corner
nooks and crannies every part of a place: *I searched all the **nooks** and crannies.*

noon *noun* (*no plural*)
twelve o'clock in the middle of the day: *I met him at **noon**.* ➲ SYNONYM **midday**

no one *pronoun*
no person or not anybody: *There was **no one** in the classroom.* ◇ ***No one** saw me go into the house.* ➲ SYNONYM **nobody**

noose (say **nooss**) *noun* (*plural* **nooses**)
a circle that is tied at one end of a rope that gets tighter as the rope is pulled: *They used a **noose** to catch the bull.*

nor (say **naw**) *conjunction*
used after 'neither' and 'not' to mean 'also not': *Neither Tom **nor** I eat meat.* ◇ *If he doesn't go, **nor** will she.* ◇ *'I don't like eggs.' '**Nor** do I.'*

norm (say **nawm**) *noun*
1 (often **the norm**) (*no plural*) a situation or way of behaving that is usual or normal: *Hot weather is the **norm** for this time of the year.*
2 norms (*plural noun*) standards of behaviour that are typical of or accepted by a particular group or society: ***norms** of good behaviour*
3 (*plural* **norms**) a required or agreed standard: *education **norms** for children of particular ages*

normal (say **nawm**-l) *adjective*
1 usual and ordinary and not different or special: *I will be home at the **normal** time.*
2 not suffering from any mental disorder: *People who commit such crimes aren't **normal**.*
➲ OPPOSITE **abnormal**

normally (say **nawm**-uh-lee) *adverb*
1 usually: *I **normally** go to bed at about ten o'clock.*
2 in the usual or ordinary way: *He isn't behaving **normally**.*

north (say **nawth**) *noun* (*no plural*) (abbr. N)
the direction to your left when you watch the sun rise, or a place in this direction: *the **north** of the country*
► **north** (*adjective, adverb*): *a **north** wind* (= that comes from the north) ◇ *We travelled **north** to Zimbabwe.*

north-east (say nawth-**eest**) *noun* (*no plural*) (abbr. NE)
the direction between north and east, or a place in this direction: *He lives in the **north-east**.*
► **north-east** (*adjective, adverb*): ***north-east** America* ► **north-eastern** (*adjective*): ***north-eastern** regions*

northern (say **nawth**-uhn) *adjective*
connected with, in or from the north: *Hluhluwe is in **northern** KwaZulu-Natal.*

North Pole *noun* (*no plural*)
the point on the Earth's surface which is furthest north ➲ See illustration at **globe**
➲ See **South Pole**

north-west (say nawth-**west**) *noun* (*no plural*) (abbr. NW)
the direction between north and west, or a place in this direction: *a strong wind from the **north-west***
► **north-west** (*adjective, adverb*): ***north-west** Johannesburg* ► **north-western** (*adjective*): ***north-western** France*

nose (*rhymes with* **froze**) *noun* (*plural* **noses**)
1 the part of your face above your mouth that you use for breathing and smelling: *Blow your **nose**!* (= Clear your **nose** by blowing through it.)
➲ See illustration at **face**[1]
2 the front part of a plane

nostalgia (say noss-**tal**-juh) *noun* (*no plural*)
a feeling of pleasure and sadness that you feel when you think about happy times in the past: *She was filled with **nostalgia** when she saw the photos.*
► **nostalgic** (*adjective*) ► **nostalgically** (*adverb*)

nostril (say **noss**-tril) *noun* (*plural* **nostrils**)
one of the two holes in your nose ➲ See illustration at **face**[1]

nosy (say **noh**-zee) *adjective* (**nosier, nosiest**)
too interested in other people's lives, in a way which is annoying: *'Where are you going?' 'Don't be so **nosy**!'*

not *adverb*
used for forming negative sentences or phrases: *I'm **not** hungry.* ◇ *They did **not** arrive.* ◇ *I can come tomorrow, but **not** on Tuesday.* ◇ *'Are you angry with me?' 'No, I'm **not**.'*
not at all
1 no, definitely not: *'Are you tired?' '**Not** at all.'*
2 used as a reply when somebody has thanked you for something: *'Thanks for your help.' 'Oh, **not** at all.'*

SPEAKING We often use **n't** instead of **not**: *John **isn't*** (= is not) here. I ***haven't*** (= have not) got any sisters.

notable (say **noht**-uhb-l) *adjective*
interesting or important enough to receive attention: *This town is **notable** for its views.* ➲ SYNONYM **remarkable**
▸ **notably** *(adverb)*

notation (say noh-**tay**-shuhn) *noun (plural* **notations***)*
a system of symbols that represent something, such as in mathematics, science or music

notch (say **noch**) *noun (plural* **notches***)*
1 a cut on the surface of something, sometimes to help you count: *There is a **notch** on his stick for each fish he's caught.*
2 a level on a scale of quality: *This food is a **notch** above normal.*

note¹ *(rhymes with* **vote***) noun (plural* **notes***)*
1 words that you write quickly to help you remember something: *I made a **note** of her address.* ◇ *The teacher told us to take **notes**.*
2 a short letter: *She sent me a **note** to thank me for the present.*
3 a piece of paper money: *He gave me a R20 **note**.*
4 a short piece of extra information about something in a book: *Look at the **note** on page 39.*
5 one sound in music, or the written symbol for one sound: *I can play a few **notes**.*

note² *(rhymes with* **vote***) verb* **(noting, noted)**
to notice and remember something: *Please **note** that the shop will be closed on Monday.*
note something down to write something so that you can remember it: *The police officer **noted** down my name.*

notebook (say **noht**-buuk) *noun (plural* **notebooks***)*
1 a small book that you can write in
2 a very small computer that you can carry with you and use anywhere

notepad (say **noht**-pad) *noun (plural* **notepads***)*
pieces of paper that you can write on, joined together in a block

notepaper (say **noht**-pay-puh) *noun (no plural)*
paper that you write letters on

nothing (say **nuth**-ing) *pronoun*
no thing, or not anything: *There's **nothing** in this bottle – it's empty.* ◇ *I've finished all my work and I've got **nothing** to do.* ◇ *Don't leave the baby there with **nothing** on* (= not wearing any clothes) *– he'll get cold.*
be or **have nothing to do with a person or thing** to have no connection with a person or thing: *That question has **nothing** to do with the problem.* ◇ *Keep out of this – it's **nothing** to do with you.*
for nothing
1 for no money: *You can have these books for **nothing**.* ➲ SYNONYM **free²** 2
2 without a good result: *I went to the station for **nothing** – she wasn't on the train.*
nothing but only: *He eats **nothing** but salad.*
nothing like not the same as somebody or something in any way: *She's **nothing** like her brother.*

notice¹ (say **noh**-tiss) *noun*
1 *(plural* **notices***)* a piece of writing that tells people something: *The **notice** on the wall says 'NO SMOKING'.*
2 *(no plural)* a warning that something will happen, or the amount of time before it happens: *We only had two weeks' **notice** of the exam.* ◇ *We left for town at short **notice** and I forgot my coat.* ◇ *He's handed in his **notice*** (= he has said officially that he will leave his job).
take no notice to not pay attention to something: *Take no **notice** of what she said.*
➲ SYNONYM **ignore**

notice² (say **noh**-tiss) *verb* **(noticing, noticed)**
to see or pay attention to a person or thing: *Did you **notice** what she was wearing?* ◇ *I **noticed** that he was driving a new car.*

noticeable (say **noh**-tiss-uhb-l) *adjective*
easy to see: *I've got a mark on my shirt. Is it **noticeable**?*

noticeboard (say **noh**-tiss-bawd) *noun (plural* **noticeboards***)*
a board on a wall for information: *The teacher put the exam results on the **noticeboard**.*

notify (say **noh**-ti-fy) *verb* **(notifying, notified)** *(formal)*
to tell somebody officially about something: *We were **notified** about the exams.* ➲ SYNONYM **tell** 1
▸ **notification** *(noun)*

A B C D E F G H I J K L M N O P Q R S T U V W X Y Z

notion (say **noh**-shuhn) *noun* (*plural* **notions**)
an idea: *I had a **notion** that they were planning something.*

notorious (say noh-**taw**-ri-uhss) *adjective*
well known for being bad: *a **notorious** criminal*
▶ **notoriously** (*adverb*): *This road is **notoriously** dangerous.*

nougat (say **noo**-gaa) *noun* (*no plural*)
a soft sweet with nuts in it

nought (say **nawt**) *noun* (*plural* **noughts**)
the number 0: *We say 0.5 as '**nought** point five'.*
➲ SYNONYM **zero**

noun (*rhymes with* **brown**) *noun* (*plural* **nouns**) (*grammar*)
a word that is the name of a person, place, thing or an idea: *'Anne', 'Kimberley', 'cat' and 'happiness' are all **nouns**.* ➲ See Study pages 4 and 5

nourish (say **nu**-rish) *verb* (**nourishing, nourished**)
to give a person or thing the right food so that they can grow and be healthy: *Eat balanced meals to **nourish** your body.*
➲ SYNONYMS **feed**[1] 1, **sustain** 1
▶ **nourishment** (*noun*): *There is **nourishment** for plants in the soil.* ▶ **nourishing** (*adjective*): *a delicious and **nourishing** meal*

novel[1] (say **nov**-l) *noun* (*plural* **novels**)
a book that tells a story about people and things that are not real: *'David Copperfield' is a **novel** by Charles Dickens.*

novel[2] (say **nov**-l) *adjective*
new, different and interesting: *a **novel** idea*

novelist (say **nov**-uh-list) *noun* (*plural* **novelists**)
a person who writes novels

November (say noh-**vem**-buh) *noun*
the eleventh month of the year
ⓘ ORIGIN: through Old English, from Latin *novem* meaning 'nine'. November was the ninth month of the Roman year.

novice (say **nov**-iss) *noun* (*plural* **novices**)
a person who is new to and without experience in a certain job or sport: *She is a **novice** at soccer.* ➲ SYNONYM **beginner**

now[1] (*rhymes with* **cow**) *adverb*
1 at this time: *I can't see you **now** – can you come back later?* ◇ *Don't wait – do it **now**!* ◇ *From **now** on* (= after this time) *your teacher will be Mr Hancock.*
2 used when you start to talk about something new, or to make people listen to you: *I've finished writing this letter. **Now**, what shall we have for dinner?* ◇ *Be quiet, **now**!*

now[2] (*rhymes with* **cow**) *conjunction* (also **now that**)
because something has happened: ***Now** that Mark has arrived we can start dinner.*

nowadays (say **now**-uh-dayz) *adverb*
at this time: *A lot of people work with computers **nowadays**.*

nowhere (say **noh**-wair) *adverb, pronoun*
at, in or to no place, or not anywhere: *There's **nowhere** to stay in this village.* ◇ *I'm going **nowhere**!*
nowhere near not at all: *His English is **nowhere** near as good as yours.*

noxious (say **nok**-shuhs) *adjective*
harmful or unpleasant: *a **noxious** weed* ◇ *a **noxious** gas* ◇ *a **noxious** idea*

nozzle (say **noz**-l) *noun* (*plural* **nozzles**)
the narrow tube at the end of a pipe that controls the liquid or gas that comes out

NQF (say en-kew-**ef**) *abbreviation*
National Qualifications Framework

nuclear (say **nyoo**-kli-uh) *adjective*
1 using the energy that is made from reactions within the central part (the **nucleus**) of an atom: ***nuclear** energy* ◇ ***nuclear** weapons*
2 that has to do with the nucleus of an atom: ***nuclear** physics*

nucleated (say nyoo-kli-**ayt**-d) *adjective*
formed around a central area: *Rural settlements are either **nucleated** or dispersed.*

nucleus (say **nyoo**-kli-uhss) *noun* (*plural* **nuclei**)
the centre of a cell or an atom ➲ See illustration at **cell** 1

nude (say **nyood**) *adjective*
not wearing any clothes ➲ SYNONYM **naked**

nudge (say **nuj**) *verb* (**nudging, nudged**)
to touch or push a person or thing with your elbow: ***Nudge** me if I fall asleep in the film.*
▶ **nudge** (*noun*): *She gave me a **nudge**.*

nugget (say **nug**-it) *noun* (*plural* **nuggets**)
1 a rough piece of gold as it is found in the ground
2 a small piece of something such as food: *chicken **nuggets*** ◇ ***nuggets** of information*

nuisance (say **nyoo**-suhnss) *noun* (*plural* **nuisances**)
a person or thing that causes you trouble: *I've lost my keys. What a **nuisance**!*

numb (say **num**) *adjective* (**number, numbest**)
not able to feel anything: *My fingers were **numb** with cold.*

number¹ (say **num**-buh) *noun* (*plural* **numbers**)
1 (abbr. No. or no.) a word or symbol that represents a quantity, for example 'two' or '130': *Choose a* ***number*** *between ten and one hundred.* ◇ *My phone* ***number*** *is 096 56767.* ◇ *I live at* ***no.*** *47.* ➲ See Study page 20
2 a group of more than one person or thing: *A large* ***number*** *of our learners come from Malawi.* ◇ *There are a* ***number*** *of ways to cook an egg.*

number² (say **num**-buh) *verb* (**numbering, numbered**)
to give a number to something: ***Number*** *the pages from one to ten.*

number plate *noun* (*plural* **number plates**)
the flat piece of metal on the front and back of a vehicle that has numbers and letters on it (its **registration number**)

numeral (say **nyoo**-muh-ruhl) *noun* (*plural* **numerals**)
a word or symbol that represents a number: *The Roman* ***numeral*** *for 12 is XII.*

numerate (say **nyoo**-muh-ruht) *adjective*
having a good basic knowledge of mathematics ➲ See **literate**
▸ **numeracy** (*noun*): *He did very well in the* ***numeracy*** *test.*

numerator (say **nyoo**-muh-ray-tuh) *noun* (*plural* **numerators**) (*maths*)
the number above the line in a fraction: *In the fraction $\frac{3}{4}$, 3 is the* ***numerator.***
➲ See **denominator**

numerical (say nyoo-**me**-rik-l) *adjective* (also **numeric**)
relating to or shown by numbers: *put something in* ***numerical*** *order*
▸ **numerically** (*adverb*): *I sorted the data both alphabetically and* ***numerically.***

numerous (say **nyoo**-muh-ruhss) *adjective* (*formal*)
many: *He wrote* ***numerous*** *books.*

nun *noun* (*plural* **nuns**)
a woman who lives in a religious group with other women, usually in a special building (called a **convent**). ➲ See **monk**

nurse¹ (say **nurss**) *noun* (*plural* **nurses**)
a person whose job is to look after people who are sick or hurt: *My sister works as a* ***nurse*** *in a hospital.*

nurse² (say **nurss**) *verb* (**nursing, nursed**)
to look after somebody who is sick or hurt: *I* ***nursed*** *my father when he was ill.*

nursery (say **nurss**-uh-ree) *noun* (*plural* **nurseries**)
1 a place where small children and babies are cared for when their parents are at work
2 a place where people grow and sell plants

nursery rhyme *noun* (*plural* **nursery rhymes**)
a song or poem for young children

nursing (say **nur**-sing) *noun* (*no plural*)
the job of being a nurse: *He has decided to go into* ***nursing*** *when he leaves school.*

nurture (say **nur**-tshuh) *verb* (**nurturing, nurtured**)
to protect and look after a person or thing while they are growing or developing: *The club* ***nurtures*** *young soccer players.*
▸ **nurture** (*noun*)

nut *noun* (*plural* **nuts**)
1 a dry fruit that has a hard outside part with a seed inside. Many types can be eaten: ***walnuts, hazelnuts*** *and* ***peanuts***
2 a small metal ring that you screw onto a **bolt¹** 2 to fix things together

nutrient (say **nyoo**-tri-uhnt) *noun* (*plural* **nutrients**)
a substance that a living thing needs to live and grow: *Plants get minerals and other* ***nutrients*** *from the soil.*

nutrition (say nyoo-**trish**-uhn) *noun* (*no plural*)
1 the food that you eat and the way it affects your health: *Good* ***nutrition*** *and exercise are important for our health.*
2 the study of food and the way it affects health
▸ **nutritional** (*adjective*): *This meal is highly* ***nutritional.*** ◇ ***nutritional*** *supplements*
🛈 **ORIGIN:** 14th–15th century, from Latin *nutrire* meaning 'to feed, nourish'

nutritious (say nyoo-**trish**-uhss) *adjective*
(used about food) good for you: *tasty and* ***nutritious*** *meals*

nuzzle (say **nuz**-l) *verb* (**nuzzling, nuzzled**)
to press or rub somebody gently with the nose: *My dog* ***nuzzled*** *my leg.*

NW *abbreviation* **north-west**

nylon (say **ny**-lon) *noun* (*no plural*)
very strong material that is made by machines and is used for making clothes, rope, brushes and other things: *a* ***nylon*** *fishing line*

nymph (say **nimf**) *noun* (*plural* **nymphs**)
1 (in old stories) a spirit, in the form of a young woman or girl, who lives in places such as rivers or forests: *a water* ***nymph***
2 a young insect that is nearly the same as the adult: *a dragonfly* ***nymph*** ➲ See illustration at **metamorphosis**

Oo

oak (say **ohk**) *noun* (*plural* **oaks**) (also **oak tree**)
a large tree that has hard wood and produces small nuts (called **acorns**)

oar (say **aw**) *noun* (*plural* **oars**)
a long stick with a flat end that you use for moving a boat through water (called **rowing**)

oasis (say oh-**ay**-siss) *noun* (*plural* **oases**)
a place in a desert that has trees and water

oath (*rhymes with* **both**) *noun* (*plural* **oaths**)
a formal promise: *He swore an **oath** of loyalty.*

oats (say **ohtss**) *plural noun*
a plant with seeds that we use as food for people and animals: *We make porridge from **oats**.*

OBE (say oh-bee-**ee**) *abbreviation*
outcomes-based education

obedient (say uh-**bee**-di-uhnt) *adjective*
doing what somebody tells you to do: *She was an **obedient** child.* ➲ OPPOSITE **disobedient**
▸ **obedience** (*noun*): *complete **obedience***
▸ **obediently** (*adverb*)

obese (say oh-**beess**) *adjective*
(used about people) very fat, in a way that is not healthy

obey (say oh-**bay**) *verb* (**obeying, obeyed**)
to do what somebody tells you to do, or to follow an order or a rule: *He always **obeyed** his parents.* ◇ *You must **obey** the law.* ➲ OPPOSITE **disobey**

obituary (say ob-**bit**-yuu-uh-ree) *noun* (*plural* **obituaries**)
a piece of writing about a person's life that is printed in a newspaper after they have died

object¹ (say **ob**-jikt) *noun* (*plural* **objects**)
1 a thing that you can see and touch: *There was a small round **object** on the table.*
2 what you plan to do: *His **object** in life is to become rich.* ➲ SYNONYMS **aim¹**, **purpose**
3 (*grammar*) the person or thing that is affected by an action: *In the sentence 'Jane painted the door', the **object** is 'the door'.* ➲ See **subject¹** 3

object² (say ob-**jekt**) *verb* (**objecting, objected**)
to not like something, or to not agree with something: *I **objected** to their plan.*

objection (say ob-**jek**-shuhn) *noun* (*plural* **objections**)
a reason why you do not like something or do not agree with something: *I have no **objections** to the plan.*

objective¹ (say uhb-**jek**-tiv) *noun* (*plural* **objectives**)
something that you are trying to achieve
➲ SYNONYM **aim¹**

objective² (say uhb-**jek**-tiv) *adjective*
not influenced by your own personal feelings and only considering the facts: *Be **objective** and tell us what happened.* ➲ OPPOSITE **subjective**
▸ **objectively** (*adverb*): *Look at the situation **objectively**.*

obligation (say ob-li-**gay**-shuhn) *noun* (*plural* **obligations**)
something that you must do: *We have an **obligation** to help.*

obligatory (say uh-**blig**-uh-tree) *adjective* (*formal*)
that you must do because it is the law or a rule: *It is **obligatory** to wear your seat belt when driving.* ➲ SYNONYM **compulsory**

oblige (say uh-**blije**) *verb* (**obliging, obliged**)
1 to force somebody to do something: *The law **obliges** parents to send their children to school.*
2 (*formal*) to be helpful and do what someone asks you to do: *If you need help, I'll be happy to **oblige**.*

obliged (say uh-**blije**-d) *adjective*
forced to do something, or feeling that you must do something: *We felt **obliged** to offer our help.*

oblique (say uh-**bleek**) *adjective*
1 at a slope, or at an angle that is not horizontal or vertical: *That roof beam must be placed at an **oblique** angle to the wall.*
2 not expressed or done in a direct way: *She gave an **oblique** answer to my question.*
▸ **obliquely** (*adverb*): *The sun's rays shone **obliquely** into the kitchen window.*

obliterate (say uh-**blit**-uh-rayt) *verb* (**obliterating, obliterated**) (*formal*) to remove all signs of something by destroying or covering it completely: *Houses were **obliterated** in the fire.*

oblivious (say uh-**bliv**-i-uhss) *adjective*
not noticing or realizing something: *She was **oblivious** of the trouble she had caused.* ◇ *He's **oblivious** to the noise.*

oblong (say **ob**-long) *noun* (*plural* **oblongs**)
1 a shape with two long sides, two short sides

and four angles of 90° ➲ SYNONYM **rectangle**
2 a shape that is longer that it is wide, for example an **oval** or a **rectangle**
▸ **oblong** (*adjective*): *This page is* ***oblong****.*

obnoxious (say uhb-**nok**-shuhss) *adjective*
extremely unpleasant: *He really is an* ***obnoxious*** *person.*

obscene (say uhb-**seen**) *adjective*
1 relating to sex in a way that most people find disgusting and which causes offence: ***obscene*** *language* ◇ *He told an* ***obscene*** *joke.*
2 a very large amount or size that some people feel is unacceptable: *an* ***obscene*** *amount of money*
▸ **obscenity** (*noun*): *He shouted* ***obscenities*** *at them.*

obscure[1] (say uhb-**skyoor**) *adjective*
1 not easy to see or understand: *His reasons are* ***obscure****.*
2 not well known: *an* ***obscure*** *poet*
▸ **obscurity** (*noun*): *She disappeared into* ***obscurity****.*

obscure[2] (say uhb-**skyoor**) *verb* (**obscuring, obscured**)
to make something difficult to see or understand: *He* ***obscured*** *his face when photographers arrived.* ➲ SYNONYM **mask[2]**

observant (say uhb-**zurv**-uhnt) *adjective*
good at noticing things: *That's very* ***observant*** *of you!*

observation (say ob-zuh-**vay**-shuhn) *noun*
1 (*no plural*) when you watch a person or thing carefully: *The police kept the house under* ***observation****.* ◇ *His powers of* ***observation*** *are excellent.*
2 (*plural* **observations**) something that you notice: *Do the experiment, then list your* ***observations****.*

observatory (say uhb-**zurv**-uh-tree) *noun* (*plural* **observatories**)
a building from which scientists can watch and study the stars, the weather and other objects in space and on land

observe (say uhb-**zurv**) *verb* (**observing, observed**) (*formal*)
1 to watch a person or thing carefully: ***Observe*** *how different materials behave when you heat them.*
2 to see or notice a person or thing: *The police* ***observed*** *a man leaving the house.*

obsess (say uhb-**sess**) *verb* (**obsessing, obsessed**)
(usually passive) to completely fill your mind: *Debbie is* ***obsessed*** *with football.*

obsession (say uhb-**sesh**-n) *noun* (*plural* **obsessions**)
a person or thing that you think about all the time: *Cars are his* ***obsession****.*

obsolete (say **ob**-suh-leet) *adjective*
no longer useful because something better has been invented: *Your tape player is* ***obsolete****.*
➲ SYNONYM **outdated**

obstacle (say **ob**-stuhk-l) *noun* (*plural* **obstacles**)
something that makes it difficult for you to do something or go somewhere: *Not speaking English was an* ***obstacle*** *in her studies.*
ⓘ **ORIGIN:** 13th–15th century, through Old French from Latin *obstare* meaning 'to stand in the way'

obstinate (say **ob**-sti-nuht) *adjective*
not changing your ideas or not doing what other people want you to do: *He's too* ***obstinate*** *to say he's sorry.* ➲ SYNONYM **stubborn**

obstruct (say uhb-**strukt**) *verb* (**obstructing, obstructed**)
to be in the way so that somebody or something cannot go past: *Please move your car – you're* ***obstructing*** *the traffic.*
▸ **obstruction** (*noun*): *an* ***obstruction*** *in the road*

obtain (say uhb-**tayn**) *verb* (**obtaining, obtained**) (*formal*)
to get something: *Where can I* ***obtain*** *tickets for the play?* ➲ SYNONYM **acquire, get**

obtrusive (say uhb-**troo**-siv) *adjective*
noticeable in an unpleasant way: *Your phone has an* ***obtrusive*** *ring tone.*
▸ **obtrusively** (*adverb*)

obtuse (say uhb-**tyooss**) *adjective* (*formal*)
slow to understand something, or not wanting to understand something: *He's being* ***obtuse****.*

obtuse angle *noun* (*plural* **obtuse angles**)
an angle between 90 degrees and 180 degrees
➲ See illustration at **angle** ➲ See **acute angle**

obvious (say **ob**-vi-uhss) *adjective*
easy to see or understand: *It's* ***obvious*** *that she's not happy.* ➲ SYNONYM **clear[1]** 1
▸ **obviously** (*adverb*): *There has* ***obviously*** *been a mistake.*

occasion (say uh-**kay**-zhuhn) *noun* (*plural* **occasions**)
1 a time when something happens: *I've been to Paris on three or four* ***occasions****.*
2 a special time: *A wedding is a big family* ***occasion****.*

occasional (say uh-**kay**-zhuhn-l) *adjective*
happening sometimes, but not very often: *We get the* ***occasional*** *visitor.*

occasionally (say uh-**kay**-zhuh-nuh-lee) *adverb*
sometimes, but not often: *I go to Polokwane occasionally.*

occupant (say **ok**-yuu-puhnt) *noun* (*plural* **occupants**)
a person who is in something such as a building or car at a particular time: *There were two **occupants** in the car.*

occupation (say ok-yuu-**pay**-shuhn) *noun*
1 (*plural* **occupations**) (*formal*) a job: *What is your mother's **occupation**?*
2 (*plural* **occupations**) something that you do in your free time: *Fishing is his favourite **occupation**.*
3 (*no plural*) when a country or army takes or has control of an area or building: *the British **occupation** of the Cape*
4 (*no plural*) (*formal*) the fact of living in a house, flat or room: *The new house is now ready for **occupation**.*

occupy (say **ok**-yuu-py) *verb* (**occupying, occupied**)
1 to fill a space or period of time: *The bed seemed to **occupy** most of the room.*
2 to keep somebody busy: *She **occupied** herself reading.*
3 (*formal*) to live or work in a room or building: *Who **occupies** these offices?*
4 to take or have control of an area or building: *Protestors **occupied** the TV station.*
▸ **occupied** (*adjective*): *This homework will keep me **occupied*** (= busy) *all week.* ◇ *Excuse me – is this seat **occupied*** (= is someone else sitting here) *?*

occur (say uh-**kur**) *verb* (**occurring, occurred**)
(*formal*) to happen: *The accident **occurred** this morning.*
occur to somebody to come into somebody's mind: *It **occurred** to me that you might like to come.*

SPELLING Be careful! You spell **occur** with one **r** and **occurrence** with **rr**.

occurrence (say uh-**ku**-ruhnss) *noun* (*plural* **occurrences**)
something that happens or exists: *two **occurrences** of fighting at school*

ocean (say **oh**-shuhn) *noun* (*plural* **oceans**)
a very big sea: *the Atlantic **Ocean***

ochre (say **oh**-kuh) *noun* (*no plural*)
a pale yellow-brown colour
▸ **ochre** (*adjective*)

o'clock (say uh-**klok**) *adverb*
used after the numbers one to twelve for saying the time: *I left home at six **o'clock** and arrived at school at half past seven.*

octa- (say **ok**-tuh) *prefix* (also **oct-**)
eight, or having eight: *an **octahedron***
ℹ ORIGIN: from Greek *oktō* meaning 'eight'

octagon (say **ok**-tuh-guhn) *noun* (*plural* **octagons**) (*maths*)
a flat closed shape with eight straight sides
▸ **octagonal** (*adjective*): *an **octagonal** coin*

octahedron (say ok-tuh-**hee**-druhn) *noun* (*plural* **octahedra** or **octahedrons**) (*maths*)
a solid shape with eight flat surfaces

octal (say **ok**-tuhl) *adjective* (*maths*)
relating to a number system that uses 8 as its base: *The **octal** digits range from 0 to 7.*

octave (say **ok**-tiv) *noun* (*plural* **octaves**) (*music*)
the set of eight musical notes that Western music is based on

octet (say ok-**tet**) *noun* (*plural* **octets**)
1 a group of eight singers or musicians
2 music written for eight singers or musicians

octo- (say **ok**-toh) *prefix* (also **oct-**)
eight, or having eight: *An **octopus** has eight 'arms'.*

October (say ok-**toh**-buh) *noun*
the tenth month of the year
ℹ ORIGIN: through Old English, from Latin *octo* meaning 'eight'. October was the eighth month of the Roman year.

octopus (say **ok**-tuh-puhss) *noun* (*plural* **octopuses**)
a sea animal with eight long parts (called **tentacles**).

octopus

odd (say **od**) *adjective* (**odder, oddest**)
1 strange or unusual: *It's **odd** that he left without telling anybody.* ➲ SYNONYM **peculiar**
2 (*maths*) not able to be divided by two: *1, 3, 5 and 7 are all **odd** numbers.* ➲ OPPOSITE **even**[2] 3
3 not with the pair or set it belongs to, or not matching: *You're wearing **odd** socks!*
the odd one out one that is different from all

the others: *'Apple', 'orange', 'cabbage' – which is the **odd** one out?*

oddly (say **od**-lee) *adverb*
in a strange or unusual way: *She behaved very **oddly**.*

odds (say **odz**) *plural noun*
the odds used for saying how likely something is: *The **odds** are that he'll win* (= he'll probably win). ◇ *The **odds** are against us* (= we will probably not succeed).

ode (*rhymes with* **road**) *noun* (*plural* **odes**)
a poem that is written for a special occasion or for a particular person or thing: *an **ode** to Beethoven*

odometer (say oh-**dom**-i-tuh) *noun* (*plural* **odometers**)
an instrument that records and shows the distance you have travelled in a vehicle: *My car's **odometer** shows that I have already covered a distance of 300 kilometres.*

odour (say **oh**-duh) *noun* (*plural* **odours**) (*formal*)
a smell, usually an unpleasant one: *There's a bad **odour** in the kitchen.*

oesophagus (say i-**sof**-uh-guhss) *noun* (*plural* **oesophaguses** or **oesophagi**)
the tube that carries food from your mouth to your stomach ➲ SYNONYM **gullet** ➲ See illustration at **alimentary canal**

of (say **ov**) *preposition*
1 belonging to or connected with a person or thing: *the back **of** the chair* ◇ *the arrival **of** the president*
2 used after an amount or number: *a litre **of** water* ◇ *the fourth **of** July* ◇ *one **of** the girls*
3 used for saying what something is or what something is made of: *a cup **of** tea* ◇ *some pieces **of** wood* ◇ *Is this shirt made **of** cotton?*
4 used for giving your opinion about somebody's behaviour: *That's very kind **of** you.*
5 used with some adjectives and verbs: *I'm proud **of** you.* ◇ *This perfume smells **of** roses.*

off[1] (say **of**) *preposition, adverb*
1 down or away from something: *He fell **off** the roof.* ◇ *We got **off** the bus.*
2 used for talking about removing something: *If you're hot, take your coat **off**.* ◇ *Clean the paint **off** the wall.*
3 not connected or not working: *Make sure the lights are **off** before you go.* ➲ OPPOSITE **on** 5
4 away from a place, or at a distance in space or time: *My birthday is not far **off**.* ◇ *I must be **off** soon* (= leave).
5 not at work or school: *I had the day **off** yesterday.*

off[2] (say **of**) *adjective*
not fresh enough to eat or drink: *The milk's **off**.*

offal (say **of**-l) *noun* (*no plural*)
the stomach and other organs of an animal used for food

offence (say uh-**fenss**) *noun*
1 (*plural* **offences**) an illegal action: *He has committed an **offence**.* ➲ SYNONYM **crime**
2 (*no plural*) when a person is angry or unhappy because of what somebody has said or done: *She took **offence** when I refused his help.*

offend (say uh-**fend**) *verb* (**offending, offended**)
to make somebody feel angry or unhappy, or to hurt somebody's feelings: *I hope they won't be **offended** if I don't come.*

offensive[1] (say uh-**fen**-siv) *adjective*
1 rude in a way that makes somebody feel upset, angry or insulted: ***offensive** language* ➲ OPPOSITE **defensive** 1
2 (only before a noun) used for or connected with attacking: ***offensive** weapons*
3 connected with the team that has control of the ball, or with the act of scoring points in a game: ***offensive** play* ➲ OPPOSITE **defensive** 3

offensive[2] (say uh-**fen**-siv) *noun* (*plural* **offensives**)
a military attack
on the offensive being the first to attack, not waiting for others to attack you: *They went on the **offensive**.*

offer[1] (say **of**-uh) *verb* (**offering, offered**)
to say or show that you will do or give something if another person wants it: *She **offered** me some cake.* ◇ *I **offered** to help her.*

offer[2] (say **of**-uh) *noun* (*plural* **offers**)
1 the act of offering to do or give something if another person wants it: *Thanks for the **offer**, but I don't need any help.*
2 an amount of money that you say you will give for something: *They've made an **offer** for the house.*
on offer for sale or available: *The college has a wide range of courses on **offer**.*

office (say **of**-iss) *noun* (*plural* **offices**)
1 a place where people work, usually at desks: *I work in an **office**.*
2 (often used in compound nouns) a room or building used for a particular purpose, especially to provide information or a service: *the tourist/ticket **office*** ➲ See **post office**

officer (say **of**-i-suh) *noun* (*plural* **officers**)
1 a person in the army, navy or air force who gives orders to other people: *a naval **officer***
2 a person who does important work, especially

for the government: *a prison **officer** ◇ police **officers***

official¹ (say uh-**fish**-l) *adjective*
connected with government or with a particular organization or a person in authority: *an **official** government report ◇ an **official** announcement*
▸ **officially** (*adverb*): *He has now heard **officially** that he's got the job.*

official² (say uh-**fish**-l) *noun* (*plural* **officials**)
a person who does important work, especially for the government: *government **officials***

offload (say of-**lohd**) *verb* (**offloading, offloaded**)
1 to **unload** cargo from a truck, train, plane or ship
2 to get rid of something that you do not need or want by passing it on to someone else: *Oil tankers **offloading** waste into the sea threatens our sea birds. ◇ It's nice to have someone you can **offload** your problems onto.*

offset (say **of**-set) *verb* (**offsetting, offset**)
to make the effect of something less strong, or to balance it: *The cost was **offset** by the benefits.*

offshoot (say **of**-shoot) *noun* (*plural* **offshoots**)
a smaller thing that develops from something else, especially a small organization that develops from a larger one

offshore (say of-**shaw**) *adjective*
1 moving away from the land towards the sea: *an **offshore** breeze*
2 in the sea some distance from the land: *an **offshore** oil rig*
3 in another country: ***offshore** banking*
➲ See **onshore**

offside (say of-**side**) *adjective*
(used about a player in football or hockey) in a position, usually ahead of the ball, that is not allowed by the rules of the game

offspring (say **of**-spring) *noun* (*plural* **offspring**) (*formal*)
a child or children, or the young of an animal: *The lioness guarded her **offspring**.*

often (say **of**-uhn or **of**-tuhn) *adverb*
many times: *We **often** play football on Sundays. ◇ I don't write to him very **often**. ◇ How **often** do you visit her?*
every so often sometimes, but not often: *Every so **often** she phones me.*

ogre (say **oh**-guh) *noun* (*plural* **ogres**)
(in stories) a very large, cruel and frightening creature that eats people ➲ SYNONYMS **giant¹** 1, **monster**

oh (say **oh**) *exclamation*
1 used for showing a strong feeling, like surprise or fear: ***Oh** no! I've lost my keys!*
2 used before other words, for example when you are thinking what to say: *'What time is it?' 'Oh, about two o'clock.'*
Oh dear used for showing that you are surprised or unhappy: ***Oh dear** – have you hurt yourself?*
Oh well used when you are not happy about something, but you cannot change it: *'I'm too busy to go out tonight.' '**Oh well**, I'll see you tomorrow then.'*

ohm (*rhymes with* **home**) *noun* (*plural* **ohms**) (symbol Ω)
a unit for measuring electrical **resistance** 3: *The resistance of the copper wire is three **ohms**.*
🛈 ORIGIN: 19th century, named after Georg Ohm (1789–1854), a German scientist who discovered various laws of electricity

oil (say **oyl**) *noun* (*no plural*)
1 a thick liquid that comes from under the ground or the sea. We use it for energy and to make machines work smoothly. ➲ See **fossil fuel**
2 a thick liquid that comes from plants or animals and that we use in cooking: *Fry the onions in **oil**.*

oilfield (say **oyl**-feeld) *noun* (*plural* **oilfields**)
an area where there is oil under the ground or under the sea

oil painting *noun* (*plural* **oil paintings**)
a picture that has been done with paint made from oil

oil rig *noun* (*plural* **oil rigs**)
a large platform in the sea with equipment for getting oil out from under the sea

oil slick *noun* (*plural* **oil slicks**)
an area of oil that is floating on the surface of the sea, usually after a ship carrying oil has had an accident

oil well *noun* (*plural* **oil wells**)
a hole that is made deep in the ground or under the sea in order to get oil

oily (say **oy**-lee) *adjective* (**oilier, oiliest**)
like oil or covered with oil: *an **oily** liquid ◇ **oily** hands*

ointment (say **oynt**-muhnt) *noun* (*plural* **ointments**)
a smooth substance that you put on sore skin or on an injury to help it get better

OK¹ (say oh-**kay**) *exclamation* (also **okay**) (*informal*)
yes: *'Shall we go to the party?' '**OK**.'*
➲ SYNONYM **all right** 3

OK² (say oh-**kay**) *adjective, adverb* (also **okay**) (*informal*)
1 safe and well, calm or happy: *'How's your mum?' '**OK**, thanks.'*
2 all right, or acceptable: *Is it **okay** to sit here?*

old (*rhymes with* **gold**) *adjective* (**older**, **oldest**)
1 having lived for a long time: *My grandfather is very **old**.* ◇ *My sister is **older** than me.* ➲ OPPOSITE **young¹**
2 made or bought a long time ago: *an **old** house* ➲ OPPOSITE **new** 1
3 used to show the age of a person or thing: *He's nine years **old**.* ◇ *How **old** are you?* ◇ *a six-year-**old** girl*
4 done or had before now: *My **old** job was more interesting than this one.* ➲ OPPOSITE **new** 2
5 known for a long time: *Jane is an **old** friend – we were at school together.* ➲ OPPOSITE **new** 2

Old English *noun* (*no plural*)
the English language used between the 5th and 11th centuries, also called Anglo-Saxon

old-fashioned (say ohld-**fash**-uhnd) *adjective*
not modern: *My parents are rather **old-fashioned**.* ◇ ***old-fashioned*** clothes

Old French *noun* (*no plural*)
the French language used until the 14th century

Old Norse (say ohld **nawss**) *noun* (*no plural*)
the language used in Norway, Iceland, Denmark and Sweden until the 14th century

oligarchy (say **ol**-i-gaa-kee) *noun*
1 (*no plural*) a form of government in which only a small group of people hold all the power
2 (*plural* **oligarchies**) the people who hold power in an oligarchy
3 (*plural* **oligarchies**) a country governed by an oligarchy

olive (say **ol**-iv) *noun* (*plural* **olives**)
a small green or black fruit that people either eat or get oil from

Olympic Games (say uh-lim-pik **gaymz**) *plural noun* (also **the Olympics**)
an international sports competition that is organized every four years in a different country

ombudsman (say **om**-budz-muhn) *noun* (*plural* **ombudsmen**)
a government official who deals with complaints made by ordinary people against public organizations: *the press **ombudsman*** ◇ *the banking **ombudsman***
ⓘ **ORIGIN:** 20th century, from Swedish *ombusdman* meaning 'legal representative'

omelette (say **om**-luht) *noun* (*plural* **omelettes**)
a dish made of eggs mixed together and then fried: *a cheese **omelette***

omen (say **oh**-muhn) *noun* (*plural* **omens**)
a sign of something that will happen in the future: *The rain clouds are a good **omen**.*

ominous (say **om**-i-nuhss) *adjective*
suggesting that something bad is going to happen: *There were **ominous** black clouds in the sky.* ➲ SYNONYM **sinister**

omission (say uh-**mish**-uhn) *noun* (*plural* **omissions**)
1 something that has been left out or not included: *There was an **omission** in the list of names.*
2 the act of not including a person or thing or not doing something

omit (say uh-**mit**) *verb* (**omitting, omitted**)
(*formal*) to not include something: ***Omit** question 2 and do question 3.*

omni- (say **om**-ni) *prefix*
all, or all things: *An **omnivore** eats meat and plants.*
ⓘ **ORIGIN:** from Latin *omnis* meaning 'all'

omnipotent (say om-**ni**-puh-tuhnt) *adjective*
very powerful and able to do anything: *an **omnipotent** god*
▸ **omnipotence** (*noun*)

omniscient (say om-**niss**-i-uhnt) *adjective*
knowing everything: *She believes God is **omniscient**.*
▸ **omniscience** (*noun*)

omnivore (say **om**-ni-vaw) *noun* (*plural* **omnivores**)
an animal that eats both plants and other animals: *Many people are **omnivores**.*
➲ See **carnivore, herbivore, insectivore**
▸ **omnivorous** (*adjective*): *an **omnivorous** diet*

on (say **on**) *preposition, adverb*
1 used for showing where something is: ***on** the table* ◇ *The number is **on** the door.* ◇ *I saw a good film **on** TV.* ◇ *I've got a cut **on** my hand.*
2 used for showing when: *My birthday is **on** 6 May.* ◇ *I'll see you **on** Monday.* ◇ *I saw her **on** her return from New York.*
3 used with ways of travelling and types of travel: *He got **on** the train.* ◇ *I came here **on** foot* (= walking).
4 used for showing that a person or thing continues: *You can't stop here – drive **on**.*
5 working, or being used: *All the lights were **on**.* ➲ OPPOSITE **off¹** 3
6 using something: *I bought it **on** the Internet.* ◇ *I was **on** the phone to Jania.*
7 about: *a book **on** cars*

A B C D E F G H I J K L M N O P Q R S T U V W X Y Z

8 covering your body: *Put your coat **on**.*
9 happening: *What's **on** tonight?*
on and on without stopping: *He went* (= talked) ***on** and **on** about his girlfriend.*

once[1] (say **wunss**) *adverb*
1 one time: *I've been to Namibia **once**.* ◇ *He phones us **once** a week* (= once every week).
2 at some time in the past: *This house was **once** a school.*
at once
1 immediately: *Come here at **once**!* ➲ SYNONYM **now[1] 1**
2 at the same time: *I can't do two things at **once**!*
for once this time only: *For **once** I agree.*
once again, **once more** again, or one more time: *Can you explain it to me **once** more?*
once or twice a few times, but not often: *I've only met them **once** or twice.*
once upon a time (used at the beginning of a children's story) a long time ago: ***Once** upon a time there was a beautiful princess …*

once[2] (say **wunss**) *conjunction*
as soon as, or when: ***Once** you've finished your homework you can go out.*

one[1] (say **wun**) *number, adjective*
1 the number 1: ***One** and **one** make two (1 + 1 = 2).* ◇ *Only **one** person spoke.* ➲ The adjective is **first[1]**
2 a person or thing, especially when they are part of a group: ***One** of my friends is ill.* ◇ *I've lost **one** of my books.*
3 only: *You are the **one** person I can trust.*
4 used for talking about a particular time, without saying exactly when: *I'll come over **one** evening.*
one by one
1 first one, then the next, and so on: *Please come in **one** by one.*
2 separately

one[2] (say **wun**) *pronoun*
1 used instead of the name of a person or thing: *I've got some bananas. Do you want **one**?* ◇ *'Can I borrow a book?' 'Yes. Which **one**?'* ◇ *The questions are hard – leave the **ones** you can't do.*
2 (*formal*) people in general, or I: ***One** feels quite helpless.*

> USAGE **You** and **I** are the words that we usually use for sense 2. **One** is formal and rather old-fashioned: ***You** feel helpless. **I** feel helpless.*

one another *pronoun*
each other: *We looked at **one another**.*

oneself (say wun-**self**) *pronoun* (*formal*)
used with 'one' for saying that an action involves the person doing it: *One has to ask **oneself** if such action is necessary.*
by oneself
1 alone, or without other people
2 without help

onion (say **un**-yuhn) *noun* (*plural* **onions**)
a round vegetable with many layers and a strong smell. Chopping them can make you cry.

online (say on-**line**) *adjective, adverb*
controlled by or connected to a computer or to the Internet: ***Online** shopping is both cheap and convenient.* ◇ *Bookings can be made **online**.*

onlooker (say **on**-luuk-uh) *noun* (*plural* **onlookers**)
a person who watches something happening: *The **onlookers** saw him escape.*

only[1] (say **ohn**-lee) *adjective*
with no others: *She's the **only** girl in her class.*

only[2] (say **ohn**-lee) *adverb*
and nobody or nothing else, or no more than: *I invited twenty people to the party, but **only** five came.* ◇ *We can't have dinner now. It's **only** four o'clock!* ◇ *We **only** waited five minutes.*
only just
1 not long ago: *We've **only** just arrived.*
2 almost not: *We **only** just had enough money to pay for the meal.*

only[3] (say **ohn**-lee) *conjunction* (*informal*)
but: *I like this bag, **only** it's too expensive.*

onomatopoeia (say on-uh-mat-uh-**pee**-uh) *noun* (*no plural*)
making a word that sounds like the thing it is naming or describing: *'Sizzle', 'whizz' and 'cackle' are examples of **onomatopoeia**.* ➲ See Study page 17
▸ **onomatopoeic** (*adjective*): *'Whoosh' is **onomatopoeic**.*

onset (say **on**-set) *noun* (*no plural*)
the beginning or start of something: *the **onset** of winter*

onshore (say **on**-shaw) *adjective*
1 moving from the sea towards the land: *The wind is **onshore** today.*
2 on the land: *an **onshore** oilfield*
➲ See **offshore**

onslaught (say **on**-slawt) *noun* (*plural* **onslaughts**)
a sudden or violent attack: *an **onslaught** against the leader*

onto (say **on**-too) *preposition* (also **on to**)
on to a place or person or thing: *The bottle fell **onto** the floor.* ◇ *The cat jumped **onto** the table.*

onus (say **oh**-nuhss) *noun* (*no plural*)
(usually **the onus**) something that is your responsibility or duty: *The **onus** is on you to improve your marks.*

onwards (say **on**-wuhdz) *adverb* (also **onward**)
1 and after: *I shall be at home from eight o'clock **onwards**.*
2 forward or further: *The soldiers marched **onwards** until they came to a bridge.*

ooze (say **ooz**) *verb* (**oozing, oozed**)
1 (used about a thick liquid) come out slowly from something: *Blood was **oozing** from the wound.*
2 to show a lot of a particular quality: *She walked into the party **oozing** confidence.*

opal (say **oh**-puhl) *noun* (*plural* **opals**)
a stone that shines with many colours and is often used in jewellery

opaque (say oh-**payk**) *adjective*
1 allowing no light to pass through: ***opaque** material* ➲ OPPOSITE **transparent**
2 difficult to understand and not clear: *He gave us **opaque** instructions that we couldn't follow.*

open[1] (say **oh**-puhn) *adjective*
1 not closed, so that people or things can go in or out: *Leave the windows **open**.* ◇ *The book lay **open** on the table.* ◇ *an **open** box*
2 available or able to be used or done: *The bank is **open** from 9 a.m. to 3 p.m.* ◇ *The competition is only **open** to children.*
3 not hiding your thoughts and feelings: *She's a very **open** person.*
4 away from towns and people, or without many buildings or trees: *We were in the **open** veld.*
5 not yet decided: *'Where shall we go on Friday?' 'Let's leave it **open**.'*
in the open air outside: *We had our lunch in the **open** air.*

open[2] (say **oh**-puhn) *verb* (**opening, opened**)
1 to move, or to move something, so that it is not closed or covered: *The door **opened** and a man came in.* ◇ ***Open** your eyes!* ◇ ***Open** your books at page 10.* ➲ OPPOSITES **close**[1] 1, **shut**[1]
2 to make it possible for people to enter a place: *Banks don't **open** on Sundays.* ◇ *The president **opened** the new hospital.* ➲ OPPOSITE **close**[1] 2, **shut**[1]
3 to start something, or to start: *I'd like to **open** a bank account.* ◇ *How do you **open** a file in this program?* ◇ *The story **opens** with a murder.*

open[3] (say **oh**-puhn) *noun* (*no plural*)
out in the open outside, or in the countryside: *Children need to play out in the **open**.*
into the open not hidden or secret: *They brought the secret out into the **open**.*

open-air (say oh-puhn-**air**) *adjective*
outside: *an **open-air** concert*

opener (say **ohp**-nuh) *noun* (*plural* **openers**)
a small tool that you use for opening tins or bottles: *a tin-**opener***

opening (say **ohp**-ning) *noun* (*plural* **openings**)
1 a space in something where people or things can go in and out: *The cattle got out through an **opening** in the fence.* ➲ SYNONYM **hole**
2 a ceremony to celebrate the start of a public event or the first time a new building, road or place is used: *the **opening** of the Olympic Games*

openly (say **oh**-puhn-lee) *adverb*
not secretly, or without trying to hide anything: *She told me **openly** that she didn't agree.*

opera (say **op**-ruh) *noun* (*plural* **operas**)
a play where the actors sing most of the words to music: *Do you like **opera**?* ◇ *We went to see an **opera** by Verdi.*

operate (say **op**-uh-rayt) *verb* (**operating, operated**)
1 to work, or to make something work: *I don't know how this machine **operates**.* ◇ *These switches **operate** the heating.*
2 to cut into somebody's body to take out or repair a part inside: *Doctors will **operate** on her leg tomorrow.*

WORD BUILDING A doctor who **operates** on people in hospital (as in meaning 2 above) is called a **surgeon**. A surgeon's work is called **surgery**.

operation (say op-uh-**ray**-shuhn) *noun* (*plural* **operations**)
1 cutting into someone's body to take out or repair a part inside: *He had an **operation** on his eye.*
2 an event that needs a lot of people or planning: *a military **operation***

operator (say **op**-uh-ray-tuh) *noun* (*plural* **operators**)
1 a person who makes a machine work: *a machine **operator***
2 a person who works for a telephone company and helps to connect people making calls: *What number do you dial for the **operator**?*
3 a person or company that runs a particular business: *a tour **operator*** ◇ *a bus **operator***

opinion (say uh-**pin**-yuhn) *noun* (*plural* **opinions**)
what you think about something: *In my **opinion**, she's wrong.* ◇ *What's your **opinion** of his work?* ◇ *She had strong **opinions** on everything.* ➲ SYNONYM **view**[1] 1

A B C D E F G H I J K L M N **O** P Q R S T U V W X Y Z

opium (say **oh**-pi-uhm) *noun* (*no plural*)
the liquid substance from the **poppy** flower, used as a powerful drug to stop pain and make you sleep
▸ **opiate** (*noun*): *Heroin is an **opiate**.*

opponent (say uh-**poh**-nuhnt) *noun* (*plural* **opponents**)
the person against you in a fight or competition: *The first team beat their **opponents** easily.*

opportunist (say op-uh-**tyoo**-nist) *noun* (*plural* **opportunists**)
a person who makes use of an opportunity to get something: *He's an **opportunist** – always looking for ways to make money.*
▸ **opportunist** (*adjective*): *an **opportunist** crime* ▸ **opportunistic** (*adjective*): *an **opportunistic** infection*

opportunity (say op-uh-**tyoo**-nuh-tee) *noun* (*plural* **opportunities**)
a chance to do something, or a time when you can do something that you want to do: *I didn't get the **opportunity** to visit them.* ◇ *It was a golden* (= perfect) ***opportunity** and I decided to take it.* ➲ SYNONYM **chance** 2

oppose (say uh-**pohz**) *verb* (**opposing**, **opposed**)
to try to stop or change something because you do not like it: *People **opposed** the new law.*

opposed (say uh-**pohzd**) *adjective*
disagreeing strongly with something and trying to stop it: *I am **opposed** to the plan.*
as opposed to (*formal*) words that you use to show that you are talking about one thing, not something different: *She teaches at the college, as **opposed** to the university.*

opposite[1] (say **op**-uh-zit) *noun* (*plural* **opposites**)
a word or thing that is as different as possible from another word or thing: *'Hot' is the **opposite** of 'cold'.*

opposite[2] (say **op**-uh-zit) *adjective, adverb, preposition*
1 across from where a person or thing is, or on the other side: *The church is on the **opposite** side of the road from my flat.* ◇ *You sit here, and I'll sit **opposite**.* ◇ *The bank is **opposite** the supermarket.*
2 as different as possible: *North is the **opposite** direction to south.*

SPELLING Remember! You spell **opposite** with **pp**.

opposition (say op-uh-**zish**-uhn) *noun* (*no plural*)
1 the act of disagreeing with something and trying to stop it: *There was a lot of **opposition** to the plan.*
2 the opposition the person or team who you compete against in sport or business: *He's gone to work for the **opposition**.*
3 the Opposition the politicians or the political parties that are in Parliament but not in the government: *the leader of the **Opposition***

oppress (say uh-**press**) *verb* (**oppressing**, **oppressed**)
to treat a group of people in an unfair way by not allowing them the same freedom and rights as others: *The regime* (= a government that has not been elected fairly) *is accused of **oppressing** religious minorities.*
▸ **oppressed** (*adjective*): *an **oppressed** minority* (= a group of people of a particular culture or religion who are outnumbered by another group in the same country) ▸ **oppression** (*noun*): *a struggle against **oppression***

oppressive (say uh-**press**-iv) *adjective*
1 controlling by force and allowing no freedom: ***oppressive** laws*
2 (used especially about the weather) causing you to feel very uncomfortable: ***oppressive** heat*

opt (say **opt**) *verb* (**opting**, **opted**)
to choose to do something: *She **opted** for a career in medicine.*

optical (say **op**-tik-l) *adjective*
1 relating to sight: *an **optical** illusion*
2 used to help you see something more clearly: *an **optical** telescope*
3 (*technology*) that operates with light: ***optical** fibre*

optician (say op-**tish**-uhn) *noun* (*plural* **opticians**)
a person who examines your eyes to find out how well you can see, and who sells glasses (spectacles)

optimism (say **op**-ti-miz-m) *noun* (*no plural*)
the feeling that good things will happen
➲ OPPOSITE **pessimism**

optimist (say **op**-ti-mist) *noun* (*plural* **optimists**)
a person who thinks that good things will happen ➲ OPPOSITE **pessimist**
▸ **optimistic:** *an **optimistic** personality*

option (say **op**-shuhn) *noun* (*plural* **options**)
a thing that you can choose: *You have the **option** of studying isiXhosa or Afrikaans.*
➲ SYNONYM **choice**

optional (say **op**-shuhn-l) *adjective*
that you can choose or not choose: *an **optional** subject at school* ➲ OPPOSITE **compulsory**

opulent (say **op**-yuu-luhnt) *adjective*
very expensive and noticeable in a way that is intended to impress other people: *Their **opulent** mansion showed off their wealth.*
➲ SYNONYMS **luxurious**, **ostentatious**
▶ **opulence** (*noun*) ▶ **opulently** (*adverb*)

or (say **aw**) *conjunction*
1 a word that joins possibilities: *Is it blue **or** green?* ◇ *Are you coming **or** not?* ◇ *You can have soup, salad **or** sandwiches.* ◇ *She hasn't phoned **or** written for weeks.*
2 if not: *Go now, **or** you'll be late.*
➲ SYNONYM **otherwise**[2]

oral (say **o**-ruhl) *adjective*
spoken, not written: *an **oral** exam*
▶ **orally** (*adverb*): *She presented her work **orally**.*

orange[1] (say **o**-rinj) *noun* (*plural* **oranges**)
1 a round fruit with a colour between red and yellow, and a thick skin: ***orange** juice*
2 a colour between red and yellow

orange[2] (say **o**-rinj) *adjective*
with a colour that is between red and yellow: ***orange** paint*

orator (say **o**-ruh-tuh) *noun* (*plural* **orators**)
a person who makes speeches: *Our principal is a good **orator**.*
▶ **oratory** (*noun*): *He studied **oratory**.*

orbit (say **aw**-bit) *noun* (*plural* **orbits**)
the regularly repeated path of a planet around a star, or the regularly repeated path of a moon or a satellite around a planet
▶ **orbit** (*verb*): *The spacecraft is **orbiting** the moon.*

orchard (say **aw**-chuhd) *noun* (*plural* **orchards**)
a piece of land where fruit trees grow

orchestra (say **aw**-kuhss-truh) *noun* (*plural* **orchestras**)
a big group of people who play different musical instruments together, led by a **conductor** 1

orchid (say **aw**-kid) *noun* (*plural* **orchids**)
a beautiful type of plant that has flowers of unusual shapes and bright colours

ordeal (say **aw**-deel) *noun* (*plural* **ordeals**)
a very bad or unpleasant thing that happens to somebody: *He was lost in the mountains with no food – it was a terrible **ordeal**.*

order[1] (say **aw**-duh) *noun*
1 (*no plural*) the way that you place people or things together: *in alphabetical **order*** ◇ *List the jobs in **order** of importance.*
2 (*no plural*) when everything is in the right place or everybody is doing the right thing: *Our teacher likes **order** in the classroom.* ◇ *Are these papers in **order*** (= correct and tidy)? ➲ OPPOSITE **disorder** 1
3 (*plural* **orders**) words that tell somebody to do something: *She gave the **order** to start the exam.* ◇ *Soldiers have to obey **orders**.*
➲ SYNONYM **command**[1] 1
4 (*plural* **orders**) when you ask a company to send or supply goods to you: *I'd like to place an **order** for some books.*
5 (*plural* **orders**) when you ask for food or drink in a restaurant or bar: *The waiter took our **order**.*
in order to so that you can do something: *We arrived early in **order** to buy our tickets.*
out of order (used about a machine or device) not working: *I couldn't ring you – the phone was out of **order**.*

order[2] (say **aw**-duh) *verb* (**ordering**, **ordered**)
1 to tell somebody that they must do something: *The student was **ordered** to leave the classroom.* ➲ SYNONYM **command**[2]
2 to ask a company to send or supply goods to you: *The shop didn't have your book in stock – I **ordered** it.*
3 to ask for food or drink in a restaurant or bar: *I **ordered** some coffee.*
4 to organize or arrange information in a certain way: ***Order** them according to age, starting with the oldest.*

orderly (say **aw**-duh-lee) *adjective*
1 neat and carefully arranged: *an **orderly** arrangement of chairs* ➲ SYNONYM **organized**
2 well behaved and peaceful: *an **orderly** crowd*

ordinal number (say aw-din-l **num**-buh) *noun* (*plural* **ordinal numbers**) (*maths*)
a number showing a thing's position in a series: *'First', 'third' and '4th' are **ordinal numbers**.* ➲ See Study page 20 ➲ See **cardinal number**

ordinary (say **aw**-duhn-ree) *adjective*
not special or unusual: *He was wearing a suit, but I was in my **ordinary** clothes.*
➲ SYNONYM **normal** 1
out of the ordinary unusual: *Did you see anything out of the **ordinary**?*
➲ SYNONYM **strange**

ordinate (say **aw**-di-nuht) *noun* (*plural* **ordinates**) (*maths*)
a point on the vertical line of a **graph**
➲ See **coordinate**[1]

ore (say **aw**) *noun* (*plural* **ores**)
rock or earth from which you get metal: *iron ore*

organ (say **aw**-guhn) *noun* (*plural* **organs**)
1 a part of an organism's body that carries out a special function for the whole body, for example the heart: *the body's internal **organs***
2 a large musical instrument with pipes through which air is forced. It is played using a **keyboard**: *She plays the **organ** in church.*

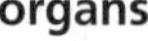

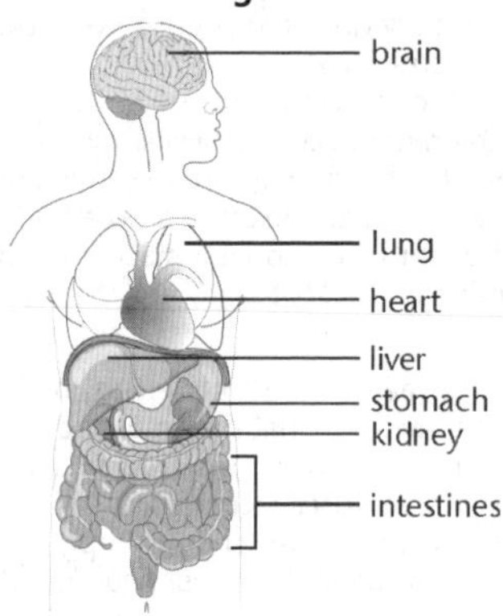

some important human organs

organic (say aw-**gan**-ik) *adjective*
1 produced by or from living things: *Improve the soil by adding **organic** matter.*
2 grown in a natural way, without using chemicals: ***organic** vegetables*
▸ **organically** (*adverb*): *Our vegetables are grown **organically**.*

organism (say **aw**-guh-niz-m) *noun* (*plural* **organisms**)
a living thing. Plants, animals and **bacteria** are examples of organisms.

organization (say aw-guh-nize-**ay**-shuhn) *noun* (also **organisation**)
1 (*plural* **organizations**) a group of people who work together for a special purpose: *He works for an **organization** that helps old people.*
2 (*no plural*) the activity of planning or arranging something, or the way that something is planned or arranged: *She's busy with the **organization** of her daughter's wedding.*

organize (say **aw**-guh-nize) *verb* (**organizing**, **organized**) (also **organise**)
to plan or arrange something: *Our teacher has **organized** a visit to the museum.*
▸ **organizer** (*noun*) (also **organiser**): *the **organizers** of the concert*

organized (say **aw**-guh-nize-d) *adjective* (also **organised**)
with everything planned or arranged: *She's very **organized**.* ➲ OPPOSITE **disorganized**

orgasm (say **aw**-gaz-m) *noun* (*plural* **orgasms**)
the point of greatest sexual pleasure: *to have an **orgasm***

orgy (say **aw**-jee) *noun* (*plural* **orgies**)
1 a party that involves a lot of drinking and sexual activity
2 a period of doing something in a wild way, without control: *an **orgy** of eating* ➲ SYNONYM **binge**

Orient (say **o**-ri-uhnt) *noun* (**the Orient**) (*formal*)
the part of the world that is east of Europe, especially China and Japan
▸ **oriental** (also **Oriental**) (*adjective*) (*old-fashioned*): ***oriental** carpets* ◇ ***oriental** art*

orient (say **o**-ri-uhnt) *verb* (**orienting**, **oriented**)
= **orientate**

orientate (say **o**-ri-uhn-tayt) *verb* (**orientating**, **orientated**)
to find out where you are in relation to the places around you: *Check the street map and **orientate** yourself.*
▸ **orientated** or **oriented** (*adjective*)

orientation (say o-ri-uhn-**tay**-shuhn) *noun*
1 (*plural* **orientations**) a person or thing's position or direction relative to something else: *the house's **orientation** to the sun.*
2 (*no plural*) the act of getting to know a new place or situation: *an **orientation** programme for new learners*

orifice (say **o**-ri-fiss) *noun* (*plural* **orifices**)
a hole or opening, especially in the body: *A mouth is an **orifice** of the body.* ◇ *the nasal* (= of the nose) ***orifice***

origami (say o-ri-**gaa**-mi) *noun* (*no plural*)
the Japanese art of folding paper into shapes for decoration: *an **origami** dragon*
🛈 **ORIGIN**: from Japanese *origami* meaning 'folding paper'

origin (say **o**-ri-juhn) *noun* (*plural* **origins**)
1 the point from which something starts or the cause of something: *the **origins** of life on Earth*
2 a person's social and family background: *Her family is of Scottish **origin**.*

original (say o-**rij**-i-nuhl) *adjective*
1 first or earliest: *I have the car now, but my sister was the **original** owner.*
2 new and different: *His poems are very **original**.*
3 real, not copied: ***original** paintings*
▸ **original** (*noun*): *This painting is a copy – the **original** is in the museum.*

originally (say o-**rij**-i-nuh-lee) *adverb*
in the beginning: *The school was **originally** very small.* ◇ *I'm from Zambia **originally**.*

ornament (say **aw**-nuh-muhnt) *noun* (*plural* **ornaments**)
a thing that we have because it is beautiful, not because it is useful: *glass **ornaments***
▸ **ornamental** (*adjective*): *There is an **ornamental** lake in the garden.*

ornate (say aw-**nayt**) *adjective*
with complicated designs as decoration: *an **ornate** gate*

orphan (say **aw**-fuhn) *noun* (*plural* **orphans**)
a child whose parents are dead

orphanage (say **aw**-fuh-nij) *noun* (*plural* **orphanages**)
a home for children whose parents are dead

orthodox (say **aw**-thuh-dokss) *adjective*
1 that most people do, believe or accept: *It was an **orthodox** decision.* ➲ SYNONYM **conventional**
2 (in certain religions) following the traditional views: *an **orthodox** Jew*

orthopaedics (say aw-thuh-**pee**-dikss) *noun* (*no plural*)
the area of medicine relating to conditions, injuries and diseases of the bones and muscles
▸ **orthopaedic** (*adjective*): *an **orthopaedic** surgeon* ◇ ***orthopaedic** shoes*

orthophoto (say **aw**-thuh-foh-toh) *noun* (*plural* **orthophotos**) (*geography*)
a photograph of the ground taken from the air and then corrected so that distances can be measured accurately on it using a scale

oscillate (say **oss**-i-layt) *verb* (**oscillating**, **oscillated**)
1 (*technology*) to keep moving from one position to another and back: *The needle **oscillates** on the gauge.*
2 to keep changing from one state to another: *Her feelings **oscillated** between joy and sadness.*
3 (*science*) to increase and decrease the value and direction of something over time in a regular way
▸ **oscillating** (*adjective*): *an **oscillating** sprinkler* ▸ **oscillation** (*noun*)

osmosis (say oz-**moh**-siss) *noun* (*no plural*)
the gradual passing of a liquid through a thin layer of material (called a **membrane**): *Water passes into the roots of a plant by **osmosis**.*

ossicle (say **oss**-ik-l) *noun* (*plural* **ossicles**)
any small bone, especially in the ear

ostentatious (say oss-tuhn-**tay**-shuhss) *adjective*
expensive or noticeable in a way that is intended to impress other people: *an **ostentatious** chandelier* ➲ SYNONYM **opulent**
▸ **ostentation** (*noun*)

ostracize (say **oss**-truh-size) *verb* (**ostracizing**, **ostracized**) (also **ostracise**) (*formal*)
to not allow a person into a social group, or to refuse to meet or talk to somebody: *Ed was **ostracized** at his new school.* ➲ SYNONYM **alienate**
▸ **ostracism** (*noun*)

ostrich (say **oss**-trich) *noun* (*plural* **ostriches**)
a very big bird from Africa that cannot fly but can run fast because it has long legs

other (say **u*th***-uh) *adjective, pronoun*
as well as or different from the one or ones I have said: *I am 12 but the **other** learners in my class are 13.* ◇ *I can only find one shoe. Have you seen the **other** one?* ◇ *I saw her on the **other** side of the road.* ◇ *We arrived at nine o'clock, but the **others*** (= the *other* people) *were late.*
other than except or apart from: *I haven't told anybody **other** than you.*
some... or other (*informal*) words that show you are not sure: *I can't find my glasses. I know I put them somewhere or **other**.*
the other day not many days ago: *I saw your brother the **other** day.* ➲ SYNONYM **recently**

otherwise[1] (say **u*th***-uh-wize) *adverb*
1 in all other ways: *The house is a bit small, but **otherwise** it's very nice.*
2 in a different way: *Most people agreed, but Rachel thought **otherwise**.*

otherwise[2] (say **u*th***-uh-wize) *conjunction*
if not: *Hurry up, **otherwise** you'll be late.* ➲SYNONYM **or** 2

otter (say **ot**-uh) *noun* (*plural* **otters**)
a mammal with brown fur, living in and near water, that eats fish and other small animals

ouch (say **owch**) *exclamation*
used when you suddenly feel pain: ***Ouch**! That hurts!*

ought to (say **awt** *tuu*) *modal verb*
1 words that you use to tell or ask somebody what is the right thing to do: *It's late – you **ought to** go home.* ◇ *You **oughtn't to** argue.* ➲SYNONYM **should** 1
2 words that you use to say what you think will happen or what you think is true: *He has worked hard, so he **ought to** pass the exam.* ◇ *That film **ought to** be good.* ➲ SYNONYM **should** 3 ➲ See note at **modal verb**

A B C D E F G H I J K L M N O P Q R S T U V W X Y Z

ounce (*rhymes with* **pounce**) *noun* (*plural* **ounces**) (abbr. oz)
a measure of mass (= 28,35 grams) used in Britain and some other countries: *four* ***ounces*** *of flour*

our (say **ow**-uh) *adjective*
belonging to us: *This is* ***our*** *house.*

ours (say **ow**-uhz) *pronoun*
something that belongs to us: *Your car is the same as* ***ours.***

ourselves (say ow-uh-**selvz**) *pronoun, plural noun*
1 used when you and another person or other people do an action and are also affected by it: *We made* ***ourselves*** *some coffee.*
2 a word that makes 'we' stronger: *We built the house* ***ourselves.***
by ourselves
1 alone, and without other people: *We went on holiday by* ***ourselves.***
2 without help

out (say **owt**) *adjective, adverb*
1 away from the inside of a place: *When you go* ***out****, please close the door.* ◇ *She opened the box and took* ***out*** *a picture.*
2 not at home or not in the place where you work: *I phoned Steve but he was* ***out.*** ◇ *I went* ***out*** *to a movie last night.*
3 not burning or shining: *The fire went* ***out.***
4 not hidden, but visible (= that you can see) : *Look! The sun is* ***out!*** ◇ *All the flowers are* ***out*** (= open).
5 in a loud voice: *She cried* ***out*** *in pain.*
➲ See **out of**

outbreak (say **owt**-brayk) *noun* (*plural* **outbreaks**)
the sudden start of something bad: *the* ***outbreak*** *of war*

outburst (say **owt**-burst) *noun* (*plural* **outbursts**)
a sudden expression of a strong feeling, especially anger: *Her angry* ***outburst*** *gave us a fright.*

outcast (say **owt**-kaast) *noun* (*plural* **outcasts**)
a person who is no longer accepted by a group of people or society: *a social* ***outcast***

outcome (say **owt**-kum) *noun* (*plural* **outcomes**)
1 the result or effect of something that takes place: *What was the* ***outcome*** *of the vote?*
2 a result of learning: knowledge or skills that a learner develops at school: *What are the learning* ***outcomes*** *for this subject?*

outcry (say **owt**-kry) *noun* (*plural* **outcries**)
a strong protest by a large number of people because they disagree with something: *There was an* ***outcry*** *about the price increase.*
➲ SYNONYM **protest**[1]

outdated (say owt-**day**-tid) *adjective*
not useful any more or old-fashioned: *My computer is* ***outdated.*** ➲ SYNONYM **obsolete**

outdoor (say **owt**-daw) *adjective*
happening, existing or used outside a building: *an* ***outdoor*** *activity* ◇ *Bring* ***outdoor*** *clothing.*
➲ OPPOSITE **indoor**

outdoors (say owt-**dawz**) *adverb*
not in a building: *In summer we sometimes eat* ***outdoors.*** ➲ SYNONYM **outside**[1] ➲ OPPOSITE **indoors**

outer (say **owt**-uh) *adjective*
on the outside, or far from the centre: *Remove the* ***outer*** *leaves from the cabbage.* ◇ *the* ***outer*** *layer* ➲ OPPOSITE **inner**

outfit (say **owt**-fit) *noun* (*plural* **outfits**)
a set of clothes that you wear together: *I've bought a new* ***outfit*** *for the party.*

outgrow (say owt-**groh**) *verb* (**outgrowing, outgrew, has outgrown**)
to become too big or too old for something: *She's* ***outgrown*** *her school uniform again.*

outing (say **owt**-ing) *noun* (*plural* **outings**)
an organized visit that lasts for less than a day: *The Grade 6s are going on an* ***outing*** *to the zoo.*
➲ SYNONYMS **excursion, trip**[1]

outlaw (say **owt**-law) *noun* (*plural* **outlaws**)
(*old-fashioned*)
a person who has done something illegal and is hiding from the police
🛈 ORIGIN: through Old English *ūtlaga* meaning 'outlaw', from Old Norse *ūtlagi*

outlay (say **owt**-lay) *noun* (*plural* **outlays**)
money that is spent, especially to start a business: *What is your financial* ***outlay?***

outlet (say **owt**-let) *noun* (*plural* **outlets**)
1 a pipe through which gas or liquid can escape
2 a shop or business that sells goods of a certain type: *a fast-food* ***outlet***
3 a way of expressing and making use of strong feelings, ideas or energy: *a creative* ***outlet***

outlier (say **owt**-ly-uh) *noun* (*plural* **outliers**)
1 a person or thing that is separate from the main body or system
2 (*maths*) a number that is much higher or lower than the closest number in a set of results

outline[1] (say **owt**-line) *noun* (*plural* **outlines**)
a line that shows the shape or edge of something: *It was dark, but we could see the* ***outline*** *of the building.* ◇ *Draw the* ***outline.***

outline[2] (say **owt**-line) *verb* (**outlining, outlined**)
to tell somebody the most important facts or ideas about something: *He **outlined** the plan.*

outlook (say **owt**-luuk) *noun* (*plural* **outlooks**)
what will probably happen: *The **outlook** for the economy is not good.*

outnumber (say owt-**num**-buh) *verb* (**outnumbering, outnumbered**)
to have a greater number of people or players than another team or an enemy: *They **outnumbered** us, but we still won.*

out of *preposition*
1 words that show where from: *She took a cake **out of** the box.* ◇ *She got **out of** bed.* ➲ OPPOSITE **into**
2 not in: *Fish can't live **out of** water.*
3 using something, or from: *He made a table **out of** some old pieces of wood.*
4 from a number or set: *Nine **out of** ten people think that the government is right.*
5 because of a particular feeling: *I was just asking **out of** curiosity.*
6 without: *We're **out of** coffee.* ◇ *She's been **out of** work for six months.*

out of date *adjective*
1 old and therefore no longer useful or wanted: *This map is **out of date**.*
2 not allowed or valid any more: *Your driving licence is **out of date**.*

outpost (say **owt**-pohst) *noun* (*plural* **outposts**)
1 a small town or group of buildings in a lonely part of a country
2 a small military camp away from the main army

output (say **owt**-puut) *noun*
1 (*no plural*) the number or amount of things that a person or thing has made or done: *What was the factory's **output** last year?*
2 (*plural* **outputs**) something that is made or done: *Compare the inputs and the **outputs**.*

outrage (say **owt**-rayj) *noun*
1 (*plural* **outrages**) something that is very bad or wrong and that causes you to feel great anger: *It's an **outrage** that theft happens in schools.*
2 (*no plural*) great anger: *I felt **outrage** when I was robbed.* ➲ SYNONYM **fury**
▸ **outrageous** (*adjective*): ***outrageous** behaviour* ▸ **outrageously** (*adverb*)

outright (say **owt**-rite) *adjective, adverb*
1 open and direct, or in an open and direct way: *She asked him **outright** what he wanted.*
2 complete and clear, or completely and clearly: *They had an **outright** lead in the league.* ◇ *an **outright** lie*
3 immediately, not gradually: *We bought the house **outright** without a loan.*

outset (say **owt**-set) *noun* (*no plural*)
the beginning of something: *We worked together from the **outset**.* ➲ SYNONYM **start**[2] 1

outside[1] (say owt-**side**) *noun* (*plural* **outsides**)
the part of something that is away from the middle: *the **outside** of the packet* ◇ *We've only seen the building from the **outside**.*
➲ OPPOSITE **inside**[2]

outside[2] (say **owt**-side) *adjective*
away from the middle of something: *the **outside** walls of the house* ◇ *an **outside** toilet*
➲ OPPOSITE **inside**[1]

outside[3] (say owt-**side**) *preposition, adverb*
in or to a place that is not inside a building: *I left my bicycle **outside** the shop.* ◇ *Come **outside** and see the garden!* ➲ OPPOSITE **inside**[1]

outskirts (say **owt**-skurtss) *plural noun*
the edges of a town or city: *They live on the **outskirts** of town.*

outspoken (say owt-**spoh**-kuhn) *adjective*
saying exactly what you think or feel although you may shock or upset people: *He is **outspoken** in his criticism.*

outstanding (say owt-**stand**-ing) *adjective*
very good and much better than others: *Her work is **outstanding**.* ➲ SYNONYM **excellent**

outward (say **owt**-wuhd) *adjective*
1 connected with the way things seem to be: *Her **outward** appearance was cheerful but she was in fact very unhappy.*
2 travelling away from a place that you will return to later: *There were no delays on the **outward** journey.* ➲ OPPOSITE **inward** 2
▸ **outwardly** (*adverb*): *He seemed **outwardly** calm but in fact he was angry.*

outwards (say **owt**-wuhdz) *adverb* (also **outward**)
towards the outside: *The windows open **outwards**.* ➲ OPPOSITE **inwards**

outwit (say owt-**wit**) *verb* (**outwitting, outwitted**)
to do something cleverer than somebody else to gain an advantage: *We **outwitted** the other team.*

ova (say **oh**-vuh) plural of **ovum**

oval (say **oh**-vuhl) *noun* (*plural* **ovals**)
1 a flat closed shape like the outline of an egg, with one end more pointed than the other: *Draw an **oval**.*
2 a flat closed shape like a flattened circle, with

A B C D E F G H I J K L M N **O** P Q R S T U V W X Y Z

both ends the same as each other
▸ **oval** (*adjective*): *an* ***oval*** *mirror*

oval

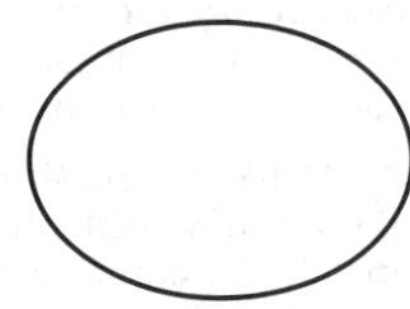

an oval (sense 1) an oval (sense 2)

ovary (say **oh**-vuh-ree) *noun* (*plural* **ovaries**) (*biology*)
1 one of the pair of female organs where eggs develop and are stored
2 the part of a plant where the female cells **(called ovules)** that become the seeds develop and are stored ➲ See illustration at **flower**
▸ **ovarian** (*adjective*): ***ovarian*** *cancer*

oven (say **uv**-uhn) *noun* (*plural* **ovens**)
the part of a stove shaped like a box with a door on the front. You bake or roast food in it: *Take the bread out of the* ***oven****.*

over¹ (say **oh**-vuh) *adverb, preposition*
1 on a person or thing so that it covers them: *She put a blanket* ***over*** *the sleeping child.*
2 above something, or higher than something: *A plane flew* ***over*** *our heads.* ◇ *There is a picture* ***over*** *the fireplace.*
3 across, or to the other side of something: *The dog jumped* ***over*** *the wall.*
4 to or in a place: *Come* ***over*** *and see us on Saturday.* ◇ *Come* ***over*** *here!*
5 down or sideways: *I fell* ***over*** *in the street.* ◇ *He leaned* ***over*** *to speak to her.*
6 so that the other side is on top: *You may turn your papers* ***over*** *and begin.*
7 more than a number, price or amount: *She lived in Spain for* ***over*** *20 years.* ◇ *This game is for children of ten and* ***over****.*
8 not used, or remaining: *There are a lot of cakes left* ***over*** *from the party.*
9 used for saying that somebody repeats something: *He said the same thing* ***over*** *and* ***over*** *again* (= many times). ◇ *You'll have to start all* ***over*** *again* (= from the beginning).
all over everywhere, and in every part: *Have you seen my glasses? I've looked all* ***over****.* ◇ *She travels all* ***over*** *the world.*

over² (say **oh**-vuh) *adjective*
finished: *The exams are* ***over*** *now.*

over³ (say **oh**-vuh) *noun* (*plural* **overs**)
(in cricket) a set of six balls delivered **(bowled)** by the same person

over- (say **oh**-vuh) *prefix*
more than is good, or too much: *He's been* ***overeating****.* ◇ *You're being* ***over-optimistic*** *– she won't pass all her exams.*

overall¹ (say oh-vuh-**rawl**) *adjective*
including everything: *The* ***overall*** *cost of the repairs will be about R350.* ➲ SYNONYM **total¹** 2
▸ **overall** (*adverb*): *How much will it cost* ***overall****?*

overall² (say **oh**-vuh-rawl) *noun* (*plural* **overalls**)
a kind of light coat that you wear over your clothes to keep them clean when you are working: *The laboratory assistant was wearing a white* ***overall****.*

overalls (say **oh**-vuh-rawlz) *plural noun*
a loose piece of clothing like a shirt and pants in one piece made of heavy cloth that workers doing dirty work wear over their other clothing: *The mechanic was wearing a pair of blue* ***overalls****.*

overboard (say **oh**-vuh-bawd) *adverb*
over the side of a boat and into the water: *She fell* ***overboard****.*
go overboard (*informal*) to be too excited or enthusiastic about a person or thing: *Don't go* ***overboard*** *about studying: you need to have some fun too.*

overcame (say oh-vuh-**kaym**) form of **overcome**

overcast (say oh-vuh-**kaast**) *adjective*
covered in cloud: *It is* ***overcast*** *today, so it might rain.*

overcoat (say **oh**-vuh-koht) *noun* (*plural* **overcoats**)
a long warm coat: *Although it was a hot day, he was wearing an* ***overcoat****.*

overcome (say oh-vuh-**kum**) *verb* (**overcoming, overcame, has overcome**)
to find an answer to a difficult thing in your life, or to control something: *He* ***overcame*** *his fear of flying.*

overcrowd (say oh-vuh-**krowd**) *verb* (**overcrowding, overcrowded**)
to fill a space more than it should be filled, usually with people
▸ **overcrowding** (*noun*): ***Overcrowding*** *at soccer matches can become dangerous.*

overcrowded (say oh-vuh-**krowd**-id) *adjective*
too full of people: *The trains are* ***overcrowded*** *in the mornings.*

overdo (say oh-vuh-**doo**) *verb* (**overdoing, overdid, has overdone**)
1 to use or do too much of something: *Don't* ***overdo*** *your exercise.*

2 to cook food for too long: *The meat was **overdone**.*

overdraft (say **oh**-vuh-draaft) *noun* (*plural* **overdrafts**)
an amount of money that the bank allows you to spend over and above the amount in your bank account

overdue (say oh-vuh-**dyoo**) *adjective*
not done by the expected time: *I was very busy and my assignment was **overdue**.*
➲ SYNONYM **late** 2

overflow (say oh-vuh-**floh**) *verb* (**overflowing**, **overflowed**)
to be so full that the contents flow over the top of something: *Someone left the tap on and the water **overflowed**.*

overgraze (say oh-vuh-**grayz**) *verb* (**overgrazing**, **overgrazed**)
to allow animals, such as cows, to feed on grass and other plants in an area of land for too long so that the grass disappears and the land can no longer be used as before
▸ **overgrazing** (*noun*): ***Overgrazing** can increase soil erosion.*

overgrown (say oh-vuh-**grohn**) *adjective*
covered with plants that have grown too big: *The house was empty and the garden was **overgrown**.*

overhaul (say oh-vuh-**hawl**) *verb* (**overhauling**, **overhauled**)
to look at something carefully and repair it if necessary: *He **overhauled** the engine.*
▸ **overhaul** (*noun*)

overhead (say **oh**-vuh-hed) *adjective*
above your head: *an **overhead** light*
▸ **overhead** (*adverb*): *A plane flew **overhead**.*

overheads (say **oh**-vuh-heds) *plural noun*
money that must be spent to keep a business running, such as payment for rent and water: *Keep your **overheads** low.*

overhear (say oh-vuh-**heer**) *verb* (**overhearing**, **overheard**)
to hear what somebody is saying when they are speaking to another person: *I **overheard** her saying that she was unhappy.*

overjoyed (say oh-vuh-**joyd**) *adjective*
very happy ➲ SYNONYM **thrilled**

overlap (say oh-vuh-**lap**) *verb* (**overlapping**, **overlapped**)
(used about a part of one thing) to partly cover another thing, or to happen partly at the same time as another thing: *The tiles on the roof **overlap**.* ◇ *We couldn't watch two programmes from different TV channels because their showing times **overlapped**.*

overlook (say oh-vuh-**luuk**) *verb* (**overlooking**, **overlooked**)
1 to not see or notice something: *He **overlooked** one important fact.*
2 to have a view over something: *My room **overlooks** the garden.*

overnight (say oh-vuh-**nite**) *adjective, adverb*
for or during the night: *an **overnight** journey* ◇ *They stayed at our house **overnight**.*

overpower (say oh-vuh-**pow**-uh) *verb* (**overpowering**, **overpowered**)
to be too strong for somebody, or to use your strength to beat somebody: *The wind **overpowered** the cyclists.* ◇ *The wrestler **overpowered** his opponent.*

overrate (say oh-vuh-**rayt**) *verb* (**overrating**, **overrated**)
(usually passive) to think that a person or thing is better than they are: *The film is **overrated**.*

overrule (say oh-vuh-**rool**) *verb* (**overruling**, **overruled**)
to use your authority to change what somebody has already decided: *The teacher **overruled** our plans.* ◇ *The judgement was **overruled**.*

overseas (say oh-vuh-**seez**) *adjective, adverb*
in, to or from another country across the sea: *There are many **overseas** students in Britain.* ◇ *She travels **overseas** a lot.*

oversee (say oh-vuh-**see**) *verb* (**overseeing**, **oversaw**, **has overseen**)
to watch a person or thing and make sure that a given job is done properly: *I'll **oversee** your project.* ➲ SYNONYM **supervise**

overshoot (say oh-vuh-**shoot**) *verb* (**overshooting**, **overshot**)
to shoot or pass beyond what you are aiming for: *The plane **overshot** the runway.*

oversight (say **oh**-vuh-site) *noun* (*no plural*)
1 something that you do not notice when you should have noticed it: *The mistake was an **oversight**.*
2 the job of overseeing something

oversleep (say oh-vuh-**sleep**) *verb* (**oversleeping**, **overslept**)
to sleep too long and not wake up at the right time: *I **overslept** and was late for work.*

overtake (say oh-vuh-**tayk**) *verb* (**overtaking**, **overtook**, **has overtaken**)
to go past a person or thing that is going more slowly: *The car **overtook** a bus.*

A B C D E F G H I J K L M N O P Q R S T U V W X Y Z

overthrow (say oh-vuh-**throh**) *verb* (**overthrowing, overthrew, overthrown**)
to force a leader or government to give up power: *The government was **overthrown** by the opposition.*
▸ **overthrow** (*noun*)

overtime (say **oh**-vuh-time) *noun* (*no plural*)
extra time that you spend at work: *I have done a lot of **overtime** this week.*

overturn (say oh-vuh-**turn**) *verb* (**overturning, overturned**)
1 to turn something over so that it is upside down: *The waves **overturned** the boat*
2 to officially decide that a decision is wrong and change it: *The court **overturned** the ban.*

overview (say **oh**-vuh-vyoo) *noun* (*plural* **overviews**)
a general description of something without the details: *Give an **overview** of your project.*

overweight (say oh-vuh-**wayt**) *adjective*
too heavy or fat: *The doctor said I was **overweight** and that I should eat less.*
➲ OPPOSITE **underweight**

overwhelm (say oh-vuh-**welm**) *verb* (**overwhelming, overwhelmed**)
1 to cause somebody to feel such strong emotions that they do not know how to react: *Your speech **overwhelmed** me.*
2 to defeat someone because you are stronger or bigger: *The wrestler **overwhelmed** his opponent.* ➲ SYNONYM **overpower**
▸ **overwhelmed** (*adjective*): *I was **overwhelmed** by the applause.*

overwhelming (say oh-vuh-**wel**-ming) *adjective*
very great or strong: *an **overwhelming** feeling of loneliness*

oviparous (say oh-**vip**-uh-ruhss) *adjective* (*biology*)
relating to animals that produce young animals by laying eggs that **hatch**[1] later: ***oviparous** animals such as birds and fish* ➲ See **viviparous**

ovulate (say **ov**-yuu-layt) *verb* (**ovulating, ovulated**)
to release an egg from the **ovary**: *Women **ovulate** about once a month.*

ovule (say **ov**-yool) *noun* (*plural* **ovules**)
(in plants that produce seeds) the part of the **ovary** that contains the female cells that become the seeds ➲ See illustration at **flower**

ovum (say **oh**-vuhm) *noun* (*plural* **ova**) (*biology*)
a female sex cell or egg

owe (*rhymes with* **go**) *verb* (**owing, owed**)
1 to have to pay money to somebody: *I lent you R10 last week and R10 the week before, so you **owe** me R20.*
2 to have something because of a particular person or thing: *He **owes** his life to the man who pulled him out of the river.*

owing to *preposition*
because of, as a result of: *The train was late **owing to** the bad weather.*

owl (*rhymes with* **fowl**) *noun* (*plural* **owls**)
a bird that flies at night and catches small animals to eat

own[1] (say **ohn**) *adjective, pronoun*
used for emphasizing that something belongs to a particular person: *I have my **own** room now that my sister has left home.* ◇ *I want a home of my **own**.*
get your own back on somebody to do something bad to somebody who has done something bad to you: *He said he would get his **own** back on me for breaking his watch.*
on your own
1 alone: *She lives on her **own**.*
2 without help: *I can't move this box on my **own** – can you help me?*

own[2] (say **ohn**) *verb* (**owning, owned**)
to have something that is yours: *We don't **own** our flat – we rent it.* ◇ *I don't **own** a car.*
own up to say that you have done something wrong: *Nobody **owned** up to breaking the window.*

owner (say **ohn**-uh) *noun* (*plural* **owners**)
a person who has something that belongs to them: *Who is the **owner** of this red book?*

ownership (say **ohn**-uh-ship) *noun* (*no plural*)
the state of owning something: *She took **ownership** of the car.*

ox (say **okss**) *noun* (*plural* **oxen**)
a bull that has been castrated (= had part of its sex organs removed) and that is used for pulling or carrying heavy things

oxbow (say **okss**-boh) *noun* (*plural* **oxbows**) (*geography*)
1 a bend in a river that almost forms a circle
2 (also **oxbow lake**) a lake that forms when this bend is separated from the river

oxide (say **ok**-side) *noun* (*plural* **oxides**) (*science*)
a compound of **oxygen** and another chemical element: *iron **oxide***

oxidize (say **ok**-si-dize) *verb* (**oxidizing, oxidized**) (also **oxidise**) (*science*)
to combine or to make a substance combine with **oxygen**: *The metal* ***oxidized*** *and became rusty.*
▸ **oxidation** (*noun*): ***oxidation*** *reaction*
◇ ***oxidation*** *number*

oxygen (say **ok**-si-juhn) *noun* (*no plural*) (symbol O)
a gas in the air and in water that animals and plants need to take in to live

oxymoron (say ok-si-**maw**-ruhn) *noun* (*plural* **oxymorons**)
a phrase that combines two words that seem to mean the opposite of each other, for example 'a deafening silence' ➲ See Study page 17

oyster (say **oyss**-tuh) *noun* (*plural* **oysters**)
a large flat shellfish. Some types can be eaten and others produce shiny white jewels (called **pearls**).

ozone (say **oh**-zohn) *noun* (*no plural*) (*science*)
a poisonous gas that has a strong smell that is a form of **oxygen**

ozone-friendly *adjective*
(used about cleaning products, for example) not containing chemicals that could harm the **ozone layer**: *Most aerosol sprays are now* ***ozone-friendly****.*

ozone layer *noun* (*no plural*)
the layer of **ozone** high above the surface of the Earth, which helps to protect the Earth from the dangerous effects of the sun ➲ See illustration at **atmosphere**

Pp

p (say **pee**) *abbreviation* (*plural* **pp**) **page**

pace[1] (say **payss**) *noun*
1 (*no plural*) how fast you do something or how fast something happens: *We started at a steady pace.*
2 (*plural* **paces**) a step: *Take two **paces** forward.*
keep pace with somebody or **something** to go as fast as somebody or something: *She couldn't keep **pace** with the other runners.*

pace[2] (say **payss**) *verb* (**pacing**, **paced**)
to walk around nervously or angrily: *She **paced** up and down outside.*

pacifist (say **pass**-i-fist) *noun* (*plural* **pacifists**)
a person who believes that wars are wrong and that you should not fight in them
▸ **pacifism** (*noun*): *Gandhi believed in **pacifism**.*

pacify (say **pass**-i-fy) *verb* (**pacifying**, **pacified**)
to make a person who is angry or upset be calm or quiet

pack[1] (say **pak**) *noun* (*plural* **packs**)
1 a set of things: *I bought a **pack** of five exercise books.* ◇ *an information **pack***
2 a set of 52 cards for playing games
3 a group of wild dogs or similar animals: *a **pack** of wolves*

pack[2] (say **pak**) *verb* (**packing**, **packed**)
1 to put things into a bag or suitcase before you go somewhere: *Have you **packed** your suitcase?* ◇ *Don't forget to **pack** your toothbrush.*
2 to put things into a box, bag or container: ***Pack** all these books into boxes.*
pack up to stop doing something: *At two o'clock we **packed** up and went home.*
➲ OPPOSITE **unpack**

package (say **pak**-ij) *noun* (*plural* **packages**)
something that is wrapped in paper, cardboard or plastic ➲ SYNONYM **parcel**

packaging (say **pak**-ij-ing) *noun* (*no plural*)
material like paper, cardboard or plastic that is used to wrap things that you buy or that you send

packed (say **pakt**) *adjective*
full: *The train was **packed**.*

packet (say **pak**-uht) *noun* (*plural* **packets**)
a small bag that you buy things in: *a **packet** of biscuits* ◇ *an empty chip **packet***

pact (say **pakt**) *noun* (*plural* **pacts**)
an important agreement to do something: *They made a **pact** not to tell anyone.*

pad *noun* (*plural* **pads**)
1 a thick flat piece of soft material: *Footballers wear **pads** on their legs to protect them.* ◇ *I used a **pad** of cotton wool to clean the cut.*
2 pieces of paper that are joined together at one end: *a writing **pad***

padded (say **pad**-uhd) *adjective*
covered with or containing a layer of thick soft material: *a **padded** jacket*

paddle[1] (say **pad**-l) *noun* (*plural* **paddles**)
a piece of wood with a flat end, that you use for moving a small boat through water

paddle[2] (say **pad**-l) *verb* (**paddling**, **paddled**)
1 to move a small boat through water with a **paddle**[1]: *We **paddled** up the river.*
2 to walk in water that is not deep: *The children were **paddling** in the sea.*

paddy (say **pad**-ee) *noun* (*plural* **paddies**)
a field covered with water in which people grow rice
ℹ ORIGIN: 17th century, from Malay *pādī*

padlock (say **pad**-lok) *noun* (*plural* **padlocks**)
a lock that you use on things like gates and bicycles

paediatrics (say peed-i-**at**-rikss) *noun* (*no plural*)
the area of medicine that deals with children's health and diseases
▸ **paediatric** (*adjective*): ***paediatric** nurse* ◇ ***paediatric** cough mixture*
▸ **paediatrician** (*noun*): *The **paediatrician** treated my daughter's ear infection.*

pagan (say **payg**-n) *adjective*
relating to a religion often older than the main religions of the world, with a number of different gods: *Valentine's Day was originally a **pagan** festival.*
▸ **pagan** (*noun*): ***pagans** who worshipped the sun*

page (say **payj**) *noun* (*plural* **pages**) (abbr. p)
one or both sides of a piece of paper in a book, magazine or newspaper: *Please turn to **page** 120.* ◇ *What **page** is the story on?*

pageant (say **paj**-uhnt) *noun* (*plural* **pageants**)
1 a competition in which the people who take part are judged on certain qualities or skills: *a beauty **pageant***
2 a type of entertainment at which people dress in clothes from long ago and perform scenes from history

pagoda (say puh-**goh**-duh) *noun* (*plural* **pagodas**) a religious building in East Asia shaped like a tower with many levels, each with an upwardly curving roof

paid (say **payd**) form of **pay**[1]

pain (say **payn**) *noun*
1 (*plural* **pains**) an unpleasant feeling that you have in your body when you are hurt or ill: *Where is the **pain**? ◇ I've got **pains** in my legs.*
2 (*no plural*) unhappiness: *Her eyes were full of **pain**.*
be a pain or **be a pain in the neck** (*informal*) a person, thing or situation that makes you angry or annoyed: *She can be a real **pain** when she's in a bad mood.*

painful (say **payn**-fuhl) *adjective* giving pain: *I've cut my leg – it's very **painful**.*
▸ **painfully** (*adverb*)

painkiller (say **payn**-kil-uh) *noun* (*plural* **painkillers**) a medicine that makes pain less strong: *She's taking **painkillers**.* ➲ SYNONYM **analgesic**

painless (say **payn**-luhss) *adjective* not causing pain: *a **painless** injection*

paint[1] (say **paynt**) *noun* (*no plural*) a coloured liquid that you put on things with a brush, to change the colour or to make a picture: *red **paint** ◇ Is the **paint** dry yet?*

paint[2] (say **paynt**) *verb* (**painting, painted**)
1 to put **paint** on something to change the colour: *We **painted** the walls grey.*
2 to make a picture of somebody or something using **paints**: *Can I **paint** a picture of you? ◇ My sister **paints** well.*

paintbrush (say **paynt**-brush) *noun* (*plural* **paintbrushes**) a brush that you use for painting

painter (say **paynt**-uh) *noun* (*plural* **painters**)
1 a person whose job is to paint things like walls or houses
2 a person who paints pictures: *Picasso was a famous **painter**.* ➲ SYNONYM **artist**

painting (say **paynt**-ing) *noun* (*plural* **paintings**) a picture that somebody makes with paint: *a **painting** by Rembrandt ◇ She did a **painting** of the bridge.*

pair *noun* (*plural* **pairs**)
1 two things of the same kind that you use together: *a **pair** of shoes ◇ a new **pair** of earrings*
2 a thing with two parts that are joined together: *a **pair** of glasses ◇ a **pair** of scissors ◇ I bought two **pairs** of trousers.*
3 two people or animals together: *a **pair** of ducks* ➲ See **couple** 2
in pairs with two things or people together: *The learners are working **in pairs**. ◇ Shoes are sold only **in pairs**.*
▸ **pair** (*verb*): ***Pair** each sock with another sock of the same colour.*

pal *noun* (*plural* **pals**) (*informal*) a friend

palace (say **pal**-uhss) *noun* (*plural* **palaces**) a large beautiful house where a king or a queen lives: *The Queen of England lives at Buckingham **Palace**.*

palaeolithic (say pa-li-uh-**lith**-ik) *adjective* relating to the early part of the **Stone Age**: *Archaeologists have found stone tools dating back to the **palaeolithic** period.*

palaeontologist (say pay-li-on-**tol**-uh-jist) *number* (*plural* **palaeontologists**) a person who studies forms of life that existed hundreds of thousands of years ago by looking at **fossils**
▸ **palaeontology** (*noun*): *He studied **palaeontology**.*

palate (say **pal**-uht) *noun* (*plural* **palates**)
1 the top part of the inside of your mouth
2 a person's sense of taste: *This cheese does not suit my **palate**.*

palatial (say puh-**lay**-shuhl) *adjective* (used about a building) large and impressive like a palace

pale (say **payl**) *adjective* (**paler, palest**)
1 with not much colour in your face: *Are you ill? You look **pale**. ◇ She has very **pale** skin.* ➲ SYNONYM **white**[1] 3
2 with a light colour, or not strong or dark: *a **pale** blue dress* ➲ OPPOSITE **dark**[1] 2

palindrome (say **pal**-in-drohm) *noun* (*plural* **palindromes**) a word or phrase that reads the same backwards as forwards: *'Madam' and 'nurses run' are **palindromes**.*

palm (say **paam**) *noun* (*plural* **palms**) the flat part of the front of your hand ➲ See illustration at **hand**[1]

palm tree *noun* (*plural* **palm trees**) a tall tree that grows in hot countries and has many large leaves at the top
ℹ ORIGIN: through Old English *palm(a)*, from Latin *palma* meaning 'palm of a hand', because the leaves are the same shape as a hand with the fingers spread out

palpitate (say **pal**-pi-tayt) *verb* (**palpitating, palpitated**)
1 (used about the heart) to beat faster or not in a regular way

A B C D E F G H I J K L M N O P Q R S T U V W X Y Z

2 (used about a person) to shake with fear or excitement
▸ **palpitation** (*noun*): *heart **palpitations***

palsy (say **pawl**-zee) *noun* (*no plural*)
a medical condition in which you lose control of your muscles and movement: *cerebral **palsy***

pampas (say **pam**-puhss) *plural noun*
large areas of land in South America that is covered in grass and has no trees

pamper (say **pam**-puh) *verb* (**pampering, pampered**)
to take care of a person very well and make them feel as comfortable as possible: *We **pampered** our mother on her birthday.*

pamphlet (say **pam**-fluht) *noun* (*plural* **pamphlets**)
a very thin book with a paper cover that gives information about something

pan[1] *noun* (*plural* **pans**)
1 a metal pot with a handle, which you usually use for cooking: *a frying **pan*** ◇ *a **saucepan***
2 (*S. African*) a shallow lake that dries out easily: *Etosha **pan***

pan[2] *verb* (**panning, panned**)
1 to move a video or film camera in a particular direction to follow a person or to give a wide view: *The camera **panned** from the singer back to the judges.*
2 to wash soil or small stones in a pan to separate out valuable minerals: ***pan** for gold*
3 (*informal*) to criticize something severely: *The newspaper **panned** the new movie.*

pan- (say **pan**) *prefix*
including all of something or connected with the whole of something: ***pan-African***

panacea (say pan-uh-**see**-uh) *noun* (*plural* **panaceas**)
something that cures all diseases and troubles: *Some people believe that chicken soup is a **panacea**.*

pancake (say **pan**-kayk) *noun* (*plural* **pancakes**)
a very thin round thing that you eat. You make **pancakes** with flour, eggs and milk and cook them in a frying pan

panda (say **pan**-duh) *noun* (*plural* **pandas**)
a large black-and-white wild animal that lives in China
ⓘ **ORIGIN**: 20th century, from Nepali, the language of Nepal

pandemic (say pan-**dem**-ik) *noun* (*plural* **pandemics**)
a disease that spreads over a whole country or the whole world ➲ See **endemic** 2, **epidemic**

pandemonium (say pan-duh-**moh**-ni-uhm) *noun* (*no plural*)
a state of great noise and confusion: ***Pandemonium** broke out after a shark was spotted in the water.*

pander (say **pan**-duh) *verb* (**pandering, pandered**)
pander to a person or **thing** to do or say exactly what a person wants, especially when this is not reasonable: *He **panders** to his boss.*

pane (say **payn**) *noun* (*plural* **panes**)
a piece of glass in a window: *a **windowpane***

panel (say **pan**-l) *noun* (*plural* **panels**)
1 a flat piece of wood, metal or glass that is part of a door, wall or ceiling
2 a group of people who give their opinions about something or discuss something: *Do you have any questions for our **panel**?* ◇ *a **panel** of experts*
3 a flat part on a machine, where there are things to help you control it: *the TV's control **panel***

pang *noun* (*plural* **pangs**)
a sudden strong and painful feeling: *hunger **pangs*** ◇ *a **pang** of jealousy*

panga (say **pang**-guh) *noun* (*plural* **pangas**)
a large heavy knife used for cutting grass and weeds ➲ **SYNONYM machete**
ⓘ **ORIGIN**: 20th century, from Kiswahili, a language of East Africa

Pangaea (say pan-**jee**-uh) *noun* (*no plural*)
one huge continent that many scientists believe existed millions of years ago and that split up into the continents we have today

panic (say **pan**-ik) *verb* (**panicking, panicked**)
to have a sudden feeling of fear that you cannot control and that makes you do things without thinking carefully: *Don't **panic**!*
▸ **panic** (*noun*): *There was **panic** in the shop when the fire started.*
ⓘ **ORIGIN**: 17th century, through French from Greek *panikos*, from the name of the Greek god Pan, who surprised and terrified people by making strange sounds in the woods and fields

panic-stricken (say **pan**-ik-strik-n) *adjective*
very frightened in a way that stops you thinking clearly: ***Panic-stricken** shoppers fled from the scene.*

panorama (say pan-uh-**raa**-muh) *noun* (*plural* **panoramas**)
a view over a wide area of land or sea
▸ **panoramic** (*adjective*): *a **panoramic** view*

pant *verb* (**panting, panted**)
to take in and let out air quickly through your

mouth, for example after running or because you are very hot: *The dog was **panting**.*

panther (say **pan**-thuh) *noun* (*plural* **panthers**)
a wild animal like a big cat with black fur

panties (say **pan**-teez) *plural noun*
a piece of underwear for girls and women that covers the lower part of the body but not the legs ➲ SYNONYM **knickers**

pantomime (say **pan**-tuh-mime) *noun* (*plural* **pantomimes**)
a funny play for children, with singing and dancing

pants *plural noun*
1 trousers
2 a small piece of clothing that you wear under your other clothes, around the middle of your body to cover your bottom ➲ See **panties**, **underpants**

pap (say **pup**) *noun* (*no plural*) (*S. African*)
porridge made with **mealiemeal**
ℹ ORIGIN: 19th century, through Afrikaans, from Dutch *pap* meaning 'porridge'

paper (say **pay**-puh) *noun*
1 (*no plural*) thin material for writing or drawing on or for wrapping things in: *a sheet of **paper*** ◇ *a **paper** bag*
2 (*plural* **papers**) a newspaper: *Have you seen today's **paper**?*
3 papers (*plural noun*) important pieces of **paper** with writing on them: *Her desk was piled high with **papers**.*
4 (*plural* **papers**) a group of questions in an exam: *The English **paper** was easy.*

paperback (say **pay**-puh-bak) *noun* (*plural* **paperbacks**)
a book with a paper cover ➲ See **hardback**

paper clip *noun* (*plural* **paper clips**)
a small metal object that you use for holding pieces of paper together

paperwork (say **pay**-puh-wurk) *noun* (*no plural*)
the written work that you have to do as part of your job: *Teachers have far too much **paperwork**.*

papier mâché (say pay-puh **mash**-ay) *noun* (*no plural*) (*art*)
strips of paper dipped in a mixture of flour and water that becomes hard when dry and is used to make puppets, models and decorations
ℹ ORIGIN: from French, meaning 'chewed paper'

papyrus (say puh-**py**-ruhss) *noun* (*no plural*)
1 a tall thin plant that grows in or near water
2 paper made from the stems of the papyrus plant, used in ancient Egypt for drawing or writing on

par (say **paa**) *noun* (*no plural*)
(in golf) the standard number of times a player should hit the ball in order to complete a particular hole or series of holes
above (or below) par better (or worse) than usual or expected
on par with a person or **thing** of an equal standard to another person or thing

parable (say **pa**-ruhb-l) *noun* (*plural* **parables**)
a short story that teaches a lesson: *Jesus used **parables** to illustrate his message.*

parabola (say puh-**rab**-uh-luh) *noun* (*plural* **parabolas**)
a curved line that has a shape like the path of an object that is thrown through the air and falls down again

parabola

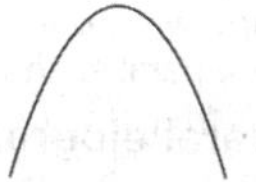

parachute (say **pa**-ruh-shoot) *noun* (*plural* **parachutes**)
a device that you have on your back when you jump out of a plane and that opens so that you fall to the ground slowly

parade (say puh-**rayd**) *noun* (*plural* **parades**)
a line of people who are walking together for a special reason, while other people watch them: *a military **parade***

paradise (say **pa**-ruh-dise) *noun* (*no plural*)
the place where some people think good people go after they die ➲ SYNONYM **heaven**

paradox (say **pa**-ruh-dokss) *noun* (*plural* **paradoxes**)
a situation or statement with two parts that seem strange or impossible together: *It's a **paradox** that the country produces so much food, yet its people are starving.* ➲ See Study page 17
▸ **paradoxical** (*adjective*)

paraffin (say **pa**-ruh-fin) *noun* (*no plural*)
a type of oil that people burn to produce heat or light

paragraph (say **pa**-ruh-graaf) *noun* (*plural* **paragraphs**)
a group of lines of writing. A **paragraph** always begins on a new line.

A B C D E F G H I J K L M N O P Q R S T U V W X Y Z

parallel (say **pa**-ruh-lel) *adjective*
Parallel lines are lines that are always the same distance from each other.

> SPELLING Remember! You spell **parallel** with one **r** and **ll**.

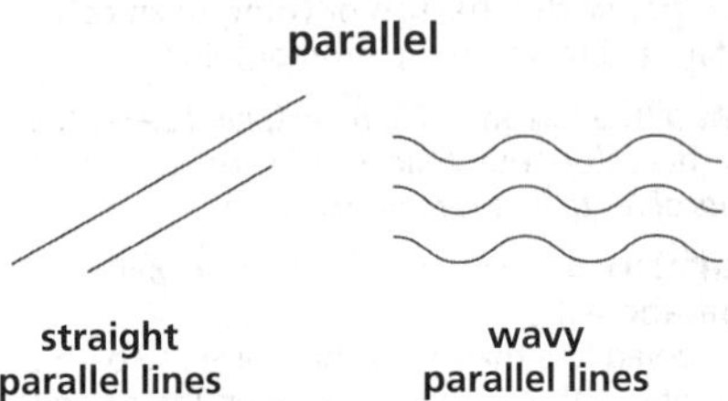

parallelogram (say pa-ruh-**lel**-uh-gram) *noun* (*plural* **parallelograms**)
a flat closed shape with four straight sides. The opposite sides are parallel and equal in length.

parallelogram

two parallelograms

paralyse (say **pa**-ruh-lize) *verb* (**paralysing, paralysed**)
to make a person unable to move all or part of their body: *After the accident she was **paralysed** from the waist down.*
▸ **paralysis** (*noun*): *complete **paralysis***

paramedic (say pa-ruh-**med**-ik) *noun* (*plural* **paramedics**)
a person who is not a doctor or a nurse, but who looks after people who are hurt or ill until they get to a hospital

paramount (say **pa**-ruh-mownt) *adjective*
most important: *Safety is **paramount** in car design.*

paranoid (say **pa**-ruh-noyd) *adjective*
wrongly believing that people are trying to harm you or are saying bad things about you
▸ **paranoia:** *He suffers from **paranoia**.*

paraphernalia (say pa-ruh-fuh-**nay**-li-uh) *noun* (*no plural*)
a large number of different objects that you need for a particular purpose: *fishing **paraphernalia***

paraphrase (say **pa**-ruh-frayz) *verb* (**paraphrasing, paraphrased**)
to express what a person has said or written using different words so that it is easier to understand
▸ **paraphrase** (*noun*): *a **paraphrase** of the story*

paraplegic (say pa-ruh-**plee**-jik) *noun* (*plural* **paraplegics**)
a person who is permanently unable to move or feel the lower half of their body
➲ See **quadriplegic**
▸ **paraplegic** (*adjective*) ▸ **paraplegia** (*noun*): *He has a type of **paraplegia**.*

parasite (say **pa**-ruh-site) *noun* (*plural* **parasites**)
an animal, plant or other living thing that lives on or in another plant or animal and gets its food from it. Parasites sometimes cause disease.
▸ **parasitic** (*adjective*): *Ticks are **parasitic** animals.*
ⓘ ORIGIN: 16th century, through Latin from Greek *parasitos* meaning '(person) eating at another person's table', from *para* meaning 'alongside' + *sitos* meaning 'food'

parasol (say **pa**-ruh-sol) *noun* (*plural* **parasols**)
(*old-fashioned*) an umbrella that you use to protect yourself from harsh sunlight
➲ See **umbrella**

parastatal (say pa-ruh-**stayt**-l) *adjective*
(used about a business) owned or controlled by the government
▸ **parastatal** (*noun*): *Telkom, Eskom, the SAA and the SABC are South African **parastatals**.*

parcel (say **paas**-l) *noun* (*plural* **parcels**)
something with paper around it, that you send or carry: *She sent a **parcel** of books to her aunt.*
➲ SYNONYM **package**

parched (say **paacht**) *adjective*
1 dried out by very hot weather: ***parched** fields*
2 (*informal*) very thirsty: *Our throats are **parched**.*

parchment (say **paach**-muhnt) *noun* (*plural* **parchments**)
thin flat material made from the skins of sheep or goats and used in the past for writing on

pardon[1] (say **paa**-duhn) *exclamation*
1 What did you say?: *'You're very quiet.' '**Pardon**?' 'I said, you're very quiet.'*
2 I'm sorry: ***Pardon** me, I didn't see you standing there.*

pardon[2] (say **paa**-duhn) *verb* (**pardoning, pardoned**) (*formal*)
to officially decide not to punish somebody for something bad that they have done: *Two hundred prisoners were **pardoned** by the king.*
➲ SYNONYM **forgive**

A B C D E F G H I J K L M N O **P** Q R S T U V W X Y Z

pare (say **pair**) *verb* (**paring, pared**)
1 to cut away the outer layer of something: *She **pared** off the skin of the apple with a knife.*
2 to gradually reduce the size or amount of a something: *The training budget has been **pared** back.*

parent (say **pair**-ruhnt) *noun* (*plural* **parents**)
a mother or father: *Her **parents** live in Italy.*

parenthesis (say puh-**ren**-thuh-siss) *noun* (*plural* **parentheses**)
1 a word, phrase or sentence that is added to a speech or piece of writing, especially in order to give extra information
2 a bracket: *(This sentence is in **parentheses**.)*

parenthood (say **pair**-ruhnt-huud) *noun* (*no plural*)
being a parent

parish (say **pa**-rish) *noun* (*plural* **parishes**)
an area that has its own church and priest

park[1] (say **paak**) *noun* (*plural* **parks**)
1 an open area in a town or city, often with grass and trees, where anybody can go to walk, play games or relax: *We had a picnic in the **park**.*
2 a large area of land that is used for a special purpose: *a national **park*** ◇ *a theme **park***

park[2] (say **paak**) *verb* (**parking, parked**)
to stop and leave a vehicle somewhere for a time: *You can't **park** in this street.* ◇ *My car is **parked** opposite the bank.*
▸ **parking** (*noun*): *There's no **parking** here.*

parliament (say **paa**-luh-muhnt) *noun* (*plural* **parliaments**)
the group of people who make the laws in a country, or the buildings in which they make these laws: *Our **parliament** meets in Cape Town.*
▸ **parliamentary** (*adjective*): *a **parliamentary** debate*
ORIGIN: 13th–15th century, from Old French *parlement* meaning 'speaking'

parlour (say **paa**-luh) *noun* (*plural* **parlours**)
1 (*old-fashioned*) a sitting room in a private house
2 a shop that provides particular goods or services: *a beauty **parlour*** ◇ *an ice-cream **parlour***

parody (say **pa**-ruh-dee) *noun* (*plural* **parodies**)
a piece of writing, speech or music that copies the style of a person or a thing in a funny way: *a **parody** of a spy novel*
▸ **parody** (*verb*)

parole (say puh-**rohl**) *noun* (*no plural*)
permission given to a prisoner to leave prison before his or her sentence has been completed, on condition that they behave well: *He's going to be released on **parole**.*

parrot (say **pa**-ruht) *noun* (*plural* **parrots**)
a type of tropical bird with a curved beak and usually with bright feathers: *My pet **parrot** has been trained to copy what people say.*

parsley (say **paass**-lee) *noun* (*no plural*)
a type of plant (called a **herb**) with small green leaves that you use in cooking

part[1] (say **paat**) *noun* (*plural* **parts**)
1 some, but not all of something, or one of the pieces of something: *We spent **part** of the day on the beach.* ◇ *Which **part** of Brazil do you come from?*
2 a piece of a machine: *Is there a shop near here that sells bicycle **parts**?*
3 the person you are in a play or film: *She played the **part** of the queen.*
take part in something to do something together with other people: *All the students took **part** in the concert.*

part[2] (say **paat**) *verb* (**parting, parted**) (*formal*)
to go away from each other: *We **parted** at the airport.*
part with something to give something to somebody else: *He was sad to **part** with his car.*

partial (say **paa**-shuhl) *adjective*
not complete: *The concert was only a **partial** success.*
▸ **partially** (*adverb*)

participant (say paa-**tiss**-i-puhnt) *noun* (*plural* **participants**)
a person who does something together with other people: *Each of the **participants** in the race will receive a prize.*

participate (say paa-**tiss**-i-payt) *verb* (**participating, participated**) (*formal*)
to do something together with other people: *Everyone in our group **participated** in the discussion.*
▸ **participation** (*noun*): *Your **participation** is important.*

participle (say paa-**tiss**-ip-l) *noun* (*plural* **participles**) (*grammar*)
a form of a verb: *The present **participle** of 'eat' is 'eating' and the past **participle** is 'eaten'.*
➲ See Study pages 6, 7 and 8

particle (say **paa**-tik-l) *noun* (*plural* **particles**)
1 a very small thing or a piece of a thing: *a dust **particle*** ◇ *Electrons and protons are sub-atomic **particles**.*
2 (*grammar*) a small word that has a function in a sentence, but cannot be placed easily into another word class, such as a noun or adverb. In the sentence 'I did not want to cross the road', 'not' and 'to' are particles.

particular (say puh-**tik**-yuu-luh) *adjective*
1 one only, and not any other: *You need a **particular** kind of flour to make bread.*
2 more than usual: *The road is very icy, so take **particular** care when you are driving.*
➲ SYNONYM **special**
3 If you are **particular**, you want something to be exactly right: *He's very **particular** about the food he eats.*
in particular more than others: *Is there anything in **particular** you want to do this weekend?* ➲ SYNONYM **especially**

particularly (say puh-**tik**-yuu-luh-lee) *adverb*
more than usual or more than others: *I'm **particularly** tired today.* ◇ *I don't **particularly** like fish.* ➲ SYNONYM **especially**

parting (say **paat**-ing) *noun* (*plural* **partings**)
1 a time when people leave each other: *We had a sad **parting** at the airport.*
2 a line in your hair that you make by brushing or combing it in different directions: *He has a side **parting**.*

partition (say paa-**tish**-n) *noun* (*plural* **partitions**)
1 a screen or a temporary wall that divides a room into two or more parts
2 the division of a country into two or more countries
▸ **partition** (*verb*): *Thin wooden planks **partition** the spaces.*

partly (say **paat**-lee) *adverb*
not completely but in some way: *The window was **partly** open.* ◇ *The accident was **partly** my fault.*

partner (say **paat**-nuh) *noun* (*plural* **partners**)
1 a person who you are doing an activity with, such as dancing or playing a game
2 your husband, wife, boyfriend or girlfriend
3 one of the people who owns a business

partnership (say **paat**-nuh-ship) *noun* (*plural* **partnerships**)
being partners: *The two sisters went into **partnership** and opened a shop.*

part of speech *noun* (*plural* **parts of speech**) (*grammar*)
one of the groups that words are divided into, for example 'noun', 'verb', 'adjective' ➲ See Study page 4

part-time (say **paat**-time) *adjective*, *adverb*
for only a part of the day or week: *I've got a **part-time** job as a babysitter.* ◇ *He works **part-time**.* ➲ See **full-time**

party (say **paat**-ee) *noun* (*plural* **parties**)
1 a time when friends meet, usually in somebody's home, to eat, drink and enjoy themselves: *a birthday **party*** ◇ *We're having a **party** this Saturday. Can you come?*
2 (*politics*) a group of people who have the same ideas about politics and who are trying to win elections to parliament, etc.: *Which political **party** will you vote for?*
3 a group of people who are travelling or working together: *a **party** of tourists*

pascal (say **pass**-kuhl) *noun* (*plural* **pascals**) (symbol Pa)
a unit for measuring pressure
❶ ORIGIN: 20th century, named after Blaise Pascal (1623–1662), a French mathematician and scientist

pass[1] (say **paass**) *verb* (**passing**, **passed**)
1 to go by somebody or something: *She **passed** me in the street.*
2 to give something to somebody: *Could you **pass** me the salt, please?*
3 (in some sports) to kick, hit or throw the ball to somebody on your team
4 If time **passes**, it goes by: *A week **passed** before his letter arrived.*
5 to spend time: *How did you **pass** the time in hospital?*
6 to do well enough in an examination or test: *Did you **pass** your driving test?* ➲ OPPOSITE **fail** 1
pass away to die: *The old man **passed** away in his sleep.*
pass out to suddenly become unconscious
➲ SYNONYM **faint**[2]
▸ **passing** (*noun*): *the **passing** of time* ◇ *The players have to work on their **passing**.*

pass[2] (say **paass**) *noun* (*plural* **passes**)
1 kicking, throwing or hitting a ball to somebody in a game
2 doing well enough in an exam: *I got a **pass** in English.*
3 a road or way through mountains: *the Swartberg **Pass***
4 a special piece of paper or card that says you can go somewhere or do something: *You need a **pass** to get into the factory.*

passage (say **pass**-ij) *noun* (*plural* **passages**)
1 a narrow way, for example between two buildings
2 a short part of a book, a speech or a piece of music: *We studied a **passage** from the story for homework.*

passenger (say **pass**-in-juh) *noun* (*plural* **passengers**)
a person who is travelling in a car, bus, train or plane but not driving or flying it: *The plane was carrying 200 **passengers**.*

passion (say **pash**-uhn) *noun* (*plural* **passions**) a very strong feeling, usually of love, but sometimes of anger or hate

passionate (say **pash**-uhn-uht) *adjective* having or showing very strong feelings: *a **passionate** kiss*

passion-fruit (say **pash**-uhn-froot) *noun* (*plural* **passion-fruit**) another word for **granadilla**

passive[1] (say **pass**-iv) *noun* (*no plural*) (*grammar*) the form of a verb that shows that the action is done by a person or thing to another person or thing: *In the sentence 'The car was stolen', the verb is in the **passive**.* ➲ OPPOSITE **active** 2

passive[2] (say **pass**-iv) *adjective* accepting what happens without trying to change anything or go against it: *a **passive** role*

Passover (say **paass**-oh-vuh) *noun* (*no plural*) the Jewish festival to **commemorate** the escape of the Jewish people from Egypt a long time ago ➲ See **Jew**

passport (say **paass**-pawt) *noun* (*plural* **passports**) an official document with your name and photograph in or on it, which identifies you as a citizen of a particular country and which you have to show when you go into or leave a country

password (say **paass**-wurd) *noun* (*plural* **passwords**) a secret word that allows you to go into a place or start using a computer: *Never tell anybody your **password**.*

past[1] (say **paast**) *adjective*
1 connected with or belonging to the time that has gone: *We will forget your **past** mistakes.*
2 just before now: *He has been ill for the **past** week.* ➲ SYNONYM **last[1]** 2

past[2] (say **paast**) *noun* (*no plural*)
1 the time before now, and the things that happened then: *We learn about the **past** in history lessons.* ◇ *Life was different in the **past**.*
2 the past (also **the past tense**) (*grammar*) the form of a verb that you use to talk about the time before now: *The **past** tense of the verb 'go' is 'went'.* ➲ See **present[2]** 2–3

past[3] (say **paast**) *preposition, adverb*
1 a word that shows how many minutes after the hour: *It's two minutes **past** four.* ◇ *It's half **past** seven.*
2 from one side to the other of somebody or something, or on the other side of somebody or something: *Go **past** the library, then turn left.* ◇ *The bus went **past** without stopping.*

pasta (say **pass**-tuh) *noun* (*no plural*) an Italian food that is made from flour, water and sometimes eggs, which comes in many different shapes: *Macaroni and spaghetti are types of **pasta**.*

paste[1] (say **payst**) *noun* (*plural* **pastes**) a soft wet substance, usually made from powder and liquid, and sometimes used for sticking paper to things: *Mix the flour with milk to make a **paste**.*

paste[2] (say **payst**) *verb* (**pasting, pasted**)
1 to stick something to something else using **paste**: ***Paste** the picture into your book.*
2 (*computing*) to copy or move writing or pictures into a computer document from somewhere else: *You can cut and **paste** the graph into your essay.*

pastel (say **pass**-tuhl) *noun* (*plural* **pastels**)
1 a soft type of **crayon**
2 a soft pale colour
► **pastel** (*adjective*): ***pastel** green curtains*

pasteurize (say **paass**-tshuh-rize) *verb* (**pasteurizing, pasteurized**) (also **pasteurise**) to heat and then cool food, especially milk, in order to destroy harmful **bacteria**
► **pasteurization** (*noun*) (also **pasteurisation**)
ℹ ORIGIN: 19th century, from the name of Louis Pasteur (1822–1895), a French scientist and chemist

pastime (say **paass**-time) *noun* (*plural* **pastimes**) something that you like doing when you are not working: *Painting is her favourite **pastime**.* ➲ SYNONYM **hobby**

pastor (say **paass**-tuh) *noun* (*plural* **pastors**) a **minister** 2 in charge of certain Christian churches

pastoral (say **paass**-tuh-ruhl) *adjective*
1 (relating to the work of a priest or teacher) giving help and advice on personal matters
2 showing the **countryside** in a romantic way

past participle *noun* (*plural* **past participles**) (*grammar*) the form of a verb that in English is used with 'have' or 'has' to make a tense (called the **perfect tense**): *'Gone' is the **past participle** of 'go'.* ➲ See Study page 6

pastry (say **payss**-tree) *noun*
1 (*no plural*) a mixture of flour, fat and water that is rolled flat and used for making a special type of food (called a **pie**)
2 (*plural* **pastries**) a small cake made with pastry

past tense *noun* (*no plural*) (*grammar*) the forms of a verb that you use to talk about the time before now: *The **past tense** of 'talk' is 'talked'.* ➲ See Study page 6

pasture (say **paass**-tshuh) *noun* (*plural* **pastures**)
land covered with grass where farm animals such as cows and sheep can feed: *The cows will get fat on the green **pasture**.*

pat *verb* (**patting, patted**)
to touch somebody or something lightly with your hand flat: *She **patted** the dog on the head.*
▸ **pat** (*noun*): *a **pat** on the shoulder*

patch (say **pach**) *noun* (*plural* **patches**)
1 a small piece of something that is not the same as the other parts: *a black cat with a white **patch** on its back*
2 a piece of cloth that you use to cover a hole in things like clothes: *I sewed a **patch** on my jeans.*

patchwork (say **pach**-wurk) *noun* (*no plural*)
a type of sewing in which small pieces of material of different colours and patterns are sewn together: *a **patchwork** quilt*

pâté (say **pat**-ay) *noun* (*no plural*)
food that is made by making meat, fish or vegetables into a smooth, thick mixture that is served cold and spread on bread, etc.: *duck pâté*

patella (say puh-**tel**-uh) *noun* (*plural* **patellae**)
= **kneecap**

patent (say **pay**-tuhnt) *noun* (*plural* **patents**)
the official right to be the only person to make, use or sell a product: *He took out a **patent** on his invention.*
▸ **patent** (*verb*): *The company **patented** their new design.*

paternal (say puh-**turn**-l) *adjective*
1 like a father or connected with being a father: *paternal love*
2 A **paternal** relation is part of your father's family: *my **paternal** grandmother* (= my father's mother) ➲ See **maternal**

paternity (say puh-**turn**-i-tee) *noun* (*no plural*)
the fact of being the father of a child: ***paternity** leave* (= days that the father of a new baby may be away from work) ➲ See **maternity**

path (say **paath**) *noun* (*plural* **paths**)
a way across a piece of land, where people can walk: *a **path** through the veld*

pathetic (say puh-**thet**-ik) *adjective*
1 (*informal*) very bad or weak: *That was a **pathetic** performance – they deserved to lose!*
2 making you feel pity or sadness: *the **pathetic** cries of hungry children*

pathological (say path-uh-**loj**-ik-uhl) *adjective*
1 connected with pathology
2 caused by or connected with disease or illness: ***pathological** depression*
3 caused by feelings that you cannot control: *a **pathological** liar*
4 (*informal*) not reasonable or sensible: *a **pathological** fear*

pathology (say puh-**thol**-uh-jee) *noun* (*plural* **pathologies**)
the study of diseases of the body: *clinical **pathology** ◇ a **pathology** report*
▸ **pathologist** (*noun*): *The **pathologist** detected the bone disease in her body.*

patience (say **pay**-shunss) *noun* (*no plural*)
staying calm and not getting angry when you are waiting for something, or when you have problems: *Learning to play the piano takes **patience**. ◇ She drove so slowly that he lost **patience** with her* (= became angry with her).

patient¹ (say **pay**-shunt) *adjective*
able to stay calm and not get angry when you are waiting for something or when you have problems: *Just sit there and be **patient**. Your mum will be here soon.* ➲ OPPOSITE **impatient**
▸ **patiently** (*adverb*)

patient² (say **pay**-shunt) *noun* (*plural* **patients**)
a sick person who a doctor or nurse is looking after

patio (say **pat**-i-oh) *noun* (*plural* **patios**)
a flat hard area outside a house where people can sit and eat

patriarch (say **pay**-tri-aak) *noun* (*plural* **patriarchs**)
an older man who is the head of a family or community and who is respected by them
➲ See **matriarch**
▸ **patriarchal** (*adjective*): *a **patriarchal** society*
▸ **patriarchy** (*noun*)

patriot (say **pay**-tri-uht) *noun* (*plural* **patriots**)
a person who loves his or her country and is ready to defend it

patriotic (say pay-tri-**ot**-ik) *adjective*
having or showing a great love for your country

patrol (say puh-**trohl**) *noun* (*plural* **patrols**)
a group of people or vehicles that go round a place to see that everything is all right: *an army patrol*
on patrol the act of going round a place to see that everything is all right: *There are 30 police officers on **patrol**.*
▸ **patrol** (*verb*): *A guard **patrols** at night.*
🛈 **ORIGIN:** 17th century, through German from French *patrouiller* meaning 'paddle in the mud'

patron (say **pay**-truhn) *noun* (*plural* **patrons**)
1 a person who supports artists, writers and musicians: *a **patron** of the arts*
2 a famous person who supports an organization such as a charity: *The queen was the **patron** of many charities.* ➲ See **sponsor**[1]

patronize (say **pat**-ruh-nize) *verb* (**patronizing, patronized**) (also **patronise**)
to treat a person in a way which seems friendly, but which shows that you think you are better, more intelligent or more experienced: *Don't **patronize** me, I'm not a child!*

patter (say **pat**-uh) *noun* (*no plural*)
quick light sounds: *I heard the **patter** of children's feet on the stairs.*
▸ **patter** (*verb*): *Rain **pattered** on the window.*

pattern (say **pat**-uhn) *noun* (*plural* **patterns**)
1 shapes and colours on something: *The curtains had a **pattern** of flowers and leaves.*
2 the way in which something happens or develops: *Her days all followed the same **pattern**.*
3 a thing that you copy when you make something: *I bought some material and a **pattern** to make a new skirt.*

patterned (say **pat**-uhnd) *adjective*
with shapes and colours on it: *a **patterned** shirt*

paunch (say **pawnch**) *noun* (*plural* **paunches**)
a big fat stomach: *His **paunch** hung over the top of his trousers.*

pauper (say **paw**-puh) *noun* (*plural* **paupers**)
(*old-fashioned*) a very poor person
ℹ **ORIGIN:** 15th century, from Latin *pauper* meaning 'poor'

pause (say **pawz**) *verb* (**pausing, paused**)
to stop talking or doing something for a short time: *He **paused** for a moment before answering my question.*
▸ **pause** (*noun*): *There was a long **pause** before she spoke.*

pave (say **payv**) *verb* (**paving, paved**)
to cover an area of ground with flat stones (called **paving stones**) or bricks: *We have **paved** the area near the house.*
▸ **paved** (*adjective*): *a **paved** driveway*

pavement (say **payv**-muhnt) *noun* (*plural* **pavements**)
the part at the side of a road where people can walk

pavilion (say puh-**vil**-i-uhn) *noun* (*plural* **pavilions**)
a building at a sports ground used by players and spectators (= people watching an event)

paw (*rhymes with* **more**) *noun* (*plural* **paws**)
the foot of an animal, for example a dog or a cat

pawn (*rhymes with* **born**) *noun* (*plural* **pawns**)
1 (in the game of chess) one of eight pieces of the smallest size and the least value
2 a person who is controlled by other more powerful people: *He was nothing but a **pawn** in their hands.*

pawpaw (say **paw**-paw) *noun* (*plural* **pawpaws**)
a sweet tropical fruit with thin, smooth, orange-coloured skin and many black seeds
ℹ **ORIGIN:** 17th century, from Spanish and Portuguese *papaya*, from Carib, a South American language

pay[1] *verb* (**paying, paid**)
to give somebody money for something, for example something they are selling you or work that they do: *How much did you **pay** for your car?* ◇ *I **paid** the builder for mending the roof.* ◇ *a **well-paid** job*
pay somebody back to hurt somebody who has hurt you: *One day I'll **pay** her back for lying to me!*
pay somebody or **something back** to give back the money that somebody has lent to you: *Can you lend me R10? I'll **pay** you **back*** (= pay it back to you) *next week.* ➲ **SYNONYM repay**

pay[2] *noun* (*no plural*)
the money that you get for working: *There are millions of workers on low **pay**.*

> **WORD BUILDING** **Pay** is the general word for money that you **earn** (get regularly for work that you have done). If you are paid daily or weekly, your pay is usually called **wages**. If you are paid each month, you get a **salary**.

PAYE (say pee-ay-wy-**ee**) *noun* (*no plural*)
a system in which your employer takes tax that you owe the government from the money you earn ℹ **PAYE** is short for 'pay as you earn'.

payment (say **pay**-muhnt) *noun*
1 (*no plural*) paying or being paid: *This money is in **payment** for your work.*
2 (*plural* **payments**) an amount of money that you pay: *I make monthly **payments** of R50.*

PC (say pee-**see**) *noun* (*plural* **PCs**)
a computer that is designed for one person to use at work or at home ℹ **PC** is an abbreviation of 'personal computer'.

PE (say pee-**ee**) *noun* (*no plural*)
sport and exercise that are done as part of a subject at school: *We have **PE** on Tuesdays.*
ℹ **PE** is an abbreviation of 'physical education'.

pea (say **pee**) *noun* (*plural* **peas**)
a very small round green vegetable. **Peas** grow in long, thin cases (called **pods**).

peace (say **peess**) *noun* (*no plural*)
1 a time when there is no war or fighting between people or countries: *The two countries eventually made **peace**.*
2 the state of being quiet and calm: *the **peace** and quiet of the mountains* ◇ *Go away and leave me in **peace**!*

peaceful (say **peess**-fuhl) *adjective*
1 with no fighting: *a **peaceful** demonstration*
2 quiet and calm
▸ **peacefully** (*adverb*): *She's sleeping **peacefully**.*

peach (say **peech**) *noun* (*plural* **peaches**)
a soft round fruit with a yellow and red skin and a large stone in the centre

peacock (say **pee**-kok) *noun* (*plural* **peacocks**)
a large male bird with beautiful long blue and green feathers in its tail

peahen (say **pee**-hen) *noun* (*plural* **peahens**)
the female of the **peacock**

peak (say **peek**) *noun* (*plural* **peaks**)
1 the time when something is highest, biggest or most: *The traffic is at its **peak** between five and six in the evening.*
2 the pointed top of a mountain: *He climbed to the **peak**.* ➲ See illustration at **mountain**
3 the front part of a hat that sticks out above your eyes

peanut (say **pee**-nut) *noun* (*plural* **peanuts**) (also **groundnut**)
a small nut that you can eat and that grows underground in a thin shell: *salted **peanuts***

peanut butter *noun* (*no plural*)
a thick soft substance made from peanuts, which you eat on bread

pear (say **pair**) *noun* (*plural* **pears**)
a fruit that is green, yellow or brown on the outside and white on the inside

pearl (say **purl**) *noun* (*plural* **pearls**)
a small round white thing that grows inside a type of shellfish (called an **oyster**). **Pearls** are valuable and are used to make **jewellery**: *a **pearl** necklace*

peasant (say **pez**-uhnt) *noun* (*plural* **peasants**)
a poor farmer, usually one who works on a small piece of land to produce food for his or her family

peat (say **peet**) *noun* (*no plural*)
a natural substance that is formed in a **wetland** (= an area of land covered by water) from a mass of dead plants. Dry peat can be burned as a fuel or put on the garden to make plants grow better.

pebble (say **peb**-l) *noun* (*plural* **pebbles**)
a small round stone

pecan (say **pee**-kuhn) *noun* (*plural* **pecans**)
a type of nut with a smooth brown oval shell
🛈 **ORIGIN**: 18th century, through French *pacane* from Illinois, a Native North American language

peck (say **pek**) *verb* (**pecking**, **pecked**)
When a bird **pecks** something, it eats or bites it quickly: *The hens were **pecking** at the corn.*

peculiar (say pi-**kyoo**-li-uh) *adjective*
strange or not usual: *What's that **peculiar** smell?*
➲ **SYNONYM odd** 1

pedal¹ (say **ped**-l) *noun* (*plural* **pedals**)
a part of a bicycle or other machine that you move with your feet

pedal² (say **ped**-l) *verb* (**pedalling**, **pedalled**)
to turn or press the **pedals** on a bicycle or other machine

pedantic (say pi-**dan**-tik) *adjective*
too concerned about rules and details or showing off technical knowledge

peddle (say **ped**-l) *verb* (**peddling**, **peddled**)
1 to sell (especially small goods) from place to place: *He **peddles** socks and dishcloths on the street.*
2 to sell (illegal drugs or stolen goods): *The police caught them **peddling** drugs.*
3 to spread and try to make acceptable (an idea or story): *I discovered he was **peddling** lies about me.*

pedestal (say **ped**-i-stuhl) *noun* (*plural* **pedestals**)
the base on which a statue or column stands

pedestrian (say puh-**dess**-tri-uhn) *noun* (*plural* **pedestrians**)
a person who is walking in the street

pedigree (say **ped**-i-gree) *noun* (*plural* **pedigrees**)
an official record of the animals from which an animal has been bred: *That racehorse has a long and excellent **pedigree**.*
▸ **pedigree** or **pedigreed** (*adjective*): ***pedigree** dogs*

peel¹ *verb* (**peeling**, **peeled**)
1 to take the outside part off a fruit or vegetable: *Can you **peel** the potatoes?*
2 to come off in thin pieces: *The paint is **peeling** off the walls.*

peel² *noun* (*plural* **peels**)
the outside part of some fruit and vegetables: *orange* ***peel*** ◇ *potato* ***peel***

peep *verb* (**peeping, peeped**)
to look at something quickly or secretly: *I* ***peeped*** *through the window and saw her.*
▸ **peep** (*noun*): *Have a quick* ***peep****.*

peer¹ *verb* (**peering, peered**)
to look closely at something because you cannot see well: *I* ***peered*** *outside but I couldn't see anything because it was dark.*

peer² *noun* (*plural* **peers**)
a person who is of the same age or position in society as you: *Learners are under a lot of* ***peer*** *pressure to be trendy.*

peg *noun* (*plural* **pegs**)
1 a small thing on a wall or door where you can hang things: *Your coat is on the* ***peg****.*
2 a small wooden or plastic thing that holds wet clothes on a line when they are drying: *a clothes* ***peg***

pelican (say **pel**-i-kuhn) *noun* (*plural* **pelicans**)
a large water bird with a big beak that it uses to catch and hold fish

pellet (say **pel**-uht) *noun* (*plural* **pellets**)
1 a small hard ball, often of a soft material that has become hard: *We feed our dog* ***pellets****.*
2 a very small round bullet: *shotgun* ***pellets***

pelt¹ *verb* (**pelting, pelted**)
1 to throw (things at a person or another thing): *The boys* ***pelted*** *each other with acorns.*
2 (used about rain) to fall very heavily: *The rain was* ***pelting*** *down.*

pelt² *noun* (*plural* **pelts**)
the skin of an animal, especially with the hair still on it ➲ See **hide²** 1

pelvis (say **pel**-viss) *noun* (*plural* **pelvises**)
the ring of bones to which your legs are joined ➲ See illustration at **skeleton**
▸ **pelvic** (*adjective*): *pelvic cavity*

pen *noun* (*plural* **pens**)
1 a thing that you use for writing with a coloured liquid (called **ink**)
2 a small piece of ground with a fence around it for keeping farm animals in

penalize (say **pee**-nuh-lize) *verb* (**penalizing, penalized**) (also **penalise**)
1 to punish a person for breaking a law or rule: *Our teacher* ***penalizes*** *us for spelling errors.*
2 to cause a person to be at a disadvantage: *Schools should not* ***penalize*** *learners whose parents cannot pay school fees.*

penalty (say **pen**-uhl-tee) *noun* (*plural* **penalties**)
1 (in sport) a punishment for one team and an advantage for the other team because a player has broken a rule: *Beckham stepped forward to take the* ***penalty****.*
2 a punishment: *The* ***penalty*** *for travelling without a ticket is R300* (= you must pay R300).

pence (say **penss**) plural of **penny**

pencil (say **pen**-suhl) *noun* (*plural* **pencils**)
a thin object that you use for writing or drawing. **Pencils** are usually made of wood and have a black or coloured point. ➲ See **pen**

pendant (say **pen**-duhnt) *noun* (*plural* **pendants**)
a small attractive object that you wear on a chain around your neck
ℹ **ORIGIN:** 13th–15th century, through Old French *pendant* meaning 'hanging', from Latin *pendre*

pendulum (say **pen**-dyuu-luhm) *noun* (*plural* **pendulums**)
a chain or stick with a heavy weight at the bottom that moves regularly from side to side to work a clock

penetrate (say **pen**-i-trayt) *verb* (**penetrating, penetrated**)
to go through or into something: *The knife* ***penetrated*** *deep into his chest.*

penfriend (say **pen**-frend) *noun* (*plural* **penfriends**)
a person who you make friends with by writing letters but who you have probably never met

penguin (say **peng**-gwin) *noun* (*plural* **penguins**)
a black-and-white bird that lives on the coasts of southern countries with cold seas. **Penguins** swim but they cannot fly.

penicillin (say pen-i-**sil**-in) *noun* (*no plural*)
a drug that is used to stop infections and to treat illnesses

peninsula (say puh-**nin**-shyuh-luh) *noun* (*plural* **peninsulas**)
a piece of land that is almost surrounded by water: *the Cape* ***Peninsula***

penis (say **pee**-niss) *noun* (*plural* **penises**)
the part of a man's or a male animal's body that is used for getting rid of waste liquid and for having sex

penknife (say **pen**-nife) *noun* (*plural* **penknives**)
a small knife that you can carry in your pocket

penny (say **pen**-ee) *noun* (*plural* **pence** or **pennies**) (abbr. p)
a small coin that people use in Britain. There

are 100 **pence** in a **pound**: *These pencils cost 40* ***pence*** *each.* ◇ *Can you lend me* ***50p****?*

pension (say **pen**-shuhn) *noun* (*plural* **pensions**) money that you get from a government or a company when you are old and do not work any more (when you are **retired**)
▸ **pensioner** (*noun*): *Many* ***pensioners*** *live in poverty.*

penta- (say **pen**-tuh) *prefix* (used in nouns, adjectives and adverbs) five or having five: ***pentathlon*** (= a sports competition with five different events)

pentagon (say **pen**-tuh-guhn) *noun*
1 (*plural* **pentagons**) (*maths*) a flat closed shape with five straight sides
2 the Pentagon (*no plural*) a large five-sided building near Washington, DC in the USA that contains the main offices of the military forces
▸ **pentagonal** (*adjective*): *a* ***pentagonal*** *prism*

pentagram (say **pen**-tuh-gram) *noun* (*plural* **pentagrams**) a five-pointed star

pentahedron (say pen-tuh-**hee**-druhn) *noun* (*plural* **pentahedra** or **pentahedrons**) (*maths*) a solid shape with five flat surfaces

pentameter (say pen-**tam**-i-tuh) *noun* (*plural* **pentameters**) a line of poetry with five **stressed** syllables, or the rhythm of poetry that has five **stressed** syllables to a line

penumbra (say pen-**um**-bruh) *noun* (*plural* **penumbrae** or **penumbras**) the outer part or lighter part of a shadow
➲ See **umbra**

people (say **peep**-l) *plural noun* more than one person: *How many* ***people*** *came to the meeting?* ◇ *lots of* ***people***

pepper (say **pep**-uh) *noun*
1 (*no plural*) powder with a hot taste that you put on food: *salt and* ***pepper***
2 (*plural* **peppers**) a hollow, usually red, green or yellow fruit that is almost empty inside and that you eat as a vegetable either raw or cooked

peppermint (say **pep**-uh-mint) *noun*
1 (*no plural*) a plant with a strong fresh taste and smell. It is used to make things like sweets and medicines.
2 (*plural* **peppermints**) a sweet with the flavour of **peppermint**

per (say **pur**) *preposition* for or in each: *These apples cost R9,50* ***per*** *kilo.* ◇ *He was driving at 60 kilometres* ***per*** *hour.*

ⓘ **ORIGIN**: from Latin *per* meaning 'through, by means of'

per annum (say pur **an**-uhm) *adverb* for or in each year: *Growth has slowed to 2%* ***per annum*** *over the past five years.*

per capita (say pur **kap**-i-tuh) *adjective, adverb* for each person: ***Per capita*** *income rose sharply last year.* ◇ *In our town we use less electricity* ***per capita*** *than people in Durban do.*

perceive (say puh-**seev**) *verb* (**perceiving**, **perceived**) (*formal*)
1 to understand or think of something or somebody in a particular way: *The police* ***perceived*** *the investigation to be important.*
2 to notice or understand something

per cent (say pur **sent**) *noun* (*no plural*) (symbol %) in each hundred: *90* ***per cent*** *of the people who work here are men* (= in 100 people there are 90 men). ◇ *You get* ***10%*** *off if you pay cash.*
▸ **percentage** (*noun*): *'What* ***percentage*** *of students passed the exam?' 'Oh, about eighty per cent.'*

perception (say pur-**sep**-shuhn) *noun*
1 (*no plural*) the ability to notice or understand something
2 (*plural* **perceptions**) a particular way of looking at or understanding something: *That's my* ***perception*** *of the problem.*

perceptive (say pur-**sep**-tiv) *adjective* quick to notice or understand things

perch (say **purch**) *verb* (**perching**, **perched**) to sit on something narrow or uncomfortable: *The bird* ***perched*** *on a branch.* ◇ *We* ***perched*** *on high stools.*
▸ **perch** (*noun*): *The parrot sat on its* ***perch****.*

percolate (say **pur**-kuh-layt) *verb* (**percolating**, **percolated**)
1 (of a liquid, gas, etc.) to move gradually through a surface that has very small holes or spaces in it: *Water is* ***percolating*** *down through the rocks.*
2 (used about coffee) to be made in a pot (called a **percolator**) in which boiling water is forced up a central tube and then comes down again through the coffee

percussion (say puh-**kush**-n) *noun* (*no plural*) (*music*) drums and other instruments that you play by hitting them

perennial (say puh-**ren**-i-uhl) *adjective*
1 happening often or lasting a long time: *a* ***perennial*** *problem* ◇ *A* ***perennial*** *river flows all year round.*

2 (used about plants) living for two or more years

perfect (say **pur**-fikt) *adjective*
1 so good that it cannot be better, or with nothing wrong: *Her English is* ***perfect***. ◇ ***perfect*** *weather* ➲ See Study page 6 ➲ SYNONYM **ideal**[1]
2 = **perfect tense**

perfection (say puh-**fek**-shuhn) *noun* (*no plural*)
the state of being perfect: *She has done her work to* ***perfection***.

perfectly (say **pur**-fikt-lee) *adverb*
1 completely: *I'm* ***perfectly*** *all right.* ➲ SYNONYM **quite** 2
2 in a perfect way: *She played the piece of music* ***perfectly***.

perfect tense *noun* (*no plural*) (*grammar*)
the form of the verb that is made with 'has', 'have' or 'had' and the **past participle**: *'I have finished' is in the* ***perfect tense***.
➲ See Study pages 6–8.

perform (say puh-**fawm**) *verb* (**performing, performed**)
1 to do something such as a piece of work or a task: *Doctors* ***performed*** *a difficult operation to save her life.*
2 to be in something such as a play or a concert: *The band is* ***performing*** *tonight.* ◇ *The play will be* ***performed*** *next week.*

performance (say puh-**fawm**-uhnss) *noun*
1 (*plural* **performances**) a time when a play is shown or music is played in front of a lot of people: *We went to the evening* ***performance*** *of the play.*
2 (*no plural*) how well you do something: *I was pleased with my* ***performance***.

performer (say puh-**fawm**-uh) *noun* (*plural* **performers**)
a person who is in something such as a play or a concert

perfume (say **pur**-fyoom) *noun* (*plural* **perfumes**)
1 a liquid with a nice smell that you put on your body: *a bottle of* ***perfume***
➲ SYNONYMS **fragrance, scent** 2
2 a nice smell

pergola (say **pur**-guh-luh) *noun* (*plural* **pergolas**)
an arch with a frame on which climbing plants can grow

perhaps (say puh-**hapss**) *adverb*
a word that you use when you are not sure about something: *I don't know where she is –* ***perhaps*** *she's still at work.* ◇ *There were three men, or* ***perhaps*** *four.* ➲ SYNONYM **maybe**

peri- (say **pe**-ri) *prefix*
round or about: *The* ***pericardium*** *is the membrane around the heart.*
ℹ ORIGIN: from Greek *peri* meaning 'about, around'

peril (say **pe**-ril) *noun* (*formal*)
1 (*no plural*) a great danger: *The people trapped in the fire are in* ***peril***.
2 (*plural* **perils**) a thing which is very dangerous: *the* ***perils*** *of drug abuse*

perimeter (say puh-**rim**-i-tuh) *noun* (*plural* **perimeters**)
1 the outside edge of something: *The farmer built a fence around the* ***perimeter*** *of his farm.*
2 the distance around the edge of an area: *The* ***perimeter*** *of the rectangle is 24 centimetres.*
ℹ ORIGIN: 14th–15th century, through Latin from Greek *perimetros*, from *peri-* meaning 'around' + *metron* meaning 'measure'

period (say **peer**-ri-uhd) *noun* (*plural* **periods**)
1 an amount of time: *This is a difficult* ***period*** *for him.* ◇ *What* ***period*** *of history are you studying?*
2 a lesson in school: *We have five* ***periods*** *of English a week.*
3 the time when a woman loses blood from her body each month

periodic (say peer-ri-**od**-ik) *adjective* (also **periodical**)
happening fairly regularly

periodic table *noun* (*no plural*) (*science*)
a list of all the chemical elements, arranged according to the number of parts with a positive electric charge **(protons)** that they each have in their **nucleus**

periphery (say puh-**rif**-uh-ree) *noun* (*plural* **peripheries**) (*formal*)
1 the outer edge of a particular area: *factories on the* ***periphery*** *of town*
2 the less important part of a thing: *smaller parties on the* ***periphery*** *of the political scene*
▸ **peripheral** (*adjective*): *of* ***peripheral*** *importance* ◇ ***peripheral*** *computer equipment*

periscope (say **pe**-ri-skohp) *noun* (*plural* **periscopes**)
an instrument with a long tube containing mirrors that allow you to see over the top of something, used especially in a ship that can operate under water **(a submarine)**

perish (say **pe**-rish) *verb* (**perishing, perished**)
(*formal*) to die or to be destroyed: *More than 100 people* ***perished*** *in the fire.*

perjury (say **pur**-juh-ree) *noun* (*no plural*) (*formal*)
the act of telling a lie in a court of law: *The witness committed* ***perjury***.
▸ **perjure** (*verb*): *She admitted she had* ***perjured*** *herself while giving evidence.*

perk (say **purk**) *noun* (*plural* **perks**) (*informal*) something extra that you get from your employer other than money: *Travelling abroad is one of the **perks** of the job.*

perky (say **purk**-ee) *adjective* (**perkier**, **perkiest**) enthusiastic and full of energy: *a **perky** little dog*

perlemoen (say **pair**-luh-muun) *noun* (*plural* **perlemoen**) (*S. African*) a large shellfish that you can eat and that has two shells with inner surfaces made of a shiny and colourful substance ➲ SYNONYM **abalone**
ℹ ORIGIN: through Afrikaans *perlemoer* from Dutch *perlenmoeder* meaning 'mother-of-pearl', the name given to the smooth shiny surface inside some shells

perm (say **purm**) *noun* (*plural* **perms**) the treatment of hair with special chemicals to make it curly: *I think I'm going to have a **perm**.*
▸ **perm** (*verb*): *Have you had your hair **permed**?*

permafrost (say **purm**-uh-frost) *noun* (*no plural*) a layer of soil or rock that is permanently frozen in very cold regions of the world

permanent (say **purm**-uh-nuhnt) *adjective* continuing for ever or for a very long time without changing: *I'm looking for a **permanent** job.* ➲ See **temporary**
▸ **permanently** (*adverb*)

permeable (say **purm**-i-uhb-l) *adjective* allowing a liquid or gas to pass through: *A frog's skin is **permeable** to water.*
▸ **permeability** (*noun*): *Sand has a high **permeability**.*

permeate (say **purm**-i-ayt) *verb* (**permeating**, **permeated**) to spread into every part of something: *The water **permeates** the gravel.* ◇ *The smell of garlic **permeated** the entire restaurant.*

permissible (say puh-**miss**-uhb-l) *adjective* (*formal*) that is allowed by law or by a set of rules: *It is not **permissible** for cars to travel in the bus lane.*

permission (say puh-**mish**-uhn) *noun* (*no plural*) allowing somebody to do something: *She gave me **permission** to leave early.* ◇ *You may not leave the school without **permission**.* ➲ SYNONYM **consent**[1]

permissive (say puh-**miss**-iv) *adjective* allowing people the freedom to do things that not everyone finds acceptable: *a **permissive** parent*

permit[1] (say puh-**mit**) *verb* (**permitting**, **permitted**) (*formal*) to let somebody do something: *You are not **permitted** to smoke in the hospital.* ➲ SYNONYM **allow**

permit[2] (say **pur**-mit) *noun* (*plural* **permits**) a piece of paper that says you can do something or go somewhere: *Have you got a work **permit**?*

peroxide (say puh-**rok**-side) *noun* (*no plural*)
1 (*science*) a chemical compound with a single oxygen–oxygen **bond**[1] 3
2 (also **hydrogen peroxide**) a colourless liquid that is used to kill bacteria and to make hair a lighter colour

perpendicular (say pur-puhn-**dik**-yuh-luh) *adjective*
1 at an angle of 90° to something: ◇ *a **perpendicular** line. The roads are **perpendicular** to each other.*
2 pointing straight up: *I had great difficulty climbing the **perpendicular** cliff.*

perpetual (say puh-**pet**-shuu-uhl) *adjective*
1 continuing for a long period of time without stopping: *During the winter far northern countries are in **perpetual** darkness.*
2 frequently repeated in a way that is annoying: *the **perpetual** hooting of the taxis*

perplex (say puh-**plekss**) *verb* (**perplexing**, **perplexed**) (usually in the passive) to make a person confused or worried: *We were **perplexed** by our dog's sudden aggressive behaviour.*

persecute (say **pur**-si-kyoot) *verb* (**persecuting**, **persecuted**)
1 to treat a person in a cruel and unfair way, especially because of their race, religion or political beliefs: *The police **persecuted** the government's opponents.*
2 to deliberately annoy a person and make their life unpleasant: *The film star is being **persecuted** by photographers.*

persevere (say pur-si-**veer**) *verb* (**persevering**, **persevered**) to continue trying to do something that is difficult: *If you **persevere** with your studies, you could go to university.*
▸ **perseverance** (*noun*)

Persian (say **pur**-zhuhn) *noun* (*no plural*) the language spoken in Iran (a country called Persia in the past)

persist (say puh-**sist**) *verb* (**persisting**, **persisted**)
1 to keep on doing something in spite of its being difficult or people going against you: *It*

was very hot but the runner ***persisted*** *and finished the race.*
2 to continue to exist: *If the symptoms* ***persist****, please see a doctor.*
▸ **persistence** (*noun*)

persistent (say puh-**siss**-tuhnt) *adjective*
1 determined to continue doing something even though people tell you to stop: *She's a very* ***persistent*** *child – she just never gives up.*
2 lasting for a long time: *a* ***persistent*** *cough*

person (say **pur**-suhn) *noun* (*plural* **people**)
a man, woman or child: *I think she's the best* ***person*** *for the job.* ◇ *We've invited a few* ***people*** *to dinner.*
in person seeing somebody, not just speaking on the telephone or writing a letter: *I want to speak to her in* ***person****.*

personal (say **pur**-suhn-l) *adjective*
of or for one person: *That letter is* ***personal*** *and you have no right to read it.* ◇ *Please keep all your* ***personal*** *belongings with you.*

personal computer (*plural* **personal computers**) = **PC**

personality (say pur-suh-**nal**-i-tee) *noun* (*plural* **personalities**)
1 the qualities that a person has which make him or her different from other people: *Mark has a great* ***personality****.*
2 a famous person: *a television* ***personality***

personally (say **pur**-suh-nuhl-ee) *adverb*
1 You say **personally** when you are saying what you think about something: ***Personally****, I like her, but a lot of people don't.*
2 done by you yourself, and not by somebody else acting for you: *I will deal with this problem* ***personally****.*

personification (say per-son-if-ik-**ay**-shuhn) *noun* (*plural* **personifications**)
a comparison in which an object is given human qualities, for example in 'the wind danced through the leaves' and 'the groaning trees': *Look for* ***personification*** *in the poem.* ➲ See Study page 17

personify (say puh-**son**-i-fy) *verb* (**personifying, personified**)
1 to be an example of a particular quality: *She is kindness* ***personified****.*
2 to describe a thing as if it were a person, as in 'the frowning clouds' or 'the angry sea'

personnel (say pur-suh-**nel**) *plural noun*
the people who work for a large business or organization: *military* ***personnel***

perspective (say puh-**spek**-tiv) *noun* (*plural* **perspectives**)
1 the ability to think about problems and decisions in a reasonable way without exaggerating them: *Try to keep your problems in* ***perspective****.*
2 a point of view: *Look at the issue from her* ***perspective****, not just yours.*
3 the art of drawing on a flat surface so that some things appear farther away than others

perspire (say puh-**spy**-uh) *verb* (**perspiring, perspired**)
to lose liquid through your skin: *She always* ***perspires*** *while she is jogging.* ➲ SYNONYM **sweat**
▸ **perspiration** (*noun*): ***Perspiration*** *ran down his forehead.*

persuade (say puh-**swayd**) *verb* (**persuading, persuaded**)
to make somebody think or do something by talking to them: *The shop assistant* ***persuaded*** *me to buy the most expensive pair of jeans.*
➲ OPPOSITE **dissuade**

persuasion (say puh-**sway**-zhuhn) *noun* (*no plural*)
the process of making somebody think or do something: *After a lot of* ***persuasion*** *she agreed to come.*

perturb (say puh-**turb**) *verb* (**perturbing, perturbed**) (*formal*)
to make a person worried or upset: *We are* ***perturbed*** *by all the litter in our street.*

peruse (say puh-**rooz**) *verb* (**perusing, perused**) (*formal*)
to read carefully or thoroughly
▸ **perusal** (*noun*): *The contract was signed after careful* ***perusal****.*

perverse (say puh-**vurss**) *adjective*
showing a deliberate desire to behave in a way that is not reasonable or acceptable: *He gets* ***perverse*** *pleasure from shocking his parents.*

pervert (say puh-**vurt**) *verb* (**perverting, perverted**)
1 to change a system or process in a bad way
2 to cause a person to act or think in a way that is not moral or acceptable: *The gang culture has* ***perverted*** *many young people.*
▸ **perverted** (*adjective*): *a* ***perverted*** *mind*

pessimism (say **pess**-i-miz-m) *noun* (*no plural*)
thinking that bad things will happen, or the quality of often thinking this way ➲ OPPOSITE **optimism**

pessimist (say **pess**-i-mist) *noun* (*plural* **pessimists**)
a person who always thinks that bad things will

A B C D E F G H I J K L M N O P Q R S T U V W X Y Z

happen or that something will not be successful ➲ OPPOSITE **optimist**
▸ **pessimistic** (*adjective*): *Don't be so pessimistic! Everything will be OK.*

pest *noun* (*plural* **pests**)
1 an insect or animal that damages plants or food
2 (*informal*) a person or thing that annoys you or makes you a little angry: *My little sister's a real* ***pest!***

pester (say **pess**-tuh) *verb* (**pestering**, **pestered**)
to annoy somebody by asking them for something many times: *Don't* ***pester*** *me! I'm busy.*

pesticide (say **pess**-ti-side) *noun* (*plural* **pesticides**)
a chemical substance you use to kill animals, especially insects, or plants that are harmful to people or their crops or animals: *crops sprayed with* ***pesticide*** ◇ *I used* ***pesticide*** *to get rid of the rats and cockroaches in my kitchen.*

pet *noun* (*plural* **pets**)
1 an animal that you keep in your home: *I've got two* ***pets*** *– a cat and a goldfish.*
2 a child who a teacher or a parent likes best: *She's the teacher's* ***pet.***

petal (say **pet**-l) *noun* (*plural* **petals**)
one of the coloured parts of a flower
➲ See illustration at **flower**

petition (say puh-**tish**-n) *noun* (*plural* **petitions**)
a special letter from a group of people that asks for something: *Hundreds of people signed the* ***petition*** *for a new pedestrian crossing.*

petrify (say **pet**-ri-fy) *verb* (**petrifying**, **petrified**)
1 (*informal*) to frighten or make rigid: *She was* ***petrified*** *of swimming.*
2 to turn material that was once living into stone by the replacing of minerals: *Wood can* ***petrify*** *over many thousands of years.*

petrol (say **pet**-ruhl) *noun* (*no plural*)
a liquid that you put in a car or similar vehicle to make it go: *to fill a car up with* ***petrol***
ℹ ORIGIN: 14th–15th century, from Latin *petra* meaning 'rock' + *oleum* meaning 'oil'. The word originally meant oil which is found in rocks under the ground.

petroleum (say puh-**troh**-li-uhm) *noun* (*no plural*)
mineral oil or natural gas that is found under the ground or sea and is used to make petrol, plastic and other chemical products: *a* ***petroleum*** *refinery*

petty (say **pet**-ee) *adjective*
1 small and unimportant: ***petty*** *cash* (= a small amount of money kept in an office for small payments) ◇ ***petty*** *crime* (= that is not very serious)
2 unkind or unpleasant to other people, especially for reasons that seem unimportant: ***petty*** *jealousy*

pH (say pee-**aych**) *noun* (*no plural*) (*science*)
a measurement of the amount of acid or base in a substance. A pH value below 7 shows an **acid** and a pH value of above 7 shows a **base** or **alkali**: *On the* ***pH*** *scale, pure water has a value of 7.* ℹ **pH** is short for 'potential of Hydrogen'.

phantom (say **fan**-tuhm) *noun* (*plural* **phantoms**)
a spirit of a dead person that people think they see ➲ SYNONYM **ghost**

pharaoh (say **fair**-roh) *noun* (*plural* **pharaohs**) (*history*)
a ruler of ancient Egypt

pharmaceutical (say faa-muh-**syoo**-tik-l) *adjective*
relating to the production of medicines and drugs: *the* ***pharmaceutical*** *industry*

pharmacist (say **faa**-muh-sist) (*plural* **pharmacists**) = **chemist** 1

pharmacy (say **faa**-muh-see) *noun* (*plural* **pharmacies**)
a shop, or part of a shop, that sells medicines and drugs ➲ See **chemist** 2

pharynx (say **fa**-rinkss) *noun* (*plural* **pharynges**)
the soft area at the back of the mouth and nose and at the top of the throat

phase (say **fayz**) *noun* (*plural* **phases**)
a time when something is changing or growing: *She's going through a difficult* ***phase.***

phenomenal (say fuh-**nom**-in-l) *adjective*
very great or impressive: *a* ***phenomenal*** *success*

phenomenon (say fuh-**nom**-i-nuhn) *noun* (*plural* **phenomena**)
a fact or an event in nature or society, especially one that is not fully understood: *Scientists say the* ***phenomenon*** *has been occurring for more than a century.*

> USAGE Be careful! Remember that **phenomena** is the plural. You say **one phenomenon** and **many phenomena**.

philander (say fi-**lan**-duh) *verb* (**philandering**, **philandered**) (*old-fashioned*)
(of a man) to have sexual relationships with many different women

▸ **philanderer** (*noun*): *Don't fall in love with that* ***philanderer****; he will break your heart.*

philanthropy (say fi-**lan**-thruh-pee) *noun* (*no plural*) (*formal*)
the practice of helping the poor and those in need, especially by giving money

philharmonic (say fi-laa-**mon**-ik) *adjective*
(used in the names of orchestras) giving all its time and resources to music: *Cape* ***Philharmonic*** *Orchestra*

philosopher (say fuh-**loss**-uh-fuh) *noun* (*plural* **philosophers**)
a person who studies **philosophy**

philosophy (say fuh-**loss**-uh-fee) *noun*
1 (*no plural*) the study of ideas about the meaning of life
2 (*plural* **philosophies**) a set of beliefs that a person has about life: *Enjoy yourself and don't worry about tomorrow – that's my* ***philosophy****!*
🛈 ORIGIN: 13th–15th century, through Old French *philosophie*, through Latin from Greek *philosophia* meaning 'love of wisdom'

phlegm (say **flem**) *noun* (*no plural*)
the thick substance that forms in your throat, often when you have a cold

phlegmatic (say fleg-**mat**-ik) *adjective*
not easily made angry or upset: *a* ***phlegmatic*** *temperament*

phloem (say **floh**-uhm) *noun* (*no plural*) (*biology*)
the material in a plant containing very small tubes that carry sugars and other substances from the leaves to the rest of the plant

phobia (say **foh**-bi-uh) *noun* (*plural* **phobias**)
a strong fear of something, which is often difficult to explain: *A common* ***phobia*** *is the fear of spiders.*
▸ **phobic** (*adjective*): *She is* ***phobic*** *about rats.*

WORD BUILDING **Phobia** is often used in compound words, such as **arachnophobia** (fear of spiders), **claustrophobia** (fear of being in an enclosed place) and **xenophobia** (fear of foreigners).

phone[1] (say **fohn**) *noun* (*plural* **phones**) (also **telephone**)
an instrument that you use for talking to somebody who is in another place: *The* ***phone****'s ringing – can you answer it?*
be on the phone to be using the phone: *She was on the* ***phone*** *for an hour.*

phone[2] (say **fohn**) *verb* (**phoning, phoned**)
to speak to somebody by phone: *I* ***phoned*** *him last night.* ◇ *Could you* ***phone*** *back later?*
➲ SYNONYM **call[1]** 3

phone book *noun* (*plural* **phone books**) (also **telephone book, telephone directory**)
a book of people's names, addresses and telephone numbers

phone call *noun* (*plural* **phone calls**) (also **telephone call**)
an act of using the telephone or a conversation on the telephone: *I need to make a* ***phone call.***

phonecard (say **fohn**-kaad) *noun* (*plural* **phonecards**)
a small plastic card that you can use to pay for a call to somebody from a public telephone

phone number *noun* (*plural* **phone numbers**) (also **telephone number**)
the number of a particular phone that you use when you want to make a call to it: *What's your* ***phone number?***

phonetics (say fuh-**net**-ikss) *noun* (*no plural*)
the study of the sounds that people make when they speak

phosphate (say **foss**-fayt) *noun* (*plural* **phosphates**)
any chemical compound containing **phosphorus**: ***Phosphates*** *are important nutrients for plants and animals.*

phosphorus (say **foss**-fuh-ruhss) *noun* (*no plural*) (symbol P)
a chemical element found in several different forms, including as a poisonous substance that shines in the dark

photo (say **foh**-toh) *noun* (*plural* **photos**) (*informal*) = **photograph**

photocopier (say **foh**-toh-kop-i-uh) *noun* (*plural* **photocopiers**)
a machine that makes copies of documents by photographing them and then printing out the copies

photocopy (say **foh**-toh-kop-ee) *noun* (*plural* **photocopies**)
a copy of something on paper that you make with a **photocopier**
▸ **photocopy** (*verb*): ***Photocopy*** *this letter.*

photogenic (say foh-toh-**jee**-nik) *adjective*
(of a person) looking attractive in photographs: *a* ***photogenic*** *Hollywood couple*

photograph (say **foh**-tuh-graaf) *noun* (*plural* **photographs**) (also **photo**)
a picture that you take with a camera: *I took a* ***photo*** *of Table Mountain.*
▸ **photograph** (*verb*): *The winner was* ***photographed*** *holding his prize.*
🛈 ORIGIN: 19th century, from Greek *photo-* meaning 'relating to light' + *graphē* meaning 'writing, drawing'

photographer (say fuh-**tog**-ruh-fuh) *noun* (*plural* **photographers**)
a person who takes photographs, especially as a job

photographic (say foh-tuh-**graf**-ik) *adjective*
connected with photographs or photography: ***photographic*** *equipment*

photography (say fuh-**tog**-ruh-fee) *noun* (*no plural*)
the art, process or job of taking photographs

photosynthesis (say foh-toh-**sin**-thuh-siss) *noun* (*no plural*)
the process by which green plants and some bacteria use energy from light to turn carbon dioxide and water into food and oxygen
▸ **photosynthesize** (*verb*) (also **photosynthesise**)

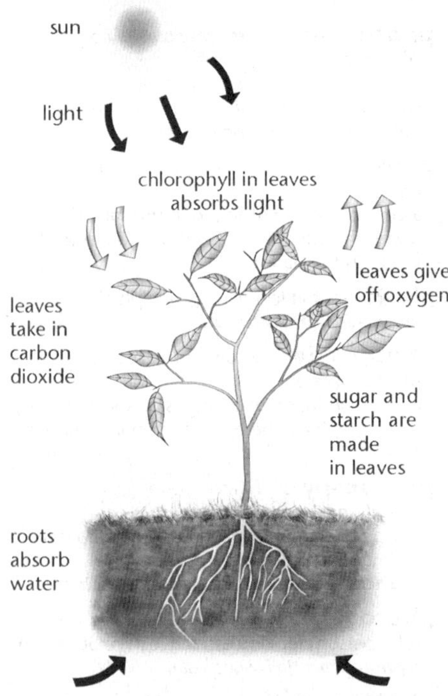

photovoltaic (say foh-toh-vol-**tay**-ik) *adjective*
producing electricity using light from the sun: ***photovoltaic*** *cells*

phrasal verb (say **frayz**-l **vurb**) *noun* (*plural* **phrasal verbs**) (*grammar*)
a verb that joins with another word or words to make a verb with a new meaning: *'Look after' and 'take off' are* ***phrasal verbs****.*

phrase (say **frayz**) *noun* (*plural* **phrases**) (*grammar*)
a group of words without a **finite** verb, which you use together as part of a sentence: *'First of all' and 'a bar of chocolate' are* ***phrases****.*

physical (say **fiz**-ik-l) *adjective*
connected with things that you feel or do with your body: ***physical*** *exercise*
▸ **physically** (*adverb*): *I'm not* ***physically*** *fit.*

physical education *noun* (*no plural*) (abbr. PE)
sport and exercise that are done as part of a subject at school

physician (say fi-**zish**-n) *noun* (*plural* **physicians**)
a medical doctor, especially one who is a specialist in general medicine

physicist (say **fiz**-i-sist) *noun* (*plural* **physicists**)
a person who studies or knows a lot about **physics**

physics (say **fiz**-ikss) *noun* (*no plural*)
the scientific study of matter and energy: *We are learning about light, electricity and atoms in* ***physics*** *this term.*

physiotherapy (say fiz-i-oh-**the**-ruh-pee) *noun* (*no plural*)
the treatment of injury or disease by exercise, rubbing the muscles and by other physical means, such as heat
▸ **physiotherapist** (*noun*): *The* ***physiotherapist*** *massaged my injured shoulder.*

physique (say fi-**zeek**) *noun* (*plural* **physiques**)
the size and shape of a person's body: *Top swimmers have good* ***physiques****.*

phytoplankton (say **fy**-toh-plank-tuhn) *noun* (*no plural*)
tiny plants, such as **algae**, that float near the surface of fresh or salt water

pi (say **py**) *noun* (*no plural*) (symbol π)
the number showing the constant relationship between the **circumference** (= the distance around it) of a circle and its **diameter** (= the distance across it). The value of pi is approximately equal to 3,14159 ...
ℹ **ORIGIN**: from Greek. The letter pi (Π) is the sixteenth letter of the Greek alphabet.

pianist (say **pi**-uh-nist) *noun* (*plural* **pianists**)
a person who plays the piano

piano (say pi-**an**-oh) *noun* (*plural* **pianos**)
a big musical instrument that you play by pressing black and white bars (called **keys**): *Can you play the **piano**?*

pick[1] (say **pik**) *verb* (**picking**, **picked**)
1 to take the person or thing you like best: *They **picked** him as their captain.* ➲ SYNONYM **choose**
2 to take a flower, fruit or vegetable from the place where it grows: *I've **picked** some flowers for you.*
pick on somebody (*informal*) to treat somebody in an unfair or cruel way: *She gets **picked** on by the other kids.*
pick somebody or **something out** to be able to see somebody or something among a lot of others: *Can you **pick** out my father in this photo?*
pick somebody up to come to get somebody, especially in a car: *My father **picks** me up from school.*
pick somebody or **something up** to take and lift somebody or something: *She **picked** up the kitten and stroked it.*
pick something up to learn something without really studying it: *Did you **pick** up any Japanese while you were in Tokyo?*

pick[2] (say **pik**) *noun* (*no plural*)
the one or ones that you choose, usually because they are the best
take your pick to choose what you like: *We've got juice or milk. Take your **pick**.*

pickaxe (say **pik**-akss) *noun* (*plural* **pickaxes**) (also **pick**)
a large sharp metal tool with a wooden handle which is used for breaking rocks or hard ground

picket (say **pik**-uht) *noun* (*plural* **pickets**)
a person or a group of people who stand outside a building to protest something
▸ **picket** (*verb*): *A group of workers who were seeking higher wages **picketed** outside Parliament.*

pickle (say **pik**-l) *noun* (*plural* **pickles**)
a vegetable put in salt water or **vinegar** so that it keeps for a long time
▸ **pickle** (*verb*): *onions **pickled** in vinegar*

pickpocket (say **pik**-pok-uht) *noun* (*plural* **pickpockets**)
a person who steals things from people's pockets

pickup (say **pik**-up) *noun* (*plural* **pickups**) (also **pickup truck**)
a type of vehicle for carrying goods that has an open part with low sides at the back ➲ See **truck**

picnic (say **pik**-nik) *noun* (*plural* **picnics**)
a meal outside, away from home: *We had a **picnic** by the river.*
▸ **picnic** (*verb*): *We **picnicked** at the beach yesterday.*
❶ ORIGIN: 18th century, from French *pique-nique*. The origin of this word is not known earlier.

pico- (say **pee**-koh) *prefix*
(used in nouns and adjectives, especially in units of measurement) one millionth of one millionth (1 in 10^{12}): ***picometre***

pictograph (say **pik**-tuh-graaf) *noun* (*plural* **pictographs**) (also **pictogram**)
1 a picture or symbol representing a word, phrase, object or idea
2 (*maths*) a diagram that uses pictures or symbols to represent amounts or numbers of a particular thing

pictorial (say pik-**taw**-ri-uhl) *adjective*
expressed in pictures: *a **pictorial** record of the journey*

picture[1] (say **pik**-tshuh) *noun* (*plural* **pictures**)
a drawing, painting or photograph: *Julie drew a **picture** of her dog.* ◇ *I took a **picture*** (= a photograph) *of the house.*

picture[2] (say **pik**-tshuh) *verb* (**picturing**, **pictured**)
to imagine something in your mind: *I can just **picture** them lying on the beach.*

pie (say **py**) *noun* (*plural* **pies**)
a type of food made of meat, fruit or vegetables covered with pastry, and baked: *an apple **pie***

piece (say **peess**) *noun* (*plural* **pieces**)
1 a part of something: *Would you like another **piece** of cake?* ◇ *a **piece** of broken glass*
2 one single thing: *Have you got a **piece** of paper?* ◇ *That's an interesting **piece** of news.*
3 a coin: *a 50c **piece***
fall to pieces to become very old and in bad condition, or to break: *The chair fell to **pieces** when I sat on it.*
in pieces broken: *The teapot lay in **pieces** on the floor.*

SPELLING Remember! **i** comes before **e** in **piece**. Use the phrase **a piece of pie** to help you remember.

pie chart *noun* (*plural* **pie charts**)
a diagram to represent data, consisting of a circle divided into parts to show the size of particular parts in relation to the whole

pier (say **peer**) *noun* (*plural* **piers**)
a long structure that is built from the land into

the sea, where people can walk or get on and off boats

pierce (say **peerss**) *verb* (**piercing, pierced**)
to make a hole in something with a sharp point: *The needle **pierced** her skin.* ◇ *I'm going to have my ears **pierced**.*

piercing (say **peer**-sing) *adjective*
A **piercing** sound is very loud and unpleasant: *a **piercing** cry*

pig *noun* (*plural* **pigs**)
1 a fat animal that people keep on farms for its meat
2 a rude word for a person who eats too much

WORD BUILDING With meaning 1 above, we call a female pig a **sow** and a male pig a **boar**. We call a young pig a **piglet**. Meat from a pig is called **pork**, **bacon** or **ham**.

pigeon (say **pi**-juhn) *noun* (*plural* **pigeons**)
a grey bird that you often see in towns

piggyback (say **pig**-ee-bak) *noun* (*plural* **piggybacks**) (also **piggyback ride**)
the way of carrying a person, especially a child, on your back: *He gave his daughter a **piggyback** when her legs got tired.*

piglet (say **pig**-luht) *noun* (*plural* **piglets**)
a young pig

pigment (say **pig**-muhnt) *noun* (*plural* **pigments**)
a substance that gives colour to things: *skin **pigment*** ◇ *The artist mixed different **pigments** together to get the colour she wanted.*
▶ **pigmentation** (*noun*): *Human beings have a range of skin **pigmentation**.*

pigsty (say **pig**-sty) *noun* (*plural* **pigsties**) (also **sty**)
a small building where pigs live

pigtail (say **pig**-tayl) *noun* (*plural* **pigtails**)
hair that you twist together **(plait)** and tie at the sides or at the back of your head

pilchard (say **pil**-chuhd) *noun* (*plural* **pilchards**)
a small silver fish that swims in the sea in large groups and that you can eat

pile¹ *verb* (**piling, piled**)
to put a lot of things on top of one another: *She **piled** the boxes on the table.*

pile² *noun* (*plural* **piles**)
a lot of things on top of one another, or a large amount of something: *a **pile** of earth* ◇ *Clothes lay in **piles** on the floor.*

WHICH WORD? **Pile** or **heap**?
■ A **pile** may be tidy or untidy. A **heap** is untidy.

pilfer (say **pil**-fuh) *verb* (**pilfering, pilfered**)
to steal things in small quantities, especially from the place where you work: *He was caught **pilfering** stationery.*

pilgrim (say **pil**-grim) *noun* (*plural* **pilgrims**)
a person who travels a long way to a place because it has a special religious meaning

pilgrimage (say **pil**-grim-ij) *noun* (*plural* **pilgrimages**)
a journey that a **pilgrim** makes

pill (say **pil**) *noun* (*plural* **pills**)
a small round hard piece of medicine that you swallow: *Take one of these **pills** before every meal.* ➲ SYNONYM **tablet**

pillar (say **pil**-uh) *noun* (*plural* **pillars**)
a tall strong piece of stone, wood or metal that holds up a building

pillow (say **pil**-oh) *noun* (*plural* **pillows**)
a soft thing that you put your head on when you are in bed

pillowcase (say **pil**-oh-kayss) *noun* (*plural* **pillowcases**)
a cover for a **pillow**

pilot (say **pile**-uht) *noun* (*plural* **pilots**)
a person who flies a plane

pimple (say **pimp**-l) *noun* (*plural* **pimples**)
a small raised red spot on your skin

PIN (say **pin**) *noun* (*plural* **PINs**)
a number given to you, for example by a bank, so that you can use a plastic card to take out money from a cash machine ℹ **PIN** is an abbreviation of 'personal identification number'.

pin¹ *noun* (*plural* **pins**)
a small thin piece of metal with a flat part at one end and a sharp point at the other. You use a **pin** for holding things together or fixing one thing to another. ➲ See **drawing pin**, **safety pin**

pin² *verb* (**pinning, pinned**)
1 to fix things together with a pin or pins: *Could you **pin** this notice to the board?*
2 to hold somebody or something so that they cannot move: *He tried to get away, but they **pinned** him against the wall.*

pinch¹ *verb* (**pinching, pinched**)
1 to press somebody's skin tightly between your thumb and finger: *Don't **pinch** me – it hurts!*

2 (*informal*) to steal something: *Who's **pinched** my pen?*

pinch² *noun* (*plural* **pinches**)
1 the act of pressing somebody's skin tightly between your thumb and finger: *He gave me a **pinch** on the arm to wake me up.*
2 an amount of something you can hold between your thumb and finger: *Add a **pinch** of salt to the soup.*

pincushion (say **pin**-kuu-shuhn) *noun* (*plural* **pincushions**)
a small cushion used for sticking pins in when they are not being used

pine¹ *noun* (*plural* **pines**) (also **pine tree**)
a tall tree with thin sharp leaves (called **needles**) that do not fall off in winter

pine² *verb* (**pining**, **pined**)
to be very unhappy because a person has died or gone away: *We still **pine** for our father, who passed away last year.*

pineapple (say **pine**-ap-l) *noun* (*plural* **pineapples**)
a big fruit that is yellow inside and has a rough brown skin

ping-pong (say **ping**-pong) *noun* (*no plural*)
a game where players hit a small light ball over a net on a big table ➲ SYNONYM **table tennis**

pink *adjective* (**pinker**, **pinkest**)
with a light red colour: *a **pink** sweater*
▸ **pink** (*noun*): *She was dressed in **pink**.*

pinnacle (say **pin**-ik-l) *noun* (*plural* **pinnacles**)
1 the most important or successful part of something: *the **pinnacle** of her career*
2 a high pointed rock on a mountain: *The climbers reached the **pinnacle**.*

pins and needles *plural noun*
a feeling that you sometimes get in a part of your body when you have not moved it for a long time

pint (say **pynt**) *noun* (*plural* **pints**) (abbr. pt)
a unit for measuring the volume of liquids (= 0,57 litres), used in Britain and the USA. There are eight **pints** in a **gallon**: *a **pint** of beer ◇ two **pints** of milk*

pioneer (say py-uh-**neer**) *noun* (*plural* **pioneers**)
a person who goes somewhere or does something before other people: *the **pioneers** of the American West*

pious (say **py**-uhss) *adjective*
very religious: *The church was filled with **pious** believers.*

pip *noun* (*plural* **pips**)
the seed of some fruits. Lemons, oranges and apples have **pips**.

pipe (*rhymes with* **wipe**) *noun* (*plural* **pipes**)
1 a long tube that takes something such as water, oil or gas from one place to another: *A water **pipe** is leaking under the ground.*
2 a tube with a small bowl at one end that is used for smoking tobacco: *My grandfather smoked a **pipe**.*

pipeline (say **pipe**-line) *noun* (*plural* **pipelines**)
a line of pipes that carry oil or gas a long way
in the pipeline Something that is **in the pipeline** is being planned or prepared and will happen soon.

piquant (say **pee**-kont) *adjective*
with a sharp spicy taste: *chicken pieces with a **piquant** sauce*

pirate (say **py**-ruht) *noun* (*plural* **pirates**)
a person on a ship who robs other ships

pistil (say **piss**-til) *noun* (*plural* **pistils**)
the female organs of a flower, which receive the **pollen** and produce seeds ➲ See **stamen**
➲ See illustration at flower

pistol (say **piss**-tuhl) *noun* (*plural* **pistols**)
a small gun that you hold in one hand

piston (say **piss**-tuhn) *noun* (*plural* **pistons**)
a round mechanical device in engines and other machines that slides up and down and transfers force from one part of the machine to another

pit *noun* (*plural* **pits**)
1 a deep hole in the ground
2 a deep hole that people make in the ground to take out coal ➲ SYNONYM **mine²** 1

pitch¹ (say **pich**) *noun*
1 (*plural* **pitches**) a piece of ground where you play certain games and sports: *a cricket **pitch** ◇ a football **pitch***
2 (*no plural*) how high or low a sound is

> WORD BUILDING You also play **hockey** and **rugby** on a **pitch**. You play **tennis** and **squash** on a **court**.

pitch² (say **pich**) *verb* (**pitching**, **pitched**)
to put up a tent: *We **pitched** our tent under a big tree.*

pitfall (say **pit**-fawl) *noun* (*plural* **pitfalls**)
a danger or difficulty, especially one that is hidden or not obvious: *the **pitfalls** of starting your own business*

A B C D E F G H I J K L M N O **P** Q R S T U V W X Y Z

pith *noun* (*no plural*)
1 the soft centre in the stem or branch of a plant or tree
2 the soft white substance inside the skin of an orange or lemon

pithy (say **pith**-ee) *adjective*
expressed in a clear, direct manner: *a **pithy** comment*

pitiful (say **pit**-i-fuhl) *adjective*
causing you to feel pity or sadness: *the **pitiful** howls of a dog locked up alone*

pitiless (say **pit**-i-luhss) *adjective*
with no pity for other people's suffering: *The people suffered under the **pitiless** tyrant.*

pity[1] (say **pit**-ee) *noun* (*no plural*)
1 a feeling of sadness for a person or an animal that is in pain or that has problems: *I feel no **pity** for him – it's his own fault.*
2 something that makes you feel a little sad or disappointed: *It's a **pity** you can't come to the party.* ➲ SYNONYM **shame** 2
take pity on somebody to help somebody because you feel sad for them: *I took **pity** on her and gave her some money.*

pity[2] (say **pit**-ee) *verb* (**pitying, pitied**)
to feel sad for somebody who is in pain or who has problems: *I really **pity** people who haven't got anywhere to live.*

pivot (say **piv**-uht) *noun* (*plural* **pivots**)
1 (*technology*) the central point on which a thing turns or balances ➲ See illustration at **lever**
2 the central or most important person or thing: *The church was the **pivot** of community life.*
▸ **pivot** (*verb*): *He **pivoted** on his heels and walked out.*

pixie (say **pik**-see) *noun* (*plural* **pixies**)
(in stories) a creature like a small person with pointy ears and magical powers.

pizza (say **pee**-tsuh) *noun* (*plural* **pizzas**)
a flat round piece of bread with tomatoes, cheese and other things on top that is cooked in an oven

placard (say **plak**-aad) *noun* (*plural* **placards**)
a large written or printed notice put up in a public place or carried during a **demonstration** 1: *The protesting staff waved **placards**.*

placate (say pluh-**kayt**) *verb* (**placating, placated**)
to make a person less angry about something: *The principal tried to **placate** the angry parents.*

place[1] (say **playss**) *noun* (*plural* **places**)
1 a particular area or position: *Put the book back in the right **place**.*
2 a particular building, town or country: *Mexico is a very interesting **place**.* ◇ *Do you know a good **place** to have lunch?*
3 a seat or space for one person: *An old man was sitting in my **place**.*
4 the position that you have in a race, competition or test: *Alice finished in second **place**.*
in place where it should be or in the right place: *Glue the picture in **place**.*
in place of somebody or **something** instead of somebody or something: *You can use milk in **place** of cream.*
take place to happen: *The wedding of John and Sara will take **place** on 22 May.*

place[2] (say **playss**) *verb* (**placing, placed**)
(*formal*) to put something somewhere: *The waiter **placed** the meal in front of me.*

placenta (say pluh-**sen**-tuh) *noun* (*plural* **placentas**)
the organ that supplies food and **oxygen** and removes waste for a baby growing inside its mother's body

placid (say **plass**-id) *adjective*
1 (of a person or an animal) not easily excited or upset: *a **placid** dog that is good with children*
2 (of water or the weather) calm and peaceful, with little movement: *a **placid** sea on a windless day*

plagiarize (say **play**-ji-uh-rize) *verb* (**plagiarizing, plagiarized**) (also **plagiarise**)
to copy another person's ideas, work or words and pretend that they are your own

plague (say **playg**) *noun* (*plural* **plagues**)
1 a disease that spreads quickly and kills many people
2 large numbers of an animal or insect that move into an area and cause great damage: *a **plague** of locusts*

plain[1] (say **playn**) *adjective* (**plainer, plainest**)
1 easy to see, hear or understand: *It's **plain** that he's unhappy.* ➲ SYNONYM **clear[1]** 1
2 simple and ordinary: ***plain** food*
3 with no pattern or all one colour: *She wore a **plain** blue dress.*
4 not pretty: *She was a **plain** child.*

plain[2] (say **playn**) *noun* (*plural* **plains**)
a large piece of flat land

plainly (say **playn**-lee) *adverb*
in a way that is easy to see, hear or understand: *They were **plainly** very angry.* ➲ SYNONYM **clearly** 2

plait (say **plat**) *verb* (**plaiting, plaited**)
to cross three long pieces of hair over and under each other to make one thick piece: *She **plaited** her hair.* ➲ SYNONYM **braid**
▸ **plait** (*noun*): *She wears her hair in **plaits**.*

plan¹ *noun* (*plural* **plans**)
1 something that you have decided to do and how you are going to do it: *What are your holiday **plans**?* ◇ *They have **plans** to build a new school.*
2 a map showing a building or a town: *a street **plan** of London*
3 a drawing that shows how a new building, room or machine will be made: *Have you seen the **plans** for the new shopping centre?*

plan² *verb* (**planning, planned**)
to decide what you are going to do and how you are going to do it: *They're **planning** a holiday in Australia next summer.* ◇ *I'm **planning** to go to university.*

plane¹ (say **playn**) *noun* (*plural* **planes**) (also **aeroplane**)
a vehicle with wings that can fly through the air: *I like travelling by **plane**.* ◇ *What time does your **plane** land?* ◇ *Our **plane** took off late.*

WORD BUILDING A plane **lands** and **takes off** at an **airport**.

plane² (say **playn**) *adjective* (*maths*)
(of a surface) completely flat and level: *a horizontal **plane***

planet (say **plan**-uht) *noun* (*plural* **planets**)
a large round object in space that moves around the sun or another star: *Earth, Mars and Venus are **planets**.*

plank *noun* (*plural* **planks**)
a long flat piece of wood

plankton (say **plangk**-tuhn) (*plural noun*)
tiny plants and animals that float near the surface of fresh or salt water: ***Plankton** provide food for fish and whales.*

plant¹ (say **plaant**) *noun* (*plural* **plants**)
1 a living thing that grows in the ground and usually has leaves, a stem and roots: *Don't forget to water the **plants**.* ◇ *a tomato **plant***
2 a very large factory: *a car **plant***

plant

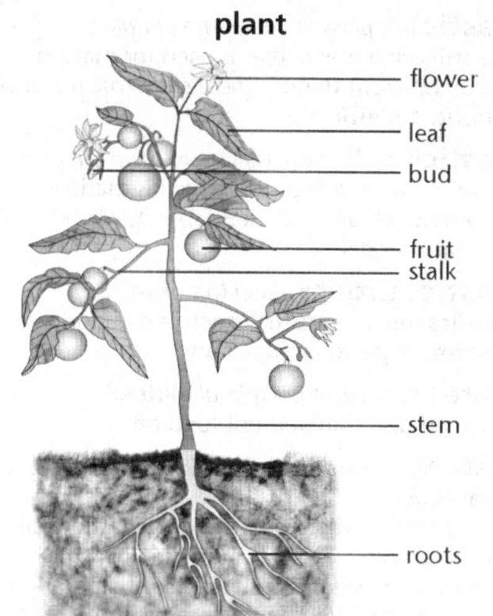

plant² (say **plaant**) *verb* (**planting, planted**)
to put plants or seeds in the ground: *We **planted** some roses in the garden.*

plantation (say plaan-**tay**-shuhn) *noun* (*plural* **plantations**)
a piece of land where trees or crops like tea, bananas or rubber are grown: *a sugar **plantation***

plaque (say **plaak**) *noun*
1 (*plural* **plaques**) a flat piece of stone or metal with words in memory of a famous person or event
2 (*no plural*) a soft substance that forms on teeth and encourages the growth of harmful bacteria

plasma (say **plaz**-muh) *noun* (*no plural*)
1 the liquid part of the blood, which carries the blood cells
2 a gas of electrically charged particles: *My **plasma** television has excellent picture quality.*

plaster¹ (say **plaass**-tuh) *noun*
1 (*no plural*) a substance that is used for covering walls inside buildings
2 (*no plural*) a hard covering around a broken bone or the substance that the covering is made of: *My leg was in **plaster**.*
3 (*plural* **plasters**) a small piece of sticky material that you put over a cut on your body to keep it clean

plaster² (say **plaass**-tuh) *verb* (**plastering, plastered**)
1 to cover a wall with **plaster¹** 1 to make it smooth
2 to cover a surface with a large amount of something: ***Plaster** yourself with sunblock!*

A B C D E F G H I J K L M N O P Q R S T U V W X Y Z

plastic (say **plass**-tik) *noun* (*no plural*)
an artificial material that is used for making many different things: *These chairs are made of **plastic**.* ◇ ***plastic** cups*

Plasticine™ (say **plass**-ti-seen) *noun* (*no plural*)
a soft substance like clay, which is made in different colours and used especially by children to make models

plastic surgery *noun* (*no plural*)
medical operations that doctors can do to improve a person's appearance

plate (say **playt**) *noun* (*plural* **plates**)
a round dish that you put food on

plateau (say pluh-**toh**) *noun* (*plural* **plateaux** or **plateaus**)
1 a large flat area of high land ➲ See illustration at **mountain**
2 a state where there is little change or development: *House prices seem to have reached a **plateau**.*

platelet (say **playt**-luht) (*plural* **platelets**)
a small blood cell that helps you to stop bleeding when you cut yourself: ***Platelets** help blood to clot.*

platform (say **plat**-fawm) *noun* (*plural* **platforms**)
1 the part of a railway station where people get on and off trains: *Our train leaves from **platform** 5.*
2 a surface that is higher than the floor, where people stand so that other people can see and hear them: *The principal went up to the **platform** to make her speech.*

platinum (say **plat**-i-nuhm) *noun* (*no plural*)
(symbol Pt)
a strong valuable silver-grey metal that is often used for making expensive jewellery: *a **platinum** wedding ring*

platonic (say pluh-**ton**-ik) *adjective*
(of a relationship) friendly but not sexual
ⓘ ORIGIN: 16th century, from *Platon*, the Greek name for Plato, a philosopher who lived in Greece in the fifth century BC

platteland (say **plut**-uh-lunt) *noun* (*no plural*)
(*S. African*)
the rural areas: *One day I would like to live on a farm in the **platteland**.*
ⓘ ORIGIN: 20th century, from Afrikaans *platteland* from *plat* meaning 'flat' + *land* meaning 'land'

play¹ (say **play**) *verb* (**playing, played**)
1 to have fun or to do something to enjoy yourself: *The children were **playing** with their toys.*
2 to take part in a game or sport: *I like **playing** tennis.* ◇ *Do you know how to **play** chess?*
3 to make music with a musical instrument: *My sister **plays** the piano very well.*
4 to put a record, CD or DVD in a machine and listen to it: *Shall I **play** the CD again?*
5 to act the part of somebody in a play: *Who wants to **play** the policeman?*

USAGE When we talk about using a musical instrument, we usually say, for example, **play the piano** and **play the guitar**: *I'm learning to **play** the guitar. She **played** the violin.*

play² *noun*
1 (*plural* **plays**) a story that you watch in the theatre or on television, or listen to on the radio: *We went to see a **play** at the National Theatre.*
2 (*no plural*) games or what children do for fun: *work and **play***

player (say **play**-uh) *noun* (*plural* **players**)
1 a person who plays a game or sport: *football **players***
2 a person who plays a musical instrument: *a trumpet **player***

playful (say **play**-fuhl) *adjective*
full of fun or not serious: *a **playful** puppy* ◇ *a **playful** remark*

playground (say **play**-grownd) *noun* (*plural* **playgrounds**)
an area where children can play, for example at school

playing card *noun* (*plural* **playing cards**)
(also **card**)
one of a set of 52 cards with numbers and pictures on them that you use for playing games: *a pack of **playing cards***

playing field *noun* (*plural* **playing fields**)
a large area of grass where people play sports like football

play script (say **play**-skript) *noun* (*plural* **play scripts**)
a written version of a play, especially for use by actors to prepare for a performance

playwright (say **play**-rite) *noun* (*plural* **playwrights**)
a person who writes plays for the theatre, television or radio ➲ SYNONYM **dramatist**

plea (say **plee**) *noun* (*plural* **pleas**)
asking for something with strong feeling: *He made a **plea** for help.*

plead (say **pleed**) *verb* (**pleading, pleaded**)
1 to ask for something in a very strong way: *He **pleaded** with his parents to buy him a guitar.*

2 to say in a court of law that you did or did not do a crime: *She **pleaded** not guilty to murder.*

pleasant (say **plez**-uhnt) *adjective*
nice, enjoyable or friendly: *The weather here is very **pleasant**.* ◇ *He's a very **pleasant** person.*
➲ OPPOSITE **unpleasant**
▸ **pleasantly** (*adverb*): *a **pleasantly** cool room*

please¹ (say **pleez**) *exclamation*
a word that you use when you ask for something politely: *What's the time, **please**?* ◇ *Two cups of coffee, **please**.* ◇ *'Would you like a cake?' 'Yes, **please**.'*

please² (say **pleez**) *verb* (**pleasing, pleased**)
to make somebody happy: *I wore my best clothes to **please** my mother.*

pleased (say **pleezd**) *adjective*
happy: *He wasn't very **pleased** to see me.* ◇ *Are you **pleased** with your new watch?* ➲ See note at **glad**

pleasure (say **ple*zh***-uh) *noun*
1 (*no plural*) the feeling of being happy or enjoying something: *She gets a lot of **pleasure** from her music.*
2 (*plural* **pleasures**) something that makes you happy: *It was a **pleasure** to meet you.*
it's a pleasure You say 'it's a pleasure' as a polite way of answering somebody who thanks you: *'Thank you for your help.' 'It's a **pleasure**.'*
with pleasure You say 'with pleasure' to show in a polite way that you are happy to do something: *'Can you help me move these boxes?' 'Yes, with **pleasure**.'*

pleat (say **pleet**) *noun* (*plural* **pleats**)
a fold that is part of a skirt, a shirt or a pair of trousers, for example

pledge (say **plej**) *noun* (*plural* **pledges**)
a formal promise or agreement
▸ **pledge** (*verb*): *The government has **pledged** to support the flood victims.*

plentiful (say **plen**-ti-fuhl) *adjective*
available in large amounts or numbers: *Grapes are **plentiful** this time of the year.* ➲ OPPOSITE **scarce**

plenty (say **plen**-tee) *pronoun*
a lot, or as much or as many as you need: *'Do we need more chairs?' 'No, there are **plenty**.'* ◇ *We've got **plenty** of time to get there.*

pliable (say **ply**-uhb-l) *adjective*
1 easy to bend or shape
2 (of a person) easy to influence

pliers (say **ply**-uhz) *plural noun*
a tool for holding things tightly or for cutting wire: *Have you got a pair of **pliers**?*

pliers

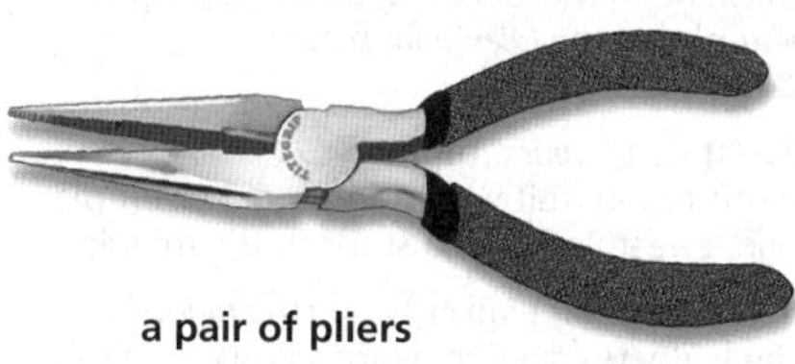

a pair of pliers

plight (say **plite**) *noun* (*plural* **plights**) (*formal*)
a bad or difficult state or situation: *the **plight** of war refugees*

plinth (say **plinth**) *noun* (*plural* **plinths**)
a block of stone on which a statue or column stands

plod *verb* (**plodding, plodded**)
to walk slowly in a heavy tired way: *We **plodded** up the hill in the rain.*

plop *noun* (*plural* **plops**)
a sound like that of a small object dropping into water
▸ **plop** (*verb*): *The frogs **plopped** into the water.*

plot¹ *noun* (*plural* **plots**)
1 what happens in a story, play or film: *This book has a very exciting **plot**.*
2 a secret plan to do something bad: *a **plot** to kill the President*
3 a small piece of land that you use or you plan to use for a special purpose: *She bought a small **plot** to build a house on.*

plot² *verb* (**plotting, plotted**)
to make a secret plan to do something bad: *They **plotted** to rob the bank.*

plough (say **plow**) *noun* (*plural* **ploughs**)
a large farm tool that is pulled across a field to dig the soil
▸ **plough** (*verb*): *The farmer **ploughed** his fields.*

ploy *noun* (*plural* **ploys**)
words or actions that you have planned carefully to get an advantage over another person: *a clever marketing **ploy***

pluck (say **pluk**) *verb* (**plucking, plucked**)
to remove something by pulling it quickly: *He **plucked** the letter from her hands.* ◇ *We needed to **pluck** the feathers from the chicken.*

plug¹ (say **plug**) *noun* (*plural* **plugs**)
1 a device with metal pins that joins a lamp or a machine to a place in the wall (called a **socket**) where there is a supply of electricity
2 a round object that you put in the hole in a bath or sink, to keep the water in

A B C D E F G H I J K L M N O **P** Q R S T U V W X Y Z

plug² (say **plug**) *verb* (**plugging, plugged**)
to fill a hole, so that nothing can get out: *He **plugged** the hole in the pipe with an old rag.*
plug something in to join a lamp or a machine to the electricity, using a **plug¹**: *Can you **plug** in the television, please?*
➲ OPPOSITE **unplug**

plum *noun* (*plural* **plums**)
a soft round fruit with smooth red or purple skin, sweet flesh and a stone in the middle

plumage (say **ploo**-mij) *noun* (*no plural*)
the feathers covering a bird's body

plumber (say **plum**-uh) *noun* (*plural* **plumbers**)
a person whose job is to put in and repair things like water pipes and baths
ℹ ORIGIN: 14th–15th century, through Old French from Latin *plumbarius* from *plumbum* meaning 'lead' (a soft metal). The word originally meant 'a person who works with lead', since pipes used to be made of lead.

plumbing (say **plum**-ing) *noun* (*no plural*)
1 the pipes that carry water into and around a building: *The builders are putting in the **plumbing**.*
2 the work of a **plumber**

PRONUNCIATION Don't pronounce the b in **plumber** and **plumbing**.

plume (say **ploom**) *noun* (*plural* **plumes**)
1 a cloud of steam or smoke that rises into the air
2 a large feather or a bunch of feathers, often worn as decoration

plummet (say **plum**-uht) *verb* (**plummeting, plummeted**) (*formal*)
to fall suddenly and quickly from a high level or position: *The spacecraft **plummeted** into the sea.* ◇ *The bad news caused share prices to **plummet**.*

plump *adjective* (**plumper, plumpest**)
a bit fat, but in a pleasant way: *a **plump** baby*

plunder (say **plun**-duh) *verb* (**plundering, plundered**)
to steal things from a place using force, especially during a time of war or disorder: *The enemy soldiers **plundered** the village.*
▸ **plunder** (*noun*): *the **plunder** of our seas by foreign fishing vessels*

plunge (say **plunj**) *verb* (**plunging, plunged**)
1 to jump or fall suddenly into something: *She **plunged** into the pool.*
2 to push something suddenly and strongly into something else: *I **plunged** my hand into the water.*

plural (say **ploor**-ruhl) *noun* (*plural* **plurals**) (*grammar*)
the form of a word that shows there is more than one: *The **plural** of 'child' is 'children'.*
➲ See Study page 5 ➲ OPPOSITE **singular**
▸ **plural** (*adjective*): *Most **plural** nouns in English end in 's'.*

plus (*rhymes with* **bus**) *preposition*
1 added to: *Two **plus** three is five (2 + 3 = 5).*
➲ See **minus¹** 1
2 and: *All of our class **plus** half of Grade 6 are going.*

plush (*rhymes with* **rush**) *adjective*
comfortable and expensive: *a **plush** hotel*

ply (*rhymes with* **fly**) *verb* (**plying, plied**)
to try to sell goods or services to people, especially on the street: *the taxi drivers were **plying** their trade outside the station*

plywood (say **ply**-wuud) *noun* (*no plural*) (*technology*)
board made by sticking several thin layers of wood together

p.m. (say pee-**em**) *abbreviation*
You use **p.m.** after a time to show that it is between midday and midnight: *The plane leaves at 3 **p.m.*** ℹ **p.m.** is short for 'post meridiem', which means 'after midday' in Latin.
➲ See **a.m.**

WORD BUILDING We use **a.m.** for times between midnight and midday.

pneumatic (say nyoo-**mat**-ik) *adjective*
filled with air or worked by air under pressure: *a **pneumatic** tyre* ◇ *a **pneumatic** drill*

pneumonia (say nyoo-**moh**-ni-uh) *noun* (*no plural*)
a serious illness of the lungs

poach (say **pohch**) *verb* (**poaching, poached**)
1 to kill and steal animals, birds or fish without permission, or from another person's land
2 to cook food gently in liquid: *My mum **poached** eggs for breakfast.*
▸ **poacher** (*noun*): *The elephant had been shot by **poachers**.*

PO Box (say pee-**oh** bokss) *noun* (*plural* **PO Boxes**)
a box at a post office for keeping the letters of a person or office: *The address is **PO Box 63**, Giyani 0826.* ℹ **PO** is short for 'Post Office'.

pocket (say **pok**-uht) *noun* (*plural* **pockets**)
the part of a piece of clothing that you can put things in: *I put the key in my **pocket**.*
pick somebody's pocket to steal money from somebody's **pocket** or bag

pocket money *noun* (*no plural*)
money that parents give to a child each week or month to buy things: *How much **pocket money** do you get?*

pod *noun* (*plural* **pods**)
a long thin case that some plants have, which is filled with seeds: *Peas grow in **pods**.*

podium (say **poh**-di-uhm) *noun* (*plural* **podiums**)
a small platform for a speaker or performer to stand on: *The athlete was on the **podium** to receive her prize.*

poem (say **poh**-uhm) *noun* (*plural* **poems**)
words arranged in lines in an artistic way, often with sounds repeated at the ends of lines: *He wrote **poems** about the beauty of the countryside.*

poet (say **poh**-uht) *noun* (*plural* **poets**)
a person who writes poems

poetic (say poh-**et**-ik) *adjective*
like poetry or as in a poem: ***poetic** language*

poetry (say **poh**-uh-tree) *noun* (*no plural*)
poems in general or a collection of poems: *Wordsworth wrote beautiful **poetry**.*

poignant (say **poyn**-yuhnt) *adjective*
causing sadness or pity: *a **poignant** story about a lost friend*

point[1] (say **poynt**) *noun* (*plural* **points**)
1 a fact, an idea or an opinion: *You made some interesting **points*** (= said some interesting things) *in your essay.* ➲ See **point of view**
2 the purpose of, or the reason for, doing something: *The **point** of going to school is to learn.* ◇ *What's the **point** of going to her house? She's not there.*
3 a particular moment in time: *It started to rain. At that **point** we decided to go home.*
4 a particular place: *No parking beyond this **point**.*
5 a small round mark (.) that many countries use when writing part of a number (called a **decimal**): *2.5* (= two ***point** five*)
6 the sharp end of something: *the **point** of a needle*
7 a single mark in some games or sports, which you add to others to get the score: *Our team scored six **points**.*
be on the point of doing something If you are on the **point** of doing something, you are going to do it very soon: *I was on the **point** of leaving when he arrived.*

point[2] (say **poynt**) *verb* (**pointing, pointed**)
1 to show where something is, using for example your finger or a stick: *He **pointed** at the bank across the road.* ◇ *I saw a sign **pointing** towards the library.*
2 to hold something towards somebody or something: *She **pointed** a gun at his head.*
point something out to tell or show somebody something: *Eva **pointed** out that my bag was open.*

pointed (say **poynt**-uhd) *adjective*
with a sharp end: *a long **pointed** nose*

pointless (say **poynt**-luhss) *adjective*
with no use or purpose: *It's **pointless** telling him anything – he never listens.*

point of view *noun* (*plural* **points of view**)
an opinion or way of thinking about something: *The book was written from the father's **point of view**.*

poise (say **poyz**) *noun* (*no plural*)
1 a calm, confident way of behaving: *The teacher made a mistake, but kept her **poise**.*
2 the ability to move or stand in an elegant way with good control of your body: *the **poise** of a ballet dancer*
▶ **poise** (*verb*): *The cat **poised**, ready to leap* (= to jump high or a long way).

poison[1] (say **poy**-zuhn) *noun* (*plural* **poisons**)
something that will kill or make living things very sick if they come into contact with it: *rat **poison*** ◇ *They experimented with different **poisons**.*

poison[2] (say **poy**-zuhn) *verb* (**poisoning, poisoned**)
to use **poison** to kill or hurt somebody or something

poisonous (say **poy**-zuh-nuhss) *adjective*
Something that is **poisonous** will kill or make living things very sick if they come into contact with it: *Some mushrooms are **poisonous**.*
➲ SYNONYM **toxic**

poke (say **pohk**) *verb* (**poking, poked**)
1 to push somebody or something hard with your finger or another long thin thing: *She **poked** me in the eye with a pencil.*
2 to push something quickly somewhere: *Jeff **poked** his head out of the window.*
▶ **poke** (*noun*): *I gave her a **poke** to wake her up.*

poker (say **pohk**-uh) *noun*
1 (*no plural*) a game that people play with cards, usually for money
2 (*plural* **pokers**) a metal stick that you use for moving the wood in a fire

polar (say **poh**-luh) *adjective*
of, connected with or near the areas around the top and bottom of the Earth (called the **North Pole** and the **South Pole**): *the **polar** regions*

A B C D E F G H I J K L M N O **P** Q R S T U V W X Y Z

polar bear *noun* (*plural* **polar bears**)
a large wild animal that has thick white fur and lives near the North Pole

pole (say **pohl**) *noun* (*plural* **poles**)
1 a long thin piece of wood or metal. **Poles** are often used to hold something up: *a flag* ***pole*** ◇ *tent* ***poles***
2 one of two places at the top and bottom of the Earth: *the North* ***Pole*** ◇ *the South* ***Pole***

police (say puh-**leess**) *plural noun*
the official organization whose job is to make sure that people do not break the laws of a country: *Have the* ***police*** *found the murderer?* ◇ *a* ***police*** *car*
▸ **police** (*verb*): *The guards* ***policed*** *the train.*

police constable *noun* (*plural* **police constables**) (abbr. PC)
an ordinary police officer

police force *noun* (*plural* **police forces**)
all the police officers in a country or part of a country

policeman (say puh-**leess**-muhn) *noun* (*plural* **policemen**)
a man who is a police officer

police officer *noun* (*plural* **police officers**)
a man or woman who works in the police

police station *noun* (*plural* **police stations**)
an office where police officers work: *They took the men to the* ***police station*** *for questioning.*

policewoman (say puh-**leess**-wuum-uhn) *noun* (*plural* **policewomen**)
a woman who is a police officer

policy (say **pol**-i-see) *noun* (*plural* **policies**)
1 the plans of a government or organization: *What is the government's* ***policy*** *on education?*
2 a document that shows an agreement that you have made with an insurance company: *an insurance* ***policy***

polio (say **poh**-li-oh) *noun* (*no plural*)
a serious disease that affects nerve cells and leads to the loss of power in muscles

polish[1] (say **pol**-ish) *noun* (*no plural*)
a cream or liquid that you put on something to make it shine: *shoe* ***polish***

polish[2] (say **pol**-ish) *verb* (**polishing, polished**)
to make something shine by rubbing it, usually after you have put **polish** on it: *Have you* ***polished*** *your shoes?*

polite (say puh-**lite**) *adjective*
speaking or behaving in a way that shows respect and good manners: *It is* ***polite*** *to say 'please' when you ask for something.*
➲ OPPOSITES **impolite, rude** 1
▸ **politely** (*adverb*) ▸ **politeness** (*noun*): *He offered her his seat out of* ***politeness.***

political (say puh-**lit**-ik-l) *adjective*
connected with politics or the government: ***political*** *parties* ◇ *his* ***political*** *beliefs*
▸ **politically** (*adverb*)

politician (say pol-uh-**tish**-n) *noun* (*plural* **politicians**)
a person who works in politics: ***Politicians*** *of all parties supported us.*

politics (say **pol**-uh-tikss) *noun* (*no plural*)
1 the work and ideas that are connected with government: *Are you interested in* ***politics?***
2 the study of government: *She studied* ***Politics*** *at university.* ➲ See **congress** 2, **election**, **party** 2

poll (*rhymes with* **hole**) *noun* (*plural* **polls**)
1 a way of discovering opinions by asking a group of people questions: *A recent* ***poll*** *showed that 73% were unhappy with the government.*
2 an election or the number of votes in an election: *The country will go to the* ***polls*** (= vote) *in June.*

pollen (say **pol**-uhn) *noun* (*no plural*)
the yellow powder in flowers that is taken to other flowers by insects or by the wind

pollinate (say **pol**-i-nayt) *verb* (**pollinating, pollinated**)
to move **pollen** from the male part to the female part of a flower in a plant so that it can produce seeds
▸ **pollination** (*noun*): ***Pollination*** *is an important step in the sexual reproduction of flowering plants.*

pollute (say puh-**loot**) *verb* (**polluting, polluted**)
to make the air, rivers or soil dirty and dangerous: *Many rivers are* ***polluted*** *with chemicals from factories.*
▸ **polluted** (*adjective*): *a* ***polluted*** *river*

pollution (say puh-**loo**-shuhn) *noun* (*no plural*)
1 the action of making the air, rivers or soil dirty and dangerous: *We must stop the* ***pollution*** *of our beaches.*
2 dirty and dangerous chemicals and gases that harm the environment

poly- (say **pol**-ee) *prefix*
(used in nouns, adjectives and adverbs) many: ***polygamy*** ◇ ***polymer***
ⓘ ORIGIN: from Greek *polus* meaning 'much' and *polloi* meaning 'many'

polyester (say pol-i-**ess**-tuh) *noun* (*no plural*)
a strong artificial plastic material used for making clothes, carpets and other products

polygamy (say puh-**lig**-uh-mee) *noun* (*no plural*)
the custom of having more than one wife at the same time ➲ See **monogamy**

polygon (say **pol**-i-guhn) *noun* (*plural* **polygons**) (*maths*)
a flat closed shape with three or more straight sides: *Triangles and hexagons are* ***polygons****.*
▸ **polygonal** (*adjective*): *a* ***polygonal*** *structure*
ⓘ **ORIGIN**: 16th century, through Latin from Greek *polugōnos* meaning 'having many angles'

polyhedron (say pol-i-**hee**-druhn) *noun* (*plural* **polyhedra** or **polyhedrons**) (*maths*)
a solid shape with many flat surfaces: *Prisms and cubes are* ***polyhedrons****.*

polymer (say **pol**-i-mur) *noun* (*plural* **polymers**) (*science*)
a chemical compound that is made of a chain of large **molecules**: *Plastics and proteins are polymers.*

polynomial (say pol-i-**noh**-mi-uhl) *noun* (*plural* **polynomials**) (*maths*)
an expression with more than one term: $3x^4+6y^3-xy+1$ *is a* ***polynomial****.* ➲ See **monomial**

polyrhythm (say **pol**-i-ri*th*-m) *noun* (*plural* **polyrhythms**) (*music*)
a rhythm which makes use of two or more different rhythms at the same time
▸ **polyrhythmic** (*adjective*): *the* ***polyrhythmic*** *structure of African music*

polystyrene (say pol-i-**sty**-reen) *noun* (*no plural*)
soft white plastic that is used for packing things so that they do not get broken

pomegranate (say pom-uh-**gran**-uht) *noun* (*plural* **pomegranates**)
a shiny round fruit that you can eat and that has many bright red seeds inside

pomp *noun* (*no plural*)
the impressive nature of a large official occasion or ceremony: *the* ***pomp*** *and ceremony of the opening of Parliament*

pompous (say **pom**-puhss) *adjective*
showing that you think you are more important than other people, for example by using long words that sound impressive: *a* ***pompous*** *official who loves his own voice*

USAGE The word **pompous** is used in a critical way.

pond *noun* (*plural* **ponds**)
a small area of water: *We have a fish* ***pond*** *in our garden.*

ponder (say **pon**-duh) *verb* (**pondering, pondered**) (*formal*)
to think about something carefully or for a long time: *He* ***pondered*** *over her question for a while before answering.*

pont *noun* (*plural* **ponts**) (*S. African*)
a **ferry** with a flat bottom, which is pulled across a river along a cable

pony (say **poh**-nee) *noun* (*plural* **ponies**)
a small horse

ponytail (say **poh**-ni-tayl) *noun* (*plural* **ponytails**)
long hair that you tie together at the back of your head so that it hangs down

poodle (say **pood**-l) *noun* (*plural* **poodles**)
a type of dog with thick curly fur that is sometimes cut into a special pattern

pool[1] *noun*
1 (*plural* **pools**) a small area of still water, for example in a river or between rocks at the sea: *a rock* ***pool***
2 (*plural* **pools**) = **swimming pool**
3 (*plural* **pools**) a small area of liquid or light on the ground: *She was lying in a* ***pool*** *of blood.*
4 (*no plural*) a game in which two players try to hit coloured balls with numbers on them into pockets on the edge of a large table, using a long stick (called a **cue**)

pool[2] *verb* (**pooling, pooled**)
to collect money or ideas together from different people: *First we'll work in pairs, then we'll* ***pool*** *our ideas.*

poor *adjective* (**poorer, poorest**)
1 not having enough money to live a comfortable life: *She was too* ***poor*** *to buy clothes for her children.* ➲ The noun is **poverty** ➲ **OPPOSITE** **rich** 1
2 a word that you use when you feel sad because somebody has problems: ***Poor*** *Tina! She's feeling ill.*
3 bad: *My grandfather is in very* ***poor*** *health.*

poorly (say **poor**-lee) *adverb*
in a way that is not good enough: *The street is* ***poorly*** *lit.*

pop[1] *noun*
1 (*no plural*) (also **pop music**) modern music that is most popular among young people: *What's your favourite* ***pop*** *group?* ◇ *a* ***pop*** *singer*
2 (*plural* **pops**) a short sudden sound like a small explosion: *The cork came out of the bottle with a loud* ***pop****.*

pop[2] *verb* (**popping, popped**)
1 to burst, or to make something burst, with a short sudden sound like a small explosion: *The*

A B C D E F G H I J K L M N O **P** Q R S T U V W X Y Z

*balloon will **pop** if you put a pin in it.*
2 to come or go somewhere quickly: *She's just **popped** out to the shops.* ◇ *We **popped** in on Ntswaki for a visit.*
pop up (*informal*) to appear suddenly: *In this program the menu **pops** up when you click on the link.*

popcorn (say **pop**-kawn) *noun* (*no plural*)
light white balls made by heating the seeds of a certain type of maize until they pop

pope (say **pohp**) *noun* (*plural* **popes**)
the head of the Roman Catholic Church: *Pope Benedict XVI*

poppy (say **pop**-ee) *noun* (*plural* **poppies**)
a brightly coloured wild flower that has many small black seeds you can eat

popular (say **pop**-yuu-luh) *adjective*
liked by a lot of people or by most of the people in a group: *Football is a **popular** sport in this country.* ➲ OPPOSITE **unpopular**

popularity (say pop-yuu-**la**-ruh-tee) *noun* (*no plural*)
being liked by many people or by most of the people in a group

population (say pop-yuu-**lay**-shuhn) *noun* (*plural* **populations**)
the number of people who live in a place: *What is the **population** of your country?*

porcelain (say **pawss**-luhn) *noun* (*no plural*)
a hard white shiny substance formed by baking clay at very high temperatures and used for expensive cups and plates

porch (say **pawch**) *noun* (*plural* **porches**)
a small area just outside the door of a house or a church, which is covered by a roof and often has walls

porcupine (say **paw**-kyuu-pine) *noun* (*plural* **porcupines**)
an animal covered with long thin sharp points (called **quills**) which it can lift up to protect itself when it is attacked

pore (say **paw**) *noun* (*plural* **pores**)
a tiny opening in a surface through which gases, liquids or fine solids can pass: *We sweat through the **pores** in our skin.*

pork (say **pawk**) *noun* (*no plural*)
meat from a pig: ***pork** sausages*
🛈 **ORIGIN**: 13th–15th century, through Old French *porc*, from Latin *porcus* meaning 'pig'

pornography (say paw-**nog**-ruh-fee) *noun* (*no plural*) (also *informal* **porn**)
books, films, etc. that describe or show naked people or sexual acts in a way that makes a person feel sexually excited
▸ **pornographic** (*adjective*): ***pornographic** magazines*

porous (say **paw**-ruhss) *adjective*
allowing gases, liquid or fine solids to pass through: *Sandy soil is more **porous** than clay soil.*

porpoise (say **paw**-puhss) *noun* (*plural* **porpoises**)
a sea mammal that has a small rounded head and lives in groups. A porpoise is similar to a **dolphin** but smaller.

porridge (say **po**-rij) *noun* (*no plural*)
a soft food made by boiling grain with liquid: *mealie **porridge***

port (say **pawt**) *noun* (*plural* **ports**)
a town or city by the sea, where ships arrive and leave: *Richards Bay is a large **port** in KwaZulu-Natal.*

portable (say **pawt**-uhb-l) *adjective*
able to be moved or carried easily: *a **portable** television*

porter (say **pawt**-uh) *noun* (*plural* **porters**)
1 a person whose job is to carry people's bags in places like railway stations and hotels
2 a person whose job is to look after the entrance of a hotel or other large building

portfolio (say pawt-**foh**-li-oh) *noun* (*plural* **portfolios**)
1 a large thin flat case for carrying maps and drawings
2 examples of work that a learner has produced over a period of time and that shows their progress
3 (*economics*) a collection of things that you **invest** your money in
4 (*politics*) the position or duties of a Minister

porthole (say **pawt**-hohl) *noun* (*plural* **portholes**)
a small round window in the side of a ship

portion (say **paw**-shuhn) *noun* (*plural* **portions**)
a part of something that one person gets: *a large **portion** of chips* ◇ *He gave a **portion** of the money to each of his children.*

portly (say **pawt**-lee) *adjective*
(especially of a man) rather fat: *The **portly** man squeezed into the seat next to me.*

portrait (say **pawt**-ruht) *noun* (*plural* **portraits**)
a painting or picture of a person

portray (say puh-**tray**) *verb* (**portraying, portrayed**)
1 to show a person or a thing in a picture, or to describe a person or a thing in writing
2 to describe a person or a thing in a particular

way: *The press **portrayed** Jake as the victim.*
3 to act the part of a person in a play or a film: *Queen Elizabeth is **portrayed** by Cate Blanchett.* ➲ SYNONYM **depict**

Portuguese (say pawt-yoo-**geez**) *noun* (*no plural*)
the language spoken in Portugal

pose (say **pohz**) *verb* (**posing, posed**)
1 to create a thing that a person has to deal with: *The number of visitors **poses** a threat to the mountain.*
2 to sit or stand in a particular position for a photograph or painting: *I hate **posing** for the camera!*
3 to pretend to be someone or something you are not: *The thief got into the house by **posing** as a telephone company employee.*
4 to behave in a way that is intended to impress people: *He's got a surfboard but he can't surf, he's just **posing**.*
▸ **pose** (*noun*): *The players struck a formal **pose** for their team photo.*

posh *adjective* (**posher, poshest**) (*informal*)
1 expensive and of good quality: *a **posh** restaurant*
2 typical of or used by people who belong to a high social class: *a **posh** accent.*

position (say puh-**zish**-n) *noun* (*plural* **positions**)
1 the place where somebody or something is: *Show me the **position** of your village on the map.*
2 the way that somebody or something is sitting, standing or facing: *in an upright **position*** ◇ *She was still in the same **position** when I came back.*
3 how things are at a certain time: *He's in a difficult **position** – he hasn't got enough money.*
4 a job: *There have been over a hundred applications for the **position** of Sales Manager.*
▸ **position** (*verb*): *Mary **positioned** herself by the door so she could get out quickly.*

positive (say **poz**-uh-tiv) *adjective*
1 thinking or talking about the good parts of a situation: *It's important to have a **positive** attitude.* ◇ *The teacher was very **positive** about my work.* ➲ OPPOSITE **negative**[1] 2
2 good or useful: *The government's support has had a **positive** effect on the industry.*
3 completely certain: *Are you **positive** that you locked the door?* ➲ SYNONYM **sure** 1
4 (used about a number) more than zero: *a **positive** number*
5 (used about a medical or scientific test) showing that something has happened or is present: *The result of the pregnancy test was **positive*** (= she is pregnant). ➲ OPPOSITE **negative**[1] 5

possess (say puh-**zess**) *verb* (**possessing, possessed**) (*formal*)
to have or own something: *He lost everything that he **possessed** in the fire.*

possession (say puh-**zesh**-n) *noun*
1 (*no plural*) (*formal*) the fact of having or owning something: *The **possession** of drugs is a crime.*
2 possessions (*plural noun*) the things that you have or own ➲ SYNONYM **belongings**

SPELLING Remember! You spell **possession** with **ss** and **ss**.

possessive (say puh-**zess**-iv) *adjective*
1 not wanting to share a thing: *Jules is very **possessive** about his toys.*
2 demanding a person's total attention and love: *If you're too **possessive** of your girlfriend, she will leave you.*
3 (*grammar*) used to describe words that show who or what a person or things belongs to: *'My', 'your' and 'her' are **possessive** adjectives.* ◇ *'Mine', 'yours' and 'hers' are **possessive** pronouns.* ➲ See Study page 11

possibility (say poss-uh-**bil**-i-tee) *noun* (*plural* **possibilities**)
something that might happen: *There's a **possibility** that it will rain, so take your umbrella.*

possible (say **poss**-ib-l) *adjective*
able to happen or to be done: *Is it **possible** to get to Upington by train?* ◇ *I'll phone you as soon as **possible**.* ➲ OPPOSITE **impossible**

possibly (say **poss**-ib-lee) *adverb*
1 perhaps: *'Will you be free tomorrow?' '**Possibly**.'*
2 in a way that can be done: *I'll come as soon as I **possibly** can.*

post[1] (say **pohst**) *verb* (**posting, posted**)
1 to send a letter or package by post: *Could you **post** this letter for me?*
2 to send somebody to a place to do a job: *Her company has **posted** her to Japan for two years.*

post[2] (say **pohst**) *noun* (*plural* **posts**)
1 (*no plural*) the official system for sending and receiving letters and packages: *I sent your present by **post**.*
2 (*no plural*) all the letters and packages that you send or receive: *Did you get any **post** this morning?*
3 (*plural* **posts**) a job, especially an important one in a large organization: *a government **post***
4 (*plural* **posts**) a piece of wood or metal that stands in the ground to hold something or to show where something is: *a **signpost*** ◇ *a lamp **post*** ◇ *The sign had fallen off the **post**.*

A B C D E F G H I J K L M N O P Q R S T U V W X Y Z

post- (say **pohst**) *prefix*
(used in nouns, verbs and adjectives) after: *postgraduate* ◇ *post-mortem* ➲ See **pre-**
🛈 **ORIGIN**: from Latin *post* meaning 'after, behind'

postage (say **pohss**-tij) *noun* (*no plural*)
money that you pay to send a letter or package

postal (say **pohss**-tuhl) *adjective*
connected with sending and receiving letters and packages: ***postal** collections*

postal code *noun* (*plural* **postal codes**) (also **postcode**)
a group of numbers or numbers and letters that you write at the end of an address, for example in *PO Box 123, Durban 4000*

postbox (say **pohst**-bokss) *noun* (*plural* **postboxes**) (also **letter box** or **mailbox**)
a box in the street where you put letters that you want to send

postcard (say **pohst**-kaad) *noun* (*plural* **postcards**)
a card with a picture on one side, which you write on and send by post: *She sent me a **postcard** from California.*

poster (say **pohss**-tuh) *noun* (*plural* **posters**)
a big piece of paper on a wall, with a picture or words on it

posterior (say poss-**teer**-ri-uh) *adjective* (*formal*)
located behind a thing or at the back of a thing: *the **posterior** part of the brain* ➲ **OPPOSITE** **anterior**

postgraduate (say pohst-**grad**-yuu-uht) *adjective*
connected with students at a university who have already finished a degree, or the courses they are studying: *a **postgraduate** diploma*
▸ **postgraduate** (*noun*): *My brother is a **postgraduate** at UCT.*

postman (say **pohst**-muhn) *noun* (*plural* **postmen**) (also **postal worker**)
a person whose job is to deliver letters and packages to people's homes

post-mortem (say pohst-**maw**-tuhm) *noun* (*plural* **post-mortems**)
a medical examination of a dead body to find out how the person died
🛈 **ORIGIN**: 18th century, from Latin *post-mortem* meaning 'after death'

post-natal (say **pohst**-nay-tuhl) *adjective*
relating to the time soon after a child has been born: *a **post-natal** check-up* ➲ See **antenatal**

post office *noun* (*plural* **post offices**)
a building where you go to send letters and packages and to buy stamps

postpone (say pohst-**pohn**) *verb* (**postponing**, **postponed**)
to say that something will happen later than you planned: *The match was **postponed** because of bad weather.*
▸ **postponement** (*noun*): *a one-week **postponement***

postscript (say **pohst**-skript) *noun* (*plural* **postscripts**) (abbr. PS)
an extra message that you add at the end of a letter, after your signature

posture (say **poss**-tshuh) *noun* (*no plural*)
the way that a person sits, stands or walks: *Poor **posture** can lead to backache.*

pot *noun* (*plural* **pots**)
1 a deep round container for cooking: *a big **pot** of soup*
2 a container that you use for a special thing: *a **teapot** ◇ a **pot** of paint ◇ a plant **pot***

potable (say **pot**-uhb-l) *adjective* (*formal*)
(used about water) safe to drink

potassium (say puh-**tass**-i-uhm) *noun* (*no plural*) (symbol K)
a soft silver-white metal that is only found in compounds with other elements in nature. It is an important mineral for the development of plants and animals.

potato (say puh-**tay**-toh) *noun* (*plural* **potatoes**)
a white vegetable with a brown or red skin that grows underground: *a baked **potato** ◇ mashed **potato***
🛈 **ORIGIN**: 16th century, through Spanish *patata*, from Taino *batata* meaning 'sweet potato'. Taino is a language that used to be spoken in the Caribbean. The English word originally meant 'sweet potato' and later came to mean the potato we know today.

potato chip *noun* (*plural* **potato chips**)
= **chip**[1] 1

potent (say **poh**-tuhnt) *adjective*
strong or powerful: *a **potent** drug*

potential[1] (say puh-**ten**-shuhl) *adjective*
possible or likely to happen or exist: ***potential** winners*
▸ **potentially** (*adverb*): *a **potentially** dangerous situation*

potential[2] (say puh-**ten**-shuhl) *noun* (*no plural*)
qualities or possibilities that exist and can be developed: *She has great **potential** as a musician.*

potential energy *noun* (*no plural*) (*science*)
the energy that an object has because of its position, its shape or its structure: *An object that*

*has been lifted, a coiled spring, and a ball at the top of a slope all have **potential energy**.*

potjie (say **poy**-kee) *noun* (*plural* **potjies**) (*S. African*)
a round iron pot with a lid and three legs, used to cook food slowly over a fire
🛈 **ORIGIN**: 20th century, from Afrikaans *potjie*, meaning 'little pot'

potter[1] (say **pot**-uh) *verb* (**pottering, pottered**)
to do small jobs or things that you enjoy without hurrying: *I spent the morning **pottering** about the garden*

potter[2] (say **pot**-uh) *noun* (*plural* **potters**)
a person who makes bowls, plates etc. from clay by hand

pottery (say **pot**-uh-ree) *noun* (*no plural*)
1 cups, plates and other things that are made from clay: *This shop sells beautiful **pottery**.*
2 the activity of making cups, plates and other things from clay: *Her hobby is **pottery**.*

pouch (say **powch**) *noun* (*plural* **pouches**)
1 a small leather bag
2 a pocket of skin on the stomach of the female of animals like the **kangaroo** in which they carry their babies

poultry (say **pohl**-tree) *plural noun*
birds such as chickens that people keep on farms for their eggs or their meat

pounce (say **pownss**) *verb* (**pouncing, pounced**)
1 to jump on somebody or something suddenly: *The cat **pounced** on the bird.*
2 to quickly notice something that somebody has said or done, especially in order to criticize it: *He was quick to **pounce** on any mistakes I made.*

pound[1] (say **pownd**) *noun* (*plural* **pounds**)
1 (symbol £) money that people use in Britain. There are 100 **pence** in a **pound**: *a ten-**pound** note ◇ I spent **£40** today.*
2 (abbr. lb) a measure of mass (= 0,454 kilograms) used in Britain and some other countries: *two **pounds** of sugar*
3 a place where the police keep vehicles that have been taken away from their owners

pound[2] (say **pownd**) *verb* (**pounding, pounded**)
1 to hit a thing hard many times making a lot of noise: *We were woken up by somebody **pounding** on the door.*
2 (used about your heart) to beat quickly and loudly: *Her heart was **pounding** with excitement.*
3 to hit a thing many times to beak it into smaller pieces: ***Pound** the seeds into a fine powder.*

pour (say **paw**) *verb* (**pouring, poured**)
1 to make liquid flow out of or into something: *She **poured** water into the teapot. ◇ He **poured** me a cup of tea.*
2 to flow quickly: *Oil **poured** out of the damaged ship.*
3 to rain very hard: *It's **pouring**. ◇ It **poured** with rain all day.*

pout (say **powt**) *verb* (**pouting, pouted**)
to push out your bottom lip or both lips to show that you are annoyed or unhappy: *The child **pouted** when his mother wouldn't give him what he wanted.*

poverty (say **pov**-uh-tee) *noun* (*no plural*)
the state of being poor: *There are many people living in **poverty** in this city.*
🛈 **ORIGIN**: 13th–15th century, through Old French *poverte*, from Latin *pauper* meaning 'poor'

powder (say **pow**-duh) *noun* (*plural* **powders**)
a dry substance like flour that is made of a lot of very small pieces: *washing **powder*** (= for washing clothes) ◇ *Crush the spices to a **powder**.*

power (say **pow**-wuh) *noun*
1 (*no plural*) the energy or strength that somebody or something has: *The President has a lot of **power**. ◇ The ship was helpless against the **power** of the storm.*
2 (*plural* **powers**) a strong person or country: *a meeting of world **powers***
3 (*no plural*) energy that can be collected and used for doing things such as making machines work or for making electricity: *solar **power***
4 (*no plural*) (*science*) the work that is done in a certain period of time: *The speakers of my sound system produce 80 watts of **power**.*
5 (*plural* **powers**) (*maths*) a way of writing the number of times a quantity is multiplied by itself: *4 to the **power** of 3 is* 4^3 *(=4×4×4=64)*

powerful (say **pow**-wuh-fuhl) *adjective*
1 having a lot of strength or power: *The car has a very **powerful** engine.*
2 having a strong effect: *a **powerful** drug*

powerless (say **pow**-wuh-luhss) *adjective*
not able to do anything: *I was **powerless** to help.*

power point *noun* (*plural* **power points**)
a place in a wall where you can connect a lamp or machine to the electricity ➲ **SYNONYM socket**

power station *noun* (*plural* **power stations**)
a place where electricity is made

PR (say pee-**aar**) *abbreviation* **public relations**

practical (say **prak**-tik-l) *adjective*
1 connected with doing or making things, not just with ideas: *We did a **practical** investigation of how heat affects materials.* ◇ *Have you got any **practical** experience of teaching?*
2 sensible, suitable or likely to be successful: *Your plan isn't **practical**.*
➲ OPPOSITE **impractical**
3 good at making and repairing things: *She's a very **practical** person.*

practically (say **prak**-tik-lee) *adverb*
almost or very nearly: *Don't go out – lunch is **practically** ready!*

practice (say **prak**-tiss) *noun* (*no plural*)
doing something many times so that you will do it well: *You need lots of **practice** when you're learning to play a musical instrument.*
out of practice not good at something, because you have not done it for a long time

WHICH WORD? **Practice** or **practise**?
■ Be careful! Don't confuse **practice**, which is a noun, with **practise**, which is a verb: *You need a lot of **practice**. You should **practise** every day.*

practise (say **prak**-tiss) *verb* (**practising, practised**)
to do something many times so that you will do it well: *If you want to play the piano well, you must **practise** every day.* ➲ See note at **practice**

practitioner (say prak-**tish**-uh-nuh) *noun* (*plural* **practitioners**) (*formal*)
a person who works in a profession like medicine or law, or who performs a skilled activity like translating ➲ See **GP**

pragmatic (say prag-**mat**-ik) *adjective*
dealing with problems in a practical way rather than by strictly following ideas or principles: *a **pragmatic** approach*

prairie (say **prair**-ree) *noun* (*plural* **prairies**)
a large area of flat land, especially in North America, that is covered in grass and has few trees

praise (say **prayz**) *verb* (**praising, praised**)
to say that somebody or something is good: *She was **praised** for her hard work.*
▸ **praise** (*noun*): *The book has received a lot of **praise**.*
praise singer = **imbongi**

pram *noun* (*plural* **prams**)
a thing that a baby lies or sits in to go out. It has wheels so that you can push it.

prance (say **praanss**) *verb* (**prancing, pranced**)
to move about with quick exaggerated steps so that people will notice you: *The pop star **pranced** around on stage.*

prank (say **prangk**) *noun* (*plural* **pranks**)
a trick you play on a person as a joke: *He is an adult man but he still loves childish **pranks**.*

prawn (*rhymes with* **born**) *noun* (*plural* **prawns**)
a small sea animal that is pink after it has been cooked

pray *verb* (**praying, prayed**)
to speak to God or a god: *They **prayed** to God for help.*
🛈 ORIGIN: 13th–15th century, through Old French *preier*, from Latin *precari* meaning 'plead, ask earnestly'

prayer (say **prair**) *noun*
1 (*plural* **prayers**) words that you say when you speak to God or a god: *They said a **prayer** for world peace.*
2 (*no plural*) the act of praying: *the power of **prayer*** ◇ *They knelt in **prayer**.*

pre- (say **pree**) *prefix*
(used in verbs, nouns and adjectives) before: ***prepay*** ◇ ***preview*** ◇ ***pre-war*** ➲ See **post-**
🛈 ORIGIN: from Latin *prae-* meaning 'before'

preach (say **preech**) *verb* (**preaching, preached**)
1 to talk about a religious subject, especially in a church
2 to give somebody advice on how to behave, on what is considered morally acceptable, etc., in a way that they find boring or annoying: *I'm sorry, I didn't mean to **preach**.*

preacher (say **preech**-uh) *noun* (*plural* **preachers**)
a person who gives religious talks in public: *Our **preacher** tonight is Reverend Jones.*

precarious (say **pri**-kair-ri-uhss) *adjective*
dangerous or not safe or certain: *That ladder looks **precarious**.* ◇ *His life was quite **precarious** after he lost his job.*

precaution (say pri-**kaw**-shuhn) *noun* (*plural* **precautions**)
something that you do so that bad things will not happen: *I took the **precaution** of locking all the windows when I went out.*

precede (say pri-**seed**) *verb* (**preceding, preceded**)
to happen, come or go before a person or thing: *Look at the table on the **preceding** page.* ◇ *During the weeks **preceding** the big race there were many cyclists training on the roads.*

precedent (say **press**-i-duhnt) *noun* (*plural* **precedents**)
an earlier action or decision that is considered

as an example or a rule to follow in a similar situation later: *If one learner is allowed to come late, it sets a **precedent** that the other learners may want to follow.* ➲ See **unprecedented**

precious (say **presh**-uhss) *adjective*
1 very valuable or expensive: *Diamonds are **precious** stones.*
2 that you consider to be very special: *My family is very **precious** to me.*

precipice (say **press**-i-puhss) *noun* (*plural* **precipices**)
a very steep side of a mountain or cliff

precipitation (say pri-sip-uh-**tay**-shuhn) *noun* (*no plural*)
1 water from the atmosphere that falls to the ground, such as rain and snow: *Hail, mist, sleet, rain and snow are all forms of **precipitation**.*
2 the amount of water falling from the atmosphere: *We had 35 millimetres of **precipitation** yesterday.*
3 the process in which a solid separates from a solution

precipitous (say pri-**sip**-i-tuhss) *adjective*
1 high or steep enough to be dangerous: ***precipitous** cliffs*
2 sudden or dramatic: *a **precipitous** decline in sales*
3 done very quickly, without enough thought or care: ***precipitous** action*

precise (say pri-**sise**) *adjective*
exactly right: *I gave him **precise** instructions on how to get to my house.*

precisely (say pri-**sise**-lee) *adverb*
exactly: *They arrived at two o'clock **precisely**.*

precision (say pri-**sizh**-uhn) *noun* (*no plural*)
the quality of being clear or exact: *The plans were drawn with great **precision**.*

precocious (say pri-**koh**-shuhss) *adjective*
(used about children) having developed certain abilities and ways of behaviour at a much younger age than usual: *a **precocious** child who started her acting career at the age of five* ◇ *Don't be **precocious**; a girl of ten can't wear high heels!*

USAGE This word is often used in a critical way.

precursor (say pri-**kur**-suh) *noun* (*plural* **precursors**)
a person or thing which comes before another of the same kind: *The industrial revolution was a **precursor** to the industrialized world.*

predator (say **pred**-uh-tuh) *noun* (*plural* **predators**)
an animal that kills and eats other animals: *Lions and eagles are both **predators**.*
▸ **predatory** (*adjective*): *a **predatory** bird* ◇ ***predatory** behaviour*

predecessor (say **pree**-di-sess-uh) *noun* (*plural* **predecessors**)
1 the person who did a job or was in a position before the current person: *The new president changed many of the policies of his **predecessor**.*
➲ **OPPOSITE successor**
2 a thing that has been followed or replaced by another

predetermine (say pree-duh-**tur**-min) *verb* (**predetermining, predetermined**) (*formal*)
to decide, agree or arrange in advance the **outcome** of something: *The referee can stop a tennis match if the heat reaches a **predetermined** level.*

predicament (say pri-**dik**-uh-muhnt) *noun* (*plural* **predicaments**)
an unpleasant and difficult situation that is hard to get out of: *a financial **predicament***

predicate (say **pred**-i-kuht) *noun* (*plural* **predicates**) (*grammar*)
the part of a sentence containing the verb and stating something about the subject, for example *went home* in *John went home*

predict (say pri-**dikt**) *verb* (**predicting, predicted**)
to say what you think will happen: *She **predicted** that it would rain, and she was right.*
▸ **prediction** (*noun*): *The results confirmed our **predictions**.* ▸ **predictable** (*adverb*): *a **predictable** outcome*
🛈 **ORIGIN:** 17th century, from Latin *prae-* meaning 'beforehand' + *dicere* meaning 'say'

predominate (say pri-**dom**-i-nayt) *verb* (**predominating, predominated**)
to be most important or greatest in number: *Blue **predominates** the cover of the book.* ◇ *The interests of the school should not **predominate** over the needs of the learners.*

preen *verb* (**preening, preened**)
1 (of a bird) to clean and smooth its feathers with its beak
2 (usually disapproving) to spend a lot of time making yourself look attractive and then admiring your appearance: *Stop **preening** yourself in the mirror like that!*

prefabricated (say pree-**fab**-ri-kayt-d) *adjective*
(especially of a building) made in sections that can be put together later: ***prefabricated** classrooms*

preface (say **pref**-uhss) *noun* (*plural* **prefaces**)
an introduction to a book that explains what it is about or why is was written

A B C D E F G H I J K L M N O **P** Q R S T U V W X Y Z

prefect (say **pree**-fekt) *noun* (*plural* **prefects**)
an older student in a school who has duties such as making sure that younger students behave

prefer (say pri-**fur**) *verb* (**preferring, preferred**)
to like one thing or person better than another: *Would you **prefer** tea or coffee?* ◇ *I would **prefer** to stay at home.* ◇ *He **prefers** going out to studying.*

preferable (say **pref**-ruhb-l) *adjective*
better or more suitable: *I think living in the country is **preferable** to living in the city.*
▸ **preferably** (*adverb*): *Phone me on Sunday, but **preferably** not too early!*

preference (say **pref**-uh-ruhnss) *noun* (*plural* **preferences**)
a feeling that you like one thing or person better than another: *We have lemonade and orange juice – do you have a **preference**?*

prefix (say **pree**-fikss) *noun* (*plural* **prefixes**) (*grammar*)
a group of letters that you add to the beginning of a word to make another word: *The **prefix** 'im-' means 'not', so 'impossible' means 'not possible'.* ➲ See Study page 12 ➲ See **suffix**

pregnancy (say **preg**-nuhn-see) *noun* (*plural* **pregnancies**)
the state of being pregnant: *Many women feel sick during **pregnancy**.*

pregnant (say **preg**-nuhnt) *adjective*
If a woman is **pregnant**, she has a baby growing in her body: *She's five months **pregnant**.*

prehistoric (say pree-hiss-**to**-rik) *adjective*
from the time in the past before events were written down: *a **prehistoric** burial site* (= a place where dead bodies were put in the ground)

prejudice (say **prej**-uh-diss) *noun* (*plural* **prejudices**)
a strong idea that you do not like somebody or something, for a reason that is wrong or unfair: *She was a victim of racial **prejudice**.*

prejudiced (say **prej**-uh-dist) *adjective*
having a strong idea that you do not like somebody or something, for a reason that is wrong or unfair: *He is **prejudiced** against me because I'm a woman.*

preliminary (say pri-**lim**-i-nuh-ree) *adjective*
coming or happening before something else that is more important: ***preliminary** results*
▸ **preliminary** (*noun*): *Bafana Bafana got through the **preliminaries** safely.*

prelude (say **prel**-yood) *noun* (*plural* **preludes**)
1 a short piece of music, especially an introduction to a longer piece
2 an action or an event that happens before something more important or serves as an introduction to it: *The performance by the dancers served as a **prelude** to the main event.*

premature (say prem-uh-**tyoor**) *adjective*
1 happening before the normal or expected time: *Her baby was born a month **premature**.*
2 acting or happening too soon: *It's **premature** to talk of success at this stage.*

premeditated (say pree-**med**-i-tayt-d) *adjective*
(used especially of a crime) planned in advance: *a **premeditated** attack*

premier[1] (say **pree**-mi-uh) *adjective*
best or most important: *the **Premier** Soccer League*

premier[2] (say **pree**-mi-uh) *noun* (*plural* **premiers**)
(in South Africa) the leader of the government of a **province**

premiere (say **prem**-i-ay) *noun* (*plural* **premieres**)
the first public performance of a film or play: *Special guests attended the **premiere** of the play.*

premises (say **prem**-iss-uhz) *plural noun*
the building and the land around it that a business owns or uses: *commercial **premises***

premium (say **pree**-mi-uhm) *noun* (*plural* **premiums**)
an amount of money that you pay regularly to a company for insurance against accidents, damage or **theft**

premonition (say prem-uh-**nish**-n) *noun* (*plural* **premonitions**)
a feeling that something unpleasant is going to happen in the future: *a **premonition** of disaster*

preoccupied (say pree-**ok**-yuu-pide) *adjective*
not paying attention to a person or a thing because you are thinking or worrying about another person or thing: *He is too **preoccupied** with his work to think of his family.*

preparation (say prep-uh-**ray**-shuhn) *noun*
1 (*no plural*) making something ready: *I packed my bags in **preparation** for the journey.*
2 preparations (*plural noun*) what you do to get ready for something: *They began to make **preparations** for the wedding last year.*

prepare (say pri-**pair**) *verb* (**preparing, prepared**)
to make somebody, something or yourself ready: *He is in the kitchen **preparing** the dinner.* ◇ *I **prepared** well for the exam.*

prepared (say pri-**paird**) *adjective*
ready, or able to deal with something: *I wasn't **prepared** for all these problems.*
prepared to do something happy to do something: *I'm not **prepared** to give you any money.* ➲ SYNONYM **willing**

preposition (say prep-uh-**zish**-n) *noun* (*plural* **prepositions**) (*grammar*)
a word that you use to show where, when or how, etc. A **preposition** is usually followed by a noun or pronoun: *In the sentence 'He travelled from Johannesburg to Munich', 'from' and 'to' are **prepositions**.* ➲ See Study pages 4 and 9

preposterous (say pri-**poss**-tuh-ruhss) *adjective*
1 unreasonable and without **common sense**: *a **preposterous** suggestion*
2 ridiculous or **absurd**: *You look **preposterous** in those silly clothes.*

prescribe (say pri-**skribe**) *verb* (**prescribing, prescribed**)
to say that somebody must take a medicine: *The doctor **prescribed** some tablets.*

prescription (say pri-**skrip**-shuhn) *noun* (*plural* **prescriptions**)
a piece of paper that a doctor gives to you with the name of your medicine on it

presence (say **prez**-uhnss) *noun* (*no plural*)
the fact of being in a place: *an experiment to test for the **presence** of oxygen* ◇ *Mother did not allow arguing in her **presence*** (= when she was there).

present¹ (say **prez**-uhnt) *adjective*
1 in a place: *The whole class was **present**.* ➲ OPPOSITE **absent**
2 being or happening now: *What is your **present** job?* ➲ SYNONYM **current¹**

PRONUNCIATION Notice how you pronounce the noun, the adjective and the verb.

present² (say **prez**-uhnt) *noun*
1 (*plural* **presents**) something that you give to somebody or get from somebody: *What can I get him as a birthday **present**?* ➲ SYNONYM **gift**
2 (*no plural*) the time now: *I can't help you at **present** – I'm too busy.* ➲ See **past²**
3 the present (*no plural*) (also **the present tense**) (*grammar*) the form of a verb that you use to talk about what is happening or what exists now

present³ (say pri-**zent**) *verb* (**presenting, presented**)
to give something to somebody, especially in a formal ceremony: *The prizes were **presented** to the winners.* ◇ *They **presented** their teacher with some flowers.*

presentation (say prez-uhn-**tay**-shuhn) *noun* (*plural* **presentations**)
1 the act of giving something to somebody, especially in a formal ceremony: *The **presentation** of prizes took place at 7.30.*
2 a meeting where somebody shows or explains something to the people listening: *Each student gave a **presentation**.*

presenter (say pri-**zent**-uh) *noun* (*plural* **presenters**)
a person whose job is to introduce programmes on television or radio

presently (say **prez**-uhnt-lee) *adverb*
1 soon: *He will be here **presently**.*
2 now: *She's **presently** working in a cafe.*

present participle *noun* (*plural* **present participles**) (*grammar*)
the form of a verb that ends in *-ing*: *'Walking' is the **present participle** of 'walk'.*
➲ See Study pages 6–8

present tense *noun* (*no plural*) (also **the present**) (*grammar*)
the forms of a verb that you use to talk about what is happening or what exists now: *'She is a teacher' and 'We are learning about insects' are sentences in the **present tense**.*
➲ See Study page 6

preservation (say prez-uh-**vay**-shuhn) *noun* (*no plural*)
the act of keeping something safe or in good condition: *the **preservation** of rare birds*

preserve (say pri-**zurv**) *verb* (**preserving, preserved**)
to keep something safe or in good condition: *They managed to **preserve** most of the paintings.*

president (say **prez**-i-duhnt) *noun* (*plural* **presidents**)
1 the leader of a country that does not have a king or queen (called a **republic**): *the **President** of the United States of America*
2 (in the USA) the person with the highest position in an organization or a company
▸ **presidential** (*adjective*): *the **presidential** elections*

press¹ *noun*
1 the press (*no plural*) newspapers and magazines and the people who write them: *She told her story to the **press**.*
2 (*plural* **presses**) a machine for printing things like books and newspapers
3 (*plural* **presses**) the act of pushing something: *Give the doorbell a **press**.*

press² *verb* (**pressing, pressed**)
1 to push something: *If you **press** this button,*

A B C D E F G H I J K L M N O **P** Q R S T U V W X Y Z

the door will open. ◇ *She **pressed** her face against the window.*
2 to make clothes flat and smooth using an iron: *This suit needs **pressing**.*

press-up (say **press**-up) *noun* (*plural* **press-ups**)
a type of exercise in which you lie on your front and push your body up with your arms: *I do twenty **press-ups** every morning.*

pressure (say **presh**-uh) *noun*
1 (*no plural*) the amount of force that presses on a particular area: *The **pressure** of the water caused the dam wall to crack.*
2 (*plural* **pressures**) the force that a gas or liquid has when it is contained inside something: *He has high blood **pressure*** (= the force with which blood travels round your body). ◇ *You should check the tyre **pressure*** (= the amount of air in the car tyres) *regularly.*
3 (*plural* **pressures**) a feeling of worry because of the things you have to do: *financial **pressures*** ◇ *She's under a lot of **pressure** at work.*

prestige (say pruhss-**teej**) *noun* (*no plural*)
the respect felt for a person because of their success or social position: *There is a lot of **prestige** attached to that job.*

presume (say pri-**zyoom**) *verb* (**presuming, presumed**)
to think that something is true, even though you are not certain: *She's not home yet so I **presume** she's still at work.*

pretend (say pri-**tend**) *verb* (**pretending, pretended**)
to try to make somebody believe something that is not true: *He **pretended** to be asleep.* ◇ *I **pretended** that I was enjoying myself.*

pretty[1] (say **prit**-ee) *adverb* (*informal*) to some extent or fairly: *It's **pretty** cold today.*

pretty[2] (say **prit**-ee) *adjective* (**prettier, prettiest**)
nice to look at or attractive: *a **pretty** little girl* ◇ *These flowers are very **pretty**.* ➲ See note at **beautiful**

prevail (say pri-**vayl**) *verb* (**prevailing, prevailed**)
1 to exist or be common in a particular place or at a particular time: *We were horrified at the conditions **prevailing** in the refugee camp.*
2 (*formal*) to win or be accepted, especially after a fight or discussion: *In the end justice **prevailed** over their evil deeds.*
▸ **prevailing** (*adjective*): *In summer the **prevailing** wind is from the south-east.*

prevalent (say **prev**-uh-luhnt) *adjective* (*formal*)
most common in a particular place or at a particular time: *The **prevalent** atmosphere was one of distrust.*

prevent (say pri-**vent**) *verb* (**preventing, prevented**)
to stop somebody from doing something, or to stop something happening: *Her parents want to **prevent** her from getting married.* ◇ *It is easier to **prevent** disease than to cure it.*

prevention (say pri-**ven**-shuhn) *noun* (*no plural*)
stopping somebody from doing something or stopping something from happening: *crime **prevention*** ◇ *the **prevention** of cruelty to animals*

preview (say **pree**-vyoo) *noun* (*plural* **previews**)
1 a chance to see a play, a film or a show before it is shown to the general public
2 a chance to see what something will be like before it happens or is shown: *Click on the print **preview** button.*

previous (say **pree**-vi-uhss) *adjective*
coming or happening before or earlier: *Who was the **previous** owner of the car?*
▸ **previously** (*adverb*)

prey (say **pray**) *noun* (*no plural*)
an animal or bird that another animal or bird kills for food: *Zebra are **prey** for lions.*

price (say **prise**) *noun* (*plural* **prices**)
how much money you pay to buy something: *'How much is it?' 'The **price** is R15.'* ◇ ***Prices** in this country are very high.*

priceless (say **prise**-luhss) *adjective*
extremely valuable: ***priceless** jewels*

prick (say **prik**) *verb* (**pricking, pricked**)
to make a very small hole in something, or to hurt somebody, with a sharp point: *I **pricked** my finger on a needle.*
▸ **prick** (*noun*): *She felt the **prick** of a needle.*

prickle (say **prik**-l) *noun* (*plural* **prickles**)
a sharp point on a plant or an animal: *A cactus and a porcupine both have **prickles**.*
▸ **prickly** (*adjective*): *a **prickly** cactus*

pride *noun* (*no plural*)
1 the feeling that you are proud of something that you or others have got or have done: *She showed us her painting with great **pride**.*
2 the feeling that you are better than other people

priest (say **preest**) *noun* (*plural* **priests**)
a person who leads people in their religion: *a Catholic **priest*** ◇ *a Buddhist **priest***

prim *adjective*
(used about a person) always behaving in a careful and formal way and easily shocked by anything that is rude: *a **prim** and proper lady*

prima donna (say pree-muh **don**-uh) *noun* (*plural* **prima donnas**)
1 (*music*) the chief female singer in an opera
2 (disapproving) a person who is very talented and important in their own eyes and who behaves badly when they cannot get what they want
ORIGIN: 18th century, from Italian *prima donna*, meaning 'first lady'

primary (say **prime**-uh-ree) *adjective*
first or most important: *The **primary** aim of this course is to improve your spoken English.*

primary school *noun* (*plural* **primary schools**)
a school, usually for learners from Grade R or Grade 1 to Grade 7 ➲ See **secondary school**

primate (say **pry**-mayt) *noun* (*plural* **primates**)
any animal that belongs to the group that includes humans, monkeys and **apes**: *All **primates** have flexible hands.*

prime (*rhymes with* **time**) *adjective*
1 main, most important or most suitable: *the **prime** candidate for the job*
2 of the best quality: *a **prime** cut of beef*
3 having all the typical characteristics of a thing: *a **prime** example*

prime minister *noun* (*plural* **prime ministers**)
the leader of the government in some countries, for example in Britain

prime number *noun* (*plural* **prime numbers**) (*maths*)
a number that can be divided only by itself and by one. Examples of **prime numbers** are 3 and 17.

primitive (say **prim**-i-tuhv) *adjective*
very simple or not developed: ***primitive** beliefs* ◇ *The cooking facilities were very **primitive**.*

prince (say **prinss**) *noun* (*plural* **princes**)
1 a man in a royal family, especially the son of a king or queen: *the **Prince** of Wales*
2 a man from a royal family who is the ruler of a small country

princess (say prin-**sess**) *noun* (*plural* **princesses**)
a woman in a royal family, especially the daughter of a king or queen or the wife of a prince

principal[1] (say **prin**-sip-l) *adjective*
most important: *My **principal** reason for going to Rome was to learn Italian.*

SPELLING Be careful! Don't confuse **principal** and **principle**, which sound similar but have different meanings.

principal[2] (say **prin**-sip-l) *noun* (*plural* **principals**)
a person who is in charge of a school or college

principally (say **prin**-sip-lee) *adverb*
mainly or mostly: *She sometimes travels to Europe, but she works **principally** in Africa.*

principle (say **prin**-sip-l) *noun* (*plural* **principles**)
1 a rule about how you should live: *He has very strong **principles**.* ◇ *I refuse to lie about it; it's against my **principles**.*
2 a rule or fact about how something happens or works: *scientific **principles***

SPELLING Be careful! Don't confuse **principle** and **principal**, which sound similar but have different meanings.

print[1] (say **print**) *verb* (**printing**, **printed**)
1 to put words or pictures onto paper using a machine. Books, newspapers and magazines are **printed**.
2 to write with letters that are not joined together: *Please **print** your name and address clearly.*

print[2] (say **print**) *noun*
1 (*no plural*) letters that a machine makes on paper: *The **print** is too small to read without my glasses.*
2 (*plural* **prints**) a mark where something has pressed on something: *muddy **footprints** on the carpet* ◇ *The police are looking for **prints*** (= fingerprints).
3 (*plural* **prints**) a copy on paper of a painting or a photograph

printer (say **print**-uh) *noun* (*plural* **printers**)
1 a machine that prints words from a computer
2 a person or company that prints things such as books or newspapers

printout (say **print**-owt) *noun* (*plural* **printouts**)
information from a computer that is printed onto paper

prior (say **pry**-uh) *adjective*
coming before in time, order or importance: ***prior** approval* ◇ ***prior** arrangement* ◇ ***prior** knowledge*

priority (say pry-**o**-ruh-tee) *noun*
1 (*plural* **priorities**) something that you think is more important than other things and that you must do first: *Education is a top **priority**.*
2 (*no plural*) being more important than somebody or something or coming before somebody or something else: *We give **priority** to families with small children.* ◇ *Emergency cases take **priority** over other patients in hospital.*

prise (say **prize**) *verb* (**prising, prised**)
to use force to open or remove a thing: *We had to **prise** open the swollen door.*

prism (say **priz**-uhm) *noun* (*plural* **prisms**)
1 (*maths*) a solid object with ends that are parallel and of the same size and shape, and with sides whose opposite edges are equal and parallel
2 (*technology*) a transparent glass or plastic object with flat surfaces, which separates light that passes through it into seven different colours

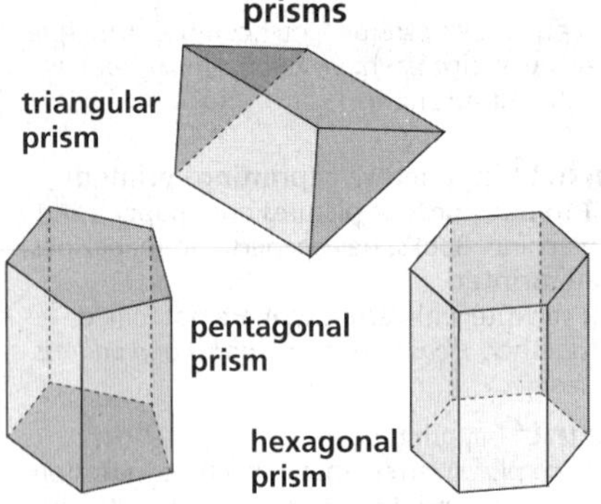

prison (say **priz**-uhn) *noun* (*plural* **prisons**)
a place where criminals must stay as a punishment: *He was sent to **prison** for robbing a bank.* ◇ *She was in **prison** for 15 years.*
➲ SYNONYM **jail**

prisoner (say **priz**-uh-nuh) *noun* (*plural* **prisoners**)
a person who is in prison as a punishment or a person who is not free: *How many **prisoners** are in the jail?* ◇ *He was taken **prisoner** by rebel soldiers.* ➲ SYNONYM **captive**

pristine (say **priss**-teen) *adjective*
1 fresh and clean or as if new: *The car is in a **pristine** condition.*
2 unspoilt or in its original condition: *a **pristine** beach free of litter*

private (say **pry**-vuht) *adjective*
1 for one person or a small group of people only, and not for anybody else: *You shouldn't read his letters – they're **private**.* ◇ *This is **private** property.*
2 without other people there: *I had a **private** meeting with the teacher.*
3 not connected with your job: *She never talks about her **private** life at work.*
4 not controlled or paid for by the government: *a **private** hospital* ◇ ***private** schools*
in private without other people there: *Can I speak to you in **private**?*
▸ **privately** (*adverb*)

privatize (say **pry**-vuh-tize) *verb* (**privatizing, privatized**) (also **privatise**)
to sell a business, industry or service owned by the government to a private company
➲ OPPOSITE **nationalize**

privilege (say **priv**-uh-lij) *noun* (*plural* **privileges**)
something special that only one person or a few people may do or have: *The Grade 7 learners have special **privileges**.*
▸ **privileged** (*adjective*): *I feel very **privileged** to be playing for the first team.*

prize[1] *noun* (*plural* **prizes**)
something that you give to the person who wins a game, race or competition: *I won first **prize** in the painting competition.* ◇ *Did you win a **prize**?*

prize[2] *verb* (**prizing, prized**)
to consider a thing to be very valuable: *She **prizes** honesty above all else.*

pro (say **proh**) *noun* (*plural* **pros**) (*informal*)
1 a person who plays sport for money: *She became a **pro** when she turned 18.*
2 a person who does something very well: *He's a real **pro** in the kitchen.* ❶ **Pro** is short for 'professional'.

pro- (say **proh**) *prefix*
(used in adjectives) in favour of or supporting: ***pro-democracy*** ◇ ***pro-choice***
❶ ORIGIN: from Latin

probability (say prob-uh-**bil**-i-tee) *noun* (*plural* **probabilities**)
1 a measure of how likely it is that something will happen, expressed in words or numbers: *There is a 75% **probability** that it will rain today.*
2 the state that something is likely to happen: *It seemed that war was a **probability**.*

probable (say **prob**-uhb-l) *adjective*
likely to happen or to be true: *It is **probable** that he will be late.* ➲ OPPOSITE **improbable**

probably (say **prob**-uhb-lee) *adverb*
almost certainly: *I will **probably** see you on Thursday.*

problem (say **prob**-luhm) *noun* (*plural* **problems**)
1 something that is difficult or that makes you worry: *She has a lot of **problems**. Her husband is ill and her son is in prison.* ◇ *There is a **problem** with my telephone.*
2 a question that you must answer by thinking about it: *I can't solve this maths **problem**.*

PRONUNCIATION Notice that this is pronounced **prob**-luhm (not **prohb**-lem). The first syllable rhymes with **rob**, not **no**.

proboscis (say pruh-**boh**-siss) *noun* (*plural* **probosces** or **proboscises**)
a long tube connected to the head or mouth of an animal, usually used for feeding: *Mosquitoes use their* ***proboscis*** *for sucking blood.* ◇ *an elephant's* ***proboscis***

procedure (say pruh-**see**-dyuh) *noun* (*plural* **procedures**)
the usual or correct way of doing a thing: *What's the* ***procedure*** *for booking the hall?*

proceed (say pruh-**seed**) *verb* (**proceeding, proceeded**) (*formal*)
1 to continue doing something: *We don't want to* ***proceed*** *with this project.*
2 to do something next, after having done something else first: *After supper, he* ***proceeded*** *to tell us a story.*

process (say **proh**-sess) *noun* (*plural* **processes**)
a number of actions, one after the other, for doing or making something: *He explained the* ***process*** *of building a boat.* ◇ *Learning a language is usually a slow* ***process****.*

procession (say pruh-**sesh**-n) *noun* (*plural* **processions**)
a line of people, cars, etc. that are moving slowly along, usually as part of a ceremony: *We watched the carnival* ***procession****.*

procrastinate (say pruh-**krass**-ti-nayt) *verb* (**procrastinating, procrastinated**) (*formal*)
put off doing a thing that you should do, usually because you do not want to do it: *Stop* ***procrastinating*** *– soon you will run out of time!*

procure (say pruh-**kyoor**) *verb* (**procuring, procured**) (*formal*)
to obtain a thing, especially with great effort: *I managed to* ***procure*** *two tickets for the match.*

prod[1] *verb* (**prodding, prodded**)
1 to push or press a person or a thing with your finger or a pointed object: *He* ***prodded*** *the body under the blankets.*
2 to try to make somebody do something, especially when they do not want to do it: *Joan works quite hard, but she does require* ***prodding*** *occasionally.*

prod[2] *noun* (*plural* **prods**)
1 the act of pushing a person or a thing with your finger or with a pointed object
2 an act of making somebody do something or of reminding somebody to do something
3 an instrument like a long stick: *a cattle* ***prod***

prodigy (say **prod**-uh-jee) *noun* (*plural* **prodigies**)
a young person who is unusually good at something: *She was a swimming* ***prodigy*** *as a teenager.*

produce[1] (say pruh-**dyooss**) *verb* (**producing, produced**)
1 to make or grow something: *This factory* ***produces*** *cars.* ◇ *What does the farm* ***produce****?*
2 to make something happen: *His hard work* ***produced*** *good results.*
3 to bring something out to show it: *She* ***produced*** *a ticket from her pocket.*
4 to organize something like a play or film: *The play was* ***produced*** *by Peter Gordon.*

produce[2] (say **prod**-yooss) *noun* (*no plural*)
food that you grow on a farm or in a garden to sell: *fresh farm* ***produce***

producer (say pruh-**dyoo**-suh) *noun* (*plural* **producers**)
1 a person who organizes something like a play or a film: *a television* ***producer***
2 a company or country that makes or grows something: *Brazil is an important* ***producer*** *of coffee.*

product (say **prod**-ukt) *noun* (*plural* **products**)
something that people make or grow to sell: *The company has just launched a new* ***product****.*

production (say pruh-**duk**-shuhn) *noun*
1 (*no plural*) the action of making or growing something: *the* ***production*** *of oil*
2 (*plural* **productions**) a play, film, concert or show: *an excellent* ***production***

productive (say pruh-**duk**-tiv) *adjective*
doing, achieving or producing a lot: *The meeting was very* ***productive***
▸ **productivity** (*noun*): *The* ***productivity*** *of the land depends on the rain.*

profession (say pruh-**fesh**-n) *noun* (*plural* **professions**)
a job that needs a lot of studying and special training: *She's a doctor by* ***profession****.*

> SPELLING Remember! You spell **profession**, **professional** and **professor** with one **f** and **ss**.

professional[1] (say pruh-**fesh**-uhn-l) *adjective*
1 connected with a profession: *I got* ***professional*** *advice from a lawyer.*
2 doing something for money as a job: *a* ***professional*** *footballer*
3 showing that you are well trained and skilful: *a* ***professional*** *performance*

professional[2] (say pruh-**fesh**-uhn-l) *noun* (*plural* **professionals**)
1 a person who does an activity or plays a sport for money as a job ➲ OPPOSITE **amateur**
2 a person who has a job that needed a lot of studying and special training: *doctors and other health* ***professionals***

professor (say pruh-**fess**-uh) *noun* (*plural* **professors**)
a university teacher of the highest level: *This is **Professor** Olivier.* ◇ *He's a **professor** of Psychology at the university.*

proficient (say pruh-**fish**-uhnt) *adjective*
skilled or able to do a particular thing well: *We are looking for someone who is **proficient** in isiXhosa.*

profile (say **proh**-file) *noun* (*plural* **profiles**)
1 the shape of a person's face when you see it from the side
2 a description of a person or thing that gives useful information: *a **profile** of the killer* ◇ *a job **profile***

profit[1] (say **prof**-it) *noun* (*plural* **profits**)
money that you get when you sell something for more than it cost to buy or make: *They made a **profit** of R10 that day.* ➲ OPPOSITE **loss** 2

profit[2] (say **prof**-it) *verb* (**profiting, profited**) (*formal*)
to get an advantage from something or to give a person an advantage: *Commuters ought to **profit** from a drop in the petrol price.*

profitable (say **prof**-it-uhb-l) *adjective*
If something is **profitable**, it brings you money: *a **profitable** business* ➲ SYNONYM **lucrative**

profound (say pruh-**fownd**) *adjective*
1 very great or that you feel very strongly: *The result of the election had a **profound** effect on the country.*
2 needing or showing a lot of knowledge or thought: *a **profound** statement about the meaning of life*

progeny (say **proj**-uh-nee) *noun* (*no plural*)
all your children and their children, etc.: *He died without **progeny**.*

prognosis (say prog-**noh**-siss) *noun* (*plural* **prognoses**)
1 an opinion, based on medical experience, of the likely development of a disease or an illness
2 (*formal*) a judgement about how a thing is likely to develop in the future: *The **prognosis** about climate change is gloomy.*

program[1] (say **proh**-gram) *noun* (*plural* **programs**) (*computing*)
a set of instructions that you give to a computer: *Load the **program** into the computer.*

> SPELLING Be careful! Don't confuse **program** and **programme**, which have different meanings. Note that in American spelling, **program** is used for all senses of the word.

program[2] (say **proh**-gram) *verb* (**programming, programmed**) (*computing*)
to give a set of instructions to a computer

programme (say **proh**-gram) *noun* (*plural* **programmes**)
1 something on television or radio: *Did you watch that **programme** about Japan on TV?*
2 a piece of paper or a little book that tells people at a play or concert what they are going to see or hear
3 a plan of things to do: *What is your **programme** for tomorrow?*

programmer (say **proh**-gram-uh) *noun* (*plural* **programmers**) (also **computer programmer**)
a person whose job is to write programs for a computer

progress[1] (say proh-**gress**) *verb* (**progressing, progressed**)
1 to improve or develop: *Learners can **progress** at their own speed.*
2 to continue or move forward: *She became more tired as the evening **progressed**.*
ⓘ ORIGIN: 14th–15th century, from Latin *progressus* meaning 'moving forward' from *pro-* meaning 'forward' + *gradi* meaning 'to walk'

progress[2] (say **proh**-gress) *noun* (*no plural*)
1 improvement or development: *He has made good **progress** in maths this year.*
2 movement forward: *She watched the tortoise's slow **progress** across the road.*
in progress happening now: *Quiet please – there's an examination in **progress**.*

progression (say pruh-**gresh**-n) *noun* (*plural* **progressions**)
movement forward or a development from one stage to another: ***progression** from the beginner to intermediate class*

progressive (say pruh-**gress**-iv) *adjective*
1 using modern methods and ideas: *a **progressive** school*
2 happening or developing steadily: *There's a **progressive** decline in malnutrition.*
3 (*grammar*) connected with the form of a verb that describes an action that continues for a period of time, for example in the sentence 'It is raining' ➲ See Study pages 6 and 7

prohibit (say pruh-**hib**-uht) *verb* (**prohibiting, prohibited**) (*formal*)
to say that people must not do something: *Smoking is **prohibited** in banks and shops.* ➲ SYNONYM **forbid**
▸ **prohibition** (*noun*)

project[1] (say **proj**-ekt) *noun* (*plural* **projects**)
1 a piece of work that you do at school. You find out a lot about something and write about

it: *We did a **project** on pollution.*
2 a big plan to do something: *a **project** to build a new airport* ◇ *The research **project** will be funded by the government.*

PRONUNCIATION Notice that this is pronounced **proj**-ekt (not **proh**-jekt).

project² (say pruh-**jekt**) *verb* (**projecting, projected**)
1 (usually passive) to plan a thing that will happen in the future: *The book's release is **projected** for March.*
2 (usually passive) to guess or calculate the size, cost or amount of a thing: *the company's **projected** sales for the year ahead*
3 to make light or an image appear on a flat surface or a screen
4 to present yourself in a certain way, especially one that creates a good impression: *The team **projects** an air of confidence.*
5 (*formal*) to stick out: *The balcony **projects** from the wall.*
6 to throw something upwards or away from you: *Actors learn to **project** their voice.*

projection (say pruh-**jek**-shuhn) *noun* (*plural* **projections**)
1 a guess about a future situation based on the present situation: *sales **projections** for the next five years*
2 the act of making a light or an image appear on a surface
3 a solid shape or object as it is represented on a flat surface: *A map **projection** turns the spherical surface of the Earth into a flat map.*

projector (say pruh-**jek**-tuh) *noun* (*plural* **projectors**)
a machine that shows films or pictures on a wall or screen

prolific (say pruh-**lif**-ik) *adjective*
(especially of a writer, as artist or a sportsperson) producing a lot: *a **prolific** goal scorer*

prologue (say **proh**-log) *noun* (*plural* **prologues**)
a piece of writing or a speech that introduces a play, novel or poem ➲ See **epilogue**

prolong (say pruh-**long**) *verb* (**prolonging, prolonged**)
to make something last longer: *The treatment could **prolong** the patient's life.*

promenade (say **prom**-uh-naad) *noun* (*plural* **promenades**)
a wide path that people walk along beside the sea in a town on the coast

prominent (say **prom**-i-nuhnt) *adjective*
1 easy to see, for example because it is bigger than usual: ***prominent** teeth*
2 important and famous: *a **prominent** writer*

promiscuous (say pruh-**miss**-kyuu-uhss) *adjective*
(disapproving) having sex with many people: ***promiscuous** behaviour* ◇ *a **promiscuous** lifestyle*

promise¹ (say **prom**-iss) *verb* (**promising, promised**)
to say that you will certainly do or not do something: *She **promised** to give me the money today.* ◇ *I **promise** that I'll come.* ◇ ***Promise** me you won't be late!*

promise² (say **prom**-iss) *noun* (*plural* **promises**)
when you say that you will certainly do or not do something: *He kept his **promise*** (= did what he said he would). ◇ *You broke your **promise** – how can I trust you?*

promising (say **prom**-i-sing) *adjective*
showing signs of becoming very good or successful: *a **promising** young artist*

promontory (say **prom**-uhn-tree) *noun* (*plural* **promontories**) (*geography*)
a long narrow area of high land that goes out into the sea

promote (say pruh-**moht**) *verb* (**promoting, promoted**)
1 to encourage something, or to help something to happen or develop: *The band is **promoting** sales of their new album.* ◇ *The organization **promotes** literacy in young learners.*
2 to move a learner to a higher grade at the end of the year or to give somebody a more important job: *He has been **promoted** to Grade 6.* ◇ *She worked hard, and after a year she was **promoted** to manager.* ➲ OPPOSITE **demote**
3 to sell a product or make it more popular by advertising it or offering it at a special price
▸ **promotion** (*noun*): *The new job is a **promotion** for me.*

prompt¹ (say **prompt**) *adjective*
quick: *She gave me a **prompt** answer.*

prompt² (say **prompt**) *verb* (**prompting, prompted**)
1 to make a person decide to do something or to cause something to happen: *What **prompted** his angry mood?*
2 to encourage somebody to speak by asking questions: *The learner remembered the answer when the teacher **prompted** him.*

promptly (say **prompt**-lee) *adverb*
1 without delay: *She replied to her emails **promptly**.*
2 exactly at the correct time or at the time agreed on: *We arrived **promptly** at two o'clock.*

A B C D E F G H I J K L M N O P Q R S T U V W X Y Z

3 almost immediately: *She **promptly** burst into tears when he insulted her.*

prong *noun* (*plural* **prongs**)
1 each of the two or more long pointed parts of a fork
2 each of the separate parts of an attack or argument that approach a place of subject from different positions: *a three-**pronged** attack*

pronoun (say **proh**-nown) *noun* (*plural* **pronouns**) (*grammar*)
a word that you use in place of a noun: *'He', 'it', 'me' and 'them' are all **pronouns**.* ➲ See Study pages 4 and 11

pronounce (say pruh-**nownss**) *verb* (**pronouncing, pronounced**)
to make the sound of a letter or word: *How do you **pronounce** your name?* ◇ *You don't **pronounce** the 'b' at the end of 'comb'.*

pronunciation (say pruh-nun-si-**ay**-shuhn) *noun* (*plural* **pronunciations**)
how you say a word or words: *What's the correct **pronunciation** of this word?* ◇ *His **pronunciation** is very good.*

PRONUNCIATION Be careful! Notice the difference in the way **pronounce** and **pronunciation** are said.

SPELLING There is a also a tricky difference in the way **pronounce** and **pronunciation** are spelt.

proof *noun* (*no plural*)
something that shows that an idea is true: *Do you have any **proof** that you are the owner of this car?* ➲ The verb is **prove**

prop[1] *noun* (*plural* **props**)
1 a stick or other object that you use to support a thing or to keep a thing in position: *Rescue workers used **props** to stop the tunnel from falling in.*
2 an object used by actors during the performance of a play or film: *We need a table and a pile of books as **props**.*

prop[2] *verb* (**propping, props**)
to support a person or a thing or keep a person or a thing in position by putting them against or on a thing: *He **propped** the window open with a piece of wood.*
prop up to support (a thing) that would otherwise fall

propaganda (say prop-uh-**gan**-duh) *noun* (*no plural*)
(usually disapproving) statements or ideas that are often false or exaggerated and are used to gain support for a political leader or party: *They sent out **propaganda** reports praising the actions of party leaders.*

propagate (say **prop**-uh-gayt) *verb* (**propagating, propagated**)
1 to produce young animals or plants
2 (used about light and sound) to send out or travel: *Sound can **propagate** through water.*
3 to spread characteristics, beliefs or practices: *After their sports victory, excitement **propagated** throughout the school.*
▸ **propagation** (*noun*): *the **propagation** of waves*

propel (say pruh-**pel**) *verb* (**propelling, propelled**)
to move, drive or push a person or thing forward or in a particular direction: *We use energy to **propel** our trains, planes and cars.*

propeller (say pruh-**pel**-uh) *noun* (*plural* **propellers**)
a part that is connected to the engine on a ship, helicopter or plane. It turns round very fast to make the ship, helicopter or plane move. ➲ See illustration at **ship**

proper (say **prop**-uh) *adjective*
1 right or correct: *I haven't got the **proper** tools to mend the car.*
2 (*informal*) real: *He hasn't got any **proper** friends.*

properly (say **prop**-uh-lee) *adverb*
well or correctly: *Close the door **properly**.* ◇ *I can't see **properly** without my glasses.*

property (say **prop**-uh-tee) *noun*
1 (*no plural*) something that you have or own: *This book is the **property** of James Waters.*
2 (*plural* **properties**) a building and the land around it

prophecy (say **prof**-uh-see) *noun* (*plural* **prophecies**)
a statement about what is going to happen in the future: *The power of the three witches' **prophecy** on Macbeth eventually destroyed him.*

prophesy (say **prof**-uh-sy) *verb* (**prophesying, prophesied**)
to say what you think will happen in the future: *Some have **prophesied** that China will become the second largest world economy.*

prophet (say **prof**-uht) *noun* (*plural* **prophets**)
a person that religious people believe their God has chosen to give messages to them

proportion (say pruh-**paw**-shuhn) *noun*
1 (*plural* **proportions**) a part of something: *A large **proportion** of* (= many) *people smoke.*
2 (*no plural*) the amount or size of something compared to the whole: *'What is the **proportion***

of girls who have completed their work?' 'Three out of every six girls have finished. So it's about 50–50.' ◇ *At her work the* ***proportion*** *of men to women is 2:1.* ➲ SYNONYM **ratio**
3 (*plural* **proportions**) the size or shape of something: *a ship of large* ***proportions***
▸ **proportional** (*adjective*)

proposal (say pruh-**pohz**-l) *noun* (*plural* **proposals**)
1 a plan or idea about how to do something: *a* ***proposal*** *to build a new station*
2 when you ask somebody to marry you

propose (say pruh-**pohz**) *verb* (**proposing, proposed**)
1 (*formal*) to say what you think should happen or be done: *I* ***propose*** *that we meet again on Monday.* ➲ SYNONYM **suggest**
2 to ask somebody to marry you: *He* ***proposed*** *to her!*

proprietor (say pruh-**pry**-uh-tuh) *noun* (*plural* **proprietors**) (*formal*)
the owner of a business, hotel or restaurant

propulsion (say pruh-**pul**-shuhn) *noun* (*no plural*) (*science*)
the force that drives a thing forward: *jet* ***propulsion***

prosaic (say proh-**zay**-ik) *adjective*
1 having or using the style of prose rather than that of poetry
2 (usually disapproving) ordinary and without imagination: ***prosaic*** *day-to-day concerns*

prose (say **prohz**) *noun* (*no plural*)
writing that is not poetry: *He wrote poetry and* ***prose***.

prosecute (say **pross**-i-kyoot) *verb* (**prosecuting, prosecuted**)
to say officially in a court of law that somebody has done something illegal: *He was* ***prosecuted*** *for theft.*

prospect¹ (say **pross**-pekt) *noun* (*plural* **prospects**)
1 the possibility that something will happen: *The planned march raised the* ***prospect*** *of clashes with the police.*
2 a thought about what may or will happen in the future: *The* ***prospect*** *of becoming a mother made her very happy.*
3 prospects (*plural noun*) chances of being successful in the future: *The* ***prospects*** *of peace in the Middle East are poor.*

prospect² (say pruh-**spekt**) *verb* (**prospecting, prospected**)
to search an area for minerals or oil: *Thousands of hopeful people rushed into the area to* ***prospect*** *for gold.*

prosper (say **pross**-puh) *verb* (**prospering, prospered**)
to develop in a successful way or to be successful, especially with money: *Her business* ***prospered*** *when more people moved into the area.*

prosperous (say **pross**-puh-ruhss) *adjective*
rich and successful

prostitute (say **pross**-ti-tyoot) *noun* (*plural* **prostitutes**)
a person, especially a woman, who earns money by having sex with people

protagonist (say pruh-**tag**-uh-nist) *noun* (*plural* **protagonists**) (*formal*)
(in literature) the main character in a play, film or book

protea (say proh-**teer**) *noun* (*plural* **proteas**)
one of a group of flowering plants, mostly growing in South Africa, but also in other areas in the southern parts of the world
🛈 **ORIGIN:** from the name of *Proteus*, a Greek sea god who could change into many different shapes, so named because there are many different types of protea

protect (say pruh-**tekt**) *verb* (**protecting, protected**)
to keep somebody or something safe: *Parents try to* ***protect*** *their children from danger.* ◇ *Wear a hat to* ***protect*** *your head against the sun.*

protection (say pruh-**tek**-shuhn) *noun* (*no plural*)
keeping somebody or something safe: *He was put under police* ***protection***.

protein (say **proh**-teen) *noun* (*plural* **proteins**)
a substance in foods such as meat, fish and beans. **Protein** helps you to grow and stay healthy.

protest¹ (say **proh**-test) *noun* (*plural* **protests**)
an action that shows publicly that you do not like or approve of something: *She took part in a* ***protest*** *against the war.*

protest² (say pruh-**test**) *verb* (**protesting, protested**)
to say or show strongly that you do not like something: *They* ***protested*** *against the government's plans.*

Protestant (say **prot**-uhss-tuhnt) *noun* (*plural* **Protestants**)
A member of one of many Christian Churches that are not ruled by or part of the Roman Catholic Church

protocol (say **proh**-tuh-kol) *noun*
1 (*no plural*) (*formal*) a system of fixed rules and behaviour used at official meetings, usually between governments

A B C D E F G H I J K L M N O P Q R S T U V W X Y Z

2 (*plural* **protocols**) (*politics*) the first or original version of a written agreement, especially one between countries
3 (*plural* **protocols**) (*computing*) a set of rules that control the way information is sent between computers
4 (*plural* **protocols**) (*science*) a plan for carrying out experiments

proton (say **proh**-ton) *noun* (*plural* **protons**) (*science*)
one of the three types of **particles** that form all atoms. Protons have a positive electric charge.
➲ See **electron**, **neutron**

protoplasm (say **proh**-tuh-plaz-m) *noun* (*no plural*)
the material substance of the living part of a cell

prototype (say **proh**-tuh-tipe) *noun* (*plural* **prototypes**)
the first model or design of a thing from which other forms will be developed

protractor (say pruh-**trak**-tuh) *noun* (*plural* **protractors**)
a circular or semi-circular device for measuring the size of an angle

proud (say **prowd**) *adjective* (**prouder**, **proudest**)
1 pleased about something that you or others have done, or about something that you have: *She is very **proud** of her new shoes.*
2 thinking that you are better than other people: *He was too **proud** to say he was sorry.*
➲ The noun is **pride**
▸ **proudly** (*adverb*): *'I made this myself,' he said **proudly**.*

prove (say **proov**) *verb* (**proving**, **proved**, **has proved** or **has proven**)
to show that something is true: *The blood on his shirt **proves** that he is the murderer.* ➲ The noun is **proof**

proverb (say **prov**-uhb) *noun* (*plural* **proverbs**)
a short sentence that people often say, that gives help or advice: *'Waste not, want not' is an English **proverb**.*

provide (say pruh-**vide**) *verb* (**providing**, **provided**)
to give something to somebody who needs it: *I'll **provide** the food for the party.* ◇ *The company has **provided** me with a car.*

provided (say pruh-**vide**-uhd) *conjunction* (also **providing**)
only if: *I'll go **provided** that the children can come with me.*

province (say **prov**-uhnss) *noun* (*plural* **provinces**)
a part of a country: *South Africa has nine **provinces**.*
▸ **provincial** (*adjective*): *the **provincial** government*

provision (say pruh-**vizh**-uhn) *noun* (*no plural*)
when something is given to somebody who needs it: *The government is responsible for the **provision** of health care.*

provisional (say pruh-**vizh**-uhn-l) *adjective*
only for the present time and that is likely to be changed in the future: *The **provisional** date for the meeting is 23 March.*

provoke (say pruh-**vohk**) *verb* (**provoking**, **provoked**)
to cause particular feelings or behaviour: *The TV show **provoked** a lively discussion.*

prow (*rhymes with* **cow**) *noun* (*plural* **prows**)
the front part of a boat or ship ➲ See **bow**

> WORD BUILDING The back part of a ship is the **stern**.

prowl (*rhymes with* **fowl**) *verb* (**prowling**, **prowled**)
(used about an animal that is hunting or a person who is waiting for a chance to do something bad) to move around an area quietly so that nobody sees or hears you: *I heard someone **prowling** around outside.*

proximity (say prok-**sim**-i-tee) *noun* (*no plural*)
(*formal*) the state of being near to a person or a thing in distance or time: *The **proximity** of our home to town is very convenient.*

prudent (say **proo**-duhnt) *adjective* (*formal*)
sensible and careful when passing judgement and making decisions, while avoiding unnecessary risks: *It is **prudent** to get advice before investing your money.*

prune[1] (say **proon**) *noun* (*plural* **prunes**)
a dried **plum** with a black wrinkled appearance and often eaten cooked

prune[2] (say **proon**) *verb* (**pruning**, **pruned**)
1 to cut branches or stems off a tree or bush to make it grow better or give it a better shape: *The best time to **prune** fruit trees is in the winter.*
2 to make a thing smaller by removing parts: *Staff numbers were **pruned**.*

pry (*rhymes with* **fly**) *verb* (**prying**, **pried**)
to try to find out about other people's lives: *Stop **prying** into my private life!* ➲ SYNONYM **snoop**

PS (say pee-**ess**) *abbreviation*
You write **PS** at the end of a letter, after your

name, when you want to add something: *… Love from Paul. PS I'll see you on Monday.* ❶ **PS** is short for the word 'postscript', based on Latin words meaning 'after the writing'.

psalm (say **saam**) *noun* (*plural* **psalms**) a **sacred** song, especially one in the Book of Psalms in the Bible and used in church services

pseudo- (say **syoo**-doh) *prefix* (used in nouns, adjectives and adverbs) false or pretended: ***pseudonym*** ◇ ***pseudoscience*** ❶ ORIGIN: from Greek *pseudos* meaning 'being false, not the truth'

pseudonym (say **syoo**-duh-nuhm) *noun* (*plural* **pseudonyms**) a name used by a person, especially a writer, instead of their real name

psychiatrist (say sy-**ky**-uh-trist) *noun* (*plural* **psychiatrists**) a doctor who helps people who have a mental illness

psychological (say sy-kuh-**loj**-ik-l) *adjective*
1 connected with the mind or how it works: *the **psychological** development of children*
2 connected with **psychology**

psychologist (say sy-**kol**-uh-jist) *noun* (*plural* **psychologists**)
1 a person who studies **psychology**
2 a trained person who treats people with **psychological** problems

psychology (say sy-**kol**-uh-jee) *noun* (*no plural*) the study of the mind and how it works ❶ ORIGIN: 17th century, from Latin *psychologia* from Greek *psukhē* meaning 'breath' and 'soul, mind' + *-logia* meaning 'study'

psychopath (say **sy**-koh-path) *noun* (*plural* **psychopaths**) a person who never feels guilty if they hurt other people or do bad things

PTA (say pee-tee-**ay**) *noun* (*plural* **PTAs**) a group run by parents and teachers in a school, which organizes social events and helps the school in different ways ❶ **PTA** is short for 'parent-teacher association'.

PTO (say pee-tee-**oh**) *abbreviation* written at the bottom of a page to tell you to turn to the next page ❶ **PTO** is short for 'please turn over'.

(Pty) Ltd (say pee-tee-wy **lim**-it-uhd) *abbreviation* used in the name of some companies: *Max Gates and Fencing **(Pty) Ltd*** ❶ **(Pty) Ltd** is short for 'Proprietary Limited'.

pub *noun* (*plural* **pubs**) a place where adults go to drink and meet their friends: *They've gone to the **pub** for a drink.*

puberty (say **pyoo**-buh-tee) *noun* (*no plural*) the time when you develop physically from a child to an adult

pubic (say **pyoo**-bik) *adjective* relating to the area of your body around the sexual organs: ***pubic** bone* ◇ ***pubic** hair*

public[1] (say **pub**-lik) *adjective* connected with everybody or for everybody: *a **public** telephone* ◇ *Smoking is not allowed in **public** places.*
▸ **publicly** (*adverb*): *She wouldn't speak **publicly** about the crime she had committed.*

public[2] (say **pub**-lik) *noun*
the public (*no plural*) everybody or people in general: *The museum is open to the **public** daily.*
in public when other people are there: *I don't want to talk about it in **public**.*

publication (say pub-li-**kay**-shuhn) *noun*
1 (*no plural*) when a book or magazine is made and sold: *He became very rich after the **publication** of his first book.*
2 (*plural* **publications**) a book or magazine

publicity (say pub-**liss**-uh-tee) *noun* (*no plural*) giving information about something so that people know about it: *There was a lot of **publicity** for the new film.*

public relations (*plural noun*) (abbr. PR) the business of providing information about somebody or something, in order to give people a good impression of them: *She works in **public relations**.*

public transport *noun* (*no plural*) buses and trains that everybody can use: *I usually travel by **public transport**.*

publish (say **pub**-lish) *verb* (**publishing, published**)
1 to prepare and print a book, magazine or newspaper for selling: *This dictionary was **published** by Oxford University Press.*
2 to make information available to the public, especially on the Internet
▸ **publisher** (*noun*): *The **publisher** is OUP.*

pudding (say **puud**-ing) *noun* (*plural* **puddings**) something sweet that you eat at the end of a meal: *'What's for **pudding**?' 'Fruit.'* ➲ SYNONYM **dessert**

puddle (say **pud**-l) *noun* (*plural* **puddles**) a small pool of rain or other liquid on the ground

A B C D E F G H I J K L M N O P Q R S T U V W X Y Z

puff[1] (say **puf**) *verb* (**puffing, puffed**)
1 (*informal*) to breathe quickly or loudly, especially after you have been running: *She was **puffing** as she ran up the hill.*
2 to smoke a cigarette, pipe or cigar: *He sat **puffing** his cigar.*
3 (used about air, smoke, wind or dust) to blow or come out in clouds: *Smoke was **puffing** out of the chimney.* ◇ *Please don't **puff** smoke in my face.*

puff[2] (say **puf**) *noun* (*plural* **puffs**)
a small amount of air, wind or smoke that is blown from somewhere: *a **puff** of smoke*

puff-adder (say puf-**ad**-uh) *noun* (*plural* **puff-adders**)
a common poisonous snake. In South Africa puff-adders have a black and gold pattern on their skin.

pugnacious (say pug-**nay**-shuhss) *adjective* (*formal*)
eager or quick to argue or fight: *a **pugnacious** politician* ◇ *The cricket player scored a **pugnacious** century.*

pula (say **poo**-luh) *noun* (*plural* **pula**)
the unit of money used in Botswana

pull (say **puul**) *verb* (**pulling, pulled**)
1 to move somebody or something strongly towards you: *She **pulled** the drawer open.*
2 to go forward, moving something behind you: *The cart was **pulled** by two horses.*
3 to move something somewhere: *He **pulled** up his trousers.*
pull somebody's leg (*informal*) to try to make somebody believe something that is not true, for fun: *I didn't really see an elephant – I was only **pulling** your leg!*
pull yourself together to control your feelings after being upset: ***Pull** yourself together and stop crying.*
pull down to destroy a building: *The old school has been **pulled** down.*
pull in to drive a car to the side of the road and stop: *I **pulled** in to look at the map.*
pull up to stop a car: *The driver **pulled** up at the traffic lights.*

pulley (say **puul**-ee) *noun* (*plural* **pulleys**) (*technology*)
a piece of equipment, consisting of a wheel and a rope, that is used for lifting heavy things

pullover (say **puul**-oh-vuh) *noun* (*plural* **pullovers**)
a warm piece of clothing with sleeves, that you wear on the top part of your body. **Pullovers** are often made of wool.

pulmonary (say **pul**-muh-nuh-ree) *adjective*
relating to the lungs: ***pulmonary** congestion*

pulp (*rhymes with* **gulp**) *noun* (*no plural*)
a soft wet substance made especially by crushing a thing: *Use a fork to press the avocado into a **pulp**.*

pulpit (say **puul**-pit) *noun* (*plural* **pulpits**)
a raised enclosed platform in a church from which the **preacher** speaks to the people

pulse (say **pulss**) *noun* (*plural* **pulses**)
the beating of your heart that you feel in different parts of your body, especially in your wrist: *The nurse felt* (= measured) *his **pulse**.*

puma (say **pyoo**-muh) *noun* (*plural* **pumas**)
a large American wild cat with yellowish-brown or grey fur and that looks similar to a female lion

pump[1] *noun* (*plural* **pumps**)
a machine that moves a liquid or gas into or out of something: *a bicycle **pump*** ◇ *a petrol **pump***

pump[2] *verb* (**pumping, pumped**)
to force a gas or a liquid to go in a particular direction: *Your heart **pumps** blood around your body.*
pump something up to fill something with air, using a **pump**: *I **pumped** up my bicycle tyres.*

pumpkin (say **pump**-kin) *noun* (*plural* **pumpkins**)
a very large round vegetable with a thick orange skin

pun (*rhymes with* **run**) *noun* (*plural* **puns**)
a funny use of a word that has two meanings, or that sounds the same as another word ➲ See Study page 17

punch *verb* (**punching, punched**)
1 to hit somebody or something hard with your closed hand (your **fist**): *He **punched** me on the nose.*
2 to make a hole in something with a special tool: *The ticket collector **punched** my ticket.*
▸ **punch** (*noun*): *a **punch** on the chin*

punctual (say **punk**-tyuu-uhl) *adjective*
arriving or doing something at the right time: *Please try to be **punctual** for your classes.*
▸ **punctually** (*adverb*): *They arrived **punctually** at seven o'clock.*

punctuate (say **punk**-tyuu-ayt) *verb* (**punctuating, punctuated**)
to put full stops, question marks and other **punctuation marks** in your writing

punctuation (say punk-tyuu-**ay**-shuhn) *noun* (*no plural*)
using **punctuation marks** when you are writing, or all the **punctuation marks** that you have used in your writing ➲ See Study page 16

punctuation mark *noun phrase* (*plural* **punctuation marks**)
one of the marks that you use in your writing, for example a full stop, comma or question mark

puncture (say **punk**-tshuh) *noun* (*plural* **punctures**)
a hole in a tyre, that lets the air go out: *My bike has a **puncture**.*
▸ **puncture** (*verb*): *A piece of glass **punctured** the tyre.*

pungent (say **pun**-juhnt) *adjective*
(used about a smell) very strong and often unpleasant: *the **pungent** smell of a stable that hasn't been cleaned for months*

punish (say **pun**-ish) *verb* (**punishing, punished**)
to make somebody suffer because they have done something wrong: *The children were **punished** for telling lies.*
🛈 **ORIGIN:** 13th–15th century, through Old French *punir* meaning 'punish', from Latin *poena* meaning 'penalty'

punishment (say **pun**-ish-muhnt) *noun* (*plural* **punishments**)
an act or a way of punishing somebody: *What is the **punishment** for murder in your country?* ◇ *The child was sent to bed as a **punishment** for being naughty.*

punnet (say **pun**-uht) *noun* (*plural* **punnets**)
a small light container in which fruit or vegetables are sold

puny (say **pyoo**-nee) *adjective* (**punier, puniest**)
very small and weak: *Tyrannosaurus rex* had *puny arms, compared to the rest of its body.*

pup (*rhymes with* **cup**) *noun* (*plural* **pups**)
1 = **puppy**
2 the young of some animals: *Baby seals and wolves are called **pups**.*

pupa (say **pyoo**-puh) *noun* (*plural* **pupae**) (*biology*)
the resting stage of an insect while it is changing into an adult, usually inside a hard case: *The **pupa** was slowly turning into a moth inside its cocoon.* ➲ SYNONYM **chrysalis** ➲ See **larva** ➲ See illustration at **metamorphosis**

pupil (say **pyoo**-puhl) *noun* (*plural* **pupils**)
1 a person who is learning at school: *There are 30 **pupils** in the class.* ➲ See **learner**
2 the round black hole in the middle of your eye ➲ See illustration at **eye**

puppet (say **pup**-uht) *noun* (*plural* **puppets**)
a small model of a person or animal that you move by pulling strings or by putting your hand or finger inside

puppy (say **pup**-ee) *noun* (*plural* **puppies**)
a young dog

purchase¹ (say **pur**-chuhss) *noun* (*plural* **purchases**) (*formal*)
the action of buying something, or something that you have bought: *She made several **purchases** and then left the store.*

purchase² (say **pur**-chuhss) *verb* (**purchasing, purchased**) (*formal*)
to buy something: *The company has **purchased** three new shops.*

pure (say **pyoor**) *adjective* (**purer, purest**)
1 not mixed with anything else: *This shirt is **pure** cotton.*
2 clean and healthy: ***pure** mountain air*
3 complete or total: *What she said was **pure** nonsense.*

purely (say **pyoor**-lee) *adverb*
only or completely: *He doesn't like his job – he does it **purely** for the money.*

purgatory (say **pur**-guh-tree) *noun* (*no plural*) (also **Purgatory**)
(in Roman Catholic teaching) a place where souls of the dead have to suffer for the **sin** they did before being allowed into Heaven

purge (say **purj**) *verb* (**purging, purged**)
to remove (people that you do not want) from an organization, usually violently or abruptly: *The new leader **purged** supporters of the previous leader from the party.*
▸ **purge** (*noun*): *The president carried out a **purge** of his political enemies.*

purify (say **pyoo**-ri-fy) *verb* (**purifying, purified**)
to remove dirty or harmful substances from something: ***Purify** the water by boiling it.*

puritan (say **pyoo**-ri-tuhn) *noun* (*plural* **puritans**)
(*usually disapproving*) a person who thinks it is wrong to enjoy yourself
▸ **puritan** (*adjective*): *a **puritan** attitude to life*

purity (say **pyoo**-ri-tee) *noun* (*no plural*)
the state of being pure: *The smoke from the fire has affected the **purity** of the air.*

purple (say **purp**-l) *adjective*
with a colour between red and blue
▸ **purple** (*noun*): *She often wears **purple**.*

purpose (say **pur**-puhss) *noun* (*plural* **purposes**)
the reason for doing something: *What is the **purpose** of your visit?*
on purpose not by accident: *'You've broken my pen!' 'I'm sorry, I didn't do it on **purpose**.'*
▸ **purposeful** (*adjective*): *a **purposeful** look*
▸ **purposefully** (*adverb*): *He walked **purposefully** towards me.*

purposely (say **pur**-puhss-lee) *adverb*
on purpose

purr (say **pur**) *verb* (**purred, purring**)
When a cat **purrs**, it makes a low sound that shows it is happy.

purse (say **purss**) *noun* (*plural* **purses**)
a small bag made of leather, plastic or material for carrying money and credit cards, used especially by women

pursue (say puh-**syoo**) *verb* (**pursuing, pursued**) (*formal*)
to follow somebody or something because you want to catch them: *The police **pursued** the stolen car for several kilometres.* ➲ SYNONYM **chase**

pus (*rhymes with* **fuss**) *noun* (*no plural*)
a thick yellowish liquid produced in infected and red, sore, swollen parts of the body

push (say **puush**) *verb* (**pushing, pushed**)
1 to use force to move somebody or something forward or away from you: *The car broke down so we had to **push** it to a garage.* ◇ *He **pushed** me over!*
2 to press something with your finger: ***Push** the red button to stop the bus.*
▸ **push** (*noun*): *She gave him a **push** and he fell.*

pushchair (say **puush**-chair) *noun* (*plural* **pushchairs**)
a chair on wheels in which a young child is pushed along

pussy (say **puuss**-ee) *noun* (*plural* **pussies**)
a word for 'cat' that children use

put (say **puut**) *verb* (**putting, put**)
1 to move something to a place or position: *She **put** the book on the table.* ◇ *He **put** his bags down.* ◇ *She **put** the box away in the cupboard.*
2 to write something: ***Put** your name at the top of the page.*
put somebody off to make somebody not like someone or something: *The accident **put** me off driving.*
put something off to not do something until later: *He **put** off his holiday because the children were ill.* ➲ SYNONYM **delay**[1]
put something on
1 to take clothes and wear them: ***Put** on your coat.* ◇ ***Put** your shoes on.*
2 to make a piece of electrical equipment start to work: *I **put** on the lights and the TV.* ◇ *Shall we **put** some music on?*
put something out to stop a fire or to stop a light shining: *She **put** out the fire with some water.* ◇ ***Put** the lights out please.*
put up with somebody or something to have pain or problems without complaining: *It's very hot but we just have to **put** up with it.*

putrid (say **pyoo**-trid) *adjective*
1 (used about dead animals and plants) smelling bad after being dead for some time
2 (*informal*) very unpleasant: *a **putrid** piece of writing*

putt (*rhymes with* **but**) *verb* (**putting, putted**)
(used in golf) to hit the ball gently when it is near the hole
▸ **putt** (*noun*): *The South African needed to sink his final **putt**.*

putty (say **put**-ee) *noun* (*no plural*)
a soft substance which becomes hard when dry, used to fix glass into window frames

puzzle[1] (say **puz**-l) *noun* (*plural* **puzzles**)
1 something that is difficult to understand or explain: *Her reason for leaving the team is a **puzzle** to me.*
2 a game that is difficult and makes you think a lot ➲ See **crossword, jigsaw**

puzzle[2] (say **puz**-l) *verb* (**puzzling, puzzled**)
to make you feel that you cannot understand or explain something: *The child's illness **puzzled** his doctors.*

puzzled (say **puz**-uhld) *adjective*
not able to understand or explain something: *She had a **puzzled** look on her face.*

puzzling (say **puz**-ling) *adjective*
difficult to understand or explain

PVA (say pee-vee-**ay**) *noun* (*no plural*)
a chemical substance used in paints and for sticking things together ❶ **PVA** is an abbreviation of 'polyvinyl acetate'.

PVC (say pee-vee-**see**) *noun* (*no plural*)
a strong plastic material that is used to make pipes, floor coverings, clothes and other products ❶ **PVC** is an abbreviation of 'polyvinyl chloride'.

pyjamas (say puh-**jaa**-muhz) *plural noun*
a loose jacket and trousers that you wear when you go to sleep
❶ ORIGIN: 19th century, from Urdu and Persian, from *pāy* meaning 'leg' + *jāma* meaning 'clothing'. Urdu is a language spoken by many people in Pakistan and India.

pylon (say **pile**-uhn) *noun* (*plural* **pylons**)
a tall metal tower that supports heavy electrical wires high above the ground

pyramid (say **pi**-ruh-mid) *noun* (*plural* **pyramids**)
1 a solid shape with a flat bottom and three or four sides in the shape of triangles that come to a point at the top
2 a very large stone structure built in the shape of a pyramid by ancient Egyptians. Egyptians buried dead kings and queens in **pyramids**.

pyramid

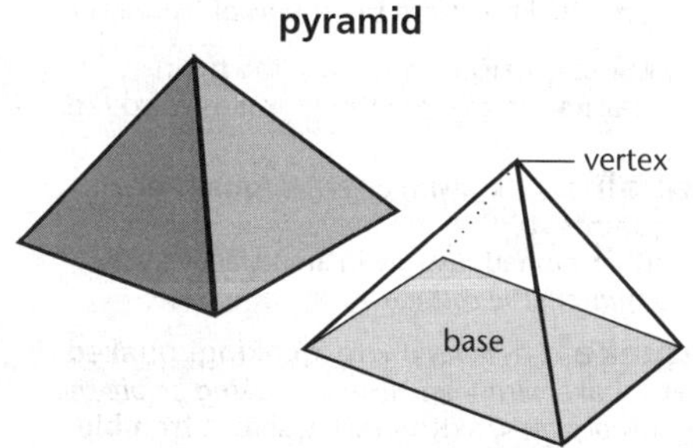

pyre (say **py**-uh) *noun* (*plural* **pyres**)
a large pile of wood on which a dead body is burned in a funeral ceremony

Pythagorean (say py-thag-uh-**ree**-uhn) *adjective*
relating to Pythagoras, his mathematics or his thinking: *a **Pythagorean** triangle* ◇ ***Pythagorean** geometry*
ORIGIN: from the name of the Greek philosopher, Pythagoras, who lived in the sixth century BC

python (say **py**-thuhn) *noun* (*plural* **pythons**)
a very large snake that kills animals by squeezing them hard

Qq

quack (say **kwak**) *noun* (*plural* **quacks**)
the sound that a duck makes
▸ **quack** (*verb*): *The duck **quacked** noisily.*

quadrangle (say kwod-**rang**-guhl) *noun* (*plural* **quadrangles**)
1 (*maths*) any closed flat shape having four angles and four straight sides ➲ SYNONYM **quadrilateral**
2 a square or rectangular open area with buildings round it: *At school we spend our breaks in the **quadrangle**.*

quadrant (say **kwod**-ruhnt) *noun* (*plural* **quadrants**)
1 (*maths*) a quarter of the area of a circle or a quarter of the distance around a circle
➲ See illustration at **circle**[1]
2 one of four equal sections of an object that you are studying
3 an instrument for measuring angles, especially to check your position at sea or to look at stars
🛈 ORIGIN: 14th–15th century, from Latin *quadrans* meaning 'quarter', from *quattuor* meaning 'four'

quadri- (say **kwod**-ri) *prefix*
four or having four: *A **quadrilateral** has four sides.*
🛈 ORIGIN: from Latin *quattuor* meaning 'four'

quadrilateral (say kwod-ri-**lat**-ruhl) *noun* (*plural* **quadrilaterals**) (*maths*)
a flat closed shape with four straight lines: *Squares and parallelograms are **quadrilaterals**.*
▸ **quadrilateral** (*adjective*)

quadriplegic (say kwod-ri-**plee**-jik) *noun* (*plural* **quadriplegics**)
a person who is permanently unable to feel or use their arms and legs ➲ See **paraplegic**
▸ **quadriplegic** (*adjective*) ▸ **quadriplegia** (*noun*): *He suffers from **quadriplegia**.*

quadruped (say **kwod**-ruh-ped) *noun* (*plural* **quadrupeds**)
any animal that walks on four legs: *Humans and insects are not **quadrupeds**, but cows are.*
➲ See **biped**

quadruple (say **kwod**-roop-l) *verb* (**quadrupling**, **quadrupled**)
to multiply or be multiplied by four: *My income has **quadrupled** since I first started working.*

quagga (say **kwu**-*khuh*) *noun* (*plural* **quagga** or **quaggas**)
an animal like a **zebra** that does not exist anymore
🛈 ORIGIN: from South African Dutch, probably from Khoikhoi, from the sound of its braying

> PRONUNCIATION Pronounce the **gg** in **quagga** like the **g** in the Afrikaans word **lag**.

quaint (say **kwaynt**) *adjective* (**quainter**, **quaintest**)
old-fashioned, usually in an attractive way: *a **quaint** little cottage*

quake[1] (say **kwayk**) *verb* (**quaking**, **quaked**)
to shake with fear: *He was **quaking** before the school play.* ➲ SYNONYMS **quiver**[1], **tremble**
quaking in your boots to be nervous about something: *She was **quaking** in her boots before the interview.*

quake[2] (say **kwayk**) *noun* (*plural* **quakes**)
(*informal*) = **earthquake**

qualification (say kwol-i-fi-**kay**-shuhn) *noun* (*plural* **qualifications**)
an examination that you have passed, or training or knowledge that you need to do a special job: *He left school with no **qualifications**.*

qualified (say **kwol**-i-fide) *adjective*
having passed the exams or done the training necessary to do a particular job: *She's a **qualified** nurse.* ➲ OPPOSITE **unqualified**

qualify (say **kwol**-i-fy) *verb* (**qualifying**, **qualified**)
to get the right knowledge and training and pass exams so that you can do a certain job: *She has **qualified** as a doctor.*

quality (say **kwol**-i-tee) *noun*
1 (*no plural*) how good or bad something is: *The **quality** of her work is excellent.* ◇ *This furniture isn't very good **quality**.*
2 (*plural* **qualities**) something that is typical of a person or thing: *the **qualities** of a manager*

quandary (say **kwon**-duh-ree) *noun* (*plural* **quandaries**)
the state of not being able to decide what to do in a difficult situation

quantity (say **kwon**-ti-tee) *noun* (*plural* **quantities**)
how much of something there is: *I bought only*

*a small **quantity** of cheese.* ➲ SYNONYM **amount¹** 1

quantum (say **kwon**-tuhm) *noun* (*plural* **quanta**)
1 a particular quantity or amount of something
2 an element of matter or energy that cannot be divided: *a **quantum** of energy* ◇ ***quantum** mechanics*

quarantine (say **kwo**-ruhn-teen) *noun* (*no plural*)
a period of time when a person, animal or thing that is carrying or may be carrying an infectious disease is kept away from other people or animals: *When we emigrated, I had to place my dog into **quarantine** for six months before it could live with us.*
► **quarantine** (*verb*): *to **quarantine** a patient*

quarrel¹ (say **kwo**-ruhl) *noun* (*plural* **quarrels**)
an argument or a disagreement with somebody: *He had a **quarrel** with his wife about money.*

quarrel² (say **kwo**-ruhl) *verb* (**quarrelling**, **quarrelled**)
to argue or disagree with somebody: *They often **quarrel** about money.* ◇ *The children are always **quarrelling**.*

quarry (say **kwo**-ree) *noun*
1 (*plural* **quarries**) a place where people cut stone or sand out of the ground
2 (*no plural*) a person or animal that is being hunted

quarter (say **kwaw**-tuh) *noun* (*plural* **quarters**)
1 one of four equal parts of something: *a **quarter** of a cup* ◇ *The film starts in three **quarters** of an hour.*
2 three months: *You get a bill every **quarter**.*
3 a part of a town: *the old **quarter***
(a) quarter past 15 minutes after the hour: *It's **quarter** past two.* ◇ *I'll meet you at a **quarter** past.*
(a) quarter to 15 minutes before the hour: *It's **quarter** to nine.*
ⓘ **ORIGIN**: 13th–15th century, through Old French *quartier*, from Latin *quartarius* meaning 'fourth part of a measure' from *quattuor* meaning 'four'

quarter-final (say kwaw-tuh-**fine**-uhl) *noun* (*plural* **quarter-finals**)
one of the four matches between the eight players or teams left in a competition
➲ See **semi-final**

quartet (say kwaw-**tet**) *noun* (*plural* **quartets**)
1 four people who sing or play music together
2 a piece of music written for four people to sing or play together ➲ See **duet**, **quintet**, **trio**

quartz (say **kwawtss**) *noun* (*no plural*)
a hard shiny mineral found in many rocks and used in electrical instruments and clocks: ***quartz** crystal*

quaver (say **kway**-vuh) *verb* (**quavering**, **quavered**)
to shake while speaking: *His voice **quavered**.*
► **quavery** (*adjective*): *She asked in a **quavery** voice.*

quay (say **kee**) *noun* (*plural* **quays**)
a place in a port where ships go so that people can move things on and off them

queen (say **kween**) *noun* (*plural* **queens**)
1 a woman from a royal family who rules a country: ***Queen** Elizabeth II, the **Queen** of England.*
2 the wife of a king
3 one of the four playing cards in a pack which has a picture of a queen on it: *the **queen** of hearts*

queer (say **kweer**) *adjective* (**queerer**, **queerest**) (*old-fashioned*)
strange or unusual: *He had a **queer** feeling.*

quell (say **kwel**) *verb* (**quelling**, **quelled**) (*formal*)
to end something: *The army came to **quell** the violence.* ◇ *I'll **quell** the rumours.*

quench (say **kwench**) *verb* (**quenching**, **quenched**)
quench your thirst to drink as much as you need so that you stop feeling thirsty

query¹ (say **kweer**-ree) *noun* (*plural* **queries**)
a question: *Phone me if you have any **queries**.*

query² (say **kweer**-ree) *verb* (**querying**, **queried**)
to ask a question about something that you think is wrong: *We **queried** the bill but the waitress said it was correct.*

quest (say **kwest**) *noun* (*plural* **quests**) (*formal*) a long search for something that is difficult to find: *We went on a **quest**.* ◇ *the **quest** for happiness*

question¹ (say **kwess**-tshuhn) *noun* (*plural* **questions**)
1 something that you ask: *They asked me a lot of **questions**.* ◇ *She didn't answer my **question**.* ◇ *What is the answer to **question** 3?*
2 something that you need to deal with or something that is being discussed: *The **question** is, how can we raise the money?* ◇ *It's a **question** of time – we are very late.*
in question that we are talking about: *On the day in **question** I was in Nairobi.*
out of the question not possible: *I won't give him money. It's out of the **question**.*

A B C D E F G H I J K L M N O P Q R S T U V W X Y Z

question[2] (say **kwess**-tshuhn) *verb* (**questioning**, **questioned**)
1 to ask somebody questions about something: *The police **questioned** him about the stolen car.*
2 to feel or express doubt about something: *She said she was the child's mother so I didn't **question** her right to be there.*

question mark *noun* (*plural* **question marks**)
the sign (**?**) that you write at the end of a question ➲ See Study page 16

questionnaire (say **kwess**-tshuh-nair) *noun* (*plural* **questionnaires**)
a list of questions for people to answer so that information can be collected from the answers: *Please fill in* (= write the answers on) *the **questionnaire**.*

question tag *noun* (*plural* **question tags**) (*grammar*)
words such as 'is it?' or 'didn't you?' that you put on the end of a sentence to make it into a question: *In the sentence 'You're English, aren't you?', 'aren't you' is a **question tag**.*

queue[1] (say **kyoo**) *noun* (*plural* **queues**)
a line of people who are waiting to do something: *We stood in a **queue** for the tickets.*

queue[2] (say **kyoo**) *verb* (**queuing**, **queued**) (also **queue up**)
to stand in a **queue**[1]: *We **queued** for a bus.*

quibble (say **kwib**-l) *noun* (*plural* **quibbles**)
a small complaint: *My one **quibble** is that the food was cold.*
▸ **quibble** (*verb*): *Stop **quibbling** about the price!*

quiche (say **keesh**) *noun* (*plural* **quiches**)
a type of food made of pastry filled with egg and milk and other foods such as cheese and onion. **Quiche** is cooked in the oven and you can eat it hot or cold.

quick (say **kwik**) *adjective, adverb* (**quicker**, **quickest**)
taking little time: *It's **quicker** to travel by plane than by train.* ◇ *Can I make a **quick** telephone call?* ➲ SYNONYM **fast**[1] 1 ➲ OPPOSITE **slow**[1] 1
▸ **quickly** (*adverb*): *Come as **quickly** as you can!*

quiet[1] (say **kwy**-uht) *adjective* (**quieter**, **quietest**)
1 making very little noise: *Be **quiet** – the baby's asleep.* ◇ *a **quiet** voice* ➲ OPPOSITE **noisy**
2 without many people or without many things happening: *Our town is very **quiet** on Sundays.*
▸ **quietly** (*adverb*): *Please close the door **quietly**.*

quiet[2] (say **kwy**-uht) *noun* (*no plural*)
when there is no noise: *I need **quiet** when I'm working.*

quill (say **kwil**) *noun* (*plural* **quills**)
1 (also **quill feather**) (*science*) a large feather from the wing or tail of a bird
2 (*science*) one of the thin sharp points on the body of a **porcupine**
3 (also **quill pen**) (*old-fashioned*) a pen made from a quill feather

quilt (say **kwilt**) *noun* (*plural* **quilts**)
a bed cover with soft material inside

quintet (say kwin-**tet**) *noun* (*plural* **quintets**)
1 five people who sing or play music together
2 a piece of music written for five people to sing or play together ➲ See **duet**, **quartet**, **trio**

quip (say **kwip**) *verb* (**quipping**, **quipped**)
to make a quick and funny comment
▸ **quip** (*noun*)

quirk (say **kwurk**) *noun* (*plural* **quirks**)
1 a part of somebody's nature or behaviour that is strange: *He has funny **quirks**.*
2 a strange thing that happens by chance: *It was a **quirk** of nature.*
▸ **quirky** (*adjective*): *her **quirky** sense of humour*

quit (say **kwit**) *verb* (**quitting**, **quit**) (*informal*)
1 to stop doing something: *We've nearly finished – we shouldn't **quit** now!*
2 to leave a job or place: *She's **quit** her job as coach.*

quite (say **kwite**) *adverb*
1 rather or not very: *It's **quite** warm today, but it's not hot.* ◇ *He plays the guitar **quite** well.* ➲ SYNONYM **fairly** 1
2 completely: *Dinner is not **quite** ready.*
quite a few or quite a lot a fairly large amount or number: ***quite** a lot of cake* ◇ *There were **quite** a few people at the party.*

quiver[1] (say **kwiv**-uh) *verb* (**quivering**, **quivered**)
to shake slightly: *Her lip **quivered** and then she started to cry.* ➲ SYNONYM **tremble**

quiver[2] (say **kwiv**-uh) *noun* (*plural* **quivers**)
a container for holding arrows: *a **quiver** of arrows*

quiz (say **kwiz**) *noun* (*plural* **quizzes**)
a game where you try to answer questions: *a **quiz** on television*

quota (say **kwoh**-tuh) *noun* (*plural* **quotas**)
the limited number of people or quantity of things that are officially allowed: *We have already reached our **quota** – we cannot take any more people.*

quotation (say kwoh-**tay**-shuhn) *noun* (*plural* **quotations**) (also **quote**)
words that you say or write, which another person said or wrote before: *That's a* ***quotation*** *from a poem by Keats.*

quotation marks *plural noun* (also **quotes**)
the signs (" ") or (' ') that you use in writing before and after the exact words that someone has said ➲ See Study page 16
➲ SYNONYM **inverted commas**

quote (say **kwoht**) *verb* (**quoting**, **quoted**)
to repeat exactly something that another person said or wrote: *She* ***quoted*** *from the Bible.* ◇ *Don't* ***quote*** *me, but she's wrong.*

quotient (say **kwoh**-shuhnt) *noun* (*plural* **quotients**) (*maths*)
a number that is the result of dividing one number by another: *In the equation 12 ÷ 4 = 3, the* ***quotient*** *is 3.*

Qur'an *noun* (*no plural*) = **Koran**

Rr

R *abbreviation* (*plural* **R**)
Rand

rabbi (say **rab**-*y*) *noun* (*plural* **rabbis**)
a Jewish religious leader and teacher of Jewish law

rabbit (say **rab**-it) *noun* (*plural* **rabbits**)
a small mammal that has brown, grey or white fur and long ears. **Rabbits** live in holes under the ground.

rabies (say **ray**-beez) *noun* (*no plural*)
a serious disease that people can get if a dog or another animal with the disease bites them: *The dog had* ***rabies****.*

race¹ (say **rayss**) *noun* (*plural* **races**)
1 a competition to see who or what can run, drive, ride, etc. fastest: *a horse* ***race*** ◇ *Who won the* ***race****?*
2 a group of people of the same kind, for example with the same colour skin, language or customs: *People of many different* ***races*** *live together in this country.*

race² (say **rayss**) *verb* (**racing**, **raced**)
1 to run, drive, swim, fly or ride in a competition to see who or what is the fastest: *The cars* ***raced*** *round the track.* ◇ *I'll* ***race*** *you to the other end of the pool.*
2 to move, or to move somebody or something, very fast: *He* ***raced*** *up the stairs.* ◇ *The police* ***raced*** *to the scene of the crime.*

racial (say **raysh**-l) *adjective*
connected with people's race or happening between people of different races: ***racial*** *differences*

racing (say **rayss**-ing) *noun* (*no plural*)
the sport of taking part in races: *motor* ***racing***

racism (say **rayss**-i-zuhm) *noun* (*no plural*)
the belief that some groups **(races)** of people are better than others
▸ **racist** (*noun*): *He's a terrible* ***racist****.*
▸ **racist** (*adjective*): *He made a* ***racist*** *comment.*

rack (say **rak**) *noun* (*plural* **racks**)
a kind of shelf, made of bars, that you put things on: *I got on the train and put my bag on the luggage* ***rack****.*

racket (say **rak**-uht) *noun* (*plural* **rackets**) (also **racquet**)
a thing that you use for hitting the ball in tennis and similar sports

radar (say **ray**-daa) *noun* (*no plural*)
a way of finding where a ship or an aircraft is and how fast it is travelling by using radio waves

radial (say **ray**-di-uhl) *adjective*
1 relating to rays or the **radius** of a circle: ***radial*** *heat*
2 having lines or rays that spread out from a central point: *a* ***radial*** *tyre*

radiant (say **ray**-di-uhnt) *adjective*
1 showing great happiness: *a* ***radiant*** *smile*
2 sending out light or heat: *the* ***radiant*** *heat of the sun*

radiate (say **ray**-di-ayt) *verb* (**radiating**, **radiated**)
1 to send out light, heat or other waves: *The sun* ***radiates*** *heat.*
2 to go out in all directions from a central point: *Narrow streets* ***radiate*** *from the village square.*
3 to clearly show a particular quality or emotion through your appearance or behaviour: *She* ***radiated*** *self-confidence in the interview.*

radiation (say ray-di-**ay**-shuhn) *noun* (*no plural*)
energy that is transported through space in the form of waves, rays, or **particles**. Some radiation is dangerous: *Scientists have recorded high levels of* ***radiation*** *near the nuclear power station.*

radiator (say **ray**-di-ay-tuh) *noun* (*plural* **radiators**)
1 a part of a car that has water in it to keep the engine cool
2 a metal thing with hot water inside that makes a room warm

radical (say **rad**-ik-l) *adjective*
1 (used about changes in something) very large: *We made* ***radical*** *changes to our project.*
2 wanting great social or political change: *He has* ***radical*** *views on politics.*
▸ **radical** (*noun*): *She's a* ***radical****.*

radicle (say **rad**-ik-l) *noun* (*plural* **radicles**)
the first root of a developing seed

radio (say **ray**-di-oh) *noun*
1 (*no plural*) the activity of sending or receiving sounds that travel a long way through the air by special waves: *The captain of the ship sent a message by* ***radio****.*

2 (*plural* **radios**) a piece of equipment that brings voices or music from far away so that you can hear them: *We listened to an interesting programme on the **radio**.* ◇ *Can you turn on the **radio**?*

radioactive (say ray-di-oh-**ak**-tiv) *adjective*
sending out powerful and dangerous energy: *the disposal of **radioactive** waste*

radish (say **rad**-ish) *noun* (*plural* **radishes**)
a small round red vegetable that is white inside and has a very strong taste

radius (say **ray**-di-uhss) *noun* (*plural* **radii**)
the length of a straight line from the centre of a circle to the outside ➲ See illustration at **circle**[1] ➲ See **diameter**

raffle (say **raf**-l) *noun* (*plural* **raffles**)
a way of making money for a charity by selling tickets with numbers on them. Later some numbers are chosen and the tickets with these numbers on them win prizes.

raft (say **raaft**) *noun* (*plural* **rafts**)
a flat boat with no sides and no engine

rafter (say **raaf**-tuh) *noun* (*plural* **rafters**)
one of the long pieces of wood that supports a roof

rag *noun* (*plural* **rags**)
1 a small piece of old cloth that you use for cleaning
2 rags (*plural noun*) clothes that are very old and torn: *She was dressed in **rags**.*

rage (say **rayj**) *noun* (*no plural*)
very strong anger: *Sue stormed out of the room in a **rage**.*

raid (say **rayd**) *noun* (*plural* **raids**)
a sudden attack on a place: *a bank **raid***
▸ **raid** (*verb*): *Police **raided** the house looking for drugs.*

rail (say **rayl**) *noun*
1 (*plural* **rails**) a long piece of wood or metal that is fixed to the wall or to something else: *Hang your towel on the **rail** in the bathroom.*
2 rails (*plural noun*) the long pieces of metal that trains travel on
3 (*no plural*) trains as a way of travelling: *We decided to travel by **rail**.*

railings (say **rayl**-ingz) *plural noun*
a fence made of long pieces of metal

railway (say **rayl**-way) *noun* (*plural* **railways**)
1 (also **railway line**) the metal lines that trains travel on from one place to another
2 a train service that carries people and things: *a **railway** timetable*

railway station *noun* (*plural* **railway stations**)
a place where trains stop so that people can get on and off

rain[1] (say **rayn**) *noun* (*no plural*)
the water that falls from the sky: ***Rain** is forecast for the weekend.*

rain[2] (say **rayn**) *verb* (**raining, rained**)
When it **rains**, water falls from the sky: *It's **raining**.* ◇ *It **rained** all day.*

rainbow (say **rayn**-boh) *noun* (*plural* **rainbows**)
a half circle of colours in the sky when the sun shines on rain

raincoat (say **rayn**-koht) *noun* (*plural* **raincoats**)
a long light coat that you wear when it rains

raindrop (say **rayn**-drop) *noun* (*plural* **raindrops**)
one drop of rain

rainfall (say **rayn**-fawl) *noun* (*no plural*)
the amount of rain that falls in a particular place over a particular period of time: *Our town has an average **rainfall** of 600 millimetres per year.* ◇ *She lives in a low **rainfall** area.*

rainforest (say **rayn**-fo-ruhst) *noun* (*plural* **rainforests**)
a forest in a hot part of the world where there is a lot of rain: *the Amazon **rainforest***

rainy (say **rayn**-ee) *adjective* (**rainier, rainiest**)
with a lot of rain: *a **rainy** day*

raise (say **rayz**) *verb* (**raising, raised**)
1 to move something or somebody up: ***Raise** your hand if you want to ask a question.*
➲ OPPOSITE **lower**[2] 1
2 to make something bigger, higher or stronger: *They've **raised** the price of petrol.* ◇ *She **raised** her voice* (= spoke more loudly).
➲ OPPOSITE **lower**[2] 2
3 to get money from other people for a particular purpose: *We **raised** R10 000 for the hospital.*
4 to start to talk about something: *He **raised** an interesting question.*
5 to look after a child or an animal until they are an adult: *It's difficult to **raise** a family with so little money.*

raisin (say **ray**-zin) *noun* (*plural* **raisins**)
a small dried grape, used in cakes, etc.

rake (say **rayk**) *noun* (*plural* **rakes**)
a garden tool with a long handle and a row of teeth at the bottom, used for collecting leaves or making the ground flat
▸ **rake** (*verb*): ***Rake** up the dead leaves.*

rally (say **ral**-ee) *noun* (*plural* **rallies**)
1 a group of people walking or standing together to show that they feel strongly about something: *a peace* ***rally***
2 a race for cars or motorcycles on public roads
3 (in tennis or similar sports) a series of hits of the ball before a point is won

RAM (say **ram**) *noun* (*no plural*) (*computing*)
computer memory in which data can be changed or removed and can be looked at in any order: *32 megabytes of* ***RAM*** ⓘ **RAM** is short for 'random access memory'.

ram[1] *noun* (*plural* **rams**)
a male sheep

ram[2] *verb* (**ramming**, **rammed**)
to crash into something or push something with great force: *The car* ***rammed*** *into the tree.*

Ramadan (say **rum**-uh-daan) *noun* (*no plural*)
the period of one month each year when Muslims do not eat or drink anything from early morning until the sun goes down in the evening ➲ See **Eid**, **Labarang**
ⓘ **ORIGIN:** from Arabic *ramaḍān*, from *ramaḍa* meaning 'be hot'. Originally Ramadan was at a hot time of the year.

ramble (say **ramb**-l) *verb* (**rambling**, **rambled**)
1 to walk in the countryside for pleasure: *We* ***rambled*** *around this weekend.*
2 to talk for a long time in a confused way: *He* ***rambled*** *on about his visit to the dentist.*

ramp *noun* (*plural* **ramps**)
a path that you use instead of steps to go up or down: *I pushed the wheelchair up the* ***ramp***.

rampart (say **ram**-paat) *noun* (*plural* **ramparts**)
a high wall with a path along the top, usually built around a castle or a town to help defend it

ramshackle (say **ram**-shak-l) *adjective*
(usually used about a building) old and falling apart: *a* ***ramshackle*** *house* ➲ **SYNONYMS** **derelict**, **dilapidated**

ran form of **run**[1]

ranch (say **raanch**) *noun* (*plural* **ranches**)
a very large farm, especially in the USA or Australia, where cows, horses or sheep are kept
ⓘ **ORIGIN:** 19th century, from Spanish *rancho* meaning 'a group of people eating together'

rancid (say **ran**-sid) *adjective*
(used about food containing fat) smelling bad because it is no longer fresh: *The butter's gone* ***rancid***.

Rand (say **rand** or **ront**) *noun* (*plural* **Rand** or **Rands**) (also **rand**) (abbr. R)
the unit of money used in South Africa. There are 100 cents in a **Rand**: *I paid R12,60 for my pen.* ◇ *Where can I exchange* ***Rands*** *for US dollars?*
ⓘ **ORIGIN:** from *the Rand*, short for *the Witwatersrand*, a goldfield area near Johannesburg

random (say **ran**-duhm) *adjective*
without any special plan: *She chose a few books at* ***random***.

rang form of **ring**[2]

range[1] (say **raynj**) *noun* (*plural* **ranges**)
1 the amount between the highest and the lowest: *The age* ***range*** *of the children is between eight and twelve.*
2 different things of the same kind: *This shop sells a* ***range*** *of bicycles.*
3 a line of mountains or hills: *a mountain* ***range***
4 how far you can see, hear, shoot, travel or go: *Young animals stay within close* ***range*** *of their mothers.*

range[2] (say **raynj**) *verb* (**ranging**, **ranged**)
to be at different points between two things: *The ages of the learners in the class* ***range*** *from thirteen to seventeen.*

rank[1] (say **rangk**) *noun* (*plural* **ranks**)
1 how important somebody is in a group of people, for example in an army: *General is one of the highest* ***ranks*** *in the army.*
2 a group or line of things or people: *a taxi* ***rank***

rank[2] (say **rangk**) *verb* (**ranking**, **ranked**)
to give something or somebody a position on a scale or to have a position of this kind: ***Rank*** *the three meals in order of cost.*

ransack (say **ran**-sak) *verb* (**ransacking**, **ransacked**)
to search a place, making it untidy and causing damage, usually because you are looking for something: *My flat was* ***ransacked*** *by burglars.*

ransom (say **ran**-suhm) *noun* (*plural* **ransoms**)
the money that you must pay so that criminals will free a person who they have taken: *The kidnappers demanded a* ***ransom*** *of two million rand.*

rap[1] *noun*
1 (*plural* **raps**) a quick knock: *I heard a* ***rap*** *on the door.*
2 (*no plural*) (*music*) a type of modern music in which singers speak the words of a song very quickly: *a* ***rap*** *song*

rap[2] *verb* (**rapping**, **rapped**)
1 to hit something quickly and lightly, making a noise: *She* ***rapped*** *on the door.*
2 (*music*) to speak the words of a **rap** song

rape (say **rayp**) *verb* (**raping**, **raped**)
to force somebody to have sex when they do not want to
▸ **rape** (*noun*): *He was sent to prison for* ***rape***.

rapid (say **rap**-id) *adjective*
happening or moving very quickly: *She made* ***rapid*** *progress and was soon the best in the class.* ➲ OPPOSITE **slow**[1] 1
▸ **rapidly** (*adverb*): *The ice melted* ***rapidly***.

rapport (say ruh-**paw**) *noun* (*no plural*)
a friendly relationship in which people understand each other very well: *The teacher established a good* ***rapport*** *with the class.*

PRONUNCIATION Don't pronounce the **t** at the end of **rapport**.

rapture (say **rap**-tshuh) *noun* (*no plural*)
a feeling of extreme happiness: *I felt such* ***rapture*** *when I heard the news.*
▸ **rapturous** (*adjective*)

rare (say **rair**) *adjective* (**rarer**, **rarest**)
1 If something is **rare**, you do not find or see it often: *Pandas are* ***rare*** *animals.* ◇ *It's* ***rare*** *to get 100% for an exam.* ➲ SYNONYM **uncommon**
2 Meat that is **rare** is not cooked for very long, so that the inside is still red.

rarely (say **rair**-lee) *adverb*
not very often: *We* ***rarely*** *go to the beach.* ➲ SYNONYM **seldom**

rascal (say **raass**-kuhl) *noun* (*plural* **rascals**)
a person, especially a child, who enjoys playing tricks on people: *you naughty* ***rascal***!

rash[1] *noun* (*plural* **rashes**)
a lot of small red spots on your skin

rash[2] *adjective* (**rasher**, **rashest**)
If you are **rash**, you do things too quickly and without thinking about the possible result: *You were very* ***rash*** *to leave your job before you had found a new one.*

rasp (say **raasp**) *noun* (*plural* **rasps**)
1 a metal tool, like a file, used for rubbing metal or wood to make it smooth
2 a rough sound: *His voice came out as a* ***rasp***.
▸ **rasp** (*verb*)

raspberry (say **raaz**-buh-ree) *noun* (*plural* **raspberries**)
a small soft red fruit that grows on bushes: ***raspberry*** *jam*

Rastafarian (say rass-tuh-**fair**-ri-uhn) *adjective*
relating to a religious movement that started in Jamaica
▸ **Rastafarian** (also **Rasta**) (*noun*)

rat *noun* (*plural* **rats**)
an animal like a big mouse

ratchet (say **rach**-uht) *noun* (*plural* **ratchets**)
a wheel with teeth around the edge and a metal piece that fits between the teeth

rate[1] (say **rayt**) *noun* (*plural* **rates**)
1 the speed of something or how often something happens: *The crime* ***rate*** *was lower in 2008 than in 2007.*
2 the amount that something costs or that somebody is paid: *The basic* ***rate*** *of pay is R10 an hour.*
at any rate (*informal*) anyway or whatever happens: *I hope to be back before ten o'clock – I won't be late at any* ***rate***.

rate[2] (say **rayt**) *verb* (**rating**, **rated**)
1 to say how good you think something is: ***Rate*** *your fitness on a scale of one to ten.* ◇ *Which of these things do you* ***rate*** *as the most important?* ➲ SYNONYMS **assess**, **evaluate**
2 to be thought of as a certain standard: *We were* ***rated*** *the top school in Limpopo.*

rather (say **raa**-thuh) *adverb*
more than a little but not very: *I was* ***rather*** *tired after the long journey.* ◇ *It's* ***rather*** *a small room.* ➲ SYNONYM **quite** 1
rather than in the place of or instead of: *Could I have tea* ***rather*** *than coffee?*
would rather would prefer to do something: *I would* ***rather*** *go by train than by bus.*

USAGE If you use **rather** with a positive word, it sounds as if you are surprised and pleased: *The new teacher is* ***rather*** *nice.*

ratify (say **rat**-i-fy) *verb* (**ratifying**, **ratified**)
to make an agreement official by voting for or signing it

ratio (say **ray**-shi-oh) *noun* (*plural* **ratios**)
the relationship between the size of two numbers, amounts or objects: *For every 3 children in my class, there are 4 books. The* ***ratio*** *of children to books is 3:4 or* $\frac{3}{4}$. ➲ See **proportion** 2

ration[1] (say **rash**-uhn) *noun* (*plural* **rations**)
a small amount of something that you are allowed to have when there is not enough for everybody to have what they want: *food* ***rations***

ration[2] (say **rash**-uhn) *verb* (**rationing**, **rationed**)
to control the amount of something that somebody is allowed to have, for example because there is not enough for everyone to have as much as they want: *Eggs were* ***rationed*** *during the war.*

A B C D E F G H I J K L M N O P Q R S T U V W X Y Z

rational (say **rash**-nuhl) *adjective*
sensible or based on facts: *There must be a **rational** explanation for why he's behaving like this.* ➲ OPPOSITE **irrational**

rationale (say rash-uh-**naal**) *noun* (*plural* **rationales**)
the reason for a decision or course of action: *What is the **rationale** behind this decision?*

rational number *noun* (*plural* **rational numbers**)
a number that can be expressed as a fraction: *The numbers –6 and* $\frac{1}{2}$ *are **rational numbers**.*

rattle¹ (say **rat**-l) *verb* (**rattling**, **rattled**)
to make a sound like hard things hitting each other or to shake something so that it makes this sound: *The windows were **rattling** all night in the wind.* ◇ *She **rattled** the money in the tin.*

rattle² (say **rat**-l) *noun* (*plural* **rattles**)
1 the noise of hard things hitting each other: *the **rattle** of empty bottles*
2 a toy that a baby can shake to make a noise

raucous (say **raw**-kuhss) *adjective*
sounding loud and unpleasant: *There was **raucous** shouting outside.*

ravage (say **rav**-ij) *verb* (**ravaging**, **ravaged**)
to damage something very badly: *a country **ravaged** by war* ◇ *Bad weather **ravaged** the coast.*
▸ **ravages** (*noun*): *the **ravages** of time*

rave¹ (say **rayv**) *verb* (**raving**, **raved**)
1 (*informal*) to say very good things about something or somebody: *Everyone's **raving** about her latest CD!*
2 to speak angrily or wildly

rave² (say **rayv**) *noun* (*plural* **raves**)
a large party at which people dance to electronic music

ravenous (say **rav**-uh-nuhss) *adjective*
very hungry

ravine (say ruh-**veen**) *noun* (*plural* **ravines**)
a deep narrow valley with steep sides ➲ See illustration at **mountain**

ravishing (say **rav**-ish-ing) *adjective*
very beautiful: *You look **ravishing** in that dress!*

raw *adjective* (**rawer**, **rawest**)
1 not cooked: ***raw** meat*
2 in its natural state or not yet made into anything: ***raw** sugar*

ray *noun* (*plural* **rays**)
a line of light or heat: *the sun's **rays***

raze (say **rayz**) *verb* (**razing**, **razed**)
to completely destroy something such as a building or a town: *The house was **razed** to the ground.*

razor (say **rayz**-uh) *noun* (*plural* **razors**)
a sharp instrument that people shave with: *an electric **razor***

razor blade *noun* (*plural* **razor blades**)
the thin metal part of a **razor** that cuts

Rd *abbreviation* **road**

RDP (say aar-dee-**pee**) *abbreviation* (*S. African*)
reconstruction and development programme

re (say **ree**) *preposition*
about. We usually use **re** at the beginning of a letter to say what the letter is about
🛈 ORIGIN: from Latin *re-*, *red-* meaning 'again, back'

re- (say **ree**) *prefix*
You can add **re-** to the beginning of some words to give them the meaning 'again': *We had to **rebuild** the fence after the storm.* ◇ *Your homework is all wrong. Please **redo** it.*

reach¹ (say **reech**) *verb* (**reaching**, **reached**)
1 to arrive somewhere: *It was dark when we **reached** home.* ◇ *Have you **reached** the end of the book yet?*
2 to put out your hand to do or get something: *I **reached** for the telephone.*
3 to be able to touch something: *I can't **reach** that book on the top shelf.*

reach² (say **reech**) *noun* (*no plural*)
the distance that you can stretch your arm
beyond reach, **out of reach** too far away to touch: *Keep this medicine out of children's **reach**.*
within reach near enough to touch or go to: *Is the beach within **reach** of the hotel?*

react (say ree-**akt**) *verb* (**reacting**, **reacted**)
1 to say or do something because something has happened: *How did Mbali **react** to the news?*
2 to become ill after eating, breathing or touching a particular substance
3 (used about a chemical substance) to change after coming into contact with another substance

reaction (say ree-**ak**-shuhn) *noun* (*plural* **reactions**)
1 what you say or do because of something that has happened: *What was his **reaction** to the news?*
2 a bad effect that your body experiences because of something that you have eaten, touched or breathed: *She had a bad **reaction** to something in the food.*
3 a chemical change produced by two or more substances coming into contact with each other

reactor (say ree-**ak**-tuh) *noun* (*plural* **reactors**)
1 a container or device in which a chemical reaction takes place
2 a very large machine that produces nuclear energy: *a nuclear* ***reactor***

read (say **reed**) *verb* (**reading, read**)
1 to look at words and understand them: *Have you* ***read*** *this book? It's very interesting.*
2 to say words that you can see: *I* ***read*** *a story to the children.* ◇ *The teacher* ***read*** *out the list of names.*
▸ **reading** (*noun*): *My interests are* ***reading*** *and football.*

reader (say **reed**-uh) *noun* (*plural* **readers**)
1 a person who reads something
2 a book for practising reading at school

readily (say **red**-i-lee) *adverb*
quickly and easily: *Most vegetables are* ***readily*** *available at this time of year.*

ready (say **red**-ee) *adjective*
1 prepared and able to do something: *I'll be* ***ready*** *to leave in five minutes.* ◇ *I must go and get* ***ready*** *for school.*
2 finished so that you can have or use it: *Dinner will be* ***ready*** *soon.*
3 happy to do something: *He's always* ***ready*** *to help.* ➲ SYNONYM **willing**

ready-made (say red-ee-**mayd**) *adjective*
already prepared and ready to use: ***ready-made*** *meals*

real (say **ree**-uhl) *adjective*
1 not false or a copy: *This ring is* ***real*** *gold.*
2 big or complete: *I've got a* ***real*** *problem.*
3 existing and not just imagined: *The film is about events that happened in* ***real*** *life.*
4 actually true and not only what people think is true: *The name he gave to the police wasn't his* ***real*** *name.*

realism (say **ree**-uh-liz-m) *noun* (*no plural*)
1 behaviour that shows that you accept the facts of a situation and are not influenced by your feelings
2 showing things as they are, especially in art and literature ➲ See **symbolism**

realistic (say ree-uh-**liss**-tik) *adjective*
1 sensible and accepting what is possible in a particular situation: *We have to be* ***realistic*** *about our chances of winning.*
2 showing things as they really are: *a* ***realistic*** *drawing*
3 not real but appearing to be real: *The monsters in the film were very* ***realistic.***

reality (say ree-**al**-i-tee) *noun*
1 (*no plural*) the way that something really is, not how you would like it to be: *I enjoyed my holiday, but now it's back to* ***reality.*** ◇ *She looked very confident but in* ***reality*** *she was extremely nervous.*
2 (*plural* **realities**) a thing that is actually experienced or seen, not just imagined: *the harsh* ***realities*** *of life*

realize (say **ree**-uh-lize) *verb* (**realizing, realized**) (also **realise**)
to understand or know something: *When I got home, I* ***realized*** *that I had lost my key.* ◇ *I didn't* ***realize*** *you were American.*
▸ **realization** (*noun*) (also **realisation**): *the* ***realization*** *of what he had done*

really (say **ree**-uh-lee) *adverb*
1 actually or in fact: *Do you* ***really*** *love him?*
2 very or very much: *I'm* ***really*** *hungry.* ◇ *'Do you like this music?' 'Not* ***really.'***
3 a word that shows you are interested or surprised: *'I'm going to China next year.' '****Really?****'*

SPELLING Remember! You spell **really** with **ll**.

reap (say **reep**) *verb* (**reaping, reaped**)
1 to cut and collect a crop: *We* ***reaped*** *the wheat this month.*
2 to get something, especially something good, as a direct result of something that you have done: *Work hard now and you'll* ***reap*** *the benefits later on.*

rear¹ (say **reer**) *noun* (*no plural*)
the back part of something: *The kitchen is at the* ***rear*** *of the house.* ➲ OPPOSITE **front**

rear² (say **reer**) *adjective*
at the back of something: *the* ***rear*** *window of a car*

rear³ (say **reer**) *verb* (**rearing, reared**)
to care for and educate young children: *She* ***reared*** *three children without any help.*
➲ SYNONYM **raise** 5

reason (say **ree**-zuhn) *noun* (*plural* **reasons**)
a cause or an explanation for why you do something or why something happens: *The* ***reason*** *I didn't come to the party was that I was ill.* ◇ *Is there any* ***reason*** *why you were late?* ◇ *She gave no* ***reasons*** *for her decision.*

reasonable (say **reez**-nuhb-l) *adjective*
1 fair and ready to listen to what other people say: *I tried to be* ***reasonable*** *even though I was very angry.*
2 fair or right in a particular situation: *I think R100 is a* ***reasonable*** *price.*
➲ OPPOSITE **unreasonable**

reasonably (say **reez**-nuh-blee) *adverb*
1 quite, but not very: *The food was* ***reasonably*** *good.* ➲ SYNONYM **fairly** 1

A B C D E F G H I J K L M N O P Q R S T U V W X Y Z

2 in a reasonable way: *Don't get angry – let's talk about this **reasonably**.*

reassure (say ree-uh-**shyoor**) *verb* (**reassuring, reassured**)
to say or do something to make somebody feel safer or happier: *The doctor **reassured** her that she was not seriously ill.*
▸ **reassurance** (*noun*): *He needs **reassurance**.*

rebel[1] (say **reb**-l) *noun* (*plural* **rebels**)
a person who fights or acts out against the people in control, for example the government

rebel[2] (say ri-**bel**) *verb* (**rebelling, rebelled**)
to fight or act out against the people in control, for example the government or your parents: *She **rebelled** against her parents by refusing to speak to them.*

PRONUNCIATION Notice that you pronounce the noun and the verb differently.

rebellion (say ri-**bel**-i-uhn) *noun* (*plural* **rebellions**)
a time when some of the people in a country fight against their government: *Hundreds of people died in the **rebellion**.*

rebuke (say ri-**byook**) *verb* (**rebuking, rebuked**) (*formal*) to speak angrily to someone because they have done something wrong
➲ See **reprimand**, **scold**
▸ **rebuke** (*noun*)

recall (say ri-**kawl**) *verb* (**recalling, recalled**) (*formal*) to remember something: *I don't **recall** the name of the hotel.*

recap (say ree-**kap**) *verb* (**recapping, recapped**) (*informal*)
short for **recapitulate**

recapitulate (say ree-kap-**it**-yuu-layt) *verb* (**recapitulating, recapitulated**) (*formal*)
to repeat or look again at the main points of something to make sure you understand them
➲ See **recap**

recede (say ri-**seed**) *verb* (**receding, receded**)
1 to move away and begin to disappear: *The flood waters **receded** after the rain stopped.*
2 (used about a hope, fear, chance) to become smaller or less strong: *Her fear **receded** when she turned the light on.*
3 (used about a man's hair) to stop growing and to fall out from the front of his head: *He's got a **receding** hairline.*

receipt (say ri-**seet**) *noun* (*plural* **receipts**)
a piece of paper that shows you have paid for something: *Can I have a **receipt**?*

PRONUNCIATION Don't pronounce the **p** in **receipt.**

receive (say ri-**seev**) *verb* (**receiving, received**) (*formal*)
to get or accept something that somebody has given or sent to you: *Did you **receive** my letter?*

SPELLING **ie** or **ei**? When the sound rhymes with **be**, the rule is **i before e, except after c**, so **receive** is spelt with **ei.**

receiver (say ri-**seev**-uh) *noun* (*plural* **receivers**)
the part of a telephone that you use for listening and speaking

recent (say **ree**-suhnt) *adjective*
that happened or began only a short time ago: *Is this a **recent** photo of your brother?*

recently (say **ree**-suhnt-lee) *adverb*
not long ago: *She was top of the class until quite **recently**.*

receptacle (say ri-**sep**-tuh-kuhl) *noun* (*plural* **receptacles**)
a container for something: *Put your recycling into the appropriate **receptacle**.*

reception (say ri-**sep**-shuhn) *noun*
1 (*no plural*) the place where you go first when you arrive at a hotel or an office building: *You can get your room key from **reception**.*
2 (*plural* **receptions**) a big important party: *The wedding **reception** will be held at the hotel.*
3 (*no plural*) the way people react to something: *The visiting team got a hostile **reception**.*
4 (*no plural*) the quality of radio or television signals: *TV **reception** is very poor where we live.*

receptionist (say ri-**sep**-shuh-nist) *noun* (*plural* **receptionists**)
a person in a hotel or an office whose job is to answer the telephone and to help people when they arrive

recession (say ri-**sesh**-n) *noun* (*plural* **recessions**)
a period of time when the economy of a country is not successful: *We are in a **recession**.* ◇ *This is the worst **recession** in years.*

recipe (say **ress**-uh-pee) *noun* (*plural* **recipes**)
a piece of writing that tells you how to cook something

recipient (say ri-**sip**-i-uhnt) *noun* (*plural* **recipients**) (*formal*) a person who receives something

reciprocate (say ri-**sip**-ruh-kayt) *verb* (**reciprocating, reciprocated**)
1 to behave or feel towards someone in the same way that they behave or feel towards you: *My feelings for her were* ***reciprocated.***
2 (*technology*) to move backwards and forwards in a straight line: *a* ***reciprocating*** *movement*
▸ **reciprocation** (*noun*)
▸ **reciprocal** (*adjective*): *Our arrangement for giving lifts is* ***reciprocal.***

recite (say ri-**site**) *verb* (**reciting, recited**)
to say a piece of writing aloud from memory, especially a poem or a list: *Learners* ***recite*** *the poem in groups.*

reckless (say **rek**-luhss) *adjective*
doing dangerous things without thinking about what could happen: ***reckless*** *driving*

reckon (say **rek**-uhn) *verb* (**reckoning, reckoned**)
1 to use numbers to find an answer: *We* ***reckoned*** *the journey would take about half an hour.* ➲ SYNONYM **calculate**
2 (*informal*) to believe something because you have thought about it: *It's very late. I* ***reckon*** *she isn't coming.*

reclaim (say ri-**klaym**) *verb* (**reclaiming, reclaimed**)
1 to get back something that has been lost or taken away: *Go to Lost Property to* ***reclaim*** *your belongings.*
2 to make sea or wetland (= land that is often covered with water) available for use: *The land behind the harbour has been* ***reclaimed.***
▸ **reclamation** (*noun*)

recline (say ri-**kline**) *verb* (**reclining, reclined**)
to sit or lie back in a relaxed and comfortable way
▸ **reclining** (*adjective*): *We've got a* ***reclining*** *chair.*

recognition (say rek-uhg-**nish**-uhn) *noun* (*no plural*)
1 knowing what something is or who somebody is when you see it or them: *I said hello to her, but there was no sign of* ***recognition*** *on her face.*
2 knowing that something exists or is true: *There is* ***recognition*** *that something needs to be done about crime.*

recognize (say **rek**-uhg-nize) *verb* (**recognizing, recognized**) (also **recognise**)
1 to know again somebody or something that you have seen or heard before: *I didn't* ***recognize*** *you without your glasses.*
2 to know that something exists or is true: *They* ***recognize*** *that there is a problem.*
3 to accept something officially: *My qualifications are not* ***recognized*** *in other countries.*
▸ **recognizable** (*adjective*) (also **recognisable**): *the most* ***recognizable*** *soccer star*

recollect (say rek-uh-**lekt**) *verb* (**recollecting, recollected**)
to remember something, especially by making an effort: *I can't* ***recollect*** *the exact number.*
▸ **recollection** (*noun*): *I have no* ***recollection*** *of that event.*

recommend (say rek-uh-**mend**) *verb* (**recommending, recommended**)
1 to tell somebody that a person or thing is good or useful: *Can you* ***recommend*** *a good book to read?*
2 to tell somebody in a helpful way what you think they should do: *I* ***recommend*** *that you see a doctor.* ➲ SYNONYM **advise**

SPELLING Remember! You spell **recommend** with one **c** and **mm**.

recommendation (say rek-uh-men-**day**-shuhn) *noun* (*plural* **recommendations**)
saying that something is good or useful: *I read this book on her* ***recommendation.***

reconcile (say rek-uhn-**sile**) *verb* (**reconciling, reconciled**)
1 (used about people) to become friends again after an argument: *They* ***reconciled*** *after their fight.*
2 to find a way of dealing with two ideas or situations that seem to be opposite to each other: *She had to* ***reconcile*** *her love for shopping with her tight budget.*
3 to accept a situation because there is nothing you can do to change it: *I have to* ***reconcile*** *myself to the fact that we get homework every day.*
▸ **reconciliation** (*noun*): *They hoped for a* ***reconciliation.***

reconnaissance (say ri-**kon**-i-suhnss) *noun* (*no plural*)
the study of an area for military reasons: *They did* ***reconnaissance*** *at night.*

reconstruct (say ree-kuhn-**strukt**) *verb* (**reconstructing, reconstructed**)
1 to build something again after it has been destroyed
2 to make up a full picture of something using all the facts: *The police* ***reconstructed*** *the crime scene.*
▸ **reconstruction** (*noun*): ***reconstruction*** *after the war*

record[1] (say **rek**-awd) *noun* (*plural* **records**)
1 notes about things that have happened: *Keep*

A B C D E F G H I J K L M N O P Q R S T U V W X Y Z

*a **record** of all the books you read.*
2 a thin round piece of plastic that makes music when you play it on a special machine: *a **record** company* ◇ *Put another **record** on.*
3 the best, fastest, highest or lowest that has been done in a sport: *She holds the school **record** for long jump.* ◇ *He did it in **record** time* (= very fast). ◇ *She's hoping to break the **record** for the 100 metres* (= to do it faster than anyone has done before).

PRONUNCIATION Notice that you pronounce the noun and the verb differently.

record² (say ri-**kawd**) *verb* (**recording, recorded**)
1 to write notes about or make pictures of things that happen so you can remember them later: ***Record** your observations in your Science notebook.* ◇ *In his diary he **recorded** the events of the holiday.* ➲ SYNONYM **tape²**
2 to put music or a film on a tape, a CD or a DVD so that you can listen to or watch it later: *I **recorded** a programme from the TV.*

record-breaking (say **rek**-awd-brayk-ing) *adjective*
the best, fastest, highest, most or least ever: *We did the journey in **record-breaking** time.*

recorder (say ri-**kawd**-uh) *noun* (*plural* **recorders**)
1 a musical instrument that children often play. You blow through it and cover the holes in it with your fingers to make different sounds.
2 a machine for recording sounds or pictures: *a video **recorder*** ➲ See **tape recorder**

recording (say ri-**kawd**-ing) *noun* (*plural* **recordings**)
sounds or pictures on a tape, CD or film: *a new **recording** of Mozart's 'Don Giovanni'*

recount (say ri-**kownt**) *verb* (**recounting, recounted**) (*formal*) to tell a story or describe an event: *He **recounted** the events of the day.*
➲ SYNONYM **narrate**

re-count (say **ree**-kownt) *verb* (**re-counting, re-counted**)
to count something again: *The votes were **re-counted**.*
▸ **re-count** (*noun*): *He asked for a **re-count**.*

recover (say ri-**kuv**-uh) *verb* (**recovering, recovered**)
1 to become well or happy again after you have been ill or sad: *She is slowly **recovering** from her illness.*
2 to get back something that was lost: *Police never **recovered** the stolen car.*

recovery (say ri-**kuv**-uh-ree) *noun* (*no plural*)
1 when you feel well or happy again after you have been ill or sad: *He made a quick **recovery** after his operation.*
2 getting something back that was lost, stolen or missing

recreation (say rek-ri-**ay**-shuhn) *noun* (*no plural*)
relaxing and enjoying yourself when you are not working: ***recreation** activities such as swimming and yoga* ➲ SYNONYM **leisure**

recruit¹ (say ri-**kroot**) *verb* (**recruiting, recruited**)
to find new people to join a company or an organization: *The army is **recruiting** new officers.*

recruit² (say ri-**kroot**) *noun* (*plural* **recruits**)
a person who has just joined the army, the navy or the police: *the training of new **recruits***

rectangle (say rek-**tang**-guhl) *noun* (*plural* **rectangles**)
a flat closed shape with two long sides, two short sides and four angles of 90 degrees
▸ **rectangular** (*adjective*): *This page is **rectangular**.*
ⓘ ORIGIN: 16th century, from Latin *rectangulum*, from *rectus* meaning 'straight' + *angulus* meaning 'an angle'

rectify (say **rek**-ti-fy) *verb* (**rectifying, rectified**)
(*formal*) to correct something that is wrong: *I'll **rectify** the situation.*

rector (say **rek**-tuh) *noun* (*plural* **rectors**)
1 a priest in some Christian churches
2 the person in charge of certain universities and religious institutions

rectum (say **rek**-tuhm) *noun* (*plural* **rectums** or **recta**)
the end section of the tube that holds solid waste before it leaves your body
▸ **rectal** (*adjective*): ***rectal** bleeding*

recuperate (say ri-**koo**-puh-rayt) *verb* (**recuperating, recuperated**) (*formal*)
to get well again after an illness or injury
➲ SYNONYM **recover**
▸ **recuperation** (*noun*)

recur (say ri-**kur**) *verb* (**recurring, recurred**)
to happen again or to happen many times: *My flu keeps **recurring**.*
▸ **recurrence** (*noun*) ▸ **recurrent** (*adjective*)

recuse (say ri-**kyooz**) *verb* (**recusing, recused**)
(usually used about a judge) to excuse yourself from judging a case in court because you may have a conflict of interest: *The judge **recused** himself from the case because his nephew was among the accused.*

recycle (say ree-**sike**-uhl) *verb* (**recycling, recycled**)
to do something to materials such as paper and glass so that they can be used again: *Old newspapers can be **recycled**.*

recycled (say ree-**sike**-uhld) *adjective*
Something that is **recycled** has been used before: ***recycled** paper*

red *adjective* (**redder, reddest**)
1 having the colour of blood: *She's wearing a bright **red** dress.* ◇ ***red** wine*
2 Red hair has a colour between red, orange and brown.
▸ **red** (*noun*): *Lucy was dressed in **red**.*

red-handed (say red-**hand**-uhd) *adjective*
to catch someone red-handed to find somebody while they are actually doing something wrong: *I caught her **red-handed** while she was reading my diary.*

redress (say ri-**dress**) *verb* (**redressing, redressed**) (*formal*) to make a situation right again: *It is necessary to **redress** the inequalities in the sports teams.*
▸ **redress** (*noun*): *The commission's main objective is **redress**.*

reduce (say ri-**dyooss**) *verb* (**reducing, reduced**)
to make something smaller or less: *I bought this shirt because the price was **reduced** from R120 to R45.* ◇ ***Reduce** speed now.* ➲ OPPOSITE **increase**[1] 1

reduction (say ri-**duk**-shuhn) *noun* (*plural* **reductions**)
making something smaller or less: *price **reductions*** ◇ *There has been a **reduction** in unemployment.*

redundant (say ri-**dun**-duhnt) *adjective*
1 without a job because you are not needed any more: *When the factory closed, 300 people were made **redundant**.*
2 not needed or wanted: *The painting has too much **redundant** detail.*

reed *noun* (*plural* **reeds**)
a tall plant, like grass, that grows in or near water

reef *noun* (*plural* **reefs**)
1 a long line of rocks, sand and other material lying just below or near the surface of the sea: *a coral **reef***
2 a line of rock containing metals or minerals: *a gold **reef***

reek *verb* (**reeking, reeked**)
to smell strongly of something unpleasant: *It **reeks** of fish in here!*

reel[1] (say **ree**-uhl) *noun* (*plural* **reels**)
a thing with round sides that holds something, for example cotton for sewing or film for cameras: *a **reel** of cotton*

reel[2] *verb* (**reeling, reeled**)
1 to walk without being in full control of your legs, for example because you are drunk or because you have been hit
2 to feel very shocked or upset about something
reel something in to wind up a **reel** to bring something closer to you: *to **reel** in a fish*

ref *noun* (*plural* **refs**) (*informal*) short for **referee**

refer (say ri-**fur**) *verb* (**referring, referred**)
refer to somebody or something
1 to look in a book or ask somebody for information: *If you don't understand a word, you may **refer** to your dictionary.*
➲ SYNONYM **consult** 2
2 to describe or be connected with somebody or something: *The word 'child' here **refers** to anybody under the age of sixteen.*
3 to talk about somebody or something: *When I said that some people are stupid, I wasn't **referring** to you!*

referee (say ref-uh-**ree**) *noun* (*plural* **referees**)
the official person in sports such as football who controls the match and prevents players from breaking the rules ➲ See **umpire**

reference (say **ref**-ruhnss) *noun*
1 (*plural* **references**) what somebody says or writes about something: *The book is full of **references** to her childhood in India.*
2 (*no plural*) looking at something for information: *Keep these instructions for future **reference**.*
3 (*plural* **references**) If somebody gives you a **reference**, they write about you to somebody who may give you a new job: *Did the principal give you a good **reference**?*

reference book *noun* (*plural* **reference books**)
a book that you use to find information: *A dictionary is a **reference book**.*

referendum (say ref-uh-**ren**-duhm) *noun* (*plural* **referendums** or **referenda**)
an occasion when people in a country can vote on a particular political question: *South Africa had a **referendum** in 1992.*

refill[1] (say ri-**fil**) *verb* (**refilling, refilled**)
to fill something again: *Can I **refill** your glass?*

refill[2] (say **ri**-fil) *noun* (*plural* **refills**)
something that you use to fill something else again: *a **refill** of coffee* ◇ *a **refill** for a pen*

refine (say ri-**fine**) *verb* (**refining, refined**)
1 to make a substance pure and free from other substances: *Oil is **refined** before we can use it.*
2 to improve something by changing small details: *I will **refine** my speech before giving it.*

refined (say ri-**fined**) *adjective*
1 (used about a substance) that has been made pure by having other substances taken out of it: ***refined** sugar*
2 (used about a person) speaking or behaving in a way that shows respect, good manners and a high level of social and cultural development: *She's **refined** and elegant.*
3 improved and producing a better result than before: *The engine sounds more **refined**.*

refinery (say ri-**fine**-uh-ree) *noun* (*plural* **refineries**)
a factory where a substance is made pure by having other substances taken out of it: *an oil **refinery***

reflect (say ri-**flekt**) *verb* (**reflecting, reflected**)
1 to show a picture of somebody or something in a mirror, water or glass: *She could see herself **reflected** in the mirror.*
2 to send back light, heat or sound: *The windows **reflected** the bright morning sunlight.*
3 to show something: *His music **reflects** his interest in African culture.*

reflection (say ri-**flek**-shuhn) *noun*
1 (*plural* **reflections**) a picture that you see in a mirror or on a shiny surface: *He admired his **reflection** in the mirror.*
2 (*no plural*) sending back light, heat or sound
3 (*plural* **reflections**) a thing that shows what somebody or something is like: *Your clothes are a **reflection** of your personality.*

reflex (say **ree**-flekss) *noun*
1 (also **reflex action**) (*plural* **reflexes**) a sudden movement or action that you make without thinking about it: *She put her hands out as a **reflex** to stop her fall.*
2 (**reflexes**) the ability to act quickly when necessary: *A good tennis player needs to have excellent **reflexes**.*
reflex angle an angle of more than 180° but less than 360°

reflexive (say ri-**flekss**-iv) *adjective* (*grammar*)
showing that the person who performs an action is also affected by it. For example, in the sentence 'He cut himself' 'himself' is a **reflexive** pronoun. ➲ See Study page 11

reform¹ (say ri-**fawm**) *verb* (**reforming, reformed**)
to change something to make it better: *The government wants to **reform** the education system in this country.*

reform² (say ri-**fawm**) *noun* (*plural* **reforms**)
a change to something to make it better: *economic **reform***

refract (say ri-**frakt**) *verb* (**refracting, refracted**) (*science*)
(used about water or glass) to make a ray of light change direction when it goes through a substance at an angle
▸ **refraction** (*noun*)

refrain (say ri-**frayn**) *verb* (**refraining, refrained**) (*formal*)
to stop doing something: *Please **refrain** from chewing gum.*

refresh (say ri-**fresh**) *verb* (**refreshing, refreshed**)
to make somebody feel less tired, less hot or full of energy again: *A sleep will **refresh** you after your long journey.*

refreshed (say ri-**fresht**) *adjective*
If you feel **refreshed**, you feel less tired, less hot or full of energy again: *I felt **refreshed** after a good night's sleep.*

refreshing (say ri-**fresh**-ing) *adjective*
making you feel less tired or less hot: *a cool, **refreshing** drink*

refreshment (say ri-**fresh**-muhnt) *noun* (*no plural*)
the act of making somebody feel stronger and less tired: *We needed **refreshment** so we went on holiday.*

refreshments (say ri-**fresh**-muhntss) *plural noun*
food and drinks that are available in a place like a cinema or a theatre, or at a public event: *Light **refreshments** will be served during the break.*

refrigerator (say ri-**frij**-uh-ray-tuh) *noun* (*plural* **refrigerators**) = **fridge**

refuge (say **ref**-yooj) *noun* (*plural* **refuges**)
a place where you are safe from somebody or something: *We took **refuge** from the hot sun under a tree.*

refugee (say ref-yuu-**jee**) *noun* (*plural* **refugees**)
a person who must leave their country because of danger, for example a war

refund (say **ree**-fund) *noun* (*plural* **refunds**)
money that is paid back to you, because you have paid too much or because you are not happy with something you have bought: *The watch didn't work properly so I took it back to the shop and got a **refund**.*
▸ **refund** (*verb*): *We will **refund** your money in full.*

refusal (say ri-**fyooz**-l) *noun* (*plural* **refusals**)
saying 'no' when somebody asks you to do or have something: *a **refusal** to pay*

refuse¹ (say ri-**fyooz**) *verb* (**refusing, refused**)
to say 'no' when somebody asks you to do or have something: *I asked Matthew to help, but he **refused**.* ◇ *The shop assistant **refused** to give me my money back.*

refuse² (say **ref**-yooss) *noun* (*no plural*) (*formal*)
things that you throw away
➲ SYNONYMS **garbage**, **rubbish** 1, **trash**

regain (say ri-**gayn**) *verb* (**regaining, regained**)
to get something back that you had lost: *to **regain** power* ◇ *to **regain** consciousness*

regal (say **ree**-guhl) *adjective*
1 suitable for or typical of a king or queen
2 very impressive: *She looked **regal** in her wedding dress.*

regard¹ (say ri-**gaad**) *verb* (**regarding, regarded**)
to think about somebody or something in a certain way: *I **regard** her as my best friend.*
➲ SYNONYM **view²** 1

regard² (say ri-**gaad**) *noun*
1 (*no plural*) (*formal*) attention to or care for somebody or something: *She shows no **regard** for other people's feelings.* ◇ *There is no news yet with **regard** to the exam results.*
2 (*no plural*) what you feel when you admire or respect somebody or something: *I have great **regard** for his work* (= I think it is very good).
3 regards (*plural noun*) used to send good wishes to somebody at the end of a letter or an email, or when you ask somebody to give your good wishes to another person who is not there: *With kind **regards**, Yours …* ◇ *Please give my **regards** to your parents.*

regarding (say ri-**gaad**-ing) *preposition* (*formal*)
about somebody or something: *We will ask the teacher for more information **regarding** the trip.*
➲ SYNONYM **concerning**

regardless (say ri-**gaad**-luhss) *adverb*
in spite of problems or difficulties: *The weather was terrible, but we carried on **regardless**.*

regatta (say ri-**gat**-uh) *noun* (*plural* **regattas**)
an event at which there are boat races

reggae (say **reg**-ay) *noun* (*no plural*) (*music*)
a type of West Indian popular music with strong rhythms

regime (say ray-***zheem***) *noun* (*plural* **regimes**)
a method or system of government, especially one that has not been elected fairly: *the apartheid **regime***

regiment (say **rej**-i-muhnt) *noun* (*plural* **regiments**)
a fairly large group of soldiers in an army

region (say **ree**-juhn) *noun* (*plural* **regions**)
a part of a country or of the world: *tropical **regions** of the world*

regional (say **ree**-juhn-l) *adjective*
belonging to a certain region

register¹ (say **rej**-iss-tuh) *verb* (**registering, registered**)
1 to put a name on an official list: *You must **register** for the courses you want to take at college.*
2 to show a number or amount: *The thermometer **registered** 30 °C.*

register² (say **rej**-iss-tuh) *noun* (*plural* **registers**)
1 an official list of names: *The teacher keeps a **register** of all the learners in the class.*
2 the type of language (formal or informal) that you use in a piece of writing or when you speak: *When you write your letter of application, make sure you use the correct **register**.*

registration (say rej-iss-**tray**-shuhn) *noun* (*no plural*)
putting a name on an official list: *the **registration** of births, marriages and deaths*

registration number *noun* (*plural* **registration numbers**)
the numbers and letters on a number plate on the front and back of a car or other vehicle

regret¹ (say ri-**gret**) *verb* (**regretting, regretted**)
to feel sorry about something that you did or did not do: *He **regrets** not working harder for the test.* ◇ *I don't **regret** what I said to her.*

regret² (say ri-**gret**) *noun* (*plural* **regrets**)
a sad feeling about something that you did or did not do: *Do you have any **regrets** about selling your bike?*

regular (say **reg**-yuu-luh) *adjective*
1 happening again and again with the same amount of space or time in between: *a **regular** heartbeat* ◇ *A light flashed at **regular** intervals.*
➲ OPPOSITE **irregular** 2
2 going somewhere or doing something often: *I'm a **regular** customer at that restaurant.*
3 usual: *Who is your **regular** doctor?*
4 (*grammar*) A word that is **regular** has the usual verb forms or plural: *'Work' is a **regular** verb; the past tense form is 'worked'.* ➲ OPPOSITE **irregular** 3
► **regularly** (*adverb*)

A B C D E F G H I J K L M N O P Q S T U V W X Y Z

regulation (say reg-yuu-**lay**-shuhn) *noun* (*plural* **regulations**)
an official rule that controls what people do: *You can't smoke here – it's against the safety **regulations**.*

regurgitate (say ri-**gur**-ji-tayt) *verb* (**regurgitating, regurgitated**)
1 to bring up food that has been swallowed back into the mouth again: *The bird **regurgitates** half-digested fish to feed its young.*
2 to repeat something you have heard or read without really thinking about it or understanding it: *She's just **regurgitating** whatever her father says.*

rehab (say **ree**-hab) *noun* (*no plural*) (*informal*) the process of trying to cure a person who has a problem with drugs or alcohol: *a **rehab** clinic* ◇ *She's in **rehab**.* ℹ **Rehab** is short for 'rehabilitation'.

rehabilitate (say ree-huh-**bil**-i-tayt) *verb* (**rehabilitating, rehabilitated**)
1 to help somebody to live a normal life again after something such as an illness or time in prison: *Some prisoners are **rehabilitated** before being released.*
2 to return something such as an environment to its original state: *We are **rehabilitating** the wetlands.*
▸ **rehabilitation** (*noun*): ***rehabilitation** of the community and their environment*

rehearsal (say ri-**hurss**-l) *noun* (*plural* **rehearsals**)
a time when you practise something such as a play or a piece of music before you do it in front of other people: *There's a **rehearsal** for the play tonight.*

rehearse (say ri-**hurss**) *verb* (**rehearsing, rehearsed**)
to practise something such as a play or a piece of music before you do it in front of other people: *We are **rehearsing** for the concert.*

reign[1] (say **rayn**) *noun* (*plural* **reigns**)
a time when a king or queen rules a country: *The **reign** of King Sobhuza II began in 1921.*

reign[2] (say **rayn**) *verb* (**reigning, reigned**)
to be king or queen of a country: *Queen Victoria **reigned** for over sixty years.*

reimburse (say ree-im-**burss**) *verb* (**reimbursing, reimbursed**) (*formal*) to pay somebody back for something: *We'll **reimburse** you for the food you bought.*
▸ **reimbursement** (*noun*)

rein (say **rayn**) *noun* (*plural* **reins**)
a long thin piece of leather that is fastened to a horse's head and used by the person riding it to control it ➲ See illustration at **horse**

reindeer (say **rayn**-deer) *noun* (*plural* **reindeer**)
a big animal that lives in very cold countries. **Reindeer** are brown and have long horns on their heads.
ℹ ORIGIN: 14th–15th century, from Old Norse *hreindýri* meaning 'reindeer'

reinforce (say ree-in-**fawss**) *verb* (**reinforcing, reinforced**)
to make something stronger: *You can **reinforce** this behaviour by rewarding your puppy.* ◇ *Concrete can be **reinforced** with steel bars.*

reject (say ri-**jekt**) *verb* (**rejecting, rejected**)
to say that you do not want somebody or something: *He **rejected** my offer of help.*
▸ **rejection** (*noun*): *She got a **rejection** from the university.*

rejoice (say ri-**joyss**) *verb* (**rejoicing, rejoiced**)
to feel or show great happiness: *We **rejoiced** when we heard the news.* ➲ SYNONYM **celebrate**
▸ **rejoicing** (*noun*): *There was much **rejoicing**.*

rejuvenate (say ri-**joo**-vuh-nayt) *verb* (**rejuvenating, rejuvenated**)
to make something or somebody look or feel younger: *Use this cream to **rejuvenate** your skin.*
▸ **rejuvenating** (*adjective*): *a **rejuvenating** bath* ▸ **rejuvenation** (*noun*)

relate (say ri-**layt**) *verb* (**relating, related**)
1 to show or to make a connection between two or more things: *I found it difficult to **relate** the two ideas in my mind.*
2 to give a spoken or written report of something or to tell a story: *He **related** the history of the Bhaca people.*
relate to somebody or **something** to be connected to somebody or something: *We don't need to read this book because it doesn't **relate** to our project.*

related (say ri-**layt**-id) *adjective*
1 in the same family: *'Are those two boys **related**?' 'Yes, they're brothers.'*
2 connected with something or somebody in some way: *drug-**related** crime*

relation (say ri-**lay**-shuhn) *noun*
1 (*no plural*) a connection between two things: *There is no **relation** between the size of the countries and the number of people who live there.*
2 (*plural* **relations**) a person in your family ➲ SYNONYM **relative**[1]

relationship (say ri-**lay**-shuhn-ship) *noun* (*plural* **relationships**)
1 the way people, groups or countries behave with each other or how they feel about each

other: *I have a good **relationship** with my parents.* ◇ *The book is about the **relationship** between a boy and a girl.*
2 the way in which two or more things relate to each other: *A graph is a diagram that shows the **relationship** between two sets of numbers.* ◇ *Is there a **relationship** between violence on TV and the increase in crime?*
3 a family connection: *'What is your **relationship** to Nyeleti?' 'She's married to my cousin.'*

relative[1] (say **rel**-uh-tiv) *noun* (*plural* **relatives**)
a person in your family ➲ SYNONYM **relation** 2

WORD BUILDING Your **relatives** include **aunts**, **brothers**, **cousins**, **grandchildren**, **grandparents**, **nephews**, **nieces**, **parents** (mother and father), **sisters** and **uncles**.

relative[2] (say **rel**-uh-tiv) *adjective*
when compared to something else: *He's small **relative** to other boys his age.*

relatively (say **rel**-uh-tiv-lee) *adverb*
quite, especially when compared to others: *This room is **relatively** small* (= other rooms are bigger).

relax (say ri-**lakss**) *verb* (**relaxing**, **relaxed**)
1 to rest and be calm: *After a hard day at work I spent the evening **relaxing** in front of the television.*
2 to become less worried or angry: *I'll only **relax** when I know you're safe.*
3 to become less tight or to make something become less tight: *Let your body **relax**.*
4 to allow rules, laws, etc. to become less strict: *The council has **relaxed** the ban on dogs in city parks.*

relaxation (say rel-ak-**say**-shuhn) *noun* (*no plural*)
time spent resting and being calm: *You need more rest and **relaxation**.*

relaxed (say ri-**lakst**) *adjective*
calm and not worried: *She felt **relaxed** after her holiday.* ➲ OPPOSITE **tense**[1] 1

relaxing (say ri-**lakss**-ing) *adjective*
helping you to rest and become less worried: *a quiet, **relaxing** holiday*

relay (say **ree**-lay) *noun* (*plural* **relays**) (also **relay race**)
a race in which each member of a team does part of the race: *I run second in our **relay** team.*

release[1] (say ri-**leess**) *noun* (*no plural*)
when a person or an animal is allowed to go free: *the **release** of the elephants into the park*

release[2] (say ri-**leess**) *verb* (**releasing**, **released**)
1 to let somebody or something go free: *He was **released** from prison last month.* ◇ *Plants **release** oxygen into the environment when photosynthesis takes place.*
2 to stop holding something so that it can move, fly or fall: ***Release** the balloon and see how far it goes.*

relent (say ri-**lent**) *verb* (**relenting**, **relented**)
1 to finally agree to something that you had refused: *My parents **relented** and let me go out.*
2 to become less strong: *When will this rain **relent**?*

relevant (say **rel**-uh-vuhnt) *adjective*
important or connected with what you are talking or writing about: *If you are writing about wild animals, a story about your puppy is not **relevant**!* ➲ OPPOSITE **irrelevant**
▸ **relevance** (*noun*): *Please explain the **relevance** of your idea.*

SPELLING Be careful! Notice how to spell **relevant** and **irrelevant**.

reliable (say ri-**ly**-uhb-l) *adjective*
that you can trust or depend on: *My car is very **reliable**.* ◇ *He is a **reliable** person.* ➲ OPPOSITE **unreliable** ➲ The verb is **rely**

relic (say **rel**-ik) *noun* (*plural* **relics**)
an object or tradition from the past: ***relics** of early settlements*

relied (say ri-**lide**) form of **rely**

relief (say ri-**leef**) *noun* (*no plural*)
1 the good feeling you have when pain or worry stops: *It was a great **relief** to pass the exam.*
2 food, clothes or money that is given to people who need it: *Many countries sent **relief** to the victims of the floods.*

relies (say ri-**lize**) form of **rely**

relieve (say ri-**leev**) *verb* (**relieving**, **relieved**)
to make a bad feeling or a pain stop or get better: *These pills should **relieve** the pain.*

relieved (say ri-**leevd**) *adjective*
feeling happy because a problem or danger has gone away: *I was **relieved** to hear that you weren't hurt in the accident.*

religion (say ri-**li**-juhn) *noun*
1 (*no plural*) believing in a god or gods and the activities connected with this
2 (*plural* **religions**) one of the ways of believing in a god or gods: *Christianity, Islam and other world **religions***

religious (say ri-**li**-juhss) *adjective*
1 connected with religion: *a **religious** leader*
2 having a strong belief in a religion: *My parents are very **religious**.*

A B C D E F G H I J K L M N O P Q R S T U V W X Y Z

relinquish (say ri-**ling**-kwish) *verb* (**relinquishing, relinquished**) (*formal*)
to give something up: *He **relinquished** his position as treasurer.* ◊ *She **relinquished** her hold on the rope.*

relish (say **rel**-ish) *verb* (**relishing, relished**)
to enjoy something or to look forward to something very much: *I **relish** the thought of seeing you again.*
▸ **relish** (*noun*): *I look forward to it with **relish**.*

reluctance (say ri-**luk**-tuhnss) *noun* (*no plural*)
not wanting to do something: *He agreed to help me with my project, but with great **reluctance**.*

reluctant (say ri-**luk**-tuhnt) *adjective*
If you are **reluctant** to do something, you do not want to do it: *He was **reluctant** to give me the money.*
▸ **reluctantly** (*adverb*)

rely (say ri-**ly**) *verb* (**relying, relied**)
rely on somebody or **something**
1 to need somebody or something: *I **rely** on my parents for money.*
2 to feel sure that somebody or something will do what they say they will do: *You can **rely** on him to help you.* ➲ The adjective is **reliable**

remain (say ri-**mayn**) *verb* (**remaining, remained**) (*formal*)
1 to stay in the same way: *I asked her a question but she **remained** silent.*
2 to stay after other people or things have gone: *After the fire, very little **remained** of the house.*

remainder (say ri-**mayn**-duh) *noun*
1 (*no plural*) the people or things that are left when everything else has been dealt with: *Half the learners will pick up litter; the **remainder** will sweep.*
2 (*plural* **remainders**) (*maths*) the number that is left after dividing two amounts that do not divide exactly

remaining (say ri-**mayn**-ing) *adjective*
continuing to exist or stay after other people or things have gone or been used: *They spent the **remaining** two days of their holiday on the beach.*

remains (say ri-**maynz**) *plural noun*
what is left when most of something has gone: *the **remains** of an old church*

remark[1] (say ri-**maak**) *noun* (*plural* **remarks**)
something that you say: *You shouldn't make rude **remarks** about the food.* ➲ SYNONYM **comment**[1]

remark[2] (say ri-**maak**) *verb* (**remarking, remarked**)
to say something: *'It's cold today,' he **remarked**.* ➲ SYNONYM **comment**[2]

remarkable (say ri-**maak**-uhb-l) *adjective*
unusual and surprising in a good way: *a **remarkable** discovery* ➲ SYNONYM **notable**
▸ **remarkably** (*adverb*): *She speaks Afrikaans **remarkably** well.*

remedial (say ri-**mee**-di-uhl) *adjective*
1 aimed at improving or correcting a situation or a condition
2 helping people who have difficulty learning something: ***remedial** Maths lessons*

remedy (say **rem**-uh-dee) *noun* (*plural* **remedies**)
something that makes you better when you are sick or in pain: *He gave me a **remedy** for toothache.*

remember (say ri-**mem**-buh) *verb* (**remembering, remembered**)
to keep something in your mind or bring something back into your mind: *Can you **remember** her name?* ◊ *I **remember** posting the letter.* ◊ *Did you **remember** to go to the library?* ➲ OPPOSITE **forget**

remind (say ri-**mynd**) *verb* (**reminding, reminded**)
1 to help somebody remember something that they must do: *Please **remind** me to buy some bread on the way home.*
2 to cause somebody to remember somebody or something: *The film about the Karoo **reminded** me of my childhood there.*

reminder (say ri-**myn**-duh) *noun* (*plural* **reminders**)
something that makes you remember something: *Eddie kept the ring as a **reminder** of happier days.*

reminisce (say rem-i-**niss**) *verb* (**reminiscing, reminisced**)
to talk about pleasant things that happened in the past: *We **reminisced** about our first house.*

remnant (say **rem**-nuhnt) *noun* (*plural* **remnants**)
a piece of something that is left after the rest has gone: *We have a **remnant** of the dress she was wearing.*

remorse (say ri-**mawss**) *noun* (*no plural*)
the feeling you have when you are sorry for doing something wrong: *She was filled with **remorse** for what she had done.* ➲ See **guilt** 1

remote (say ri-**moht**) *adjective* (**remoter, remotest**)
far away from where other people live: *a **remote** island in the Pacific Ocean*

remote control *noun*
1 (*no plural*) a way of controlling something from a distance: *The doors can be opened by **remote control**.*
2 (*plural* **remote controls**) (also *informal* **remote**) a piece of equipment that you use for controlling something from a distance: *Pass me the TV **remote control** – I'll see what's on the other channel.*

remotely (say ri-**moht**-lee) *adverb*
at all or in any way: *I'm not **remotely** interested in your opinions.*

removal (say ri-**moov**-l) *noun* (*no plural*)
when you take something off or away: *the **removal** of a car that was blocking the exit*

remove (say ri-**moov**) *verb* (**removing, removed**)
to take off or to take away: *Please **remove** your shoes before entering the temple.* ◇ *The statue was **removed** from the museum.*

Renaissance (say ri-**nay**-suhnss) *noun* (*no plural*) (also **the Renaissance**)
the period in Europe during the 14th, 15th and 16th centuries when people used the ideas and culture of ancient Greece and Rome in art and literature
🛈 **ORIGIN**: from French *renaissance*, from *re-* meaning 'back, again' + *naissance* meaning 'birth'

renal (say **reen**-l) *adjective*
relating to or involving the **kidneys**: ***renal** failure*

rendezvous (say **ron**-day-voo) *noun* (*plural* **rendezvous**)
1 a meeting that you have arranged with somebody: *We have a **rendezvous** at 8 p.m.*
2 a place where people often meet
▶ **rendezvous** (*verb*): *We'll **rendezvous** at my house.*

renew (say ri-**nyoo**) *verb* (**renewing, renewed**)
to get or give something new in the place of something old: *If you want to stay in the country for another month, you must **renew** your visa.*

renewable (say ri-**nyoo**-uhb-l) *adjective*
1 (used about sources of energy) that will always exist: *Wind is a **renewable** resource.*
2 that can be continued or replaced with a new one for another period of time: *Your membership is **renewable**.*

rennet (say **ren**-it) *noun* (*no plural*)
a substance that makes milk thick and sour and is used in making cheese

renovate (say **ren**-uh-vayt) *verb* (**renovating, renovated**)
to repair an old building and put it back into good condition: *We'll **renovate** our house this year.*
▶ **renovation** (*noun*): *The house is getting a **renovation**.* ▶ **renovations** (*noun*): *We're doing **renovations** to our house.*

rent[1] *noun* (*no plural*)
the money that you pay to live in a place or to use something that belongs to another person: *How much is your **rent**?*

rent[2] *verb* (**renting, rented**)
1 to pay to live in a place or to use something that belongs to another person: *I **rent** a house on the edge of town.*
2 to let somebody live in a place or use something that belongs to you, if they pay you: *He **rents** rooms in his house to students.*

rep *noun* (*plural* **reps**) (also **representative**)
(*informal*) a person whose job is to travel around an area selling their company's products: *a sales **rep***

repaid (say ri-**payd**) form of **repay**

repair[1] (say ri-**pair**) *noun* (*plural* **repairs**)
something you do to fix something that is broken or damaged: *The school is closed for **repairs** to the roof.*

repair[2] (say ri-**pair**) *verb* (**repairing, repaired**)
to make something that is broken or damaged good again: *Can you **repair** my bike?*
➲ **SYNONYMS** **mend**, **fix**[1] 3

reparation (say rep-uh-**ray**-shuhn) *noun* (*plural* **reparations**) (*formal*) the act of giving something to somebody to show that you are sorry for suffering that you have caused

repatriate (say ree-**pat**-ri-ayt) *verb* (**repatriating, repatriated**)
to send somebody back to their own country
▶ **repatriation** (*noun*)

repay (say ri-**pay**) *verb* (**repaying, repaid**)
1 to pay back money to somebody: *to **repay** a loan*
2 to do something for somebody to show your thanks: *How can I **repay** you for all your help?*

repayment (say ri-**pay**-muhnt) *noun* (*no plural*)
paying somebody back, or the money that you pay them: *monthly **repayments***

repeal (say ri-**peel**) *verb* (**repealing, repealed**)
(*formal*) to make a law no longer valid

A B C D E F G H I J K L M N O P Q R S T U V W X Y Z

repeat (say ri-**peet**) *verb* (**repeating, repeated**)
1 to say or do something again: *He didn't hear my question, so I **repeated** it.*
2 to say what another person has said: ***Repeat** this sentence after me.*
▸ **repeat** (*noun*): *I think I've seen this programme before – it must be a **repeat**.*

repeated (say ri-**peet**-uhd) *adjective*
happening or done many times: *There have been **repeated** accidents on this stretch of road.*
▸ **repeatedly** (*adverb*): *I've asked him **repeatedly** not to leave his bicycle here.*

repel (say ri-**pel**) *verb* (**repelling, repelled**)
1 to send or push something or somebody back or away: *Burn citronella candles to **repel** mosquitoes.*
2 to make somebody feel disgusted: *The smell from the fridge **repelled** her.*

repent (say ri-**pent**) *verb* (**repenting, repented**) (*formal*)
to feel and show that you are sorry for something bad that you have done
▸ **repentance** (*noun*) ▸ **repentant** (*adjective*)

repetition (say rep-uh-**tish**-n) *noun*
1 (*no plural*) saying or doing something again: *to learn by **repetition***
2 (*plural* **repetitions**) something that has been done or said before: *Let's avoid a **repetition** of what happened last week.*

repetitive (say ri-**pet**-uh-tiv) *adjective*
1 not interesting because the same thing is repeated many times: *This music is **repetitive**.*
2 repeated often: *a **repetitive** pattern of behaviour*

replace (say ri-**playss**) *verb* (**replacing, replaced**)
1 to take the place of somebody or something: *Teachers will never be **replaced** by computers in the classroom.*
2 to put a new or different person or thing in the place of another: *The watch was broken so the shop **replaced** it with a new one.*
3 to put something back in the place where it was before: *Please **replace** the books on the shelf when you have finished with them.*

replacement (say ri-**playss**-muhnt) *noun* (*plural* **replacements**)
a new or different person or thing that takes the place of another: *Our teacher is leaving next month so we will have a **replacement**.*

replay (say ree-**play**) *verb* (**replaying, replayed**)
to play something again, for example something that you have recorded: *They **replayed** the dramatic catch.*
▸ **replay** (*noun*): *The **replay** was shown on TV.*

replenish (say ri-**plen**-ish) *verb* (**replenishing, replenished**)
to fill something up again: *Please **replenish** the water supply.*
▸ **replenishment** (*noun*)

replica (say **rep**-li-kuh) *noun* (*plural* **replicas**)
an exact copy of something

reply[1] (say ri-**ply**) *verb* (**replying, replied**)
to say or write something as an answer to somebody or something: *I wrote to her but she hasn't **replied**.* ➲ SYNONYMS **answer**[1] 1, **respond**

reply[2] (say ri-**ply**) *noun* (*plural* **replies**)
an answer: *Have you had a **reply** to your letter?* ◇ *What did you say in **reply** to his question?*

report[1] (say ri-**pawt**) *verb* (**reporting, reported**)
to give people information about something that has happened: *We **reported** the accident to the police.*

report[2] (say ri-**pawt**) *noun* (*plural* **reports**)
1 something that somebody says or writes about something that has happened: *Did you read the newspaper **report** about the earthquake?*
2 something that teachers write about a learner's work
🛈 **ORIGIN:** 14th–15th century, through Old French *report*, from Latin *reportare* meaning 'bring back'

reported speech *noun* (*no plural*) (also **indirect speech**) (*grammar*)
saying what somebody has said, rather than repeating their exact words. In **reported speech**, 'I'll come later' becomes 'He said he'd come later'. ➲ See **direct speech**

reporter (say ri-**pawt**-uh) *noun* (*plural* **reporters**)
a person who writes in a newspaper or speaks on the radio or television about things that have happened ➲ See **journalist**

repossess (say ree-puh-**zess**) *verb* (**repossessing, repossessed**)
to take something back when a person cannot pay for it in full: *The bank **repossesses** cars and houses.*
▸ **repossessed** (*adjective*): *a **repossessed** car*

represent (say rep-ri-**zent**) *verb* (**representing, represented**)
1 to speak or do something in place of another person or other people: *It is an honour for soccer players to **represent** their country.*
2 to be an example or a sign of something: *The yellow lines on the map **represent** roads.*

representative (say rep-ri-**zen**-tuh-tiv) *noun* (*plural* **representatives**)
a person who speaks or does something for a group of people: *a class **representative*** ◇ *There were **representatives** from every country in Africa at the meeting.*

repress (say ri-**press**) *verb* (**repressing, repressed**)
1 to control an emotion or to try to prevent it from being shown or felt: *He **repressed** his joy.*
2 to limit the freedom of a group of people: *In the past women were **repressed**.*
▸ **repression** (*noun*): *to suffer **repression***

reprimand (say **rep**-ri-maand) *verb* (**reprimanding, reprimanded**)
to tell somebody officially that they have done something wrong ➲ SYNONYMS **rebuke**, **scold**
▸ **reprimand** (*noun*): *to receive a **reprimand***

reproach (say ri-**prohch**) *verb* (**reproaching, reproached**)
to tell somebody that they have done something wrong: *He was **reproached** for being late.*
▸ **reproach** (*noun*): *Her behaviour was beyond **reproach**.*

reproduce (say ree-pruh-**dyooss**) *verb* (**reproducing, reproduced**)
1 to make a copy of something
2 When people, animals or plants **reproduce**, they have young ones.

reproduction (say ree-pruh-**duk**-shuhn) *noun* (*no plural*)
1 producing babies or young animals or plants: *We are studying plant **reproduction** at school.*
2 the production of copies of something: *Digital recording gives excellent sound **reproduction**.*

reptile (say **rep**-tile) *noun* (*plural* **reptiles**)
any animal with cold blood that lays eggs. Snakes, crocodiles, lizards and tortoises are **reptiles**.
🛈 ORIGIN: 14th–15th century, from Latin *reptilis*, from *rept-* meaning 'crawled'

republic (say ri-**pub**-lik) *noun* (*plural* **republics**)
a country where people elect the government and the leader: *the **Republic** of South Africa*
➲ See **monarchy**

repugnant (say ri-**pug**-nuhnt) *adjective* (*formal*)
making you feel disgusted: *This idea is **repugnant** to me.* ➲ SYNONYM **repulsive**

repulse (say ri-**puls**) *verb* (**repulsing, repulsed**)
1 to make you feel disgusted: *The scene in the movie **repulsed** me.*
2 to force somebody or something back: *The police **repulsed** the rioters.*
▸ **repulsion** (*noun*)

repulsive (say ri-**pul**-siv) *adjective*
making you feel disgusted: *What a **repulsive** smell!* ◇ *That's a **repulsive** sight.*

reputable (say **rep**-yuh-tuhb-l) *adjective*
that is known to be good and can be trusted: *Buy a phone from a **reputable** dealer.*
➲ OPPOSITE **disreputable** 1

reputation (say rep-yuu-**tay**-shuhn) *noun* (*plural* **reputations**)
what people think or say about somebody or something: *a bad **reputation*** ◇ *Our school has a **reputation** for producing excellent learners.*

request[1] (say ri-**kwest**) *noun* (*plural* **requests**)
asking for something in a polite or formal way: *They made a **request** for money.*

request[2] (say ri-**kwest**) *verb* (**requesting, requested**) (*formal*)
to ask for something in a formal way: *Passengers are **requested** not to smoke.*

require (say ri-**kwy**-uh) *verb* (**requiring, required**) (*formal*)
to need something: *Do you **require** anything else?*

WHICH WORD? **Require** or **need**? **Need** is the word that we usually use. **Require** is quite formal.

requirement (say ri-**kwy**-uh-muhnt) *noun* (*plural* **requirements**)
something that you need or that you must have

rescue[1] (say **ress**-kyoo) *verb* (**rescuing, rescued**)
to save somebody or something from danger: *She **rescued** the child when he fell into the river.*

rescue[2] (say **ress**-kyoo) *noun* (*no plural*)
saving somebody or something from danger: *The police came to his **rescue**.*

research[1] (say ri-**surch**) *noun* (*no plural*)
the careful study of something to find out more about it: *scientific **research***

research[2] (say ri-**surch**) *verb* (**researching, researched**)
to study something carefully to find out more about it: *We **researched** the history of our community using books from the library.* ◇ *Scientists are **researching** the causes of the disease.*
▸ **researcher** (*noun*)

A B C D E F G H I J K L M N O P Q **R** S T U V W X Y Z

resemblance (say ri-**zem**-bluhnss) *noun* (*plural* **resemblances**)
looking like somebody or something else: *There's no **resemblance** between my two brothers.*

resemble (say ri-**zem**-buhl) *verb* (**resembling, resembled**)
to look like somebody or something else: *Lisa **resembles** her mother.*

USAGE **Look like** are the words that we usually use.

resent (say ri-**zent**) *verb* (**resenting, resented**)
to feel angry about something because you think it is not fair: *I **resented** the way she talked about me behind my back.*

resentment (say ri-**zent**-muhnt) *noun* (*no plural*)
a feeling of anger about something that you think is not fair

reservation (say rez-uh-**vay**-shuhn) *noun* (*plural* **reservations**)
an arrangement for a room, seat, table or another thing that you have asked somebody to keep for you: *I phoned the restaurant and made a **reservation** for a table for two.*
➲ SYNONYM **booking**

reserve[1] (say ri-**zurv**) *verb* (**reserving, reserved**)
1 to keep something for a special reason or to use later: *Those seats are **reserved** for the Grade 7 parents.*
2 to ask for a seat, table or room to be kept for you at a future time: *I would like to **reserve** a single room for tomorrow night, please.*
➲ SYNONYM **book**[2]

reserve[2] (say ri-**zurv**) *noun* (*plural* **reserves**)
1 something that you keep to use later: ***reserves** of food*
2 an area of land where the animals and plants are protected by law: *a nature **reserve***
3 a person who will play in a game if another person cannot play
in reserve for using later: *Don't spend all the money – keep some in **reserve**.*

reserved (say ri-**zurvd**) *adjective*
If you are **reserved**, you keep your feelings hidden from other people.

reservoir (say **rez**-uhv-waa) *noun* (*plural* **reservoirs**)
a big lake where a town or city keeps water to use later
ⓘ ORIGIN: 17th century, from French *réservoir* from *réserver* meaning 'to reserve, keep'

residence (say **rez**-i-duhnss) *noun*
1 (*plural* **residences**) (*formal*) a large house, usually where an important or famous person lives: *The President's official **residence** was in Cape Town.*
2 (*no plural*) having your home in a particular place: *The family applied for permanent **residence** in the United States.*

resident (say **rez**-i-duhnt) *noun* (*plural* **residents**)
a person who lives in a place: *a **resident** of Soweto*

residential (say rez-i-**den**-shuhl) *adjective*
A **residential** area is one where there are houses rather than offices or factories.

residue (say **rez**-i-dyoo) *noun* (*plural* **residues**)
what is left after the main part of something is taken or used: *There is a **residue** of washing powder on the clothes.*
▸ **residual** (*adjective*)

resign (say ri-**zine**) *verb* (**resigning, resigned**)
to leave your job: *The principal of that school **resigned** last month.*
resign yourself to something to accept something that you do not like but that you cannot change: *There were a lot of people at the bank so Vani **resigned** herself to a long wait.*

PRONUNCIATION Don't say the **g** in **resign**. Notice the differences in the way you say **resign** and **resignation**.

resignation (say rez-ig-**nay**-shuhn) *noun* (*plural* **resignations**)
saying that you want to leave your job: *a letter of **resignation*** ◇ *to hand in your **resignation*** (= to give your employer a letter saying that you want to leave your job)

resilient (say ri-**zil**-i-uhnt) *adjective*
strong enough to deal with something bad that happens, such as an illness, a change or a shock: *He is **resilient** and recovers quickly.*
▸ **resilience** (*noun*)

resin (say **rez**-in) *noun* (*plural* **resins**)
a sticky substance produced from plants or from artificial materials: ***Resin** can be used to make perfumes and varnishes.*

resist (say ri-**zist**) *verb* (**resisting, resisted**)
1 to try to stop something happening or to fight against somebody or something: *Teenagers need to try to **resist** pressure from their peers.* ◇ *If a material is stiff, it can **resist** bending.*
2 to stop yourself doing or having something that you want to do or have: *I can't **resist** chocolate.*

resistance (say ri-**ziss**-tuhnss) *noun* (*no plural*)
1 when people try to stop something happening or are fighting against somebody or something: *There was a lot of* ***resistance*** *to the new road from the local community.* ◇ *Some groups supported passive* ***resistance*** *to apartheid.*
2 (*science*) a force that prevents movement or that stops another force: *air* ***resistance*** ◇ *thermal* ***resistance***
3 (*science*) (symbol R) the degree to which a material does not allow electricity to flow through it: *Electrical* ***resistance*** *is measured in ohms.*

resistor (say ri-**ziss**-tuh) *noun* (*plural* **resistors**)
an electrical device that does not allow electricity to flow freely through it

resolution (say rez-uh-**lyoo**-shuhn) *noun* (*plural* **resolutions**)
something that you decide to do or not to do: *Aisha made a* ***resolution*** *to study harder.*

resolve (say ri-**zolv**) *verb* (**resolving, resolved**) (*formal*)
to decide to do or not to do something: *He* ***resolved*** *never to steal again.*

resort[1] (say ri-**zawt**) *noun* (*plural* **resorts**)
a place where a lot of people go on holiday: *a popular seaside* ***resort***
a last resort the only person or thing left that can help: *Nobody else will lend me the money, so I am asking you as a last* ***resort****.*

resort[2] (say ri-**zawt**) *verb* (**resorting, resorted**)
to do or use something unpleasant because you have no choice: *We* ***resorted*** *to hiding the keys.*

resound (say ri-**zownd**) *verb* (**resounding, resounded**)
1 (used about a sound) to fill a space: *The phone's ring* ***resounded*** *through the library.*
2 (used about a place) to be filled with sound: *The office* ***resounds*** *with the sound of typing.*

resounding (say ri-**zownd**-ing) *adjective*
1 very great: *a* ***resounding*** *success*
2 very loud: *a* ***resounding*** *roar*

resource (say ri-**sawss** or ri-**zawss**) *noun* (*plural* **resources**)
something that a person, an organization or a country has and can use: *Coal is one of our most important natural* ***resources****.*

respect[1] (say ri-**spekt**) *noun* (*no plural*)
1 thinking that somebody or something is very good or clever: *I have a lot of* ***respect*** *for your father.*
2 being polite to somebody or something: *You should treat older people with more* ***respect****.*
🛈 **ORIGIN:** 14th–15th century, from Latin *respectus*, from *respicere* meaning 'look back at', from *re-* meaning 'back' + *specere* meaning 'look at'

respect[2] (say ri-**spekt**) *verb* (**respecting, respected**)
to have a good opinion of somebody or something: *I* ***respect*** *her for her honesty.*
➲ SYNONYM **admire**

respectable (say ri-**spek**-tuhb-l) *adjective*
If a person or thing is **respectable**, people think they are good or correct: *She comes from a* ***respectable*** *family.*
▸ **respectably** (*adverb*): *He was* ***respectably*** *dressed.*

respectful (say ri-**spekt**-fuhl) *adjective*
If you are **respectful**, you are polite to other people and in different situations: *The crowd listened in* ***respectful*** *silence.*
▸ **respectfully** (*adverb*)

respective (say ri-**spek**-tiv) *adjective*
belonging separately to each of the people being mentioned: *the three mothers and their* ***respective*** *children*
▸ **respectively** (*adverb*)

respiration (say ress-pi-**ray**-shuhn) *noun* (*no plural*)
1 (*formal*) the process of breathing
2 (*biology*) the process by which living things produce energy from food. Respiration usually involves taking in **oxygen** and releasing **carbon dioxide**: *cellular* ***respiration***
▸ **respiratory** (*adjective*): *the* ***respiratory*** *system* ◇ ***respiratory*** *diseases*

respond (say ri-**spond**) *verb* (**responding, responded**) (*formal*)
to do or say something to answer somebody or something: *I said 'hello', but he didn't* ***respond****.*
➲ SYNONYM **reply[1]**

response (say ri-**sponss**) *noun* (*plural* **responses**)
an answer to somebody or something: *I wrote to them but I've had no* ***response****.*
➲ SYNONYM **reply[2]**

responsibility (say ri-spon-suh-**bil**-uh-tee) *noun* (*plural* **responsibilities**)
a duty to deal with or take care of somebody or something, so that it is your fault if something goes wrong: *Who will take* ***responsibility*** *for the new learners?* ◇ *The dog is my brother's* ***responsibility****.*

responsible (say ri-**spon**-suhb-l) *adjective*
1 having the duty to take care of somebody or something, so that it is your fault if something goes wrong: *The driver is* ***responsible*** *for the lives of the people on the bus.*

2 being the person who made something bad happen: *Who was **responsible** for the accident?*
3 A **responsible** person is somebody that you can trust: *We need a **responsible** person to look after our baby sister.* ➲ OPPOSITE **irresponsible**
▸ **responsibly** (*adverb*): *He always behaves **responsibly**.*

responsive (say ri-**spon**-siv) *adjective*
paying attention and reacting in a suitable way to something: *The students were **responsive** to the lecture.*

rest[1] *noun*
1 (*plural* **rests**) a time when you relax, sleep or do nothing: *After walking for an hour, we stopped for a **rest**.*
2 the rest (*no plural*) the part that is left or the ones that are left: *I ate half my lunch, and left the **rest**.* ◇ *She watched TV and the **rest** of us went for a walk.*

rest[2] *verb* (**resting**, **rested**)
1 to relax, sleep or do nothing after an activity or an illness: *We worked all morning and then **rested** for an hour before starting work again.*
2 to be on something or to put something on or against another thing: *His arms were **resting** on the table.*

restaurant (say **ress**-tront) *noun* (*plural* **restaurants**)
a place where you buy a meal and eat it

> SPELLING Be careful! Notice how to spell and pronounce **restaurant**.

restful (say **rest**-fuhl) *adjective*
making you feel relaxed and calm: *a **restful** holiday*

restitution (say ress-ti-**tyoo**-shuhn) *noun* (*no plural*) (*formal*)
1 the act of giving something back to the person it was taken from
2 (in law) payment that is given for something that a person has suffered

restless (say **rest**-luhss) *adjective*
not able to stay still or relax because you are bored or nervous: *I get tired and **restless** on long journeys.*

restore (say ri-**staw**) *verb* (**restoring**, **restored**)
to make something as good as it was before: *The old painting has been **restored**.*
▸ **restoration** (*noun*): *The **restoration** of the house took a year.*

restrain (say ri-**strayn**) *verb* (**restraining**, **restrained**)
1 to control somebody or something: *I couldn't **restrain** my anger.*
2 to stop somebody or something from doing something

restrict (say ri-**strikt**) *verb* (**restricting**, **restricted**)
to allow only a certain amount, size or sort: *Our house is very small, so we had to **restrict** the number of people we invited to the party.*
➲ SYNONYM **limit[2]**

restriction (say ri-**strik**-shuhn) *noun* (*plural* **restrictions**)
a rule to control somebody or something: *If it doesn't rain soon we may have water **restrictions**.*

restroom (say **rest**-ruum) *noun* (*plural* **restrooms**)
a room with a toilet in a public place, for example a restaurant or a theatre

result[1] (say ri-**zult**) *noun*
1 (*no plural*) something that happens because of something else: *The accident was a **result** of bad driving.* ◇ *I woke up late and as a **result** I was late for school.*
2 (*plural* **results**) the score at the end of a game, competition or exam: *football **results*** ◇ *When will you know your exam **results**?*

result[2] (say ri-**zult**) *verb* (**resulting**, **resulted**)
result in something to make something happen ➲ SYNONYM **cause[2]**: *The accident **resulted** in the death of two drivers.*

resume (say ri-**zyoom**) *verb* (**resuming**, **resumed**) (*formal*)
to start something again after stopping for a period of time: *We **resumed** the lesson after the interruption.*

resurrect (say rez-uh-**rekt**) *verb* (**resurrecting**, **resurrected**)
to bring back something that has not been used or has not existed for a long time: *We **resurrected** our old costumes from the nativity play.*

resurrection (say rez-uh-**rek**-shuhn) *noun* (*no plural*)
bringing back something that has not been used or has not existed for a long time

resuscitate (say ri-**suss**-i-tayt) *verb* (**resuscitating**, **resuscitated**)
to bring a person back to life, especially after they have stopped breathing or their heart has stopped beating
▸ **resuscitation** (*noun*): *She used mouth-to-mouth **resuscitation** to save him after he almost drowned.*

retail (say **ree**-tayl) *noun* (*no plural*)
the selling of goods to the public: *I want to work in **retail**.* ➲ See **wholesale**
▸ **retailer** (*noun*)

retain (say ri-**tayn**) *verb* (**retaining, retained**) (*formal*)
to keep something: *Fresh vegetables* ***retain*** *more flavour.*
▸ **retainer** (*noun*)

retaliate (say ri-**tal**-i-ayt) *verb* (**retaliating, retaliated**)
to react to something that somebody does to you, by doing something unpleasant to them: *He* ***retaliated*** *by punching his brother.*
▸ **retaliation** (*noun*): *She slapped him in* ***retaliation*** *for his hitting her.*

retch (say **rech**) *verb* (**retching, retched**)
to make sounds and movements as if you are going to vomit

rethink (say re-**thingk**) *verb* (**rethinking, rethought**)
to think about something again because you probably need to change it: *to* ***rethink*** *a plan* ◇ *The government has been forced to* ***rethink*** *its economic policy.*

reticent (say **ret**-i-suhnt) *adjective*
not wanting to tell people about things: *She is* ***reticent*** *about her achievements.*
▸ **reticence** (*noun*)

retina (say **ret**-i-nuh) *noun* (*plural* **retinas** or **retinae**)
the layer at the back of your eye that is sensitive to light and sends an image of what you see to your brain ➲ See illustration at **eye**

retinue (say **ret**-i-nyoo) *noun* (*plural* **retinues**)
a group of people such as assistants who follow an important person around

retire (say ri-**ty**-uh) *verb* (**retiring, retired**)
to stop working, usually because you reach a certain age: *My grandfather* ***retired*** *at 65.*
▸ **retired** (*adjective*): *a* ***retired*** *teacher*

retirement (say ri-**ty**-uh-muhnt) *noun* (*no plural*)
the time in a person's life when they have stopped working, usually because they have reached a certain age: *We wished her a long and happy* ***retirement****.*

retort[1] (say ri-**tawt**) *verb* (**retorting, retorted**)
to reply quickly to what somebody says, often in an angry or amused way: *'Never!' she* ***retorted****.*

retort[2] (say ri-**tawt**) *noun* (*plural* **retorts**)
1 a quick angry or amusing reply: *an angry* ***retort***
2 (*science*) a glass container with a long narrow neck, used for heating liquids

retrace (say ri-**trayss**) *verb* (**retracing, retraced**)
to repeat a past journey or series of events: ***Retrace*** *your steps to find your keys.*

retract (say ri-**trakt**) *verb* (**retracting, retracted**) (*formal*)
to say that something you have said is not true: *She* ***retracted*** *her statement.*

retreat (say ri-**treet**) *verb* (**retreating, retreated**)
to move back or away from somebody or something, for example because you have lost a fight: *The enemy is* ***retreating****.*
▸ **retreat** (*noun*): *The army is now in* ***retreat****.*

retribution (say ret-ri-**byoo**-shuhn) *noun* (*no plural*) (*formal*)
punishment for a crime

retrieve (say ri-**treev**) *verb* (**retrieving, retrieved**)
to get something back from where it was left or lost: *We* ***retrieved*** *the necklace from behind the cupboard.*
▸ **retrieval** (*noun*)

retrospect (say **ret**-ruh-spekt) *noun*
in retrospect thinking about something in the past, often seeing it differently from how you saw it at the time: *In* ***retrospect****, I shouldn't have left my homework till the last minute.*

retrospective (say ret-ruh-**spek**-tiv) *adjective*
1 looking again at the past: *a* ***retrospective*** *discussion*
2 (used about laws and decisions) meant to take effect from a date in the past

retrovirus (say ret-ruh-**vy**-ruhss) *noun* (*plural* **retroviruses**)
a type of **virus**: *HIV is a* ***retrovirus****.*
▸ **retroviral** (*adjective*): *a* ***retroviral*** *disease*

return[1] (say ri-**turn**) *verb* (**returning, returned**)
1 to come or go back to a place: *They* ***returned*** *from Italy last week.*
2 to give, put, send or take something back: *Will you* ***return*** *this book to the library?*

return[2] (say ri-**turn**) *noun*
1 (*no plural*) coming or going back to a place: *They met me at the airport on my* ***return*** *to South Africa.*
2 (*no plural*) giving, putting, sending or taking something back: *the* ***return*** *of the stolen money*
3 (*plural* **returns**) (also **return ticket**) a ticket to travel to a place and back again: *One* ***return*** *to Langa, please.* ➲ OPPOSITE **single**[2] 2
in return as a way of thanking somebody for something they have done for you or paying them for something they have given you: *I bought you a present in* ***return*** *for all your help.*
many happy returns words that you say to wish somebody a happy birthday

A B C D E F G H I J K L M N O P Q **R** S T U V W X Y Z

reunion (say ree-**yoo**-ni-uhn) *noun* (*plural* **reunions**)
a meeting of people who have not seen one another for a long time: *We had a family **reunion** on my aunt's birthday.*

reunite (say ree-yoo-**nite**) *verb* (**reuniting, reunited**)
to come together or to bring people together again: *The missing child was found and **reunited** with his parents.*

Rev. *abbreviation* (also **Revd**) **Reverend**

rev (say **rev**) *verb* (**revving, revved**)
to increase the speed of an engine or motor: *She **revved** her car loudly before she pulled away from the traffic lights.*
▸ **rev** (*noun*): *The engine **revs** need to be kept high.*

reveal (say ri-**veel**) *verb* (**revealing, revealed**)
to tell something that was a secret or show something that was hidden: *She refused to **reveal** the names of the gang members to the police.*

revel (say **rev**-uhl) *verb* (**revelling, revelled**)
to have fun in a lively, noisy way, especially at a party
revel in something to enjoy something very much: *He likes being famous, and **revels** in the attention he gets.*
▸ **revel** (*noun*): *New Year's Eve **revels***
▸ **revelry** (*noun*): *sounds of **revelry***

revelation (say rev-uh-**lay**-shuhn) *noun*
1 (*plural* **revelations**) something that was unknown and is now made known: *He makes a startling **revelation** in his autobiography.*
2 (*no plural*) a thing or person that surprises you and makes you change your mind about something: *I had a **revelation**!*

revenge (say ri-**venj**) *noun* (*no plural*)
something bad that you do to somebody who has done something bad to you: *He wants to take his **revenge** on his enemies.*

revenue (say **rev**-uhn-yoo) *noun* (*no plural*)
money regularly received by a government, company or person: *What is your main source of **revenue**?*

Reverend (say **rev**-uh-ruhnd) *noun* (*plural* **Reverends**) (abbr. Rev. or Revd)
the title of a priest in some Christian churches

reverent (say **rev**-uh-ruhnt) *adjective* (*formal*)
showing respect ➲ OPPOSITE **irreverent**
▸ **reverence** (*noun*): *The ritual showed **reverence** for the dead.*

reversal (say ri-**vurss**-l) *noun* (*plural* **reversals**)
the act of changing something to the opposite of what it was before: *The decision was a **reversal** of the previous one.*

reverse[1] (say ri-**vurss**) *verb* (**reversing, reversed**)
1 to turn something the other way round: *Writing is **reversed** if you look at it in a mirror.*
2 to go backwards in a car or truck, or to make a car or truck go backwards: *Dad **reversed** the car into the garage.*

reverse[2] (say ri-**vurss**) *noun* (*no plural*)
1 the control in a car or other vehicle that allows it to move backwards: *Leave the car in **reverse** while it's parked on this hill.*
2 the complete opposite of what somebody just said, or of what you expect: *Of course I don't dislike you – quite the **reverse**.*

review[1] (say ri-**vyoo**) *noun* (*plural* **reviews**)
1 a piece of writing, usually in a newspaper or magazine that says what somebody thinks about a book, film or play: *We had to write a **review** of a book we'd read.* ◊ *The film got very good **reviews**.*
2 looking at something or thinking about something again to see if it needs changing: *There will be a **review** of your salary after six months.*

review[2] (say ri-**vyoo**) *verb* (**reviewing, reviewed**)
1 to look at something or think about something again to see if it needs changing: *Your salary will be **reviewed** after one year.*
2 to write about a new book, film or play, giving your opinion of it: *The play was **reviewed** in the newspaper.*

revise (say ri-**vize**) *verb* (**revising, revised**)
1 to change something to make it better or more correct: *The writer **revised** the book.*
2 to study again something that you have learnt, before an exam or test: *I'm **revising** for the Geography test.*

revision (say ri-**vizh**-uhn) *noun* (*no plural*)
studying something again that you have already learnt, in order to prepare for an exam: *I need to do some **revision** for the History exam.*

revive (say ri-**vive**) *verb* (**reviving, revived**)
1 to make somebody or something well or strong again: *They tried to **revive** him, but he was already dead.*
2 to become well or strong again: *I've **revived**!*
▸ **revival** (*noun*):

revolt (say ri-**vohlt**) *verb* (**revolting, revolted**)
to fight against the people in control: *The army is **revolting** against the government.*
▸ **revolt** (*noun*): *The army quickly stopped the **revolt**.*

revolting (say ri-**vohlt**-ing) *adjective*
extremely unpleasant or so bad that it makes you feel sick: *This meat tastes **revolting**.*
➲ SYNONYM **disgusting**

revolution (say rev-uh-**loo**-shuhn) *noun* (*plural* **revolutions**)
1 a fight by people against their government in order to put a new government in its place: *The French **Revolution** began in 1789.*
2 a big change in the way of doing things: *the Industrial **Revolution***
3 one complete turn around a central point, for example, in a car engine

revolutionary (say rev-uh-**loo**-shuhn-ree or rev-uh-**loo**-shuhn-uh-ree) *adjective*
1 connected with a political **revolution** 1
2 very new and different or producing great changes: *a **revolutionary** plan to increase the use of solar power*

revolutionize (say rev-uh-**loo**-shuhn-ize) *verb* (**revolutionizing, revolutionized**) (also **revolutionise**)
to change something completely to improve it: *The moving assembly line **revolutionized** car production.*

revolve (say ri-**volv**) *verb* (**revolving, revolved**)
to move in a circle around a central point: *The Earth **revolves** around the sun.*

revolving and rotating

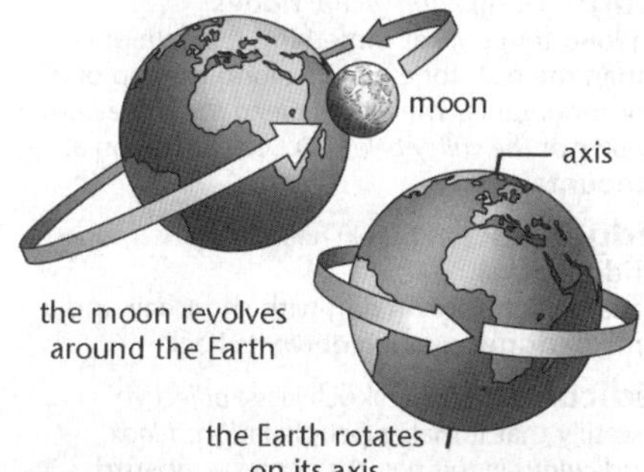

WHICH WORD? **Revolve** or **rotate**? Note the difference in the meanings of these words.

revolver (say ri-**vol**-vuh) *noun* (*plural* **revolvers**)
a type of small gun that has a container for bullets. The container turns around so that shots can be fired quickly without the user having to stop to put more bullets in

revulsion (say ri-**vul**-shuhn) *noun* (*no plural*)
a feeling of disgust: *It filled me with **revulsion**.*

reward[1] (say ri-**wawd**) *noun* (*plural* **rewards**)
a present or money that somebody gives you because you have done something good or worked hard: *She is offering a R250 **reward** to anyone who finds her dog.*

reward[2] (say ri-**wawd**) *verb* (**rewarding, rewarded**)
to give something to somebody because they have done something well or worked hard: *His parents bought him a bike to **reward** him for passing his exam.*

rewind (say ree-**wynd**) *verb* (**rewinding, rewound**)
to make a video or a tape go backwards: *Please **rewind** the tape after watching the film.*

rhapsody (say **rap**-suh-dee) *noun* (*plural* **rhapsodies**)
1 the expression of great happiness
2 a piece of music that is full of feeling and is not regular in form

rhetoric (say **ret**-uh-rik) *noun* (*no plural*) (*formal*)
a way of speaking or writing that is meant to impress or influence people but is not always sincere: *I'm tired of politicians' **rhetoric**.*
▸ **rhetorical** (*adjective*)

rheumatism (say **roo**-muh-tiz-m) *noun* (*no plural*)
an illness that causes pain in the muscles and where your bones join together (your **joints**)

rhino (say **ry**-noh) *noun* (*plural* **rhinos**) (*informal*)
short for **rhinoceros**

rhinoceros (say ry-**noss**-uh-ruhss) *noun* (*plural* **rhinoceroses**)
a large wild mammal from Africa or Asia, with thick skin and a horn on its nose

rhizome (say **ry**-zohm) *noun* (*plural* **rhizomes**)
a horizontal **stem** often under the surface of the soil that has both roots and leaves

rhombus (say **rom**-buhss) *noun* (*plural* **rhombuses**)
a flat closed shape with four sides of equal length: *Unlike a square, the angles of a **rhombus** do not have to be 90°.*

rhyme[1] (say **rime**) *noun* (*plural* **rhymes**)
1 a word that **rhymes** with another word, for example 'bell' and 'well' ➲ See Study page 17
2 a short piece of writing in which the lines end with the same sounds: *a children's **rhyme***

SPELLING Be careful when you spell **rhyme**.

rhyme[2] (say **rime**) *verb* (**rhyming, rhymed**)
1 to have the same sound or to end with the same sound as another word: *'Chair' **rhymes** with 'bear'.*

A B C D E F G H I J K L M N O P Q **R** S T U V W X Y Z

A B C D E F G H I J K L M N O P Q R S T U V W X Y Z

2 to have lines that end with the same sounds: *This poem doesn't **rhyme**.*
ORIGIN: 13th–15th century, through Old French and Latin, from Greek *rhuthmos*, related to *rhein* meaning 'to flow'

rhythm (say ri*th*-uhm) *noun* (*plural* **rhythms**)
a regular pattern of sounds that come again and again: *This music has a good **rhythm**.*

SPELLING Be careful when you spell **rhythm**.

rib *noun* (*plural* **ribs**)
one of the bones around your chest
➲ See illustration at **skeleton**

ribbon (say **rib**-n) *noun* (*plural* **ribbons**)
a long thin piece of material for tying things or making something look pretty: *She wore a pink **ribbon** in her hair.*

rice (say **rise**) *noun* (*no plural*)
short thin white or brown grain from a plant that grows on wet land in hot countries. We cook and eat **rice**: *Would you like **rice** or potatoes with your chicken?*

rich *adjective* (**richer**, **richest**)
1 having a lot of money: *a **rich** family* ◇ *It's a favourite resort for the **rich*** (= people who are rich). ➲ OPPOSITE **poor** 1
2 containing a lot of something: *Oranges are **rich** in vitamin C.*
3 Food that is **rich** has a lot of fat or sugar in it and makes you feel full quickly: *a **rich** chocolate cake*

Richter scale (say ri*kh*-tuh skayl) *noun* (*no plural*)
a system for measuring how strong an **earthquake** is: *an earthquake measuring 7 on the **Richter scale***
ORIGIN: 20th century, named after Charles Richter (1900–1985), an American geologist

rickets (say **rik**-uhtss) *noun* (*no plural*)
a disease in children who do not get enough **vitamin** D or sunlight, making their bones become soft and badly formed, especially in their legs

rickety (say **rik**-uh-tee) *adjective*
not made strongly or likely to break: *Be careful on the **rickety** bridge.*

rickshaw (say **rik**-shaw) *noun* (*plural* **rickshaws**)
a small light passenger vehicle with two wheels, usually pulled by a person walking or on a bicycle
ORIGIN: 19th century, short for *jinricksha* from Japanese, from *jin* meaning 'man' + *riki* meaning 'strength' + *sha* meaning 'vehicle'

ricochet (say **rik**-uh-shay) *verb* (**ricocheting**, **ricocheted**)
(used about a moving object) to move away quickly after hitting something hard: *The stone **ricocheted** off the car.*

rid *adjective*
get rid of somebody or **something** to make yourself free of somebody or something that you do not want, or to throw something away: *This dog is following me – I can't get **rid** of it.* ◇ *I got **rid** of my old coat and bought a new one.*

ridden (say **rid**-n) form of **ride**[2]

riddle (say **rid**-l) *noun* (*plural* **riddles**)
a difficult question that has a clever or funny answer: *Here's a **riddle**: What has four legs but can't walk? The answer is a chair!*

ride[1] *noun* (*plural* **rides**)
a journey on a horse or bicycle, or in a car, bus or train: *We went for a **ride** in the woods.* ◇ *I had a **ride** in his new car.*

ride[2] *verb* (**riding**, **rode**, **has ridden**)
1 to sit on a horse or bicycle and control it as it moves: *Don't **ride** your bike on the grass!* ◇ *I'm learning to **ride** a horse.*
2 to travel in a car, bus or train: *We **rode** in the back of the car.*

rider (say **ride**-uh) *noun* (*plural* **riders**)
a person who rides a horse or a bicycle

ridge (say **rij**) *noun* (*plural* **ridges**)
a long thin part of something that is higher than the rest, for example along the top of hills or mountains: *We walked along the **ridge** looking down at the valley below.* ➲ See illustration at **mountain**

ridgeback (say **rij**-bak) *noun* (*plural* **ridgebacks**)
a large light-brown dog with short hair and a mark **(ridge)** running down its back

ridiculous (say ri-**dik**-yuh-luhss) *adjective*
so silly that it makes people laugh: *I look **ridiculous** in this hat.* ➲ SYNONYM **absurd**

riding (say **ride**-ing) *noun* (also **horse riding**) (*no plural*)
the sport of **riding** a horse

riempie (say **rim**-pee) *noun* (*plural* **riempies**) (*S. African*)
a narrow piece of soft leather used especially to make the seats of chairs
ORIGIN: 19th century, from Afrikaans and Dutch *riem* meaning 'leather, long thin piece of leather'

rife *adjective* (*formal*)
(used especially about bad things) very common: *Rumours are **rife** that she was fired.*

rifle (say **rife**-uhl) *noun* (*plural* **rifles**)
a long gun that you hold against your shoulder to shoot with

rift *noun* (*plural* **rifts**)
1 (*geography*) a very large crack or opening in the ground or a rock: *a **rift** valley*
2 a serious disagreement between friends or relatives that stops their relationship from continuing: *Jen's boyfriend caused a **rift** between the sisters.*

rig *verb* (**rigging, rigged**)
to control or organize something in an unfair way so that you get the results you want: *The cricket match had been **rigged**.*

right[1] (say **rite**) *adjective*
1 good, fair or what the law allows: *It's not **right** to leave young children alone in the house.*
2 correct or true: *That's not the **right** answer.* ◇ *'Are you Mr Johnson?' 'Yes, that's **right**.'*
3 best: *Is she the **right** person for the job?* ➲ OPPOSITE **wrong**[1] 2
4 on or of the side of the body that faces east when a person faces north: *Most people write with their **right** hand.* ➲ OPPOSITE **left**[2]

right[2] (say **rite**) *adverb*
1 exactly: *She was sitting **right** next to me.*
2 all the way: *Go **right** to the end of the road.*
3 immediately: *Wait here – I'll be **right** back.* ◇ *Phone the doctor **right** away.*
4 correctly: *Have I spelt your name **right**?* ➲ OPPOSITE **wrong**[2]
5 to the **right** side: *Turn **right** at the end of the street.* ➲ OPPOSITE **left**[2]

right[3] (say **rite**) *noun*
1 (*no plural*) what is good or fair: *Young children have to learn the difference between **right** and wrong.* ➲ OPPOSITE **wrong**[3]
2 (*plural* **rights**) what you are allowed to do, especially by law: *In South Africa, everyone has the **right** to vote at the age of 18.*
3 (*no plural*) the **right** side or direction: *We live in the first house on the **right**.*

right angle *noun* (*plural* **right angles**)
(*maths*)
an angle of 90 degrees. A square has four **right angles**.

right-hand (say **rite**-hand) *adjective*
of or on the right: *The supermarket is on the **right-hand** side of the road.* ➲ OPPOSITE **left-hand**

right-handed (say rite-**hand**-uhd) *adjective*
If you are **right-handed**, you use your right hand more easily than your left hand, for example for writing. ➲ OPPOSITE **left-handed**

rightly (say **rite**-lee) *adverb*
correctly: *If I remember **rightly**, the party was on 15 June.*

rigid (say **rij**-id) *adjective*
1 not able or not wanting to be changed: *The school has very **rigid** rules.*
2 hard and not easy to bend or move: *She was **rigid** with fear.* ◇ *A framework structure makes a beam **rigid**.*

rigorous (say **rig**-uh-ruhss) *adjective*
done very carefully and with great attention to detail: *I had a **rigorous** training plan.*

rim *noun* (*plural* **rims**)
the edge of something round: *the **rim** of a cup*

rind (say **rynd**) *noun* (*plural* **rinds**)
the thick hard skin of some fruits, or some types of cheese and meat: *lemon **rind***

rinderpest (say **rin**-duh-pest) *noun* (*no plural*)
a disease that kills **cattle**
ⓘ ORIGIN: 19th century, from German, from *Rinder* meaning 'cattle' + *Pest* from Latin *pestis* meaning 'plague'

ring[1] *noun* (*plural* **rings**)
1 a circle of metal that you wear on your finger: *a wedding **ring***
2 a circle: *We danced around in a **ring**.*
3 the sound that a bell makes: *There was a **ring** at the door.*

ring[2] *verb* (**ringing, rang, has rung**)
1 to telephone somebody: *She **rang** up yesterday and invited me to her party.* ◇ *I'll give you a **ring** on Sunday.* ➲ SYNONYMS **call**[1] 3, **phone**[2]
2 to make a sound like a bell: *The telephone is **ringing**.*
ring somebody back to telephone somebody again: *He isn't here now – can you **ring** back later?*

ring tone *noun* (*plural* **ring tones**)
the sound a cellphone makes when somebody is calling you: *You can download **ring tones** from the Internet.*

rink *noun* (*plural* **rinks**) short for **ice rink**

rinse (say **rinss**) *verb* (**rinsing, rinsed**)
to wash something with water to take away dirt or soap: *Wash your hair and **rinse** it well.*

riot (say **ry**-uht) *noun* (*plural* **riots**)
when a group of people fight and make a lot of noise and trouble: *Police were called in to control a **riot** in the street.*
▸ **riot** (*verb*): *The prisoners are **rioting**.*

A B C D E F G H I J K L M N O P Q R S T U V W X Y Z

rip *verb* (**ripping**, **ripped**)
to pull or tear something quickly and suddenly: *I **ripped** my shirt on a nail.* ◇ *Johan **ripped** the letter open.* ◇ *She **ripped** the photo up and threw away the pieces.*
rip somebody off (*informal*) to cheat somebody by making them pay too much for something: *Tourists complained that they had been **ripped** off by local taxi drivers.*

ripe *adjective* (**riper**, **ripest**)
Fruit that is **ripe** is ready to eat: *These bananas aren't **ripe** – they're still green.*

rip-off (say **rip**-of) *noun* (*plural* **rip-offs**)
(*informal*) something that costs a lot more than it should: *R700 for a T-shirt! What a **rip-off**!*

ripple[1] (say **rip**-l) *noun* (*plural* **ripples**)
a small wave or movement on the surface of water

ripple[2] (say **rip**-l) *verb* (**rippling**, **rippled**)
to move in small waves: *The sea **rippled** and sparkled in the sun.*

rise[1] (say **rize**) *verb* (**rising**, **rose**, **has risen**)
1 to become higher or more: *Prices have **risen** by 20%.* ➲ SYNONYM **increase**[1] 2
2 to get up from a sitting or lying position: *She **rose** to her feet.*
3 to move up into the sky: *The sun **rises** in the east and sets* (= goes down) *in the west.* ◇ *Smoke was **rising** from the chimney.*

rise[2] (say **rize**) *noun* (*plural* **rises**)
an increase in the amount, number or level of something: *There has been a sharp **rise** in the price of oil.* ◇ *a pay **rise***

risk[1] *noun* (*plural* **risks**)
the possibility that something bad may happen, or a dangerous situation: *Smoking can increase the **risk** of heart disease.*
at risk in danger: *Children are most at **risk** from this disease.*
take a risk or **risks** to do something when you know that something bad may happen because of it: *Don't take **risks** when you're driving.*
▸ **risky** (*adjective*): *Jumping off the boat was a **risky** thing to do.*

risk[2] *verb* (**risking**, **risked**)
1 to put something or yourself in danger: *He **risked** his life to save the child from the burning house.*
2 to do something when you know that something bad may happen because of it: *If you don't work harder, you **risk** failing the exam.*

rite *noun* (*plural* **rites**)
a ceremony performed by a particular group of people, often for religious purposes: *funeral **rites***
rite of passage a ceremony or event that marks a stage in someone's life

ritual (say **rit**-shuhl) *noun* (*plural* **rituals**)
an action, ceremony or process that is always done the same way: *Masks are used in some **rituals**.*
▸ **ritual** (*adjective*) ▸ **ritualistic** (*adjective*)

rival (say **ry**-vuhl) *noun* (*plural* **rivals**)
a person who wants to do better than you or who is trying to take what you want: *Tinyiko and Puluso are **rivals** for the manager's job.*

river (say **riv**-uh) *noun* (*plural* **rivers**)
a long wide line of water that flows into the sea: *the **River** Amazon*

road (say **rohd**) *noun* (*plural* **roads**) (abbr. Rd)
the way from one place to another, where cars can go: *Is this the **road** to the city centre?* ◇ *Her address is 34a Windsor **Road**, East London 5201.* ◇ *Mountain **Rd*** (= on a road sign or an envelope)
by road in a car, taxi or bus: *It's a long journey by **road** – the train is faster.*

> WORD BUILDING **Street** is another word for a road in a town. A narrow road is often called a **lane**. A **highway** or **freeway** is a fast road which you use to travel around or between cities.

roadworks (say **rohd**-wurkss) *plural noun*
work that involves repairing or building roads

roam (say **rohm**) *verb* (**roaming**, **roamed**)
to walk or travel with no special plan: *Dogs were **roaming** the streets looking for food.*

roar (say **rawr**) *verb* (**roaring**, **roared**)
to make a loud deep sound: *The lion **roared**.* ◇ *Everybody **roared** with laughter.*
▸ **roar** (*noun*): *the **roar** of the plane's engines* ◇ *The lion gave a loud **roar**.*

roast (say **rohst**) *verb* (**roasting**, **roasted**)
to cook or be cooked in an oven or over a fire: ***Roast** the chicken in a hot oven.*
▸ **roast** (*adjective*): ***roast** beef and roast potatoes*
ℹ ORIGIN: 13th–15th century, through Old French *rostir* meaning 'to roast'

rob *verb* (**robbing**, **robbed**)
to take something that is not yours from a person or place: *They **robbed** a bank.* ➲ See note at **steal**

robber (say **rob**-uh) *noun* (*plural* **robbers**)
a person who steals things from a person or a place: *a bank **robber*** ➲ See note at **thief**

robbery (say **rob**-uh-ree) *noun* (*plural* **robberies**)
taking something that is not yours from a

person or a place: *What time did the **robbery** take place?*

robe (say **rohb**) *noun* (*plural* **robes**)
a long loose piece of clothing that you wear on your body, for example at a special ceremony: *The Muslim pilgrims wore long white **robes**.*

robin (say **rob**-in) *noun* (*plural* **robins**)
a small brown bird with an orange front

robot (say **roh**-bot) *noun* (*plural* **robots**)
1 a machine that can work like a person: *This car was built by **robots**.*
2 (*S. African*) a set of traffic lights: *When you reach the **robot**, turn right.*

rock[1] (say **rok**) *noun*
1 (*no plural*) the very hard material that is in the ground and in mountains
2 (*plural* **rocks**) a big piece of rock: *The ship hit the **rocks**.*
3 (*no plural*) (also **rock music**) a type of loud modern music with a strong beat played on electric guitars and drums: *a **rock** concert*

rock[2] (say **rok**) *verb* (**rocking, rocked**)
to move slowly backwards and forwards or from side to side, or to make somebody or something do this: *The boat was **rocking** gently on the lake.* ◇ *I **rocked** the baby until she went to sleep.*

rock and roll *noun* (*no plural*) (also **rock 'n' roll**)
a type of music with a strong rhythm that was most popular in the 1950s

rocket (say **rok**-uht) *noun* (*plural* **rockets**)
1 a vehicle that is used for travelling into space: *to launch a **rocket*** ◇ *a space **rocket***
2 a weapon that travels through the air and carries a bomb ➲ SYNONYM **missile** 1
3 an object that shoots high into the air and then explodes with pretty coloured lights (a type of **firework**)

rock music *noun* (also **rock**) = **rock**[1] 3

rocky (say **rok**-ee) *adjective* (**rockier, rockiest**)
with a lot of rocks: *a **rocky** path*

rod *noun* (*plural* **rods**)
a long thin straight piece of wood or metal: *a fishing **rod***

rode (say **rohd**) form of **ride**[2]

rodent (say **rohd**-uhnt) *noun* (*plural* **rodents**)
a type of small mammal that has strong sharp front teeth, for example a mouse or a rabbit

rogue[1] (say **rohg**) *adjective*
behaving differently from other similar people or things, often causing damage: *A **rogue** elephant charged the car.* ◇ *a **rogue** reporter*

rogue[2] (say **rohg**) *noun* (*plural* **rogues**)
a person who behaves badly

role (say **rohl**) *noun* (*plural* **roles**)
1 what a person does, for example in an organization or a relationship: *Your **role** is to welcome guests as they arrive.*
2 a person's part in a play or a film: *He played the **role** of the King.*

role play *noun* (*plural* **role plays**)
an activity in which a person acts a part in a situation: *We did a **role play** about arguments.*
▸ **role-play** (*verb*): *We **role-played** the situation.*

roll[1] (say **rohl**) *noun* (*plural* **rolls**)
1 something made into a long round shape by turning it around itself many times: *a **roll** of material* ◇ *a **roll** of film*
2 a small round piece of bread made for one person: *a **roll** and butter*

roll[2] (say **rohl**) *verb* (**rolling, rolled**)
1 to move along by turning over and over, or to make something move in this way: *The pencil **rolled** off the table onto the floor.*
2 to turn your body over when you are lying down: *She **rolled** over onto her back.*
3 to move on wheels: *The car **rolled** down the hill.*
4 to make something into a long round shape or the shape of a ball: *Can you help me to **roll** up this carpet?*
5 to make something flat by moving something heavy on top of it: ***Roll** the pastry out flat.*

Rollerblade™ (say **rohl**-uh-blayd) *noun* (*plural* **Rollerblades**)
a boot with a line of small wheels on the bottom ➲ See **roller skate**
▸ **Rollerblading** (*noun*): *to go **Rollerblading***

roller coaster (say **rohl**-uh kohss-tuh) *noun* (*plural* **roller coasters**)
a metal track that goes up and down and around bends, and that people ride on in a small train for fun

roller skate *noun* (*plural* **roller skates**) (also **skate**)
a boot with small wheels on the bottom
➲ See **Rollerblade™**
▸ **roller skate** (also **skate**) (*verb*): *She **roller skates** really well.* ▸ **roller skating** (also **skating**) (*noun*): *Let's go **roller skating**.*

ROM (say **rom**) *noun* (*no plural*)
computer memory that contains instructions or data that you can read but that you cannot change or remove ℹ **ROM** is short for 'read-only memory'.

A B C D E F G H I J K L M N O P Q R S T U V W X Y Z

Roman Catholic (say **roh**-muhn **kath**-lik) *noun* (*plural* **Roman Catholics**)
a member of the Christian church that has the Pope as its head: *She's a **Roman Catholic**.*
► **Roman Catholic** (*adjective*): *a **Roman Catholic** priest*

romance (say roh-**manss**) *noun* (*plural* **romances**)
1 a time when two people are in love: *a **romance** between a doctor and a nurse*
2 a story about love: *She writes **romances**.*

Roman number (say **roh**-muhn **num**-buh) *noun* (*plural* **Roman numbers**)
one of the letters used by the ancient Romans to represent numbers, such as I, V and X. **Roman numbers** are still used today in some situations, as in 'King Henry VIII' (King Henry the 8th): *My watch has **Roman numbers**.*
➲ See Study page 20 ➲ See **Arabic number**

romantic (say roh-**man**-tik) *adjective*
about love or full of feelings of love: *a **romantic** film*

romp (say **romp**) *verb* (**romping, romped**)
(used about children and animals) to play in a happy and noisy way: *The children are **romping** with the puppies.* ➲ SYNONYM **frolic**

rondavel (say ron-**daav**-l) *noun* (*plural* **rondavels**) (*S. African*)
a traditional circular **hut** (= a simple building with one room)
🛈 ORIGIN: 19th century, from Afrikaans *rondawel*, possibly from *ronde* meaning 'round' + *wal* meaning 'wall'

roof (*rhymes with* **proof**) *noun* (*plural* **roofs** or **rooves**)
the structure that covers the top of a building or car

rooibos (say **roy**-bawss) *noun* (*no plural*)
a South African plant that is dried and used to make a type of tea
🛈 ORIGIN: 20th century, from Afrikaans *rooibos* meaning 'red bush'

rook (say **ruuk**) *noun* (*plural* **rooks**)
(in the game of chess) a piece shaped like a castle

room (say **ruum**) *noun*
1 (*plural* **rooms**) one of the spaces in a building that has walls around it: *How many **rooms** are there in the new house?* ◇ *a **classroom*** ◇ *A lounge, a bedroom, a bathroom and a kitchen are all **rooms**.*
2 (*no plural*) space or enough space: *There's no **room** for the dog in the car.*

roost (say **roost**) *noun* (*plural* **roosts**)
a place where birds rest
► **roost** (*verb*): *Birds are **roosting** in the tree.*

root (*rhymes with* **boot**) *noun* (*plural* **roots**)
the part of a plant that is under the ground
➲ See illustration at **plant**[1]
🛈 ORIGIN: through Old English *rōt* meaning 'root', from Old Norse *rót*

rope (say **rohp**) *noun* (*plural* **ropes**)
very thick strong string

rosary (say **roh**-zuh-ree) *noun* (*plural* **rosaries**)
a string of small round pieces of wood, plastic or glass (called **beads**) used by some religious people for counting prayers

rose[1] (say **rohz**) form of **rise**[2]

rose[2] (say **rohz**) *noun* (*plural* **roses**)
a flower with a sweet smell. It grows on a bush that has sharp points (called **thorns**) on it

rosette (say roh-**zet**) *noun* (*plural* **rosettes**)
a decoration made from a **ribbon** (= long thin piece of material) that you wear on your clothes or win as a prize

Rosh Hashanah (say rosh huh-**shaa**-nuh) *noun* (*no plural*)
the Jewish New Year festival celebrated in September
🛈 ORIGIN: from Hebrew *Rosh Hashanah* meaning 'head (beginning) of the year'

roster (say **ross**-tuh) *noun* (*plural* **rosters**)
a list of people who share a task and the times that they will do it, or a list of people and the tasks they will do: *Put your name on the **roster** for cleaning the room.*

rosy (say **rohz**-ee) *adjective* (**rosier, rosiest**)
pink and looking healthy: ***rosy** cheeks*

rot *verb* (**rotting, rotted**)
to become bad and soft, as things do when they die: *the smell of **rotting** fruit* ➲ SYNONYMS **decay, decompose**

rotate (say roh-**tayt**) *verb* (**rotating, rotated**)
1 to turn in circles around a central point: *The Earth **rotates** on its axis.* ➲ See illustration at **revolve**
2 to happen in turn or in a particular order, or to make something do this: *We **rotate** our chores so we don't have to do the same ones all the time.*
► **rotation** (*noun*): *the **rotation** of the Earth*

rote (say **roht**) *noun* (*no plural*)
repeating something from memory: *We learnt the poem by **rote**.*
► **rote** (*adjective*): ***rote** learning*

rotten (say **rot**-n) *adjective*
bad or old and not fresh: *These eggs are **rotten** – they smell horrible!*

rotund (say roh-**tund**) *adjective*
1 (used about a person) large and fat
2 round in shape

rough (say **ruf**) *adjective* (**rougher**, **roughest**)
1 not smooth or flat: *It was difficult to walk on the **rough** ground.*
2 not exactly correct: *Can you give me a **rough** idea how much it will cost?*
3 made or done quickly: *a **rough** drawing*
4 not gentle or calm: ***rough** seas*

roughage (say **ruf**-ij) *noun* (*no plural*)
the parts of food that cannot be **digested** but that help other food and waste products to pass through the bowels ➲ SYNONYM **fibre**

roughly (say **ruf**-lee) *adverb*
1 about or not exactly: *The journey should take **roughly** two hours.* ➲ SYNONYM **approximately** ➲ OPPOSITE **exactly** 1
2 not gently: *He pushed me away **roughly**.*

round[1] (say **rownd**) *adjective* (**rounder**, **roundest**)
having the shape of a circle or a ball: *a **round** table*

round[2] (say **rownd**) *adverb*, *preposition* (also **around**)
1 on or to all sides of something, often in a circle: *The Earth moves **round** the sun.* ◇ *The bird flew **round** and **round** the room.*
2 in the opposite direction or in another direction: *I turned **round** and went home.*
3 in or to different parts of a place: *We travelled **round** Namibia last summer.*
4 to or on the other side of something: *There's a bank just **round** the corner.*
5 from one person or place to another: *Pass these photos **round** the class.*
6 (*informal*) to or at somebody's house: *Come **round*** (= to my house) *at eight o'clock.*
round about nearly, but not exactly: *It will cost **round** about R90.*
go round to be enough for everybody: *Are there enough cakes to go **round**?*

round[3] (say **rownd**) *noun* (*plural* **rounds**)
1 one part of a game or competition: *the third **round** of the boxing match*
2 a lot of visits, one after another, for example as part of your job: *The postman starts his **round** at seven o'clock.*
3 drinks for all the people in a group: *I'll buy this **round**. What would you all like?*

roundabout (say **rownd**-uh-bowt) *noun* (*plural* **roundabouts**)
1 a place where roads meet, where cars must drive round in a circle
2 a round platform for children to play on. They sit or stand on it and somebody pushes it round.

round trip *noun* (*plural* **round trips**)
a journey to a place and back again: *It's a ten-kilometre **round trip** to the centre of town.*

rouse (say **rowz**) *verb* (**rousing**, **roused**)
1 (*formal*) to make somebody wake up: *He **roused** her from a deep sleep.*
2 to make somebody feel very angry, excited or interested
▶ **rousing** (*adjective*): *a **rousing** speech*

route (say **root**) *noun* (*plural* **routes**)
a way from one place to another: *What is the quickest **route** from Johannesburg to Durban?*

routine (say **roo**-teen) *noun* (*plural* **routines**)
your usual way of doing things: *Make exercise a part of your daily **routine**.*

row[1] (*rhymes with* **go**) *noun* (*plural* **rows**)
1 a line of people or things: *a **row** of houses* ◇ *We sat in the front **row** of the theatre* (= the front line of seats).
2 (in a written table) a list of words, pictures or numbers from left to right across a page: *Draw a table with five **rows** and two columns.*
in a row one after another or with no break: *It rained non-stop for four days in a **row**.*

row[2] (*rhymes with* **go**) *verb* (**rowing**, **rowed**)
to move a boat through water using long pieces of wood with flat ends (called **oars**): *We **rowed** across the lake.*

PRONUNCIATION Notice the different pronunciations in the three entries for **row**.

row[3] (*rhymes with* **cow**) *noun*
1 (*plural* **rows**) a noisy talk between people who do not agree about something: *She had a **row** with her boyfriend.* ➲ SYNONYMS **argument** 1, **quarrel**[1]
2 (*no plural*) a loud noise: *The children were making a terrible **row**.*

rowing boat *noun* (*plural* **rowing boats**)
a small boat that you move through water using long thin pieces of wood with flat ends (called **oars**)

royal (say **roy**-uhl) *adjective*
connected with a king or queen: *the **royal** family*

royalty (say **roy**-uhl-tee) *noun* (*no plural*)
kings, queens and their families

A B C D E F G H I J K L M N O P Q R S T U V W X Y Z

rpm (say aar-pee-**em**) *noun* (*no plural*) (also **r/min**) a measurement of the speed of an engine or a record when it is playing: *My car's engine spins at 2 500* ***rpm.*** ❶ **rpm** is short for 'revolutions per minute'.

RSA (say aar-ess-**ay**) *abbreviation* Republic of South Africa

RSVP (say aar-ess-vee-**pee**) *abbreviation* (used on invitations) please reply ❶ **RSVP** is short for the French words 'répondez s'il vous plaît'.

rub *verb* (**rubbing**, **rubbed**) to move something backwards and forwards on another thing: *I* ***rubbed*** *my hands together to keep them warm.*
rub something out to take writing or marks off something by using a rubber or a cloth: *I* ***rubbed*** *the word out and wrote it again.*
▸ **rub** (*noun*): *Give your shoes a* ***rub.***

rubber (say **rub**-uh) *noun*
1 (*no plural*) a strong material that we use to make things such as car tyres
2 (*plural* **rubbers**) a small piece of **rubber** that you use for taking away marks that you have made with a pencil ➲ SYNONYM **eraser**

rubber band *noun* (*plural* **rubber bands**) (also **elastic band**) a thin circle of rubber that you use for holding things together

rubbish (say **rub**-ish) *noun* (*no plural*)
1 things that you do not want any more: *old boxes, bottles and other* ***rubbish*** ◇ *Throw this* ***rubbish*** *in the bin.* ➲ SYNONYMS **garbage**, **refuse**[2], **trash**
2 (*informal*) something that you think is bad, stupid or wrong: *You're talking* ***rubbish!*** ➲ SYNONYMS **nonsense**, **trash**

rubble (say **rub**-l) *noun* (*no plural*) pieces of broken brick, cement and stone, especially from a damaged building or road

ruby (say **roo**-bee) *noun* (*plural* **rubies**) a dark red stone that is used in jewellery

rucksack (say **ruk**-sak) *noun* (*plural* **rucksacks**) a bag that you carry on your back, for example when you are walking or climbing ➲ SYNONYM **backpack**[1]

rudder (say **rud**-uh) *noun* (*plural* **rudders**) a flat piece of wood or metal at the back of a boat or a plane. It moves to make the boat or the plane go left or right. ➲ See illustration at **ship**

rude (say **rood**) *adjective* (**ruder**, **rudest**)
1 not polite: *It's* ***rude*** *to walk away when someone is talking to you.* ➲ SYNONYM **impolite**
2 connected with sex or using the toilet, in a way that might offend people: ***rude*** *words*
▸ **rudely** (*adverb*): *'Shut up!' she said* ***rudely.***
▸ **rudeness** (*noun*): *I would like to apologize for my* ***rudeness.***

rudiments (say **roo**-duh-muhntss) *plural noun* **the rudiments** (*formal*) the most basic or important facts of something: *Learn the* ***rudiments*** *of cooking.*
▸ **rudimentary** (*adjective*): *It was only a* ***rudimentary*** *shelter.*

rueful (say **roo**-fuhl) *adjective* expressing sadness: *She had a* ***rueful*** *expression.*

ruffle (say **ruf**-l) *verb* (**ruffling**, **ruffled**)
1 to make something untidy: *She* ***ruffled*** *his hair.*
2 to make somebody annoyed or upset: *My exam results* ***ruffled*** *me.*

rug *noun* (*plural* **rugs**)
1 a small piece of thick material that you put on the floor ➲ See **carpet**, **mat** 1
2 a thick piece of material that you put round your body to keep you warm

rugby (say **rug**-bee) *noun* (*no plural*) a game like football for two teams, usually of 15 players each, using an oval ball. In **rugby**, you can kick and carry the ball.

rugged (say **rug**-uhd) *adjective* **Rugged** land is not smooth; it has a lot of rocks and not many plants on it.

ruin[1] (say **roo**-in) *verb* (**ruining**, **ruined**) to damage something badly so that it is no longer good, or to destroy something completely: *I spilled coffee on my jacket and* ***ruined*** *it.* ◇ *The rain* ***ruined*** *our picnic.*

ruin[2] (say **roo**-in) *noun* (*plural* **ruins**) a building that has been badly damaged: *The old farmhouse is now little more than a* ***ruin.***
in ruins badly damaged or destroyed: *The city was in* ***ruins*** *after the war.*

rule[1] (say **rool**) *verb* (**ruling**, **ruled**) to control a country: *He* ***ruled*** *for many years.*

rule[2] (say **rool**) *noun*
1 (*plural* **rules**) something that tells you what you must or must not do: *It's against the school* ***rules*** *to smoke.* ◇ *to break a* ***rule*** (= do something that you should not do)
2 (*no plural*) government: *The country is under military* ***rule.***

ruler (say **roo**-luh) *noun* (*plural* **rulers**)
1 a long piece of plastic, metal or wood that you use for drawing straight lines or for measuring things
2 a person who rules a country

rum *noun* (*no plural*)
a strong alcoholic drink that is made from the sugar plant

rumble (say **rumb**-l) *verb* (**rumbling, rumbled**)
to make a long deep sound: *I'm so hungry that my stomach is* ***rumbling***.
▶ **rumble** (*noun*): *the* ***rumble*** *of thunder*

rummage (say **rum**-ij) *verb* (**rummaging, rummaged**)
to move things and make them untidy while you are looking for something: *I* ***rummaged*** *through my clothes looking for pants.*

rumour (say **roo**-muh) *noun* (*plural* **rumours**)
something that a lot of people are talking about that is perhaps not true: *There's a* ***rumour*** *that our teacher is leaving.*

rump *noun* (*plural* **rumps**)
the back end of an animal: ***rump*** *steak*

run[1] *verb* (**running, ran, has run**)
1 to move very quickly on your legs: *I was late, so I* ***ran*** *to the bus stop.* ◇ *The dog* ***ran*** *after* (= chased) *a rabbit.*
2 to go somewhere: *The buses don't* ***run*** *on Sundays.* ◇ *The river* ***runs*** *into the sea.*
3 to work or to control something and make it work: *Who* ***runs*** *the business?* ◇ *The car had stopped but the engine was still* ***running***.
run away to go quickly away from a place: *She* ***ran*** *away from home when she was fourteen.*
➲ SYNONYM **escape**[1] 1

run[2] *noun* (*plural* **runs**)
1 moving very quickly on your legs: *I go for a* ***run*** *every morning.*
2 a point in the games of **cricket** and **baseball**: *Our team won by two* ***runs***.

rung[1] form of **ring**[2]

rung[2] *noun* (*plural* **rungs**)
one of the steps of a ladder

runner (say **run**-uh) *noun* (*plural* **runners**)
a person who runs

runner-up (say **run**-ur-up) *noun* (*plural* **runners-up**)
a person or team that comes second in a race or competition

running[1] (say **run**-ing) *noun* (*no plural*)
the sport of running: *Let's go* ***running*** *tomorrow morning.*

running[2] (say **run**-ing) *adjective*
one after another: *We won the competition for three years* ***running***.

runny (say **run**-ee) *adjective* (**runnier, runniest**)
1 If you have a **runny** nose, a lot of liquid comes out of it, for example because you have a cold.
2 If a substance is **runny**, it has more liquid than is usual: *Porridge should not be too* ***runny***.

runway (say **run**-way) *noun* (*plural* **runways**)
a long piece of ground where planes take off and land

rural (say **roor**-ruhl) *adjective*
in or related to the areas of land away from towns and cities: *Many* ***rural*** *households use wood as fuel for heating and cooking.* ◇ *a* ***rural*** *community* ➲ See **urban**

rush[1] *verb* (**rushing, rushed**)
1 to move or do something very quickly or too quickly: *The children* ***rushed*** *out of school.* ◇ *We* ***rushed*** *to finish the work on time.*
2 to take somebody or something quickly to a place: *She was* ***rushed*** *to hospital.*

rush[2] *noun* (*no plural*)
1 a sudden quick movement: *At the end of the film there was a* ***rush*** *for the exits.*
2 a situation when you need to move or do something very quickly: *I can't stop now – I'm in a* ***rush***. ➲ SYNONYM **hurry**[2]

rush hour *noun* (*plural* **rush hours**)
the time when the roads are busy because a lot of people are going to or coming from work

rust *noun* (*no plural*)
a red-brown substance that you sometimes see on metal that has been wet
▶ **rust** (*verb*): *My bike* ***rusted*** *because I left it out in the rain.* ▶ **rusty** (*adjective*): *a* ***rusty*** *nail*

rustic (say **russ**-tik) *adjective*
typical of the countryside: *We stayed in a* ***rustic*** *cabin with no electricity.*

rustle (say **russ**-l) *verb* (**rustling, rustled**)
to make a sound like dry leaves moving together, or to make something make this sound: *Stop* ***rustling*** *your newspaper – I can't hear the film!*
▶ **rustle** (*noun*): *the* ***rustle*** *of leaves*

rut *noun* (*plural* **ruts**)
a deep track that a wheel makes in the ground
be in a rut to have a boring life that is difficult to change: *I gave up my job because I felt I was stuck in a* ***rut***.

ruthless (say **rooth**-luhss) *adjective*
(used about people) hard and cruel, or determined to get what you want even if it means treating other people unfairly: *He was a* ***ruthless*** *leader.*
▶ **ruthlessly** (*adverb*) ▶ **ruthlessness** (*noun*)

rye (say **ry**) *noun* (*no plural*)
a grain you use to make flour and alcoholic drinks, or as food for animals

A
B
C
D
E
F
G
H
I
J
K
L
M
N
O
P
Q
R
S
T
U
V
W
X
Y
Z

Ss

S (say **ess**) *abbreviation* **south** or **southern**

SA (say ess-**ay**) *abbreviation*
South Africa

SAAF (say **ess**-ay-ay-ef) *abbreviation*
South African Air Force

sabbath (say **sab**-uth) *noun* (*plural* **sabbaths**) (also **the Sabbath**)
the day of the week for rest and prayer in certain religions (Friday evening to Saturday evening for Jews, Sunday for most Christians)
ORIGIN: from Old English, through Latin *sabbatum*, through Greek from Hebrew *sabat* meaning 'to rest'

SABC (say ess-ay-bee-**see**) *abbreviation*
South African Broadcasting Corporation

sabotage (say **sab**-uh-taaj) *verb* (**sabotaging, sabotaged**)
to damage or destroy things like machinery, roads or bridges to prevent an enemy or a competitor being successful: *A group of terrorists threatened to* ***sabotage*** *the gas pipe.*
▸ **sabotage** (*noun*): *acts of* ***sabotage***

sac (say **sak**) *noun* (*plural* **sacs**)
a bag-shaped part of an animal or plant: *egg* ***sac*** ◇ *pollen* ***sac***

sack¹ (say **sak**) *noun* (*plural* **sacks**)
a big strong bag for carrying heavy things: *a* ***sack*** *of potatoes*
get the sack (*informal*) to lose your job: *She got the* ***sack*** *for being late.*

sack² (say **sak**) *verb* (**sacking, sacked**)
to say that somebody must leave their job: *The manager* ***sacked*** *her because she was always late.*
➲ SYNONYMS **fire**² 2, **dismiss** 1

sacred (say **sayk**-ruhd) *adjective*
with a special religious meaning: *A mosque and a church are* ***sacred*** *buildings.*
ORIGIN: 14th–15th century, through Old French *sacre* meaning 'make holy', from Latin *sacer* meaning 'holy'

sacrifice (say **sak**-ri-fise) *verb* (**sacrificing, sacrificed**)
1 to stop doing or having something important so that you can get something else or help somebody: *Many people* ***sacrificed*** *their lives in the struggle to end apartheid.*
2 to kill an animal as a present to a god: *They* ***sacrificed*** *a lamb.*
▸ **sacrifice** (*noun*): *His family made many* ***sacrifices*** *to pay for him to go to university.*

sad *adjective* (**sadder, saddest**)
unhappy or making you feel unhappy: *We are very* ***sad*** *to hear that you are leaving.* ◇ *a* ***sad*** *story* ➲ OPPOSITE **happy** 1
▸ **sadly** (*adverb*): *She looked* ***sadly*** *at the empty house.* ▸ **sadness** (*noun*): *Thoughts of him filled her with* ***sadness***.

WORD BUILDING See the Word Building note at **unhappy**.

saddle (say **sad**-l) *noun* (*plural* **saddles**)
a seat on a horse or bicycle ➲ See illustration at **horse**

sadist (say **sayd**-uhst) *noun* (*plural* **sadists**)
a person who gets pleasure, sometimes sexual, from hurting another person

safari (say suh-**faa**-ree) *noun* (*plural* **safaris**)
a journey to look at or hunt wild animals, usually in Africa

safe¹ (say **sayf**) *adjective* (**safer, safest**)
1 not in danger or not hurt: *Don't go out alone at night – you won't be* ***safe***.
2 not dangerous: *Is it* ***safe*** *to swim in this river?* ◇ *Always keep medicines in a* ***safe*** *place.*
safe and sound not hurt or broken: *The child was found* ***safe*** *and sound.*
▸ **safely** (*adverb*)

safe² (say **sayf**) *noun* (*plural* **safes**)
a strong metal box with a lock where you keep money or things like jewellery

safety (say **sayf**-tee) *noun* (*no plural*)
being safe: *He is worried about the* ***safety*** *of his children.*

safety belt *noun* (*plural* **safety belts**)
a long thin piece of material that you put around your body in a car or a plane to keep you safe in an accident ➲ SYNONYM **seat belt**

safety pin *noun* (*plural* **safety pins**)
a pin that you use for joining pieces of cloth together. It has a cover over the point so that it is not dangerous.

sag *verb* (**sagging, sagged**)
to bend or hang down: *The bed is very old and it* ***sags*** *in the middle.*

saga (say **saa**-guh) *noun* (*plural* **sagas**)
a very long story or a long series of events: *The*

saga of the weapons cargo carried by the Chinese ship continued for months.

said (say **sed**) form of **say**[2]

sail[1] (say **sayl**) *verb* (**sailing, sailed**)
1 to travel on water: *The ship **sailed** along the coast.*
2 to control a boat with sails: *We **sailed** the yacht down the river.*
▸ **sailing** (*noun*): *My favourite pastime is **sailing**.*

sail[2] (say **sayl**) *noun* (*plural* **sails**)
a large piece of cloth on a boat that catches the wind and moves the boat along ➲ See illustration at **yacht**

sailor (say **sayl**-uh) *noun* (*plural* **sailors**)
a person who sails ships or boats as their job or as a sport

saint (say **saynt**) *noun* (*plural* **saints**) (abbr. St)
(in the Christian religion) a dead person who lived their life in a very good way: ***Saint** Mary*

USAGE The usual way of writing **saint** before names is **St**: *St (say* **sint**) *George's Church.*

sake (say **sayk**) *noun*
for goodness' sake, for Heaven's sake (*informal*) something that you say to show you are annoyed
for the sake of somebody or **something**
1 to help somebody or something: *The couple stayed together for the **sake** of their children.*
2 because of somebody or something

salad (say **sal**-uhd) *noun* (*plural* **salads**)
a dish of cold vegetables that have not been cooked: *a **salad** of lettuce, tomato and cucumber*
ⓘ ORIGIN: 14th–15th century, from Old French *salade*, based on Latin *sal* meaning 'salt'. Originally a salad was a dish of food with salt on it.

salami (say suh-**laa**-mee) *noun* (*plural* **salamis**)
a type of large spicy sausage, originally from Italy, usually eaten cold in slices

salary (say **sal**-uh-ree) *noun* (*plural* **salaries**)
money that you receive every month for the work that you do
ⓘ ORIGIN: 13th–15th century, through Old French *salarie*, from Latin *salarium*, the word for an allowance that Roman soldiers were given for buying salt, based on *sal* meaning 'salt'

sale (say **sayl**) *noun*
1 (*no plural*) the selling of something
2 (*plural* **sales**) a time when a shop sells things for less money than usual: *In the **sale**, everything is half-price.*
for sale If something is **for sale**, its owner wants to sell it: *Is this house for **sale**?*
on sale If something is **on sale**, you can buy it in shops: *The magazine is on **sale** at most newsagents.*

salesman (say **saylz**-muhn) *noun* (*plural* **salesmen**)
a man whose job is to sell things

salesperson (say **saylz**-pur-suhn) *noun* (*plural* **salespeople**)
a man or a woman whose job is to sell things

saleswoman (say **saylz**-wuu-muhn) *noun* (*plural* **saleswomen**)
a woman whose job is to sell things

saline (say **say**-line) *adjective*
containing salt: *a **saline** solution*

saliva (say suh-**ly**-vuh) *noun* (*no plural*)
the liquid in your mouth that helps you to swallow food ➲ SYNONYM **spit**[2] 1

salmon (say **sam**-uhn) *noun* (*plural* **salmon**)
a big fish with pink meat that lives in the sea and in rivers

PRONUNCIATION Don't pronounce the **l** in **salmon**.

salmonella (say sal-muh-**nel**-uh) *noun* (*no plural*)
a type of **bacterium** that causes food poisoning and other diseases

salon (say **sal**-on) *noun* (*plural* **salons**)
a shop where you can have beauty or hair treatment or where you can buy expensive clothes

salt (say **solt** or **sawlt**) *noun* (*no plural*)
a white substance that comes from sea water and from the earth. We put it on food to make food taste better: *Add a little **salt** and pepper.*
▸ **salty** (*adjective*): *Sea water tastes **salty**.*

salute (say suh-**loot**) *verb* (**saluting, saluted**)
to make the special sign that soldiers make, by lifting your hand to the side of your head: *The soldiers **saluted** as the President walked past.*
▸ **salute** (*noun*): *The soldier gave a **salute**.*

salvage (say **sal**-vij) *verb* (**salvaging, salvaged**)
to manage to rescue a thing from being lost or damaged, or to rescue a situation from disaster: ***Salvage** parts from your old computer that could still be of use.* ◇ *Let's work together to **salvage** our economy.*
▸ **salvage** (*noun*): *a **salvage** operation*

salvation (say sal-**vay**-shuhn) *noun* (*no plural*)
1 a thing or person that saves or protects another person or thing from danger, disaster or loss: *The people are suffering and they need immediate **salvation**.*

A B C D E F G H I J K L M N O P Q R S T U V W X Y Z

2 (in religion) being saved from the power of evil: *to pray for the* ***salvation*** *of the world*

same¹ (say **saym**) *adjective*
the same not different, or not another: *Emma and I like the* ***same*** *kind of music.* ◇ *I've lived in the* ***same*** *town all my life.* ◇ *He went to the* ***same*** *school as I did.*

same² (say **saym**) *pronoun*
the same not a different person or thing: *Do these two words mean the* ***same****?* ◇ *I'd like some jeans the* ***same*** *as yours.*
all the same or **just the same** in spite of this: *I understand why you're angry. All the* ***same****, I think you should say sorry.*

samoosa (say suh-**moo**-suh) *noun* (*plural* **samoosas**)
a triangular fried pastry containing spiced mince or vegetables

samp *noun* (*no plural*)
crushed mealies, or **porridge** cooked from it
🛈 **ORIGIN:** 17th century, through North American English, from Algonquian *nasamp* meaning 'made soft with water'. Algonquian is a language spoken in North America.

sample¹ (say **saam**-puhl) *noun* (*plural* **samples**)
a small amount of something that shows what the rest is like: *a free* ***sample*** *of perfume* ◇ *a blood* ***sample*** ➲ See **specimen** 2

sample² (say **saam**-puhl) *verb* (**sampling, sampled**)
1 to taste a small amount of food
2 to test part of a thing or question part of a group of people to find out what the rest is like

San (say **san** or **sun**) *noun* (*plural* **San**) (also **Bushman**)
a member of the people who have lived in southern Africa since ancient times. Traditionally the **San** lived by hunting and collecting food from the **veld**: *He found paintings done by the* ***San*** *on the walls of caves.* ◇ *Small groups of* ***San*** *live in Botswana.*
🛈 **ORIGIN:** from Nama *sān* meaning 'collector of food' and 'indigenous people, settlers'

sanction¹ (say **sang**-shuhn) *noun* (*plural* **sanctions**)
1 a threat of punishment for breaking a rule or law
2 (usually **sanctions**) an official order that limits contact or business with a country in order to make it do something, such as treating its own people fairly: *Economic* ***sanctions*** *were imposed on the country.*
3 (*formal*) official permission or approval for an action

sanction² (say **sang**-shuhn) *verb* (**sanctioning, sanctioned**)
1 (*formal*) to give official permission for something: *The Church refuses to* ***sanction*** *birth control.*
2 to punish a person or a thing

sanctity (say **sank**-ti-tee) *noun* (*no plural*)
1 the state of being very important and worth protecting: *the* ***sanctity*** *of human life*
2 the state of being sacred: *the* ***sanctity*** *of mosques*

sanctuary (say **sank**-tshuh-ree) *noun*
1 (*no plural*) a place where a person can be safe from enemies: *The refugees fled to the church looking for* ***sanctuary****.*
2 (*plural* **sanctuaries**) a place where birds or animals are protected from being hunted

sand¹ (say **sand**) *noun* (*no plural*)
powder made of very small pieces of rock, that you find on beaches and in deserts: *Concrete is a mixture of* ***sand****, stone and cement.*
► **sandy** (*adjective*): *a* ***sandy*** *beach*

sand² (say **sand**) *verb* (**sanding, sanded**)
to smooth or polish a thing with **sandpaper**, either by hand or with a machine

sandal (say **sand**-l) *noun* (*plural* **sandals**)
a light open shoe that you wear in warm weather
🛈 **ORIGIN:** 13th–15th century, through Latin from Greek *sandalion* meaning 'small wooden shoe'

SANDF (say ess-ay-en-dee-**ef**) *abbreviation*
South African National Defence Force

sandpaper (say **sand**-pay-puh) *noun* (*no plural*)
stiff paper with sand stuck to one side that is used for rubbing surfaces to make them smooth

sandstone (say **sand**-stohn) *noun* (*no plural*)
a type of rock made from sand grains held together with other minerals: ***Sandstone*** *is a sedimentary rock.*

sandwich (say **sand**-wich) *noun* (*plural* **sandwiches**)
two pieces of bread with other food between them: *a cheese* ***sandwich***
🛈 **ORIGIN:** 18th century, named after the Earl of Sandwich (1718–1792), who was said to prefer eating this food to getting up from card games for meals

sane (say **sayn**) *adjective* (**saner, sanest**)
with a normal healthy mind ➲ **OPPOSITE insane**

sang form of **sing**

sangoma (say sun-**gaw**-muh) *noun* (*plural* **sangomas**)
(in southern Africa) a traditional healer: *You can visit the **sangoma** for herbal remedies or to discuss your problems.*
ORIGIN: 19th century, from isiZulu *isangoma* meaning 'diviner (a person who finds out the truth using special powers)'

sanitary (say **san**-uh-tree) *adjective*
connected with the protection of health, especially the way human waste is removed and clean drinking water is supplied: ***sanitary** pads or towels ◇ They are not at risk of getting the disease because their **sanitary** conditions are good.*

sanitation (say san-i-**tay**-shuhn) *noun* (*no plural*)
the equipment and systems that keep places clean, especially by removing human waste

sanity (say **san**-uh-tee) *noun* (*no plural*)
1 the state of having a normal healthy mind: *The prisoners on Robben Island played soccer as a way to survive and find **sanity**.*
2 the state of being sensible and reasonable

sank (say **sangk**) form of **sink**[1]

Santa Claus (say san-tuh **klawz**) *noun* = **Father Christmas**
ORIGIN: from Dutch *Sante Klaas* meaning 'Saint Nicholas'. People think that Saint Nicholas may have been a bishop in the 4th century AD in Turkey, who was famous for his kindness and generosity. Dutch colonists took the tradition of Santa Claus to the USA in the 17th century.

sap *noun* (*no plural*)
the liquid in a plant or tree

sapling (say **sap**-ling) *noun* (*plural* **saplings**)
a young tree

sapphire (say **saf**-fy-uh) *noun* (*plural* **sapphires**)
a bright blue precious stone

SAPS (say ess-ay-pee-**ess** or **saps**) *abbreviation*
South African Police Service

sarcasm (say saa-**kaz**-m) *noun* (*no plural*)
saying the opposite of what you mean because you want to be rude to somebody or to show them you are angry ➲ See Study page 17
▸ **sarcastic** (*adjective*): *There's no need to be sarcastic.*

sardine (say saa-**deen**) *noun* (*plural* **sardines**)
a very small sea fish that you can eat. You often buy **sardines** in tins.

sari (say **saa**-ree) *noun* (*plural* **saris**)
a long piece of material that women, particularly Indian women, wear around their bodies as a dress
ORIGIN: 19th century, from Hindi *sāṛī*

sarong (say suh-**rong**) *noun* (*plural* **sarongs**)
a long piece of material folded around the body from the waist or the chest, worn by Malaysian and Indonesian men and women

SARS (say **saaz**) *abbreviation*
South African Revenue Service

sash *noun* (*plural* **sashes**)
a long piece of material that is worn round the waist or across the shoulder, often as part of a uniform

sat form of **sit**

satanic (say say-**tan**-ik) *adjective*
1 connected with the **worship** 2 of devils: *satanic rituals*
2 evil: *The matric learner went on a **satanic** murder spree.*

satchel (say **sach**-uhl) *noun* (*plural* **satchels**)
a bag that children use for carrying books to and from school

satellite (say **sat**-uh-lite) *noun* (*plural* **satellites**)
1 a piece of electronic equipment that people send into space. **Satellites** travel round the Earth and send back pictures or television and radio signals: ***satellite** television*
2 a large natural object that moves around a planet in space: *The moon is a **satellite** of the Earth.*
ORIGIN: 16th century, through French *satellite*, from Latin *satelles* meaning 'attendant'. When the word first came into English it meant 'a follower'. Later it came to mean one object that always moves near or around another one, especially in the sky.

satellite dish *noun* (*plural* **satellite dishes**)
a piece of equipment that people put on the outside of their houses so that they can receive television signals from a **satellite**

satin (say **sat**-in) *noun* (*no plural*)
very shiny smooth cloth

satire (say **sat**-y-uh) *noun*
1 (*no plural*) using humour to attack somebody or something that you think is bad or silly: *political **satire***
2 (*plural* **satires**) a piece of writing or a play or film that uses **satire**: *The play is a **satire** on political life.*

satisfaction (say sat-iss-**fak**-shuhn) *noun* (*no plural*)
being pleased with what you or other people have done: *She finished painting the picture and looked at it with **satisfaction**.*

A B C D E F G H I J K L M N O P Q R S T U V W X Y Z

satisfactory (say sat-iss-**fak**-tuh-ree) *adjective*
good enough, but not very good: *Her work is not **satisfactory**.* ➲ OPPOSITE **unsatisfactory**

satisfied (say **sat**-iss-fide) *adjective*
pleased because you have had or done what you wanted: *The teacher was not **satisfied** with my work.* ➲ OPPOSITE **dissatisfied**

satisfy (say **sat**-iss-fy) *verb* (**satisfying**, **satisfied**)
to give somebody what they want or need, or to be good enough to make somebody pleased: *Nothing he does **satisfies** his father.*

satisfying (say **sat**-iss-fy-ing) *adjective*
Something that is **satisfying** makes you pleased because it is what you want: *a **satisfying** result*

saturate (say **sat**-yuh-rayt) *verb* (**saturating**, **saturated**)
1 to make a thing extremely wet
2 to fill something so completely that it is impossible to add any more: *The market is **saturated** with cheap goods.*
▸ **saturation** (*noun*)

Saturday (say **sat**-uh-day) *noun*
the day of the week after Friday and before Sunday ➲ See note at **day**

sauce (say **sawss**) *noun* (*plural* **sauces**)
a thick liquid that you eat on or with other food: *pasta with tomato **sauce***

saucepan (say **sawss**-puhn) *noun* (*plural* **saucepans**) (also **pan**)
a round metal container for cooking

saucer (say **saw**-suh) *noun* (*plural* **saucers**)
a small round plate that you put under a cup

sauna (say **saw**-nuh) *noun* (*plural* **saunas**)
a room that is hot and filled with steam where people sit to relax and feel healthy: *a hotel with a swimming pool and a **sauna***
🛈 ORIGIN: 19th century, from Finnish, the language of Finland

saunter (say **sawn**-tuh) *verb* (**sauntering**, **sauntered**)
walk without hurrying: *He **sauntered** by, looking as if he had all the time in the world.*

sausage (say **soss**-ij) *noun* (*plural* **sausages**)
a mixture of meat and spices that is pressed into a long, thin skin: *garlic **sausage** ◇ **sausages** and chips*
🛈 ORIGIN: 14th–15th century, through Old French *saussiche*, from Latin *salsicia* meaning 'a food preserved with salt', based on *sal* meaning 'salt'

savage (say **sav**-ij) *adjective*
wild or violent: *He was the victim of a **savage** attack by a large dog.*

savannah (say suh-**van**-uh) *noun* (*plural* **savannahs**) (also **savanna**)
a wide flat open area of land, especially in Africa, that is covered in grass with a few trees and other plants ➲ See **prairie**
🛈 ORIGIN: 16th century, through Spanish *sabana*, from Taino *zavana*. Taino is a language that used to be spoken in the Caribbean.

save (say **sayv**) *verb* (**saving**, **saved**)
1 to take somebody or something away from danger: *She **saved** me from the fire. ◇ The doctor **saved** her life.*
2 (also **save up**) to keep or not spend money so that you can buy something later: *I've **saved** enough money to buy a bike. ◇ I'm **saving** up for a new dress.*
3 to keep something to use in the future: ***Save** some of the meat for tomorrow.*
4 to use less of something: *She **saves** money by making her own clothes.*
5 to prevent somebody from scoring a goal, for example in football
6 (*computing*) to store information in a computer by giving it a special instruction: *Don't forget to **save** the file before you close it.*

savings (say **sayv**-ingz) *plural noun*
money that you are keeping to use later: *I keep my **savings** in the bank.*

saviour (say **say**-vi-uh) *noun* (*plural* **saviours**)
a person who rescues someone or something from a dangerous or difficult situation: *He is seen as the **saviour** of the rural* (= in or related to the areas of land away from towns and cities) *poor.*

savour (say **say**-vuh) *verb* (**savouring**, **savoured**)
1 to enjoy the full taste or flavour of something, especially by eating or drinking it slowly: *to **savour** a meal*
2 to enjoy a feeling or an experience deeply or thoroughly: *to **savour** every moment*

savoury (say **say**-vuh-ree) *adjective*
(used about food) having a taste that is salty and not sweet: *a **savoury** snack*
▸ **savoury** (*noun*): *a plate of **savouries***

saw[1] form of **see**

saw[2] *noun* (*plural* **saws**)
a metal tool for cutting wood
▸ **saw** (*verb*): *She **sawed** a branch off the tree.*

sawdust (say **saw**-dust) *noun* (*no plural*)
powder that falls when you cut wood with a saw

saxophone (say **sak**-suh-fohn) *noun* (*plural* **saxophones**) a musical instrument made of metal that you play by blowing into it
ORIGIN: from the name of Adolphe *Sax* (1814–1894), who made musical instruments + Greek *-phone* meaning 'sound, voice'

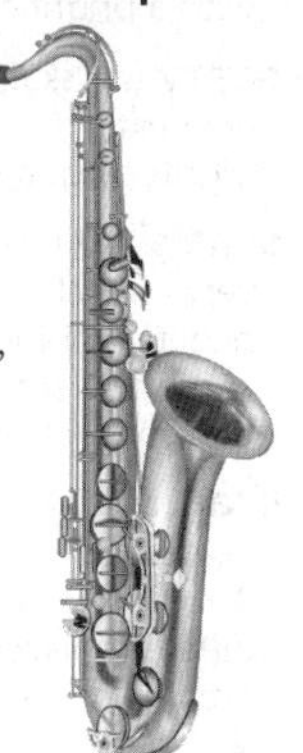
saxophone

say¹ *noun* (*no plural*)
have a say to have the right to help decide something: *I'd like to have a **say** in who we invite to the party.*

say² *verb* (**saying, said**)
1 to make words with your mouth: *You **say** 'please' when you ask for something.* ◇ *'This is my room,' he **said**.* ◇ *She **said** that she was cold.*
2 to give information in writing, numbers or pictures: *The clock **says** half past three.*

WHICH WORD? **Say** or **tell**?
- We use **say** with meaning 1 above with the actual words that someone says: *'I'm ready,' he **said**.*
- We use **say** before **that** in reported speech: *He **said that** he was ready.*
- Notice that you **say** something **to** somebody: *Mandla **said to** to Ntswaki, 'I am ready'.*
- But you **tell** somebody something (without **to**): *Mandla **told** Ntswaki that he was ready.*

saying (say **say**-ing) *noun* (*plural* **sayings**) a sentence that people often say, which gives advice about something: *'Love is blind' is an old **saying**.*

scab (say **skab**) *noun* (*plural* **scabs**) a hard covering that grows over your skin where it is cut or broken

scaffolding (say **skaf**-uhl-ding) *noun* (*no plural*) metal bars or pieces of wood joined together, where people such as painters can stand when they are working on high parts of a building

scald (say **skawld**) *verb* (**scalding, scalded**) to burn somebody or something with very hot liquid

scale (say **skayl**) *noun* (*plural* **scales**)
1 the size or level of something: *In the morning we saw the full **scale** of the damage caused by the storm.*
2 a set of levels or numbers used for measuring something: *Their work is assessed on a **scale** from 1 to 10.*
3 scales (*plural noun*) a machine for showing how heavy people or things are: *bathroom scales*
4 how distances are shown on a map: *This map has a **scale** of one centimetre to ten kilometres.*
5 one of the flat hard things that cover the body of animals such as fish and snakes

scalene (say **skay**-leen) *adjective* In a **scalene** triangle all three sides have different lengths. ➲ See illustration at **triangle**

scalp (say **skalp**) *noun* (*plural* **scalps**) the skin on the top of your head, under your hair

scamper (say **skam**-puh) *verb* (**scampering, scampered**) (used especially about a child or a small animal) to run quickly with short light steps: *Baby chicks and children **scamper** about.*

scan (say **skan**) *verb* (**scanning, scanned**)
1 to look at or read every part of something quickly until you find what you are looking for: *She **scanned** the list until she found her own name.*
2 to pass light over a picture or a document using an electronic machine (called a **scanner**) in order to copy it and put it in the memory of a computer

scandal (say **skan**-duhl) *noun*
1 (*plural* **scandals**) something that shocks people and makes them talk about it because they think it is bad: *a drug **scandal***
2 (*no plural*) unkind talk about shocking things that people have done or are thought to have done: *newspapers full of **scandal***

scanner (say **skan**-uh) *noun* (*plural* **scanners**)
1 (*computing*) a piece of equipment that copies words or pictures from paper into a computer
2 a machine that gives a picture of the inside of something. Doctors use one kind of **scanner** to look inside people's bodies.

A B C D E F G H I J K L M N O P Q R S T U V W X Y Z

scanty (say **skan**-tee) *adjective* (**scantier**, **scantiest**)
too small in size or amount: ***scanty** clothing* ◇ *Information about the plan is **scanty**.*

scapegoat (say **skayp**-goht) *noun* (*plural* **scapegoats**)
a person who is blamed for other people's mistakes or the bad things they have done: *Immigrants have become **scapegoats** for South Africa's social problems.*

scapula (say **skap**-yuu-luh) *noun* (*plural* **scapulae** or **scapulas**) = **shoulderblade**
➲ See illustration at **skeleton**

scar (say **skaa**) *noun* (*plural* **scars**)
a mark that is left on your skin by an old cut or wound: *The operation didn't leave a very big **scar**.*
▶ **scar** (*verb*): *His face was badly **scarred** by the accident.*

scarce (say **skairss**) *adjective* (**scarcer**, **scarcest**)
difficult to find or not enough: *Food for birds and animals is more **scarce** in the winter.*
➲ OPPOSITE **plentiful**
▶ **scarcity** (*noun*): *She explained why there is a **scarcity** of food during a drought.*

scarcely (say **skairss**-lee) *adverb*
almost not or only just: *He was so frightened that he could **scarcely** speak.* ➲ SYNONYMS **hardly**, **barely**

scare[1] (say **skair**) *verb* (**scaring**, **scared**)
to make somebody feel afraid: *That noise **scared** me!* ➲ SYNONYM **frighten**
❶ ORIGIN: 13th–15th century, from Old Norse *skirra* meaning 'frighten', from *skjarr* meaning 'timid'

scare[2] (say **skair**) *noun* (*plural* **scares**)
1 a feeling of being frightened: *You gave me a **scare**!*
2 a situation where many people are afraid or worried about something: *a health **scare***

scarecrow (say **skair**-kroh) *noun* (*plural* **scarecrows**)
a thing that looks like a person, that gardeners and farmers put on their land to frighten birds

scared (say **skaird**) *adjective*
frightened of something or afraid that something bad might happen: *Claire is **scared** of the dark.* ◇ *Don't be **scared**!* ◇ *I'm **scared**.*

> Notice that we say **scared of**, not 'scared for': *Are you **scared of** dogs?*

scarf (say **skaaf**) *noun* (*plural* **scarves**)
a piece of material that you wear around your neck or head

scarlet (say **skaa**-luht) *adjective*
with a bright red colour

scary (say **skair**-ree) *adjective* (**scarier**, **scariest**) (*informal*)
frightening: *a **scary** ghost story*

scathing (say **skay*th***-ing) *adjective*
very critical or expressing a very strong negative opinion about a person or a thing: *The report was **scathing** of the way the police handled the crowd of protesters.*

scatter (say **skat**-uh) *verb* (**scattering**, **scattered**)
1 to throw things so that they fall in a lot of different places: ***Scatter** the seeds over the ground.*
2 to move quickly in different directions: *The crowd **scattered** when it started to rain.*

scavenge (say **skav**-inj) *verb* (**scavenging**, **scavenged**)
to look among waste and rubbish for food and things that can be used again

scenario (say si-**naa**-ri-oh) *noun* (*plural* **scenarios**)
1 a description of what happens in a play or a film
2 one way that things may happen in the future: *There are four possible **scenarios**; their impacts range from very positive to very negative.*

scene (say **seen**) *noun* (*plural* **scenes**)
1 a place where something happened: *The police arrived at the **scene** of the crime.*
2 part of a play or film: *Act 1, **Scene** 2 of 'Hamlet'*
3 what you see in a place: *He painted **scenes** of life in the countryside.*

scenery (say **seen**-uh-ree) *noun* (*no plural*)
1 the things like mountains, rivers and forests that you see around you in the countryside: *beautiful **scenery***
2 things on the stage of a theatre that make it look like a real place

scenic (say **seen**-ik) *adjective*
having beautiful scenery: *Montagu is a **scenic** two-hour drive from Cape Town.*

scent (say **sent**) *noun*
1 (*plural* **scents**) a smell: *These flowers have no **scent**.*
2 (*no plural*) a liquid with a nice smell that you put on your body: *a bottle of **scent*** ➲ SYNONYM **perfume** 1
▶ **scented** (*adjective*): *These **scented** candles smell wonderful!*

sceptical (say **skep**-tik-l) *adjective*
having doubts that something is true or that

something will happen: *I am **sceptical** about his chances of winning.*

schedule (say **shed**-yool or **sked**-yool) *noun* (*plural* **schedules**)
a plan or list of times when things will happen or be done: *I've got a busy **schedule** next week.* ◇ *We're behind **schedule*** (= late) *with the project.* ◇ *Filming began on **schedule*** (= at the planned time).

scheme[1] (say **skeem**) *noun* (*plural* **schemes**)
a plan or a system for doing or organizing something: *a feeding **scheme*** ◇ *a local **scheme** for recycling newspapers*

scheme[2] (say **skeem**) *verb* (**scheming, schemed**)
to make secret plans to do something: *The President's enemies were **scheming** against him.*

schism (say **skiz**-m) *noun* (*plural* **schisms**)
strong disagreement between groups within an organization that causes the organization to split

schizophrenia (say skit-soh-**free**-ni-uh) *noun* (*no plural*)
a serious mental illness in which a person confuses the real world and the world of the imagination and often behaves in strange and unexpected ways
▸ **schizophrenic** (*adjective*): *The **schizophrenic** patient went to the hospital to receive his medication.*

scholar (say **skol**-uh) *noun* (*plural* **scholars**)
1 a person who knows a lot about a subject because they have studied it in detail: *a famous history **scholar***
2 a student who has been given a scholarship to study at a school, college or university: *a Mandela Rhodes **scholar***

scholarship (say **skol**-uh-ship) *noun* (*plural* **scholarships**)
money that is given to good students to help them to continue studying: *Jabu won a **scholarship** to university.*

school (say **skool**) *noun*
1 (*plural* **schools**) a place where children go to learn: *Alida is at primary **school**.* ◇ *Which **school** do you go to?*
2 (*no plural*) being at **school**: *I hate **school**!* ◇ *He left **school** when he was sixteen.* ◇ ***School** starts at nine o'clock.*
3 (*plural* **schools**) a place where you go to learn a special thing: *a language **school***
4 (*plural* **schools**) a large group of fish or sea mammals that swim together: *a **school** of dolphins*

> USAGE You usually talk about **school** without 'the' or 'a': *I enjoyed being at **school**.* ◇ *Do you walk to **school**?*
> You use 'a' or 'the' when you talk about a certain school: *Saddiq goes to the **school** that his father went to.* ◇ *She teaches at a **school** for deaf children.*

schoolboy (say **skool**-boy) *noun* (*plural* **schoolboys**)
a boy who goes to school

schoolchild (say **skool**-chyld) *noun* (*plural* **schoolchildren**)
a boy or girl who goes to school

schooldays (say **skool**-dayz) *plural noun*
the time in your life when you are at school

schoolgirl (say **skool**-gurl) *noun* (*plural* **schoolgirls**)
a girl who goes to school

science (say **sy**-uhnss) *noun*
1 (*no plural*) the study of and knowledge about the physical world and natural laws: *I'm interested in **science**.*
2 (*plural* **sciences**) one of the subjects into which science can be divided: *Biology, chemistry and physics are all **sciences**.*

science fiction *noun* (*no plural*)
books, films, etc. about things like travel in space, life on other planets or life in the future

scientific (say sy-uhn-**tif**-ik) *adjective*
connected with or involving science: *We need more money for **scientific** research.*
▸ **scientifically** (*adverb*)

scientist (say **sy**-uhn-tist) *noun* (*plural* **scientists**)
a person who studies science or works with science

sci-fi (say **sy**-fy) *noun* (*no plural*) (*informal*) short for **science fiction**

scintillating (say **sin**-ti-layt-ing) *adjective*
very clever, amusing or interesting: *a **scintillating** performance*

scissors (say **siz**-uhz) *plural noun*
a tool for cutting that has two flat sharp parts that are joined together: *These **scissors** aren't sharp enough to cut the paper.* ◇ *I need two pairs of **scissors**.*

> USAGE Be careful! You cannot say 'a scissors'. You say a **pair of scissors**: *I need **a pair of scissors*** (or: *I need **some scissors***).

scoff (say **skoff**) *verb* (**scoffing, scoffed**)
to speak about a person or a thing in a way that shows you think he or she or it is stupid or

ridiculous: *Most people will **scoff** at that wage in disgust.*

scold (say **skohld**) *verb* (**scolding, scolded**)
to tell somebody in an angry way that they have done something wrong: *His mother **scolded** him for being so naughty.*

scone (say **skon**) *noun* (*plural* **scones**)
a small round cake often eaten with butter, jam and cream spread on it

scoop[1] (say **skoop**) *noun* (*plural* **scoops**)
1 a tool like a large spoon with a deep bowl, used for picking up ice cream, flour, etc.
2 the amount that you can pick up with a scoop: *two **scoops** of ice cream*
3 an exciting piece of news that is reported by one newspaper, television or radio station before it is reported anywhere else

scoop[2] (say **skoop**) *verb* (**scooping, scooped**)
1 to use a **scoop**, a spoon or your hands to take something up or out: *I **scooped** some ice cream out of the bowl.*
2 to move or lift somebody or something with a quick continuous movement: *He **scooped** the child up in his arms.*

scoot (say **skoot**) *verb* (**scooted, scooting**)
1 to go somewhere on a **scooter**
2 (*informal*) to go or leave somewhere quickly: *He **scooted** up the stairs.*

scooter (say **skoot**-uh) *noun* (*plural* **scooters**)
1 a light motorcycle with a small engine
2 a child's toy with two wheels, which you stand on and move by pushing one foot against the ground

scope (say **skohp**) *noun* (*no plural*)
1 the chance or opportunity to do a thing: *There is plenty of **scope** for improvement in your marks.*
2 the variety of subjects that are being discussed or considered: *The judge has had the **scope** of her inquiry extended.*

scorch (say **skawch**) *verb* (**scorching, scorched**)
1 to burn and damage the surface of a thing: *I **scorched** my dress when I was ironing it.*
2 to cause to become dry and brown, especially from the heat of the sun: ***scorched** grass*

score[1] (say **skaw**) *noun* (*plural* **scores**)
1 the number of points, goals, etc. that you win in a game or competition: *The winner got a **score** of 320.* ◇ *What's the **score** now?*
2 the written or printed form of a piece of music showing what each instrument is to play or what each voice is to sing

score[2] (say **skaw**) *verb* (**scoring, scored**)
to get points, goals, etc. in a game or competition: *Brazil **scored** three goals against Kenya.*

scoreboard (say **skaw**-bawd) *noun* (*plural* **scoreboards**)
a large board that shows the score during a game or competition

scorn (say **skawn**) *noun* (*no plural*)
a strong feeling that somebody or something is stupid or not good enough: *He was full of **scorn** for my idea.*
▸ **scornful** (*adjective*): *She gave him a **scornful** look.*

scorpion (say **skaw**-pi-uhn) *noun* (*plural* **scorpions**)
a small animal that has a poisonous sting in its long curved tail

scorpion

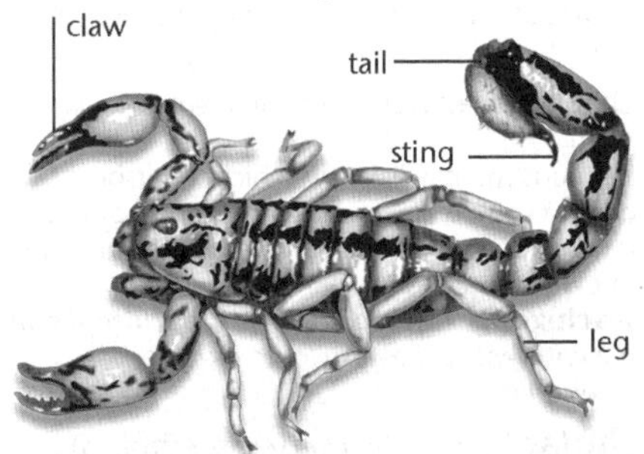

scour (say **skow**-uh) *verb* (**scouring, scoured**)
1 to clean a thing by rubbing it hard with rough material: *The pan was so dirty that I had to **scour** it.*
2 to search a place very carefully to find a thing: ***scour** the Internet*

scourge (say **skurj**) *noun* (*plural* **scourges**)
a person or thing that causes a lot of trouble or suffering: *the **scourge** of crime* ◇ *Aids is a **scourge**.*

Scout (say **skowt**) *noun* (*plural* **Scouts**)
1 the Scouts (*plural noun*) a special club for boys, and sometimes girls too, which does a lot of activities with them, for example camping
2 a boy or girl who is a member of the **Scouts**

scout[1] (say **skowt**) *verb* (**scouting, scouted**)
1 to search for a person or a thing in various places: *We spent weekends **scouting** around for a house to buy.*
2 to look for sportspeople, actors, musicians or models with **talent** to offer them work

scout[2] (say **skowt**) *noun* (*plural* **scouts**)
1 a soldier, an aircraft, etc. sent ahead to get information about the enemy's position, strength, etc.
2 a person who looks for sportspeople, actors, musicians or models with **talent** to offer them work: *a talent **scout***

scowl (say **skowl**) *verb* (**scowling**, **scowled**)
to look at somebody in an angry way: *His teacher **scowled** at him for being late.*
▶ **scowl** (*noun*): *She looked up at me with a **scowl**.*

scramble (say **skram**-buhl) *verb* (**scrambling**, **scrambled**)
to move quickly up or over something, using your hands to help you: *They **scrambled** over the wall.*

scrambled eggs *plural noun*
eggs that you mix together with milk and cook in a pan

scrap (say **skrap**) *noun*
1 (*plural* **scraps**) a small piece of something: *a **scrap** of paper*
2 (*no plural*) something you do not want any more but that is made of material that can be used again: ***scrap** paper* ◇ ***scrap** metal*

scrapbook (say **skrap**-buuk) *noun* (*plural* **scrapbooks**)
a large book with empty pages that you can stick pictures or newspaper articles in

scrape (say **skrayp**) *verb* (**scraping**, **scraped**)
1 to move a rough or sharp thing across something: *I **scraped** the mud off my shoes with a stick.*
2 to hurt or damage something by moving it against a rough or sharp thing: *I fell and **scraped** my knee on the wall.*

scratch[1] (say **skrach**) *verb* (**scratching**, **scratched**)
1 to move your nails across your skin: *She **scratched** her head.*
2 to cut or make a mark on something with a sharp thing: *The cat **scratched** me!*

scratch[2] (say **skrach**) *noun* (*plural* **scratches**)
a cut or mark that a sharp thing makes: *Her hands were covered in **scratches** from the cat.*
from scratch from the beginning: *I threw away the letter I was writing and started again from **scratch**.*

scrawl (say **skrawl**) *verb* (**scrawling**, **scrawled**)
to write something quickly in an untidy and careless way: *Someone had **scrawled** his name all over the wall.*
▶ **scrawl** (*noun*): *Her signature was an illegible **scrawl**.*

scrawny (say **skraw**-nee) *adjective* (**scrawnier**, **scrawniest**)
(of people or animals) very thin in a way that is not attractive: *a **scrawny** stray dog*

scream[1] (say **skreem**) *verb* (**screaming**, **screamed**)
to make a loud high cry that shows you are afraid or hurt: *She saw the snake and **screamed**.* ◇ *He **screamed** for help.*

scream[2] (say **skreem**) *noun* (*plural* **screams**)
a loud high cry: *a **scream** of pain*

scree (say **skree**) *noun* (*plural* **screes**)
a steep area of loose rocks, often at the base of a mountain or cliff: *a **scree** slope*

screech (say **skreech**) *verb* (**screeching**, **screeched**)
to make a loud high sound: *The car's brakes **screeched** as it stopped suddenly.*
▶ **screech** (*noun*): *The **screech** of the owl kept us awake.*

screen (say **skreen**) *noun* (*plural* **screens**)
1 the flat square part of a television or computer where you see pictures or words
➲ See illustration at **computer**
2 the flat thing on the wall of a cinema, where you see films
3 a kind of thin wall that you can move around. **Screens** are used to keep away cold, light, sound, etc. or to stop people from seeing something: *The nurse put a **screen** around the bed.*

screw[1] (say **skroo**) *noun* (*plural* **screws**)
a small thin piece of metal with a sharp end, that you use for fixing things together. You push it into something by turning it with a tool (called a **screwdriver**).

screw[2] (say **skroo**) *verb* (**screwing**, **screwed**)
1 to fix something to another thing using a **screw**[1]: *The cupboard is **screwed** to the wall.*
2 to turn something to fix it to another thing: *Screw the lid on the jar.*
screw something up to make paper or material into a ball with your hand: *He **screwed** up the letter and threw it in the bin.*

screwdriver (say **skroo**-drive-uh) *noun* (*plural* **screwdrivers**)
a tool for turning **screws**

scribble (say **skrib**-l) *verb* (**scribbling**, **scribbled**)
to write something or make marks on paper quickly and without care: *The children **scribbled** in my book.*

script (say **skript**) *noun* (*plural* **scripts**)
the written form of a play or film

scripture (say **skrip**-tshuh) *noun* (*plural* **scriptures**)
the book or books that a particular religion is based on
ORIGIN: 13th–15th century, from Latin *scriptura* meaning 'writings', from *script-* meaning 'written'

scroll[1] (say **skrohl**) *verb* (**scrolling**, **scrolled**)
to move what you can see on a computer screen up or down so that you can look at different parts of it: ***Scroll** down to the bottom of the document.*

scroll[2] (say **skrohl**) *noun* (*plural* **scrolls**)
a long roll of paper with writing on it: *the Dead Sea **scrolls***

scrotum (say **skroh**-tuhm) *noun* (*plural* **scrotums** or **scrota**)
the bag of skin that contains the two round male sex organs **(testicles)**

scrub[1] (say **skrub**) *verb* (**scrubbing**, **scrubbed**)
to rub something hard to clean it, usually with a brush and soap and water: *He **scrubbed** the floor.*

scrub[2] (say **skrub**) *noun* (*no plural*)
1 an act of cleaning a thing by rubbing it hard, often with a brush: *The kitchen floor needs a good **scrub**.*
2 small trees and bushes that grow in an area that has very little rain: *hardy Karoo **scrub***

scruff (say **skruf**) *noun* (*plural* **scruffs**)
the back of a person's or an animal's neck: *The dog carried her puppy by the **scruff** of its neck.*

scruffy (say **skruf**-ee) *adjective* (**scruffier**, **scruffiest**)
untidy and perhaps dirty: *She was wearing **scruffy** jeans.*

scrum (say **skrum**) *noun* (*plural* **scrums**)
the part of a game of rugby when players from both sides link together in a group, with their heads down, and push against each other, trying to get the ball that has been thrown at their feet

scrumptious (say **skrump**-shuhss) *adjective* (*informal*) tasting very good: *The stylish restaurant is famous for its **scrumptious** lunches and dinners.*

scruple (say **skroop**-l) *noun* (*plural* **scruples**)
(usually in the plural) a feeling that stops you from doing a thing that you think is morally wrong: *companies that have no **scruples** about ignoring contracts*

scrupulous (say **skroop**-yuh-luhss) *adjective*
1 very careful or paying great attention to detail: *You should always be **scrupulous** about hygiene.*
2 careful to do what is right or honest: *He was **scrupulous** in all his business dealings.*
▸ **scrupulously** (*adverb*)

scrutinize (say **skroo**-ti-nize) *verb* (**scrutinizing**, **scrutinized**) (also **scrutinise**)
to look at or examine a thing carefully: ***Scrutinize** any contract before you sign it.*

scuba-diving (say skoo-buh-**dive**-ing) *noun* (*no plural*)
swimming underwater using special equipment for breathing: *You should never go **scuba-diving** alone.*

scuff (say **skuf**) *verb* (**scuffing**, **scuffed**)
to make a dirty mark on a surface, for example by kicking something: *His new school shoes were **scuffed** after a week.*

scuffle (say **skuf**-l) *noun* (*plural* **scuffles**)
a short, not very violent fight: *The touring players were involved in a **scuffle** in a bar.*
SYNONYM **tussle**

sculptor (say **skulp**-tuh) *noun* (*plural* **sculptors**)
a person who makes shapes and forms from materials such as stone or wood

sculpture (say **skulp**-tshuh) *noun* (*art*)
1 (*no plural*) making shapes and forms from materials such as stone or wood
2 (*plural* **sculptures**) a shape or form made from a material such as stone or wood

scum (say **skum**) *noun* (*no plural*)
1 a layer of dirty bubbles that float on a liquid
2 (*informal*) an insulting word for people who you have no respect for: *I have no sympathy for the **scum** who murder and rape.*

scurry (*rhymes with* **hurry**) *verb* (**scurrying**, **scurried**)
to run quickly with short steps: *Everyone **scurried** for cover when it suddenly started pouring.*

scurvy (say **skur**-vee) *noun* (*no plural*)
a disease caused by the lack of **vitamin** C: *Some sailors used to get **scurvy** from not eating enough fresh fruit and vegetables.*

scuttle (say **skut**-l) *verb* (**scuttling**, **scuttled**)
1 to run quickly with short steps or with the body close to the ground: *The cockroach **scuttled** across the floor.*
2 to deliberately cause a scheme to fail: *Some parties are unhappy with the deal and have threatened to **scuttle** it.*
3 to sink a ship deliberately by making holes in the side or bottom of it

scythe (say **sithe**) *noun* (*plural* **scythes**)
a tool with a long handle and a long curved **blade**, used for cutting long grass and, in the past, grain ➲ See **sickle**

SE *abbreviation* **south-east**

sea (say **see**) *noun*
1 (*no plural*) the salt water that covers large parts of the Earth: *We had a swim in the **sea**.* ◇ *The **sea** is rough today.*
2 (*plural* **seas**) a large area of salt water: *He sailed across many **seas**.* ◇ *the **Sea** of Galilee* ➲ See **ocean**
at sea travelling on the sea: *We spent three weeks at **sea**.*

seabed (say **see**-bed) *noun* (*no plural*)
the floor of the sea

seafood (say **see**-food) *noun* (*no plural*)
fish and small animals from the sea that we eat, especially **shellfish** (= animals with shells that live in water)

seagull (say **see**-gul) *noun* (*plural* **seagulls**)
a big grey or white bird with a loud cry, that lives near the sea

sea-horse (say **see**-hawss) *noun* (*plural* **sea-horses**)
a small fish that swims in an upright position and has a head that looks like a horse's head

sea-horse

seal¹ (say **seel**) *noun* (*plural* **seals**)
an animal with short fur and flippers, which lives in and near the sea and eats fish

seal² (say **seel**) *verb* (**sealing, sealed**)
to close something tightly by sticking two parts together: *She **sealed** the envelope.*

sea-level (say **see**-lev-l) *noun* (*no plural*)
the average level of the sea, used for measuring the height of places on land: *Our city is 650 metres above **sea-level**.* ◇ *Some people predict that global warming will cause a rise in **sea-level**.*

seam (say **seem**) *noun* (*plural* **seams**)
a line where two pieces of cloth are joined together

search¹ (say **surch**) *verb* (**searching, searched**)
to look carefully because you are trying to find somebody or something: *I **searched** everywhere for my pen.*

search² (say **surch**) *noun* (*plural* **searches**)
when you try to find somebody or something: *I found my key after a long **search**.* ◇ *We drove round the town in **search** of a cheap hotel.* ◇ *The **search** for the murder weapon goes on.*

searchlight (say **surch**-lite) *noun* (*plural* **searchlights**)
a powerful lamp of which the **beam¹** 1 can be directed in any direction and which is used to find people and vehicles at night

seashell (say **see**-shel) *noun* (*plural* **seashells**)
the empty shell of a small animal that lives in the sea

seashore (say **see**-shaw) *noun*
the seashore (*no plural*) the land next to the sea: *We were looking for seashells on the **seashore**.*

seasick (say **see**-sik) *adjective*
If you are **seasick**, you feel ill in your stomach because the boat or ship you are on is moving a lot.

season (say **see**-zuhn) *noun* (*plural* **seasons**)
1 one of the four parts of the year that we call spring, summer, autumn and winter
2 one of the periods of different weather during the year: *The hot rainy **season** is the growing **season**.*
3 a special time of the year for something: *the cricket **season*** ◇ *What are you doing during the holiday **season**?* ◇ *Which fruits are in **season** now?*
► **seasonal** (*adjective*): *The stream was swollen by heavy **seasonal** rains.*
🛈 **ORIGIN:** 13th–15th century, through Old French *saison*, from Latin *satio(n-)* meaning 'time for sowing, planting seeds'. In Old French the word came to mean 'the right time' for anything.

seasoning (say **see**-zuhn-ing) *noun* (*plural* **seasonings**)
salt, herbs or spices added in small amounts to food to make it taste better

seat (say **seet**) *noun* (*plural* **seats**)
something that you sit on: *the back **seat** of a car* ◇ *We had **seats** at the front of the theatre.* ◇ *Please take a **seat*** (= sit down).

seat belt *noun* (*plural* **seat belts**)
a long thin piece of material that you put round your body in a car, bus or plane to keep you safe in an accident ➲ **SYNONYM** **safety belt**

A B C D E F G H I J K L M N O P Q R S T U V W X Y Z

seaweed (say **see**-weed) *noun* (*no plural*)
a type of **alga** that grows in the sea. There are many different types of **seaweed**, and many look similar to plants.

secant (say **see**-kuhnt) *noun* (*plural* **secants**)
a line cutting a curve at two or more points

secluded (say si-**klood**-uhd) *adjective*
far away from other people, houses or roads; sheltered, very quiet and private: *a **secluded** beach*

second¹ (say **sek**-uhnd) *adjective, adverb*
2nd or next after first: *February is the **second** month of the year.* ◇ *She came **second** in the race.*

second² (say **sek**-uhnd) *noun* (*no plural*)
2nd or a person or thing that comes next after the first: *Today is the **second** of April* (= 2 April). ◇ *I was the first to arrive, and he was the **second**.*

second³ (say **sek**-uhnd) *noun* (*plural* **seconds**)
1 a measure of time. There are 60 **seconds** in a minute.
2 a very short time: *Wait a **second**!* ◇ *I'll be ready in a **second**.*

second⁴ (say **sek**-uhnd) *verb* (**seconding, seconded**)
1 to support a person's suggestion or idea at a meeting so that it can be discussed and voted on
2 to provide support to a person running, cycling or swimming a long-distance race

secondary school (say **sek**-uhnd-ree skool) *noun* (*plural* **secondary schools**) = **high school**

second class *noun* (*no plural*)
the part of a train, boat or plane that it is cheaper to travel in: *We sat in **second class**.*
▸ **second-class** (*adjective*): *a **second-class** ticket*

second-hand (say sek-uhnd-**hand**) *adjective, adverb*
used by another person before: ***second-hand** books* ◇ *I bought this car **second-hand**.*
➲ SYNONYM **used²**

secondly (say **sek**-uhnd-lee) *adverb*
a word that you use when you are giving the second thing in a list: *Firstly, it's too expensive and, **secondly**, we don't really need it.*

secrecy (say **seek**-ruh-see) *noun* (*no plural*)
not telling other people: *They worked in **secrecy**.*

secret¹ (say **seek**-ruht) *noun* (*plural* **secrets**)
something that you do not or must not tell other people: *I can't tell you where I'm going – it's a **secret**.* ◇ *Can you keep a **secret*** (= not tell other people)*?*
in secret without other people knowing: *They met in **secret**.*

secret² (say **seek**-ruht) *adjective*
If something is **secret**, other people do not or must not know about it: *They kept their wedding **secret*** (= they did not tell anybody about it). ◇ *a **secret** meeting*

secretarial (say sek-ruh-**tair**-ri-uhl) *adjective*
connected with the work of a secretary: *a **secretarial** college*

secretary (say **sek**-ruh-tree) *noun* (*plural* **secretaries**)
1 a person who types letters, answers the telephone and does other things in an office
2 (in the USA and the UK) an important person in the government: *the **Secretary*** (= head of the department) *for Defence*

secrete (say si-**kreet**) *verb* (**secreting, secreted**) (*biology*)
(used about a part of a plant, animal or person) to produce a liquid: *Insulin is **secreted** by the pancreas.*

secretive (say **seek**-ruh-tiv) *adjective*
If you are **secretive**, you do not like to tell other people about yourself, your plans or the things that you do: *He is very **secretive** about his job.*

secretly (say **seek**-ruht-lee) *adverb*
without other people knowing: *We are **secretly** planning a big party for her.*

sect (say **sekt**) *noun* (*plural* **sects**)
(sometimes disapproving) a small group of people with beliefs or practices that separate them from the rest of the group to which they belong

section (say **sek**-shuhn) *noun* (*plural* **sections**)
one of the parts of something: *This **section** of the road is closed.*

sector (say **sek**-tuh) *noun* (*plural* **sectors**)
1 a part of the business activity of a country: *the public/private **sector*** ◇ *The manufacturing **sector** has declined in recent years.*
2 a part of a particular area: *the different **sectors** of a war zone*
3 (*maths*) a part of a circle that is between two straight lines drawn from the centre to the edge ➲ See illustration at **circle**

secular (say **sek**-yuu-luh) *adjective*
not concerned with religion or the church: ***secular** music* ◇ *Turkey's strict **secular** laws separate religion and state.*

secure (say si-**kyoor**) *adjective*
1 If you are **secure**, you feel safe and you are not worried: *Do you feel **secure** about the future?* ➲ OPPOSITE **insecure** 1
2 safe: *Don't climb that ladder – it's not very **secure*** (= it may fall). ◇ *Her job is **secure*** (= she will not lose it).
3 well locked or protected so that it is difficult for people to enter or leave: *This gate isn't very **secure**.*
▶ **securely** (*adverb*): *Are all the windows **securely** closed?*
ℹ ORIGIN: 16th century, from Latin *securus*, from *se-* meaning 'without' + *cura* meaning 'care'. When the word first came into English, it meant 'feeling no worry'.

security (say si-**kyoo**-ruh-tee) *noun* (*no plural*)
1 the feeling of being safe: *Children need love and **security**.*
2 things that you do to keep a place safe: *We need better **security** on our trains.*

sedan (say si-**dan**) *noun* (*plural* **sedans**)
a car with a closed body and a closed boot that is separated from the part in which the driver and passengers sit

sedate[1] (say si-**dayt**) *adjective*
quiet, especially in a way that lacks excitement: *Adults who don't like speed will be glad to hear there are more **sedate** rides at the park.*

sedate[2] (say si-**dayt**) *verb* (**sedating, sedated**)
to give a drug or medicine to a person or animal to make them feel calm or to make them sleep: *The hospital said the patient was heavily **sedated** but in a stable* (= not likely to change) *condition.*

sedative (say **sed**-uh-tiv) *noun* (*plural* **sedatives**)
a drug or medicine that makes you feel calm or want to sleep ➲ SYNONYM **tranquillizer**

sedentary (say **sed**-uhn-tree) *adjective*
1 (of work or activities) involving a lot of sitting down: *a **sedentary** job or lifestyle*
2 (of people) spending a lot of time sitting down or not being active: *He became more and more **sedentary** in later life.*
3 (of animals or people) staying or living in the same place or area throughout life: *Rhinos are largely **sedentary** animals.*

sediment (say **sed**-i-muhnt) *noun* (*no plural*)
the solid pieces of material that settle at the bottom of a liquid

sedimentary (say sed-i-**men**-tree) *adjective*
relating to rocks that are formed from layers of sand, stones and mud that usually collect at the bottom of lakes, rivers and the sea and then harden: *Sandstone and shale are **sedimentary** rocks.*

seduce (say si-**dyooss**) *verb* (**seducing, seduced**)
1 to persuade a person do a thing they would not normally agree to do: *Special offers **seduce** customers into spending their money.*
2 to persuade a person to have sex with you

see *verb* (**seeing, saw, has seen**)
1 to know or notice something using your eyes: *It was so dark that I couldn't **see** anything.* ◇ *Can you **see** that plane?*
2 to watch a film, play or television programme: *I'm going to **see** a film tonight.*
3 to find out about something: *Go and **see** what time the train leaves.*
4 to visit or meet somebody: *We're going to **see** my grandma.* ◇ *I'll **see** you later.*
5 to understand something: *'Your essay is not long enough.' 'I **see**.'*
seeing that, seeing as (*informal*) because: ***Seeing** that you've got nothing to do, you can help me!*
see you, see you later (*informal*) goodbye: *'Bye Dave!' '**See** you!'*
see somebody off to go to an airport or a station to say goodbye to somebody who is leaving

WHICH WORD? **See, look** or **watch**?
- When you **see** something (meaning 1 above), you know about it with your eyes, without trying: *I **saw** a bird fly past the window.*
- When you **watch** something, you look at it for some time: *They **watched** a television programme.*
- When you **look at** something, you turn your eyes towards it because you want to **see** it: *She **looked** carefully **at** all the pictures.*

seed *noun* (*plural* **seeds**)
the small hard part of a plant from which a new plant grows
ℹ ORIGIN: from Old English *sǣd*, related to Dutch *zaad*

seedling (say **seed**-ling) *noun* (*plural* **seedlings**)
a very young plant growing from a seed

seek *verb* (**seeking, sought**) (*formal*)
to try to find or get something: *You should **seek** help for such a serious problem.*

seem *verb* (**seeming, seemed**)
to give the impression of being or doing

A B C D E F G H I J K L M N O P Q R S T U V W X Y Z

A B C D E F G H I J K L M N O P Q R S T U V W X Y Z

something: *She **seems** tired.* ◇ *My mother **seems** to like you.* ◇ *Helen **seems** like* (= seems to be) *a nice girl.*

seen form of **see**

seep *verb* (**seeping**, **seeped**)
(used about a liquid) to flow very slowly through something: *Water started **seeping** in through the cracks in the wall.*

see-saw (say **see**-saw) *noun* (*plural* **see-saws**)
a piece of equipment for children to play on that is made of a long wooden plank supported by a short pole in the centre. The plank moves up and down when a child sits on each end.

segment (say **seg**-muhnt) *noun* (*plural* **segments**)
1 a section or part of something: *I divided the page into three **segments**.* ◇ *a **segment** of a circle*
2 one of the sections of a fruit such as an orange or a lemon
▸ **segmented** (*adjective*): *a worm with a **segmented** body* (= with different sections joined together)

segregate (say **seg**-ri-gayt) *verb* (**segregating**, **segregated**)
to separate one group of people or things from the rest: *The two groups of football fans were **segregated** to avoid trouble.*

seine (say **sayn**) *noun* (*plural* **seines**) (also **seine net**)
a type of fishing net that hangs down in the water and is pulled together at the ends to catch the fish

seismic (say **size**-mik) *adjective*
relating to sudden movements in the Earth's surface: *a **seismic** wave*
▸ **seismology** (*noun*): ***Seismology** is the study of earthquakes.*

seismograph (say **size**-muh-graaf) *noun* (*plural* **seismographs**)
an instrument for measuring and recording information about an **earthquake** (= a sudden movement and violent shaking in and under the Earth's surface)

seize (say **seez**) *verb* (**seizing**, **seized**)
to take somebody or something quickly and firmly: *The thief **seized** her bag and ran away.*
➲ SYNONYM **grab**

seldom (say **sel**-duhm) *adverb*
not often: *We **seldom** visit out grandma – she lives two thousand kilometres away!*
➲ SYNONYM **rarely**

select (say si-**lekt**) *verb* (**selecting**, **selected**)
to choose somebody or something from a group of people or things, usually according to a system: *The captain **selected** the best team of players.* ◇ ***Select** examples that will illustrate your report well.*

selection (say si-**lek**-shuhn) *noun*
1 (*no plural*) the act of choosing somebody or something from a group of people or things, usually according to a system: *The manager is responsible for team **selection**.*
2 (*plural* **selections**) a group of people or things that somebody has chosen, or a group of things that you can choose from: *The shop has a good **selection** of CDs.*

self *noun* (*plural* **selves**)
a person's own nature or qualities: *It's good to see you back to your old **self** again* (= well or happy again). ◇ *I have confidence in **myself** and my abilities.*
ℹ ORIGIN: from Old English

self- (say **self**) *prefix*
by yourself or for yourself: *He is **self-taught** – he never went to university.*

self-confident (say self-**kon**-fi-duhnt) *adjective*
sure about yourself and what you can do
▸ **self-confidence** (*noun*): *She lost a lot of her **self-confidence** when she failed that exam.*

self-conscious (say self-**kon**-shuhss) *adjective*
worried about what other people think of you: *She walked into her new school feeling very **self-conscious**.*

self-control (say self-kuhn-**trohl**) *noun* (*no plural*)
the ability to control yourself and your emotions

self-defence (say self-di-**fenss**) *noun* (*no plural*)
the use of force to protect yourself: *I only hit him in **self-defence** – he hit me first.*

self-employed (say self-im-**ployd**) *adjective*
working for yourself, not for somebody else: *He's a **self-employed** electrician.*

selfish (say **sel**-fish) *adjective*
thinking too much about what you want and not about what other people want: *I'm sick of your **selfish** behaviour!* ➲ OPPOSITE **unselfish**
▸ **selfishly** (*adverb*): *He behaved very **selfishly**.*
▸ **selfishness** (*noun*): *Her **selfishness** made me very angry.*

self-pity (say self-**pit**-ee) *noun* (*no plural*)
when you think too much about your own problems and feel sorry for yourself

self-service (say self-**sur**-viss) *adjective*
In a **self-service** shop or restaurant you take what you want and then pay for it: *This is a **self-service** restaurant.*

sell (say **sel**) *verb* (**selling, sold**)
to give something to somebody who pays you money for it: *I **sold** my guitar for R350.* ◇ *She **sold** me a ticket.* ◇ *Bookshops usually **sell** books, newspapers and magazines.* ➲ See **buy**
sell out, be sold out to be sold completely so that there are no more left: *I went to buy a newspaper, but they had all **sold** out.* ◇ *The concert was **sold** out weeks ago.*
sell out of something to **sell** all that you have of something: *I'm afraid we've **sold** out of milk.*

Sellotape™ (say **sel**-uh-tayp) *noun* (*no plural*)
a type of clear tape that you use for sticking things like paper and cardboard together

selves (say **selvz**) plural of **self**

semen (say **seem**-uhn) *noun* (*no plural*)
the liquid that is produced by the male sex organs and that contains the **sperm** cells necessary for producing young animals

semester (say si-**mess**-tuh) *noun* (*plural* **semesters**)
one of the two periods that the university year is divided into ➲ See **term** 2

semi- (say **sem**-i) *prefix*
half or part: *She's **semi-retired** now* (= she works only some of the time).
🛈 **ORIGIN:** from Latin

semicircle (say **sem**-i-surk-l) *noun* (*plural* **semicircles**)
half a circle: *The children sat in a **semicircle**.*
➲ See illustration at **circle**[1]
🛈 **ORIGIN:** 16th century, from Latin *semicirculus* from *semi-* meaning 'half' + *circulus* meaning 'small ring', from *circus* meaning 'ring'

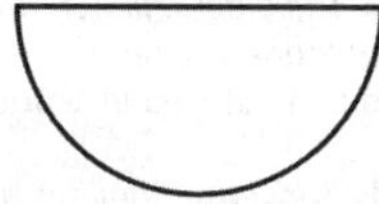

semicolon (say sem-i-**koh**-luhn) *noun* (*plural* **semicolons**)
a mark (;) that you use in writing to separate parts of a sentence ➲ See Study page 16

semiconductor (say sem-i-kuhn-**duk**-tuh) *noun* (*plural* **semiconductors**)
a material that allows heat or electricity to pass through it or along it under particular conditions: *Silicon is a substance that is often used as a **semiconductor**.*

semi-detached (say sem-i-di-**tach**-t) *adjective*
A **semi-detached** house is joined to another house on one side.

semi-final (say sem-i-**fine**-uhl) *noun* (*plural* **semi-finals**)
one of the two games that are played in a competition to find out who will play in the last part of the competition (the **final**)

seminar (say **sem**-i-naa) *noun* (*plural* **seminars**)
1 a class at a university in which a lecturer discusses a topic with a small group of students
2 a conference or other meeting for training or discussion

Semitic (say suh-**mit**-ik) *adjective*
1 relating to a family of languages that includes Hebrew, Arabic and Aramaic.
2 relating to the people who speak these languages

senator (say **sen**-uh-tuh) *noun* (*plural* **senators**)
one of a group of elected politicians who make laws in some countries, for example in the USA

send *verb* (**sending, sent**)
1 to make something go somewhere, especially a letter or a message: *I am **sending** a message to Fahiema.* ◇ *Have you **sent** your parents a postcard?*
2 to make somebody go somewhere: *My company is **sending** me to Delhi.* ◇ *He was **sent** to prison for ten years.*
send for somebody or something to ask for somebody or something to come to you: ***Send** for an ambulance!*
send something off to post something: *I'll **send** the letter off today.*

senile (say **see**-nile) *adjective*
having a decrease in mental function because of old age

senior (say **see**-ni-uh) *adjective*
1 more important than others: *a **senior** officer in the army*
2 older than others: *a **senior** pupil* ➲ **OPPOSITE junior**

Senior Certificate *noun* (*no plural*)
the qualification achieved at the end of Grade 12, the final year of study at a South African school

senior citizen *noun* (*plural* **senior citizens**)
a person who has reached the age when you can stop work

WORD BUILDING Some people think it is polite to say **senior citizens** or **pensioners** instead of **old people**.

Senior Phase *noun* (*no plural*)
Grade 7 to Grade 9 in South African schools

A B C D E F G H I J K L M N O P Q R **S** T U V W X Y Z

A B C D E F G H I J K L M N O P Q R S T U V W X Y Z

sensation (say sen-**say**-shuhn) *noun* (*plural* **sensations**)
1 a physical feeling: *I felt a burning* ***sensation*** *on my skin.*
2 great excitement or interest: *The film caused a* ***sensation.***

sensational (say sen-**say**-shuhn-l) *adjective*
very exciting or interesting: ***sensational*** *news*

sense[1] (say **senss**) *noun*
1 (*plural* **senses**) the power to see, hear, smell, taste or touch: *Dogs have a very good* ***sense*** *of smell.*
2 (*no plural*) the ability to feel or understand something: *The boy had no* ***sense*** *of right and wrong.* ◇ *I like her – she's got a great* ***sense*** *of humour.*
3 (*no plural*) the ability to think carefully about something and to do the right thing: *Did anybody have the* ***sense*** *to call the police?*
4 (*plural* **senses**) a meaning: *This word has four* ***senses.***
make sense to be possible to understand: *What does this sentence mean? It doesn't make* ***sense*** *to me.*

sense[2] (say **senss**) *verb* (**sensing**, **sensed**)
to understand or feel something: *I* ***sensed*** *that he was worried.*

senseless (say **senss**-luhss) *adjective*
1 having no meaning or purpose: *an act of* ***senseless*** *violence*
2 unconscious: *The two boxers beat each other* ***senseless.***

sensible (say **sen**-suhb-l) *adjective*
able to think carefully about something and to do the right thing: *a* ***sensible*** *answer* ◇ *It wasn't very* ***sensible*** *of you to run away.* ➲ OPPOSITE **silly**
▸ **sensibly** (*adverb*): *I hope you'll act* ***sensibly.***

sensitive (say **sen**-suh-tiv) *adjective*
1 understanding other people's feelings and being careful about them: *He's a very* ***sensitive*** *man.* ➲ OPPOSITE **insensitive**
2 easily becoming worried or unhappy about something, or about things in general: *Don't say anything about her hair – she's very* ***sensitive*** *about it.* ➲ OPPOSITE **insensitive**
3 easily hurt or damaged: *She's got very* ***sensitive*** *skin.*
▸ **sensitivity** (*noun*): *a* ***sensitivity*** *to dust* ◇ *She has no* ***sensitivity*** *to people's feelings.*

sensory (say **sen**-suh-ree) *adjective* (*biology*)
(usually before a noun) relating to the physical senses (sight, hearing, smell, taste or touch) or **sensation** 1: ***sensory*** *organs* ◇ ***sensory*** *deprivation* (= being prevented from sensing a thing)

sensual (say **sen**-shuu-uhl) *adjective*
connected with physical, especially sexual, pleasure
▸ **sensuality** (*noun*)

sent form of **send**

sentence[1] (say **sen**-tuhnss) *noun* (*plural* **sentences**)
1 a group of words that tells you something or asks a question. When you write a **sentence**, you always begin with a capital letter and usually end with a full stop, like this: *This* ***sentence*** *has a capital letter and a full stop.*
2 the punishment that a judge gives to somebody in a court of law: *Twenty years in prison was a very harsh* ***sentence.***

sentence[2] (say **sen**-tuhnss) *verb* (**sentencing**, **sentenced**)
to tell somebody in a court of law what their punishment will be: *The judge* ***sentenced*** *the man to two years in prison.*

sentimental (say sen-ti-**men**-tuhl) *adjective*
producing or showing feelings such as romantic love or pity that are too strong or not appropriate: *a* ***sentimental*** *love story* ◇ *I'm so* ***sentimental*** *– I always cry at weddings!*

sentry (say **sen**-tree) *noun* (*plural* **sentries**)
a soldier who stands outside a building and guards it

sepal (say **see**-puhl) *noun* (*plural* **sepals**) (*biology*)
the green leaf-like part at the base of a flower that supports the **petals** ➲ See illustration at **flower**

separate[1] (say **sep**-ruht) *adjective*
1 away from something, or not together or not joined: *The cup broke into three* ***separate*** *pieces.* ◇ *In my school, the older children are* ***separate*** *from the younger ones.*
2 not the same: *We stayed in* ***separate*** *rooms in the same hotel.*
▸ **separately** (*adverb*): *Shall we go* ***separately*** *or together?*

SPELLING Be careful when you spell **separate**.

PRONUNCIATION Notice that the adjective **separate** is pronounced differently from the verb.

separate[2] (say **sep**-uh-rayt) *verb* (**separating**, **separated**)
1 to stop being together: *My parents* ***separated*** *when I was a baby.*
2 to divide people or things, or to keep people or things away from each other: *The teacher* ***separated*** *the class into two groups.* ➲ SYNONYM **split**[1] 1

3 to be between two things: *The Mediterranean Sea **separates** Europe and Africa.*
▸ **separation** (*noun*): ***Separation** from your family and friends can make you unhappy.*

Sepedi (say si-**ped**-i) *noun*
a version of **Sesotho sa Leboa** spoken by the Pedi people

September (say sep-**tem**-buh) *noun*
the ninth month of the year
ℹ **ORIGIN**: through Old English, from Latin *septem* meaning 'seven'. September was the seventh month of the Roman year.

septic (say **sep**-tik) *adjective*
(of a wound or part of the body) infected with poisonous bacteria
septic tank an underground tank in which human waste collects and is broken down by bacteria

septum (say **sep**-tum) *noun* (*plural* **septa**)
a thin layer or wall separating two spaces: *A **septum** separates the two nostrils*

sepulchre (say **sep**-uhl-kuh) *noun* (*plural* **sepulchres**)
a small room, built of stone or cut into rock, in which a dead person is buried

sequel (say **see**-kwuhl) *noun* (*plural* **sequels**)
1 a book or film that continues the story of the one before
2 something that happens after, or is the result of, an earlier event: *The screaming might have died down, but there is a **sequel** to all of this.*

sequence (say **see**-kwuhnss) *noun* (*plural* **sequences**)
a number of things that happen or come one after another: *a strange **sequence** of events* ◇ *Complete the following **sequence**: 2, 4, 8…*
▸ **sequence** (*verb*): *Scientists discovered the way our DNA is **sequenced**.*

sequin (say **see**-kwin) *noun* (*plural* **sequins**)
a small shiny round piece of metal or plastic that is sewn onto clothing as decoration

serenade (say se-ruh-**nayd**) *noun* (*plural* **serenades**)
a piece of music sung or played outside, especially by a man at night under the window of his **beloved**
▸ **serenade** (*verb*): *A guitar player **serenaded** the restaurant's guests.*

serene (say suh-**reen**) *adjective*
calm and peaceful: *a **serene** woman* ◇ *The lake was **serene**.* ➲ **SYNONYM tranquil**

serf (say **surf**) *noun* (*plural* **serfs**)
(mainly in the past) a farm worker who is not free and is forced to live and work on the land of a land-owner in return for certain rights: *medieval **serfs***

sergeant (say **saa**-juhnt) *noun* (*plural* **sergeants**)
an officer in the army or the police

serial (say **seer**-ri-uhl) *noun* (*plural* **serials**)
a story that is told in parts on television or radio, or in a magazine ➲ See **series** 2

series (say **seer**-reez) *noun* (*plural* **series**)
1 a number of things of the same kind that come one after another: *I heard a **series** of shots and then silence.*
2 a number of television or radio programmes, often on the same subject, that come one after another: *The first episode of the new **series** is on Saturday.* ◇ *a TV **series** on dinosaurs* ➲ See **serial**

serious (say **seer**-ri-uhss) *adjective*
1 very bad: *That was a **serious** mistake.* ◇ *They had a **serious** accident.*
2 important: *a **serious** decision*
3 not funny: *a **serious** film*
4 If you are **serious**, you are not joking or playing: *Are you **serious** about going to live in Maputo?* ◇ *You look very **serious**. Is something wrong?*
▸ **seriousness** (*noun*): *The boy didn't understand the **seriousness** of his crime.*

seriously (say **seer**-ri-uhss-lee) *adverb*
in a serious way: *She's **seriously** ill.* ◇ *Smoking can **seriously** damage your health.*
take somebody or **something seriously** to show that you know somebody or something is important: *Don't take what he says too **seriously** – he's always joking.*

sermon (say **sur**-muhn) *noun* (*plural* **sermons**)
a talk that a priest gives in church

serpent (say **sur**-puhnt) *noun* (*plural* **serpents**)
(*formal*) a snake, especially a large one

serrated (say suh-**rayt**-d) *adjective*
having a row of V-shaped points along the edge: *a knife with a **serrated** edge*

servant (say **surv**-uhnt) *noun* (*plural* **servants**)
a person who works in another person's house, doing work like cooking and cleaning

> **USAGE** Many people do not like using the word **servant** and prefer to say **domestic worker** or **char**.

serve (say **surv**) *verb* (**serving, served**)
1 to give food or drink to somebody: *We **serve** breakfast from 7.30 to 9.00 a.m.*
2 to help somebody in a shop to buy things: *Excuse me, Madam. Are you being **served**?*
3 to do work for other people: *She became a nurse because she wants to **serve** the community.*

it serves you right words that you use to tell somebody that it is right that a bad thing has happened to them: *'I feel ill.' 'It **serves** you right for eating so much!'*

service[1] (say **surv**-iss) *noun*
1 (*plural* **services**) a system or an organization that does useful work for all the people in a country or an area: *This town has a good bus **service**. ◇ the health **service***
2 (*no plural*) the work that somebody does for customers in a shop, restaurant or hotel: *The food was good but the **service** was slow.*
3 (*plural* **services**) a business whose work is doing something for customers but not producing goods, or the work that such a business does: *banking and financial **services** ◇ Tourism is a **service** industry.*
4 (*no plural*) help or work that you do for somebody: *She left the company after ten years of **service**.*
5 (*plural* **services**) the time when somebody checks a car or machine to see that it is working well: *She took her car to the garage for a **service**.*
6 (*plural* **services**) a meeting in a church with prayers and singing: *We went to the evening **service**.*

service[2] (say **surv**-iss) *verb* (**servicing**, **serviced**)
1 to examine and, if necessary, repair a car or machine
2 to supply an area with services such as running water and electricity, and to maintain such services

service station *noun* (*plural* **service stations**)
a place at the side of a big road where you can stop to buy petrol and food and use the toilets

serviette (say sur-vee-**et**) *noun* (*plural* **serviettes**)
a piece of cloth or paper that you use when you are eating to clean your mouth and hands and to keep your clothes clean ➲ SYNONYM **napkin**

Sesotho (say si-**soo**-too) *noun* (*no plural*)
the Southern Sotho language spoken mainly in the Free State and an official language of South Africa and Lesotho

Sesotho sa Leboa (say si-**soo**-too saa li-**baw**-waa) *noun* (*no plural*)
the Northern Sotho language spoken mainly in the Limpopo province

session (say **sesh**-n) *noun* (*plural* **sessions**)
a period of time spent doing a particular activity: *The first swimming **session** is at nine o'clock.*

set[1] *noun* (*plural* **sets**)
1 a group of things of the same kind, or a group of things that you use together: *a **set** of six glasses ◇ a tool **set** ◇ a data **set***
2 the scenery of a play or film
3 (*maths*) a group of things that have a shared quality

set[2] *verb* (**setting**, **set**)
1 to decide where, what or when something will be, or to arrange something: *Let's **set** a date for the party. ◇ I **set** my alarm clock for seven o'clock. ◇ Our teacher **set** us a lot of homework. ◇ The film is **set** in India in the 1920s. ◇ She **set** up the business in 1999.*
2 to make something burn: *They **set** the house on fire.*
3 When the sun **sets**, it seems to go down below the **horizon**. ➲ OPPOSITE **rise**[1] 3
4 to become hard or solid: *Wait for the cement to **set**.*
set the table to put knives, forks, plates and other things on the table before you eat
set off, **set out** to start a journey: *We **set** off for school at seven o'clock.*

set square *noun* (*plural* **set squares**) (*maths*)
an instrument for drawing lines and angles, made from a flat piece of plastic or metal in the shape of a triangle with one angle of 90°

Setswana (say se-**tswaa**-nuh) *noun* (*no plural*)
the language of the Tswana people

settee (say set-**ee**) *noun* (*plural* **settees**) another word for **sofa** or **couch**

setting (say **set**-ing) *noun* (*plural* **settings**)
the place where something is or where something happens: *The house is in a beautiful **setting** on top of a hill.*

settle (say **set**-l) *verb* (**settling**, **settled**)
1 to go to live in a new place and stay there: *They left Malawi and **settled** in Botswana.*
2 to come down and rest somewhere: *The bird **settled** on a branch.*
3 to decide something after talking to somebody, or to end a discussion or an argument: *Have you **settled** your argument with Rajit?*
4 to pay something: *I **settled** our bill.*
settle down
1 to sit down or lie down so that you are comfortable: *I **settled** down in front of the TV.*
2 to become calm and quiet: *The children **settled** down and went to sleep.*
3 to begin to have a calm life in one place: *When are you going to **settle** down?*

settlement (say **set**-uhl-muhnt) *noun* (*plural* **settlements**)
1 an agreement about something after talking

or arguing: *After days of talks, the two sides reached a **settlement**.*
2 a group of homes, especially in a place where no people have lived before: *a **settlement** on the edge of the desert*

settler (say **set**-luh) *noun* (*plural* **settlers**)
a person who goes to live permanently in a new place or region: *the 1820 British **Settlers***

seven (say **sev**-uhn) *number*
7

seventeen (say sev-uhn-**teen**) *number*
17

seventeenth (say sev-uhn-**teenth**) *adjective, adverb, noun*
17th

seventh (say **sev**-uhnth) *adjective, adverb, noun*
1 7th
2 one of seven equal parts of something; $\frac{1}{7}$

seventieth (say **sev**-uhn-ti-uth) *adjective, adverb, noun*
70th

seventy (say **sev**-uhn-tee) *number*
1 70
2 the seventies (*plural noun*) the numbers 70 to 79 or the years 1970 to 1979: *She was born in the **seventies*** (= in the 1970s).
in your seventies between the ages of 70 and 79

several (say **sev**-ruhl) *adjective, pronoun*
more than two but not many: *I've read this book **several** times.* ◇ *I have **several** exams next week.* ◇ *This is one of **several**.*

severe (say si-**veer**) *adjective* (**severer, severest**)
1 not kind or gentle: *a **severe** punishment*
2 very bad: *She suffers from **severe** headaches.*
► **severely** (*adverb*): *They punished him **severely**.* ◇ *She was **severely** injured in the accident.*

sew (*rhymes with* **go**) *verb* (**sewing, sewed, has sewed** or **has sewn**)
to use a needle and cotton to join pieces of material together or to join something to material: *He **sewed** a button on his shirt.* ◇ *Can you sew?*

PRONUNCIATION Notice how to say **sew**. It sounds the same as **so**.

sewage (say **syoo**-ij or **soo**-ij) *noun* (*no plural*)
the waste material from people's bodies that is carried away from toilets in a **sewer**

sewer (say **soo**-uh) *noun* (*plural* **sewers**)
a large underground pipe that carries human waste in water to a place where it can be treated

sewerage (say **syoo**-uh-rij) *noun* (*no plural*)
the system by which **sewage** is carried away from buildings and is cleaned and made safe by having chemicals added to it

sewing (say **soh**-ing) *noun* (*no plural*)
1 the activity of sewing
2 something that you sew

sewing machine *noun* (*plural* **sewing machines**)
a machine that you use for sewing

sewn (say **sohn**) form of **sew**

sex (say **sekss**) *noun*
1 (*plural* **sexes**) the state of being a male or a female: *the male **sex*** ◇ *What **sex** is your dog?* ◇ *Fill in your **sex** (male or female) on the application form.*
2 (*no plural*) (also **sexual intercourse, intercourse**) the physical activity of sex, usually describing the act of a man putting his **penis** inside a woman's **vagina**: *Think carefully before you have **sex** with him.*

sexism (say **sek**-siz-m) *noun* (*plural* **sexism**)
the unfair treatment of people, especially women, on the basis of their sex, or the attitude that causes this: *We must understand how **sexism** keeps certain groups of women vulnerable* (= weak and easy to hurt).

sexual (say **sek**-shuu-uhl) *adjective*
connected with sex: *a campaign for **sexual** equality* ◇ *the **sexual** organs*
sexual abuse using somebody sexually in a wrong or bad way
► **sexually** (*adverb*): *to be **sexually** active*

sexual intercourse (say **sek**-sh*uu*-uhl **in**-tuh-kawss) *noun* (*no plural*) (also **intercourse** or **sex**) (*formal*)
the physical activity of sex, usually describing the act of a man putting his **penis** into a woman's **vagina**. **Sexual intercourse** can result in a woman becoming pregnant and having a baby: *They were having **sexual intercourse**.*

sexuality (say seks-yuu-**al**-i-tee) *noun* (*no plural*)
the nature of a person's sexual activities or desires: *Our **sexuality** is linked to the way we see ourselves as boys and girls.*

sexy (say **sek**-see) *adjective* (**sexier, sexiest**)
1 sexually attractive or exciting: *The Pussycat Dolls are known just as much for their **sexy** image as they are for their music.*
2 (*informal*) very exciting or appealing: *The device is **sexy** and smart.*

A B C D E F G H I J K L M N O P Q R S T U V W X Y Z

shabby (say **shab**-ee) *adjective* (**shabbier, shabbiest**)
old and untidy or dirty because it has been used a lot: *This coat's getting a bit **shabby**.*
▸ **shabbily** (*adverb*): *She was **shabbily** dressed.*

shack (say **shak**) *noun* (*plural* **shacks**)
a small building, usually made of wood or metal, that has not been built well: *Every great city, from ancient Rome to New York, was at some point ringed by **shacks**.*

shackle (say **shak**-l) *verb* (**shackling, shackled**)
(often figurative) restrain or restrict a person or a thing (= to allow only limited movement, as with a chain tied between a person's ankles or wrists): *The rule of law is intended to **shackle** rulers to prevent them from posing a threat to citizens.*
▸ **shackle** (*noun*): *We need to uplift* (= lift up, raise) *our people from the **shackles** of poverty.*

shade[1] (say **shayd**) *noun*
1 (*no plural*) a place where it is dark and cool because the sun doesn't shine there: *We sat in the **shade** of a big tree.*
2 (*plural* **shades**) a thing that keeps strong light from your eyes: *I bought a new **shade** for the lamp.*
3 (*plural* **shades**) how light or dark a colour is: *I want a shirt in a darker **shade** of red.*
4 shades (*plural noun*) (*informal*) = **sunglasses**

shade[2] (say **shayd**) *verb* (**shading, shaded**)
to stop light from shining on something: *He **shaded** his eyes with his hand.*

shading (say **shayd**-ing) *noun* (*no plural*)
1 the darkening of an illustration with parallel lines or lines that **intersect**
2 material used to provide shade, especially for plants

shadow (say **shad**-oh) *noun* (*plural* **shadows**)
a dark shape that you see near somebody or something that is in front of the light: *Your **shadow** gets longer and longer as the sun goes down.*
🛈 **ORIGIN**: from Old English *scead(u)we* meaning 'shade', related to Dutch *schaduw*. These words are from an older word related to Greek *skotos* meaning 'darkness'.

shady (say **shayd**-ee) *adjective* (**shadier, shadiest**)
not in the sun: *We sat in a **shady** part of the garden.*

shaft (say **shaaft**) *noun* (*plural* **shafts**)
1 the long narrow part of a tool or weapon, by which it is held: *the **shaft** of a javelin* (= a long pointed stick that people throw as a sport) ◇ *the **shaft** of a golf club*
2 (*technology*) a long turning rod that connects parts of a machine so that power can pass between them
3 a long narrow hole, usually vertical, in which a thing can move up or down or enter or leave: *a lift **shaft** ◇ a mine **shaft***

shaggy (say **shag**-ee) *adjective* (**shaggier, shaggiest**)
1 (about hair, fur or material) long, thick and untidy: *The yak has a long **shaggy** coat.*
2 covered in long, thick and untidy hair or fur: *a **shaggy** dog*

shake (say **shayk**) *verb* (**shaking, shook, has shaken**)
1 to move quickly from side to side or up and down, or to make something do this: *The house **shakes** when trains go past. ◇ He was **shaking** with fear. ◇ **Shake** the bottle before opening it. ◇ An explosion **shook** the windows.*
2 to disturb or upset somebody or something: *The boy's parents were **shaken** by his death.*
shake hands to hold somebody's hand and move it up and down when you meet them
shake your head to move your head from side to side to say 'no'

shaken (say **shayk**-n) form of **shake**

shaky (say **shayk**-ee) *adjective* (**shakier, shakiest**)
1 shaking because you are ill or frightened: *You've got **shaky** hands.*
2 not firm or not strong: *That ladder looks a little **shaky**.*

shale (say **shayl**) *noun* (*no plural*)
a type of rock made from layers of hardened clay and mud

shall (say **shal**) *modal verb*
1 a word that you use with a verb when you are asking, offering, or suggesting something to do: *What time **shall** I come? ◇ **Shall** I close the window? ◇ **Shall** we go now?*
2 (*formal*) a word that you use instead of 'will' with 'I' and 'we' to show the future: *I **shall** see you tomorrow.* ➲ See **modal verb**

USAGE In formal and old-fashioned English **shall** is used to form the future tense after **I** and **we** in sentences like these: *I **shall** go now. ◇ We **shall** see you later.* In modern English **shall** and **will** are both seen as correct: *I **will** go now. ◇ We **will** see you later.*

shallow (say **shal**-oh) *adjective* (**shallower, shallowest**)
not deep or with not much water: *This part of the river is **shallow** – we can walk across.*

sham *noun* (*plural* **shams**)
a person who pretends to be someone or something they are not or a thing that is not what it is presented as: *The consultation* (= discussion before a course of action is undertaken) *that was carried out was a **sham**.*
▶ **sham** (*adjective*): ***sham** elections*

shaman (say **sha**-muhn or **shay**-muhn) *noun* (*plural* **shamans**)
a member of certain tribes who is believed to move between the seen world and the unseen spirit world and to practise magic to heal, predict and control natural events

shame (say **shaym**) *noun* (*no plural*)
1 the unhappy feeling that you have when you have done something wrong or stupid: *I was filled with **shame** after I lied to my parents.* ➲ The adjective is **ashamed**
2 a fact or situation that makes you feel sad or disappointed: *It's a **shame** you can't come to the party.* ◇ *'Sally's not well.' 'What a **shame**!'*
➲ SYNONYM **pity**[1] 2

shameless (say **shaym**-luhss) *adjective*
doing bad things without caring what other people think: *She is **shameless** – she copied somebody else's work!*

shampoo (say sham-**poo**) *noun* (*no plural*)
a special liquid for washing your hair: *a bottle of **shampoo***
▶ **shampoo** (*verb*): *How often do you **shampoo** your hair?*

shan't (say **shaant**) short for **shall not**

shanty (say **shan**-tee) *noun* (*plural* **shanties**)
a small, crudely built **shack**
shanty town an area, usually on the edge of a big city, where poor people live in bad conditions in homes they have built themselves

shape[1] (say **shayp**) *noun*
1 (*plural* **shapes**) what you see if you draw a line round something, or the form of something: *Circles, squares and triangles are all different **shapes**.* ◇ *I bought a bowl in the **shape** of a fish.*
2 (*no plural*) the physical condition of somebody or something: *He was in bad **shape** after the accident.* ◇ *I like to keep in **shape*** (= keep fit) *by exercising.*
out of shape
1 not having the right shape: *My sweater went out of **shape** when I washed it.*
2 (used about a person) not in good physical condition: *I didn't realize how out of **shape** I was!*

shape[2] (say **shayp**) *verb* (**shaping**, **shaped**)
to give a certain shape to something: *She **shaped** the clay into a pot.*

shaped (say **shaypt**) *adjective*
having a certain shape: *a heart-**shaped** box of chocolates* ◇ *He gave me a birthday card **shaped** like a cat.*

shapeless (say **shayp**-luhss) *adjective*
not having a clear shape: *a **shapeless** jacket*

shapely (say **shayp**-lee) *adjective* (**shapelier**, **shapeliest**)
(especially of a woman's body) having an attractive shape, with proportions pleasing to the eye: *She showed a **shapely** pair of legs as she walked away.*

share[1] (say **shair**) *verb* (**sharing**, **shared**)
1 to divide something between two or more people: ***Share** these sweets with your friends.* ◇ *We **shared** a large pizza among three of us.*
2 to have or use something with another person: *I **share** a bedroom with my sister.*

share[2] (say **shair**) *noun*
1 (*no plural*) a part of something bigger that each person has: *Here is your **share** of the money.* ◇ *I did my **share** of the work.*
2 (*plural* **shares**) one of equal parts which the value of a company is divided into. People who want to own part of the company buy **shares** in it: *a fall in **share** prices*

shark (say **shaak**) *noun* (*plural* **sharks**)
a big fish that lives in the sea. Some **sharks** have sharp teeth and are dangerous.

sharp[1] (say **shaap**) *adjective* (**sharper**, **sharpest**)
1 with an edge or point that cuts or makes holes easily: *a **sharp** knife* ◇ *a **sharp** needle*
➲ OPPOSITE **blunt** 1
2 strong and sudden: *a **sharp** bend in the road* ◇ *I felt a **sharp** pain in my leg.*
3 clear and easy to see: *We saw the **sharp** outline of the mountains against the sky.*
4 able to see, hear or learn well: *She's got a very **sharp** mind.* ◇ ***sharp** eyes*
5 sudden and angry: ***sharp** words*
▶ **sharply** (*adverb*): *The road bends **sharply** to the left.* ◇ *'Go away!' he said **sharply**.*

sharp[2] (say **shaap**) *adverb*
1 exactly: *Be here at six o'clock **sharp**.*
2 with a big change of direction: *Turn **sharp** right at the next corner.*

sharpen (say **shaap**-n) *verb* (**sharpening**, **sharpened**)
to make something sharp or sharper: *They **sharpened** all the knives.*

sharpener (say **shaap**-nuh) *noun* (*plural* **sharpeners**)
a thing that you use for making something sharp: *a pencil **sharpener***

A B C D E F G H I J K L M N O P Q R S T U V W X Y Z

shatter (say **shat**-uh) *verb* (**shattering, shattered**)
to break into very small pieces or to break something into very small pieces: *The glass hit the floor and **shattered**.* ◇ *The explosion **shattered** the windows.*

shave (say **shayv**) *verb* (**shaving, shaved**)
to cut hair off your face or body by cutting it very close with a special knife (called a **razor**): *He **shaves** every morning.*
▸ **shave** (*noun*): *I haven't had a **shave** today.*

shaver (say **shayv**-uh) *noun* (*plural* **shavers**)
an electric tool that you use for shaving
➲ See **razor**

shawl (*rhymes with* **crawl**) *noun* (*plural* **shawls**)
a big piece of cloth that a woman wears round her shoulders, or that you put round a baby

she (say **shee**) *pronoun* (*plural* **they**)
a woman or girl who the sentence is about: *'Where's your sister?' '**She's** (= she is) at work.'*

sheaf (say **sheef**) *noun* (*plural* **sheaves**)
1 a **bundle** of grain stalks tied together after reaping
2 objects tied in a **bundle**, especially papers

shear (say **sheer**) *verb* (**shearing, sheared, has shorn**)
to cut the wool off a sheep or to cut off hair or grass with a large pair of scissors

shears (say **sheerz**) *plural noun*
a tool like a very large pair of scissors that you use for cutting things in the garden

sheaves plural of **sheaf**

shebeen (say shuh-**been**) *noun* (*plural* **shebeens**)
1 a place that sells alcohol without a licence to do so, often seen as rather **disreputable** 1
2 (in South African townships) an informal drinking place
ℹ **ORIGIN:** 18th century, from Irish *shebeen* from *seibe* meaning 'mugful'. Irish is a language spoken in Ireland.

shed[1] *noun* (*plural* **sheds**)
a small building where you keep things or animals: *We keep our tools in the garden **shed**.*

shed[2] (say **shed**) *verb* (**shedding, shed**)
to lose something because it falls off: *Some trees **shed** their leaves at the end of summer.*

she'd (say **sheed**) short for **she had; she would**

sheen *noun* (*no plural*)
a soft gleam on the surface of a thing: *He fondly remembers the **sheen** of her velvet jacket.*

sheep *noun* (*plural* **sheep**)
an animal that people keep on farms for its meat and its wool

sheer *adjective*
1 complete: ***sheer** nonsense*
2 very steep: *It was a **sheer** drop to the sea.*

sheet *noun* (*plural* **sheets**)
1 a big piece of thin material for a bed: *I put some clean **sheets** on the bed.*
2 a thin flat piece of something like paper, glass or metal: *a **sheet** of writing paper*

sheikh (say **shayk** or **she*kh***) *noun* (*plural* **sheikhs**)
1 an Arab ruler, in particular the head of a tribe, family or village
2 a leader in a Muslim community
ℹ **ORIGIN:** 16th century, from Arabic *šayk* meaning 'old man, sheikh'

shelf *noun* (*plural* **shelves**)
a long flat piece of wood on a wall or in a cupboard, where things can stand: *Put the plates on the **shelf**.* ◇ ***bookshelves***

shell *noun* (*plural* **shells**)
the hard outside part of birds' eggs and nuts and of some animals ➲ See **seashell**

she'll (say **shee**-uhl) short for **she will**

shellfish (say **shell**-fish) *noun* (*plural* **shellfish**)
a kind of animal that lives in water and that has a shell

shelter[1] (say **shel**-tuh) *noun*
1 (*no plural*) protection from bad weather or danger: *We took **shelter** from the rain under a tree.* ◇ *People ran for **shelter** when the bombs started to fall.*
2 (*plural* **shelters**) a place that protects you from bad weather or danger: *a bus **shelter*** (= for people who are waiting at a bus stop)

shelter[2] (say **shel**-tuh) *verb* (**sheltering, sheltered**)
1 to make somebody or something safe from bad weather or danger: *The trees **shelter** the house from the wind.*
2 to go to a place where you will be safe from bad weather or danger: *Let's **shelter** from the rain under that tree.*

shelves (say **shelvz**) plural of **shelf**

shepherd (say **shep**-uhd) *noun* (*plural* **shepherds**)
a person who looks after sheep

sheriff (say **she**-rif) *noun* (*plural* **sheriffs**)
an officer of the law in a United States county

(= a political and administrative division of a state)

PRONUNCIATION Pronounce the **e** in **sheriff** like the **e** in **get**.

she's (say **sheez**) short for **she is; she has**

shield[1] (say **shee**-uhld) *noun* (*plural* **shields**)
a big piece of metal, wood or leather that soldiers carried in front of their bodies when they were fighting in wars long ago. Some police officers carry **shields** now.

shield[2] (say **shee**-uhld) *verb* (**shielding, shielded**)
to keep somebody or something safe from danger or from being hurt: *She **shielded** her eyes from the sun with her hand.*

shift[1] *verb* (**shifting, shifted**)
to move something from one place to another: *Can you help me to **shift** the bed? I want to sweep the floor.*

shift[2] *noun* (*plural* **shifts**)
1 a change in what people think about something: *There has been a **shift** in the public's attitude.*
2 a period of time worked by a group of workers who start work when another group finishes: *I'm on the night **shift**.*

shifty (say **shif**-tee) *adjective* (**shiftier, shiftiest**)
(used about a person or their appearance) giving the impression that you cannot trust them: ***shifty** eyes*

shipment (say **ship**-muhnt) *noun*
1 (*no plural*) the carrying of goods from one place to another
2 (*plural* **shipments**) a quantity of goods that are sent from one place to another

Shi'ite (say **shee**-ite) *noun* (*plural* **Shi'ites**)
a follower of the Shia branch of Islam ➲ See **Sunni**

shimmer (say **shim**-uh) *verb* (**shimmering, shimmered**)
to shine with a soft light that seems to be moving: *The moonlight **shimmered** on the sea.*

shin *noun* (*plural* **shins**)
the bone in the front part of your leg from your knee to your foot ➲ See illustration at **body**

shin bone *noun* (*plural* **shin bones**) (also **tibia**)
the front and larger bone of the two bones in the lower part of the leg between the knee and the ankle ➲ See illustration at **skeleton**

shine (*rhymes with* **fine**) *verb* (**shining, shone**)
1 to give out light: *The sun is **shining**.*
2 to be bright: *Her eyes **shone** with happiness.*
3 to direct a light at somebody or something: *Don't **shine** your torch in my eyes!*

shiny (say **shine**-ee) *adjective* (**shinier, shiniest**)
causing a bright effect when in the sun or in light: *The new shampoo leaves your hair soft and **shiny**.* ◇ *He's got a **shiny** new car.*

ship *noun* (*plural* **ships**)
a big boat for carrying people and goods on the sea: *We went to India by **ship**.*
▸ **ship** (*verb*): *Some types of cars are **shipped** to South Africa.*

shipping (say **ship**-ing) *noun* (*no plural*)
ships in general or the carrying of goods by ships: *a **shipping** company* ◇ *The port is now open to **shipping**.*

ship

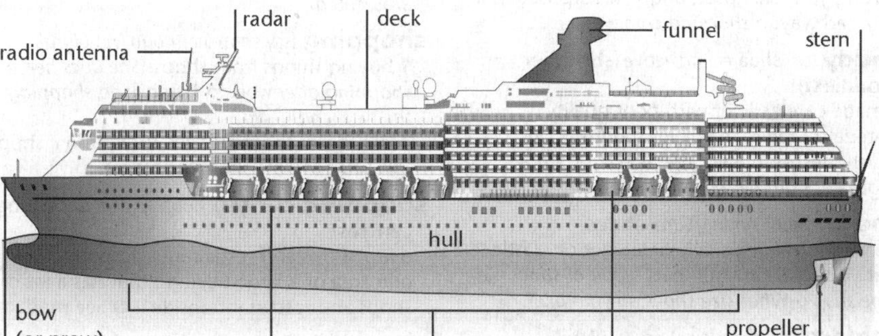

A B C D E F G H I J K L M N O P Q R **S** T U V W X Y Z

A B C D E F G H I J K L M N O P Q R S T U V W X Y Z

shipshape (say **ship**-shayp) *adjective*
in good order or trim and neat: *The car was packed and **shipshape** for our road trip.*

shipwreck (say **ship**-rek) *noun* (*plural* **shipwrecks**)
an accident at sea when a ship breaks up in bad weather or on rocks
be shipwrecked to be on a ship when it has an accident and breaks up: *They were **shipwrecked** off the coast of Portugal.*

shirk (say **shurk**) *verb* (**shirking, shirked**)
to avoid or **neglect** your duty or responsibility: *Don't **shirk** your duty!*

shirt (say **shurt**) *noun* (*plural* **shirts**)
a thin piece of clothing that you wear on the top part of your body: *a short-sleeved **shirt** ◇ a football **shirt***

shiver (say **shiv**-uh) *verb* (**shivering, shivered**)
to shake because you are cold, frightened or ill: *We were **shivering** with cold.*
▸ **shiver** (*noun*): *Sue gave a **shiver** and pulled her coat around her.*

shoal (*rhymes with* **hole**) *noun* (*plural* **shoals**)
a large group of fish that feed and swim together

shock[1] (say **shok**) *noun* (*plural* **shocks**)
1 a very bad surprise: *The news of his death came as a **shock** to all of us.*
2 a sudden pain when electricity goes through your body: *Don't touch that wire – you'll get an electric **shock**.*

shock[2] (say **shok**) *verb* (**shocking, shocked**)
to give somebody a very bad surprise, or to upset somebody: *I was **shocked** by his behaviour.*
▸ **shocked** (*adjective*): *Don't look so **shocked** – I did warn you!*

shocking (say **shok**-ing) *adjective*
making you feel upset, angry or surprised in a very bad way: *a **shocking** crime*

shoddy (say **shod**-ee) *adjective* (**shoddier, shoddiest**)
1 made carelessly or with poor quality materials: *I refuse to pay for **shoddy** goods.*
2 dishonest or unfair: *She received **shoddy** treatment from her boyfriend.*

shoe (say **shoo**) *noun* (*plural* **shoes**)
a covering made usually of leather or plastic that you wear on your feet: *a pair of **shoes** ◇ a **shoe** shop ◇ What size **shoes** do you take?*

shoelace (say **shoo**-layss) *noun* (*plural* **shoelaces**) (also **lace**)
a long thin piece of material like string that you tie to close a shoe: *Tie your **shoelaces**.*

shone (say **shon**) form of **shine**

shook (say **shuuk**) form of **shake**

shoot[1] (*rhymes with* **boot**) *verb* (**shooting, shot**)
1 to fire a gun or another weapon: *He **shot** an arrow from his bow.*
2 to hurt or kill a person or an animal with a gun: *She **shot** a bird. ◇ The police officer was **shot** in the arm.*
3 to move quickly or suddenly: *The car **shot** past us.*
4 to make a film: *They are **shooting** a film about the war.*

shoot[2] (say **shoot**) *noun* (*plural* **shoots**)
a new part of a plant: *The first **shoots** appear in spring.*

shop[1] *noun* (*plural* **shops**)
a building where you buy things: *a **bookshop** ◇ Do you need anything from the **shops**?*

shop[2] (say **shop**) *verb* (**shopping, shopped**)
to go to buy things from shops: *I'm **shopping** for some new clothes.*
▸ **shopper** (*noun*): *The streets were full of **shoppers**.*

> USAGE We usually say **go shopping** when we are planning to go: *I'm **going shopping** later this afternoon.*

shop assistant *noun* (*plural* **shop assistants**)
a person who works in a shop but is not the owner or manager

shopkeeper (say **shop**-keep-uh) *noun* (*plural* **shopkeepers**)
a person who owns a small shop

shoplifting (say **shop**-lift-ing) *noun* (*no plural*)
the crime of stealing things from shops: *He was accused of **shoplifting**.*
▸ **shoplifter** (*noun*): ***Shoplifters** will be prosecuted.*

shopping (say **shop**-ing) *noun* (*no plural*)
1 buying things from shops: *She does her **shopping** after work. ◇ I usually go **shopping** at the weekend.*
2 the things that you have bought in a shop: *Will you carry my **shopping** for me?*

shopping centre *noun* (*plural* **shopping centres**)
a few shops and restaurants close together in one area or a large building that has a lot of shops and restaurants inside it ➲ See **mall**

shore[1] (say **shaw**) *noun* (*plural* **shores**)
the land next to the sea or a lake: *The swimmer kept close to the **shore**.*

shore² (say **shaw**) *verb* (**shoring, shored**)
shore up
1 to support a thing by placing thick wooden planks or metal poles against or under it: *The workers had to **shore** up the building, which was in danger of collapse.*
2 to help support a thing that is weak or going to fail: *The measures were aimed at **shoring** up failing banks.*

shorn (say **shawn**) form of **shear**

short (say **shawt**) *adjective* (**shorter, shortest**)
1 a small distance from one end to the other: *Her hair is very **short**.* ◇ *We live a **short** distance from the beach.* ➲ OPPOSITE **long¹** 1
2 less tall than most people: *a **short** fat man* ◇ *I'm too **short** to reach the top shelf.* ➲ OPPOSITE **tall**
3 lasting for only a little time: *a **short** holiday* ◇ *The film was very **short**.* ➲ OPPOSITE **long¹** 3
be short of something to not have enough of something: *I'm **short** of money this month.*
for short as a **short** way of saying or writing something: *My sister's name is Deborah, but we call her 'Deb' for **short**.*
short for something a **short** way of saying or writing something: *'Tom' is **short** for 'Thomas'.*
ⓘ ORIGIN: from Old English *sceort*, related to English *shirt* and *skirt*

shortage (say **shaw**-tij) *noun* (*plural* **shortages**)
a situation when there is not enough of something: *a water **shortage*** ◇ *There is a **shortage** of good teachers.*

short cut *noun* (*plural* **short cuts**)
a shorter way to get somewhere: *We took a **short cut** to school across the field.*

shorten (say **shawt**-n) *verb* (**shortening, shortened**)
to become shorter or to make something shorter: *The trousers were too long, so I **shortened** them.* ➲ OPPOSITE **lengthen**

shortly (say **shawt**-lee) *adverb*
soon: *The doctor will see you **shortly**, Mr Smith.* ◇ *We left **shortly** after six o'clock.*

shorts (say **shawtss**) *plural noun*
1 short trousers that end above your knees: *a pair of **shorts***
2 (also **boxer shorts, boxers**) a piece of loose clothing that men wear under their trousers

short-sighted (say shawt-**site**-uhd) *adjective*
1 able to see things clearly only when they are near to you: *I have to wear glasses for driving because I'm **short-sighted**.*
2 not considering what is likely to happen in the future: *a **short-sighted** policy*

short-tempered (say shawt-**tem**-puhd) *adjective*
that gets angry quickly: *Heavy traffic makes everyone **short-tempered** and hostile.*

shot¹ form of **shoot¹**

shot² (say **shot**) *noun* (*plural* **shots**)
1 the action of firing a gun, or the noise that this makes: *He fired a **shot**.*
2 the action of kicking or hitting a ball in a sport like football: *a **shot** at goal*
3 a photograph: *This is a good **shot** of you.*

shotgun (say **shot**-gun) *noun* (*plural* **shotguns**)
a long gun that shoots a lot of small metal bullets and is often used for shooting small animals and birds

should (say **shuud**) *modal verb*
1 a word that you use to tell or ask somebody what is the right thing to do: *If you feel ill, you **should** stay in bed.* ◇ *You **shouldn't** eat so much chocolate.* ◇ *I'm tired. I **shouldn't** have gone to bed so late.* ➲ SYNONYM **ought to**
2 a word that you use to give or ask somebody for advice: *You **should** read this book – it's excellent* ◇ ***Should** I invite him to the party?*
3 a word that you use to say what you think will happen or what you think is true: *They **should** be here soon.*
4 the word that we use for 'shall' in the past, when we say what somebody said: *We asked if we **should** help her.* ➲ See **modal verb**

USAGE Be careful! Notice how **should** is used in certain tenses: *I **should have** gone.* (not 'I should of gone.') *We **should have** swum.* (not 'We should of swum.')

USAGE The negative form of **should** is **should not** or the short form, **shouldn't** (*say* **shuud**-uhnt).

shoulder (say **shohl**-duh) *noun* (*plural* **shoulders**)
the part of your body between your neck and your arm ➲ See illustration at **body**

shoulderblade (say **shohl**-duh-blayd) *noun* (*plural* **shoulderblades**) (also **scapula**)
one of the two large flat bones at the top of the back ➲ See illustration at **skeleton**

shouldn't (say **shuud**-uhnt) short for **should not**

should've (say **shuud**-uhv) short for **should have**

A B C D E F G H I J K L M N O P Q R S T U V W X Y Z

A B C D E F G H I J K L M N O P Q R **S** T U V W X Y Z

shout (say **showt**) *verb* (**shouting, shouted**)
to speak very loudly: *Don't* ***shout*** *at me!* ◇ *'Go back!' she* ***shouted****.*
▸ **shout** (*noun*): *We heard a* ***shout*** *for help.*

shove (say **shuv**) *verb* (**shoving, shoved**)
to push somebody or something in a rough way: *They* ***shoved*** *him through the door.*

shovel[1] (say **shuv**-l) *noun* (*plural* **shovels**)
a tool that you use for picking up and moving earth or sand

shovel[2] (say **shuv**-l) *verb* (**shovelling, shovelled**)
to move something with a **shovel**: *He* ***shovelled*** *the earth into the hole.*

show[1] (say **shoh**) *verb* (**showing, showed, has shown** or **has showed**)
1 to let somebody see something: *She* ***showed*** *me her holiday photos.* ◇ *You have to* ***show*** *your ticket on the train.* ◇ *He has* ***shown*** *me round the school.*
2 to make something clear or to explain something to somebody: *Can you* ***show*** *me how to use the computer?* ◇ *Research* ***shows*** *that most people get too little exercise.*
3 to appear or be seen: *The anger* ***showed*** *in his face.*
show off to talk loudly or do something silly to make people notice you: *She was* ***showing*** *off by driving too fast.*
show something off to let people see something that is new or beautiful: *He wanted to* ***show*** *off his new jacket.*

show[2] (say **shoh**) *noun* (*plural* **shows**)
1 something that you watch at the theatre or on television: *a comedy* ***show*** ◇ *Did you enjoy the* ***show****?*
2 a group of things in one place that people go to see: *a flower* ***show*** ◇ *The paintings are on* ***show*** *at the National Gallery.*

shower (*rhymes with* **power**) *noun* (*plural* **showers**)
1 a place where you can wash by standing under water that falls from above you: *There's a* ***shower*** *in the bathroom.*
2 the act of washing yourself in a shower: *I had a* ***shower*** *after the tennis match.*
3 rain that falls for a short time: *The day will be cloudy, with occasional heavy* ***showers****.*

shown (say **shohn**) form of **show**[1]

showroom (say **shoh**-ruum) *noun* (*plural* **showrooms**)
a large open room in a shop where customers can look at items such as cars, furniture and electrical goods that are on sale

shrank form of **shrink**

shrapnel (say **shrap**-nuhl) *noun* (*no plural*)
small pieces of metal that fly around when a bomb explodes

shred *noun* (*plural* **shreds**)
a small thin piece of material that has been cut or torn off: ***shreds*** *of paper*

shrewd (say **shrood**) *adjective* (**shrewder, shrewdest**)
able to make good decisions because you understand people or situations well: *She's a very* ***shrewd*** *businesswoman.*

shriek (say **shreek**) *verb* (**shrieking, shrieked**)
to make a loud high cry: *She* ***shrieked*** *with fear when she saw the snake.*
▸ **shriek** (*noun*): *He gave a* ***shriek*** *of pain.*
🛈 **ORIGIN:** 15th century. The word came from imitating the sound.

shrill *adjective* (**shriller, shrillest**)
A **shrill** sound is high and loud: *a* ***shrill*** *whistle*

shrimp *noun* (*plural* **shrimps** or **shrimp**)
a small sea animal with a shell and a lot of legs that turns pink when you cook it. **Shrimps** are similar to prawns but smaller.

shrine (*rhymes with* **fine**) *noun* (*plural* **shrines**)
a special place that is important to people for religious reasons

shrink *verb* (**shrinking, shrank** or **shrunk**)
to become smaller or to make something smaller: *My jeans* ***shrank*** *when I washed them.*

shrivel (say **shriv**-uhl) *verb* (**shrivelling, shrivelled**)
to become smaller, especially because of dry conditions: *The plants* ***shrivelled*** *up and died in the hot weather.*

shroud (say **shrowd**) *noun* (*plural* **shrouds**)
a cloth or sheet that is put around a dead body before it is buried

shrub *noun* (*plural* **shrubs**)
a plant like a small low tree

shrug *verb* (**shrugging, shrugged**)
to move your shoulders to show that you do not know or do not care about something: *I asked her where Sam was but she just* ***shrugged****.*
▸ **shrug** (*noun*): *He answered my question with a* ***shrug****.*

shrunk form of **shrink**

shudder (say **shud**-uh) *verb* (**shuddering, shuddered**)
to shake because you are cold or frightened, or because of a strong feeling: *He* ***shuddered*** *when he saw the snake.*
▸ **shudder** (*noun*): *She felt a* ***shudder*** *of fear.*

shuffle (say **shuf**-l) *verb* (**shuffling, shuffled**)
1 to walk slowly without lifting your feet off the ground: *The old man **shuffled** along the road.*
2 to mix playing cards before a game: *She **shuffled** the cards carefully before dealing them.*

shun *verb* (**shunning, shunned**)
to avoid, ignore or reject a person or a thing: *The actor liked to be private and **shunned** publicity.*

shunt *verb* (**shunting, shunted**)
1 to move a railway train from one track to another
2 to make a person go from one place to another, often to a less important place or position: *The officials **shunted** the applicants from one office to the next.*

shut[1] *verb* (**shutting, shut**)
1 to move something so that it is not open: *Could you **shut** the door, please?* ◇ *The door **shut** behind me.* ➲ SYNONYM **close**[1] 1
2 to stop being open, so that people cannot go there: *The shops **shut** at 5.00 p.m.* ◇ *The factory **shut** down* (= closed and stopped working) *last year.* ➲ SYNONYM **close**[1] 2
shut up (*informal*) to stop talking: ***Shut** up and listen!*

SPEAKING The expression **shut up** is quite rude. It is more polite to say **'Be quiet'**.

shut[2] *adjective*
not open: *The restaurant is **shut** today.* ◇ *Is the door **shut**?* ➲ SYNONYM **closed**

shutter (say **shut**-uh) *noun* (*plural* **shutters**)
1 a wooden or metal thing that covers the outside of a window: *Close the **shutters** at night.*
2 the part at the front of a camera that opens for a very short time to let light in so that a photograph can be taken

shuttle (say **shut**-l) *noun* (*plural* **shuttles**)
1 a plane, bus or train that travels regularly between two places
2 = **space shuttle**

shy (say **shy**) *adjective* (**shyer, shyest**)
not able to talk easily to people you do not know: *He was too **shy** to speak to her.* ◇ *a **shy** smile*
▸ **shyness** (*noun*): *As a child she suffered from terrible **shyness**.*

SI *abbreviation*
International System
SI unit a unit based on the international system for units of measurement: *The **SI** unit for distance is a metre.*
🛈 ORIGIN: from French *Système International*

sibling (say **sib**-ling) *noun* (*plural* **siblings**)
(*formal*) a brother or a sister

USAGE **Brother** and **sister** are the words that we usually use. **Sibling** is quite formal.

sick (say **sik**) *adjective* (**sicker, sickest**)
not well: *She's looking after her **sick** mother.* ◇ *He's been off **sick*** (= away because of illness) *all week.* ➲ SYNONYM **ill**
be sick When you **are sick**, food comes up from your stomach and out of your mouth. ➲ SYNONYM **vomit**
be sick of something to have had or done too much of something, so that you do not want it any longer: *I'm **sick** of watching TV – let's go out.*
feel sick to feel that food is going to come up from your stomach ➲ See **nausea**

sickle (say **sik**-l) *noun* (*plural* **sickles**)
a tool with a short handle and a long curved **blade**, used for cutting long grass and, in the past, grain ➲ See **scythe**

sickness (say **sik**-nuhss) *noun* (*no plural*)
being ill: *He could not work for a long time because of **sickness**.*

side[1] *noun* (*plural* **sides**)
1 one of the flat outside parts of something: *A box has six **sides**.* ◇ *A triangle has three **sides**.*
2 the part of something that is not the front, back, top or bottom: *Go to the door at the **side** of the house.* ◇ *There's a scratch on the **side** of Mom's new car.*
3 the part of something that is near the edge and away from the middle: *I stood at the **side** of the road.*
4 the right or left part of something: *He lay on his **side**.* ◇ *They walked **side** by **side*** (= next to each other). ◇ *We drive on the left **side** of the road in South Africa.*
5 one of two groups of people who fight, argue or play a game against each other: *I thought you were on my **side*** (= agreed with me). ◇ *Did the South African cricket **side** win?*
take sides to show that you agree with one person and not the other in a fight or an argument

side[2] *verb* (**siding, sided**)
side with to support a person in an argument: *I am **siding** with you on this issue but not on that one.*

sideboard (say **side**-bawd) *noun* (*plural* **sideboards**)
a type of cupboard that you use for storing plates and dishes in the room where you eat (called a **dining room**)

sidetrack (say **side**-trak) *verb* (**sidetracking, sidetracked**)
(usually passive) to make a person forget what they are doing or talking about and start doing or talking about a less important thing: *Concentrate on your work: don't get **sidetracked** so easily!*

sideways (say **side**-wayz) *adjective, adverb*
1 to or from the side: *She looked **sideways** at the girl next to her.*
2 with one of the sides first: *We carried the table **sideways** through the door.*

siege (say **seej**) *noun* (*plural* **sieges**)
a situation when an army stays outside a town or police stay outside a building for a long time so that no one can get in or out: *the **siege** of Mafikeng*

siesta (say see-**ess**-tuh) *noun* (*plural* **siestas**)
a short sleep or rest that people take in the afternoon, especially in hot countries
ORIGIN: 17th century, through Spanish from Latin *sexta (hora)* meaning 'sixth hour'. For the ancient Romans, the sixth hour of the day was midday, when it was time to have a rest.

sieve (say **siv**) *noun* (*plural* **sieves**)
a type of kitchen tool that you use to remove lumps from food such as flour or soup

sift *verb* (**sifting, sifted**)
1 to pass flour, sugar or a similar substance through a **sieve** to remove any lumps
2 to examine a thing very carefully: *It took weeks to **sift** through all the evidence.*

sigh (say *sy*) *verb* (**sighing, sighed**)
to let out a deep breath, for example because you are sad, tired or pleased
▶ **sigh** (*noun*): *'I wish I had more money,' he said with a **sigh**.*

sight (say **site**) *noun*
1 (*no plural*) the ability to see: *She has poor **sight*** (= she cannot see well). ➲ SYNONYMS **eyesight**, **vision** 1
2 (*no plural*) seeing somebody or something: *We had our first **sight** of London from the plane.*
3 (*plural* **sights**) something that you see: *The mountains were a beautiful **sight**.*
4 sights (*plural noun*) the interesting places, especially in a town or city, that are often visited by tourists: *When you come to Cape Town I'll show you the **sights**.*
5 (*no plural*) a position where you can see somebody or something: *We watched until they were out of **sight*** (= we could not see them). ◇ *Eventually the town came into **sight*** (= we could see it).
at first sight when you see somebody or something for the first time: *He fell in love with her at first **sight**.*
catch sight of somebody or **something** to see somebody or something suddenly: *I caught **sight** of her in the crowd.*
lose sight of somebody or **something** to no longer be able to see somebody or something: *After an hour at sea we lost **sight** of land.*

sightseeing (say **site**-see-ing) *noun* (*no plural*)
the activity of visiting interesting buildings and places as a tourist: *to go **sightseeing*** ◇ *Did you have a chance to do any **sightseeing**?*
▶ **sightseer** (*noun*): *The town was full of **sightseers**.* ➲ SYNONYM **tourist**

sign[1] (say **sine**) *noun* (*plural* **signs**)
1 a mark, shape or movement that has a special meaning: *In mathematics, a cross is a plus **sign**.* ◇ *I put up my hand as a **sign** for him to stop.*
2 something that tells you that something exists, is happening or may happen in the future: *Dark clouds are a **sign** of rain.*
3 a thing with writing or a picture on it that tells you something: *a road **sign*** ◇ *The **sign** said 'No Smoking'.*

sign[2] (say **sine**) *verb* (**signing, signed**)
1 to write your name in your own way on something: ***Sign** here, please.* ◇ *I **signed** the application form.* ➲ The noun is **signature**
2 to communicate with somebody using special hand movements, called **sign language**

signal (say **sig**-nuhl) *noun* (*plural* **signals**)
a light, sound or movement that tells you something without words: *A red light is a **signal** for cars to stop.*
▶ **signal** (*verb*): *The policeman **signalled** to the children to cross the road.*

signature (say **sig**-ni-tshuh) *noun* (*plural* **signatures**)
your name as you usually write it, for example at the end of a letter ➲ The verb is **sign**[2] 1

significance (say sig-**nif**-i-kuhnss) *noun* (*no plural*)
the importance or meaning of something: *What is the **significance** of this discovery?*

significant (say sig-**nif**-i-kuhnt) *adjective*
important or with a special meaning: *The police say it is **significant** that there were no signs of a struggle.* ➲ OPPOSITE **insignificant**

signify (say **sig**-ni-fy) *verb* (**signifying, signified**) (*formal*)
1 to mean or be a sign of something: *This hot dry wind **signifies** that a storm is building up.*
2 to express or indicate something: *They **signified** their agreement by raising their hands.*

sign language *noun* (*no plural*)
a language that uses movements of the hands. It is used especially by people who cannot hear.

signpost (say **sine**-pohst) *noun* (*plural* **signposts**)
a sign beside a road that shows the way to a place and how far it is

silence (say **sy**-luhnss) *noun*
1 (*no plural*) a situation in which there is no sound: *I can only work in complete **silence**.*
2 (*plural* **silences**) a time when nobody speaks or makes a noise: *There was a long **silence** before she answered the question.* ◇ *We ate our dinner in **silence**.*

silent (say **sy**-luhnt) *adjective*
1 with no sound: *Everyone was asleep, and the house was **silent**.*
2 If you are **silent**, you are not speaking: *I asked him a question and he was **silent** for a moment before he answered.*
▶ **silently** (*adverb*)

silhouette (say sil-*uu*-**et**) *noun* (*plural* **silhouettes**)
the dark solid shape of a person or a thing seen against a light background

silica (say **sil**-i-kuh) *noun* (*no plural*)
a glass-like mineral found in sand, clay and many rocks

silicon (say **sil**-i-kuhn) *noun* (*no plural*) (symbol Si)
the second most common chemical element found on Earth. It is found in sand and many rocks and is used in electronic equipment: *a **silicon** chip*

silicone (say **sil**-i-kohn) *noun* (*no plural*)
an artificial compound that comes in forms such as rubber, oil and plastic: ***silicone** gel*

silk *noun* (*no plural*)
a type of thin smooth cloth that is made from the threads that a **silkworm** makes: *a **silk** shirt* ◇ *This scarf is made of **silk**.*

silkworm (say **silk**-wurm) *noun* (*plural* **silkworms**)
a small white **caterpillar** that produces threads that can be made into silk

silky (say **silk**-ee) *adjective* (**silkier**, **silkiest**)
soft, smooth and shiny, like **silk**: ***silky** hair*

sill (say **sil**) (*plural* **sills**) short for **windowsill**

silly (say **sil**-ee) *adjective* (**sillier**, **silliest**)
not sensible or clever: *Don't be so **silly**!* ◇ *It was **silly** of you to leave the door open.*

> **WORD BUILDING** See the Word Building note at **stupid**.

silo (say **sy**-loh) *noun* (*plural* **silos**)
1 a tall tower on a farm used to store grain
2 an underground pit in which a military rocket is kept ready to be fired

silt *noun* (*no plural*)
1 fine pieces of sand, soil or mud that collect at the sides or the bottom of areas of water, such as in rivers, lakes and oceans
2 a mineral substance with a grain size bigger than clay and smaller than sand
▶ **silt** (*verb*): *The dam **silted** up.*

silver[1] (say **sil**-vuh) *noun* (*no plural*)
1 (symbol Ag) a shiny grey metal that is valuable: *a **silver** necklace*
2 things that are made of silver, for example knives, forks and dishes: *The thieves stole some valuable **silver**.*

silver[2] (say **sil**-vuh) *adjective*
with the colour of silver: ***silver** paper*

similar (say **sim**-i-luh) *adjective*
the same in some ways but not completely the same: *Rats are **similar** to mice, but they are bigger.* ◇ *Rowena and her sister look very **similar**.*
▶ **similarly** (*adverb*)

similarity (say sim-uh-**la**-ri-tee) *noun* (*plural* **similarities**)
a way that people or things are the same: *There are a lot of **similarities** between the two countries.*
➲ OPPOSITE **difference**

simile (say **sim**-i-lee) *noun* (*plural* **similes**)
a phrase that compares one thing to another, using the words *like* or *as*; for example *a face like a mask* or *as white as the sand on Clifton beach*: *'My sister's like a tiger when she gets angry' is a **simile**.* ➲ See Study page 17
➲ See **metaphor**
❶ **ORIGIN**: 14th–15th century, from Latin *similis* meaning 'like, similar to'

> **WHICH WORD? Simile** or **metaphor**?
> Compare the example sentences used in the entries for **simile** and **metaphor**. Notice the difference:
> ■ '*My sister's like a tiger*' is a simile.
> ■ '*My sister's a tiger*' is a metaphor.

simmer (say **sim**-uh) *verb* (**simmering**, **simmered**)
to cook gently in water that is almost boiling: ***Simmer** the vegetables for ten minutes.*

simple (say **simp**-l) *adjective* (**simpler**, **simplest**)
1 easy to do or understand: *'How do you open this?' 'I'll show you – it's **simple**.'* ◇ *I like books written in **simple** English.* ➲ OPPOSITE **complicated**

A B C D E F G H I J K L M N O P Q R S T U V W X Y Z

A B C D E F G H I J K L M N O P Q R **S** T U V W X Y Z

2 without a lot of different parts or extra things: *a **simple** meal* ◇ *She wore a **simple** black dress.* ➲ SYNONYM **plain**[1] 2
3 (*informal*) not clever: *Think, and don't be so **simple**!*
4 (*grammar*) used to describe the tenses of a verb that are formed without using another verb such as be, do or have. The sentence 'She loves him' is in the present **simple** tense: *the **simple** present tense* ◇ *the past **simple** tense*
➲ See Study pages 6 and 7

USAGE Some people talk about the **present simple** tense while others say the **simple present**. Both are correct.

simplicity (say sim-**pliss**-uh-tee) *noun* (*no plural*)
the quality of being simple: *I like the **simplicity** of these paintings.*

simplify (say **sim**-pli-fy) *verb* (**simplifying, simplified**)
to make something easier to do or understand: *The story was **simplified** so that everyone could understand it.*

simply (say **sim**-plee) *adverb*
1 a word that you use when you want to show how easy or basic something is: ***Simply** add water and stir.* ➲ SYNONYM **just**[1] 6
2 in a simple way: *Please explain it more **simply**.*
3 really: *The weather was **simply** terrible – it rained every day!*

simulate (say **sim**-yuu-layt) *verb* (**simulating, simulated**)
to **imitate** certain conditions that exist in real life using computers or models, usually for study or training purposes: *The astronauts trained in a machine that **simulates** conditions in space.*

simultaneous (say sim-uhl-**tay**-ni-uhss) *adjective*
happening at exactly the same time: *There were three **simultaneous** bombings in three different cities.*
▸ **simultaneously** (*adverb*)

sin *noun* (*plural* **sins**)
something that your religion says you should not do, because it is very bad: *Stealing is a **sin**.*
▸ **sin** (*verb*): *He told the priest that he had **sinned**.*

since (say **sinss**) *adverb, preposition, conjunction*
1 from a time in the past until a later time in the past or until now: *He has been ill **since** Sunday.* ◇ *I haven't seen him **since** 2003.* ◇ *She has lived here **since** she was a child.* ◇ *I broke my leg last year and haven't been able to walk much **since**.*
2 because: ***Since** it's your birthday, I made you a cake.* ➲ SYNONYM **as** 5
3 at a time after another time in the past: *They got married five years ago and have **since** had three children.*

WHICH WORD? **For** or **since**?
- We use **for** to say how long something has continued, for example in **hours**, **days** or **years**: *She has been ill **for** three days.*
- We use **since** with points of time in the past, for example a **time** on the clock, a **date** or an **event**: *I have been waiting **since** six o'clock.*

sincere (say sin-**seer**) *adjective*
being honest and meaning what you say: *Were you being **sincere** when you said that you loved me?* ➲ OPPOSITE **insincere**
▸ **sincerity** (*noun*): *I doubted his **sincerity** when he said he wanted to marry her.*

sincerely (say sin-**seer**-lee) *adverb*
in a sincere way: *I am **sincerely** grateful to you.*
Yours sincerely words that you write at the end of a formal letter, before your name

sine (*rhymes with* **mine**) *noun* (*plural* **sines**) (*maths*) (abbr. sin)
the **ratio** of the length of the side opposite one of the angles in a right-angled triangle (a triangle with a 90° angle) to the length of the longest side: *The **sine** of a 30° angle is $\frac{1}{2}$.* ➲ See **cosine**, **tangent** 2, **hypotenuse**

sinew (say **sin**-yoo) *noun* (*plural* **sinews**)
a strong band in your body that joins a muscle to a bone ➲ SYNONYM **tendon**

sinful (say **sin**-fuhl) *adjective*
committing **sin**; immoral: *a **sinful** way of life*

sing *verb* (**singing, sang, has sung**)
to make music with your voice: *She **sang** a song.* ◇ *The birds were **singing**.*

singe (say **sinj**) *verb* (**singeing, singed**)
to burn the surface of a thing slightly, or to be burned in this way: *The heat of the flames **singed** the hairs off the back of my hand.*

singer (say **sing**-uh) *noun* (*plural* **singers**)
a person who sings, or whose job is singing, especially in public: *an opera **singer***

single[1] (say **sing**-guhl) *adjective*
1 only one: *He gave her a **single** red rose.*
2 a word that makes 'every' stronger: *You answered every **single** question correctly.*
3 not married: *Is she married or **single**?*
4 for one person: *I would like to book a **single** room, please.* ◇ *a **single** bed* ➲ See **double**[2] 1
5 for a journey to a place, but not back again:

*How much is a **single** ticket to Hillbrow, please?* ➲ See **return²** 3

single² (say **sing**-guhl) *noun* (*plural* **singles**)
1 a CD, tape or record that has only one song on each side, or the main song on this CD, tape or record: *Have you heard Joss Stone's new **single**?* ➲ See **album** 1
2 a ticket for a journey to a place, but not back again: *A **single** to town, please.* ➲ See **return²** 3

single-handed (say sing-guhl-**hand**-uhd) *adjective, adverb*
on your own with nobody helping you: *He planted the tree **single-handed**.*
▸ **single-handedly** (*adverb*)

single-minded (say sing-guhl-**mynd**-uhd) *adjective*
having one clear aim or goal which you are determined to achieve: *Her quest for success was **single-minded**.*

single parent *noun* (*plural* **single parents**)
a person who looks after his or her child or children alone, without help from the other parent

singular (say **sing**-gyuh-luh) *noun* (*no plural*) (*grammar*)
the form of a word that you use for one person or thing: *The **singular** of 'men' is 'man'.* ➲ See Study page 5 ➲ See **plural**
▸ **singular** (*adjective*): *'Table' is a **singular** noun.*

sinister (say **sin**-i-stuh) *adjective*
seeming evil or dangerous, or making you feel that something bad will happen: *There's something **sinister** about him. He scares me.*
🛈 **ORIGIN:** 14th–15th century, from Old French *sinistre* or Latin *sinister* meaning 'left, the left side'. People used to believe that the left side of the body was unlucky.

sink¹ (say **singk**) *verb* (**sinking, sank, has sunk**)
1 to go down under water: *If you throw a stone into water, it **sinks**.* ◇ *The fishing boat **sank** to the bottom of the sea.* ➲ See **float¹** 1
2 to make a ship go down under water: *The ship was **sunk** by a torpedo.*
3 to go down: *The sun **sank** slowly behind the hills.*

sink² (say **singk**) *noun* (*plural* **sinks**)
the place in a kitchen where you wash dishes

sinus (say **sy**-nuhss) *noun* (*plural* **sinuses**)
an air-filled hole, especially the spaces in the bones of your face that are connected to your nose: *a **sinus** infection* ◇ *I have a terrible cold and my **sinuses** are blocked.*

sip *verb* (**sipping, sipped**)
to drink something slowly, taking only a little each time: *She **sipped** her coffee.*
▸ **sip** (*noun*): *Can I have a **sip** of your lemonade?*

siphon (say **sy**-fuhn) *verb* (**siphoning, siphoned**)
1 to remove a liquid from a container, often into another container, through a tube: *They **siphoned** petrol out of the car's tank into a bottle.*
2 to take money from an organization illegally over a long time

sir (say **sur**) *noun* (*no plural*)
1 a polite way of speaking to a man, instead of using his name: *'Can I help you, **sir**?' asked the shop assistant.* ➲ See **madam** 1
2 Sir a word that you can use at the beginning of a business letter to a man: *Dear **Sir** …* ➲ See **madam** 2
3 Sir the title that is used before the name of a man who has received one of the highest British honours: ***Sir** Bob Geldof* ➲ See **lady** 2

siren (say **sy**-ruhn) *noun* (*plural* **sirens**)
a machine that makes a long loud sound to warn people about something. Police cars and fire engines have **sirens**.

sisal (say **sy**-suhl) *noun* (*no plural*)
strong thin threads from the leaves of a Central American plant that you use for making rope, floor-covering and other products

sissy (say **siss**-ee) *noun* (*plural* **sissies**)
a cowardly, weak person: *Don't be such a **sissy** – jump into the river with us!*

sister (say **siss**-tuh) *noun* (*plural* **sisters**)
1 a girl or woman who has the same parents as you: *I've got two **sisters** and one brother.* ◇ *Those two girls are **sisters**.*
2 Sister a nurse who has an important job in a hospital
3 Sister a female member of a religious group
🛈 **ORIGIN:** from Old English *suster*, related to Dutch *zuster*

sister-in-law (say **siss**-tuh-in-law) *noun* (*plural* **sisters-in-law**)
1 the sister of your wife or husband
2 the wife of your brother

Siswati (say si-**swaa**-ti) *noun* (*no plural*) (also **Swazi**)
the language of the Swazi people

sit *verb* (**sitting, sat**)
1 to rest your weight on your bottom, for example in a chair: *We **sat** in the garden all afternoon.* ◇ *Come and **sit** next to me.* ◇ *She was **sitting** on the sofa.*
2 (*formal*) to do an examination: *The students will **sit** their exams in June.*

sit down to move your body downwards so you are sitting: *She came into the room and* ***sat*** *down.*

site (*rhymes with* **kite**) *noun* (*plural* **sites**)
1 a place where a building is, was, or will be: *a building* ***site*** ◇ *This house was built on the* ***site*** *of an old theatre.*
2 a place where something happened: *the* ***site*** *of a famous battle*
3 short for **website**

sitting room *noun* (*plural* **sitting rooms**)
another word for **living room**

situated (say **sit**-yuu-ayt-d) *adjective*
in a place: *The hotel is* ***situated*** *on a hill.*

situation (say sit-yuu-**ay**-shuhn) *noun* (*plural* **situations**)
the things that are happening in a certain place or at a certain time: *We are in a difficult* ***situation*** *at the moment.*

six (say **sikss**) *number*
6

sixteen (say sikss-**teen**) *number*
16

sixteenth (say sikss-**teenth**) *adjective, adverb, noun*
1 16th
2 one of sixteen equal parts of something; $\frac{1}{16}$

sixth (say **siksth**) *adjective, adverb, noun*
1 6th
2 one of six equal parts of something; $\frac{1}{6}$

sixtieth (say **sikss**-ti-uth) *adjective, adverb*
60th

sixty (say **sikss**-tee) *number*
1 60
2 the sixties (*plural noun*) the numbers 60 to 69 or the years 1960 to 1969: *He grew up in the* ***sixties*** (= in the 1960s).
in your sixties between the ages of 60 and 69: *My mum's in her* ***sixties****.*

size (*rhymes with* **prize**) *noun*
1 (*no plural*) how big or small something is: *My bedroom is the same* ***size*** *as yours.* ◇ *This table is four times the* ***size*** (= as big as) *of that one.*
2 (*plural* **sizes**) an exact measurement in which something is made: *Have you got these shoes in a bigger* ***size****?*

sizzle (say **siz**-l) *verb* (**sizzling, sizzled**)
1 to make the sound of food frying in hot fat
2 (*informal*) to be very hot: *It was a* ***sizzling*** *hot day.*

sjambok (say **shum**-bawk) *noun* (*plural* **sjamboks**)
a long stiff whip: *The police chased the rioters* (= people causing trouble) *with* ***sjamboks****.*
ⓘ **ORIGIN**: 18th century, through South African Dutch and Malay *tjambok*, from Urdu *chabuk* meaning 'horsewhip'. Malay is the language of Malaysia. Urdu is a language spoken in Pakistan and India.

skate¹ (say **skayt**) *verb* (**skating, skated**)
1 (also **ice-skate**) to move on ice, wearing **skates**: *Can you* ***skate****?* ◇ *They* ***skated*** *across the frozen lake.*
2 short for **roller skate**

skate² (say **skayt**) *noun* (*plural* **skates**)
1 a boot with a long sharp piece of metal under it that you wear for moving on ice ➲ SYNONYM **ice-skate**
2 a boot with wheels on the bottom, that you wear for moving quickly on smooth ground ➲ SYNONYM **roller skate**

skateboard (say **skayt**-bawd) *noun* (*plural* **skateboards**)
a long piece of wood or plastic on wheels. You stand on it as it moves over the ground.
▸ **skateboarding** (*noun*): *He goes* ***skateboarding*** *every weekend.*

skeleton (say **skel**-i-tuhn) *noun* (*plural* **skeletons**)
the bones of a whole animal or person

human skeleton

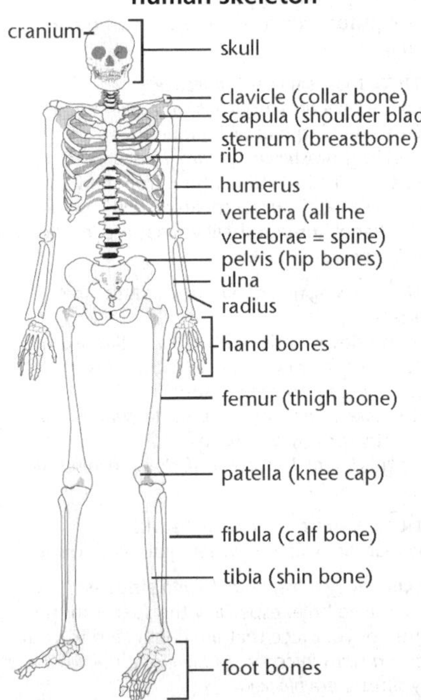

sketch (say **skech**) *noun* (*plural* **sketches**)
a picture that you draw quickly: *The artist is making **sketches** for his next painting.*
▶ **sketch** (*verb*): *She quickly **sketched** the view from the window.*

sketchy *adjective* (**sketchier**, **sketchiest**)
not having many or enough details: ***sketchy** notes*

skew (say **skyoo**) *adjective*
neither parallel nor at right angles to a line; **crooked**: *a **skew** angle* ◇ *His glasses were **skew** because a hinge had bent.*

skewer (say **skyoo**-uh) *noun* (*plural* **skewers**)
a long thin sharp piece of metal or wood that is pushed through pieces of meat and vegetables to hold them together while cooking
▶ **skewer** (*verb*): *pieces of chicken, pineapple, onion and red pepper **skewered** together*

ski (say **skee**) *noun* (*plural* **skis**)
one of a pair of long flat pieces of wood, metal or plastic that you fix to boots so that you can move over snow: *a pair of **skis***
▶ **ski** (*verb*): *Can you **ski**?* ◇ *We went **skiing** in Austria.* ▶ **skier** (*noun*): *Marie's a good **skier**.*

skid *verb* (**skidding**, **skidded**)
If a vehicle such as a car or a lorry **skids**, it moves suddenly and in a dangerous way to the side, for example because the road is wet: *The truck **skidded** on the icy road.*

skies (say **skize**) plural of **sky**

skilful (say **skil**-fuhl) *adjective*
very good at doing something: *a very **skilful** tennis player*
▶ **skilfully** (*adverb*)

skill (say **skil**) *noun*
1 (*no plural*) the ability to do something well: *Flying a plane takes great **skill**.*
2 (*plural* **skills**) a thing that you can do well: *What **skills** do you need for this job?*
🛈 **ORIGIN**: from Old English *scele* meaning 'knowledge', from Old Norse *skil* meaning 'the ability to judge well, knowledge'

skilled (say **skild**) *adjective*
good at something because you have learned about or done it for a long time: ***skilled** workers*

skim *verb* (**skimming**, **skimmed**)
1 to remove something from the surface of a liquid: *to **skim** the cream off milk*
2 to move quickly over or past a thing, almost touching it or touching it slightly: *The plane came in low, **skimming** the tops of the trees.*
3 to read a thing quickly to get the main idea, without paying attention to the details and without reading every word: *I only have time to **skim** through the newspaper before I leave for work in the morning.*

skimpy (say **skim**-pee) *adjective* (**skimpier**, **skimpiest**)
1 (of clothes) short and not covering much of your body
2 using or having less than is needed: ***skimpy** knowledge*

skin *noun* (*plural* **skins**)
1 the substance that covers the outside of a person or an animal's body: *She has dark **skin**.* ◇ *animal **skins***
2 the outside part of some fruits and vegetables: *the **skin** of an apple*
🛈 **ORIGIN**: from Old English *scinn* meaning 'skin', from Old Norse *skinn*

skinny (say **skin**-ee) *adjective* (**skinnier**, **skinniest**)
too thin: *He's so **skinny** – he doesn't eat enough.*
➲ See note at **thin**

skip *verb* (**skipping**, **skipped**)
1 to move along quickly with little jumps from one foot to the other: *The children were **skipping** along the road.*
2 to jump many times over a rope that is turning
3 to not do or have something that you should do or have: *I **skipped** my class today and went swimming instead.*
▶ **skip** (*noun*): *She gave a **skip** and a jump and was off down the street.*

skipper (say **skip**-uh) *noun* (*plural* **skippers**) (*informal*)
the captain of a boat or ship, or of a sports team: *The **skipper** of the cricket team hit an unbeaten hundred.*

skipping rope *noun* (*plural* **skipping ropes**)
a rope that you use for **skipping**

skirt[1] (say **skurt**) *noun* (*plural* **skirts**)
a piece of clothing for a woman or girl that hangs from the waist and covers part or all of the legs

skirt[2] (say **skurt**) *verb* (**skirting**, **skirted**)
to go around the edge of a thing
skirt around to avoid talking about a thing in a direct way: *Jason **skirted** around the issue of his school report.*

skit *noun* (*plural* **skits**)
a funny piece of writing or film, especially a **parody**: *The movie Johnny English is a **skit** on secret agent thrillers.*

skittish (say **skit**-ish) *adjective*
nervous and easily frightened; **volatile**: *The*

A B C D E F G H I J K L M N O P Q R S T U V W X Y Z

horses were ***skittish*** *at the start of the race.* ◇ *The banking crisis has made the markets very* ***skittish****.*

skittles (say **skit**-ls) *plural noun*
a game in which players try to knock down all nine of the bottle-shaped objects set up at the end of an alley by throwing or rolling a ball at them

skollie (say **skol**-ee) *noun* (*plural* **skollies**)
(*informal*) a criminal involved in small crime or a **hooligan**: *There were some* ***skollies*** *hanging around at the corner.*
🛈 **ORIGIN:** from Afrikaans, probably from Dutch *schoelje* meaning 'a dishonest person'

skull (say **skul**) *noun* (*plural* **skulls**)
the bones of the head of a person or an animal ➲ See illustration at **skeleton** ➲ See **cranium**

skunk (*rhymes with* **bunk**) *noun* (*plural* **skunks**)
a mammal, typically with black and white fur, that can make a bad smell

sky (say **sky**) *noun* (*plural* **skies**)
the space above the Earth where you can see the sun, moon and stars: *a beautiful blue* ***sky*** ◇ *There are no clouds in the* ***sky****.*
🛈 **ORIGIN:** 13th–15th century, from Old Norse *ský* meaning 'cloud'

skyline (say **sky**-line) *noun* (*plural* **skylines**)
the shape that is made by tall buildings against the sky: *the Johannesburg* ***skyline***

skyscraper (say **sky**-skrayp-uh) *noun* (*plural* **skyscrapers**)
a very tall building: *He works on the 49th floor of a* ***skyscraper****.*

slab *noun* (*plural* **slabs**)
a thick flat piece of something: *stone* ***slabs*** ◇ *a big* ***slab*** *of cheese*

slack (say **slak**) *adjective* (**slacker**, **slackest**)
1 loose: *Suddenly the rope went* ***slack****.*
➲ **OPPOSITE tight**
2 not busy: *Business has been very* ***slack****.*

slag *noun* (*no plural*)
the waste material that is left after metal has been removed from **ore**

slain (say **slayn**) form of **slay**

slam *verb* (**slamming**, **slammed**)
to close something or put something down with a loud noise: *She* ***slammed*** *the door angrily.* ◇ *He* ***slammed*** *the book on the table and went out.*

slander (say **slaan**-duh) *noun* (*no plural*)
the act of saying something about a person or organization that is not true and that would give people a bad opinion of them ➲ See **defame, libel**
▸ **slander** (*verb*): *The policeman felt he had been* ***slandered*** *by the accusations.*
▸ **slanderous** (*adjective*): ***slanderous*** *and untrue statements*

slang *noun* (*no plural*)
informal words that people use when they are talking. You do not use **slang** when you need to be polite, and you do not usually use it in writing: *In South African English, 'oke' is* ***slang*** *for 'man', and 'chick' is slang for 'girl'.*

slant (say **slaant**) *verb* (**slanting**, **slanted**)
Something that **slants** has one side higher than the other or does not stand up straight: *My handwriting* ***slants*** *to the left.*
▸ **slant** (*noun*): *Please straighten the mirror. It's hanging at a* ***slant****.*

slap *verb* (**slapping**, **slapped**)
to hit somebody with the flat inside part of your hand: *He* ***slapped*** *me on the face.*
▸ **slap** (*noun*): *She gave me a* ***slap*** *across the face.*

> **USAGE** It is not standard English to say 'She slapped him through the face.' Instead say: *She slapped him* ***across*** *the face.*

slapdash (say **slap**-dash) *adjective, adverb*
careless, or done too quickly and carelessly: ***slapdash*** *building methods*

slapstick (say **slap**-stik) *noun* (*no plural*)
a type of humour that is based on simple jokes in which actors fall over or hit each other and behave in a noisy and excited way: ***slapstick*** *comedy*

slash *verb* (**slashing**, **slashed**)
1 to make or try to make a long deep cut in something with a violent movement: *Vandals* ***slashed*** *the tyres of seven cars.*
2 to reduce something very much: *The company has* ***slashed*** *its workforce by 50%.*

slate (say **slayt**) *noun*
1 (*no plural*) a kind of smooth stone that can be broken into thin flat pieces
2 (*plural* **slates**) a thin flat piece of such stone used for covering roofs and floors

slaughter (say **slaw**-tuh) *verb* (**slaughtering**, **slaughtered**)
1 to kill an animal for food
2 to kill a lot of people in a cruel way
▸ **slaughter** (*noun*): *We must stop the* ***slaughter*** *of innocent women and children in the war.*

slave[1] (say **slayv**) *noun* (*plural* **slaves**)
a person who belongs to another person and must work for that person for no money

slave trade the buying and selling of people as **slaves**: *The Atlantic **slave** trade ended in the 1800s.*
▶ **slavery** (*noun*): *When did **slavery** end in the United States of America?*

slave² (say **slayv**) *verb* (**slaving**, **slaved**)
to work very hard: *I've been **slaving** away all day.*

slay *verb* (**slaying**, **slew**, **has slain**)
(*old-fashioned*) to kill in a violent way: *He **slew** the dragon with a lance.*

sledge (say **slej**) *noun* (*plural* **sledges**)
a small vehicle in which you travel over snow and which slides on flat pieces of metal or wood instead of moving on wheels
➲ See **sleigh**

sleek *adjective* (**sleeker**, **sleekest**)
1 smooth and shiny because it is healthy: *the **sleek** skin of a dolphin* ◇ *She has long **sleek** hair.*
2 having an elegant, smooth shape: *a **sleek** new car*

sleep¹ *verb* (**sleeping**, **slept**)
to rest with your eyes closed and your mind and body not active, as you do at night: *I **sleep** for eight hours every night.* ◇ *Did you **sleep** well?*

WORD BUILDING We use **go to sleep** or **fall asleep** to talk about starting to sleep. *She got into bed and **went to sleep**.* ◇ *He **fell asleep** in front of the fire.*

sleep² *noun* (*no plural*)
the natural condition of rest when your eyes are closed and your mind and body are not active or conscious: *I didn't get any **sleep** last night.*
go to sleep to start to sleep: *'Sh! Go to **sleep** now.'*

sleeper (say **sleep**-uh) *noun* (*plural* **sleepers**)
1 somebody who is asleep or somebody who sleeps in a particular way: *a light **sleeper*** (= somebody who wakes up easily)
2 one of the heavy pieces of wood or concrete that are put under a railway track to support the rails: *furniture made from old railway **sleepers***
3 one of the parts of a train that has beds for passengers, or a bed on a train: *The train is air-conditioned, with **sleepers** and a restaurant carriage.*

sleeping bag *noun* (*plural* **sleeping bags**)
a big warm bag that you sleep in when you go camping

sleepless (say **sleep**-luhss) *adjective*
without sleep: *I had a **sleepless** night.*

sleepy (say **sleep**-ee) *adjective* (**sleepier**, **sleepiest**)
1 tired and ready to sleep: *I felt **sleepy** after that big meal.*
2 quiet, with not many things happening: *a **sleepy** little village*

sleet *noun* (*no plural*)
snow and rain together

sleeve (say **sleev**) *noun* (*plural* **sleeves**)
the part of a coat, dress or shirt, for example, that covers your arm: *a shirt with short **sleeves***

sleigh (say **slay**) *noun* (*plural* **sleighs**)
a large vehicle in which you travel over snow and which slides on flat pieces of metal or wood instead of moving on wheels. A **sleigh** is usually pulled by animals.

slender (say **slen**-duh) *adjective* (**slenderer**, **slenderest**)
thin, in an attractive way: *She has long, **slender** legs.*

slept form of **sleep¹**

sleuth (say **slooth**) *noun* (*plural* **sleuths**)
(*old-fashioned*)
a person whose job is to find out who did a crime ➲ SYNONYM **detective**

slew (say **sloo**) form of **slay**

slice (say **slise**) *noun* (*plural* **slices**)
a thin piece that you cut off bread, meat or other food: *Would you like a **slice** of cake?* ◇ *She cut the bread into **slices**.*
▶ **slice** (*verb*): ***Slice** the onions.*

slick (say **slik**) *adjective* (**slicker**, **slickest**)
1 done skilfully and well, and without seeming to involve much effort: *a **slick** show*
2 clever at persuading people but perhaps not completely honest: *a **slick** salesman*

slide¹ *verb* (**sliding**, **slid**)
to move smoothly or to make something move smoothly across something: *The car **slid** on the muddy road.*

slide² *noun* (*plural* **slides**)
1 a long metal structure that children play on. They climb up steps, sit down, and then **slide¹** down the other side.
2 a small photograph that you show on a screen, using a special machine (called a **projector**): *a **slide** show*
3 (*maths*) the movement of a shape so that it still faces the same direction: *A **slide** is a transformation that moves a shape in a horizontal, vertical or diagonal direction.*
slide rule a long narrow instrument like a ruler that is used for calculating numbers

A B C D E F G H I J K L M N O P Q R S T U V W X Y Z

slight (say **slite**) *adjective* (**slighter**, **slightest**) small, or not important or serious: *I've got a **slight** problem.* ◇ *a **slight** headache*

slightly (say **slite**-lee) *adverb* a little: *I'm feeling **slightly** better today.*

slim[1] *adjective* (**slimmer**, **slimmest**) thin, but not too thin: *a tall **slim** man* ➲ See note at **thin**

slim[2] *verb* (**slimming**, **slimmed**) to become thinner: *I've been trying to **slim**.*

SPELLING **Lose weight** is the term that we usually use: *I've been trying to **lose weight**.*

slime *noun* (*no plural*) a thick liquid that looks or smells bad: *The pond was covered in green **slime**.*
▸ **slimy** (*adjective*): *The snail left a **slimy** trail.*

sling[1] *noun* (*plural* **slings**) a piece of cloth that you wear to hold up an arm that is hurt: *She's got her arm in a **sling**.*

sling[2] *verb* (**slinging**, **slung**) (*informal*) to throw something without care: *He got angry and **slung** the book at me.*

slink (say **slingk**) *verb* (**slinking**, **slunk**) to move somewhere slowly and quietly because you do not want anyone to see you, often when you feel guilty, embarrassed or afraid

slip[1] *verb* (**slipping**, **slipped**)
1 to move smoothly over something by accident and fall or almost fall: *He **slipped** in the mud and broke his leg.*
2 to go quickly and quietly so that nobody sees you: *She **slipped** out of the room.*
3 to put something in a place quickly and quietly: *He **slipped** the money into his pocket.*
slip up (*informal*) to make a mistake

slip[2] *noun* (*plural* **slips**)
1 a small piece of paper: *Write your address on this **slip** of paper.*
2 a small mistake: *It was just a **slip**.*
a slip of the tongue something that you say that you did not mean to say

slipper (say **slip**-uh) *noun* (*plural* **slippers**) a light soft shoe that you wear in the house: *a pair of **slippers***

slippery (say **slip**-uh-ree) *adjective* so smooth or wet that you cannot move on it or hold it easily: *a **slippery** floor* ◇ *The road was wet and **slippery**.*

slip-slop (say **slip**-slop) *noun* (*plural* **slip-slops**) (*S. African*) another word for **flip-flop**

slit[1] *noun* (*plural* **slits**) a long thin hole or opening: *Cut a **slit** in the cardboard.*

slit[2] (say **slit**) (**slitting**, **slit**) to make a long thin hole or cut: *He **slit** the melon with a knife.*

slither (say **sli*th***-uh) *verb* (**slithering**, **slithered**) to move by sliding from side to side along the ground like a snake: *I saw a snake **slithering** down a rock.*

sliver (say **sliv**-uh) *noun* (*plural* **slivers**) a small, thin piece of something that has been cut or broken off a larger piece, or a small narrow piece of something: ***slivers** of smoked salmon* ◇ *a **sliver** of light*

slob *noun* (*plural* **slobs**) (*informal*) a lazy, untidy person: *My brother's such a **slob** – he never tidies his room.*

slog *verb* (**slogging**, **slogged**) (*informal*)
1 to work hard and long at something difficult or boring: *I've been **slogging** away at this homework for hours.*
2 to walk or move slowly in a certain direction with a lot of effort: *We **slogged** back to our campsite.*
▸ **slog** (*noun*): *As a learner you cannot avoid the hard **slog**.*

slogan (say **sloh**-guhn) *noun* (*plural* **slogans**) a short sentence or group of words that is easy to remember. **Slogans** are used to make people believe something or buy something: *anti-government **slogans*** ◇ *an advertising **slogan***
🛈 ORIGIN: 16th century, from Scottish Gaelic *sluagh-ghairm* meaning 'a war-cry'. Later it referred to words used by a political party or another group. Scottish Gaelic is a language spoken in Scotland.

slope[1] (say **slohp**) *noun* (*plural* **slopes**)
1 a piece of ground that has one end higher than the other, like the side of a hill: *We walked down the mountain **slope**.* ➲ See illustration at **mountain**
2 (*maths*) a number that represents how steep a line or surface is: *We can calculate the **slope** of a line by dividing its vertical distance by its horizontal distance.* ➲ SYNONYM **gradient** 1

slope[2] (say **slohp**) *verb* (**sloping**, **sloped**) to have one end higher than the other: *The field **slopes** down to the river.* ◇ *a **sloping** roof*

sloppy (say **slop**-ee) *adjective* (**sloppier**, **sloppiest**)
1 showing a lack of care or effort: *a **sloppy** piece of work*
2 (used about clothes) loose, comfortable and without much shape: *a **sloppy** sweater*

slot *noun* (*plural* **slots**)
a long thin hole that you push something through: *Put your money in the* ***slot*** *and take your ticket.*

sloth (*rhymes with* **both**) *noun*
1 (*plural* **sloths**) a South and Central American mammal that lives in trees and moves very slowly
2 (*no plural*) (*formal*) the bad habit of not wanting to work or make an effort

slot machine *noun* (*plural* **slot machines**)
1 a **gambling** machine that you put coins into and that gives money back if particular pictures appear together on the screen
2 a machine that gives you things such as drinks or sweets when you put money in it

slouch (say **slowch**) *verb* (**slouching, slouched**)
to sit, stand or walk in a lazy way, with your head and shoulders hanging down: *Try not to* ***slouch*** *over your desk.*

slovenly (say **sluv**-uhn-lee) *adjective* (*old-fashioned*)
careless and untidy: ***slovenly*** *in appearance*

slow¹ (say **sloh**) *adjective* (**slower, slowest**)
1 not moving or doing something quickly: *a* ***slow*** *train* ◇ *She hasn't finished her work yet – she's very* ***slow***.
2 If a clock or watch is **slow**, it shows a time that is earlier than the real time: *My watch is five minutes* ***slow***. ➲ OPPOSITE **fast¹**
▸ **slowly** (*adverb*): *The old lady walked* ***slowly*** *up the hill.*

slow² (say **sloh**) *adverb* (**slower, slowest**)
in a slow way: ***slow***-*moving traffic* ◇ *Please drive* ***slower***.

slow³ (say **sloh**) *verb* (**slowing, slowed**)
slow down, slow somebody or **something down** to start to go more slowly, or to make somebody or something start to go more slowly: *The train* ***slowed*** *down as it came into the station.* ◇ *Don't talk to me when I'm working – it* ***slows*** *me down.*

slug *noun* (*plural* **slugs**)
a small soft animal that moves slowly and eats plants

sluggish (say **slug**-ish) *adjective*
moving or working more slowly, or less active than normal: ***sluggish*** *economic growth*

sluice (say **slooss**) *noun* (*plural* **sluices**) (also **sluice gate**)
a type of gate or other device that you can open or close to control the flow of water out of or into a canal, dam, lake, etc.: *The* ***sluices*** *on the dam were opened to release some of the water.*

slum *noun* (*plural* **slums**)
a poor part of a city where people live in old dirty buildings

slumber (say **slum**-buh) *verb* (**slumbering, slumbered**) (*old-fashioned*)
to be asleep
▸ **slumber** (*noun*): *blissful* ***slumber***

slump *verb* (**slumping, slumped**)
1 (used about prices, sales and the economy) to fall suddenly and by a large amount: *Shares* ***slumped*** *to their lowest ever level.*
2 to fall or sit down suddenly because you are ill, weak or tired: *Suddenly the old man* ***slumped*** *to the floor.*

slung form of **sling²**

slunk (say **slungk**) form of **slink**

slur (*rhymes with* **fur**) *verb* (**slurring, slurred**)
1 to pronounce words in a way that is not clear, for example because you are drunk
2 (of words) to be pronounced in a way that is not clear

slush *noun* (*no plural*)
1 snow or ice that has begun to melt
2 soft wet mud
3 a drink made of very small pieces of ice with the flavour of fruit added to it
4 (*informal*) something you say or write that shows feelings that are so strong and emotional that it seems silly
▸ **slushy** (*adjective*): *a* ***slushy*** *earth track* ◇ *The story has a* ***slushy*** *ending.*

sly (say *sly*) *adjective*
A person who is **sly** tricks people or does things secretly. ➲ SYNONYM **cunning**

smack (say **smak**) *verb* (**smacking, smacked**)
to hit somebody with the inside part of your hand: *They never* ***smack*** *their children.*
▸ **smack** (*noun*): *She gave her son a* ***smack***.

small (say **smawl**) *adjective* (**smaller, smallest**)
1 little or not big: *This dress is too* ***small*** *for me.* ◇ *My house is* ***smaller*** *than yours.*
2 young: *They have two* ***small*** *children.*

WORD BUILDING There are many words that you can use instead of **small**, but check their exact meanings first. Examples are: **diminutive, little, microscopic, mini, miniature, minor** 1, **minute, skimpy** and **tiny**.

smallpox (say **smawl**-pokss) *noun* (*no plural*)
a serious infectious disease that causes a high

A B C D E F G H I J K L M N O P Q R **S** T U V W X Y Z

A B C D E F G H I J K L M N O P Q R S T U V W X Y Z

temperature and leaves marks on your skin. In past times many people died from smallpox.

smart (say **smaat**) *adjective* (**smarter**, **smartest**)
1 clean and tidy or right for a special or an important time: *a **smart** new suit* ◇ *He looks very **smart** in his new jacket.*
2 clever: *She's not as **smart** as her sister.*
► **smartly** (*adverb*)

smash *verb* (**smashing**, **smashed**)
1 to break something into many pieces: *The boys **smashed** the window with their ball.*
2 to break into many pieces: *The plate fell on the floor and **smashed**.*
► **smash** (*noun*): *The glass hit the floor with a **smash**.*

smear (say **smeer**) *verb* (**smearing**, **smeared**)
to spread a soft substance on something, making it dirty: *The child had **smeared** chocolate all over his clothes.*
► **smear** (*noun*): *She had **smears** of paint on her dress.*

smell (say **smel**) *verb* (**smelling**, **smelt** or **smelled**, **has smelt** or **has smelled**)
1 to have a particular smell: *Dinner **smells** good!* ◇ *The perfume **smells** of roses.*
2 to notice something with your nose: *Can you **smell** smoke?*
3 to have a bad smell: *Your feet **smell**!*
► **smell** (*noun*): *There's a **smell** of gas here.*

smelly (say **smel**-ee) *adjective* (**smellier**, **smelliest**)
having a bad smell: ***smelly** socks*

smelt[1] *verb* (**smelting**, **smelted**)
to heat and melt rock containing metal (called **ore**) in order to get the metal out

smelt[2] form of **smell**

smile (say **smile**) *verb* (**smiling**, **smiled**)
to move your mouth to show that you are happy or that you think something is funny: *He **smiled** at me.*
► **smile** (*noun*): *She had a big **smile** on her face.*

smirk (say **smurk**) *verb* (**smirking**, **smirked**)
to smile in a silly or unpleasant way which shows that you are pleased with yourself or think you are clever
► **smirk** (*noun*): *His **smirk** was annoying.*

smith *noun* (*plural* **smiths**)
a person who makes or repairs things made of metal ➲ SYNONYM **blacksmith**

smock (say **smok**) *noun* (*plural* **smocks**)
1 a piece of clothing like a long shirt that you wear over other clothes so that they do not get dirty
2 a loose dress or top

smog *noun* (*no plural*)
dirty poisonous air that can cover a whole city. **Smog** is usually a mixture of smoke and fog.

smoke[1] (say **smohk**) *noun* (*no plural*)
the grey, white or black gas that you see in the air when something is burning: *cigarette **smoke*** ◇ *The room was full of **smoke**.*

smoke[2] (say **smohk**) *verb* (**smoking**, **smoked**)
1 to breathe in smoke through a cigarette, cigar or pipe and let it out again: *They were **smoking** cigars.*
2 to use cigarettes etc. as a habit: *Do you **smoke**?*
► **smoker** (*noun*): *She is a **non-smoker**.*
► **smoking** (*noun*): ***Smoking** is a bad habit.*

smoked (say **smohkt**) *adjective*
Smoked food is put over a wood fire to give it a special taste: ***smoked** salmon*

smoky (say **smohk**-ee) *adjective* (**smokier**, **smokiest**)
full of smoke: *a **smoky** room*

smooth (say **smoo*th***) *adjective* (**smoother**, **smoothest**)
1 having a completely flat surface: *Babies have such **smooth** skin.* ◇ *The surface should be completely **smooth**.* ➲ OPPOSITE **rough** 1
2 with no big pieces in it: *Beat the sauce until it is **smooth**.* ➲ OPPOSITE **lumpy**
3 A **smooth** movement or journey is even and comfortable: *The roads were good so we had a very **smooth** journey.* ➲ OPPOSITE **bumpy**
► **smooth** (*verb*): *She **smoothed** the wet clay with her fingers.* ► **smoothly** (*adverb*): *The plane landed **smoothly**.* ► **smoothness** (*noun*): *a feeling of **smoothness***

smother (say **smu*th***-uh) *verb* (**smothering**, **smothered**)
1 to kill somebody by covering their face so that they cannot breathe
2 to cover a thing with too much of something: *He **smothered** his cake with cream.*

smoulder (say **smohl**-duh) *verb* (**smouldering**, **smouldered**)
to burn slowly without a flame: *The ashes of the fire were still **smouldering** in the morning.*

SMS (say ess-em-**ess**) *noun* (*plural* **SMSes**)
a short message that you send in writing from one cellphone to another: *She sent me an **SMS**.*
ⓘ **SMS** is short for 'short message service'.
► **SMS** (*verb*): *I will **SMS** you after lunch.*

WORD BUILDING See the list of shortened words that many people use in SMSes on Study page 21. But be careful! Don't use these short cuts in schoolwork or in other formal writing.

smudge (say **smuj**) *verb* (**smudging, smudged**)
If something **smudges** or you **smudge** it, it becomes dirty or untidy because you have touched it: *Leave the painting to dry or you'll **smudge** it.* ◇ *Mum's lipstick has **smudged**.*
▸ **smudge** (*noun*): *There's a **smudge** on your cheek.*

smug *adjective* (**smugger, smuggest**)
too pleased with yourself, in a way that annoys other people: *He gave her a **smug** look.*

smuggle (say **smug**-l) *verb* (**smuggling, smuggled**)
to take things secretly into or out of a country when this is against the law: *They were trying to **smuggle** drugs into the country.*
▸ **smuggler** (*noun*): *drug **smugglers***

snack (say **snak**) *noun* (*plural* **snacks**)
a small quick meal: *We had a **snack** on the train.*

snag *noun* (*plural* **snags**)
a small problem: *It's a beautiful bike – the only **snag** is, it's very expensive.*

snail (say **snayl**) *noun* (*plural* **snails**)
a small soft animal with a hard shell on its back. **Snails** move very slowly.

snake (say **snayk**) *noun* (*plural* **snakes**)
a reptile with a long thin body and no legs: *Are these **snakes** poisonous?*

snap[1] *verb* (**snapping, snapped**)
1 to break something suddenly with a sharp noise, or to be broken in this way: *He **snapped** the pencil in two.* ◇ *Suddenly, the rope **snapped**.*
2 to say something in a quick angry way: *'Go away – I'm busy!' she **snapped**.*
3 to try to bite somebody or something: *The dog **snapped** at my leg.*

snap[2] *noun* (*plural* **snaps**)
1 a sudden sound of something breaking
2 (also **snapshot**) a photograph: *She showed us her holiday **snaps**.*

snapshot (say **snap**-shot) *noun* (*plural* **snapshots**) (also **snap**)
a photograph that is taken quickly and in an informal way

snare (say **snair**) *noun* (*plural* **snares**)
a device used to catch animals, consisting of a piece of wire or string tied in a circle that pulls tight as the animal tries to get free
▸ **snare** (*verb*): *The boys **snared** a rabbit.*

snarl (say **snaal**) *verb* (**snarling, snarled**)
When an animal **snarls**, it shows its teeth and makes a low angry sound: *The dogs **snarled** at the stranger.*

snatch (say **snach**) *verb* (**snatching, snatched**)
to take something with a quick rough movement: *A thief **snatched** her handbag and ran away.* ➲ SYNONYM **grab**

sneak (say **sneek**) *verb* (**sneaking, sneaked**)
to go somewhere very quietly so that nobody sees or hears you: *She **sneaked** out of the house without telling her parents.*

sneer (*rhymes with* **gear**) *verb* (**sneering, sneered**)
to speak or smile in an unkind way to show that you do not like somebody or something, or that you think they are not good enough: *I told her about my idea, but she just **sneered** at it.*
▸ **sneer** (*noun*): *His lips curled in a **sneer**.*

sneeze (say **sneez**) *verb* (**sneezing, sneezed**)
to have air come out of your nose and mouth with a sudden loud noise in a way that you cannot control, for example because you have a cold: *Pepper makes you **sneeze**.*
▸ **sneeze** (*noun*): *She gave a loud **sneeze**.*

sniff (say **snif**) *verb* (**sniffing, sniffed**)
1 to make a noise by suddenly taking in air through your nose. People sometimes **sniff** when they have a cold or when they are crying: *I wish you'd stop **sniffing**!*
2 to smell something: *The dog **sniffed** the meat.*
▸ **sniff** (*noun*): *I heard a loud **sniff**.*
ⓘ ORIGIN: 13th–15th century. The word came from imitating the sound.

snigger (say **snig**-uh) *verb* (**sniggering, sniggered**)
to laugh secretly and softly in an unkind way which shows that you do not respect somebody
▸ **snigger** (*noun*): ***sniggers** of derision*

snip *verb* (**snipping, snipped**)
to cut something with a short quick action using scissors
▸ **snip** (*noun*): *He cut the cord with one **snip** of the scissors.*

snob *noun* (*plural* **snobs**)
a person who likes people with a high social position and thinks they are better than other people: *He's such a **snob** – he's always talking about his rich family.*

snoek (say **snuuk**) *noun* (*plural* **snoek**)
a large fish that lives in the southern oceans of the world and that we eat as food
ⓘ ORIGIN: 18th century, through South African Dutch, from Dutch *snoek*

A B C D E F G H I J K L M N O P Q R S T U V W X Y Z

snooker (say **snook**-uh) *noun* (*no plural*)
a game in which two players try to hit coloured balls into pockets on the edge of a large table, using a long stick (called a **cue**)

snoop *verb* (**snooping, snooped**) (*informal*) to investigate or look around secretly in order to find out something ➲ SYNONYM **pry**
▸ **snoop** (*noun*): *She had a **snoop** around her brother's room.*

snooze (say **snooz**) *verb* (**snoozing, snoozed**) (*informal*) to sleep for a short time ➲ See **siesta**
▸ **snooze** (*noun*): *I had a **snooze** after lunch.*

snore (say **snaw**) *verb* (**snoring, snored**)
to make a noise in your nose and throat when you are asleep: *He was **snoring** loudly.*

snorkel (say **snawk**-l) *noun* (*plural* **snorkels**)
a short tube that a person who is swimming just below the surface of the water can use to breathe through
▸ **snorkelling** (*noun*): *to go **snorkelling***

snort (say **snawt**) *verb* (**snorting, snorted**)
to make a noise by blowing air through the nose: *The horse **snorted**.*

snout (say **snowt**) *noun* (*plural* **snouts**)
the long nose and area around the mouth of some types of animal: *a pig's **snout***

snow (say **snoh**) *noun* (*no plural*)
soft white pieces of frozen water that fall from the sky when it is very cold
▸ **snow** (*verb*): *It often **snows** in Lesotho in winter.* ◇ *It's **snowing**!*
🛈 ORIGIN: from Old English *snaw*, related to Dutch *sneeuw*

snowball (say **snoh**-bawl) *noun* (*plural* **snowballs**)
a ball of snow made by people to throw: *The kids were having a **snowball** fight* (= throwing snowballs at each other).

snowflake (say **snoh**-flayk) *noun* (*plural* **snowflakes**)
one piece of falling snow

snowman (say **snoh**-man) *noun* (*plural* **snowmen**)
the figure of a person, which people make out of snow

snowy (say **snoh**-ee) *adjective* (**snowier, snowiest**)
with a lot of snow: ***snowy** weather*

snub *verb* (**snubbing, snubbed**)
to treat somebody rudely, for example by ignoring them
▸ **snub** (*noun*): *He denied that his decision not to attend the meeting was a **snub**.*

snug *adjective* (**snugger, snuggest**)
1 warm and comfortable: *The children were **snug** in bed.* ➲ SYNONYM **cosy**
2 fitting somebody or something closely: *Make sure the dog's collar is not too **snug**.*
▸ **snugly** (*adverb*)

snuggle (say **snug**-l) *verb* (**snuggling, snuggled**)
to get into a warm, comfortable position, usually next to another person: *I **snuggled** down under the blanket to get warm.*

so¹ (say **soh**) *adverb*
1 a word that makes an adjective or adverb stronger, especially when this produces a particular result: *This bag is **so** heavy that I can't carry it.* ◇ *I'm **so** tired I can't keep my eyes open.* ◇ *Why are you **so** late?*
2 You use 'so' instead of saying words again: *'Is he coming?' 'I think **so*** (= I think that he is coming).' ◇ *'I got it wrong, didn't I?' 'I'm afraid **so*** (= you did get it wrong).'
3 also: *She is a teacher and **so** is her husband.* ◇ *'I like this music.' '**So** do I.'*
and so on and other things like that: *The shop sells pens, paper and **so** on.*
not so … as words that show how two people or things are different: *He's not **so** tall as his brother.*
or so words that you use to show that a number is not exactly right: *Forty or **so** people came to the party.*

WHICH WORD? **So** or **such**?
- In meaning 1 above, you use **so** before an adjective that is used without a noun: *It was **so** cold that we stayed at home.* ◇ *This book is **so** exciting.*
- You use **such** before a noun that has an adjective in front of it: *It was **such** a cold night that we stayed at home.* ◇ *This is **such** an exciting book.*

USAGE In meaning 3 above, in negative sentences, we use **neither** or **nor**: *Lydia can't swim and **neither** can I.* ◇ *If Solly doesn't go, **nor** will Ava.*

so² (say **soh**) *conjunction*
1 with the result that: *The shop is closed **so** I can't buy any bread.*
2 (also **so that**) in order that: *I'll give you a map **so** you can find my house.* ◇ *Speak louder **so** that everybody can hear you.*
so what? (*informal*) why is that important or interesting?: *'It's late.' '**So** what? There's no school tomorrow.'*

soak (say **sohk**) *verb* (**soaking, soaked**)
1 to make somebody or something very wet:

Soak the plants thoroughly once a week.
2 to be in a liquid or to let something stay in a liquid: *Leave the dishes to **soak** in hot water.*
soak something up to take in a liquid: ***Soak** the water **up** with a cloth.*

soaked (say **sohkt**) *adjective*
very wet: *You're **soaked**! Come in and get dry.*

soaking (say **soh**-king) *adjective*
very wet: *This towel is **soaking**.*

soap (say **sohp**) *noun* (*no plural*)
a substance that you use with water for washing and cleaning: *a bar of **soap***
▸ **soapy** (*adjective*): ***soapy** water*

soap opera *noun* (*plural* **soap operas**) (also *informal* **soap**)
a story about the lives of a group of people, which is on television or radio every day or several times each week: *Do you watch the **soaps**?*

soar (say **saw**) *verb* (**soaring**, **soared**)
1 to fly high in the sky: *The kite **soared** up into the sky.*
2 to go up very fast: *Prices are **soaring**.*

sob *verb* (**sobbing**, **sobbed**)
to cry loudly, making short sounds: *She **sobbed** and tears ran down her cheeks.*
▸ **sob** (*noun*): *I could hear her **sobs** through the wall.*

sober (say **soh**-buh) *adjective*
1 not drunk
2 serious or not funny: *He gave a **sober** speech about the dangers of drugs.*

so-called (say **soh**-kawld) *adjective*
a word that you use to show that you do not think another word is correct: *Her **so-called** friends did not help her* (= they are not really her friends).

soccer (say **sok**-uh) *noun* (*no plural*) another word for **football**
ORIGIN: 19th century, a shortening of *Assoc.* + *-er. Assoc.* is short for *Association Football*, a formal name for the game in Britain.

sociable (say **soh**-shuhb-l) *adjective*
friendly and enjoying being with other people

social (say **soh**-shuhl) *adjective*
1 connected with society and the way it is organized: *the **social** problems of big cities*
2 connected with being with other people: *She has a busy **social** life* (= she goes out with friends a lot). ◇ ***social** skills*
social science or **social sciences**
1 the study of people in society
2 a subject that you study at school in which you learn history and geography

socialism (say **soh**-shuh-liz-m) *noun* (*no plural*)
an economic and political system that is based on the belief that all people are equal and that money and property should be equally divided

socialize (say **soh**-shuh-lize) *verb* (**socializing**, **socialized**) (also **socialise**)
to meet and spend time with people in a friendly way: *I enjoy **socializing** with friends.*

social science *noun* (*plural* **social sciences**)
the study of people in society and in their environment: *History, human geography, archaeology and psychology are examples of **social sciences**.*

social security *noun* (*no plural*)
money that a government pays to somebody who is poor, for example because they have no job

social worker *noun* (*plural* **social workers**)
a person whose job is to help people who have problems, for example because they are poor or ill

society (say suh-**sy**-uh-tee) *noun*
1 (*no plural*) a large group of people who live in the same country or area and have the same ideas about how to live: *They carried out research into the roles of men and women in today's **society**.*
2 (*plural* **societies**) a group of people who are interested in the same thing: *a music **society***

sock (say **sok**) *noun* (*plural* **socks**)
a piece of clothing that you wear on your foot and lower leg, inside your shoe: *a pair of **socks***

socket (say **sok**-uht) *noun* (*plural* **sockets**)
a place in a wall where you can connect electrical equipment to a power supply
➲ SYNONYM **power point**

soda (say **soh**-duh) *noun* (*no plural*) (also **soda water**)
water with bubbles in it that is used for mixing with other drinks: *whisky and **soda***

sodden (say **sod**-n) *adjective*
extremely wet: *The game was played in rainy weather on a **sodden** field.*

sodium (say **soh**-di-uhm) *noun* (*no plural*) (symbol Na)
a soft silver white metal that is only found in compounds with other elements, such as salt: *Salt is a compound of the elements **sodium** and chlorine.*

sofa (say **soh**-fuh) *noun* (*plural* **sofas**)
a long soft seat for more than one person: *The two friends were sitting on the* ***sofa***. ➲ SYNONYM **couch**[1]
🛈 ORIGIN: 17th century, through French, based on Arabic *ṣuffa*

soft *adjective* (**softer**, **softest**)
1 that moves when you press it, or is not hard or firm: *Warm butter is* ***soft***. ◇ *a* ***soft*** *bed*
2 smooth and nice to touch: ***soft*** *skin* ◇ *My cat's fur is very* ***soft***.
3 not bright or strong: *the* ***soft*** *light of a candle*
4 quiet or gentle: ***soft*** *music* ◇ *He has a very* ***soft*** *voice.*
5 kind and gentle, or not strict: *She's too* ***soft*** *with her class and they don't do any work.*
▸ **softness** (*noun*): *I felt the* ***softness*** *of the baby's skin.*

soft drink *noun* (*plural* **soft drinks**) another word for **cooldrink**

soften (say **sof**-uhn) *verb* (**softening**, **softened**)
to become softer or to make something softer: *This cream* ***softens*** *the skin.*

PRONUNCIATION Don't pronounce the **t** in **soften**.

softly (say **soft**-lee) *adverb*
gently or quietly: *She spoke very* ***softly***.

software (say **soft**-wair) *noun* (*no plural*)
programs for a computer: *The teacher has just loaded some new* ***software*** *onto the computers.*

soggy (say **sog**-ee) *adjective* (**soggier**, **soggiest**)
very wet

soil[1] (say **soyl**) *noun* (*no plural*)
what plants and trees grow in ➲ SYNONYM **earth**[1] 2

soil[2] (say **soyl**) *verb* (**soiling**, **soiled**) (*formal*) to make something dirty: *The carpets have become* ***soiled*** *and need to be cleaned.*

solace (say **sol**-uhss) *noun* (*no plural*)
something that makes you feel happier when you are sad or disappointed: *Your letters were a source of great* ***solace*** *to me.*

solar (say **soh**-luh) *adjective*
1 connected with the sun: *a* ***solar*** *eclipse*
2 using the sun's energy: ***solar*** *energy* ◇ *a* ***solar*** *heating panel*

solar power (say soh-luh-**pow**-uh) *noun* (*no plural*)
the technology we use to get energy from the sun as a source of heat or electricity

solar power

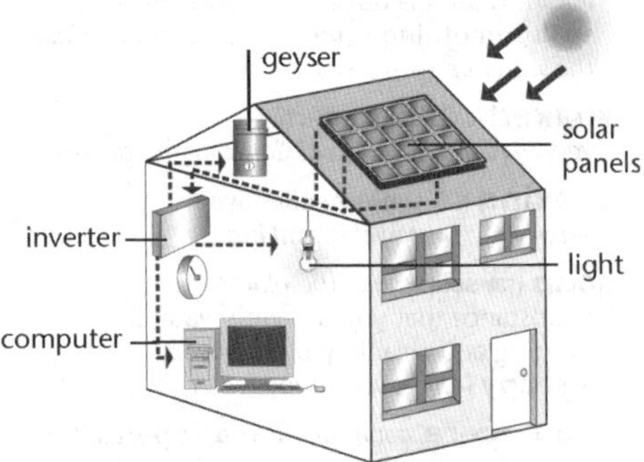

supplementary power provided by solar panels in a domestic house

solar system *noun* (*no plural*)
the sun and the planets that move around it

sold (*rhymes with* **gold**) form of **sell**

solder (say **sol**-duh) *verb* (**soldering**, **soldered**)
to join pieces of metal or wire together using a mixture of metals that is heated and melted: *We* ***soldered*** *two pipes together.*

soldier (say **sohl**-juh) *noun* (*plural* **soldiers**)
a person in an army
🛈 ORIGIN: 13th–15th century, through Old French *soldier*, from *soulde* meaning '(soldier's) pay', from Latin *solidus*, a gold coin used by the Romans

sole[1] (say **sohl**) *adjective*
only: *His* ***sole*** *interest is football.*

sole[2] (say **sohl**) *noun*
1 (*plural* **soles**) the bottom part of your foot or of a shoe: *These boots have leather* ***soles***. ➲ See illustration at **foot**
2 (*plural* **sole**) a flat sea fish that you can eat

solely (say **sohl**-lee) *adverb*
only, and not involving anybody or anything else: *I agreed to come* ***solely*** *because of Frank.*

solemn (say **sol**-uhm) *adjective*
serious: *slow,* ***solemn*** *music*
▸ **solemnly** (*adverb*): *'I've got some bad news for you,' he said* ***solemnly***.

solicit (say suh-**liss**-it) *verb* (**soliciting**, **solicited**) (*formal*)
1 to ask somebody for advice, help or money: *They tried to* ***solicit*** *support for the proposal.*
2 to go to somebody and offer sex in return for money: *The police arrested a prostitute who was caught* ***soliciting*** *a client in the street.*

solid[1] (say **sol**-id) *adjective*
1 hard, not like a liquid or a gas: *Water becomes* ***solid*** *when it freezes.*
2 with no empty space inside or made of the same material inside and outside: *a* ***solid*** *rubber ball* ◇ *This ring is* ***solid*** *gold.*

solid[2] (say **sol**-id) *noun* (*plural* **solids**)
1 not a liquid or gas: *Milk is a liquid and cheese is a* ***solid****.*
2 an object that has length, width and height, not a flat shape: *A cube is a* ***solid****.*

solidify (say suh-**lid**-i-fy) *verb* (**solidifying, solidified**)
to make or become hard or solid
▸ **solidification** (*noun*)

solitary (say **sol**-uh-tree) *adjective*
without others: *She went for a long* ***solitary*** *walk.* ➲ SYNONYM **lone** 1

solitude (say **sol**-i-tyood) *noun* (*no plural*)
the state of being alone or away from other people: *I enjoy the peace and* ***solitude*** *of the Kalahari.*

solo[1] (say **soh**-loh) *adjective, adverb*
on your own or without other people: *She flew* ***solo*** *across the Atlantic.*

solo[2] (say **soh**-loh) *noun* (*plural* **solos**)
a piece of music for one person to sing or play: *a guitar* ***solo***

solstice (say **sol**-stiss) *noun* (*plural* **solstices**)
either of the two times of the year when the sun reaches its highest or lowest point in the sky at midday, marked by the longest and shortest days: *the summer or winter* ***solstice***
➲ See **equinox**

soluble (say **sol**-yuhb-l) *adjective*
1 referring to a substance that can dissolve in another substance, especially in water: *water-****soluble*** *vitamins* ◇ *Enamel paint is* ***soluble*** *in turpentine. It is not* ***soluble*** *in water.*
➲ OPPOSITE **insoluble** 1
2 (of a problem or difficulty) able to be solved
➲ OPPOSITE **insoluble** 2
▸ **solubility** (*noun*): *Salt has a high* ***solubility*** *in water.*

solute (say **sol**-yoot) *noun* (*plural* **solutes**)
(*science*)
a substance, usually a solid, that can dissolve in another substance: *In a solution of salt and water, salt is the* ***solute****.*

solution (say suh-**loo**-shuhn) *noun* (*plural* **solutions**)
1 the answer to a question or problem: *I can't find a* ***solution*** *to this problem.*
2 a way of solving a problem or of dealing with a difficult situation
3 (*science*) a mixture in which a substance has dissolved in another substance: *We made a* ***solution*** *of sugar and water.*

WORD BUILDING There are several words we can use to talk about chemical **solutions** (as in meaning 3 above). Sugar is **soluble** in water. The sugar **dissolves** in water to make a **solution**. The water is called the **solvent** and the sugar is called the **solute**.

solve (say **solv**) *verb* (**solving, solved**)
to find the answer to a question or problem: *The police are still trying to* ***solve*** *the crime.* ◇ *I* ***solved*** *the maths problem quite easily.*

solvent[1] (say **sol**-vuhnt) *noun* (*plural* **solvents**)
(*science*)
a substance, usually a liquid, that dissolves another substance: *In a solution of salt and water, water is the* ***solvent****.*

solvent[2] (say **sol**-vuhnt) *adjective*
1 (*business*) If a person or business is **solvent**, they have enough money to pay their debts.
➲ OPPOSITE **insolvent**
2 able to dissolve other substances: *the* ***solvent*** *action of certain chemicals*

sombre (say **som**-buh) *adjective*
1 dark in colour or not bright: *elderly gentlemen dressed in* ***sombre*** *suits*
2 sad and serious: *a* ***sombre*** *mood*

some (say **sum**) *adjective, pronoun*
1 a number or an amount of something: *I bought* ***some*** *tomatoes and* ***some*** *butter.* ◇ *This cake is nice. Do you want* ***some****?*
2 part of a number or an amount of something: ***Some*** *of the children can swim, but the others can't.*
3 I do not know who or which: *There's* ***some*** *man at the door who wants to see you.*
some more a little more or a few more: *Have some more coffee.*
some time quite a long time: *We waited for some time but she did not come.*

somebody (say **sum**-buh-dee) *pronoun* (also **someone**)
a person, especially one that you do not know: *There's* ***somebody*** *at the door.* ◇ ***Someone*** *has broken the window.* ◇ *Ask* ***somebody*** *else* (= another person) *to help you.*

somehow (say **sum**-how) *adverb*
in some way that you do not know: *We must find her* ***somehow****.*

A B C D E F G H I J K L M N O P Q R S T U V W X Y Z

someone (say **sum**-wun) another word for **somebody**

somersault (say **sum**-uh-sawlt) *noun* (*plural* **somersaults**)
a movement when you turn your body with your feet going over your head: *The children were doing **somersaults** on the carpet.*

something (say **sum**-thing) *pronoun*
a thing, especially one you cannot name: *There's **something** under the table. What is it?* ◇ *I want to tell you **something**.* ◇ *Would you like **something** else* (= another thing) *to eat?*
something like the same as somebody or something in some ways, but not in every way: *A rat is **something** like a mouse, but bigger.*

sometime (say **sum**-time) *adverb*
at a time that you do not know exactly: *I'll phone **sometime** tomorrow.*

sometimes (say **sum**-time-z) *adverb*
not very often: *He **sometimes** writes to me.* ◇ ***Sometimes** I walk to school and **sometimes** I go by bus.*

somewhere (say **sum**-wair) *adverb*
at, in or to a place that you do not know exactly: *They live **somewhere** near Kimberley.* ◇ *'Did she go to Durban last year?' 'No, I think she went **somewhere** else* (= to another place).'

son (say **sun**) *noun* (*plural* **sons**)
a boy or man who is somebody's child: *They have a **son** and two daughters.*

sonar (say **soh**-nuh) *noun* (*no plural*)
equipment or a system for finding objects under water using sound waves ➲ See **radar**

song *noun*
1 (*plural* **songs**) a piece of music with words that you sing: *a pop **song***
2 (*no plural*) music that a person or a bird makes: *The story is told through **song** and dance.*

songololo (say sawng-guh-**law**-law) *noun* (*plural* **songololos**) (also **shongololo**) (*S. African*)
a small creature with a long thin body divided into many sections, each with two pairs of legs ➲ SYNONYM **millipede**
🛈 ORIGIN: from isiXhosa and isiZulu, from *s(h)onga* meaning 'roll up', which is what a songololo does if you touch it

sonic (say **son**-ik) *adjective*
relating to sound and sound waves: *a **sonic** boom*

son-in-law (say **sun**-in-law) *noun* (*plural* **sons-in-law**)
the husband of your daughter

sonnet (say **son**-it) *noun* (*plural* **sonnets**)
a poem that has fourteen lines and a fixed pattern of rhyme (= lines with the same sound at the end as other lines)

soon (*rhymes with* **moon**) *adverb* (**sooner**, **soonest**)
not long after now, or not long after a certain time: *Dad will be home **soon**.* ◇ *She arrived **soon** after two o'clock.* ◇ *Goodbye! See you **soon**!*
as soon as at the same time that: *Phone me as soon as you get home.*
sooner or later at some time in the future: *Don't worry – I'm sure he'll write to you **sooner** or later.*

soot (*rhymes with* **foot**) *noun* (*no plural*)
black powder that comes from smoke

soothe (say **soo*th***) *verb* (**soothing**, **soothed**)
to make somebody feel calmer and less unhappy: *The baby was crying, so I tried to **soothe** her by singing to her.*
► **soothing** (*adjective*): ***soothing** music*

sophisticated (say suh-**fiss**-ti-kay-tid) *adjective*
1 having a lot of experience of the world and social situations or knowing about things like fashion and culture: *She's a very **sophisticated** young woman.*
2 (used about machines, systems, etc.) clever and complicated: *highly **sophisticated** computer systems*

sopping (say **sop**-ing) *adjective*, *adverb*
full of water or completely wet: *It rained all night and our tents got **sopping** wet.*

soprano (say suh-**praa**-noh) *noun* (*music*)
1 (*no plural*) the highest type of singing voice
2 (*plural* **sopranos**) a woman, girl or boy with the highest type of singing voice

sorcerer (say **saw**-suh-ruh) *noun* (*plural* **sorcerers**)
a person who has magical or evil powers

sordid (say **saw**-did) *adjective*
1 unpleasant, or not honest or moral: *We discovered the truth about his **sordid** past.*
2 very dirty and unpleasant: ***sordid** living conditions*

sore (say **saw**) *adjective*
If a part of your body is **sore**, it gives you pain: *My feet were **sore** after the long walk.* ◇ *I've got a **sore** throat.*

sorghum (say **saw**-guhm) *noun* (*no plural*)
a grain you use to make flour, alcoholic drinks or as food for animals

sorrow (*rhymes with* **borrow**) *noun* (*no plural*)
sadness ➲ OPPOSITE **joy**

sorry (say **so**-ree) *adjective* (**sorrier**, **sorriest**)
1 feeling sad: *I'm **sorry** to hear you have been so unwell.*
2 a word that you use when you feel bad about something you have done: *I'm **sorry** I didn't phone you.* ◇ ***Sorry** I'm late!* ◇ *I'm **sorry** for losing your pen.*
3 a word that you use to say 'no' politely: *I'm **sorry** – I can't help you.*
4 a word that you use when you did not hear what somebody said and you want them to say it again: *'My name is Ashwin Davids.' '**Sorry**? Ashwin who?'*
feel sorry for somebody to feel sad because somebody has problems: *I felt **sorry** for her and gave her some money.*

sort[1] (say **sawt**) *noun* (*plural* **sorts**)
a group of things or people that are the same in some way: *What **sort** of music do you like best – pop or classical?* ◇ *We found all **sorts** of shells on the beach.* ➲ SYNONYMS **kind[1]**, **type[1] 1**
sort of (*informal*) words that you use when you are not sure about something: *It's **sort** of long and thin, a bit like a sausage.*

sort[2] (say **sawt**) *verb* (**sorting**, **sorted**)
to put things into groups: *The machine **sorts** the eggs into large ones and small ones.*
sort something out
1 (*informal*) to make something tidy: *I **sorted** out my clothes and put the old ones in a bag.*
2 to find an answer to a problem: *I haven't found a flat yet but I hope to **sort** something out soon.*

SOS (say ess-oh-**ess**) *noun* (*no plural*)
a call for help from a ship or a plane that is in danger: *We've received an **SOS** from a boat.*

sosatie (say suh-**saa**-tee) *noun* (*plural* **sosaties**) (*S. African*)
small pieces of meat, vegetables, etc. that are cooked on a thin stick (called a **skewer**)
➲ SYNONYM **kebab**
🛈 ORIGIN: 19th century, through Afrikaans and South African Dutch *sasaatje* from Javanese *sesate*. Javanese is the language of Java.

Sotho (say **soo**-too) *noun* (*no plural*) (also **Sotho-Tswana**)
a group of southern African languages that includes Sesotho, Setswana and Sesotho sa Leboa

sought (say **sawt**) form of **seek**

soul (say **sohl**) *noun*
1 (*plural* **souls**) the part of a person that some people believe does not die when the body dies: *Christians believe that your **soul** goes to heaven when you die.*
2 (*no plural*) (also **soul music**) a kind of music that was made popular by African American musicians: *a **soul** singer*
not a soul not one person: *I looked everywhere, but there wasn't a **soul** in the building.*

sound[1] (say **sownd**) *noun* (*plural* **sounds**)
something that you hear: *I heard the **sound** of a baby crying.* ◇ *Light travels faster than **sound**.*

sound[2] (say **sownd**) *verb* (**sounding**, **sounded**)
to seem a certain way when you hear it: *He **sounded** angry when I spoke to him on the phone.* ◇ *That **sounds** like a good idea.* ◇ *She told me about the book – it **sounds** interesting.*

sound[3] (say **sownd**) *adjective* (**sounder**, **soundest**)
1 right and good: *She gave me some **sound** advice.*
2 healthy or strong: ***sound** teeth*

sound[4] (say **sownd**) *adverb*
sound asleep sleeping very well: *The children are **sound** asleep.*
▸ **soundly** (*adverb*): *I slept very **soundly** last night.*

soundtrack (say **sownd**-trak) *noun* (*plural* **soundtracks**)
1 the recorded music and sound in a film or computer game
2 a recording of the music that has been used in a film and that is sold on CD

soup (say **soop**) *noun* (*no plural*)
liquid food that you make by cooking things like vegetables or meat in water: *tomato **soup***

sour (say **sow**-uh) *adjective*
1 with a sharp taste like a lemon: *If the lemonade is too **sour**, put some sugar in it.*
2 tasting bad because it is no longer fresh: *This cream has gone **sour**.*

source (say **sawss**) *noun* (*plural* **sources**)
a place, person or thing where something comes or starts from or where something is obtained: *What is their main **source** of income?* ◇ *The river's **source** is in the Drakensberg.* ◇ *Our information comes from many **sources**.*

south (say **sowth**) *noun* (*no plural*) (abbr. S)
the direction that is on your right when you watch the sun come up in the morning
▸ **south** (*adjective, adverb*): *the **south** coast* ◇ *Birds fly **south** in the winter.*

South African War *noun* (also **Anglo-Boer War**) (*history*)
one of the wars fought between Britain and the Boer republics in South Africa, especially the war of 1899–1902, but also that of 1880–1881

A B C D E F G H I J K L M N O P Q R S T U V W X Y Z

south-east (say sowth-**eest**) *noun* (*no plural*) (abbr. SE)
the direction between south and east, or a place in this direction: *The wind is coming from the **south-east**.*
▸ **south-east** (*adjective, adverb*): ***south-east** Botswana* (= the south-eastern part of Botswana)
▸ **south-eastern** (*adjective*): *the **south-eastern** areas of the country*

southern (say ***suth**-uhn*) *adjective*
connected with, in or from the south: *Bredasdorp is in the **southern** Cape.*

South Pole *noun* (*no plural*)
the point on the Earth's surface which is furthest south ➲ See illustration at **globe** ➲ See **North Pole**

south-west (say sowth-**west**) *noun* (*no plural*) (abbr. SW)
the direction between south and west, or a place in this direction: *The wind is coming from the **south-west**.*
▸ **south-west** (*adjective, adverb*): *Our house faces **south-west**.* ▸ **south-western** (*adjective*)

souvenir (say soo-vuh-**neer**) *noun* (*plural* **souvenirs**)
something that you keep to remember a place or a special event: *I brought back this hat as a **souvenir** of Lesotho.*

sovereign[1] (say **sov**-rin) *noun* (*plural* **sovereigns**)
a king or a queen ➲ SYNONYM **monarch**

sovereign[2] (say **sov**-rin) *adjective*
1 (used about a country) not controlled by any other country
2 having the highest possible authority
▸ **sovereignty** (*noun*)

sow[1] (*rhymes with* **go**) *verb* (**sowing**, **sowed**, **has sown** or **has sowed**)
to put seeds in the ground: *The farmer **sowed** his land with wheat.*

PRONUNCIATION Notice that the verb, **sow**, is pronounced differently from the noun.

sow[2] (*rhymes with* **cow**) *noun* (*plural* **sows**)
an adult female pig

soya bean (say **soy**-uh been) *noun* (*plural* **soya beans**)
a type of bean that you can cook and eat or use to make different foods such as flour, oil and a kind of milk

space (say **spayss**) *noun*
1 (*no plural*) a place that is big enough for somebody or something to go into or onto: *Is there **space** for me in your car?* ➲ SYNONYM **room** 2
2 (*plural* **spaces**) an empty place between things: *a parking **space*** ◇ *There is a **space** here for you to write your name.*
3 (*no plural*) (also **outer space**) the area outside the Earth's atmosphere where all the other planets and stars are: ***space** travel*

spacecraft (say **spayss**-kraaft) *noun* (*plural* **spacecraft**)
a vehicle that travels in space

spaceship (say **spayss**-ship) *noun* (*plural* **spaceships**)
a vehicle that travels in space, carrying people

space shuttle *noun* (*plural* **space shuttles**) (also **shuttle**)
a vehicle carrying people which can travel into space and land like a plane when it returns to Earth

spacious (say **spay**-shuss) *adjective*
with a lot of space inside: *a **spacious** kitchen*

spade (say **spayd**) *noun*
1 (*plural* **spades**) a tool that you use for digging
2 spades (*plural noun*) the playing cards that have the shape ♠ on them: *the queen of **spades***

spaghetti (say spuh-**get**-i) *noun* (*no plural*)
a kind of food made from flour and water that looks like long pieces of string: *Shall we have some **spaghetti**?*
ORIGIN: from Italian *spaghetti*, meaning 'small string'

spam *noun* (*no plural*) (*informal*) advertisements that companies send by email to people who have not asked for them

span[1] *noun* (*plural* **spans**)
1 the length of time that something continues: *The project has a time **span** of several months.*
2 the width of something from one side to the other: *The bird's wings have a **span** of almost a metre.*

span[2] *verb* (**spanning**, **spanned**)
1 to continue for a particular length of time: *His career **spanned** more than 50 years.*
2 to form a bridge over something: *The river is **spanned** by a beautiful iron bridge.*

Spanish (say **span**-ish) *noun* (*no plural*)
the language that is spoken in Spain and many Central and South American countries

spank *verb* (**spanking**, **spanked**)
to hit somebody on their bottom with the flat inside part of your hand as a punishment
▸ **spank** (*noun*) ▸ **spanking** (*noun*)

spanner (say **span**-uh) *noun* (*plural* **spanners**)
a tool that you use for turning **nuts** and **bolts** ➲ SYNONYM **wrench**[2] 3

spanspek (say spun-**spek**) *noun* (*plural* **spanspeks**) (*S. African*)
a type of **melon** that we eat
ⓘ ORIGIN: through Afrikaans from Dutch *Spaansche spek* meaning 'Spanish bacon', the name in the West Indies for a type of melon

spare[1] (say **spair**) *adjective*
1 If something is **spare**, you do not need it now, but you keep it because you may need to use it in future: *Have you got a **spare** tyre in your car?* ◇ *You can stay with us tonight. We've got a **spare** room.*
2 Spare time is time when you are not working: *What do you do in your **spare** time?*

spare[2] (say **spair**) *verb* (**sparing**, **spared**)
to be able to give something to somebody: *I can't **spare** the time to help you today.* ◇ *Can you **spare** any change?*

spare[3] (say **spair**) *noun* (*plural* **spares**)
something that you do not need now, but that you keep because you may need to use it in future: *I've got four new tyres on the car and a **spare** in the boot.*

spare part *noun* (*plural* **spare parts**)
a part for a machine, an engine, etc., that you can use to replace an old part which is damaged or broken

spark (say **spaak**) *noun* (*plural* **sparks**)
a very small piece of something that is burning

sparkle (say **spaak**-l) *verb* (**sparkling**, **sparkled**)
to shine with a lot of very small points of light: *The sea **sparkled** in the sunlight.* ◇ *Her eyes **sparkled** with excitement.*
▸ **sparkle** (*noun*): *the **sparkle** of diamonds*

sparkling (say **spaak**-ling) *adjective*
1 shining with a lot of very small points of light: ***sparkling** blue eyes*
2 Sparkling wine or water has a lot of small bubbles in it. ➲ SYNONYM **fizzy**

sparrow (*rhymes with* **barrow**) *noun* (*plural* **sparrows**)
a small brown bird

sparse (say **spaass**) *adjective* (**sparser**, **sparsest**)
small in quantity or amount, or not crowded: *The koppies are covered with **sparser** vegetation than the plains.*
▸ **sparsely** (*adverb*): *a **sparsely** populated area*

spartan (say **spaa**-tuhn) *adjective* (*formal*) very simple and not comfortable: ***spartan** accommodation facilities*
ⓘ ORIGIN: from *Sparta*, the name of an ancient city in Greece, whose powerful warriors had tough physical training, with no comforts

spasm (say **spaz**-m) *noun* (*plural* **spasms**)
a sudden movement of a muscle that you cannot control: *She had painful muscle **spasms** in her leg.*

spat form of **spit**[1]

spate (say **spayt**) *noun* (*no plural*)
a large number of similar things or events happening in a short period of time: *There has been a **spate** of burglaries in the area recently.*

spatial (say **spay**-shuhl) *adjective* (*formal*) relating to the position of something, or involving or happening in space: ***Spatial** orientation is important if you are a racing driver.*

spatter (say **spat**-uh) *verb* (**spattering**, **spattered**)
to throw small drops of liquid over a surface or cover a person or thing with small drops of something wet
▸ **spatter** (*noun*): *How do you remove paint **spatters** from clothes?*

spawn (*rhymes with* **lawn**) *verb* (**spawning**, **spawned**)
1 (used about fish and frogs) to produce eggs
2 to cause something to happen or exist, or to produce something in large quantities: *The Internet has **spawned** many new ways of communicating.*
▸ **spawn** (*noun*): *The pool was full of frog **spawn**.*

spay *verb* (**spaying**, **spayed**)
to perform an operation on a female animal so that she cannot have any babies: *The vet **spayed** my cat by removing her ovaries.*

spaza (say **spaa**-zuh) *noun* (*plural* **spazas**) (also **spaza shop**) (*S. African*)
a small shop or cafe, often based in a private home
ⓘ ORIGIN: from township slang *spaza* meaning 'camouflaged'

SPCA (say ess-pee-see-**ay**) *abbreviation*
Society for the Prevention of Cruelty to Animals

speak (say **speek**) *verb* (**speaking**, **spoke**, **spoken**)
1 to say things or to talk to somebody: *Please **speak** more slowly.* ◇ *Can I **speak** to Lindiwe Mali, please?* (= words that you say on the telephone) ◇ *The principal **spoke** for over an hour.* ➲ The noun is **speech**
2 to know and use a language: *I can **speak** Sesotho and English.*

A B C D E F G H I J K L M N O P Q R S T U V W X Y Z

speak up to talk louder: *Can you **speak** up? I can't hear you!*

speaker (say **speek**-uh) *noun* (*plural* **speakers**)
1 a person who is talking to a group of people
2 the part of something such as a radio or CD player where the sound comes out

spear (say **speer**) *noun* (*plural* **spears**)
a long stick with a sharp point at one end, used for hunting or fighting

special (say **spesh**-uhl) *adjective*
1 not usual or ordinary, or important for a reason: *It's my birthday today so we are having a **special** dinner.*
2 for a particular person or thing: *He goes to a **special** school for deaf children.*
▸ **speciality** (*noun*): *This food is the chef's **speciality*** (= a very good food that the chef is famous for).

specialist (say **spesh**-uh-list) *noun* (*plural* **specialists**)
a person who knows a lot about something: *She's a **specialist** in Chinese art.*

specialize (say **spesh**-uh-lize) *verb* (**specializing**, **specialized**) (also **specialise**)
specialize in something to study or know a lot about one special thing: *He **specialized** in criminal law.*

specially (say **spesh**-uh-lee) *adverb* (also **especially**)
1 for a particular person or thing: *I made this cake **specially** for you.*
2 more than usual or more than others: *The food was not **specially** good.* ➲ SYNONYM **particularly**

species (say **spee**-sheez) *noun* (*plural* **species**)
a group of animals or plants that are the same and can breed together: *a rare **species** of frog*

specific (say spuh-**sif**-ik) *adjective*
1 exact and clear: *She gave us **specific** instructions on how to get there.*
2 particular: *Is there anything **specific** that you want to talk about?*
▸ **specifically** (*adverb*): *I **specifically** asked you to buy butter, not margarine.*

specification (say **spess**-i-fik-ay-shuhn) *noun* (*plural* **specifications**)
detailed information about how something is or how it should be made

specify (say **spess**-i-fy) *verb* (**specifying**, **specified**)
to say something clearly or in detail: *He said he'd be arriving in the morning, but didn't **specify** the time.*

specimen (say **spess**-i-muhn) *noun* (*plural* **specimens**)
1 one example of a group of things: ***specimens** of different types of rock*
2 a small amount or part of something that shows what the rest is like: *The doctor took a **specimen** of blood for testing.* ➲ SYNONYM **sample[1]**

speck (say **spek**) *noun* (*plural* **specks**)
a very small bit of something: ***specks** of dust*

speckle (say **spek**-l) *noun* (*plural* **speckles**)
a small spot or mark: *The beetles are black with **speckles** of yellow.*
▸ **speckled** (*adjective*): *red **speckled** beans*

spectacle (say **spek**-tuh-kuhl) (*plural* **spectacles**)
a performance or an event that is exciting or impressive to look at: *The carnival was a magnificent **spectacle**.*

spectacles (say **spek**-tuh-kuhlz) *plural noun* (*formal*)
pieces of special glass that you wear over your eyes to help you see better: *a pair of **spectacles*** ➲ SYNONYM **glasses**

spectacular (say spek-**tak**-yuh-luh) *adjective*
wonderful to see: *There was a **spectacular** view from the top of the mountain.* ➲ SYNONYM **breathtaking**
▸ **spectacularly** (*adverb*): *This is a **spectacularly** beautiful area.*

spectator (say spek-**tay**-tuh) *noun* (*plural* **spectators**)
a person who is watching an event, especially a sports event: *There were 2 000 **spectators** at the football match.*

spectre (say **spek**-tuh) *noun* (*plural* **spectres**)
1 something unpleasant that people are afraid might happen in the future: *the **spectre** of unemployment*
2 (*old-fashioned*) a ghost

spectrum (say **spek**-truhm) *noun* (*plural* **spectra**)
1 the set of colours that make up light such as sunlight: *The colours of the **spectrum** are red, orange, yellow, green, blue, indigo and violet.*
2 a set of related qualities, ideas or activities: *the whole **spectrum** of human emotions*

speculate (say **spek**-yuu-layt) *verb* (**speculating**, **speculated**)
1 to make a guess about something without having all the necessary facts or information
2 (*business*) to buy things such as property or shares with the aim of making money but with the risk of losing it
▸ **speculation** (*noun*): *reports based on **speculation** and rumours* ▸ **speculator** (*noun*): *a **speculator** in the world's commodity markets*

▸ **speculative** (*adjective*): *a **speculative** theory* ◇ ***speculative** buying of company shares*

sped form of **speed²**

speech *noun*
1 (*plural* **speeches**) a talk that you give to a group of people: *The President made a **speech**.*
2 (*no plural*) the power to speak, or the way that you speak: *He has problems with his **speech**.*

speed¹ *noun* (*plural* **speeds**)
how fast something goes: *a **high-speed** train* (= that goes very fast) ◇ *The car was travelling at a **speed** of 80 kilometres an hour.*

speed² *verb* (**speeding**, **sped** or **speeded**)
1 to go or move very quickly: *She **sped** past me on her bike.*
2 to drive too fast: *The police stopped the driver who was **speeding**.*
speed up, **speed something up** to go faster or to make something go faster: *What can we do to **speed** up the process?*

speed limit *noun* (*plural* **speed limits**)
the fastest that you are allowed to travel on a road: *The **speed limit** on highways is 120 kilometres an hour.*

speedometer (say spee-**dom**-i-tuh) *noun* (*plural* **speedometers**)
an instrument in a vehicle that tells you how fast you are travelling

spell¹ (say **spel**) *verb* (**spelling**, **spelt** or **spelled**)
to use the correct letters in the correct order to make a word: *'How do you **spell** your name?' 'A-Z-I-Z.'* ◇ *You have **spelt** this word wrongly.*

spell² (say **spel**) *noun* (*plural* **spells**)
(in stories) magic words that make somebody change or that make them do what you want: *The witch cast a **spell** on the prince.*

spelling (say **spel**-ing) *noun*
1 (*plural* **spellings**) the correct way of writing a word: *Look in your dictionary to find the right **spelling**.*
2 (*no plural*) the ability to spell correctly: *You need to work on your **spelling**.*

spelt form of **spell¹**

spend *verb* (**spending**, **spent**)
1 to pay money for something: *Louise **spends** a lot of money on clothes.*
2 to pass time: *I **spent** the summer in the Eastern Cape.* ◇ *He **spent** a lot of time sleeping.*

sperm (say **spurm**) *noun*
1 (*plural* **sperm** or **sperms**) a cell that is produced in the sex organs of a male and that can join with a female egg to produce young
2 (*no plural*) the liquid that contains sperms
➲ SYNONYM **semen**

SPF (say ess-pee-**ef**) *noun* (*plural* **SPFs**)
the degree to which a sun cream protects your skin from the sun's rays: *The sunblock that I bought has an SPF of 30.* ❶ **SPF** is short for 'sun protection factor'.

sphere (say **sfeer**) *noun* (*plural* **spheres**)
any solid round object that is like a ball: *The Earth is a **sphere**.*
▸ **spherical** (*adjective*)

sphinx (say **sfinkss**) *noun* (*plural* **sphinxes**)
an ancient Egyptian stone statue with a human head and the body of a lion lying down

spice (say **spise**) *noun* (*plural* **spices**)
seeds or other parts of a plant, sometimes ground into a powder, that you can put in food to give it a stronger taste: *We use a lot of **spices**, such as chilli and pepper.*
▸ **spicy** (*adjective*): ***spicy** food*
❶ **ORIGIN**: 13th–15th century, from Old French *espice*, from Latin *species* meaning 'sort, kind'

spider (say **spide**-uh) *noun* (*plural* **spiders**)
a small animal that catches and eats insects, and has eight legs: ***Spiders** spin webs to catch insects.*

spied (say **spide**) form of **spy²**

spies (say **spize**)
1 plural of **spy¹**
2 form of **spy²**

spike *noun* (*plural* **spikes**)
a piece of metal or wood with a sharp point: *The fence has **spikes** along the top.*

spiky (say **spike**-ee) *adjective* (**spikier**, **spikiest**)
1 having sharp points: ***spiky** leaves*
2 **Spiky** hair sticks straight up in the air.

spill (say **spil**) *verb* (**spilling**, **spilt** or **spilled**)
If you **spill** a liquid, it flows out of something by accident: *I've **spilt** my coffee!*
▸ **spill** (*noun*): *There was a large oil **spill** from a tanker off the east coast last week.*

spin *verb* (**spinning**, **spun**)
1 to turn round quickly or to turn something round quickly: *She **spun** round as he entered the room.* ◇ ***Spin** the wheel.*
2 to make thread from wool or cotton: *She **spun** and dyed the wool herself.*
3 If a spider **spins** a **web**, it produces thread from its own body to make it.

spinach (say **spin**-ich) *noun* (*no plural*)
a vegetable with big green leaves

spinal (say **spine**-uhl) *adjective*
relating to the bones of your back: ***spinal** cord*

spindle (say **spind**-l) *noun* (*plural* **spindles**)
a stick that has a cut in the top through which thin pieces of wool or cotton are pulled and twisted together to make thread

spine *noun* (*plural* **spines**)
1 the row of small bones that are connected together down the middle of the back of a person or an animal ➲ SYNONYM **backbone**
➲ See illustration at **skeleton**
2 one of the sharp points like needles on some plants and animals: *Porcupines use their **spines** to protect themselves.*
3 the narrow part of the cover of a book that you can see when it is on a shelf

spineless (say **spine**-luhss) *adjective* (*informal*)
weak, easily frightened and not sure about what to do ➲ OPPOSITE **brave**

spiral (say **spy**-ruhl) *noun* (*plural* **spirals**)
a long shape that goes round and round as it goes up: *A spring is a **spiral**.*
▸ **spiral** (*adjective*): *a **spiral** staircase*

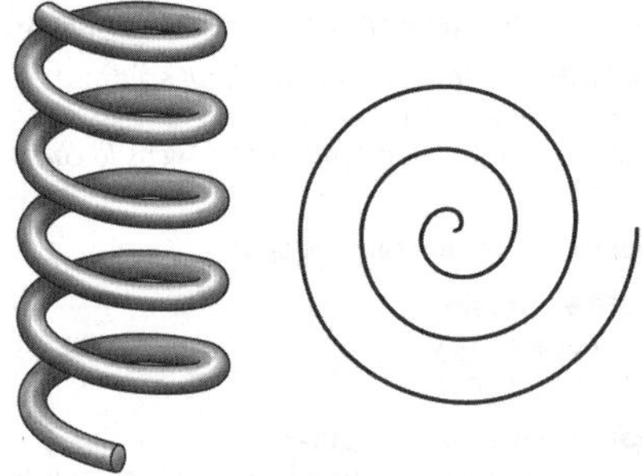

examples of spirals

spire (say **spy**-uh) *noun* (*plural* **spires**)
a tall pointed tower on top of a church
🛈 ORIGIN: from Old English *spir* meaning 'tall thin stem of a plant'

spirit (say **spi**-rit) *noun*
1 (*plural* **spirits**) the part of a person that is not the body. Some people think that your **spirit** does not die when your body dies.
2 spirits (*plural noun*) strong alcoholic drinks such as **whisky** 1
3 spirits (*plural noun*) the way that a person feels: *She's in high **spirits*** (= happy) *today.*

spirited (say **spi**-ri-tid) *adjective*
1 full of energy, enthusiasm and determination: *A **spirited** performance by the team earned them victory.*
2 having a particular mood or attitude: *nasty and mean-**spirited** remarks*

spiritual (say **spi**-rit-yuu-uhl) *adjective*
connected with deep feelings and beliefs rather than the physical body: *Our society often neglects people's **spiritual** needs.*

spit¹ *verb* (**spitting**, **spat**)
to send liquid or food out from your mouth: *He **spat** on the ground.* ◇ *The baby **spat** her food out.*

spit² *noun*
1 (*no plural*) the liquid in your mouth that helps you to swallow food ➲ SYNONYM **saliva**
2 (*plural* **spits**) a narrow pointed stick that holds meat over a fire: *We cooked lamb on a **spit** for the party.*
3 (*plural* **spits**) a narrow piece of land that stretches out into the sea: *a sand **spit***

spite *noun* (*no plural*)
when somebody deliberately says or does unkind things: *She broke my watch out of **spite**.*
in spite of something even though something is true, or not noticing or caring about something ➲ SYNONYM **despite**: *I slept well in **spite** of the noise.* ◇ *In **spite** of the bad weather, we went out.*

spiteful (say **spite**-fuhl) *adjective*
saying or doing unkind things in order to hurt or upset somebody ➲ SYNONYM **vindictive**

splash¹ *verb* (**splashing**, **splashed**)
to throw drops of liquid over somebody or something, or to make this happen: *The car **splashed** us as it drove past.* ◇ *The children were **splashing** around in the pool.*

splash² *noun* (*plural* **splashes**)
1 the sound that a person or thing makes when they fall into water: *Tom jumped into the river with a big **splash**.*
2 a small amount of liquid: *There were **splashes** of paint on the floor.*

splatter (say **splat**-uh) *verb* (**splattering**, **splattered**)
to fly about in large drops and hit somebody or something noisily, or to throw or drop water, paint, etc. on somebody or something in large drops: *Rain **splattered** on the roof.* ◇ *They **splattered** paint all over the walls.*

splendid (say **splen**-did) *adjective*
very beautiful or very good: *a **splendid** palace* ◇ *What a **splendid** idea!*

splendour (say **splen**-duh) *noun* (*no plural*)
the state or quality of being very impressive or beautiful, or something that is impressive and beautiful: *the **splendour** of the Maluti Mountains*

splinter (say **splin**-tuh) *noun* (*plural* **splinters**)
a small thin sharp piece of wood, metal or glass that has broken off a bigger piece: *I've got a **splinter** in my finger.*

split[1] *verb* (**splitting**, **split**)
1 to divide or separate, or to make this happen: *I **split** the wood with an axe.* ◇ *The teacher told us to **split** into groups.*
2 to tear or break apart, or to make this happen: *His jeans **split** when he sat down.*
split up to stop being together: *She has **split** up with her boyfriend.*

split[2] *noun* (*plural* **splits**)
a long cut or hole in something: *There's a big **split** in my jeans.*

splutter (say **splut**-uh) *verb* (**spluttering**, **spluttered**)
1 to speak quickly but not clearly because you are angry, embarrassed or confused: *She was **spluttering** with rage.*
2 to make a series of short sharp sounds: *The engine **spluttered** and stopped.*
▸ **splutter** (*noun*)

spoil (say **spoyl**) *verb* (**spoiling**, **spoilt** or **spoiled**)
1 to make something less good than before: *The mud **spoiled** my shoes.* ◇ *Did the bad weather **spoil** your holiday?*
2 to give a child too much so that they think they can always have what they want: *She **spoils** her grandchildren.*

spoilt (say **spoylt**) *adjective*
(used about a child) rude and badly behaved because people give them everything they ask for: *a **spoilt** child*

spoke[1] (say **spohk**) form of **speak**

spoke[2] (say **spohk**) *noun* (*plural* **spokes**)
one of the thin bars that join the middle part of a wheel to the outside part ➲ See illustration at **wheel**[1]

spoken (say **spohk**-n) form of **speak**

spokesperson (say **spohkss**-pur-suhn) *noun* (*plural* **spokespeople** or **spokepersons**) (also **spokesman**, **spokeswoman**)
a person who has been chosen to tell somebody what a group of people or an organization has decided

sponge (say **spunj**) *noun* (*plural* **sponges**)
1 a soft thing with a lot of small holes in it that you use for washing yourself or cleaning things
2 (also **sponge cake**) a soft light cake: *a chocolate **sponge***

spongy (say **spun**-jee) *adjective* (**spongier**, **spongiest**)
soft, like a **sponge** 1: *The ground was quite **spongy**.*

sponsor[1] (say **spon**-suh) *noun* (*plural* **sponsors**)
1 a person, company or organization that gives money so that an event will take place: *The race organizers are trying to attract **sponsors**.*
2 a person who agrees to pay money to a charity if somebody else completes a particular activity: *I need **sponsors** for a bike ride to Polokwane in aid of cancer research.*

sponsor[2] (say **spon**-suh) *verb* (**sponsoring**, **sponsored**)
1 to give money so that an event will take place: *The local football team was **sponsored** by a large company.* ◇ *The government **sponsored** peace talks with the rebels.*
2 to agree to pay money to a charity if somebody else completes a particular activity: *a **sponsored** walk to raise money for children in need*

spontaneous (say spon-**tay**-ni-uhss) *adjective*
done or happening suddenly and without being planned in advance: *a **spontaneous** burst of applause* ➲ SYNONYM **impromptu**
▸ **spontaneity** (*noun*): *the **spontaneity** of children's art*
▸ **spontaneously** (*adverb*): *Nyembezi smiled **spontaneously** when she thought of him.*

spook (say **spuuk**) *verb* (**spooking**, **spooked**)
(*informal*) to do something that makes a person or an animal feel surprised or frightened, or to become frightened: *The noise of the motorbike **spooked** the horse and it ran off.*
▸ **spooky** (*adjective*): *a **spooky** horror film*

spoon (*rhymes with* **moon**) *noun* (*plural* **spoons**)
an object with a round end that you use for eating, serving or mixing food: *a wooden **spoon*** ◇ *You need a knife, fork and **spoon**.*
ℹ ORIGIN: from Old English *spon* meaning 'chip of wood', probably because spoons used to be made of wood

spoonful (say **spoon**-fuul) *noun* (*plural* **spoonfuls**)
the amount that you can put in one spoon: *a **spoonful** of sugar*

spoor (say **spoo**-uh) *noun* (*no plural*)
a mark that an animal or person makes on the ground: *I saw lots of animal **spoor** around the camp.*
▸ **spoor** (*verb*): ***spooring** game in the bush*
ℹ ORIGIN: 19th century, from Dutch *spor*

sporadic (say spuh-**rad**-ik) *adjective*
not done or happening regularly: ***Sporadic** outbreaks of cholera occur in many parts of the world.* ➲ SYNONYM **occasional**
▸ **sporadically** (*adverb*): *I exercise **sporadically**.*

A B C D E F G H I J K L M N O P Q R **S** T U V W X Y Z

spore (say **spaw**) *noun* (*plural* **spores**)
one of the very small cells, like seeds, that are produced by some plants and other organisms: *Ferns, fungi and mosses reproduce by means of **spores**.*

sport (say **spawt**) *noun* (*plural* **sports**)
a physical game or activity that you do to keep your body strong or because you enjoy it: *She does a lot of **sport**.* ◇ *Football, swimming, karate, rugby, baseball and tennis are all **sports**.*

sportsperson (say **spawtss**-pur-suhn) *noun* (*plural* **sportspeople** or **sportspersons**) (also **sportsman**, **sportswoman**)
a person who plays sport

sporty (say **spaw**-tee) *adjective* (**sportier**, **sportiest**)
liking or good at sport

spot¹ *noun* (*plural* **spots**)
1 a small round mark: *a red dress with white **spots***
2 a small red mark on your skin: *A lot of teenagers get **spots** on their faces.*
3 a place: *This is a good **spot** for a picnic.*
4 a small dirty mark on something: *'I've got a **spot** on my new shirt!'*

spot² *verb* (**spotting**, **spotted**)
to see somebody or something suddenly: *She **spotted** her friend in the crowd.*

spotless (say **spot**-luhss) *adjective*
completely clean: *She keeps the house **spotless**.*

spotted (say **spot**-id) *adjective*
with small round marks on it: *a **spotted** shirt*

spotty (say **spot**-ee) *adjective* (**spottier**, **spottiest**)
with small red marks on your skin: *He's got a very **spotty** face.*

spouse (say **spowss** or **spowz**) *noun* (*plural* **spouses**) (*formal*) your husband or wife

spout¹ (say **spowt**) *noun* (*plural* **spouts**)
the narrow part of a container that you pour liquid through

spout² (say **spowt**) *verb* (**spouting**, **spouted**)
1 (used about a liquid) to flow very fast or with great force, or to make this happen: *He turned on the tap and water began to **spout** from the hose.*
2 (*informal*) to talk about something for a long time, in a way that is boring or annoying

sprain (say **sprayn**) *verb* (**spraining**, **sprained**)
to hurt part of your body by turning it suddenly: *She fell and **sprained** her ankle.*

sprang form of **spring²**

sprawl (*rhymes with* **crawl**) *verb* (**sprawling**, **sprawled**)
1 to sit, lie or fall with your arms and legs spread out in different directions
2 to cover or stretch over a large area
▸ **sprawl** (*noun*): *urban **sprawl*** ▸ **sprawling** (*adjective*): *a **sprawling** maze of narrow alleys*

spray¹ *noun* (*no plural*)
1 liquid in very small drops that flies through the air: ***spray** from the sea*
2 liquid in a container that comes out in very small drops when you press a button: *a can of **hairspray***

spray² *verb* (**spraying**, **sprayed**)
to make very small drops of liquid fall on something: *Somebody has **sprayed** paint on my car.*

spread (say **spred**) *verb* (**spreading**, **spread**)
1 to open something so that you can see all of it: *The bird **spread** its wings and flew away.* ◇ ***Spread** out the map on the table.*
2 to put a soft substance all over something: *I **spread** butter on the bread.*
3 to reach more people or places, or to make something do this: *Fire quickly **spread** to other parts of the building.* ◇ *Rats **spread** disease.*
▸ **spread** (*noun*): *Doctors are trying to stop the **spread** of the disease.*

spreadsheet (say **spred**-sheet) *noun* (*plural* **spreadsheets**) (*computing*)
a computer program for working with rows of numbers, used especially for doing accounts

sprightly (say **sprite**-lee) *adjective* (**sprightlier**, **sprightliest**)
active, strong and full of energy: *a **sprightly** 70-year-old granny*

spring¹ *noun*
1 (*no plural*) the part of the year (called a **season**) that comes after winter, when plants start to grow: *flowers that bloom in **spring***
2 (*plural* **springs**) a long thin piece of metal that is bent round and round. A **spring** will go back to the same size and shape after you push or pull it.
3 (*plural* **springs**) a place where water comes out of the ground: *a mountain **spring***

spring² *verb* (**springing**, **sprang**, **has sprung**)
to jump or move suddenly: *He **sprang** to his feet.* ◇ *Everyone **sprang** into action.*

springbok (say **spring**-bok) *noun* (*plural* **springbok** or **springboks**)
1 a medium-sized brown-and-white antelope that lives in southern Africa. The **springbok** is the national animal of South Africa. ➲ See

illustration at **antelope**
2 Springbok a member of South Africa's national rugby team
🛈 ORIGIN: 18th century, through South African Dutch, from Dutch *springen* meaning 'to jump' + *bok* meaning 'buck, antelope'

spring onion *noun* (*plural* **spring onions**)
a very small onion with long leaves, often eaten raw

sprinkle (say **sprink**-l) *verb* (**sprinkling, sprinkled**)
to shake small pieces of something or drops of a liquid on another thing: ***Sprinkle** some sugar on the fruit.*

sprint *verb* (**sprinting, sprinted**)
to run a short distance very fast

sprout[1] (say **sprowt**) *verb* (**sprouting, sprouted**)
to start to grow: *New leaves are **sprouting** on the trees.*

sprout[2] (say **sprowt**) *noun* (*plural* **sprouts**)
1 a plant that is just beginning to grow from a seed: *Bean **sprouts** are often eaten in salads without being cooked.*
2 short for **Brussels sprout**

spruit (say **sprayt**) *noun* (*plural* **spruits**)
a very small river that is often only filled after rain
🛈 ORIGIN: 19th century, through Afrikaans from Dutch *spruit* meaning 'offshoot'

sprung form of **spring[2]**

spun form of **spin**

spur *noun* (*plural* **spurs**)
1 a small piece of metal attached to the heel of a rider's boot that is pushed into a horse's side to make it go faster
2 (*geography*) a mountain or hill that sticks out from the main mountain or line of mountains
3 something that encourages you to take action or make a greater effort: *Our trip to Madagascar is a good **spur** to learn some French.*
on the spur of the moment suddenly or without planning: *We all say things on the **spur** of the moment that we regret later.*

spurt *verb* (**spurting, spurted**)
1 (used about a liquid) to flow out suddenly and strongly, or to make a liquid do this: *Blood **spurted** from the wound.* ➲ SYNONYM **squirt**
2 to increase your speed or effort suddenly: *The taxi **spurted** past us.*
▸ **spurt** (*noun*): ***spurts** of water* ◇ *a growth **spurt***

spy[1] (*rhymes with* **fly**) *noun* (*plural* **spies**)
a person who tries to learn secrets about another country, person or company

spy[2] (*rhymes with* **fly**) *verb* (**spying, spied**)
to watch a country, person or company and try to learn their secrets: *He **spied** for his government for more than ten years.*
spy on somebody or something to watch somebody or something secretly: *Have you been **spying** on me?*

squabble (say **skwob**-l) *verb* (**squabbling, squabbled**)
to argue about something that is not important: *The children were **squabbling** over the last piece of cake.*
▸ **squabble** (*noun*): *a silly **squabble***

squad (say **skwod**) *noun* (*plural* **squads**)
a small group of people who work together: *South Africa's cricket **squad*** ◇ *a **squad** of police officers*

squalid (say **skwol**-id) *adjective*
very dirty, untidy and unpleasant: *a **squalid** refugee camp*

squander (say **skwon**-duh) *verb* (**squandering, squandered**)
to waste time, money, etc.: *We must not **squander** the chance to reach a peaceful solution.*

square[1] (say **skwair**) *adjective*
1 with four straight sides that are the same length: *a **square** table*
2 (abbr. sq) used for talking about the area of something: *If a room is 5 metres long and 4 metres wide, its area is 20 **square** metres.*
3 (used about something that is **square** in shape) having sides of a particular length: *The picture is 20 centimetres **square*** (= each side is 20 centimetres long).

square[2] (say **skwair**) *noun* (*plural* **squares**)
1 a flat closed shape with four straight sides of equal length and four right angles
2 an open space in a town with buildings around it: *Let's meet in the **square**.*
3 (*maths*) the number that you get when you multiply another number by itself: *Four is the **square** of two* (= 2 x 2 = 4).

squared (say **skwaird**) *adjective*
1 (*maths*) (used about a number) multiplied by itself: *Four **squared** is sixteen (= 4 x 4 = 16).*
2 made square or marked with squares

squash[1] (say **skwosh**) *noun*
1 (*no plural*) a game where two players hit a small ball against the wall in a special room: *the **squash** courts*
2 (*no plural*) a drink made from fruit juice and sugar. You add water before you drink it: *a glass of orange **squash***
3 (*plural* **squashes**) a type of vegetable that grows on the ground with a hard skin and

A B C D E F G H I J K L M N O P Q R S T U V W X Y Z

yellow or orange flesh inside: *Pumpkin is a type of* ***squash****.*

squash[2] (say **skwosh**) *verb* (**squashing, squashed**)
1 to press something hard and make it flat: *She sat on my hat and* ***squashed*** *it.*
2 to push a lot of people or things into a small space: *We* ***squashed*** *five people into the back of the car.*

squat (say **skwot**) *verb* (**squatting, squatted**)
1 to sit with your feet on the ground, your legs bent and your bottom just above the ground: *I* ***squatted*** *down to light the fire.*
2 to live on land that is not yours, or in an empty building, without permission

squatter (say **skwot**-uh) *noun* (*plural* **squatters**)
a person who is living on land that is not theirs, or in an empty building, without permission

squawk (say **skwawk**) *verb* (**squawking, squawked**)
1 to make a loud harsh noise: *young chicks* ***squawking*** *for food*
2 (*informal*) to complain loudly
▸ **squawk** (*noun*): *the* ***squawk*** *of a hen*

squeak (say **skweek**) *verb* (**squeaking, squeaked**)
to make a short high sound as a mouse does: *The door was* ***squeaking****, so I put some oil on its hinges.*
▸ **squeak** (*noun*): *the* ***squeak*** *of a mouse*
▸ **squeaky** (*adjective*): *He's got a* ***squeaky*** *voice.*
🛈 **ORIGIN:** 14th–15th century. The word came from imitating the sound.

squeal (say **skweel**) *verb* (**squealing, squealed**)
to make a loud high sound: *The children* ***squealed*** *with excitement.*
▸ **squeal** (*noun*): ***squeals*** *of delight*

squeeze (say **skweez**) *verb* (**squeezing, squeezed**)
1 to press something hard: ***Squeeze*** *the lemons and add the juice to the mixture.* ◇ *She* ***squeezed*** *his hand.*
2 to go into a small space or to push too much into a small space: *Fifty people* ***squeezed*** *into the small room.*
▸ **squeeze** (*noun*): *She gave my arm a* ***squeeze****.*

squid (say **skwid**) *noun* (*plural* **squid** or **squids**)
a sea animal that we eat, with a soft body and ten long parts (called **tentacles**)

> **WORD BUILDING** When we eat **squid**, we call it **calamari**.

squiggle (say **skwig**-l) *noun* (*plural* **squiggles**)
(*informal*) a short line that turns in many directions

squint (say **skwint**) *verb* (**squinting, squinted**)
1 to look at something with your eyes almost closed: *to* ***squint*** *in bright sunlight*
2 to have a physical problem in which one eye looks to the side as the other looks forward
▸ **squint** (*noun*)

squirm (say **skwurm**) *verb* (**squirming, squirmed**)
to turn your body from side to side, especially because you are nervous, uncomfortable or embarrassed
▸ **squirm** (*noun*)

squirrel (say **skwi**-ruhl) *noun* (*plural* **squirrels**)
a small grey or brown animal with a big thick tail. **Squirrels** live in trees and eat nuts.

squirt (say **skwurt**) *verb* (**squirting, squirted**)
(used about a liquid) to suddenly come out and go onto something or towards something, or to make this happen: *I bit into the orange and juice* ***squirted*** *out.* ◇ *He* ***squirted*** *me with water.*

St *abbreviation*
1 saint: *St Anthony*
2 street: *Tambo St*

stab *verb* (**stabbing, stabbed**)
to push a knife or another sharp thing into somebody or something: *He was* ***stabbed*** *in the back.*
🛈 **ORIGIN:** 14th–15th century. The origin of this word is not known.

stability (say stuh-**bil**-uh-tee) *noun* (*no plural*)
the state or condition of being steady and unlikely to change, fall or move: *peace and* ***stability*** ◇ *The ladder is slightly wider at the bottom for greater* ***stability****.* ➲ The adjective is **stable**[1] ➲ **OPPOSITE instability**

stabilize (say **stay**-buh-lize) *verb* (**stabilizing, stabilized**) (also **stabilise**)
to become or to make something steady and unlikely to change, fall or break: *Food prices have* ***stabilized*** *in recent months.*
▸ **stabilization** (*noun*) (also **stabilisation**): *the* ***stabilization*** *of sand dunes*

stable[1] (say **stayb**-l) *adjective*
not likely to move, fall or change: *Don't stand on that chair – it's not very* ***stable****.* ➲ **OPPOSITE unstable**

stable[2] (say **stayb**-l) *noun* (*plural* **stables**)
a building where you keep horses

stack[1] (say **stak**) *noun* (*plural* **stacks**)
a lot of things on top of one another: *a* ***stack*** *of books* ➲ **SYNONYM pile**[2]

stack[2] (say **stak**) *verb* (**stacking, stacked**)
to put things on top of one another: *I* ***stacked*** *the chairs after the concert.*

stadium (say **stay**-di-uhm) *noun* (*plural* **stadiums** or **stadia**)
a place with seats around it where you can watch sport: *a football* ***stadium***
ORIGIN: 14th–15th century, through Latin from Greek *stadion*. In Greek, *stadion* was a measure of length (about 185 metres, which was the length of a stadium). When the word came into English, it still had the meaning of a measure of length and it got its present meaning only in the 19th century.

staff (say **staaf**) *plural noun*
the people who work in an organization: *The hotel* ***staff*** *were very friendly.*

stage (say **stayj**) *noun* (*plural* **stages**)
1 a certain time in a longer set of things that happen: *The first* ***stage*** *of the race is through the town.* ◇ *At this* ***stage*** *I don't know what I'll do when I leave school.*
2 the part of a theatre where the actors, dancers or singers perform: *The* ***stage*** *was brightly lit.* ◇ *At the end of the play all the actors came on* ***stage****.*

stagger (say **stag**-uh) *verb* (**staggering, staggered**)
to walk as if you are going to fall: *He* ***staggered*** *across the room with the heavy box.* ➲ SYNONYM **totter**

stagnant (say **stag**-nuhnt) *adjective*
1 (used about water or air) not flowing or moving and therefore having an unpleasant smell: *pools of water that lie* ***stagnant***
2 not active, developing or making progress: *a* ***stagnant*** *economy*

stain (say **stayn**) *verb* (**staining, stained**)
to leave a dirty mark that is difficult to remove on something: *The blood* ***stained*** *my shirt red.*
▸ **stain** (*noun*): *She had blood* ***stains*** *on her shirt.*

stainless (say **stayn**-luhss) *adjective*
not damaged or dirty: *a* ***stainless*** *reputation*
stainless steel a type of metal that does not rust

stair *noun*
1 stairs (*plural noun*) steps that lead up and down inside a building: *I ran up the* ***stairs*** *to the bedroom.* ➲ See **downstairs, upstairs**
2 (*plural* **stairs**) one of the steps in a set of stairs: *How many* ***stairs*** *are there up to the top floor?*

staircase (say **stair**-kayss) *noun* (*plural* **staircases**) (also **stairway**)
a big set of stairs

stake (say **stayk**) *noun*
1 (*plural* **stakes**) a wooden or metal pole with a sharp point at one end that you push into the ground to mark or support something
2 (*plural* **stakes**) a share or interest in something, especially a part of a company that you own, that makes you want to know if it succeeds or fails
3 stakes (*plural noun*) the things that you might win or lose in a game or in a particular situation: *We play cards for money, but never for very high* ***stakes****.*
at stake in danger or at risk of being lost: *He thought very carefully about the decision because he knew his future was at* ***stake****.*

stakeholder (say **stayk**-hohl-duh) *noun* (*plural* **stakeholders**)
a person who is very involved in something such as a business or movement and who is interested in whether it succeeds or fails

stalactite (say **stal**-uhk-tite) *noun* (*plural* **stalactites**)
a thin piece of rock hanging down from the roof of a **cave**[1] ➲ See **stalagmite**

stalagmite (say **stal**-uhg-mite) *noun* (*plural* **stalagmites**)
a thin piece of rock pointing upwards from the floor of a **cave**[1] ➲ See **stalactite**

stalactites and stalagmites

stale (say **stayl**) *adjective* (**staler, stalest**)
not fresh: ***stale*** *bread* ◇ ***stale*** *air*

stalk[1] (say **stawk**) *noun* (*plural* **stalks**)
one of the long thin parts of a plant that the flowers, leaves or fruit grow on ➲ See illustration at **plant**[1]

stalk[2] (say **stawk**) *verb* (**stalking, stalked**)
1 to move slowly and quietly towards an

A B C D E F G H I J K L M N O P Q R S T U V W X Y Z

animal in order to catch or kill it: *a leopard **stalking** its prey*
2 to follow a person over a period of time in a frightening or annoying way: *She was **stalked** by an ex-boyfriend for three months.*
3 to walk in an angry or proud way

stall (say **stawl**) *noun* (*plural* **stalls**)
a big table with goods on it that somebody wants to sell, for example in a street or market: *a fruit **stall***

stallion (say **stal**-i-uhn) *noun* (*plural* **stallions**)
a male horse, especially one that is kept for breeding ➲ See **gelding**, **mare**

stamen (say **stay**-muhn) *noun* (*plural* **stamens**)
a small thin male part in the middle of a flower that produces a fine powder (**pollen**) ➲ See **pistil** ➲ See illustration at **flower**

stamina (say **stam**-i-nuh) *noun* (*no plural*)
the energy and strength that allow you to do something that involves a lot of physical or mental effort for a long time

stammer (say **stam**-uh) *verb* (**stammering, stammered**)
to say the same sound many times when you are trying to say a word: *'B-b-b-but wait for me,' she **stammered**.* ➲ SYNONYM **stutter**

stamp¹ *noun* (*plural* **stamps**)
1 (also **postage stamp**) a small piece of paper that you put on a letter to show that you have paid to send it: *Could I have three **stamps**, please?*
2 a small piece of wood or metal that you press on paper to make marks or words: *a date **stamp***

stamp² *verb* (**stamping, stamped**)
1 to put your foot down very hard: *She **stamped** on the spider and killed it.*
2 to walk by putting your feet down hard and loudly: *He **stamped** angrily out of the room.*
3 to press a small piece of wood or metal on paper to make marks or words: *They **stamped** my passport at the airport.*

stampede (say stam-**peed**) *noun* (*plural* **stampedes**)
a sudden quick movement of a large number of animals or people in the same direction, for example because they are frightened or excited
▸ **stampede** (*verb*): *Many people were injured when a large crowd **stampeded** to get into the stadium.*
🛈 ORIGIN: 19th century, through Mexican Spanish from Spanish *estampida* meaning 'crash, uproar'

stand¹ *noun* (*plural* **stands**)
1 a table or small shop where you can buy things or get information: *a **news-stand*** (= where you can buy newspapers and magazines)
2 a piece of furniture that you can put things in or on: *an umbrella **stand***
3 a large structure where people can watch sport from seats arranged in rows that are low near the front and high near the back ➲ See **grandstand**

stand² *verb* (**standing, stood**)
1 to be on your feet: *'**Stand** still, please!' ◇ She was **standing** by the door.*
2 (also **stand up**) to get up on your feet: *The teacher asked us all to **stand** up.*
3 to put something somewhere: *I **stood** the ladder against the wall.*
can't stand somebody or **something** to hate somebody or something: *I can't **stand** this music.*
stand by somebody to help somebody when they need it: *Her parents **stood** by her when she was in trouble.*
stand for something to be a short way of saying or writing something: *SA **stands** for 'South Africa'.*
stand up for somebody or something to say that somebody or something is right, or to support somebody or something: *Everyone else said I was wrong, but my sister **stood** up for me.*
stand up to somebody to argue or fight with a more powerful person who is attacking you

standard¹ (say **stan**-duhd) *noun*
1 (*no plural*) how good somebody or something is: *Her work is of a very high **standard**.*
2 standards (*plural noun*) a level of behaviour that people think is acceptable: *Many people are worried about falling **standards** in modern society.*

standard² (say **stan**-duhd) *adjective*
normal or not special: *Clothes are sold in **standard** sizes.*

standardize (say **stan**-duh-dize) *verb* (**standardizing, standardized**) (also **standardise**)
to make things that are different the same: *The company is **standardizing** the services they offer across the world.*
▸ **standardization** (*noun*) (also **standardisation**): *the **standardization** of rules*

standard of living *noun* (*plural* **standards of living**)
how rich or poor you are: *They have a low **standard of living*** (= they are poor).

stank (say **stangk**) form of **stink¹**

stanza (say **stan**-zuh) *noun* (*plural* **stanzas**)
a group of lines that are arranged together to form a separate unit within a poem

staple[1] (say **stayp**-l) *adjective*
most important or main: *Mealiemeal is their **staple** food.* ◇ *Wool is Australia's **staple** export product.*

staple[2] (say **stayp**-l) *noun* (*plural* **staples**)
a small thin piece of metal that you use for fastening pieces of paper together. You press the **staples** through the paper, using a **stapler**.
▸ **staple** (*verb*): ***Staple** the pieces of paper together.*

stapler (say **stayp**-luh) *noun* (*plural* **staplers**)
a tool that you use for fixing pieces of paper together with metal **staples**

star[1] (say **staa**) *noun* (*plural* **stars**)
1 a large ball of burning gas in space that you see as a point of light in the sky at night: *It was a clear night and the **stars** were shining brightly.*
2 a shape, decoration, etc. with five or six points sticking out in a regular pattern: *a horse with a white **star** on its forehead*
3 a famous person, for example an actor or a singer: *a film **star***

star[2] (say **staa**) *verb* (**starring, starred**)
1 to be the main actor in a play or film: *He has **starred** in many films.*
2 to have somebody as a star: *The film **stars** Julia Roberts.*

starch (say **staach**) *noun* (*no plural*)
1 a white substance containing **carbohydrate** that is in foods such as rice, potatoes and wheat
2 a substance that is used to make cloth **stiff**

stare (say **stair**) *verb* (**staring, stared**)
to look at somebody or something for a long time: *Everybody **stared** at her hat.* ◇ *He was **staring** out of the window.*

WHICH WORD? **Stare** or **gaze**?
- You usually **stare** at somebody or something if you are surprised or shocked. It is rude to **stare** at people.
- You often **gaze** at somebody or something that you love or admire.

starfish (say **staa**-fish) *noun* (*plural* **starfish**)
a flat sea animal in the shape of a star

stark (say **staak**) *adjective* (**starker, starkest**)
1 very empty or plain and therefore unpleasant or not attractive: *a **stark** landscape*
2 unpleasant and impossible to avoid: *He now faces the **stark** reality of life in prison.*
3 very different to something in a way that is easy to see: *the **stark** contrast between rich and poor people*
4 complete: ***stark** nonsense*

starling (say **staa**-ling) *noun* (*plural* **starlings**)
a noisy bird, common in most parts of the world

start[1] (say **staat**) *verb* (**starting, started**)
1 to begin to do something: *I **start** work at nine o'clock.* ◇ *It **started** raining.* ◇ *She's **starting** to cry.*
2 to begin to happen, or to make something begin to happen: *The film **starts** at 7.30.* ◇ *The police do not know who **started** the fire.*
3 to begin to work or move, or to make something begin to work or move: *The engine won't **start**.* ◇ *I can't **start** the car.*
start off to begin: *The teacher **started** off by asking us our names.*

start[2] (say **staat**) *noun* (*no plural*)
1 the beginning or first part of something: *She arrived after the **start** of the lesson.*
2 the act of starting something: *There's lots of work to do, so let's make a **start**.*
for a start (*informal*) words that you use when you give your first reason for something: *'Why can't we go on holiday?' 'Well, for a **start**, we don't have any money.'*

startle (say **staat**-l) *verb* (**startling, startled**)
to make somebody suddenly surprised or frightened: *You **startled** me when you knocked on the window.*

starve (say **staav**) *verb* (**starving, starved**)
to die because you do not have enough to eat: *Millions of people are **starving** in some parts of the world.*
be starving (*informal*) to be very hungry: *When will dinner be ready? I'm **starving**!*
▸ **starvation** (*noun*): *The child died of **starvation**.*

state[1] (say **stayt**) *noun* (*plural* **states**)
1 how somebody or something is: *The house was untidy and in a terrible **state**.* ◇ *She is not in a very good **state** of mind* (= she is not very happy).
2 a country and its government: *Many schools are owned by the **state**.*
3 (also **State**) a part of a country: *The Free **State***
4 the States (*plural noun*) (*informal*) the United States of America

state[2] (say **stayt**) *verb* (**stating, stated**)
to formally say or write something: *I **stated** in my letter that I was looking for a job.*

statement (say **stayt**-muhnt) *noun* (*plural* **statements**)
something that you say or write, especially formally: *The driver made a **statement** to the police about the accident.*

A B C D E F G H I J K L M N O P Q R S T U V W X Y Z

static (say **stat**-ik) *adjective*
1 not moving, changing or developing: ***static** population growth*
2 (*science*) relating to forces that do not cause movement or relating to objects that are not moving ➲ OPPOSITE **dynamic** 3

station¹ (say **stay**-shuhn) *noun* (*plural* **stations**)
1 (also **railway station**) a place where trains stop so that people can get on and off
2 a place where buses or coaches start and end their journeys: *the bus **station***
3 a building for some special work: *the police **station** ◇ the fire **station** ◇ a petrol **station***
4 a television or radio company

station² (say **stay**-shuhn) *verb* (**stationing, stationed**)
1 to send somebody to work in a particular place for a period of time: *SANDF soldiers **stationed** in Burundi*
2 to stand or sit somewhere so that you can watch what is going on around you: *The dog **stationed** itself at the door and waited for its owner.*

stationary (say **stay**-shuhn-ree) *adjective*
not moving: *a **stationary** vehicle*

stationer (say **stay**-shuh-nuh) *noun* (*plural* **stationers**)
a person who owns or manages a shop that sells **stationery**

stationery (say **stay**-shuhn-ree) *noun* (*no plural*)
paper, pens and other things that you use for writing

> SPELLING Be careful! Don't confuse **stationery** and **stationary**, which sound the same but have different meanings. Remember that a station**er** sells station**ery**.

station-wagon (say **stay**-shuhn-wag-uhn) *noun* (*plural* **station-wagons**)
a car with a door at the back and a long area for luggage behind the back seat

statistic (say stuh-**tiss**-tik) *noun*
1 statistics (*plural noun*) numbers that have been collected to provide information about something: *These **statistics** show that 54% of South Africans live in urban areas.*
2 (*plural* **statistics**) a piece of information shown in numbers: *An interesting **statistic** is that 60% of households have a cellphone.*
▸ **statistical** (*adjective*): ***statistical** information*
▸ **statistically** (*adverb*)

statue (say **stat**-shoo) *noun* (*plural* **statues**)
a model of a person or an animal, made from stone or metal

stature (say **stat**-tshuh) *noun* (*no plural*) (*formal*)
1 the height of a person: *She was tall in **stature**.*
2 how important and respected somebody is because of their skill or because of what they have done: *The novelist's reputation has grown in **stature**.*

status (say **stay**-tuhss) *noun* (*no plural*)
1 the legal position of a person, group or country: *What is your marital **status**?* (= are you married or single?)
2 your social or professional position in relation to other people in a society or an organization: *Domestic workers don't have a very high **status** in this country.*
3 a high social position: *The new job gave him much more **status**.*
4 the situation that somebody or something is in at a particular time: *What is the **status** of my order?*

statute (say **stat**-yoot) *noun* (*plural* **statutes**) (*formal*)
an official law or rule: *the **statutes** of the constitution*

staunch (say **stawnch**) *adjective* (**stauncher, staunchest**)
believing in somebody or something or supporting somebody or something very strongly: *He is one of the team's **staunchest** supporters.*

stay¹ *verb* (**staying, stayed**)
1 to be in the same place and not go away: ***Stay** here until I come back. ◇ I **stayed** in bed until ten o'clock. ◇ 'Please **stay** behind after the lesson.' ◇ I'm **staying** in this evening* (= I'm staying at home).
2 to continue in the same way and not change: *I tried to **stay** awake.*
3 to live somewhere for a short time: *I **stayed** with my friend in Nelspruit. ◇ Which hotel are you **staying** at?*
stay up to not go to bed: *We **stayed** up until after midnight.*

> WHICH WORD? **Stay** or **live**?
> - When you are in a place for a while but it is not your home, you **stay** there. *We **stayed** with my aunt in Mthatha for a month, but we **live** in East London.*
> - When a place is your home, you **live** there: *I **live** in Grahamstown. We **live** in that house. Where do you **live**?*

stay² *noun* (*plural* **stays**)
a short time when you live somewhere: *Did you enjoy your **stay** in Tshwane?*

STD (say ess-tee-**dee**) *noun* (*plural* **STDs**)
an infectious disease that you can get by having

sex with an infected person. ℹ **STD** is short for 'sexually transmitted disease'.

steady (say **sted**-ee) *adjective* (**steadier**, **steadiest**)
1 developing or changing at a regular speed: *a* ***steady*** *increase*
2 not changing or stopping: *Father now has a* ***steady*** *job.* ◇ *His breathing was* ***steady***.
3 not moving or shaking: *a* ***steady*** *ladder*
▸ **steadily** (*adverb*): *Prices are falling* ***steadily***.

steak (say **stayk**) *noun* (*plural* **steaks**)
a wide flat piece of meat, especially meat from a cow (called **beef**): *I'd like* ***steak*** *and chips, please.*
ℹ **ORIGIN**: 13th–15th century, from Old Norse *steik*

steal (say **steel**) *verb* (**stealing**, **stole**, **has stolen**)
to secretly take something that is not yours: *He* ***steals*** *cars.* ◇ *Who* ***stole*** *my sweets?* ◇ *Her money has been* ***stolen***.
▸ **stealing** (*noun*): ***Stealing*** *is a crime.*

WORD BUILDING A person who steals is called a **thief**. A thief **steals** things, but **robs** people and places: *They* ***stole*** *my camera.* ◇ *That woman* ***robbed*** *me.* ◇ *I've been* ***robbed***. ◇ *They* ***robbed*** *a bank.*

stealthy (say **stel**-thee) *adjective* (**stealthier**, **stealthiest**)
done quietly, slowly and carefully: *The intruder's movements were* ***stealthy***.

steam¹ (say **steem**) *noun* (*no plural*)
the gas that water becomes when it gets very hot: *There was* ***steam*** *coming from my coffee.*

steam² (say **steem**) *verb* (**steaming**, **steamed**)
1 to send out **steam¹**: *Our damp clothes* ***steamed*** *in the heat*
2 to cook something in **steam¹**: *I* ***steamed*** *vegetables for supper*

steam engine (say **steem**-en-jin) *noun* (*plural* **steam engines**)
an engine that uses hot steam to make it work

steel *noun* (*no plural*)
very strong metal that is used for making things such as knives, tools and machines

steep *adjective* (**steeper**, **steepest**)
A **steep** hill, mountain or road goes up quickly from a low place to a high place: *I can't cycle up the hill – it's too* ***steep***.
▸ **steeply** (*adverb*): *The path climbed* ***steeply*** *up the side of the mountain.*

steeple (say **steep**-l) *noun* (*plural* **steeples**)
a tall pointed tower on a church

steer (*rhymes with* **gear**) *verb* (**steering**, **steered**)
to make a car, boat, bicycle, etc. go left or right by turning a wheel or handle

steering wheel *noun* (*plural* **steering wheels**)
the wheel that you turn to make a car go left or right

Stem (say **stem**) *noun* ➲ See **Die Stem**

stem *noun* (*plural* **stems**)
1 the long thin part of a plant that rises from the ground and that smaller branches grow from
2 a thin part of a plant that grows from a branch and supports a leaf, flower, or fruit
➲ See illustration at **plant¹**

stench *noun* (*plural* **stenches**)
a strong and very unpleasant smell

stencil (say **sten**-suhl) *noun* (*plural* **stencils**)
1 a thin sheet of metal, plastic or card with a design cut out of it that you put onto a surface and paint over, so that the design is left on the surface
2 the pattern or the design that is produced in this way

step¹ *noun* (*plural* **steps**)
1 a movement when you move your foot up and put it down in another place to walk, run or dance: *She took a* ***step*** *forward and then stopped.*
2 a place to put your foot when you go up or down: *These* ***steps*** *go down to the garden.*
3 one thing in a list of things that you must do: *What is the first* ***step*** *in planning a holiday?*
step by step doing one thing after another, usually in a slow and deliberate way: *This book shows you how to play the guitar,* ***step by step***.

step² *verb* (**stepping**, **stepped**)
to move your foot up and put it down in another place when you walk, run or dance: *You* ***stepped*** *on my foot!*

step- *prefix*
You can add **step-** to the beginning of some words to show that a person is related to you because one of your parents married again: *my* ***stepsister*** *and my* ***stepbrother***

stepchild (say **step**-chyld) *noun* (*plural* **stepchildren**)
the child from an earlier marriage of your husband or your wife

stepfather (say **step**-faa-*thuh*) *noun* (*plural* **stepfathers**)
a man who has married your mother but who is not your father ➲ See note at **stepmother**

A B C D E F G H I J K L M N O P Q R **S** T U V W X Y Z

stepladder (say **step**-lad-uh) *noun* (*plural* **stepladders**)
a type of ladder with two parts, one with steps. The parts are joined together at the top so that it can stand on its own and be folded up when you are not using it.

stepmother (say **step**-mu*th*-uh) *noun* (*plural* **stepmothers**)
a woman who has married your father but who is not your mother

WORD BUILDING The child of your stepmother or stepfather is called your **stepbrother** or **stepsister**.

steppe (say **step**) *noun* (*plural* **steppes**)
a large area of flat land, especially in Eastern Europe and Central Asia, that is covered in grass and has few trees

stepping stone (say **step**-ing-stohn) *noun* (*plural* **stepping stones**)
1 a stone in a river with its surface above the water level that you can step on in order to cross the river
2 something that helps you to make progress towards a goal

stereo (say **ste**-ri-oh) *noun*
1 (*plural* **stereos**) a machine for playing CDs, tapes or records, with two parts (called **speakers**) that let you hear separate sounds from each: *a car* ***stereo***
2 (*no plural*) the system for playing recorded music, speech, etc. in which the sound is divided into two parts: *This programme is broadcast in* ***stereo***.
▸ **stereo** (*adjective*): *a* ***stereo*** *cassette player*

stereotype (say **ste**-ri-uh-tipe) *noun* (*plural* **stereotypes**)
a fixed set of ideas or an impression about what a particular type of person or thing is like, which is often not true in reality
▸ **stereotype** (*verb*): *People should stop* ***stereotyping*** *teenagers.* ▸ **stereotypical** (*adjective*): ***stereotypical*** *views*

sterile (say **ste**-rile) *adjective*
1 not able to produce young animals or babies
2 completely clean and free from bacteria: *The equipment in a doctor's surgery must be* ***sterile***.
3 not producing any useful result: *a* ***sterile*** *argument*
4 lacking in imagination or original thought: *a* ***sterile*** *drama performance*

sterilize (say **ste**-ruh-lize) *verb* (**sterilizing**, **sterilized**) (also **sterilise**)
1 to make something completely clean and free from bacteria
2 to perform an operation that makes a person or animal not able to have babies: *My dog has been* ***sterilized***, *so she can no longer have puppies.*

sterling (say **stur**-ling) *noun* (*no plural*)
the system of money that is used in Britain, which uses the pound as its basic unit: *You can pay in pounds* ***sterling*** *or in American dollars.*

stern[1] (say **sturn**) *adjective* (**sterner**, **sternest**)
serious and strict with people, or not smiling or friendly: *a* ***stern*** *expression*

stern[2] (say **sturn**) *noun* (*plural* **sterns**)
the back part of a ship or boat ➲ See illustration at **ship**

sternum (say **stur**-nuhm) *noun* (*plural* **sternums** or **sterna**) = **breastbone** ➲ See illustration at **skeleton**

stethoscope (say **steth**-uh-skohp) *noun* (*plural* **stethoscopes**)
an instrument a doctor uses to listen to your breathing, your heart and other sounds in your body

stew (say **styoo**) *noun* (*plural* **stews**)
food that you make by cooking meat or vegetables in liquid for a long time: *beef* ***stew***
▸ **stew** (*verb*): *We* ***stewed*** *fruit for breakfast.*

steward (say **styoo**-uhd) *noun* (*plural* **stewards**)
a man whose job is to look after people on a plane or a ship

stewardess (say styoo-uh-**dess**) *noun* (*plural* **stewardesses**)
a woman whose job is to look after people on a plane or a ship

stick[1] (say **stik**) *verb* (**sticking**, **stuck**)
1 to push a pointed thing into something: ***Stick*** *a fork into the meat to see if it's cooked.*
2 to join something to something else with a sticky substance or to become joined in this way: *I* ***stuck*** *a stamp on the envelope.*
3 to be fixed in one place or to not be able to move: *This door always* ***sticks***.
stick out to come out of the side or top of something so that you can see it easily: *The boy's head was* ***sticking*** *out of the window.*
stick something out to push something out: *Don't* ***stick*** *your tongue out!*
stick to something to continue with something and not change it: *We're* ***sticking*** *to our plan.*
stick up for somebody or something to say that somebody or something is right: *Everyone else said I was wrong, but she* ***stuck*** *up for me.*

stick² (say **stik**) *noun* (*plural* **sticks**)
1 a long thin piece of wood: *We found some* ***sticks*** *and made a fire.*
2 (also **walking stick**) a long thin piece of wood you use to help you walk: *The old man walked with a* ***stick****.*
3 a long thin object that is used in some sports to hit or control the ball: *a hockey* ***stick***
4 a long thin piece of something: *a* ***stick*** *of chalk* ◇ *a candy* ***stick***

sticker (say **stik**-uh) *noun* (*plural* **stickers**)
a small piece of paper with a picture or words on it that you can stick onto things

sticky (say **stik**-ee) *adjective* (**stickier**, **stickiest**)
able to stick to things or covered with a substance that can stick to things: *Glue is* ***sticky****.* ◇ ***sticky*** *fingers*

stiff (say **stif**) *adjective* (**stiffer**, **stiffest**)
1 (used about material or paper, etc.) not easy to bend or move: ***stiff*** *cardboard*
2 (used about parts of the body) not easy to move: *My legs were* ***stiff*** *after the run.*
3 (used about a liquid) very thick or almost solid: *Beat the egg whites until they are* ***stiff****.*
▸ **stiffness** (*noun*): *The* ***stiffness*** *in my legs is bothering me.*

stigma (say **stig**-muh) *noun*
1 (*no plural*) bad and often unfair feelings that people in general have about a particular illness, way of behaving, etc.: *the* ***stigma*** *attached to being bankrupt* ◇ *They were not able to escape the* ***stigma*** *of the scandal.*
2 (*plural* **stigmas**) the top part of the female organs of a flower (called the **pistil**) that receives the **pollen** ➲ See illustration at **flower**

stile *noun* (*plural* **stiles**)
a step or set of steps that you can use to climb over a fence or wall

stiletto (say sti-**let**-oh) *noun* (*plural* **stilettos** or **stilettoes**)
1 a high pointed heel on a woman's shoe
2 a type of small knife with a narrow pointed blade (called a **dagger**)

still¹ (say **stil**) *adverb*
1 a word that you use to show that something has not changed: *Do you* ***still*** *live in Underberg?* ◇ *Is it* ***still*** *raining?*
2 although that is true: *She felt ill, but she* ***still*** *went to the party.*
3 a word that you use to make another word stronger: *It was cold yesterday, but today it's colder* ***still****.*

still² (say **stil**) *adjective*
1 without moving: *Please stand* ***still*** *while I take a photo.* ◇ *The water was perfectly* ***still****.*
2 (used about a drink) not containing any bubbles or gas: ***still*** *mineral water* ➲ OPPOSITES **fizzy**, **sparkling** 2
▸ **stillness** (*noun*): *the* ***stillness*** *of the night*

stilts (say **stiltss**) *plural noun*
1 a pair of poles with places to rest your feet on, on which you can walk: *Have you tried walking on* ***stilts****?*
2 wooden or metal poles that support a building or another structure above land or water: *houses built on* ***stilts***

stimulant (say **stim**-yuu-luhnt) *noun* (*plural* **stimulants**)
a drug or other substance that makes you feel more active and awake: *Caffeine is a* ***stimulant****.*

stimulate (say **stim**-yuu-layt) *verb* (**stimulating**, **stimulated**)
1 to make something active or more active, or to encourage something to increase or develop faster: *Exercise* ***stimulates*** *the blood circulation.* ◇ *The government has decided to cut taxes in order to* ***stimulate*** *the economy.*
2 to make somebody feel interested and excited about something
▸ **stimulating** (*adjective*): *a* ***stimulating*** *educational experience*

sting¹ *verb* (**stinging**, **stung**)
1 If an insect or a plant **stings** you, it hurts you by pushing a small sharp part into your skin: *I've been* ***stung*** *by a bee!*
2 to feel a sudden sharp pain: *The smoke made my eyes* ***sting****.*

sting² *noun* (*plural* **stings**)
1 the sharp part of some insects that can hurt you: *A wasp's* ***sting*** *is in its tail.* ➲ See illustration at **scorpion**
2 a hurt place on your skin where an insect or a plant has **stung** you: *a bee* ***sting***

stingy (say **stin**-jee) *adjective* (**stingier**, **stingiest**) (*informal*)
1 not liking to give or to spend money: *She's very* ***stingy*** *with money.*
2 small in size or amount: *a* ***stingy*** *meal*

stink¹ (say **stingk**) *verb* (**stinking**, **stank**, **has stunk**) (*informal*)
to have a very bad smell: *That fish* ***stinks****!*

stink² (say **stingk**) *noun* (*plural* **stinks**) (*informal*)
a very bad smell: *What a terrible* ***stink****!*

stipulate (say **stip**-yuu-layt) *verb* (**stipulating**, **stipulated**) (*formal*)
to officially and formally say what must be done: *The Constitution* ***stipulates*** *that the President is elected for five years.*
▸ **stipulation** (*noun*): *a* ***stipulation*** *in a contract*

A B C D E F G H I J K L M N O P Q R S T U V W X Y Z

stir (say **stur**) *verb* (**stirring, stirred**)
1 to move a spoon or another thing round and round to mix something: *He put sugar in his coffee and **stirred** it.*
2 to move a little or to make something move a little: *The wind **stirred** the leaves.*

stirrup (say **sti**-ruhp) *noun* (*plural* **stirrups**)
one of the two metal objects that are attached to a **saddle** on a horse, and used to support the rider's feet ➲ See illustration at **horse**

stitch[1] (say **stich**) *noun* (*plural* **stitches**)
1 a small line or circle of thread that joins or decorates cloth: *a neat row of small **stitches***
2 a circle of wool that you put round a needle when you are knitting
3 a circle of special thread that doctors use to sew the edges of a cut together: *The cut needed eight **stitches**.*

stitch[2] (say **stich**) *verb* (**stitching, stitched**)
to sew something: *I **stitched** a button on my skirt.*

stock[1] (say **stok**) *noun*
1 (*no plural*) things that a shop keeps ready to sell: *We have a large **stock** of tables.* ◇ *I'll see if we have your size in **stock**.* ◇ *I'm afraid that book's out of **stock** now.* ➲ SYNONYM **merchandise**
2 (*plural* **stocks**) (*business*) a share in a company or business that somebody has bought, or the value of those shares: ***stocks** and shares* ➲ See **stock exchange**
3 (*no plural*) (also **livestock**) animals that are kept on a farm: *cattle, sheep, and other **stock***

stock[2] (say **stok**) *verb* (**stocking, stocked**)
to keep something ready to sell: *I'm afraid we don't **stock** umbrellas.*

stockbroker (say **stok**-broh-kuh) *noun* (*plural* **stockbrokers**) (*business*)
a person whose job is to buy and sell shares in companies for other people

stock exchange *noun* (also **stock market**) (*no plural*) (*business*)
a place where people buy and sell shares in companies, or the business of doing this: *the London **Stock Exchange***

stockfish (say **stok**-fish) *noun* (*plural* **stockfish**)
a grey fish (also called **hake**) that is popular as food

stocking (say **stok**-ing) *noun* (*plural* **stockings**)
one of a pair of thin pieces of clothing that fit tightly over a woman's feet and legs: *a pair of **stockings***

stockist (say **stok**-ist) *noun* (*plural* **stockists**)
a shop that sells a particular kind of product: *The video game is now available from your local **stockist**.*

stocky (say **stok**-ee) *adjective* (**stockier, stockiest**)
not very tall but broad and physically strong: *A **stocky** man walked past.*

stodgy (say **stoj**-ee) *adjective* (**stodgier, stodgiest**)
1 (used about food) heavy and causing you to feel very full, and usually with little or no flavour
2 (*informal*) boring and serious, or having old-fashioned attitudes

stoep (say **stuup**) *noun* (*plural* **stoeps**) (*S. African*)
a platform that is joined to the side or the front of a house, which has a roof but no outside wall ➲ SYNONYM **veranda**
🛈 ORIGIN: through South African Dutch, from Dutch *stoep* meaning 'step, porch, small paved area in front of a house'

stoical (say **stoh**-ik-l) *adjective* (also **stoic**) (*formal*)
suffering pain, difficulty or bad luck without complaining or getting upset
▸ **stoically** (*adverb*): *She is **stoically** cheerful despite her illness.* ▸ **stoicism** (*noun*): *They accepted his decision with **stoicism**.*

stoke (say **stohk**) *verb* (**stoking, stoked**)
1 to add fuel to a fire so that it burns with greater heat: *She **stoked** the fire to keep the room warm.*
2 to make people feel an emotion such as anger more strongly: *They accused the opposition party of **stoking** up the violence.*

stokvel (say **stawk**-fel) *noun* (*plural* **stokvels**) (*S. African*)
a system of regularly collecting money among a group of people. The money is given to a different member of the group, one after the other, at each group meeting.
🛈 ORIGIN: 20th century, from English *stock-fair* from *stock* meaning 'farm animals' + *fair* meaning 'fair, market'. English settlers in the 19th century sold their cattle at stock-fairs held in one place after another. The change in spelling came from a mistake in pronunciation that made people think that the word was Afrikaans.

stole, stolen (say **stohl**, **stoh**-luhn) forms of **steal**

stoma (say **stoh**-muh) *noun* (*plural* **stomas** or **stomata**)
1 a very small opening in the leaf or stem of a plant that allows gases to pass through
2 an opening in your body, especially one made by a doctor during an operation

stomach (say **stum**-uhk) *noun* (*plural* **stomachs**)
1 the part inside your body where food goes after you eat it ➲ See illustrations at **alimentary canal**, **organ**
2 the front part of your body below your chest and above your legs

stomach ache (say **stum**-uhk ayk) *noun* (*plural* **stomach aches**)
a pain in your stomach: *I've got a **stomach ache**.*

stomata (say stoh-**muh**-tuh) plural of **stoma**

stone (say **stohn**) *noun*
1 (*no plural*) the very hard material that is found in the ground. **Stone** is sometimes used for building: *a **stone** wall*
2 (*plural* **stones**) a small piece of **stone**: *The children were throwing **stones** into the river.*
3 (*plural* **stones**) the hard seed in the middle of some types of fruit: *Peaches, plums, cherries and olives all have **stones**.* ➲ See **pip**
4 (*plural* **stones**) a small piece of beautiful rock that is very valuable: *A diamond is a precious **stone**.*

stony (say **stohn**-ee) *adjective* (**stonier**, **stoniest**)
containing a lot of stones or covered with a lot of stones: ***stony** ground*

stood (say **st*uu*d**) form of **stand**[2]

stool (*rhymes with* **pool**) *noun* (*plural* **stools**)
a small seat with no back: *kitchen **stools***

stoop (*rhymes with* **troop**) *verb* (**stooping**, **stooped**)
to bend your body forward and down: *She **stooped** to pick up the baby.*
▸ **stoop** (*noun*): *He walks with a **stoop**.*

stop[1] *verb* (**stopping**, **stopped**)
1 to finish moving or working, or to become still: *The train **stopped** at every station.* ◇ *The clock has **stopped**.* ◇ *I **stopped** to post a letter.*
2 to not do something any more or to finish: ***Stop** making that noise!*
3 to make somebody or something finish moving or doing something: *Ring the bell to **stop** the bus.*
stop somebody (from) doing something to not let somebody do something: *My dad **stopped** me from going out.*

stop[2] *noun* (*plural* **stops**)
1 the moment when somebody or something finishes moving: *The train came to a **stop**.*
2 a place where buses or trains **stop** so that people can get on and off: *I'm getting off at the next **stop**.*
put a stop to something to make something finish: *A teacher put a **stop** to the fight.*

stopwatch (say **stop**-woch) *noun* (*plural* **stopwatches**)
a special watch that you can start and stop when you want to, used to measure exactly how long something takes

storage (say **staw**-rij) *noun* (*no plural*)
1 the activity of keeping things that are not being used in a safe place or the place where these things are kept: *This room is being used for **storage** at the moment.*
2 (*computing*) = **memory** 3
▸ **storage** (*adjective*): *a **storage** area for empty crates* ◇ ***storage** costs*

store[1] (say **staw**) *noun* (*plural* **stores**)
1 a shop, especially a large one: *a health food **store*** ◇ *There are many big **stores** in Johannesburg.*
2 things that you are keeping to use later, or the place where you keep them: *a secret **store** of food*

store[2] (say **staw**) *verb* (**storing**, **stored**)
to keep something to use later: *The information is **stored** on a computer.*

storey (say **staw**-ree) *noun* (*plural* **storeys**)
one level in a building: *The building has four **storeys**.* ➲ See **floor** 2

> SPELLING Be careful! Don't confuse **storey** and **story**, which sound the same but have different meanings.

stork (say **stawk**) *noun* (*plural* **storks**)
a large bird with a long neck, beak and legs. Storks often make their homes (**nests**) on top of buildings.

storm[1] (say **stawm**) *noun* (*plural* **storms**)
very bad weather with strong winds and rain: *a **thunderstorm***

> WORD BUILDING When there is a storm, you may hear **thunder** and see **lightning** in the sky. **Cyclones**, **hurricanes**, **tornadoes** and **typhoons** are large violent storms.

storm[2] (say **stawm**) *verb* (**storming**, **stormed**)
to move in a way that shows you are angry: *He **stormed** out of the room.*

stormy (say **stawm**-ee) *adjective* (**stormier**, **stormiest**)
with strong wind and rain: *a **stormy** night*

story (say **staw**-ree) *noun* (*plural* **stories**)
1 words that tell you about people and things that are not real: *Hans Christian Andersen wrote **stories** for children.* ◇ *a ghost **story***

A B C D E F G H I J K L M N O P Q R S T U V W X Y Z

2 words that tell you about things that really happened: *My grandmother told me **stories** about when she was a child.*

SPELLING Be careful! Don't confuse **story** and **storey**, which have different meanings.

stout (say **stowt**) *adjective* (**stouter**, **stoutest**)
1 (used about a person) heavily built or fairly fat
2 thick, strong and unlikely to break: ***stout** boots* ➲ SYNONYM **sturdy**

stove (say **stohv**) *noun* (*plural* **stoves**)
1 a piece of kitchen equipment for cooking. It has places for heating pans on the top and an oven for cooking food inside it: *an electric **stove***
2 a closed metal box in which you burn wood and coal to heat a room: *a wood-burning **stove***

straddle (say **strad**-l) *verb* (**straddling**, **straddled**)
1 to sit or stand with one leg on either side of something: *to **straddle** a chair*
2 to be or exist on both sides of something, or to cross, or have parts in, different places: *The game park **straddles** the borders of Botswana, Zimbabwe and South Africa.*

straight[1] (say **strayt**) *adverb* (**straighter**, **straightest**)
1 not in a curve or at an angle: *Look **straight** in front of you.* ◇ *Go **straight** on until you come to the bank, then turn left.*
2 without stopping or doing anything else: *Come **straight** home.* ◇ *She walked **straight** past me.*
straight away immediately: *I'll do it **straight** away.*

straight[2] (say **strayt**) *adjective* (**straighter**, **straightest**)
1 with no curve or bend: *Use a ruler to draw a **straight** line.* ◇ *His hair is curly and mine is **straight**.*
2 with one side as high as the other: *This picture isn't **straight**.*
3 honest and direct: *a **straight** answer to a **straight** question*
get something straight to make sure that you understand something completely: *Let's get this **straight**. Are you sure you left your bike at the gate?*

straighten (say **strayt**-n) *verb* (**straightening**, **straightened**)
to become or to make something straight

straightforward (say strayt-**faw**-wuhd) *adjective*
easy to understand or do: *a **straightforward** question*

strain[1] (say **strayn**) *noun* (*plural* **strains**)
1 physical force: *The rope broke under the **strain**.*
2 worry or problems caused by worry: *His illness put a great **strain** on their marriage.*
3 an injury to part of your body, caused by making it work too hard: *back **strain***

strain[2] (say **strayn**) *verb* (**straining**, **strained**)
1 to try very hard: *Her voice was so quiet that I had to **strain** to hear her.*
2 to hurt a part of your body by making it work too hard: *Don't read in the dark. You'll **strain** your eyes.*
3 to pour a liquid through something with small holes in it, to remove any solid bits

strait (say **strayt**) *noun*
1 (*plural* **straits**) a narrow piece of sea between two areas of land, which connects two larger seas: *the **Strait** of Gibraltar* ➲ See **isthmus**
2 straits (*plural noun*) a bad or very difficult situation, especially one caused by having no money: *The company is in financial **straits**.*

strand[1] *noun* (*plural* **strands**)
one piece of thread or hair

strand[2] *verb* (**stranding**, **stranded**)
1 to drive something such as a ship onto rocks or land so that it cannot move, or to become stuck on land in such a way: *Whales that **strand** on the shore often die.*
2 to leave or put somebody in a place that they cannot get away from: *The strike will **strand** travellers at airports.*

stranded (say **strand**-uhd) *adjective*
left in a place that you cannot get away from: *The car broke down and I was **stranded** on a lonely road.*

Strandloper (say **strunt**-loor-puh) *noun* (*plural* **Strandlopers**) (*S. African*)
a member of a group of **Khoisan** people who lived on the west coast of South Africa long ago
🛈 ORIGIN: 19th century, from Dutch *strandlooper*, from *strand* meaning 'beach' + *looper* meaning 'walker'

strange (say **straynj**) *adjective* (**stranger**, **strangest**)
1 unusual or surprising: *Did you hear that **strange** noise?*
2 that you do not know: *We were lost in a **strange** town.*

strangely (say **straynj**-lee) *adverb*
in a surprising or an unusual way: *He was acting very **strangely**.* ◇ *She was **strangely** quiet.*

stranger (say **strayn**-juh) *noun* (*plural* **strangers**)
1 a person who you do not know

2 a person who is in a place that they do not know: *I'm a **stranger** to this city.*

strangle (say **strang**-guhl) *verb* (**strangling**, **strangled**)
to kill somebody by pressing their neck very tightly ➲ SYNONYM **throttle**

strap[1] *noun* (*plural* **straps**)
a long flat piece of material that you use for carrying something or for keeping something in place: *a leather watch **strap***

strap[2] *verb* (**strapping**, **strapped**)
to hold something in place with a **strap[1]**: *I **strapped** the bag onto the back of my bike.*

strata (say **straa**-tuh) plural of **stratum**

strategic (say struh-**tee**-jik) *adjective* (also **strategical**)
1 useful and helping you to achieve a plan: *They made a **strategic** decision to sell off part of the company.*
2 relating to plans that are necessary for a country to achieve success in politics, the defence of the country, or war: ***strategic** warfare*
3 (used about weapons) designed to be fired over long distances at the enemy's country, rather than to be used to win a particular battle: ***strategic** nuclear weapons*
▸ **strategically** (*adverb*): *The island is **strategically** important.*

strategy (say **strat**-uh-jee) *noun* (*plural* **strategies**)
a plan or planning: *What's your **strategy** for passing the exam?* ➲ SYNONYM **tactic** 1

stratified (say **strat**-i-fide) *adjective*
arranged in layers or grades: ***stratified** rocks*
▸ **stratification** (*noun*): *the **stratification** of society*

stratosphere (say **strat**-uh-sfeer) *noun*
the stratosphere the layer of the atmosphere that contains the **ozone layer** ➲ See illustration at **atmosphere** ➲ See **ionosphere**, **mesosphere**, **thermosphere**, **troposphere**

stratum (say **straa**-tuhm) *noun* (*plural* **strata**)
1 (*science*) a layer, especially a layer or series of layers of rock, soil, etc.
2 (*formal*) a level of society or social class: *officials and other influential **strata***

straw *noun*
1 (*no plural*) dried plants that animals sleep on or that people use for making things like hats and floor coverings: *a **straw** hat*
2 (*plural* **straws**) a thin paper or plastic tube that you can drink through

the last straw, the final straw the last of several bad things or the thing that finally makes a situation impossible for you

strawberry (say **straw**-buh-ree) *noun* (*plural* **strawberries**)
a soft red fruit with seeds near the surface

stray[1] *adjective*
A **stray** animal is lost or does not have a home: *a **stray** dog*
▸ **stray** (*noun*): *There are many **strays** in our town.*

stray[2] *verb* (**straying**, **strayed**)
1 to go away from the place where you should be: *The sheep **strayed** onto the road.*
2 to not keep to the subject that you should be thinking about or discussing: *My thoughts **strayed** for a few minutes.*

streak[1] (say **streek**) *noun* (*plural* **streaks**)
a long thin line that is a different colour from the surface it is on: *a **streak** of lightning ◇ She's got **streaks** of grey in her hair.*

streak[2] (say **streek**) *verb* (**streaking**, **streaked**)
1 to mark or to become marked with long thin lines: *Tears **streaked** her face.*
2 to move very quickly: *He **streaked** ahead of the other athletes.*
3 (*informal*) to run quickly through a public place with no clothes on

stream[1] (say **streem**) *noun* (*plural* **streams**)
1 a small river: *a mountain **stream***
2 moving liquid, or moving things or people: *a **stream** of blood ◇ I've had a steady **stream** of visitors.*
🛈 ORIGIN: from Old English *stream*, related to Dutch *stroom*

stream[2] (say **streem**) *verb* (**streaming**, **streamed**)
to move like water: *Tears were **streaming** down his face.*

streamline (say **streem**-line) *verb* (**streamlining**, **streamlined**)
1 to give something like a car or boat a long smooth shape so that it can go fast through air or water
2 to make an organization or a way of doing things work better by making it simpler

street *noun* (*plural* **streets**) (abbr. St)
a road in a city, town or village with buildings along the sides: *I saw her walking down the **street**. ◇ I live in Main **Street**. ◇ 91 Pepper **St**, Bloemfontein*

strength (*rhymes with* **length**) *noun*
1 (*no plural*) how strong or powerful you are: *I don't have the **strength** to lift this box – it's too*

A B C D E F G H I J K L M N O P Q R S T U V W X Y Z

heavy. ➲ SYNONYM **might**[2] ➲ The adjective is **strong**
2 (*plural* **strengths**) a good quality or an ability that a person or thing has: *Our team has many **strengths** and only one weakness.*

strengthen (say **streng**-thuhn) *verb* (**strengthening, strengthened**)
to become or to make somebody or something stronger: *The wind had **strengthened** overnight.*

strenuous (say **stren**-yuu-uhss) *adjective*
needing or using a lot of effort or energy
▸ **strenuously** (*adverb*): *She **strenuously** denied that she had anything to do with the crime.*

stress[1] *noun* (*no plural*)
1 a feeling of worry because of problems in your life: *Mum's been suffering from **stress** since Dad's been ill.*
2 saying one word or part of a word more strongly than another: *In the word 'dictionary', the **stress** is on the first part of the word.*
➲ SYNONYM **emphasis**

stress[2] *verb* (**stressing, stressed**)
1 to say something strongly to show that it is important: *I must **stress** how important this meeting is.*
2 to say one word or part of a word more strongly than another: *You should **stress** the first part of the word 'happy'.* ➲ SYNONYM **emphasize**

stressful (say **stress**-fuhl) *adjective*
causing a lot of worry: *a **stressful** job*

stretch[1] (say **strech**) *verb* (**stretching, stretched**)
1 to pull something to make it longer or wider, or to become longer or wider: *The T-shirt **stretched** when I washed it.*
2 to push your arms and legs out as far as you can: *Joe got out of bed and **stretched**.* ◇ *The cat **stretched** out in front of the fire and went to sleep.*
3 to cover a large area of land or a long period of time: *The beach **stretches** for miles.*

stretch[2] (say **strech**) *noun* (*plural* **stretches**)
a piece of land or water: *This is a beautiful **stretch** of countryside.*

stretcher (say **strech**-uh) *noun* (*plural* **stretchers**)
a kind of bed for carrying somebody who is ill or hurt: *They carried him to the ambulance on a **stretcher**.*

strict (say **strikt**) *adjective* (**stricter, strictest**)
If you are **strict**, you make people do what you want and do not allow them to behave badly: *Her parents are very **strict** – she has to be home before ten o'clock.* ◇ ***strict** rules*

strictly (say **strikt**-lee) *adverb*
1 definitely or in a strict way: *Smoking is **strictly** forbidden.*
2 exactly: *That is not **strictly** true.*

stride *verb* (**striding, strode**)
to walk with long steps: *The police officer **strode** across the road.*
▸ **stride** (*noun*): *He walked with long **strides**.*

strife (*rhymes with* **life**) *noun* (*no plural*) (*formal*)
very angry and sometimes violent fighting between people or groups

strike[1] *verb* (**striking, struck**)
1 (*formal*) to hit somebody or something: *A stone **struck** me on the back of the head.*
2 to stop working because you want more money or are angry about something: *The nurses are **striking** for better pay.*
3 to come suddenly into your mind: *It suddenly **struck** me that she looked like my sister.*
4 If a clock **strikes**, it rings a bell a certain number of times so that people know what time it is: *The clock **struck** nine.*
strike a match to make fire with a match

WORD BUILDING For meaning 1 above, **hit** is the more usual word. But you always use **strike** when you talk about lightning: *The tree was **struck** by lightning.*

strike[2] *noun* (*plural* **strikes**)
a time when people are not working because they want more money or are angry about something: *There are no trains today because the drivers are on **strike**.*

striking (say **strike**-ing) *adjective*
If something is **striking**, you notice it because it is very unusual or interesting: *That's a very **striking** hat.*

string *noun* (*plural* **strings**)
1 very thin rope that you use for tying things: *I tied up the parcel with **string**.* ◇ *The key was hanging on a **string**.*
2 a line of things on a piece of thread: *a **string** of blue beads*
3 a piece of thin wire on a musical instrument: *guitar **strings*** ➲ See illustration at **violin**

stringed (say **string**-d) *adjective*
(used about musical instruments) having strings: *a nylon-**stringed** guitar*

stringent (say **strin**-juhnt) *adjective*
very strict or requiring attention to detail: ***stringent** safety rules* ◇ ***stringent** hygiene standards*

strip[1] *verb* (**stripping, stripped**)
1 (also **strip off**) to take off your clothes or to take off another person's clothes: *She **stripped** off and ran into the sea.* ◇ *They were **stripped** and searched by the police officers.*
2 to take off something that is covering something: *I **stripped** the wallpaper off the walls.*

strip[2] *noun* (*plural* **strips**)
a long thin piece of something: *a **strip** of paper*

stripe *noun* (*plural* **stripes**)
a long thin line of colour: *Zebras have black and white **stripes**.*
▶ **striped** (*adjective*): *He wore a blue and white **striped** shirt.*

strive (*rhymes with* **dive**) *verb* (**striving, strove, has striven**)
(*formal*) to try very hard to do or get something: *to **strive** for perfection* ◇ *We **strive** to train and employ disabled people.*

strode (say **strohd**) form of **stride**

stroke[1] (say **strohk**) *noun*
1 (*plural* **strokes**) a movement that you make with your arms, for example when you are swimming or playing sports such as **tennis**
2 (*plural* **strokes**) a sudden serious illness when the brain stops working properly: *He had a **stroke**.*
3 (*no plural*) a sudden successful action or event: *It was a **stroke** of luck finding your ring again so quickly.*
4 (*plural* **strokes**) a gentle movement of your hand over a surface: *He gave the cat a **stroke**.*

stroke[2] (say **strohk**) *verb* (**stroking, stroked**)
to move your hand gently over somebody or something to show love: *She **stroked** his hair.*

stroll (say **strohl**) *verb* (**strolling, strolled**)
to walk somewhere in a slow relaxed way: *We **strolled** along the beach.*
▶ **stroll** (*noun*): *We went for a **stroll** by the river.*

strong *adjective* (**stronger, strongest**)
1 A **strong** person has a powerful body, and can carry heavy things: *I need somebody **strong** to help me move this table.*
2 A **strong** object does not break easily: *Don't stand on that chair – it's not very **strong**.*
3 A **strong** opinion or belief is not easy to change: *There was **strong** opposition to the plan.*
4 powerful: ***strong** winds* ◇ *The current was very **strong**.*
5 having a big effect on the mind or the body: *a **strong** smell of oranges* ◇ *I like **strong** tea* (= with not much milk in it).
➲ opposite **weak**
➲ The noun is **strength**
▶ **strongly** (*adverb*): *I **strongly** believe that he is wrong.*

strove (say **strohv**) form of **strive**

struck (say **struk**) form of **strike[1]**

structure (say **struk**-tshuh) *noun*
1 (*no plural*) the way that something is made: *We are studying the **structure** of a bird's wing.*
2 (*plural* **structures**) a building or another thing that people have made with many parts: *The new post office is a tall glass and brick **structure**.*
▶ **structure** (*verb*): *You must **structure** your essay logically and clearly.*

struggle (say **strug**-l) *verb* (**struggling, struggled**)
1 to try very hard to do something that is not easy: *We **struggled** to lift the heavy box.*
2 to move your arms and legs a lot when you are fighting or trying to get free: *She **struggled** with her attacker.*
▶ **struggle** (*noun*): *It was a **struggle** to get him to agree to come.*

strum *verb* (**strumming, strummed**)
to play a guitar by moving your fingers up and down over the strings

strut (*rhymes with* **but**) *verb* (**strutting, strutted**)
to walk in a proud and confident way: *The geese **strutted** towards the pond.* ➲ SYNONYM **swagger**

stub[1] *noun* (*plural* **stubs**)
1 a short part of something such as a pencil that is left after the rest has been used
2 the part of a cheque or ticket that you keep as a record when you give the other part to somebody else ➲ SYNONYM **counterfoil**

stub[2] *verb* (**stubbing, stubbed**)
to hurt your toe by accidentally hitting it against something
stub out to make a cigarette or cigar stop burning by pushing it against something hard

stubble (say **stub**-l) *noun* (*no plural*)
1 the short hairs growing on a man's face when he has not shaved for some time
2 the short parts of crops such as wheat that are left in the ground after the rest has been cut down

stubborn (say **stub**-uhn) *adjective*
A **stubborn** person does not change their ideas easily or do what other people want them to do: *She's too **stubborn** to say sorry.* ➲ SYNONYM **obstinate**
▶ **stubbornly** (*adverb*): *He **stubbornly** refused to apologize.* ▶ **stubbornness** (*noun*): *Her **stubbornness** is very irritating.*

A B C D E F G H I J K L M N O P Q R S T U V W X Y Z

stuck[1] (say **stuk**) form of **stick**[1]

stuck[2] (say **stuk**) *adjective*
1 not able to move: *This drawer is **stuck** – I can't open it.* ◇ *I was **stuck** in town with no money.*
2 not able to do something because it is difficult: *If you get **stuck**, ask your teacher for help.*

stud *noun* (*plural* **studs**)
1 a small piece of metal that sticks out from the rest of the surface that it is fixed to, used especially for decoration: *a belt decorated with **studs***
2 a piece of jewellery that you push through a small hole in your ear or other part of your body: *diamond **studs***
3 one of the small pieces of plastic or metal that stick out from the bottom part of a shoe or boot, that help you stand on soft or wet ground
4 a farm where animals of high quality are kept for breeding: *a **stud** farm* ◇ *racehorses from a famous **stud***

student (say **styoo**-duhnt) *noun* (*plural* **students**)
a person who is studying at a college or university: *She is a history **student**.*

WHICH WORD? **Student**, **learner** or **pupil**?
- We usually call people who are at school **learners** or **pupils**.
- We usually call someone who is at a college or university a **student**.

studio (say **styoo**-di-oh) *noun* (*plural* **studios**)
1 a room where an artist works
2 a room where people make films, radio and television programmes or records: *a television **studio***

studious (say **styoo**-di-uhss) *adjective*
spending a lot of time studying or reading: *She is so **studious**! She spends hours in the library every day.*

study[1] (say **stud**-ee) *verb* (**studying**, **studied**)
1 to spend time learning about something: *He **studied** French at university.*
2 to look at something carefully: *We must **study** the map before we leave.*

study[2] (say **stud**-ee) *noun* (*plural* **studies**)
1 the activity of learning about something: *Biology is the **study** of living things.* ◇ *He's doing a course in Business **Studies**.*
2 a room in a house where you go to study, read or write

stuff[1] (say **stuf**) *noun* (*no plural*) (*informal*)
any material, substance or group of things: *What's this blue **stuff** on the carpet?* ◇ *Put your **stuff** in this bag.*

stuff[2] (say **stuf**) *verb* (**stuffing**, **stuffed**)
1 to fill something with something: *The pillow was **stuffed** with feathers.*
2 (*informal*) to push something quickly into another thing: *He took the money quickly and **stuffed** it into his pocket.*

stuffy (say **stuf**-ee) *adjective* (**stuffier**, **stuffiest**)
If a room is **stuffy**, it has no fresh air in it: *Open the window – it's very **stuffy** in here.*

stumble (say **stumb**-l) *verb* (**stumbling**, **stumbled**)
to hit your foot against something when you are walking or running, and almost fall: *The old lady **stumbled** as she was going upstairs.*

stump *noun* (*plural* **stumps**)
1 the small part that is left when something is cut off or broken: *a tree **stump***
2 (in cricket) one of three upright wooden sticks that form the **wicket** 1

stun *verb* (**stunning**, **stunned**)
1 to hit a person or an animal on the head so hard that they cannot see, think or make a sound for a short time
2 to make somebody very surprised or shocked: *His sudden death **stunned** his family and friends.*

stung form of **sting**[1]

stunk (say **stungk**) form of **stink**[1]

stunning (say **stun**-ing) *adjective*
very beautiful, impressive or surprising: *a **stunning** dress* ◇ *a **stunning** victory*

stunt *noun* (*plural* **stunts**)
something dangerous or difficult that a person does, especially as part of a film: *James Bond films are full of exciting **stunts**.*

stupendous (say styoo-**pen**-duhss) *adjective*
very large or extremely impressive: *a **stupendous** achievement*

stupid (say **styoo**-pid) *adjective*
not intelligent or sensible: *Don't be so **stupid**!* ◇ *What a **stupid** question!* ◇ *This child's not **stupid**.* ◇ *He's a **stupid** man.* ➲ OPPOSITE **clever**
▸ **stupidity** (*noun*): *There are no limits to his **stupidity**!* ▸ **stupidly** (*adverb*): *I **stupidly** forgot to close the door.*

WORD BUILDING There are many words that you can use instead of **stupid**, but check their exact meanings first. Examples are: **absurd**, **crazy**1 (informal), **dim**2 (informal), **dumb**2 (informal), **foolish**, **idiotic**, **ignorant**, **irrational**, **mad**2 (informal), **rash**[2],

reckless, **ridiculous**, **senseless**1, **silly**, **simple**3 (informal), **thick**6 (informal) and **unwise**.

stupor (say **styoo**-puh) *noun* (*no plural*)
the state or condition of being nearly unconscious or unable to think properly because of being very tired or drunk, for example

sturdy (say **stur**-dee) *adjective* (**sturdier**, **sturdiest**)
1 strong and healthy: ***sturdy** legs*
2 strong and not easy to break: ***sturdy** shoes* ◇ *a **sturdy** branch* ➲ SYNONYM **stout**

stutter (say **stut**-uh) *verb* (**stuttering**, **stuttered**)
to say the same sound many times when you are trying to say a word: *'I d-d-don't understand,' he **stuttered**.* ➲ SYNONYM **stammer**

sty (*rhymes with* **fly**) (*plural* **sties**)
1 short for **pigsty**
2 an infection on the eyelid that makes it red and painful

style (say **stile**) *noun* (*plural* **styles**)
1 a way of doing, making or saying something: *I don't like his **style** of writing.*
2 the shape or kind of something: *a new **hairstyle*** ◇ *This shop has all the latest **styles**.*
3 (*biology*) the part of a flower that carries the **stigma** ➲ See illustration at **flower**

stylish (say **stile**-ish) *adjective*
fashionable and attractive: *You look very **stylish** in that hat!*
▶ **stylishly** (*adverb*): *She was very **stylishly** dressed.*

sub- *prefix*
1 under, beneath or below: ***submarine*** ◇ ***subsoil***
2 not as important as somebody or something else: ***subordinate***
3 making a smaller part of something: ***sub-plot***
🛈 **ORIGIN**: from Latin *sub* meaning 'under, close to'

subconscious (say sub-**kon**-shuhss) *noun* (*no plural*)
the part of your mind that has thoughts and feelings that you are not fully aware of but that can affect the way you behave
▶ **subconscious** (*adjective*): *Many advertisements work at a **subconscious** level.*
▶ **subconsciously** (*adverb*): *He was **subconsciously** relieved that he did not have to make the decision.*

subdivide (say sub-di-**vide**) *verb* (**subdividing**, **subdivided**)
to divide or be divided into several smaller parts
▶ **subdivision** (*noun*)

subdue (say suhb-**dyoo**) *verb* (**subduing**, **subdued**)
to get control of somebody or something, or to defeat somebody: *to **subdue** fears* ◇ *to **subdue** an uprising*

subject[1] (say **sub**-jikt) *noun* (*plural* **subjects**)
1 the person or thing that you are talking or writing about: *What is the **subject** of your talk?*
2 something you study at school, university or college: *Maths is my favourite **subject**.*
3 (*grammar*) the word in a sentence that does the action of the verb: *In the sentence 'Ntsako ate the cake', 'Ntsako' is the **subject**.* ➲ See **object**[1] 3
4 a person who belongs to a certain country, especially one with a king or queen: *British **subjects***

subject[2] (say suhb-**jekt**) *verb* (**subjecting**, **subjected**)
to bring a country or group of people under your control, especially by using force: *The Roman Empire **subjected** much of Europe to its rule.*

subjective (say suhb-**jek**-tiv) *adjective*
based on your own personal opinions or feelings rather than on facts or evidence
➲ OPPOSITE **objective**[2]
▶ **subjectively** (*adverb*): *The products were **subjectively** rated on a scale of one to ten.*

sublime (say suh-**blime**) *adjective*
so good or so beautiful that it makes you admire something very much
▶ **sublimely** (*adverb*): *The resort is in a **sublimely** beautiful location.*

submarine (say sub-muh-**reen**) *noun* (*plural* **submarines**)
a ship that can travel underwater

submerge (say suhb-**murj**) *verb* (**submerging**, **submerged**)
to go or to make something go under the surface of water or some other liquid: ***Submerge** the parts in acid to remove the rust.*
▶ **submerged** (*adjective*): *The ship struck a **submerged** rock.*

submissive (say suhb-**miss**-iv) *adjective*
ready to obey other people and do whatever they tell you to do: ***submissive** behaviour*

submit (say suhb-**mit**) *verb* (**submitting**, **submitted**)
1 to give something such as a document to somebody so that it can be studied, considered

A B C D E F G H I J K L M N O P Q R **S** T U V W X Y Z

or approved: *Don't forget to **submit** your CV together with your application.*
2 to accept somebody else's authority or stop trying to fight something because you cannot win

subordinate (say suh-**baw**-di-nuht) *adjective*
having less power or authority than somebody else, or being less important than something else: *the **subordinate** status of rural women*
▸ **subordinate** (*noun*): *She is a good boss and looks after her **subordinates**.*

sub-plot (say **sub**-plot) *noun* (*plural* **sub-plots**)
a story that is related to, but less important than, the main story in a book, play or film

subscribe (say suhb-**skribe**) *verb* (**subscribing, subscribed**)
1 to get a newspaper, magazine or service regularly, usually by paying for it in advance: ***Subscribing** to satellite TV is expensive.* ◇ ***Subscribe** to our free monthly email letter.*
2 (*formal*) to agree with or support an idea, belief or opinion: *Our company **subscribes** to the idea that the customer is always right.*
▸ **subscriber** (*noun*): *a magazine **subscriber***

subscription (say suhb-**skrip**-shuhn) *noun* (*plural* **subscriptions**)
money that you pay, for example to get the same magazine each month or to join a club: *I have a **subscription** to a wildlife magazine.*

subsequent (say **sub**-si-kwuhnt) *adjective*
(*formal*) coming or happening after or later than something else: *a sustainable future for **subsequent** generations*
▸ **subsequently** (*adverb*): *The rumours were **subsequently** found to be untrue.*

subservient (say suhb-**sur**-vi-uhnt) *adjective*
1 too ready to obey or serve other people
2 (*formal*) less important than something else: *Individual security is **subservient** to national security.*

subset (say **sub**-set) *noun* (*plural* **subsets**)
a set contained within another set: *The group of girls is a **subset** of the set of all the children in my class.*

subside (say suhb-**side**) *verb* (**subsiding, subsided**)
1 to become weaker, calmer or quieter: *The storm seems to be **subsiding**.* ◇ *Her fear **subsided**.* ◇ *The fever will eventually **subside**.*
2 to move or go down to a lower level: *He hoped the rain would stop and the water **subside**.* ◇ *The wall had **subsided** and sunk further into the ground.*

subsidy (say **sub**-suh-dee) *noun* (*plural* **subsidies**)
1 money that the government pays to an industry to keep down the prices at which its goods or services are sold to the public: *a transport **subsidy***
2 money that the government gives to an organization or charity to help it to function: *annual **subsidies** for the theatres*
▸ **subsidize** (*verb*) (also **subsidise**): *The government **subsidizes** housing loans.*

subsist (say suhb-**sist**) *verb* (**subsisting, subsisted**) (*formal*)
to manage to live with very little food or money: *Many people in Africa **subsist** on less than a dollar a day.*
▸ **subsistence** (*noun*): ***subsistence** wages*

subsistence farming (say suhb-**siss**-tuhnss **faam**-ing) *noun* (*no plural*)
farming that produces enough food to feed the farmer's family, but not enough to sell to other people
▸ **subsistence farmer** (*noun*)

subsoil (say **sub**-soyl) *noun* (*no plural*)
a layer of soil between the **topsoil** and the rock beneath it

substance (say **sub**-stuhnss) *noun* (*plural* **substances**)
1 any solid, liquid or gas: *chemical **substances*** ◇ *Stone is a hard **substance**.*
2 the main or most important part of something: *I agree with the **substance** of your argument.*

substantial (say suhb-**stan**-shuhl) *adjective*
1 large in amount, size, value or importance: *The storm caused **substantial** damage.* ◇ *a **substantial** discount*
2 strongly made or built: *A **substantial** stone fort was built to protect the town.*

substitute (say **sub**-sti-tyoot) *noun* (*plural* **substitutes**)
a person or thing that you put in the place of another: *One player was injured, so a **substitute** came on.*
▸ **substitute** (*verb*): *You can **substitute** margarine for butter.*

subtitles (say **sub**-ty-tuhlz) *plural noun*
words at the bottom of a film or television programme that tell you what people are saying: *The film was in isiZulu with English **subtitles**.*

subtle (say **sut**-l) *adjective* (**subtler, subtlest**)
not large, bright or easy to notice: ***subtle***

colours ◇ *There has been a **subtle** change in her behaviour.*

PRONUNCIATION Don't pronounce the **b** in **subtle**

subtotal (say **sub**-toh-tuhl) *noun* (*plural* **subtotals**)
the sum of part of a group of numbers that you are adding up: *The **subtotal** on this invoice excludes VAT and delivery costs.*

subtract (say suhb-**trakt**) *verb* (**subtracting, subtracted**)
to take a number away from another number: *If you **subtract** 6 from 9, you get 3.* ➲ OPPOSITE **add** 2
▶ **subtraction** (*noun*): *The children are learning how to do **subtraction**.* ➲ See **addition** 1

subtrahend (say **sub**-truh-hend) *noun* (*plural* **subtrahends**) (*maths*)
the amount that is taken away from another amount: *In the equation 9 – 6 = 3, the **subtrahend** is 6.* ➲ See **minuend**

subtropical (say sub-**trop**-ik-l) *adjective*
in or related to the regions with a warm climate that are near the tropical parts of the world: ***subtropical** vegetation* ◇ *a **subtropical** storm*
▶ **the subtropics** (*noun*): *It hardly ever snows in **the subtropics**.*

suburb (say **sub**-urb) *noun* (*plural* **suburbs**)
an area where people live that is outside the central part of a town or city: *We live in the **suburbs**.* ◇ *the northern **suburbs***
▶ **suburban** (*adjective*): ***suburban** areas*

subway (say **sub**-way) *noun* (*plural* **subways**)
1 a path that goes under a busy road, so that people can cross safely
2 a railway system that exists in tunnels under the ground: *a **subway** station* ➲ SYNONYM **underground**[2]

succeed (say suhk-**seed**) *verb* (**succeeding, succeeded**)
to do or get what you wanted to do or get: *She finally **succeeded** in getting a job.* ◇ *I tried to get a ticket for the concert but I didn't **succeed**.* ➲ OPPOSITE **fail** 2

success (say suhk-**sess**) *noun*
1 (*no plural*) doing or getting what you wanted, or doing well: *I wish you **success** with your studies.* ◇ *Hard work is the key to **success**.*
2 (*plural* **successes**) somebody or something that does well or that people like a lot: *That film was a great **success**.* ➲ OPPOSITE **failure** 1

successful (say suhk-**sess**-fuhl) *adjective*
If you are **successful**, you have got or done what you wanted, or you have become popular, rich, etc.: *a **successful** actor* ◇ *The party was very **successful**.* ➲ OPPOSITE **unsuccessful**
▶ **successfully** (*adverb*): *She completed her studies **successfully**.*

SPELLING Remember! You spell **success** and **successful** with **cc** and **ss**.

successive (say suhk-**sess**-iv) *adjective*
following one after the other in a series: *This is the team's third **successive** victory.*
▶ **successively** (*adverb*): ***successively** lower levels*

successor (say suhk-**sess**-uh) *noun* (*plural* **successors**)
a person or thing that comes after somebody or something else and takes up the same position ➲ OPPOSITE **predecessor**

succulent[1] (say **suk**-yuu-luhnt) *adjective*
1 (of a plant) that grows in dry climates and stores water in its thick leaves and stems
2 containing a lot of juice and tasting good: ***succulent** mangoes*

succulent[2] (say **suk**-yuu-luhnt) *noun* (*plural* **succulent**)
a plant, growing in dry climates, that stores water in its thick leaves and stems: *Cacti and aloes are **succulents**.*

succumb (say suh-**kum**) *verb* (**succumbing, succumbed**) (*formal*)
1 to stop fighting against something: *to **succumb** to temptation*
2 to die: *She **succumbed** to cancer.*

such *adjective*
1 a word that makes another word stronger: *He wears **such** strange clothes.* ◇ *It was **such** a nice day that we decided to go to the beach.* ➲ See note at **so**[1]
2 like this or that: *'Can I speak to Mrs Pule?' 'I'm sorry. There's no **such** person here.'*
such as words that you use to give an example ➲ SYNONYM **like**[2] 3: *Too many sweet foods **such as** chocolate are not good for you.*

suck (say **suk**) *verb* (**sucking, sucked**)
1 to pull something into your mouth, using your lips: *The baby **sucked** milk from its bottle.*
2 to hold something in your mouth and touch it a lot with your tongue: *She was **sucking** a sweet.*

sucker (say **suk**-uh) *noun* (*plural* **suckers**)
1 (*informal*) a person who trusts and believes people too easily and who is therefore easy to trick
2 a part of some plants, animals or insects that

A B C D E F G H I J K L M N O P Q R S T U V W X Y Z

is used for helping them stick onto a surface
➲ See illustration at **octopus**

suckle (say **suk**-l) *verb* (**suckling, suckled**)
1 to feed a baby milk from the mother's breast
2 to drink milk from the mother's breast
▸ **suckling** (*noun*): *The calf is a **suckling**. It still drinks from its mother's udder.*

sucrose (say ***suuk***-rohz) *noun* (*no plural*)
the form of sugar that comes from sugar **cane**[1] 1 ➲ See **glucose**

suction (say **suk**-shuhn) *noun* (*no plural*)
1 the action of removing air or liquid from a space in order to pull something else into that space or in order to cause something to stick to a surface
2 the force with which air or liquid is removed in order to pull something else into that space: *A vacuum cleaner works by **suction**.*

sudden (say **sud**-uhn) *adjective*
happening quickly when you do not expect it: *His death was very **sudden**.* ◇ *a **sudden** change in the weather* ➲ OPPOSITE **gradual**
all of a sudden suddenly: *We were watching TV when all of a **sudden** the lights went out.*

suddenly (say **sud**-uhn-lee) *adverb*
quickly and unexpectedly: *He got up and left very **suddenly**.* ◇ ***Suddenly** there was a loud noise.*

suds (say **sudz**) *plural noun*
bubbles that you get when you mix soap and water

sue (say **soo**) *verb* (**suing, sued**)
to go to a court of law and ask for money from a person who has done something bad to you: *Cigarette smokers **sued** the tobacco company.*

suede (say **swayd**) *noun* (*no plural*)
a type of soft leather with a rough surface: ***suede** boots*
🛈 ORIGIN: 17th century, from French *(gants de) Suède* meaning '(gloves of) Sweden'

suffer (say **suf**-uh) *verb* (**suffering, suffered**)
to feel pain, sadness or another unpleasant feeling: *She **suffers** from bad headaches.* ◇ *It's not right for children to **suffer**.*
▸ **suffering** (*noun*): *The people of that country have experienced so much **suffering**.*

sufficient (say suh-**fish**-uhnt) *adjective*
as much or as many as you need or want: *We had **sufficient** food to last two weeks.*
➲ SYNONYM **enough** ➲ OPPOSITE **insufficient**

suffix (say **suf**-ikss) *noun* (*plural* **suffixes**)
letters that you add to the end of a word to make another word: *If you add the **suffix** '-ly' to the adjective 'quick', you make the adverb 'quickly'.* ➲ See Study page 12 ➲ See **prefix**

suffocate (say **suf**-uh-kayt) *verb* (**suffocating, suffocated**)
to die or to make somebody die because there is no air to breathe

suffrage (say **suf**-rij) *noun* (*no plural*)
the right to vote in political elections: *universal suffrage* (= the right of all adult citizens to vote in an election)

sugar (say **sh*uu***-guh) *noun*
1 (*no plural*) a sweet substance, often in the form of small white or brown **crystals**, which comes from certain plants: *Do you take **sugar** in your coffee?*
2 (*plural* **sugars**) the amount of **sugar** that a small spoon can hold: *Two **sugars**, please.*
🛈 ORIGIN: 13th–15th century, through Old French *sukere*, through Italian *zucchero*, from Arabic *sukkar*

suggest (say suh-**jest**) *verb* (**suggesting, suggested**)
to say what you think somebody should do or what should happen: *I **suggest** that you stay here tonight.* ◇ *She **suggested** going for a walk.* ◇ *What do you **suggest**?*

suggestion (say suh-**jess**-tshuhn) *noun* (*plural* **suggestions**)
a plan or an idea that somebody thinks of for somebody else to discuss and consider: *I don't know what to buy Mum for her birthday. Have you got any **suggestions**?* ◇ *May I make a **suggestion**?*

suicide (say **soo**-i-side) *noun* (*plural* **suicides**)
the act of killing yourself: *He committed **suicide** at the age of 45.*
▸ **suicidal** (*adjective*): *She is feeling depressed and may be **suicidal*** (= wanting to kill herself).

suit[1] (say **soot**) *noun* (*plural* **suits**)
1 a jacket and trousers, or a jacket and skirt, that you wear together and that are made from the same material
2 one of the four sets of **playing cards**: *The four **suits** are hearts, clubs, diamonds and spades.*

suit[2] (say **soot**) *verb* (**suiting, suited**)
1 If something **suits** you, it looks good on you: *Does this hat **suit** me?*
2 to be right for you or to be what you want or need: *Would it **suit** you if I came at five o'clock?*

suitable (say **soo**-tuhb-l) *adjective*
right for somebody or something: *This film isn't **suitable** for children – it is very violent.*
➲ OPPOSITE **unsuitable**
▸ **suitably** (*adverb*): *He wasn't **suitably** dressed for a party.* ▸ **suitability** (*noun*): *I'm not sure about her **suitability** for the job.*

suitcase (say **soot**-kayss) *noun* (*plural* **suitcases**)
a large bag with flat sides in which you carry your clothes when you travel

suite (say **sweet**) *noun* (*plural* **suites**)
1 a set of rooms, especially in a hotel, which are used for a particular purpose: *the honeymoon **suite***
2 a set of two or more pieces of furniture for a particular room: *a lounge **suite***
3 (*computing*) a set of computer programs that are designed to work together: *a software **suite** for small businesses*

sulfur *noun* ➲ See **sulphur**

sulk *verb* (**sulking, sulked**)
to not speak because you are angry about something: *She's been **sulking** all day because her mum wouldn't let her go to the party.*
▸ **sulky** (*adjective*): *I can't stand **sulky** teenagers.*

sullen (say **sul**-uhn) *adjective*
looking bad-tempered and not wanting to speak to people: *a **sullen** expression*

sulphur (say **sul**-fuh) *noun* (also **sulfur**) (*no plural*) (symbol S)
a natural yellow substance that smells like bad eggs

SPELLING For many years this word was spelt in two ways: **sulphur** and **sulfur**. Scientists have agreed that in scientific writing the word must be spelt **sulfur**, not **sulphur**.

sulphuric acid (say sul-fyoo-rik **ass**-id) *noun* (*no plural*) (also **sulfuric acid**)
a strong colourless acid used in the chemical industry

sultan (say **sul**-tuhn) *noun* (*plural* **sultans**)
a king or ruler in some Muslim countries

sultry (say **sul**-tree) *adjective* (**sultrier, sultriest**)
1 (used about the weather) hot and making you uncomfortable
2 attractive in a way that causes feelings of sexual desire: *Kim is one of Hollywood's **sultriest** stars.*

sum[1] *noun* (*plural* **sums**)
1 an amount of money: *R200 000 is a large **sum** of money.*
2 the answer that you have when you add numbers together: *The **sum** of two and five is seven (2 + 5 = 7).*
3 a simple piece of work with numbers, for example adding or dividing: *Children have to learn how to do **sums**.*

sum[2] *verb* (**summing, summed**)
sum up
1 to describe or tell something again using fewer words: *The main arguments can be **summed** up in one sentence.*
2 to judge and describe in a few words how good, bad or important somebody or something is: *He **summed** the situation up immediately.*

summarize (say **sum**-uh-rize) *verb* (**summarizing, summarized**) (also **summarise**)
to describe the most important facts or main points of what somebody has said or written in a shorter form: ***Summarize** chapters 1 to 3 in one paragraph.*

summary (say **sum**-uh-ree) *noun* (*plural* **summaries**)
a short way of telling something by giving only the most important facts: *'To end the news, here is a **summary** of the top stories …'* ◇ *The teacher asked us to write a **summary** of the story we had read.* ➲ SYNONYM **synopsis**
🛈 ORIGIN: 14th–15th century, from Latin *summarius*, from *summa* meaning 'total, sum total'

summative (say **sum**-uh-tiv) *adjective*
relating to a process that teachers use to judge how much learners have learnt during a particular time: ***summative** assessment*

summer (say **sum**-uh) *noun* (*no plural*)
the part of the year (called a **season**) that comes between spring and autumn. **Summer** is the warmest season of the year: *the **summer** holidays* ◇ *I am going to visit my family in the **summer**.*

summit (say **sum**-it) *noun* (*plural* **summits**)
the top of a mountain

summon (say **sum**-uhn) *verb* (**summoning, summoned**) (*formal*) to order a person to come to a place: *The boys were **summoned** to the principal's office.*

summons (say **sum**-uhns) *noun* (*plural* **summonses**)
1 an order to appear in a court of law: *He received a **summons** to appear in court the following week.*
2 (*formal*) an order to come and see somebody: *to obey a royal **summons***

sumptuous (say **sump**-tsh*uu*-uhss) *adjective*
very expensive or looking very impressive or beautiful: *a **sumptuous** dinner at a fashionable restaurant*
▸ **sumptuously** (*adverb*): *a **sumptuously** flowering garden*

sun *noun* (*no plural*)
1 the sun the star that shines in the sky during the day and that gives us light and heat: *The **sun** is shining.*

A B C D E F G H I J K L M N O P Q R **S** T U V W X Y Z

A B C D E F G H I J K L M N O P Q R **S** T U V W X Y Z

2 light and heat from the sun: *You should put on sunblock to protect your skin from the **sun**.*

sunbathe (say **sun**-bay*th*) *verb* (**sunbathing, sunbathed**)
to lie in the sun so that your skin becomes darker: *We **sunbathed** on the beach.*
▸ **sunbathing** (*noun*): ***Sunbathing** is bad for your skin.*

sunblock (say **sun**-blok) *noun* (*no plural*)
a cream or liquid that you put on your skin to protect it from **sunburn** by completely blocking out the sun's rays

sunburn (say **sun**-burn) *noun* (*no plural*)
red painful skin that you get when you have been in the hot sun for too long ➲ See **suntan**
▸ **sunburned** (also **sunburnt**) (*adjective*): ***sunburned** shoulders*

Sunday (say **sun**-day) *noun*
the day of the week after Saturday and before Monday. People think of **Sunday** as either the first or the last day of the week. ➲ See note at **day**

sundial (say **sun**-dy-uhl) *noun* (*plural* **sundials**)
a simple instrument that measures time during the day by the position of the sun: *The shadow of the pointer on the **sundial** showed that it was four o'clock in the afternoon.*

sundry (say **sun**-dree) *adjective* (*formal*) of various kinds, but considered as a single group: *parrots of **sundry** colours ◇ books, paper, pens and **sundry** items*
all and sundry (*informal*) everybody: *Welcome to all and **sundry**.*

sunflower (say **sun**-flow-uh) *noun* (*plural* **sunflowers**)
a very tall plant with large yellow flowers and many seeds. **Sunflower** seeds and their oil are used in cooking: ***sunflower** oil ◇ **sunflower** seeds*

sung form of **sing**

sunglasses (say **sun**-glaa-suhz) *plural noun* (also *informal* **shades**)
glasses with dark glass in them that you wear in strong light: *a pair of **sunglasses***

sunk form of **sink**[1]

sunlight (say **sun**-lite) *noun* (*no plural*)
the light from the sun: *The room was full of **sunlight**.*
▸ **sunlit** (*adjective*): *a **sunlit** room*

Sunni (say *suu*-nee or **sun**-ee) *noun* (*plural* **Sunnis**)
a follower of the Sunni branch of Islam ➲ See **Shi'ite**

sunny (say **sun**-ee) *adjective* (**sunnier, sunniest**)
bright and warm with light from the sun: *a **sunny** day ◇ Tomorrow will be warm and **sunny**.*

sunrise (say **sun**-rize) *noun* (*no plural*)
the time in the morning when the sun comes up: *They got up before **sunrise**.* ➲ SYNONYM **dawn**

sunset (say **sun**-set) *noun* (*no plural*)
the time in the evening when the sun goes down: *The park closes at **sunset**.* ➲ SYNONYM **dusk**

sunshine (say **sun**-shine) *noun* (*no plural*)
the light and heat from the sun: *We sat outside in the **sunshine**.*

sunstroke (say **sun**-strohk) *noun* (*no plural*)
an illness you can get by spending too much time in the hot sun: *Drinking lots of water and wearing a hat can prevent you from getting **sunstroke**.*

suntan (say **sun**-tan) *noun* (*no plural*) (also **tan**)
When you have a **suntan**, your skin is browner than usual because you have been in the hot sun: *I'm trying to get a **suntan**.* ➲ See **sunburn**
▸ **suntanned** (also **tanned**) (*adjective*): ***suntanned** arms*

super (say **soo**-puh) *adjective* (*informal*)
very good: *That was a **super** meal.* ➲ SYNONYM **lovely**
🛈 ORIGIN: from Latin *super* meaning 'above, beyond'

super- (say **soo**-puh) *prefix*
1 larger, better or more important than others of the same kind: ***superhuman** ◇ a **superpower***
2 over, above or beyond: ***superimpose** ◇ **supernatural***

superb (say soo-**purb**) *adjective*
very good or beautiful: *a **superb** holiday ◇ The view from the window is **superb**.*
▸ **superbly** (*adverb*)

supercilious (say soo-puh-**sil**-i-uhss) *adjective* (*formal*)
showing that you think you are better or more important than other people: *a **supercilious** smile* ➲ SYNONYM **haughty**
▸ **superciliously** (*adverb*)

superficial (say soo-puh-**fish**-l) *adjective*
1 not understanding or thinking about something in a deep or complete way: *a **superficial** knowledge of a subject*
2 relating to or affecting the surface of something, or lying close to the surface: *a **superficial** wound ◇ **superficial** veins*

3 not caring about serious or important things or deep emotions: *She thinks fashion models are superficial.*
▶ **superficiality** (*noun*) ▶ **superficially** (*adverb*)

superfluous (say soo-**pur**-fluu-uhss) *adjective* (*formal*)
not useful or needed, or more than is needed: *Don't include **superfluous** information in your report.* ➲ SYNONYM **unnecessary**

PRONUNCIATION Notice how to say this word, especially which part should be stressed.

superhuman (say soo-puh-**hyoo**-muhn) *adjective*
greater than is usual for human beings: ***superhuman** strength*

superimpose (say soo-puh-rim-**pohz**) *verb* (**superimposing, superimposed**)
to put one thing on or over another thing so that what is underneath can still be seen: *The logo consists of a head of a lion **superimposed** on the shape of the African continent.*

superintendent (say soo-puh-rin-**ten**-duhnt) *noun* (*plural* **superintendents**)
1 a person who manages and controls a large building: *a hospital **superintendent***
2 a police officer with a high position: *Detective **Superintendent** Nkosi*

superior (say soo-**peer**-i-uh) *adjective*
1 better or more important than another person or thing: *I think fresh fruit is **superior** to tinned fruit.* ➲ OPPOSITE **inferior**
2 thinking you are better than other people
▶ **superiority** (*noun*): *an air of **superiority***
ℹ ORIGIN: 14th–15th century, from Old French *superiour*, from Latin *superior*, from *super* meaning 'above, beyond'

superlative (say soo-**pur**-luh-tiv) *noun* (*plural* **superlatives**) (*grammar*)
the form of an adjective or adverb that shows the most of something: *'Most intelligent', 'best' and 'fastest' are all **superlatives**.* ➲ See Study pages 10 and 11
▶ **superlative** (*adjective*): *'Youngest' is the **superlative** form of 'young'.* ➲ See **comparative**

supermarket (say **soo**-puh-maa-kit) *noun* (*plural* **supermarkets**)
a big shop where you can buy food, drinks and other goods for your home

WORD BUILDING When you shop in a **supermarket** you put the things you want to buy in a **basket** or a **trolley**. You pay for them all at the **till** or **checkout**.

supernatural (say soo-puh-**nat**-shruhl) *adjective*
that cannot be explained by science or the laws of nature, or relating to magic: *a **supernatural** force ◇ a creature with **supernatural** powers*

superpower (say **soo**-puh-**pow**-wuh) *noun* (*plural* **superpowers**)
one of the countries in the world that has greater military, economic or political power than most other nations, for example the USA

supersonic (say soo-puh-**son**-ik) *adjective*
faster than the speed of sound: *a **supersonic** aeroplane*

superstar (say **soo**-puh-staa) *noun* (*plural* **superstars**)
a person such as a singer or film star who is very famous and successful: *Madonna is a global **superstar**.*

superstition (say soo-puh-**sti**-shuhn) *noun* (*plural* **superstitions**)
a belief in good and bad luck and other things that cannot be explained: *People say that walking under a ladder brings bad luck, but it's just a **superstition**.*
▶ **superstitious** (*adjective*): *A lot of people are **superstitious** about the number thirteen.*

supervise (say **soo**-puh-vize) *verb* (**supervising, supervised**)
to watch somebody or something in order to see that people are working or behaving correctly: *It was his job to **supervise** the builders.*
➲ SYNONYM **oversee**
▶ **supervision** (*noun*): *Children must not use the pool without **supervision**.* ▶ **supervisor** (*noun*): *a factory **supervisor***

supper (say **sup**-uh) *noun* (*plural* **suppers**)
the last meal of the day: *We had **supper** and then went to bed.*

supple (say **sup**-l) *adjective* (**suppler, supplest**)
that bends or moves easily: *I'm **supple** and can touch my toes.* ➲ SYNONYM **flexible** 2
➲ OPPOSITE **stiff** 2
▶ **suppleness** (*noun*) ▶ **supplely** (*adverb*)

supplement (say **sup**-li-muhnt) *verb* (**supplementing, supplemented**)
to add to something: *You can **supplement** the work with extra reading.*
▶ **supplement** (*noun*): *a vitamin **supplement**.*
▶ **supplementary** (*adjective*): ***supplementary** exercises*

supply[1] (say suh-**ply**) *noun* (*plural* **supplies**)
a store or an amount of something that you need: *Food **supplies** were dropped by helicopter. ◇ The water **supply** was cut off.*

A B C D E F G H I J K L M N O P Q R S T U V W X Y Z

supply² (say suh-**ply**) *verb* (**supplying**, **supplied**)
to give or sell something that somebody needs: *The school **supplies** us with books.* ◇ *The lake **supplies** water to thousands of homes.*
▸ **supplier** (*noun*): *a **supplier** of computers*

support¹ (say suh-**pawt**) *verb* (**supporting**, **supported**)
1 to give strength, help or encouragement to someone or something: *Everybody else said I was wrong but he **supported** me.* ◇ *Which football team do you **support**?* ◇ *A local company is **supporting** the computer project.*
2 to help somebody to live by giving things such as money, a home or food: *She has three children to **support**.*
3 to hold somebody or something up so that they do not fall: *The bridge isn't strong enough to **support** heavy lorries.*
4 to help to show that something is true: *In your report, use examples that **support** your point of view.*
▸ **supportive** (*adjective*): *Thank you for being such a **supportive** friend.*

support² (say suh-**pawt**) *noun*
1 (*no plural*) help and encouragement that you give to a person or thing: *Thank you for all your **support**.*
2 (*plural* **supports**) something that holds up another thing: *a roof **support***

supporter (say suh-**pawt**-uh) *noun* (*plural* **supporters**)
a person who supports a political party or a sports team: *football **supporters***

suppose (say suh-**pohz**) *verb* (**supposing**, **supposed**)
1 to think that something is probably true or will probably happen: *'Where's Tsakani?' 'I don't know – I **suppose** she's still in the library.'*
2 a word that you use when you agree with something but are not happy about it: *'Can I borrow your pen?' 'Yes, I **suppose** so – but don't lose it.'*
be supposed to
1 If you **are supposed to** do something, you should do it: *You were **supposed** to help me with the work.*
2 (*informal*) If something **is supposed to** be true, people say it is true: *This is **supposed** to be a good book.*

supposing (say suh-**pohz**-ing) *conjunction*
if something happens or is true: ***Supposing** we miss the bus, how will we get to the airport?*

suppress (say suh-**press**) *verb* (**suppressing**, **suppressed**)
1 to stop something by using force: *The police **suppressed** the protesters.* ➲ SYNONYM **subdue**
2 to stop yourself from expressing your feelings: *She **suppressed** her giggles.*
3 to stop something from being seen or known: *to **suppress** the truth*
▸ **suppression** (*noun*)

supreme (say soo-**preem**) *adjective*
highest or most important: *the **Supreme** Court* (= the highest court in the land)

supremely (say soo-**preem**-lee) *adverb*
extremely: *He is **supremely** confident that he can win.*

sure (say **shoor**) *adjective, adverb* (**surer**, **surest**)
1 knowing that something is true or right: *I'm **sure** I've seen that man before.* ◇ *If you're not **sure** how to do it, ask your teacher.* ➲ SYNONYMS **certain** 1, **positive** 3
2 If you are **sure** to do something, you will certainly do it: *If you work hard, you're **sure** to pass the exam.*
for sure without any doubt: *I think he's coming to the party but I don't know for **sure**.*
make sure to check something so that you are certain about it: *Make **sure** you don't leave your bag on the bus.*
sure (*informal*) yes: *'Can I borrow this book?' '**Sure**.'*
sure enough as I thought: *I said they would be late, and **sure** enough they were.*

surely (say **shoor**-lee) *adverb*
a word that you use when you think that something must be true, or when you are surprised: *This will **surely** cause problems.* ◇ ***Surely** you know where your brother works!*

surf¹ (say **surf**) *noun* (*no plural*)
the white part on the top of waves in the sea

surf² (say **surf**) *verb* (**surfing**, **surfed**) (also **go surfing**)
to stand or lie on a long piece of wood or plastic (called a **surfboard**) and ride on a wave: *We went **surfing** in Margate.*
surf the Net, **surf the Internet** to use the Internet: *He spends hours every day **surfing** the Net.*
▸ **surfer** (*noun*): *The beach is popular with **surfers**.*

surface (say **sur**-fuhss) *noun* (*plural* **surfaces**)
1 the outside part of something: *the Earth's **surface*** ◇ *The road has a very uneven **surface**.*
2 the top part of an area of water: *She dived below the **surface**.*
▸ **surface** (*verb*): *She dived into the water and, after a few moments, she **surfaced*** (= came to the top).

A B C D E F G H I J K L M N O P Q R S T U V W X Y Z

surfboard (say **surf**-bawd) *noun* (*plural* **surfboards**)
a long piece of wood or plastic that you sit or lie on to ride on a wave

surfing (say **surf**-ing) *noun* (*no plural*)
the sport of riding on waves while standing on a **surfboard**: *His favourite hobby is **surfing**.*

surge (say **surj**) *noun* (*plural* **surges**)
1 a sudden strong movement by a large number of people or things: *a **surge** forward* ◇ *a **surge** in prices*
2 a sudden strong feeling: *a **surge** of excitement*
▸ **surge** (*verb*): *The crowd **surged** towards the gate.*

surgeon (say **sur**-juhn) *noun* (*plural* **surgeons**)
a doctor who cuts your body to take out or repair a part inside, as part of a medical operation: *a brain **surgeon***
ⓘ **ORIGIN**: 13th–15th century, through Old French *serurgien*, through Latin from Greek *kheirourgia* meaning 'surgery' from *kheir* meaning 'hand' + *ergon* meaning 'work'

surgery (say **sur**-juh-ree) *noun*
1 (*no plural*) cutting a person's body to take out or repair a part inside: *He needed **surgery** after the accident.*
2 (*plural* **surgeries**) a place or time when a doctor or dentist sees patients: *The doctor's **surgery** is open from 9.00 till 4.30.*

surly (say **sur**-lee) *adjective* (**surlier**, **surliest**)
unfriendly and rude: *He was **surly** today.*
▸ **surliness** (*noun*)

surmise (say suh-**mize**) *verb* (**surmising**, **surmised**) (*formal*)
to guess something based on evidence: *From their beaks, we can **surmise** that sparrows eat seeds.*

surname (say **sur**-naym) *noun* (*plural* **surnames**)
the name that a family has: *Her name is Jane Compton; Compton is her **surname**.*

surpass (say suh-**paass**) *verb* (**surpassing**, **surpassed**) (*formal*)
to do something better than somebody or something else, or better than expected: *You **surpassed** our expectations.* ➲ **SYNONYMS** **better**[3], **exceed**
▸ **surpassing** (*adjective*)

surplus (say **sur**-pluhss) *noun* (*plural* **surpluses**)
an amount that is extra or more than you need: *a budget **surplus*** ◇ *There is a food **surplus** in some countries* ➲ **OPPOSITE** **deficit**
▸ **surplus** (*adjective*): *There are **surplus** funds in your account.*

surprise[1] (say suh-**prize**) *noun*
1 (*no plural*) the feeling that you have when something that you did not expect happens suddenly: *He looked up in **surprise** when I walked in.* ◇ *To my **surprise**, everyone agreed with me.*
2 (*plural* **surprises**) something that happens when you do not expect it: *Don't tell him about the party – it's a **surprise**!*
take somebody by surprise to happen when somebody does not expect it: *The news took me completely by **surprise**.*

surprise[2] (say suh-**prize**) *verb* (**surprising**, **surprised**)
to do something that somebody does not expect: *I arrived early to **surprise** her.* ◇ *We **surprised** him on his birthday with a new soccer ball.*

surprised (say suh-**prize**-d) *adjective*
If you are **surprised**, you feel or show surprise: *I was **surprised** to see him yesterday – I thought he was still in hospital.*

surprising (say suh-**prize**-ing) *adjective*
If something is **surprising**, it makes you feel surprise: *The news was **surprising**.*
▸ **surprisingly** (*adverb*): *The exam was **surprisingly** easy.*

surrender (say suh-**ren**-duh) *verb* (**surrendering**, **surrendered**)
to stop fighting and allow yourself to be captured because you cannot win: *After six hours on the roof, the man **surrendered** to the police.*
▸ **surrender** (*noun*): *We will not even consider **surrender**.*

surreptitious (say su-ruhp-**tish**-uhss) *adjective*
done secretly: *I took a **surreptitious** peep at her work.*
▸ **surreptitiously** (*adverb*): *He **surreptitiously** passed me a note.*

surround (say suh-**rownd**) *verb* (**surrounding**, **surrounded**)
to be or go all around something: *The lake is **surrounded** by trees.*

surroundings (say suh-**rownd**-ingz) *plural noun*
everything around you, or the place where you live: *I don't like seeing animals in a zoo – I prefer to see them in their natural **surroundings**.*
➲ See **environment** 1

surveillance (say suh-**vay**-luhnss) *noun* (*no plural*)
the careful watching of somebody who may have done something wrong: *They are under **surveillance** by the police.* ◇ ***surveillance** cameras*

survey[1] (say **sur**-vay) *noun* (*plural* **surveys**)
1 asking questions to find out what people

think or do: *to carry out a* ***survey*** ◇ *We did a* ***survey*** *of people's favourite TV programmes.*
2 the action of examining an area of land and making a map of it: *an aerial* ***survey***

survey[2] (say suh-**vay**) *verb* (**surveying, surveyed**)
1 to examine something carefully: *She* ***surveyed*** *all the children in her new class.*
2 to take exact measurements in order to calculate the position, form or size of something, usually an area of land: *I* ***surveyed*** *my property to determine its exact boundaries.*

surveyor (say suh-**vay**-uh) *noun* (*plural* **surveyors**)
a person who takes exact measurements in order to calculate the position, form or size of something, usually an area of land: *a land* ***surveyor*** ◇ *a quantity* ***surveyor***

survive (say suh-**vive**) *verb* (**surviving, survived**)
to continue to live in or after a difficult or dangerous time: *Camels can* ***survive*** *for many days without water.* ◇ *Only one person* ***survived*** *the plane crash.*
▸ **survival** (*noun*): *Food and water are necessary for* ***survival***. ▸ **survivor** (*noun*): *The government sent help to the* ***survivors*** *of the earthquake.*

susceptible (say suh-**sep**-tuhb-l) *adjective*
easily affected by something: *This plant is* ***susceptible*** *to frost.*

suspect[1] (say suh-**spekt**) *verb* (**suspecting, suspected**)
1 to think that something is true, but not be certain: *He wasn't at college today – I* ***suspect*** *that he's ill.*
2 to think that somebody has done something wrong but not be certain: *They* ***suspect*** *Helen of stealing the money.* ➲ The adjective is **suspicious** ➲ The noun is **suspicion**

suspect[2] (say **suss**-pekt) *noun* (*plural* **suspects**)
a person who you think has done something wrong: *The police have arrested two* ***suspects***.

suspend (say suh-**spend**) *verb* (**suspending, suspended**)
1 to hang something from something else: *Coloured flags were* ***suspended*** *from the ceiling.*
2 to stop or delay something for a time: *The bus service was* ***suspended*** *during the strike.*
3 to officially stop somebody doing their job, going to school, etc. for a time: *The learner was* ***suspended*** *while the complaint was investigated.*
ⓘ **ORIGIN:** 13th–15th century, from Old French *suspendre* or Latin *suspendere*, from *sub-* meaning 'from below' + *pendere* meaning 'hang'

suspense (say suh-**spenss**) *noun* (*no plural*)
a feeling of excitement or worry that you have when you are waiting for news or for something to happen: *Don't keep me in* ***suspense*** *– did you pass the exam?*

suspension (say suh-**spen**-shuhn) *noun*
1 (*plural* **suspensions**) the act of officially removing somebody from their job, school, team, etc. for a time, usually as a punishment: ***suspension*** *from school* ◇ *The rugby players are appealing against their* ***suspensions***.
2 (*no plural*) the act of delaying something for a time: *the* ***suspension*** *of bus services*
3 (*no plural*) the parts that are connected to the wheels of a car, etc. that make it more comfortable to ride in
4 (*plural* **suspensions**) (*science*) a liquid with very small pieces of solid matter floating in it, or the state of such a liquid

suspicion (say suh-**spish**-uhn) *noun* (*plural* **suspicions**)
1 a feeling that somebody has done something wrong: *He was arrested on* ***suspicion*** *of murder.*
2 an idea that is not totally certain: *We have a* ***suspicion*** *that she is unhappy.* ➲ The verb is **suspect**[1]

suspicious (say suh-**spish**-uhss) *adjective*
1 If you are **suspicious**, you do not believe somebody or something, or you feel that something is wrong: *The police are* ***suspicious*** *of her story.*
2 A person or thing that is **suspicious** makes you feel that something is wrong: *Anyone who sees anything* ***suspicious*** *should contact the police.*
▸ **suspiciously** (*adverb*)

sustain (say suh-**stayn**) *verb* (**sustaining, sustained**)
1 to keep something or somebody alive and healthy: *Earth is the only planet we know that can* ***sustain*** *life.*
2 to make something continue for some time without becoming less: *Can you* ***sustain*** *a conversation with an adult?*
3 (*formal*) to experience something bad: *He* ***sustained*** *an injury to his knee.*

sustainable (say suh-**stayn**-uhb-l) *adjective*
1 involving the use of natural products and energy in a way that does not harm the environment: *the development of* ***sustainable*** *fuel*
2 that can continue or be continued for a long time: *a* ***sustainable*** *eating plan* ➲ **OPPOSITE unsustainable**
▸ **sustainability** (*noun*)

sustenance (say **suss**-tuh-nuhnss) *noun* (*no plural*) (*formal*)
the food and drink that people, animals and plants need to stay alive: *They relied on wild fruits for* ***sustenance****.*

SW *abbreviation* **south-west**

swab (say **swob**) *noun* (*plural* **swabs**)
1 a piece of soft material used by a doctor or a nurse for cleaning a place where your body has been hurt, or for taking a substance from your body to test it: *She used a* ***swab*** *of cotton to clean the cut.*
2 the act of taking a substance from a person's body to test it: *a throat* ***swab***
▶ **swab** (*verb*)

swagger (say **swag**-uh) *verb* (**swaggering, swaggered**)
to walk in a way that shows you are too confident or proud: *He* ***swaggered*** *across the room swinging his car keys.* ➲ SYNONYM **strut**
▶ **swagger** (*noun*): *She walked with a* ***swagger****.*

swallow¹ (say **swol**-oh) *verb* (**swallowing, swallowed**)
to make food or drink move down your throat from your mouth: *I can't* ***swallow*** *these pills without water.*

swallow² (say **swol**-oh) *noun* (*plural* **swallows**)
a small bird with a long tail

swam form of **swim**

swamp¹ (say **swomp**) *noun* (*plural* **swamps**)
an area of soft wet ground or ground that is covered with water

swamp² (say **swomp**) *verb* (**swamping, swamped**)
1 to cover or fill something with water: *As glaciers melt they raise sea levels and* ***swamp*** *coastal areas.*
2 to have more of something than you can deal with or to give somebody more of something than they can deal with: *I can't go out tonight, I'm* ***swamped*** *with work.*

swan (say **swon**) *noun* (*plural* **swans**)
a big white bird with a very long neck. **Swans** live on rivers and lakes.

swap (say **swop**) *verb* (**swapping, swapped**) (also **swop**)
to change one thing for another thing or to give one thing and get another thing for it: *Do you want to* ***swap*** *chairs with me* (= you have my chair and I'll have yours)*?* ◇ *I* ***swapped*** *my CD for Tom's* (= I had his and he had mine).
▶ **swap** (*noun*): *Why don't we do a swap?*

swarm¹ (say **swawm**) *noun* (*plural* **swarms**)
a big group of flying insects: *a* ***swarm*** *of bees*

swarm² (say **swawm**) *verb* (**swarming, swarmed**)
to fly or move quickly in a big group: *The supporters* ***swarmed*** *into the stadium.*

swastika (say **swoss**-ti-kuh) *noun* (*plural* **swastikas**)
an ancient symbol of a cross with the ends bent at a right angle: *A* ***swastika*** *is used as a symbol for Nazi Germany.*

swat (say **swot**) *verb* (**swatting, swatted**)
to hit something, especially an insect, with something flat: ***Swat*** *the flies near the food!*

sway *verb* (**swaying, swayed**)
to move slowly from side to side: *The trees were* ***swaying*** *in the wind.*

Swazi (say **swah**-zi) another word for **Siswati**

swear (say **swair**) *verb* (**swearing, swore, has sworn**)
1 to say rude or bad words: *Don't* ***swear*** *at your mother!*
2 to make a serious promise: *He* ***swears*** *that he is telling the truth.*
▶ **swearing** (*noun*)

swear word *noun* (*plural* **swear words**)
a rude or bad word that may upset people

sweat (say **swet**) *verb* (**sweating, sweated**)
to produce liquid through your skin because you are hot, ill or afraid: *The room was so hot that everyone was* ***sweating****.* ➲ SYNONYM **perspire**
▶ **sweat** (*noun*): *He wiped the* ***sweat*** *from his forehead.*

sweater (say **swet**-uh) *noun* (*plural* **sweaters**)
a warm knitted piece of clothing made of wool or cotton, which has long sleeves and which you wear on the top part of your body

sweatshirt (say **swet**-shurt) *noun* (*plural* **sweatshirts**)
a warm piece of clothing made of thick cotton, which has long sleeves, and which you wear on the top part of your body

sweaty (say **swet**-ee) *adjective* (**sweatier, sweatiest**)
covered with sweat: ***sweaty*** *socks* ◇ *I'm all hot and* ***sweaty*** *– I need a shower.*

sweep *verb* (**sweeping, swept**)
1 to clean something by moving dirt or rubbish away with a broom: *I've* ***swept*** *the floor.*
2 to push something along or away quickly and strongly: *The bridge was* ***swept*** *away by the floods.*
sweep up, sweep something up to remove dirt or rubbish using a brush: *I* ***swept*** *up the broken glass.*

A B C D E F G H I J K L M N O P Q R S T U V W X Y Z

sweet[1] *adjective* (**sweeter, sweetest**)
1 containing or tasting of sugar: *Honey is **sweet**.*
2 with a good smell: *the **sweet** smell of roses*
3 attractive or pretty: *What a **sweet** little girl!*
➲ SYNONYM **cute**
4 having or showing a kind character: *It was **sweet** of you to help me.*

sweet[2] *noun* (*plural* **sweets**)
1 a small piece of sweet food: *He bought a packet of **sweets** for the children.*
2 sweet food that you eat at the end of a meal: *Do you want a **sweet**?* ➲ SYNONYM **dessert**

sweetcorn (say **sweet**-kawn) *noun* (*no plural*)
the sweet yellow seeds of a tall plant (called **maize**) that you eat as a vegetable

sweetheart (say **sweet**-haat) *noun* (*no plural*)
a word that you use when speaking to a person that you love: *Do you want a drink, **sweetheart**?*

sweetly (say **sweet**-lee) *adverb*
in a pretty, kind or nice way: *She smiled **sweetly**.*

swell[1] (say **swel**) *verb* (**swelling, swelled, has swollen** or **has swelled**)
swell up to become bigger or thicker than normal: *After he hurt his ankle it **swelled** up.*

swell[2] (say **swel**) *noun* (*plural* **swells**)
the slow movement, up and down, of the sea: *There are huge **swells** today.*

swelling (say **swel**-ing) *noun* (*plural* **swellings**)
a place on the body that is bigger or fatter than it usually is: *He's got a **swelling** on his leg where an insect stung him.* ➲ See **swollen**

sweltering (say **swel**-tuh-ring) *adjective*
uncomfortably hot: *It's a **sweltering** day.*

swept form of **sweep**

swerve (say **swurv**) *verb* (**swerving, swerved**)
to change direction suddenly so that you do not hit somebody or something: *The driver **swerved** when he saw the child in the road.*

swift *adjective* (**swifter, swiftest**)
quick or fast: *We made a **swift** decision.*
▸ **swiftly** (*adverb*): *She ran **swiftly** up the stairs.*

swim *verb* (**swimming, swam, has swum**)
to move your body through water: *Can you swim?* ◇ *I **swam** across the lake.*
▸ **swim** (*noun*): *Let's go for a **swim**.*
▸ **swimmer** (*noun*): *He's a good **swimmer**.*
▸ **swimming** (*noun*): ***Swimming** is my favourite sport.*
🛈 ORIGIN: from Old English *swimman*, related to Dutch *zwemmen*

> USAGE When you talk about spending time swimming as a sport, you usually say **go swimming**: *I **go swimming** every day.*

swimming costume *noun* (*plural* **swimming costumes**) (also **swimsuit**)
a piece of clothing that you wear for swimming

swimming pool *noun* (*plural* **swimming pools**) (also **pool**)
a place that is built for people to swim in: *an open-air **swimming pool***

swimsuit (say **swim**-soot) *noun* (*plural* **swimsuits**) another word for **swimming costume**

swing[1] *verb* (**swinging, swung**)
1 to move backwards and forwards or from side to side through the air, or to make somebody or something do this: *Monkeys were **swinging** from the trees.* ◇ *He **swung** his arms as he walked.*
2 to move in a curve: *The door **swung** open.*

swing[2] *noun* (*plural* **swings**)
a seat that hangs down and that children can sit on to move backwards and forwards through the air

swipe *verb* (**swiping, swiped**) (*informal*)
1 to hit or try to hit something by swinging either your arm or an object that you are holding: *He **swiped** at the ball and missed.*
2 to steal something

swirl (say **swurl**) *verb* (**swirling, swirled**)
to make or cause something to make fast circular movements: *The tea **swirled** in my cup when I stirred it.*
▸ **swirl** (*noun*) *a **swirl** of wind*

switch[1] (say **swich**) *noun* (*plural* **switches**)
a small thing that you press to turn electricity on or off: *Where is the light **switch**?*

switch[2] (say **swich**) *verb* (**switching, switched**)
to change to something different: *I **switched** to another seat because I couldn't see the film.*
switch something off to make a light or a machine stop working by pressing a **switch**[1]: *I **switched** the TV off.* ◇ *Don't forget to **switch** off the lights!*
switch something on to make a light or a machine work by pressing a **switch**: ***Switch** the radio on.*

switchboard (say **swich**-bawd) *noun* (*plural* **switchboards**)
the place in a large company where somebody answers telephone calls and sends them to the right people

swivel (say **swiv**-l) *verb* (**swivelling, swivelled**)
to turn around a central point, or to make something do this: *She **swivelled** in her chair.*

swollen[1] (say **swoh**-luhn) form of **swell**[1]

swollen[2] (say **swoh**-luhn) *adjective*
(used about a part of the body) thicker or fatter than it usually is: *a **swollen** ankle* ➲ See **swelling**

PRONUNCIATION Notice how to say **swollen**: the first part rhymes with '**so**'.

swoop (*rhymes with* **loop**) *verb* (**swooping**, **swooped**)
to fly down quickly: *The eagle **swooped** down low and caught the mouse.*

swop *verb* = **swap**

sword (say **sawd**) *noun* (*plural* **swords**)
a weapon that looks like a very long sharp knife

PRONUNCIATION Don't pronounce the **w** in **sword**.

swore, sworn (say **swaw**, **swawn**) forms of **swear**

swot[1] *verb* (**swotting**, **swotted**) (*informal*)
to study hard before an exam: *She is **swotting** for her test next week.*

swot[2] *noun* (*plural* **swots**) (*informal*)
a person who spends too much time studying

swum form of **swim**

swung form of **swing**[1]

sycophant (say **sik**-uh-fant) *noun* (*plural* **sycophants**) (*formal*)
a person who says nice things that are not sincere to somebody because they want something from this person
▸ **sycophantic** (*adjective*)

syllable (say **sil**-uhb-l) *noun* (*plural* **syllables**)
a part of a word that has one vowel sound when you say it. 'Swim' has one **syllable** and 'system' has two **syllables**.

syllabus (say **sil**-uh-buhss) *noun* (*plural* **syllabuses** or **syllabi**)
a list of all the things that you must study in a course or subject

symbiosis (say sim-by-**oh**-siss) *noun* (*plural* **symbioses**)
a close relationship between two different kinds of living things so that both can help each other
▸ **symbiotic** (*adjective*): *There is a **symbiotic** relationship between bees and flowers. Bees need nectar from flowers and flowers need bees for pollination.*

symbol (say **simb**-l) *noun* (*plural* **symbols**)
a mark, sign or picture that has a special meaning: *O is the **symbol** for oxygen.* ◇ *A dove is the **symbol** of peace.*

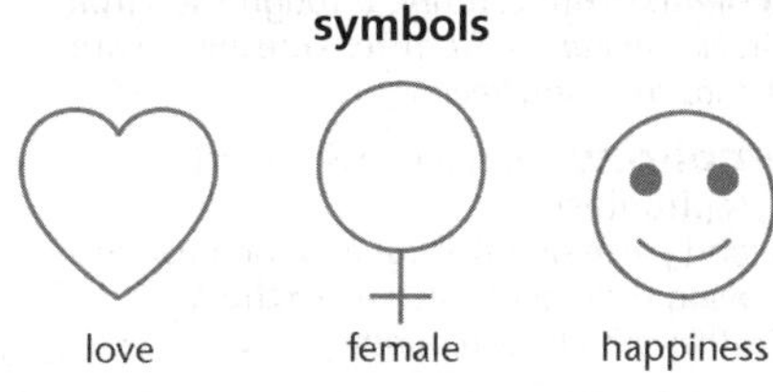

symbolism (say **sim**-buh-liz-m) *noun* (*no plural*)
the use of symbols to represent things, especially in art and literature ➲ See **realism** 2

symmetrical (say si-**met**-rik-l) *adjective* (also **symmetric**)
having two halves that match each other exactly in size, shape, etc.: ***symmetrical** patterns* ➲OPPOSITE **asymmetrical**

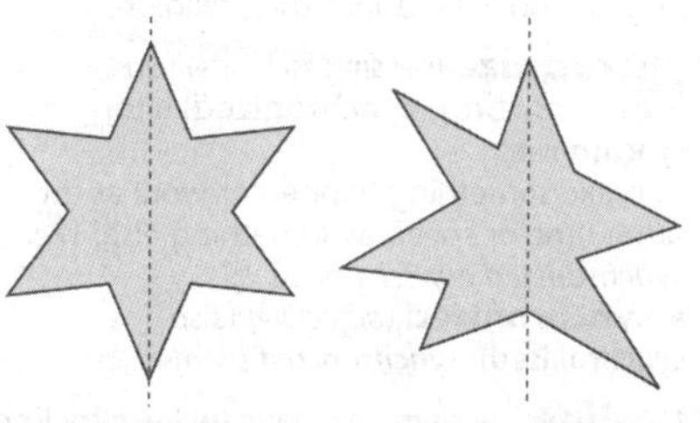

symmetry (say **sim**-uh-tree) *noun* (*no plural*)
the quality of having two halves on either side of a dividing line that match each other exactly in shape and size

sympathetic (say sim-puh-**thet**-ik) *adjective*
showing that you understand other people's feelings when they have problems: *Everyone was very **sympathetic** when I was ill.* ➲ OPPOSITE **unsympathetic**
▸ **sympathetically** (*adverb*): *He smiled **sympathetically**.*

sympathize (say **sim**-puh-thize) *verb* (**sympathizing**, **sympathized**) (also **sympathise**)
to show that you understand somebody's feelings when they have problems: *I **sympathize** with you – I've got a lot of work to do too.*

A B C D E F G H I J K L M N O P Q R S T U V W X Y Z

sympathy (say **sim**-puh-thee) *noun* (*no plural*)
understanding of another person's feelings and problems: *We all felt* ***sympathy*** *for the victims of the accident.*
ⓘ **ORIGIN:** 16th century, through Latin from Greek *sumpathēs*, from *sun-* meaning 'with' + *pathos* meaning 'feeling'

symphony (say **sim**-fuh-nee) *noun* (*plural* **symphonies**)
a long piece of music for a lot of musicians playing together (called an **orchestra**): *Beethoven's fifth* ***symphony***

symptom (say **simp**-tuhm) *noun* (*plural* **symptoms**)
a change in your body that shows that you have an illness: *A sore throat is often a* ***symptom*** *of a cold.*

synagogue (say **sin**-uh-gog) *noun* (*plural* **synagogues**)
a building where Jewish people go to say prayers and learn about their religion

synchronize (say **sing**-kruh-nize) *verb* (**synchronizing**, **synchronized**) (also **synchronise**)
to make something happen or work at the same time or speed as something else: *We* ***synchronized*** *our schedules.*
▸ **synchronized** (*adjective*) (also **synchronised**): ***synchronized*** *swimming*

syncline (say **sing**-kline) *noun* (*plural* **synclines**) (*geography*)
folded layers of rock shaped like a valley ➲ See illustration at **anticline**

syndrome (say **sin**-drohm) *noun* (*plural* **syndromes**)
1 a group of signs or changes in the body that are typical of an illness or condition: *Down's* ***Syndrome*** ◇ *Acquired Immunodeficiency* ***Syndrome*** *(Aids)*
2 a set of opinions or a way of behaving that is typical of a particular person, attitude or social problem

synonym (say **sin**-uh-nim) *noun* (*plural* **synonyms**)
a word or phrase that means the same as another word or phrase in the same language: *'Big' and 'large' are* ***synonyms.*** ➲ **OPPOSITE** **antonym**

synopsis (say si-**nop**-sis) *noun* (*plural* **synopses**)
a short description of the main points of something such as a story or play: *We wrote a* ***synopsis*** *of the novel.* ➲ **SYNONYM** **summary**

synoptic (say si-**nop**-tik) *adjective*
relating to a large or general view of something: *The* ***synoptic*** *charts showed the weather conditions over a large area.*

synthesis *noun*
1 (*plural* **syntheses**) the act of combining separate ideas, beliefs, facts, styles, etc., often to create something new: *a* ***synthesis*** *of traditional and modern values* ➲ See Study page 19
2 (*no plural*) (*biology*) the natural chemical production of a substance in animals and plants: *protein* ***synthesis***
3 (*no plural*) the artificial production of a substance that is present naturally in animals and plants: *the* ***synthesis*** *of penicillin*
4 (*no plural*) the production of sounds, music or speech by electronic means: *speech* ***synthesis***

synthesizer (say **sin**-thuh-sy-zuh) *noun* (*plural* **synthesizers**) (also **synthesiser**)
an electronic musical instrument that can produce many different sounds

synthetic (say sin-**thet**-ik) *adjective*
made by people and not natural: *Nylon is a* ***synthetic*** *material, but wool is natural.*
➲ **SYNONYM** **artificial**

syphilis (say **sif**-i-liss) *noun* (*no plural*)
a serious disease that someone can get from having sexual contact with an infected person

syringe (say si-**rinj**) *noun* (*plural* **syringes**)
a plastic or glass tube with a needle that is used for taking blood out of the body or putting medicine into the body

syrup (say **si**-ruhp) *noun* (*no plural*)
a thick sweet liquid made by boiling sugar with water or fruit juice: *peaches in* ***syrup***
ⓘ **ORIGIN:** 14th–15th century, from Old French *sirop*, from Arabic *šarāb* meaning 'beverage'

system (say **siss**-tuhm) *noun* (*plural* **systems**)
1 a set of ideas or ways of doing or organizing something: *'Do you have a* ***system*** *for organizing the books in your bookshelf?' 'Yes, I order them alphabetically.'* ◇ *We have a new computerized* ***system*** *in the library.*
2 a group of things or parts that work together: *the transport* ***system*** ◇ *the health* ***system***

systematic (say siss-tuh-**mat**-ik) *adjective*
done using a fixed plan or system: *You should be* ***systematic*** *when checking your work.*
➲ **SYNONYM** **methodical**
▸ **systematically** (*adverb*)

systemic (say siss-**tem**-ik) *adjective*
affecting or connected with an entire system, especially the human body: ***systemic*** *therapy* ◇ *a* ***systemic*** *poison*

Tt

t *abbreviation* (*plural* **t**) **ton** 1

table (say **tayb**-l) *noun* (*plural* **tables**)
1 a piece of furniture with a flat top on legs: *a coffee **table***
2 a list of facts or numbers. A **table** is usually arranged in rows and columns: *a **table** with three columns and five rows* ◇ *There is a **table** of irregular verbs at the back of this dictionary.*

tableau (say **tab**-loh) *noun* (*plural* **tableaux**)
a group of models or actors who represent a scene from a story or from history: *End your performance with a **tableau** of the scene.*

tablecloth (say **tay**-buhl-kloth) *noun* (*plural* **tablecloths**)
a cloth that you put over a table when you have a meal

tablespoon (say **tay**-buhl-spoon) *noun* (*plural* **tablespoons**)
a big spoon that you use for putting food on plates

tablet (say **tab**-luht) *noun* (*plural* **tablets**)
a small hard piece of medicine that you swallow: *Take two of these **tablets** before every meal.* ➲ SYNONYM **pill**

table tennis *noun* (also *informal* **ping pong**) (*no plural*)
a game where players use a small round bat to hit a small light ball over a net on a big table

tabloid (say **tab**-loyd) *noun* (*plural* **tabloids**)
1 a newspaper with small pages, usually half the size of larger newspapers
2 (sometimes disapproving) a newspaper of this size with short articles and a lot of pictures and stories about famous people, often thought of as less serious than other newspapers

taboo (say tuh-**boo**) *noun* (*plural* **taboos**)
something that you must not say or do because it might shock or offend people or make them embarrassed: *That is **taboo** in some cultures.* ◇ *It's a **taboo**.*
🛈 ORIGIN: 18th century, from Tongan *tabu* meaning 'set apart, forbidden'. Tongan is a Polynesian language. The word was introduced into English by Captain James Cook, an English ship's captain and explorer who made several scientific expeditions to the Pacific.

tabular (say **tab**-yuh-luh) *adjective*
arranged or presented in a table: *Give your results in **tabular** form.*

tabulate (say **tab**-yuh-layt) *verb* (**tabulating, tabulated**)
to arrange or present information in a table: ***Tabulate** your results.*

tack (say **tak**) *noun* (*plural* **tacks**)
a type of short nail with a large head that you use to fasten paper to a board: *Use **tacks** to put the pictures up.* ➲ See **drawing pin**

tackie (say **tak**-ee) *noun* (*plural* **tackies**) (also **takkie**) (*S. African, informal*)
a light shoe made of strong cloth with a rubber sole

tackle[1] (say **tak**-l) *verb* (**tackling, tackled**)
1 to try to deal with a difficult problem or situation: *How shall we **tackle** this problem?*
2 to try to take the ball from or to stop somebody in a game such as football
3 to try to catch and hold somebody: *The police officer **tackled** one of the robbers as he ran out.*

tackle[2] (say **tak**-l) *noun* (*plural* **tackles**)
1 an act of trying to get the ball from somebody or stopping somebody in a game like football: *a rugby **tackle***
2 the equipment used in a particular sport or activity, especially fishing: *all my fishing **tackle***

tacky (say **tak**-ee) *adjective* (**tackier, tackiest**) (*informal*)
1 cheap and of bad quality: *a shop selling **tacky** souvenirs*
2 (used about paint, for example) sticky and not quite dry

tact (say **takt**) *noun* (*no plural*)
knowing how and when to say things so that you do not hurt or insult people: *She handled the situation with great **tact**.*

tactful (say **takt**-fuhl) *adjective*
careful not to say or do things that may make people unhappy or angry: *That wasn't a very **tactful** thing to say!* ➲ OPPOSITE **tactless**
▸ **tactfully** (*adverb*)

tactic (say **tak**-tik) *noun*
1 (*plural* **tactics**) the particular method or plan that you use to achieve something: *What **tactic** did you use to win?* ➲ SYNONYM **strategy**
2 tactics (*plural noun*) the skilful arrangement and use of military forces in order to win a battle
▸ **tactical** (*adjective*)

A B C D E F G H I J K L M N O P Q R S **T** U V W X Y Z

tactile (say **tak**-tile) *adjective*
1 relating to or connected with the sense of touch
2 able to be touched or felt ➲ SYNONYM **tangible**
3 using your touch

tactless (say **takt**-luhss) *adjective*
saying or doing things that may make people unhappy or angry: *It was **tactless** of you to ask how old she was.* ➲ OPPOSITE **tactful**

tadpole (say **tad**-pohl) *noun* (*plural* **tadpoles**)
a young form of a **frog** when it has a tail and swims in water. Young **tadpoles** have no legs, but these develop as they grow: *A **tadpole** is in the larval stage of its metamorphosis.* ➲ See illustration at **life cycle**

tag *noun* (*plural* **tags**)
a small piece of paper or material fixed to something which tells you about it: *I looked at the price **tag** to see how much the dress cost.* ➲ SYNONYM **label**[1]

tail (say **tayl**) *noun* (*plural* **tails**)
1 the long thin part at the end of an animal's body: *The dog wagged its **tail**.*
2 the part at the back of something: *the **tail** of an aeroplane*
3 tails (*plural noun*) the side of a coin that does not have the head of a person or the symbol for the country (called **the coat of arms**) on it. ➲ See **head** 6

tailings (say **tay**-lingz) *plural noun*
waste material that is left when the metal is taken out of **ore**

tailor (say **tay**-luh) *noun* (*plural* **tailors**)
a person whose job is to make clothes for men

take (say **tayk**) *verb* (**taking**, **took**, **has taken**)
1 to hold something: ***Take** this money – it's yours.* ◇ *She **took** my hand and led me outside.* ➲ See note at **bring**
2 to remove something from a place or a person, often without asking them: *Somebody has **taken** my bike.* ◇ *I **took** the scissors away from the child.*
3 to eat or drink something: *Don't forget to **take** your medicine.*
4 to accept something: ***Take** my advice and forget about him.*
5 to need an amount of time or space: *The journey **took** four hours.* ◇ *The bed **takes** up half the room.*
6 to travel in a bus, train, etc.: *I **took** a taxi to the hospital.*
take after somebody to be like or look like an older member of your family: *She **takes** after her mother.*
take off When a plane **takes off**, it leaves the ground and starts to fly. ➲ OPPOSITE **land**[2] 1
take something off
1 to remove clothes from your body: ***Take** off your coat.*
2 to have time as a holiday, not working: *I am **taking** a week off in June.*
take over, **take something over** to get control of something or look after something when another person stops: *Robert **took** over the business when his father died.*
ⓘ **ORIGIN**: through Old English *tacan* meaning 'get by force, capture', from Old Norse *taka* meaning 'grasp, get hold of'

takeaway (say **tayk**-uh-way) *noun* (*plural* **takeaways**)
1 a restaurant that sells hot food that you take out with you to eat somewhere else: *a Chinese **takeaway***
2 food that you buy at this kind of restaurant: *Let's have a **takeaway** tonight.*
▸ **takeaway** (*adjective*): *a **takeaway** pizza*

take-off (say **tayk**-of) *noun* (*plural* **take-offs**)
the time when a plane leaves the ground and starts to fly ➲ OPPOSITE **landing** 2

tale (say **tayl**) *noun* (*plural* **tales**)
a story, usually about things that are not true: *fairy **tales***

talent (say **tal**-uhnt) *noun* (*plural* **talents**)
a natural ability to do something very well: *She has a **talent** for drawing.*
▸ **talented** (*adjective*): *a **talented** musician*

talk[1] (say **tawk**) *verb* (**talking**, **talked**)
to speak to somebody or to say words: *She is **talking** to her friend on the telephone.* ◇ *We **talked** about our holiday.*

talk[2] (say **tawk**) *noun* (*plural* **talks**)
1 when two or more people **talk** about something: *Dave and I had a long **talk** about the problem.* ◇ *The two countries are holding **talks** to try to end the war.*
2 when a person speaks to a group of people: *Professor Wilson gave an interesting **talk** on Chinese art.*

talkative (say **tawk**-uh-tiv) *adjective*
A person who is **talkative** likes to talk a lot.

tall (say **tawl**) *adjective* (**taller**, **tallest**)
1 higher than other people or things: *a **tall** tree* ◇ *He is **taller** than his brother.* ➲ OPPOSITE **short** 1–2
2 You use **tall** to say or ask about the height of someone or something: *How **tall** are you?* ◇ *She's 1,62 metres **tall**.* ➲ See note at **high**[1]

tally[1] (say **tal**-ee) *verb* (**tallying**, **tallied**)
1 to agree or match: *These names don't **tally** with the list.*
2 to count things: ***Tally** up the votes.*

tally[2] (say **tal**-ee) *noun* (*plural* **tallies**)
a total amount or number: *What is the **tally** of votes?*

Talmud (say **tal**-muud) *noun* (*no plural*)
a collection of important Jewish writing and laws
ORIGIN: from Hebrew *talmūḏ* meaning 'instruction'

talon (say **tal**-uhn) *noun* (*plural* **talons**)
a long sharp curved nail on the feet of some birds, especially ones that kill animals for food

tambourine (say tam-buh-**reen**) *noun* (*plural* **tambourines**)
a musical instrument that has a circular frame covered in a skin or plastic, with metal discs around the edge. You play a **tambourine** by shaking or hitting it.

tame[1] (say **taym**) *adjective* (**tamer**, **tamest**)
A **tame** animal is not wild and is not afraid of people: *The birds are so **tame** they will eat from your hand.*

tame[2] (say **taym**) *verb* (**taming**, **tamed**)
to make a wild animal easy to control or to make something **tame**[1]

tamper (say **tam**-puh) *verb* (**tampering**, **tampered**)
to make changes to something, especially to damage it, without permission: *Who's been **tampering** with my phone?* ➲ SYNONYM **meddle**

tampon (say **tam**-pon) *noun* (*plural* **tampons**)
a tightly rolled piece of cotton that a woman puts into her body to take in and hold the blood that she loses once a month

tan[1] *verb* (**tanning**, **tanned**)
1 If your skin **tans**, it becomes darker because you have spent time in the sun: *My skin **tans** really easily.*
2 to make animal skin into leather by treating it with chemicals
▸ **tanned** (*adjective*)

tan[2] *noun* (*plural* **tans**) (also **suntan**)
the darker brown colour that your skin goes when you have spent time in the sun: *to get a **tan***

tandem (say **tan**-duhm) *noun* (*plural* **tandems**)
a bicycle for two people with one sitting behind the other

tangent (say **tan**-juhnt) *noun* (*plural* **tangents**)
1 (*maths*) a straight line that touches a curve but does not cross it
2 (also **tan**) (*maths*) a **ratio** between angles and sides of a right-angled triangle ➲ See **cosine**, **sine**, **trigonometry**
3 a different topic from the one you were talking about: *He went off at a **tangent** during class.*

tangerine (say tan-juh-**reen**) *noun* (*plural* **tangerines**)
a fruit like a small sweet orange, with a skin that is easy to take off
ORIGIN: 19th century, from *Tanger*, the former name of Tangier, a city in Morocco, where the fruit originally came from

tangible (say **tan**-juhb-l) *adjective*
that can be clearly seen or felt to exist: *The excitement in the crowd was **tangible**.*
➲ OPPOSITE **intangible**

tangle (say **tang**-guhl) *noun* (*plural* **tangles**)
many things that have become twisted together so that you cannot easily separate the different parts: *My hair is full of **tangles**.*
▸ **tangle** (*verb*): *Does your hair **tangle** easily?*
▸ **tangled** (*adjective*): *The string is all **tangled**.*

tango (say **tang**-goh) *noun* (*plural* **tangos**)
a fast South American dance with a strong rhythm for two people, or the music for this dance: *Can you do the **tango**?* ➲ See **waltz**

tangram (say **tang**-gram) *noun* (*plural* **tangrams**)
a game (called a **puzzle**) in which you use different shapes to make up a square

tank (say **tangk**) *noun* (*plural* **tanks**)
1 a large container for holding liquid or gas: *a fuel **tank*** (= in a car)
2 a strong heavy vehicle with big guns. **Tanks** are used by armies in wars.

tanker (say **tang**-kuh) *noun* (*plural* **tankers**)
a ship or lorry that carries oil, petrol or gas in large amounts: *an oil **tanker***

tantalize (say **tan**-tuh-lize) *verb* (**tantalizing**, **tantalized**) (also **tantalise**)
to know about something that you want but cannot have: *Those cakes have **tantalized** me all morning.*
▸ **tantalizing** (*adjective*) (also **tantalising**)

tantrum (say **tan**-truhm) *noun* (*plural* **tantrums**)
a sudden short period of angry, unreasonable behaviour, especially in a child: *to throw a **tantrum***

tap[1] *verb* (**tapping**, **tapped**)
to hit or touch somebody or something quickly and lightly: *She **tapped** me on the shoulder.* ◇ *I **tapped** on the window.*

tap[2] *noun* (*plural* **taps**)
1 a thing that you turn to make something like water or gas come out of a pipe: *Turn the **tap** off.*
2 a light hit with your hand or fingers: *They heard a **tap** at the door.*

tape[1] (say **tayp**) *noun* (*plural* **tapes**)
1 a long thin piece of plastic material that is used for recording sound, music or moving pictures so that you can listen to or watch it or them later: *I have got the concert on **tape**.* ◇ *Will you play your new music **tape**?*
2 a long thin piece of material or paper, used for sticking things together: *sticky **tape***

tape[2] (say **tayp**) *verb* (**taping, taped**)
to put sound, music or moving pictures on **tape**[1] 1 so that you can listen to or watch it later: *I **taped** the film that was on TV last night.*
➲ SYNONYM **record**[2] 2

tape measure *noun* (*plural* **tape measures**)
a long thin piece of plastic, cloth or metal for measuring things

taper (say **tay**-puh) *verb* (**tapering, tapered**)
1 to make or become narrower: *These candles **taper** towards the one end.*
2 to slowly get smaller or less: *My enthusiasm for completing the project **tapered** off.*

tape recorder *noun* (*plural* **tape recorders**)
a machine that you use for recording and playing sound or music on tape

tapestry (say **tap**-uhss-tree) *noun* (*plural* **tapestries**)
a piece of heavy cloth with pictures made from coloured thread on it

tapeworm (say **tayp**-wurm) *noun* (*plural* **tapeworms**)
a long flat creature with a soft body and no legs that lives inside the **intestines** of humans and animals

tar (say **taa**) *noun* (*no plural*)
a black substance that is thick and sticky when it is hot, and hard when it is cold. **Tar** is used for making the surface of roads.

target[1] (say **taa**-git) *noun* (*plural* **targets**)
1 a result that you are trying to achieve: *Our **target** is to finish the job by Friday.*
2 a person, place or thing that you try to hit when you are shooting or attacking: *The bomb hit its **target**.*

target[2] (say **taa**-git) *verb* (**targeting, targeted**)
1 to try to have an effect on a particular group of people: *This book **targets** teenagers.*
2 to try to attack something: *He **targets** the mice in the kitchen.*

tariff (say **ta**-rif) *noun* (*plural* **tariffs**)
1 a tax that has to be paid for goods coming into the country
2 a list of prices, especially in a hotel

tart (say **taat**) *noun* (*plural* **tarts**)
an open pie filled with sweet food such as fruit: *Would you like a piece of apple **tart**?*

tartan (say **taa**-tuhn) *noun*
1 (*no plural*) a pattern of squares and lines of different colours and widths that cross each other, which is used especially on cloth and had its origin in Scotland: *a **tartan** skirt*
2 (*plural* **tartans**) a **tartan** pattern connected with a particular group of families in Scotland: *the MacLeod **tartan***

tartrazine (say **taa**-truh-zeen) *noun* (*no plural*)
an artificial substance you add to food to give it a yellow colour

task (say **taask**) *noun* (*plural* **tasks**)
a piece of work that you must do: *I had the **task** of cleaning the floors.*

taste[1] (say **tayst**) *noun*
1 (*plural* **tastes**) the feeling or quality that a certain food or drink gives in your mouth: *Sugar has a sweet **taste** and lemons have a sour **taste**.* ◇ *I don't like the **taste** of this cheese.*
2 (*no plural*) the ability to recognize the flavour of food and drink with your mouth: *When you have a cold, you often lose your sense of **taste**.*
3 (*plural* **tastes**) a little bit of food or drink: *Have a **taste** of the fish to see if you like it.*
4 (*no plural*) being able to choose nice things: *She has good **taste** in clothes.*

taste[2] (say **tayst**) *verb* (**tasting, tasted**)
1 to have a certain flavour: *This cake **tastes** of oranges.* ◇ *Honey **tastes** sweet.*
2 to feel or recognize the flavour of a certain food or drink in your mouth: *Can you **taste** onions in this soup?*
3 to eat or drink a little of something, to test its flavour: ***Taste** this cheese to see if you like it.*

tasteful (say **tayst**-fuhl) *adjective*
attractive and of good quality, and showing that you can choose nice things: ***tasteful** furniture* ➲ OPPOSITE **tasteless** 2
► **tastefully** (*adverb*): *The room was **tastefully** decorated.*

tasteless (say **tayst**-luhss) *adjective*
1 having little or no flavour: *a bowl of **tasteless** soup* ➲ OPPOSITE **tasty**
2 of bad quality and not attractive, showing that you cannot choose nice things: ***tasteless** furniture* ➲ OPPOSITE **tasteful**

tasty (say **tayst**-ee) *adjective* (**tastier, tastiest**)
good to eat: *The soup was very **tasty**.*

tattered (say **tat**-uhd) *adjective*
old and torn, or in a bad condition: ***tattered** shoes* ➲ SYNONYMS **scruffy**, **tatty**

tattoo[1] (say tuh-**too**) *noun* (*plural* **tattoos**)
a picture on somebody's skin, made with a needle and coloured liquid: *She has a **tattoo** of a tiger on her shoulder.*
ℹ ORIGIN: 18th century, from *ta-tau* or *ta-tu*, from a Polynesian language

tattoo[2] (say tuh-**too**) *verb* (**tattooing, tattooed**)
to mark somebody's skin with a picture, made with a needle and coloured ink: *He had a snake **tattooed** on his arm.*

tatty (say **tat**-ee) *adjective* (**tattier, tattiest**) (*informal*)
in a bad condition: *a **tatty** shirt*
➲ SYNONYMS **scruffy**, **tattered**

taught (say **tawt**) form of **teach**

taunt (say **tawnt**) *verb* (**taunting, taunted**)
to try to make somebody angry or upset by saying unpleasant or cruel things: *The boys **taunted** the new girl.*
▸ **taunt** (*noun*): *cruel **taunts***

taut (say **tawt**) *adjective*
(used about a rope or wire) stretched very tight: *Keep the rope **taut**.*

tavern (say **tav**-uhn) *noun* (*plural* **taverns**)
(*old-fashioned*) a place where you can buy drinks and meals ➲ SYNONYM **pub**

tax[1] (say **takss**) *noun* (*plural* **taxes**)
money that you have to pay to the government. You pay **tax** from the money you earn or when you buy things: *There is a **tax** on cigarettes in this country.*

tax[2] (say **takss**) *verb* (**taxing, taxed**)
to make somebody pay **tax**[1]

taxi (say **tak**-si) *noun* (*plural* **taxis**) (also **cab**)
a car that you can travel in if you pay the driver: *I took a **taxi** to the airport.* ◇ *I came by **taxi**.*

TB *abbreviation* **tuberculosis**

tea (say **tee**) *noun* (*no plural*)
1 a brown drink that you make with hot water and the dry leaves of a special plant: *Would you like a cup of **tea**?*
2 the dry leaves of a special plant that you use to make tea to drink
ℹ ORIGIN: 17th century, probably through Malay from Chinese *te*

tea bag *noun* (*plural* **tea bags**)
a small paper bag with tea leaves inside it. You use it to make tea.

teach (say **teech**) *verb* (**teaching, taught**)
1 to give lessons to learners, for example in a school or college: *He **teaches** Mathematics to Grades 6 and 7.*
2 to show somebody how to do something: *My mother **taught** me how to drive.*
▸ **teaching** (*noun*): ***Teaching** is my profession.*

teacher (say **tee**-chuh) *noun* (*plural* **teachers**)
a person whose job is to teach: *He's my English **teacher**.*

teak (say **teek**) *noun* (*no plural*)
strong hard wood used to make furniture: *a **teak** table*

team (say **teem**) *noun* (*plural* **teams**)
1 a group of people who play a sport or a game together against another group: *Which **team** do you play for?* ◇ *a netball **team***
2 a group of people who work together: *a **team** of doctors*

teamwork (say **teem**-wurk) *noun* (*no plural*)
the ability of people to work together in a team: *We used **teamwork** to build the hut.*

teapot (say **tee**-pot) *noun* (*plural* **teapots**)
a container for making and pouring tea

tear[1] (say **tair**) *verb* (**tearing, tore, has torn**)
1 to damage something by pulling it apart or making an untidy hole in it: *She **tore** her dress on a nail.* ◇ *I **tore** the piece of paper in half.* ◇ *I can't use this bag – it's **torn**.*
2 to come apart or to break: *Paper **tears** easily.*
3 to take something from somebody or something in a quick and violent way: *He **tore** the bag out of her hands.*
4 to move somewhere very fast: *She **tore** down the street.*
tear something up to destroy something by pulling it into small pieces: *I **tore** the letter **up** and threw it away.*

tear[2] (say **tair**) *noun* (*plural* **tears**)
an untidy hole in something like paper or material: *You've got a **tear** in your jeans.*

tear[3] (say **teer**) *noun* (*plural* **tears**)
a drop of water that comes from your eye when you cry: *I was in **tears*** (= crying) *at the end of the film.* ◇ *She read the letter and burst into **tears*** (= suddenly started to cry).

PRONUNCIATION Notice the difference between the pronunciation of **tear**[2] and **tear**[3].

tearful (say **teer**-fuhl) *adjective*
crying or nearly crying: *Why is she so **tearful**?*

tease (say **teez**) *verb* (**teasing, teased**)
to laugh at somebody in a friendly way or in

order to upset them: *Don't take any notice of him – he's only **teasing** you.*

teaspoon (say **tee**-spoon) *noun* (*plural* **teaspoons**)
a small spoon that you use for putting sugar into tea or coffee

teat (say **teet**) *noun* (*plural* **teats**)
1 the rubber part at the end of a bottle that the baby sucks to get milk
2 a part of the female body that babies suck to get milk ➲ SYNONYM **nipple**

tea towel *noun* (*plural* **tea towels**)
a small cloth that you use for drying things such as plates and cups after you wash them

technical (say **tek**-nik-l) *adjective*
related to the machines and materials used in science and in making things: *The train was delayed due to a **technical** problem.*

technician (say tek-**ni**-shuhn) *noun* (*plural* **technicians**)
a person who works with machines or instruments: *a laboratory **technician***

technikon (say **tek**-ni-kon) *noun* (*plural* **technikons**)
the old name for a **university of technology**

technique (say tek-**neek**) *noun* (*plural* **techniques**)
a special way of doing something: *new **techniques** for learning languages*

technology (say tek-**nol**-uh-jee) *noun* (*no plural*)
1 knowing about science and about how things work, and using this to build and make things: *developments in computer **technology***
2 the study of machinery, engineering and how things work
▸ **technological** (*adjective*): *a **technological** problem*

tectonic (say tek-**ton**-ik) *adjective*
relating to the structure and movement of the surface layer of the Earth: ***tectonic** activity* ◇ ***tectonic** uplift*
plate tectonics : ***Plate tectonics** is a theory that the Earth's crust is made up of huge slowly moving plates.*

teddy bear (say **ted**-ee bair) *noun* (*plural* **teddy bears**) (also **teddy**)
a toy for children that looks like a bear
🛈 ORIGIN: 20th century, from Teddy (Theodore) Roosevelt (1858–1919), a USA president who enjoyed bear hunting

tedious (say **tee**-di-uhss) *adjective*
very long and not interesting: *a **tedious** journey*
➲ SYNONYMS **boring, tiresome**

teenager (say **teen**-ay-juh) *noun* (*plural* **teenagers**)
a person who is between 13 and 19 years old
➲ SYNONYM **adolescent**
▸ **teenage** (*adjective*): *This book is a favourite with **teenage** boys.*

teens (say **teenz**) *plural noun*
the time when you are between the ages of 13 and 19: *She is in her **teens**.*

teeth (say **teeth**) plural of **tooth**

teetotal (say tee-**toh**-tuhl) *adjective*
(used about a person) never drinking alcohol: *He's **teetotal** and won't drink.*
▸ **teetotaller** (*noun*): *She's a **teetotaller**.*

tele- (say **tel**-i) *prefix*
1 over a long distance: ***telescope***
2 done over the telephone: ***telesales***

telecommunications (say tel-i-kuh-myoo-ni-**kay**-shunz) *plural noun*
the technology of sending signals, pictures and messages over long distances by radio, telephone or television: *the **telecommunications** industry*

telegram (say **tel**-i-gram) *noun* (*plural* **telegrams**)
a message that is sent by a system that uses electrical signals and is then printed and given to somebody

telegraph (say **tel**-i-graaf) *noun* (*plural* **telegraphs**)
a method of sending messages (called **telegrams**) over long distances, using wires that carry electrical signals

telepathy (say tuh-**lep**-uh-thee) *noun* (*no plural*)
the communication of thoughts between people's minds without using speech, writing or other normal methods: *My dog knew by **telepathy** that we were going for a walk.*

telephone[1] (say **tel**-i-fohn) *noun* (*plural* **telephones**) (also **phone**)
a piece of equipment that you use for talking to somebody who is in another place: *What's your **telephone** number?* ◇ *I made a **telephone** call.* ◇ *The **telephone**'s ringing.*
on the telephone using a **telephone** to speak to somebody: *He's on the **telephone** to his mother.* ➲ See **cellphone**

telephone[2] (say **tel**-i-fohn) *verb* (**telephoning, telephoned**) (*formal*)
to use a **telephone** to speak to somebody: *I must **telephone** my parents.* ➲ SYNONYMS **call**[1] 3, **phone**[2]

telephone directory *noun* (*plural* **telephone directories**)
a book of people's names, addresses and telephone numbers

telescope (say **tel**-i-skohp) *noun* (*plural* **telescopes**)
an instrument in the shape of a tube with a special piece of glass (called a **lens**) inside it. You look through it to make things that are far away appear bigger and nearer.

telescope

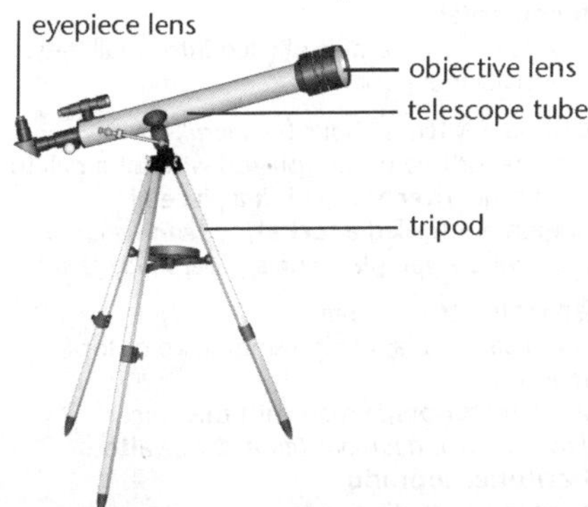

television (say tel-i-**vizh**-uhn) *noun* (abbr. TV)
1 (*plural* **televisions**) a piece of electrical equipment with a screen that shows moving pictures with sound: *to turn the **television** on*
2 (*no plural*) things that you watch on a television: *I watched **television** last night.* ◇ *What's on **television**?* ◇ *a **television** programme*
3 (*no plural*) a way of sending pictures and sounds so that people can watch them on television: *satellite **television***
ORIGIN: 20th century, from Greek *tēle-* meaning 'far off' + Latin *vision* from *videre* meaning 'to see'

tell (say **tel**) *verb* (**telling, told**)
1 to give information to somebody by speaking or writing: *I **told** her my new address.* ◇ *This book **tells** you how to make bread.* ◇ *He **told** me that he was tired.*
2 to say what somebody must do: *Our teacher **told** us to read this book.*
3 to know, guess or understand something: *I can **tell** that she's been crying because her eyes are red.* ◇ *I can't **tell** the difference between him and his brother. They look exactly the same!*
tell somebody off to speak to somebody in an angry way because they have done something wrong: *I **told** the children off for making so much noise.*

teller (say **tel**-uh) *noun* (*plural* **tellers**)
a person in a bank who deals with customers: *I have to see a **teller** to deposit money.*

temper (say **tem**-puh) *noun* (*plural* **tempers**)
1 If you have a **temper**, you get angry very easily: *She must learn to control her **temper**.*
2 the way you are feeling at a certain time: *Why are you in a bad **temper**?* ➲ SYNONYM **mood**
lose your temper to suddenly become angry: *She lost her **temper** with a customer and shouted at him.*

temperament (say **tem**-pruh-muhnt) *noun* (*plural* **temperaments**)
a person or animal's character, especially as it affects the way they behave and feel: *Andy has a fiery **temperament**.* ◇ *My dog has a good **temperament**.* ➲ SYNONYMS **character** 1, **personality** 1

temperamental (say tem-pruh-**men**-tuhl) *adjective*
often and suddenly changing the way you behave or feel: *My sister is so **temperamental**.* ➲ SYNONYM **moody**

temperate (say **tem**-puh-ruht) *adjective*
(used about a climate), not very hot and not very cold

temperature (say **tem**-pruh-tshuh) *noun* (*plural* **temperatures**)
how hot or cold a thing or a place is: *a high/low **temperature*** ◇ *On a hot day, the **temperature** can reach 35 °C.*
have a temperature to feel very hot because you are ill
take somebody's temperature to see how hot somebody is, using a special instrument (called a **thermometer**)

SPELLING Notice how to spell and say **temperature**.

tempest (say **tem**-pist) *noun* (*plural* **tempests**)
a violent storm

tempestuous (say tem-**pess**-tyuu-uhss) *adjective*
1 very stormy
2 full of strong emotions: *We have a **tempestuous** relationship.* ➲ SYNONYM **turbulent**

template (say **tem**-playt) *noun* (*plural* **templates**)
1 a thing that is used as a model for producing other similar examples: *I keep a **template** of a letter on my computer.*
2 a shape cut out of a hard material, used as a model for producing exactly the same shape many times in another material: *Use a **template** to make the pattern on the wall.*

A B C D E F G H I J K L M N O P Q R S T U V W X Y Z

temple (say **temp**-l) *noun* (*plural* **temples**)
1 a building where people go to say prayers to a god or gods
2 one of the flat parts on each side of your forehead ➲ See illustration at **face**[1]

tempo (say **tem**-poh) *noun*
1 (*no plural*) the speed of an activity or event
2 (*plural* **tempos**) the speed of a piece of music: *Use a quicker **tempo** in your rhythms.*

temporarily (say **tem**-pruh-ruh-lee) *adverb*
for a short time only: *The road is **temporarily** closed for repairs.*

temporary (say **tem**-pruh-ree) *adjective*
Something that is **temporary** lasts for a short time: *I had a **temporary** job in the summer holidays.* ➲ OPPOSITE **permanent**

tempt *verb* (**tempting**, **tempted**)
to make somebody want to do or have something, especially something that is wrong: *He saw the money on the table, and he was **tempted** to take it.* ➲ SYNONYM **entice**

temptation (say temp-**tay**-shuhn) *noun*
1 (*no plural*) a feeling that you want to do something that you know is wrong: *I couldn't resist the **temptation** to open the letter.*
2 (*plural* **temptations**) a thing that makes you want to do something wrong: *Don't leave the money on your desk – it's a **temptation** to thieves.*

tempting (say **tempt**-ing) *adjective*
Something that is **tempting** makes you want to do or have it: *That cake looks very **tempting**!*

ten *number*
10
🛈 ORIGIN: from Old English *ten*, *tien* meaning 'ten', related to Dutch *tien* and Latin *decem*

tenacious (say tuh-**nay**-shuss) *adjective*
not likely to give up or let something go
➲ SYNONYMS **determined**, **persistent**
▶ **tenaciously** (*adverb*): *She held on **tenaciously**.* ▶ **tenacity** (*noun*): *He showed great **tenacity**.*

tenant (say **ten**-uhnt) *noun* (*plural* **tenants**)
a person who pays money (called **rent**) to live in or use a place

tend *verb* (**tending**, **tended**)
to usually do or be something: *Men **tend** to be taller than women.*

tendency (say **ten**-duhn-see) *noun* (*plural* **tendencies**)
something that a person or thing usually does: *He has a **tendency** to be late.*

tender (say **ten**-duh) *adjective*
1 kind, gentle and loving: *a **tender** look*
2 **Tender** meat is soft and easy to cut or bite.
➲ OPPOSITE **tough** 4
3 If a part of your body is **tender**, it hurts when you touch it. ➲ SYNONYM **sore**
▶ **tenderly** (*adverb*): *He touched her arm **tenderly**.* ▶ **tenderness** (*noun*): *a feeling of **tenderness***

tendon (say **ten**-duhn) *noun* (*plural* **tendons**)
a strong band in your body that joins a muscle to a bone ➲ SYNONYM **sinew**

tenement (say **ten**-uh-muhnt) *noun* (*plural* **tenements**)
a large building that is divided into small flats, especially in a poor area

tennis (say **ten**-iss) *noun* (*no plural*)
a game for two or four players who hit a ball to each other over a net using a piece of equipment (called a **racket**): *a **tennis** court* (= a place where you play tennis) ◇ *Let's play **tennis**.*

tenor (say **ten**-uh) *noun*
1 (*no plural*) a fairly high singing voice for a man
2 (*plural* **tenors**) a man with this voice: *Pavarotti was a famous **tenor**.* ➲ See **alto**, **baritone**, **soprano**
▶ **tenor** (*adjective*): *a **tenor** saxophone*

tense[1] (say **tenss**) *adjective*
1 worried or nervous and not able to relax: *I always feel very **tense** before exams.*
➲ OPPOSITE **relaxed**
2 pulled tightly, not relaxed: ***tense** muscles*

tense[2] (say **tenss**) *noun* (*plural* **tenses**) (*grammar*)
the form of a verb that shows whether something happens in the past, present or future ➲ See Study page 6

tensile (say **ten**-sile) *adjective* (*technology*)
1 used to describe how much something can stretch without breaking: *the **tensile** strength of a rope*
2 able to be pulled or stretched

tension (say **ten**-shuhn) *noun*
1 (*no plural*) being worried or nervous and not able to relax: ***Tension** can give you headaches.*
2 (*plural* **tensions**) bad feeling and lack of trust between people, countries, etc.
3 (*no plural*) (used about rope, muscle, etc.) the state of being stretched tight, or how tightly something is stretched: *muscular **tension***

tent *noun* (*plural* **tents**)
a kind of small house made of cloth. You sleep in a **tent** when you go camping: *We put up our **tent**.*

tentacle (say **ten**-tik-l) *noun* (*plural* **tentacles**)
one of the long thin parts like legs on the body of some sea animals: *An octopus has eight* ***tentacles.*** ➲ See illustration at **octopus**

tentative (say **ten**-tuh-tiv) *adjective*
1 (used about plans) uncertain and not definite: *We have a* ***tentative*** *arrangement to meet.*
2 not confident about what you are saying or doing: *She made a* ***tentative*** *move towards him.*
➲ SYNONYM **hesitant**

tenth (say **tenth**) *adjective, adverb, noun*
1 10th: *on the* ***tenth*** *day*
2 one of ten equal parts of something; $\frac{1}{10}$

tepid (say **tep**-id) *adjective*
(used about liquids) slightly warm: *The bath water is* ***tepid.***

term (say **turm**) *noun* (*plural* **terms**)
1 a word or group of words connected with a special subject: *'Program' is a computing* ***term.***
2 one of the four periods that the school year is divided into: *The first* ***term*** *is from January to March.*

terminal[1] (say **turm**-in-l) *noun* (*plural* **terminals**)
a building where people begin and end their journeys by bus, train, plane or ship: *I went to the airport* ***terminal*** *to fetch my visitors.*

terminal[2] (say **turm**-in-l) *adjective*
(used about illness) slowly causing death: ***terminal*** *cancer*
▸ **terminally** (*adverb*): *He's* ***terminally*** *ill.*

terminate (say **turm**-i-nayt) *verb* (**terminating, terminated**) (*formal*) to end or to make something end: *I'll* ***terminate*** *my membership.*
▸ **termination** (*noun*)

terminology (say turm-i-**nol**-uh-jee) *noun* (*no plural*)
the special words and expressions that are used in a particular subject, profession or activity: *What* ***terminology*** *must I use?*

terminus (say **turm**-i-nuhss) *noun* (*plural* **termini** or **terminuses**)
the last stop or station at the end of a bus route or railway line: *a bus* ***terminus***

termite (say **tur**-mite) *noun* (*plural* **termites**)
a small insect that lives in large groups, mainly in warm countries. Termites mostly eat dead plant material and some can cause serious damage to the wood in buildings.

terms (say **turmz**) *plural noun*
the things that people must agree to when they make an arrangement or an agreement: *Under the* ***terms*** *of the contract he had to complete all work by the end of the year.*

terrace (say **te**-ruhss) *noun* (*plural* **terraces**)
1 a flat place outside a house or restaurant: *We had our lunch on the* ***terrace.*** ➲ See **veranda**
2 a line of houses that are joined together

terrain (say tuh-**rayn**) *noun* (*plural* **terrains**)
an area of land, especially concerning its physical features: *rocky* ***terrain*** ◇ *an all-****terrain*** *vehicle*

terrestrial (say tuh-**ress**-tri-uhl) *adjective*
1 of the Earth: ***terrestrial*** *life*
2 living on land or connected with land: *Humans are* ***terrestrial;*** *they don't live in the sea, trees or the air.* ➲ See **aerial²**, **aquatic**
🛈 ORIGIN: 14th–15th century, from Latin *terrestris*, from *terra* meaning 'earth'. When the word first came into English, it meant 'ordinary, everyday'.

terrible (say **te**-ruh-buhl) *adjective*
very bad: *She had a* ***terrible*** *accident.* ◇ *The food in that restaurant is* ***terrible!***

terribly (say **te**-ruh-blee) *adverb*
1 very: *I'm* ***terribly*** *sorry!*
2 very badly: *He played* ***terribly.*** ➲ SYNONYM **awfully**

terrier (say **te**-ri-uh) *noun* (*plural* **terriers**)
a type of small dog

terrific (say tuh-**rif**-ik) *adjective* (*informal*) very good: *What a* ***terrific*** *idea!*

terrified (say **te**-ri-fide) *adjective*
very frightened: *He is* ***terrified*** *of dogs.*

terrify (say **te**-ri-fy) *verb* (**terrifying, terrified**)
to make somebody feel very frightened: *Spiders* ***terrify*** *me!*

territory (say **te**-ruh-tree) *noun* (*plural* **territories**)
the land that belongs to one country: *This part of the country was once British* ***territory.***

terror (say **te**-ruh) *noun* (*no plural*)
very great fear: *He screamed in* ***terror*** *as the rats came towards him.*

terrorism (say **te**-ruh-riz-m) *noun* (*no plural*)
when a group of people use violence to try to influence a government and make it do what they want: *the fight against* ***terrorism***
➲ See **guerrilla**

terrorist (say **te**-ruh-rist) *noun* (*plural* **terrorists**)
a person who uses violence, for example by putting a bomb in a public place, in order to try to make a government do what they want: *a* ***terrorist*** *attack*

A B C D E F G H I J K L M N O P Q R S T U V W X Y Z

terrorize (say **te**-ruh-rize) *verb* (**terrorizing, terrorized**) (also **terrorise**)
to make somebody frightened by using or threatening to use violence against them: *Bullies are **terrorizing** the school.*

tertiary (say **tur**-shuh-ree) *adjective*
1 third in order
2 (used about education) at university level: *After school you can get a **tertiary** education.*

tessellate (say **tess**-i-layt) *verb* (**tessellating, tessellated**)
to fit similar shapes together exactly, making a pattern: *I had great difficulty **tessellating** the triangular tiles in my new bathroom.*
► **tessellation** (*noun*)

shapes that tessellate

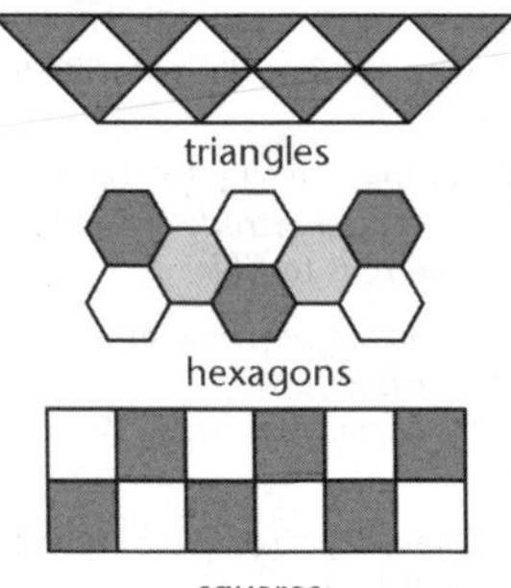

test¹ *noun* (*plural* **tests**)
an exam that you do in order to show what you know or what you can do: *We have a spelling **test** every Friday.* ◇ *Did you pass your driving **test**?*

test² *verb* (**testing, tested**)
1 to ask somebody questions to find out what they know or what they can do: *The teacher **tested** us on our spelling.*
2 to use or look at something carefully to find out how good it is or if it works well: *I don't think medicines should be **tested** on animals.* ◇ *The doctor **tested** my eyes.*

testament (say **tess**-tuh-muhnt) *noun*
1 (*no plural*) something that shows that something exists or is true: *His action is **testament** to his loyalty.* ➲ SYNONYM **evidence**
2 (*plural* **testaments**) one of the two parts that the **Bible** 1 is divided into: *the Old **Testament*** ◇ *the New **Testament***

testicle (say **tess**-tik-l) *noun* (*plural* **testicles**)
one of the two round male sex organs that produce **sperm**
► **testicular** (*adjective*): ***testicular** cancer*

testify (say **tess**-ti-fy) *verb* (**testifying, testified**)
to make a formal statement that something is true, especially in a court of law: *She **testified** against the mugger.*

testimonial (say tess-ti-**moh**-ni-uhl) *noun* (*plural* **testimonials**)
a formal statement about someone's character or qualifications: *I have a **testimonial** in my CV.*

testimony (say **tess**-ti-muh-nee) *noun*
1 (*plural* **testimonies**) a formal statement that something is true, especially one that is made in a court of law: *We heard witness **testimonies** in court.*
2 (*no plural*) (*formal*) something that shows that something exists or is true: *Her blisters are **testimony** to the distance she walked.*
➲ SYNONYM **testament** 1

test tube *noun* (*plural* **test tubes**)
a long thin glass tube that you use in scientific experiments

tether (say **te*th***-uh) *noun* (*plural* **tethers**)
a rope used to tie an animal to something
at the end of one's tether having no more patience for something: *I'm at the end of my **tether** with you!*
► **tether** (*verb*): *The cow was **tethered** to the pole.*

tetragon (say **tet**-ruh-guhn) *noun* (*plural* **tetragons**) (*maths*)
any closed flat shape having four angles and four straight sides ➲ SYNONYMS **quadrangle, quadrilateral**

tetrahedron (say tet-ruh-**hee**-druhn) *noun* (*plural* **tetrahedra** or **tetrahedrons**) (*maths*)
a solid shape with four flat surfaces, sometimes called a triangular **pyramid**

text¹ (say **tekst**) *noun*
1 (*no plural*) the words in a book, newspaper or magazine: *This book has a lot of pictures but not much **text**.*
2 (*plural* **texts**) a book, a poem or a short piece of writing that you study: *Read the **text** and answer the questions.*

text² (say **tekst**) *verb* (**texting, texted**)
to send someone a message on a cellphone: *He **texted** me to say he'd arrived in Nairobi.*

textbook (say **tekst**-buuk) *noun* (*plural* **textbooks**)
a book that teaches you about something: *a biology **textbook***

textile (say **tekss**-tile) *noun* (*plural* **textiles**)
any cloth made in a factory: *the **textile** industry*
➲ SYNONYMS **fabric, material¹** 1

text message (*plural* **text messages**) = **SMS**

texture (say **tekss**-tshuh) *noun* (*plural* **textures**) the way that something feels when you touch it: *Silk has a smooth* ***texture****.* ◇ *a rough* ***texture***

than (say *than*) *conjunction, preposition* You use 'than' when you compare people or things: *I'm older* ***than*** *him.* ◇ *You speak isiXhosa much better* ***than*** *she does.*

thank (say **thangk**) *verb* (**thanking, thanked**) to tell somebody that you are pleased because they gave you something or helped you: *I* ***thanked*** *her for my birthday present.* ➲ See **thanks, thank you**

thankful (say **thangk**-fuul) *adjective* happy that something good has happened or that something bad has not happened: *We were* ***thankful*** *that our house wasn't burnt in the fire.*
▸ **thankfully** (*adverb*): *There was an accident, but* ***thankfully*** *nobody was hurt.*

thanks (say **thangkss**) *plural noun* a word that shows you are pleased because somebody gave you something, helped you or was kind to you: *Please give my* ***thanks*** *to your sister for her help.*
thanks to somebody or **something** because of somebody or something: *We're late,* ***thanks*** *to you!* ➲ See **thank, thank you**

thank you *noun* (*no plural*) words that show you are pleased because somebody gave you something, helped you or was kind to you: ***Thank you*** *for your letter.* ◇ *'How are you?' 'I'm fine,* ***thank you****.'* ➲ SYNONYM **thanks**
no, thank you or **no, thanks** words that you use to say that you do not want something: *'Would you like some more tea?' 'No,* ***thank you****.'*

SPELLING Remember that **thank you** is two words.

that¹ (say *that*) *adjective, pronoun* (*plural* **those**) the one there or then: *'Who is* ***that*** *boy in the garden?'* ***'That'****s my brother.'* ◇ *She got married two years ago. At* ***that*** *time, she was a teacher.* ◇ *Who are* ***those*** *girls?* ◇ *I used* ***those****.*

that² (say *that*) *pronoun* which, who or whom: *A lion is an animal* ***that*** *lives in Africa.* ◇ *The tourists* ***that*** *I met were very nice.* ◇ *I'm reading the book* ***that*** *you gave me.*

that³ (say *that*) *conjunction* a word that you use to join two parts of a sentence: *She said* ***that*** *she was unhappy.* ◇ *I'm sure* ***that*** *he will come.* ◇ *I was so hungry* ***that*** *I ate all the food.*

that⁴ (say *that*) *adverb* as much as that: *The next village is ten kilometres from here. I can't walk* ***that*** *far.*

thatch (say **thach**) *noun* (*no plural*) a roof covering made of a type of grass or leaves: *The roof is made of* ***thatch****.*
▸ **thatch** (*verb*): *They are* ***thatching*** *the roof.*
▸ **thatched** (*adjective*): *Our house has a* ***thatched*** *roof.*

thaw (say **thaw**) *verb* (**thawing, thawed**) to warm something that is frozen so that it becomes soft or liquid, or to get warmer so that it becomes soft or liquid: *I took the meat out of the freezer to let it* ***thaw****.* ➲ OPPOSITE **freeze**

the (say *thuh* or *thee*) *article*
1 a word that you use before the name of somebody or something when it is clear what person or thing you mean: *I bought a shirt and some trousers.* ***The*** *shirt is blue.* ◇ ***The*** *sun is shining.* ◇ ***The*** *apple is sour.*
2 a word that you use before numbers and dates: *Monday* ***the*** *sixth of May*
3 a word that you use to talk about a group of people or things of the same kind: ***the*** *Americans* (= all American people) ◇ *Do you play* ***the*** *piano?*
4 a word that you use before the names of rivers, seas, etc. and some countries: ***the*** *Limpopo* (= the Limpopo River) ◇ ***the*** *Atlantic* (= the Atlantic Ocean) ◇ ***the*** *United States of America*
the ..., the ... words that you use to talk about two things happening together because of each other: ***The*** *more you eat,* ***the*** *fatter you get.*

PRONUNCIATION You pronounce **the** as ***thee*** when it is followed by a vowel sound, for example ***thee*** **ash,** ***thee*** **end.**

theatre (say **thee**-uh-tuh) *noun* (*plural* **theatres**)
1 a building where you go to see plays: *I'm going to the* ***theatre*** *this evening.*
2 (also **operating theatre**) a room in a hospital where medical operations are performed

theft (say **theft**) *noun* (*no plural*) the crime of stealing something from a person or a place: *She was sent to prison for* ***theft****.* ◇ *I told the police about the* ***theft*** *of my car.* ➲ See **thief**

their (say *thair*) *adjective* of or belonging to them: *Who is* ***their*** *teacher?*

SPELLING Be careful! Don't confuse **their** and **there**. These words sound the same but have very different meanings: *Those are* ***their*** *shoes, not mine.* ◇ *He's over* ***there*** *near the door.*

theirs (say *thairz*) *pronoun*
something that belongs to them: *Our house is smaller than* ***theirs****.*

them (say *them*) *pronoun, plural noun*
1 a word that shows more than one person, animal or thing: *I wrote* ***them*** *a letter and then I phoned* ***them****.* ◇ *I'm looking for my keys. Have you seen* ***them****?*
2 him or her: *If anybody phones, tell* ***them*** *I'm busy.*

theme (say **theem**) *noun* (*plural* **themes**)
something that you talk or write about: *The* ***theme*** *of his speech was 'the future of our planet'.*

themselves (say *thehm*-**selvz**) *pronoun, plural noun*
1 a word that shows the same people, animals or things that you have just talked about: *They bought* ***themselves*** *a new car.*
2 a word that makes 'they' stronger: *Did they build the house* ***themselves****?*
by themselves
1 alone, or without other people: *The children went out by* ***themselves****.*
2 without help: *They cooked dinner by* ***themselves****.*

then (say *then*) *adverb*
1 at that time: *I was born in 1999. We lived in Gauteng* ***then****, but now we live in Limpopo.* ◇ *I'm going tomorrow. Can you wait until* ***then****?*
2 next, or after that: *We had supper and* ***then*** *we watched a movie.*
3 if that is true: *If you miss that train,* ***then*** *you'll have to get a bus.*

theology (say thee-**ol**-uh-jee) *noun* (*no plural*)
the study of religion: *a* ***theology*** *student*
► **theological** (*adjective*)

theorem (say **thee**-uh-ruhm) *noun* (*plural* **theorems**) (*maths*)
a statement you can show to be true: *Pythagoras'* ***theorem***

theoretical (say thee-uh-**ret**-ik-l) *adjective*
based on ideas and principles, not on practical experience: *We looked at* ***theoretical*** *examples in class.* ➲ See **practical** 1
► **theoretically** (*adverb*): ***Theoretically****, we can still win.*

theory (say **thee**-uh-ree) *noun*
1 (*plural* **theories**) an idea or set of ideas that tries to explain something: *There are a lot of different* ***theories*** *about how life began.*
2 (*no plural*) the general idea or principles of a particular subject: *political* ***theory*** ◇ *the* ***theory*** *and practice of language teaching*
3 (*plural* **theories**) an opinion or a belief that has not been shown to be true

therapeutic (say the-ruh-**pyoo**-tik) *adjective*
1 helping you to relax and feel better: *Going for a walk is* ***therapeutic****.*
2 helping to cure an illness: ***therapeutic*** *drugs*

therapy (say **the**-ruh-pee) *noun* (*no plural*)
a way of helping people who are ill in their body or mind, usually without drugs: *speech* ***therapy***

there (say *thair*) *adverb, pronoun*
1 a word that you use with verbs such as 'be', 'seem' and 'appear' to show that something is true or that something is happening: ***There*** *is a man at the door.* ◇ *Is* ***there*** *a film on TV tonight?* ◇ ***There*** *aren't any shops in this village.*
2 in, at or to that place: *Don't put the box* ***there*** *– put it here.* ◇ *Have you been to Mafikeng? I'm going* ***there*** *next week.*
3 a word that makes people look or listen: *Oh look,* ***there****'s Linda.*
there you are words that you say when you give something to somebody: *'****There*** *you are,' she said, giving me a cake.*

> SPELLING Be careful! Don't confuse **there** and **their**. These words sound the same but have very different meanings: *He's over* ***there*** *near the door.* ◇ *Those are* ***their*** *shoes, not mine.*

thereafter (say *thair*-**aaf**-tuh) *adverb*
after that

thereby (say *thair*-**by**) *adverb*
in that way

therefore (say *thair*-faw) *adverb*
for that reason: *He was sick and* ***therefore*** *did not come to soccer practice.*

thermal[1] (say **thurm**-l) *adjective*
relating to or connected with heat: ***thermal*** *energy*

thermal[2] *noun* (*plural* **thermals**)
a rising column of warm air in the atmosphere: ***Thermals*** *help gliders to soar through the air.*

thermo- (say **thur**-moh) *prefix*
relating to heat: *A* ***thermometer*** *measures temperature.*

thermometer (say thuh-**mom**-i-tuh) *noun* (*plural* **thermometers**)
an instrument that shows how hot or cold something is
ORIGIN: 17th century, through French *thermomètre* from Greek *thermo-* meaning 'of heat' + *-metrum* meaning 'measure'

thermometer

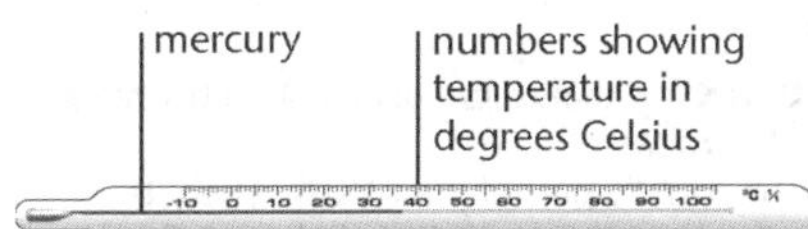

thermosphere (say **thur**-muh-sfeer) *noun*
the thermosphere the large warm layer of the atmosphere where there is very little gas ➲ See illustration at **atmosphere** ➲ See **ionosphere**, **mesosphere**, **stratosphere**, **troposphere**

thermostat (say **thur**-muh-stat) *noun* (*plural* **thermostats**)
a device that controls the temperature in a house or a machine by switching the heat on or off when necessary

thesaurus (say thi-**saw**-ruhss) *noun* (*plural* **thesauruses**)
a book that has lists of words and phrases with similar meanings

these (say ***th*eez**) *adjective, pronoun*
a word that you use to talk about people or things that are here or now: ***These** books are mine.* ◇ *Do you want **these**?*

USAGE **These** is the plural form of **this**.

PRONUNCIATION Be careful how you say **these**. Don't confuse it with **this** (which is pronounced *th*iss).

they (say ***th*ay**) *pronoun, plural noun*
1 the people, animals or things that the sentence is about: *Kulani and Mseni came at two o'clock and **they** left at six o'clock.* ◇ *'Where are my keys?' '**They're*** (= they are) *on the table.'*
2 a word that you use instead of 'he' or 'she': *Someone phoned for you – **they** said they would phone again later.*
3 people: ***They** say it will be cold this winter.*

they'd (say ***th*ayd**) short for **they had; they would**

they'll (say ***th*ayl**) short for **they will**

they're (say ***th*ay**-uh) short for **they are**

they've (say ***th*ayv**) short for **they have**

thick (say **thik**) *adjective* (**thicker**, **thickest**)
1 far from one side to the other: *The walls are very **thick**.* ◇ *It's cold tonight, so put a **thicker** blanket on your bed.* ➲ OPPOSITE **thin** 1
2 You use **thick** to say or ask how far something is from one side to the other: *The wall is 23 centimetres **thick**.*
3 with a lot of people or things close together: ***thick** dark hair* ➲ OPPOSITES **thin** 3, **fine**[1] 5
4 If a liquid is **thick**, it does not flow easily: *This paint is too **thick**.* ➲ OPPOSITE **runny** 2
5 difficult to see through: ***thick** smoke*
6 (*informal*) stupid, not clever
▸ **thickness** (*noun*): *Make sure the paint is the right **thickness**.*

thicket (say **thik**-uht) *noun* (*plural* **thickets**)
a thick group of bushes and trees: *There's a dense **thicket** on the edge of the park.*

thief (say **theef**) *noun* (*plural* **thieves**)
a person who steals something: *A **thief** stole my car.*

WORD BUILDING A **thief** is a general word for a person who steals things, usually secretly and without violence. The name of the crime is **theft**.
A **robber** steals from a bank, shop, etc. and often uses violence or threats. The crime is **robbery**.
A **burglar** takes things from your house when you are out or asleep. The crime is **burglary**.
A **shoplifter** steals things from shops while pretending to shop. The crime is **shoplifting**.

thigh (say **thy**) *noun* (*plural* **thighs**)
the part of your leg above your knee ➲ See illustration at **body**

thin (say **thin**) *adjective* (**thinner**, **thinnest**)
1 not far from one side to the other: *The walls in this house are very **thin**.* ◇ *I cut the bread into **thin** slices.* ➲ OPPOSITE **thick** 1
2 not fat: *He's tall and **thin**.* ➲ OPPOSITE **fat**[1]
3 not close together: *My father's hair is getting **thin**.* ➲ OPPOSITE **thick** 3
4 If a liquid is **thin**, it flows easily like water: *The soup was very **thin**.* ➲ SYNONYM **runny** ➲ OPPOSITE **thick** 4

WORD BUILDING We say **slim** to talk about people who are **thin** (in meaning 2 above) in an attractive way: *How do you stay so lovely and slim?* If you say somebody is **skinny**, you mean that he or she is too **thin**.

thing (say **thing**) *noun* (*plural* **things**)
1 an object: *What's that red **thing**?*
2 things (*plural noun*) objects, clothes or tools that belong to you or that you use for something: *Pack your **things** for the journey.*

A B C D E F G H I J K L M N O P Q R S T U V W X Y Z

3 what happens or what you do: *A strange **thing** happened to me yesterday.* ◇ *That was a difficult **thing** to do.*
4 an idea or a subject: *We talked about a lot of **things**.*

think (say **thingk**) *verb* (**thinking, thought**)
1 to have an opinion about something or to believe something: *I **think** it's going to rain.* ◇ *'Do you **think** Sara will come tomorrow?' 'Yes, I **think** so.'* (= I ***think** that she will come*) ◇ *What do you **think** of this music?*
2 to use your mind: ***Think** before you answer the question.* ➲ The noun is **thought**[1]
think of doing something to try to decide whether or not to do something: *He's **thinking** of leaving his job.*

thinly (say **thin**-lee) *adverb*
in a way that makes a thin piece of something: *Slice the potatoes **thinly**.*

third (say **thurd**) *adjective, adverb, noun*
1 3rd: *on his **third** birthday*
2 one of three equal parts of something; $\frac{1}{3}$

thirst (say **thurst**) *noun* (*no plural*)
the feeling you have when you want to drink something

thirsty (say **thurss**-tee) *adjective* (**thirstier, thirstiest**)
If you are **thirsty**, you want to drink something: *I'm **thirsty**. Can I have a drink of water, please?* ➲ See **hungry**

thirteen (say thur-**teen**) *number*
13
▸ **thirteenth** (*adjective, adverb*): *It's my **thirteenth*** (= 13th) *birthday today.*

thirtieth (say **thur**-ti-uth) *adjective, adverb*
30th

thirty (say **thur**-tee) *number*
1 30
2 the thirties (*plural noun*) the numbers 30 to 39 or the years 1930 to 1939: *He grew up in the **thirties*** (= in the 1930s).
in your thirties between the ages of 30 and 39

this[1] (say ***thiss***) *adverb*
so: *The road is not usually **this** busy* (= not as busy as it is now).

> **PRONUNCIATION** Be careful how you say **this**. Don't confuse it with **these** (which is pronounced ***theez***).

this[2] (say ***thiss***) *adjective, pronoun*
1 a word that you use to talk about a person or thing that is close to you in time or space: ***This** is my sister.* ◇ *How much does **this** cost?* ◇ *Come and look at **these** photos.*
2 a word that you use with periods of time that are connected to the present time: *I am on holiday **this** week.* ◇ *What are you doing **this** evening* (= today in the evening) *?*

thistle (say **thiss**-l) *noun* (*plural* **thistles**)
a plant with sharp pointed leaves and purple flowers

thorax (say **thaw**-rakss) *noun* (*plural* **thoraxes** or **thoraces**)
1 the middle part of your body where the bones around your chest **(ribs)** are ➲ See illustration at **body**
2 the middle section of an insect's body to which the legs and wings are connected ➲ See illustration at **insect**

thorn (say **thawn**) *noun* (*plural* **thorns**)
a sharp point that grows on a plant: ***Thorn** trees and rose bushes have **thorns**.*

thorough (say **thu**-ruh) *adjective*
careful and complete: *We gave the room a **thorough** clean.*

thoroughbred (say **thu**-ruh-bred) *noun* (*plural* **thoroughbreds**)
an animal, especially a horse, of high quality that has parents that are the same type: *They breed **thoroughbreds** on their farm.*
▸ **thoroughbred** (*adjective*)

thoroughfare (say **thu**-ruh-fair) *noun* (*plural* **thoroughfares**)
a public road or path that is open at both ends and is a route between two places

thoroughly (say **thu**-ruh-lee) *adverb*
1 carefully and completely: *He cleaned the room **thoroughly**.*
2 very, very much or completely: *I **thoroughly** enjoyed the film.*

those (say ***thohz***) *adjective, pronoun*
a word that you use to talk about people or things that are not here and now, but there or then: *I don't know **those** boys.* ◇ *Her grandfather was born in 1850. In **those** days, there were no cars.* ◇ *Can I have one of **those** sweets?*

> **USAGE** **Those** is the plural form of **that**.

though[1] (say ***thoh***) *conjunction*
1 in spite of something: *I was very cold, **though** I was wearing my coat.* ◇ ***Though** she was in a hurry, she stopped to talk.* ◇ *He went to the party, even **though** he was tired.* ➲ SYNONYM **although**
2 but: *I thought it was right, **though** I wasn't sure.*

as though in a way that makes you think something: *I'm so hungry – I feel as* ***though*** *I haven't eaten for days!*

though² (say **thoh**) *adverb*
however: *I like him very much. I don't like his brother,* ***though****.*

thought¹ (say **thawt**) form of **think**

thought² (say **thawt**) *noun*
1 (*no plural*) thinking: *After a lot of* ***thought****, I decided not to take the job.*
2 (*plural* **thoughts**) an idea: *Have you had any* ***thoughts*** *about what you want to do?*

thoughtful (say **thawt**-fuhl) *adjective*
1 thinking carefully: *She listened with a* ***thoughtful*** *look on her face.*
2 thinking about other people: *It was very* ***thoughtful*** *of you to cook us dinner.*
➲ SYNONYMS **considerate, kind²**

thoughtless (say **thawt**-luhss) *adjective*
not thinking about other people: *It was very* ***thoughtless*** *of them to leave the room in such a mess.* ➲ SYNONYM **inconsiderate**

thousand (say **thow**-zuhnd) *number*
1 000: *a* ***thousand*** *people* ◇ *two* ***thousand*** *and fifteen* ◇ *There were* ***thousands*** *of birds on the lake.*
▸ **thousandth** (*adjective, adverb, pronoun*): *That money is worth only one-****thousandth*** *(= 1 000th) of its value a year ago.*
🛈 **ORIGIN:** from Old English *thusend*, related to Dutch *duizend*

thrash (say **thrash**) *verb* (**thrashing, thrashed**)
1 to hit someone many times as a punishment: *Our neighbour* ***thrashed*** *my brother.*
2 to move or make something move about wildly without any control: *She was* ***thrashing*** *around in the pool.*
3 (*informal*) to beat someone very easily in a game or competition: *We* ***thrashed*** *the other school at athletics.*
▸ **thrashing** (*noun*): *She gave me a* ***thrashing*** *for lying.*

thread¹ (say **thred**) *noun* (*plural* **threads**)
a long thin piece of cotton, wool, etc.: *I need a needle and* ***thread****.*

thread² (say **thred**) *verb* (**threading, threaded**)
to put **thread¹** through the hole in a needle: *to* ***thread*** *a needle*

threadbare (say **thred**-bair) *adjective*
(used about material and clothes) old and very thin ➲ SYNONYM **tattered**

threat (say **thret**) *noun* (*plural* **threats**)
1 a promise that you will hurt somebody if they do not do what you want
2 a person or thing that may damage or hurt somebody or something: *Pollution is a* ***threat*** *to the lives of animals and people.*

threaten (say **thret**-uhn) *verb* (**threatening, threatened**)
1 to say that you may hurt or punish somebody if they do not do what you want: *They* ***threatened*** *to leave him at home if he didn't behave.* ◇ *She* ***threatened*** *him with a knife.*
2 to seem ready to do something bad: *The dark clouds* ***threatened*** *rain.*

three (say **three**) *number*
3 ➲ The adjective is **third**

three-dimensional (say three-dy-**men**-shuhn-l) *adjective* (abbr. 3-D)
(used about an object or space) having or appearing to have length, width and depth: *A sphere and a cube are* ***three-dimensional*** *figures.*
➲ See **two-dimensional**

WORD BUILDING A block is **three-dimensional**. Its faces or surfaces are **two-dimensional**. The surfaces intersect to produce **edges**. These edges or lines are **nought-dimensional**. The edges intersect to produce **points** or **vertices**. These points are considered nought-dimensional – they have no length, width or depth.

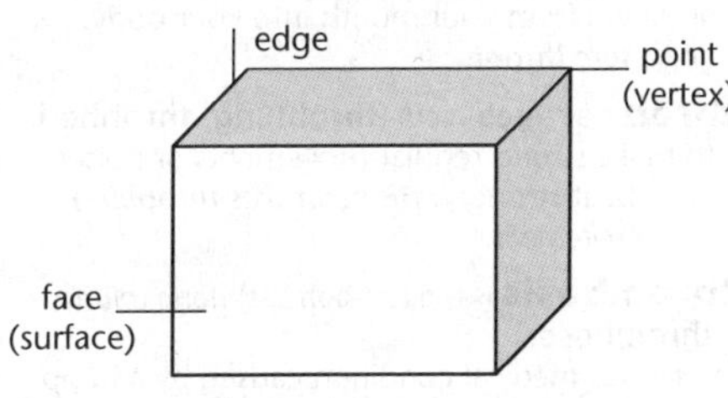

a three-dimensional block

thresh (say **thresh**) *verb* (**threshing, threshed**)
to separate grains of corn or rice from the rest of the plant using a machine or special tool
▸ **threshing** (*noun*): *Let's start today's threshing.* ▸ **threshing** (*adjective*): *a* ***threshing*** *machine* ▸ **thresher** (*noun*)

threshold (say **thresh**-hohld) *noun* (*plural* **thresholds**)
1 the ground at the entrance to a room or building: *Step across the* ***threshold****.*
2 the level at which something starts to happen or you start to feel something: *I have a low pain* ***threshold****.*
3 the time when you are just about to start or find something: *Scientists are on the* ***threshold*** *of a discovery.*

A B C D E F G H I J K L M N O P Q R S T U V W X Y Z

threw (say **throo**) form of **throw**

thrifty (say **thrif**-tee) *adjective* (**thriftier, thriftiest**)
careful not to spend too much money: *Try to be **thrifty** with your pocket money.*

thrill[1] (say **thril**) *noun* (*plural* **thrills**)
a sudden strong feeling of excitement: *It gave me a big **thrill** to meet my favourite cricketer.*

thrill[2] (say **thril**) *verb* (**thrilling, thrilled**)
to make somebody feel very excited or pleased: *This band has **thrilled** audiences all over the world.*

thrilled (say **thrild**) *adjective*
very happy and excited: *We are all **thrilled** that you won the prize.* ➲ SYNONYM **overjoyed**

thriller (say **thril**-uh) *noun* (*plural* **thrillers**)
an exciting book, film or play, especially one about crime or **spying**

thrilling (say **thril**-ing) *adjective*
very exciting: *a **thrilling** adventure*

thrive (say **thrive**) *verb* (**thriving, thrived**)
to grow or develop well: *My plants are **thriving**.* ➲ SYNONYM **flourish**
▸ **thriving** (*adjective*): *a **thriving** market*

throat (say **throht**) *noun* (*plural* **throats**)
1 the front part of your neck
2 the part inside your neck that takes food and air down from your mouth into your body: *I've got a sore **throat**.*

throb (say **throb**) *verb* (**throbbing, throbbed**)
to make strong regular movements or noises, or to beat strongly: *His heart was **throbbing** with excitement.*

thrombosis (say throm-**boh**-siss) *noun* (*plural* **thromboses**)
a serious medical condition caused by a lump of thick blood formed in a **blood vessel**

throne (*rhymes with* **groan**) *noun* (*plural* **thrones**)
a special chair where a king or queen sits

throttle (say **throt**-l) *verb* (**throttling, throttled**)
to hold someone tightly by the throat and stop them from breathing ➲ SYNONYM **strangle**

through (say **throo**) *preposition, adverb*
1 from one side or end of something to the other side or end: *What can you see **through** the window?* ◇ *She opened the gate and we walked **through**.*
2 from the beginning to the end of something: *We travelled **through** the night.*
3 connected by telephone: *Can you put me **through** to Johan van Eeden, please?* ◇ *I tried to phone you but I couldn't get **through**.*
4 because of somebody or something: *She got the job **through** her father.*

throughout (say throo-**owt**) *preposition, adverb*
1 in every part of something: *We painted the house **throughout**.* ◇ *She is famous **throughout** the world.*
2 from the beginning to the end of something: *They talked **throughout** the film.*

throw (say **throh**) *verb* (**throwing, threw, has thrown**)
1 to move your arm quickly to send something through the air: ***Throw** the ball to Alex.* ◇ *The child **threw** a stone at the cat.*
2 to move your body or part of it quickly: *He **threw** his arms up.*
throw something away or **out** to get rid of rubbish or something that you do not want: *Don't **throw** that box away.*
▸ **throw** (*noun*): *What a good **throw**!*

> USAGE Be careful when you use this word! You say: *He **threw** mud **at** me.* Don't say 'He threw me with mud.'

> WHICH WORD? **Throw** or **put**?
> - **Throwing** something is a strong, quick action: ***Throw** the ball!* ◇ *Please **throw** an apple to me.* ◇ *He angrily **threw** his shoe across the room.*
> - Use **put** or other suitable verbs (not **throw**) for actions such as these: ***Put** onions in the pot, then **add** the beans and then **pour** in a cup of water.* ◇ ***Put** R5 into the machine and take your ticket.*

thrush (say **thrush**) *noun*
1 (*plural* **thrushes**) any of a large family of small and medium-sized birds: *A robin is a type of **thrush**.*
2 (*no plural*) an infection caused by a fungus, often occurring as white marks in the mouth and throat

thrust (say **thrust**) *verb* (**thrusting, thrust**)
to push somebody or something suddenly and strongly: *She **thrust** the money into my hand.*
▸ **thrust** (*noun*): *He killed the man with a **thrust** of the knife.*

thud[1] (say **thud**) *noun* (*plural* **thuds**)
the sound that a heavy thing makes when it hits something: *The book hit the floor with a **thud**.*

thud[2] (say **thud**) *verb* (**thudding, thudded**)
1 to fall or hit something with a low dull sound: *The bullet **thudded** into the soldier's chest.*
2 (especially of the heart) to beat strongly

thug (say **thug**) *noun* (*plural* **thugs**)
a rough and violent man

thumb (say **thum**) *noun* (*plural* **thumbs**)
the short thick finger at the side of your hand
➲ See illustration at **hand**[1]
the thumbs up or **down** a sign or expression that shows approval or disapproval: *Dad's given my new boyfriend the* ***thumbs up*** *– he likes him!*

PRONUNCIATION Don't pronounce the **b** in **thumb**.

thump (say **thump**) *verb* (**thumping, thumped**)
1 to hit somebody or something hard with your hand or a heavy thing: *He* ***thumped*** *on the door.*
2 to make a loud sound by hitting or beating hard: *Her heart was* ***thumping*** *with fear.*
▸ **thump** (*noun*)
ⓘ ORIGIN: 16th century. The word came from imitating the sound.

thunder[1] (say **thun**-duh) *noun* (*no plural*)
a loud noise in the sky when there is a storm: *There was* ***thunder*** *and lightning.* ➲ See note at **storm**[1]

thunder[2] (say **thun**-duh) *verb* (**thundering, thundered**)
1 When it **thunders**, there is a loud noise in the sky during a storm: *It* ***thundered*** *all night.*
2 to make a very loud deep noise: *The trucks* ***thundered*** *along the road.*

thunderstorm (say **thun**-duh-stawm) *noun* (*plural* **thunderstorms**)
a storm with a lot of rain, **thunder**[1] and **lightning** in the sky ➲ See note at **storm**[1]

Thursday (say **thurz**-day) *noun*
the day of the week after Wednesday and before Friday ➲ See note at **day**

thus (say *thuss*) *adverb* (*formal*)
1 in this way: *Hold the pen between your finger and thumb,* ***thus.***
2 because of this: *He was very busy and was* ***thus*** *unable to come to the meeting.*

tibia (say **tib**-i-uh) *noun* (*plural* **tibiae**) = **shin bone** ➲ See illustration at **skeleton**

tic (say **tik**) *noun* (*plural* **tics**)
a sudden movement of a muscle, often in the face or head, that you cannot control and that keeps repeating: *She has a nervous* ***tic.***

tick[1] (say **tik**) *verb* (**ticking, ticked**)
1 (used about a clock) to make short repeated sounds: *I could hear a clock* ***ticking.***
2 to make a mark like this ✓ next to something: ***Tick*** *the right answer.*

tick[2] (say **tik**) *noun* (*plural* **ticks**)
1 a small mark like this ✓: *Put a* ***tick*** *next to the correct answer.*
2 one of the short repeated sounds that a clock makes
3 a small creature with eight legs that sucks blood from other animals or people

ticket (say **tik**-it) *noun* (*plural* **tickets**)
a piece of paper or card that you buy to travel, or to go into a cinema, theatre, etc.: *a theatre* ***ticket*** ◇ *May I have one return* ***ticket*** *to town, please?*
ticket office a place where you buy tickets

tickle (say **tik**-l) *verb* (**tickling, tickled**)
1 to touch somebody lightly with your fingers to make them laugh: *She* ***tickled*** *the baby's feet.*
2 to have the feeling that something is touching you lightly: *My nose* ***tickles.***

tidal (say **tide**-uhl) *adjective*
connected with or depending on the **tides**: ***tidal*** *forces* ◇ *a* ***tidal*** *pool*

tide *noun* (*plural* **tides**)
the movement of the sea towards the land and away from the land: *The* ***tide*** *is coming in.* ◇ *The* ***tide*** *is going out.*

WORD BUILDING **High tide** is when the sea is nearest the land, and **low tide** is when the sea is furthest from the land.

tidy[1] (say **tide**-ee) *adjective* (**tidier, tidiest**)
1 with everything in the right place: *Her room is very* ***tidy.*** ➲ SYNONYM **neat**
2 liking to have everything in the right place: *a* ***tidy*** *boy* ➲ OPPOSITE **untidy**
▸ ***tidily*** (*adverb*): *Put the books back* ***tidily*** *when you've finished with them.* ▸ **tidiness** (*noun*)

tidy[2] (say **tide**-ee) *verb* (**tidying, tidied**) (also **tidy up**)
to make something tidy: *I* ***tidied*** *the house before my parents arrived.* ◇ *Can you help me to* ***tidy up?***

tie[1] (say *ty*) *verb* (**tying, tied**)
1 to fasten or fix something using rope, string, etc.: *I* ***tied*** *my hair back with a ribbon.* ◇ *She* ***tied*** *a scarf round her neck.*
2 to end a game or competition with the same number of points for both teams or players: *France* ***tied*** *with Egypt for second place.*
tie something or somebody up to put a piece of string or rope around something to hold it in place or around somebody to stop them from moving: *I* ***tied*** *up the parcel with string.* ◇ *The robbers* ***tied*** *up the owner of the shop.*

A B C D E F G H I J K L M N O P Q R S **T** U V W X Y Z

tie² (say **ty**) *noun*
1 (*plural* **ties**) a long thin piece of cloth that you wear round your neck with a shirt
2 (*no plural*) when two teams or players have the same number of points at the end of a game or competition: *The match ended in a* ***tie***.
➲ See **draw²**
3 ties (*plural noun*) a connection between people or organizations: *Our school has* ***ties*** *with a school in Florida.*

tiff (say **tif**) *noun* (*plural* **tiffs**)
a short argument or disagreement with someone: *They are having a* ***tiff***. ➲ SYNONYMS **quarrel¹**, **row³**

tiger (say **ty**-guh) *noun* (*plural* **tigers**)
a wild animal like a large cat, with yellow fur and black stripes. **Tigers** live in Asia.

WORD BUILDING A female tiger is called a **tigress** and a young tiger is called a **cub**.

tight (say **tite**) *adjective* (**tighter**, **tightest**)
1 fixed firmly so that you cannot move it easily: *a* ***tight*** *knot* ◇ *I can't open this jar of jam – the lid is too* ***tight***. ➲ OPPOSITE **loose** 2
2 Tight clothes fit very closely in a way that is often uncomfortable: ***tight*** *trousers* ◇ *These shoes are too* ***tight***.
▸ **tight** (also **tightly**) (*adverb*): *Hold* ***tight***! ◇ *I tied the string* ***tightly*** *around the box.*

tighten (say **tite**-uhn) *verb* (**tightening**, **tightened**)
to become tighter or to make something tighter: *Can you* ***tighten*** *this screw?* ➲ OPPOSITE **loosen**

tightrope (say **tite**-rohp) *noun* (*plural* **tightropes**)
a rope or wire high above the ground. People (called **acrobats**) walk along or do tricks on **tightropes** as a form of entertainment.

tights (say **tite**-ss) *plural noun*
a thin piece of clothing that fits tightly over the feet and legs: *a pair of* ***tights***

tigress (say **ty**-gruhss) *noun* (*plural* **tigresses**)
➲ See note at **tiger**

tik (say **tik**) *noun* (*no plural*) (*S. African, informal*)
a strong and dangerous illegal drug that increases your energy, prevents sleep and causes violent behaviour ➲ SYNONYM **methamphetamine**
🛈 **ORIGIN**: 20th century, from the crackling sound that tik makes when it is heated, usually in a thin glass container or a light bulb

tile *noun* (*plural* **tiles**)
a flat, usually square object. We use **tiles** for covering roofs, walls and floors.
▸ **tile** (*verb*): *Dad is* ***tiling*** *the bathroom.*

till¹ (say **til**) *conjunction, preposition* (*informal*)
= **until**

till² (say **til**) *noun* (*plural* **tills**)
a drawer or machine for money in a shop

till³ (say **til**) *verb* (**tilling**, **tilled**)
to prepare land for planting crops: ***Till*** *the fields.*

tilt *verb* (**tilting**, **tilted**)
to have one side higher than the other or to move something so that it has one side higher than the other: *She* ***tilted*** *the tray and all the cups fell off.*

timber (say **tim**-buh) *noun* (*no plural*)
wood that we use for building and making things

timbre (say **taam**-buh) *noun* (*plural* **timbres**) (*formal*)
the quality of sound that is produced by a particular voice or musical instrument

time¹ (say **time**) *noun*
1 (*no plural*) a period of seconds, minutes, hours, days, weeks, months or years: ***Time*** *passes quickly when you're busy.* ◇ *I haven't got* ***time*** *to help you – I'm late!* ◇ *It takes a long* ***time*** *to learn a language.* ◇ *I spend a lot of* ***time*** *playing tennis.*
2 (*plural* **times**) a certain point in the day or night that you say in hours and minutes: *'What's the* ***time****?' 'It's twenty past six.'* ◇ *Can you tell me the* ***times*** *of buses to George, please?*
3 (*plural* **times**) a certain moment or occasion: *I've seen this film four* ***times***. ◇ *Come and visit us next* ***time*** *you're here.* ◇ *I see my cousin from* ***time*** *to* ***time***.
4 (*plural* **times**) an experience or something that you do: *We had a great* ***time*** *on holiday.* ◇ *Have a good* ***time***!
5 (*plural* **times**) certain years in history: *In Shakespeare's* ***time***, *few people could read.*
at a time together or on one occasion: *The lift can carry six people at a* ***time***.
in a week's, **two months'**, **a year's time** after a week, two months, a year: *I'll see you in two weeks'* ***time***.
in time or **in good time** at the right time or early: *I finished my homework in* ***time*** *for supper.* ◇ *I want to get to the station in good* ***time***.
on time not late or early: *My train was on* ***time***.
spare time, **free time** time when you do not have to work or study: *What do you do in your spare* ***time***?
take your time to do something slowly
tell the time to read the **time** from a clock or watch: *Can you tell the* ***time***?

time² *verb* (**timing, timed**)
1 to plan something so that it will happen when you want: *The bomb was **timed** to explode at six o'clock.*
2 to measure how much **time** it takes to do something: *We **timed** the journey – it took half an hour.*

times¹ (say **tymz**) *preposition* (symbol x)
multiplied by: *Three **times** four is twelve (3 x 4 = 12).*

times² (say **tymz**) *plural noun*
a word that you use to show how much bigger, smaller, more expensive, etc. one thing is than another: *This town is ten **times** bigger than the place where I grew up.*

timetable (say **time**-tayb-l) *noun* (*plural* **timetables**)
a list of times when something happens: *a train **timetable*** ◇ *a school **timetable*** (= showing when lessons start and finish)

timid (say **tim**-id) *adjective*
shy and easily frightened
► **timidly** (*adverb*): *She opened the door **timidly** and came in.*

timpani (say **tim**-puh-nee) *plural noun*
a set of drums that you play in an orchestra

tin *noun*
1 (*no plural*) (symbol Sn) a soft silver-white metal that is often mixed with other metals
2 (*plural* **tins**) a metal container for food and drink that keeps it fresh: *a biscuit **tin*** ◇ *I opened a **tin** of beans.* ➲ SYNONYM **can²**
► **tinned** (*adjective*): ***tinned** peaches*

tinge (say **tinj**) *noun* (*plural* **tinges**)
a small amount of a colour or a feeling: *There's a green **tinge** to this paint.*
► **tinged** (*adjective*): *Her joy was **tinged** with sadness.*

tingle (say **ting**-guhl) *verb* (**tingling, tingled**)
to feel as if a large number of small points are pushing into a part of your body: *My feet are **tingling** because I was sitting on them.*
► **tingle** (*noun*): *a **tingle** of excitement*

tinkle (say **tingk**-l) *verb* (**tinkling, tinkled**)
to make a light high ringing sound, like that of a small bell: *The doorbell **tinkled**.*
► **tinkle** (*noun*): *I heard a **tinkle**.*

tin-opener (say **tin**-ohp-nuh) *noun* (*plural* **tin-openers**)
a tool for opening tins

tint *noun* (*plural* **tints**)
a small amount of a colour: *The paint has a blue **tint**.* ➲ See **tinge**
► **tint** (*verb*): ***tinted** windows.*

tiny (say **ty**-nee) *adjective* (**tinier, tiniest**)
very small: *Ants are **tiny** insects.* ➲ SYNONYM **minute²**

tip¹ *noun* (*plural* **tips**)
1 the pointed or thin end of something: *the **tips** of your fingers*
2 a small amount of extra money that you give to somebody who serves you, for example in a restaurant: *I left a **tip** on the table for the waiter.*
3 a small piece of advice: *She gave me some useful **tips** on how to pass the exam.*

tip² *verb* (**tipping, tipped**)
1 to move so that one side goes up or down, or to move something so that one side goes up or down: *Don't **tip** your chair back.*
2 to turn something so that the things inside fall out: *She opened a tin of peaches and **tipped** them into a bowl.*
3 to give somebody an extra amount of money to thank them for something they have done for you as part of their job: *Do you **tip** taxi drivers in your country?*
tip over, tip something over to turn over or to make something turn over: *The boat **tipped** over and we all fell into the water.* ◇ *Don't **tip** your cup over!*

tipsy (say **tip**-see) *adjective* (**tipsier, tipsiest**)
slightly drunk: *He was **tipsy** at the party.*

tiptoe (say **tip**-toh) *verb* (**tiptoeing, tiptoed**)
to walk quietly on your toes: *He **tiptoed** into the bedroom.*
on tiptoe standing or walking on your toes with the rest of your feet off the ground: *She stood on **tiptoe**.*

tirade (say ty-**rayd**) *noun* (*plural* **tirades**)
a long angry speech: *a **tirade** of criticism*

tire (say **ty**-uh) *verb* (**tiring, tired**)
to feel that you need to rest or sleep, or to make somebody feel this: *These exercises **tire** me out!*

tired (say **ty**-uhd) *adjective*
needing to rest or sleep: *I've been working all day and I'm **tired** out* (= extremely tired). ◇ *He's feeling **tired**.*
be tired of something to have had or done too much of something, so that you do not want it any longer: *I'm **tired** of watching TV – let's go out.*
► **tiredness** (*noun*)

tiresome (say **ty**-uh-suhm) *adjective* (*formal*)
that makes you angry or bored: *This homework is **tiresome**.* ➲ SYNONYM **tedious**

tiring (say **ty**-uh-ring) *adjective*
making you feel tired: *a **tiring** journey*

A B C D E F G H I J K L M N O P Q R S **T** U V W X Y Z

A B C D E F G H I J K L M N O P Q R S T U V W X Y Z

tissue (say **ti**-shoo) *noun*
1 (*plural* **tissues**) a thin piece of soft paper that you use to clean your nose: *a box of* ***tissues***
2 (*no plural*) a group of similar cells that together perform a particular function in an organism: *muscle* ***tissue***

tissue paper *noun* (*no plural*)
thin paper that you use for wrapping things

titbit (say **tit**-bit) *noun* (*plural* **titbits**)
1 a nice but very small piece of food
2 an interesting piece of information

title[1] (say **tite**-l) *noun* (*plural* **titles**)
1 the name of something, for example a book, film or picture: *What is the* ***title*** *of this poem?*
2 a word like 'Mr', 'Mrs' or 'Doctor' that you put before a person's name

title[2] (say **tite**-l) *verb* (**titling**, **titled**)
give a name to something such as a book or a film: *This book is* ***titled*** *'The Season of Joy'.*
➲ See **entitled**

TNT (say tee-en-**tee**) *noun* (*no plural*)
a highly explosive substance ❶ **TNT** is short for 'trinitrotoluene'.

to (say ***tuu*** or **tuh**) *preposition, adverb*
1 a word that shows direction: *She went* ***to*** *Swaziland.* ◇ *This bus goes* ***to*** *the city centre.*
2 a word that shows the person or thing that receives something: *I gave the book* ***to*** *Puleng.* ◇ *Be kind* ***to*** *animals.*
3 a word that shows the end or limit of something: *The museum is open from 9.30* ***to*** *5.30.* ◇ *Jeans cost from R70* ***to*** *R450.*
4 on or against something: *They were sitting back* ***to*** *back.*
5 a word that shows how something changes: *The sky changed from blue* ***to*** *grey.*
6 a word that you use for comparing things: *I prefer football* ***to*** *tennis.*
7 a word that shows how many minutes it is before the hour: *It's two minutes* ***to*** *six.*
8 a word that you use before verbs to make the **infinitive** (= the simple form of a verb): *I want* ***to*** *go home.*

toad *noun* (*plural* **toads**)
a small cold-blooded animal with rough skin that lives in or near water ➲ See **frog**

toadstool (say **tohd**-stool) *noun* (*plural* **toadstools**)
a type of organism (called a **fungus**) that is usually poisonous, with a round top and a thin stem ➲ See **mushroom[1]**, **fungus**

toast (say **tohst**) *noun*
1 (*no plural*) a thin piece of bread that you have cooked so that it is brown: *I had a slice of* ***toast*** *and jam for breakfast.*
2 (*plural* **toasts**) the act of holding up a glass of wine and wishing somebody happiness or success before you drink: *They drank a* ***toast*** *to the winner.*
▸ **toast** (*verb*): ***toasted*** *sandwiches* ◇ *We all* ***toasted*** *the bride and groom* (= at a wedding).

toaster (say **tohss**-tuh) *noun* (*plural* **toasters**)
a machine for making **toast**

tobacco (say tuh-**bak**-oh) *noun* (*no plural*)
special dried leaves that people smoke in cigarettes and pipes, or the plant on which these leaves grow
❶ **ORIGIN:** 16th century, from Spanish *tabaco*, perhaps from Carib or Taino, languages of South America and the Caribbean. Spanish colonists and traders brought the word to Europe.

toboggan (say tuh-**bog**-uhn) *noun* (*plural* **toboggans**)
a type of flat board with flat pieces of metal underneath which people use for travelling down hills on snow for fun ➲ See **sledge**
❶ **ORIGIN:** 19th century, through Canadian French *tabaganne*, from Micmac *topaan* meaning 'sled'. Micmac is a language spoken by a small group of people in Canada.

today (say tuh-**day**) *adverb, noun* (*no plural*)
1 this day or on this day: ***Today*** *is Friday.* ◇ *What shall we do* ***today?***
2 the present time or at the present time: *Many people* ***today*** *have cellphones.* ➲ **SYNONYM nowadays**

toddler (say **tod**-luh) *noun* (*plural* **toddlers**)
a young child who has just started to walk

toe (say **toh**) *noun* (*plural* **toes**)
1 one of the five parts at the end of your foot ➲ See illustration at **foot**
2 the part of a shoe or sock that covers the end of your foot

toenail (say **toh**-nayl) *noun* (*plural* **toenails**)
the hard part at the end of your toe ➲ See illustration at **foot**

toffee (say **tof**-ee) *noun* (*plural* **toffees**)
a hard brown sweet made from sugar and butter

toga (say **toh**-guh) *noun* (*plural* **togas**)
a long piece of material that men in ancient Rome wore around their bodies

together (say tuh-**ge*th***-uh) *adverb*
1 with each other or close to each other: *My brother and sister usually walk home* ***together.*** ◇ *Stand with your feet* ***together.***
2 so that two or more things are joined to or mixed with each other: *Tie the ends of the rope*

together. ◇ *Add these numbers* ***together.*** ◇ *Mix the eggs and sugar* ***together.***

toil (say **toyl**) *verb* (**toiling, toiled**) (*formal*)
to work very hard or for a long time at something: *I* ***toiled*** *in the garden through summer.*
▸ **toil** (*noun*)

toilet (say **toy**-luht) *noun* (*plural* **toilets**)
1 a large bowl with a seat that you use when you need to empty waste from your body
2 a room that contains a **toilet**: *I'm going to the toilet.*

WORD BUILDING For meaning 2 above, in their houses people usually say **the toilet** or **the bathroom** or, informally, **the loo**. In public places, the toilets are often called the **Ladies** or the **Gents**.

toilet paper *noun* (*no plural*)
soft thin paper that you use to clean yourself after going to the toilet

token (say **toh**-kuhn) *noun* (*plural* **tokens**)
1 a piece of paper, plastic or metal that you use instead of money to pay for something
2 a small thing that you use to show something else: *This gift is a* ***token*** *of our friendship.*

tokoloshe (say **tok**-uh-losh) *noun* (*plural* **tokoloshes**) (*S. African*)
(in African stories) a creature that causes trouble or harms people, usually at night
ⓘ ORIGIN: from isiZulu *utokoloshe* or isiXhosa *uthikoloshe*, a name given to a magical creature that lives in rivers

told (say **tohld**) form of **tell**

tolerant (say **tol**-uh-ruhnt) *adjective*
letting people do or believe things even though you do not like, understand or agree with them: *We must be* ***tolerant*** *of other people's beliefs.* ➲ OPPOSITE **intolerant**
▸ **tolerance** (*noun*): ***tolerance*** *of other religions*

tolerate (say **tol**-uh-rayt) *verb* (**tolerating, tolerated**)
to let people do something even though you do not like or understand it: *He won't* ***tolerate*** *rudeness.*

toll (*rhymes with* **hole**) *noun* (*plural* **tolls**)
1 money that you pay to use a particular road (called a **toll road**)
2 the amount of damage done or the number of people killed or injured by something: *the death* ***toll*** ◇ *The drought has taken its* ***toll*** *on us.*

tomato (say tuh-**maa**-toh) *noun* (*plural* **tomatoes**)
a soft red fruit that you cook or eat cold in salads: ***tomato*** *soup*
ⓘ ORIGIN: 17th century, from French, Spanish and Portuguese *tomate*, from Nahuatl *tomatl*. Nahuatl is a language spoken in Mexico and Central America.

tomato sauce *noun* (*no plural*)
a cold sauce made from tomatoes
➲ See **ketchup**

tomb (say **toom**) *noun* (*plural* **tombs**)
a structure made of stone where the body of an important person is buried

tomboy (say **tom**-boy) *noun* (*plural* **tomboys**)
a young girl who enjoys the same games and activities that are traditionally seen as boys' games: *My sister is a* ***tomboy.***

tombstone (say **toom**-stohn) *noun* (*plural* **tombstones**)
a large flat stone on the place where a person is buried (their **grave**), showing their name and the dates when they lived

tomcat (say **tom**-kat) *noun* (*plural* **tomcats**)
a male cat

tomorrow (say tuh-**mo**-roh) *adverb*, *noun* (*no plural*)
the day after today or on the day after today: *Let's go swimming* ***tomorrow.*** ◇ *I'll see you* ***tomorrow*** *morning.* ◇ *We are going home the day after* ***tomorrow.***

SPELLING Remember! You spell **tomorrow** with one **m** and **rr**.

ton (say **tun**) *noun* (also **tonne**)
1 (*plural* **tons**) a unit for measuring **mass**. One ton is equal to 1 000 kilograms: *three* ***tons*** *of wheat*
2 tons (*plural noun*) (*informal*) a lot: *He's got* ***tons*** *of money.*

USAGE For meaning 1 above, in South Africa a **ton** means a **metric ton**. In some other countries the number of kilograms in a **ton** is slightly different.
In maths and science, the usual spelling is **tonne**.

tone (say **tohn**) *noun* (*plural* **tones**)
the way that something sounds: *I knew she was angry by the* ***tone*** *of her voice.*

tongs (say **tongz**) *plural noun*
a tool with two parts joined at one end that you use for holding things or picking things up

tongue (say **tung**) *noun* (*plural* **tongues**)
1 the soft part inside your mouth that moves when you talk or eat
2 (*formal*) a language: *your mother* ***tongue***

A B C D E F G H I J K L M N O P Q R S T U V W X Y Z

tonic (say **ton**-ik) *noun*
1 (*plural* **tonics**) a medicine or something that you do that makes you feel stronger, especially after an illness or when you are very tired: *The chemist gave me a **tonic**.* ◇ *This weekend is like a **tonic** for me.*
2 (*no plural*) (also **tonic water**) water with bubbles and a bitter taste, often added to alcoholic drinks: *a gin and **tonic***

tonight (say tuh-**nite**) *noun* (*no plural*)
the evening or night of today: ***Tonight** is the last night of our holiday.*
▸ **tonight** (*adverb*): *I'm going to a party **tonight**.*

tonne (say **tun**) *noun* (*plural* **tonnes**) = **metric ton** ➲ See note at **ton**

tonsil (say **ton**-sil) *noun* (*plural* **tonsils**)
one of the two soft lumps in your throat at the back of your mouth: *She went to hospital to have her **tonsils** out.*

tonsillitis (say ton-si-**lite**-uhss) *noun* (*no plural*)
an illness in which the tonsils become very sore and swollen

too *adverb*
1 more than you want or need: *These shoes are **too** big.* ◇ *She put **too** much milk in my coffee.*
2 also: *Green is my favourite colour but I like blue **too**.*

WHICH WORD? **Too** or **very**?
- Be careful when you use **too**. It means 'more than something should be'. If a person is **too kind**, it means that they are being more kind than they should be: *You're being **too** kind and you're spoiling her.*
- If you want to emphasize something, use **very**: *She's a **very** kind, wonderful person.*

took (say **tuuk**) form of **take**

tool *noun* (*plural* **tools**)
a piece of equipment that you hold in your hand and use to do a special job: *Hammers, saws, drills and screwdrivers are **tools**.*

tooth *noun* (*plural* **teeth**)
1 one of the hard white things in your mouth that you use for eating: *I brush my **teeth** after every meal.*
2 one of the long narrow pointed parts of an object such as a comb

WORD BUILDING A **dentist** is a person whose job is to look after teeth. If a **tooth** is bad, the dentist may **fill** it (put a substance in the hole) or **take** it **out**. People who have lost their own teeth can wear **false teeth**, also called **dentures**.

toothache (say **tooth**-ayk) *noun* (*no plural*)
a pain in your tooth: *I've got **toothache**.*

toothbrush (say **tooth**-brush) *noun* (*plural* **toothbrushes**)
a small brush for cleaning your teeth

toothpaste (say **tooth**-payst) *noun* (*no plural*)
a substance that you put on your **toothbrush** and use for cleaning your teeth

top[1] *noun* (*plural* **tops**)
1 the highest part of something: *There's a church at the **top** of the hill.* ➲ OPPOSITE **bottom** 1
2 a cover that you put on something to close it: *Where's the **top** of this bottle?*
3 a piece of clothing that you wear on the **top** part of your body: *I like your **top** – is it new?*
on top on its highest part: *The cake had cream on **top**.*
on top of something on or over something: *A tree fell on **top** of my car.*

top[2] (say **top**) *adjective*
1 highest: *Put this book on the **top** shelf.*
2 best: *She's one of the country's **top** athletes.*

topaz (say **toh**-paz) *noun* (*no plural*)
a clear stone that comes in different colours and is used in jewellery

topic (say **top**-ik) *noun* (*plural* **topics**)
something that you talk, learn or write about: *The **topic** of the discussion was music.*
➲ SYNONYM **subject**[1] 1

topical (say **top**-ik-l) *adjective*
relating to something that is happening now and that people are interested in: *Choose something **topical** for your project.*

topography (say tuh-**pog**-ruh-fee) *noun* (*no plural*)
the physical characteristics of an area of land, especially its rivers and mountains
▸ **topographical** (*adjective*): ***topographical** maps*

topple (say **top**-l) *verb* (**toppling**, **toppled**)
1 to become less steady and fall down: *The tower of blocks **toppled** over.*
2 to cause a leader or government to lose their position of power ➲ SYNONYM **overthrow**

topsoil (say **top**-soyl) *noun* (*no plural*)
the top layer of soil, often consisting of a lot of dead plant matter

Torah (say **taw**-raa or taw-**raa**) *noun* (*no plural*)
(in Judaism) the book that Jews believe contains the laws of God, and that is contained in the first part of the **Bible**

torch (say **tawch**) *noun* (*plural* **torches**)
1 a small electric light that you can carry in your hand: *Did you pack spare batteries for your torch?*
2 a long piece of wood with burning material at one end which people carry to give light: *a burning* ***torch*** ◊ *the Olympic* ***torch***

tore, torn (say **taw**, **tawn**) forms of **tear**[1]

torment[1] (say taw-**ment**) *verb* (**tormenting, tormented**)
to cause great pain and suffering to somebody or something: *Stop* ***tormenting*** *the puppy.*
➲ SYNONYM **torture**[2]

torment[2] (say **taw**-ment) *noun* (*plural* **torments**) (*formal*)
something that causes great pain and suffering to somebody or something

tornado (say taw-**nay**-doh) *noun* (*plural* **tornadoes**)
a violent storm with a very strong wind that blows in a circle
ℹ ORIGIN: 16th century, probably from Spanish *tronada* meaning 'thunderstorm'

torpedo (say taw-**pee**-doh) *noun* (*plural* **torpedoes**)
a type of bomb in the shape of a long tube that is fired from a ship or a **submarine** and that explodes when it hits its target

torque (say **tawk**) *noun* (*no plural*) (*technology*)
the force that causes machinery to turn round **(rotate)**: *The more* ***torque*** *a car has, the bigger the load it can carry in the same gear.*

torrent (say **to**-ruhnt) *noun* (*plural* **torrents**)
a strong fast flow of water: *The rain was coming down in* ***torrents***.
▸ **torrential** (*adjective*): ***torrential*** *rain*

torrid (say **to**-rid) *adjective*
1 very hot and dry: *a* ***torrid*** *climate*
2 very difficult: *The boxer gave his opponent a* ***torrid*** *time.*

torso (say **taw**-soh) *noun* (*plural* **torsos**)
the main part of your body, not your head, legs or arms

tortoise (say **taw**-tuhss) *noun* (*plural* **tortoises**)
a slow-moving animal with a hard shell on its back, that lives on land. Tortoises are **reptiles**.
➲ See **turtle**

torture[1] (say **taw**-tshuh) *noun* (*no plural*)
the act of making somebody feel great pain, often to make them give information: *His confession was obtained under* ***torture***.

torture[2] (say **taw**-tshuh) *verb* (**torturing, tortured**)
to cause great pain to somebody, often to make them give information: *They* ***tortured*** *the prisoners.*

toss *verb* (**tossing, tossed**)
1 to throw something quickly and without care: *I* ***tossed*** *the paper into the bin.*
2 to move quickly up and down or from side to side, or to make something do this: *The boat was being* ***tossed*** *by the huge waves.*
3 to decide something by throwing a coin in the air and seeing which side shows when it falls: *We* ***tossed*** *a coin to see who would pay for the meal.*
▸ **toss** (*noun*): *a* ***toss*** *of the coin*

tot *noun* (*plural* **tots**)
1 (*informal*) a small child
2 a small alcoholic drink: *a* ***tot*** *of gin*

total[1] (say **toh**-tuhl) *adjective*
1 complete: *There was* ***total*** *silence in the classroom.*
2 if you count everything or everybody: *What was the* ***total*** *number of people at the meeting?*

total[2] (say **toh**-tuhl) *noun* (*plural* **totals**)
the number you have when you add everything together: *Enter the* ***total*** *at the bottom of the page.*

totalitarian (say toh-tal-i-**tair**-ri-uhn) *adjective*
relating to a type of government which demands that people obey it completely
▸ **totalitarian** (*noun*)

totally (say **toh**-tuh-lee) *adverb*
completely: *I* ***totally*** *agree.* ➲ SYNONYM **wholly**

totter (say **tot**-uh) *verb* (**tottering, tottered**)
to stand or move in a way that is not steady, as if you are going to fall because you are ill or drunk ➲ SYNONYM **stagger**

touch[1] (say **tuch**) *verb* (**touching, touched**)
1 to put your hand or finger on somebody or something: *Don't* ***touch*** *the kettle – it's hot!* ◊ *She* ***touched*** *the baby on its cheek.*
2 to be so close to another thing or person that there is no space in between: *Her coat was so long that it* ***touched*** *the ground.*

touch[2] (say **tuch**) *noun*
1 (*plural* **touches**) the action of putting a hand or finger on somebody or something: *I felt the* ***touch*** *of her hand on my arm.*
2 (*no plural*) the feeling in your hands and skin that tells you about something: *We had to feel our way by* ***touch***.
be or keep in touch with somebody to meet, phone or write to somebody often: *Are you still in* ***touch*** *with her?* ◊ *Let's keep in* ***touch***.

A B C D E F G H I J K L M N O P Q R S T U V W X Y Z

A B C D E F G H I J K L M N O P Q R S T U V W X Y Z

get in touch with somebody to write to, or phone somebody: *I'm trying to get in **touch** with my cousin.*
lose touch with somebody to stop meeting, phoning or writing to somebody: *I've lost **touch** with all my old friends from school.*

touching (say **tuch**-ing) *adjective*
that makes you feel emotions such as sadness or love: *He wrote me a **touching** poem.*
➲ SYNONYM **moving**
▸ **touched** (*adjective*): *I was **touched** that you thought of me.*

touchline (say **tuch**-line) *noun* (*plural* **touchlines**)
the line on the border of a soccer or rugby field

touchy (say **tuch**-ee) *adjective* (**touchier**, **touchiest**)
1 easily upset or made angry: *She's **touchy** about her hair.* ◇ *Don't be so **touchy**, it was a joke!* ➲ SYNONYM **sensitive** 2
2 (used about a subject or situation) that may easily upset people or make them angry: *The traffic is a **touchy** subject.*

tough (say **tuf**) *adjective* (**tougher**, **toughest**)
1 difficult: *This is a **tough** job.* ➲ SYNONYM **hard**[1] 2
2 strict or firm: *He's very **tough** on his children.* ➲ SYNONYM **hard**[1] 4 ➲ OPPOSITE **soft** 5
3 very strong: *You need to be **tough** to go climbing in winter.*
4 **Tough** meat is difficult to cut and eat. ➲ OPPOSITE **tender** 2
5 difficult to break or tear: *a **tough** pair of boots*

tour (say **toor**) *noun* (*plural* **tours**)
1 a journey to see a lot of different places: *We went on a **tour** of the country.*
2 a short visit to see a place such as a building or city: *They gave us a **tour** of the house.*
▸ **tour** (*verb*): *We **toured** Namibia for three weeks.*

tourism (say **toor**-riz-m) *noun* (*no plural*)
the business of arranging holidays for people: *The country earns a lot of money from **tourism**.*

tourist (say **toor**-rist) *noun* (*plural* **tourists**)
a person who visits a place on holiday

tournament (say **toor**-nuh-muhnt) *noun* (*plural* **tournaments**)
a sports competition with a lot of players or teams: *a tennis **tournament***

tourniquet (say **toor**-ni-kay) *noun* (*plural* **tourniquets**)
a piece of cloth that is tied tightly around an arm or leg to stop a cut or injury from bleeding

tout (say **towt**) *verb* (**touting**, **touted**)
to sell something, often quite aggressively: *They were **touting** souvenirs.*
▸ **tout** (*noun*): *Watch out for **touts**.*

tow (say **toh**) *verb* (**towing**, **towed**)
to pull a vehicle behind another vehicle using a rope or chain: *My car was **towed** to a garage.*

towards (say tuh-**wawdz**) *preposition* (also **toward**)
1 in the direction of somebody or something: *We walked **towards** the river.* ◇ *I couldn't see her face – she had her back **towards** me.*
2 near a time or a date: *Let's meet **towards** the end of the week.* ◇ *It gets cooler **towards** evening.*
3 to somebody or something: *The people in the village are always very friendly **towards** tourists.*
4 to help pay for something: *She gave me R10 **towards** Sam's birthday present.*

towel (say **tow**-uhl) *noun* (*plural* **towels**)
a piece of cloth that you use for drying yourself: *I washed my hands and dried them on a **towel**.*

tower[1] (say **tow**-uh) *noun* (*plural* **towers**)
a tall narrow building or a tall part of a building: *a church **tower*** ◇ *a 50 metre radio **tower***

tower[2] (say **tow**-uh) *verb* (**towering**, **towered**)
to be taller than something else: *My brother **towers** over his girlfriend.*
▸ **towering** (*adjective*): *a **towering** building*

town (*rhymes with* **gown**) *noun* (*plural* **towns**)
a place where there are many houses, shops and other buildings: *Worcester is a **town** in the Western Cape.* ◇ *I'm going into **town** to do some shopping.*

WORD BUILDING A **town** is bigger than a **village** but smaller than a **city**.

township (say **town**-ship) *noun* (*plural* **townships**)
1 (*S. African*) a part of a city that was set aside for black people to live in during the time of apartheid ➲ See **location**
2 a small town

toxic (say **tokss**-ik) *adjective*
containing poison: ***Toxic** waste had been dumped on the site.* ➲ SYNONYM **poisonous**

toxin (say **tokss**-in) *noun* (*plural* **toxins**)
a poisonous substance, especially one that is produced by plants, animals and other organisms

toy *noun* (*plural* **toys**)
an object for a child to play with: *soft **toys***

toyi-toyi (say **toy**-toy) *noun* (*plural* **toyi-toyis**) (*S. African*)
a dance where you lift your legs high, often done during protests and marches
▸ **toyi-toyi** (*verb*): *We* ***toyi-toyied*** *outside the school.*
ⓘ ORIGIN: from isiNdebele, and Shona, a language spoken in Zimbabwe

trace[1] (say **trayss**) *verb* (**tracing, traced**)
1 to look for and find somebody or something: *The police* ***traced*** *the gang to a house in a suburb.*
2 to put thin paper over a picture and draw over the lines to make a copy

trace[2] (say **trayss**) *noun* (*plural* **traces**)
a mark or sign which shows that a person or thing has been in a place: *The police could not find any* ***trace*** *of the missing child.*

trachea (say truh-**kee**-uh) *noun* (*plural* **tracheas** or **tracheae**)
the tube in your throat that carries air to your lungs ➲ SYNONYM **windpipe** ➲ See illustration at **lung**

track[1] (say **trak**) *noun* (*plural* **tracks**)
1 a rough path or road: *We drove along a* ***track*** *through the bush.*
2 tracks (*plural noun*) a line of marks that an animal, a person or a vehicle makes on the ground: *We saw the animal's* ***tracks*** *in the mud.*
3 the metal lines that a train runs on: *The train had gone off the* ***tracks.***
4 a special road for races: *a racing* ***track***
5 one song or piece of music on a tape, CD or record: *Which is your favourite* ***track?***
lose track of somebody or **something** to not have information about what is happening or where somebody or something is: *I lost all* ***track*** *of time* (= forgot what time it was).

track[2] (say **trak**) *verb* (**tracking, tracked**)
to follow signs or marks to find somebody or something
track somebody or **something down** to find somebody or something after looking in several different places: *The police have so far failed to* ***track*** *down the attacker.*

tracksuit (say **trak**-soot) *noun* (*plural* **tracksuits**)
a special jacket and trousers that you wear for sport

traction (say **trak**-shuhn) *noun* (*no plural*)
1 the force that stops something, for example the wheels of a vehicle, sliding along a surface: *My new walking shoes have great* ***traction*** *to stop me from slipping.*
2 the action of pulling something over a surface: *electric railway* ***traction***
3 a way of treating a broken bone in the body that involves using special equipment to pull the bone gradually back into place: *He spent six weeks in* ***traction*** *after he broke his leg.*

tractor (say **trak**-tuh) *noun* (*plural* **tractors**)
a big strong vehicle that people use on farms to pull heavy things

trade[1] (say **trayd**) *noun*
1 (*no plural*) the buying and selling of things: ***trade*** *between Africa and Europe*
2 (*plural* **trades**) a particular type of business: *the building* ***trade***
3 (*plural* **trades**) a job for which you need special skills, especially with your hands: *to learn a* ***trade*** ◇ *He is a plumber by* ***trade.***

trade[2] (say **trayd**) *verb* (**trading, traded**)
to buy and sell things: *Japan* ***trades*** *with many different countries.*

trademark (say **trayd**-maak) *noun* (*plural* **trademarks**) (abbr. TM)
a special mark or name that a company puts on the things it makes and that other companies must not use

trader (say **trayd**-uh) *noun* (*plural* **traders**)
a person who buys and sells things, especially goods in a market or company shares

tradesman (say **traydz**-muhn) *noun* (*plural* **tradesmen**)
1 a person whose job requires special practical skills and training, for example a **plumber**, **builder**, or **carpenter**
2 a person who sells things

trade union *noun* (*plural* **trade unions**) (also **union**)
a group of workers who have joined together to try to get better pay and working conditions

tradition (say truh-**dish**-n) *noun* (*plural* **traditions**)
something that people in a certain place have done or believed for a long time: *In some countries it's a* ***tradition*** *to give chocolate eggs at Easter.*

traditional (say truh-**dish**-uh-nuhl) *adjective*
being part of the beliefs, customs, or way of life of a group of people, that have not changed for a long time: ***traditional*** *music*
▸ **traditionally** (*adverb*)

traffic (say **traf**-ik) *noun* (*no plural*)
all the cars and other vehicles that are on a road: *There was a lot of* ***traffic*** *on the way to school this morning.*

traffic jam *noun* (*plural* **traffic jams**)
a long line of cars and other vehicles that cannot move or can only move slowly

A B C D E F G H I J K L M N O P Q R S T U V W X Y Z

traffic lights *plural noun*
lights that change from red to orange to green, to tell cars and other vehicles when to stop and when to go ➲ See **robot** 2

tragedy (say **tra**-juh-dee) *noun* (*plural* **tragedies**)
1 a very sad thing that happens: *The child's death was a* ***tragedy***.
2 a serious and sad play: *Shakespeare's 'King Lear' is a* ***tragedy***. ➲ See **comedy**

tragic (say **tra**-jik) *adjective*
very sad: *a* ***tragic*** *accident*
▸ **tragically** (*adverb*): *He died* ***tragically*** *at the age of 25.*

trail[1] (say **trayl**) *noun* (*plural* **trails**)
1 a line of marks that show which way a person or thing has gone: *There was a* ***trail*** *of blood across the floor.*
2 a path in the country: *We followed the* ***trail*** *through the forest.*

trail[2] (say **trayl**) *verb* (**trailing**, **trailed**)
to pull something along behind you or to be pulled along behind somebody or something: *Her skirt was too long and it* ***trailed*** *along the ground.*

trailer (say **tray**-luh) *noun* (*plural* **trailers**)
1 a container with wheels that a vehicle pulls along: *The car was towing a boat on a* ***trailer***.
2 a short piece from a film that shows you what it is about

train[1] (say **trayn**) *noun* (*plural* **trains**)
a vehicle that is pulled by an engine along a railway line: *I'm going home by* ***train***. ◇ *We caught the 7.15* ***train*** *from the station.*

WORD BUILDING You get **on** and **off** trains at a **station**. A **goods train** or a **freight train** carries things in **wagons** and a **passenger train** carries people in **coaches** or **carriages**.

train[2] (say **trayn**) *verb* (**training**, **trained**)
1 to teach a person or an animal to do something: *He was* ***trained*** *as a pilot.*
2 to make yourself ready for something by studying or doing something a lot: *Ann is* ***training*** *to be a doctor.* ◇ *She's* ***training*** *for the Olympics.*

trainer (say **trayn**-uh) *noun*
1 (*plural* **trainers**) a person who teaches people or animals to do something
2 trainers (*plural noun*) soft shoes that you wear for doing sport or with informal clothes

training (say **trayn**-ing) *noun* (*no plural*)
the process of getting ready for a sport or job: *She is in* ***training*** *for the Olympic Games.*

trait (say **trayt**) *noun* (*plural* **traits**)
a quality that forms part of your personality: *Fairness is a good* ***trait***.

traitor (say **tray**-tuh) *noun* (*plural* **traitors**)
a person who harms their own country in order to help another country

trajectory (say truh-**jek**-tuh-ree) *noun* (*plural* **trajectories**)
the path of a moving object through space: *the* ***trajectory*** *of a bullet*

tram *noun* (*plural* **trams**)
an electric bus that runs along metal tracks (called **rails**) in the road

tramp[1] *noun* (*plural* **tramps**)
a homeless person with no job, who goes from place to place ➲ SYNONYM **vagrant**

tramp[2] *verb* (**tramping**, **tramped**)
to walk with slow heavy steps, especially for a long time: *We* ***tramped*** *through the snow.*
➲ SYNONYM **trudge**

trample (say **tramp**-l) *verb* (**trampling**, **trampled**)
to walk on something and damage it with your feet: *Don't* ***trample*** *on the flowers!*

trampoline (say tram-puh-**leen**) *noun* (*plural* **trampolines**)
a piece of equipment for jumping up and down on

trance (say **traanss**) *noun* (*plural* **trances**)
a mental state in which you do not notice what is going on around you: *He was in a* ***trance***.

tranquil (say **trang**-kwil) *adjective* (*formal*)
calm and quiet ➲ SYNONYMS **peaceful**, **serene**

tranquillizer (say **trang**-kwi-lize-uh) *noun* (*plural* **tranquillizers**) (also **tranquilliser**)
a drug or medicine that makes you feel calm or sleepy ➲ SYNONYM **sedative**

trans- (say **traanss**) *prefix*
1 (used to make adjectives) across or beyond: ***transatlantic***
2 (used in verbs) into another place or state: ***transplant*** ◇ ***transform***
ⓘ ORIGIN: from Latin *trans* meaning 'across'

transact (say **traan**-zakt) *verb* (**transacting**, **transacted**)
to do business: *He* ***transacted*** *the sale of our house.*

transaction (say traan-**zak**-shuhn) *noun* (*plural* **transactions**)
a piece of business that is done between people: *Every* ***transaction*** *must have a receipt.*

transfer (say traanss-**fur**) *verb* (**transferring, transferred**)
to move somebody or something to a different place: *I want to **transfer** R100 from this account to my savings account.*
▶ **transfer** (*noun*): *The player asked for a **transfer** to a different team.*

transform (say traanss-**fawm**) *verb* (**transforming, transformed**)
to change a person or thing completely: *Electricity has **transformed** people's lives.*

transformation (say traanss-faw-**may**-shuhn) *noun*
1 (*plural* **transformations**) a complete change in somebody or something: *The insect's **transformation** from a caterpillar to a butterfly was amazing.*
2 (*no plural*) the process of social and political change to help all people obtain equal rights

transformer (say traanss-**fawm**-uh) *noun* (*plural* **transformers**)
a device for increasing or reducing the electrical force **(voltage)** that goes into a piece of electrical equipment

transfusion (say traanss-**fyoo**-zhuhn) *noun* (*plural* **transfusions**)
the giving of new blood to a person's body to replace blood that is lost during a medical operation or because of injury or illness: *a blood **transfusion***

transient (say **traan**-zi-uhnt) *adjective*
lasting only a short time ➲ SYNONYM **temporary**

transistor (say traan-**ziss**-tuh) *noun* (*plural* **transistors**)
1 a small electronic part inside something such as a radio, a television or a computer
2 (also **transistor radio**) a radio that uses **transistors**. A transistor radio receives radio programmes.

transition (say traan-**zish**-uhn) *noun* (*plural* **transitions**)
a change from one state to another: *the **transition** from childhood to being an adult*
▶ **transitional** (*adjective*): *a **transitional** phase*

transitive (say **traan**-suh-tiv) *adjective* (*grammar*)
A **transitive** verb has an object: *In the sentence 'Jan opened the door', 'opened' is a **transitive** verb.* ➲ OPPOSITE **intransitive**

translate (say traanss-**layt**) *verb* (**translating, translated**)
to change what somebody has said or written in one language to another language: *Can you **translate** this letter into English for me?*
▶ **translation** (*noun*): *a **translation** from English into Siswati* ▶ **translator** (*noun*): *She works as a **translator**.*

translucent (say traanss-**loo**-suhnt) *adjective*
allowing light, but not clear images, to pass through: *The frosted glass in my bathroom window is **translucent**. I can't see through it clearly.* ➲ See **opaque, transparent**

transmission (say traanss-**mish**-uhn) *noun*
1 (*plural* **transmissions**) the act or process of sending out energy, electronic signals, radio waves, light waves, etc.: *a radio **transmission*** ◇ *a **transmission** line*
2 (*no plural*) the act or process of sending or spreading something from one person or place to another: *the **transmission** of HIV*
3 (*plural* **transmissions**) the system in a car, etc. by which power is passed from the engine to the wheels

transmit (say traanss-**mit**) *verb* (**transmitting, transmitted**)
1 to send out energy, electronic signals, radio waves, light waves, etc.: *The soccer match was **transmitted** live all over the world.*
2 to send or spread something from one person or place to another: *a sexually **transmitted** disease*
🛈 ORIGIN: 14th–15th century, from Latin *transmittere* from *trans-* meaning 'across' + *mittere* meaning 'send'

transmitter (say traanss-**mit**-uh) *noun* (*plural* **transmitters**)
a piece of equipment that sends out energy, electronic signals, radio waves, light waves, etc.

transparency (say traanss-**pa**-ruhn-see) *noun*
1 (*plural* **transparencies**) a thin clear piece of plastic that you can write or draw on to look at with a special machine (called a **projector**) that shines light on it
2 (*no plural*) (used about people or governments) the state of being transparent or not hiding anything: *Our principal believes in **transparency** in school management.*

transparent (say traanss-**pa**-ruhnt) *adjective*
If something is **transparent**, you can see through it: *Glass is **transparent**.* ➲ OPPOSITE **opaque**

transplant¹ (say traanss-**plaant**) *verb* (**transplanting, transplanted**)
1 to move a growing plant and plant it somewhere else
2 to perform a medical operation in which you take out part of a person's body and put it into another person

transplant² (say **traanss**-plaant) *noun* (*plural* **transplants**)
a medical operation in which an organ is taken out of somebody's body and put into another person's body: *a heart **transplant***

transport (say **traanss**-pawt) *noun* (*no plural*)
a way of carrying people or things from one place to another: *road **transport*** ◇ *I travel to school by public **transport*** (= bus or train).
▸ **transport** (*verb*): *The goods were **transported** by train.*

transversal (say traanz-**vurss**-l) *adjective*
lying or placed across a thing
▸ **transversal** (*noun*) (also **transversal line**): *The **transversal** crossed three other lines*

transverse (say **traanz**-vurss) *adjective*
lying or placed across a thing, especially at an angle of 90°: *a **transverse** wave* ◇ *A **transverse** bar joins the two poles.*

transvestite (say traanz-**vess**-tite) *noun* (*plural* **transvestites**)
a person, especially a man, who enjoys dressing like a member of the opposite sex

trap¹ *noun* (*plural* **traps**)
1 a thing that you use for catching animals: *The rabbit's leg was caught in a **trap**.*
2 a plan to trick somebody: *I knew the question was a **trap**, so I didn't answer it.*

trap² *verb* (**trapping**, **trapped**)
1 to keep a person or an animal in a place that they cannot escape from: *They were **trapped** in the burning building.*
2 to catch or trick somebody or something: *The lawyer asked clever questions and **trapped** him.*

trapdoor (say **trap**-daw) *noun* (*plural* **trapdoors**)
a small door in a floor or ceiling

trapeze (say truh-**peez**) *noun* (*plural* **trapezes**)
a wooden or metal bar hanging from two ropes high above the ground, used by performers (called **acrobats**) ➲ See **acrobat**

trapezium (say truh-**peez**-i-uhm) *noun* (*plural* **trapeziums** or **trapezia**) (*maths*)
a flat closed shape with four straight sides with only one pair of opposite sides parallel

trapezium

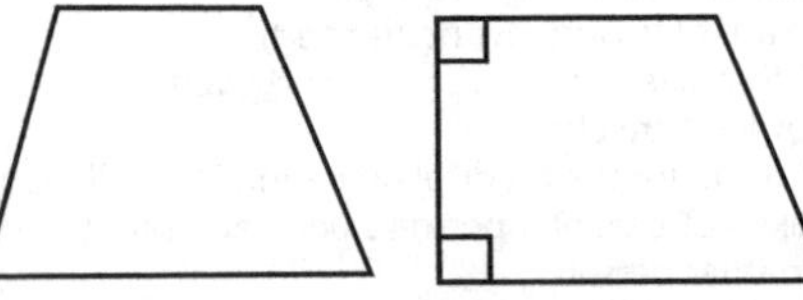

examples of trapeziums

trapezoid (say **trap**-uh-zoyd) *noun* (*plural* **trapezoids**) (*maths*)
a flat closed shape with four straight sides and no sides parallel

trash *noun* (*no plural*)
1 things that you do not want any more: *Throw this **trash** in the bin.* ➲ SYNONYMS **garbage**, **refuse²**, **rubbish**
2 (*informal*) something that you think is bad, stupid or wrong: *You're talking **trash**.*
➲ SYNONYM **nonsense**, **rubbish**

trauma (say **traw**-muh) *noun* (*plural* **traumas**)
1 any serious injury to your body: *The accident caused brain **trauma**.*
2 a state of great shock or sadness caused by a particular event: *psychological **trauma*** ◇ ***traumas** caused by war*
▸ **traumatic** (*adjective*): *a **traumatic** experience*
▸ **traumatize** (*verb*) (also **traumatise**): *The violent attack **traumatized** her.*

travel (say **trav**-l) *verb* (**travelling**, **travelled**)
to go from one place to another: *I would like to **travel** round the world.* ◇ *I **travel** to school by bus.* ◇ *She **travelled** 800 km in one day.*
▸ **travel** (*noun*)

travel agent *noun* (*plural* **travel agents**)
a person who works in a company called a **travel agency** (that plans holidays and journeys for people)

traveller (say **trav**-luh) *noun* (*plural* **travellers**)
a person who is travelling

traverse (say truh-**vurss**) *verb* (**traversing**, **traversed**)
1 to travel across something: *She **traversed** along the side of the mountain.*
2 to continue across or over something: *The plank **traverses** the gap.*
▸ **traverse** (*noun*): *a difficult **traverse***

trawler (say **traw**-luh) *noun* (*plural* **trawlers**)
a large fishing boat

tray *noun* (*plural* **trays**)
a flat object that you use for carrying food or drinks

TRC (say tee-aar-**see**) *noun* (*no plural*)
an organization that investigated crimes that were committed during **apartheid** ❶ **TRC** is short for 'Truth and Reconciliation Commission'.

treacherous (say **trech**-uh-ruhss) *adjective*
1 (used about a person) that you cannot trust and who may do something to harm you: *He was cowardly and **treacherous**.*
2 dangerous: *a **treacherous** coastline*
▸ **treachery** (*noun*): *Her **treachery** shocked us.*

treacle (say **treek**-l) *noun* (*no plural*)
a thick, dark, sticky liquid that is made from sugar ➲ SYNONYM **molasses**

tread (say **tred**) *verb* (**treading, trod, has trodden**)
to put your foot down while you are walking: *He* ***trod*** *on my foot.*

treadmill (say **tred**-mil) *noun* (*plural* **treadmills**)
an exercise machine that you can walk or run on without going anywhere

treason (say **treez**-n) *noun* (*no plural*)
the crime of harming your country by helping its enemies

treasure[1] (say **tre*zh***-uh) *noun*
1 (*no plural*) a collection of gold, silver, jewellery or other things that are worth a lot of money: *They were searching for buried* ***treasure.***
2 (*plural* **treasures**) something or somebody that you consider to be to be very special or valuable

treasure[2] (say **tre*zh***-uh) *verb* (**treasuring, treasured**)
to consider something or somebody to be very special or valuable: *I'll* ***treasure*** *these memories.*

treasurer (say **tre*zh***-uh-ruh) *noun* (*plural* **treasurers**)
a person who looks after the money of a club or an organization

treasury (say **tre*zh***-uh-ree) *noun* (*plural* **treasuries**)
1 the money that is kept and used by a club or organization
2 Treasury the government department that controls public money

treat[1] (say **treet**) *verb* (**treating, treated**)
1 to behave in a certain way towards somebody or something: *How does your older brother* ***treat*** *you?* ◇ ***Treat*** *these glasses with care.*
2 to think about something in a certain way: *They* ***treated*** *my idea as a joke.*
3 to try to make a sick or injured person well again: *The doctors* ***treated*** *several people for burns.*
4 to give yourself or another person something special or enjoyable: *Mum* ***treated*** *us to an ice cream.*
5 to put a chemical substance onto something, for example to protect it from damage or to clean it: *I* ***treated*** *the wood with oil to protect it.*

treat[2] (say **treet**) *noun* (*plural* **treats**)
something special or enjoyable that makes somebody happy: *My parents took me to the theatre as a* ***treat*** *for my birthday.*

treatment (say **treet**-muhnt) *noun*
1 (*plural* **treatments**) the things that a doctor does to try to make a sick or injured person well again: *a new* ***treatment*** *for cancer*
2 (*no plural*) the way that you behave towards somebody or something: *Their* ***treatment*** *of the animals was very cruel.*

treaty (say **tree**-tee) *noun* (*plural* **treaties**)
a written agreement between countries: *The two countries signed a peace* ***treaty.***

treble (say **treb**-l) *verb* (**trebling, trebled**)
to become or to make something three times as much or as many: *Prices have* ***trebled*** *in the last ten years.* ➲ SYNONYM **triple**

tree *noun* (*plural* **trees**)
a tall plant that can live for a long time. Trees have a central part (called a **trunk**) and most have many branches: *a pine* ***tree*** ◇ *Apples grow on* ***trees.***

trek *noun* (*plural* **treks**)
a long difficult journey, especially done by walking: *We went for a* ***trek*** *in the valley.*
➲ SYNONYM **hike**
▸ **trek** (*verb*): *We* ***trekked*** *through the mountains.*
ⓘ ORIGIN: 19th century, from South African Dutch *trek, trekken* meaning 'to pull, travel'

tremble (say **tremb**-l) *verb* (**trembling, trembled**)
to shake, for example because you are cold, afraid or ill: *She was* ***trembling*** *with fear.*

tremendous (say truh-**men**-duhss) *adjective*
1 very big or very great: *The new trains travel at a* ***tremendous*** *speed.*
2 (*informal*) very good: *The match was* ***tremendous.***
▸ **tremendously** (*adverb*): *The film was* ***tremendously*** *exciting.*

tremor (say **trem**-uh) *noun* (*plural* **tremors**)
a slight shaking movement: *an earth* ***tremor*** ◇ *a* ***tremor*** *in her voice*

tremulous (say **trem**-yuh-luhss) *adjective*
shaking slightly: *He spoke with a* ***tremulous*** *voice.*

trench *noun* (*plural* **trenches**)
a long narrow hole that is dug in the ground, for example to put pipes or wires in

trend *noun* (*plural* **trends**)
a change to something different: *new* ***trends*** *in science*

trendy (say **tren**-dee) *adjective* (**trendier**, **trendiest**) (*informal*) fashionable: *a* ***trendy*** *shirt*

trepidation (say trep-i-**day**-shuhn) *noun* (*no plural*)
a feeling of worry and fear, often before something is about to happen

trespass (say **tress**-puhss) *verb* (**trespassing**, **trespassed**)
to go on somebody's land without asking them if you can
▸ **trespasser** (*noun*): *A sign on the gate said 'No* ***Trespassers****'.*

trestle (say **tress**-l) *noun* (*plural* **trestles**)
1 a frame made with a board resting on two pairs of legs: *Put the food on the* ***trestle*** *table.*
2 the pairs of legs a board rests on: *Are the* ***trestles*** *wobbly?*

tri- (say **try**) *prefix*
three or having three: *A* ***tricycle*** *has three wheels.*
ⓘ **ORIGIN**: from Latin *tres* and Greek *treis* meaning 'three'

trial (say **try**-uhl) *noun* (*plural* **trials**)
1 the process in a court of law when a judge or a **magistrate** can decide if a person has done something wrong, and what the punishment will be: *He was on* ***trial*** *for murder.*
2 the act or process of testing something to see if it is good or bad: *They are conducting* ***trials*** *of a new drug* (= they are testing a new medicine).

triangle (say **try**-ang-guhl) *noun* (*plural* **triangles**)
a flat closed shape with three straight sides
▸ **triangular** (*adjective*): ***triangular*** *shapes*
ⓘ **ORIGIN**: 14th–15th century, from Old French *triangle* or Latin *triangulus* meaning 'having three corners'

triangles

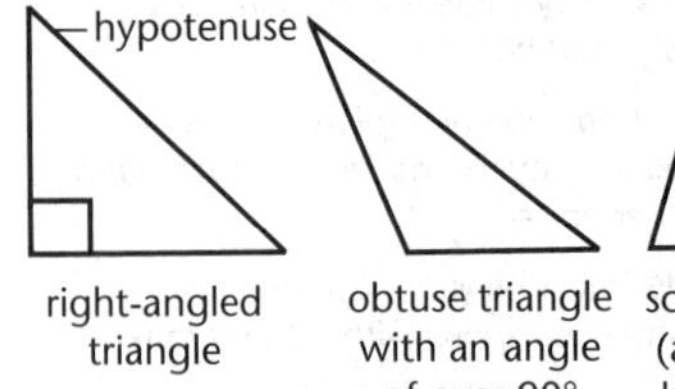

examples of triangles

triangulate (say try-**ang**-gyuu-layt) *verb* (**triangulating**, **triangulated**) (*technology*)
1 to use triangles to measure an area
2 to divide an area into triangles
▸ **triangulation** (*noun*)

tribe (say **tribe**) *noun* (*plural* **tribes**)
a small group of people who have the same language and customs: ***tribes*** *living in the Amazon rainforest*
▸ **tribal** (*adjective*): ***tribal*** *dances*

tribunal (say try-**byoo**-nuhl) *noun* (*plural* **tribunals**)
a type of court with the authority to decide who is right in particular types of disagreement: *the competition* ***tribunal***

tributary (say **trib**-yoo-tree) *noun* (*plural* **tributaries**)
a small river that flows into a larger river

tribute (say **trib**-yoot) *noun* (*plural* **tributes**)
something that you do, say or give to show that you respect or admire somebody: *They built a statue in London as a* ***tribute*** *to Nelson Mandela.*

triceps (say **try**-sepss) *noun* (*plural* **triceps**)
the large muscle at the back of your upper arm
➲ See **biceps**

trick¹ (say **trik**) *noun* (*plural* **tricks**)
1 a clever plan that makes somebody believe something that is not true: *They used a* ***trick*** *to get past the guards.*
2 something clever that you have learned to do: *Do you know any card* ***tricks****?*
play a trick on somebody to do something that makes somebody look silly, in order to make other people laugh: *The children played a* ***trick*** *on their teacher by hiding her books.*

trick² (say **trik**) *verb* (**tricking**, **tricked**)
to do something that is not honest to get what you want from somebody: *He* ***tricked*** *the old lady into giving him all her money.* ➲ **SYNONYM** **fool²**

trickle (say **trik**-l) *verb* (**trickling**, **trickled**)
to move slowly like a thin line of water: *Tears* ***trickled*** *down her cheeks.*
▸ **trickle** (*noun*): *a* ***trickle*** *of blood*

tricky (say **trik**-ee) *adjective* (**trickier**, **trickiest**)
difficult or hard to do: *a* ***tricky*** *question*

tricycle (say **try**-sik-l) *noun* (*plural* **tricycles**)
a toy similar to a bicycle, that has one wheel in front and two at the back

trident (say **try**-duhnt) *noun* (*plural* **tridents**)
a type of weapon (called a **spear**) with three points instead of one

tried (say **tride**) form of **try¹**

tries (say **trize**) plural of **try²**

trigger¹ (say **trig**-uh) *noun* (*plural* **triggers**)
the part of a gun that you pull with your finger to fire it

trigger² (say **trig**-uh) *verb* (**triggering, triggered**)
to cause something to happen suddenly: *Burning toast* ***triggered*** *the fire alarm.*

trigonometry (say trig-uh-**nom**-uh-tree) *noun* (*no plural*) (also *informal* **trig**) (*maths*)
the area of mathematics that deals with the relationship between functions of angles, especially the relationships between the sides and angles of 90° triangles ➲ See **cosine, sine, tangent** 2
▶ **trigonometric** (*adjective*): ***trigonometric*** *ratios*

trillion (say **tril**-yuhn) *number*
1 000 000 000 000; one million million or 10^{12}: *In one year, light travels almost 10* ***trillion*** *kilometres.*

trilogy (say **tril**-uh-jee) *noun* (*plural* **trilogies**)
a group of three novels, films or plays that form a set: *Have you read the 'Lord of the Rings'* ***trilogy****?*

trim *verb* (**trimming, trimmed**)
to cut a small amount off something to make it tidy: *He* ***trimmed*** *my hair.*
▶ **trim** (*noun*): *My hair needs a* ***trim****.*

trinket (say **tring**-kuht) *noun* (*plural* **trinkets**)
a piece of jewellery or a small decoration that is not worth much money

trinomial (say try-**noh**-mi-uhl) *noun* (*plural* **trinomials**) (*maths*)
an expression with three terms: $5x^2 + 7y - 4$ *is a* ***trinomial****.*

trio (say **tree**-oh) *noun* (*plural* **trios**)
1 a group of three people or things
2 a group of three people who play music or sing together ➲ See **duet, quartet, quintet**
3 a piece of music written for three people to sing or play together

trip¹ *noun* (*plural* **trips**)
a journey to a place and back again: *We went on a* ***trip*** *to the mountains.*

trip² *verb* (**tripping, tripped**)
1 to hit your foot against something so that you fall or nearly fall: *She* ***tripped*** *over the step.*
2 to make somebody fall or nearly fall: *He put out his foot and* ***tripped*** *me.*

tripe *noun* (*no plural*)
1 the stomach of an animal such as a cow or sheep that is used as food
2 (*informal*) nonsense: *You're talking* ***tripe****!*

triple¹ (say **trip**-l) *adjective*
with three parts, happening three times or containing three times as much as usual: *a* ***triple*** *murder* (= in which three people were killed)

triple² (say **trip**-l) *verb* (**tripling, tripled**)
to become or to make something three times as much or as many: *Sales have* ***tripled*** *this year.* ➲ SYNONYM **treble**

triplet (say **trip**-luht) *noun* (*plural* **triplets**)
one of three people who have the same mother and were born at the same time: *My pregnant aunt is expecting* ***triplets****.*

tripod (say **try**-pod) *noun* (*plural* **tripods**)
a piece of equipment with three legs that supports something such as a camera or **telescope** ➲ See illustration at **telescope**

trite *adjective*
(used about a phrase or saying) used too much and losing its meaning: *That's such a* ***trite*** *thing to say!* ➲ SYNONYM **banal**

triumph (say **try**-umf) *noun* (*plural* **triumphs**)
great success: *The race ended in* ***triumph*** *for the home team.*

triumphant (say try-**um**-fuhnt) *adjective*
very happy because you have won or succeeded at something
▶ **triumphantly** (*adverb*): *The winning team ran* ***triumphantly*** *round the stadium.*

trivial (say **triv**-i-uhl) *adjective*
not important: *She gets angry about* ***trivial*** *things.*

trod, trodden (say **trod**, **trod**-uhn) forms of **tread**

troll (say **trohl**) *noun* (*plural* **trolls**)
(in children's stories) an ugly and cruel creature that usually lives in a cave or under a bridge

trolley (say **trol**-ee) *noun* (*plural* **trolleys**)
a thing on wheels that you use for carrying things: *a supermarket* ***trolley***

trombone (say **trom**-bohn) *noun* (*plural* **trombones**)
a large musical instrument. You play it by blowing and moving a long tube up and down.

troop¹ *noun*
1 (*plural* **troops**) a large group of people or animals: *a* ***troop*** *of baboons*
2 troops (*plural noun*) soldiers, especially in large groups

troop² *verb* (**trooping, trooped**)
to move in a large group of people: *The class* ***trooped*** *in after break.*

trophic (say **troh**-fik or **trof-ik**) *adjective* (*biology*)
relating to food or **nutrition**: *In many*

ecosystems, plants such as grass form the first ***trophic*** *level in the food chain.*

trophy (say **troh**-fee) *noun* (*plural* **trophies**)
a thing, for example a silver cup, that you get when you win a competition: *a tennis* ***trophy***

tropic (say **trop**-ik) *noun*
1 (*plural* **tropics**) one of the two lines on a map that go round the Earth and that are 23°27′ north and south of the **equator**: *The* ***Tropic*** *of Cancer is in the northern hemisphere and the* ***Tropic*** *of Capricorn is in the southern hemisphere.*
2 the tropics the part of the world that is between these two lines, and where the climate is wet and hot: *In* ***the tropics*** *it rains most of the year.*
▸ **tropical** (*adjective*): ***tropical*** *rainforests* ◇ ***tropical*** *islands*

troposphere (say **trop**-uh-sfeer) *noun*
the troposphere the lowest layer of the atmosphere where the Earth's weather takes place ➲ See illustration at **atmosphere** ➲ See **ionosphere**, **mesosphere**, **stratosphere**, **thermosphere**

trot *verb* (**trotting**, **trotted**)
to run with short quick steps: *The horse* ***trotted*** *along the road.*

troubadour (say **troo**-buh-daw) *noun* (*plural* **troubadours**)
a poet or singer in France in the 11th to 13th centuries who usually sang about love ➲ See **minstrel**

trouble[1] (say **trub**-l) *noun*
1 (*plural* **troubles**) difficulty, problems or worry: *We had a lot of* ***trouble*** *finding the book you wanted.* ◇ *He got into* ***trouble*** *with the police.* ◇ *I'll be in* ***trouble*** *if I'm late home again.*
2 (*no plural*) extra work: *'Thanks for your help!' 'Oh, it was no* ***trouble****.'*
3 (*plural* **troubles**) a situation in which people are fighting or arguing: *There was* ***trouble*** *at the station during the bus strike.*
4 (*no plural*) pain or illness: *He's got heart* ***trouble****.*

trouble[2] (say **trub**-l) *verb* (**troubling**, **troubled**)
1 to worry somebody: *I was* ***troubled*** *by the news.*
2 (*formal*) a word that you use when you need to disturb somebody by asking them something: *I'm sorry to* ***trouble*** *you, but you're in my seat.* ➲ SYNONYM **bother**[1]

troublemaker (say **trub**-uhl-mayk-uh) *noun* (*plural* **troublemakers**)
a person who deliberately causes trouble

trough (say **trof**) *noun* (*plural* **troughs**)
a long open container that holds food or water for animals: *a water* ***trough***

troupe (say **troop**) *noun* (*plural* **troupes**)
a group of actors or singers who perform together

SPELLING Be careful! Don't confuse **troupe** with **troop**, which has a different meaning.

trousers (say **trow**-zuhz) *plural noun* (also **pants**)
a piece of clothing for your legs and the lower part of your body: *Where are my new* ***trousers****?* ◇ *I have two pairs of* ***trousers****.*

USAGE Be careful! You cannot say 'a trousers'. You can say **a pair of trousers**: *I bought a new* ***pair of trousers*** or *I bought some new trousers.*

trout (say **trowt**) *noun* (*plural* **trouts**)
a fish that lives in rivers and that you can eat

trowel (say **trow**-uhl) *noun* (*plural* **trowels**)
1 a small garden tool that you use for digging
2 a small tool that you use in building for spreading cement

truant (say **troo**-uhnt) *noun* (*plural* **truants**)
a child who stays away from school when they should be there
play truant to stay away from school when you should be there

truce (say **trooss**) *noun* (*plural* **truces**)
an agreement to stop fighting for a short time

truck (say **truk**) *noun* (*plural* **trucks**)
a big vehicle for carrying heavy things: *a* ***truck*** *driver* ➲ See **lorry**, **bakkie**

trudge (say **truj**) *verb* (**trudging**, **trudged**)
to walk with slow heavy steps because you are ill or tired: *He* ***trudged*** *up the stairs.* ➲ SYNONYM **tramp**[2]
▸ **trudge** (*noun*)

true (say **troo**) *adjective* (**truer**, **truest**)
1 right or correct: *Is it* ***true*** *that you are leaving?* ◇ *A banana is a fruit:* ***true*** *or false?* ➲ OPPOSITES **untrue**, **false** 1
2 real: *A* ***true*** *friend will always help you.* ◇ *It's a* ***true*** *story* (= it really happened). ➲ The noun is **truth**
come true to happen in the way that you hoped or imagined: *Her dream came* ***true****.*

truism (say **troo**-iz-m) *noun* (*plural* **truisms**)
a statement that is obviously true but does not say very much: *A* ***truism*** *in rugby is that if you've got the ball the other team can't score.*

truly (say **troo**-lee) *adverb*
really: *I'm **truly** sorry.*
Yours truly (*formal*) words that you can use at the end of a formal letter before you write your name

trumpet (say **trum**-pit) *noun* (*plural* **trumpets**)
a musical instrument that is made of metal and that you blow. There are three buttons on it, which you press to make different notes.

trumpet

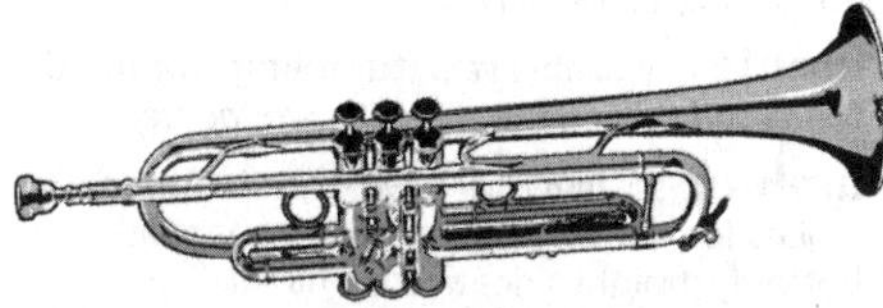

truncheon (say **trun**-chuhn) *noun* (*plural* **truncheons**)
a short thick stick that some police officers carry as a weapon ➲ SYNONYM **baton** 1

trundle (say **trund**-l) *verb* (**trundling, trundled**)
to move, or to make something heavy move slowly and noisily: *The truck **trundled** up the road.*

trunk *noun* (*plural* **trunks**)
1 the thick part of a tree, that grows up from the ground
2 the long nose of an elephant
3 a large strong box for carrying things when you travel

trust[1] *noun* (*no plural*)
the belief that somebody is honest and good and will not hurt you in any way: *Put your **trust** in God.*

trust[2] *verb* (**trusting, trusted**)
to believe that somebody is honest and good and will not hurt you in any way: *I just don't **trust** him.* ◇ *You can **trust** her to do the job well.*

trustworthy (say **trust**-wurth-ee) *adjective*
A **trustworthy** person is somebody that you can trust.

truth (say **trooth**) *noun*
1 (*no plural*) being true or what is true: *There is no **truth** in these rumours.* ◇ *We need to find out the **truth** about what happened.* ◇ *Are you telling me the **truth**?*
2 (*plural* **truths**) a fact that is believed by most people to be true: *universal **truths***

truthful (say **trooth**-fuhl) *adjective*
1 true: *a **truthful** answer*
2 A person who is **truthful** tells the truth.
▸ **truthfully** (*adverb*): *You must answer me **truthfully**.* ▸ **truthfulness** (*noun*): *I have doubts about the **truthfulness** of her story.*

try[1] (say **try**) *verb* (**trying, tried**)
1 to make an effort to do something: *I **tried** to remember her name but I couldn't.* ◇ *I'm not sure if I can help you, but I'll **try**.* ➲ SYNONYM **attempt**
2 to use or do something to find out if you like it: *Have you ever **tried** Japanese food?*
3 to ask somebody questions in a court of law to decide if they have done something wrong: *He was **tried** for murder.*
try something on to put on a piece of clothing to see if you like it and if it fits: *I **tried** on the jeans but they were too small.*

try[2] (say **try**) *noun* (*plural* **tries**)
1 (used in rugby) when a player puts the ball down behind the line on the field to score points: *I scored the winning **try**.*
2 an effort to do something: *I can't open this door – will you have a **try**?*

tsar (say **zaa**) *noun* (*plural* **tsars**) (also **tzar**, **czar**)
the title of the leader of Russia in the past
▸ **tsarina** (also **tzarina**, **czarina**) (*noun*): *The **tsarina** was the tsar's wife.*

tsetse (say **tset**-see) *noun* (*plural* **tsetses**) (also **tsetse fly**)
an African fly that bites humans and animals and can spread a serious disease, called **sleeping sickness**
ⓘ ORIGIN: 19th century, from Setswana *tsètsè*

T-shirt (say **tee**-shurt) *noun* (*plural* **T-shirts**)
a type of shirt with short sleeves and no **collar** (= the folded part that fits round your neck)

Tshivenda (say tshi-**ven**-duh) *noun* (*no plural*) (also **Venda**)
the language of the Venda people

Tsonga (say **tsawng**-guh) *noun* another word for **Xitsonga**

tsotsi (say **tsawt**-si) *noun* (*plural* **tsotsis**) (*S. African*)
a young urban criminal
ⓘ ORIGIN: 20th century, possibly from a Sesotho variation of *zoot suit*, a man's suit that was fashionable in the 1940s and 1950s

tsunami (say tsoo-**naa**-mi) *noun* (*plural* **tsunamis**)
a very large wave in the sea, usually caused by an **earthquake**

tub *noun* (*plural* **tubs**)
1 a large round container: *She did her hand washing in a **tub**.*
2 a small, usually round container with a lid, which is used for holding food: *a **tub** of margarine*

tuba (say **tyoo**-buh) *noun* (*plural* **tubas**)
a large metal musical instrument that you blow into to make a deep, low sound

tubby (say **tub**-ee) *adjective* (**tubbier**, **tubbiest**) (*informal*)
short and a bit fat ➲ SYNONYMS **chubby**, **plump**

tube (say **tyoob**) *noun*
1 (*plural* **tubes**) a long thin pipe for liquid or gas
2 (*plural* **tubes**) a long thin soft container with a hole and a lid at one end: *a **tube** of toothpaste*
3 (*no plural*) (*informal*) the underground railway in London: *Shall we go by bus or by **tube**?*

tuber (say **tyoo**-buh) *noun* (*plural* **tubers**)
a short thick round part of a plant, such as a potato, which grows under the ground

tuberculosis (say tyuu-**bur**-kyuu-loh-siss) *noun* (*no plural*) (abbr. TB)
a serious infectious disease that often affects the lungs

tubular (say **tyoob**-yuh-luh) *adjective*
long, round and empty, like a tube: ***tubular** flowers*

tuck (say **tuk**) *verb* (**tucking**, **tucked**)
to put or push the edges of something inside or under something else: *He **tucked** his shirt into his trousers.*
tuck somebody in, **tuck somebody up** to make somebody feel comfortable in bed by pulling the covers around them: *I'll come and **tuck** you in later.*

tuckshop (say **tuk**-shop) *noun* (*plural* **tuckshops**)
a small shop, usually in a school, that sells sweets and other food ➲ See **spaza**

Tuesday (say **tyooz**-day) *noun*
the day of the week after Monday and before Wednesday ➲ See note at **day**

tuft (say **tuft**) *noun* (*plural* **tufts**)
a small amount of something such as hair or grass growing together

tug[1] *verb* (**tugging**, **tugged**)
to pull something hard and quickly: *I **tugged** at the rope and it broke.*

tug[2] *noun* (*plural* **tugs**)
1 a sudden hard pull: *The little girl gave my hand a **tug**.*
2 (also **tugboat**) a small strong boat that pulls big ships

tuition (say tyoo-**ish**-n) *noun* (*no plural*)
teaching, especially to a small group: *A lot of students have extra **tuition** before their exams.*

tulip (say **tyoo**-lip) *noun* (*plural* **tulips**)
a brightly coloured flower that grows in spring and is shaped like a cup

tumble (say **tumb**-l) *verb* (**tumbling**, **tumbled**)
to fall suddenly: *He **tumbled** down the steps.*

tumbler (say **tum**-bluh) *noun* (*plural* **tumblers**)
a glass for drinking out of, which has a flat bottom, straight sides and no handle

tummy (say **tum**-ee) *noun* (*plural* **tummies**)
(*informal*) the part of your body between your chest and your legs ➲ SYNONYMS **belly**, **stomach**

tumour (say **tyoo**-muh) *noun* (*plural* **tumours**)
a mass of cells that do not grow normally in the body, and which may or may not be harmful: *a benign* (= not usually dangerous) ***tumour*** ◇ *a malignant* (= dangerous) ***tumour***

tumult (say **tyoo**-muhlt) *noun* (*plural* **tumults**)
1 confusion, usually with a lot of noise and often caused by a large number of people: *There was **tumult** at the soccer match.*
➲ SYNONYM **commotion**
2 a state in which your thoughts or feelings are confused
▸ **tumultuous** (*adjective*)

tuna (say **tyoo**-nuh) *noun* (*plural* **tuna**)
a large fish that lives in the sea and that you can eat: *a tin of **tuna** in vegetable oil*

tundra (say **tun**-druh) *noun* (*no plural*)
the low flat Arctic regions where no trees grow and where the soil deep below the surface of the ground is always frozen

tune[1] (say **tyoon**) *noun* (*plural* **tunes**)
a group of musical notes that make a nice sound when you play or sing them together: *I know the **tune** but I don't know the words.*
➲ SYNONYM **melody**

tune[2] (say **tyoon**) *verb* (**tuning**, **tuned**)
to make small changes to a musical instrument so that it makes the right sounds: *She **tuned** her guitar before playing it.*

tungsten (say **tung**-stuhn) *noun* (*no plural*) (symbol W)
a very hard metal used in light bulbs and in making steel

tunic (say **tyoo**-nik) *noun* (*plural* **tunics**)
a piece of women's loose clothing, like a dress without sleeves

tunnel[1] (say **tun**-l) *noun* (*plural* **tunnels**)
a long hole under the ground or the sea for a road or railway

tunnel[2] (say **tun**-l) *verb* (**tunnelling, tunnelled**)
to make a tunnel through something: *Moles are **tunnelling** through the garden.*

turban (say **tur**-buhn) *noun* (*plural* **turbans**)
a covering that some men wear on their heads. You make a **turban** by folding a long piece of material round your head.
ORIGIN: 16th century, through French from Turkish *tülbent*, from Persian

turbine (say **tur**-bine) *noun* (*plural* **turbines**)
a machine or engine that receives its power from a wheel that is turned by the energy of a moving gas or liquid, such as water or steam: *a wind **turbine** ◇ a steam **turbine***

turbulent (say **tur**-byuh-luhnt) *adjective*
1 in which there is a lot of change and disorder and sometimes violence: *a **turbulent** relationship* ➲ SYNONYM **tempestuous**
2 (used about water or air) moving in a violent way: *There were **turbulent** winds during our flight.*
▸ **turbulence** (*noun*): ***turbulence** in the stock market ◇ **turbulence** during a flight*

turf[1] *noun* (*no plural*)
short thick grass with a layer of soil underneath it: *We bought **turf** for our garden.*

turf[2] *verb* (**turfing, turfed**)
to cover the ground with turf
turf out (*informal*) to force somebody or something out of a place: *We **turfed** out the rubbish.*

turgid (say **tur**-jid) *adjective*
1 (used about language, writing etc.) boring, complicated and difficult to understand: *a **turgid** speech*
2 containing more water than usual: ***turgid** cells ◇ a **turgid** river* ➲ SYNONYM **swollen**[2]

turkey (say **tur**-kee) *noun* (*plural* **turkey**)
a big bird that people keep on farms for their meat. **Turkeys** are often eaten at **Christmas** meals.
ORIGIN: 16th century. The bird was given this name because people thought they looked like guinea fowls, which at the time, were also called turkeys. Guinea fowls were called turkeys because people mistakenly thought they came from Turkey, but in fact they came from Africa.

Turkish (say **tur**-kish) *noun* (*no plural*)
the language spoken in Turkey

turmeric (say **tur**-muh-rik) *noun* (*no plural*)
yellow spice that you put on food to add flavour

turmoil (say **tur**-moyl) *noun* (*no plural*)
a state of confusion or noise: *political **turmoil** ◇ We were shocked after the **turmoil**.*

turn[1] *verb* (**turning, turned**)
1 to move round, or to move something round: *The wheels are **turning**. ◇ **Turn** the key. ◇ She **turned** round and walked away.*
2 to move in a different direction: ***Turn** left at the traffic lights.*
3 to become different or to make somebody or something change: *Water **turns** into ice when it gets very cold. ◇ The sun **turned** her hair blonde.*
4 to find a certain page in a book: ***Turn** to page 97.*
turn something down
1 to make something produce less sound or heat by moving a switch: *The TV is too loud – can you **turn** it down, please?*
2 to say no to what somebody wants to do or to give you: *They offered me the job but I **turned** it down.*
turn something off to move the handle or switch that controls something, so that it stops: ***Turn** the tap off. ◇ She **turned** off the lights and the TV.*
turn something on to move the handle or switch that controls something, so that it starts: *Could you **turn** the light on?*
turn over or **turn something over** to move or move something so that the other side is on top: *She **turned** over and went back to sleep. ◇ Please **turn** over to the next page.*
turn something up to make something produce more sound or heat by moving a switch: ***Turn** up the TV, please.*

turn[2] *noun* (*plural* **turns**)
1 the action of turning something round: *Put the pencil into the sharpener and give it a few **turns**.*
2 a change of direction: *Take a left **turn** at the end of this road.*
3 the time when you can or should do something: *It's your **turn** to do the washing-up!*
in turn one after the other: *He spoke to each of the learners in **turn**.*
take turns at something, take it in turns to do something to do something one after the other: *The two learners took it in **turns** to use the computer.*

turning (say **turn**-ing) *noun* (*plural* **turnings**)
a place where one road joins another road: *Take the first **turning** on the right.*

A B C D E F G H I J K L M N O P Q R S **T** U V W X Y Z

A B C D E F G H I J K L M N O P Q R S T U V W X Y Z

turnip (say **tur**-nip) *noun* (*plural* **turnips**)
a round white vegetable that grows under the ground

turpentine (say **tur**-puhn-tine) *noun* (*no plural*)
a clear liquid with a strong smell that you use to remove paint or make paint thinner

turquoise (say **tur**-kwoyz or **tur**-kwaaz) *noun* (*no plural*)
1 a green or blue-green precious stone: *a necklace made of* ***turquoise***
2 the colour of this stone: *the* ***turquoise*** *sea*

turret (say **tu**-ruht) *noun* (*plural* **turrets**)
1 a small tower at the top of a large building such as a castle
2 a small metal tower on a ship, plane or **tank** that can usually turn around and from which guns are fired

turtle (say **turt**-l) *noun* (*plural* **turtles**)
an animal that has a hard shell on its back and that lives in the sea or in rivers, lakes, etc. **Turtles** are reptiles. ➲ See **tortoise**

tusk *noun* (*plural* **tusks**)
a long pointed tooth that grows beside the mouth of an animal such as an elephant or a **warthog**

tussle (say **tuss**-l) *noun* (*plural* **tussles**)
a fight between two people for the same thing: *There was a* ***tussle*** *for the last biscuit.*
➲ SYNONYM **scuffle**
▸ **tussle** (*verb*)

tutor (say **tyoo**-tuh) *noun* (*plural* **tutors**)
a teacher who teaches one person or a small group

TV (say tee-**vee**) *noun* (*plural* **TVs**) **television**

twang *verb* (**twanging, twanged**)
to make the sound that is made when you pull a tight elastic or wire and let it go suddenly: *I* ***twanged*** *the strings on my guitar.*
▸ **twang** (*noun*)

tweak (say **tweek**) *verb* (**tweaking, tweaked**)
1 to twist and pull something suddenly: *She* ***tweaked*** *his ear.*
2 (*informal*) to improve something by making small changes to it: ***Tweak*** *your project to make it work better.*
▸ **tweak** (*noun*): *I gave it some* ***tweaks****.*

tweezers (say **twee**-zuhz) *plural noun*
a small tool made of two pieces of metal joined at one end. You use **tweezers** for holding or pulling out very small things: *She pulled the splinter out of my finger with a pair of* ***tweezers****.*

twelfth (say **twelfth**) *adjective, adverb*
12th: *He's playing in his* ***twelfth*** *match of the season.*

twelve (say **twelv**) *number*
12

twentieth (say **twen**-ti-uth) *adjective, adverb*
20th: *It's his* ***twentieth*** *birthday.*

twenty (say **twen**-tee) *number*
1 20
2 the twenties (*plural noun*) the numbers 20 to 29 or the years 1920 to 1929: *She grew up in the* ***twenties*** (= in the 1920s).
in your twenties between the ages of 20 and 29

twice (say **twise**) *adverb*
two times: *I have been to Japan* ***twice****.* ◇ *He ate* ***twice*** *as much as I did.*

twig *noun* (*plural* **twigs**)
a small thin branch of a tree

twilight (say **twy**-lite) *noun* (*no plural*)
the time after the sun has gone down and before it gets completely dark ➲ See **dusk**

twin *noun* (*plural* **twins**)
1 one of two people who have the same mother and were born at the same time: *David and John are* ***twins****.* ◇ *I have a* ***twin*** *sister.*
2 one of two things that are the same: *a room with* ***twin*** *beds*

twine[1] *noun* (*no plural*)
strong string made by twisting two or more smaller strings together: *Look at rope,* ***twine*** *or knitting wool and see how it is made.*

twine[2] *verb* (**twining, twined**)
to twist something around something else or to cause this to happen: *The rose* ***twined*** *around the frame.*

twinkle (say **twink**-l) *verb* (**twinkling, twinkled**)
to shine with a small bright light that comes and goes: *Stars* ***twinkled*** *in the night sky.*

twirl (say **twurl**) *verb* (**twirling, twirled**)
to turn round and round quickly or to make somebody turn around quickly: *He* ***twirled*** *her on the dance floor.*
▸ **twirl** (*noun*)

twist *verb* (**twisting, twisted**)
1 to change the shape of something by turning it in different directions, or to turn in many directions: *She* ***twisted*** *the wire into the shape of a bird.* ◇ *The path* ***twists*** *and turns through the forest.*
2 to turn something with your hand: ***Twist*** *the lid off the jar.*

3 to turn something round and round many times: *They **twisted** the sheets into a rope and escaped through the window.*
4 to hurt part of your body by suddenly turning it in a way that is not natural: *She fell and **twisted** her ankle.*
▸ **twist** (*noun*): *the **twists** and turns of the river* ◇ *She gave the handle a hard **twist**.*

twitch (say **twich**) *verb* (**twitching, twitched**)
to make a sudden quick movement with a part of your body: *Rabbits **twitch** their noses.*

twitter (say **twit**-uh) *verb* (**twittering, twittered**)
(used about birds) to make many quick high sounds: *Birds are **twittering** in the tree.*

Twitter™ (say **twit**-uh) *noun* (*no plural*)
the name of a **website** that people join and use to send short messages to friends through the **Internet** or as **SMS**es on cellphones

two (say **too**) *number*
2 ➲ The adjective is **second**[1]
in two into **two** pieces: *The cup fell on the floor and broke in **two**.*

two-dimensional *adjective* (abbr. 2-D)
having length and width, but no depth: *a flat **two-dimensional** shape* ◇ ***two-dimensional** art*
➲ See **three-dimensional**

tycoon (say ty-**koon**) *noun* (*plural* **tycoons**)
a person who is very successful in business or industry and who has become rich and powerful: *an oil **tycoon*** ➲ SYNONYM **magnate**
ⓘ ORIGIN: 19th century, from Japanese *taikun* meaning 'great lord'

tying (say **ty**-ing) form of **tie**[1]

type[1] (say **tipe**) *noun*
1 (*plural* **types**) a group of things that are the same in some way: *An almond is a **type** of nut.* ◇ *What **type** of music do you like?* ➲ SYNONYMS **kind**[1], **sort**[1]
2 (*no plural*) the letters that a machine makes on paper: *The **type** was so small I couldn't read it.*

type[2] (say **tipe**) *verb* (**typing, typed**)
to write something using a machine that has keys, such as a computer or a **typewriter**: *Her secretary **types** all her letters.* ◇ *Can you **type**?*

typewriter (say **tipe**-rite-uh) *noun* (*plural* **typewriters**)
a machine with keys that you use for writing: *an electric **typewriter***

typhoid fever (say ty-foyd **fee**-vuh) *noun* (*no plural*)
a serious infectious disease that you can get from bacteria in dirty water and food

typhoon (say ty-**foon**) *noun* (*plural* **typhoons**)
a violent storm with strong winds in a **tropical** area ➲ See note at **storm**[1]

typhus (say **ty**-fuhss) *noun* (*no plural*)
an infectious disease spread by lice and fleas, causing high body temperatures, weakness and skin sores

typical (say **tip**-ik-l) *adjective*
Something that is **typical** is a good example of its kind: *We had a **typical** English breakfast – bacon, eggs, toast and tea.*
▸ **typically** (*adverb*): *This food is **typically** South African.*

typist (say **tipe**-uhst) *noun* (*plural* **typists**)
a person who works in an office typing letters and documents

typography (say ty-**pog**-ruh-fee) *noun* (*no plural*)
the process of arranging letters and words and printing them

tyranny (say **ti**-ruh-nee) *noun* (*no plural*)
the cruel and unfair use of power by a person or small group of people to control a country
▸ **tyrannical** (*adjective*): *a **tyrannical** ruler*

tyrant (say **ty**-ruhnt) *noun* (*plural* **tyrants**)
a person with a lot of power who uses it in a cruel way ➲ SYNONYM **despot**
▸ **tyrannical** (*adjective*): *a **tyrannical** ruler*

tyre (say **ty**-uh) *noun* (*plural* **tyres**)
a circle of rubber around the outside of a wheel, for example on a car or bicycle: *I think we've got a flat **tyre** (= a **tyre** with not enough air inside it).* ➲ See illustration at **car**

A
B
C
D
E
F
G
H
I
J
K
L
M
N
O
P
Q
R
S
T
U
V
W
X
Y
Z

Uu

ubiquitous (say yoo-**bik**-kwi-tuhss) *adjective* (*formal*)
something or someone that seems to be everywhere: *The influence of the great woman is **ubiquitous**.*

ubuntu (say *uu*-**b*uu***n-tuu) *noun* (*no plural*)
the quality of being a good human being, which involves accepting other people as part of our lives and being generous towards them: ***Ubuntu** means different things to different people.*
🛈 **ORIGIN**: 20th century, from isiXhosa and isiZulu *ubuntu*, meaning 'humanity, goodness'

udder (say **ud**-uh) *noun* (*plural* **udders**)
the part of a female animal, especially of a cow, sheep or goat, that hangs under its body and produces milk

UFO (say yoo-ef-**oh**) *noun* (*plural* **UFOs**)
a strange object that some people think they have seen in the sky and that may come from another planet. 🛈 **UFO** is short for 'unidentified flying object'.

ugly (say **ug**-lee) *adjective* (**uglier**, **ugliest**)
not pleasant to look at: *an **ugly** face* ◇ *The house was really **ugly**.* ➲ **OPPOSITE** **beautiful** 1

WHICH WORD? It is not polite to say somebody is **ugly**. It is better to say **unattractive**.

WORD BUILDING There are many words that you can use instead of **ugly**, but check their exact meanings first. Examples are: **disgusting**, **ghastly**, **gross** 4, **grotesque**, **hideous**, **inelegant**, **repulsive**, **unattractive**, **unpleasant** and **unsightly**.

UIF (say yoo-*y*-**ef**) *noun* (*no plural*)
an insurance which pays money to people who have lost their jobs 🛈 **UIF** is short for 'unemployment insurance fund'.

UK (say yoo-**kay**) *abbreviation*
United Kingdom (England, Scotland, Wales and Northern Ireland as a political unit)

ulcer (say **ul**-suh) *noun* (*plural* **ulcers**)
a painful area on your skin or inside your body: *a mouth **ulcer***

ulterior (say ul-**teer**-ri-uh) *adjective*
that you keep secret or hide: *Why is he suddenly being so nice to me? Does he have an **ulterior** motive?*

ultimate (say **ul**-ti-muht) *adjective*
happening at the end of a long process: *The **ultimate** goal was independence.*
▸ **ultimately** (*adverb*): ***Ultimately**, you are the one who must decide.*

ultimatum (say ul-ti-**may**-tuhm) *noun* (*plural* **ultimatums** or **ultimata**)
a final warning to somebody to do what you have asked, before you take action against them: *The landlord gave us an **ultimatum** – pay the rent or move out of the house.*

ultra- (say **ul**-truh) *prefix*
extremely: *an **ultra-modern** house*
🛈 **ORIGIN**: from Latin *ultra* meaning 'beyond'

ultrasound (say **ul**-truh-sownd) *noun*
1 (*no plural*) sound that is higher than humans can hear
2 (*plural* **ultrasounds**) a medical process using sound waves that produces an image of what is inside your body: *The **ultrasound** showed that she was expecting twins.*

ultraviolet (say ul-truh-**vy**-uh-luht) *adjective* (abbr. UV)
Ultraviolet light cannot be seen and makes your skin go darker: *You must protect your skin from harmful **ultraviolet** rays.*

ululate (say **yool**-yuu-layt) *verb* (**ululating**, **ululated**)
to sing in a special way to show that you are happy or sad or that you respect a person: *The women **ululated** when Nelson Mandela appeared.*
▸ **ululation** (*noun*)

umbilical cord *noun* (*plural* **umbilical cords**)
the tube that connects a baby to its mother before it is born and is cut at the moment of birth

umbra (say **um**-bruh) *noun* (*plural* **umbras** or **umbrae**)
the darkest part of a shadow ➲ See **penumbra**

umbrella (say um-**bre**-luh) *noun* (*plural* **umbrellas**)
an object that you open and hold over your head to keep you dry when it rains or to protect you from the sun: *It started to rain, so I put my **umbrella** up.*

Umkhonto we Sizwe (say *uum*-**kawn**-taw we-**siz**-we) *noun* (abbr. MK)
an armed organization that fought against the

government of South Africa during the time of **apartheid**, from 1961 to 1990: ***Umkhonto we Sizwe** was the armed division of the ANC during its struggle for democracy.*
ℹ **ORIGIN**: from isiXhosa, meaning 'Spear of the Nation'

umkhwetha (say *uum*-**kwair**-tuh) *noun* (*plural* **abakhwetha**)
a Xhosa boy who takes part in a traditional ceremony in which he is **circumcised** and accepted as an adult man
ℹ **ORIGIN**: 19th century, from isiXhosa *umkhwetha*, meaning 'an initiate'

umpire (say **um**-py-uh) *noun* (*plural* **umpires**)
a person who watches a game such as tennis or cricket to make sure the players obey the rules
➲ See **referee**
▸ **umpire** (*verb*): *The match was **umpired** by an Italian.*

UN *abbreviation* **United Nations**

un- *prefix*
You can add **un-** to the beginning of some words to give them the opposite meaning, for example: ***unhappy*** (= not happy) ◇ ***untrue*** (= not true) ◇ ***undress*** (= to take clothes off)
ℹ **ORIGIN**: from Old English

unable (say un-**ayb**-l) *adjective*
not able to do something: *Dana was **unable** to come to school because she was ill.* ➲ The noun is **inability**

unacceptable (say un-uhk-**sep**-tuhb-l) *adjective*
If something is **unacceptable**, you cannot accept or allow it: *This behaviour is completely **unacceptable**.* ➲ OPPOSITE **acceptable**

unambiguous (say un-am-**big**-*yuu*-uhss) *adjective*
not **ambiguous**

unanimous (say *yuu*-**nan**-i-muhss) *adjective*
with the agreement of every person: *The decision was **unanimous**.*

unarmed (say un-**aamd**) *adjective*
not carrying a gun or any weapon: *an **unarmed** police officer* ➲ OPPOSITE **armed**

unattractive (say un-uh-**trak**-tiv) *adjective*
not nice to look at ➲ OPPOSITE **attractive** ➲ See note at **ugly**

unavoidable (say un-uh-**voyd**-uhb-l) *adjective*
If something is **unavoidable**, you cannot stop it or get away from it: *This tragic accident was **unavoidable**.*

unaware (say un-uh-**wair**) *adjective*
not knowing about or not noticing somebody or something: *I was **unaware** of the danger.*

unbearable (say un-**bair**-ruhb-l) *adjective*
If something is **unbearable**, you cannot accept it because it is so bad: *Everyone left the room because the noise was **unbearable**.* ➲ SYNONYM **intolerable**
▸ **unbearably** (*adverb*): *It was **unbearably** hot.*

unbelievable (say un-bi-**leev**-uhb-l) *adjective*
1 used to emphasize how good, bad or extreme something is: *We had an **unbelievable** holiday; it was great!* ➲ SYNONYM **incredible** 1
2 difficult to believe and probably not true

unbiased (say un-**by**-uhst) *adjective*
not **biased**: *an **unbiased** report*

unborn (say un-**bawn**) *adjective*
not yet born: *an **unborn** child*

unbroken (say un-**broh**-kuhn) *adjective*
not **broken**: *an **unbroken** record*

uncanny (say un-**kan**-ee) *adjective* (**uncannier**, **uncanniest**)
something very strange, which you cannot easily explain: *She has an **uncanny** ability to know what I am going to say next.*

uncertain (say un-**sur**-tuhn) *adjective*
not sure or not decided: *an **uncertain** future* ◇ *I'm **uncertain** about what to do.* ➲ SYNONYM **unsure** ➲ OPPOSITE **certain** 1
▸ **uncertainty** (*noun*): *This decision should put an end to all the **uncertainty**.*

uncle (say **ung**-kuhl) *noun* (*plural* **uncles**)
1 the brother of your mother or father, or the husband of your aunt: ***Uncle** Paul*
2 a word used by a child or a young person to address or refer to an older man

unclear (say un-**kleer**) *adjective*
not **clear**[1]: *The meaning of the message is **unclear**.*

uncomfortable (say un-**kumf**-tuhb-l) *adjective*
1 not pleasant to wear, sit on, lie on, etc.: *The chair was hard and **uncomfortable**.*
2 not able to sit, lie or stand in a way that feels pleasant
3 feeling or causing worry or embarrassment: *I felt **uncomfortable** when they started arguing in front of me.* ➲ OPPOSITE **comfortable**

uncommon (say un-**kom**-uhn) *adjective*
not usual: *This tree is **uncommon** in this area.* ➲ SYNONYM **rare** 1

uncompromising (say un-**kom**-pruh-mize-ing) *adjective*
refusing to discuss or change a decision

unconscious (say un-**kon**-shuhss) *adjective*
1 If you are **unconscious**, you are in a kind of sleep and you do not know what is happening:

A B C D E F G H I J K L M N O P Q R S T U V W X Y Z

She hit her head and was ***unconscious*** *for three days.*
2 If you are **unconscious** of something, you do not know about it: *He seemed* ***unconscious*** *that I was watching him.* ➲ OPPOSITE **conscious**
▶ **unconsciousness** (*noun*): *She slipped into* ***unconsciousness*** *after the accident.*

uncontrollable (say un-kuhn-**troh**-luhb-l) *adjective*
If a feeling is **uncontrollable**, you cannot control or stop it: *I suddenly got an* ***uncontrollable*** *urge to sneeze.*
▶ **uncontrollably** (*adverb*): *He started laughing* ***uncontrollably****.*

uncooked (say un-**kuu**kt) *adjective*
not **cooked**

uncountable noun (say un-**kown**-tuhb-l **nown**) *noun* (*plural* **uncountable nouns**) (*grammar*)
nouns that have no plural and cannot be used with 'a' or 'an', for example *advice* or *furniture*. ➲ See Study page 5 ➲ OPPOSITE **countable noun**

uncouth (say un-**kooth**) *adjective*
behaving in a rude or unacceptable way

uncover (say un-**kuv**-uh) *verb* (**uncovering, uncovered**)
1 to take away something that is on top of another thing: *While I was digging, I* ***uncovered*** *an old box in the ground.* ➲ OPPOSITE **cover**[1] 1
2 to find out something that was secret: *Police* ***uncovered*** *a plot to steal the painting.*

undeniable (say un-di-**ny**-uhb-l) *adjective*
clear, true or certain: *It is* ***undeniable*** *that girls mature faster than boys.*

under (say **un**-duh) *preposition, adverb*
1 in or to a place that is lower than or below something: *The cat is* ***under*** *the table.* ◇ *We sailed* ***under*** *the bridge.* ◇ *The boat filled with water, then went* ***under****.*
2 less than something: *If you are* ***under*** *17 you are not allowed to drive a car.*
3 covered by something: *I'm wearing a vest* ***under*** *my shirt.* ➲ SYNONYM **underneath**
4 controlled by somebody or something: *The team are playing well* ***under*** *their new captain.*

under- (say **un**-duh) *prefix*
1 You can add **under-** to the beginning of some words to show that something is **under** another thing: ***underwater*** (= below the surface of the water) ◇ ***underwear*** (= clothes that you wear under your other clothes)
2 You can add **under-** to the beginning of some words to show that something is not enough: ***undercooked*** (= not cooked enough) ◇ ***underpaid*** (= not paid enough)

underage (say un-duh-**ayj**) *adjective*
too young to be allowed by law to do something: ***underage*** *drinking*

underarm (say un-duh-**aam**) *adjective*
1 connected with a person's **armpit**: *an* ***underarm*** *deodorant* ◇ ***underarm*** *sweating*
2 an **underarm** throw or hit of a ball is done with the hand kept below the level of the shoulder

undercurrent (say **un**-duh-ku-ruhnt) *noun* (*plural* **undercurrents**)
a feeling that people do not talk about openly: *The learners obeyed the new rules but there was an* ***undercurrent*** *of anger.*

undercut (say un-duh-**kut**) *verb* (**undercutting, undercut**)
to sell something at a lower price than other shops: *This supermarket always* ***undercuts*** *fruit prices.*

underdone (say un-duh-**dun**) *adjective*
not completely cooked: *Do you like your meat* ***underdone*** *or well cooked?*

undergo (say un-duh-**goh**) *verb* (**undergoing, underwent, has undergone**)
to have a difficult or unpleasant experience: *Our teacher is in hospital* ***undergoing*** *an operation.*

undergraduate (say un-duh-**grad**-yuu-uht) *adjective*
connected with students at a university who are studying certain courses for their first degree, or the courses they are doing: *an* ***undergraduate*** *course* ➲ See **graduate**[1], **degree**
▶ **undergraduate** (*noun*): *My sister is an* ***undergraduate*** *at the University of Pretoria.*

underground[1] (say **un**-duh-grownd or un-duh-**grownd**) *adjective, adverb*
under the ground: *an* ***underground*** *car park* ◇ *Earthworms live* ***underground****.*

underground[2] (say **un**-duh-grownd) *noun* (also **the Underground**) (*no plural*)
an **underground** railway system in a city: *I go to work by* ***underground****.* ➲ SYNONYM **subway** 2

undergrowth (say **un**-duh-grohth) *noun* (*no plural*)
bushes and other plants that grow under trees: *There was a path through the* ***undergrowth****.*

underhand (say un-duh-**hand**) *adjective*
1 secret or not honest: *an* ***underhand*** *deal*
2 throwing or hitting a ball in a certain way

underline (say un-duh-**line**) *verb* (**underlining, underlined**)
to draw a line under a word or words. *This sentence is underlined.*

underlying (say un-duh-**ly**-ing) *adjective*
something that is important but not obvious: *We need to find the* ***underlying*** *cause of this problem.*

undermine (say un-duh-**mine**) *verb* (**undermining, undermined**)
to make something weaker or to make somebody less confident: *The scandal has* ***undermined*** *the people's confidence in the leader.*

underneath (say un-duh-**neeth**) *preposition, adverb*
under or below something: *The dog was lying* ***underneath*** *the car.* ◇ *She wore a black jacket with a red jumper* ***underneath*** *it.*

undernourished (say un-duh-**nu**-risht) *adjective*
in bad health because you do not eat enough of the right kind of food ➲ See **malnourished**

underpants (say **un**-duh-pantss) *plural noun* (also *informal* **pants**)
a piece of clothing that a man or boy wears under his trousers: *a pair of* ***underpants*** ➲ See **panties, pants, underwear**

underprivileged (say un-duh-**priv**-uh-lijd) *adjective*
having less money or fewer rights and opportunities than other people

understand (say un-duh-**stand**) *verb* (**understanding, understood**)
1 to know what something means or why something happens: *I didn't* ***understand*** *what the teacher said.* ◇ *He doesn't* ***understand*** *isiNdebele.* ◇ *I don't* ***understand*** *why you're so angry.* ➲ SYNONYM **comprehend**
2 to know something because somebody has told you about it: *I* ***understand*** *that the plane from Windhoek will be late.* ➲ SYNONYM **believe** 1
make yourself understood to make people understand you: *My Afrikaans isn't very good but I can usually make myself* ***understood.***

understanding[1] (say un-duh-**stand**-ing) *noun* (*no plural*)
knowing about something: *He's got a good* ***understanding*** *of computers.*

understanding[2] (say un-duh-**stand**-ing) *adjective*
ready to listen to other people's problems and try to understand them: *My parents are very* ***understanding.*** ➲ SYNONYM **sympathetic**

understatement (say **un**-duh-stayt-muhnt) *noun* (*plural* **understatements**)
a statement that makes something seem less important than it really is: *To say that I am happy is an* ***understatement.*** *I am absolutely delighted!*

understood (say un-duh-**stuud**) form of **understand**

undertake (say un-duh-**tayk**) *verb* (**undertaking, undertook, has undertaken**)
1 to decide to do something and start doing it: *The community has* ***undertaken*** *to clean up the park.*
2 to agree to do something

undertaker (say **un**-duh-tayk-uh) *noun* (*plural* **undertakers**)
a person whose job is to prepare the bodies of dead people to be buried or **cremated**, and to organize funerals

underwater (say un-duh-**waw**-tuh) *adjective, adverb*
below the surface of water: *an* ***underwater*** *camera* ◇ *Can you swim* ***underwater?***

underwear (say **un**-duh-wair) *noun* (*no plural*)
clothes that you wear next to your body, under your other clothes ➲ See **panties, pants, underpants**

underweight (say un-duh-**wayt**) *adjective*
weighing less than is normal or correct: *an* ***underweight*** *baby* ➲ OPPOSITE **overweight**

underwent (say un-duh-**went**) form of **undergo**

underworld (say **un**-duh-wurld) *noun* (*no plural*)
1 people who are involved in organized crime
2 in old stories (called **myths**), the place under the surface of the Earth, where dead people and spirits live

undesirable (say un-di-**zy**-ruhb-l) *adjective*
unpleasant or not wanted ➲ OPPOSITE **desirable**

undid form of **undo**

undo (say un-**doo**) *verb* (**undoing, undid, has undone**)
to open something that was tied or fixed: *I can't* ***undo*** *this zip.* ◇ *Don't* ***undo*** *your jacket – I've just done it up!*

undone (say un-**dun**) *adjective*
not tied or fixed: *Your shoelaces are* ***undone.***

undoubtedly (say un-**dowt**-uhd-lee) *adverb*
certainly or without doubt: *She is* ***undoubtedly*** *very intelligent.*

A B C D E F G H I J K L M N O P Q R S T U V W X Y Z

undress (say un-**dress**) *verb* (**undressing, undressed**)
to take off your clothes or those of another person: *He **undressed** and got into bed.* ◇ *She **undressed** her baby.* ➲ OPPOSITE **dress**² 1
▸ **undressed** (*adjective*): *I got **undressed** and had a shower.*

undue (say un-**dyoo**) *adjective*
more than is necessary or reasonable: *The police try not to use **undue** force when arresting a suspect.*
▸ **unduly** (*adverb*): *She didn't seem **unduly** worried.*

undulate (say **un**-dyuu-layt) *verb* (**undulating, undulated**)
1 to move like a wave, up and down: *His body **undulated** to the music.*
2 to have a shape that reminds you of moving waves
▸ **undulating** (*adjective*): ***undulating** hills and valleys*

unearth (say un-**urth**) *verb* (**unearthing, unearthed**)
1 to find something or dig up something from under the ground: *Archaeologists have **unearthed** the skeleton of a dinosaur.*
2 to find information, etc. after searching for it carefully: *The newspaper has **unearthed** some worrying facts about corruption.*

uneasy (say un-**ee**-zee) *adjective*
worried that something is wrong: *I started to feel **uneasy** when the children were late coming home.*
▸ **uneasily** (*adverb*): *She looked **uneasily** around the room.*

unemployed (say un-im-**ployd**) *adjective*
If you are **unemployed**, you can work but you do not have a job: *She has been **unemployed** for over a year.*

unemployment (say un-im-**ploy**-muhnt) *noun* (*no plural*)
1 the state of not being able to find a job: ***Unemployment** depresses most people.*
2 the number of people who are unemployed: *If the factory closes, **unemployment** in the town will increase.* ➲ OPPOSITE **employment**

unequal (say un-**ee**-kwuhl) *adjective*
1 not **equal** in size or amount
2 not fair: *the **unequal** distribution of water resources* ➲ The noun is **inequality**

uneven (say un-**eev**-uhn) *adjective*
1 not smooth or flat: *The driver had to go slowly because the road was so **uneven**.* ➲ The adjective is **even**². ➲ OPPOSITE **even**¹ 1
2 not always of the same level or quality: *an **uneven** performance* (= with some good parts and some bad parts)
3 not fair or equal: *an **uneven** distribution of resources*
▸ **unevenly** (*adverb*): *Wealth in the country is **unevenly** distributed.*

unexpected (say un-ek-**spek**-tid) *adjective*
surprising because you did not expect it: *an **unexpected** visit*
▸ **unexpectedly** (*adverb*): *She arrived **unexpectedly**.*

unfair (say un-**fair**) *adjective*
not treating or dealing with people fairly or equally: *It was **unfair** to give chocolates to some of the children and not to the others.* ➲ OPPOSITE **fair**¹ 1
▸ **unfairly** (*adverb*): *He left his job because the boss was treating him **unfairly**.*

unfaithful (say un-**fayth**-fuhl) *adjective*
not **faithful**

unfamiliar (say un-fuh-**mil**-i-uh) *adjective*
that you do not know or recognize: *I woke up in an **unfamiliar** room.* ➲ OPPOSITE **familiar**

unfashionable (say un-**fash**-nuhb-l) *adjective*
not popular or in a popular style at a particular time: ***unfashionable** clothes* ➲ OPPOSITE **fashionable**

unfasten (say un-**faa**-suhn) *verb* (**unfastening, unfastened**)
to open something that was tied or fixed: *to **unfasten** your seatbelt* ➲ OPPOSITE **fasten**

PRONUNCIATION Don't pronounce the **t** in **unfasten**.

unfavourable (say un-**fay**-vuh-ruhb-l) *adjective*
not **favourable**
▸ **unfavourably** (*adverb*)

unfit (say un-**fit**) *adjective*
1 not good enough or not right for something: *This house is **unfit** for people to live in.*
2 not healthy or strong: *She never does any exercise – that's why she's so **unfit**.* ➲ OPPOSITE **fit**²

unfold (say un-**fohld**) *verb* (**unfolded, unfolding**)
to open something to make it flat or to open out and become flat: *Marie **unfolded** the newspaper.* ◇ *The sofa **unfolds** to make a bed.* ➲ OPPOSITE **fold**¹ 1

unforeseen (say un-faw-**seen**) *adjective*
not **expected**: *an **unforeseen** problem*

unfortunate (say un-**faw**-tshuh-nuht) *adjective*
not **lucky**: *It's **unfortunate** that you were ill on your birthday.* ➲ OPPOSITE **fortunate**

unfortunately (say un-**faw**-tshuh-nuht-lee) *adverb*
a word that you use to show that you are not happy about a situation or fact: *I'd like to give you some money, but **unfortunately** I haven't got any.* ➲ See **fortunate**

unfounded (say un-**fown**-did) *adjective*
not supported by facts: *The allegations that he made are **unfounded**.*

unfriendly (say un-**frend**-lee) *adjective*
not friendly, or not kind or helpful to other people

ungrateful (say un-**grayt**-fuhl) *adjective*
If you are **ungrateful**, you do not show thanks when somebody helps you or gives you something: *Don't be so **ungrateful**! I spent all morning looking for this present.* ➲ OPPOSITE **grateful**

unhappy (say un-**hap**-ee) *adjective* (**unhappier**, **unhappiest**)
not happy or satisfied: *He was very **unhappy** when his wife left him.* ◇ *I was **unhappy** with the salary they offered me.* ➲ SYNONYM **sad**
▸ **unhappily** (*adverb*): *'I failed the exam,' she said **unhappily**.* ▸ **unhappiness** (*noun*): *He has had a lot of **unhappiness** in his life.*

WORD BUILDING There are many words that you can use instead of **unhappy**, but check their exact meanings first. Examples are: **crestfallen**, **dejected**, **depressed**, **desolate**2, **disappointed**, **down**^{2}2, **downcast**1, **fed up** (informal) **forlorn**, **gloomy**2, **glum**, **heartbroken**, **lonely**1, **melancholy**, **miserable**1, **sad**, **sombre**2, **sorry**1, **upset** and **wretched**1.

unhealthy (say un-**hel**-thee) *adjective* (**unhealthier**, **unhealthiest**)
1 not well or often ill: *an **unhealthy** child*
2 that can make you ill: ***unhealthy** food*
➲ OPPOSITE **healthy**

unhelpful (say un-**help**-fuhl) *adjective*
not wanting to help somebody or not useful: *The shop assistant was rather **unhelpful**.*
➲ OPPOSITE **helpful**

uni- (say **yoo**-ni) *prefix*
one or single: ***uniform*** ◇ ***unilateral***
ⓘ ORIGIN: from Latin *unus* meaning 'one'

unicellular (say yoo-ni-**sel**-yuh-luh) *adjective* (*biology*)
having or consisting of only one cell: *Bacteria are **unicellular** organisms.*

unicorn (say **yoo**-ni-kawn) *noun* (*plural* **unicorns**)
(in children's stories) an animal that looks like a horse with a horn on its forehead

uniform^1 (say **yoo**-ni-fawm) *noun* (*plural* **uniforms**)
the special clothes that everybody in the same job, school or organization wears: *Police officers wear dark blue **uniforms**.*

uniform^2 (say **yoo**-ni-fawm) *adjective*
the same in all parts, not changing: *blocks of stone of **uniform** size* ◇ *a row of **uniform** houses*
▸ **uniformity** (*noun*)

unify (say **yoo**-ni-fy) *verb* (**unifying**, **unified**)
to join separate parts together to make them one unit or to make them similar: *The states were **unified** into one country.*
▸ **unification** (*noun*)

unilateral (say yoo-ni-**lat**-ruhl) *adjective*
done or made by one person or country without the agreement of others: *a **unilateral** declaration of independence*
▸ **unilaterally** (*adverb*)

unimportant (say un-im-**paw**-tuhnt) *adjective*
not **important**

uninhabited (say un-in-**hab**-i-tid) *adjective*
where nobody lives: *an **uninhabited** island*

uninhibited (say un-in-**hib**-i-tid) *adjective*
behaving in a free and natural way without worrying what other people think of you

union (say **yoo**-ni-uhn) *noun*
1 (*plural* **unions**) (also **trade union**) a group of workers who have joined together to talk to their managers about things such as pay and the way they work: *a mineworkers' **union***
2 (*plural* **unions**) a group of people or countries that have joined together: *the African **Union***
3 (*no plural*) coming together: *The **union** of the colonies of South Africa took place in 1910.*

unionist (say **yoo**-ni-uhn-ist) *noun* (*plural* **unionists**)
a member of an organization called a **trade union**

unique (say yuu-**neek**) *adjective*
not like anybody or anything else: *Everybody in the world is **unique**.*

unison (say **yoo**-ni-suhn) *noun*
in unison saying or doing the same thing at the same time: *'Yes, please!' they shouted in **unison**.*

unit (say **yoo**-nit) *noun* (*plural* **units**)
1 one complete thing or group that may be part of something larger: *The book has twelve **units**.*

A B C D E F G H I J K L M N O P Q R S T U V W X Y Z

2 a measurement of a fixed quantity: *A metre is a **unit** of length and a kilogram is a **unit** of mass.*

unitary (say **yoo**-nuh-tree) *adjective*
when the power in a country or organization is controlled by a central body ➲ See **federal**

unite (say *yuu*-**nite**) *verb* (**uniting, united**)
to join together to do something together or to put two things together: *We must **unite** to defeat our enemies.*
▸ **united** (*adjective*): *the **United** States of America*

United Nations *noun* (*no plural*) (abbr. UN)
an organization that tries to solve world problems in a peaceful way and to give help to countries that need it

unity (say **yoo**-nuh-tee) *noun* (*no plural*)
a situation in which people agree and work together: *family **unity*** ◇ *Is there **unity** in the government?*
🛈 **ORIGIN:** 13th–15th century, through Old French from Latin *unus* meaning 'one'

universal (say yoo-ni-**vurss**-l) *adjective*
connected with, done by or for everybody: *The environment is a **universal** issue.*
▸ **universally** (*adverb*): *to be **universally** accepted*

universe *noun* (*no plural*)
the Earth and all the stars, planets and everything else in space
🛈 **ORIGIN:** 14th–15th century, from Old French *univers* or Latin *universum* meaning 'combined into one, whole'

university (say yoo-ni-**vur**-suh-tee) *noun* (*plural* **universities**)
a place where people go to study more difficult subjects after they have left school: *I'm hoping to go to **university** next year.* ◇ *My sister is at **university** studying Chemistry.*

> **WORD BUILDING** If you are studying at a university you are a **student**. If you pass all your exams at a university, you **graduate**, meaning you get a **degree**.

university of technology *noun* (*plural* **universities of technology**)
a type of college or university that mainly teaches practical subjects: *I'm going to a **university of technology** after school.* ➲ See **technikon**

unjust (say un-**just**) *adjective*
not fair or right: *This tax is **unjust** because poor people pay as much as rich people.* ➲ SYNONYM **unfair**
▸ **unjustly** (*adverb*): *He was **unjustly** accused of a crime he didn't commit.*

unkempt (say un-**kempt**) *adjective*
not well cared for, untidy: *He always looks dirty and **unkempt**.* ➲ SYNONYM **dishevelled**

unkind (say un-**kynd**) *adjective*
unpleasant and not friendly: *It was **unkind** of you to laugh at her.* ➲ OPPOSITE **kind**²

unknown (say un-**nohn**) *adjective*
1 that you do not know: *an **unknown** face* ➲ SYNONYM **unfamiliar**
2 not famous: *an **unknown** actor* ➲ OPPOSITES **famous**, **well known**

unleaded (say un-**led**-id) *adjective*
Unleaded petrol is less harmful to the environment than some types of petrol, because it does not contain any **lead**² 1.

unleavened (say un-**lev**-uhnd) *adjective*
(used to describe bread) flat and heavy because it does not have anything in it (such as **yeast**) to make it rise

unless (say un-**less**) *conjunction*
if not or except if: *You will be late **unless** you leave now.* ◇ ***Unless** you work harder, you'll fail the exam.*

unlike (say un-**like**) *preposition*
different from: *She is **unlike** anyone I've ever met.* ➲ OPPOSITE **like**² 1

unlikely (say un-**like**-lee) *adjective* (**unlikelier, unlikeliest**)
If something is **unlikely**, it will probably not happen: *It is **unlikely** that it will rain.* ◇ *He is **unlikely** to pass the exam.* ➲ OPPOSITE **likely**

unload (say un-**lohd**) *verb* (**unloading, unloaded**)
to take things that have been carried somewhere off or out of a car, truck, ship or plane: *I **unloaded** the shopping from the car.* ◇ *They **unloaded** the ship at the dock.*

unlock (say un-**lok**) *verb* (**unlocking, unlocked**)
1 to open something with a key: *I **unlocked** the door and went in.*
2 to discover something and make it known: *The divers hoped to **unlock** some of the secrets of the shipwreck.*

unlucky (say un-**luk**-ee) *adjective* (**unluckier, unluckiest**)
having or bringing bad luck: *They were **unlucky** to lose because they played very well.* ◇ *Some people think the number 13 is **unlucky**.* ➲ OPPOSITE **lucky**
▸ **unluckily** (*adverb*): ***Unluckily**, I missed the bus.*

unmarried (say un-**ma**-rid) *adjective*
not married, or without a husband or wife
➲ SYNONYM **single**[1] 3

unmistakable (say un-miss-**tayk**-uhb-l) *adjective*
If something is **unmistakable**, it is easy to recognize and will not be confused with anything else: *She is **unmistakable** in that big red hat.*

unnatural (say un-**nat**-yuu-ruhl) *adjective*
different from what is normal or expected: *There was an **unnatural** silence.* ➲ OPPOSITE **natural**

unnecessary (say un-**ness**-uh-suh-ree) *adjective*
not needed, or more than is needed: *All this fuss is totally **unnecessary**.* ➲ OPPOSITE **necessary**
▸ **unnecessarily** (*adverb*)

SPELLING Remember! You spell **unnecessary** with **nn**, one **c** and **ss**.

unoccupied (say un-**ok**-yuu-pide) *adjective*
not **occupied**: *The flat is currently **unoccupied**.*

unofficial (say un-uh-**fish**-l) *adjective*
not accepted or approved by a person or people in authority: ***Unofficial** reports say that four people died in the explosion.*
▸ **unofficially** (*adverb*): *We heard **unofficially** that our teacher is leaving.*

unpack (say un-**pak**) *verb* (**unpacking**, **unpacked**)
to take all the things out of a bag, suitcase, etc.: *Have you **unpacked** your suitcase?* ◇ *We arrived at the hotel, **unpacked**, and then went to the beach.*

unpaid (say un-**payd**) *adjective*
not yet paid: ***unpaid** bills*

unpleasant (say un-**plez**-uhnt) *adjective*
not pleasant or not nice: *There was an **unpleasant** smell of bad fish.* ◇ *He has an **unpleasant** face – he always looks angry.*
▸ **unpleasantly** (*adverb*): *It was **unpleasantly** hot in that room.*

unplug (say un-**plug**) *verb* (**unplugging**, **unplugged**)
to take out a piece of electrical equipment (called a **plug**) from the electricity supply: *Please don't **unplug** the TV – I've just plugged it in.*

unpopular (say un-**pop**-yuu-luh) *adjective*
not **popular**: *He's **unpopular** at work because he's lazy.*

unprecedented (say un-**press**-i-den-tid) *adjective*
something that was never done or known before: *The Internet has given us **unprecedented** access to information.*

unpredictable (say un-pri-**dik**-tuhb-l) *adjective*
If something is **unpredictable**, you cannot say how it will change in the future: *The weather is very **unpredictable** at this time of year.* ➲ See **predict**

unprofessional (say un-pruh-**fesh**-uhn-l) *adjective*
below the standard that other people expect of you: *They behaved in an **unprofessional** manner.*

unqualified (say un-**kwol**-i-fide) *adjective*
not **qualified**

unrealistic (say un-ree-uh-**liss**-tik) *adjective*
not **realistic**: ***unrealistic** expectations*
▸ **unrealistically:** *The prices are **unrealistically** high.*

unreasonable (say un-**reez**-nuhb-l) *adjective*
expecting too much: *an **unreasonable** request*
➲ OPPOSITE **reasonable** 1

unreliable (say un-ri-**ly**-uhb-l) *adjective*
If something or somebody is **unreliable**, you cannot trust or depend on it or them: *an **unreliable** car* ◇ *Don't lend her money – she's very **unreliable** and you might not get it back.*
➲ OPPOSITE **reliable**

unrest (say un-**rest**) *noun* (*no plural*)
a situation in which people are angry or unhappy and ready to protest or fight: *There was **unrest** in the country after the elections.*

unrivalled (say un-**ry**-vuhld) *adjective*
much better than any other of the same type: *The museum has an **unrivalled** collection of African art.*

unruly (say un-**roo**-lee) *adjective*
difficult to control: *an **unruly** crowd*
▸ **unruliness** (*noun*): *the **unruliness** of the crowd*

unsafe (say un-**sayf**) *adjective*
1 dangerous or not safe: *Don't climb on that wall – it's **unsafe**.*
2 (of people) in danger of being harmed: *I felt **unsafe** when I went for a walk at night.*

unsatisfactory (say un-sat-iss-**fak**-tuh-ree) *adjective*
not good enough or not acceptable: *Your work is **unsatisfactory**. Please do it again.* ➲ OPPOSITE **satisfactory**

unsavoury (say un-**say**-vuh-ree) *adjective*
not pleasant or not morally acceptable: *Some of his friends are rather **unsavoury** characters.*

unscathed (say un-**skaythd**) *adjective*
not hurt, without injury: *She was lucky to escape* ***unscathed*** *from the accident.*

unseen (say un-**seen**) *adjective*
1 not **seen** or that cannot be seen: *She slipped out of the room* ***unseen****.*
2 something not seen before: ***unseen*** *difficulties* ◇ *You will get an* ***unseen*** *comprehension text in the exam.*

unselfish (say un-**sel**-fish) *adjective*
not **selfish**
▸ **unselfishly** (*adverb*)

unsettled (say un-**set**-uhld) *adjective*
1 changing often and making people uncertain about what will happen: ***unsettled*** *weather* ◇ *We are living in* ***unsettled*** *times.*
2 not calm or relaxed
3 not paid: *an* ***unsettled*** *account*

unsightly (say un-**site**-lee) *adjective*
very ugly and unpleasant to look at: *an* ***unsightly*** *building*

unskilled (say un-**skild**) *adjective*
not **skilled**: *an* ***unskilled*** *worker*

unsociable (say un-**soh**-shuhb-l) *adjective*
not **sociable**

unsound (say un-**sownd**) *adjective*
1 based on facts or ideas that are wrong: *He gave me some* ***unsound*** *advice.*
2 in poor condition or weak: *an* ***unsound*** *bridge* ◇ *of* ***unsound*** *mind*

unstable (say un-**stayb**-l) *adjective*
1 Something that is **unstable** may fall, move or change: *an* ***unstable*** *government* ◇ *This bridge is* ***unstable****.*
2 (used about a person's moods or behaviour) likely to change suddenly or often ➲ OPPOSITE **stable**[1] ➲ The noun is **instability**

unsteady (say un-**sted**-ee) *adjective*
not **steady**: *Be careful. This ladder is* ***unsteady****!*

unsuccessful (say un-suhk-**sess**-fuhl) *adjective*
If you are **unsuccessful**, you have not done what you wanted and tried to do: *I tried to repair the bike but I was* ***unsuccessful****.*
➲ OPPOSITE **successful**
▸ **unsuccessfully** (*adverb*): *He tried* ***unsuccessfully*** *to lift the box.*

unsuitable (say un-**soot**-uhb-l) *adjective*
not suitable, or not right for somebody or something: *This film is* ***unsuitable*** *for children.*

unsure (say un-**shoor**) *adjective*
not sure about something: *We were* ***unsure*** *what to do.* ➲ SYNONYM **uncertain** ➲ OPPOSITE **certain** 1
be unsure of yourself lacking confidence in yourself

unsustainable (say un-suhss-**tayn**-uhb-l) *adjective*
not **sustainable**

unsympathetic (say un-sim-puh-**thet**-ik) *adjective*
If you are **unsympathetic**, you are not kind to somebody who is hurt or sad, and you show that you do not understand their feelings and problems. ➲ OPPOSITE **sympathetic**

untidy (say un-**tide**-ee) *adjective* (**untidier**, **untidiest**)
not tidy or not with everything in the right place: *Your room is always so* ***untidy****!*
➲ SYNONYM **messy**
▸ **untidiness** (*noun*): *I hate* ***untidiness****!*

untie (say un-*ty*) *verb* (**untying, untied**)
to remove a knot or to take off the string or rope that is holding something: *Can you* ***untie*** *this knot?* ◇ *I* ***untied*** *the parcel.*

until (say un-**til**) *conjunction, preposition* (also *informal* **till**)
up to a certain time or event: *The shop is open* ***until*** *6.30.* ◇ *Stay in bed* ***until*** *you feel better.* ◇ *I can't come* ***until*** *tomorrow.*

> SPELLING Remember! You spell **until** with one **l** (but you spell **till** with **ll**).

untold (say un-**tohld**) *adjective*
very great or so big that you cannot count or measure it: *Their wealth is* ***untold****.* ◇ ***untold*** *suffering*

untrue (say un-**troo**) *adjective*
not true or correct: *What you said was completely* ***untrue****.* ➲ SYNONYM **false** 1

unused (say un-**yoozd**) *adjective*
1 not **used**: *an* ***unused*** *section of the railway line*
2 not having experience of something: *He is* ***unused*** *to driving big lorries.*

unusual (say un-**yoo**-*zhuu*-uhl) *adjective*
If something is **unusual**, it does not often happen or you do not often see it: *It's* ***unusual*** *to see a cat without a tail.* ◇ *What an* ***unusual*** *name!* ➲ OPPOSITE **usual**
▸ **unusually** (*adverb*): *It was an* ***unusually*** *wet summer.*

unwanted (say un-**won**-tid) *adjective*
not **wanted**: *an* ***unwanted*** *gift*

unwelcome (say un-**wel**-kuhm) *adjective*
If somebody or something is **unwelcome**, you are not happy to have or see them: *an* ***unwelcome*** *visitor* ➲ OPPOSITE **welcome**[2] 1

unwell (say un-**wel**) *adjective*
ill or not well: *I'm **unwell** today.*

unwieldy (say un-**weel**-dee) *adjective*
difficult to move or carry because it is so big ➲ SYNONYM **cumbersome** 1

unwilling (say un-**wil**-ing) *adjective*
If you are **unwilling** to do something, you are not ready or happy to do it: *He was **unwilling** to lend me any money.* ➲ OPPOSITE **willing**
▸ **unwillingly** (*adverb*)

unwind (say un-**wy**nd) *verb* (**unwinding**, **unwound**)
1 to open out something that has been wrapped into a ball or around something else: *to **unwind** a ball of string*
2 to start to relax, after working hard or worrying about something: *Watching television helps me **unwind** after a busy day.*

unwise (say un-**wize**) *adjective*
showing that you do not make good decisions: *It would be **unwise** to tell anybody about our plan yet.* ➲ SYNONYM **foolish**
▸ **unwisely** (*adverb*): *Perhaps **unwisely**, I agreed to help her.*

unworthy (say un-**wur*th***-ee) *adjective* (*formal*)
not **worthy**

unwound form of **unwind**

unwrap (say un-**rap**) *verb* (**unwrapping**, **unwrapped**)
to take off the paper or cloth that is around something: *I **unwrapped** the parcel.*
➲ OPPOSITE **wrap**

up *preposition, adverb*
1 in or to a higher place: *We climbed **up** the mountain.* ◇ *Put your hand **up** if you know the answer.* ➲ OPPOSITE **down**[1] 1
2 from sitting or lying to standing: *Stand **up**, please.* ◇ *What time do you get **up*** (= out of bed)*?* ◇ *'Is Joe **up*** (= out of bed)*?' 'No, he's still asleep.'*
3 to the place where somebody or something is: *She came **up** to me and asked me the time.*
4 a word we use to show an increase in something: *Prices are going **up**.* ◇ *Please turn the radio **up** – I can't hear it.* ➲ OPPOSITE **down**[1] 3
5 into pieces: *Cut the meat **up**.*
6 so that it is finished: *Eat **up**, I want you to finish this food.*
7 in a certain direction: *We walked **up** the road.*
➲ OPPOSITE **down**[1] 4
be up to somebody to be the person who should do or decide something: *'What shall we do this evening?' 'I don't mind. It's **up** to you.'*
up to
1 until or as far as: ***Up** to now, she has worked very hard.*
2 as much or as many as: ***Up** to 300 people came to the meeting.*
ⓘ ORIGIN: from Old English *up(p)*, *uppe*, related to Dutch *op*

upbringing (say **up**-bring-ing) *noun* (*no plural*)
the way your parents treat you and teach you how to behave when you are growing up: *She had a strict **upbringing**.*

update (say up-**dayt**) *verb* (**updating**, **updated**)
to make something more modern or add new things to it: *The information on our website is **updated** every week.*
▸ **update** (*noun*): *a news **update***

upgrade (say up-**grayd**) *verb* (**upgrading**, **upgraded**)
to change something so that it is better: *I've just **upgraded** my PC.*
▸ **upgrade** (*noun*): *to install an **upgrade***

upheaval (say up-**heev**-l) *noun* (*plural* **upheavals**)
a sudden big change, especially one that causes trouble

uphill (say up-**hil**) *adverb*
going up, towards the top of a hill: *It's difficult to ride a bicycle **uphill**.* ➲ OPPOSITE **downhill**

uphold (say up-**hohld**) *verb* (**upholding**, **upheld**)
to support a decision or a principle or the law: *The police have to **uphold** the law.* ◇ *The judge's ruling was **upheld**.*

upholster (say up-**hohl**-stuh) *verb* (**upholstering**, **upholstered**)
to cover a piece of furniture such as a **sofa** with cloth
▸ **upholstered** (*adjective*): *an **upholstered** chair*

upkeep (say **up**-keep) *noun* (*no plural*)
the cost and process of keeping something or someone in good condition: *Who is paying for the **upkeep** of the farm and the animals?*

upon (say uh-**pon**) *preposition* (*formal*)
on: *He sat **upon** a rock.* ◇ *The decision was based **upon** the doctor's evidence.*

upper (say **up**-uh) *adjective*
in a higher place than something else: *the **upper** lip* ➲ OPPOSITE **lower**[1]

upper case *noun* (*no plural*)
the large form of letters, for example A, B, C (not a, b, c): *'SABC' is written in **upper case**.*
➲ SYNONYM **capital** 3 ➲ OPPOSITE **lower case**

uppermost (say **up**-uh-mohst) *adjective*
in the highest or most important position: *Safety was **uppermost** in my mind as we crossed the river.*

upright (say **up**-rite) *adjective, adverb*
standing straight up, not lying down: *Put the ladder **upright** against the wall.*

uprising (say **up**-rize-ing) *noun* (*plural* **uprisings**)
a situation in which a group of people fight against the government of their country because they want it to change

uproar (say **up**-raw) *noun* (*no plural*)
a lot of noise or shouting because people are angry about something: *The meeting ended in **uproar**.* ◇ *The film caused an **uproar** when it was released.*

upset[1] (say up-**set**) *adjective*
1 unhappy or worried: *The children were very **upset** when their dog died.*
2 ill: *I've got an **upset** stomach.*
▸ **upset** (*noun*): *She has a stomach **upset**.*

upset[2] (say up-**set**) *verb* (**upsetting, upset**)
1 to make somebody feel unhappy or worried: *You **upset** him when you said he was fat.*
2 to make something go wrong: *The bad weather **upset** our plans for the weekend.*
3 to knock something so that it turns over and things fall out: *I **upset** a glass of milk all over the table.*

upsetting (say up-**set**-ing) *adjective*
making you feel unhappy or worried: *The experience was very **upsetting** for all of us.*

upside down *adverb*
with the top part at the bottom: *The picture is **upside down**.*

upstairs (say up-**stairz**) *adverb*
to or on a higher floor of a building: *I went **upstairs** to bed.* ➲ OPPOSITE **downstairs**
▸ **upstairs** (*adjective*): *An **upstairs** window was open.*

upstream (say up-**streem**) *adverb, adjective*
in the direction from which a river flows: *He found it hard work swimming **upstream**.* ◇ *an **upstream** slope*

uptight (say up-**tite**) *adjective* (*informal*) nervous and not relaxed: *She gets very **uptight** when she has to perform in front of the class.*

up to date *adjective*
modern or using new information: *Is this information **up to date**?*

upwards (say **up**-wuhdz) *adverb* (also **upward**)
up, or towards a higher place: *We climbed **upwards**, towards the top of the mountain.*
➲ OPPOSITE **downwards**

uranium (say yuu-**ray**-ni-uhm) *noun* (*no plural*) (symbol U)
a metal that can be used to produce nuclear energy: ***Uranium** is highly radioactive.*

urban (say **ur**-buhn) *adjective*
in or related to a town or city: ***urban** areas*
➲ See **rural**
🛈 ORIGIN: 17th century, from Latin *urbanus* from *urbs* meaning 'city'

urbanize (say **ur**-buh-nize) *verb* (**urbanizing, urbanized**) (also **urbanise**)
to make an area into a city or town with many roads, houses and businesses
▸ **urbanized** (*adjective*) (also **urbanised**): *This is an **urbanized** community that has moved from rural areas and settled in the city.*
▸ **urbanization** (*noun*) (also **urbanisation**)

urchin (say **ur**-chin) *noun* (*plural* **urchins**)
1 a young, badly dressed child
2 a type of shellfish which is also called a **sea urchin**

urea (say yuu-**ree**-uh) *noun* (*no plural*)
a substance that contains **nitrogen** and is found in the liquid waste that is passed from your body

ureter (say yuu-**ree**-tuh or **yuu**-ruh-tuh) *noun* (*plural* **ureters**)
the tube that liquid waste from the body passes through to get from the **kidneys** to the **bladder**

urethra (say yuu-**reeth**-ruh) *noun* (*plural* **urethras**)
the tube that carries liquid waste out of the body. In males, the male sex cells **(sperm)** also flow through it.

urge[1] (say **urj**) *verb* (**urging, urged**)
to try to make somebody do something: *I **urged** him to stay for dinner.*

urge[2] (say **urj**) *noun* (*plural* **urges**)
a strong feeling that you want to do something: *I had a sudden **urge** to laugh.*

urgency (say **ur**-juhn-see) *noun* (*no plural*)
the need to do something quickly because it is very important

urgent (say **ur**-juhnt) *adjective*
so important that you must do it or answer it quickly: *The doctor received an **urgent** telephone call.*
▸ **urgently** (*adverb*): *I must see you **urgently**.*

urinate (say **yoor**-ri-nayt) *verb* (**urinating, urinated**)
to pass liquid waste **(urine)** from the body

urine (say **yoor**-in) *noun* (*no plural*)
the yellow liquid waste that is passed from your body

URL (say yoo-aar-**el**) *noun* (*plural* **URLs**) (*computing*)
the address of a **World Wide Web** page ⓘ **URL** is short for 'Uniform Resource Locator'.

urn (*rhymes with* **turn**) *noun* (*plural* **urns**)
1 a container, used especially to hold the powder (called **ashes**) that is left when a dead person's body has been burnt **(cremated)**
2 a large metal container used for making a large quantity of tea or coffee and for keeping it hot

US (say yoo-**ess**) *abbreviation* short for **USA**

us (say **uss**) *pronoun, plural noun*
another person or other people and me, or you and me: *We were pleased when she invited **us** to dinner.* ◇ *Come with **us**.*

USA (say yoo-ess-**ay**) *abbreviation*
the United States of America

usable (say **yooz**-uhb-l) *adjective*
that can be used

usage (say **yoo**-sij) *noun* (*no plural*)
1 the way that something is used or the amount of something that is used: *The municipality is monitoring the water **usage** in the area.*
2 the way in which words are normally used in a language

use¹ (say **yooz**) *verb* (**using, used**)
1 to do a job with something: *Could I **use** your telephone?* ◇ *Do you know how to **use** this machine?* ◇ *Wood is **used** to make paper.*
2 to take something: *Don't **use** all the milk.*
use something up to **use** something until you have no more: *I've **used** up all the coffee, so I need to buy some more.*

> USAGE
> - We say **use** when we talk about using a tool to do something: *I **used** a knife to cut the meat.*
> - We say **used to** when we talk about an action that happened often in the past: *We **used to** eat a big meal every Sunday.*

use² (say **yooss**) *noun*
1 (*no plural*) using something or being used: *This pool is for the **use** of hotel guests only.* ◇ *If you don't want that box, I can make **use** of it.* ◇ *It's no **use** talking to her; she never listens.*
2 (*plural* **uses**) what you can do with something: *This machine has many **uses**.*
3 (*no plural*) the opportunity to **use** something, for example something that belongs to somebody else: *I've got the **use** of Manny's car while he's on holiday.*

used¹ (say **yoost**) *adjective*
be used to something to know something well because you have seen, heard, tasted or done it a lot: *I'm **used** to walking because I don't have a car.*
get used to something to begin to know something well after a time: *I'm getting **used** to my new job.*

used² (say **yoozd**) *adjective*
that had another owner before: *The garage sells **used** cars.* ➲ SYNONYM **second-hand**
➲ OPPOSITE **new** 1

used to *modal verb*
words that tell us about something that happened often or that was true in the past: *She **used to** smoke when she was young.* ◇ *I **used to** be afraid of dogs, but now I like them.*

> USAGE To form questions we use **did** with **use to**: *Did she **use** to smoke when she was young?* We form negatives with **didn't use to**: *I didn't **use** to like fish, but I do now.*

useful (say **yooss**-fuhl) *adjective*
good and helpful for doing something: *This bag will be **useful** for carrying my books.*

useless (say **yooss**-luhss) *adjective*
1 not good for anything: *A car is **useless** without petrol.*
2 that does not do what you hoped: *It was **useless** asking my brother for money – he didn't have any.*
► **uselessness** (*noun*): *a feeling of **uselessness***

user (say **yoo**-zuh) *noun* (*plural* **users**)
a person who uses something: *computer **users***

user-friendly (say yoo-zuh-**frend**-lee) *adjective*
easy to understand and use: *Computers are much more **user-friendly** now than they used to be.*

USSR (say yoo-ess-ess-**aar**) *abbreviation* (*history*)
the Union of Soviet Socialist Republics

usual (say **yoo**-*zhuu*-uhl) *adjective*
that happens most often: *He arrived home later than **usual**.* ➲ SYNONYM **normal**
as usual in the way that happens most often: *My sister was late, as **usual**.*

usually (say **yoo**-*zhuu*-uh-lee) *adverb*
in the way that is usual: *I'm **usually** home by six o'clock.*

A B C D E F G H I J K L M N O P Q R S T U V W X Y Z

utensil (say yoo-**ten**-sil) *noun* (*plural* **utensils**)
a tool that is used in the home: *cooking* ***utensils***

uterus (say **yoo**-tuh-ruhss) *noun* (*plural* **uteri**)
(*biology*)
the part of a female person or other mammal where a baby develops before it is born
➲ SYNONYM **womb**

utilize (say **yoo**-tuh-lize) *verb* (**utilizing**, **utilized**)
(also **utilise**) (*formal*)
to make use of: *The scientists are studying ways of* ***utilizing*** *natural resources.*
▸ **utilization** (*noun*) (also **utilisation**)

utmost (say **ut**-mohst) *noun* (*no plural*)
the greatest amount possible
do your utmost : *I will do my* ***utmost*** *to help you.*
▸ **utmost** (*adjective*): *This is a message of the* ***utmost*** *importance.*

Utopia (say yoo-**toh**-pi-uh) *noun* (*plural* **Utopias**)
a place that exists only in the imagination and where everything is perfect
▸ **Utopian** (*adjective*)
ℹ ORIGIN: 16th century, based on Greek *ou* meaning 'not' + *topos* meaning 'place', made up by Sir Thomas More (1478–1535) and used in a book called *Utopia*

utter[1] (say **ut**-uh) *adjective*
complete: *He felt an* ***utter*** *fool.*

utter[2] (say **ut**-uh) *verb* (**uttering**, **uttered**)
(*formal*)
to say something or make a sound with your mouth: *She did not* ***utter*** *a word.*

utterly (say **ut**-uh-lee) *adverb*
completely or very: *That's* ***utterly*** *impossible!*

U-turn (say **yoo**-turn) *noun* (*plural* **U-turns**)
the movement that you make when you are driving in which you turn around and drive in the opposite direction

UV (say yoo-**vee**) *abbreviation* **ultraviolet**

Vv

V *abbreviation* (*plural* **V**) **volt**

v *abbreviation* (also **vs**) **versus**

vacancy (say **vay**-kuhn-see) *noun* (*plural* **vacancies**)
1 a job that nobody is doing: *We have a vacancy for a secretary in our office.*
2 a room in a hotel that nobody is using: *The sign outside the hotel says 'no **vacancies**'* (= the hotel is full).

vacant (say **vay**-kuhnt) *adjective*
1 empty or not being used: *a **vacant** room*
2 If a job in a company is **vacant**, nobody is doing it and it is available for somebody to do.

vacate (say vuh-**kayt**) *verb* (**vacating**, **vacated**) to leave a place such as a building or room, or to leave a job or position, so that it is available for somebody else

vacation (say vuh-**kay**-shuhn) *noun* (*plural* **vacations**)
a period of time when you do not go to work or school and are on holiday: *We had a week's **vacation** by the sea.*

vaccinate (say **vak**-si-nayt) *verb* (**vaccinating**, **vaccinated**)
to put a **vaccine** into a person's or an animal's body using a needle, to stop them getting a disease: *Have you been **vaccinated** against measles?* ➲ SYNONYM **inoculate**

vaccination (say vak-si-**nay**-shuhn) *noun* (*plural* **vaccinations**)
when a **vaccine** is put into a person's or an animal's body with a needle, to stop them getting a disease: *a **vaccination** against measles*

vaccine (say vak-**seen**) *noun* (*plural* **vaccines**)
a substance that is put into a person's or an animal's body using a needle, to stop them getting a disease: *All children should have the polio vaccine.*

vacuole (say **vak**-yuu-ohl) *noun* (*plural* **vacuoles**)
a space inside a plant or animal cell containing substances for the cell to use ➲ See illustration at **cell** 1

vacuum[1] (say **vak**-yuum) *noun* (*plural* **vacuums**)
a space with no air, gas or anything else in it

vacuum[2] (say **vak**-yuum) *verb* (**vacuuming**, **vacuumed**) (*informal*) to clean a carpet or the floor with a **vacuum cleaner**

vacuum cleaner *noun* (*plural* **vacuum cleaners**)
a machine that cleans carpets and other surfaces by sucking up dirt

vagabond (say **vag**-uh-bond) *noun* (*plural* **vagabonds**)
a person who has no permanent home or job ➲ SYNONYM **vagrant**

vagina (say vuh-**jine**-uh) *noun* (*plural* **vaginas**)
the part of a woman's or a female animal's body that leads to the place where a baby grows (called the **womb**)

vagrant (say **vay**-gruhnt) *noun* (*plural* **vagrants**)
a person who moves from place to place, has no home or job and asks other people for money ➲ SYNONYMS **tramp[1]**, **vagabond**

vague (say **vayg**) *adjective* (**vaguer**, **vaguest**)
not clear or not exact: *I couldn't find the house because he gave me very **vague** directions.*
► **vaguely** (*adverb*): *I **vaguely** remember what happened.*

vain (say **vayn**) *adjective* (**vainer**, **vainest**)
1 too proud of what you can do or how you look ➲ The noun is **vanity**
2 useless or without success: *They made a **vain** attempt to save his life.*
in vain without success: *I tried in **vain** to sleep.*

valiant (say **val**-yuhnt) *adjective* (*formal*) full of courage and not afraid: *a **valiant** effort*
► **valiantly** (*adverb*)

valid (say **val**-id) *adjective*
acceptable or able to be used: *Your bus ticket is **valid** for one week.* ➲ OPPOSITE **invalid[1]**

valley (say **val**-ee) *noun* (*plural* **valleys**)
the low land between mountains or the land that a river flows through ➲ See illustration at **mountain**

valuable (say **val**-yuu-uhb-l) *adjective*
1 worth a lot of money: *Is this ring **valuable**?*
2 very useful: *The book contains some **valuable** information.*
► **valuables** (*noun*): *jewellery and other **valuables***

value[1] (say **val**-yoo) *noun*
1 (*plural* **values**) how much money you can sell something for: *The thieves stole goods with a total **value** of R100 000.*
2 (*no plural*) how much something is worth compared with its price: *The meal was good*

A B C D E F G H I J K L M N O P Q R S T U V W X Y Z

value at only R35,00.
3 (*no plural*) how useful or important something is: *Their help was of great **value**.*
4 values (*plural noun*) the principles and beliefs about what is the right and wrong way for people to behave: *We should respect traditional **values**.*

value[2] (say **val**-yoo) *verb* (**valuing, valued**)
1 to think that something is very important: *I **value** my freedom.*
2 to say how much money something is worth: *The house was **valued** at R500 000.*

valve (say **valv**) *noun* (*plural* **valves**)
a part in a pipe or tube which lets air, liquid or gas flow in one direction only

vampire (say **vam**-py-uh) *noun* (*plural* **vampires**)
(in stories) a person who drinks people's blood

van *noun* (*plural* **vans**)
a kind of big car or small truck for carrying things

vanadium (say vuh-**nay**-di-uhm) *noun* (*no plural*) (symbol V)
a hard grey metal used for increasing the strength of steel

vandal (say **vand**-l) *noun* (*plural* **vandals**)
a person who deliberately damages somebody else's property: ***Vandals** have damaged the benches in the park.*
▸ **vandalism:** *They were arrested for **vandalism**.*
🛈 **ORIGIN:** from Latin *Vandalus*. The Vandals were a people from northern Europe who invaded and destroyed Rome and parts of Europe in the fourth and fifth centuries.

vandalize (say **van**-duh-lize) *verb* (**vandalizing, vandalized**) (also **vandalise**)
to deliberately damage or destroy somebody else's property

vane (say **vayn**) *noun* (*plural* **vanes**)
a flat blade that is moved by wind or water, and is part of the machinery in a windmill or windpump ➲ See illustration at **windpump**

vanilla (say vuh-**ni**-luh) *noun* (*no plural*)
a substance from a plant that gives a taste to some sweet foods: ***vanilla** ice cream*

vanish (say **van**-ish) *verb* (**vanishing, vanished**)
to go away or to stop being seen: *The thief ran into the crowd and **vanished**.* ➲ SYNONYM **disappear**

vanity (say **van**-uh-tee) *noun* (*no plural*)
being too proud of what you can do or how you look ➲ The adjective is **vain**

vantage point (say **vaan**-tij poynt) *noun* (*plural* **vantage points**)
a place from which you have a good view of something: *You can see the whole town from this **vantage point**.*

vapour (say **vay**-puh) *noun* (*no plural*)
a substance, especially one that is normally a liquid or a solid, in the form of a gas: *water **vapour***

variable[1] (say **vair**-ri-uhb-l) *adjective*
changing often or not staying the same: *The wind is **variable** at this time of the year.*
▸ **variability** (*noun*)

variable[2] (say **vair**-ri-uhb-l) *noun* (*plural* **variables**)
a situation, quantity or number that can change or be changed: *It is difficult to work out a budget because there are so many **variables** in the project.* ◇ *In this experiment the temperature will remain constant but the pressure will be a **variable**.*

variation (say vair-ri-**ay**-shuhn) *noun* (*plural* **variations**)
1 a change or difference in the amount or level of something: *price **variations*** ◇ *There is little **variation** in prices from shop to shop.*
2 a different version of the same thing: *Roller hockey is a **variation** of ice hockey.*

varied[1] (say **vair**-reed) *adjective*
including a lot of different things: *I try to make my lessons as **varied** as possible.*

varied[2] (say **vair**-reed) form of **vary**

varies (say **vair**-reez) form of **vary**

variety (say vuh-**ry**-uh-tee) *noun*
1 (*no plural*) a lot of different things: *There's a wide **variety** of dishes on the menu.*
2 (*no plural*) the fact that you are not always doing the same things: *There's a lot of **variety** in my new job.*
3 (*plural* **varieties**) a type of something: *This **variety** of apple is very sweet.*

various (say **vair**-ri-uhss) *adjective*
several different: *We sell this shirt in **various** colours and sizes.*

varnish (say **vaa**-nish) *noun* (*no plural*)
a clear paint with no colour that you put on something to protect it and make it shine
▸ **varnish** (*verb*): *The doors are then stained and **varnished**.*

varsity (say **vaa**-si-tee) *noun* (*plural* **varsities**)
(*informal*) university

vary (say **vair**-ree) *verb* (**varying, varied**)
1 to be different from each other: *The price*

varies according to the quality.
2 to change according to the situation: *Class sizes **vary** from 25 to 40.*
3 to make something different by changing it often in some way: *We try to **vary** the course to suit learners' needs.*

vase (say **vaaz**) *noun* (*plural* **vases**)
a container that you put cut flowers in

vast (say **vaast**) *adjective*
very big: *Australia is a **vast** country.*
➲ SYNONYMS **enormous, huge**

WORD BUILDING See the note at **big**.

VAT (say vee-ay-**tee** or **vat**) *noun* (*no plural*)
a tax which we pay on goods and services
ⓘ **VAT** is short for 'value added tax'.

vat *noun* (*plural* **vats**)
a large container for holding liquids: *a wine **vat***

vault[1] (say **vawlt**) *noun* (*plural* **vaults**)
1 a special room in a bank with strong walls and doors where money and valuable things are kept
2 a room under a church where dead people are buried
3 a high roof or ceiling in a church or other building

vault[2] (say **vawlt**) *verb* (**vaulting, vaulted**)
to jump over something using your hands or a pole to help you: *He **vaulted** over the fence.*

VCR (say vee-see-**aar**) *noun* (*plural* **VCRs**)
a machine connected to a television, that you use for recording or showing programmes
ⓘ **VCR** is short for 'video cassette recorder'.

VDU (say vee-dee-**yoo**) *noun* (*plural* **VDUs**)
a computer screen ⓘ **VDU** is short for 'visual display unit'.

veal (say **veel**) *noun* (*no plural*)
meat from a young cow (**a calf**)

vector (say **vek**-tuh) *noun* (*plural* **vectors**)
1 (*science*) a measurement or quantity that has both size and direction: *A **vector** is often represented as an arrow.*
2 (*biology*) an organism that carries a particular disease from one living thing to another: *Mosquitoes are the **vectors** in malaria.*

veer (*rhymes with* **gear**) *verb* (**veering, veered**)
to change direction suddenly: *The car **veered** off the road.*

vegan (say **vee**-guhn) *noun* (*plural* **vegans**)
a person who does not eat meat or any other foods that come from animals, such as eggs or milk

vegetable (say **vej**-tuhb-l) *noun* (*plural* **vegetables**)
a plant or part of a plant that we eat: *The learners grow **vegetables** such as cabbages, beans and carrots.*

SPELLING Notice how to spell and say **vegetable**.

vegetarian (say vej-uh-**tair**-ri-uhn) *noun* (*plural* **vegetarians**)
a person who does not eat meat or fish
▸ **vegetarian** (*adjective*): *a **vegetarian** restaurant*

vegetation (say vej-uh-**tay**-shuhn) *noun* (*no plural*)
1 plants in general: *There is no **vegetation** at all in that part of the desert.*
2 the plant life of a particular region: *tropical **vegetation***

vegetative (say **vej**-i-tay-tiv) *adjective*
relating to reproduction in plants that is **asexual** 2 (= without using seeds)

vehicle (say **veer**-kuhl) *noun* (*plural* **vehicles**) (*formal*)
a machine such as a car, bus, lorry or bicycle used for transporting people or things: *Are you the owner of this **vehicle**?*

PRONUNCIATION Notice how to say this word. Don't pronounce the **h** in **vehicle**.

veil (say **vayl**) *noun* (*plural* **veils**)
a piece of material that a woman puts over her head and face

vein (say **vayn**) *noun* (*plural* **veins**)
one of the small tubes in your body that carry blood to the heart ➲ See **artery**

Velcro™ (say **vel**-kroh) *noun* (*no plural*)
two bands of special material that stick together to fasten things such as clothes, shoes and bags

veld (say **felt**) *noun* (*no plural*)
land that is not being used for growing crops, usually covered with wild grass and bush: *We went for a long walk through the **veld**.* ◇ *Many small animals die in **veld** fires.*
ⓘ ORIGIN: 18th century, from Dutch *veld*, meaning 'field, battle-field'

USAGE Be careful! **Veld** has no plural. We say: *She walked across **the veld*** or *She walked across **an area of veld***, but not 'She walked across a veld'.

A B C D E F G H I J K L M N O P Q R S T U V W X Y Z

velocity (say vuh-**loss**-i-tee) *noun* (*no plural*) (*science*)
the speed at which something moves in a particular direction: *The car was travelling at a constant* ***velocity*** *of 90 km/h in an easterly direction.*

velskoen (say **fel**-skuun) *noun* (*plural* **velskoens** or **velskoene**) (also **veldskoen**)
a rough boot or shoe made of soft leather
🛈 **ORIGIN:** through Afrikaans *veldskoen* from Dutch *veldschoen* meaning 'shoe for wearing outside', or from South African Dutch *velschoen* meaning 'shoe made from an animal's skin'

velvet (say **vel**-vuht) *noun* (*no plural*)
cloth that is soft and thick on one side: *red* ***velvet*** *curtains*

Venda (say **ven**-duh) ➲ See **Tshivenda**

vendor (say **ven**-duh) *noun* (*plural* **vendors**)
a person who is selling something: *a street* ***vendor*** ***selling mealies***

veneer (say vuh-**neer**) *noun*
1 (*plural* **veneers**) a thin layer of wood or plastic that you stick over a cheaper material to make it look more attractive
2 (*no plural*) a way of behaving which hides somebody's real character: *a* ***veneer*** *of politeness*

vengeance (say **ven**-juhnss) *noun* (*no plural*)
the act of punishing or harming somebody who has done something bad to you, your family or your friends: *an act of* ***vengeance***
with a vengeance very strong and greater than expected

venison (say **ven**-i-suhn) *noun* (*no plural*)
meat from a wild buck or antelope
🛈 **ORIGIN:** 13th–15th century, from Old French *veneso(u)n*, from Latin *venatio(n-)* meaning 'hunting'

Venn diagram (say **ven** dy-uh-gram) *noun* (*plural* **Venn diagrams**) (*maths*)
a diagram that shows the relationships between different sets of things, using circles that cross each other
🛈 **ORIGIN:** 20th century, named after John Venn (1834–1923), an English scientist and philosopher

venom (say **ven**-uhm) *noun* (*no plural*)
1 the poisonous liquid that some snakes, spiders and other animals produce when they bite or sting you
2 extreme anger or hatred: *She gave him a look of pure* ***venom.***
► **venomous** (*adjective*): *a* ***venomous*** *snake*

vent[1] *noun* (*plural* **vents**)
an opening in a wall or a machine that allows gases or liquids to come in and go out: *an air* ***vent***

vent[2] *verb* (**venting**, **vented**) (*formal*)
to do or say something that shows strong emotion, especially anger: *Don't* ***vent*** *your anger on me!*

ventilate (say **ven**-ti-layt) *verb* (**ventilating**, **ventilated**)
to allow air to move through a building
► **ventilation** (*noun*): *poor* ***ventilation***

ventral (say **ven**-truhl) *adjective*
relating to the bottom or lower side or surface of something, especially of an animal: *a shark's* ***ventral*** *fin* ➲ See illustration at **fish**[1] ➲ See **dorsal**

ventricle (say **ven**-trik-l) *noun* (*plural* **ventricles**)
a space in the heart or brain: *the third* ***ventricle*** *of the brain* ➲ See illustration at **heart**

ventriloquist (say ven-**tril**-uh-kwist) *noun* (*plural* **ventriloquists**)
a performer who can speak without moving their lips so that their voice sounds as if it is coming from another place

venture[1] (say **ven**-tshuh) *noun* (*plural* **ventures**)
a new project or business activity, especially one that involves some risk

venture[2] (say **ven**-tshuh) *verb* (**venturing**, **ventured**) (*formal*)
1 to do something or go somewhere new or dangerous: *Don't* ***venture*** *out in the desert by yourself.*
2 to say something that other people might criticize: *I was too scared to* ***venture*** *an opinion.*

venue (say **ven**-yoo) *noun* (*plural* **venues**)
a place where people meet for an organized event such as a concert: *The film will be shown at four different* ***venues.***

veranda (say vuh-**ran**-duh) *noun* (*plural* **verandas**) (also **verandah**)
a covered area with an open front which is joined to a house on the ground floor
➲ **SYNONYM** **stoep**

verb (say **vurb**) *noun* (*plural* **verbs**) (*grammar*)
a word that tells you what somebody does or what happens. 'Go', 'sing', 'do' and 'be' are all **verbs**. ➲ See study pages 6–8

verbal (say **vurb**-l) *adjective*
1 expressed in words which you speak but do not write down: *a **verbal** agreement*
2 relating to words or the use of words: *good **verbal** skills*
► **verbally** (*adverb*): *She passed the message on **verbally**.*

verbose (say vur-**bohss**) *adjective* (*formal*)
using more words than you need to use
➲ SYNONYM **long-winded**

verdict (say **vur**-dikt) *noun* (*plural* **verdicts**)
a decision in a court of law about whether somebody is guilty or not: *The judge returned a **verdict** of 'not guilty'.*

verge[1] (say **vurj**) *noun* (*plural* **verges**)
a narrow piece of land at the side of the road that is usually covered in grass
on the verge of something about to happen or very likely to happen: *Scientists are on the **verge** of discovering a cure for the disease.*

verge[2] (say **vurj**) *verb* (**verging, verged**)
to be very close to becoming or being something: *His behaviour often **verges** on rudeness.*

verify (say **ve**-ri-fy) *verb* (**verifying, verified**)
to check and make sure that something is true or accurate: *Can you **verify** that the flight number is correct?*
► **verification** (*noun*)

vermilion (say vuh-**mil**-i-uhn) *adjective*
with a bright red colour: *a **vermilion** scarf*
► **vermilion** (*noun*): *The pattern has stripes of **vermilion** and purple.*

vermin (say **vur**-min) *plural noun*
small wild animals such as rats that carry disease and destroy plants and food

versatile (say **vur**-suh-tile) *adjective*
1 having many skills and able to do many different things: *a **versatile** actor*
2 (used about an object) having many different uses: *a **versatile** tool*

verse (say **vurss**) *noun*
1 (*no plural*) words arranged in lines with a definite rhythm, often with sounds repeated at the ends of lines: *The play is written in **verse**.*
➲ SYNONYM **poetry**
2 (*plural* **verses**) a group of lines in a song or poem: *This song has five **verses**.* ➲ See **stanza**

version (say **vur**-zhuhn) *noun* (*plural* **versions**)
1 a form of something that is different in some way: *the latest **version** of the software*
2 what one person says or writes about something that happened: *His **version** of the accident is different from mine.*

versus (say **vur**-suhss) *preposition* (abbr. v, vs)
on the other side in a sport or competition: *There's a good rugby match on TV tonight – South Africa **versus** Australia.* ➲ SYNONYM **against** 1

vertebra (say **vur**-ti-bruh) *noun* (*plural* **vertebrae**)
any of the small bones that are connected together to form the line of bones in your back (called the **spine**) ➲ See illustration at **skeleton**
► **vertebral** (*adjective*): *the **vertebral** column*

vertebrate (say **vur**-ti-bruht) *noun* (*plural* **vertebrates**)
an animal that has a line of bones (called the **spine**) going down its back: *Mammals, birds, reptiles, amphibians and fish are **vertebrates**.*
➲ See **invertebrate**

vertex (say **vur**-tekss) *noun* (*plural* **vertices** or **vertexes**)
1 the highest point of something: *the **vertex** of a pyramid* ◇ *the **vertex** of an arch*
➲ See illustration at **cone** 1
2 the point where lines or edges meet: *A cube has eight **vertices**.*
➲ See illustration at **three-dimensional**

vertical (say **vur**-tik-l) *adjective*
going straight up or down at an angle of 90° from a level surface: *a **vertical** line*
➲ See illustration at **horizontal**
➲ See **perpendicular**

vertices (say **vur**-ti-seez) plural of **vertex**

vertigo (say **vur**-ti-goh) *noun* (*no plural*)
a feeling that everything is turning round and round and that you are going to fall: *People who are scared of heights sometimes get **vertigo**.*

very[1] (say **ve**-ree) *adverb*
You use 'very' before another word to make it stronger: ***Very** few people know that.* ◇ *She speaks **very** quietly.* ◇ *I like chocolate **very** much.* ◇ *I'm not **very** hungry.*

very[2] (say **ve**-ree) *adjective*
exact or same: *You are the **very** person I wanted to see!* ◇ *We climbed to the **very** top of the mountain.*

vessel (say **vess**-l) *noun* (*plural* **vessels**)
1 a ship or a large boat
2 (*old-fashioned*) a container for liquids: *a drinking **vessel***

vest *noun* (*plural* **vests**)
a piece of clothing that you wear under your other clothes on the top part of your body
➲ See **underwear**

A B C D E F G H I J K L M N O P Q R S T U V W X Y Z

vet *noun* (*plural* **vets**) (also *formal* **veterinary surgeon** or **veterinarian**)
1 a doctor for animals
2 short for **veteran** 1

veteran (say **vet**-uh-ruhn) *noun* (*plural* **veterans**)
1 a person who has been in the army, navy or air force during a war: *a **veteran** of World War II* ◇ *an MK **veteran***
2 a person who has a lot of experience in a particular job or activity: *a **veteran** journalist*

veterinary (say **vet**-rin-ree) *adjective*
relating to the medical treatment of sick animals: *a **veterinary** clinic*

veto (say **vee**-toh) *verb* (**vetoing**, **vetoed**)
to refuse to give permission for a plan or an action when other people have agreed to it: *The President **vetoed** the proposal.*
▸ **veto** (*noun*): *the President's power of **veto***

via (say **vy**-uh or **vee**-uh) *preposition*
going through a place: *We flew from Cape Town to Nairobi **via** Johannesburg.*
🛈 **ORIGIN**: 18th century, from Latin *via* meaning 'way, road'

viable (say **vy**-uhb-l) *adjective*
that can be done and will be successful: *Is your plan economically **viable**?*
▸ **viability** (*noun*)

vibrate (say vy-**brayt**) *verb* (**vibrating**, **vibrated**)
to move very quickly from side to side or up and down: *The house **vibrates** every time a train goes past.*
▸ **vibration** (*noun*): *the **vibrations** coming from the car's engine*

vicar (say **vik**-uh) *noun* (*plural* **vicars**)
a priest in some Christian churches

vice (say **vise**) *noun*
1 (*no plural*) criminal activities involving sex or drugs: *detectives from the **vice** squad*
2 (*plural* **vices**) a moral weakness or bad habit
➲ **OPPOSITE** **virtue** 2

vice- (say **vise**) *prefix*
next to the leader in importance or position and able to represent the leader: *He's **vice-captain** of the team.* ◇ *the **vice-president***

vice versa (say vise **vur**-suh) *adverb*
in the opposite way to what has just been said: *Mpho likes chicken and Moegsien likes fish – or is it **vice versa**?*
🛈 **ORIGIN**: 17th century, from Latin *vice versa* meaning 'with the position reversed'

vicinity (say vuh-**sin**-i-tee) *noun* (*plural* **vicinities**)
in the vicinity (*formal*) in the same area or near a place: *There are three parks in the **vicinity** of the school.*

vicious (say **vish**-uhss) *adjective*
violent and cruel: *a **vicious** attack*

victim (say **vik**-tim) *noun* (*plural* **victims**)
a person or animal that is hurt, damaged or killed by somebody or something: *the innocent **victims** of crime*

Victorian (say vik-**taw**-ri-uhn) *adjective*
relating to the time of the British queen Victoria (1837–1901): *a **Victorian** house built in 1890*

victorious (say vik-**taw**-ri-uhss) *adjective*
successful in a fight, game or war: *the **victorious** team*

victory (say **vik**-tuh-ree) *noun* (*plural* **victories**)
success against an opponent in a fight, game or war: *the team's 23–12 **victory** against Nigeria*

video (say **vid**-i-oh) *noun* (*plural* **videos**)
1 (also **videotape**) tape in a plastic box (called a **cassette**) on which a film, television programme or real event is recorded: *You can get this film on **video** or on DVD.* ◇ *We stayed at home and watched a **video**.* ◇ *They made a **video** of the wedding.*
2 (also **video recorder**) a machine connected to a television that you use for recording or showing programmes: *Have you set the **video**?*
➲ **SYNONYM** **VCR**

video game *noun* (*plural* **video games**)
a game that you play using a television or a computer screen

vie (say **vy**) *verb* (**vying**, **vied**)
to try hard to do something more successfully than somebody else: *The children are **vying** for the attention of their parents.*

view[1] (say **vyoo**) *noun* (*plural* **views**)
1 what you believe or think about something: *He has strong **views** on marriage.* ◇ *In my **view**, she has done nothing wrong.* ➲ **SYNONYM** **opinion**
2 what you can see from a particular place: *There were beautiful **views** of the mountains all around.* ◇ *At the top of the hill, the lake came into **view*** (= could be seen).
in view of something because of something: *In **view** of the bad weather we decided to cancel the match.*
on view in a place for people to see: *Her paintings are on **view** at the museum.*

view[2] (say **vyoo**) *verb* (**viewing**, **viewed**) (*formal*)
1 to think about something in a particular way: *She **views** holidays as a waste of time!*
➲ **SYNONYM** **regard**[1]

2 to watch or look at something: *The tourists **viewed** the city from the top of the mountain.*

viewer (say **vyoo**-uh) *noun* (*plural* **viewers**)
a person who watches a television programme

viewfinder (say **vyoo**-fine-duh) *noun* (*plural* **viewfinders**)
a device on a camera that you look through to see what you are photographing

vigilant (say **vij**-i-luhnt) *adjective*
careful and watching for possible danger: *The police told us to be **vigilant** after the attacks.*
▸ **vigilance** (*noun*): *Protecting our democracy requires constant **vigilance**.*

vigorous (say **vig**-uh-ruhss) *adjective*
strong and full of energy: ***vigorous** exercise*
▸ **vigorously** (*adverb*): *She shook my hand **vigorously**.*

vigour (say **vig**-uh) *noun* (*no plural*)
physical or mental strength and energy: *They started off the job with **vigour** and enthusiasm.*

Viking (say **vike**-ing) *noun* (*plural* **Vikings**)
people who came from Scandinavian countries and attacked parts of northern Europe in the 8th-11th centuries

vile *adjective* (**viler**, **vilest**)
very bad or unpleasant: *What a **vile** smell!*
➲ SYNONYM **horrible**

villa (say **vil**-uh) *noun* (*plural* **villas**)
a house with a garden in the countryside, especially in southern Europe

village (say **vil**-ij) *noun* (*plural* **villages**)
a very small town in the countryside: *She lives in a **village** in the mountains.* ➲ See note at **town**
🛈 ORIGIN: 14th–15th century, through Old French from Latin *villa* meaning 'country house'

villager (say **vil**-i-juh) *noun* (*plural* **villagers**)
a person who lives in a village

villain (say **vil**-uhn) *noun* (*plural* **villains**) (*formal*)
a bad person, usually in a book, play or film

vindictive (say vin-**dik**-tiv) *adjective*
wanting or trying to hurt somebody without good reason: *a **vindictive** person* ◇ *a **vindictive** comment* ➲ SYNONYM **spiteful**
▸ **vindictiveness** (*noun*)

vine *noun* (*plural* **vines**)
the plant that grapes grow on

vinegar (say **vin**-i-guh) *noun* (*no plural*)
a liquid with a strong sour taste that is used in cooking: *I mixed some oil and **vinegar** to put on the salad.*

vineyard (say **vin**-yuhd) *noun* (*plural* **vineyards**)
a piece of land where grapes are grown to make wine

PRONUNCIATION Notice how to say this word.

vinyl (say **vy**-nuhl) *noun* (*no plural*)
a strong type of plastic that can bend easily and that you use to cover walls and floors

viola (say vi-**oh**-luh) *noun* (*plural* **violas**)
a musical instrument like a large **violin**

violence (say **vy**-uh-luhnss) *noun* (*no plural*)
1 behaviour that causes physical harm or damage to somebody or something: *There's too much **violence** on TV.*
2 force or power: *the **violence** of the storm*

violent (say **vy**-uh-luhnt) *adjective*
1 using physical force to hurt, kill or damage somebody or something: *Her husband was a **violent** man.* ◇ *The protest march started peacefully but later turned **violent**.*
2 involving a lot of force and energy: *a **violent** storm*
▸ **violently** (*adverb*): *He died **violently**.*

violet (say **vy**-uh-luht) *noun*
1 (*plural* **violets**) a small purple flower
2 (*no plural*) a colour that is between dark blue and purple
▸ **violet** (*adjective*): *a **violet** ribbon*

violin (say **vy**-uh-lin) *noun* (*plural* **violins**)
a musical instrument that you hold under your chin and play by moving a stick (called a **bow**) across the strings

violin

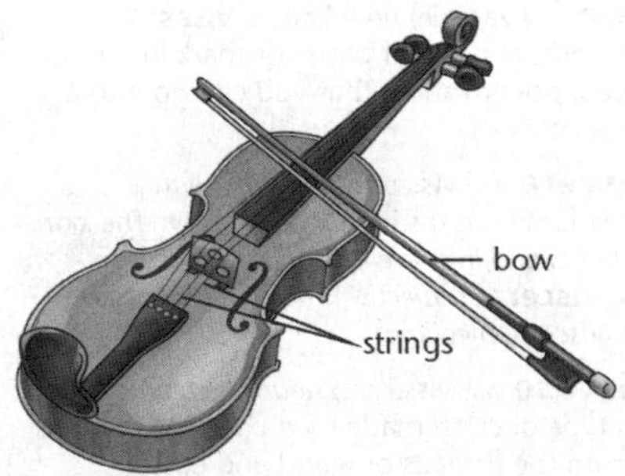

VIP (say vee-y-**pee**) *noun* (*plural* **VIPs**)
a person who is famous or important
🛈 **VIP** is short for 'very important person'.

virgin[1] (say **vur**-jin) *noun* (*plural* **virgins**)
a person who has never had sex
▸ **virginity** (*noun*)

virgin[2] (say **vur**-jin) *adjective*
that has not yet been used or damaged and is in its original state: *a **virgin** forest*

virtual (say **vur**-tshuu-uhl) *adjective*
1 being almost or very nearly something: *He married a **virtual** stranger.*
2 made to appear to exist by a computer

virtually (say **vur**-tshuu-uh-lee) *adverb*
almost: *The two boys look **virtually** the same.*

virtual reality *noun* (*no plural*) (*computing*)
computer images that seem to be all around you and seem almost real

virtue (say **vur**-tshoo) *noun*
1 (*no plural*) behaviour that shows high moral standards: *to lead a life of **virtue***
2 (*plural* **virtues**) a good quality or habit: *He has many **virtues**.* ➲ OPPOSITE **vice** 2

virulent (say **vi**-ruh-luhnt) *adjective*
1 (used about a disease or a poison) very strong and dangerous: *a **virulent** form of flu*
2 very strong and full of hate or anger: ***virulent** criticism*

virus (say **vy**-ruhss) *noun* (*plural* **viruses**)
1 (*science*) a living thing that is too small to see without a special instrument (a **microscope**). **Viruses** can can make you ill: *a flu **virus***
2 (*computing*) a program that enters your computer and stops it from working properly
🛈 ORIGIN: 14th–15th century, from Latin *virus* meaning 'slimy liquid, poison'. When the word first came into English, it meant 'snake's poison' because at the time, people believed that when they were sick, the human body produced a dangerous substance that could infect others, in the same way as snake venom does.

visa (say **vee**-zuh) *noun* (*plural* **visas**)
an official piece of paper or mark in your **passport** to show that you can go into a country

viscera (say **viss**-uh-ruh) *plural noun*
the large organs inside your body: *The kidneys, uterus and liver are examples of **viscera**.*
▸ **visceral** (*adjective*): *the **visceral** organs* ◇ ***visceral** bleeding*

viscose (say **viss**-kohz) *noun* (*no plural*)
a type of cloth made by a chemical process from the threads of wood and cotton

viscous (say **viss**-kuhss) *adjective*
relating to liquids that are thick and do not flow easily: *a layer of **viscous** oil*
▸ **viscosity** (*noun*): *Glue has a high **viscosity**.*

visibility (say viz-uh-**bil**-uh-tee) *noun* (*no plural*)
how far you can see clearly in particular light or weather conditions: *In the fog **visibility** was down to 50 metres.*

visible (say **viz**-uhb-l) *adjective*
If something is **visible**, you can see it: *Stars are **visible** only at night.* ➲ OPPOSITE **invisible**

vision (say **vi*zh***-uhn) *noun*
1 (*no plural*) the ability to see: *He wears glasses because he has poor **vision**.* ➲ SYNONYM **sight** 1
2 (*plural* **visions**) something that you imagine: *the government's **vision** of providing four million job opportunities by 2014*
3 (*plural* **visions**) an experience of seeing a person, thing or situation in a dream: *The sangoma had a **vision** of a beautiful village in the sky.*

visionary (say **vi*zh***-uhn-ree) *adjective*
having good and imaginative plans for the future: *a **visionary** leader*
▸ **visionary** (*noun*)

visit (say **viz**-it) *verb* (**visiting**, **visited**)
to go to see a person or place for a short time: *When you go to London, you must **visit** the Science Museum.* ◇ *She **visited** me in hospital.*
▸ **visit** (*noun*): *This is my first **visit** to Gauteng.* ◇ *He promised to pay us a **visit** next year.*

visitor (say **viz**-i-tuh) *noun* (*plural* **visitors**)
a person who goes to see another person or a place for a short time: *The old lady never has any **visitors**.* ◇ *Millions of **visitors** come to Africa every year.*

vista (say **viss**-tuh) *noun* (*plural* **vistas**)
a beautiful view of a place

visual (say **vi*zh***-yuu-uhl) *adjective*
connected with seeing: *Painting and cinema are **visual** arts.*
▸ **visually** (*adverb*): *A **visually** impaired person cannot see well.*

visualize (say **vi*zh***-yuu-uh-lize) *verb* (**visualizing**, **visualized**) (also **visualise**)
to imagine or have a picture in your mind of somebody or something: *I find it hard to **visualize** what the house will look like when it is finished.* ◇ *I **visualized** him as a small person but he is quite big.*

vital (say **vy**-tuhl) *adjective*
very important or necessary: *It's **vital** that she sees a doctor – she's very ill.*
▸ **vitally** (*adverb*): ***vitally** important*
🛈 ORIGIN: 14th–15th century, through Old French from Latin *vitalis*, from *vita* meaning 'life'

vitality (say vy-**tal**-uh-tee) *noun* (*no plural*)
the state of being strong and full of energy

vitamin (say **vit**-uh-min) *noun* (*plural* **vitamins**)
one of the substances in food that you need to be healthy: *Oranges are rich in* ***vitamin*** *C.*

vitreous (say **vit**-ri-uhss) *adjective*
hard and transparent, like glass

viva (say **vee**-vuh) *exclamation*
a word that you shout to show approval or support: ***Viva*** *Mandela!*

vivacious (say vi-**vay**-shuhss) *adjective*
(used about a person, usually a woman) full of energy and happy

vivid (say **viv**-id) *adjective*
1 creating a very clear picture in your mind: *I had a very* ***vivid*** *dream last night.*
2 having a strong bright colour: ***vivid*** *yellow*
▸ **vividly** (*adverb*): *I remember my first day at school* ***vividly****.* ◇ *a* ***vividly*** *coloured kingfisher*

viviparous (say vi-**vip**-uh-ruhss) *adjective* (*biology*)
1 relating to animals that produce live babies from their bodies, without forming eggs: *Most mammals are* ***viviparous****.* ➲ See **oviparous**
2 relating to plants that produce seeds that start growing while still joined to the parent plant

vlei (say **flay**) *noun* (*plural* **vleis**) (*S. African*)
a lake that is not very deep or a **wetland**
🛈 **ORIGIN**: 19th century, through Afrikaans and South African Dutch, from Dutch *vallei* meaning 'valley'

vocabulary (say vuh-**kab**-yuh-luh-ree) *noun*
1 (*plural* **vocabularies**) all the words that somebody knows or that are used in a particular book or subject: *He has an amazing* ***vocabulary*** *for a five-year-old.*
2 (*no plural*) all the words in a language: *New words are always entering the* ***vocabulary****.*

vocal (say **vohk**-l) *adjective*
1 relating to the human voice: ***vocal*** *music*
2 expressing your opinions loudly and freely: *She is a* ***vocal*** *supporter of children's rights.*

vocal cords *plural noun*
the thin bands of muscle at the back of your throat that move to produce your voice

vocation (say voh-**kay**-shuhn) *noun* (*no plural*)
the type of work or way of life that you think is especially suitable for you: *Teaching is my true* ***vocation****.*

vocational *adjective*
relating to the skills and knowledge that you need to do a particular job: ***vocational*** *training*

vociferous (say vuh-**sif**-uh-ruhss) *adjective* (*formal*) expressing your opinions in a loud and strong way
▸ **vociferously** (*adverb*): *They* ***vociferously*** *opposed the initiative.*

vodka (say **vod**-kuh) *noun* (*no plural*)
a strong, clear alcoholic drink

voetstoots (say **fuutss**-toortss) *adjective, adverb* (*S. African*)
(used about something that you buy) as it is, without being able to return it: *The car was sold* ***voetstoots*** *so the buyer could not complain afterwards about things that didn't work properly.*
🛈 **ORIGIN**: 20th century, through Afrikaans, from Dutch *met de voet te stoten* meaning 'to push with the foot'

voice (say **voyss**) *noun*
1 (*plural* **voices**) the sounds that you make when you speak or sing: *My father has a very deep* ***voice****.*
2 (*no plural*) the ability to speak: *She had a bad cold and lost her* ***voice****.*
at the top of your voice very loudly: *'Help!' he shouted at the top of his* ***voice****.*
3 (*no plural*) the right to express your opinion and influence decisions: *The workers should have a* ***voice*** *in the decision.*

voicemail (say **voyss**-mayl) *noun* (*no plural*)
an electronic system that lets you leave or listen to telephone messages: *Have you checked your* ***voicemail****?*

void[1] (say **voyd**) *adjective*
that can no longer be accepted or used: *The ticket is* ***void****.*

void[2] (say **voyd**) *noun* (*no plural*) (*formal*) a large empty space: *His death left a* ***void*** *in our lives.*

volatile (say **vol**-uh-tile) *adjective*
1 that can change suddenly and unexpectedly: *a* ***volatile*** *situation* ◇ *He has a* ***volatile*** *personality.*
2 (used about a substance) that can easily change into a gas
▸ **volatility** (*noun*)

volcano (say vol-**kay**-noh) *noun* (*plural* **volcanoes** or **volcanos**)
a mountain with a hole in the top where fire, gas and hot liquid rock (called **lava**) sometimes come out
▸ **volcanic** (*adjective*): ***volcanic** rocks*

volcano

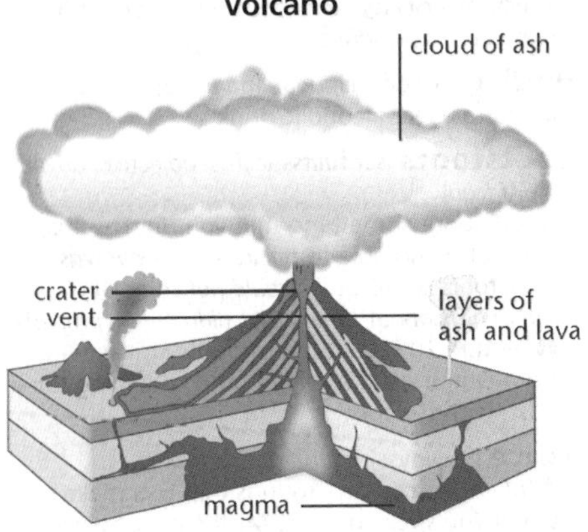

volley (say **vol**-ee) *noun* (*plural* **volleys**)
1 (in some sports) a hit or kick of the ball before it touches the ground: *a backhand **volley***
2 a number of things such as bullets or arrows that you throw or shoot at the same time: *The police fired a **volley** of rubber bullets.*
▸ **volley** (*verb*): *Federer **volleyed** the ball over the net.*

volleyball (say **vol**-ee-bawl) *noun* (*no plural*)
a game where two teams hit a ball backwards and forwards over a high net with their hands: *We played **volleyball** on the beach.*

volt (say **vohlt**) *noun* (*plural* **volts**) (*science*) (abbr. V)
a unit for measuring the force that causes an electric current to flow: *Mains electricity carries 220–240 **volts**, and a small torch battery usually has 1,5 **volts**.*
🛈 **ORIGIN:** 19th century, named after Alessandro Volta (1745–1827), an Italian scientist, who first produced an electric current

voltage (say **vohlt**-ij) *noun* (*plural* **voltages**)
a measure of the electrical force or pressure that causes electrical current to flow, measured in **volts**: *a high-**voltage** cable* ◇ *high **voltages***

voltmeter (say **vohlt**-mee-tuh) *noun* (*plural* **voltmeters**)
an instrument for measuring **voltage**

volume (say **vol**-yoom) *noun*
1 (*no plural*) the amount of space that something contains or fills: *What is the **volume** of this box?*
2 (*no plural*) the amount of sound that something produces: *I can't hear the radio. Can you turn the **volume** up?*
3 (*plural* **volumes**) a book, especially one of a set or series: *The dictionary is in two **volumes**.*

voluntarily (say **vol**-uhn-truh-lee) *adverb*
because you want to, not because you must: *She left the job **voluntarily**.*

voluntary (say **vol**-uhn-tree) *adjective*
1 If something is **voluntary**, you do it because you want to, not because you must: *She took a **voluntary** decision to leave the job.* ➲ OPPOSITE **involuntary**
2 without payment: *He does **voluntary** work at a children's hospital.*

volunteer[1] (say vol-uhn-**teer**) *noun* (*plural* **volunteers**)
a person who offers or agrees to do something without being forced or paid to do it: *They're asking for **volunteers** to help at the Christmas party.*

volunteer[2] (say vol-uhn-**teer**) *verb* (**volunteering**, **volunteered**)
to say that you will do a job without being forced or without being paid to do it: *I **volunteered** to do the washing-up.*

voluptuous (say vuh-**lup**-tshuu-uhss) *adjective*
(especially of a woman's body) having a shape that is sexually attractive

vomit (say **vom**-it) *verb* (**vomiting**, **vomited**)
When you **vomit**, food comes up from your stomach and out of your mouth. ➲ See **retch**, **sick**
▸ **vomit** (*noun*): *The dog left a pile of **vomit** on the floor.*

Voortrekker (say **foor**-trek-uh) *noun* (*plural* **Voortrekkers**) (*history*)
a member of a group of people who took part in an event in South African history in the 1830s called the Great Trek
🛈 **ORIGIN:** through Afrikaans, from Dutch *voor* meaning 'ahead, in front' + *trekken* meaning 'to travel'

voracious (say vuh-**ray**-shuss) *adjective*
1 eating large quantities of food: *a **voracious** predator*
2 doing something often or wanting a lot of new information and knowledge: *a **voracious** reader*

vortex (say **vaw**-tekss) *noun* (*plural* **vortexes** or **vortices**)
a mass of gas or liquid that turns around very fast and pulls things into its centre ➲ See **whirlpool**, **whirlwind**

vote (say **voht**) *noun*
1 (*plural* **votes**) when you choose somebody or something by writing on a piece of paper or by putting up your hand: *There were 96* ***votes*** *for the plan, and 25 against.*
2 the vote (*no plural*) the legal right to express your choice or opinion in an election: *There are some countries in the world where women do not have the* ***vote****.*
▸ **vote** (*verb*): *Who did you* ***vote*** *for in the election?*

voter (say **voh**-tuh) *noun* (*plural* **voters**)
a person who votes in a political election

voucher (say **vow**-tshuh) *noun* (*plural* **vouchers**)
a piece of paper that you can use instead of money to pay for something

vow *noun* (*plural* **vows**)
a formal and serious promise to do something: *wedding* ***vows***
▸ **vow** (*verb*): *He* ***vowed*** *never to return.*

vowel (say **vow**-uhl) *noun* (*plural* **vowels**)
1 one of the letters *a, e, i, o* or *u*
2 a sound represented by one of the letters *a, e, i, o, u* or *y*, or by a set of letters such as *ea, ow* or *oy*. ➲ See **consonant**

voyage (say **voy**-ij) *noun* (*plural* **voyages**)
a long journey on a ship or in a spacecraft: *a* ***voyage*** *from Cape Town to Mombasa*

vs *abbreviation* (also **v**) **versus**

vulgar (say **vul**-guh) *adjective*
1 not showing good judgement about what is attractive or appropriate: ***vulgar*** *furnishings*
2 rude or about things like sex or using the toilet: ***vulgar*** *jokes*

vulnerable (say **vul**-nuh-ruhb-l) *adjective*
easily hurt or harmed physically or emotionally: *Homeless children in the city are* ***vulnerable*** *to many dangers.*
▸ **vulnerability** (*noun*): *the children's* ***vulnerability*** *to abuse*

vulture (say **vul**-tshuh) *noun* (*plural* **vultures**)
a type of bird that eats dead animals

vulva (say **vul**-vuh) *noun* (*plural* **vulvas**)
the outer parts of the female sex organs

vuvuzela (say vuu-vuu-**zel**-uh) *noun* (*plural* **vuvuzelas**) (*S. African*)
a type of simple trumpet that makes a loud noise and that is blown by people at soccer matches and other events

vygie (say **fay**-*khee*) *noun* (*plural* **vygies**) (*S. African*)
a plant with thick leaves and bright flowers that open in the sun ➲ SYNONYM **mesembryanthemum**
ℹ ORIGIN: 20th century, through Afrikaans *vygie* meaning 'little fig'. The fruits of the vygie look like small figs.

PRONUNCIATION Pronounce the **g** in this word like the **g** in the Afrikaans word **lag**.

Ww

W *abbreviation*
1 **west** or **western**[1]
2 (*plural* **W**) **watt**

wad (say **wod**) *noun* (*plural* **wads**)
1 a pile of paper money, documents or papers that you keep together: *a **wad** of R20 notes*
2 a mass of soft material: *She used a **wad** of cotton wool to stop the bleeding.*

waddle (say **wod**-l) *verb* (**waddling, waddled**)
to walk like a duck walks, with short steps and moving your body from side to side

wade (say **wayd**) *verb* (**wading, waded**)
to walk through water: *Can we **wade** across the river, or is it too deep?*

wafer (say **way**-fuh) *noun* (*plural* **wafers**)
a very thin, dry biscuit

waffle[1] (say **wof**-l) *noun*
1 (*plural* **waffles**) a flat cake with a pattern on it that people often eat with cream, ice cream or a sweet sauce (called **syrup**)
2 (*no plural*) (*informal*) language that uses a lot of words but that does not say anything important: *There is a lot of **waffle** in this report!*

waffle[2] (say **wof**-l) *verb* (**waffling, waffled**)
(*informal*) to talk or write a lot without saying anything important or interesting: *He is always **waffling** on about something!*

waft (say **woft**) *verb* (**wafting, wafted**)
to move or make something move gently through the air: *The scent of lavender **wafted** through the room.* ➲ SYNONYM **float**[1] 2

wag *verb* (**wagging, wagged**)
to move or make something move from side to side or up and down: *The dog **wagged** its tail.*

wage (say **wayj**) *verb* (**waging, waged**)
to begin and then continue a war or battle against somebody or something: *We are **waging** a battle against drugs.*

wages (say **wayj**-uhz) *plural noun*
the money that you receive every week for the work that you do: *low **wages*** ◇ *Our **wages** are paid every Friday.*

wagon (say **wag**-uhn) *noun* (*plural* **wagons**)
1 a vehicle with four wheels that a horse pulls
2 a part of a train where things such as coal are carried

waif (say **wayf**) *noun* (*plural* **waifs**)
a small, thin person, usually a child, who does not have a home

wail (say **wayl**) *verb* (**wailing, wailed**)
to make a long sad noise or complain in a loud voice: *The little boy started **wailing** for his mother.*
▸ **wail** (*noun*): *a **wail** of sadness*

waist (say **wayst**) *noun* (*plural* **waists**)
1 the narrow part around the middle of your body ➲ See illustration at **body**
2 the part of a piece of clothing that is shaped to fit around your **waist**.

waistcoat (say **wayst**-koht) *noun* (*plural* **waistcoats**)
a piece of clothing like a jacket with no sleeves

wait[1] (say **wayt**) *verb* (**waiting, waited**)
to stay in one place and not do anything until something happens or until somebody or something comes: *If I'm late, please **wait** for me.* ◇ *Have you been **waiting** long?* ◇ *The doctor kept me **waiting*** (= made me wait) *for half an hour.* ◇ *I'll be home late so don't **wait** up for me.*
can't wait used when somebody is very excited about something that is going to happen: *I can't **wait** to see you again!*

wait[2] (say **wayt**) *noun* (*plural* **waits**)
a period of time when you must wait: *We had a long **wait** for the bus.*

waiter (say **wayt**-uh) *noun* (*plural* **waiters**)
a man who brings food and drink to your table in a restaurant

waiting room *noun* (*plural* **waiting rooms**)
a room where people can sit and wait, for example to see a doctor or to catch a train

waitress (say **wayt**-ruhss) *noun* (*plural* **waitresses**)
a woman who brings food and drink to your table in a restaurant

waitron (say **wayt**-ron) *noun* (*plural* **waitrons**)
a man or a woman who brings food and drink to your table in a restaurant

waive (say **wayv**) *verb* (**waiving, waived**)
(*formal*)
1 to officially say that a rule need not be obeyed
2 to officially decide to give up your right to something: *The actor **waived** the usual fee for the charity event.*

wake (say **wayk**) *verb* (**waking, woke, has woken**) (also **wake up**)
1 to stop sleeping: *What time did you **wake** up this morning?*
2 to make somebody stop sleeping: *The noise **woke** me up.* ◇ *Don't **wake** the baby.*

walk[1] (say **wawk**) *verb* (**walking, walked**)
1 to move by putting one foot in front of the other on the ground, but without running: *I usually **walk** to work.* ◇ *We **walked** twenty kilometres today.*
2 to go somewhere with somebody, for example to make sure that they get there safely: *I'll **walk** you home if you don't want to go on your own.*
walk out to leave suddenly because you are angry: *He **walked** out of the meeting.*

walk[2] (say **wawk**) *noun* (*plural* **walks**)
1 going somewhere on foot: *The beach is a short **walk** from our house.* ◇ *I took the dog for a **walk**.* ◇ *It was a lovely day so we went for a **walk** in the park.*
2 a place or path for walking: *Visitors to the reserve can enjoy informative nature **walks**.*

walker (say **wawk**-uh) *noun* (*plural* **walkers**)
1 a person who walks
2 a frame that supports a person who needs help when they walk

wall (say **wawl**) *noun* (*plural* **walls**)
1 a side of a building or room: *There's a picture on the **wall**.*
2 a vertical structure made of stones or bricks that is built around an area of land: *He went through a gate in the **wall**.* ◇ *She sat on the garden **wall**.*
🛈 **ORIGIN**: through Old English, from Latin *vallum* meaning 'the outside wall of a castle or city' from *vallus* meaning 'stake, sharpened post'. The walls of a city or castle were built for protection and the first city walls were probably made from a row of stakes (sharpened sticks).

wallaby (say **wol**-uh-bee) *noun* (*plural* **wallabies**)
an Australian mammal that is similar to, but smaller than, a **kangaroo**

wallet (say **wol**-it) *noun* (*plural* **wallets**)
a small flat case for money and bank cards: *A pickpocket stole my **wallet**.*

wallow (say **wol**-oh) *verb* (**wallowing, wallowed**)
1 to lie down and roll around in water or mud: *Hippos **wallow** in the mud, but I prefer **wallowing** in the bath!*
2 to let yourself enjoy a situation or feeling without making any effort to change it: *Don't allow yourself to **wallow** in self-pity.*

wallpaper (say **wawl**-pay-puh) *noun* (*no plural*)
special paper that you use for covering the walls of a room
▶ **wallpaper** (*verb*): *We **wallpapered** the bedroom ourselves.*

walnut (say **wawl**-nut) *noun* (*plural* **walnuts**)
a type of nut that we eat

walrus (say **wawl**-ruhss) *noun* (*plural* **walruses** or **walrus**)
a large mammal similar to a **seal[1]** with two long teeth (**tusks**) that lives in or near the sea in northern regions

waltz (say **wolss**) *noun* (*plural* **waltzes**)
1 an elegant dance that you do with a partner
2 a piece of music for this dance
▶ **waltz** (*verb*): *She **waltzed** with her father at her wedding.*

wand (say **wond**) *noun* (*plural* **wands**)
a thin stick that you hold in your hand when you do a magic trick: *wave a magic **wand***

wander (say **won**-duh) *verb* (**wandering, wandered**)
1 to walk slowly with no special plan: *We **wandered** around the town until the shops opened.*
2 to stop concentrating on what you are doing and think about other things: *The lecture was so boring that my attention began to **wander**.*

wane (say **wayn**) *verb* (**waning, waned**)
1 to become weaker or less important: *My enthusiasm **waned** as I became tired.*
2 (used about the moon) to look smaller each day after being full and round ➲ **OPPOSITE** **wax[2]** 3

want (say **wont**) *verb* (**wanting, wanted**)
to wish to have or do something: *Do you **want** a chocolate?* ◇ *I **want** to go to the park.* ◇ *She **wanted** me to give her some money.*
▶ **want** (*noun*): *What are people's **wants** and needs?*

> **WHICH WORD?** **Would like** or **want**?
> **Would like** is more polite than **want**: ***Would** you **like** a cup of tea?*

war (say **waw**) *noun*
1 (*no plural*) fighting between countries or between groups of people: ***War** had broken out (= started).* ◇ *The two countries have been at **war** (= fighting) for five years.*
2 (*plural* **wars**) a period of fighting between different countries or between groups of people: *the frontier **wars***

ward[1] (say **wawd**) *noun* (*plural* **wards**)
1 a room in a hospital that has beds for the

A B C D E F G H I J K L M N O P Q R S T U V W X Y Z

patients: *He worked as a nurse on the children's **ward**.*
2 one of the areas into which a city or district is divided for elections: *Who is your **ward** councillor?*

ward² (say **wawd**) *verb* (**warding, warded**)
ward somebody or **something off** to protect yourself against somebody or something

warden (say **wawd**-n) *noun* (*plural* **wardens**)
a person whose job is to look after a place and the people in it: *the **warden** of a youth hostel*

wardrobe (say **wawd**-rohb) *noun* (*plural* **wardrobes**)
1 a cupboard where you hang your clothes
2 your own collection of clothes: *I need a new summer **wardrobe**.*

warehouse (say **wair**-howss) *noun* (*plural* **warehouses**)
a big building where people keep things before they sell them: *a furniture **warehouse***

warfare (say **waw**-fair) *noun* (*no plural*)
the activity of fighting a war: *naval **warfare***

warm¹ (say **wawm**) *adjective* (**warmer, warmest**)
1 having a pleasant temperature that is fairly high, between cool and hot: *It's **warm** by the fire.*
2 Warm clothes are clothes that stop you feeling cold: *Take **warm** clothes on the trip.*
3 friendly and kind: *My aunt is a very **warm** person.* ➲ OPPOSITE **cold¹** 2
▸ **warmly** (*adverb*): *The child was **warmly** dressed.* ◇ *He thanked me **warmly**.*

WHICH WORD? **Warm** or **hot**?
Read the meaning of **warm** above. Water that you use for making tea or coffee is **hot** or **boiling**, not **warm**.

warm² (say **wawm**) *verb* (**warming, warmed**)
warm up, warm somebody or **something up** to become warmer, or to make somebody or something warmer: *I **warmed** up the soup.* ◇ *I sat in front of the fire to **warm** up.*

warm-blooded (say wawm-**blud**-uhd) *adjective*
relating to animals that have a blood temperature that does not change if the temperature of the surroundings changes: *Mammals and birds are **warm-blooded**.* ➲ See **cold-blooded**

warmth (say **wawmth**) *noun* (*no plural*)
1 a pleasant temperature that is not too hot: *the **warmth** of the sun*
2 the quality of being kind and friendly: *the **warmth** of his smile*

warn (say **wawn**) *verb* (**warning, warned**)
to tell somebody about danger or about something bad that may happen: *I **warned** him not to go too close to the fire.*

warning (say **wawn**-ing) *noun* (*plural* **warnings**)
something that tells you about danger or about something bad that may happen: *There is a **warning** on every packet of cigarettes.* ◇ *The storm came without **warning**.*

warp¹ (say **wawp**) *verb* (**warping, warped**)
1 to make or become bent into the wrong shape: *The window frame was so badly **warped** that I couldn't close the window.*
2 to start behaving in a strange or shocking way because of something that has happened to you: *The war **warped** his mind.*
▸ **warped** (*adjective*): *a **warped** door frame* ◇ *You have a **warped** sense of humour!*

warp² (say **wawp**) *noun* (*no plural*)
the set of threads that is fixed along the longest part of a machine that is used for making cloth (called a **loom**), under and over which another set of threads is passed ➲ See **weft**

warrant (say **wo**-ruhnt) *noun* (*plural* **warrants**)
an official document giving somebody permission to do something: *The police have issued a **warrant** for his arrest.*

warren (say **wo**-ruhn) *noun* (*plural* **warrens**)
a group of connected holes and tunnels under the ground where wild rabbits live

warrior (say **wo**-ri-uh) *noun* (*plural* **warriors**)
a person who fights in battles, especially in past times

warship (say **waw**-ship) *noun* (*plural* **warships**)
a ship used for fighting battles on the sea

wart (say **wawt**) *noun* (*plural* **warts**)
a small hard dry lump that sometimes grows on your skin: *I went to the doctor to have the **wart** on my hand removed.*

warthog (say **wawt**-hog) *noun* (*plural* **warthogs**)
an African wild pig with two large outer teeth (**tusks**) and lumps on its face

wary (say **wair**-ree) *adjective* (**warier, wariest**)
careful because you are not sure, or because you are afraid of something or somebody: *You should be **wary** of products that promise to make you lose weight quickly.*
▸ **warily** (*adverb*): *She looked at him **warily**.*

was (say **woz**) form of **be**

wash¹ (say **wosh**) *verb* (**washing, washed**)
1 to clean somebody, something or yourself

with water and usually soap: *Have you **washed** the car?* ◇ ***Wash** your hands before you eat.* ◇ *I **washed** and dressed quickly.*
2 (used about water) to flow somewhere: *The waves **washed** over my feet.*
wash somebody or **something away** (used about water) to move or carry somebody or something to another place: *The house was **washed** away by the flood.*
wash up to clean the dishes after a meal: *I **washed** up after dinner.*

wash² (say **wosh**) *noun* (*no plural*)
1 cleaning something with water: *I had a quick **wash** before dinner.*
2 clothes that are being washed or that are going to be washed: *All my socks are in the wash!*

washable (say **wosh**-uhb-l) *adjective*
that can be washed without being damaged

washbasin (say **wosh**-bay-sin) *noun* (*plural* **washbasins**) (also **basin**)
a large bowl for water in a bathroom where you wash your hands and face

washing (say **wosh**-ing) *noun* (*no plural*)
clothes that you must wash or that you have washed: *I've done the **washing**.* ◇ *Shall I hang the **washing** outside to dry?* ➲ SYNONYM **laundry**

washing machine *noun* (*plural* **washing machines**)
a machine that washes clothes

washing-up (say wosh-ing-**up**) *noun* (*no plural*)
1 the work of washing the plates, knives, forks, and pots after a meal: *I'll do the **washing-up**.*
2 the dishes and knives, forks and spoons that need washing after a meal

wasn't (say **woz**-uhnt) short for **was not**

wasp (say **wosp**) *noun* (*plural* **wasps**)
a flying insect that can sting people

waste¹ (say **wayst**) *verb* (**wasting, wasted**)
to use too much of something or not use something in a good way: *She **wastes** a lot of money on sweets.* ◇ *He **wasted** his time at university – he didn't do any work.* ◇ *We shouldn't **waste** natural resources.*

waste² (say **wayst**) *noun* (*no plural*)
1 not using something in a useful way: *It's a **waste** to throw away all this food!* ◇ *This watch was a **waste** of money – it's broken already!*
2 things that people throw away because they are not useful or not needed: *A lot of **waste** from the factories goes into this river.*

waste³ (say **wayst**) *adjective*
not useful or needed: ***Waste** paper should be recycled.*

watch¹ (say **woch**) *verb* (**watching, watched**)
1 to look at somebody or something for some time: *We **watched** television all evening.* ◇ ***Watch** how I do this.* ➲ See note at **see**
2 to look after something or somebody: *Could you **watch** my bags while I buy a ticket?*
watch out to be careful because of somebody or something dangerous: ***Watch** out! There's a car coming.*

watch² (say **woch**) *noun*
1 (*plural* **watches**) a type of small clock that you wear on your wrist so you know what time it is: *She kept looking at her **watch** nervously.*
➲ See note at **clock**
2 (*no plural*) the action of watching something in case of danger or problems: *The soldier was keeping **watch** at the gate.*

water¹ (say **waw**-tuh) *noun* (*no plural*)
1 the liquid that falls from clouds as rain and is in rivers, lakes and seas: *I'd like a glass of **water**.* ◇ *After the heavy rain a lot of the fields were under **water**.*
2 an area of water such as a river, a lake or the sea: *Don't go too near the edge or you'll fall in the **water**.*

water² (say **waw**-tuh) *verb* (**watering, watered**)
1 to give water to plants: *Have you **watered** the garden?*
2 When your eyes water, they fill with tears: *The smoke made my eyes **water**.*
3 When your mouth **waters**, it produces a liquid (called **saliva**): *The smell of fried chicken makes my mouth **water**.*

watercolour (say **waw**-tuh-kul-uh) *noun*
1 watercolours (*plural noun*) paints that you mix with water, not oil
2 (*plural* **watercolours**) a picture that you paint with **watercolours**: *an exhibition of **watercolours***

waterfall (say **waw**-tuh-fawl) *noun* (*plural* **waterfalls**)
a place where water falls from a high place to a low place ➲ See illustration at **mountain**

waterlogged (say **waw**-tuh-logd) *adjective*
extremely wet or full of water: *The ground was **waterlogged** after the heavy rains.*

watermark (say **waw**-tuh-maak) *noun* (*plural* **watermarks**)
a symbol or design on paper which you can see when you hold it up to the light: *Can you see the **watermark** on this R50 note?*

A B C D E F G H I J K L M N O P Q R S T U V W X Y Z

watermelon (say **waw**-tuh-mel-uhn) *noun* (*plural* **watermelons**)
a big round fruit with a thick green skin. It is pink inside with a lot of black seeds.

waterproof (say **waw**-tuh-proof) *adjective*
If something is **waterproof**, it does not let water go through it: *a **waterproof** jacket*

waters (say **waw**-tuhz) *plural noun*
the water in a particular sea or lake or near a particular country: *South African coastal **waters***

watershed (say **waw**-tuh-shed) *noun* (*plural* **watersheds**)
1 (*geography*) an area of high land where streams on one side flow into one river and streams on the other side flow into a different river
2 an event or time when an important change happens: *The year 1994 was a **watershed** in the history of South Africa.*

waterskiing (say **waw**-tuh-skee-ing) *noun* (*no plural*)
the sport of moving fast over the surface of water on long boards (called **waterskis**), pulled by a boat

water table *noun* (*plural* **water tables**)
the level in the ground below which the soil is completely wet with water

watertight (say **waw**-tuh-tite) *adjective*
1 made so that water cannot get in or out: *a **watertight** container*
2 (used about an excuse or explanation) that you can find nothing wrong with: *a **watertight** alibi.*

waterway (say **waw**-tuh-way) *noun* (*plural* **waterways**)
a canal or river that boats can travel along

watt (say **wot**) *noun* (*plural* **watts**) (abbr. W)
a unit for measuring electrical power: *a 60-**watt** light bulb*
ORIGIN: 19th century, named after James Watt (1736–1819), a Scottish engineer

wattle (say **wot**-l) *noun* (*plural* **wattles**)
an Australian tree with small cream or yellow flowers: *Some people use the branches and wood of **wattles** to build houses.*

wave¹ (say **wayv**) *noun* (*plural* **waves**)
1 one of the lines of water that moves across the top of the sea or another water surface: ***Waves** crashed against the cliffs.*
2 a movement of your hand from side to side in the air, to say hello or goodbye, or to make a sign to somebody: *As she turned the corner, she gave me a **wave**.* ◇ *I felt a **wave** of anger.*
3 a gentle curve in your hair
4 (*science*) the form that some types of energy such as heat, light and sound take when they move: *radio **waves***
5 a sudden increase in a type of behaviour or feeling: *a crime **wave*** ◇ *I felt a **wave** of anger.*

wave² (say **wayv**) *verb* (**waving**, **waved**)
1 to move your hand from side to side in the air to say hello or goodbye, or to make a sign to somebody: *She **waved** to me as the train left the station.* ◇ *Who are you **waving** at?*
2 to move something quickly from side to side in the air: *The children **waved** flags as the President's car drove past.*
3 to move up and down or from side to side: *The flags were **waving** in the wind.*

wavelength (say **wayv**-length) *noun* (*plural* **wavelengths**) (*science*)
the distance between a point on one wave and the same point on the next wave: *Radio waves have a greater **wavelength** than X-rays.*
be on the same wavelength (*informal*) able to understand somebody because you have the same way of thinking: *We get on OK, but we're not really on the same **wavelength**.*

wavelength

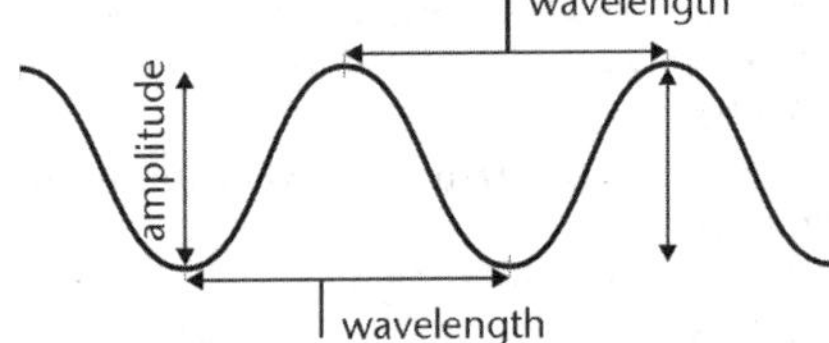

waver (say **wayv**-uh) *verb* (**wavering**, **wavered**)
1 to become uncertain about what you think about somebody or something: *His support for the political party has never **wavered**.*
2 to move in a way that is not firm or steady: *Her hand **wavered** as she took the cup.*

wavy (say **wayv**-ee) *adjective* (**wavier**, **waviest**)
having curves or not straight: *a **wavy** line* ◇ *She has **wavy** black hair.*

wax¹ (say **wakss**) *noun* (*no plural*)
a solid substance that becomes soft when it is heated, used for making candles or polish: ***wax** floor polish*

wax² (say **wakss**) *verb* (**waxing**, **waxed**)
1 to put **wax¹** onto something to make it shine
2 to remove hair from a part of your body using **wax¹**: *She **waxes** her legs.*
3 (used about the moon) to look bigger every day until it looks full or round again ➲ OPPOSITE **wane** 2

way *noun*
1 (*plural* **ways**) a method or style of doing something: *What is the best **way** to learn a language?* ◇ *He smiled in a friendly **way**.*
2 (*plural* **ways**) a road or path that you must follow to go to a place: *Can you tell me the **way** to the station, please?* ◇ *I lost my **way** and I had to look at the map.* ◇ *We stopped for a meal on the **way** to the beach.* ◇ *Get out of the **way**! There's a car coming!*
3 (*plural* **ways**) a direction, or where somebody or something is going or looking: *Come this **way**.* ◇ *She was looking the other **way**.* ◇ *Is this picture the right **way** up?*
4 (*no plural*) distance: *It's a long **way** from here to Cairo.*
by the way words that you say when you are going to talk about something different: *By the **way**, I had a letter from Palisa yesterday.*
give way
1 to stop and let somebody or something go before you: *You must give **way** to traffic coming from the right.*
2 to agree with somebody when you did not agree before
3 to break: *The ladder gave **way** and Ben fell to the ground.*
in the way in front of somebody so that you stop them from seeing something or moving: *I can't see – you're in the **way**.*
way of life how people live: *Is the **way** of life in Europe different from that in Africa?*
🛈 **ORIGIN:** from Old English *weg*, related to Dutch *weg*

WC (say dub-uhl-yoo-**see**) *noun* (*plural* **WCs**) (*old-fashioned*)
a toilet 🛈 **WC** is short for 'water closet'.

we (say **wee**) *pronoun*
the person who is speaking and another person or other people, or you and I: *Sipho and I went out last night – **we** went to the theatre.* ◇ *Are **we** late?*

weak (say **week**) *adjective* (**weaker**, **weakest**)
1 not powerful or strong: *She felt very **weak** after her long illness.* ◇ *He is too **weak** to be a good leader.*
2 Something that is **weak** can break easily: *The bridge is too **weak** to carry heavy traffic.*
3 (used about a drink) containing a lot of water or not strong in taste: *I like my tea quite **weak**.*
➲ **OPPOSITE strong** 5
▸ **weakly** (*adverb*): *She smiled **weakly** at them.*

weaken (say **week**-uhn) *verb* (**weakening, weakened**)
to become less strong or to make somebody or something less strong: *He was **weakened** by the illness.* ➲ **OPPOSITE strengthen**

weakling (say **week**-ling) *noun* (*plural* **weaklings**)
a person who is physically weak

weakness (say **week**-nuhss) *noun*
1 (*no plural*) the state of not being strong: *He thought that crying was a sign of **weakness**.*
2 (*plural* **weaknesses**) something that is wrong or bad in a person or thing: *It is important to know your strengths and **weaknesses**.*
➲ **OPPOSITE strength**

wealth (say **welth**) *noun* (*no plural*)
a lot of money, land or property: *He is a man of great **wealth**.*
▸ **wealthy** (*adjective*): *a **wealthy** family*

wean (say **ween**) *verb* (**weaning, weaned**)
to start feeding a baby or young animal solid food instead of its mother's milk: *It takes time for babies to be **weaned** onto food.*

weapon (say **wep**-n) *noun* (*plural* **weapons**)
something such as a gun that is used for fighting or killing people: *nuclear **weapons*** ◇ *The police still haven't found the murder **weapon**.*

wear[1] (say **wair**) *verb* (**wearing, wore, has worn**)
1 to have clothes, jewellery, etc. on your body: *She was **wearing** a red dress.* ◇ *I **wear** glasses.*
2 to become or make something become thinner, smoother or weaker because of being used or rubbed a lot: *These tyres are badly **worn**.*
wear off to become less strong: *The pain is **wearing** off.*
wear out to become thin or damaged because you have used it a lot, or to make something do this: *Children's shoes usually **wear** out very quickly.*
wear somebody out to make somebody very tired: *She **wore** herself out with work.*

wear[2] (say **wair**) *noun* (*no plural*)
1 clothes that are suitable for a particular purpose or occasion: ***sportswear*** ◇ *leisure **wear***
2 long use which damages something: *This carpet is showing signs of **wear**.*

weary (say **weer**-ree) *adjective* (**wearier, weariest**)
very tired: *a **weary** traveller*
▸ **wearily** (*adverb*): *She sank **wearily** into a chair.* ▸ **weariness** (*noun*): *a feeling of **weariness***

weasel (say **weez**-l) *noun* (*plural* **weasels**)
a small wild mammal with light brown fur, a long thin body and short legs

weather[1] (say **we*th***-uh) *noun* (*no plural*)
how much sun, rain or wind there is at a certain

time and place, or how hot or cold it is: *What's the **weather** like where you are?* ◇ *We had bad **weather** last week.* ➲ See **climate**

SPELLING Be careful! Don't confuse **weather** and **whether**, which sound similar but have very different meanings.

weather² (say we*th*-uh) *verb* (**weathering, weathered**)
1 to change or make something change because of the effect of the air, rain, sun or wind over a long time: *rocks that have **weathered** and become smooth*
2 to come through a difficult time or experience safely: *We've **weathered** the exams.*

weather forecast *noun* (*plural* **weather forecasts**)
a description on television, radio or in a newspaper that tells you what the weather will be like: *The **weather forecast** says it will be sunny and dry tomorrow.*

weave (say **weev**) *verb* (**weaving, wove, has woven**)
to make things such as cloth or baskets by putting threads or other long thin pieces of material over and under each other: *These mats are **woven** by hand.*
▸ **weaving** (*noun*): *reeds used for basket **weaving***

web *noun*
1 (*plural* **webs**) a thin net that a spider makes to catch insects ➲ SYNONYM **cobweb**
2 the Web (*no plural*) (*computing*) the system of computers that makes it possible for you to see information from all over the world on a computer ➲ SYNONYM **World Wide Web**

webbed (say **webd**) *adjective*
having skin joining the toes of an animal's foot: *Ducks have **webbed** feet.*

webcam (say **web**-kam) *noun* (*plural* **webcams**) (*computing*)
a camera that is connected to a computer and that records moving pictures. You can watch what the **webcam** records on a **website** as it is happening.

web page *noun* (*plural* **web pages**) (*computing*)
a computer file on a **website** that you can see on your computer screen: *We learnt how to create and register a new **web page**.*

website (say **web**-site) *noun* (*plural* **websites**) (*computing*)
a place on the Internet that you can look at to find out information about something: *I found this information on their **website**.* ◇ *Visit our **website** to learn more.*

we'd (say **weed**) short for **we had; we would**

wedding (say **wed**-ing) *noun* (*plural* **weddings**)
a time when two people, usually a man and a woman, get married: *Fahiema and Naseef invited me to their **wedding**.* ◇ *a **wedding** dress*

WORD BUILDING At a **wedding**, two people **get married**. A woman who is getting married is called a **bride** and a man is called a **groom** (or **bridegroom**).

wedge¹ (say **wej**) *noun* (*plural* **wedges**)
1 a piece of wood or other material with one thicker end and one thin pointed end, that you can fit into a space, for example to separate two things: *We keep the door open with a **wedge**.*
2 something that is shaped like a triangle: *a **wedge** of cheese*

wedge² (say **wej**) *verb* (**wedging, wedged**)
1 to force something into a small or narrow space: *The cupboard is **wedged** in the corner.*
2 to stop something from moving by using a **wedge¹** 1: *to **wedge** a door open*

Wednesday (say **wenz**-day) *noun*
the day of the week after Tuesday and before Thursday ➲ See note at **day**

weed¹ *noun* (*plural* **weeds**)
a wild plant that grows where you do not want it: *The garden of the old house was full of **weeds**.*

weed² *verb* (**weeding, weeded**)
to pull **weeds** out of the ground

week *noun* (*plural* **weeks**)
1 a period of seven days, usually from Sunday to Saturday: *I'm going on holiday next **week**.* ◇ *I play tennis twice a **week**.* ◇ *I saw him two **weeks** ago.*
2 the five days from Monday to Friday, when people go to work: *I work during the **week** but not at weekends.*

WORD BUILDING We call a period of two weeks a **fortnight**.

weekday (say **week**-day) *noun* (*plural* **weekdays**)
any day except Saturday or Sunday: *I work only on **weekdays**.*

weekend (say week-**end**) *noun* (*plural* **weekends**)
Saturday and Sunday: *What are you doing at the **weekend**?*

weekly (say **week**-lee) *adjective*, *adverb*
happening or coming every week or once a week: *a **weekly** magazine* ◇ *I am paid **weekly**.*

weep *verb* (**weeping**, **wept**) (*formal*)
to cry, usually because you are very sad

weft *noun* (*no plural*)
the set of threads that you pass under and over the threads that go up and down on a machine used for making cloth (called a **loom**) ➲ See **warp**[2]

weigh (say **way**) *verb* (**weighing**, **weighed**)
1 to measure how heavy somebody or something is using scales: *The shop assistant **weighed** the tomatoes.*
2 to have or show a certain weight: *'How much do you **weigh**?' 'I **weigh** 55 kilos.'*

weight (say **wayt**) *noun*
1 (*no plural*) how heavy somebody or something is: *Do you know the **weight** of the parcel?* ◇ *I'm getting fat – I need to lose **weight*** (= get thinner)*!*
2 (*no plural*) (*science*) the pull of **gravity** on a mass: ***Weight** is measured on a scale, in newtons.* ➲ See **mass**, **gravity**
3 (*plural* **weights**) a piece of metal that weighs a particular amount and is used to measure the mass of something
4 (*plural* **weights**) a heavy object: *a **paperweight*** ◇ *He lifts **weights** in the gym.*

USAGE In science, **weight** and **mass** mean different things, but in everyday language people often use the word **weight** to mean **mass**.

weightlifting (say **wayt**-lift-ing) *noun* (*no plural*)
a sport in which people lift heavy metal weights

weird (say **weerd**) *adjective* (**weirder**, **weirdest**)
very strange: *I had a **weird** dream.* ➲ SYNONYM **bizarre**
▸ **weirdly** (*adverb*): *a **weirdly** shaped rock*

welcome[1] (say **wel**-kuhm) *verb* (**welcoming**, **welcomed**)
to show that you are happy to see somebody or to get or accept something: *He came to the door to **welcome** us.* ◇ *We **welcome** your comments.*
▸ **welcome** (*noun*): *They gave us a great **welcome**.*

welcome[2] (say **wel**-kuhm) *adjective*
1 If somebody or something is **welcome**, you are happy to see them or it: *The cool drinks were **welcome** on such a hot day.* ◇ ***Welcome** to our home!* ➲ OPPOSITE **unwelcome**
2 (*informal*) used to say that you are happy for somebody to do something if they want to: *If you come back again, you're **welcome** to stay with us.*
make somebody welcome to show a visitor that you are happy to see them
you're welcome polite words that you say when somebody has said 'thank you': *'Thank you.' 'You're **welcome**.'*

weld *verb* (**welding**, **welded**)
to join pieces of metal by heating them and pressing them together

welfare (say **wel**-fair) *noun* (*no plural*)
1 the health and happiness of a person: *The school looks after the **welfare** of its students.*
2 help and care for poor or unemployed people who have problems with health, money and education: ***welfare** services*

well[1] (say **wel**) *adverb* (**better**, **best**)
1 in a good or right way: *You speak English very **well**.* ◇ *These shoes are very **well** made.* ◇ *He did **well** in his exams.* ➲ OPPOSITE **badly** 1
2 completely or properly: *I don't know her very **well**.* ◇ *Shake the bottle **well** before you open it.*
as well also: *'I'm going out.' 'Can I come as **well**?'* ➲ SYNONYM **too**
as well as and also: *She has a flat in town as **well** as a house in the Eastern Cape.*
may or **might as well** words that you use to say that you will do something, often because there is nothing else to do: *If you've finished your work, you may as **well** go home.*
well done! words that you say to somebody who has done something good: *'I got the job!' '**Well** done!'*

well[2] (say **wel**) *adjective* (**better**, **best**)
healthy: *'How are you?' 'I'm very **well**, thanks.'* ➲ OPPOSITE **ill**

well[3] (say **wel**) *noun* (*plural* **wells**)
a deep hole for getting water or oil from under the ground: *an oil **well***

we'll (say **wee**-uhl) short for **we will**, **we shall**

well behaved *adjective*
behaving in a way that most people think is good: *Their children are very **well behaved**.*

wellington (say **wel**-ing-tuhn) *noun* (*plural* **wellingtons**) (also **wellington boot**, **wellingtons**) (also *informal* **welly**)
one of a pair of long rubber boots that you wear to keep your feet and part of your legs dry ➲ SYNONYM **gumboot**

well known *adjective*
famous: *This writer is **well known**.* ➲ OPPOSITE **unknown**

A B C D E F G H I J K L M N O P Q R S T U V **W** X Y Z

well off *adjective*
rich: *They must be very* ***well off*** *– their house is enormous.*

went form of **go**[1]

wept form of **weep**

were (say **wur**) form of **be**

we're (say **weer**) short for **we are**

weren't (say **wurnt**) short for **were not**

werewolf (say **weer**-wuulf) *noun* (*plural* **werewolves**)
(in stories) a person who sometimes changes into a **wolf**

west *noun* (*no plural*)
1 (abbr. W) the direction you look in to see the sun go down: *Which way is* ***west****?*
2 the West the countries of North America and Western Europe
▸ **west** (*adjective, adverb*): *I live on the* ***west*** *coast.* ◇ *The town is five kilometres* ***west*** *of here.*

western[1] (say **wess**-tuhn) *adjective* (abbr. W)
in or belonging to the west of a place: *The* ***western*** *parts of the country will be very cold.*

western[2] (say **wess**-tuhn) *noun* (*plural* **westerns**)
a film or book about life in the west of the USA in the past

wet *adjective* (**wetter**, **wettest**)
1 covered in water or another liquid: *This towel is* ***wet*** *– can I have a dry one?* ◇ *There was a strong smell of* ***wet*** *paint.*
2 with a lot of rain: *a* ***wet*** *day* ➲ OPPOSITE **dry**[1] 1–2

wetland (say **wet**-luhnd) *noun* (*plural* **wetlands**)
an area of land that is mostly covered with water: *It is important to conserve our country's* ***wetlands****, such as swamps, marshes and vleis.*

we've (say **weev**) short for **we have**

whale (say **wayl**) *noun* (*plural* **whales**)
a very large mammal that lives in the sea and looks like a very big fish
🛈 ORIGIN: from Old English *hwæl*

whale

wharf (say **wawf**) *noun* (*plural* **wharves** or **wharfs**)
a platform built next to the sea or a river where boats or ships go so that people can move things on and off them

what (say **wot**) *pronoun, adjective*
1 a word that you use when you ask about somebody or something: ***What's*** *your name?* ◇ ***What*** *are you reading?* ◇ ***What*** *time is it?* ◇ ***What*** *kind of music do you like?*
2 the thing that, or anything or everything that: *I don't know* ***what*** *this word means.* ◇ *Tell me* ***what*** *to do.*
3 a word that you use to show surprise or other strong feelings: ***What*** *a terrible day!* ◇ ***What*** *beautiful flowers!*
what about ...? words that you use when you suggest something: ***What*** *about going to a film tonight?*
what ... for? for **what** purpose or reason?: ***What*** *did you do that for?* (= Why did you do that?) ◇ ***What's*** *this machine for?*
what is ... like? words that you use when you want to know more about somebody or something: *'****What's*** *her brother like?' 'He's very nice.'*
what's up? what is wrong?: *You look sad.* ***What's*** *up?*

whatever (say wot-**ev**-uh) *adjective, pronoun, adverb*
1 any or every: *These animals eat* ***whatever*** *food they can find.*
2 anything or everything: *I'll do* ***whatever*** *I can to help you.*
3 it does not matter what: ***Whatever*** *you do, don't be late.*
4 (*informal*) a word that you say to show that you do not mind what you do or have: *'What shall we do tomorrow?' '****Whatever****.'*

what's (say **wotss**) short for **what is; what has**

wheat (say **weet**) *noun* (*no plural*)
a plant that farmers grow for its grain or the grain that can be made into flour

wheel[1] (say **weel**) *noun* (*plural* **wheels**)
1 a thing like a circle that turns round to move something such as a car or a bicycle: *His favourite toy is a dog on* ***wheels****.*
2 the **wheel** that you turn to make a car go left or right ➲ SYNONYM **steering wheel**

wheel

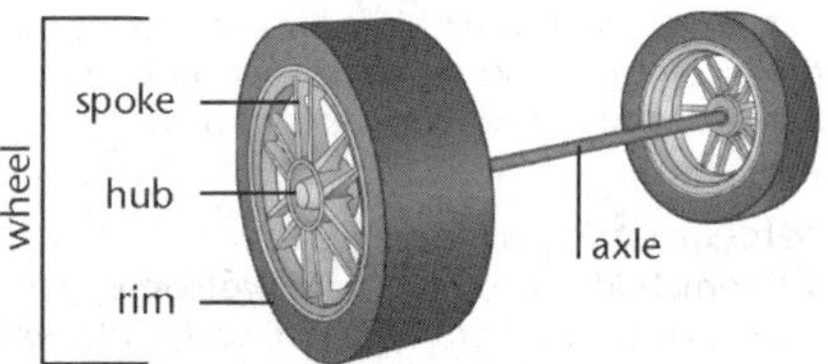

wheel[2] (say **weel**) *verb* (**wheeling, wheeled**)
1 to push along something that has wheels: *I* ***wheeled*** *my bicycle up the hill.*

2 to move somebody or something on a vehicle that has wheels: *The patient was **wheeled** back to the ward.*

wheelbarrow (say **weel**-ba-roh) *noun* (*plural* **wheelbarrows**)
a container with a single wheel at the front and two handles for lifting and pushing it with at the back, that you use outside for carrying things

wheelchair (say **weel**-chair) *noun* (*plural* **wheelchairs**)
a chair with wheels for somebody who cannot walk

when (say **wen**) *adverb, conjunction*
1 at what time: ***When** did she arrive?* ◇ *I don't know **when** his birthday is.*
2 as soon as: *He came **when** I called him.*
3 at the time that: *It was raining **when** we left school.* ◇ *I saw her **when** she was here in May.*

whenever (say wen-**ev**-uh) *conjunction*
1 at any time that: *Come and see us **whenever** you want.*
2 every time that: ***Whenever** I see her, she talks about her boyfriend.*

where (say **wair**) *adverb, conjunction*
1 in or to what place: ***Where** do you live?* ◇ ***Where** is she going?*
2 in or at which: *This is the street **where** I live.*

whereas (say **wair**-az) *conjunction*
a word that you use to show how two people, ideas, etc. are different: *He likes travelling, **whereas** I don't.*

whereby (say wair-**by**) *adverb* (*formal*) by which or according to which: *They have an agreement **whereby** they share the costs.*

wherever (say wair-**ev**-uh) *adverb, conjunction*
1 at, in or to any place: *Sit **wherever** you like.*
2 a way of saying 'where' more strongly: ***Wherever** did I put my keys?*

whether (say **we*th***-uh) *conjunction*
1 a word that we use to talk about choosing between two things: *I don't know **whether** to go or not.*
2 if: *She asked me **whether** I was American.*

SPELLING Be careful! Don't confuse **whether** and **weather**, which sound similar but have different meanings.

whey (say **way**) *noun* (*no plural*)
the thin liquid part of sour milk that is left when you take out the solid parts (called **curd**) ➲ See **curd**

which (say **wich**) *pronoun, adjective*
1 what person or thing: ***Which** colour do you like best – blue or green?* ◇ ***Which** flat do you live in?*
2 a word that shows exactly what thing or things you are talking about: *Did you read the poem **which** Louise wrote?*
3 a word that you use before you say more about something: *Her new dress, **which** she bought in Durban, is beautiful.*

whichever (say wich-**ev**-uh) *adjective, pronoun*
any person or thing, or the one that: *Here are two books – take **whichever** you want.*

whiff (say **wif**) *noun* (*plural* **whiffs**)
a smell that you smell for a short time: *I caught a **whiff** of the food that was being cooked.*

while[1] (say **wile**) *conjunction* (also *formal* **whilst**)
1 during the time that: *The telephone rang **while** I was having a shower.*
2 at the same time as: *I listen to the radio **while** I'm eating my breakfast.*

while[2] (say **wile**) *noun* (*no plural*)
a period of time: *Let's sit here for a **while**.* ◇ *I'm going home in a **while*** (= soon).

whilst (say **wylst**) (*formal*) another word for **while**[1]

whim (say **wim**) *noun* (*plural* **whims**)
a sudden idea or decision to do something: *He bought the new car on a **whim**.*

whimper (say **wim**-puh) *verb* (**whimpering, whimpered**)
to cry softly, because you are hurt or afraid: *'Don't leave me alone,' he **whimpered**.*
► **whimper** (*noun*): *The dog gave a **whimper**.*

whine (say **wine**) *verb* (**whining, whined**)
1 to make a long high sad sound: *The dog was **whining** outside the door.*
2 to complain about things in an annoying way: *'It's not fair!' she **whined**.*
► **whine** (*noun*)

whinge (say **winj**) *verb* (**whinging, whinged**) (*informal*)
to complain about things in an annoying way: *She's always **whingeing** about how much homework she has to do.*

whip[1] (say **wip**) *noun* (*plural* **whips**)
a long piece of leather or rope with a handle, used for making animals move or for hitting people

whip[2] (say **wip**) *verb* (**whipping, whipped**)
1 to hit an animal or a person with a **whip**[1]: *The rider **whipped** the horse to make it go faster.*
2 to mix food very quickly with a fork, for example, until it is light and thick: ***whipped** cream*

A B C D E F G H I J K L M N O P Q R S T U V W X Y Z

whirl (say **wurl**) *verb* (**whirling, whirled**)
to move, or to make somebody or something move, round and round very quickly: *The dancers* ***whirled*** *around the room.*

whirlpool (say **wurl**-pool) *noun* (*plural* **whirlpools**)
an area of water in the sea or a river that moves very quickly round in a circle

whirlwind (say **wurl**-wind) *noun* (*plural* **whirlwinds**)
a very strong wind that forms a tall column of air moving round and round in a circle as it travels across the land or sea

whirr (say **wurr**) *verb* (**whirring, whirred**)
to make a continuous low sound: *The fan* ***whirred*** *all night.*
▸ **whirr** (*noun*): *the* ***whirr*** *of machinery*

whisk[1] (say **wisk**) *verb* (**whisking, whisked**)
1 to mix eggs or cream very quickly with a fork or a **whisk**[2]
2 to take a person or thing somewhere very quickly: *The President was* ***whisked*** *away in a helicopter.*

whisk[2] (say **wisk**) *noun* (*plural* **whisks**)
a kitchen tool that you use for mixing eggs or cream very quickly

whisker (say **wiss**-kuh) *noun* (*plural* **whiskers**)
one of the long hairs that grow near the mouth of cats, mice and some other animals

whisky (say **wiss**-kee) *noun*
1 (*no plural*) a strong alcoholic drink that is made from grain
2 (*plural* **whiskies**) a glass of **whisky**

whisper (say **wiss**-puh) *verb* (**whispering, whispered**)
to speak very quietly to somebody, so that other people cannot hear what you are saying: *He* ***whispered*** *so that he would not wake the baby up.*
▸ **whisper** (*noun*): *She spoke in a* ***whisper****.*

whistle[1] (say **wiss**-l) *noun* (*plural* **whistles**)
1 a small device that makes a long high sound when you blow it: *The referee blew his* ***whistle*** *to end the match.*
2 the long high sound that you make when you blow air out between your lips or when you blow a **whistle**

whistle[2] (say **wiss**-l) *verb* (**whistling, whistled**)
1 to make a long high sound by blowing air out between your lips or through a **whistle**[1] 1: *He* ***whistled*** *a tune to himself.*
2 to move or go very fast with a high sound: *A bullet* ***whistled*** *past my head.*

white[1] (say **wite**) *adjective* (**whiter, whitest**)
1 with the colour of milk or snow: *He wore a* ***white*** *shirt and a blue tie.*
2 belonging to a race of people with pale skins
3 without much colour in your face: *She went* ***white*** *with fear.* ➲ SYNONYM **pale** 1
4 White coffee is made with milk: *I'd like a* ***white*** *coffee.*
5 White wine is wine with a light colour.

white[2] (say **wite**) *noun*
1 (*no plural*) the colour of milk or snow: *She was dressed in* ***white****.*
2 (*plural* **whites**) a person who belongs to a race of people with pale skins
3 (*plural* **whites**) the clear liquid surrounding the middle part of an egg (the **yolk**) that becomes white when it is cooked: *Add the* ***whites*** *of two eggs.*

whitewash (say **wite**-wosh) *noun* (*no plural*)
a white liquid that you use for painting walls
▸ **whitewash** (*verb*): *I* ***whitewashed*** *the walls.*

whizz (say **wiz**) *verb* (**whizzing, whizzed**)
(*informal*) to move very quickly: *The bullet* ***whizzed*** *past his head.*

who (say **hoo**) *pronoun*
1 a word we use in questions to ask about the name, position, etc. of one or more people: ***Who*** *is that girl?* ◇ *I don't know* ***who*** *did it.*
2 a word that shows exactly which person or people you are talking about: *I like people* ***who*** *say what they think.* ◇ *The woman* ***who*** *I work for is very nice.*
3 a word that you use before you say more about something: *My mother,* ***who*** *is over 80, still drives a car.*

who'd (say **hood**) short for **who had; who would**

whoever (say hoo-**ev**-uh) *pronoun*
1 the person that, or any person or people who: ***Whoever*** *broke the glass must pay for it.*
2 a way of saying 'who' more strongly: ***Whoever*** *could have done that?*

whole[1] (say **hohl**) *adjective*
1 complete: *He ate the* ***whole*** *cake!* ◇ *We are going to Australia for a* ***whole*** *month.*
2 not broken or cut into pieces: *The supermarket sells* ***whole*** *chickens and chicken pieces.*
ⓘ ORIGIN: from Old English *hāl*. This word is related to Dutch *heel*.

PRONUNCIATION We don't say the **w** in **whole**.

whole² (say **hohl**) *noun* (*no plural*)
1 a thing that is complete: *Two halves make a whole.*
2 all of something: *I spent the **whole** of the weekend in bed.*
on the whole generally, but not always completely true: *On the **whole**, I think it's a good idea.*

wholesale (say **hohl**-sayl) *adjective, adverb*
relating to buying and selling goods in large quantities: ***wholesale** prices* ◇ *Buying goods **wholesale** is usually cheaper than buying them retail.* ➲ See **retail**
▸ **wholesaler** (*noun*)

wholesome (say **hohl**-suhm) *adjective*
1 good for your health: ***wholesome** food*
2 having a good moral effect: ***wholesome** entertainment*

who'll (say **hool**) short for **who will**

wholly (say **hoh**-lee) *adverb* (*formal*) completely: *He is not **wholly** to blame for the situation.* ➲ SYNONYM **totally**

whom (say **hoom**) *pronoun* (*formal*)
a word we use instead of 'who' as the object of a verb or a preposition: *To **whom** did you give the money?* ◇ *She's the woman **whom** I met in Greece.*

USAGE **Whom** is very formal. **Who** is the word that we usually use, and it is accepted as correct in modern English when referring to the subject or the object: *There's the man **who** I helped.*

whooping cough (say **hoop**-ing kof) *noun* (*no plural*)
a serious infectious disease that affects mainly children, and that makes people cough loudly and be unable to breathe easily

whorl (say **wurl**) *noun* (*plural* **whorls**)
1 something that moves or goes around in a circle
2 (*biology*) an arrangement of leaves, flowers or branches that forms a circle around a stem

who's (say **hooz**) short for **who is; who has**

SPELLING Be careful! Don't confuse **who's** and **whose**, which sound the same but have different meanings.

whose (say **hooz**) *adjective, pronoun*
1 used to ask who something belongs to: *Whose car is this?*
2 used to say exactly which person or thing you mean, or to give extra information about a person or thing: *That's the boy **whose** sister is a singer.*

who've (say **hoov**) short for **who have**

why (say **wy**) *adverb*
for what reason: ***Why** are you late?* ◇ *I don't know **why** she's angry.*
why not? words that you use to make or agree to a suggestion: ***Why** not ask Lerato to go with you?*

wick (say **wik**) *noun* (*plural* **wicks**)
the piece of string that burns in the middle of a candle

wicked (say **wik**-uhd) *adjective*
1 very bad: *a story about a **wicked** witch* ➲ SYNONYM **evil**
2 (*informal*) slightly unkind or bad, but in a way that is funny or enjoyable: *a **wicked** sense of humour* ◇ *a **wicked** joke*

wicker (say **wik**-uh) *noun* (*no plural*)
long thin sticks of wood that we use to make baskets and furniture: *a **wicker** chair*

wicket (say **wik**-uht) *noun* (*plural* **wickets**)
1 (in cricket) a set of three wooden upright sticks with pieces of wood lying across the top, at which the player who throws the ball (the **bowler**) aims
2 the rectangular area of ground between the two **wickets**

wicketkeeper (say **wik**-it-keep-uh) *noun* (*plural* **wicket-keepers**)
(in cricket) a player who stands behind the **batsman** at the wicket, and tries to catch the ball

wide¹ *adjective* (**wider, widest**)
1 far from one side to the other: *We drove down a **wide** road.* ➲ SYNONYM **broad** ➲ OPPOSITE **narrow** 1
2 You use **wide** to say or ask how far something is from one side to the other: *The table was two metres **wide**.* ◇ *How **wide** is the river?*
3 completely open: *The children's eyes were **wide** with excitement.*
4 including or involving a large number or variety of different people or things: *a **wide** range of goods*
➲ The noun is **width**

wide² *adverb*
completely or as far or as much as possible: *Open your mouth **wide**.* ◇ *I'm **wide** awake!* ◇ *She stood with her feet **wide** apart.*

widely (say **wide**-lee) *adverb*
by a lot of people, or in or to a lot of places: *Her*

*books are **widely** read.* ◇ *He has travelled **widely** in Asia.*

widen (say **wide**-uhn) *verb* (**widening, widened**)
to become wider or to make something wider: *They are **widening** the road.*

widespread (say **wide**-spred) *adjective*
If something is **widespread**, it is happening in many places: *The disease is becoming more **widespread**.*

widow (say **wid**-oh) *noun* (*plural* **widows**)
a woman whose husband has died and who has not married again

widower (say **wid**-oh-uh) *noun* (*plural* **widowers**)
a man whose wife has died and who has not married again

width (say **width**) *noun* (*plural* **widths**)
how far it is from one side of something to the other or how wide something is: *The room is five metres in **width**.* ◇ *We swam five **widths** in the pool.* ➲ SYNONYM **breadth** ➲ The adjective is **wide**[1] ➲ See illustration at **length**

wield (say **weeld**) *verb* (**wielding, wielded**)
1 to have and use power, authority or influence: *She **wields** enormous power in the company.*
2 to hold and be ready to use a weapon: *The thief was **wielding** a knife.*

wife *noun* (*plural* **wives**)
the woman that a man is married to ➲ See **husband**

Wi-Fi™ (say **wy**-fy) *noun* (*no plural*)
a group of technical standards for sending information over **wireless**[1] networks ❶ **Wi-Fi** is short for 'Wireless Fidelity'.

wig *noun* (*plural* **wigs**)
a covering for your head made of real or false hair: *The actress wore a black **wig**.*

wiggle (say **wig**-l) *verb* (**wiggling, wiggled**)
to move from side to side or up and down with quick movements: *She **wiggled** her toes in the sand.*
▸ **wiggle** (*noun*): *to walk with a **wiggle***

wild (say **wyld**) *adjective* (**wilder, wildest**)
1 Wild plants and animals live or grow in nature, not with people: *You shouldn't pick **wild** flowers.*
2 excited or not controlled: *She was **wild** with anger.* ◇ *The crowd went **wild** with excitement.*
▸ **wildly** (*adverb*): *The crowd cheered and waved **wildly**.*

wildebeest (say **vil**-duh-bee-uhst) *noun* (*plural* **wildebeest** or **wildebeests**)
a large African antelope with horns similar to those of a cow
❶ ORIGIN: 19th century, through South African Dutch *wildebeest* from Dutch *wilde* meaning 'wild' + *beest* meaning 'beast'

wilderness (say **wil**-duh-nuhss) *noun* (*no plural*)
a large area of land that has never been used for building on or for farming: *The Antarctic is still mostly a **wilderness**.*

wildlife (say **wyld**-life) *noun* (*no plural*)
wild animals and plants that live in a natural environment

wilful (say **wil**-fuhl) *adjective*
1 doing exactly what you want to do, no matter what other people say or think: *a **wilful** child*
2 done on purpose, although the person doing it knows that it is wrong: *to cause **wilful** damage*
▸ **wilfully** (*adverb*): *He **wilfully** set the house on fire.*

will[1] (say **wil**) *modal verb*
1 a word that shows the future: *Do you think she **will** come tomorrow?*
2 a word that you use when you agree or promise to do something: *I **will** carry your bag.*
3 a word that you use when you ask somebody to do something: ***Will** you open the window, please?*

> USAGE The short form of **will** is **'ll**. We often use this, as in: ***You'll*** (= you will) *be late. **He'll*** (= he will) *drive you to the station.* The negative form of **will** is **will not** or the short form **won't** (*say* **wohnt**): *They **won't** be there.*

will[2] (say **wil**) *noun*
1 (*no plural*) the power of your mind that makes you choose, decide and do things: *She has a very strong **will** and nobody can stop her doing what she wants.*
2 (*no plural*) what somebody wants to happen: *She made Joe get into the car against his **will*** (= when he did not want to).
3 (*plural* **wills**) a document that says who will have your money, house or property when you die: *My grandmother left me R2 000 in her **will**.*

willing (say **wil**-ing) *adjective*
ready and happy to do something: *I'm **willing** to work at weekends.* ➲ OPPOSITE **unwilling**
▸ **willingly** (*adverb*): *I'll **willingly** help you.*
▸ **willingness** (*noun*): *He showed no **willingness** to help.*

wilt *verb* (**wilting**, **wilted**)
(used about plants and flowers) to bend and start to die because of heat or lack of water

win *verb* (**winning**, **won**)
1 to be the best or the first in a game, race or competition: *Who **won** the race?* ◇ *Tshililo **won** and I was second.* ➲ OPPOSITE **lose** 3
2 to receive something because you did well or tried hard: *I **won** a prize in the competition.* ◇ *Who **won** the gold medal?*
▸ **win** (*noun*): *Our team has had five **wins** this year.*

winch *noun* (*plural* **winches**)
a machine that lifts or pulls heavy objects with a rope or chain
▸ **winch** (*verb*): *They **winched** the car up onto the trailer.*

wind¹ (say **wind**) *noun* (*plural* **winds**)
air that moves: *The **wind** blew his hat off.* ◇ *Strong **winds** caused a lot of damage to buildings.*

wind² (*rhymes with* **find**) *verb* (**winding**, **wound**)
1 A road or river that **winds** has a lot of bends and turns: *The path **winds** through the forest.*
2 to make something long go round and round another thing: *The nurse **wound** the bandage around my knee.*
3 to turn a key or handle to make something work or move: *The clock will stop if you don't **wind** it up.* ◇ *The driver **wound** her car window down.*

windfall (say **wind**-fawl) *noun* (*plural* **windfalls**)
an amount of money that you win or receive unexpectedly

windmill (say **wind**-mil) *noun* (*plural* **windmills**)
a tall building or structure with long flat parts that turn when the wind blows. People use **windmills** to take water out of the ground, make flour from grain or make electricity.
➲ See **mill**

window (say **win**-doh) *noun* (*plural* **windows**)
an opening in a building or in a car door, for example, with glass in it: *It was cold, so I closed the **window**.* ◇ *She looked out of the **window**.*
❶ ORIGIN: 13th–15th century, from Old Norse *vindauga*, from *vindr* meaning 'wind' + *auga* meaning 'eye'

windowpane (say **win**-doh-payn) *noun* (*plural* **windowpanes**)
a piece of glass in a window

windowsill (say **win**-doh-sil) *noun* (*plural* **windowsills**) (also **window ledge**)
a shelf under a window

windpipe (say **wind**-pipe) *noun* (*plural* **windpipes**)
the tube in your throat that carries air to your lungs ➲ SYNONYM **trachea** ➲ See illustration at **lung**

windpump (say **wind**-pump) *noun* (*plural* **windpumps**)
a tall structure that uses the power of the wind to bring water up out of the ground

windpump

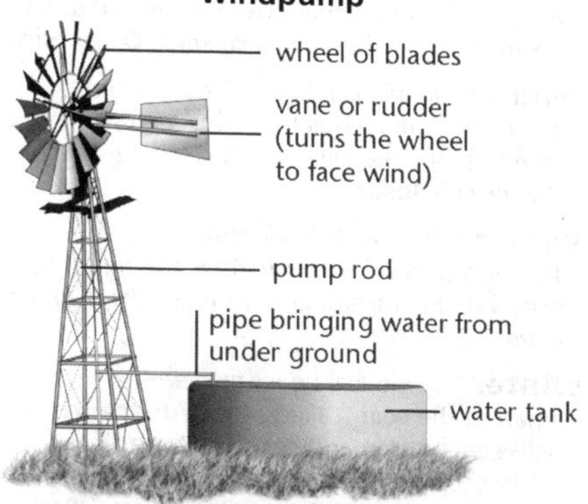

windscreen (say **wind**-skreen) *noun* (*plural* **windscreens**)
the big window at the front of a car ➲ See illustration at **car**

windscreen wiper (say wind-skreen **wipe**-uh) *noun* (*plural* **windscreen wipers**)
a thing that cleans rain and dirt off the **windscreen** while you are driving

windsurfer (say **wind**-surf-uh) *noun* (*plural* **windsurfers**)
1 a special board with a sail. You stand on it as it moves over the water.
2 a person who rides on a board like this

windsurfing (say **wind**-surf-ing) *noun* (*no plural*)
the sport of moving over water while standing on a special board with a sail: *We like to go **windsurfing** at the weekend.*

windy (say **win**-dee) *adjective* (**windier**, **windiest**)
with a lot of wind: *It's very **windy** today!*

wine *noun* (*plural* **wines**)
an alcoholic drink made from grapes: *South African **wines*** ◇ *She ordered a glass of white **wine**.*

wing *noun* (*plural* **wings**)
1 one of the two parts that a bird, a bat or an insect uses to fly: *The chicken ran around flapping its **wings**.* ➲ See illustration at **bird**, **insect**

A B C D E F G H I J K L M N O P Q R S T U V W X Y Z

2 one of the two long parts at the sides of a plane that support it in the air
3 a group of people in a political party or other organization that have their own beliefs and opinions: *the conservative **wing** of the National Party*
4 a section of a large building: *the maternity **wing** of the hospital*

wink *verb* (**winking**, **winked**)
to close and open one eye quickly as a friendly or secret sign to somebody: *She **winked** at me.*
▸ **wink** (*noun*): *He gave me a **wink**.* ➲ See **blink**

winner (say **win**-uh) *noun* (*plural* **winners**)
a person or an animal that wins a game, race or competition: *The **winner** was given a prize.*
➲ OPPOSITE **loser**

winning (say **win**-ing) *adjective*
The **winning** person or team is the one that wins a game, race or competition: *the **winning** team*

winter (say **win**-tuh) *noun* (*no plural*)
a part of the year (called a **season**) that comes between autumn and spring. **Winter** is the coldest season: *The nights are very cold in **winter**.* ◇ *the wet **winters** in Cape Town* ➲ See **season**

wipe *verb* (**wiping**, **wiped**)
1 to make something clean or dry with a cloth: *The waitress **wiped** the table.* ◇ *I washed my hands and **wiped** them on a towel.*
2 to take away something by rubbing it: *She **wiped** the writing off the blackboard.* ◇ *I **wiped** up the milk on the floor.*
wipe something out to destroy something completely: *The bombs **wiped** out whole towns.*
▸ **wipe** (*noun*): *He gave the table a quick **wipe**.*

wire (say **wy**-uh) *noun* (*plural* **wires**)
a long thin piece of metal: *The box was fastened with a piece of **wire**.* ◇ *a **wire** fence* ◇ *The telephone **wires** had been cut.*

wireless[1] (say **wy**-uh-luhss) *adjective*
using radio waves to send and receive electronic signals, not wires: *a **wireless** network*

wireless[2] (say **wy**-uh-luhss) *noun* (*plural* **wirelesses**) (*old-fashioned*) a radio

wisdom (say **wiz**-duhm) *noun* (*no plural*)
knowing and understanding a lot about many things and able to make sensible decisions: *Some people think that old age brings **wisdom**.*
➲ The adjective is **wise**
🛈 ORIGIN: from Old English *wisdom*

wise (say **wize**) *adjective* (**wiser**, **wisest**)
knowing and understanding a lot about many things: *a **wise** old man* ◇ *Do you think this is wise?*
▸ **wisely** (*adverb*): *Many people **wisely** stayed at home in the bad weather.*

wish[1] *noun* (*plural* **wishes**)
1 a feeling that you want to do or have something: *I have no **wish** to go.*
2 an act of trying to make something happen by saying you want it to happen or hoping that it will happen: *Close your eyes and make a **wish**!*
best wishes words that you write at the end of a letter, before your name, to show that you hope somebody is well and happy: *See you soon. **Best** wishes, Lucy.*

wish[2] *verb* (**wishing**, **wished**)
1 to want something that is not possible or that will probably not happen: *I **wish** I could fly!* ◇ *I **wish** I had passed the exam!* ◇ *I **wish** we were rich.*
2 to say to yourself that you want something and hope that it will happen: *You can't have everything you **wish** for.*
3 to say that you hope somebody will have something: *I **wished** her a happy birthday.*
4 (*formal*) (used in requests) to want to do or have something: *I **wish** to see the manager.*

> USAGE **Wish** is a very formal word to use in requests (sense 4). **Want** or **would like** are the words that we usually use: *I **want** to see the manager.* ◇ *I **would like** to see you at 4.30.*

wisp *noun* (*plural* **wisps**)
1 a small amount of smoke or cloud
2 a few pieces of hair that are together
▸ **wispy** (*adjective*): ***wispy** white clouds* ◇ ***wispy** grey hair*

wistful (say **wist**-fuhl) *adjective*
feeling or showing sadness because you cannot have what you want
▸ **wistfully** (*adjective*): *She looked **wistfully** at the cakes in the shop.*

wit *noun* (*no plural*)
speaking or writing in a clever and funny way

witch (say **wich**) *noun* (*plural* **witches**)
(in stories) a woman who has magic powers
➲ See **wizard**

with (say **with**) *preposition*
1 a word that shows people or things are together: *I live **with** my parents.* ◇ *Mix the flour **with** milk.* ◇ *I agree **with** you.* ◇ *Come **with** me.*
2 having or carrying: *He's an old man **with** grey hair.* ◇ *I want to live in a house **with** a garden.* ◇ *I passed a woman **with** an enormous suitcase.*
3 using: *I cut it **with** a knife.* ◇ *Fill the bottle **with** water.*
4 against: *I played tennis **with** my sister.*

5 because of: *Her hands were blue **with** cold.*
6 a word that shows that something fills or covers something: *His hands were covered **with** oil.*

USAGE For sense 1, remember that **with** should not be at the end of sentences like these: *Please come **with me**!* (not 'Please come with!') *Did he go **with you**?* (not 'Did he go with?') *Take the blanket **with you**!* (not 'Take the blanket with').

withdraw (say with-**draw**) *verb* (**withdrawing, withdrew, has withdrawn**)
1 to move back or away: *The army **withdrew** from the town.*
2 to say that you will not take part in something: *Rob has **withdrawn** from the race.*
3 to take something out or away: *I **withdrew** R100 from my bank account.*

wither (say wi*th*-uh) *verb* (**withering, withered**)
If a plant **withers**, it becomes dry and dies: *The plants **withered** in the hot sun.*

withhold (say with-**hohld**) *verb* (**withholding, withheld**)
to refuse to give something to somebody: *He is **withholding** information from the police.*

within (say with-**in**) *preposition*
1 before the end of: *I'll be back **within** an hour.*
2 not further than: *We live **within** a mile of the station.*
3 (*formal*) inside: *There are 400 prisoners **within** the prison walls.*

without (say with-**owt**) *preposition, adverb*
1 not having, showing or using something: *It's cold – don't go out **without** your coat.* ◇ *I drink coffee **without** sugar.*
2 not being with somebody or something: *He left **without** me.*
without doing something not doing something: *They left **without** saying goodbye.*

withstand (say with-**stand**) *verb* (**withstanding, withstood**)
to be strong enough not to break or to give up: *Glass can **withstand** very high temperatures.* ◇ *The house **withstood** the earthquake.*

witness (say **wit**-nuhss) *noun* (*plural* **witnesses**)
1 a person who sees something happen and can tell other people about it later: *There were two **witnesses** to the accident.*
2 a person who goes to a court of law to tell people what they know or what they have seen: *a **witness** for the defence*
▸ **witness** (*verb*): *She **witnessed** a murder.*

witty (say **wit**-ee) *adjective* (**wittier, wittiest**)
clever and funny: *a **witty** answer*

wives (say **wyvz**) plural of **wife**

wizard (say **wiz**-uhd) *noun* (*plural* **wizards**)
(in stories) a man who has magic powers ➲ See **witch**

wobble (say **wob**-l) *verb* (**wobbling, wobbled**)
to move a little from side to side: *That chair **wobbles** when you sit on it.*
▸ **wobbly** (*adjective*): *a **wobbly** table*

woe (*rhymes with* **go**) *noun*
1 (*no plural*) (*formal*) great sadness: *full of **woe***
2 woes (*plural noun*) the problems that somebody has: *You don't have to listen to all my **woes**.*
woe betide somebody (*old-fashioned*) used as a warning that there will be trouble if a person does or does not do a particular thing: ***Woe** betide anybody who doesn't come to practice this afternoon!*

woke, woken forms of **wake**

wolf (say **wuulf**) *noun* (*plural* **wolves**)
a wild animal like a big dog

woman (say **wuu**-muhn) *noun* (*plural* **women**)
an adult female person: *men, **women** and children* ◇ *Would you prefer to see a **woman** doctor?*

womb (say **woom**) *noun* (*plural* **wombs**)
the part of a woman's body where a baby grows ➲ SYNONYM **uterus**

won (say **wun**) form of **win**

wonder[1] (say **wun**-duh) *verb* (**wondering, wondered**)
to want to know about something: *I **wonder** what that noise is.* ◇ *I **wonder** why he didn't come.*
I wonder if ... words that you use to ask a question politely: *I **wonder** if I could use your phone.*

wonder[2] (say **wun**-duh) *noun*
1 (*no plural*) a feeling that you have when you see or hear something very strange, surprising or beautiful: *The children stared in **wonder** at the elephants.*
2 (*plural* **wonders**) something that gives you this feeling: *Read about the **wonders** of modern medicine!*
it's a wonder ... it is surprising that ...: *It's a **wonder** you weren't killed in the accident.*
no wonder not surprising: *She didn't sleep last night, so no **wonder** she's tired.*

wonderful (say **wun**-duh-fuhl) *adjective*
very good, impressive or enjoyable: *What a*

A B C D E F G H I J K L M N O P Q R S T U V W X Y Z

wonderful present! ◇ *This food is **wonderful**.*
➲ SYNONYM **fantastic**

WORD BUILDING See the Word Building notes at **good1**, **nice** and **magnificent**.

won't (say **wohnt**) short for **will not**

wood (say **wuud**) *noun*
1 (*no plural*) the hard substance that trees are made of: *Put some more **wood** on the fire.* ◇ *The table is made of **wood**.*
2 (*plural* **woods**) a big group of trees, smaller than a forest: *a large **wood*** ◇ *a walk in the **woods***

woodcut (say **wuud**-kut) *noun* (*plural* **woodcuts**)
a picture that is made by cutting a design into the surface of a piece of wood and then making a print with it

wooden (say **wuud**-uhn) *adjective*
made of wood: *The toys are kept in a **wooden** box.*

woodwind (say **wuud**-wind) *noun* (*no plural*)
the group of musical instruments that you play by blowing into them: *Flutes and clarinets are **woodwind** instruments.*

woodwork (say **wuud**-wurk) *noun* (*no plural*)
1 the activity or skill of making things out of wood
2 the parts of a building that are made of wood

wool (say **wuul**) *noun* (*no plural*)
1 the soft thick hair of sheep
2 thread or cloth that is made from the hair of sheep: *The cat was playing with a ball of **wool**.* ◇ *This jumper is made of pure **wool**.*

woollen (say **wuul**-uhn) *adjective*
made of wool: ***woollen** socks*

woolly (say **wuul**-ee) *adjective*
made of wool or like wool: *a **woolly** hat*

word (say **wurd**) *noun*
1 (*plural* **words**) a sound that you make, or a letter or group of letters that you write, which has a meaning: *What's the isiXhosa **word** for 'dog'?* ◇ *Do you know the **words** of this song?*
2 (*plural* **words**) something that you say: *Can I have a few **words** with you?* ◇ *Don't say a **word** about this to anybody.*
3 (*no plural*) a promise: *She gave me her **word** that she wouldn't tell anyone.* ◇ *Tiyani said she would come, and she kept her **word*** (= did what she had promised).
in other words saying the same thing in a different way: *He doesn't like hard work – in other **words**, he's lazy!*
take somebody's word for it to believe what somebody says
word for word using exactly the same words: *She repeated **word** for **word** what you told her.*

word processor (say **wurd proh**-sess-uh) *noun* (*plural* **word processors**)
1 a small computer used to create, store or print pieces of text ➲ See **computer**, **PC**
2 a computer program that you use to create, store or print a piece of text, usually typed in from a **keyboard**

wore (say **waw**) form of **wear**[1]

work[1] (say **wurk**) *verb* (**working**, **worked**)
1 to be busy doing or making something: *You will need to **work** hard if you want to pass the exam.* ◇ *I'm going to **work** on my essay this evening.*
2 to do something as a job and get money for it: *My friend **works** for the SABC.* ◇ *I **work** at the car factory.*
3 to go or function correctly or properly: *We can't watch TV – the television isn't **working**.*
4 to make something do something: *Can you show me how to **work** the photocopier?*
5 to have the result you wanted: *I don't think your plan will **work**.*
work out
1 to have the result you wanted: *I hope things **work** out for you.*
2 to do exercises to keep your body strong and well: *She **works** out every day.*
work something out to find the answer to something: *We **worked** out the cost of the holiday.* ◇ *Why did she do it? I can't **work** it out.*

work[2] (say **wurk**) *noun*
1 (*no plural*) the job that you do to earn money or the place where you have a job: *I'm looking for **work**.* ◇ *What time do you start **work**?* ◇ *He's been out of **work*** (= without a job) *for six months.* ◇ *I phoned him at **work**.*
2 (*no plural*) doing or making something: *Digging is hard **work**.*
3 (*no plural*) something that you make or do: *The teacher marked our **work**.*
4 (*plural* **works**) a book, painting or piece of music: *He's read the complete **works** of Shakespeare.* ◇ *A number of priceless **works** of art were stolen from the gallery.*
5 works (*plural noun*) a place where people make things with machines: *My grandfather worked at the **steelworks**.*
6 works (*plural noun*) the activity of building or repairing something: *The **roadworks** are causing traffic jams.*
7 (*no plural*) (*science*) the use of force to move an object over a distance: ***Work** is measured in joules.*

get to work to start doing something: *Let's get to **work** on this washing-up.*

workable (say **wurk**-uhb-l) *adjective*
able to be done or used successfully: *a **workable** plan ◇ a **workable** solution*

workbook (say **wurk**-buuk) *noun* (*plural* **workbooks**)
a book in which you write answers to questions, that you use when you are studying something

worker (say **wurk**-uh) *noun* (*plural* **workers**)
1 a person who works: *an office **worker** ◇ The factory **workers** all went on strike.*
2 a person who works in a particular way: *He's a very inaccurate **worker**.*

workforce (say **wurk**-fawss) *noun* (*plural* **workforces**)
1 all the people who work in an organization, a company or an industry
2 the total number of people in a country who are able to work: *About twelve per cent of the **workforce** are unemployed at the moment.*

USAGE We can use a singular or a plural verb with **workforce**: *The **workforce are** unemployed. ◇ The **workforce is** unemployed.*

workman (say **wurk**-muhn) *noun* (*plural* **workmen**)
a man who works with his hands to build or repair something

worksheet (say **wurk**-sheet) *noun* (*plural* **worksheets**)
a piece of paper where you write answers to questions, which you use when you are studying something

workshop (say **wurk**-shop) *noun* (*plural* **workshops**)
1 a place where people make or repair things
2 a time when people meet and work together to learn about something: *We went to a drama **workshop**.*

world (say **wurld**) *noun*
1 (*no plural*) the Earth with all its countries and people: *There was a map of the **world** on the classroom wall. ◇ Which is the biggest city in the **world**?*
2 (*no plural*) a part of the Earth and the people and things that exist there: *the English-speaking **world***
3 (*no plural*) human society: *the modern **world***
4 (*plural* **worlds**) a particular area of activity or the people who are involved in it: *the **world** of sport*

world-famous (say wurld-**fay**-muhss) *adjective*
known everywhere in the world: *John is a **world-famous** writer.*

worldwide (say **wurld**-wide) *adjective, adverb*
existing or happening everywhere in the world: *Pollution is a **worldwide** problem. ◇ They sell their computers **worldwide**.*

World Wide Web *noun* (*no plural*) (also **the Web**) (*computing*) (abbr. WWW)
the system of computers that makes it possible to see information from all over the world on your computer ➲ See **Internet**

worm (say **wurm**) *noun*
1 (*plural* **worms**) a small animal with a long thin body and no legs: *an **earthworm***
2 worms (*plural noun*) a number of worms that live inside the body of an animal and that may cause a disease or an infection: *Our dog has **worms**.*

worn (say **wawn**) form of **wear**[1]

worn out *adjective*
1 old and damaged because you have used it a lot: *These shoes are completely **worn out**.*
➲ SYNONYM **tatty**
2 very tired: *He's **worn out** after his long journey.*
➲ See **exhaust**[2]

worried (say **wo**-reed) *adjective*
unhappy because you think that something bad will happen or has happened: *Danya is **worried** that she's going to fail the exam. ◇ I'm **worried** about my brother – he looks ill.*

worry[1] (say **wo**-ree) *verb* (**worrying, worried**)
1 to feel that something bad will happen or has happened, or to make somebody feel this: *Mum **worries** when we're late. ◇ Don't **worry** if you don't know the answer. ◇ There's nothing to **worry** about.*
2 to disturb somebody: *I'm sorry to **worry** you.*

worry[2] (say **wo**-ree) *noun*
1 (*no plural*) a feeling that something bad will happen or has happened: *Her face showed signs of **worry**.*
2 (*plural* **worries**) something that makes you feel worried: *I have a lot of **worries**.*

wors (say **vawss**) *noun* (*no plural*) (*S. African*)
short for **boerewors**
ORIGIN: through Afrikaans, from Dutch *worst* meaning 'sausage'

worse[1] (say **wurss**) *adjective* (**bad, worse, worst**)
1 not as good or as well as something else: *The weather today is **worse** than yesterday.*
2 more ill: *If you get **worse**, you must go to the doctor.* ➲ OPPOSITE **better**[1]

A B C D E F G H I J K L M N O P Q R S T U V W X Y Z

worse² (say **wurss**) *adverb* (**badly, worse, worst**)
in a less pleasant or useful way: *The first team lost badly, but the second team did even* ***worse****.*
➲ OPPOSITE **better²**

worship (say **wur**-ship) *verb* (**worshipping, worshipped**)
1 to show that you believe in God or a god by saying prayers: *Christians usually* ***worship*** *in churches.*
2 (*informal*) to love or admire somebody very much: *She* ***worships*** *her grandchildren.*
▸ **worship** (*noun*): *A mosque is a place of* ***worship****.*

worst¹ (say **wurst**) *adjective* (**bad, worse, worst**)
1 the least pleasant or suitable: *This is the* ***worst*** *day of my life.*
2 the least skilful or successful: *He's the* ***worst*** *player in the team!* ➲ OPPOSITE **best¹**

worst² (say **wurst**) *adverb* (**badly, worse, worst**)
in a way that is worse than all others: *Everyone played badly, but I played* ***worst*** *of all.*
➲ OPPOSITE **best¹**

worst³ (say **wurst**) *noun* (*no plural*)
something or somebody that is as bad as they can be: *I'm the* ***worst*** *in the class at grammar.*
if the worst comes to the worst if something very bad happens: *If the* ***worst*** *comes to the* ***worst*** *and I fail the exam, I'll take it again next year.*

worth¹ (say **wurth**) *adjective*
1 having a particular value: *This house is* ***worth*** *R700 000.*
2 good or useful enough to do or have: *Is this film* ***worth*** *seeing?* ◇ *It's not* ***worth*** *asking Lyn for money – she never has any.*

worth² (say **wurth**) *noun* (*no plural*)
1 value: *The painting is of little* ***worth****.*
2 how much or how many of something an amount of money will buy: *I'd like 50 rands'* ***worth*** *of petrol, please.*

worthless (say **wurth**-luhss) *adjective*
having no value or use: *A cheque is* ***worthless*** *if you don't sign it.*

worthwhile (say **wurth**-wile) *adjective*
good or useful enough for the time, money or energy that you spend: *Getting into the team made all the training* ***worthwhile****.*

worthy (say **wur*th***-ee) *adjective* (**worthier, worthiest**)
good or useful enough for something or to have something: *He felt he was not* ***worthy*** *of the prize.*

would (say **wuud**) *modal verb*
1 a word that you use to talk about a situation that is not real: *If I had a million rand, I* ***would*** *buy a big house.*
2 a word that you use to ask something in a polite way: ***Would*** *you close the door, please?*
3 a word that you use with 'like' or 'love' to ask or say what somebody wants: ***Would*** *you like a cup of tea?* ◇ ***I'd*** (= I would) *love to go to Africa.*
4 the past form of 'will': *He said he* ***would*** *come.* ◇ *They* ***wouldn't*** *tell us where she was.*
5 a word that you use to talk about something that happened many times in the past: *When I was young, my grandparents* ***would*** *visit us every Sunday.*

USAGE Be careful! Notice how **would** is used in certain tenses: *I* ***would have*** *gone.* (not 'I would of gone.') *We* ***would have*** *swum.* (not 'We would of swum.')

USAGE The short form of **would** is **'d**. We often use this, as in: ***I'd*** (= I would) *like to meet her.* ***They'd*** (= they would) *help if they had the time.* The negative form of **would** is **would not** or the short form **wouldn't** (*say* **wuud**-uhnt): *He* ***wouldn't*** *help me.*

wouldn't (say **wuud**-uhnt) short for **would not**

would've (say **wuud**-uhv) short for **would have**

wound¹ (say **woond**) *verb* (**wounding, wounded**)
to hurt somebody with a weapon: *The bullet* ***wounded*** *him in the leg.*
▸ **wounded** (*adjective*): *She nursed the* ***wounded*** *soldier.*

wound² (say **woond**) *noun* (*plural* **wounds**)
damage to your body made by something such as a gun or a knife: *He had knife* ***wounds*** *in his chest.*

wound³ (say **wownd**) form of **wind²**

wove, woven forms of **weave**

wow (*rhymes with* **cow**) *exclamation* (*informal*)
a word that shows surprise and admiration: ***Wow****! What a lovely car!*

wrap (say **rap**) *verb* (**wrapping, wrapped**)
to put paper or cloth around somebody or something: *The baby was* ***wrapped*** *in a blanket.* ◇ *She* ***wrapped*** *the glasses up in paper.*
➲ OPPOSITE **unwrap**

wrapper (say **rap**-uh) *noun* (*plural* **wrappers**)
a piece of paper or plastic that covers something like a sweet or a packet of cigarettes: *Don't throw your* ***wrappers*** *on the floor!*

wrapping (say **rap**-ing) *noun* (*plural* **wrappings**)
a piece of paper or plastic that covers a present or something that you buy: *I took the shirt out of its* ***wrapping***. ◇ *They enjoy making their own gift* ***wrappings***.

wrapping paper *noun* (*no plural*)
special paper that you use to wrap presents

wreath (say **reeth**) *noun* (*plural* **wreaths**)
an arrangement of flowers or leaves in the shape of a circle: *She put a* ***wreath*** *on the grave.*

wreck[1] (say **rek**) *noun* (*plural* **wrecks**)
a ship, car or plane that has been very badly damaged in an accident: *a* ***shipwreck*** ◇ *The car was a* ***wreck***, *but no one was hurt.*

wreck[2] (say **rek**) *verb* (**wrecking, wrecked**)
1 to break or destroy something completely: *The fire had completely* ***wrecked*** *the hotel.*
2 to spoil or upset something: *Our holiday was* ***wrecked*** *by the rain.*

wreckage (say **rek**-ij) *noun* (*no plural*)
the broken parts of something that has been badly damaged: *A few survivors were pulled from the* ***wreckage*** *of the train.*

wrench[1] (say **rench**) *verb* (**wrenching, wrenched**)
1 to pull or turn something strongly or suddenly: *They* ***wrenched*** *the door open.*
2 to move or turn a part of your body suddenly and hurt yourself: *I have* ***wrenched*** *my arm.*

wrench[2] (say **rench**) *noun*
1 (*plural* **wrenches**) a sudden violent pull or turn: *He managed to open the door with a quick* ***wrench***.
2 (*no plural*) the sadness you feel because you have to leave somebody or something: *Leaving my old school was a huge* ***wrench***.
3 (*plural* **wrenches**) a tool that you use to hold or turn an object ➲ SYNONYM **spanner**

wrestle (say **ress**-l) *verb* (**wrestling, wrestled**)
to fight by trying to throw somebody to the ground, especially as a sport
▸ **wrestler** (*noun*): *He used to be a professional* ***wrestler***. ▸ **wrestling** (*noun*): *a* ***wrestling*** *match*

wretched (say **rech**-id) *adjective*
1 very unhappy or sick: *I'm feeling* ***wretched*** *today.*
2 very bad or unpleasant: *The prisoners lived in* ***wretched*** *conditions.*
3 (*informal*) a word that people use to show that they are angry: *That* ***wretched*** *dog has dug up the garden again!*

wriggle (say **rig**-l) *verb* (**wriggling, wriggled**)
1 to turn your body quickly from side to side: *The teacher told the children to stop* ***wriggling***.
2 to move somewhere by turning your body quickly from side to side: *The worm* ***wriggled*** *back into the soil.*

wring (say **ring**) *verb* (**wringing, wrung**)
to press and twist something that is wet with your hands to squeeze out the liquid: *He* ***wrung*** *the towel out and put it outside to dry.*

wrinkle (say **rink**-l) *noun* (*plural* **wrinkles**)
a small line in something, for example in the skin of your face: *My grandmother has a lot of* ***wrinkles***.
▸ **wrinkled** (*adjective*): *His face is very* ***wrinkled***.

wrist (say **rist**) *noun* (*plural* **wrists**)
the part of your body where your arm joins your hand ➲ See illustration at **hand[1]**

write (say **rite**) *verb* (**writing, wrote, has written**)
1 to make letters or words on paper using a a pen or a pencil: ***Write*** *your name at the top of the page.* ◇ *He can't read or* ***write***.
2 to create a story, book, song, piece of music, etc.: *Shakespeare* ***wrote*** *plays.* ◇ *I've* ***written*** *a poem for you.*
3 to write and send a letter to somebody: *My mother* ***writes*** *to me every week.* ◇ *I* ***wrote*** *her a postcard.*
4 to take an exam: *The learners start* ***writing*** *on Monday.*
write something down to write something on paper, so that you can remember it: *I* ***wrote*** *down his telephone number.*

writer (say **rite**-uh) *noun* (*plural* **writers**)
a person who writes books, stories, etc.: *Es'kia Mphahlele was a famous* ***writer***.

writing (say **rite**-ing) *noun* (*no plural*)
1 the activity or skill of putting words on paper: *Today we're going to practise our* ***writing***.
2 the way a person writes: *I can't read your* ***writing*** *– it's so small.* ➲ SYNONYM **handwriting**
3 words that somebody puts on paper: *a piece of* ***writing***
in writing written on paper: *They have offered me the job on the telephone but not in* ***writing***.

writing paper *noun* (*no plural*)
paper for writing letters on

written[1] (say **rit**-uhn) form of **write**

written[2] (say **rit**-uhn) *adjective*
using writing, not speech: *a* ***written*** *contract* ◇ *a* ***written*** *exam*

wrong[1] (say **rong**) *adjective*
1 not true or not correct: *She gave me the **wrong** key, so I couldn't open the door.* ◇ *The time on this clock is **wrong**.* ➲ OPPOSITE **right**[1] 2
2 not the best: *We took the **wrong** road and got lost.* ➲ OPPOSITE **right**[1] 3
3 not as it should be, or not working well: *There's something **wrong** with the car – it won't start.* ◇ *'What's **wrong** with Ntswaki?' 'She's got a cold.'*
4 bad, or not what the law allows: *Stealing is **wrong**.* ◇ *I haven't done anything **wrong**.* ➲ OPPOSITE **right**[1] 1
ⓘ ORIGIN: through Old English *wrang*, from Old Norse *rangr* meaning 'wrong' or 'unjust'

wrong[2] (say **rong**) *adverb*
not correctly or not right: *You've spelt my name **wrong**.* ◇ *You're doing it **wrong**.* ➲ OPPOSITE **right**[2] 4
go wrong
1 to not happen as you hoped or wanted: *All our plans went **wrong**.*
2 to stop working well: *My watch keeps going **wrong**.*

wrong[3] (say **rong**) *noun (no plural)*
what is bad or not right: *Babies don't know the difference between right and **wrong**.* ➲ OPPOSITE **right**[3] 1

wrongly (say **rong**-lee) *adverb*
not correctly: *He was **wrongly** accused of stealing the money.*

wrote (say **roht**) form of **write**

wrung (say **rung**) form of **wring**

wry (*rhymes with* **cry**) *adjective* (**wrier** or **wryer**, **wriest** or **wryest**)
showing both amusement and disappointment: *'Never mind,' he said with a **wry** smile.*
▶ **wryly** (*adverb*): *'How nice,' she commented **wryly**.*

WWW (say **dub**-uhl-yoo **dub**-uhl-yoo **dub**-uhl-yoo) *abbreviation* **World Wide Web**

Xx

xenophobia (say zen-uh-**foh**-bi-uh) *noun* (*no plural*)
a fear or hatred of people or things from other cultures or countries
▸ **xenophobic** (*adjective*): ***xenophobic** attacks*

Xhosa (say **kaw**-zuh) = **isiXhosa**

PRONUNCIATION The **Xh** in **Xhosa** is pronounced as a click. Listen to a speaker of the language saying it.

Xitsonga (say shee-**tsawng**-guh) *noun* (*no plural*) (also **Tsonga**)
the language of the Tsonga people

PRONUNCIATION The **X** in **Xitsonga** is pronounced as **sh**. Listen to a speaker of the language saying it.

Xmas (say **ekss**-muhss) *noun* (*no plural*) (*informal*)
short for **Christmas**

USAGE **Xmas** is used mainly in informal writing. *Happy **Xmas** and New Year!*

X-ray (say **ekss**-ray) *noun* (*plural* **X-rays**)
a photograph of the inside of your body that is made by using a special light that you cannot see: *The doctor took an **X-ray** of my shoulder.*
▸ **X-ray** (*verb*): *She had her leg **X-rayed**.*

xylem (say **zy**-luhm) *noun* (*no plural*) (*biology*)
the material in plants that carries water and food upwards from the roots

xylophone (say **zy**-luh-fohn) *noun* (*plural* **xylophones**)
a musical instrument with metal or wooden bars that you hit with small hammers

xylophone

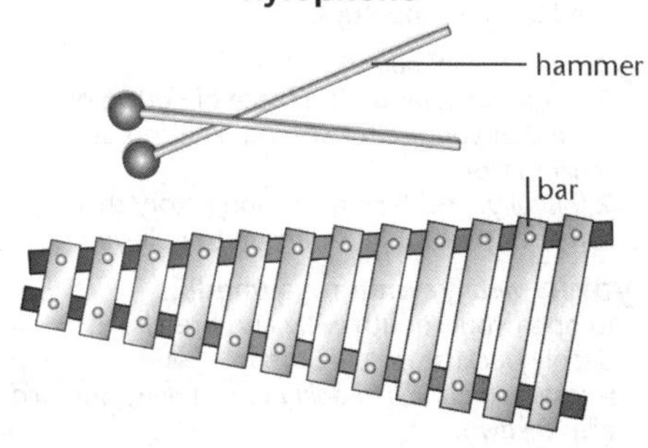

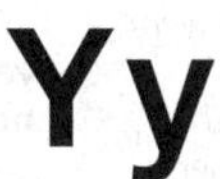

Yy

yacht (say **yot**) *noun* (*plural* **yachts**)
1 a boat with sails that people go on for pleasure: *a **yacht** race*
2 a big boat with an engine that people go on for pleasure: *a millionaire's **yacht***
ORIGIN: 16th century, from Dutch *jaghte*, from *jaghtschip* meaning 'fast pirate ship', from *jag(h)t* meaning 'hunting' + *schip* meaning 'ship'

PRONUNCIATION Notice how to say this word.

yacht

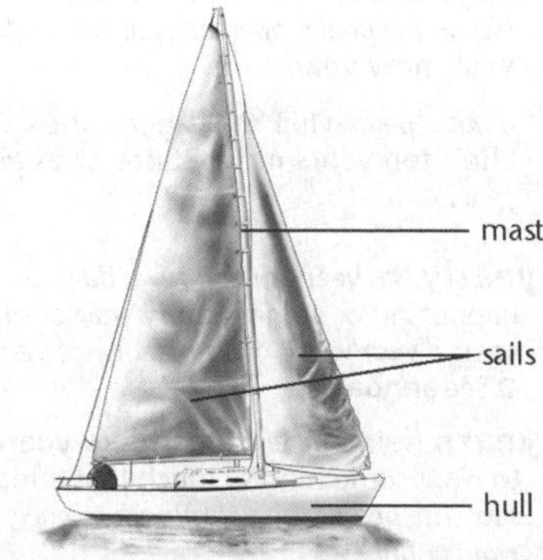

yak *noun* (*plural* **yaks** or **yak**)
an animal of the cow family with long hair and long horns that lives in central Asia

yam *noun* (*plural* **yams**)
the root of a tropical plant that looks like a large potato and that is cooked as a vegetable

yap *verb* (**yapping, yapped**)
(used about dogs) to make short, loud noises: *That **yapping** little dog is driving me mad!*

yard (*say* **yaad**) *noun* (*plural* **yards**)
1 an area next to a building, usually with a fence or wall around it: *a **farmyard*** ◇ *The children were playing in the school **yard**.*
➲ See **courtyard**
2 a measure of length equal to 91 centimetres, used in some countries.

yarn (*say* **yaan**) *noun*
1 (*no plural*) a long, thin piece of cotton or wool that you use for sewing, knitting or making cloth
2 (*plural* **yarns**) (*informal*) a long story that somebody tells that is difficult to believe

yawn *verb* (**yawning, yawned**)
to open your mouth wide and breathe in deeply because you are tired
▸ **yawn** (*noun*): *'I'm going to bed now,' she said with a **yawn**.*

yeah (*say* **yair**) *exclamation* (*informal*) yes

year (*say* **yeer**) *noun*
1 (*plural* **years**) a period of 365 or 366 days from 1 January to 31 December. A **year** has twelve months or 52 weeks: *Where are you going on holiday this **year**?* ◇ *'In which **year** were you born?' '1973.'* ◇ *I left school last **year**.*
2 (*plural* **years**) any period of twelve months: *I've known Sizwe for three **years**.* ◇ *My brother is two **years** old.* ◇ *a five-**year**-old son*
3 (*no plural*) the level that a student is at in college or university: *They're third-**year** students.*
all year round for the whole year: *The swimming pool is open all **year** round.* ➲ See **leap year**, **new year**

> USAGE Be careful! You can say **She's ten** or **She's ten years old** (but not 'She's ten years').

yearly (*say* **yeer**-lee) *adjective, adverb*
happening or coming every year or once a year: *a **yearly** visit* ◇ *We meet twice **yearly**.*
➲ See **annual**

yearn (*say* **yurn**) *verb* (**yearning, yearned**)
to want something so much that it makes you sad: *The people are **yearning** for peace, but the war continues.*
▸ **yearning** (*noun*): *He had a **yearning** to become a priest.*

yeast (*say* **yeest**) *noun* (*no plural*)
a substance that you use to make bread rise before you bake it, and for making beer

yell (*say* **yel**) *verb* (**yelling, yelled**)
to shout loudly: *Stop **yelling** at me!*
▸ **yell** (*noun*): *He gave a **yell** of pain.*

yellow (*say* **yel**-oh) *adjective* (**yellower, yellowest**)
with the colour of a lemon or of butter: *She was wearing a **yellow** shirt.*
▸ **yellow** (*noun*): ***Yellow** is my favourite colour*

yellowwood (*say* **yel**-oh-wuud) *noun*
1 (*plural* **yellowwoods**) a medium to large tree with narrow leaves that grows in southern Africa
2 (*no plural*) the wood of a **yellowwood** tree: *a **yellowwood** kist*

yelp *verb* (**yelping, yelped**)
to give a sudden, short cry when you are in pain or shock: *The dog **yelped** in pain.*
▸ **yelp** (*noun*): *a **yelp** of pain*

yen *noun*
1 (*plural* **yen**) (symbol ¥) money that people use in Japan
2 (*plural* **yens**) a strong desire to do or have something: *I have always had a **yen** to be a pilot.*

yes (*say* **yess**) *exclamation*
a word that you use for answering a question. You use 'yes' to agree, to say that something is true, or to say that you would like something: *'Have you got the key?' '**Yes**, here it is.'* ◇ *'Would you like some coffee?' '**Yes**, please.'* ➲ OPPOSITE **no**[1] 1

yesterday (*say* **yess**-tuh-day) *adverb*
on the day before today: *Did you see her **yesterday**?* ◇ *I phoned you **yesterday** afternoon but you were out.* ◇ *I sent the letter the day before **yesterday**.* ➲ See **tomorrow**
▸ **yesterday** (*noun*)

yet *adverb, conjunction*
1 a word that you use for talking about something that has not happened but that you expect to happen: *I haven't finished the book **yet**.* ◇ *Have you seen that film **yet**?* ➲ See note at **already**
2 now or as early as this: *You don't need to go **yet** – it's only seven o'clock.*
3 in the future: *They may win **yet**.*
4 but or in spite of that: *We arrived home tired **yet** happy.*
yet again once more: *John is late **yet** again!*

yield[1] (say **yeeld**) *verb* (**yielding, yielded**)
1 to produce something such as crops or results: *The survey* ***yielded*** *some interesting information.*
2 to allow somebody to have power or control: *The government eventually* ***yielded*** *to the rebels.*
3 to allow traffic coming from a certain direction to go ahead of you or in front of you: *You have to* ***yield*** *to vehicles coming from the right.*

yield[2] (say **yeeld**) *noun* (*plural* **yields**)
an amount of something that is produced: *The maize* ***yield*** *was higher this year.*

yob *noun* (*plural* **yobs**) (*informal*) (also **yobbo**)
a young man who is rude and sometimes violent

yoga (say **yoh**-guh) *noun* (*no plural*)
a system of exercises that helps you relax both your body and your mind

yoghurt (say **yoh**-guht) *noun* (*no plural*) (also **yogurt**)
a thick liquid food made from milk: *strawberry* ***yoghurt*** ◇ *Do you want some* ***yoghurt****?*

yoke (say **yohk**) *noun* (*plural* **yokes**)
1 a frame that you put over the necks of **oxen** so that they walk next to each other and pull a heavy load together
2 something that limits your freedom or makes your life difficult

yolk (say **yohk**) *noun* (*plural* **yolks**)
the yellow part in an egg

PRONUNCIATION Don't pronounce the **l** in **yolk**. This word rhymes with **joke**.

Yom Kippur (say yom **kip**-oor) *noun* (*no plural*)
a day in September or October at the end of the Jewish New Year **(Rosh Hashanah)** during which people do not eat or drink anything

you (say **yoo**) *pronoun*
1 the person or people that I am speaking to: ***You*** *are late.* ◇ *I phoned* ***you*** *yesterday.*
2 a person or people in general: ***You*** *can buy stamps at a post office.* ➲ See note at **one**[2]

you'd (say **yood**) short for **you had; you would**

you'll (say **yoo**-uhl) short for **you will**

young[1] (say **yung**) *adjective* (**younger, youngest**)
in the early part of life, growth or development: *They have two* ***young*** *children.* ◇ *You're* ***younger*** *than I am.* ➲ OPPOSITE **old** 1

young[2] (say **yung**) *plural noun*
1 baby animals: *Birds build nests for their* ***young****.*
2 the young children and young people: *a television programme for the* ***young*** ➲ See **youth**

youngster (say **yung**-stuh) *noun* (*plural* **youngsters**)
a young person: *There isn't much for* ***youngsters*** *to do here.*

your (say **yaw**) *adjective*
1 relating or belonging to the person or people you are talking to: *Where's* ***your*** *car?* ◇ *Do you all have* ***your*** *books?* ◇ *Show me* ***your*** *hands.*
2 belonging to or connected with people in general: *You should have* ***your*** *teeth checked every six months.*

SPELLING Be careful! Don't confuse **your** and **you're**. They sound slightly different and they mean different things: *Is this* ***your*** *bag or mine?* ◇ ***You're*** *early and* ***we're*** *late.*

you're (say **yoor**) short for **you are**

yours (say **yawz**) *pronoun*
1 something that belongs to the person or people you are talking to: *Is this pen* ***yours*** *or mine?*
2 Yours a word that you write at the end of a letter: ***Yours*** *sincerely …* ◇ ***Yours*** *faithfully …*

yourself (say yaw-**self**) *pronoun* (*plural* **yourselves**)
1 a word that shows 'you' when I have just talked about you: *Did you hurt* ***yourself****?* ◇ *Buy* ***yourselves*** *some sweets.*
2 a word that makes 'you' stronger: *Did you make this cake* ***yourself****?* ◇ *'Who told you?' 'You told me* ***yourself****!'*
by yourself, by yourselves
1 alone or without other people: *Do you live by* ***yourself****?*
2 without help: *You can't carry all those bags by* ***yourself****.*

youth (say **yooth**) *noun*
1 (*no plural*) the part of your life when you are young: *She regrets that she spent her* ***youth*** *travelling and not studying.* ◇ *He was a fine musician in his* ***youth****.*
2 (*plural* **youths**) a boy or young man: *The fight was started by a gang of* ***youths****.*
3 the youth (*no plural*) young people: *We must do more for the* ***youth*** *of this country.*

you've (say **yoov**) short for **you have**

yo-yo (say **yoh**-yoh) *noun* (*plural* **yo-yos**)
a toy which is a round piece of wood or plastic with a string wound round the middle. You put the string on your finger and make the **yo-yo** go up and down.

Zz

zap *verb* (**zapping**, **zapped**) (*informal*)
to hit, destroy or kill something or somebody, usually with a weapon: *In this computer game you have to **zap** the aliens with a laser.* ◇ *The tree was **zapped** by lightning.*

zeal (say **zeel**) *noun* (*no plural*)
great energy or enthusiasm: *religious **zeal***
▸ **zealous** (*adjective*): *He was a **zealous** supporter of the revolution.*
▸ **zealously** (*adverb*)

zebra (say **zeb**-ruh) *noun* (*plural* **zebras** or **zebra**)
an African wild animal like a horse, with black and white lines on its body

zebra crossing *noun* (*plural* **zebra crossings**)
a black and white path across a road. Cars must stop there to let people cross the road safely.

zero (say **zeer**-roh) *noun* (*plural* **zeros** or **zeroes**)
1 the number 0 ➲ SYNONYM **nought**
2 0° Celsius or the **freezing point** of water: *The temperature is two degrees below **zero**.*
3 nothing or the lowest possible amount or level: *The car can go from **zero** to 100 in eight seconds.*

zest *noun* (*no plural*)
a feeling of enjoyment, excitement and enthusiasm: *He has a great **zest** for life!*

ziggurat (say **zig**-uh-rat) *noun* (*plural* **ziggurats**)
an ancient tower with a square base and levels that get smaller and smaller going up

zigzag[1] (say **zig**-zag) *noun* (*plural* **zigzags**)
a line that goes up and down, like this:

▸ **zigzag** (*adjective*): *a **zigzag** pattern*

zigzag[2] (say **zig**-zag) *verb* (**zigzagging**, **zigzagged**)
to move along in a **zigzag[1]** pattern or path: *The helicopter **zigzagged** over the town.*

zinc (say **zingk**) *noun* (*no plural*)
1 (symbol Zn) a blue-white metal
2 (*S. African*) steel or iron that has been treated with zinc to prevent it from rusting, and which is used in buildings: *a **zinc** roof* ◇ *sheets of **zinc***
➲ See **galvanize**

zip[1] *noun* (*plural* **zips**)
a long metal or plastic device with a small part that you pull to close and open things such as clothes and bags

zip[2] *verb* (**zipping**, **zipped**)
1 to close or open something with a **zip[1]**: *She **zipped** the camera bag closed.*
2 (*computing*) to make computer files smaller so that they use less space
zip something up to fasten something with a zip: *She **zipped** up her dress.*

zodiac (say **zoh**-di-ak) *noun* (*no plural*)
a diagram of the positions of the sun, the moon and the planets, which is divided into twelve equal parts that each have a name and a special symbol: *Which sign of the **zodiac** are you? I'm a Scorpio.* ➲ See **horoscope**

zone (say **zohn**) *noun* (*plural* **zones**)
an area or place that is different from those around it, for example because something special happens there: *Do not enter the danger **zone**!*

zoo *noun* (*plural* **zoos**)
a place where wild animals are kept and people can go and look at them

zoology (say zoo-**ol**-uh-jee) *noun* (*no plural*)
the scientific study of animals ➲ See **biology**, **botany**
▸ **zoological** (*adjective*): ***zoological** research,* ◇ *a **zoological** garden* ▸ **zoologist** (*noun*): *Mandy wants to be a **zoologist**, because she is interested in animal evolution.*

zoom *verb* (**zooming**, **zoomed**)
1 (*informal*) to move very fast: *The traffic **zoomed** past us.*
2 (used about a camera) to show the object that is being photographed from closer or further away, using a special lens: *The camera **zoomed** in on the insect.*

Zulu (say **zoo**-loo) = **isiZulu**

zygote (say **zy**-goht) *noun* (*plural* **zygotes**)
a cell that starts the process of forming a baby animal, produced by the joining together of a male and a female sex cell

Answers (for activities in SP22–SP32)

1 Getting to know your dictionary SP22–SP23

1 1 aunt, deposit, fairy, gambler, laboratory, pie, reality, scarecrow, vase
2 daffodil, fake, galleon, philosopher, recipe, salami, team, upgrade, varnish
3 December, fancy, July, moment, outside, pizza, sixteen, soccer, urgent

2 1 acid, blue, cable, dancer, egg
2 epic, just, mean, real, sour
3 jam, jazz, jeep, joke, juice
4 mine, miserable, Monday, monkey, month
5 undo, unload, unloved, untidy, unworthy

3 1 aware, awkward, axis
2 firework, fiscal
3 peacock, peck

4 **fayz:** phase
hoo: who
kay-oss: chaos
kween: queen
ji-**raaf:** giraffe
rek: wreck

5 1 injury: noun; injuries
2 galaxy: Greek; yes – *galaxies*
3 meditate: meditated; meditation
4 nevertheless: adverb; but/however
5 near: far; nearest
6 chemist: **kem**-ist; pharmacy
7 ghastly: adjective; horrific
8 him: pronoun; them
9 bear: three; it means that you hate the person
10 MHz: megahertz; under *hertz*
11 multi-: many, more than one; multiparty, multicoloured
12 -ism: nouns like *baptism, Hinduism, Judaism*

6 **shoulder** *noun* (*plural* **shoulders**) the part of your body between your neck and your arm

7 1 arise
2 inkosi
3 refugee
4 science fiction
5 note at *beautiful*
6 illustration at *skeleton*

2 Vocabulary SP24–SP25

1 1 kangaroo; it is not an African animal.
2 polymer; it is not a shape.
3 democrat; it has the opposite meaning to the other two words.

2 1 false: You will find a regiment in an **army**.
2 false: Spaghetti is a type of **pasta**.
3 true
4 false: A global problem is a problem that affects the whole **world**.

3 1 abduct: kidnap
2 eager: keen
3 call off: cancel
4 eraser: rubber

4 1 accurate: inaccurate
2 deny: admit
3 worse: better
4 forget: remember

5 1 library: libraries
2 wife: wives
3 nucleus: nuclei
4 photo: photos

6 1 whole
2 sails
3 course
4 weigh
5 meter
6 stationery

7 1 amount
2 accept
3 lend
4 loose

8 1 squash: to press something hard and make it flat
2 abstract: not a real thing
3 address: to make a formal speech to a group of people
4 market: to sell something using advertisements

9 1 micro-: very small; microphone
2 post-: after, later than; post-apartheid, postgraduate
3 omni-: all, all things; omnivore
4 bio-: relating to life and living things; biodegradable, biography, biology
5 ultra-: extremely; ultra-modern
6 un-: not, the opposite of; unable, uncertain, unfair

10 1 four
2 many
3 three
4 four
5 five
6 ten

11 1 value: valuable, -able
2 perform: performance, -ance; performer, -er
3 wool: woolly, -ly; woollen, -len
4 collect: collection, -tion; collector, -or
5 surprising: surprisingly, -ly

12 1 pick
2 got
3 kept in
4 make

3 Grammar SP26–SP27

1 caution (verb), caution (noun), cautious (adjective), cautiously (adverb)

help (verb), help/helping (nouns), helpful/helpless (adjectives), helpfully (adverb)

comfort (verb), comfort (noun), comfortable (adjective), comfortably (adverb)

2 1 excitement
2 promotion
3 damaging
4 racist
5 misty

3 1 verb: *I have to **practise** my song every day if I want to win the competition.*
2 noun: *She won a **medal** at the Paralympics.*
3 noun: *I can hold my **breath** for quite a long time!*
4 verb: *Weather can **affect** the maize crops.*

4 1 sang
2 were singing
3 sing
4 sung

5 1 teaches
2 live
3 understand
4 makes

6 I break the glass.; I broke the glass.; I have broken the glass.; I was breaking the glass.

Jane fries eggs.; Jane fried eggs.; Jane has fried eggs.; Jane was frying eggs.

The girls skip.; The girls skipped.;

The girls have skipped.; The girls were skipping.

They write poetry.; They wrote poetry.; They have written poetry.; They were writing poetry.

7 1 offending
2 lay, read
3 seen
4 hurries
5 will climb

8 1 Who's
2 advice
3 fewer
4 lend

9 1 easiest
2 better
3 creepiest
4 higher

10 1 to put **up with** something: to have pain or problems without complaining
2 to let somebody **down**: not to do something you promised to do
3 to try something **on**: to put on a piece of clothing to see if you like it, and if it fits you
4 to hold something **back**: to stop something from moving forwards

4 Editing SP28

1 1 I hurt my **knee** at **gym**.
2 She is so **excited**! She saw the **queen**!
3 He doesn't **know** how to **write** an email.
4 My **friend phoned** to say she was going to be an **hour** late.

2 1 **T**he most popular programmes on **TV**, besides the sports programmes**,** are the soap operas**. A**ll the **TV** stations in **S**outh **A**frica show at least one soapie. **T**he most popular soaps are **I**sidingo, **T**he **B**old and the **B**eautiful**, G**enerations**, E**goli and **S**candal**.**
2 **Y**esterday **I** went shopping with my mother and my aunt**. W**e wanted to buy some new clothes for summer**.**
'Don't be a slave to fashion**,'** my aunt said.
My mother said**, 'L**ook for something comfortable**.'** **W**hat do they know**?**

3 1 fertile, green, lush, pretty
2 excellent, fascinating, long, short, tiring
3 chatters, whispers
4 delighted, ecstatic, elated, satisfied

4 Do you like my new **sunglasses**?

That **man** is really **frightening/scary**!

That's a really **fashionable/ impressive** motorbike.

See you in the **laboratory**!

5 1 When can you **begin** work?
2 I need to speak to you **about** this project.
3 Where are you **now**?

5 Using your dictionary for research SP29

1 the history of English, parts of speech, nouns, verb tenses, prepositions, adjectives, adverbs and pronouns, building words with prefixes and suffixes, punctuation, figures of speech and sound effects, plain English, instruction words, numbers, SMS language

2 1 Afrikaans grew from Dutch, and Old English and Dutch came from the same languages.
2 Prepositions tell us when or where things are, or where they happen.
3 Change the *-y* to *-i* and add *-es*.
4 A conjunction links or joins parts of sentences.
5 Apostrophes are used to replace missing letters in contractions, and to show possession.
6 partly, half
7 *There was a deafening silence.*
8 a longer answer in which you use information you have to create a new idea
9 Twenty-second (22nd)
10 See you tomorrow. Bye for now. Love

3 1 six
2 a hundred
3 fourteen
4 XLV1
5 three
6 one million
7 eleven
8 1 000
9 a billion (one thousand million)

4 (Answers will vary.)

6 Word origins SP30

1 avocado: Nahuatl
chutney: Hindi
democracy: Greek
equator: Latin
gogga: Khoikhoi
jacket: Old French
judo: Japanese
kebab: Arabic
malaria: Italian
mango: Dravidian
month: Old English
pyjamas: Urdu and Persian
rectangle: Latin
Renaissance: French
vlei: Dutch
window: Old Norse

2 1 The words are named after people.
2 The words all come from Greek or Latin.

3 boerewors: from Afrikaans; *boere* meaning *farmers* and *wors* meaning *sausage*

breakfast: from Old English; *brecan* meaning *to break* and *faestan* meaning *to fast*

Celsius: named after a scientist, Anders Celsius, who invented the scale

impala: from the isiZulu word which names the animal

4 1 imam
2 baboon
3 daughter
4 bead

5 1 astron: astronaut, astronomer, astronomy
2 demos: democracy, democrat, democratic, demography
3 graphe: graph, graphic, graphics
4 super: superb, supercilious, superficial, superfluous, superhuman, superimpose, superintendent, supersonic, superstar
5 therme: thermometer, thermosphere, thermostat
6 transmittere: transmission, transmit, transmitter

6 ten: decem, tien
church: circe, kerk
shadow: sceaduwe, skotos
leather: lether, leer
milk: milc, melk

7 1 algorithm: the man of Kwarizm
2 assassin: someone who takes hashish
3 berserk: wild, raging warrior

4 clue: a rounded mass, a ball of thread
5 denim: material called *serge* from a town called Nîmes
6 karate: empty hand
7 maverick: named after Samuel Maverick
8 papier mâché: chewed paper
9 prima donna: first lady
10 sinister: the left side

7 Exam questions SP31

1 1 noun
2 specialist
3 particularly
4 specialise

2 1 everything
2 everyday
3 everyone
4 everywhere

3 1 account
2 account
3 accountable
4 accountant
5 accounting

8 Just for fun! SP32

1 1 sea in the middle of the Earth
2 Mars
3 Tangier
4 A clove of garlic has the same shape as the head of a spear – *gar* means *spear* in Old English.
5 Pan
6 Pipes used to be made of lead.
7 wood
8 Both words come from the Latin word *sal*, which means *salt*. Roman soldiers were paid an allowance (called a *sallarium*) to buy salt.
9 a type of war

2 Clues across
1 woman
3 put
5 mice
7 accessible
8 youd (you'd)

Clues down
1 washable
2 necessity
4 targeted
5 machine
6 sing

3 Here are a few words:

cat chat cheat clot cool cot
each etch eat echo
halo hate heal hole hoot hot hotel
lace late loch loot lot
tale teach tool